W9-BZV-858

Your opinion matters. It matters to us. It matters to your fellow Fodor's travelers, too. And we'd like to hear it. In fact, we need to hear it.

When you share your experiences and opinions, you become an active member of the Fodor's community. That means we'll not only use your feedback to make our books better, but we'll publish your names and comments whenever possible. Throughout our guides, look for "Word of Mouth," excerpts of your unvarnished feedback.

Here's how you can help improve Fodor's for all of us.

Tell us when we're right. We rely on local writers to give you an insider's perspective. But our writers and staff editors—who are the best in the business—depend on you. Your positive feedback is a vote to renew our recommendations for the next edition.

Tell us when we're wrong. We're proud that we update most of our guides every year. But we're not perfect. Things change. Hotels cut services. Museums change hours. Charming cafés lose charm. If our writer didn't quite capture the essence of a place, tell us how you'd do it differently. If any of our descriptions are inaccurate or inadequate, we'll incorporate your changes in the next edition and will correct factual errors at fodors.com immediately.

Tell us what to include. You probably have had fantastic travel experiences that aren't yet in Fodor's. Why not share them with a community of like-minded travelers? Maybe you chanced upon a beach or bistro or B&B that you don't want to keep to yourself. Tell us why we should include it. And share your discoveries and experiences with everyone directly at fodors.com. Your input may lead us to add a new listing or highlight a place we cover with a "Highly Recommended" star or with our highest rating, "Fodor's Choice."

Give us your opinion instantly at our feedback center at www.fodors.com/feedback. You may also e-mail editors@fodors.com with the subject line "Ireland Editor." Or send your nominations, comments, and complaints by mail to Ireland Editor, Fodor's, 1745 Broadway, New York, NY 10019.

You and travelers like you are the heart of the Fodor's community. Make our community richer by sharing your experiences. Be a Fodor's correspondent.

Happy traveling!

Tim Jarrell, Publisher

CONTENTS

Fodor's 2008

IRELAND

Where to Stay and Eat
for All Budgets

Must-See Sights
and Local Secrets

Ratings You Can Trust

Fodor's Travel Publications   New York, Toronto, London, Sydney, Auckland
www.fodors.com

FODOR'S IRELAND 2008
Editor: Robert I. C. Fisher

Editorial Production: Astrid deRidder
Editorial Contributors: John Daly, Alannah Hopkin, Anto Howard
Maps & Illustrations: David Lindroth, cartographer; William Wu; Bob Blake and Rebecca Baer, *map editors*
Design: Fabrizio LaRocca, *creative director*; Guido Caroti, Siobhan O'Hare, *art directors*; Tina Malaney, Chie Ushio, Ann McBride, *designers*; Melanie Marin, *senior picture editor*; Moon Sun Kim, *cover designer*
Cover Photo (Early Celtic footpath on Skellig Island): Michael St. Maur Shell/Corbis
Production/Manufacturing: Steve Slawsky

ISBN 978-1-4000-1821-5

ISSN 0071-6464

SPECIAL SALES

This book is available at special discounts for bulk purchases for sales promotions or premiums. Special editions, including personalized covers, excerpts of existing books, and corporate imprints, can be created in large quantities for special needs. For more information, write to Special Markets/Premium Sales, 1745 Broadway, MD 6-2, New York, New York 10019, or e-mail specialmarkets@randomhouse.com.

AN IMPORTANT TIP & AN INVITATION

Although all prices, opening times, and other details in this book are based on information supplied to us at press time, changes occur all the time in the travel world, and Fodor's cannot accept responsibility for facts that become outdated or for inadvertent errors or omissions. So **always confirm information when it matters,** especially if you're making a detour to visit a specific place. Your experiences—positive and negative—matter to us. If we have missed or misstated something, **please write to us.** We follow up on all suggestions. Contact the Ireland editor at editors@fodors.com or c/o Fodor's at 1745 Broadway, New York, NY 10019.

PRINTED IN THE UNITED STATES OF AMERICA
10 9 8 7 6 5 4 3 2 1

IRELAND IN FOCUS

CONTENTS

ABOUT THIS BOOK

Our Ratings

Sometimes you find terrific travel experiences and sometimes they just find you. But usually the burden is on you to select the right combination of experiences. That's where our ratings come in.

As travelers we've all discovered a place so wonderful that its worthiness is obvious. And sometimes that place is so experiential that superlatives don't do it justice: you just have to be there to know. These sights, properties, and experiences get our highest rating, **Fodor's Choice**, indicated by orange stars throughout this book.

Black stars highlight sights and properties we deem **Highly Recommended**, places that our writers, editors, and readers praise again and again for consistency and excellence.

By default, there's another category: any place we include in this book is by definition worth your time, unless we say otherwise. And we will.

Disagree with any of our choices? Care to nominate a place or suggest that we rate one more highly? Visit our feedback center at www. fodors.com/feedback.

Budget Well

Hotel and restaurant price categories from ¢ to $$$$ are defined in the opening pages of each chapter. For attractions, we always give standard adult admission fees; reductions are usually available for children, students, and senior citizens. Want to pay with plastic? **AE, D, DC, MC, V** following restaurant and hotel listings indicate if American Express, Discover, Diners Club, MasterCard, and Visa are accepted.

Restaurants

Unless we state otherwise, restaurants are open for lunch and dinner daily. We mention dress only when there's a specific requirement and reservations only when they're essential or not accepted—it's always best to book ahead.

Hotels

Hotels have private bath, phone, TV, and air-conditioning and operate on the European Plan (aka EP, meaning without meals), unless we specify that they use the Continental Plan (CP, with a Continental breakfast), Breakfast Plan (BP, with a full breakfast), or Modified American Plan (MAP, with breakfast and dinner) or are all-inclusive (including all meals and most activities). We always

list facilities but not whether you'll be charged an extra fee to use them, so when pricing accommodations, find out what's included.

Many Listings
- ★ Fodor's Choice
- ★ Highly recommended
- ✉ Physical address
- ✦ Directions
- ⬧ Mailing address
- ☎ Telephone
- 🖷 Fax
- ⊕ On the Web
- ✉ E-mail
- 🏷 Admission fee
- ☉ Open/closed times
- Ⓜ Metro stations
- ⊟ Credit cards

Hotels & Restaurants
- 🏨 Hotel
- ⌨ Number of rooms
- ♨ Facilities
- ⑩ Meal plans
- ✕ Restaurant
- ⬧ Reservations
- ↘ Smoking
- ♟ BYOB
- ✕🏨 Hotel with restaurant that warrants a visit

Outdoors
- ⛳ Golf
- ⛺ Camping

Other
- ⊙ Family-friendly
- ⇨ See also
- ✉ Branch address
- ☞ Take note

Experience Ireland

Bloody Foreland, Donegal

WORD OF MOUTH

"All of you 'Irish' dreamers, who are remembering Ireland and longing for her with every drop of Irish blood you have in you, are just awakening the poetry and music in my soul. And you know, of course, that even for those who have not a drop of Irish blood, once you spend some time with the Irish, you come home changed. Ireland slips into your heart and won't ever let go. Only there do you get to have the whole bowl of cream—or any real cream at all!"

—Melissa5

www.fodors.com/forums

WHAT'S NEW

After a decade of riding the back of its explosive "Celtic Tiger" economy, timeless Ireland has changed forever. Massive constructive cranes hover over Dublin's old Georgian houses; Riverdance has become a worldwide old-Irish mass jig; U2 reveals just how hot-cool new Irish culture is; unemployment is at a record low; and Ireland's populace (with 24% under the age of 15) now makes it one of Europe's youngest nations.

But be assured that beneath all the innovations and the new affluence, that ageless, magical, Irish thing endures. Like the Janus stones and sheela-na-gigs of its pre-Christian past, the real Ireland is two-faced, embracing the past while focusing on the future. In order to understand this country, atingle with activity, this chapter spells out the latest trends, sums up the old favorites, and bids you welcome to the "new" Ireland.

New, indeed. If this is your first trip to the Emerald Isle, don't expect to find too many red-haired colleens leading turf-laden donkeys at crossroads or thatched cottages with old crones seated out front. Instead, expect a very confident country lifted by a financial tidal wave of the past decade where the average house now costs over $500,000 and the capital city sold more BMWs than Bavaria last year. Thanks to an economic turnaround that's become the envy of its EU neighbors—in part due to Ireland's low tax incentives to multinational companies and Europe's youngest and best educated population—the country's ethos of spend, spend, spend has transformed everything from tourism to building to corporate finance. In contrast to the grim reality of the early '90s where the emigrant plane was the first option of most college graduates, the country presently groans under the weight of returning ex-pats keen to nab top-paying jobs, as well as a massive influx of Eastern European immigrants seeking their portion of the economic miracle. Polish people have led this charge with over a quarter of a million already in the country and rising.

Church attendances are falling, gym memberships are rising, most families take three foreign vacations each year, and the hunger for second homes has resulted in pub conversations that often start: "We picked up a lovely beach villa in Goa last week, but Mary's adamant that no way are we selling the Paris apartment." The Irish are still great talkers, but nowadays leisurely pub chats are sandwiched between personal training sessions, investment-club meetings, and the constant search for that perfect weekend cottage in Connemara. That's a cottage with satellite TV and Wi-Fi in every room, of course.

Are We Too Dear, Dear?

In tandem with easier comparison to other European countries through common usage of the euro comes the harsh reality of just how expensive Ireland has become in recent years. Okay, so the average house is now worth well over $500,000, but what's a cup of coffee? Quite a lot, actually—a double espresso runs three euros in some Dublin bars, but just one euro in Milan. How about dinner for two in a restaurant with a bottle of house wine? Bad again, we're afraid. What costs $60 in Paris can cost up to $100 in the Emerald Isle. Wanna talk hotel rooms, DVDs, clothes, shoes? The same upward prices. Politicians squeak that high prices are a by-product of Ireland's stellar economic success and will

shortly level out, but they said exactly the same thing three years ago when the average house cost $300,000. Ireland is no longer cheap by any standards, and that includes Tokyo, London, and New York. Yet, in spite of this, tourist numbers continue to rise by 10% every year. Ireland's got great *craic*, (chat), good vibes, mighty scenery, and a welcome to beat the best out there—but how much longer will the visitors come if they can stay two weeks in France for the price of one week in Ireland? Feeling faint? Why not try a glass of mineral water, my dear—a snip at $6.

A Hundred Thousand Polish Welcomes

Does part of your Irish itinerary include discourse with a genuine local barman full of wit and wisdom regarding his native land? You may have to search far and wide to find this endangered species in 2008 as most pubs now have at least two or three Polish people dispensing tipples. With over 250,000 Poles calling Ireland home (plus many thousands of Lithuanians, Hungarians, and Latvians), the hospitality industry has bloomed under this new immigrant wave—perhaps just as well, since most Irish people have little interest in the unsocial hours of the bar and hotel business anymore. The new emigrants are efficient, courteous, and good humored—but they've got a long way to go to match the caustic, all-knowing info you'll get from an Irish barman. There are still quite a few left, though: catch 'em while you can.

Mary (Cough), I Think I Love You (Cough, Cough)

Though famous for their rebelliousness through the centuries, the Irish took to the pub smoking ban with a meekness that prompted many acres of newsprint. Now everybody's getting on board the "no butts" bandwagon—France, the United Kingdom, and Italy are presently looking to enforce similar bans. But maybe the acceptance of the smoking ban is not entirely about the health concerns and clean air—it's also brought a whole new angle to the boy-meets-girl romance dance. Faced with die-hard smokers who threatened to stay home, pub owners rushed to fill every inch of sidewalk with special open-air sections devoted to consumers of the demon weed. Warming heaters, outdoor seating, and overhead plasma TV screens followed. Soon all the action moved outdoors—a whole new ballgame for Irish folk. Frequently, pub bands play to 50 people indoors, while 150 gaze in from the sidewalk. Around the office water cooler next morning can be heard: "I don't even like smoking, but it's where all the cute guys are." Masters of making the best of a bad situation, the Irish have turned the smoking debate into a dating agency where dubious intentions make perfect bedfellows with bad habits.

The Long and Winding Road

In direct contrast to the aesthetic good vibes at the Atlantic Edge, a nightmare presently threatens the sacred Hill of Tara in County Meath, where, much to the anger of conservationists (who have already had a few scuffles with the police), the government has green-lighted a traffic corridor off the M3 motorway that would plow directly through some of the ancient ceremonial site. The history of Tara dominates the earliest Irish annals, and along with the 25 visible monuments on the Hill, topographical surveys and researchers with the Discovery Program have detected a further 80 significant sites, many of which are now

in the path of the bulldozer. A fine example of Ireland's present progress colliding head-on with its past, the battle between sacred heritage and toll plaza is headed for Ireland's Supreme Court, where the final showdown will unfold.

Catching A Tube

As recently as five years ago, surfing was an activity pursued by a few hundred hardy souls watched pityingly by multitudes bemoaning the all-pervasive power of *Baywatch*. In 2008, however, it's the fastest growing water sport in the country. In a line stretching from Portrush to Rossnowlagh and Easkey in the Northwest down along the coast to Lahinch, Castlegregory, Inchedoney, and Garretstown in the Southwest, the day-glo colors of a new generation continue to flex their muscles against challenging world-standard waves despite the cooler temperatures. Ireland's geographical position on the edge of Europe has consistently delivered some of the best waves found on this side of the planet and the country has become a must-do on the international surf tour. Last summer, the Irish Surfing Association (*www.isasurf.ie*) became seriously energized about "Aill na Searrach" spotted at the Cliffs of Moher—the biggest and most powerful break ever seen in Ireland.

Knead Me, Mould Me ... Slowly

Up to the 1990s, Ireland took a simple line on food preparation—fry it, boil it, or roast it, within an inch of its life. As cheap fares on Ryanair shuttled Irish travelers to France and Italy for weekends, a different attitude began to prevail about food and how best to prepare it. So long spuds and gravy, *Benevento* pasta carbonara. More recently, Ireland has joined the Slow Food Movement (*www.slowfoodireland.com*), an international network of people interested in the promotion, production, and consumption of good food. Begun in Italy, the movement has strong links all over the world with a well-established presence in Ireland supporting food artisans, their handmade produce, and the skills they embody. Many of the weekend food markets springing up in Irish country towns are directly connected to this epicurean phenomenon.

Getting It Right, Eco-Style

Irish engineering and its relationship with the fragile earth has come in for a fair amount of stick in recent years—new suburbs with zero green spaces, exploding cities precariously balanced on 100-year-old sewage systems, and roads with the worst traffic chaos in Europe. If you're ever stuck for a pub opener, ask about the state of the roads then move quickly out of range from the bile that will inevitably pour forth. How pleasant then that the Atlantic Edge visitors center at the Cliffs of Moher (*www.cliffsofmoher.com*) opened to universal applause last year. The building is sunk into the contours of the land and covered by a grass hillside. The center uses renewable energy sources such as solar energy and a ground source heat pump. Visitors enter via a viewing ramp that provides access to the central floor and its themed areas exploring different elements of the cliffs: Ocean, Rock, Nature, and Man. The tour continues from the central dome via a winding tunnel that evokes the many caves of the area to a theater housing a virtual reality cliff-face adventure called, "The Ledge."

WHEN TO GO

In summer the weather is pleasant, the days are long (daylight lasts until after 10 in late June and July), and the countryside is green. But there are crowds in popular holiday spots, and prices for accommodations are at their peak. As British and Irish school vacations overlap from late June to mid-September, vacationers descend on popular coastal resorts in the south, west, and east. Unless you're determined to enjoy the short (July and August) swimming season, it's best to visit Ireland outside peak travel months. Fall and spring are good times to travel (late September can be dry and warm, although the weather can be unpredictable). Seasonal hotels and restaurants close from early or mid-November until mid-March or Easter. During this off-season, prices are lower than in summer, but your selection is limited, and many minor attractions close. St. Patrick's Week gives a focal point to a spring visit, but some Americans may find the saint's-day celebrations a little less enthusiastic than the ones back home. Dublin, however, has a weekend-long series of activities, including a parade and the Lord Mayor's Ball. If you're planning an Easter visit, don't forget that most theaters close from Thursday to Sunday of Holy Week (the week preceding Easter), and all bars and restaurants, except those serving hotel residents, close on Good Friday. Many hotels arrange Christmas packages. Mid-November to mid-February is either too cold or too wet for all but the keenest golfers, although some of the coastal links courses are playable.

DUBLIN

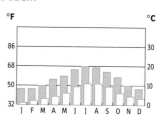

BELFAST

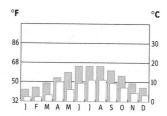

WHAT'S WHERE

1 Dublin. A transformed city since the days of O'Casey and Joyce, Ireland's capital may have replaced its legendary tenements with modern highrises but its essential spirit remains intact. One of Europe's most popular city-break destinations, it has art, culture, Georgian architecture, and, of course, hundreds of pubs where conversation and vocal dexterity continue to flourish within an increasingly multicultural mix. Get spirited (pun intended) at the Guinness Brewery, "Rock n' Stroll" your way through hip Temple Bar, and be illuminated by the *Book of Kells* at Trinity College's great library.

2 Dublin Environs. The counties outside the Pale are a treasure trove of history, monastic settlements, ancient tombs, battlefields, and peaceful valleys only an hour from the hubbub of the capital's center. From the lush greenery of Kildare and Wicklow, to the mythology and traditions of Meath and Louth, the historic timeline encompasses many of the pivotal pre-Christian and early Church locales of Ireland's past. Listen for ancient echoes at the Hill of Tara, hike into prehistory at Newgrange, discover medieval Ireland at Glendalough, and opt for opulence at the stately homes of Castletown and Russborough.

3 The Midlands. Overlooked by many visitors due to the region's relative absence of 'Wow!' factor attractions, this verdant oasis of bog and lake harks back to the simpler, and slower, life of Ireland forty years ago. Friendly, almost shy natives, old-style pubs, unspoiled vistas and walks, plus a wealth of historic ruins make for a relaxing adventure into the way we were. Tree-hug one of the great yews at Tullynally Gardens, lift your spirits at Clonmacnoise, and take a river cruise down the Shannon.

4 The Southeast. Ireland's sunniest corner (with almost double the national average), the coastal counties have long been the favored hideaway of Dublin folk on vacation. Quiet seaside villages, country houses, and some of the nation's best land make for easy access en route to Cork or Kerry. Inland, counties like Kilkenny and Tipperary offer a lion's share of history and important monuments. Follow in the footsteps of St. Patrick at the Rock of Cashel, dig the ducal lifestyle at Lismore, prowl the ancient Viking street of Wexford, and don anti-brilliance goggles at the Waterford crystal works.

ATLANTIC OCEAN

MAYO

Achill Island

Clare Island

Clew Bay

Inishturk

Inishbofin

Oileáin Árainn (Aran Islands)

Mouth of the Shannon

Tralee

Corca Dhuibne (Dingle Peninsula)

Blasket Islands

Dingle Bay

Killar

Skellig Rocks

Iveragh Peninsula

KERRY

Kenmare Bay

Beara Peninsula

Bantry Bay

Mizen Head

SCOTLAND
(United Kingdom)

Malin Head

Toraigh
(Tory Island)

Rathlin Island

Portrush

Coleraine

North Channel

Ariann Mhor
(Aranmore Island)

Letterkenny

Derry City
DERRY

Ballymena

Larne

Gweebarra
Bay

DONEGAL

Strabane

NORTHERN
IRELAND
(United Kingdom)

ANTRIM

Island Magee

Belfast Lough

Donegal
Town

Omagh

Cookstown

Lough
Neagh

Belfast

Newtownards

Donegal
Bay

Ballyshannon

Lower
Lough Erne

TYRONE

Dungannon

DOWN

Sligo
Bay

FERMANACH

Armagh City

Newcastle

Killala
Bay

LEITRIM

Upper
Lough Erne

ARMAGH

Ballina

Sligo Town

SLIGO

Monaghan
City

Newry

Lough
Conn

MONAGHAN

Dundalk

Castlebar

ROSCOMMON

Cavan

CAVAN

Dundalk Bay

Knock

Longford

LOUTH

Drogheda

Lough
Mask

LONGFORD

MEATH

Lough
Corrib

GALWAY

3

Mullingar

DUBLIN

WESTMEATH

Dublin

Galway
City

Athlone

2

Dún Laoghaire

Ballinasloe

OFFALY

Naas

1

alway Bay

Birr

KILDARE

Bray

Irish Sea

REPUBLIC OF IRELAND

Portlaoise

WICKLOW

Wicklow

Ennis

LAOIS

Athy

Nenagh

Roscrea

Arklow

CLARE

Shannon

TIPPERARY

Kilkenny
City

CARLOW

ilrush

Limerick
City

Thurles

Gorey

LIMERICK

KILKENNY

Newcastle
West

Tipperary
Town

Cashel

4

WEXFORD

stowel

Clonmel

Carrick-on-Suir

Wexford Town

Mallow

Farahy

WATERFORD

Waterford

CORK

Midleton

Youghal

St. George's Channel

Cork City

Kinsale

Cobh

Skibbereen

0   50 mi

0   50 km

WHAT'S WHERE

5 The Southwest. Traditionally, the counties of Cork, Kerry, Clare, and Limerick have accounted for over half the visitors to Ireland annually, with places like Glengariff, Killarney, Bunratty, and The Burren topping every tourist's must-see list. Busy market towns, sleepy hamlets perched on windswept peninsulas, uninhabited valleys, and the glory of Ireland's highest mountain range combine to paint a canvas that, although touristy in parts, still casts a potent spell upon the stranger. Teach yourself good taste at Ballymaloe House, sail the Skellig Islands, and kiss the Blarney Stone.

6 The West. Known to locals as "the wild West" both for their scenic splendor and cultural bohemianism, counties Galway and Mayo are a concoction of barren landscape, stunning shoreline, and towering mountain that test all senses—including your grip upon the steering wheel when negotiating the frequent hairpin bends. Outside the thriving bustle of Galway city, expect a remote and isolated otherworldliness in Connemara and Clew Bay. Test your 20/20 vision at the Cliffs of Moher, cruise the coast by the Aran Islands, and put on your "veddy best airs" at Ashford Castle hotel.

7 The Northwest. Virtually bereft of tourism in comparison to the rest of the country, Sligo, Leitrim, and Donegal are homelands of rugged, self-sufficient people and roads where wandering sheep and cows are still the norm. Weatherwise, the area gets more than its fair share of the elements—a condition more than compensated for in its friendly welcome and endless beaches where you'll walk all day without meeting a soul. Take a poetry break beside Yeats's grave near Ben Bulben, discover hidden Clencolumbkille, and immerse yourself in Irish in Sligo town.

8 Northern Ireland. Considered for decades a risky proposition to conflict-averse tourists, Northern Ireland has positively bloomed since the peace dividend of recent times, which finally nailed the coffin lid upon "the Troubles." From the beauty of Antrim's coastline to the vibrant cultural renaissance of Derry and Belfast, Northern Ireland has finally emerged from the yoke of its sectarian past into a present full of promise and possibility. Cross the Giant's Causeway, slide into a cozy snug in a pub on Belfast's Golden Mile, and trail after Eire's "wee folk" in the shimmery Glens of Antrim.

ATLANTIC OCEAN

MAYO

Achill Island

Clare Island

Clew Bay

Inishturk

Inishbofin

Oileáin Árainn (Aran Islands)

Mouth of the Shannon

Tralee

Corca Dhuibhne (Dingle Peninsula)

Blasket Islands

Dingle Bay

Killarr

Iveragh Peninsula

KERRY

Skellig Rocks

Kenmare Bay

Beara Peninsula

Bantry Bay

Mizen Head

Malin Head

Toraigh
(Tory Island)

Rathlin Island

SCOTLAND
(United Kingdom)

Portrush

Coleraine

North Channel

Ariann Mhor
(Aranmore Island)
*Gweebarra
Bay*

Letterkenny

Derry City

DERRY

Ballymena

Larne

DONEGAL

Strabane

**NORTHERN
IRELAND**

Island Magee

8 **ANTRIM**

Belfast Lough

Donegal
Town

(United Kingdom)

Belfast

*Donegal
Bay*

Ballyshannon

Omagh

Cookstown

*Lough
Neagh*

Newtownards

Lower
Lough Erne

TYRONE

Dungannon

DOWN

*Sligo
Bay*

7

FERMANACH

Armagh City

Newcastle

*Killala
Bay*

Sligo Town

LEITRIM

Upper
Lough Erne

Monaghan
City

Newry

Ballina

SLIGO

MONAGHAN

Dundalk

*Lough
Conn*

Cavan

Dundalk Bay

Castlebar

ROSCOMMON

CAVAN

LOUTH

Knock

Longford

Drogheda

*Lough
Mask*

6

LONGFORD

MEATH

GALWAY

River Shannon

Mullingar

DUBLIN

*Lough
Corrib*

WESTMEATH

Athlone

Dublin

Galway
City

Ballinasloe

Dún Laoghaire

alway Bay

OFFALY

Naas

Bray *Irish Sea*

Birr

KILDARE

REPUBLIC OF IRELAND

Portlaoise

WICKLOW

Wicklow

Ennis

LAOIS

Athy

CLARE

Nenagh

Roscrea

Arklow

Shannon

TIPPERARY

Kilkenny
City

CARLOW

ilrush

Limerick

Thurles

Gorey

LIMERICK City

KILKENNY

Newcastle
West

Tipperary
Town

Cashel

WEXFORD

stowel

Clonmel

Carrick-on-Suir

Wexford Town

5

Farahy

WATERFORD

Waterford

Mallow

CORK

Midleton

Youghal

St. George's Channel

Cork City

Cobh

Kinsale

Skibbereen

0   50 mi

0   50 km

EXPERIENCE IRELAND PLANNER

Getting Around

There was a time not so long ago when Ireland's bus and rail network left much to be desired.

While still slightly antiquated in reaching some areas (Sligo and Donegal, for example), the system has improved greatly over the past decade.

All urban centers and towns are now interconnected by bus and rail, and you shouldn't have great difficulty crisscrossing the country in any direction you desire.

But if you can, opt for a car—its greater flexibility combined with the possibility of meandering down byways and country lanes opens up a great many more vistas than any train will do.

The ability to change your itinerary midstream due to unpredictable weather or other circumstances also makes a rental the most flexible option.

Rental rates are on par with most EU countries, and offices are located at all airports, ferry terminals, and town centers.

During the summer months, it's wise to book in advance.

Finding a Place to Stay

Determining your budget is the key here—are you content with B&Bs and small hotels, or do you want to splurge on castles and grand country houses? It's best when planning your trip to Ireland to set aside a few hours of Web browsing to familiarize yourself with costs and standards. Certainly prices have risen in Ireland, but value is still there to be had with careful planning. As well as our own site—@Fodors.com—which should be your first stop, try @www.discoverireland.com and @www.goireland.com. The Irish Tourist Board's Web site—@www.ireland.ie—is a mine of information and a good overview of the whole country. For a week's stay in Ireland, consider small city-center hotels in Dublin, Cork, and Galway; use B&Bs in the country as a means of getting up-close and personal with the locals. For at least one night, consider staying in a castle or country house—it'll be costly, but very memorable. Ashford or Dromoland would be top of the castles list, with Mount Juliet, Hilton Park, and Tinakilly the leaders in the country-house stakes. Check out @www.irelandsbluebook.com for a select listing.

Feeling Festive?

If you plan to visit the biggest festivals and events in Ireland, book well in advance. In March, Ireland's major St. Patrick's event is the **Dublin Festival and Parade** (@www.stpatricksday.ie), which inclues fireworks and bands from the United States. In April, see the spectacular **World Irish Dancing Championships** (@www.clrg.ie/oireachtas.htm). In May, the **Fleadh Nua,** the annual festival of traditional Irish music, song, and dance, takes place in Ennis, County Clare. August brings a highlight of the traditional-music calendar, the **Fleadh Cheoil na hEireann** (@www.clonmelfleadh.com), held during the the last weekend of August or the first weekend in September, an extravaganza across the country. In October, the **Dublin Theatre Festival** (@www.dublintheatrefestival.com) puts on 10 international productions, 10 Irish plays, and a fringe og 60-plus plays. In October, the **Wexford Opera Festival** (@www.wexfordopera.com) is high glamour.

Meeting the Locals

The pub remains the center of all Irish social life, in spite of the smoking ban that many gloomy commentators predicted would be the death knell of the trade.

In any village or town, your local pub counter remains the best place to hear decent music, local gossip, and an overview of the world at large that's uniquely Irish.

Given Ireland's more hurried pace in recent times, the pub is no longer much of a daytime haunt (except for a good lunch on the road).

For really getting into the vibe, saunter along to the nearest hostelry anytime after 9 PM and buy a round for the few patrons nearest you at the bar—it may cost you $20, but you'll have a front-row seat for true Irish theater for the next two hours.

Meeting the locals is an opportunity that's available anywhere, really—at the post office, the local shop, at a crossroads, on a sleepy Main Street.

It all comes down to gently breaking the ice with tried-and-tested topics like: the weather (obviously), the spate of new building (it's everywhere), the price of the pint (always upwards), and how long the boom will last (nobody, not even the Good Lord himself, knows the answer to this one).

Safety Tips

Ireland is still essentially a safe country, but you do need to observe some basic precautions.

Don't leave valuables in a rental car: this is advice countless visitors neglect with sad consequences. Most car theft is opportunistic—if there's nothing visible like a pocketbook, a bag, a camera, even maps or guides within the car, most likely your petty criminal will amble past toward more available pickings.

Likewise, when parking in urban areas, use a car park—this also guards against auto clampers (a recent scourge of Irish towns, where fines to release your car cost up to €130).

Carry only the minimal amount of cash with perhaps one credit card when strolling around the streets and shops—while handbag snatching is minimal, there's no point is making yourself a possible target.

Stretching Your Dollar

At this writing, the dollar had reached a record low against the euro—$1.41 to 1 euro —with further falls expected. While nobody wants to penny-pinch on vacation, a few changes can yield savings without upsetting your holiday.

For starters, take a bus from the airport—it'll be one-quarter the cost of a cab and will get you into town twice as fast on dedicated bus corridors now operating in all cities.

Opt for B&Bs. They're well located and they'll have comfy bedrooms, good food, and an all-knowing landlady to answer all your questions. Listen carefully to her advice on bargain shopping, as she's got an inside line you'll not find on any Web site. In restaurants, opt for the house wine—people have become serious wine-drinkers in recent years and the house stuff is no longer just "plonk" for unsophisticated palates.

At lunchtime, why not try a picnic? After all, you're here to see scenery, and given that our changeable weather does allow for some dazzling sunshine most days, why not pack a few sandwiches and some drinks or coffee? Ireland is full of wonderful road pull-ins where you can park, walk a few minutes, and dine in glorious isolation to the sound of gurgling streams, lowing cows, or wind echoing across an open plain.

IRELAND TODAY

Politics

A "steady as she goes" attitude has prevailed among voters for the past 10 years, with the center-right Fianna Fail government and its three-time leader, Bertie Ahern, governing the country. On the back of the boom years, not to mention the peace treaty in Northern Ireland, it's been a case of "the devil you know" at the ballot box (despite a strong Green Party and Sinn Féin resurgence). The handshake between Bertie Ahern and Northern Ireland leader, Ian Paisley, at the Battle of the Boyne site in 2007 marked the absolute end of violence and a new dawn upon a political divide that has lasted centuries. At any bar counter, however, talk of politics will lead directly to the Irish health service and its poor state—everybody will tell you a story of taking their kid to the local emergency room and waiting five hours for someone to look at a broken finger. One recent government minister described the health portfolio as "Angola," a concise definition that spoke volumes. Ireland's a great country with a rosy future, goes the common view—just don't get sick.

Economics

Even with all the newfound wealth of the past decade, the average Irish person will traditionally lean toward a "glass half-empty" position after any initial probing. "Can it last?" is a mantra that plays across a thousand pub counters up and down the land when talk of the famous Celtic Tiger economy unfolds. With wages rising and the building boom leveling out, the specter of those IT multinationals decamping to cheaper countries is a grim prospect given full rein after the third pint. One computer company left Ireland for India last year because they could employ four similarly skilled Indians for the cost of one Irish person.

Media

As the Church confessional is no longer the purge-zone of choice for the majority of Irish people, radio and TV talk shows have stepped in to fill the void. Every topic under the sun is squeezed and caressed over the airwaves on a daily basis—lesbian nuns, love on the Web, cheap retirement in Bulgaria, mothers and daughters double-date rules, not to mention one beer-tasting show where brands from around the world are digested in an ever-downward spiral of hilarious drunkenness. Not quite Howard Stern, you understand, but eons beyond Vatican II, all the same. Newspapers include the major three dailies: the *Irish Times,* the *Irish Independent,* and the *Irish Examiner.* A host of U.K. tabloids have also entered the market in recent years, with the *Mail,* the *Sun,* and the *Mirror* being the leading lights. So-called "freesheets"—morning commuter giveaway papers containing a condensed version of the day's news plus heaps of advertising—are similarly flexing their literary muscles. No matter where you are in the country, there will always be a handy newspaper lying somewhere nearby.

People

For all their dangerous propensity to whack up the biggest credit card debt in Europe on BMW's, boob jobs, and second homes on Capri, most Irish are, at heart, as confused by life in the New Ireland as the tourist might be. The Irish work the longest hours on average in Europe, and much discussion now centers on the "work versus quality of life" dilemma. Everybody, it seems, knows somebody who's chucked in the rat race to raise Viet-

namese pot-bellied pigs somewhere in the Loire Valley or Andalucia. And despite their breezy, world-weary air, Irish people remain largely as enthusiastic and innocent about life as they ever were. One caller to a radio show summed up his ideal life: "a two-car garage, sex with my wife twice a week, a 12 handicap, and kids who won't call me a loser to my face." The average Joe is in there somewhere.

Religion

Now that priests have hit the headlines through sex scandals and criminal pedophilia over the past decade, a strange equanimity has settled between Church and Everyman. With the Church still needed for births, marriages, and funerals, even committed Mass-avoiders will observe the civilities of their parent's generation when dealing with those men in black. Priests themselves have been similarly liberated from the traditionally rigid confines of the cassock and are increasingly adopting the ancient role of good shepherd rather than their centuries-old dominance as dictatorial diviners of morality.

Sports

That enduring love affair between the Irish and their sports continues unabated regardless of any other cultural changes. Football and hurling are still enshrined as the national pastimes—but only just ahead of rugby, soccer, and horse racing. For a small nation, Ireland has consistently punched above its weight in the global arena, as exemplified by the cricket team getting to the knock-out stages of the World Games in 2007. That's cricket—the imperialist, colonial, ultra-British game—we're talking about. Every pub has a satellite dish pulling down anything from badminton in Bhutan to sumo wrestling in Tokyo. It's no surprise that

images of winning football teams reside in pride of place with JFK and the Pope on many pub walls. And it's not just the guys anymore, as the gals are fast becoming just as obsessed.

Culture

Neither the World Wide Web, cellular texting, nor Internet gaming will dent the nation's fondness for the written word. While there have been few to match the talent of Shaw, Wilde, and Joyce, the huge-selling works of Frank McCourt, Joe O'Connor, Roddy Doyle, and Pat McCabe underline the country as one of the biggest book-buying populations in Europe. In the movies, time and tide have taken us a long way from John Wayne in *The Quiet Man* to writer-directors like Neil Jordan, Jim Sheridan, and Noel Pearson and their warts-and-all visions of modern Ireland.

The Sexes

Equality in the bedroom happened 10 years ago—much more problematic has been the more recent balancing of the scales in the boardroom. Irish women have moved right up the corporate ladder since the late '90s and now challenge and frequently best their male counterparts for the big jobs. Sure, there are many glass ceilings still to shatter, but an unstoppable momentum has begun and God knows where it will all lead. Stay at home Dads? Check. What happens in Macau stays in Macau bachelorette weekends? Check. Fortysomething divorcees with teen boy toys in tow? Check. Most traditional males are hoping it's a horrible nightmare they'll soon wake from. Only time will tell.

TOP IRELAND ATTRACTIONS

(A) The Burren

A brooding, isolated expanse of limestone plateau covering most of northwest Clare, its flora and fauna flourish within a unique ecosystem encompassing hills, streams and peaceful valleys. Oliver Cromwell described it as "a savage land yielding neither water enough to drown a man, nor tree to hang him, nor soil enough to bury." The megalithic structures date back 5,000 years, older than Egypt's pyramids.

(B) The Rock of Cashel

The center of tribal and religious power for more than a thousand years, it became the seat of the Munster Kings in the 5th century. Handed over to the early Christian Church in 1101, the medieval abbey perched on a limestone mount in Tipperary contains rare Romanesque sculpture and carvings celebrating St. Patrick's visit there in 450.

(C) Yeats Country

A place where the mystic work of Ireland's most famous poet, W. B. Yeats, was conceived, this region of Ireland's northwest beckons with lyrical sights. From towering Ben Bulben to the Isle of Innisfree and Glencar waterfall, Sligo's fabled locales remain virtually intact since Yeats's time there in the 18th century. Yeats penned the simple epitaph upon his stone in Drumcliff graveyard: "Cast a cold eye on life, on death. Horseman, pass by."

(D) The Giant's Causeway

Irish mythology claims that the warrior Finn MacCool laid the Antrim causeway himself to enable easy crossing to his lover on Staffa Island off the Scottish coast, where similar basalt columns are found. Formed by volcanic eruptions more than 60 million years ago, the area is a magical mix of looming cliffs and thunder-

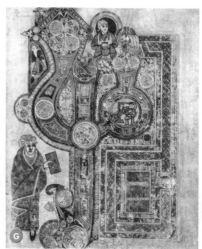

ing surf—and an awesome reminder of nature's power.

(E) Newgrange

Stonehenge and the pyramids at Giza are spring chickens compared to Newgrange, one of the most fascinating sites near Dublin. Built around 5,200 years ago, Newgrange is a passage tomb—a huge mound of earth with a stone passageway leading to a burial chamber constructed entirely of dry stone (mortar wasn't invented yet). Steeped in Celtic myth and lore, these graves were built for the Kings of Tara. Untouched for centuries, the main chamber was excavated in the 1960s and revealed itself as the world's oldest solar observatory, where the sun's rays light up the interior on December 21st each year.

(F) Glendalough

Established by St. Kevin in the 6th century, this monastic site set within an atmospheric valley of twin lakes in Wicklow suffered more than its fair share of invaders from the Vikings to Cromwell but continued to flourish as a seat of European learning up to the 14th century. The monastic remains include a superb round tower, stone churches, and decorated crosses, and are one of Ireland's most-visited attractions.

(G) Book of Kells

If you visit only one attraction in Dublin, let it be this extraordinary creation housed in Trinity College. Often called "the most beautiful book in the world," the manuscript dates to the 8th or 9th century and remains a marvel of intricacy and creativity. Fashioned by monks probably based on the Hebridean island of Iona, and worked with reed pens and iron-gall ink on a folded section of vellum, the manuscript demonstrates a sense of sublime balance and beauty in elaborate interlaces, abstractions, and "carpet-pages."

(H) The Blarney Stone

One of the country's most enduring myths, wherein kissing a stone high upon the battlements of a ruined Cork castle bestows a magical eloquence on the visitor, may also be one of its most ludicrous. Grasped by the ankles and hanging perilously upside down to pucker upon ancient rock, you'll certainly have a tall tale to tell the folks back home. Despite the difficulty, there's generally a long line waiting to scale the skeletal remains of Blarney Castle, a strangely derelict edifice in the other neatly groomed estate; try to visit in the very early morning.

(I) Lakes of Killarney

Fabled in ballad and song, the three Kerry lakes encompass a moody and powerfully scenic area where weather patterns and the ever-shifting hues of light combine to etch a constantly beguiling canvas of water and mountain. Set within Killarney National Park, the vast area includes the Gap of Dunloe, Muckross House, and Torc Waterfall.

(J) Aran Islands

Famed for their haunting beauty, these three islands set in Galway Bay have lured artists, writers, and multitudes of curious visitors for decades. On Inishmore, Inishmaan, and Inisheer you'll find a mode of life that reflects man's struggle against nature. Topped with the stone forts and crisscrossed by ancient "garden" walls, they epitomize solitude—one reason Irish bards like playwright J. M. Synge visited them many times. More recently, poet Seamus Heaney was moved to write: "Did sea define the land or land the sea…Each drew new meaning from the waves' collision."

FAQS

Does It Really Rain All the Time?

In recent years, the climate has been getting warmer with a greater degree of sunshine recorded across the country. In general, however, Ireland was never noted for its balmy climate, so it's best to bring a light raincoat and sweater. That old chestnut about having all the seasons in a day? It's generally true.

Are Transatlantic Fares Likely to Fall Soon?

Yes. Ryanair, Europe's biggest discount carrier, has plans to open up a number of Ireland–U.S. routes sometime in 2009 for prices around $150 round-trip. Having already conquered Europe with 20¢ fares, Ryanair's claims are already goading Ireland's national carrier, Aer Lingus, to contemplate slashing fares on their established Ireland–U.S. routes as well.

Where Can I Find a Complete Index of Festivals and Fleadhs on a Month-by-Month Basis?

The Fáilte Ireland Web site—⊕*www. discoverireland.ie*—has info on everything happening around the country. Every local tourist office will also have info on events in their immediate areas.

Has All the Violence in Northern Ireland Really Ended at This Point?

Yes. After many years during which one or more parties hadn't joined the peace movement, the meeting between Taoiseach Bertie Ahern and the Ulster Unionist Ian Paisley last year finally sealed the peace. Northern Ireland has been enjoying a huge economic and cultural renaissance as a result of the treaty.

With All the Modernization and Progress of Recent Years, Is It Still Possible to Find Genuine Irish "Characters"?

Naturally. Every Irish person is convinced he or she's a "character" anyway, so the tradition's not likely to die off just because many of the locals now live in spanking new apartments. In the more rural places around the West and Southwest, every bar counter will have its fair share of colorful types with outrageous views on the world. Some of those views might involve criticism of Americans, but don't take it personally; they save the darkest bile for Irish politicians.

Can You Cover All the Main Places of Interest in Ireland in a Week?

Unlikely, unless you tank up on coffee and drive all night. It's a classic mistake for first-time visitors to try to squeeze in too much. Vacations are about relaxation—don't spend it all behind the wheel. Pick a region—Cork/Kerry, Galway/Mayo, Dublin/Wicklow—and do a hub-and-spoke tour over a few days allowing plenty of free time for aimless ambling.

Are There Any Conversational Areas that Irish People are Ultra-Sensitive About?

Carry a courteous manner of polite inquiry into any Irish encounter and you will be rewarded with ample quantities of honesty, humor, and wit.

Is It Absolutely Necessary to Book Accommodations in Advance?

Apart from the high-season period of June and July, it's generally easy to find suitable accommodation wherever you are. Provided you're flexible between hotels, country houses, and B&Bs, the local tourist office should be able to sort you out at short notice.

TOP EXPERIENCES

Sonatas in Ancient Grandeur

Among the architectural grandeur that is Bantry House in Cork, the annual music festival ⊕*www.westcorkmusic.ie* allows for languid sunsets, picnics on the lawns, and sublime sounds from some of Europe's top classical musicians. The notes may be highbrow, but the vibe is indelibly Irish-mellow.

The Write Stuff

Fancy getting up close and personal with Lawrence Block, Frank McCourt, Joe O'Connor, Neil Jordan, Pat Conroy, and a host of other literary greats? Listowel Writer's Week ⊕*www.writersweek.ie* is a chaotic and seriously democratic gathering devoted to all things literary—including numerous workshops by the greats where info on writing your own masterpiece is there for the asking. This being Kerry, expect discussions to last well toward dawn.

Making "Long Bullets"

On the back roads of West Cork and Armagh, the ancient art of road bowling continues to thrive—the only places in Ireland where the game is still played. Two men, two 28-ounce balls of iron, and a 3-mi stretch of quiet country lane are the ingredients; the man with the least throws wins. Join the massive crowds that follow this slice of ancient Ireland called "long bullets" or "score" by locals—and place a bet to add to the excitement.

Acting the Goat

Puck Fair in Kerry ⊕*www.puckfair.ie* is the oldest festival in Ireland, dating back to pagan times, where a goat is made king for three days of drinking, dancing, and general abandon. Pubs stay open all night, traveler folk sell horses and cows on Main Street, and up to 100,000 peo-ple crowd this tiny town of 58 pubs for a mad three-day weekend. All in all, truly one of Ireland's most unusual festivals.

A Night on the Cobblestones

The Trinity Ball ⊕*www.trinityball.ie* happens in May just before students face end-of-year exams. The biggest enclosed party in Europe, it takes place around the ancient confines of this gorgeous Dublin city center seat of learning and offers everything from Strauss waltzes to punk, hip-hop, and good old rock 'n' roll. Tuxedos and ball gowns are the order of the day. The party officially ends at dawn—and then everybody heads to Grafton Street for breakfast.

Make Like a Bird

Happening on the May Bank Holiday Weekend, the Kinvara Cuckoo Fleadh ⊕*www.kinvara.com* is perfectly timed to welcome in the warmer evenings of early summer. A well-established and richly deserved reputation has ensured that the fleadh has become a showcase for the best in traditional music, attracting musicians from all over the country and beyond. An added bonus is having it in one of the country's prettiest towns.

Tory at the Movies

Billing itself as "Ireland's only maritime film festival," the Tory Island Film Festival ⊕*www.toryfilmfestival.com* is as unusual for its location as the kind of film fare presented. Eight miles off the Donegal coast, Tory is one of those truly undisturbed and old-fashioned places that a day's sunshine makes enchanting. The festival is well supported and a great chance to meet the rugged and wonderfully friendly folk who live hereabouts.

Food, Glorious Food

Long noted for its cuisine innovations, the Kinsale Gourmet Festival ⊕*www.kinsalerestaurants.com* is all about the happy pursuit of great food and wine plus the excitable bravado of this infectious coastal town. Buy a weekend ticket, have breakfast on a boat, lunch at a pierside pub, and dinner at any of the dozens of great eateries in this amazingly friendly town.

Have a Flutter on the Nags

Galway Race Week ⊕*www.galway races.com* is one of the country's biggest events with most of Dublin, Cork, and Limerick decamping to the City of the Tribes for a July week of celebration centered half around equine excellence and half around pub sessions. Every politician worth his salt hits the races to press the flesh, followed by legions of supporters and onlookers out for the "craic"—of which there is an endless supply.

Lark in the Park

Every June, Cork city struts its artistic stuff with the Midsummer Festival ⊕*www.cork festival.com*, a mix of music, film, and theater. Be sure to get tickets for whatever the Corcadorca Theatre Company is doing—in the past they've taken Shakespeare to the local courthouse, the city morgue, and the expansive green spaces of Fitzgerald's Park: a very different experience from a company constantly pushing the envelope.

Good for the Sole

On the last Sunday in July, join the thousands of pilgrims/adventurers who climb Mayo's Croagh Patrick ⊕*www.croaghpatrick.com*—and in your bare feet for the full purging of your misdeeds. A ghostly hill, tricky loose stones underfoot, and a Mass overlooking Clew Bay: it all adds up to an experience that is difficult but hugely rewarding.

Blooming Forth

Even though it is now reckoned that more Americans and Japanese attend the events surrounding Bloomsday ⊕*www.james-joyce.ie* than Irish people, it hasn't taken away a jot from an event that continues to grow regardless. Most Irish, if they're being honest, will probably admit to "never having actually finished *Ulysses*," but are still happy to discourse at length over devilled kidneys and other Joycean delights on the hidden meanings within this legendary work.

Clash of the Ash

Usually happening on the first Sunday in September, the All-Ireland Hurling Final ⊕*www.gaa.ie*, at Dublin's Croke Park, is a uniquely Irish sporting spectacle. Thirty highly-amped players clutching ash hurleys whack a heavy leather ball, or slíothar, at warp speeds around the pitch as they slug it out for the sport's highest prize. Raw emotions, brilliant color, and Harry Potter-ish skills like you won't see back home make it memorable.

What a Wonderful World

For jazz lovers, Cork's Jazz Festival ⊕*www.corkjazzfestival.com* in October is a perfect antidote to the approaching dark evenings of winter. George Melly, one of the music legends who visits regularly, puts it thus: "I forget where I've parked, where I'm meant to be playing, and, sometimes, even who I am—but it all works out in the end." A fair description of a festival with heart and soul.

SIMPLE PLEASURES

The Pub: Pillar of Irish Social Life

It's been said that the pub is the poor man's university. If this is true, Ireland has more than 10,000 opportunities for higher education. Even if you only order an Evian, a visit to a pub (if not two or three) is a must. The Irish public house is a national institution—down to the spectacle, at some pubs, of patrons standing at closing time for the playing of Ireland's national anthem. Samuel Beckett would often repair to a pub, believing a glass of Guinness stout was the best way to ward off depression.

Pubs remain pillars of Irish social life—places to chat, listen, learn, gossip, and, of course, enjoy a throaty sing-along. Impromptu concerts often break out, and if you're really enjoying the craic—quintessentially Irish friendly chat and lively conversation—it's good form to buy a pint for the performers.

Wherever you go, remember that when you order a Guinness, the barman first pours it three-quarters of the way, then lets it settle, then tops it off and brings it over to the bar. The customer should then wait again until the top-up has settled, at which point the brew turns a deep black. The mark of a perfect pint? As you drink the liquid down, the brew will leave thin rings on the glass to mark each mouthful.

"Fleadhs" & Festivals

From bouncing-baby competitions to traditional-music festivals, the tradition of the fleadh (festival, pronounced "flah") is alive and well in Ireland year-round. Before you leave home, check on regional Irish tourist Web sites or, upon arrival, discuss the local happenings with local tourist boards or your hotel concierge. Music festivals rule the roost—Kinvara's Cuckoo Fleadh, Galway's Festival of Irish

If you want to get a sense of Irish culture and indulge in some of its pleasures, start by familiarizing yourself with the rituals of daily life. These are a few highlights—things you can take part in with relative ease.

Popular Music, the giant Fleadh Cheoil na hÉireann, and the World Irish Dancing Championships (held every April in Ennis) are some major events.

But there are also village festivals dedicated to hill-walking, fishing, poetry, art, and food; the Mullaghmore Lobster Festival in August always proves mighty tasty.

Keep A'Clappin' & A'Tappin'

Ceol agus craic, loosely translated as "music and merriment," are not simply recreations in Ireland. They are part of the very fabric of the national identity. Ask most Irish men or women in exile what they miss most about home and, more than likely, those words "the craic" will be uttered. And the beat and rhythm that accompany Irish fun are the "4/4" of the reel and the jig.

Wherever you go you'll find that every town buzzes with its own blend of styles

and sounds. In its most exciting form, "trad" music is an impromptu affair, with a single guitar or fiddle player belting out a few tunes until other musicians—flute, whistle, uilleann pipes, concertina, and bodhrán drum—seem to arrive out of the pub's dark corners and are quickly drawn into the unstoppable force of the session.

A check of local event guides will turn up a wealth of live entertainment—if you're lucky you'll find a world-class artist in performance whose talents are unsung outside a small circle of friends and fans.

On some nights, Dublin itself—with more than 120 different clubs and music pubs to choose from—almost becomes one giant traditional-music jam session. Where to head first? Just take a walk down Grafton Street and keep your ears open.

IF YOU LIKE

The Most Beautiful Villages

Nearly everyone has a mind's-eye view of the perfect Irish village. Cozy huddles filled with charming calendar cottages, mossy churchyards, and oozing with thatched-roof-pewter-and-china-dog-atmosphere, these spots have a sense of once-upon-a-timefied tranquility that not even tour buses can ruin. Should you be after medicine for overtired nerves—a gentle peace in beautiful surroundings with a people so warm you'll be on first-name terms in five minutes—these will be your Arcadias. Many are so nestled away they remain the despair of motorists, but then no penciled itinerary is half as fun as stumbling upon these four-leaf clovers. Here are four of the most famous—but why not summon up courage, venture out on the lesser roads, and throw away the map?

Kinvara, Co. Galway. This village is picture-perfect, thanks to its gorgeous bayside locale, great walks, and numerous pubs. North of the town is spectacularly sited Dunguaire Castle, noted for its medieval-banquet evenings.

Cong, Co. Mayo. John Ford's *The Quiet Man* introduced this charmer to the world and the singular beauty of its whitewashed single-story cottages with tied-on thatched roofs.

Adare, Co. Limerick. Right out of a storybook, this celebrated village of low-slung Tudor cottages is adorned with ivied churches and a moated castle from the days when knighthood was in flower.

Lismore, Co. Tipperary. Set within some of Ireland's lushest pasturelands and lorded over by the Duke of Devonshire's castle, dreamy Lismore is popular with both romantic folk and anglers (the sparkling Blackwater here teems with salmon).

New Irish Cuisine

To the astonishment—and delight—of many visitors, Ireland is in the throes of a food revolution. Not far out of Dublin you begin to see some of the reasons all about you: livestock grazing in impossibly green fields, clear waters to spawn the freshest fish, and acres of produce thriving in the temperate climate. But it is Ireland's chefs who are the stars of the rapidly changing food scene. Having traveled the world, they're now producing a Pan-European, postmodern cuisine. This New Irish cuisine—sometimes referred to as *cuisine Irelandaise*—marries simple treatments of traditional dishes, such as Clonakilty black pudding, Clare nettle soup, Galway oysters, and Cong wild salmon, with exotic influences from Europe, North America, and the Pacific Rim. That noted, the Irish are a feisty lot not about to let newfangled food get the better of them. Food in Ireland has become more international in flavor, but there has also been a renaissance of authentically Irish cuisine based on regional cooking, thanks to the teachings and cookbooks of Myrtle Allen.

Thornton's, Dublin. Newer-than-now-nouvelle and grand-ol'-Irish ingredients collide in the kitchen of culinary wizard Kevin Thornton. Don't miss his moonshine sauce.

Ballymaloe House, Shanagarry. Presided over by Myrtle Allen, this famed outpost of Irish country-house cuisine uses marvelously fresh local produce, including seafood from the picturesque port of Ballycotton.

The Tannery, Dungarvan. Sir Andrew Lloyd Webber is just one foodie who raves over culinary wizard Paul Flynn's creations, including such gastro-pub fare as breast of wood pigeon on toasted brioche with truffle oil.

Celtic Sites

From rush hour on busy O'Connell Street in Dublin it's a long way to Tipperary's Cashel of the Kings, a group of ancient church relics—the largest in all Ireland—perched high above the plain on its famous rock. The journey is worth it, since it takes you back in time to the legendary days when Celtic Christianity conquered the isle of Eire. Beginning in the 5th century AD, hallowed shrines and monasteries sprung up across the land, often dotted with treasures sacred—the famous High Crosses, inscribed with biblical symbols and stories—and profane, such as the lofty Round Towers, lookouts for Viking raids. Just north of Dublin, around the Boyne Valley, you'll find three great sites: Tara, where "The Harp That Once Through Tara's Halls" played; Newgrange, once seat of the High Kings of Ireland; and Monasterboice, home to Muiredeach's High Cross, the finest in the land.

Clonmacnoise, Co. Offaly. This isolated monastery at the confluence of two rivers was famous throughout Europe as a center of learning. It's also a royal burial ground.

Glendalough, Co. Wicklow. A monastery founded by a hermit in the 6th century, attacked by Vikings in the 9th and 10th centuries, and plundered by English soldiers in the 12th century—your typical Irish ruins.

Rock of Cashel, Co. Tipperary. A cluster of ruins—cathedral, chapel, round tower—crowning a circular, mist-shrouded rock that rises from a plain.

Tara, Co. Meath. Fabled home of one of Ireland's titular High Kings, the ageless Hill of Tara has fired up people's imaginations from early Christians to Scarlett O'Hara.

The Most Stately Houses

Ireland's stately homes are either proud reminders of a shared history with Britain or symbols of an oppressive colonial past. If you're interested in luxurious pomp and reliving the decadence of yesteryear, there's no denying the magnificence of these country estates and lavish mansions, erected by the Anglo-Irish Protestant Ascendancy in the 17th, 18th, and 19th centuries. The wealthy settlers constructed ornate houses in various architectural styles, with Palladian designs popular in the first half of the 18th century, before the Neoclassical and neo-Gothic influences took over. In the last century, several majestic piles—notably Ashford Castle in Cong, Castle Leslie in Monaghan, and Dromoland Castle in Newmarket-on-Fergus—became hotels, so anyone can now enjoy a queen-for-a-stay fantasy.

Castle Ward, Co. Down. An architectural curiosity, in that it was built inside and out in two distinct styles, Classical and Gothic—perhaps because Viscount Bangor and his wife never could agree on anything.

IF YOU LIKE

Bantry House, Bantry, Co. Cork. Set in Italianate gardens and perched over one of Ireland's most spectacular bays, this impressive manor has a baroque, Continental air, thanks to its extensive art collection, including tapestries and fine French furniture.

Castletown House, Co. Kildare. Renaissance architect Andrea Palladio would surely have approved of this exceedingly large and grand Palladian country house.

Florence Court, Co. Down. With magnificent Georgian-period stuccoed salons, this shimmering white mansion is strikingly set against the Cuilcagh Mountains where, legend has it, you can hear the "song of the little people."

Retail Therapy

Once you get past all the traditional Irish leprechauns with MADE IN CHINA stickers on their bottoms, you'll find that Ireland has some of Europe's finest-quality goods. Objects like a Donegal tweed hat or a hand-knit Aran sweater, a Belfast linen tablecloth, or a piece of Waterford or Cavan crystal can be pricey but will last a lifetime. In Dublin look for antiques, vintage books, or au courant European and Irish fashions, many showcased at cool shops like Costume and Platform. Galway has its share of galleries and offbeat boutiques and is a great spot for book shopping, especially the Irish antiquarian section at famed Kenny's Bookshop. Keep an eye open for signs indicating crafts workshops, where independent craftspeople sell directly from their studios. The best of the North's traditional products, many made according to time-honored methods, include exquisite linen, laces, and superior handmade woolen garments. Traditional music CDs and the unadorned blackthorn walking stick are two good choices at the other end of the price scale.

John Molloy, Ardara. One of many shops in town where you can stake your claim to an heirloom Aran sweater or dream-woven Donegal tweed scarf.

O'Sullivan Antiques, Dublin. Mia Farrow and Liam Neeson are just two fans of this purveyor of 19th-century delights.

Waterford Crystal Factory and Shop, Waterford. Sunglasses might come in handy on a tour of this razzle-dazzle place.

Belleek Pottery, Co. Fermanagh. Any bride would be honored to receive a "Blessing Plate" of Parian china from this famed maker.

Natural Wonders

It's not always easy to conjure up leprechauns and druids in today's Ireland, but head to any of its famously brooding landscapes and those legendary times will seem like yesterday. With its romantic coastlines, wild bogs, and rugged seascapes, the Emerald Isle is especially rich in rugged, wildly gorgeous spectacle. Around its natural splendors, the countryside is dotted with villages where sheep outnumber residents by 100 to 1. Unfortunately, sheep don't also outnumber tourists.

The Aran Islands, Galway Bay. The islands battle dramatically with sea and storm and now welcome droves of visitors who fall under the spell of their brooding beauty.

The Skelligs, Ring of Kerry. Be warned: these spectacular pinnacles of rock soaring out of the sea will haunt you for days.

The Burren, Co. Clare. A 300-square-km (116-square-mi) expanse that is one of Ireland's strangest landscapes, the Burren stretches off as far as the eye can see in a gray, rocky, lunar landscape that becomes a wild rock garden in spring.

Cliffs of Moher, Co. Clare. One of Ireland's most breathtaking natural sights, these majestic cliffs stretch for 8 km/5 mi. At some points, the only thing separating you from the sea, 700 feet below, is a patch of slippery heather.

Giant's Causeway, Co. Antrim, Northern Ireland. There are equal measures of legend and science surrounding this rock formation—a cluster of 37,000-odd volcanic basalt pillars.

Glens of Antrim, Northern Ireland. This enchanted area is made up of nine wooded river valleys—don't miss Glenariff Forest Park, called "Little Switzerland" by Thackeray.

The Perfect Links

What makes Irish golf so great—and increasingly popular—is the natural architecture. The wild, wonderful coastline seems to be made for links golf; unlike many international courses, these courses have few forests, ponds, or short roughs. Most famous of these links courses is the celebrated Ballybunion. Fortunately, the courses can be played year-round—an asset in rainy Ireland. Pack plenty of sweaters and rain gear, and make sure you're in good shape: electric carts are available only at the most expensive courses. Golf clubs and bags can be rented almost anywhere. With the exception of the ancient Royal Belfast, all golf clubs in Ireland are happy to have visitors (and charge well for the privilege), and several tour operators have made golf excursions an art, so it's easy to have the golf trip of a lifetime. For information on the best courses in Ireland, see the Irish Greens chapter of this book.

Ballybunion Golf Club, Co. Kerry. On the Old Course, one of the country's classics, each and every hole is a pleasure.

The K Club, Co. Kildare. You'd have to be a nongolfer *and* a hermit not to have heard of this course, one of the country's most prestigious and demanding.

Portmarnock Golf Club, Co. Dublin. One of the nation's "Big Four" golf clubs (along with Ballybunion, Royal County Down, and Royal Portrush), Portmarnock is a links course near Dublin.

Royal County Down, Northern Ireland. A lunar landscape makes this course as beautiful as it is difficult.

GREAT ITINERARIES

THE EAST & THE SOUTH
5 to 10 days

Dublin's literary charm and Georgian riches, and rugged County Wicklow and the historic Meath plains are all just a few hours' drive from each other. Here you'll find the Boyne Valley, the cradle of native Irish civilization—no one will want to miss sacred Tara, Kells, Newgrange, and Glendalough, all time-burnished sites that guard the roots of Irishness. More idyllic pleasures can be found at Powerscourt, the grandest gardens in the land. In the south you'll find fishing towns and bustling markets, coastal panoramas, and—just outside of crazy Killarney (oh, and it is crazy, an emerald-green Orlando)—stunning mountain-and-lake scenery.

Dublin
1 to 3 days

Dublin's pleasures are uncontainable. James Joyce's Dublin holds treasures for all sorts. Literary types: explore Trinity College, Beckett's stomping grounds, and its legendary *Book of Kells*. Visit key Joyce sites and the Dublin Writers Museum, and indulge in the Dublin Literary Pub Crawl. Joyce fanatics: arrive a week before Bloomsday (June 16) for Bloomstime celebrations. Literary or not, stroll around the city center and take in the elegant Georgian architecture around St. Stephen's Green, austere Dublin Castle, and the national treasures in the museums around Merrion Square and pedestrianized Grafton Street. Check out Temple Bar, Dublin's hip zone, and join locals in this city-of-1,000-pubs for a foamy pint in the late afternoon. Pubs are the center of Dublin activity, and the locals never lose their natural curiosity about "strangers." You will frequently be

asked, "Are you enjoying your holiday?" "Yes" is not good enough: What they're really after is your life story, and if you haven't got a good one you might want to make one up. Pay your respects by taking a tour of the ever-popular Guinness Brewery and Storehouse. Night options: catch a show at W. B. Yeats's old haunt, the Abbey Theatre; see some Victorian music hall shows at the Olympia Theatre; or listen to traditional or alternative music at a pub or other venue. Last call arrives early at pubs, even here, so if you're still revved, go to Lesson Street and hit the nightclubs. For a dose of unmitigated Irish enthusiasm, join the roaring crowds at Croke Park and see some traditional Gaelic football and hurling.

Boyne Valley & County Wicklow
2 days

Walt Disney couldn't have planned it better. The small counties immediately to the north, south, and west of Dublin—historically known as the Pale—seem expressly designed for the sightseer. The entire region is like an open-air museum, layered with legendary Celtic sites, spectacular gardens, and elegant Palladian country estates. First head to the Boyne Valley, a short trip north of the capital. Spend the morning walking among the Iron Age ruins of the rolling Hill of Tara. After a picnic lunch on top of the hill, drive through ancient Kells—one of the centers of early Christianity in Ireland—and then to Newgrange, famous for its ancient passage graves. One thousand years older than Stonehenge, the great white-quartz structure merits two or three hours. Spend the rest of your day driving through the low hills and valleys

of County Meath and to Georgian-era Slane, a manorial town planned by the Conynghams. Dominating the town are elegant Slane Castle and 500-foot Slane Hill. Backtrack to Kells or continue to Drogheda and spend the night. The following day, head south of Dublin through the County Wicklow mountains. You might want to stop in one of the small, quiet towns along the Wicklow Way hiking trail and go for a short hike. Drive on to stately Powerscourt House, whose gardens epitomize the glory and grandeur of the Anglo-Irish aristocracy. From the profane to the sacred, head next to the "monastic city" of Glendalough and the medieval monastery of the hermit St. Kevin. Repair to Ireland's highest village, Roundwood, for lunch at the town's 17th-century inn.

West Cork & Kerry
4 days

Head about 250 km (155 mi) southwest to Cork City, filled with tall Georgian houses and old quays and perfect for a half day of walking. The place has few don't-miss attractions, but that's not the point: unlike many other towns, Cork is very much alive. As Europe's 2005 City of Culture, it has a progressive university,

art galleries, offbeat cafés, a formidable pub scene, and some of the country's best traditional music. Drive south to Kinsale, once heralded as the gourmet capital of Ireland, an old fishing town turned resort, with many good restaurants. A slow three- or four-hour drive along the coast and up through the small towns of West Cork takes you through the kind of landscape that inspired Ireland's nickname, the Emerald Isle. Spend the night in the market town of Skibbereen. Next morning, cross into County Kerry and head straight for Killarney, at the center of a scattering of azure lakes and heather-clad mountains. Although it has been almost transformed into a Celtic theme park by a flood of tourists, it's a good base for exploring your pick of three great Atlantic-pounded peninsulas: the strikingly desolate Beara Peninsula, the Ring of Kerry, and the Dingle Peninsula. All offer stunning ocean views, hilly landscapes (like the Macgillycuddy's Reeks mountains), and welcoming towns with good B&Bs. To do justice to the fabulous views of the Ring, you need a minimum of two days, especially if traveling by bus. The five-hour drive back to Dublin takes you through Limerick City and the lakes of the Midlands.

THE WEST & THE NORTH
6 to 7 days

"To hell or to Connaught" was the choice given the native population by Cromwell, and indeed the harsh, barren landscape of parts of the west and north might appear cursed to the eye of an uprooted farmer. But there's an appeal in the very wildness of Counties Clare, Galway, Mayo, Sligo, and Donegal, with their stunning, steep coastlines hammered and shaped for aeons by the Atlantic. Here, in isolated communities, you'll hear locals speaking Irish as they go about their business. The arrival of peace has opened the lush pastures of long-suffering Northern Ireland to travelers.

Galway & Clare
2 days

A three-hour drive west from Dublin leads straight to the 710-foot-high Cliffs of Moher, perhaps the single most impressive sight in Ireland. Using the waterside village of Ballyvaughan as your base, spend a day exploring the lunar landscape of the harsh, limestone Burren. In spring it becomes a mighty rock garden of exotic colors. The next morning, head north out of Ballyvaughan toward Galway City. On the way you'll pass 2-million-year-old Ailwee Cave and the picture-perfect village of Kinvara. Galway City, spectacularly overlooking Galway Bay, is rapidly growing, vibrant, and packed with culture and history. If time allows, drive west to Ros an Mhil (Rossaveal) and take a boat to the fabled Aran Islands. Spend the night in Galway City.

North & West to Donegal
2 days

Northwest of Galway City is tiny Clifden, with some of the country's best Atlantic views. From here, head east through one of the most beautiful stretches of road in Connemara—through Kylemore Valley, home of Kylemore Abbey, a huge Gothic Revival castle. After seeing the castle and its grounds, head north through tiny Leenane (the setting of the hit Broadway play, The Beauty Queen of Leenane) and on to the most attractive town in County Mayo, Westport. It's the perfect spot to spend the night: the 18th-century planned town is on an inlet of Clew Bay, and some of the west coast's finest beaches are nearby. Your drive north leads through the heart of Yeats Country in Sligo. Just north of cozy Sligo Town is the stark outline of a great hill, Ben Bulben, in whose shadow poet Yeats wanted to be buried. South of town, follow the signposted Yeats Trail around woody, gorgeously scenic Lough Gill. Continuing north, you pass Yeats's simple grave in unassuming Drumcliff, a 3000 bc tomb in Creevykeel, and small Donegal Town. Head north through Letterkenny on the tight, meandering roads, into the windswept mountains and along the jagged coastline of northern Donegal. A trip on a fishing boat to one of the many islands off the coast is a must, as is a slow drive along the coast from the Gweedore Headland, covered with heather and gorse, to the former plantation village of Dunfanaghy (Dun Fionnachaid), heart of Donegal's Irish-speaking Gaeltacht region and a friendly place to spend the night.

Northern Ireland

2 days

Begin exploring the province in historic, divided Derry City (called Londonderry by Unionists), Northern Ireland's second city. A few hours are sufficient to take in the views from the old city walls and the fascinating murals of the Catholic Bogside district. Continue on to two of the region's main attractions, the 13th-century Norman fortress of Dunluce Castle and the Giant's Causeway, shaped from volcanic rock some 60 million years ago. Heading south, sticking to coastal roads for the best scenery, you'll soon pass through the Glens of Antrim, whose green hills roll down into the sea. Tucked in the glens are a number of small, unpretentious towns with great hotels. Early in the morning, head straight to Northern Ireland's capital, Belfast. The old port city, gray and often wet, is a fascinating place, recovering from years of strife. A morning of driving through its streets will have to suffice before you head west through the rustic, pretty countryside to Lough Neagh, the largest lake in the British Isles. It's time to head back to Dublin, but if you're ahead of schedule, take the longer route that passes through the glorious Mountains of Mourne and around icy-blue Carlingford Lough.

BY CAR: SOME TIPS

Road signs are generally in both Irish and English, although in Gaeltacht (Irish speaking) areas new laws now mandate signs in Irish *only* (most such regions are located in the counties along the Western coast of the country, Donegal and Connemara in particular). Thus, if traveling in these areas, invest in a good, detailed map with both Irish and English names.

Another new law has mandated that all speed limit signs now need to be posted in kilometers—not miles—per hour (a bit of a nuisance, as most cars have speedometers in miles). Signage is currently being changed throughout Ireland.

Remember to slow down on smaller, countryside lanes and roads: traffic jams can sometimes be caused by flocks of sheep and cattle, not cars.

Brand-new divided highways are the fastest way to get from one point to another, but use caution: highways sometimes end as abruptly as they begin.

IRISH FAMILY NAMES

Doherty

O'Hara
Quinn

Friel
McLaughlin
Mooney   Gallagher   DERRY   McDonnell
O'Donnell   Gormley   Hegarty   McNeill   ANTRIM
Boyle   Quinn   Kelly   O'Neill
McSweeney   DONEGAL   Cohan   O'Neil

McGrath   Donnelly   Hagan   Lynch   White
Clery   Murphy   TYRONE   McCann
O'Neill
Flanagan   Cassidy
Corrigan   FERMANAGH   McKenna   ARMAGH   DOWN
Clancy   McManus   Hanlon   McGuinness
O'Dowd   Rafferty   O'Rourke   McCabe   Connolly   McMahon
Boland   O'Hara   Maguire   Boylan   McMahon   Hanratty
SLIGO   McDonagh   McGovern   MONAGHAN
Higgins   Molloy   CAVAN   McNally
Dugan   Jordan   Lynch   LOUTH
O'Malley   MAYO   McDermot   Sheridan   McGowan   O'Carroll
Costello   Flanagan   McManus   O'Reilly   MEATH   Plunkett
Burke   Madden   Hanley   Cusack   Dillon
Kelly   Horan   Flynn   ROSCOMMON   Hayes   Hennessey
Gormley   Kirwan   Murphy   Connolly   O'Casey
Joyce   Jennings   Moran   Quinn   WESTMEATH   Plunkett   Plunkett
O'Flaherty   Dalton   Coffey   Quinlan
GALWAY   Kelly   Madden   Dillon   Daly   DUBLIN
French   Fallon   McKeogh   Sheridan   O'Byrne
Blake   Lynch   Kenny   Malone   OFFALY   White
O'Halloran   Coghlan   Molloy   KILDARE   O'Toole
Daly   Burke   Dempsey   Fitzgerald   Kelly
O'Loughlin   Fah(e)y   Doran   Cullen   WICKLOW
Boland   Clery   O'Carroll   Dunn(e)   Kelly   O'Byrne
Clancy   Molon(e)y   Meagher   Moore
O'Dea   CLARE   O'Halloran   Kennedy   (Maher)   LAOISE   Nolan   McKeogh
McMahon   McInerney   Purcell   Fitzpatrick   CARLOW   Doyle
O'Brien   McGrath   Ryan   O'Meara   O'Neill
Lynch   McNamara   Aherne   Lynch   Fogarty   Butler   Kinsella   Redmond
O'Grady   McKeogh   Doran
Fitzgerald   Woulfe   KILKENNY   WEXFORD
Connor   Fitzgibbon   O'Brien   O'Dwyer   Tobin   Hartley
LIMERICK   Kavanagh
O'Cullane   TIPPERARY   O'Carroll   Walsh   Keating
KERRY   (Collins)   O'Casey
O'Brien
O'Shea   Moriarty   Roche   Phelan   McGrath   Power   Keane
Galvin   O'Leary   Barry   Keane
McCarthy   Callaghan   Sheridan   WATERFORD
O'Donoghue   O'Keefe   Flynn
Fitzgerald   McSweeney   Nugent   Scanlon
O'Sullivan   O'Riordan
O'Connell   Murphy
Lynch   CORK
Donovan   Cullinane
O'Mahony   Hennessey
Hogan   Driscoll

1

Antrim
Lynch
McDonnell
McNeill
O'Hara
O'Neill
Quinn

Armagh
Hanlon
McCann

Carlow
Kinsella
Nolan
O'Neill

Cavan
Boylan
Lynch
McCabe
McGovern
McGowan
McNally
O'Reilly
Sheridan

Clare
Aherne
Boland
Clancy
Daly
Lynch
McGrath
McInerney
McMahon
McNamara
Molon(e)y
O'Brien
O'Dea
O'Grady
O'Halloran
O'Loughlin

Cork
Barry
Callaghan
Cullinane
Donovan
Driscoll
Flynn
Hennessey
Hogan
Lynch
McCarthy
McSweeney
Murphy
Nugent
O'Casey

O'Cullane
(Collins)
O'Keefe
O'Leary
O'Mahony
O'Riordan
Roche
Scanlon
Sheridan

Derry
Cahan
Hegarty
Kelly
McLaughlin

Donegal
Boyle
Clery
Doherty
Friel
Gallagher
Gormley
McGrath
McLoughlin
McSweeney
Mooney
O'Donnell

Down
Lynch
McGuinness
O'Neil
White

Dublin
Hennessey
O'Casey
Plunkett

Fermanagh
Cassidy
Connolly
Corrigan
Flanagan
Maguire
McManus

Galway
Blake
Burke
Clery
Fah(e)y
French
Jennings
Joyce
Kelly
Kenny
Kirwan
Lynch

Madden
Moran
O'Flaherty
O'Halloran

Kerry
Connor
Fitzgerald
Galvin
McCarthy
Moriarty
O'Connell
O'Donoghue
O'Shea
O'Sullivan

Kildare
Cullen
Fitzgerald
O'Byrne
White

Kilkenny
Butler
Fitzpatrick
O'Carroll
Tobin

Laois
Dempsey
Doran
Dunn(e)
Kelly
Moore

Leitrim
Clancy
O'Rourke

Limerick
Fitzgerald
Fitzgibbon
McKeough
O'Brien
O'Cullane
(Collins)
O'Grady
Woulfe

Longford
O'Farrell
Quinn

Louth
O'Carroll
Plunkett

Mayo
Burke
Costello
Dugan

Gormley
Horan
Jennings
Jordan
Kelly
Madden
O'Malley

Meath
Coffey
Connolly
Cusack
Dillon
Hayes
Hennessey
Plunkett
Quinlan

Monaghan
Boylan
Connolly
Hanratty
McKenna
McMahon
McNally

Offaly
Coghlan
Dempsey
Fallon
Malone
Meagher
(Maher)
Molloy
O'Carroll
Sheridan

Roscommon
Fallon
Flanagan
Flynn
Hanley
McDermot
McKeogh
McManus
Molloy
Murphy

Sligo
Boland
Higgins
McDonagh
O'Dowd
O'Hara
Rafferty

Tipperary
Butler
Fogarty
Kennedy

Lynch
Meagher
(Maher)
O'Carroll
O'Dwyer
O'Meara
Purcell
Ryan

Tyrone
Cahan
Donnelly
Gormley
Hagan
Murphy
O'Neill
Quinn

Waterford
Keane
McGrath
O'Brien
Phelan
Power

Westmeath
Coffey
Dalton
Daly
Dillon
Sheridan

Wexford
Doran
Doyle
Hartley
Kavanagh
Keating
Kinsella
McKeogh
Redmond
Walsh

Wicklow
Cullen
Kelly
McKeogh
O'Byrne
O'Toole

ANCESTOR HUNTING

Over 46 million Americans claim Irish ancestry, and the desire to trace those long-lost roots back in the "auld sod" can run deep. Here are some pointers for how you can make your trip to Ireland a journey into your past.

Before You Go

The more you can learn about your ancestors, the more fruitful your search is going to be once you're on Irish soil. Crucial facts include:

- **The name of your ancestor**
- **Names of that ancestor's parents/spouse**
- **His or her date of birth, marriage, or death**
- **County and parish of origin in Ireland**
- **Religious denomination**

The first place to seek information is directly from members of your family. A grandparent or a great aunt with a story to tell can be the source of important clues. And relatives who don't know any family history may have documents stored away that can help with your sleuthing—old letters, wills, diaries, birth certificates, photos.

If family resources aren't leading you anywhere, try turning to the Mormon Church. They've made it their mission to collect mountains of genealogical information, much of which it makes available free of charge at familyresearch.org; plug in the name a relative, and you may find records that include parents' names and places of origin. You can also visit one of hundreds of research centers throughout the United States (addresses for which are available on the Web site).

On the Ground in Ireland

Ancestor hunters have long traveled throughout Ireland to comb parish church records, but most of these records are now available on microfilm in Dublin at the **National Library** (⊠*Kildare St.* ☎*01/603–0200* ⊕*www.nil.ie*) The library is a great place to begin your hunting; you can consult a research adviser there free of charge.

Civil records—dating back to 1865—are available at the **General Register Office** (⊠*8-11 Lombard St. E, Dublin* ☎*01/635–4423* ⊕*www.groireland.ie*). Records for Anglican marriages date from 1845. The **National Archives** (⊠*Bishop St., Dublin* ⊕*www.nationalarchives.ie*) has census records, and like the National Library, provides free genealogy consultations.

For Northern Ireland, you can find information at the **Centre for Migration Studies** (⊠*Mellon Rd., Castletown, Omagh* ☎*028/8225–6315* ⊕*www.qub.ac.uk/cms/*) at the Ulster American Folk Park and the **Public Records Office** (⊠*Balmoral Ave., Belfast* ☎*028/9025–5905* ⊕*www.proni.gov.uk*).

None of these places has actual records available online, but their Web sites provide information about genealogical research. If you'd rather not spend your vacation in a record hall, you can hire a professional to do your spadework. The Association of Professional Genealogists in Ireland (⊕*www.irishgenealogy.ie*) will present you with a "package of discovery" upon your arrival. The *Irish Times* newspaper also has ancestor-hunting resources (⊕*www.ireland.com/ancestor*). And the National Library provides references for professionals.

Dublin

WORD OF MOUTH

"I decided to take one of Dublin's hop-on/hop-off tours to get my bearings, riding through the close-packed streets, seeing modern buildings next to Georgian townhouses, ivy and glass becoming roommates. I waved at a truck driver and he smiled and waved back; Amid the noisy motorcycles, the shush of buses, and the singing of brave birds, I found the magic of Dublin. Oh, and for those that doubt it, there really IS a pub on every corner!"

—Green Dragon

WELCOME TO DUBLIN

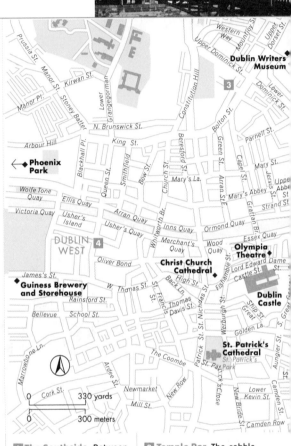

TOP REASONS TO GO

★ **Georgian Elegance:** Dublin's signature architectural style makes its most triumphant showing in Merrion, Fitzwilliam, Mountjoy, and Parnell squares.

★ **The Guinness Brewery and Storehouse:** A high-tech museum tells the story of Guinness, Dublin's black blood. At the top, the Gravity Bar has the city's best views.

★ **Toe-Tapping "Trad.":** If your head is still throbbing from last night's sing-along at the pub, head to other music-mad venues like the Olympia Theatre, where local traditional folk acts and international artists often share the stage.

★ **Temple Bar:** This hyper-trendy neighborhood has two identities: quirky shopping district by day, raucous pub quarter by night.

★ **Trinity College:** An oasis of books, granite, and grass sits at the heart of the city. Highlights are the exquisitely illustrated *Book of Kells* and the ornate Long Room.

1 The Southside. Between **Christ Church Cathedral** and **Trinity College** lies a concentration of famous sights. **Merrion Square** is the heart of the Georgian district; to its west, four major museums sit side by side. Southwest from there is quaint **St. Stephen's Green,** which connects to Trinity via stylish, pedestrian-only **Grafton Street.**

2 Temple Bar. The cobblestone streets and small lanes bounded by Wellington Quay and Dame Street have been transformed into Dublin's trendiest neighborhood. The nightlife doesn't stop at "last call," and on weekends the streets are packed with young people from all over Europe.

2

GETTING ORIENTED

Despite the hustle and bustle generated by Ireland's flourishing economy, Dublin remains an intimate capital that mixes elegant Georgian buildings, wrought-iron bridges, an army of booksellers, and more than 1,000 pubs. The heart of the city is the river Liffey, which runs east to west, splitting Dublin neatly in two. The more affluent Southside has a greater concentration of sights, and it can seem a world apart from the more working-class (though increasingly gentrified) Northside. North or south, Dublin is compact and easily navigated, making it a great walking city.

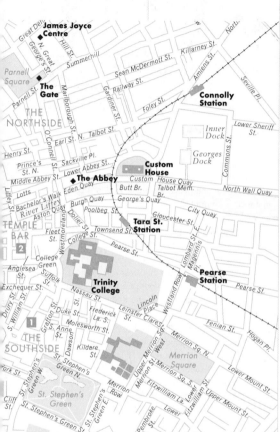

3 The Northside. Less affluent but more eloquent than the Southside, this neighborhood was once home to James Joyce; today it's the site of the **Dublin Writers Museum** and the **James Joyce Centre.** Other highlights are the grand **Custom House,** historic **O'Connell Street,** and Dublin's two great theaters, the **Abbey,** and the **Gate.**

4 Dublin West. This former industrial district stretches from **Christ Church** west to that other Dublin shrine, the **Guinness Brewery.** Imposing **Dublin Castle** houses the **Chester Beatty Library**—arguably the most impressive museum in Ireland. **Phoenix Park,** Europe's largest public city park, hugs the north bank of the Liffey.

DUBLIN PLANNER

Getting Around

Central Dublin is compact, so walking is the first choice for getting pretty much everywhere. Main thoroughfares can become crowded with pedestrians, especially at rush hour, so if you prefer less bustle, plan routes along quieter side streets. When your feet need a break, turn to public transit. There's an extensive network of buses (mainly green double-deckers), and the pleasant LUAS tram system has two lines running through the city center. You can hail a taxi, or phone a taxi company. Because they're allowed to use bus lanes, taxis get through traffic faster than private vehicles do. For the details about getting around, see "Transportation" in the Essentials section at the end of this chapter.

Day-tripping on the DART

The DART (Dublin Area Rapid Transit) train line is great for jaunts out of the city. It runs from the fishing village of Howth, at the northern tip of Dublin Bay, south to the seaside resort of Bray in Wicklow. The route hugs the coastline, providing one spectacular view after another. And with tickets running a little over €3, the price is right.

Making the Most of Your Time

The city-center area south of the Liffey is a logical place to begin your exploration of Dublin: many of the top sights are there, set among graceful squares and terraces dating from the city's elegant Georgian heyday. You haven't really seen Dublin until you've toured this area.

Begin at **O'Connell Bridge**—the closest thing Dublin has to a central landmark—and head south down Westmoreland Street to view the **Bank of Ireland,** one of Dublin's most spectacular buildings. Across the street is the genteel campus of **Trinity College,** where your priority should be the Old Library, with its staggering Long Room and Ireland's greatest art treasure, the *Book of Kells.*

From there, a stroll along **Grafton Street,** Dublin's busiest shopping avenue, brings you to lovely **St. Stephen's Green.** At the Green's northeast corner you'll find the epicenter Dublin cultural institutions: standing side by side are the **National Museum of Archaeology and History,** the **National Gallery of Ireland, the National Library,** and the **National Museum of Natural History.**

Other "must sees" on the Southside are nearby **Merrion Square,** the happening **Temple Bar** district along the Liffey's banks, and, farther west, **St. Patrick's Cathedral,** the **Guinness Brewery and Storehouse,** and the **Chester Beatty Library**—a gem of a museum. Cross the river to experience the grittier (though gentrifying) side of central Dublin. It's here that Dublin's literary heart beats strongest—the **Dublin Writers Museum** is a highlight, and the area is filled with landmarks from events in Irish literary history, both real and imagined. (⇨ Check out "Literary Dublin" later in this chapter.)

Meeting the Dubs

The most appealing thing about Dublin isn't the sights, or even the great pubs and restaurants. It's the people—the citizens, the Dubs. They're fun, funny, and irreverent, and most of them love nothing better than talking to strangers. So, to get the most out of your visit, make a point of rubbing elbows with the locals. The pub is a natural spot to do this (⇨see "A Trip to the Pub" later in this chapter), but almost any place will suffice. Ask for directions on a street corner (even if you don't need them), and you might be on your way to a brilliant conversation.

Mind the Slag

"Slagging" is the Dubliner's favorite type of humor. It consists of mildly—or not so mildly—insulting a friend or a soon-to-be-friend in sharp but jovial fashion. It's best employed to deflate vanity or hubris, but clearly marks out the victim as well-liked and worthy. Packed buses and late-night chip shops are classic slagging venues.

Dublin with a Guiding Hand

Dublin is a walkers' city, and it's a city full of storytellers. Put two and two together, and it's little surprise that Dublin is a particularly good place for guided walking tours. There are scores of informative, jovial guides eager to reveal the mysteries of "dirty, darling Dublin"—*specific recommendations are found under "Contacts & Resources" in the Essentials section at the end of this chapter*. Tours usually have a theme that falls into one of three categories: history, culture, or music. While you're learning about the city and getting to know a garrulous local, you can also swap stories and recommendations with other visitors along for the walk.

How's the Weather?

When is it best—and worst—to pay a call on the Irish capital? The summer offers a real lift, as the natives spill out of the pubs into the slew of sidewalk cafés and open-air restaurants. The week around St. Patrick's Day (March 17th) is, naturally, a nonstop festival of parades, cultural happenings, and "hooleys" (long nights of partying) throughout the city.

Christmas in Dublin seems to last a month, and the city's old-style illuminations match the genteel, warm mood of the locals. The downside quickly follows, however, for January and February are damp hangover months.

A warm sweater is a must all year round, as even summer nights can occasionally get chilly. Dublin gets its share of rain (though a lot less than other parts of Ireland), so an umbrella is a good investment—and best to make it a strong one, as the winds show no mercy to cheaper models.

Updated by
Anto Howard

IN HIS INIMITABLE, IRRESISTIBLE WAY, James Joyce immortalized the city of Dublin in *Ulysses, Dubliners,* and *A Portrait of the Artist as a Young Man,* filling these works with the people he knew, speaking in their own words, and adding many more of his own. Disappointed with the city's provincial outlook and small-town manners, he left it in 1902, at the age of 20 (his famed peers Sean O'Casey and Samuel Beckett soon followed). Later he said he chose Dublin as the setting for his work because it was a "center of paralysis" where nothing much ever changed. Which only proves that even the greats get it wrong sometimes. Indeed, if Joyce were to return to his once genteel home-town today and take a quasi-Homeric odyssey through the city (as he so famously does in *Ulysses*), would he even recognize Dublin as his "Dear Dirty Dumpling, foostherfather of fingalls and dotthergills"?

For instance, what would he make of Temple Bar—the city's erstwhile down-at-the-heels neighborhood, now crammed with restaurants and trendy hotels in its made-over state as Dublin's "Left Bank"? Or the old market area of Smithfield, whose Cinderella transformation has changed it into an impressive plaza and winter ice-skating venue? Or of the new Irishness, where every aspect of Celtic culture results in sold-out theaters, from Martin McDonagh's Broadway hit *The Beauty Queen of Leenane,* to *Riverdance,* the old Irish mass-jig recast as a Las Vegas extravaganza? Plus, the resurrected Joyce might be stirred by the songs of U2, fired up by the sultry acting of Colin Farrell, and moved by the poems of Nobel laureate Seamus Heaney. In short, Irish is cool. As for Ireland's capital, elegant shops and hotels, galleries, art-house cinemas, coffeehouses, and a stunning variety of restaurants are spring-ing up on almost every street in Dublin, transforming the genteel city that suffocated Joyce into a place almost as cosmopolitan as the Paris to which he fled.

Dublin's popularity has provoked a few of its citizens to protest that the rapid transformation of their heretofore tranquil city has changed its spirit and character. Mundane topics like "house prices" and "the bloody traffic" have found their way into pub conversation. These skeptics (skepticism long being a favorite pastime in the capital city) await the outcome of "Dublin: The Sequel"—can the "new Dublin" get beyond the rage stage without losing its very essence? Their greatest fear is the possibility that the tattered old lady on the Liffey is becom-ing like everywhere else.

Oh ye of little faith: the rare aul' gem that is Dublin is far from buried. The fundamentals—the Georgian elegance of Merrion Square, the Nor-man drama of Christ Church Cathedral, the foamy pint at an atmo-spheric pub—are still on hand to gratify. Most of all, there are the locals themselves: the nod and grin when you catch their eye on the street, the eagerness to hear half your life story before they tell you all of theirs, and their paradoxically dark but warm sense of humor.

Dublin Past & Present

Until 500 AD, Dublin was little more than a crossroads—albeit a critical one—for four of the main thoroughfares that traversed the country. It had two names: Baile Atha Cliath, meaning City of the Hurdles, bestowed by Celtic traders in the 2nd century AD; and Dubhlinn, or "dark pool," after a body of water believed to have been where Dublin Castle now stands.

In 837, Norsemen carried out the first invasion of Dublin, to be followed by new waves of warriors staking their claim to the city—from the 12th-century Anglo-Normans to Oliver Cromwell in 1651. Not until the 18th century did Dublin reach a golden age, when the patronage of wealthy nobles turned the city into one of Europe's most prepossessing capitals. But the aura of "the glorious eighteenth" was short-lived; in 1800, the Act of Union brought Ireland and Britain together in a United Kingdom, and power moved to London.

The 19th century proved to be a time of political turmoil, although Daniel O'Connell, the first Catholic lord mayor of Dublin, won early success with the introduction of Catholic Emancipation in 1829. During the late 1840s, Dublin escaped the worst effects of the famine that ravaged much of southern and western Ireland.

The city entered another period of upheaval in the first decades of the 20th century, marked by the Easter Uprising of 1916. A war for independence from Britain began in 1919, followed by establishment of the Irish Free State in December 1921 and subsequent civil war. In its aftermath Dublin entered an era of political and cultural conservatism, which continued until the late 1970s. A major turning point occurred in 1972, when Ireland joined the European Economic Community. In the 1980s, while the economy remained in recession, Irish musicians stormed the American and British barricades of rock-and-roll music, with U2 climbing to the topmost heights.

The 1990s and first years of the 21st century have truly been Ireland's boom time, set in motion to a great extent by the country's participation in the European Union. When Ireland approved the new EU treaty in 1992, it was one of the poorest member nations, qualifying it for grants of all kinds. Since then, Ireland has transformed itself into the economic envy of the world, propelled by massive investment from multinational corporations, particularly in the telecommunications, software, and service industries. In 2000 the government announced that Ireland was the world's largest exporter of software. Recent years have seen a slight leveling off after years of such rapid growth that local wags suggest the economy needs to be tested for steroids.

Today, roughly a third of the Irish Republic's 4.1 million people live in Dublin and its suburbs. It's a city of young people—astonishingly so. Students from all over Ireland attend Trinity College and the city's dozen other universities. After graduating, more and more stick around, filling the new jobs and contributing to the hubbub.

EXPLORING DUBLIN

"In Dublin's fair city, where the girls are so pretty"—so went the centuries-old ditty. Today, there are parts of the city that may not be fair or pretty, but although you may not be conscious of it while you're in the center city, Dublin *does* boast a beautiful setting: it loops around the edge of Dublin Bay and on a plain at the edge of the gorgeous, green Dublin and Wicklow mountains, which rise softly just to the south. From the famous Four Courts building in the heart of town, the sight of the city, the bay, and the mountains will take your breath away. From the city's noted vantage points, such as the South Wall, which stretches far out into Dublin Bay, you can nearly get a full measure of the city. From north to south, Dublin stretches 16 km (10 mi); in total, it covers 28,000 acres—but Dublin's heart is far more compact than these numbers indicate. Like Paris, London, and Florence, a river runs right through it. The river Liffey divides the capital into the Northside and the Southside, as everyone calls the two principal center-city areas, and virtually all the major sights are well within less than an hour's walk of one another.

Our coverage in this chapter is organized into six sections exploring the main neighborhoods of Dublin city (plus one excursion into the northern suburbs of County Dublin). The first two sections—The Southside and Southeast Dublin—focus on many of the city center's major sights: Trinity College, St. Stephen's Green, Merrion Square, and Grafton Street. The third section, Temple Bar, takes you through this revived neighborhood, still the hippest zone in the capital. The Northside section covers major cultural sights north of the Liffey and east of Capel Street, including the James Joyce Centre, Gate Theatre, Dublin Writers Museum, and the Hugh Lane Municipal Gallery of Modern Art. It also includes the majestic Customs House and the rapidly developing, high-rise Docklands area near the mouth of the river. The next section, Dublin West, picks up across Dame Street from Temple Bar and continues west though the historic, working-class Liberties neighborhood to the Guinness Brewery and Storehouse, the city's most popular attraction. In addition, it includes the two main cathedrals and the rapidly developing Smithfield district, which locals are hailing as the future "Temple Bar of the Northside." Finally, the Phoenix Park and Environs section covers the most western fringe of the Northside and the great public park itself. If you're planning to take in all the sights, you may wish to invest in the city's special tourist ticket, the **Dublin Pass**; for more information, *see* Contacts & Resources *in* the Essentials section at the end of this chapter.

If you're visiting Dublin for more than two or three days, you'll have time to explore farther afield. There's plenty to see and do a short distance from the city center—in the suburbs of County Dublin. Worthwhile destinations in these parts of the county are covered in the Side Trips section.

DUBLIN'S SOUTHSIDE: TRINITY COLLEGE TO ST. STEPHEN'S GREEN

The river Liffey provides a useful aid of orientation, flowing as it does through the direct middle of Dublin. If you ask a native Dubliner for directions—from under an umbrella, as it will probably be raining in the approved Irish manner—he or she will most likely reply in terms of "up" or "down," up meaning away from the river, and down towards it. Until recently, Dublin's center of gravity had been O'Connell Bridge, a diplomatic landmark in that it avoided locating the center either north or south of the river—strong local loyalties still prevailed among "Northsiders" and "Southsiders," and neither group would ever accept that the city's center lay elsewhere than on their own side. The 20th century, however, saw diplomacy fall by the wayside—Dublin's heart now beats loudest southward across the Liffey, due in part to a large-scale refurbishment and pedestrianization of Grafton Street, which made this already upscale shopping address the main street on which to shop, stop, and be seen. At the foot of Grafton Street is the city's most famous and recognizable landmark, Trinity College; at the top of it is Dublin's most popular strolling retreat, St. Stephen's Green, a 27-acre landscaped park with flowers, lakes, bridges, and Dubliners enjoying their time-outs.

Numbers in the margin correspond to numbers on the Dublin Southside map.

TIMING   To merely walk the streets of Dublin's compact city center would take only an hour, but it is so crammed with pleasures and treasures, you'll want to set aside at least a half a day to explore it. After all, Trinity College can easily take an hour or two. And who would ever want to rush up Grafton Street? Take a leisurely amble and then stroll through St. Stephen's Green for a fitting finale.

THE MAIN ATTRACTIONS

❷ Bank of Ireland. Across the street from the west facade of Trinity College stands one of Dublin's most striking buildings, formerly the original home of Irish Parliament. Sir Edward Lovett Pearce designed the central section in 1729; three other architects would ultimately be involved in the remainder of the building's construction. A pedimented portico fronted by six massive Corinthian columns dominates the grand facade, which follows the curve of Westmoreland Street as it meets College Green, once a Viking meeting place and burial ground. Two years after Parliament was abolished in 1801 under the Act of Union,

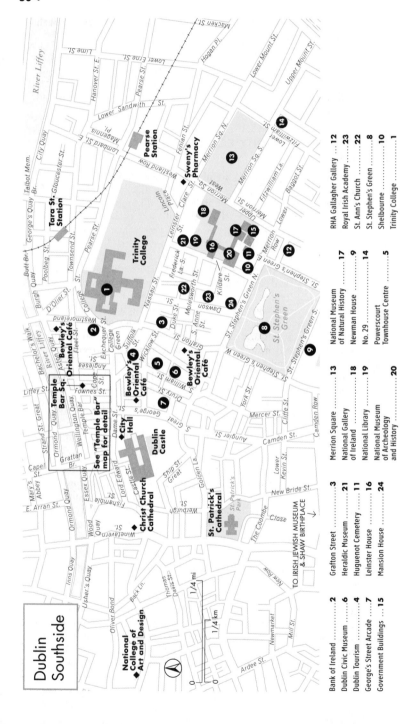

Dublin Southside

Bank of Ireland **2**
Dublin Civic Museum **6**
Dublin Tourism **4**
George's Street Arcade ... **7**
Government Buildings ... **15**

Grafton Street **3**
Heraldic Museum **21**
Huguenot Cemetery **11**
Leinster House **16**
Mansion House **24**

Merrion Square **13**
National Gallery
of Ireland **18**
National Library **19**
National Museum
of Archeology
and History **20**

National Museum
of Natural History **17**
Newman House **9**
No. 29 .... **14**
Powerscourt
Townhouse Centre **5**

RHA Gallagher Gallery ... **12**
Royal Irish Academy **23**
St. Ann's Church **22**
St. Stephen's Green **8**
Shelbourne **10**
Trinity College **1**

which brought Ireland under the direct rule of Britain, the building was bought for the equivalent of €50,790 by the Bank of Ireland. Inside, stucco rosettes adorn the coffered ceiling in the pastel-hued, colonnaded, clerestoried main banking hall, at one time the Court of Requests, where citizens' petitions were heard. Just down the hall is the original House of Lords, with an oak-panel nave, a 1,233-drop Waterford glass chandelier, and tapestries depicting the Battle of the Boyne and the Siege of Derry; ask a guard to show you in. Visitors are welcome during normal banking hours; the Dublin historian and author Éamonn Mac Thomáis conducts brief guided tours every Tuesday at 10:30, 11:30, and 1:45. Accessed via Foster Place South, the small alley on the bank's east flank, the Bank of Ireland Arts Centre frequently mounts displays of contemporary Irish art and has a permanent exhibition, "Journey Through 200 Years." ⊠*2 College Green, Southside* 🕾*01/661–5933 bank, 01/671–1488 Arts Centre* ⊕*www.visitdublin. com* 🖃*Bank free, Arts Centre €1.50* ⊙*Bank Mon.–Wed. and Fri. 10–4, Thurs. 10–5; Arts Centre Tues.–Fri. 9:30–4.*

❸ Grafton Street. It's no more than 200 yards long and about 20 feet wide, but brick-lined Grafton Street, open only to pedestrians, can claim to be the most humming street in the city, if not in all of Ireland. It's one of Dublin's vital spines: the most direct route between the front door of Trinity College and St. Stephen's Green, and the city's premier shopping street, with Dublin's most distinguished department store, Brown Thomas, as well as tried and trusted Marks & Spencer. Grafton Street and the smaller alleyways that radiate off it offer dozens of independent stores, a dozen or so colorful flower sellers, and some of the Southside's most popular watering holes. In summer, buskers from all over the world line both sides of the street, pouring out the sounds of drum, whistle, pipe, and string.

NEED A BREAK? The granddaddy of the capital's cafés, **Bewley's Oriental Café** (⊠ *78 Grafton St., Southside* 🕾*01/677–6761*) recently came within a heartbeat of extinction, after having served coffee and sticky buns to Dubliners since its founding by the Quakers in 1842. Fortunately, the old dame has been saved and turned into a combination café, pizza, and pasta joint, with a quality fish restaurant on the first floor. Best of all, the new owners have brought back some of the old grandeur associated with Bewley's, including the exotic picture wallpaper and trademark stained-glass windows, designed by the distinguished early-20th-century artist Harry Clarke. The place is worth a visit if only to sit in the super-comfortable velvet seats over a cup of quality coffee, and people-watch just like Dubliners have for well over 150 years. There's even a cute little theater upstairs with lunchtime shows. The ticket price (€14) includes homemade soup and a sandwich.

❾ Newman House. One of the greatest glories of Georgian Dublin, Newman House is actually two imposing town houses joined together. The earlier of the two, No. 85 St. Stephen's Green (1738), was originally known as Clanwilliam House. Designed by Richard Castle, favored architect of Dublin's rich and famous, it features a winged Palladian window on the Wicklow granite facade. It has two landmarks of Irish Georgian style: the Apollo Room, decorated with stuccowork depicting the sun god and his muses; and the magnificent Saloon, "the supreme example of Dublin Baroque," according to scholars Jacqueline O'Brien and Desmond Guinness. The Saloon is crowned with an exuberant ceiling aswirl with cupids and gods, created by the Brothers Lafranchini, the finest *stuccadores* (plaster-workers) of 18th-century Dublin. Next door at No. 86 (1765), the staircase, on pastel walls, is one of the city's most beautiful Rococo examples—with floral swags and musical instruments picked out in cake-frosting white. Catholic University (described by James Joyce in *A Portrait of the Artist as a Young Man*) was established in this building in 1850, with Cardinal John Henry Newman as its first rector. To explore the houses you must join a guided tour. At the back of Newman House lies Iveagh Gardens, a delightful hideaway with statues and sunken gardens that remains one of Dublin's best-kept secrets (you can enter via Earlsfort Terrace and Harcourt Street). ⊠ *85–86 St. Stephen's Green, Southside* ☎ *01/716-7422* ⊕ *www.visitdublin.com* ⊡ *House and garden €5* ☉ *Tours June–Aug., Tues.–Fri. at 2, 3, and 4.*

❺ Powerscourt Townhouse Centre. Lucky man, the Viscount Powerscourt. In the mid-18th century, not only did he build Ireland's most spectacular country house, in Enniskerry, County Wicklow (which bears the family name), but he also decided to rival that structure's grandeur with one of Dublin's largest stone mansions. Staffed with 22 servants and built of granite from the viscount's quarry in the Wicklow Hills, Powerscourt House was a major statement in the Palladian style. Designed by Robert Mack in 1771, it's a massive edifice that towers over the little street it sits on (note the top story, framed by large volutes, which was intended as an observatory). Inside, there are Rococo salons designed by James McCullagh, splendid examples of plasterwork in the Adamesque style and—surprise!—a shopping atrium, installed in and around the covered courtyard. The stores here include high-quality Irish crafts shops and numerous food stalls. The mall exit leads to the Carmelite Church of St. Teresa's and Johnson's Court. Beside the church, a pedestrian lane leads onto Grafton Street. ⊠ *59 S. William St., Southside* ☎ *01/679-7000* ⊕ *www.powerscourtcentre.com* ☉ *Mon.–Wed. and Fri. 10–6, Thurs. 10–8, Sat. 9–9, Sun. noon–6; limited shops open Sun.*

❽ St. Stephen's Green. Dubliners call it simply Stephen's Green, and green it is (year-round)—a verdant, 27-acre Southside square that was used for the public punishment of criminals until 1664. After a long period of decline, it became a private park in 1814—the first time in its history that it was closed to the public. Its fortunes changed again in 1880, when Sir Arthur Guinness (a member of the Guinness brewery family who was

Fodor'sChoice ★

2

later known as Lord Ardiluan), paid for it to be laid out anew. Flower gardens, formal lawns, a Victorian bandstand, and an ornamental lake with lots of waterfowl are all within the park's borders, connected by paths guaranteeing that strolling here or just passing through will offer up unexpected delights (such as palm trees). Among the park's many statues are a memorial to Yeats and another to Joyce by Henry Moore, and the *Three Fates,* a dramatic group of bronze female figures watching over human destiny. In the 18th century the walk on the north side of the green was referred to as the Beaux Walk because most of Dublin's gentlemen's clubs were in town houses here. Today it's dominated by the legendary Shelbourne Hotel. On the south side is the alluring Georgian-gorgeous Newman House. ☜*Free* ⊘ *Daily sunrise–sunset.*

🔟 **Shelbourne.** After a two-year, multi-million-euro refurbishment, the red-brick, white-wood-trim Shelbourne Hotel is open, and once again, it commands "the best address in Dublin" from the north side of St. Stephen's Green, as it has since 1865. The new restaurant and lounge, and the completely redesigned guest rooms and public spaces constitute a major face-lift for Dublin's most iconic hotel. Afternoon tea in the truly opulent Lord Mayor's Lounge is a true Dublin treat to be enjoyed by all. In 1921 the Irish Free State's constitution was drafted here, in a first-floor suite. Elizabeth Bowen wrote her novel *The Hotel* about this very place. ✉*27 St. Stephen's Green, Southside* ☎*01/676–6471* ⊕*www.marriott.com.*

① **Trinity College.** Founded in 1592 by Queen Elizabeth I to "civilize" (Her Majesty's word) Dublin, Trinity is Ireland's oldest and most famous college. The memorably atmospheric campus is a must; here you can track the shadows of some of the noted alumni, such as Jonathan Swift (1667–1745), Oscar Wilde (1854–1900), Bram Stoker (1847–1912), and Samuel Beckett (1906–89). Trinity College, Dublin (familiarly known as TCD), was founded on the site of the confiscated Priory of All Hallows. For centuries Trinity was the preserve of the Protestant Church; a free education was offered to Catholics—provided that they accepted the Protestant faith. As a legacy of this condition, until 1966 Catholics who wished to study at Trinity had to obtain a dispensation from their bishop or face excommunication.

Fodor'sChoice
★

Trinity's grounds cover 40 acres. Most of its buildings were constructed in the 18th and early 19th centuries. The extensive **West Front,** with a classical pedimented portico in the Corinthian style, faces College Green and is directly across from the Bank of Ireland; it was built between 1755 and 1759, and is possibly the work of Theodore Jacobsen, architect of London's Foundling Hospital. The design is repeated on the interior, so the view is the same from outside the gates and from the quadrangle inside. On the lawn in front of the inner facade stand statues of two alumni, orator Edmund Burke (1729–97) and dramatist Oliver Goldsmith (1730–74). Like the West Front, **Parliament Square** (commonly known as Front Square), the cobblestone quadrangle that lies just beyond this first patch of lawn, dates from the 18th century. On the right side of the square is Sir William Chambers's theater, or Examination Hall, dating from the mid-1780s, which contains the college's most splendid Adamesque interior, designed by Michael Stapleton. The hall houses an impressive organ retrieved from an 18th-century Spanish ship and a gilded oak chandelier from the old House of Commons; concerts are sometimes held here. The chapel, left of the quadrangle, has stucco ceilings and fine woodwork. The theater and the chapel were designed by Scotsman William Chambers in the late 18th century. The looming campanile, or bell tower, is the symbolic heart of the college; erected in 1853, it dominates the center of the square. To the left of the campanile is the Graduates Memorial Building, or GMB. Built in 1892, the slightly Gothic building now contains the offices of Philosophical and Historical societies, Trinity's ancient and fiercely competitive debating groups. At the back of the square stands old redbrick Rubrics, looking rather ordinary and out of place among the gray granite and cobblestones. Rubrics, now used as housing for students and faculty, dates from 1690, making it the oldest campus building still standing.

The **Old Library** houses Ireland's largest collection of books and manuscripts; its principal treasure is the *Book of Kells,* generally considered to be the most striking manuscript ever produced in the Anglo-Saxon world and one of the great masterpieces of early Christian art. The book, which dates to the 9th century, is a splendidly illuminated version of the Gospels. It was once thought to be lost—the Vikings looted the book in 1007 for its jeweled cover but ultimately left the manuscript behind. In the 12th century, Guardius Cambensis declared that the book was made by an angel's hand in answer to a prayer of St. Bridget; in the 20th century, scholars decided instead that the book originated on the island of Iona off Scotland's coast, where followers of St. Columba lived until the island came under siege in the early to mid-9th century. They fled to Kells, County Meath, taking the book with them. The 680-page work was re-bound in four volumes in 1953, two of which are usually displayed at a time, so you typically see no more than four original pages. (Some wags have taken to calling it the "Page of Kells.") However, such is the incredible workmanship of the *Book of Kells* that one folio alone is worth the entirety of many other painted manuscripts. On some pages, it has been determined that within a quarter inch, no fewer than 158 interlacements of a ribbon pattern of white lines on a black background can be discerned—little wonder some historians feel this book contains all the designs to be found in Celtic art. Note, too, the extraordinary colors, some of which were derived from shellfish, beetles' wings, and crushed pearls. The most famous page shows the "XPI" monogram (symbol of Christ), but if this page is not on display, you can still see a replica of it, and many of the other lavishly illustrated pages, in the adjacent exhibition—dedicated to the history, artistry, and conservation of the book—through which you must pass to see the originals.

Because of the fame and beauty of the *Book of Kells*—now the centerpiece of an exhibition called "Turning Darkness into Light"—it's all too easy to overlook the other treasures in the library. They include a beautiful early Irish harp, the *Book of Armagh,* a 9th-century copy of the New Testament that also contains St. Patrick's Confession, and the

2

legendary *Book of Durrow,* a 7th-century Gospel book from County Offaly. You may have to wait in line to enter the library if you don't get there early in the day.

The main library room, also known as the **Long Room,** is one of Dublin's most staggering sights. At 213 feet long and 42 feet wide, it contains in its 21 alcoves approximately 200,000 of the 3 million volumes in Trinity's collection. Originally

the room had a flat plaster ceiling, but in 1859–60 the need for more shelving resulted in a decision to raise the level of the roof and add the barrel-vault ceiling and the gallery bookcases. Since the 1801 Copyright Act, the college has received a copy of every book published in Britain and Ireland, and a great number of these publications must be stored in other parts of the campus and beyond. Of note are the carved Royal Arms of Queen Elizabeth I above the library entrance—the only surviving relic of the original college buildings—and, lining the Long Room, a grand series of marble busts, of which the most famous is Roubiliac's depiction of Jonathan Swift. The Trinity College Library Shop sells books, clothing, jewelry, and postcards. ⊠*Front Sq., Southside* ☎*01/896–2320* ⊕*www.tcd.ie/library* ☎€8 ⊙*May–Sept., Mon.–Sat. 9:30–5, Sun. 9:30–4:30; Oct.–Apr., Mon.–Sat. 9:30–5, Sun. noon–4:30.* Trinity College's starkly modern Arts and Social Sciences Building, with an entrance on Nassau Street, houses the **Douglas Hyde Gallery of Modern Art,** which concentrates on contemporary art exhibitions and has its own bookstore. Also in the building, down some steps from the gallery, is a snack bar serving coffee, tea, and sandwiches, where students willing to chat about life in the old college frequently gather. ⊠*Nassau St., Southside* ☎*01/896–1116* ⊕*www.douglashydegallery.com* ☎*Free* ⊙*Mon.–Wed. and Fri. 11–6, Thurs. 11–7, Sat. 11–4:45.* The **Berkeley Library,** the main student library at Trinity, was built in 1967 and named after the philosopher and alumnus George Berkeley (pronounced "Barkley," like the basketball player). The small open space in front of the library contains a spherical brass sculpture designed by Arnaldo Pomodoro. A very modern, sleek extension dominates the Nassau Street side of the campus. The library is not open to the public. ⊠*Nassau St., Southside* ☎*01/896–1661* ⊕*www.tcd.ie* ⊙*Grounds daily 8* AM*–10* PM. In the Thomas Davis Theatre in the arts building, the **"Dublin Experience,"** a 45-minute audiovisual presentation, explains the history of the city over the last 1,000 years. ⊠*Nassau St., Southside* ☎*01/608–1688* ☎*€5* ⊙*Mid May–early Oct., daily 10–5; shows every hr on the hr.*

ALSO WORTH SEEING

6 **Dublin Civic Museum.** Built between 1765 and 1771 as an exhibition hall for the Society of Artists, this building later was used as the City Assembly House, precursor of City Hall. The museum's esoteric collection includes Stone Age flints, Viking coins, old maps and prints of the city, and the sculpted head of British admiral Horatio Nelson, which used to top Nelson's Pillar, beside the General Post Office on O'Connell Street; the column was toppled by an IRA explosion in 1966 on the 50th anniversary of the Easter Uprising. The museum also holds temporary exhibitions relating to the city. ⊠*58 S. William St., Southside* ☎*01/679–4260* ⊕*www.dublincity.ie* 🎫*Free* ☉*Tues.–Sat. 10–6, Sun. 11–2.*

❹ Dublin Tourism. Medieval St. Andrew's Church, deconsecrated and fallen into ruin, has been resurrected as the home of Dublin Tourism, a private organization that provides the most complete information on Dublin's sights, restaurants, and hotels; you can even rent a car here. The office has reservations facilities for all Dublin hotels, as well as guided tours, a plethora of brochures, and a gift shop. A pleasant café upstairs serves sandwiches and drinks. ⊠*St. Andrew's Church, Suffolk St., Southside* ☎*01/605–7700, 1850/230–330 in Ireland* ⊕*www.visitdublin.com* ☉*July–Sept., Mon.–Sat. 8:30–6, Sun. 11–5:30; Oct.–June, daily 9–6.*

❼ George's Street Arcade. This Victorian covered market fills the block between Drury Street and South Great George's Street. Two dozen or so stalls sell books, prints, clothing (new and secondhand), exotic foodstuffs, and trinkets. ⊠*S. Great George's St., Southside* ☉*Mon.– Sat. 9–6.*

NEED A BREAK?

With its mahogany bar, mirrors, and plasterwork ceilings, the **Long Hall Pub** (⊠*51 S. Great George's St., Southside* ☎*01/475–1590*) is one of Dublin's most ornate traditional taverns. It's a good place to take a break for a cup of tea or a cheeky daytime pint of Guinness.

⓫ Huguenot Cemetery. One of the last such burial grounds in Dublin, this cemetery was used in the late 17th century by French Protestants who had fled persecution in their native land. The cemetery gates are rarely open, but you can view the grounds from the street—it's on the northeast corner across from the square. ⊠*27 St. Stephen's Green N, Southside.*

⓬ RHA Gallagher Gallery. The Royal Hibernian Academy, an old Dublin institution, is housed in a well-lighted building, one of the largest exhibition spaces in the city. Besides its permanent collection, the gallery holds adventurous exhibitions of the best in contemporary art, both from Ireland and abroad. ⊠*15 Ely Pl., off St. Stephen's Green, Southside* ☎*01/661–2558* ⊕*www.royalhibernianacademy.ie* 🎫*Free* ☉*Mon.–Wed., Fri., and Sat. 11–5, Thurs. 11–8, Sun. 2–5.*

SOUTHEAST DUBLIN: MUSEUMS & MARVELS

If there's one travel poster that signifies "Dublin" more than any other, it's the one that depicts 50 or so Georgian doorways—door after colorful door, all graced with lovely fanlights upheld by columns. A building boom began in Dublin in the early 18th century as the Protestant Ascendancy constructed terraced town houses for themselves, and civic structures for their city, in the style that came to be known as Georgian, after the four successive British Georges who ruled from 1714 through

1830. The Georgian architectural rage owed much to architects such as James Gandon and Richard Castle. They and others were influenced by the great Italian Andrea Palladio (1508–80), whose *Four Books of Architecture* were published in the 1720s in London and helped to precipitate the revival of his style, which swept through England and its colonies. Never again would Dublin be so "smart," its visitors' book so full of aristocratic names, its Southside streets so filled with decorum and style. "Serene red and pink houses showed beautifully designed doorways, the one spot of variation in the uniformity of facade," as architectural historian James Reynolds puts it. Today, Dublin's Southside remains a veritable shop window of the Georgian style, though there are many period sights on the Northside as well (for instance, the august interiors of the Dublin Writers Museum and Belvedere College, or James Gandon's great civic structures, the Custom House and the Four Courts, found quayside).

But Georgian splendor is just the icing on the cake of this neighborhood. For there are also four of the most fascinating and glamorous museums in Ireland, conveniently sitting cheek by jowl: the National Gallery of Ireland, the National Library, the National Museum of Natural History, and the National Museum of Archaeology and History. Priceless old master paintings, legendary Celtic treasures, mythic prehistoric "Irish elks," and George Bernard Shaw manuscripts—there is enough here to keep you occupied for days.

Numbers in the margin correspond to numbers on the Dublin Southside map.

TIMING   This area is so compact you could stroll by all of the sights in a couple of hours, if you didn't linger or set foot in the museums. But that is unthinkable—after all, the treasures at the National Gallery and the National Museum of Archaeology and History, and the green tranquility of Merrion Square are some of Dublin's most fabled attractions. In addition, many of Dublin's finest Georgian mansions line these streets (as do dozens of the city's most historic pubs). Take a full day to savor the sights here, then plan on returning to visit your favorites at greater leisure.

THE MAIN ATTRACTIONS

16 Leinster House. Commissioned by the Duke of Leinster and built in 1745, this residence—Dublin's Versailles—almost single-handedly ignited the Georgian style that dominated Dublin for 100 years. It was not only the largest private home in the city but Richard Castle's first structure in Ireland (Castle—or Casells, to use his original German spelling—was a follower of the 16th-century Italian architect Palladio and designed some of the country's most important 18th-century country houses). Inside, the grand salons were ornamented with coffered ceilings, Rembrandts, and Van Dycks—fitting settings for the parties often given by the duke's wife (and celebrated beauty), Lady Emily Lennox. The building has two facades: the one facing Merrion Square is designed in the style of a country house; the other, on Kildare Street, resembles that of a town house. The latter facade—ignoring the ground floor—was a major inspiration for Irishman James Hoban's designs for the White

House in Washington, D.C. Built in hard Ardbracan limestone, the exterior of the house makes a cold impression, and, in fact, the duke's heirs pronounced the house "melancholy" and fled. Today, the house is the seat of Dáil Éireann (the House of Representatives, pronounced dawl *e*-rin) and Seanad Éireann (the Senate, pronounced shanad *e*-rin), which together constitute the Irish Parliament. When the Dáil is not in session, tours can be arranged weekdays; when the Dáil is in session, tours are available only on Monday and Friday. The Dáil visitor gallery is included in the tour, although it can be accessed on days when the Dáil is in session and tours are not available. To arrange a visit, contact the public relations office. ⊠ *Kildare St., Southeast Dublin* ☎ *01/618–3000 public relations office* ⊕ *www.irlgov.ie* ☞ *Free.*

13 Merrion Square. Created between 1762 and 1764, this tranquil square
Fodor'sChoice a few blocks east of St. Stephen's Green is lined on three sides by some
★ of Dublin's best-preserved Georgian town houses, many of which have brightly painted front doors crowned by intricate fanlights. Leinster House, the National Museum of Natural History, and the National Gallery line the west side of the square. It's on the other sides, however, that the Georgian terrace streetscape comes into its own—the finest houses are on the north border. Even when the flower gardens here are not in bloom, the vibrant, mostly evergreen grounds, dotted with sculpture and threaded with meandering paths, are worth strolling through. Several distinguished Dubliners have lived on the square, including Oscar Wilde's parents, Sir William and "Speranza" Wilde (No. 1); Irish national leader Daniel O'Connell (No. 58); and authors W. B. Yeats (Nos. 52 and 82) and Sheridan LeFanu (No. 70). As you walk past the houses, read the plaques on the house facades, which identify former inhabitants. Until 50 years ago the square was a fashionable residential area, but today most of the houses serve as offices. At the south end of Merrion Square, on Upper Mount Street, stands the Church of Ireland St. Stephen's Church. Known locally as the "pepper canister" church because of its cupola, the structure was inspired in part by Wren's churches in London. ⊠ *Southeast Dublin* ☉ *Daily sunrise–sunset.*

18 National Gallery of Ireland. Caravaggio's *The Taking of Christ* (1602),
Fodor'sChoice Van Gogh's *Rooftops of Paris* (1886), Vermeer's *Lady Writing a Letter*
★ *with Her Maid* (circa 1670)…you get the picture. The National Gallery of Ireland—the first in a series of major civic buildings on the west side of Merrion Square—is one of Europe's finer smaller art museums—with "smaller" being a relative term: the collection holds more than 2,500 paintings and some 10,000 other works. But unlike Europe's largest art museums, the National Gallery can be thoroughly covered in a morning or afternoon without inducing exhaustion. An 1854 Act of Parliament provided for the establishment of the museum, which was helped along by William Dargan (1799–1867), who was responsible for building much of Ireland's rail network (he is honored by a statue on the front lawn). The 1864 building was designed by Francis Fowke, who was also responsible for London's Victoria & Albert Museum.

Dublin's Gorgeous Georgians

"Extraordinary Dublin!" sigh art lovers and connoisseurs of the 18th century. It was during the "gorgeous eighteenth" that this duckling of a city was transformed into a preening swan, largely by the Georgian style of art and architecture that flowered between 1714 and 1820 during the reigns of the four English Georges.

Today Dublin remains in good part a sublimely Georgian city, thanks to enduring grace notes: the commodious and uniformly laid out streets, the genteel town squares, the redbrick mansions accented with demilune fan windows. The great 18th-century showpieces are **Merrion, Fitzwilliam, Mountjoy,** and **Parnell squares. Merrion Square East,** the longest Georgian street in town, reveals scenes of decorum, elegance, polish, and charm, all woven into a "tapestry of rosy brick and white enamel," to quote the 18th-century connoisseur Horace Walpole.

Setting off the facades are fanlighted doors (often lacquered in black, green, yellow, or red) and the celebrated "patent reveal" window trims—thin plaster linings painted white to catch the light. These half-moon fanlights—as iconic of the city as clock towers are of Zurich—are often in the Neoclassical style known as the Adamesque (which was inspired by the designs of the great English architect, Robert Adam).

Many facades appear severely plain, but don't be fooled: just behind their stately front doors are entry rooms and stairways aswirl with tinted Rococo plasterwork, often the work of *stuccadores* (plasterworkers) from Italy (including the talented Lafranchini brothers). Magnificent **Newman**

House, one of the finest of Georgian houses, is open to the public. **Belvedere College** (✉ *6 Great Denmark St., Northside* ☎ *01/874–3974*) is open by appointment only.

The Palladian style—as the Georgian style was then called—began to reign supreme in domestic architecture in 1745, when the Croesus-rich earl of Kildare returned from an Italian grand tour and built a gigantic Palladian palace called **Leinster House** in the seedy section of town.

"Where I go, fashion will follow," he declared, and indeed it did. By then, the Anglo-Irish elite had given the city London airs by building the **Parliament House** (now the Bank of Ireland), the **Royal Exchange** (now City Hall), the **Custom House,** and the **Four Courts** in the new style.

But this phase of high fashion came to an end with the Act of Union: according to historian Maurice Craig, "On the last stroke of midnight, December 31, 1800, the gaily caparisoned horses turned into mice, the coaches into pumpkins, the silks and brocades into rags, and Ireland was once again the Cinderella among the nations."

It was nearly 150 years before the spotlight shone once again on 18th-century Dublin. In recent decades, the conservation efforts of the **Irish Georgian Society** (✉ *74 Merrion Sq., Southside* ☎ *01/676–7053* ⊕ *www. irishgeorgiansociety.org*) have done much to restore Dublin to its Georgian splendor. Thanks to its founders, the Hon. Desmond Guinness and his late wife, Mariga, many historic houses including that of George Bernard Shaw on Synge Street, have been saved and preserved.

A highlight of the museum is the major collection of paintings by Irish artists from the 17th through 20th centuries, including works by Roderic O'Conor (1860–1940), Sir William Orpen (1878–1931), and William Leech (1881–1968). The Yeats Museum section contains works by members of the Yeats family. Jack B. Yeats (1871–1957), the brother of writer W.B. Yeats, is by far the best-known Irish painter of the 20th century. Yeats painted portraits and landscapes in an abstract expressionist style not unlike that of the Bay Area Figurative painters of the 1950s and '60s. His *The Liffey Swim* (1923) is particularly worth seeing for its Dublin subject matter (the annual swim is still held, usually on the first weekend in September).

> ### WHAT A CHARACTER!
>
> If you want to size up a real Irish character, check out one of the National Gallery's most eye-knocking paintings, Sir Joshua Reynolds' *First Earl of Bellamont* (1773). Depicted in pink silks and ostrich plumes, Charles Coote was a notorious womanizer (leading to his nickname, the "Hibernian Seducer") and was shot in the groin for his troubles by rival Lord Townshend. Famously, Coote gave his inaugural speech as quartermaster-general of Ireland in *French*, continually referred to his County Cavan neighbors as "Hottentots," and wound up marrying the daughter of the super-rich Duke of Leinster.

The collection also claims exceptional paintings from the 17th-century French, Dutch, Italian, and Spanish schools. Among the highlights are those mentioned above and Rembrandt's *Rest on the Flight into Egypt* (1647), Poussin's *The Holy Family* (1649) and *Lamentation over the Dead Christ* (circa 1655–60), and Goya's *Portrait of Doña Antonia Zárate* (circa 1810). Don't miss the portrait of the *First Earl of Bellamont* (1773) by Sir Joshua Reynolds; the earl was among the first to introduce the Georgian fashion to Ireland, and this portrait flaunts the extraordinary style of the man himself. The French Impressionists are represented with paintings by Monet, Sisley, and Pissarro. The British collection and the Irish National Portrait collection are displayed in the north wing of the gallery, while the Millennium Wing, a standout of postmodern architecture in Dublin, houses part of the permanent collection and also stages major international traveling exhibits. The amply stocked gift shop is a good place to pick up books on Irish artists. Free guided tours are available on Saturday at 3 and on Sunday at 2, 3, and 4. ⊠ *Merrion Sq. W, Southeast Dublin* ☎ *01/661–5133* ⊕ *www.nationalgallery.ie* ⊠ *Free; special exhibits €10* ⊙ *Mon.–Wed., Fri., and Sat. 9:30–5:30, Thurs. 9:30–8:30, Sun. noon–5:30.*

NEED A BREAK?

Fitzer's (⊠ *Merrion Sq. W, Southside* ☎ *01/661–4496*), the National Gallery's self-service restaurant, is a find—one of the city's best spots for an inexpensive, top-rate lunch. The 16 to 20 daily menu items are prepared with an up-to-date take on European cuisine. It's open Monday–Saturday 10–5:30 (lunch is served noon–2:30) and Sunday 2–5.

2

⑲ **National Library.** Happily, Ireland is one of the few countries in the world where you can admit to being a writer. And few countries as geographically diminutive as Ireland have garnered as many recipients of the Nobel Prize for Literature. Along with works by W.B. Yeats (1923), George Bernard Shaw (1925), Samuel Beckett (1969), and Seamus Heaney (1995), the National Library contains first editions of every major Irish writer, including books by Jonathan Swift, Oliver Goldsmith, and James Joyce (who used the library as the scene of the great literary debate in *Ulysses*). In addition, almost every book ever published in Ireland is kept here, along with an unequaled selection of old maps and an extensive collection of Irish newspapers and magazines—more than 5 million items in all.

The library is housed in a rather stiff Neoclassical building with colonnaded porticoes and an excess of ornamentation—it's not one of Dublin's architectural showpieces. But inside, the main Reading Room, opened in 1890 to house the collections of the Royal Dublin Society, has a dramatic domed ceiling, beneath which countless authors have researched and written. The personal papers of greats such as Yeats are also on display. The library also has a free genealogical consultancy service that can advise you on how to trace your Irish ancestors. ⊠ *Kildare St., Southeast Dublin* ☎ *01/603–0200* ⊕ *www.nli.ie* ⊠ *Free* ⊙ *Mon.–Wed. 10–9, Thurs. and Fri. 10–5, Sat. 10–1.*

⑳ **National Museum of Archaeology and History.** Just south of Leinster House
★ is Ireland's National Museum of Archaeology and History, which has a fabled collection of Irish artifacts dating from 7000 BC to the present. Organized around a grand rotunda, the museum is elaborately decorated, with mosaic floors, marble columns, balustrades, and fancy ironwork. It has the largest collection of Celtic antiquities in the world, including gold jewelry, carved stones, bronze tools, and weapons.

The Treasury collection, including some of the museum's most renowned pieces, is open on a permanent basis. Among the priceless relics on display are the late Bronze Age gold collar known as the Gleninsheen Gorget; the 8th-century Ardagh Chalice, a two-handled silver cup with gold filigree ornamentation; the bronze-coated iron St. Patrick's Bell, the oldest surviving example (5th–8th centuries) of Irish metalwork; the 8th-century Tara Brooch, an intricately decorated piece made of white bronze, amber, and glass; and the 12th-century bejeweled oak Cross of Cong, covered with silver and bronze panels.

The Road to Independence Room is devoted to the 1916 Easter Uprising and the War of Independence (1919–21); displays here include uniforms, weapons, banners, and a piece of the flag that flew over the General Post Office during Easter Week, 1916. Upstairs, Viking Age Ireland is a permanent exhibit on the Norsemen, featuring a full-size Viking skeleton, swords, leather works recovered in Dublin and surrounding areas, and a replica of a small Viking boat. The newest attraction is an exhibition entitled "Kinship and Sacrifice," centering on a number of Iron Age "bog bodies" found along with other objects found in Ireland's peat bogs.

In contrast to the ebullient late-Victorian architecture of the main museum building, the design of the National Museum Annex is purely functional; it hosts temporary shows of Irish antiquities. The 18th-century Collins Barracks, near Phoenix Park *(see below)*, houses the National Museum of Decorative Arts and History, a collection of glass, silver, furniture, and other decorative arts. ⊠*Kildare St.; Annex, 7–9 Merrion Row, Southeast Dublin* ☏*01/677-7444* ⊕*www.museum.ie* 🎟*Free* ⊙*Tues.–Sat. 10–5, Sun. 2–5.*

ALSO WORTH SEEING

⑮ **Government Buildings.** The swan song of British architecture in the capital, this enormous complex, a landmark of Edwardian Baroque, was the last Neoclassical edifice to be erected by the British government. It was designed by Sir Aston Webb, who did many of the similarly grand buildings in London's Piccadilly Circus, to serve as the College of Science in the early 1900s. Following a major restoration, these buildings became the offices of the Department of the *taoiseach* (the prime minister, pronounced *tea*-shuck) and the *tánaiste* (the deputy prime minister, pronounced tawn-*ish*-ta). Fine examples of contemporary Irish furniture and carpets populate the offices. A stained-glass window, known as "My Four Green Fields," was made by Evie Hone for the 1939 New York World's Fair. It depicts the four ancient provinces of Ireland: Munster, Ulster, Leinster, and Connacht. The government offices are accessible only via 45-minute guided tours on Saturday, though they are dramatically illuminated every night. ⊠*Upper Merrion St., Southeast Dublin* ☏*01/662–4888* ⊕*www.taoiseach.gov.ie* 🎟*Free; pick up tickets from National Gallery on day of tour* ⊙*Tours Sat. 10:30–3:30.*

㉑ **Heraldic Museum.** Looking for something original for your wall? If you're a Fitzgibbon from Limerick, a Cullen from Waterford, or a McSweeney from Cork, chances are that your family designed, begged, borrowed, or stole a coat of arms somewhere in its history. The Heraldic Museum—the first in the world, founded in 1909—has hundreds of family-crest flags, coins, stamps, and silver, all highlighting the uses and evolution of heraldry in Ireland. ⊠*2 Kildare St., Southeast Dublin* ☏*01/661–4877* ⊕*www.nli.ie/h_muse.htm* 🎟*Free* ⊙*Mon.–Wed. 10–8:30, Thurs. and Fri. 10–4:30, Sat. 10–12:30; guided tours by appointment.*

㉔ **Mansion House.** The mayor of Dublin resides at the Mansion House, which dates from 1710. It was built for Joshua Dawson, who later sold the property to the government on the condition that "one loaf of double refined sugar of six pounds weight" be delivered to him every Christmas. In 1919 the Declaration of Irish Independence was adopted here. The house is not open to the public. ⊠*Dawson St., Southeast Dublin.*

⑰ **National Museum of Natural History.** The famed explorer of the African interior, Dr. Stanley Livingstone (of "Dr. Livingstone, I presume?" fame), inaugurated this museum when it opened in 1857. It's little changed from Victorian times and remains a fascinating repository of mounted mammals, birds, and other flora and fauna. The Irish Room houses the most famous exhibits: skeletons of the extinct, prehistoric, giant

"Irish elk." The International Animals Collection includes a 65-foot whale skeleton suspended from the roof. Don't miss the very beautiful Blaschka Collection, finely detailed glass models of marine creatures, the zoological accuracy of which has never been achieved again in glass. The museum is next door to the Government Buildings. ⊠*Merrion St., Southeast Dublin* ☎*01/677–7444* ⊕*www.museum.ie* ☞*Free* ⊗*Tues.–Sat. 10–5, Sun. 2–5.*

⓮ No. 29. Everything in this carefully refurbished 1794 home, known simply as Number Twenty-Nine, is in keeping with the elegant lifestyle of the Dublin middle class between 1790 and 1820, the height of the Georgian period, when the house was owned by a wine merchant's widow. From the basement to the attic—in the kitchen, nursery, servant's quarters, and the formal living areas—the National Museum has re-created the period's style with authentic furniture, paintings, carpets, curtains, paint, wallpapers, and even bell pulls. ⊠*29 Lower Fitzwilliam St., Southeast Dublin* ☎*01/702–6165* ⊕*www.esb.ie/numbertwentynine* ☞*€5* ⊗*Tues.–Sat. 10–5, Sun. 1–5.*

㉓ Royal Irish Academy. The country's leading learned society houses important documents in its 18th-century library, including a large collection of ancient Irish manuscripts, such as the 11th- to 12th-century *Book of the Dun Cow*, and the library of the 18th-century poet Thomas Moore. ⊠*19 Dawson St., Southeast Dublin* ☎*01/676–2570* ⊕*www. ria.ie* ☞*Free* ⊗*Weekdays 9:30–5.*

㉒ St. Ann's Church. St. Ann's plain, neo-Romanesque granite exterior, built in 1868, belies the rich Georgian interior of the church, which Isaac Wills designed in 1720. Highlights of the interior include polished-wood balconies, ornate plasterwork, and shelving in the chancel dating from 1723—and still in use for organizing the distribution of bread to the parish's poor. ⊠*Dawson St., Southeast Dublin* ☎*01/676-7727* ☞*Free* ⊗*Weekdays 10–4, Sun. for services.*

OFF THE BEATEN PATH

Irish Jewish Museum. Roughly 5,000 European Jews fleeing the pogroms of Eastern Europe arrived in Ireland in the late 19th and early 20th centuries. Today the Jewish population hovers around 1,800. The museum, opened in 1985 by Israeli president Chaim Herzog (himself Dublin educated), includes a restored synagogue and a display of photographs, letters, and personal memorabilia culled from Dublin's most prominent Jewish families. Exhibits trace the Jewish presence in Ireland back to 1067. In homage to Leopold Bloom, the Jewish protagonist of Joyce's *Ulysses,* every Jewish reference in the novel has been identified. The

---

MANSIONS & MOONSHINE

"We passed row after row of identical Georgian houses, all with different brightly painted doors and rounded window arches. The story is that men were too drunk after a night at the pub to know which door was the right one unless it was painted a bright, strong color (red, blue, etc.). I don't know if the story is true, but it certainly makes sense!"

—Green Dragon

museum is a 20-minute-or-so walk southwest from St. Stephen's Green. ⊠*3–4 Walworth Rd., Grand Canal* ☎*01/490–1857* ✉*Free* ⊙*May–Sept., Tues., Thurs., and Sun. 11–3:30; Oct.–Apr., Sun. 10:30–2:30.*

Sandymount Strand. South of the city center, a few blocks west of the Sydney Parade DART station, the Sandymount Strand stretches for 5 km (3 mi) from Ringsend to Booterstown. It was cherished by James Joyce and his beloved, Nora Barnacle from Galway, and it figures as one of the settings in *Ulysses*. (The beach is "at the lacefringe of the tide," as Joyce put it.) When the tide recedes, the beach extends for 1½ km (1 mi) from the foreshore, but the tide sweeps in again very quickly. A sliver of a park lies between Strand Road and the beach, the water of which is not suitable for swimming.

Shaw Birthplace. "Author of many plays" is the simple accolade to George Bernard Shaw (1856–1950) on the plaque outside his birthplace. The Nobel laureate was born here to a once prosperous family fallen on hard times. Shaw lived in this modest, Victorian terrace house until he was 10 and remembered it as having a "loveless" feel. The painstaking restoration of the little rooms highlights the cramped, claustrophobic atmosphere. All the details of a family home—wallpaper, paint, fittings, curtains, furniture, utensils, pictures, rugs—remain, and it appears as if the family has just gone out for the afternoon. You can almost hear one of Mrs. Shaw's musical recitals in the tiny front parlor. The children's bedrooms are filled with photographs and original documents and letters that throw light on Shaw's career. ⊠*33 Synge St., Southeast Dublin* ☎*01/475–0854* ⊕*www.visitdublin.com* ✉*€7* ⊙*May–Sept., Mon., Tues., Thurs. and Fri. 10–1 and 2–5, weekends 2–5.*

TEMPLE BAR: THE CHANGING FACE

Locals complain about the late-night noise, visitors sometimes say the place has the feel of a "Dublin Theme Park," but a visit to modern Dublin wouldn't be complete without spending some time in the city's most vibrant area. More than any other neighborhood in the city, Temple Bar represents the dramatic changes (good and bad) and ascending fortunes of Dublin that came about in the last decade of the 20th century. The area, which takes its name from one of the streets of its central spine, was targeted for redevelopment in 1991–92 after a long period of neglect, having survived widely rumored plans to turn it into a massive bus depot and/or a giant parking lot. Temple Bar took off as Dublin's version of New York's SoHo, Paris's Bastille, London's Notting Hill—a thriving mix of high and alternative culture distinct from what you'll find in any other part of the city. Dotting the area's narrow cobblestone streets and pedestrian alleyways are new apartment buildings (inside they tend to be small and uninspired, though bearing sky-high rents), vintage-clothing stores, postage-stamp-size boutiques selling €250 sunglasses and other expensive gewgaws, art galleries, a hotel resuscitated by U2, hip restaurants, pubs, clubs, European-style cafés, and a smattering of cultural venues.

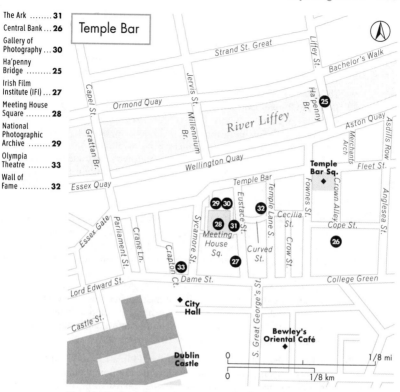

Temple Bar's regeneration was no doubt abetted by that one surefire real estate asset: location. The area is bordered by Dame Street to the south, the Liffey to the north, Fishamble Street to the west, and Westmoreland Street to the east. In fact, Temple Bar is situated so perfectly between everywhere else in Dublin that it's difficult to believe this neighborhood was once largely forsaken. It's now sometimes called the "playing ground of young Dublin," and for good reason: on weekend evenings and daily in summer it teems with young people—not only from Dublin but from all over Europe—drawn by its pubs, clubs, and lively *craic* (good conversation and fun).

Some who have witnessed Temple Bar's rapid gentrification and commercialization complain that it's losing its artistic soul—*Harper's Bazaar* said it was in danger of becoming "a sort of pseudoplace," like London's Covent Garden Piazza or Paris's Les Halles. For some years now there has been talk that the more cautiously developed Smithfield area might replace Temple Bar as the cutting edge of Dublin culture, but for the moment there's no denying that this is one of the best places to get a handle on the city.

Numbers in the margin correspond to numbers on the Temple Bar map.

TIMING You can easily breeze through Temple Bar in an hour or so, but if you've got the time, plan to spend a morning or afternoon here, drifting in and out of the dozens of stores and galleries, relaxing at a café over a cup of coffee or at a pub over a pint. If you're looking for a change from sightseeing, you can even try catching a film.

THE MAIN ATTRACTIONS

30 Gallery of Photography. Dublin's premier photography gallery has a permanent collection of early-20th-century Irish photography and also puts on monthly exhibitions of work by contemporary Irish and international photographers. The gallery is an invaluable social record of Ireland. The bookstore is the best place in town to browse for photography books and to pick up arty postcards. ⌧ *Meeting House Sq. S, Temple Bar* ☎ *01/671–4654* ⊕ *www.galleryofphotography.ie* 🎟 *Free* ⊙ *Tues.–Sat. 11–6, Sun. 1–6.*

25 Ha'penny Bridge. Every Dubliner has a story about meeting someone on this cast-iron Victorian bridge, a heavily trafficked footbridge that crosses the Liffey at a prime spot—Temple Bar is on the south side, and the bridge provides the fastest route to the thriving Mary and Henry Street shopping areas to the north. Until early in the 20th century, a halfpenny toll was charged to cross it. Congestion on the Ha'penny has been relieved with the opening of the Millennium Footbridge a few hundred yards up the river. A refurbishment, including new railings, a return to the original white color, and tasteful lighting at night has given the bridge a new lease on life.

27 Irish Film Institute (IFI). The opening of the IFI in a former Quaker meetinghouse helped to launch the revitalization of Temple Bar. It has two comfortable art-house cinemas showing revivals and new independent films, the Irish Film Archive, a bookstore for cineastes, and a popular bar and restaurant-café, all of which make this one of the neighborhood's most vital cultural institutions and *the* place to be seen. On Saturday nights in summer, the center screens films outdoors on Meeting House Square. ⌧ *6 Eustace St., Temple Bar* ☎ *01/679–5744* ⊕ *www.ifi.ie* 🎟 *Free* ⊙ *Weekdays 9:30 AM–midnight, weekends 11 AM–midnight.*

NEED A BREAK? The trendy **Irish Film Institute Café** (⌧ *6 Eustace St., Temple Bar* ☎ *01/679–5744*) is a pleasant place for a lunchtime break. Sandwiches are large and healthful, with plenty of vegetarian choices, and the people-watching is unmatched.

28 Meeting House Square. The square, which is behind the Ark and accessed via Curved Street, takes its name from a nearby Quaker meetinghouse. Today it's something of a gathering place for Dublin's youth and artists. Numerous summer events—classic movies (Saturday nights), theater, games, and family programs—take place here. (Thankfully, seats are installed.) The square is also a favorite site for the continuously changing street sculpture that pops up all over Temple Bar (artists commissioned by the city sometimes create oddball pieces, such as half of a Volkswagen protruding from a wall). Year-round, the square is a great spot to sit, people-watch, and take in the sounds of the performing buskers who swarm to the place. There's also an organic food market here every Saturday morning and a crafts and furniture market on Sunday.

> **TOO GREAT A TOLL**
>
> William Butler Yeats was one of many Dubliners who found the halfpenny toll of Ha'penny Bridge too steep. He detoured to O'Connell Bridge instead.

③③ ★ **Olympia Theatre.** One of the best places in Europe to see musical acts, the Olympia is Dublin's second-oldest theater, and one of its busiest. This classic Victorian music hall, built in 1879, has a gorgeous red wrought-iron facade. The Olympia's long-standing Friday and Saturday series, "Midnight at the Olympia," has brought numerous musical performers to Dublin, and the theater has also seen many notable actors strut across its stage, including Alec Guinness, Peggy Ashcroft, Noël Coward, and even the old-time Hollywood team of Laurel and Hardy. Big-name performers like Van Morrison often choose the intimacy of the Olympia over larger venues. It's really a hot place to see some fine performances, so if you have a chance, by all means go. Conveniently, there are two pubs here—through doors directly off the back of the theater's orchestra section. ✉ *72 Dame St., Temple Bar* ☎ *01/677–7744* ⊕ *www.mcd.ie/Olympia.*

③② ★ **Wall of Fame.** If you're strolling through Temple Bar and suddenly come upon a group of slack-jawed young people staring wide-eyed at a large wall, then you've probably stumbled upon the Wall of Fame. The whole front wall of the Temple Bar Music Centre has become a giant tribute to the giants of Irish rock music. Twelve huge photos adorn the wall, including a very young and innocent U2, a very beautiful Sinead O'Connor, and a very drunk Shane McGowan. ✉ *Curved St., Temple Bar* ☎ *01/607–9202.*

NEED A BREAK?

The creamiest, frothiest coffees in all of Temple Bar can be had at the **Joy of Coffee/Image Gallery Café** (✉ *25 E. Essex St., Temple Bar* ☎ *01/679–3393*); the wall of windows floods light onto the small gallery, where original photographs adorn the walls.

ALSO WORTH SEEING

③① ♺ **The Ark.** If you're traveling with children and looking for something fun to do, stop by the Ark, Ireland's cultural center for children, housed in a former Presbyterian church. Its theater opens onto Meeting House Square for outdoor performances in summer. A gallery and workshop space host ongoing activities. ✉ *11a Eustace St., Temple Bar* ☎ *01/670–7788* ⊕ *www.ark.ie* ✆ *Free* ☉ *Weekdays 9:30–5:30, weekends only if there's a show.*

②⑥ **Central Bank.** Everyone in Dublin seems to have an opinion on the Central Bank. Designed by Sam Stephenson in 1978, the controversial, ultramodern glass-and-concrete building suspends huge concrete slabs around a central axis. It was originally one story higher, but the top floor had to be lopped off as it was hazardous to low-flying planes. Watch out for—or just watch—the skateboarders and in-line skaters who have taken over on the little plaza in front of the building. ⊠ *Dame St., Temple Bar* ☎ *01/671–6666* ⊕ *www.centralbank.ie* ⊙ *Weekdays 10–6.*

㉙ National Photographic Archive. Formerly housed in the National Library's main building, the National Photographic Archive now has a stylish home in Temple Bar. The collection comprises approximately 600,000 photographs, most of which are Irish, making up a priceless visual history of the nation. Although most of the photographs are historical, dating as far back as the mid-19th century, there's also a large number of contemporary pictures. Subject matter ranges from topographical views to studio portraits, from political events to early tourist photographs. You can also buy a print of your favorite photo. ⊠ *Meeting House Sq., Temple Bar* ☎ *01/603–0374* ⊕ *www.nli.ie/new_archive. htm* ▣ *Free* ⊙ *Weekdays 10–5, Sat. 10–2.*

ACROSS THE LIFFEY: THE NORTHSIDE

"What do you call a Northsider in a suit? The accused." So went the old joke. But old stereotypes about the Northside being Dublin's poorer and more deprived half have been washed away beneath the wave of Celtic Tiger development. Locals and visitors alike are discovering the no-nonsense, laid-back charm of the Northside's revamped Georgian wonders, understated cultural gems, high-quality restaurants, and buzzing ethnic diversity.

If you stand on O'Connell Bridge or the pedestrian-only Ha'penny span, you'll get excellent views up and down the River Liffey, known in Gaelic as the *abha na life,* transcribed phonetically as Anna Livia by James Joyce in *Finnegan's Wake*. Here, framed with embankments like those along Paris's Seine, the river nears the end of its 128-km (80-mi) journey from the Wicklow Mountains to the Irish Sea. And near the bridges, you begin a pilgrimage into James Joyce country—north of the Liffey, in the center of town—and the captivating sights of Dublin's Northside, a mix of densely thronged shopping streets and genteelly refurbished homes.

For much of the 18th century, the upper echelons of Dublin society lived in the Georgian houses in the Northside—around Mountjoy Square—and shopped along Capel Street, which was lined with stores selling fine furniture and silver. But development of the Southside— Merrion Square in 1764, the Georgian Leinster House in 1745, and Fitzwilliam Square in 1825—changed the Northside's fortunes. The city's fashionable social center crossed the Liffey, and although some of the Northside's illustrious inhabitants stuck it out, the area gradually became run-down. The Northside's fortunes have now changed back, however. Once-derelict swaths of houses, especially on and near the Liffey, have been rehabilitated, and large shopping centers have opened on Mary and Jervis streets. The high-rise Docklands area, east of the Custom House, is the new hot place to live and the Abbey Theatre is going to move here in a few years; in addition, the beginnings of a little

Chinatown are forming on Parnell Street, and a ferry taxi on the Liffey will soon connect it with Temple Bar, while a swing bridge has already been added between City Quay and the Northside. A huge shopping mall and entertainment complex is planned for O'Connell Street, right where the defunct Carlton Cinema stands. O'Connell Street itself has been partially pedestrianized, and most impressive of all is the Spire, the street's new 395-foot-high stainless-steel monument. Precisely because the exciting redevelopment that transformed Temple Bar is still in its early stages here—because it's a place on the cusp of transition—the Northside is an intriguing part of town.

Numbers in the margin correspond to numbers on the Dublin Northside map.

The two greatest cultural institutions of the Northside—the Dublin Writers Museum and the Dublin City Gallery, The Hugh Lane—deserve several hours each. Also, a number of additional sights connected with James Joyce and *Ulysses* are in the vicinity, so devoted Joyce fans will want to devote more time to the area.

THE MAIN ATTRACTIONS

48 **Custom House.** Seen at its best when reflected in the waters of the Liffey during the short interval when the high tide is on the turn, the Custom House is the city's most spectacular Georgian building. Extending 375 feet on the north side of the river, this is the work of James Gandon, an English architect who arrived in Ireland in 1781, when the building's construction commenced (it continued for 10 years). Crafted from gleaming Portland stone, the central portico is linked by arcades to pavilions at either end. A statue of Commerce tops the copper dome, whose puny circumference, unfortunately, is out of proportion to the rest of the building. Statues on the main facade are based on allegorical themes. Note the exquisitely carved lions and unicorns supporting the arms of Ireland at the far ends of the facade. After Republicans set fire to the building in 1921, it was completely restored and reconstructed to house government offices. A visitor center traces the building's history and significance, and the life of Gandon. ⊠ *Custom House Quay, Northside* ☎ *01/888–2538* ⊕ *www.visitdublin.com* ⊠ *€1.30* ☉ *Mid-Mar.–Oct., weekdays 10–12:30, weekends 2–5; Nov.–mid-Mar., Wed.–Fri. 10–12:30, Sun. 2–5.*

40 **Dublin City Gallery, The Hugh Lane.** Built as a town house for the Earl of
★ Charlemont in 1762, this residence was so grand its Parnell Square street was nicknamed "Palace Row" in its honor. Sir William Chambers, who also built the Marino Casino for Charlemont, designed the structure in the best Palladian manner. Its delicate and rigidly correct facade, extended by two demilune (half-moon) arcades, was fashioned from the "new" white Ardmulcan stone (now seasoned to gray). Charlemont was one of the cultural locomotives of 18th-century Dublin—his walls were hung with Titians and Hogarths, and he frequently dined with Oliver Goldsmith and Sir Joshua Reynolds—so he would undoubtedly be delighted that his home is now a gallery, named after Sir Hugh Lane, a nephew of Lady Gregory (Yeats's aristocratic

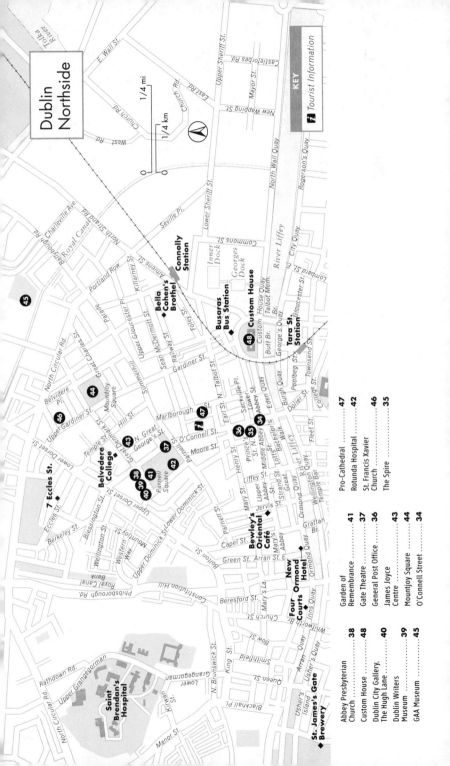

Dublin Northside

1/4 mi	
1/4 km	

KEY

i *Tourist Information*

Tolka River

Toita River

E. Wall St.
West Rd.
Church Rd.
Church Rd.
Upper Sheriff St.
Castleforbes Rd.
Mayor St.
New Wapping St.
North Wall Quay
Rogerson's Quay
Lombard St.
River Liffey
North City Quay
East Rd.

Charleville Ave.
Ballybough Rd.
North Strand Rd.
Royal Canal
North Circular Rd.

Seville Pl.
Lower Sheriff St.
Commons St.
Inner Dock
Georges Dock

Connolly Station
Amiens St.
Oriel St.
Portland Row
Killarney St.

Bella Cohen's Brothel
Railway St.
Foley St.

Busaras Bus Station
Custom House Quay
Talbot Mem. Br.

48 Custom House
Butt Br.
George's Quay
Poolbeg St.
Gloucester St.

Tara St. Station
Townsend St.
Lombard St.

Sean McDermott St.
Upper Gloucester Pl.
Gardiner St.
Summerhill
Portland Pl.

45
North Circular Rd.
Great Charles St.
Belvedere Pl.

44 Mountjoy Square
Hill St.

46
Upper Gardiner St.
Lower Dorset St.
Temple St.

Belvedere College
Great Denmark St.
43 N. Great George's St.
Marlborough St.
47
Earl St. N.
Talbot St.
Sackville Pl.
36 Lower Abbey St.
35
34 Abbey St.
Eden Quay

37
Parnell St.
O'Connell St.
Moore St.
Henry St.
Prince's St. N.
Middle Abbey St.
Bachelor's Walk

42
38 **41**
39 **40**
Parnell Square
Upper Dorset St.

7 Eccles St.
Eccles St.
Blessington St.
Berkeley St.
Wellington St.
Mountjoy St.
Western Way
Upper Dominick St. Lower Dominick St.
Bolton St.
Parnell St.

Phibsborough Rd.
Constitution Hill
Royal Canal
Beresford St.
Green St. Arran St. E.

New Ormond Hotel
Ormond Quay
Grattan Br.

Bewley's Oriental Café
Capel St.
Mary's La.
Mary's Abbey
Jervis St.
Upper Abbey St.
Strand St. Great
Liffey St.
Wellington Quay
Temple Bar
Fleet St.
College St.
D'Olier St.

Saint Brendan's Hospital
Rathdown Rd.
Upper Grangegorman
Lower Grangegorman
N. Brunswick St.
King St.
Smithfield
Queen St.
Bow St.
Church St.

Four Courts
Whitworth Br.
Inns Quay
Mary's Abbey
Green St.

Manor St.
Blackhall Pl.
Usher's Island
St. James's Gate
Kirwan St.
Arran Quay
Usher's Quay

St. James's Gate Brewery

North Circular Rd.

Abbey Presbyterian Church	38
Custom House	48
Dublin City Gallery, The Hugh Lane	40
Dublin Writers Museum	39
GAA Museum	45

Garden of Remembrance	41
Gate Theatre	37
General Post Office	36
James Joyce Centre	43
Mountjoy Square	44
O'Connell Street	34

Pro-Cathedral	47
Rotunda Hospital	42
St. Francis Xavier Church	46
The Spire	35

patron). Lane collected both Impressionist paintings and 19th-century Irish and Anglo-Irish works. A complicated agreement with the National Gallery in London (reached after heated diplomatic dispute) stipulates that a portion of the 39 French paintings amassed by Lane shuttle between London and here. Time it right and you'll be able to see Pissarro's *Printemps,* Manet's *Eva Gonzales,* Morisot's *Jour d'Été,* and, the jewel of the collection, Renoir's *Les Parapluies.*

In something of a snub to the British art establishment, the late Francis Bacon's partner donated the entire contents of the artist's studio to the gallery. The studio of arguably Britain's premier 20th-century artist has been reconstructed here in all its gaudy glory as a permanent display. It gives you a unique opportunity to observe the bravura technique of the artist responsible for such masterpieces as *Study After Velázquez* and the tragic splash-and-crash *Triptych.* Also on display are Bacon's diary, books, and apparently everything else picked up off his floor.

Between the collection of Irish paintings in the National Gallery of Ireland and the superlative works on display here, you can quickly become familiar with Irish 20th-century art. Irish artists represented include Roderic O'Conor, well known for his views of the west of Ireland; William Leech, including his *Girl with a Tinsel Scarf* and *The Cigarette*; and the most famous of the group, Jack B. Yeats (W. B.'s brother). The museum has a dozen of his paintings, including *Ball Alley* and *There Is No Night.* There's also strikingly displayed stained-glass work by early-20th-century Irish master-artisans Harry Clarke and Evie Hone. ⊠ *Parnell Sq. N, Northside* ☎ *01/222–5550* ⊕ *www. hughlane.ie* ⊠ *Gallery free; Bacon Studio €7.50, €3.50 Tues. 9:30– noon* ☉ *Tues.–Thurs. 10–6, Fri. and Sat. 10–5, Sun. 11–5.*

㊴ Dublin Writers Museum. ★ "If you would know Ireland—body and soul— you must read its poems and stories," wrote Yeats in 1891. Further investigation into the Irish way with words can be found at this unique museum, in a magnificently restored 18th-century town house on the north side of Parnell Square. The mansion, once the home of John Jameson, of the Irish whiskey family, centers on the Gallery of Writers, an enormous drawing room gorgeously decorated with paintings, Adamesque plasterwork, and a deep Edwardian lincrusta frieze. Rare manuscripts, diaries, posters, letters, limited and first editions, photographs, and other mementos commemorate the lives and works of the nation's greatest writers—and there are many of them, so leave plenty of time—including Joyce, Shaw, J. M. Synge, Lady Gregory, Yeats, Beckett, and others. On display are an 1804 edition of Swift's *Gulliver's Travels,* an 1899 first edition of Bram Stoker's *Dracula,* and an 1899 edition of Wilde's *Ballad of Reading Gaol.* There's a "Teller of Tales" exhibit showcasing Behan, O'Flaherty, and O'Faoláin. Readings are periodically held. The bookshop and café make this an ideal place to spend a rainy afternoon. If you lose track of time and stay until the closing hour, you might want to dine at Chapter One, a highly regarded restaurant in the basement, which would have had Joyce ecstatic over its currant-sprinkled scones. ⊠ *18 Parnell Sq. N, Northside* ☎ *01/872– 2077* ⊕ *www.writersmuseum.com* ⊠ *€7* ☉ *July and Aug., weekdays*

*10–6, Sat. 10–5, Sun. 11–5; Sept.–
June, Mon.–Sat. 10–5, Sun. 11–5.*

37 Gate Theatre. The show begins here as soon as you walk into the auditorium, a gorgeously Georgian masterwork designed by Richard Johnston in 1784 as an assembly room for the Rotunda Hospital

> **THE SCARS OF HISTORY**
>
> Look for the bullet marks on the pillars of the General Post Office—they're remnants of the 1916 Easter Uprising.

complex. The Gate has been one of Dublin's most important theaters since its founding in 1929 by Micháel MacLiammóir and Hilton Edwards, who also founded Galway City's An Taibhdhearc as the national Irish-language theater. The Gate stages many innovative productions by Irish as well as foreign playwrights—and plenty of foreign actors have performed here, including Orson Welles (his first paid performance) and James Mason (early in his career). ✉ *Cavendish Row, Northside* ☎ *01/874–4045* ✆ *Shows Mon.–Sat.*

36 General Post Office. One of the great civic buildings of Dublin's Georgian era, the GPO's fame is based on the role it played in the Easter Uprising. The building, with its impressive Neoclassical facade, was designed by Francis Johnston and built by the British between 1814 and 1818 as a center of communications. This gave it great strategic importance—and was one of the reasons it was chosen by the insurgent forces in 1916 as a headquarters. Here, on Easter Monday, 1916, the Republican forces, about 2,000 in number and under the guidance of Pádrig Pearse and James Connolly, stormed the building and issued the Proclamation of the Irish Republic. After a week of shelling, the GPO lay in ruins; 13 rebels were ultimately executed, including Connolly, who was dying of gangrene from a wound in a leg shattered in the fighting and had to be propped up in a chair in front of the firing squad. Most of the original building was destroyed, though the facade survived, albeit with the scars of bullets on its pillars. Rebuilt and reopened in 1929, it became a working post office with an attractive two-story main concourse. A bronze sculpture depicting the dying Cuchulainn, a leader of the Red Branch Knights in Celtic mythology, sits in the front window. The 1916 Proclamation and the names of its signatories are inscribed on the green marble plinth. ✉ *O'Connell St., Northside* ☎ *01/872–8888* ⊕ *www. anpost.ie* ✆ *Free* ✆ *Mon.–Sat. 8–8, Sun. 10:30–6.*

▌ NEED A BREAK? For a classic Dublin pub with a bustling all-day atmosphere, stop in at **Kiely's** (✉ *37/38 Middle Abbey St., Northside* ☎ *01/872-2100*). It's popular with media folk and does a great pub lunch and a smooth pint of the black stuff.

43 James Joyce Centre. Few may have read him, but everyone in Ireland has at least heard of James Joyce (1882–1941)—especially since a copy of his censored and suppressed *Ulysses* was one of the top status symbols of the early 20th century. Joyce is of course now acknowledged as one of the greatest modern authors, and his *Dubliners, Finnegan's Wake,* and *A Portrait of the Artist as a Young Man* can even be read as quirky "travel guides" to Dublin. Open to the public, this restored 18th-century Georgian town house, once the dancing academy of Professor Denis J. Maginni (which many will recognize from a reading of *Ulysses*), is a center for Joycean studies and events related to the author. It has an extensive library and archives, exhibition rooms, a bookstore, and a café. The collection includes letters from Beckett, Joyce's guitar and cane, and a celebrated edition of *Ulysses* illustrated by Matisse. The center is the main organizer of "Bloomstime," which marks the week leading up to the Bloomsday celebrations. (Bloomsday, June 16, is the single day *Ulysses* chronicles, as Leopold Bloom winds his way around Dublin in 1904.) ✉ *35 N. Great George's St., Northside* ☎ *01/878–8547* ⊕ *www.jamesjoyce.ie* ☞ *€5, guided tour €10* ⊘ *Tues.–Sat. 10–5.*

③④ O'Connell Street. Dublin's most famous thoroughfare, which is 150 feet wide, was previously known as Sackville Street, but its name was changed in 1924, two years after the founding of the Irish Free State. After the devastation of the 1916 Easter Uprising, the Northside street had to be almost entirely reconstructed, a task that took until the end of the 1920s. At one time the main attraction of the street, Nelson's Pillar, a Doric column towering over the city center and a marvelous vantage point, was blown up in 1966, on the 50th anniversary of the Easter Uprising. The 395-foot-high Spire was built in its place in 2003, and today this gigantic, stainless-steel monument dominates the street. A major clean up and repaving have returned to the street some of its old glory. The large monument at the south end of the street is dedicated to Daniel O'Connell (1775–1847), "The Liberator," and was erected in 1854 as a tribute to the orator's achievement in securing Catholic Emancipation in 1829. Seated winged figures represent the four Victories—Courage, Eloquence, Fidelity, and Patriotism—all exemplified by O'Connell. Ireland's four ancient provinces—Munster, Leinster, Ulster, and Connacht—are identified by their respective coats of arms. Look closely and you'll notice that O'Connell is wearing a glove on one hand, as he did for much of his adult life, a self-imposed penance for shooting a man in a duel. But even the great man himself is dwarfed by the newest addition to O'Connell Street, the silver Spire.

NEED A BREAK?

Conway's (✉ *Parnell St. near Upper O'Connell St., Northside* ☎ *01/873–2687*), founded in 1745, is reputed to be Dublin's second-oldest pub. Guinness-drinking men who like "a flutter on the gee gees" (to gamble on horse racing) mix with office workers on their lunch breaks availing themselves of the unpretentious pub grub. One of Dublin's oldest hotels, dating to 1817, the **Gresham** (✉ *Upper O'Connell St., Northside* ☎ *01/874–6881*) was once the bastion of Dublin high society. Its high-ceiling Georgian dining area is still a pleasant, old-fashioned spot for morning coffee or afternoon tea.

④⑦ Pro-Cathedral. Dublin's principal Catholic cathedral (also known as St. Mary's) is a great place to hear the best Irish male voices—a Palestrina choir, in which the great Irish tenor John McCormack began his career, sings in Latin here every Sunday morning at 11. The cathedral, built between 1816 and 1825, has a classical church design—on a suitably epic scale. The church's facade, with a six-Doric-pillared portico, is

Continued on page 82

LITERARY DUBLIN

A PLAYWRIGHT ON EVERY CORNER

A ramble through literary Dublin is a crash course in Irish soul.

As any visit to the Dublin Writers Museum will prove, this city packs more literary punch per square foot than practically any other spot on the planet. While the Irish capital may be relatively small in geographic terms, it looms huge as a country of the imagination. Dubliners wrote some of the greatest works of Western literature, including these immortal titles: *Ulysses, Gulliver's Travels, Dracula, The Importance of Being Earnest,* and *Waiting for Godot.* Today Dublin is a veritable literary theme park: within a few minutes' walk you can visit the birthplace of George Bernard Shaw, see where Sean O'Casey wrote *Juno and the Paycock,* and pop into the pub where Brendan Behan loved to get marinated.

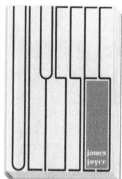

Ulysses, First American Edition

Shaw's proof copy of *Pygmalion*, his Nobel prize, and his Oscar

A Way with Words

As tellers of the tallest tales, speakers of Gaelic (reputedly the world's most perfect medium for prayers, curses, and seduction), and the finest practitioners of the art of blarney, it's little surprise that the Hibernian race produced no fewer than four Nobel prize winners: Shaw, W. B. Yeats, Samuel Beckett, and Seamus Heaney. But what is surprising is that this tiny, long-colonized island on the outskirts of Europe somehow managed to maneuver itself to the very heart of literature in the language of the invader itself, English. And at that heart's core lies Dublin.

> "All the world's a stage and most of us are desperately unrehearsed."
> —Sean O'Casey

For Better or Verse

By the 18th century, the Gaelic tradition was trumped by the boom of literature written in English, often by second- or third-generation descendants of English settlers, such as William Congreve, Richard Brinsley Sheridan, and Oliver Goldsmith. With the Easter Uprising of 1916, so many Irish writers found themselves censored that "being banned" became a matter of prestige (it also did wonders for book sales abroad, with a smuggled copy of *Ulysses* becoming the ultimate status symbol). Sadly, many writers became exiles; most famously, Joyce was joined in Paris by Beckett in 1932.

Dublin B(u)y the Book

Book lovers know that a guidebook to this city is an anthology of Irish literature in itself. Dublin's Northside is studded with landmarks immortalized in James Joyce's novels. A stone's throw from the Liffey is the Abbey Theater, a potent symbol of Ireland's great playwrights. To the south lies Trinity College, alma mater of Jonathan Swift, Bram Stoker, Oscar Wilde, and Samuel Beckett. And scattered around the city are thousands of pubs where storytelling evolved as the incurable Irish "disease." They are the perfect places to take a time-out while touring Dublin's leading literary shrines and sites.

Arrow Books

Macmillan

THE TRAIL OF TALES

Allowing you to turn the pages of the city, as it were, with your feet, a literary ramble through Dublin is a magical mystery tour through more than 400 years of Irish history.

Dublin Writers Museum, Gallery of Writers

DUBLIN WRITERS MUSEUM. The best place to start any literary tour of the city, this gloriously restored 18th-century mansion was once the home of the Jameson Whiskey family (booze and writers are never too far apart in Dublin). Its Edwardian rooms are filled with inky treasures like the 1804 edition of Swift's *Gulliver's Travels* and the 1899 first edition of Stoker's *Dracula.* ⇨ p. 64 ⊠ 18 Parnell Sq. N ☎ 01/872-2077 ⊕ www.writersmuseum.com.

GATE THEATER. Landmarked by its noble Palladian portico, this magnificent Georgian theater (built 1784) today sees the premieres of some of Ireland's most talked-about plays. Orson Welles and James Mason got their starts here. ⊠ Cavendish Row ⊠ ☎ 01/874-4045 ⊕ www.gate-theater.ie.

JAMES JOYCE CENTRE. Now an extensive library dedicated to arguably the greatest novelist of the 20th century, this sumptuously decorated 18th-century town house was featured in *Ulysses* as a dancing academy. Letters from Beckett, Joyce's guitar and cane, and a Joyce edition illustrated by Matisse are collection highlights. ⇨ p. 66. ⊠ 35 N. Great George's St. ☎ 01/878-8547 ⊕ www.jamesjoyce.ie.

SEAN O'CASEY HOUSE. A one-time construction laborer, O'Casey became Ireland's greatest modern playwright and this is the house where he wrote all his famous Abbey plays, including *Juno and the Paycock* and *The Plough and the Stars.* ⊠ 422 N. Circular Rd.

ABBEY THEATRE. Hard to believe this 1950s modernist eyesore is the fabled home of Ireland's national theater company, established on a wave of nationalist passion by Yeats and his patron, Lady Gregory, in 1904. Here premiered J.M. Synge's scandalous *Playboy of the Western World* and the working-class plays of Sean O'Casey. The foyer and bar display mementos of the theater's fabled "Abbeyists." ⊠ Lower Abbey St. ☎ 01/878-7222 ⊕ www.abbeytheater.ie.

TRINITY COLLEGE DUBLIN. This 400-year-old college has an incredible record for turning out literary giants like Swift, Goldsmith, Wilde, Synge, Stoker, and Beckett. Majestically presiding over its famous library is the 9th-century Book of Kells, mother of all Irish tomes. ⇨ pp. 46–49. ⊠ Front Sq. ☎ 01/896-2320 ⊕ www.tcd.ie.

NATIONAL LIBRARY. Joyce used the 1890 Main Reading Room, with its dramatic domed ceiling, as the scene of the great literary debate in *Ulysses.* At No. 30 Kildare Street a plaque marks a former residence of *Dracula*'s creator, Bram Stoker. ⇨ p. 54. ⊠ Kildare St. ☎ 01/603-0200 ⊕ www.nli.ie.

MERRION SQUARE. An elegant mansion, which can be toured, No. 1 Merrion Square is the former Oscar Wilde family residence. A statue of Oscar reclines in

2

Neary's Pub

the park opposite. Around the square, note the plaques that indicate former residents, including W.B. Yeats and Sheridan le Fanu, Dublin's most famous ghost-story teller ⇨ p. 52.

ST. STEPHEN'S GREEN. This pretty, flower-filled little park is home to a wonderful statue of Joyce ⇨ p. 46.

GEORGE BERNARD SHAW BIRTHPLACE. Shaw lived in this modest, Victorian terrace house until he was 10 and the painstaking restoration of the little rooms highlights a cramped, claustrophobic atmosphere Eliza Doolittle would have felt at home in. ⇨ p. 57. ✉ 33 Synge St. ☎ 01/475-0854 ⊕ www.visitdublin.com.

NEARY'S PUB. The exotic, Victorian-style interiors here were once haunted by Dublin's literary set, most notably the master bar raconteur Brendan Behan. ✉ 1 Chatham St. ☎ 01/677-7371.

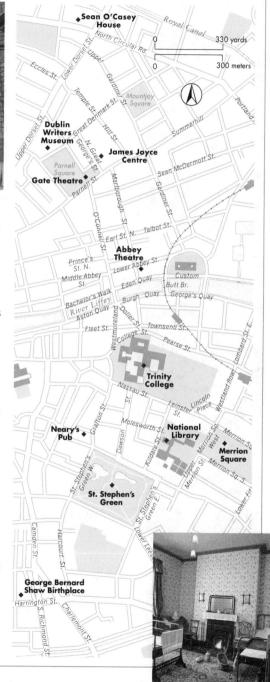

Shaw Birthplace

A DUBLIN PANTHEON

JONATHAN SWIFT

"Where fierce indignation can no longer tear his heart": Swift, one of the great satirists in the English language, willed these words be carved on his tomb at Dublin's St. Patrick's Cathedral. Swift was born on November 30th, 1667, in the Liberties area of Dublin. Life would deal him many misfortunes, but he gave as good as he got, venting his great anger with a pen sharper than any sword. His rage at the British government's mistreatment of the Irish was turned into the brilliant satire *A Modest Proposal* where he politely recommends a solution to the dual problems of hunger and overpopulation: breed babies for meat. Best remembered for the brilliant moral fable *Gulliver's Travels*, he died on October 19, 1745, and is buried in Dublin's St. Patrick's Cathedral, where he was dean.

OSCAR WILDE

The greatest wit of his age and arguably any other, Wilde was born on October 16th, 1834, at 21 Westland Row in Dublin, the son of an eminent eye doctor. He was educated at Trinity College, where he was a promising boxer and was quoted as saying his greatest challenge was learning to live up to the blue china he had installed in his rooms. Wilde moved to London in 1879, where he married, had children, and became celebrated for the plays *The Importance of Being Earnest* and *Salome* and his titillating novel *The Picture of Dorian Gray*. But his life was always more famous than his work and a scandalous affair with the aristocratic Alfred Douglas finally led to his ruin and imprisonment.

W. B. YEATS

Poet, dramatist, and prose writer, Yeats—winner of the Nobel Prize for Literature in 1923—stands as one of the greatest English-language poets of the 20th century. And yet in Ireland itself he is best remembered for his key role in the struggle for Irish freedom and the revival of Irish culture, including his part in forming the Abbey Theatre (National Theatre). Born in the seaside suburb of Sandymount in Dublin in 1865, his fascination with Celtic folklore and the stories of Cuchulainn can be seen throughout his early poems and plays. But many of his greatest poems are haunted by the dashing figure of Maud Gonne, actress, revolutionary, and unrequited love. He died in 1939 in Paris but his body was buried in Drucliffe, at the foot of Ben Bulben mountain in his beloved County Sligo.

2

GEORGE BERNARD SHAW

G. Bernard Shaw—he hated George, and never used it either personally or professionally—was born in Dublin in 1856. His father was a boozing corn merchant and his mother a professional singer. When Shaw was a boy his mother ran away with her voice coach, and it may be no coincidence that his plays are dotted with problem child/parent relationships. In 1886 he went to London where plays such as *Pygmalion* and *Saint Joan* helped propel him to international stardom. Pacifist, socialist, and feminist, Shaw was a true original, a radical in the real sense of the word, his work always challenging the norms of his day. He lived to the ripe old age of 94 and died in 1950 after falling off a ladder while trimming trees outside his house.

SEAN O'CASEY

The first working-class Irish literary great, dramatist O'Casey was born at 85 Upper Dorset Street in the inner-city Dublin slums in 1880. Problems with his eyes as a child kept him indoors where he gleaned a love of reading. An early advocate of Yeats's Celtic Revival, he later found his true faith in the socialism of union leader Jim Larkin. His trilogy of great tragicomedies—*Shadow of a Gunman*, *Juno and the Paycock*, and *The Plough and the Stars*—all deal with ordinary families caught up in the maelstrom of Irish politics and were performed at Yeats's Abbey in the 1920s. Their playful language and riotous action have made them classics ever since. He spent his later life in England and died in Devon in 1964.

BRENDAN BEHAN

Writer, fighter, drinker, and wit, Brendan Francis Behan was born in Dublin's Holles Street Hospital in 1923 into an educated, political working-class family. Urged on by his fiercely patriotic grandmother, he joined Fiánna Eireann, the youth wing of the IRA and, in 1939, was jailed for three years for possessing explosives. In prison he began to write but it wasn't until the 1950s that he hit it big with *The Quare Fellow*, a play based on his prison experiences, and later works *The Hostage* and *Borstal Boy*. But it was in the bars of Dublin that the "demon drinker" Behan delivered many of his greatest lines—alas, lost now forever. A self-proclaimed "drinker with a writing problem," he died in 1964 at the age of only 41.

REJOICE!: The Darlin' Dublin of James Joyce

If Joyce fans make one pilgrimage in their lives, let it be to Dublin on June 16th for Bloomsday. June 16th, of course, is the day Leopold Bloom toured Dublin in *Ulysses*, and commemorative events take place all week long leading up to the big day (and night).

Grown men and women stroll the streets attired in black suits and carrying fresh bars of lemon soap in their pockets, imitating the unsassuming hero of what is arguably the 20th century's greatest novel. Denounced as obscene, blasphemous, and unreadable when it was first published in 1922 (and then banned in the U.S. until 1933), this 1,000-page riff on Homer's *Odyssey* portrays three characters—Leopold Bloom, a Jewish ad salesman, his wife, Molly, and friend Stephen Daedelus—as they wander through Dublin during the span of one day, June 16th, 1904. Dedicated Joyceans flock to the weeklong event, now called "Bloomstime," for Bloomsday breakfasts (where they can enjoy, like Bloom himself, "grilled mutton kidneys... which gave to his palate a fine tang of faintly scented urine"), readings, performances, and general merriment.

But don't despair if you miss Bloomsday, because you can experience the Dublin that inspired the author's novels year-round. James Joyce (1882-1941) set all his major works—*Dubliners, A Portrait of the Artist as a Young Man, Ulysses,* and *Finnegan's Wake*—in the city where he was born and spent the first 22 years of his life. Joyce knew and remembered Dublin in such detail that he bragged (and that's the word) that if the city were destroyed, it could be rebuilt in its entirety from his written works.

Above Left: Joyce Statue, Earl Street
Above Right: Bloomsday celebrations
Left: A portrait of the author by photographer Berenice Abbott

BEGIN IN THE HEART OF THE NORTHSIDE, on Prince's Street, next to the GPO (General Post Office), where the office of the old and popular *Freeman's Journal* newspaper (published 1763–1924) was once located and where Bloom once worked. Head north up O'Connell Street down Parnell Square before turning right onto Dorset Street and then left onto Eccles Street. Leopold and Molly Bloom's fictional home stood at 7 Eccles Street, north of Parnell Square.

Head back to Dorset Street and go east. Take a right onto Gardiner Street and then a left onto Great Denmark Street and Belvedere College. Between 1893 and 1898, Joyce studied at Belvedere College (☎ 01/874–3974) under the Jesuits; it's housed in a splendid 18th-century mansion. The **James Joyce Centre** (☎ 01/878–8547 ⊕ www.jamesjoyce.ie), a few steps from Belvedere College on North Great George's Street, is the hub of Bloomsday celebrations.

Go back to Gardiner Street and then south until you come to Railway Street on your left. The site of **Bella Cohen's Brothel** (✉ 82 Railway St.) is in an area that in Joyce's day contained many houses of ill repute. A long walk back down O'Connell Street to the bridge and then a right will take you to Ormond Quay. On the western

Map labels:
7 Eccles · Eccles St. · Lower Dorset St. · Upper Dorset St. · Gardiner St. · Belvedere College · Mountjoy Square · Great Denmark St. · George's St. · James Joyce Centre · Summerhill · Bella Cohen's Brothel · Parnell Square · Gardiner St. · Railway St. · Parnell St. · O'Connell St. · Earl St. N. · Talbot St. · Prince's St. · General Post Office · New Ormond Hotel · Bachelor's Walk · River Liffey · Aston Quay · Anglesea St. · College Green · Trinity College · College Park · Grafton St. · Duke St. · Davy Byrne's Pub · National Library · Molesworth St. · Leinster St. · Lincoln Place · Sweny's Pharmacy · Leinster Lawn

0 — 330 yards
0 — 300 meters

a Gorgonzola cheese sandwich, and meets his friend Nosey Flynn. Today, the pub has gone very upscale from its pre-World War II days, but even Joyce would have cracked a smile at the sight of the shamrock-painted ceiling and the murals of Joycean Dublin by Liam Proud.

After a stop at Davy Byrne's, proceed via Molesworth Street to the **National Library**—where Bloom has a near meeting with Blazes Boylan, his wife's lover. Walk up Molesworth Street until you hit Trinity. Take a right and walk to Lincoln Place. No establishment mentioned by Joyce has changed less since his time than **Sweny's Pharmacy** (✉ Lincoln Pl.), which still has its black-and-white exterior and an interior crammed with potions and vials.

edge of the Northside, the **New Ormond Hotel** (✉ Upper Ormond Quay ☎ 01/872–1811) was an afternoon rendezvous spot for Bloom.

Across the Liffey, walk up Grafton Street to **Davy Byrne's Pub** (✉ 21 Duke St., ☎ 01/671–1298). Here, Bloom comes to settle down for a glass of Burgundy and

Davy Byrne's Pub

based on the Temple of Theseus in Athens; the interior is modeled after the Grecian-Doric style of St. Philippe du Roule in Paris. But the building was never granted full cathedral status, nor has the identity of its architect ever been discovered; the only clue to its creation is in the church ledger, which lists a "Mr. P." as the builder. ⊠ *Marlborough St., Northside* 🕾 *01/874–5441* ⊕ *www.procathedral.ie* 🖃 *Free* ⊙ *Weekdays 7:30–6:45, Sat. 7:30–7:15, Sun. 9–1:45 and 5:30–7:45.*

❸❺ The Spire. Christened the "Stiletto in the Ghetto" by local smart alecs, this needlelike monument is the most exciting thing to happen to Dublin's skyline in decades. The Spire, also known as the Monument of Light, was originally planned as part of the city's millennium celebrations. But Ian Ritchie's spectacular 395-foot-high monument wasn't erected until the beginning of 2003. Seven times taller than the nearby General Post Office, the stainless-steel structure rises from the spot where Nelson's Pillar once stood. Approximately 10 feet in diameter at its base, the softly lighted monument narrows to only 1 foot at its apex—the upper part of the Spire sways gently when the wind blows. The monument's creators envisioned it serving as a beacon for the whole of the city, and it will certainly be the first thing you see as you drive into Dublin from the airport. ⊠ *O'Connell St., Northside.*

ALSO WORTH SEEING

❸❽ Abbey Presbyterian Church. Built on the profits of sin—well, by a generous wine merchant actually—and topped with a soaring Gothic spire, this church anchors the northeast corner of Parnell Square, an area that was the city's most fashionable address during the gilded days of the 18th-century Ascendancy. Popularly known as Findlater's Church—after the merchant Alex Findlater—the church was completed in 1864 with an interior that has a stark Presbyterian mood despite stained-glass windows and ornate pews. For a bird's-eye view of the area, climb the small staircase that leads to the balcony. ⊠ *Parnell Sq., Northside* 🕾 *01/837–8600* 🖃 *Free* ⊙ *Hrs vary.*

❹❺ GAA Museum. The Irish are sports crazy, and reserve their fiercest pride for their native games. In the bowels of Croke Park, the main stadium and headquarters of the GAA (Gaelic Athletic Association), this museum gives you a great introduction to native Irish sport. The four Gaelic games (football, hurling, camogie, and handball) are explained in detail, and if you're brave enough you can have a go yourself. High-tech displays take you through the history and highlights of the games. *National Awakening* is a really smart, interesting short film reflecting the key impact of the GAA on the emergence of the Irish nation and the forging of a new Irish identity. The exhilarating *A Day in September* captures the thrill and passion of All Ireland finals day—the annual denouement of the intercounty hurling and Gaelic football seasons—which is every bit as important to the locals as the Super Bowl is to sports fans in the United States. You can even try out your own hurling skills in the interactive game area. Tours of the stadium, the fourth largest in Europe, are available. ⊠ *New Stand, Croke Park, North County Dublin* 🕾 *01/855–8176* ⊕ *http://museum.gaa.ie* 🖃 *Museum €5.50,* *museum and stadium tour €9.50* ⊙*July and Aug., Mon.–Sat. 9:30–6, Sun. noon–5; Sept.–June, Mon.–Sat. 9:30–5, Sun. noon–5.*

④ Garden of Remembrance. Opened 50 years after the Easter Uprising of 1916, the garden in Parnell Square commemorates those who died fighting for Ireland's freedom. At the garden's entrance is a large plaza; steps lead down to the fountain area, graced with a sculpture by contemporary Irish artist Oisín Kelly, based on the mythological Children of Lír, who were turned into swans. The garden serves as an oasis of tranquility in the middle of the busy city. ⊠*Parnell Sq., Northside* ⌧*Free* ⊙*Daily 9–5.*

④ Mountjoy Square. Built over the course of the two decades leading up to 1818, this Northside square was once surrounded by elegant terraced houses. Today only the northern side remains intact. The houses on the once derelict southern side have been converted into apartments. Irishman Brian Boru, who led his soldiers to victory against the Vikings in the Battle of Clontarf in 1014, was said to have pitched camp before the confrontation on the site of Mountjoy Square. Playwright Sean O'Casey lived here, at No. 35, and used the square as a setting for *The Shadow of a Gunman.*

④ Rotunda Hospital. The Rotunda, founded in 1745 as the first maternity hospital in Ireland and Britain, was designed on a grand scale by architect Richard Castle (1690–1751), with a three-story tower and a copper cupola. It's now mostly worth a visit for its chapel, which has elaborate plasterwork and, appropriately, honors motherhood; it was built by Bartholomew Cramillion between 1757 and 1758. The Gate Theatre, in a lavish Georgian assembly room, is on the O'Connell Street side of this large complex. ⊠*Parnell St., Northside* ☎*01/873–0700.*

④ St. Francis Xavier Church. One of the city's finest churches in the classical style, the Jesuit St. Francis Xavier's was begun in 1829, the year of Catholic Emancipation, and was completed three years later. The building is designed in the shape of a Latin cross, with a distinctive Ionic portico and an unusual coffered ceiling. The striking, faux-marble high altarpiece, decorated with lapis lazuli, came from Italy. The church appears in James Joyce's story "Grace." ⊠*Upper Gardiner St., Northside* ☎*01/836–3411* ⌧*Free* ⊙*Daily 7 AM–8:30 PM.*

DUBLIN WEST: CATHEDRALS & GUINNESS

A cornucopia of things quintessentially Dublin, this area is studded with treasures and pleasures ranging from the opulent 18th-century salons of Dublin Castle to time-burnished St. Patrick's Cathedral, from the Liberties neighborhood—redoubt of the city's best antiques stores—to the Irish Museum of Modern Art (housed at the strikingly renovated Royal Hospital Kilmainham). You can time-travel from the 10th-century crypt at Christ Church Cathedral—the city's oldest surviving structure—to the modern plant of the Guinness Brewery and its storehouse museum. You can also cross the Liffey for a visit to Smithfield. Bordered on the east by Church Street, on the west by Blackhall Place, to the north by King Street, and to the south by the Liffey, Smithfield is Dublin's old market area where flowers, fruit, vegetables, and even horses have been sold for generations. Chosen as a flagship for north inner-city renovation, the area has seen a major face-lift in the last few years. The beautiful cobblestones of its streets have been taken up, refinished, and replaced, and giant masts topped with gas-lights send 6-foot-high flames over Smithfield Square—now the venue for the occasional major rock concert (the square was where U2 were awarded the keys to Dublin city in 1999). Early morning is a special time in Smithfield, as the wholesale fruit and veg sellers still ply their trade in the wonderful 19th-century covered market. Traditional music bars like the Cobblestone, a favorite of the market traders, now sit side by side with modern hotels like the Park Inn, and the award-winning Old Jameson Distillery museum.

Keep in mind that Dublin is compact. The following sights aren't far from those in the other city-center neighborhoods. In fact, City Hall is just across the street from the Temple Bar, and Christ Church Cathedral is a short walk farther west. The westernmost sights covered here—notably the Royal Hospital and Kilmainham Gaol—are, however, at some distance, so if you're not an enthusiastic walker, you may want to drive or catch a cab or a bus to them.

Numbers in the margin correspond to numbers on the Dublin West & Phoenix Park map.

TIMING Allow a few hours for this area, especially if you want to include the Guinness Brewery and Storehouse and the Irish Museum of Modern Art at the Royal Hospital. Keep in mind that if you want to cover the easternmost sights—Dublin Castle, City Hall, Christ Church Cathedral, and environs—you can easily append them to a tour of Temple Bar.

THE MAIN ATTRACTIONS

61 **Chester Beatty Library.** A connoisseur's delight, this "library" is considered by many to be the most impressive museum in Ireland. After Sir Alfred Chester Beatty (1875–1968), a Canadian mining millionaire and a collector with a flawless eye, assembled one of the most significant collections of Islamic and Far Eastern art in the Western world, he donated it to Ireland. Housed in the gorgeous clock-tower building of Dublin Castle, and voted European Museum of the Year in 2002, the library is one of Dublin's real gems. Among the exhibits are clay tablets from Babylon dating from 2700 BC, Japanese wood-block prints, Chinese jade books, and Turkish and Persian paintings. The second floor, dedicated to the major religions, houses 250 manuscripts of the Koran from across the Muslim world, as well as one of the earliest Gospels. Life-size Buddhas from Burma and rhino cups from China are among the other curios on show. Guided tours of the library are available on Tuesday and Saturday at 2:30 PM. On sunny days the garden is one of the most tranquil places in central Dublin. The shop is full of unique and exotic souvenirs relating to the collection. ⊠ *Castle St., Dublin West* ☎ *01/407–0750* ⊕ *www.cbl.ie* ☜ *Free* ☉ *May–Sept., weekdays 10–5, Sat. 11–5, Sun. 1–5; Oct.–Apr., Tues.–Fri. 10–5, Sat. 11–5, Sun. 1–5.*

Fodor's Choice
★

NEED A BREAK?

Silk Road Cafe (⊠ *Chester Beatty Library, Castle St., Dublin West* ☎ *01/407–0770*) is a great-value, Middle-Eastern delight hidden away in the Chester Beatty library. The buffet-style menu is always full of exotic surprises and the light-filled room and serene atmosphere make you want to linger longer than you should. It's open Tuesday–Friday 10–4:30, Saturday 11–4:30, and Sunday 1–4:30.

52 **Christ Church Cathedral.** You'd never know from the outside that the first
★ Christianized Danish king built a wooden church at this site in 1038; because of the extensive 19th-century renovation of its stonework and trim, the cathedral looks more Victorian than Anglo-Norman. Construction on the present Christ Church—the flagship of the Church of Ireland and one of two Protestant cathedrals in Dublin (the other is St. Patrick's just to the south)—was begun in 1172 by Strongbow, a Norman baron and conqueror of Dublin for the English crown, and continued for 50 years. By 1875 the cathedral had deteriorated badly; a major renovation gave it much of the look it has today, including the addition of one of Dublin's most charming structures: a Bridge of Sighs–like affair that connects the cathedral to the old Synod Hall, which now holds the Viking multimedia exhibition, Dublinia. Remains from the 12th-century building include the north wall of the nave, the west bay of the choir, and the fine stonework of the transepts, with their pointed arches and supporting columns. Strongbow himself is buried in the cathedral, beneath an impressive effigy. The vast, sturdy **crypt,** with its 12th- and 13th-century vaults, is Dublin's oldest surviving structure and the building's most notable feature. The Treasures of Christ Church exhibition includes manuscripts, various historic artifacts, and the tabernacle used when James II worshipped here. At 6 PM on Wednesday and Thursday you can enjoy the glories of a choral evensong. ⊠ *Christ Church Pl. and Winetavern St., Dublin West* ☎ *01/677–8099* ⊕ *www. cccdub.ie* 🖃 *€5* ⊙ *June–Aug., daily 9–6; Sept.–May, daily 9:45–5.*

49 **City Hall.** Facing the Liffey from Cork Hill at the top of Parliament Street, this grand Georgian municipal building (1769–79), once the Royal Exchange, marks the southwest corner of Temple Bar. Today it's the seat of the Dublin Corporation, the elected body that governs the city. Thomas Cooley designed the building with 12 columns that encircle the domed central rotunda, which has a fine mosaic floor and 12 frescoes depicting Dublin legends and ancient Irish historical scenes. The 20-foot-high sculpture to the right is of Daniel O'Connell, "The Liberator." He looks like he's about to begin the famous speech he gave here in 1800. The building houses a multimedia exhibition—with artifacts, kiosks, graphics, and audiovisual presentations—tracing the evolution of Ireland's 1,000-year-old capital. ⊠ *Dame St., Dublin West* ☎ *01/222–2204* ⊕ *www.dublincity.ie/your_council/city_hall* 🖃 *€4* ⊙ *Mon.–Sat. 10–5:15, Sun. 2–5.*

50 **Dublin Castle.** Neil Jordan's film *Michael Collins* captured Dublin Castle's near indomitable status well: seat and symbol of the British rule of Ireland for more than seven centuries, the castle figured largely in Ireland's turbulent history early in the 20th century. It's now mainly used

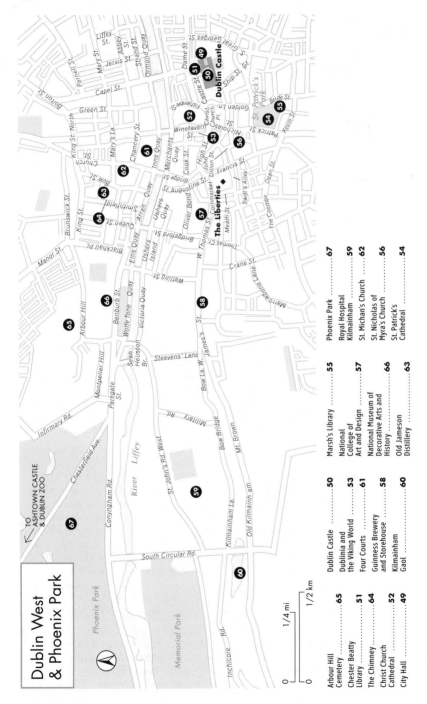

Dublin West & Phoenix Park

0   1/4 mi

0   1/2 km

TO ASHTOWN CASTLE & DUBLIN ZOO

Phoenix Park

Memorial Park

River Liffey

The Liberties ◆

Dublin Castle

for Irish and EU governmental purposes. The sprawling Great Court-yard is the reputed site of the Black Pool (Dubh Linn, pronounced *dove*-lin) from which Dublin got its name. In the Lower Castle Yard, the Record Tower, the earliest of several towers on the site, is the largest remaining relic of the original Norman buildings, built by King John between 1208 and 1220. The clock tower building now houses the Chester Beatty Library. Guided tours are available of the principal State Apartments (on the southern side of the Upper Castle Yard), formerly the residence of the English viceroys and now used by the president of Ireland to host visiting heads of state and EU ministers. The State Apartments are lavishly furnished with rich Donegal carpets and illuminated by Waterford glass chandeliers. The largest and most impressive of these chambers, St. Patrick's Hall, with its gilt pillars and painted ceiling, is used for the inauguration of Irish presidents. The Round Drawing Room, in Bermingham Tower, dates from 1411 and was rebuilt in 1777; numerous Irish leaders were imprisoned in the tower from the 16th century to the early 20th century. The blue oval Wedgwood Room contains Chippendale chairs and a marble fireplace. The Castle Vaults now hold an elegant little patisserie and bistro.

Carved oak panels and stained glass depicting viceroys' coats of arms grace the interior of the Church of the Holy Trinity (formerly called Chapel Royal), on the castle grounds. The church was designed in 1814 by Francis Johnston, who also designed the original General Post Office building on O'Connell Street. Once you're inside, look up—you'll see an elaborate array of fan vaults on the ceiling. More than 100 carved heads adorn the walls outside: among them, St. Peter and Jonathan Swift preside over the north door, St. Patrick and Brian Boru over the east.

One-hour guided tours of the castle are available every half hour, but the rooms are closed when in official use, so call ahead. The easiest way into the castle is through the Cork Hill Gate, just west of City Hall. ✉ *Castle St., Dublin West* ☎ *01/645–8813* ⊕ *www.dublincastle. ie* ☞ *State Apartments €4.50 including tour* ⊗ *Weekdays 10–4:45, weekends 2–4:45.*

61 **Four Courts.** The stately Corinthian portico and the circular central hall warrant a visit here, to the seat of the High Court of Justice of Ireland. The distinctive copper-cover dome topping a colonnaded rotunda makes this one of Dublin's most instantly recognizable buildings. The view from the rotunda is terrific. Built between 1786 and 1802, the Four Courts are James Gandon's second Dublin masterpiece—close on the heels of his Custom House, located downstream on the same side of the River Liffey. In 1922, during the Irish Civil War, the Four Courts was almost totally destroyed by shelling—the adjoining Public Records Office was gutted, and many priceless legal documents, including innumerable family records, were destroyed. Restoration took 10 years. Tours of the building are not given, but you're welcome to sit in while the courts are in session. ✉ *Inns Quay, Dublin West* ☎ *01/872–5555* ⊕ *www.courts.ie* ⊗ *Daily 10–1 and 2:15–4.*

58 **Guinness Brewery and Storehouse.** Ireland's all-dominating brewery—
Fodor'sChoice founded by Arthur Guinness in 1759 and at one time the largest stout-
★ producing brewery in the world—spans a 60-acre spread west of Christ
Church Cathedral. Not surprisingly, it's the most popular tourist destination in town—after all, the Irish national drink is Guinness stout,
a dark brew made with roasted malt. The brewery itself is closed to
the public, but the Guinness Storehouse is a spectacular attraction,
designed to woo you with the wonders of the "dark stuff." In a 1904
cast-iron-and-brick warehouse, the museum display covers six floors
built around a huge, central glass atrium. Beneath the glass floor of the
lobby you can see Arthur Guinness's original lease on the site, for a
whopping 9,000 years. The exhibition elucidates the brewing process
and its history, with antique presses and vats, a look at bottle and can
design through the ages, a history of the Guinness family, and a fascinating archive of Guinness advertisements. You might think it's all a bit
much (it's only a drink, after all), and parts of the exhibit do feel a little
over the top—readers complain about the numerous ads and promos
for the brew at nearly every turn. The star attraction is undoubtedly
the top-floor **Gravity Bar**, with 360-degree floor-to-ceiling glass walls
that offer a nonpareil view out over the city at sunset while you sip
your free pint. One of the bar's first clients was one William Jefferson
Clinton. The Guinness Shop on the ground floor is full of funky lifestyle merchandise. ⊠ *St. James' Gate, Dublin West* ☎ *01/408–4800*
⊕ *www.guinness-storehouse.com* ⊠ *€14* ⊙ *July and Aug., daily 9:30–
7; Sept.–June, daily 9:30–5.*

60 **Kilmainham Gaol.** Leaders of many failed Irish rebellions spent their last
days in this grim, forbidding structure, and it holds a special place in
the myth and memory of the country. The 1916 commanders Pádrig
Pearse and James Connolly were held before being executed in the
prison yard. Other famous inmates included the revolutionary Robert
Emmet and Charles Stewart Parnell, a leading politician. You can visit
the prison only as part of a guided tour, which leaves every hour on the
hour. The cells are a chilling sight, and the guided tour and a 30-minute
audiovisual presentation relate a graphic account of Ireland's political
history over the past 200 years—from an Irish Nationalist viewpoint.
A new exhibition displays items that haven't been seen together since
Robert Emmet's failed rebellion of 1803. A small tearoom is on the
premises. ⊠ *Inchicore Rd., Dublin West* ☎ *01/453–5984* ⊕ *www.heri-
tageireland.ie* ⊠ *€5.30* ⊙ *Apr.–Sept., daily 9:30–5; Oct.–Mar., Mon.–
Sat. 9:30–4, Sun. 10–5.*

59 **Royal Hospital Kilmainham.** This replica of Les Invalides in Paris is
★ regarded as the most important 17th-century building in Ireland.
Commissioned as a hospice for disabled and veteran soldiers by James
Butler—the duke of Ormonde and viceroy to King Charles II—the
building was completed in 1684, making it the first building erected in
Dublin's golden age. It survived into the 1920s as a hospital, but after
the founding of the Irish Free State in 1922, the building fell into disre-
pair. The entire edifice has since been restored to what it once was.

The structure's four galleries are arranged around a courtyard; there's also a grand dining hall—100 feet long by 50 feet wide. The architectural highlight is the hospital's Baroque chapel, distinguished by its extraordinary plasterwork ceiling and fine wood carvings. "There is nothing in Ireland from the 17th century that can come near this masterpiece," raved cultural historian John FitzMaurice Mills. The Royal Hospital also houses the **Irish Museum of Modern Art,** which concentrates on the work of contemporary Irish artists such as Richard Deacon, Richard Gorman, Dorothy Cross, Sean Scully, Matt Mullican, Louis Le Brocquy, and James Colman. The museum also displays works by some non-Irish 20th-century greats, including Picasso and Miró, and regularly hosts touring shows from major European museums. The Café Musée serves light fare such as soups and sandwiches. The hospital is a short ride by taxi or bus from the city center. ⊠ *Kilmainham La., Dublin West* ☎ *01/612–9900* ⊕ *www.modernart.ie* ▣ *Free* ⊙ *Royal Hospital Tues.–Sat. 10–5:30, Sun. noon–5:30; tours every ½ hr. Museum Tues. and Thurs.–Sat. 10–5:30, Wed. 10:30–5:30, Sun. noon–5:30; tours Wed. and Fri. at 2:30, Sat. at 11:30.*

㊾ **St. Patrick's Cathedral.** The largest cathedral in Dublin and also the national cathedral of the Church of Ireland, St. Patrick's is the second of the capital's two Protestant cathedrals. (The other is Christ Church, and the reason Dublin has two cathedrals is because St. Patrick's originally stood outside the walls of Dublin, while its close neighbor was within the walls and belonged to the see of Dublin.) Legend has it that in the 5th century, St. Patrick baptized many converts at a well on the site of the cathedral. The original building, dedicated in 1192 and early English Gothic in style, was an unsuccessful attempt to assert supremacy over Christ Church Cathedral. At 305 feet, this is the longest church in the country, a fact Oliver Cromwell's troops—no friends to the Irish—found useful as they made the church's nave into their stable in the 17th century. They left the building in a terrible state; its current condition is largely due to the benevolence of Sir Benjamin Guinness—of the brewing family—who started financing major restoration work in 1860.

Fodor's Choice
★

Make sure you see the gloriously heraldic Choir of St. Patrick's, hung with colorful medieval banners, and find the tomb of the most famous of St. Patrick's many illustrious deans, Jonathan Swift, immortal author of *Gulliver's Travels,* who held office from 1713 to 1745. Swift's tomb is in the south aisle, not far from that of his beloved "Stella," Mrs. Esther Johnson. Swift's epitaph is inscribed over the robing-room door. Yeats—who translated it thus: "Swift has sailed into his rest; Savage indignation there cannot lacerate his breast"—declared it the greatest epitaph of all time. Other memorials include the 17th-century Boyle Monument, with its numerous painted figures of family members, and the monument to Turlough O'Carolan, the last of the Irish bards and one of the country's finest harp players. Immediately north of the cathedral is a small park, with statues of many of Dublin's literary figures and St. Patrick's Well. "Living Stones" is the cathedral's permanent exhibition celebrating St. Patrick's place in the life of the city. If you're a music lover, you're in for a treat; matins (9:40 AM) and evensong (5:45 PM) are still sung on most days. ⊠*Patrick St., Dublin West* ☏*01/453–9472* ⊕*www.stpatrickscathedral.ie* 🎟*€5* ⊙*Mar.–Oct., Mon.–Sat. 9–6, Sun. 9–11, 12:45–3, and 4:15–6; Nov.–Feb. weekdays 9–6, Sat. 9–5, Sun. 10–11 and 12:45–3.*

FROM PEW TO VIEW

While in the shadow of St. Patrick's Cathedral, head from Patrick Close to Patrick Street; look down the street toward the Liffey for a glorious view of Christ Church.

ALSO WORTH SEEING

64 ☾ **The Chimney.** Just in front of the Park Inn Hotel stands one of the original brick chimneys, built in 1895, of the Old Jameson Distillery, which has been turned into a 185-foot-tall observation tower with a 360-degree view of Dublin. The redbrick chimney now has a two-tier, glass-enclosed platform at the top. The trip aloft in the glass elevator is just as thrilling as the view from the platform. ⊠*Smithfield Village, Dublin West* ☏*01/817–3800* ⊕*www.heritageireland.com* 🎟*€5* ⊙*Mon.–Sat. 10–5, Sun 11–5:30.*

53 ☾ **Dublinia and the Viking World.** Ever wanted a chance to put your head in the stocks? Dublin's Medieval Trust has set up an entertaining and informative reconstruction of everyday life in medieval Dublin. The main exhibits use high-tech audiovisual and computer displays; you can also see a scale model of what Dublin was like around 1500, a medieval maze, a life-size reconstruction based on the 13th-century dockside at Wood Quay, and a fine view from the tower. For a more modern take on the city, check out the James Malton series of prints of 18th-century Dublin, hanging on the walls of the coffee shop. Dublinia is in the old Synod Hall (formerly a meeting place for bishops of the Church of Ireland), joined via a covered stonework Victorian bridge to Christ Church Cathedral. An exhibition on "The Viking World" consists of a similar reconstruction of life in even earlier Viking Dublin. ⊠*St. Michael's Hill, Dublin West* ☏*01/679–4611* ⊕*www.dublinia.ie* 🎟*Exhibit €6* ⊙*Apr.–Sept., daily 10–5; Oct.–Mar., weekdays 11–4, weekends 10–4:30.*

55 **Marsh's Library.** When Ireland's first public library was founded and endowed in 1701 by Narcissus Marsh, the Archbishop of Dublin, it was made open to "All Graduates and Gentlemen." The two-story brick Georgian building has remained virtually the same since then. It houses a priceless collection of 250 manuscripts and 25,000 15th- to 18th-century books. Many of these rare volumes were locked inside cages, as were the readers who wish to peruse them. The cages were to discourage students who, often impecunious, may have been tempted to make the books their own. The library has been restored with great attention to its original architectural details, especially in the book stacks. The library is a short walk west from St. Stephen's Green and accessed through a charming little cottage garden. ⊠*St. Patrick's Close off Patrick St., Dublin West* ☏*01/454–3511* ⊕*www.marshlibrary.ie* 🎟*€2.50* ⊙*Mon. and Wed.–Fri. 10–1 and 2–5, Sat. 10:30–1.*

57 National College of Art and Design. The delicate welding of glass and iron onto the redbrick Victorian facade of this onetime factory makes this school worth a visit. A walk around the cobblestone central courtyard often gives the added bonus of viewing students working away in glass, clay, metal, and stone. ⊠*Thomas St., Dublin West* ☎*01/671–1377* ⊕*www.ncad.ie* ☜*Free* ⊗*Weekdays 9–7.*

63 Old Jameson Distillery. Founded in 1791, this distillery produced one of Ireland's most famous whiskeys for nearly 200 years, until 1966, when local distilleries merged to form Irish Distillers and moved to a purpose-built, ultramodern distillery in Middleton, County Cork. Part of the complex was converted into the group's head office, and the distillery itself became a museum. There's a short audiovisual history of the industry, which had its origins 1,500 years ago in Middle Eastern perfume making. You can also tour the old distillery, and learn about the distilling of whiskey from grain to bottle, or view a reconstruction of a former warehouse, where the colorful nicknames of former barrel makers are recorded. The 40-minute tour includes a complimentary tasting (remember: Irish whiskey is best drunk without a mixer—try it straight or with water); four attendees are invited to taste different brands of Irish whiskey and compare them against bourbon and Scotch. If you have a large group and everyone wants to do this, phone in advance to arrange it. ⊠*Bow St., Dublin West* ☎*01/807–2355* ⊕*www.jamesondistillery.ie* ☜*€9.75* ⊗*Daily 9:30–6; tours every ½ hr.*

62 St. Michan's Church. However macabre, St. Michan's main claim to fame is down in the vaults, where the totally dry atmosphere has preserved several corpses in a remarkable state of mummification. They lie in open caskets. Most of the resident deceased are thought to have been Dublin tradespeople (one was, they say, a religious crusader). Except for its 120-foot-high bell tower, this Anglican church is architecturally undistinguished. The church was built in 1685 on the site of an 11th-century Danish church (Michan was a Danish saint). Another reason to come is to see the 18th-century organ, which Handel supposedly played for the first performance of *Messiah*. Don't forget to check out the Stool of Repentance—the only one still in existence in the city. Parishioners judged to be "open and notoriously naughty livers" used it to do public penance. ⊠*Lower Church St., Dublin West* ☎*01/872–4154* ☜*€3.50* ⊗*Mid-Mar.–Oct., weekdays 10–12:45 and 2–4:30, Sat. 10–12:45, Sun. service at 10 AM; Nov.–mid-Mar., weekdays 12:30–3:30, Sat. 10–12:45, Sun. service at 10 AM.*

56 St. Nicholas of Myra's Church. A grand Neoclassical style characterizes this church, completed in 1834. The highly ornate chapel inside includes ceiling panels of the 12 apostles, and a pietà raised 20 feet above the marble altar, guarded on each side by angels sculpted by John Hogan while he was in Florence. The tiny nuptial chapel to the right has a small Harry Clarke stained-glass window. ⊠*St. Nicholas St., Dublin West* ☜*Free* ⊗*Hrs vary.*

"TAKE IT AISY": PHOENIX PARK & ENVIRONS

Far and away Dublin's largest park, Phoenix Park (the name is an anglicization of the Irish *Fionn Uisce,* meaning clear water) is a vast, green, arrowhead-shape oasis north of the Liffey, about a 20-minute walk from the city center. It's the city's main escape valve and sports center (cricket, soccer, Gaelic games, and polo), and the home of the noble creatures of the Dublin Zoo. A handful of other cultural sights near the park also merit a visit.

Numbers in the margin correspond to numbers on the Dublin West & Phoenix Park map.

TIMING Phoenix Park is *big*; exploring it on foot could easily take the better part of a day. If you're looking for a little exercise, head here: jogging, horseback riding, and bicycling are the ideal ways to explore the park. To make a full day of it, you could couple a trip to the park with visits to several of the sights in the Dublin West area; the Smithfield neighborhoods and the Old Jameson Distillery are closest, and the Guinness Brewery and Storehouse, across the river, is also fairly close.

THE MAIN ATTRACTIONS

66 **National Museum of Decorative Arts and History.** Connoisseurs of the decorative arts have always had a special fondness for Irish style, whose glories range from Bronze Age Celtic jewels to the moderne 20th-century furniture of Eileen Gray. Here, in one gigantic treasure chest, is the full panoply of the National Museum's collection of glass, silver, furniture, and other decorative arts. The setting is spectacular: the huge Collins Barracks, named for the assassinated Irish Republican leader Michael Collins (1890–1922). Built in the early 18th century, designed by Captain Thomas Burgh, these erstwhile "Royal Barracks" were stylishly renovated to become a showcase for the museum, which opened in September 1997. The displays are far ranging, covering everything from one of the greatest collections of Irish silver in the world to Irish period furniture—you'll see that the country's take on Chippendale was far earthier than the English mode. "The Way We Wore: 250 Years of Irish Clothing and Jewelry" and a thousand years of Irish coins are other highlights. Headlining the collections are some extraordinary objects, including the Fonthill Vase, the William Smith O'Brien Gold Cup, and the Lord Chancellor's Mace. ⊠ *Benburb St., Dublin West* ☎ *01/677–7444* ⊕ *www.museum.ie* 🖾 *Free* ⊗ *Tues.–Sat. 10–5, Sun. 2–5.*

67 **Phoenix Park.** Europe's largest public park, which extends about 5 km (3 mi) along the Liffey's north bank, encompasses 1,752 acres of verdant green lawns, woods, lakes, and playing fields. Sunday is the best time to visit: games of cricket, football (soccer), polo, baseball, hurling (a combination of lacrosse, baseball, and field hockey), and Irish football are likely to be in progress. Old-fashioned gas lamps line both sides of Chesterfield Avenue, the main road that bisects the park for 4 km (2½ mi), which was named for Lord Chesterfield, a lord lieutenant of Ireland, who laid out the road in the 1740s. To the right as you enter the park is the People's Garden, a colorful flower garden designed in 1864.

2

Among the park's major monuments are the Phoenix Column, erected by Lord Chesterfield in 1747, and the 198-foot obelisk, built in 1817 to commemorate the Duke of Wellington, the Irish general who defeated Napoléon for the British. (Wellington was born in Dublin but, true to the anti-Irish prejudice so prevalent in 19th-century England, balked at the suggestion that he was Irish: "If a man is born in a stable, it doesn't mean he is a horse," he is reputed to have said.) A tall white cross marks the spot where Pope John Paul II addressed more than a million people during his 1979 visit to Ireland. Wild deer can be seen grazing in the many open spaces of the park, especially near here.

You're guaranteed to see wildlife at the **Dublin Zoo** (⊠ *Dublin West* ☎ *01/677–1425* ⊕ *www.dublinzoo.ie*), the third-oldest public zoo in the world, founded in 1830, and just a short walk beyond the People's Garden. A major renovation completed in 2007 has now given new life and luster to the old place. Animals from tropical climes are kept in unbarred enclosures, and Arctic species swim in the lakes close to the reptile house. Some 700 lions have been bred here since the 1850s, one of whom became familiar to movie fans the world over when MGM used him for its trademark. (As they will tell you at the zoo, he is in fact yawning in that familiar shot: an American lion had to be hired to roar and the "voice" was dubbed.) The African Plains section houses the zoo's larger species; the Nakuru Safari is a new 25-minute tour of this area. World of Primates is a gathering of the usual suspects from tiny colobus monkeys to big gorillas. In summer the Lakeside Café serves ice cream and drinks. Admission to the Dublin Zoo is €12.50. Hours are April through September, Monday–Saturday 9:30–6:30 and Sunday 10:30–6:30; March, Monday–Saturday 9:30–6 and Sunday 10:30–6; October through February, Monday–Saturday 9:30–4:30 and Sunday 10:30–4:30. Both the president of Ireland and the U.S. ambassador have official residences in the park (the president's is known as Aras an Uachtarain), but neither building is open to the public. Also within the park is a **visitor center** (⊠ *Dublin West* ☎ *01/677–0095* ⊕ *www. heritageireland.ie*), in the 17th-century fortified Ashtown Castle; it has information about the park's history, flora, and fauna. Admission to the center is €2.75. Hours are mid-March through end of March and October, daily 10–5:30; April to September, daily 10–6; November to mid-March, Wednesday–Sunday 10–5.

NEED A BREAK?

Ryan's Pub (⊠ *28 Parkgate St., Dublin West* ☎ *01/677–6097*), one of Dublin's last remaining genuine late-Victorian-era pubs, has changed little since its last remodeling—in 1896. It's right near the entrance to Phoenix Park.

ALSO WORTH SEEING

65 **Arbour Hill Cemetery.** All 14 Irishmen executed by the British following the 1916 Easter Uprising are buried here, including Pádrig Pearse, who led the rebellion; his younger brother Willie, who played a minor role in the uprising; and James Connolly, a socialist and labor leader wounded in the battle. Too weak from his wounds to stand, Connolly was tied to a chair and then shot. The burial ground is a simple but formal area, with the names of the dead leaders carved in stone beside an inscription of the proclamation they issued during the uprising. ⊠*Arbour Hill, Dublin West* ☎*01/605–7700* ⊠*Free* ⊗*Mon.–Sat. 9–4:30, Sun. 9:30–noon.*

WHERE TO EAT

By Anto Howard

"Come in! Come in! Your dinner's poured out!" goes the old North Dublin joke. In truth, its description of Irish food as being best when hidden in soup wasn't so far off the mark. For years, "Irish cuisine" used to be nothing more than a convenient way of grouping potatoes and stout under the same heading. However, the days when critics bemoaned the *pot* luck of the Irish are thankfully gone. Today, be prepared to have your preconceptions overturned, and, on occasion, to be enthralled and very happily sated in the process. No longer does a pub crawl turn up a better meal than one in a fancy restaurant. Dubliners now forgo heading to the "local" to down a pint after work because they've made reservations at the newest eateries and hippest showplaces (of course, the pubs and the pints come later in the evening). These chowhounds are intent on enjoying the fruits of Ireland's gastronomic revolution, but Dublin's best chefs have been leading the charge.

Month after month, these euro-toques continue to come up with new and glorious ways to abuse your waistline. Skewered John Dory wrapped in nori and served with a daring mint and pea risotto? Sautéed rabbit loin with Clonakilty black pudding? Or a dazzling dessert like lavender jelly with Cooleeney Camembert sauce? As these dishes reveal, Dublin's top cooks are determined to take advantage of the fact that Ireland has some of the best "raw materials" in the world. Given that it is a small island on which one is never farther than an hour-and-a-half drive from the coast, it is not only its seaside restaurants that can claim to serve fish on the same day it's caught. In addition, the freshest Limerick hams, tastiest Cork *crubins* (pigs' trotters), and most succulent Galway Bay oysters arrive in the city every day. But since young Dubliners love to travel the world, they have also demanded Indian

> ## WORD OF MOUTH
>
> "Here's a cool marketing fact we never knew before: Do you know the Guinness Book of World Records? Of course you do. Well, it was originally created as an advertising tool. One of the execs back in the 1950s wanted to settle a bar room bet he made with someone, and didn't have a way of finding an answer—so he came up with the idea to publish a book containing every record imaginable. That way, they could sell them for use in bars around the world, so that the Guinness name would always be there to settle bets. Who knew?"
>
> —Erin74

2

curries, Thai chilis, and pan-Asian fireworks. Ethnic restaurants, as a result, have blossomed—so you can indulge your passion for superb French or Italian food one day, then enjoy fusion the next. This interest in far-flung food has heralded a new wave of internationally trained professionals who have stamped their own *blás* (Irish for "gloss") on traditional ingredients.

Many top eateries now offer affordable fixed-price lunch menus, which can be considered bargains for the cash-conscious epicurean. A recent welcome phenomenon has been the arrival of little, family-run Italian joints with great food, no fuss, and real coffee, all at a good price. The two Bar Italias on either side of the quays and the fantastically bustling Dunne and Crescenzi near Trinity are two of the best. The twin wonders of L'Gueuleton and Gruel have introduced Dublin the joys of affordable, casual, but always classy French cuisine. To the usual array of ethnic choices—including Chinese, Japanese, and Indian—Dublin is adding even more exotica, including Montys of Kathmandu, a Nepalese spot in Temple Bar, and the Philippine Bahay Kubo.

KNOW-HOW

The Irish dine later than Americans. They stay up later, too, and reservations are usually not booked before 6:30 or 7 PM and up to around 11 PM. Lunch is generally served from 12:30 to 2:30. Pubs often serve food through the day—until 8:30 or 9 PM. Most pubs are family-friendly and welcome children until 7 PM. The Irish are an informal bunch, so smart casual dress is typical. The more formal restaurants, however, do expect you to wear a jacket and tie (noted below). And remember: shorts and sneakers are out here.

A word of warning: forget about singing, you will pay for your supper in Dublin. High overhead and staffing costs have pushed up prices, especially in upscale places. Alas, Dublin recently got its first Starbucks, but there are scores of cafés serving excellent coffee, and often good sandwiches. Other eateries, borrowing trends from all around the world, serve inexpensive pizzas, focaccia, pitas, tacos, and wraps (which are fast gaining popularity over the sandwich). It's worthwhile to see if the restaurant of your choice offers an early-bird or pre- or post-theater menu, with significantly lower set prices at specific times, usually up to 7:30 PM and after the show. Value Added Tax (V.A.T.)—a 13.5% tax on food and a government excise tax on drinks—will automatically be added to your bill. Before paying, check to see whether a service charge has been included on your bill, which is often the case for groups of five or more. If so, you can pay the entire bill with a credit card; if not, it's customary to leave a tip in cash (10% to 15%) even if you're paying the main bill by credit card.

WHAT IT COSTS IN EUROS				
¢	$	$$	$$$	$$$$
AT DINNER	under €10	€10–€17	€18–€24	€25–€30	over €30

Prices are per person for a main course.

EATING WELL IN DUBLIN

It's only a decade since "ethnic" food in Dublin meant sitting at home in front of the TV with a very uninspired Chinese dish of sweet-and-sour chicken. A flood of foreign restaurants has resuscitated the once staid and boring Dublin dining scene and forced native chefs to rethink their menus and reinvent old favorites.

The abundant high-quality produce the country is famous for is finally receiving the care and attention of world-class chefs in the capital city's restaurants. Salmon is mixed with smoked haddock for fish cakes served with anchovy and parsley butter; black pudding is butter-fried and covered in an apple compote; and Irish beef is spiced and topped with a tangy avocado salsa.

Even the humble potato is being shaped and transformed into potato cakes and boxty (potato-and-flour pancake), and colcannon—a traditional Irish dish with bacon and cabbage—is getting a nouvelle spin.

Being an agricultural country with a maritime industry, Ireland benefits from a copious supply of freshly grown and readily available produce and seafood. Excellent Irish beef, pork, ham, and lamb appear on almost every menu.

Keep an eye out, too, for seasonal specials, such as wild or farmed quail and pheasant. Rich seafood harvests mean you can find fresh and smoked salmon, oysters, mussels, and shellfish in many guises—all vying with tender cuts of meat and an appetizing selection of quality vegetables.

Excellent dairy products are also essential to Irish cuisine. Dollops of fresh cream with home-baked desserts promise some exciting conclusions to these feasts—though you could also opt to finish a meal with a selection of native cheeses.

Leave room for the mature cheddars and luscious blue cheeses, the slightly sweet Dubliner, St. Tola goat's cheese from Clare, and Carrigburne Brie from Wexford—only a few of the many fine artisanal cheeses produced around the country.

While you're in Dublin, do indulge at least once in the traditional Irish breakfast, which is often served all day. It includes rashers (bacon), sausages, black-and-white pudding (types of sausage), mushrooms, tomatoes, and a fried egg—with lots of traditional homemade brown and soda breads and the famous Irish creamery butter. You'll need a pot or two of tea to wash this down. Known as an "Ulster Fry" in Northern Ireland, this breakfast is often the biggest—and best—meal of the day.

CITY CENTER: THE SOUTHSIDE

AMERICAN

$$$$ ✕ **Shanahan's on the Green.** The management describes this as an "American-style steak house," and if by that they mean big steaks—Texas-big—they deliver. Happily, quantity doesn't necessarily diminish quality and Shanahans arguably serves the best beef in the country, all certified Irish Angus, of course. In fact, the only things "American" here are those humongous portions and the basement bar, the Oval Office, full

of Americana and presidential paperwork. The building itself is an Irish Georgian glory, designed by Richard Cassels, Dublin's leading 18th-century architect. Glowing with gilded chandeliers and graced with a few marble fireplaces, this restored town house offers a sleekly elegant setting in which to chow down on some of the tenderest beef this side of Kobe (they cook it in a special high-temperature oven, searing the outside to keep the inside good and juicy). If steak doesn't float your boat, they also do a mean pan-roasted Alaskan halibut with lump-crab stuffed artichoke, cherry-vine tomatoes, and gremolata. Oreo-cookie-crust cheesecake is the perfect way to finish off the feast, but many will consider the decor—think sash windows, gilt mirrors, and plush carpets—rich enough. ⊠ *119 St. Stephen's Green, Southside* ☎ *01/407–0939* ⊕ *www.shanahans.ie* ⚏ *Reservations essential* ☰ *AE, DC, MC, V* ⊘ *No lunch Sat.–Thurs.*

CAFÉ

¢ ✗ **Busyfeet & Coco Café.** This bustling, quirky café emphasizes good, wholesome food. Organic ingredients play a prominent role on a menu that's laden with delicious salads and sandwiches. Try the grilled goat-cheese salad served with walnut-and-raisin toast and sun-dried-tomato tapenade on a bed of arugula. The delicious homemade hummus sandwich—served on poppy-seed bread, and topped with roasted red and yellow peppers, red onions, and zucchini—is a must. ⊠ *41–42 S. William St., Southside* ☎ *01/671–9514* ☰ *No credit cards.*

Fodor's Choice
★

CONTINENTAL

$$–$$$ ✗ **Locks.** Near poet Patrick Kavanagh's favorite spot on the Grand Canal, where "here by a lock Niagariously roars," a genuinely warm welcome awaits you at this adorably casual yet chic little restaurant. Dublin's favorite young chef Troy McGuire has recently taken over the kitchen and the interior has had a major revamp, with a smart beach-house look of white wood-panel walls and dark brown parquet floors. The two fireplaces will add to the sense of winter evening coziness. Inventive signature dishes include a wonderfully rich black pudding and an apple tart with Roquefort and Pommery mustard. The two small rooms above the dining room have feasting menus (think whole sucking pig with apple in mouth) for large parties. ⊠ *1 Windsor Terr., Portobello, Southside* ☎ *01/454–3391* ⚏ *Reservations essential* ☰ *AE, DC, MC, V* ⊘ *Closed Sun.*

★

FRENCH

$$$$ ✗ **Thornton's.** If there has been something of a revolution in Irish cooking in the last decade then Kevin Thornton has been the movement's Lenin, and his permanently full restaurant is the Kremlin. Forget the stretched metaphors: if you're passionate about food, this place is a must. Thornton's cooking style is light, and his dishes are small masterpieces of structural engineering, piled almost dangerously high in towers of food. A highlight is the braised suckling pig served with trotter and loin in a *poitin* (Irish moonshine made from potatoes) sauce. Desserts range from banana ice cream to warm chocolate tartlet with raspberries. Sheridans of Dublin supplies the enormous selection of cheeses. The recently restyled dining room is simple and elegant—there's little

★

Where to Eat in Dublin

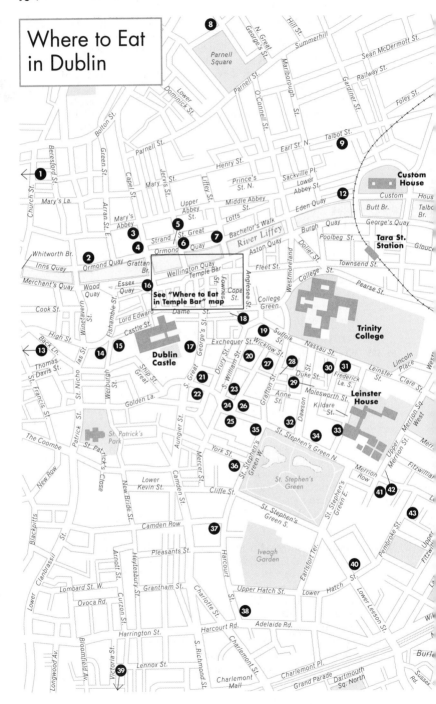

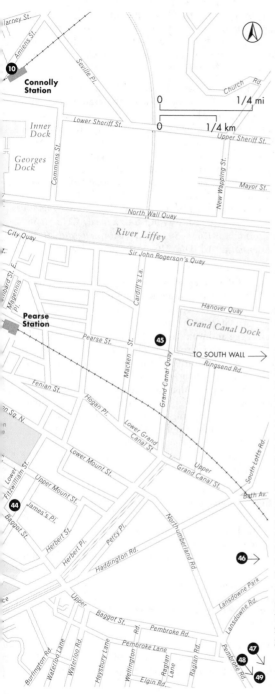

to distract you from the exquisite food—and the new Canapé Bar is the perfect spot for a pre- or post-theater snack with a glass of champagne. ✉*Fitzwilliam Hotel, St. Stephen's Green, Southside* ☎*01/478–7008* ⊕*www.thorntonsrestaurant.com* ⌁*Reservations essential* ▭*AE, DC, MC, V* ☼*Closed Sun. and Mon. No lunch Wed.*

$$$–$$$$ ✕**Brownes.** "Dress to Impress" would seem to be the motto of this established brasserie—as soon as you walk up the granite steps into the small drawing room, the eclectic, luxurious decor almost assaults you. Italian-style friezes, jewel-color walls covered in gilded mirrors, velvet-draped tall windows, and crystal chandeliers all vie for your attention. The food, in a slight contrast to the decor, is quite Irish and hearty, though with plenty of French decorative touches to keep it interesting. Favorites include lobster sausage with sour cabbage mash and bisque sauce, and roasted breast of guinea fowl filled with Durus cheese and tarragon. The floating island with Bailey's *crème anglaise* (a rich custard sauce) is the perfect way finish to a meal. ✉*22 St. Stephen's Green, Southside* ☎*01/638–3939* ⊕*www.brownesdublin.com* ⌁*Reservations essential* ▭*AE, DC, MC, V* ☼*No lunch Sat.*

$$–$$$ ✕**L'Gueuleton.** Dubliners don't do waiting, but you'll see hungry crowds
Fodor'sChoice   doing just that outside this exceptional new eatery just off George's
★   Street. Definitely the best new restaurant in Dublin, L'Gueuleton's tiny size doesn't put off the crowds who head here for authentic French food at a people's price. Start with the braised ray wings with capers or the warm poached egg and watercress salad. For a main course, the Toulouse sausages with choucroute and Lyonnaise potatoes somehow manages to be hearty and adventurous at the same time. Desserts have a devilishly childish touch to them—jelly and ice cream with a raspberry cookie is a typical example. All in all, this is most definitely worth the wait. Speaking of which: although you can't phone in a reservation, you can go there early in the evening and put your name down for a table along with your cell-phone number. They will give you a call 20 minutes before your table is ready. People also gather outside hoping to be fitted in during the evening. ✉*1 Fade St., Southside* ☎*01/675–3708* ▭*MC, V* ☼*Closed Sun.*

¢   ✕**Lemon Crêpe and Coffee Co.** Avoid this place on Fat Tuesday (known as Pancake Tuesday in Ireland) because there will be a line halfway down the street. On any other day this tiny place has the best crepes in town, and hungry Dubliners know it. The space is compact, white, and minimalist. A few sidewalk tables—complete with an outdoor heater— make this a great spot for a tasty snack while you watch Dublin saunter by. Ham, cheese, bacon, and spinach are a few of the savory filling choices. Favorite sweet fillings include banana, Nutella, cream, and the old classic, lemon juice and sugar. Take-out service is swift. ✉*66 S. William St., Southside* ☎*01/672–9044* ▭*No credit cards.*

INDIAN

$–$$ ✕**Jaipur.** Call to mind all the stereotypes of bad, production-line Indian restaurants. Then consign them to the flames, for Jaipur is something different altogether. A spacious room with a sweeping staircase and contemporary furnishings reflects Jaipur's modern, cutting-edge approach to Indian cuisine. Mixed with traditional dishes, such as chicken tikka masala, are more unusual preparations, such as *rara gosdh* (lamb slowly cooked with black-eyed peas). The delightful *karwari* is a sweet and sour butterfish in a tamarind-flavor broth redolent of coastal-south-Indian spices. Try the Jaipur Jugalbandi, a selection of five appetizers. Dishes can be toned down or spiced up to suit your palate, and service is courteous and prompt. Another plus: the wine list is well thought out. ⊠*41 S. Great George's St., Southside* ☎*01/677–0999* ⊕*www. jaipur.ie* ♨*Reservations essential* ▭*AE, MC, V.*

$–$$ ✕**Khyber Tandoori.** The Khyber Tandoori doorman, dressed in traditional colorful costume complete with a dashing white turban, has become something of a living landmark in modern Dublin. A short walk from St. Stephen's Green, this gem of a restaurant specializes in Pakistani cuisine but also serves a broad selection of Indian dishes. Try the *shami* (Syrian) kebabs—dainty, spiced patties of minced lamb and lentils—or *kabuli chicken tikka shashlik* (marinated, diced chicken with onions and red and green peppers), which comes bright red and sizzling on an iron platter. Settle in and admire the richly embroidered wall hangings and the great gusts of steam coming from the tandoori oven in the glassed-in area. ⊠*44–45 S. William St., Southside* ☎*01/670–4855* ▭*AE, DC, MC, V* ⊘*No lunch Sun.*

IRISH

¢–$ ✕**Kilkenny Kitchen.** Take a break from shopping and sightseeing at this big self-service restaurant on the upper floor of the Kilkenny Shop. Homemade soup, casseroles, cold meats, and salads are arranged on a long buffet, along with lots of tasty breads and cakes. Try to get a table by the window overlooking the playing fields of Trinity College. Lunchtime is busy, but Kilkenny is very pleasant for morning coffee or afternoon tea. ⊠*5–6 Nassau St., Southside* ☎*01/677–7075* ⊕*www. kilkennyshop.com* ▭*AE, DC, MC, V.*

ITALIAN

$$–$$$ ✕**Il Primo.** Eccentric, gregarious Dieter Bergman likes to run his little two-story Italian restaurant like an intimate dinner party. So don't be surprised if he joins you at your table for a chat. Old wooden tables and chairs give the two small dining rooms a casual feel, and the friendly, if cramped, surroundings attract a devoted clientele. The *gnocchi di patate,* potato dumplings with tomato, spinach, and ricotta, is typical of the hearty fare. For the more adventurous the *Ravioli il Primo*—open ravioli stuffed with chicken, Parma ham, and wild mushrooms and smothered in a cream sauce—is a must. The wine list is, to quote a local phrase, as long as your arm. ⊠*Montague St. off Harcourt St., Southside* ☎*01/478–3373* ▭*AE, DC, MC, V* ⊘*No lunch weekends.*

$ ✕**The Steps of Rome.** Discerning natives flock to this place for a cheap lunch, or a good takeout. Just a few steps from Grafton Street, this Italian eatery is also popular for a late-night bite. Slices of delicious, thin-crust pizza, with all the traditional toppings, are the main attraction. The *funghi* (mushroom) pizza is particularly good. The few tables are usually full, but it's worth waiting around for the classic Italian pasta dishes. Some diners just opt for the fresh salads with focaccia. Follow it all with cheesecake or tiramisu, and good strong espresso. ⊠*1 Chatham Ct., Southside* ☎*01/670–5630* ⊟*No credit cards.*

¢–$ ╳**Dunne and Crescenzi.** Nothing
Fodor's Choice   succeeds like success. So popu-
★   lar is this classy little Italian joint just off Nassau Street that they've expanded into the premises two doors down. Pity the poor little coffee shop in between trying to compete with the unpretentious brilliance of this brother-and-sister restaurant and deli. The menu couldn't be simpler: paninis (sandwiches), antipasti, a single

pasta special, and desserts. But the all-Italian kitchen staff work wonders with high-quality imported ingredients. The antipasto *misto,* an assortment of thinly sliced Parma ham, three types of salami, sun-dried tomatoes, cheeses, peppers in olive oil, and artichoke hearts makes a great light lunch. A couple of long tables make it perfect for a group, and the hundreds of bottles of wine on shelves cover every inch of the walls. ⊠*14 S. Fredrick St., Southside* ☎*01/677–3815* ⊕*www.dunneandcrescenzi.com* ⊟*AE, MC, V.*

JAPANESE

$–$$ ╳**Wagamama.** Canteen food wasn't like this at your school. Modeled on a Japanese canteen, Wagamama, with its long wooden tables and benches and high ceilings with exposed metal piping, ensures a unique communal dining experience. It attracts a young, loud crowd and is constantly busy. Formal courses aren't acknowledged—food is served as soon as it's ready, and appetizers and main courses arrive together. *Edamame*—steamed and salted green soybeans in the pod—are a delicious starter and great fun to pop open and eat. Choose from filling bowls of *cha han* (fried rice with chicken, prawns, and vegetables) or chili beef ramen, and wash it down with fresh fruit or vegetable juice. There's also a fine selection of beers and sakes for the less abstemious. ⊠*S. King St., Southside* ☎*01/478–2152* ⊟*AE, DC, MC, V.*

$–$$ ╳**Yamamori.** Dublin's young and mobile folk went noodle-mad a few years ago and Yamamori jumped to the top of the list for these ramen addicts. The open plan and family-style tables have kept it popular with the buzz crowd. The meals-in-a-bowl are a splendid slurping experience, and although you'll be supplied with a small Chinese-style soup spoon, the best approach is with chopsticks. The *yasai yaki soba,* Chinese-style noodles with Asian vegetables and egg, garnished with menma and spring onions is a favorite example. You can also get sushi and sashimi, plus delicious chicken teriyaki. ⊠*71–72 S. Great George's St., Southside* ☎*01/475–5001* ⊟*AE, MC, V.*

PAN-ASIAN

$–$$ ✕**Mao.** Everything is Asian-fusion at this bustling café, from the little Andy Warhol pastiche of Chairman Mao on the washroom door to the eclectic mix of dishes on the menu, which combine Thai, Vietnamese, and other Southeast Asian elements. Top choices include the Malaysian chicken, chili squid, and the *nasi goreng* (Indonesian fried rice with chicken and shrimp). Go early to be sure of a seat. ⊠*2 Chatham Row, Southside* ☎*01/670–4899* ⚖*Reservations not accepted* ⊟*MC, V.*

VEGETARIAN

¢–$ ✕**Nude.** One-word titles for restaurants and cafés were all the rage in Dublin about five years ago. Many of them have fallen by the wayside, but Nude, a sleek, ecofriendly fast-food café, has been such a success that owner Norman Hewson—brother of U2's Bono—has opened another branch for takeout only on Upper Leeson Street. The canteen-style tables set the extremely casual atmosphere—don't be surprised if your neighbor strikes up a conversation. You order at the counter and someone delivers to your table in double-quick time. The menu is mostly vegetarian, and everything on it is made with organic and free-range ingredients. Choose from homemade soups and vegetable wraps (hummus and peppers is a classic), smoothies, and fresh-squeezed juices. ⊠*21 Suffolk St., Southside* ☎*01/677–4804* ⊕*www.nude.ie* ⊟*DC, MC, V.*

SOUTHEAST DUBLIN

ASIAN

$–$$$ ✕**Diep le Shaker.** Don't be surprised to see people ordering champagne with their meals—there's a permanent party vibe at this flamboyant Thai restaurant, which attracts Ireland's wealthy in droves. Comfortable high-back chairs, pristine table linen, and elegant stemware make this a stylish place to dine. But half the reason for going is to see and be seen. Try the steamed scallops and ginger, or lobster in garlic pepper and Thai herbs. It's slightly off the beaten track, on a narrow lane off Pembroke Street. ⊠*55 Pembroke La., Southeast Dublin* ☎*01/661–1829* ⊕*www.diep.net* ⚖*Reservations essential* ⊟*AE, DC, MC, V* ☉*No lunch Sun.*

$–$$ ✕**Chai-Yo.** Be educated while you eat. There's always something thrilling about getting close up and watching a master at work. The Japanese teppan-yaki area at this classy pan-Asian restaurant on bustling Baggot Street, where the chef cooks your food right on your tabletop, is a feast for the eye as well as the palate. Choose from a selection of scallops, sea bass, steak, teriyaki chicken, and prawns, and watch as a beautiful grilled dish is whipped up before your eyes. The white walls and dark lacquered furnishings give Chai-Yo a serene ambience, enhanced by the delicate glassware and fine, green-washed-porcelain plates. The menu picks the best from Chinese, Thai, and Japanese dishes. The deep-fried crispy quail eggs are a tasty starter, and the king scallops in Thai chili oil with scallion and onion is the place's most popular main course. ✉ *100 Lower Baggot St., Southeast Dublin* ☎ *01/676–7652* 🖃 *AE, DC, MC, V* ☺ *No lunch Sun.*

FRENCH

$$$$
Fodor'sChoice
★

✕ **Patrick Guilbaud.** The words "Dublin's finest restaurant" often share the same breath as the name of this do-be-impressed place on the ground floor of the Merrion Hotel. The menu is described as French, but Guilbaud's genius lies in his occasional daring use of traditional Irish ingredients—so often abused and taken for granted—to create the unexpected. With the eponymous chef in charge, you can always expect superb cooking. His best dishes are simple—and flawless: Châlons duck à l'orange, Connemara lobster in season, and braised pig's trotters. Follow that, if you can, with the *assiette au chocolat* (a tray of five hot-and-cold chocolate desserts). The ambience is just as delicious—if you're into modern art, that is. There are no Georgian Gainsboroughs to be found here. Instead, you'll think you've wandered into skyscraper Manhattan, thanks to the marvelously lofty dining room and minimalist art hanging on the walls (the Roderick O'Connor and Louis LeBrocquys are all from the owner's private collection). Nearly as impressive is the 70-page wine list, the view of the Merrion's manicured gardens, and the lunch special for under €30. Soaring white vaults and empty white walls won't make you feel warm and cozy but you can always go somewhere else for that. What you won't find anywhere else is Guilbaud. ✉ *21 Upper Merrion St., Southeast Dublin* ☎ *01/676–4192* ⊕ *www.merrionhotel.com* ⌚ *Reservations essential* 🖃 *AE, DC, MC, V* ☺ *Closed Sun. and Mon.*

$$–$$$

✕ **Balzac.** A new player on the Dublin dining stage, Paul Flynn's Balzac aims to re-create the glamour and ambience of the best Parisian brasseries. The sparklingly handsome dining room with giant wall mirrors, high windowed ceiling, and glitzy candelabra, is one of the most impressive in the city. But the atmosphere is still casual, and the menu has a touch of peasant France mixed with a Parisian finish. The champagne-and-truffle risotto is sensational and serious carnivores will delight in the slow-cooked beef with Vichy carrot, parsley, and shallot salad. The lengthy wine list is second to none. ✉ *35 Dawson St., Southeast Dublin* ☎ *01/677–8611* ⊕ *www.lastampa.ie/restaurant* 🖃 *AE, DC, MC, V.*

$$–$$$

✕ **Dax.** When is a wine bar not a wine bar? When it's the city's best new restaurant. Opened as a basement wine bar by Olivier Meisonnave, the former sommelier at stellar Thornton's, Dax is quickly becoming the dining spot of choice for Dubliners who care about food. You can choose to drink or dine (tapas style) at the bar, in the lush armchairs of the open-plan lounge, or in the more formal, restrained-modern dining room. The sautéed foie gras is a standout starter, while the chestnut risotto has quickly become one of the favorite main courses. The cold meat platter is a finger-lickin' little bar dish. With Olivier in charge the wine list is the envy of many a more expensive eatery, and with a couple dozen wines poured by the glass you can dare to try something really special. ✉ *23 Pembroke St., Southeast Dublin* ☎ *01/676–1494* ⊕ *www.*

dax.ie ⚖*Reservations essential*
▱*AE, DC, MC, V* ⊘*Closed Sun
and Mon. No lunch Sat.*

IRISH

$–$$$ ✕**Ely Winebar.** Almost equidistant
from the twin dames of Dublin
hotel elegance, the Shelbourne and
the Merrion, Ely started out as a
mere wine bar—and oh, what a
selection of wines they have, many
of them by the glass. But it has

quickly grown into a wonderful little eatery with organic meat and veg
from the owner's family farm in County Clare, guaranteeing a tasty
mouthful every bite. Dishes tend to be simple—bangers and mash, a
scrumptious lamb stew, Killaha oysters with brown bread—but incred-
ibly fresh and succulent. The plate of mature Irish and Continental
cheeses is the perfect finish—with a glass of wine of course. ✉*22 Ely
Pl., Southeast Dublin* ☎*01/676–8986* ⊕*www.elywinebar.ie* ▱*AE,
DC, MC, V* ⊘*Closed Sun.*

ITALIAN

$$–$$$$ ✕**Town Bar and Grill.** Even basements can surprise, and an old wine
merchant's cellar on Kildare Street has been transformed into this cozy,
modern-Italian trattoria. The elegant, New York–vibe dining room has
a definite buzz, and numerous Irish celebrities have already made this
a regular haunt. Chef Temple Garner likes to take traditional Italian
classics and give them a little—just a little—twist. The rabbit fricassee
with white wine and sage tagliatelle is one of the most exciting starters.
For mains try the monkfish *zuppa di pesce* with chorizo, red pepper,
and saffron aioli crostini. Gingered sticky toffee pudding with *cara-
melita* (caramel ice cream with soft toffee pieces) is a nice guilty way
to finish. ✉*21 Kildare St., Southeast Dublin* ☎*01/662–4724* ⊕*www.
townbarandgrill.com* ▱*AE, DC, MC, V* ⊘*No lunch Sun.*

MODERN IRISH

$$$–$$$$ ✕**One Pico.** Grown women have been known to swoon when chef–
★ owner Eamonn O'Reilly walks into the dining room of his little res-
taurant tucked away in a quiet lane only a few minutes from Stephen's
Green. Eamonn cuts quite a dash, but it's his sophisticated, daring,
contemporary cuisine that tends to seduce visitors to One Pico. Try
the incredible escabeche of mackerel citrus couscous with black olive
tapenade to start. Dishes such as roast rump of veal with fricassee of
girolles, pearl onion, and truffle, and *pomme sarladaise* (a southern
France version of mashed potatoes) demonstrate a savvy use of native
ingredients. Follow this with the baked chèvre cheesecake garnished
with praline chocolate and orange confit. As is usual with Dublin's
luxe eateries, the fixed-price lunch menu offers great value. ✉*5–6
Molesworth Pl., off Schoolhouse La., Southeast Dublin* ☎*01/676–
0300* ⊕*www.onepico.com* ⚖*Reservations essential* ▱*AE, DC, MC,
V* ⊘*Closed Sun.*

TEMPLE BAR

AMERICAN

$-$$ ✕**Elephant & Castle.** The Elephant was long established in Temple Bar before the Tiger (Celtic, that is) changed the neighborhood forever. Large windows are great for people-watching in the city's trendiest area, but "nothing fancy" would be a good motto for the traditional American food. Charcoal-grilled burgers, salads, omelets, sandwiches, and pasta comprise the much-thumbed menu. Sunday brunch is always packed. The portions are some of the most generous in Dublin. When the service is good, the turnover tends to be quick, although you may be inclined to linger. New Yorkers take note: yes, this is a cousin of the restaurant of the same name in Greenwich Village. ⊠ *18 Temple Bar, Temple Bar* ☎ *01/679–3121* ⊜ *Reservations not accepted* ▭ *AE, DC, MC, V.*

¢–$$ ✕**Bad Ass Café.** If you want to make a Dublin native wince, mention with excitement that Sinéad O'Connor used to wait tables at this lively café in a converted warehouse between the Central Bank and Ha'penny Bridge. (A "Rock 'n Stroll" tour plaque notes O'Connor's past here.) Old-fashioned cash shuttles whiz around the ceiling of the barnlike space, which has bare floors and primary colors inside and out. You can indulge in some great people-watching behind the wall of glass here. The food—mainly pizzas, pastas, and burgers—is unexceptional, but the Bad Ass can be a lot of fun and appetites of all ages love it. ⊠ *9–11 Crown Alley, Temple Bar* ☎ *01/671–2596* ⊕ *www.badasscafe. com* ▭ *AE, MC, V.*

ECLECTIC

$$–$$$ ✕**Mermaid Café.** Hope you don't mind sharing your dinner conversation with the people next to you. The Mermaid has the simple, crowded feel of a very upmarket canteen, with large tables set close together and casual, but classy, service. One of the chef–owners dabbles in fine art, and his tastes in this area are reflected in his artistic and decorative style of bistro cooking. It's not cheap, but the food is reliable. Lunch is an exceptional value—piquant crab cakes, huge hearty seafood casseroles, five-spiced duck breast, or butternut squash risotto with grilled squash, spinach, and Parmesan. Attention to detail and a thoughtful wine list make this modest restaurant with tall windows looking onto busy Dame Street one of the most popular eateries in Temple Bar. ⊠ *69 Dame St., Temple Bar* ☎ *01/670–8236* ⊕ *www.mermaid.ie* ▭ *MC, V.*

FRENCH

$$$$ ✕**Les Frères Jacques.** Many restaurants call themselves French, but this
★ elegant eatery next to the Olympia Theatre positively reeks of Gallic panache. Old prints of Paris and Deauville hang on the green-paper walls, and the French waiters, dressed in white Irish linen and black bow ties, exude a European charm without being excessively formal. Expect traditional French cooking that nods to the seasons. Seafood is a major attraction, and lobster (fished right from the tank—a "plus" that people with delicate sensibilities will find a definite minus) is typically roasted and flambéed with Irish whiskey. Others prefer the half

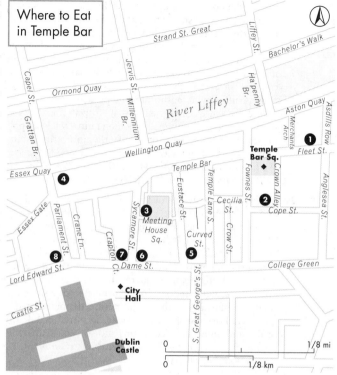

Where to Eat in Temple Bar

roasted duck, filleted and served with a pivithier of foie gras and cabbage. Also recommended are the seasonal game specialties. A piano player performs Friday and Saturday evenings and on the occasional weeknight. ⊠*74 Dame St., Temple Bar* ☎*01/679–4555* ⊕*www.les-freresjacques.com* ⌕*Reservations essential* ⊟*AE, MC, V* ⊘*Closed Sun. No lunch Sat.*

ITALIAN

$–$$$ ✕**Toscana.** A genuine trattoria in the heart of crazy Temple Bar, Toscana buzzes with chatter all evening long. A Mediterranean slant to the simple dining room includes plenty of terra-cotta, cream tones, and wood. A typical starter is the golden croquettes of mozzarella and rice served with a garlic dip. The *Penne al Salmone* is an Irish smoked salmon sautéed in butter and fresh basil and cooked in a creamy tomato sauce. The meat and pizza dishes are also always reliable and the Baileys cheesecake with chocolate sauce is a dessert that will have your taste buds tap dancing. ⊠*3 Cork Hill, Dame Street., Temple Bar* ☎*01/670–9785* ⊕*www.toscana.ie* ⊟*AE, DC, MC, V.*

MODERN IRISH

$$$$ ✕**The Tea Room.** In the Clarence Hotel, you can sit around all day and hope that Bono and the boys of U2—they own the joint after all—might turn up for a quick snack. Other stars of stage and screen often

stay at the hotel and stop in at the Tea Room. Minimalistically hued in golden oak, eggshell white, and light yellows, the high-ceiling room is a perfect stage for off-duty celebs. The contrast between this high-vaulted cocoon and busy Essex Street—whose madding crowds can be glimpsed through the double-height windows—is nowhere else as dramatic. Drama is also found on the newer-than-now nouvelle menu. You can opt for either adventurous specials—-spatchcock quail with pea puree, truffled wild mushroom, and pistachio vinaigrette, anyone?—or such consistently good, typically mouthwatering delights as the pan-fried foie gras with caramelized onion tatin, "wicked apple" cider with muscat raisins, or the risotto of Carlingford mussels and courgettes. Obviously, the menu is as chic as the customers. ⊠ *Clarence Hotel, 6–8 Wellington Quay, Temple Bar* ☎ *01/407–0813* ⊕ *www.theclarence.ie* ⌕ *Reservations essential* ▤ *AE, DC, MC, V.*

$$–$$$ ✕**Eden.** Perennially one of Dublin's hippest places, Eden is where arty
★ and media types are likely to gather to talk about, well, themselves. It has an open kitchen and a high wall of glass through which you can observe one of Temple Bar's main squares. Patio-style doors lead to an outdoor eating area—a major plus in a city with relatively few alfresco dining spots. On weekend nights in summer you can enjoy an outdoor movie in Meeting House Square while you eat. Seasonal menus are in vogue here, but standout dishes include wild Irish venison stew, and fried fillet of halibut with celeriac mash, balsamic roasted beetroot, arugula, and horseradish crème fraîche. Desserts include rhubarb crème brûlée and homemade ice creams and sorbets. ⊠ *Meeting House Sq., Temple Bar* ☎ *01/670–5372* ⊕ *www.edenrestaurant.ie* ⌕ *Reservations essential* ▤ *AE, DC, MC, V.*

NEPALESE

$–$$ ✕**Montys of Kathmandu.** Montys proudly declares itself the "only Nepalese restaurant in Dublin." Was there ever any doubt? The bland decor is nothing to write home about, but the food at this little eatery in the middle of hypermodern Temple Bar is as authentic as it is unique. *Poleko* squid (lightly spiced and barbecued in a tandoori oven and served in a sizzler) or lamb *Choila* (with fresh chilis, ginger, garlic, herbs, and a dash of red wine) are the more adventurous starters. For a main course try *Mo Mo*, dumplings served with Mo Mo chutney, a favorite street dish in Kathmandu. The wine cellar is surprisingly varied. ⊠ *28 Eustace St., Temple Bar* ☎ *01/670–4911* ⊕ *www.montys.ie* ▤ *AE, DC, MC, V* ⊙ *No lunch Sun.*

THE NORTHSIDE

ECLECTIC

$–$$ ✕**The Vaults.** Come eat under the train station. Not exactly the best sales pitch you've ever heard, but this wonderful, long-neglected space beneath Connolly Station was imaginatively revamped to create one of the city's most fashionable dining spots. Cavernous arches, smooth Portland stone floors, striking furniture, and dramatic lighting create the background for a mostly young business set. Each of the vaults is

2

decorated in its own style, ranging from hypermodern to turn-of-the-20th-century elegant. Cocktails are a specialty, although it's worth a visit for the food alone. The Italian chef makes everything from scratch, including the pizza dough. A wide-ranging menu covers light snack options alongside more substantial dishes like the house pizza, a blend of tomato, mozzarella, prawns, red onion, and herbs. Be sure to leave room for the excellent chocolate meringue with wild berries and cream. Note that dinner is served only until 8. ⊠*Harbourmaster Pl., Northside* ☎*01/605–4700* ⊕*www.thevaults.ie* ⊟*AE, MC, V* ☉*Closed Sun.*

IRISH

$–$$ ✕**The Winding Stair.** A dark cloud hung over Dublin when one of its
Fodor'sChoice favorite secondhand bookshop-cafés, The Winding Stair, was set to
★ close. But the silver lining appeared in the form of this atmospheric, buzzing little restaurant, which reemerged in the old space, replete with a downstairs bookshop and the well-worn name. Upstairs, former habitués will enjoy seeing the old bookcases around the walls (some of which are now stacked with wine). To get the real feel for the place try to get a table looking out over the Ha'penny Bridge and the slow-flowing river beneath. Traditional Irish food re-created with an adventurous twist best describes the terrific menu, which is greatly helped by organic credentials, as nearly everything on the menu is locally sourced. The bacon and cabbage with parsley sauce is a standout, as is the undyed smoked haddock with a delicious white cheddar mash. An inventive wine list and a wonderful Irish farmhouse cheese selection are two more treats on offer. If your sweet tooth is acting up try the mind-blowing bread-and-butter pudding for dessert. A new Dublin gem, for sure. ⊠*40 Lower Ormond Quay, Northside* ☎*01/872–7320* ⊕*www.winding-stair.com* ⊟*AE, DC, MC, V.*

¢ ✕**Soup Dragon.** This tiny café and take-out soup shop serves an aston-
★ ishing array of fresh soups daily. Soups come in three sizes, and you can get vegetarian soup or soups with meat- or fish-based broth. Best bets include red pepper, tomato, and goat cheese soup; fragrant Thai chicken soup; and hearty mussel, potato, and leek soup. The friendly staff makes fine coffee and delicious smoothies. The cost of soup includes bread and a piece of fruit for dessert—an excellent value. ⊠*168 Capel St., Northside* ☎*01/872–3277* ⊟*No credit cards* ☉*Closed Sun. No dinner.*

ITALIAN

¢–$$ ✕**Il Vignardo.** Sometimes when it comes to dining, the where is more
★ important than the what. Il Vignardo serves some of Dublin's tasti-est cheap and cheerful pizzas and pasta, but it's the unique decor that elevates this place a little above the rest. The dramatically vaulted ceilings, painted with creeping vines and branches, burst into bloom as they rise from Tuscan columns and evoke thoughts of Italian vineyards and sunshine. Outside, the sheltered courtyard garden, a real oasis in a city center setting, is perfect for summer dining or just a little aperitif. The extra-hot Mexican special is a great pizza, while the penne arrabiata is the best of the pastas. If you want to spend a little extra, try the *Bistecca al Diana,* an 8-ounce sirloin with cognac and Diane sauce. But

who can resist the lasagna, served up with minced Irish beef? ⊠*Hotel Isaccs, Store St., Northside* ☎*01/855–3099* ⊕*www.isaacs.ie* ⊟*AE, DC, MC, V.*

¢–$ ✕**Enoteca delle Langhe.** Officially called Quartier Bloom in tribute to
FodorsChoice   Joyce's most famous character, a charming little (very little) Italian
★   quarter has sprung up just off Ormond Quay, bringing a chorus of approval from Dubliners long starved of quality, down-to-earth Italian food. It consists of a communal plaza area, a fabulous mural that's a modern take on Leonardo da Vinci's *The Last Supper,* and a couple of places to eat, including Enoteca delle Langhe. Italian owned and operated, Langhe serves up the full enoteca experience: quality, affordable Italian wines (more than 75% are sourced from the Langhe district); a limited but enticing selection of appetizers—try the perfect bruschetta with scrumptious toppings like sun-dried tomato pesto and sautéed courgettes—warm, friendly, family-style service; and a constant buzz in the air. In summer tango dancers perform outside. ⊠*Blooms La., Northside* ☎*01/888–0834* ⊟*AE, DC, MC, V.*

MEDITERRANEAN

$$ ✕**101 Talbot.** Sardi's it's not, but the 101 has that certain buzz that only comes from restaurants popular with the artistic and literary set. Close to the Abbey and Gate theaters, so there's no danger of missing a curtain call, this comfortable upstairs restaurant showcases an ever-changing exhibition of local artists' work. The creative contemporary food—with Mediterranean and Middle Eastern influences—uses fresh local ingredients. Try the roast pork fillet marinated in orange, ginger, and soy sauce, and served with fried noodles. The cashew and red-pepper *rissole* (turnover) with chili and ginger jam, served with wild and basmati rice, also impresses. Healthful options and several vegetarian choices make this a highly versatile restaurant. ⊠*101 Talbot St., Northside* ☎*01/874–5011* ⌣*Reservations essential* ⊟*AE, DC, MC, V* ⊗*Closed Sun. and Mon.*

MODERN IRISH

$$$$ ✕**Chapter One.** If you spot the maitre d' strolling between tables and
FodorsChoice   handing out tickets, you know you're at the hugely popular prethe-
★   ater special at Chapter One. Yes, if you're at the pretheater sitting, they'll actually go pick up your tickets from the nearby Abbey or Gate theaters. The place gets its name from its location, downstairs in the vaulted, stone-wall basement of the Dublin Writers Museum; the natural stone-and-wood setting gives it a cozy cavelike feel. This contemporary French eatery is currently the culinary king of the Northside, thanks to chef-proprietor Ross Lewis's way with such dishes as veal sweetbreads, served with smoked bacon, fennel, mushroom, carrot, and gingerbread crumbs, and topped with a pistachio cream sauce. Yeats himself would have loved the sea bream with braised squid, celery, tomato, and shellfish sauce, while Synge probably would have fancied the Dublin version of Proust's madeleine: rich bread-and-butter pudding, a favorite of working-class Irish mothers for generations, here turned into an outrageously filling work of art. ⊠*18–19 Parnell Sq., Northside* ☎*01/873–2266* ⊕*www.chapteronerestaurant.com*

⚓Reservations essential ▤*AE, DC, MC, V* ⊗*Closed Sun. and Mon. No lunch Sat.*

$$–$$$ ✕**Halo.** Judges from the nearby Four Courts rest their wigs on empty seats while the fashion crowd sits over multicolor drinks at this chic restaurant in the even more chic Morrison Hotel. A recent restyling has slightly softened the severity of the soaring ceiling and minimalist feel of the dramatic two-story dining room, devised by fashion designer John Rocha. It looks its best at night: moody and mysterious. European fusion is the tag new chef Richie Wilson gives his menu. Seafood is the focus of his star dishes; the panfried pike fillet with purple potato puree and truffle sauce is a rich and warm favorite. For a starter try the pea risotto with Normandy cheese and saffron foam. As a fitting finale, desserts are miniature works of art on enormous china platters. ✉*Morrison Hotel, Ormond Quay, Northside* ☎*01/887–2421* ⊕*www.morrisonhotel.ie* ▤*AE, DC, MC, V.*

$$–$$$ ✕**Rhodes D7.** Newly opened and greatly hyped, Rhodes D7, from Brit-
★ ish celebrity chef Gary Rhodes, is an upmarket, contemporary Euro-pean-style eatery on the edge of the emerging Smithfield neighborhood. "He has built it. Will they come?" local foodies are asking. Consider-ing this chef's resume, most probably yes: Rhodes is considered the father of Mod Brit cooking (being the first to give a nouvelle spin to such old faves as fish cakes and braised oxtail); he once hosted "Hell's Kitchen," and he currently runs five restaurants in London and has a series of glossy cookbooks to his credit. Now, his adventurous tastes are set to conquer Ireland, and all at a price few in Dublin's high end are matching. The smoked eel on toast with poached egg, crispy pan-cetta, and hollandaise is a brave but rewarding starter. Entrées include staples like fish-and-chips with crème fraîche tartar, as well as more exciting options like the panfried skate with shrimp and capers, served in a lemon-butter sauce with a side of chive potatoes. The interior is a slight mishmash of styles dominated by some startlingly colorful mod-ern paintings of, among other things, cows—but you'll be too focused on your plate to care. ✉*The Capel Building, Mary's Abbey, North-side* ☎*01/804–4444* ⊕*www.rhodesd7.com* ⚓*Reservations essential* ▤*AE, DC, MC, V* ⊗*Closed Sun. No dinner Mon.*

$–$$ ✕**Harbour Master.** You just have to look out the window to understand why this big, airy restaurant and bar in the Irish Financial Services Cen-ter north of the Liffey is so popular: it overlooks the serene and calming canal basin. A lunch-only venue, it tends to be busy and buzzing with stockbrokers and lawyers, so get there a little early if possible. You can dine bistro-style at the cavernous bar, but it's better to head for the more spacious—and more relaxing—dining area. The kitchen is best on the basics, so try the panfried rib-eye steak doused in garlic-and-rosemary butter (and served up with mesclun and fries). The establish-ment also runs an adjacent bar that stays open late and serves excel-lent bar food. ✉*Custom House Docks, Northside* ☎*01/670–1688* ⊕*www.harbourmaster.ie* ▤*AE, MC, V* ⊗*No dinner.*

SOUTH DUBLIN: THE GRAND CANAL & BALLSBRIDGE

FRENCH

$–$$ ✗**French Paradox.** Like the people of the south of France that inspired
★ the place, relaxed but stylish would best describe the decor and dining
at this little restaurant above a wineshop. French Paradox has found a
real niche in the Dublin scene. Wine buffs, Francophiles, and gourmets
flock here for the hearty traditional fare and Mediterranean environment. Share the *assiette le fond de barrique,* a selection of charcuterie,
pâté, and cheese, or perhaps indulge in a smoked-duck salad or a selection from the foie gras menu. Select a nice bottle from the ground-floor
wineshop (mostly French labels) and sip it in situ for a mere €8 corkage
fee. Seating is limited. ⊠*53 Shelbourne Rd., Ballsbridge* ☎*01/660–
4068* ⊕*www.thefrenchparadox.com* ⌂*Reservations essential* ☐*AE,
MC, V* ⊙*Closed Sun.*

IRISH

$$–$$$$ ✗**Franks.** Snugly tucked into the arches under the Old Malting Tower
Bridge at Grand Canal Quay, this relaxed bar and restaurant has one
of the most unusual locations of the Dublin dining scene. The main,
bistro-style menu is strong on comfort meat dishes, including a signa-
ture steak tartare and wonderful homemade beef burgers, but there are
plenty of snack and salad dishes available if you don't fancy splurg-
ing on a full meal. During Sunday brunch, which is a big hit here, the
cozy atmosphere takes on a delightful busy hum. A great choice of
wine in full and half bottles helps keep that buzz going. ⊠*The Malt-
ing Tower, Grand Canal Quay, Grand Canal* ☎*01/662–5870* ☐*AE,
DC, MC, V.*

MODERN IRISH

$$$–$$$$ ✗**Seasons.** Although the restaurant at the Dublin branch of the vaunted
Four Seasons hotel took a little time to find its feet in and out of the
kitchen, it is starting to stake its claim in Dublin's high-end dining
scene—Sunday brunch has become a ritual for many well-to-do Dub-
lin families. Highly dramatic dishes, served in the large and slightly
overwhelming silver-service dining room, creatively incorporate local
(and often organic) ingredients. A starter of roast double breast of
quail with Moroccan spices and toasted almond puree might be fol-
lowed by seared veal loin with morel mushroom polenta, and a glazed
shallot, crisp chervil, and Parma salad. Sommelier Simon Keegan is one
of the best in the country. ⊠*Four Seasons Hotel, Simmonscourt Rd.,
Ballsbridge* ☎*01/665–4642* ⊕*www.fourseasons.com* ⌂*Reservations
essential* ☐*AE, DC, MC, V.*

$–$$ ✗**O'Connells.** When it comes to cooking, pedigree counts. Owner Tom
★ O'Connell is a brother to Ireland's favorite celebrity chef, Darina Allen,
famed for her "slow food" Ballymaloe Cookery School in Cork. Tom
follows the family blueprint by showcasing locally produced meats and
game that can be traced back to their source (in many cases, an individual farm). Add to this a focus on fresh Irish produce and baked
goods cooked in a unique wood-fire oven and you have the makings of
a feast that is deliriously, quintessentially Irish. Spiced beef is prepared

according to an old Cork recipe, salmon fillet is "hot smoked" by the restaurant itself, while Ashe's Annascaul Black Pudding is handmade on the Dingle peninsula. You can also try the spit-roasted duck or the monkfish in a lemon-and-garlic sauce—or an omelet made from organic eggs from free-range chickens, with peppers, zucchini, and a sweet chili sauce. A tremendous selection of fresh breads is on display in the open kitchen, which turns into a buffet for breakfast and lunch. The cheese board is a who's who of Irish farmhouse cheeses, including the Ferguson family's tangy Gubbeen. Serving as a cool backdrop, O'Connell's vast modern space is beautifully fitted out with sleek timber paneling and floor-to-ceiling windows. ⊠ *Merrion Rd., Ballsbridge* ☎ *01/647–3304* ⊕ *www.oconnellsballsbridge.com* ▭ *AE, DC, MC, V.*

PHILIPPINE

$-$$ ✕ **Bahay Kubo.** Don't always believe what you read. The very basic English translations on the menu fail miserably to capture the excitement and diversity of the dishes at Ireland's only Philippine restaurant. Persevere and you'll find a fine selection of authentic Philippine cooking with touches of Chinese and Malaysian cuisines. Chicken, beef, and prawns all feature heavily, with red-curry chicken in coconut milk the most popular choice with regulars. Desserts have been brought in frozen, so it's best to stick to starters and entrées and finish up with a coffee. The starched white linen and pale-wood flooring give the place an open and light feel. ⊠ *14 Bath Ave., Ballsbridge* ☎ *01/660–5572* ⌖ *Reservations essential* ▭ *AE, MC, V* ⊙ *Closed Mon. No lunch Sat.–Wed.*

DUBLIN WEST

CAFÉS

¢–$ ✕ **Gallic Kitchen.** Canny Dubliners make regular pilgrimages to Sarah Webb's bakery, where some of the best pastries in town are available daily. There's no seating in this powerhouse patisserie, but long counters allow space for perching your coffee and tucking into the finest sweet and savory treats. Pop in for a morning coffee and a pear tart; try the quiche or salmon roulade with homemade salsa for lunch; or simply take afternoon tea with a scrumptious scone. Expect queues at lunchtime, and be sure to buy in bulk for the tastiest take-out picnic in town. ⊠ *49 Francis St., Liberties* ☎ *01/454–4912* ⊕ *www.gallickitchen.com* ▭ *No credit cards* ⊙ *Closed Sun. No dinner.*

IRISH

¢   ✕ **Burdock's.** Old man Burdock has moved on and the place hasn't been the same since. But the hordes still join the inevitable queue at Dublin's famous take-out fish-and-chips shop, right next door to the Lord Edward pub. You can eat in the gardens of St. Patrick's Cathedral, a five-minute walk away. ⊠ *2 Werburgh St., Dublin West* ☎ *01/454–0306* ▭ *No credit cards.*

ITALIAN

¢–$ ✕ **Bar Italia.** We hope you're not shy about being seen eating, because
★   the front of tiny Bar Italia is a sheer wall of glass that looks out onto the Liffey and the Civic Offices at Wood Quay. If the weather is good, snag

one of the tables on the patio and grin at the office workers trudging back to work after lunch. The menu is short and simple, but everything on it is guaranteed to be fresh and cooked like your mother back in Naples would have done. The minestrone soup is, without question, the best in Ireland, and the melt-on-your-tongue gnocchi is served in a few different sauces. People travel miles to have their coffee here and the house wines never let you down. They now have a second, slightly more formal restaurant in the new "Italian Quarter," almost directly across the river on Ormond Quay. ⊠ *Essex Quay, Dublin West* ☎ *01/679–5128* ⊕ *www. baritalia.ie* ⊟ *MC, V* ⊙ *Closed Sun. No dinner.*

SEAFOOD

$$ ⋊**Lord Edward.** Culinary trends and fashions may come and go but Dublin's oldest seafood restaurant remains resolutely traditional. On the cozy top floor above a lovely old bar of the same name, the Lord Edward looks out on the front entrance of Christchurch Cathedral. They do a mean Irish stew but the stars here are definitely the seafood dishes, usually smothered in a totally unhip but delicious, calorie-packed creamy sauce. The salmon and the cod are two favorites. ⊠ *23 Christchurch Pl., Dublin West* ☎ *01/454–2420* ⊕ *www.lordedward.ie* ⊟ *AE, DC, MC, V* ⊙ *Closed Sun. No lunch Sat.*

PHOENIX PARK & ENVIRONS

ECLECTIC

$–$$$ ⋊**Nancy Hands.** It's a fine line to walk: to re-create tradition without coming across like a theme bar. Happily, Nancy Hands just about pulls it off. A galleylike room juxtaposes old wood, raw brick, and antiques with contemporary art to create a convivial, cozy dining area. The bar food is good, but the upstairs restaurant operates on a more serious level. Specialties include Flanagan's Twist—a mousseline of scallop and crab encased in fresh salmon—and a Mediterranean skewer laden with succulent chicken and beef. The menu includes Thai- and Japanese-style dishes, too. Numerous wines are served by the glass, and the selection of spirits is one of the most impressive in the country. ⊠ *30–32 Parkgate St., Dublin West* ☎ *01/677–0149* ⊕ *www.nancy-hands.ie* ⌕ *Reservations essential* ⊟ *AE, DC, MC, V.*

WHERE TO STAY

If you're lucky enough to stay at one of the classy hotels or elegant B&Bs that occupy former Georgian town houses on both sides of the Liffey, you'll quickly realize that entering one of these little domestic palaces really is a trip back in time. But this does not mean the 21st century has not arrived. "An absolute avalanche of new hotels" is how the *Irish Times* characterized Dublin's recent hotel boom. New lodgings have sprung up all over the city, including the much-talked-about Westin at College Green, the Four Seasons, and a few others in Ballsbridge, an inner "suburb" that's a 20-minute walk from the city center.

Dublin has a decent selection of inexpensive accommodations, including many moderately priced hotels with basic but agreeable rooms. Most B&Bs, long the mainstay of the economy end of the market, have upgraded their facilities and now provide rooms with private bathrooms or showers, as well as cable color televisions, direct-dial telephones, and Internet connections. The bigger hotels are all equipped with in-room data ports or Wi-Fi. If you've rented a car and you're not staying at a hotel with secure parking facilities, it's worth considering a location out of the city center, such as Dalkey or Killiney, where the surroundings are more pleasant and you won't have to worry about parking on city streets.

PRICES

Demand for rooms means that rates are high at the best hotels by the standards of any major European or North American city (and factoring in the exchange rate means a hotel room can take a substantial bite out of your budget). Service charges range from 15% in expensive hotels to zero in moderate and inexpensive ones. Be sure to inquire when you make reservations.

As a general rule of thumb, lodgings on the north side of the Liffey River tend to be more affordable than those on the south. B&Bs charge as little as €46 a night per person, but they tend to be in suburban areas—generally a 15-minute bus ride from the center of the city. This is not in itself a great drawback, and savings can be significant. Many hotels have a weekend, or "B&B," rate that's often 30% to 40% cheaper than the ordinary rate; some hotels also have a midweek special that provides discounts of up to 35%. These rates are available throughout the year but are harder to get in high season. Ask about them when booking a room (they are available only on a prebooked basis), especially if you plan a brief or weekend stay.

WHAT IT COSTS IN EUROS				
¢	$	$$	$$$	$$$$
FOR TWO PEOPLE Under €80	€80–€130	€130–€180	€180–€230	over €230

Prices are for a standard double room in high season, including V.A.T. and a service charge (often applied in larger hotels). Most hotels operate on the European Plan (EP), with no meals included in the basic room rate, or, if indicated, with Breakfast Plan (BP).

More Bang for Your Buck

You get what you pay for. For decades Dublin was synonymous with cheap but unexciting accommodation. The Celtic Tiger has transformed expectations for visitors to Dublin. When it comes to their hotels, it is indeed the best of times and the worst of times. Choice and quality have expanded exponentially, but so have prices. So it's more important than ever to get the best deal for your dollar. If location is a priority but you don't want to spend a fortune, try the moderately priced, redbrick **Central Hotel,** which lives up to its name: it's 100 yards from the front gate of Trinity College. The rooms are small but stylish, and you have easy access to the wonderful Library Bar, the most serene drinking spot in Dublin. To stay just off the ever-trendy Grafton Street for less than €150 is a real treat, and the **Grafton House** also throws in beautifully furnished rooms in a Victorian town house. Or, in Victorian-era Ballsbridge, head to the charming **Ariel Guest House,** where homemade jams and warm scones can be enjoyed under the Waterford-crystal chandelier in the sumptuous, fireplace-warmed drawing room. **Globetrotters Tourist Hostel** is the pick of its kind in the city, and it even has a cute B&B next door. Perhaps because the **Clifden Guesthouse** is on the Northside, its prices do not reflect its spacious comfort. Add in the free parking and oversize rooms and you know you've found a real bargain.

CITY CENTER: THE SOUTHSIDE

$$$$
Fodor's Choice
★
Shelbourne. Paris has the Ritz, New York has the Pierre, and Dublin has the Shelbourne. Resplendent in its broad, ornamented, pink-and-white, mid-Victorian facade, this grande dame of Stephen's Green has reopened after a no-expense-spared, head-to-toe, two-year renovation. Long famed as the Dublin home of the nation's literati, the hotel has been immortalized by authors running from Thackeray to Elizabeth Bowen. The Constitution of the Irish Free State was framed within its venerable walls, and almost as venerable a tradition was to take tea in the Lord Mayor's Lounge, just off the towering, marble-floor, cream-and-crystal lobby with its gilded pillars and brass candelabras. Having grown a little long in the tooth, however, the Shelburne recently transformed its public spaces with original, daring furniture, textiles, and colors. Today, the most sumptuous place in town has just gotten more so—too bad most of the patina is gone. The shock of the new begins in the lobby, where the Irish Chippendale chairs have given way to contempo Irish art. The Saddle Room restaurant—a "modern steak and fish" spot—now flaunts towering gold-lamé banquettes. Happily, the guest rooms are almost as luxurious as the lobby, with the marble bathrooms a real tactile pleasure. Rooms in front overlook the Green (one of Dublin's squares more blighted than most by modern development); those in the back, without a view, are quieter. ⊠ *27 St. Stephen's Green, Southside, 2* ☎ *01/663–4500, 800/543–4300 in U.S.* 🖷 *01/661–6006* ⊕ *www.marriott.com* ⇆ *246 rooms, 19 suites* ♿ *In-room: refrigerator,*

VCR, Ethernet. In-hotel: restaurant, room service, bar, laundry service, no-smoking rooms. ⊟AE, DC, MC, V

$$$$ 🏠**Westbury.** A favorite with the platinum credit-card set, this luxurious, chandelier-filled, modern hotel is just off Grafton Street, the shopping mecca of Dublin. You can join elegantly dressed Dubliners for afternoon tea in the spacious mezzanine-level main lobby, furnished with a grand piano and a great view out onto the busy streets. Alas, the utilitarian rooms—painted in pastels—don't share the lobby's elegance. More inviting are the suites, which combine European stylings with tasteful Japanese screens and prints. The flowery Russell Room serves formal lunches and dinners; the downstairs Sandbank, a seafood restaurant and bar, looks like a turn-of-the-20th-century establishment. *⊠Grafton St., Southside, 2 ☎01/679–1122 🖶01/679–7078 ⊕www.jurys-dublin-hotels.com ⮑187 rooms, 17 suites ♿In-room: refrigerator, VCR, Ethernet. In-hotel: 2 restaurants, room service, bar, laundry service, parking (no fee), no-smoking rooms ⊟AE, DC, MC, V.*

$$$$ 🏠**Westin Dublin.** If you've ever dreamed of spending the night in a bank,
★ here's your chance. Reconstructed from three 19th-century landmark buildings (including a former bank) across the road from Trinity College, the Westin is all about location. The public spaces re-create a little of the splendor of yesteryear: marble pillars, tall mahogany doorways, blazing fireplaces, and period detailing on the walls and ceilings. The bedrooms, on the other hand, are functional and small, with crisp, white Indian linen and custom-made beds the only luxurious touches. The rooms that overlook Trinity College are a little more expensive, but the chance to watch the students in a leisurely game of cricket on a summer weekend makes all the difference. The restaurant and Mint Bar are in the original vaults of the bank. *⊠College Green, Southside, 2 ☎01/645–1000 🖶01/645–1401 ⊕www.westin.com ⮑141 rooms, 22 suites ♿In-room: refrigerator, Wi-Fi. In-hotel: restaurant, room service, bars, concierge, laundry service, parking (no fee), no-smoking rooms ⊟AE, DC, MC, V.*

$$$–$$$$ 🏠**Brooks.** Even though it has nearly 100 rooms, the Brooks likes to describe itself as a boutique property, and it does manage to convey the classy, personal touch of a much smaller establishment. A two-minute walk from Grafton Street, it is the perfect place to sit and recover if the Irish rain plays havoc with your plans: public spaces and the bar are warm and full of leather chairs, high-veneer oak paneling, and decorative bookcases. The rooms exude an old-school elegance, with deep burgundy curtains, heavy bedspreads, and beds so big you could get lost in them. Each also has a high-tech, wireless audiovisual setup. Situated so near to the Gaiety Theatre, the hotel's Jasmin Bar is an ideal spot for a pre- or post-theater drink. *⊠Drury St, Southside, 2 ☎01/670–4000 🖶01/670–4455 ⊕www.sinnotthotels.com/brooks ⮑98 rooms ♿In-room: VCR, Wi-Fi. In-hotel: restaurant, room service, bar, gym, concierge, laundry service, parking (no fee), no-smoking rooms ⊟AE, DC, MC, V.*

$$–$$$ 🏨**Central Hotel.** Every modern city needs its little oasis of sanctuary,
★   and the Central's book-and-armchair-filled Library bar—warmed by a
Victorian fireplace—nicely fits the bill. Established in 1887, this grand,
old-style redbrick spot is in the heart of the city center, steps from Grafton Street, Temple Bar, and Dublin Castle. Recently renovated rooms
are snug but you'll hardly notice the dimensions thanks to the high ceilings and the cosseting and stylish furnishings—flocked bedspreads, racing paintings, and 19th-century bric-a-brac make some of these rooms
World of Interiors–worthy. The stately hotel dining room delights with
its pastel-green walls, bookcases, and gilt-frame pictures. Much less
soigné and a good deal more lively is Molly Malone's Tavern, adjacent
to the hotel, with plenty of regulars who come for the atmosphere
and the live, traditional Irish music on Friday and Saturday nights.
⊠*1–5 Exchequer St., Southside, 2* ☎*01/679–7302* 📠*01/679–7303*
⊕*www.centralhotel.ie* ↪*67 rooms, 3 suites* △*In-room: Wi-Fi. In-
hotel: restaurant, room service, bar, concierge, laundry service* ⊟*AE,
DC, MC, V.*

$$–$$$ 🏨**Drury Court Hotel.** With a hint of the Munich beer hall, the cozy,
parquet-floor rathskeller dining room is the most charming thing about
this small, good-value hotel. Public areas are purely functional but subtle greens, golds, and burgundies add a certain warmth to the rooms.
The location is ideal, a two-minute walk from Grafton Street and just
around corner from some of the city's best restaurants. Lunch is served
in the casual Digges Lane Bar, frequented by many new-money, young
Dubliners. ⊠*28–30 Lower Stephens St., Southside, 2* ☎*01/475–1988*
📠*01/478–5730* ⊕*www.drurycourthotel.com* ↪*42 rooms* △*In-
room: Ethernet. In-hotel: restaurant, room service, bar, laundry service* ⊟*AE, DC, MC, V.*

$ 🏨**Grafton House.** A stone's throw from the famous shopping street
that gave it its name, this Victorian Gothic–style building has been
tastefully transformed into one of central Dublin's best bargains. The
rooms are a little cramped, but they're brightly decorated with cheerful
pine furnishings, and the small size of the place ensures warm, friendly
service. ⊠*26–27 S. Great George's St., Southside, 2* ☎*01/679–2041*
📠*01/677–9715* ⊕*www.graftonguesthouse.com* ↪*17 rooms* △*In-
room: no a/c, dial-up. In-hotel: no-smoking rooms, no elevator* ⊟*AE,
MC, V* ⊚*BP.*

SOUTHEAST DUBLIN: AROUND MERRION SQUARE

$$$$ 🏨**Conrad Dublin International.** Ask for, no, insist on a room on the
top three floors. The best thing about the seven-story, redbrick and
smoked-glass Conrad are the spectacular views out over the city. Just
off St. Stephen's Green, the Conrad firmly aims for international business travelers. Gleaming light-color marble graces the large formal
lobby. Rooms are rather cramped but are nicely outfitted with natural-
wood furnishings, painted in sand colors and pastel greens, and have
Spanish marble in the bathrooms. A note to light sleepers: the air-conditioning–heating system can be noisy. The hotel has two restaurants:

the informal Plurabelle and the plusher Alexandra Room. ⊠*Earlsfort Terr., Southeast Dublin, 2* ☎*01/676–5555* 🖷*01/676–5424* ⊕*www. conradhotels.com* 🛏*182 rooms, 10 suites* ⚘*In-room: refrigerator, safe, VCR, Ethernet. In-hotel: 2 restaurants, room service, bars, gym, concierge, parking (no fee), no-smoking rooms* ⊟*AE, DC, MC, V.*

$$$$ 📺**Merrion.** Arthur Wellesley, the Duke of Wellington and hero of Water-
Fodor'sChoice loo, once famously commented when queried about his Irish birth:
★ "Just because a man is born in a stable doesn't make him a horse." His "stable," directly across from Government Buildings between Stephen's Green and Merrion Square, is one of the four exactingly restored Georgian town houses that make up this luxurious hotel. Some of the stately guest rooms are appointed in classic Georgian style—from the crisp linen sheets to the Carrara-marble bathrooms. Some are vaulted with delicate Adamesque plasterwork ceilings, and others are graced with magnificent, original marble fireplaces. Still, the decor is almost too spiffy—if this is the 18th century, it has been buffed to a shiny 21st-century gloss—so, to fully enjoy the historic patina, opt for a room in the Main House at the front, for its chambers have a more authentic feel. The staff is obviously accustomed to dealing with heads of state and royalty, so ladies shouldn't be surprised if they are addressed as "Madame." And all will enjoy the hotel's little spa, a perfect place to unwind. Clearly, this place must be very special, since leading Dublin restaurateur Patrick Guilbaud has moved his eponymous and fabulous restaurant here. ⊠*Upper Merrion St., Southeast Dublin, 2* ☎*01/603–0600* 🖷*01/603–0700* ⊕*www.merrionhotel.com* 🛏*122 rooms, 20 suites* ⚘*In-room: safe, refrigerator, VCR, Ethernet. In-hotel: 2 restaurants, room service, bars, pool, gym, spa, laundry service, concierge, public Wi-Fi, parking (no fee), no-smoking rooms* ⊟*AE, DC, MC, V.*

$$–$$$$ 📺**Number 31.** Sam Stephenson, Dublin's most famous and highly con-
★ troversial modernist architect, strikingly renovated two Georgian mews in the early 1960s as a private home. They are now connected via a small garden to the grand house they once served. Together they form a marvelous guesthouse a short walk from St. Stephen's Green, which gives you a choice of bedroom styles: Georgian elegance or cool modern. Owners Deirdre and Noel Comer serve made-to-order breakfasts at refectory tables in the balcony dining room. The white-tile sunken living room, with its black leather sectional sofa and modern artwork that includes a David Hockney print, may make you think you're in California. If that essay in *Wallpaper*–modern doesn't send you, you'll be happy enough ensconced in one of the period-style guest rooms, one of which—No. 21—has a ceiling so lofty and corniced even a royal would feel at home. ⊠*31 Leeson Close, Southeast Dublin, 2* ☎*01/676–5011* 🖷*01/676–2929* ⊕*www.number31.ie* 🛏*18 rooms* ⚘*In-room: no a/c, Wi-Fi. In-hotel: no elevator, laundry service, parking (no fee), no-smoking rooms* ⊟*AE, MC, V.*

$$$ 📺**La Stampa.** Definitely a good thing in a small albeit very pretty pack-
Fodor'sChoice age, this intimate town-house hotel, above the ever-popular and spec-
★ tacular Balzac restaurant and 50 yards from Trinity College, is the classiest new arrival on the Dublin scene. Each suite is individually dec-

orated with an Asian theme—lots of wood, simple color schemes, and velvet bedspreads imported from Paris add to the luxury. Balzac is a vast and soigné brasserie; even more eye-catching is Samsara, a Moroccan themed bar that is a fantasia of tin chandeliers, multihued stained glass, and oh-so-sexy ambience. For the price, there are few better spots in town. ⊠*35 Dawson St., Southeast Dublin, 2* ☎*01/677–4444* 🖷*01/677–4411* ⊕*www.lastampa.ie* ⟿*22 suites* ⌂*In-room: refrigerator, VCR, Wi-Fi. In-hotel: 3 restaurants, room service, laundry service, parking (no fee), no-smoking rooms* ⊟*AE, DC, MC, V.*

$$–$$$ ⛫**Stephen's Hall Hotel & Suites.** Get a top-floor suite at this tastefully modernized Georgian town house just off St. Stephen's Green and lord it over the whole Southside. The suites, considerably larger than the average hotel room, include one or two bedrooms, a separate sitting room, a fully equipped kitchen, and bath. The modern, motel-functional furniture is nondescript, but top-floor suites have spectacular city views, and ground-floor suites have private entrances. The Romanza restaurant serves breakfast, lunch, and dinner with an Italian flavor. ⊠*14–17 Lower Leeson St., Southeast Dublin, 2* ☎*01/661–0585* 🖷*01/661– 0606* ⊕*www.stephens-hall.com* ⟿*30 suites* ⌂*In-room: safe, kitchen, Ethernet. In-hotel:restaurant, concierge, laundry service, public Wi-Fi, no-smoking rooms* ⊟*AE, DC, MC, V.*

$–$$ ⛫**Georgian House Hotel.** The name says it all. The owners of this hotel took three classic Georgian houses near St. Stephen's Green, added a modern extension, and opened one of Dublin's best value hotels. So you get an 18th-century-Dublin experience—high ceilings, original fireplaces, antique gilded mirrors—at guesthouse prices. Within the hotel, Maguires is a cozy, unpretentious little pub. ⊠*18 Lower Baggot St., Southeast Dublin, 2* ☎*01/661–8832* 🖷*01/661–8834* ⊕*www.georgianhotel.ie* ⟿*20 rooms* ⌂*In-room: no a/c, dial-up. In-hotel: bar, no elevator, public Internet, parking (no fee)* ⊟*AE, MC, V* ⦿*BP.*

$–$$ ⛫**Kilronan House.** A good guesthouse should cheer you up when you come home at the end of a long day's touring. This large, mid-19th-century, terraced house with an elegant white facade will bring a smile to your face every time. The ground-floor sitting room is a real cozy winter treat when a big fire is on. Kilronan flaunts richly patterned wallpaper and carpets in its bright and airy guest rooms, while orthopedic beds (rather rare in Dublin hotels, let alone in guesthouses) help to guarantee a restful night's sleep. The guesthouse is a five-minute walk from St. Stephen's Green. ⊠*70 Adelaide Rd., Southeast Dublin, 2* ☎*01/475–5266* 🖷*01/478–2841* ⊕*www.dublinn.com* ⟿*12 rooms* ⌂*In-room: no a/c. In-hotel: no elevator, parking (no fee), no-smoking room* ⊟*MC, V.*

TEMPLE BAR

$$$–$$$$ ⛫**The Clarence.** If coolness is contagious you definitely want a room at Temple Bar's most prestigious hotel. You might well bump into celebrity friends of co-owners Bono and the Edge of U2. Dating to 1852, the grand old hotel was given a total, no-expense-spared overhaul by its new owners in the early 1990s. The unique shapes and Arts-and-Crafts style of the old hotel were maintained in the Octagon Bar and the sleekly fabulous Tea Room Restaurant. Guest rooms are decorated in a mishmash of earth tones accented with deep purple, gold, cardinal red, and royal blue. With the exception of those in the penthouse suite, rooms are small. The laissez-faire service seems to take its cue from the minimalist style, so if you like to be pampered, stay elsewhere. ⊠6–8 *Wellington Quay, Temple Bar,* 2 ☎*01/407–0800* 🖷*01/407–0820* ⊕*www.theclarence.ie* ⤵*43 rooms, 84 suites* ♨*In-room: refrigerator, VCR, Ethernet. In-hotel: restaurant, room service, bar, laundry service, no-smoking rooms* ▤*AE, DC, MC, V.*

$$–$$$$ ⊞**The Morgan.** In the sparkling heart of Temple Bar, the Morgan boasts about its chic design and decor, and the individually designed bedrooms and luxurious, colorful bathrooms are indeed pleasing to the eye. It is the hotel's extended-stay suites, however, that really sets it apart from the crowd. With a fully equipped kitchen and a spacious, gadget-filled living room, you can hunker down and make yourself comfortable for a week or two. The generously heated outside courtyard is perfect for cocktails. ⊠*10 Fleet St., Temple Bar,* 2 ☎*01/643–7000* 🖷*01/643–7060* ⊕*www.themorgan.com* ⤵*106 rooms* ♨*In-room: refrigerator, Wi-Fi. In-hotel: restaurant, bar, laundry service, no-smoking rooms* ▤*AE, DC, MC, V.*

$$–$$$$ ⊞**Paramount.** This medium-size hotel in the heart of trendy Temple Bar has opted to maintain its classy Victorian facade. The foyer continues this theme of solid elegance, with incredibly comfortable leather couches, bleached-blond-oak floors, and burgundy curtains. Dark woods and subtle colors decorate the bedrooms—very 1930s (if not Bogie and Bacall). If you're fond of a tipple, try the hotel's Art Deco Turks Head Bar and Chop House. ⊠*Parliament St. and Essex Gate, Temple Bar,* 2 ☎*01/417–9900* 🖷*01/417–9904* ⊕*www.paramounthotel.ie* ⤵*70 rooms* ♨*In-room: dial-up. In-hotel: restaurant, bar, laundry service, no-smoking rooms* ▤*AE, DC, MC, V.*

$–$$$ ⊞**Temple Bar.** Dublin doesn't usually do Art Deco, so the 1920s-style lobby of the Temple Bar—with its old-fashioned cast-iron fireplace, natural-wood furniture, and legions of exotic plants—is a refreshing change. Off the lobby are a small cocktail bar and the bright, airy, glass-roof Terrace restaurant, great spots to hang out and enjoy a pretheater martini. Mahogany wood and autumn green and rust colors characterize the guest rooms, nearly all of which have big double beds (which can leave them a little cramped). The Boomerang nightclub on the premises is open to both guests and the public. The hotel is in a former bank building, around the corner from Trinity College. ⊠*Fleet St., Temple Bar,* 2 ☎*01/677–3333* 🖷*01/677–3088* ⊕*www.templebarhotel.com* ⤵*129 rooms* ♨*In-hotel: restaurant, bars, public Wi-Fi, parking (fee)* ▤*AE, DC, MC, V.*

$–$$ ⊞**Parliament.** As with many Dublin hotels, the interiors of the Parliament do not quite live up to the fabulous facade of one of Dublin's finest Edwardian buildings. Inside, the atmosphere is very much functional, if tidy, and appeals to mainly a business clientele—drawn by the location near the Central Bank and Trinity College. But rooms are a good size, with a simple, slightly monotonous beige and off-white color scheme. The Forum bar keeps up the democratic theme with reliable selection of bar food. ⊠*Lord Edward St., Temple Bar, 2* ☎*01/670–8777* 🖷*01/670–8787* ⊕*www.regencyhotels.com* ☞*63 rooms* ⅄*In-hotel: bar, public Wi-Fi, no-smoking rooms* ⊟*AE, DC, MC, V.*

THE NORTHSIDE

$$$–$$$$ 🏨**Clarion Hotel IFSC.** Built with business guests in mind, this high-rise hotel has been a surprise hit with tourists. Smack in the middle of the International Financial Services Centre, the Clarion, with its office-block-like exterior, is indistinguishable from many of the financial institutions that surround it. The public spaces, however, are bright and cheery, if a little uninspired. The bedrooms—big by Dublin standards—are all straight lines and contemporary light-oak furnishings. Shades of blue and taupe do create a calm environment (the hotel claims its environment is guided by Eastern philosophy, no less), but for true serenity try to get a room at the front with great views out over the Liffey. Because the hotel mainly caters to business travelers, weekend bargains are a definite possibility—make sure you ask. ⊠*IFSC, Northside, 1* ☎*01/433–8800* 🖷*01/433–8811* ⊕*www.clarionhotelifsc.com* ☞*145 rooms, 17 suites* ⅄*In-room: refrigerator, Wi-Fi. In-hotel: restaurant, room service, bar, pool, gym, laundry service, parking (no fee), no-smoking rooms* ⊟*AE, DC, MC, V.*

$$$–$$$$ 🏨**The Morrison.** How do you make a Dublin hotel instantly trendy? Simple: get the country's top fashion guru to design the interiors. John Rocha had the last word on everything at this übermodern trendsetting hotel, down to the toiletries and staff uniforms. Past the 18th-century Georgian facade, the superstriking, *Wallpaper*-ready public areas contrast with the very unfussy, almost Scandinavian bedrooms. Some visitors complain that the place leaves them a little cold, though others claim that the Morrison is as good as a London boutique hotel, though many times the size. A new wing with 49 rooms and a private art gallery opened in 2005. Halo, the hotel's nouvelle Irish restaurant, is super-stylish and has one of the most ambitiously delicious menus in town. Halfway between the Ha'penny and Capel Street bridges, the Morrison is no more than a 10-minute walk from Trinity College. ⊠*Ormond Quay, Northside, 1* ☎*01/887–2400* 🖷*01/874–4039* ⊕*www.morrisonhotel.ie* ☞*124 rooms, 14 suites* ⅄*In-room: refrigerator, VCR, Ethernet. In-hotel: restaurant, room service, bars, concierge, laundry service, parking (no fee), no-smoking rooms* ⊟*AE, DC, MC, V.*

$$–$$$ 🏨**Royal Dublin Hotel.** No, the Queen never stayed here and O'Connell Street is not what it once was, but new life has been brought to this old lady. One of the big pluses of this beige-plush and chandelier-lighted hotel is its perfect location at the top of the thoroughfare, near the Northside's major attractions (a 10-minute walk south deposits you

at Trinity College). The public spaces are subtly lighted and decorated in slightly loud glass and brass. Rooms are spacious, and the hotel has built a solid reputation for extra-friendly service. The Georgian Room and Raffles bar try to put on posh English airs (think crisp linens), but the casual warmth of the staff undoes the stuffiness. ⊠ *O'Connell St., Northside, 1* ☎ *01/873–3666* 🖨 *01/873–3120* ⊕ *www.royaldublin. com* ⟲ *117 rooms, 3 suites* ⟐ *In-room: refrigerator, VCR, Ethernet. In-hotel: restaurant, room service, bar, laundry service, no-smoking rooms* ⊟ *AE, MC, V.*

¢–$$ 🗹**Charleville Lodge.** If Dublin's city center is a Georgian wonder, a short
Fodor'sChoice   commute out to the historic Phibsborough area of Dublin's Northside
★   will transport you to the elegantly Victorian 19th century. Here, in a row of beautifully restored terraced houses you can enjoy quality time in Charleville Lodge's dramatically lighted residents' lounge, complete with twinkling chandeliers, plush wing chairs, and a working fireplace. An antiquarian's delight, this grand salon is a great spot to chat with other travelers who have dared to stray off the beaten path. Upstairs, guest rooms are brightly colored, wide, and have refreshingly high ceilings. As for the commute, the No. 10 bus takes but five minutes and it's even a great walk in good weather. All in all, this hostelry offers a touch of luxury at great value. ⊠ *268–272 N. Circular Rd., Northside, Phibsborough, 7* ☎ *01/838–6633* 🖨 *01/838–5854* ⊕ *www.charlevillelodge. ie* ⟲ *30 rooms* ⟐ *In-room: no a/c. In-hotel: no elevator, parking (no fee), public Internet, no-smoking rooms* ⊟ *MC, V* ⑭ *BP.*

$ 🗹**Clifden Guesthouse.** The Gardiner Street area deservedly gets some bad press, as it's home to a host of cheap, poor-quality guesthouses. But there are a few diamonds in the rough, and the Clifden, although still certainly a bargain, is a cut above the rest. The Georgian building has been stylishly refurbished, and the rooms are huge, with simple furnishings and wonderfully tall, period windows. O'Connell Street is a five-minute walk away. As an added bonus, you can park here free even after you have checked out. ⊠ *32 Gardiner Pl., Northside, 1* ☎ *01/874–6364* 🖨 *01/874–6122* ⊕ *www.clifdenhouse.com* ⟲ *15 rooms* ⟐ *In-room: no a/c. In-hotel: no elevator, parking (no fee), no-smoking rooms* ⊟ *MC, V* ⑭ *BP.*

¢–$ 🗹**Globetrotters Tourist Hostel.** Globetrotters is a giant step up from many Dublin hostels, with a pleasant outdoor courtyard; clean, locking dorm rooms with en suite showers; a turf fire; comfortable bunk beds (with lamps for late-night reading); and a delicious all-you-can-eat breakfast. Plus, you're within walking distance of the city center, one block from the bus station, and two blocks from the train station. The owners also run Town House, a cute B&B in the same building. ⊠ *47–48 Lower Gardiner St., Northside, 1* ☎ *01/873–5893* 🖨 *01/878–8787* ⊕ *www. globetrottersdublin.com* ⟲ *94 dorm beds with shared bath, 38 double rooms* ⟐ *In-room: no a/c, no TV. In-hotel: restaurant, no elevator, public Internet, no-smoking rooms* ⊟ *MC, V* ⑭ *BP.*

¢–$ 🗹**Marian Guest House.** A veritable Everest of fine Irish meats, the Marian's mighty full Irish breakfast, with black pudding and smoked bacon,

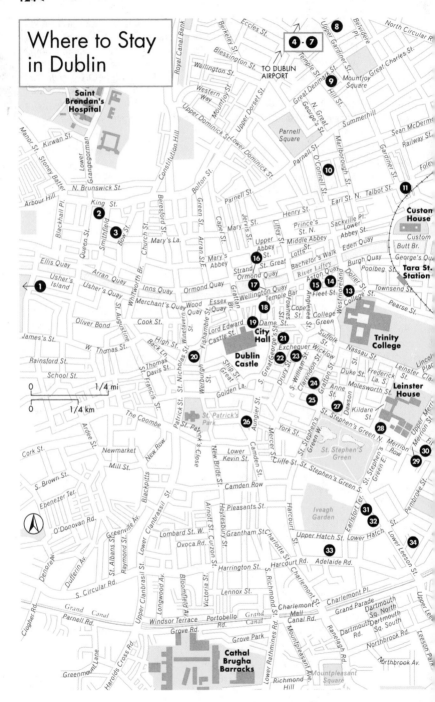

Where to Stay in Dublin

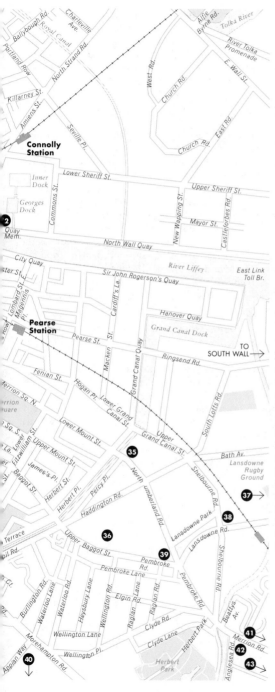

is reason enough to stay at this family-run guesthouse (the whole family can speak Irish, by the way). The place only has six rooms, so you get lots of attention and pampering. Rooms are fairly basic, but clean and pleasant. ⊠ *21 Upper Gardiner St., Northside, 1* ☎ *01/874–4129* ⊕ *www.marianguesthouse.ie* ⤳ *6 rooms* ⌂ *In-room: no a/c. In-hotel: no elevator, parking (no fee)* ☰ *MC, V* ⦿ *BP.*

SOUTH DUBLIN: THE GRAND CANAL & BALLSBRIDGE

$$$$ **Dylan.** "Sensual" is a word this new, luxury boutique hotel in an old Victorian building uses to describe itself, and it does have the feel of a place you might go for a naughty night with that someone special. The mysteriously lit exterior looks beautiful at dusk. Inside, individually designed bedrooms feature leather padded walls, textured wallpaper, hyper-modern furnishings, and seriously sexy beds (one room even has a mirror on the ceiling). It actually might be a little too much, but there's no denying the place is unique and an interesting addition to the sometimes staid Dublin scene. The Still restaurant continues the over-the-top decor with a lavish 1940s glam look, but the food is a little hit or miss. ⊠ *Eastmoreland Pl., Ballsbridge, 4* ☎ *01/660–3000* ⊟ *01/660–3005* ⊕ *www.dylan.ie* ⤳ *38 rooms, 6 suites* ⌂ *In-room: safe, refrigerator, VCR, Wi-Fi. In-hotel: restaurant, room service, bar, laundry service, no-smoking rooms* ☰ *AE, DC, MC, V.*

$$$$ **Four Seasons.** Much controversy surrounds the brash postmodern—critics would say faux-Victorian-Georgian hybrid—architecture of this hotel. The six-floor building mixes pre-20th-century design with modern glass and concrete. The impressive landscaping—it has 4 acres of gardens—aims to makes the hotel seem like an oasis; a big effort has been made to ensure that a bit of greenery can be seen from most rooms. Guest rooms are spacious, with large windows that allow light to flood in. A selection of landscapes on the hotel walls lends the place a warm touch. The lower-level spa is one of the finest in the country, with a naturally lighted lap pool. ⊠ *Simmonscourt Rd., Ballsbridge, 4* ☎ *01/665–4000* ⊟ *01/665–4099* ⊕ *www.fourseasons.com* ⤳ *157 rooms, 40 suites* ⌂ *In-room: safe, refrigerator, VCR, Ethernet. In-hotel: 2 restaurants, room service, bars, gym, pool, laundry service, concierge, parking (no fee), no-smoking rooms* ☰ *AE, DC, MC, V.*

$$$$ **Herbert Park Hotel.** For maximum pleasure secure a room overlooking the park of the same name adjacent to this independently owned hotel, which is also beside the Dodder River. Two of the suites even have large balconies with views of the park or the leafy suburbs. Relaxing shades of blue and cream predominate in the spacious rooms; all have individually controlled air-conditioning, a large desk, and two telephone lines. The hotel's large, light-filled lobby has floor-to-ceiling windows and a slanted glass roof. The spacious bar, terrace lounge, and restaurant are Japanese-inspired minimalist in style. You can dine on the restaurant terrace in warm weather. ⊠ *Merrion Rd., Ballsbridge, 4* ☎ *01/667–2200* ⊟ *01/667–2595* ⊕ *www.herbertpark-hotel.ie* ⤳ *150 rooms, 3 suites* ⌂ *In-room: safe, refrigerator, Ethernet.*

In-hotel: restaurant, bar, gym, parking (no fee), no-smoking rooms
▤AE, DC, MC, V.

$$$–$$$$ 🏠 **Burlington.** A genuine institution, Ireland's largest hotel is one of those landmarks where nearly every Irish person seems to have spent at least one night (or so they claim). In high contrast to the hotel's impersonal, 1972 glass-and-concrete facade, the staff here is famously friendly and attentive. Public rooms, especially the large bar, have mahogany counters and hanging plants that enhance the conservatory-style setting and take the edge off the uninspired building. The generous-size rooms, furnished in modern minimalist style, with neutral tones, have large picture windows. At night, Annabel's nightclub and the seasonal Irish cabaret are both lively (sometimes too lively!) spots. The Burlington has no sports and health facilities, but the Doyle hotel group, which runs it, has an arrangement that allows you to use the RiverView Sports Club in nearby Clonskeagh for €6.35 a visit. *⊠Upper Leeson St., Ballsbridge, 4 ☎01/660–5222 ⊟01/660–8496 ⊕www.jurysdoyle. com ➲504 rooms ⅄In-room: refrigerator (some), Ethernet. In-hotel: 2 restaurants, room service, bar, laundry service, public Wi-Fi, parking (no fee), no-smoking rooms.*

$$$ 🏠 **Schoolhouse Hotel.** "Ahead of its class" exclaims the terrible slogan,
★ but this converted Victorian parochial school just off the Grand Canal really is an A-plus. The rooms—each named for a famous Irish writer and hung with a corresponding portrait—are very old-school (excuse the pun) luxury, with thick rugs matching the quilted bedspreads, plus beautiful oak chairs and desks. Though its name is hardly promising, the Canteen Restaurant is actually a classy, modern-Irish eatery in a beautiful, light-filled former classroom with a barrel ceiling. *⊠2-8 Northumberland Rd., Ballsbridge, 4 ☎01/667–5014 ⊟01/667–5015 ⊕www.schoolhousehotel.com ➲31 rooms ⅄In-room: Wi-Fi. In-hotel: restaurant, bar, no elevator, laundry service, parking (no fee), no-smoking rooms ▤AE, DC, MC, V.*

$$–$$$ 🏠 **Pembroke Townhouse.** Dublin is at its most beautiful when it wears
Fodor'sChoice its Georgian face, and the Pembroke, a superb example of classic 18th-
★ century grandeur, captures the city on a very good hair day. "Townhouse" does not do justice to the splendor of the place, but does hint at the cozy, relaxed atmosphere. The fan-windowed front door leads into a stately reception area, complete with Grecian pillars. The bright, airy, high-ceiling rooms are all individually designed in a gentle clash of contemporary chic and Georgian symmetry. Nearly every wall bears a striking piece of contemporary Irish art. The hearty breakfast—including sautéed lamb's liver if desired—is served in the serene dining room. *⊠90 Pembroke Rd., Ballsbridge, 4 ☎01/660–0277 ⊟01/660–0291 ⊕www.pembroketownhouse.ie ➲48 rooms ⅄In-room: safe, Wi-Fi. In-hotel: laundry service, parking (no fee), no-smoking rooms ▤AE, DC, MC, V.*

$–$$$ 🏠 **Ariel Guest House.** The homemade preserves and oven-warm scones
★ are reason enough to stay at this redbrick 1850 Victorian guesthouse in one of Dublin's poshest tree-lined suburbs. It's a few steps from a DART

stop and a 15-minute walk from St. Stephen's Green. Restored rooms in the main house are lovingly decorated with Georgian antiques, Victoriana, and period wallpaper and drapes. The 13 rooms at the back of the house are more spartan, but all are immaculate. A Waterford-crystal chandelier hangs over the comfortable leather and mahogany furniture in the gracious, fireplace-warmed drawing room. Owner Michael O'Brien is an extraordinarily helpful and gracious host. ⊠ *52 Lansdowne Rd., Ballsbridge, 4* ☏ *01/668–5512* 🖶 *01/668–5845* ⊕ *www.ariel-house.net* ⤳ *37 rooms* ⚒ *In-room: no a/c. In-hotel: no elevator, public Wi-Fi, parking (no fee)* ▤ *MC, V* ❖ *BP.*

$–$$$ ⬚ **Mount Herbert Hotel.** The Loughran family's sprawling accommodation includes a number of large, Victorian-era houses. The hotel overlooks some of Ballsbridge's fine rear gardens and is near the main rugby stadium; the nearby DART will have you in the city center in seven minutes. The simple rooms are painted in light shades and contain little besides beds. The lounge is a good place to relax. The restaurant, which overlooks the English-style back garden (floodlighted at night) and children's play area, serves three meals a day; at dinner you can dine on steaks and stews. ⊠ *7 Herbert Rd., Ballsbridge, 4* ☏ *01/668–4321* 🖶 *01/660–7077* ⊕ *www.mountherberthotel.ie* ⤳ *172 rooms* ⚒ *In-room: no a/c, Wi-Fi. In-hotel: restaurant, bar, parking (no fee), no-smoking rooms* ▤ *AE, DC, MC, V.*

$$ ⬚ **Merrion Hall.** When your hotel is surrounded by embassies you know
★ you're in a classy part of town. Four-poster beds and whirlpool spas are some of the luxuries showered upon you at this quaintly elegant Edwardian town-house hotel in Ballsbridge. Ivy covers the secluded redbrick building, and a *Room with a View* atmosphere is created with a wonderfully stuffy afternoon tea (and also fine wines) served in the bay-windowed drawing room—a great chance to meet the other happy guests. ⊠ *7 Herbert Rd., Ballsbridge, 4* ☏ *01/668–1426* 🖶 *01/668–4280* ⊕ *www.halpinsprivatehotels.com* ⤳ *34 rooms* ⚒ *In-room: dial-up. In-hotel: no elevator, laundry service, parking (no fee), public Wi-Fi, no-smoking rooms* ▤ *AE, DC, MC, V.*

DUBLIN WEST

$–$$$ ⬚ **The Park Inn.** This strikingly modern hotel anchors the rejuvenation of the old fruit market area, known as Smithfield Village, north of the Liffey. The top floors have delightful rooftop gardens with views of the city on both sides of the Liffey. Smallish, high-tech rooms all have in-room data ports and look thoroughly up-to-date, thanks to their glass-tile walls, hot-and-cool Miami Beach colors, 1960s-mod and minimalist furnishings (chrome, anyone?), and feng shui–inspired bathrooms. The café-bar has live traditional music and contemporary Irish food, while Duck Lane is a trendy little shopping arcade that's part of the hotel complex. ⊠ *Smithfield Village, Dublin West, 7* ☏ *01/817–3838* 🖶 *01/817–3839* ⊕ *www.rezidorparkinn.com* ⤳ *70 rooms, 3 suites* ⚒ *In-room: safe, Wi-Fi. In-hotel: restaurant, room service, bar, laundry service, parking (no fee), no-smoking rooms* ▤ *AE, DC, MC, V.*

$$ ⊡ **Jurys Inn Christchurch.** Expect few frills at this functional budget hotel, part of a Jurys minichain that offers a low, fixed room rate for up to three adults or two adults and two children. (The branch at Custom House Quay operates according to the same plan.) The biggest plus is the pleasant location, facing Christ Church Cathedral and within walking distance of most city-center attractions. The rather spartan rooms are decorated in pastel colors and have utilitarian furniture. ⊠ *Christ Church Pl., Dublin West, 8* ☎ *01/454–0000* 🖷 *01/454–0012* ⊕ *www.jurysdoyle.com* ➥ *182 rooms* ✆ *In-room: Ethernet. In-hotel: restaurant, bar, laundry service, parking (fee), no-smoking rooms* 🟰 *AE, DC, MC, V.*

$–$$ ⊡ **Comfort Inn Smithfield.** On Smithfield Plaza, this new, snazzy, good-value hotel is at the heart of this hip area's growing development. The look, outside and in, is definitely functional-modern, but the beige and brown tones do soften things a bit and the public spaces are bright and cheerful. Bedrooms are big for the price and most include large floor-to-ceiling windows allowing for great light. Try to get a room at the front on a higher floor, as they have some stunning views looking out onto the plaza and to the city beyond. ⊠ *Smithfield Village, Dublin West, 8* ☎ *01/485–0900* 🖷 *01/485–0910* ⊕ *www.comfortinndublincity.com* ➥ *85 rooms, 7 suites* ✆ *In-room: Ethernet. In-hotel: restaurant, bar, parking (fee), no-smoking rooms* 🟰 *AE, DC, MC, V.*

$ ⊡ **Bewleys at Newlands Cross.** Cheap and cheerful would best sum up this four-story hotel on the southwest outskirts of the city. It's ideal if you're planning to head out of the city early (especially to points in the southwest and west) and don't want to deal with morning traffic. The hotel is emulating the formula popularized by Jurys Inns, in which rooms—here each has a double bed, a single bed, and a sofa bed— are a flat rate for up to three adults or two adults and two children. ⊠ *Newlands Cross at Naas Rd., Dublin West, 22* ☎ *01/464–0140* 🖷 *01/464–0900* ⊕ *www.bewleyshotels.com* ➥ *258 rooms* ✆ *In-room: no a/c, Wi-Fi. In-hotel: restaurant, parking (no fee), no-smoking rooms* 🟰 *AE, MC, V.*

¢–$ ⊡ **Avalon House.** Many young, independent travelers rate this cleverly ★ restored redbrick Victorian building, a five-minute walk southwest from Grafton Street and 5 to 10 minutes from some of the city's best music venues, the most appealing of Dublin's hostels. Avalon House has a mix of dormitories, rooms without bath, and rooms with bath. The dorm rooms and en suite quads all have loft areas that offer more privacy than you'd typically find in a multibed room. The Avalon Café serves food until 10 PM but is open as a common room after hours. ⊠ *55 Aungier St., Dublin West, 2* ☎ *01/475–0001* 🖷 *01/475–0303* ⊕ *www.avalon-house.ie* ➥ *40 4-bed rooms, 35 with bath; 26 twin rooms, 4 with bath; 4 single rooms with shared bath; 5 12-bed dorms, 1 10-bed dorm, and 1 26-bed dorm, all with shared bath* ✆ *In-room: no a/c, no TV. In-hotel: restaurant, public Internet* 🟰 *AE, MC, V.*

AROUND DUBLIN AIRPORT

$–$$ ⊞ **Clarion Dublin Airport.** Seen one, seen 'em all. The saying is fairly accurate when talking about airport hotels, and this Clarion is no exception. But the low-rise redbrick structure with a plain exterior has one big plus: rooms big enough to make you forget about the cookie-cutter decor. The Bistro Restaurant serves fish, meat, and vegetarian dishes; Sampans serves Chinese cuisine and is open for dinner only. There's live music in the bar on weekends. Guests have access to a nearby health club. ⊠ *Dublin Airport, County Dublin, North County Dublin* ☎ *01/808–0500* 🖷 *01/844–6002* ⊕ *www.clariondublinairport.com* 🛏 *247 rooms* ♿ *In-room: dial-up. In-hotel: restaurant, room service, bar, parking (no fee), no-smoking rooms* 🖃 *AE, DC, MC, V.*

$–$$ ⊞ **Radisson SAS Dublin Airport.** You could sleepwalk to your plane from the Radisson SAS; the hotel even has flight monitors in the lobby. Near the main terminal, and next to the main road into the city center is this modern five-story hotel that looks a little severe on the outside. But rooms are spacious and comfortable, if unexciting, but the service is exceptional. Double glazing ensures the roar of a 747 won't interrupt any beauty sleep. Interconnecting family rooms are available. ⊠ *Dublin Airport, County Dublin, North County Dublin* ☎ *01/844–6000* 🖷 *01/844–6001* ⊕ *http://airport.dublin.radissonsas.com* 🛏 *223 rooms, 6 suites* ♿ *In-room: dial-up. In-hotel: restaurant, room service, bar, parking (no fee)* 🖃 *AE, DC, MC, V.*

$ ⊞ **Skylon.** Location, location…and spacious rooms: the three reasons for choosing the Skylon. On the main road into Dublin city center from the airport stands this modern five-story hotel with a concrete-and-glass facade and generous-size rooms plainly decorated in cool, sea-bright colors. Double beds and a pair of easy chairs are almost the only furniture in the rooms. A glass-fronted lobby with a large bar and the Rendezvous Room restaurant dominate the public areas. The cooking is adequate but uninspired, with dishes such as grilled steak, poached cod, and omelets. ⊠ *Upper Drumcondra Rd., North County Dublin* ☎ *01/837–9121* 🖷 *01/837–2778* ⊕ *www.skylon.org* 🛏 *90 rooms* ♿ *In-room: Ethernet. In-hotel: restaurant, bar, parking (no fee)* 🖃 *AE, DC, MC, V.*

NIGHTLIFE & THE ARTS

Long before Stephen Dedalus's excursions into "nighttown" in James Joyce's *Ulysses,* Dublin was proud of its lively after-hours scene, particularly its thriving pubs. But the Celtic Tiger economy, the envy of all Europe, turned Dublin into one of the most happening destinations on the whole continent. Some of the old watering holes were replaced with huge, London-style "superbars," which, with the ubiquitous DJ in the corner, walk the fine line between pub and club. Most nights, the city's nightspots overflow with young cell phone–toting Dubliners and Europeans, who descend on the capital for weekend getaways. The city's 900-plus pubs are its main source of entertainment; many public houses in the city center have live music—from rock to jazz to traditional Irish.

Theater is an essential element of life in the city that was home to O'Casey, Synge, Yeats, and Beckett. Today Dublin has eight major theaters that reproduce the Irish "classics," and also present newer fare from the likes of Martin Macdonagh and Conon Macpherson. Opera, long overlooked, now has a home in the restored old Gaiety Theatre.

Check the following newspapers for informative listings: the *Irish Times* publishes a daily guide to what's happening in Dublin and the rest of the country, and has complete film and theater schedules. The *Evening Herald* lists theaters, cinemas, and pubs with live entertainment. The *Big Issue* is a weekly guide to film, theater, and musical events around the city. The *Event Guide,* a weekly free paper that lists music, cinema, theater, art shows, and dance clubs, is available in pubs and cafés around the city. In peak season, consult the free Bord Fáilte (Irish Tourist Board) leaflet "Events of the Week." The **Temple Bar Web site** (⊕*www.temple-bar.ie*) provides information about events in the Temple Bar area.

NIGHTLIFE

Dubliners have always enjoyed a night out, but in the last decade or so they have turned the pleasure into a work of art: the streets of the city center are the scene of what appears to be a never-ending party. In loud, brash dance clubs, where style and swagger rule, you're as likely to find crowds at 2 AM on a Wednesday as you are at the same time on a Saturday. In Dublin's clubs the dominant sound is hip-hop and electronic dance music, and the crowd that flocks to them every night of the week is of the trendy, under-thirty generation. Leeson Street—just off St. Stephen's Green, south of the Liffey, and known as "the strip"—is a main nightclub area aimed at the over-thirty crowd that revs up at pub closing time and stays active until 4 AM. It has, however, lost its gloss since a number of lap-dancing establishments have opened. The dress code at Leeson Street's dance clubs is informal, but jeans and sneakers are not welcome. Most of these clubs are licensed only to sell wine, and the prices can be exorbitant (up to €26 for a mediocre bottle); the upside is that most don't charge to get in.

There are plenty of alternatives to the electronic dance scene, including nightclubs where the dominant sounds range from soul to salsa—such as the weekend nightclub "Play" at the Gaiety Theatre. Although jazz isn't a big part of the nightlife here, a few regular venues do draw the best of local and international talent. And if you're looking for something more mellow, the city doesn't disappoint: there are wine bars, bistros, cafés, and all manner of other late-night eateries where you can sit, sip, and chat until 2 AM or later.

Some of Dublin's classic pubs—arguably some of the finest watering holes in the world—have been reinvented with modern interiors and designer drinks, to attract a younger, upwardly mobile crowd. Beware

Dublin Tourism's "Official Dublin Pub Guide," which has a tendency to recommend many of these bland spots. Despite the changes, however, the traditional pub has steadfastly clung to its role as the primary center of Dublin's social life. The city has nearly 1,000 pubs ("licensed tabernacles," writer Flann O'Brien calls them). And although the vision of elderly men enjoying a chin wag over a creamy pint of stout has become something of a rarity, there are still plenty of places where you can enjoy a quiet (or not so quiet) drink and a chat. Last drinks are called at 11:30 PM Monday to Thursday, 12:30 AM Friday and Saturday, and 11 PM on Sunday. Some city-center pubs have extended opening hours and don't serve last drinks until 1:45 AM.

A word of warning: although most pubs and clubs are perfectly safe, the lads can get lively—public drunkenness is very much a part of Dublin's nightlife. Whereas this is for the most part seen as the Irish form of unwinding after a long week (or, well, day), it can sometimes lead to regrettable incidents (fighting, for instance). In an effort to keep potential trouble at bay, bouncers and security guards maintain a visible presence in all clubs and many pubs around the city. At the end of the night, the city center is full of young people trying to get home, which makes for extremely long lines at taxi stands and late-night bus stops, especially on weekends. The combination of drunkenness and impatience can very occasionally lead to trouble, so practice a little caution. If you will need late-night transportation, try to arrange it with your hotel before you go out.

IRISH CABARET, MUSIC & DANCING

Bewley's Cafe Theatre (⊠ *Grafton St., Southside* ☎ *086/878-4001*), with its "Live at The Oriental Room" nights, has become the atmospheric cabaret hot spot in Dublin.

BALLSBRIDGE **Burlington Hotel** (⊠ *Upper Leeson St., Ballsbridge* ☎ *01/660–5222*) has a high-class lounge featuring a well-performed Irish cabaret—with dancing, music, and song.

JAZZ

The Bleu Note (⊠ *61-63 Capel St., Northside* ☎ *01/878–3371* ⊕ *www. bleunoteclub.com*) is the city's only dedicated jazz and blues venue. A buzzing, clubby atmosphere, it offers good music every Friday and Saturday.

International (⊠ *Wicklow St., Southside* ☎ *01/677–9250*) hosts the Dirty Jazz Club upstairs on Tuesday night.

JJ Smyth's (⊠ *12 Aungier St., City Center* ☎ *01/475–2565*) is an old-time jazz venue where the Pendulum Club on Sunday is a popular hangout for all the "jazz heads."

The Mint Bar (⊠ *Westin Hotel, College Green, City Center* ☎ *01/645–1000*), a basement venue, presents Velvet Lounge bands and guests every Saturday night.

NIGHTCLUBS

NORTHSIDE **Spirit** (✉ *57 Middle Abbey St., Northside* ☎ *01/877–9999*) attracts a party-time, young crowd, which is serious about two things: dancing and more dancing. Spirit likes to call itself a "holistic venue" and its three floors are loosely designed around the themes of Mind, Body, and Soul. Mind is the basement level full of scented candles, chill-out couches, and ambient sounds; Body is the main dance floor with full-on dance tracks; and Soul is more funky.

Lillie's Bordello (✉ *Grafton St., City Center* ☎ *01/679–9204*) is a popular spot for a trendy professional crowd, as well as for rock and film stars.

The Pod (✉ *Harcourt St., City Center* ☎ *01/478–0166*), also known as the "Place of Dance," qualifies as Dublin's most renowned dance club, especially among the younger set. Whether you get in depends as much on what you're wearing as on your age.

Renards (✉ *St. Fredrick St., Georgian Dublin* ☎ *01/677–5876*) is where you'll find upmarket thirtysomethings who like to let their hair down. The music can be a bit predictable, but you might just bump into Bono.

Rí Ra (✉ *Dame Ct., City Center* ☎ *01/677–4835*) is part of the hugely popular Globe bar. The name means "uproar" in Irish, and on most nights the place does go a little wild. It's one of the best spots in Dublin for fun, no-frills dancing. Upstairs is more low-key.

Spy (✉ *59 S. William St., City Center* ☎ *01/679–0014*) is a split-level space broken up into four distinct rooms, each with its own bar and vibe. Downstairs is an all-out dance club known as Wax.

★ **Tripod** (✉ *Old Harcourt St. Station, Harcourt St., City Center* ☎ *01/478–0166*), adjacent to the Pod and the Crawdaddy music venue, can pack in more than 1,300 people and surround them with state-of-the-art sound and light. It regularly hosts Irish and international rock acts, and celebrity DJs from Europe and the United States. It has full bar facilities.

Underground@Kennedy's (✉ *31–32 Westland Row, City Center* ☎ *01/661–1124*) is a real dive of a basement club that attracts cutting-edge European DJs and a serious dance and hip-hop crowd.

TEMPLE BAR **Temple Bar Music Centre** (✉ *Curved St., Temple Bar* ☎ *01/670–9202*) claims to provide a different sound every night, including house, tribute bands, guitar-driven rock, and Latin music.

Viper Room (✉ *5 Aston Quay, Temple Bar* ☎ *01/672–5566*), decorated in rich reds and purples, is a delightfully decadent late-night club that plays funk, chart, and rhythm and blues. Downstairs there's live jazz and salsa.

PUBS

"When I die I want to decompose in a barrel of porter and have it served in all the pubs in Dublin." Author J.P. Donleavy realized that it's impossible to think of Dublin without also thinking of its 1,000 or so "public houses." These are what give Dublin so much of its character, and they're largely to blame for the fierce loyalty Dublin inspires among locals and visitors. Some wag once asked if it was possible to cross Dublin without passing a single pub along the way. The answer was "Yes, but only if you go into every one." As a general rule, the area between Grafton and Great George's streets is a gold mine for classy pubs. Another good bet is the Temple Bar district (though some of the newer ones are all plastic and mirrors). And if it be real spit-on-the-floor hideaways you're after, head across the Liffey to the area around Parnell Square.

NORTHSIDE   **Conways** (⊠*70 Parnell St., Northside* ☎*01/873–2687*) is an old-school, "spit-and-sawdust" public house with the beat of modern live music upstairs.

The Flowing Tide (⊠*Lower Abbey St., Northside* ☎*01/874–0842*), directly across from the Abbey Theatre, draws a lively pre- and post-theater crowd. No TVs, quality pub talk, and a great pint of Guinness make it a worthwhile visit.

GUBU (⊠*Capel St., Northside* ☎*01/874–0710*), run by the hugely successful owners of the Globe, is a mixed gay and straight bar. The music is loud and dance-driven, and the downstairs pool table is an added bonus.

Liffey Bar (⊠*Morrison Hotel, Upper Ormond Quay, Northside* ☎*01/878–2999*) is a modern, stylish bar in one of Dublin's most designer-friendly hotels. The loungy bar overlooks the river it's named after and attracts a crowd that likes to dress up and talk about it.

SOUTHSIDE &   **Cassidy's** (⊠*42 Lower Camden St., Southside* ☎*01/475–1429*), is a
SOUTHEAST   quality neighborhood pub with a pint of stout so good that former
DUBLIN   president Bill Clinton dropped in for one during a visit to Dublin.

Cellar Bar (⊠*24 Upper Merrion St., Southeast Dublin* ☎*01/603–0600*), at the Merrion Hotel, is in a stylish 18th-century wine vault with bare brick walls and vaulted ceilings. It tends to draw a well-heeled crowd.

Davy Byrne's (⊠*21 Duke St., Southside* ☎*01/671–1298*) is a pilgrimage stop for Joyceans. In *Ulysses*, Leopold Bloom stops in here for a glass of Burgundy and a Gorgonzola-cheese sandwich. He then leaves the pub and walks to Dawson Street, where he helps a blind man cross the road. Unfortunately, the decor is greatly changed from Joyce's day, but it still serves some fine pub grub.

Doheny & Nesbitt (⊠*5 Lower Baggot St., Southeast Dublin* ☎*01/676–2945*), a traditional spot with snugs, dark wooden furnishings, and smoke-darkened ceilings, has hardly changed over the decades.

Pub Grub

Most pubs serve food at lunchtime, many throughout the day and into the early evening. This is an inexpensive way to eat out, and the quality of the food is often quite good.

Davy Byrne's. James Joyce immortalized this pub in *Ulysses*. Nowadays it's more akin to a cocktail bar than a Dublin pub, but it's good for fresh and smoked salmon, salads, fresh oysters, and a hot daily special. ⊠ *21 Duke St., Southside* ☎ *01/671–1298* ⊟ *AE, MC, V.*

The Odeon. The converted main building of Harcourt Street's old railway station houses this large, modern bar. Both the lunch and dinner menus include fresh-grilled panini, beef-and-Guinness stew, chicken wings, and homemade sausages. Sunday brunch is served between noon and 5. ⊠ *57 Harcourt St., Southside* ☎ *01/478–2088* ⊟ *AE, MC, V.*

The South William. A new, lively pub with a huge glass front that happens to serve gourmet pies that might be the best pub food in the known world. Try the bacon and cabbage. ⊠ *South William St., Southside* ☎ *01/672–5946* ⊟ *AE, MC, V.*

Stag's Head. The most beautiful pub in Dublin, period. Built in 1895, it's a Victorian-era mahogany masterpiece. Serving one of Dublin's best pub lunches, this place is a favorite among Trinity students. ⊠ *1 Dame Ct., Southside* ☎ *01/679–3701* ⊟ *No credit cards.*

Zanzibar. This spectacular, immense bar on the Northside looks as though it might be more at home in downtown Marrakech. Laze an afternoon away in one of the wicker chairs and enjoy hearty pastas, burgers, salads, and cocktails. ⊠ *34–35 Lower Ormond Quay, Northside* ☎ *01/878–7212* ⊟ *AE, MC, V.*

Doyle's (⊠ *9 College St., Southside* ☎ *01/671–0616*), a small, cozy pub, is a favorite with journalists from the *Irish Times* office, just across the street.

George (⊠ *89 S. Great George's St., Southside* ☎ *01/478–2983*), Dublin's two-floor main gay pub, draws an almost entirely male crowd; its nightclub stays open until 2:30 AM nightly except Tuesday. The "alternative bingo night," with star drag act Miss Shirley Temple Bar, is a riot of risqué fun.

Globe (⊠ *11 S. Great George's St., Southside* ☎ *01/671–1220*), one of the hippest café-bars in town, draws arty, trendy Dubliners who sip espresso drinks by day and pack the place at night. There's live jazz on Sunday.

Fodor'sChoice
★ **Grogans** (⊠ *15 S. William St., Southside* ☎ *01/677–9320*), also known as the Castle Lounge, is a small place packed with creative folk. Owner Tommy Grogan is known as a patron of local artists, and his walls are covered with their work.

Hogan's (⊠ *35 Great St. George's St., Southside* ☎ *01/677–5904*), a huge space on two levels, gets jammed most nights, but the old place maintains its style through it all.

★ **Horseshoe Bar** (⊠*Shelbourne, 27 St. Stephen's Green, Southside* ☎*01/676–6471*) was recently given a massive face-lift along with the rest of the Shelbourne hotel and is now the hottest ticket in town. Long a popular meeting place for Dublin's businesspeople and politicians, there's comparatively little space for drinkers around the famous semi-circular bar—but this does wonders for making friends quickly.

Kehoe's (⊠*9 S. Anne St., Southside* ☎*01/677–8312*) is popular with Trinity students and academics. The tiny back room is cozy, and the upstairs is basically the owner's living room, open to the public.

Kitty O'Shea's (⊠*Upper Grand Canal St., Southeast Dublin* ☎*01/660–9965*) has Pre-Raphaelite–style stained glass, and lots of sports paraphernalia on the walls, and is popular with sports fans of all types. Its sister pubs are in Brussels and Paris; this is the original.

Lesson Lounge (⊠*148 Upper Lesson St., Southeast Dublin* ☎*01/660–3816*) has the look of a classic old Dublin "boozer," with one notable exception: it has a television. The Lesson is known as a place to watch televised sports of all kinds, and it's always pleasant and inclusive.

★ **Library Bar** (⊠*Central Hotel, 1–5 Exchequer St., Southside* ☎*01/679–7302*) is the place to go when you're ready to get away from all the madness. The book-lined shelves, big armchairs and sofas, and blazing fireplace make this first-floor hideaway one of the most serene night-time spots in Dublin.

Long Hall Pub (⊠*51 S. Great George's St., Southside* ☎*01/475–1590*), one of Dublin's most ornate traditional taverns, has Victorian lamps, a mahogany bar, mirrors, chandeliers, and plasterwork ceilings, all more than 100 years old. The pub serves sandwiches and an excellent pint of Guinness.

McDaid's (⊠*3 Harry St., Southside* ☎*01/679–4395*) attracted boisterous Brendan Behan and other leading writers in the 1950s; its wild literary reputation still lingers, although the bar has been discreetly modernized and is altogether quieter.

Mulligan's (⊠*8 Poolbeg St., Southside* ☎*01/677–5582*) is synonymous in Dublin with a truly inspirational pint of Guinness. Until a few years ago no women were admitted. Today journalists, locals, and students of both genders flock here for the perfect pint.

Neary's (⊠*1 Chatham St., Southside* ☎*01/677–7371*), with an exotic, Victorian-style interior, was once the haunt of music-hall artists and a certain literary set, including Brendan Behan. Join the actors from the adjacent Gaiety Theatre for a good pub lunch.

O'Donoghue's (⊠*15 Merrion Row, Southside* ☎*01/676–2807*), a cheerful smoky hangout, has impromptu musical performances that often spill out onto the street.

The Old Stand (⊠*37 Exchequer St., Southside* ☎*01/677–7220*), one of the oldest pubs in the city, is named after the Old Stand stadium at Lansdowne Road, home to Irish rugby and football. The pub is renowned for great pints and fine steaks.

Ron Black's (✉37 Dawson St., Southside ☎01/677–7220) is one of three "superbars" along Dawson Street. Celtic Tiger cubs jam the place, trying to meet each other over kicking house music and six or seven drinks.

Fodor's Choice ★ **Stag's Head** (✉1 Dame Ct., Southside ☎01/679–3701) dates from 1770 and was rebuilt in 1895. Theater people from the nearby Olympia, journalists, and Trinity students gather around the unusual Connemara red marble bar. The interior is a Victorian beaut.

Toner's (✉139 Lower Baggot St., Southside ☎01/676–3090), though billed as a Victorian bar, actually goes back 200 years, with an original flagstone floor to prove its antiquity, as well as wooden drawers running up to the ceiling—a relic of the days when bars doubled as grocery shops. Oliver St. John Gogarty, who was the model for Buck Mulligan in James Joyce's *Ulysses,* accompanied W. B. Yeats here, in what was purportedly the latter's only visit to a pub.

TEMPLE BAR **Front Lounge** (✉33 Parliament St., Temple Bar ☎01/679–3988), a modern pub, caters to a mixed crowd of young professionals, both gay and straight.

Oliver St. John Gogarty (✉57 Fleet St., Temple Bar ☎01/671–1822) is a lively bar that attracts all ages and nationalities; it overflows with patrons in summer. On most nights there's traditional Irish music upstairs.

Palace Bar (✉21 Fleet St., Temple Bar ☎01/677–9290), scarcely changed since the 1940s, is tiled and rather barren looking, but is popular with journalists and writers (the *Irish Times* is nearby). The walls are lined with cartoons drawn by the illustrators who used to spend time here.

The Porterhouse (✉16–18 Parliament St., Temple Bar ☎01/679–8847) is one of the few bars in Ireland to brew its own beer. The Plain Porter has won the best stout at the "Brewing Oscars," beating out the mighty Guinness. The tasteful interior is all dark woods and soft lighting.

BALLSBRIDGE **The 51** (✉Haddington Rd., Ballsbridge ☎01/660–0150) is famous for its collection of whiskies from around the world. Its Beer Garden is always buzzing with activity in fine weather.

O'Brien's (✉Sussex Terr., Ballsbridge ☎01/668–2594), beside the Doyle Burlington Hotel, is a little antique gem of a pub, scarcely changed since the 1950s, with traditional snugs.

DUBLIN WEST **Brazen Head** (✉Bridge St., Dublin West ☎01/677–9549), Dublin's oldest pub (the site has been licensed since 1198), has stone walls and open fireplaces—it has hardly changed over the years. The pub is renowned for traditional-music performances and lively sing-along sessions on Sunday evenings. On the south side of the Liffey quays, it's a little dif-

Dublin Pubs

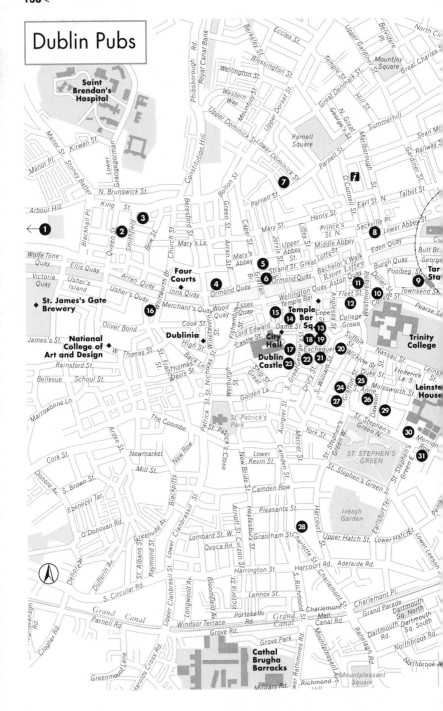

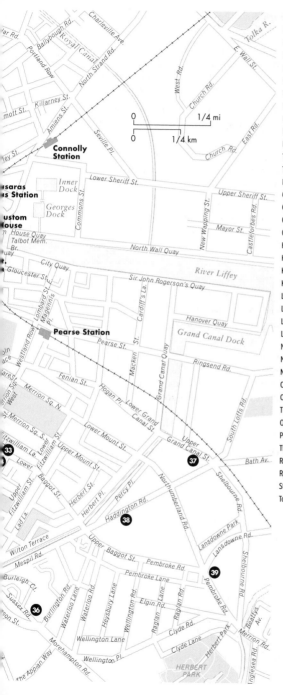

2

ficult to find—turn down Lower Bridge Street and make a right onto the old lane.

Cobblestone (⊠*N. King St., Dublin West* ☎*01/872–1799*) is a glorious house of ale in the best Dublin tradition, popular with Smithfield Market workers. Its chatty imbibers and live traditional music are attracting a more varied, younger crowd from all over town.

Company Cafe Bar (⊠*27 Ormond Quay, Dublin West* ☎*01/872–2480*) is the renamed, polished-up incarnation of one of Dublin's old reliable gay hangouts.

Dice Bar (⊠*79 Queen St., Dublin West* ☎*01/674–6710*), partly owned by one of the members of the Fun Lovin' Criminals band, may look like the dive that it is, but the DJ-driven music always rocks and the hipster folks are friendly and laid-back.

★ **Ryan's Pub** (⊠*28 Parkgate St., Dublin West* ☎*01/677–6097*) is one of Dublin's last genuine, late-Victorian-era pubs, and has changed little since its last (1896) remodeling.

THE ARTS

CLASSICAL MUSIC & OPERA

The Bank of Ireland Arts Center (⊠*Foster Pl. S, Southside* ☎*01/671–1488*) is great at lunchtime, when classical music and opera recitals take place.

SOUTHEAST DUBLIN   **National Concert Hall** (⊠*Earlsfort Terr., Southeast Dublin* ☎*01/475–1666* ⊕*www.nch.ie*), just off St. Stephen's Green, is Dublin's main theater for classical music of all kinds, from symphonies to chamber groups. The slightly austere Neoclassical building was transformed in 1981 into one of Europe's finest medium-size concert halls. It houses the cream of Irish classical musicians, the National Symphony Orchestra of Ireland. A host of guest international conductors and performers—Maxim Vengerov, Radu Lupu, and Pinchas Zukerman are just a few of the soloists who have appeared—keep the standard very high, and performances continue throughout the year. The concert year picks up speed in mid-September and sails through to June; July and August also get many dazzling troupes. The smaller, more intimate John Field and Carolan rooms are perfect for chamber music.

St. Stephen's Church (⊠*Merrion Sq., Southeast Dublin* ☎*01/288–0663*) stages a regular program of choral and orchestral events under its glorious "pepper canister" cupola.

DUBLIN WEST   **Opera Ireland** (⊠*West Wing 3, Adelaide Chambers, Peter St., Dublin West* ☎*01/478–6041* ⊕*www.operaireland.com*) performs at the Gaiety Theatre; call to find out what's on.

TEMPLE BAR   **Opera Theatre Company** (⊠*Temple Bar Music Centre, Curved St., Temple Bar* ☎*01/679–4962* ⊕*www.opera.ie*) is Ireland's only touring opera company. It performs at venues in Dublin and throughout the country.

Continued on page 146

A TRIP TO THE PUB

For any visitor to Ireland who wants to see the natives in their bare element—to witness them at full pace, no-holds-barred—a trip to a busy pub is a must. Luckily for you, the pub is above all a welcoming place, where a visitor is seen as a source of new, exotic stories and, more importantly, as an unsullied audience for the locals and their tall tales.

WELCOME TO IRELAND'S LIVING ROOM...

The term "pub" is shorthand for "public house," which is an apt name for one of Ireland's great institutions. Stepping into a pub (and there seems to be one on every corner) is the easiest way to transport yourself into the thick of Irish life.

A pub, of course, is a drinking establishment, and for better or worse the Irish have a deep, abiding relationship with drink—particularly their beloved black stout. The point, however, isn't what you drink, but where: in the warmth of the public house, in company. It's the place to tell stories, most of them true, and to hear music. It's where locals go to mark the key stages of their lives: to wet a new baby's head; to celebrate a graduation; to announce an engagement; and finally to wake a corpse.

HOW TO CHOOSE A PUB

Not all pubs are created equal. Throughout this book we recommend some of the finest, but here are a few ways to distinguish the real gold from the sparkling pyrite:

- Qualified, experienced bar staff—not grubby students dreaming of the round-the-world trip they are working to save up for. A uniform of white shirt and black trousers is often a good sign.

- At least one man over sixty (preferably with a cap of some description) drinking at the bar (not at a table). He should know the good bars by now, right?

- No TV. Or, if there is a TV it should be hidden away in a corner, only to be used for horse racing and other major sporting events.

- No recorded music. A pub is a place to talk and listen. Occasional live music is okay, especially a traditional session.

- Bathrooms are clean but not *too* clean. They are purely functional, not polished chambers for hanging out and chatting with friends about your new Blackberry.

THE QUEST FOR THE CRAIC

Pub-going at its best has a touch of magic to it: conversation flows, spirits rise, and inhibitions evaporate. There's a word in Gaelic for this happy condition: the *craic*, which roughly translates as "lively talk and good times." The craic is the sort of thing that's difficult to find only when you're looking too hard for it. Large crowds, loud music, and one pint too many can also make the craic elusive. When your companions all seem clever and handsome, and you can't imagine better company in the world, that's when you know you've found it.

PUB ETIQUETTE

Some things to keep in mind if you want to get the most out of your trip to the pub:

- First, if you want to meet people and get into the craic, belly up to the bar counter and pass up a seat at a table.

- Always place your drink order at the bar and don't heckle the barkeepers to get their attention. They're professionals—they'll see you soon enough.

- If you do take a table, bring your dirty glasses back to the bar before you leave, or when you order another round.

- In present-day Ireland, male and female pubgoers usually get equal treatment. At the most traditional places, though, it's still customary in mixed company for the man to order drinks at the bar while the woman takes a table seat.

- Don't tip the barkeepers, except at Christmas, when you can offer to buy them a drink.

- Never sip from your Guinness until it has fully settled. You'll know this from the deep black color and perfectly defined white head.

- Don't smoke in the bar; it's against the law. But feel free to gather outside in the rain and chat with the other unfortunates. It's a great spot to start a romance.

- You have to be at least 18 years old to *drink* in a pub, but kids are welcome during the day, and nondrinking minors as young as 14 are often tolerated at night.

MAKING THE ROUNDS

You may get caught up in the "rounds" system, in which each pub mate takes turns to "shout" an order. Your new friends may forget to tell you when it's your round, but any failure to "put your hand in your pocket" may lead to a reputation that will follow you to the grave. To miss your "shout" is to become known for "short arms and long pockets" and to be shunned by decent people.

LAST CALL

Technically, pubs have to stop serving at 11:30 Mon.–Thurs., 12:30 Fri.–Sat., and 11 Sun. At the end of the night, ignore the first five calls of "Time please, ladies and gentlemen!" from the barman. You'll know he's getting serious by the roar of his voice.

THE "BLACK STUFF"

Stout, a dark beer made using roasted malts or barley, originated in Ireland, and it's the country's national drink, consumed in pubs with unflagging allegiance.

Rich, creamy head.

Nearly black in color, with a very slight coffee-like aftertaste.

As you drink, the head will leave "rings of pleasure" down the side of the glass.

There are three main brands:

GUINNESS For most Irish, the name Guinness is synonymous with stout. With massive breweries in Africa and the Americas, it really is a world brand, but the "true" pint still flows from the original brewery at St. James Gate in Dublin. While some old-timers still drink the more malty bottled version, draught Guinness is now the standard. A deep, creamy texture and slightly bitter first taste is followed by a milder, more "toasty" aftertaste.

MURPHY'S The Murphy Brewery was founded by James Murphy in 1856 in Cork City. Murphy's is very much a Cork drink, and often suffers from "second city" complex in relation to its giant rival Guinness. Corkonians say Murphy's is a less bitter, more nutty flavor than the "Dublin stout."

BEAMISH Another Cork drink, a little sweeter and less dry than either Guinness or Murphy's, and so a little easier on the novice palate. Beamish and Crawford Brewery began making beer in 1792, after purchasing an existing brewery in the heart of Cork's medieval center that dates back to at least 1650 (and possibly 1500).

THE POUR

The storage and pouring of a pint of stout is almost as important as the brewing. The best quality is usually found in older bars that sell a lot of pints—meaning the beer you get hasn't been sitting in the keg too long and the pipes are well coated.

Pouring a pint consists of two stages: The glass is filled three-quarters full, then allowed to sit. After the head settles, the glass is filled to the top (stage two).

Why the painstaking ritual? Because the barkeeper knows you don't want your first sip to be a mouthful of foam. And because the flavor's that much sweeter for the waiting.

FOOD, SONG, AND ADDITIONAL DRINK

Although the majority of your companions will be drinking stout, you do have other options.

- A lager is always available—Heiniken and Carlsberg are the most popular brands.

- If you're thirsting for something stronger, take a nip of Irish whiskey, which tends to be less smoky and intensely flavored than its Scotch cousin. Jameson and Bushmills, both smooth blends, are the standard varieties, and you can usually find a single-malt as well.

- On the other hand, if the booze isn't your thing, you can always choose tea, soda, or a bottle of water. (Ballygowan is the Irish Evian.) It's fine to order nonalcoholic drinks—many people who drive do so.

- Pub food is a lunchtime thing; the prices are reasonable, and the quality can be quite good. Ask for a menu at the bar. If you're near a coast, look for seafood specialties, from oysters and mussels to smoked salmon. With beef-and-Guinness stew, you can drink your stout and eat it too.

"TRAD" MUSIC IN ITS NATURAL DOMAIN

The pub is an ideal place to hear traditional Irish music. Performances can have a spontaneous air to them, but they don't start up just anywhere. Pubs that accommodate live sessions have signs saying so; and they're more common outside Dublin than in the city. To learn more about Irish music, see "Gael Force" in chapter 7.

Top photo: Traditional Irish stew
Above: Jameson whiskey

DUBLIN WEST **Royal Hospital Kilmainham** (⊠ *Military Rd., Dublin West* ☎01/671–8666 ⊕ *www.rhk.ie*) presents frequent classical concerts in its magnificent 17th-century interior.

FILM

NORTHSIDE **Cineworld** (⊠ *Parnell Center, Parnell St., Northside* ☎01/872–8400), a 17-screen theater just off O'Connell Street, is the city center's only multiplex movie house; it shows the latest commercial features.

> **BONO RECOMMENDS**
>
> Irish rock & roll hero Bono has one prevailing test for judging a pub: "My favorite pubs are any that let you drink in after hours. As for traditional music, it's all over Temple Bar in Dublin. If in Howth Head, check out Sharon Shannon—still a genius."

Savoy Cinema (⊠ *O'Connell St., Northside* ☎01/874–6000), just across from the General Post Office, is a four-screen theater with the largest screen in the country.

TEMPLE BAR **Irish Film Institute** (⊠ *6 Eustace St., Temple Bar* ☎01/677–8788) shows classic and new independent films.

SOUTHSIDE **Screen Cinema** (⊠ *2 Townsend St., Southside* ☎01/671–4988), between Trinity College and O'Connell Street Bridge, is a popular three-screen art-house cinema.

ROCK & CONTEMPORARY MUSIC

NORTHSIDE **The Ambassador** (⊠ *1 Parnell Sq., Northside* ☎01/889–9403) was once a cinema attached to the Gate Theatre. The plush interior and seats have been removed, and the stripped-down venue now houses visiting bands and "school-disco" nights with music from the '70s and '80s.

The Point (⊠ *Eastlink Br., Northside* ☎01/836–3633 ⊕ *www.thepoint. ie*), a 6,000-capacity arena about 1 km (½ mi) east of the Custom House on the Liffey, is Dublin's premier venue for internationally renowned acts. Call or send a self-addressed envelope to receive a list of upcoming shows; tickets can be difficult to obtain, so book early.

SOUTHSIDE **Crawdaddy** (⊠ *Old Harcourt Station., Harcourt St., Southside*
★ ☎01/478–0166) is an intimate venue at the center of the hot Pod nightclub complex. A predecessor to *Rolling Stone, Crawdaddy* was the very first rock magazine in the United States. It's an homage to that bygone era of sweat, three chords, and the truth.

International Bar (⊠ *Wicklow St., Southside* ☎01/677–9250) has a long-established, tiny, get-close-to-the-band venue upstairs. It hosts theater in the afternoons.

The Village (⊠ *26 Wexford St., Southside* ☎01/475–8555), set in a striking, glass-fronted building, isn't too fussy about the kind of bands it hosts, so long as their amps are turned up full and the lead singer knows how to scream.

Whelan's (⊠ *25 Wexford St., Southside* ☎01/478–0766), just off the southeastern corner of St. Stephen's Green, is one of the city's best—and most popular—music venues. Well-known performers play everything from rock to folk to traditional music. The same owners run the Village bar and venue next door.

TEMPLE BAR **Olympia Theatre** (✉ *72 Dame St., Temple Bar* ☎ *01/677–7744*) puts on
★ "Midnight from the Olympia" shows every Friday and Saturday from midnight to 2 AM, with everything from rock to country.

Temple Bar Music Centre (✉ *Curved St., Temple Bar* ☎ *01/670–0533*) is a music venue, rehearsal space, television studio, and pub rolled into one. It buzzes with activity every day of the week. Live acts range from rock bands to world music to singer-songwriters.

DUBLIN WEST **Vicar Street** (✉ *58–59 Thomas St., Dublin West* ☎ *01/454–5533*), just across from Christ Church Cathedral, is a venue for intimate concerts. It often plays host to folk music, jazz, and comedy, as well as rock performances.

THEATER

NORTHSIDE **Abbey Theatre** (✉ *Lower Abbey St., Northside* ☎ *01/878–7222* ⊕ *www.abbeytheatre.ie*) is the fabled home of Ireland's national theater company. In 1904 W. B. Yeats and his patron, Lady Gregory, opened the theater, which became a major center for the Irish literary renaissance—the place that first staged works by J. M. Synge and Sean O'Casey, among many others. The year 2004 celebrated the 100th anniversary of this landmark theater. Plays by recent Irish drama heavyweights like Brian Friel, Tom Murphy, Hugh Leonard, and John B. Keane have all premiered here, and memorable productions of international greats like Mamet, Ibsen, and Shakespeare have also been performed. You should not, however, arrive expecting 19th-century grandeur: the original structure burned down in 1951. Unfortunately, an ugly concrete boxlike auditorium was built in its place—but what it may lack in visuals it makes up for in space and acoustics. Some say the repertoire is overly reverential and mainstream, but such chestnuts as Dion Boucicault's *The Shaughran* wound up being applauded by many. Happily, the Abbey's sister theater at the same address, the Peacock, offers more experimental drama. But the Abbey will always be relevant since much of the theatergoing public still looks to it as a barometer of Irish culture.

Gate Theatre (✉ *Cavendish Row, Parnell Sq., Northside* ☎ *01/874–4045* ⊕ *www.gate-theatre.ie*), an intimate 371-seat theater in a jewel-like Georgian assembly hall, produces the classics and contemporary plays by leading Irish writers, including Beckett, Wilde (the production of *Salome* was a worldwide hit), Shaw, and the younger generation of dramatists, such as Conor McPherson.

SOUTHSIDE **Andrew's Lane Theatre** (✉ *9–11 Andrew's La., Southside* ☎ *01/679–5720*) presents experimental productions.

Gaiety Theatre (✉ *S. King St., Southside* ☎ *01/677–1717*) is the home of Opera Ireland when it's not showing musical comedy, drama, and revues. On weekends this elegant theater is taken over by a nightclub with live music and cabaret.

Samuel Beckett Centre (⊠ *Trinity College, Southside* ☎ *01/608–2266*) is home to Trinity's drama department, as well as visiting European groups. Dance is often performed here by visiting troupes.

TEMPLE BAR **New Project Arts Centre** (⊠ *39 E. Essex St., Temple Bar* ☎ *01/671–2321*) is a theater and performance space in an ugly modern building at the center of Temple Bar. Fringe and mainstream theater, contemporary music, and experimental art have all found a home here.

The New Theatre (⊠ *43 E. Essex St., Temple Bar* ☎ *01/670–3361*) is a troupe with a political agenda, so you'll often find this newly renovated space favors Irish working-class writers like Sean O'Casey and Brendan Behan.

> ### WORD OF MOUTH
>
> "It is as difficult if not more difficult to get tickets to shows in Dublin theaters than it is to get tickets to shows in London. So good are they, most of the Dublin presentations transfer straight to Broadway and later to Hollywood scripts and the movies. Thus, I would suggest than you jump at the opportunity when you're in Dublin. After all, Irish literature and theater is one of the things that Ireland is famous for. Dramas tend to be deep—reflecting social and historic issues past and present in Ireland—and they give an insight into the country that you will be touring."
>
> —Cathy

Olympia Theatre (⊠ *72 Dame St., Temple Bar* ☎ *01/677–7744*) is Dublin's oldest and premier multipurpose theatrical venue. In addition to its high-profile musical performances, it has seasons of comedy, vaudeville, and ballet.

SPORTS

FOOTBALL

Soccer—called football in Europe—is very popular in Ireland, largely due to the euphoria resulting from the national team's successes since the late 1980s. However, the places where you can watch it aren't ideal—they tend to be small and out-of-date. **Lansdowne Road Stadium** (⊠ *62 Lansdowne Rd., Ballsbridge* ☎ *01/668–4601*), a vast rugby stadium, is the main center for international matches. The stadium is about to be knocked down and a state-of-the-art replacement built on the same spot. In the meantime, soccer and rugby games will be played at Croke Park—the first time in history so called "foreign games" will be allowed on the Gaelic Athletic Association's hallowed turf.

League of Ireland matches take place throughout the city on Friday evenings or Sunday afternoons from March to November. For details, contact the **Football Association of Ireland** (⊠ *80 Merrion Sq. S, Southeast Dublin* ☎ *01/676–6864*).

GAELIC GAMES

The traditional games of Ireland, Gaelic football and hurling, attract a huge following, with roaring crowds cheering on their county teams. Games are held at Croke Park, the stunning, high-tech national stadium for Gaelic games, just north of the city center. For details of matches, contact the **Gaelic Athletic Association** (*GAA* ✉*Croke Park, North County Dublin* ☎*01/836–3222* ⊕*www.gaa.ie*).

HORSE RACING

Horse racing—from flat to hurdle to steeplechase—is one of the great sporting loves of the Irish. The sport is closely followed and betting is popular, but the social side of attending races is equally important to Dubliners. The main course in Dublin is **Leopardstown** (✉*Leopardstown Rd., South County Dublin* ☎*01/289–3607* ⊕*www.leopardstown. com*), an ultramodern course that in February hosts the Hennessey Gold Cup, Ireland's most prestigious steeplechase. Summertime is devoted to flat racing, and the rest of the year to racing over fences. You can also nip in for a quick meal at the restaurant.

The **Curragh** (☎*045/441–205* ⊕*www.curragh.ie*), southwest of Dublin off M7, hosts the five Classics, the most important flat races of the season, from May to September. There are numerous bars here and two restaurants. **Fairyhouse** (✉*Co. Meath* ☎*01/825–6167*) hosts the Grand National, the most popular steeplechase of the season, every Easter Monday. **Punchestown** (☎*045/897–704*), outside Naas, County Kildare, is the home of the ever-popular Punchestown National Hunt Festival in April.

SHOPPING

The only known specimens of leprechauns or shillelaghs in Ireland are those in souvenir-shop windows, and shamrocks mainly bloom around the borders of Irish linen handkerchiefs and tablecloths. But in Dublin's shops you can find much more than kitschy designs. There's a tremendous variety of stores here, many of which are quite sophisticated—as a walk through Dublin's central shopping area, from O'Connell to Grafton Street, will prove. Department stores stock internationally known fashion-designer goods and housewares, and small (and often pricey) boutiques sell Irish crafts and other merchandise. Don't expect too many bargains here. And be prepared, if you're shopping in central Dublin, to push through crowds—especially in the afternoons and on weekends. Most large shops and department stores are open Monday to Saturday 9 to 6, with late hours on Thursday until 9. Although nearly all department stores are closed on Sunday, some smaller specialty shops stay open. Those with later closing hours are noted below. You're particularly likely to find sales in January, February, July, and August.

SHOPPING STREETS

Each of Dublin's dozen or so main shopping streets has a different character. Visit them all to appreciate the wide selection of items for sale here. The main commercial streets north of the river have both chain and department stores that tend to be less expensive (and less design-conscious) than their counterparts in the city center on the other side of the Liffey.

Henry Street, where cash-conscious Dubliners shop, runs westward from O'Connell Street. Arnotts department store is the anchor here; smaller, specialty stores sell CDs, footwear, and clothing. Henry Street's continuation, Mary Street, has a branch of Marks & Spencer and the Jervis Shopping Centre.

O'Connell Street, the city's main thoroughfare, is more downscale than Southside city streets (such as Grafton Street), but it is still worth a walk. One of Dublin's largest department stores, Clery's, is here, across from the GPO. On the same side of the street as the post office is Eason's, a large book, magazine, and stationery store.

Dawson Street, just east of Grafton Street between Nassau Street to the north and St. Stephen's Green to the south, is the city's primary bookstore avenue. Waterstone's and Hodges Figgis face each other from opposite sides of the street.

Francis Street and surrounding areas, such as the Coombe, have plenty of shops where you can browse. It's all part of the Liberties, the oldest part of the city and the hub of Dublin's antiques trade. If you're looking for something in particular, dealers will gladly recommend the appropriate store to you.

Grafton Street, Dublin's bustling pedestrian-only main shopping street, has two department stores: down-to-earth Marks & Spencer and *trés* chic Brown Thomas. The rest of the street is taken up by shops, many of them branches of international chains, such as the Body Shop and Bally, and many British chains. This is also the spot to buy fresh flowers, available at reasonable prices from outdoor stands. On the smaller streets off Grafton Street—especially Duke Street, South Anne Street, and Chatham Street—are worthwhile crafts, clothing, and designer housewares shops.

Nassau Street, Dublin's main tourist-oriented thoroughfare, has some of the best-known stores selling Irish goods, but you won't find many locals shopping here. Still, if you're looking for classic Irish gifts to take home, you should be sure at least to browse along here.

Temple Bar, Dublin's hippest neighborhood, is dotted with small, precious boutiques—mainly intimate, quirky shops that traffic in a small selection of trendy goods, from vintage clothes to some of the most avant-garde Irish garb anywhere in the city.

Dublin a la Mode

The success of shops like Costume and Platform has given young Irish designers the confidence to produce more original and impressive work. One of Costume's most popular designers, **Helen James,** graduated from NCAD textile design in 1992. She went straight to New York, where she worked for Donna Karan, Club Monaco, and Victoria's Secret, among others. She returned to Ireland in 2002 and developed her line of unique, hand-printed textile accessories. Many people say there is a delicate Japanese feel to her work.

Footwear has long been an area overlooked by Irish designers, but Irishwoman **Eileen Shields** been living and working in New York since 1988; for almost 10 years she designed footwear for Donna

Karan. Her own premiere collection is all about clean, bold lines. Materials include antique kid, fine suede, python, and soft patent leather. Textures are often strongly contrasting, while colors are sensual and sophisticated. You can get the shoes online at ⊕*www.eileenshields.com,* or in her store on Scarlett Row in Temple Bar.

The Tucker family has been a key player in Irish fashion since the 1960s, and daughter **Leigh Tucker** has quickly established herself as one of Dublin's classiest young designers. Fine tailoring is her trademark—the finish on her evening wear is nonpareil—and beaded French lace and draped jersey are her favorite materials. Her line can be found in boutiques across Ireland and at Costume in Dublin.

SHOPPING CENTERS

NORTHSIDE

Ilac Center (⊠*Henry St., Northside*) was Dublin's first large, modern shopping center, with two department stores, hundreds of specialty shops, and several restaurants. The stores are not as exclusive as those at some of the other centers, but there's plenty of free parking.

Jervis Shopping Centre (⊠*Jervis and Mary Sts., Northside* ☏01/878–1323) is a slightly high-end center housing some of the major British chain stores. It has a compact design and plenty of parking.

SOUTHSIDE

Powerscourt Townhouse Centre (⊠*59 S. William St., Southside*), the former town home of Lord Powerscourt, built in 1771, has an interior courtyard that has been refurbished and roofed over; a pianist often plays on the dais at ground-floor level. Coffee shops and restaurants share space with a mix of stores selling antiques and crafts. You can also buy original Irish fashions here by young designers, such as Gráinne Walsh.

Royal Hibernian Way (⊠*Off Dawson St. between S. Anne and Duke Sts., Southside* ☏01/679–5919) is on the former site of the two-centuries-old Royal Hibernian Hotel, a coaching inn that was demolished in 1983. The pricey, stylish shops—about 20 or 30, many selling fashionable clothes—are small in scale and include a branch of Leonidas, the Belgian chocolate firm.

St. Stephen's Green Centre (✉ *Northwest corner of St. Stephen's Green, Southside* ☎*01/478–0888*), Dublin's largest and most ambitious shopping complex, resembles a giant greenhouse, with Victorian-style ironwork. On three floors overlooked by a giant clock, the 100 mostly small shops sell crafts, fashions, and household goods.

Tower Design Centre (✉ *Pearse St., Southside* ☎*01/677–5655*), east of the heart of the city center (near the Waterways Visitors Centre), has more than 35 separate crafts shops in a converted 1862 sugar-refinery tower. On the ground floor are workshops devoted to heraldry and Irish pewter; the other six floors have stores that sell hand-painted silks, ceramics, hand-knit items, jewelry, and fine-art cards and prints.

Westbury Mall (✉ *Westbury Hotel, off Grafton St., Southside*) is an upmarket shopping mall where you can buy designer jewelry, antique rugs, and decorative goods.

DEPARTMENT STORES

Arnotts (✉ *Henry St., Northside* ☎*01/805–0400*), on three floors, stocks a wide selection of clothing, household accessories, and sporting goods. It is known for matching quality with value. There is a Gap section downstairs.

★ **Brown Thomas** (✉ *Grafton St., Southside* ☎*01/605–6666*), Dublin's most exclusive department store, stocks the leading designer names (including some Irish designers) in clothing and cosmetics, plus lots of stylish accessories. There's also a good selection of crystal.

Clery's (✉ *O'Connell St., Northside* ☎*01/878–6000*), once the city's most fashionable department store, is still worth a visit. You'll find all kinds of merchandise—from clothing to home appliances—on its four floors. Note that goods sold here reflect a distinctly modest, traditional sense of style.

Debenhams (✉ *Henry St., Northside* ☎*01/873–0044*), the U.K. chain store, has opened in the city center and includes a Zara section along with its own clothing and homeware lines.

Dunnes Stores (✉ *St. Stephen's Green Centre, Southside* ☎*01/478–0188* ✉*Henry St., Northside* ☎*01/872–6833* ✉*Ilac Center, Mary St., Northside* ☎*01/873–0211*) is Ireland's largest chain of department stores. All of the branches stock fashion (including the exciting Savida range), household, and grocery items, and have a reputation for value and variety.

Eason's (✉ *O'Connell St., Northside* ☎*01/873–3811* ✉*Ilac Center, Mary St., Northside* ☎*01/872–1322*) is known primarily for its large selection of books, magazines, and stationery; the larger O'Connell Street branch sells tapes, CDs, records, videos, and other audiovisual goodies.

Marks & Spencer (⊠ *Grafton St., Southside* ☎ *01/679–7855* ⊠ *Henry St., Northside* ☎ *01/872–8833*), perennial competitor to Brown Thomas, stocks everything from fashion (including lingerie) to tasty unusual groceries. The Grafton Street branch even has its own bureau de change, which doesn't charge commission.

2

OUTDOOR MARKETS

Cows Lane Market, held on weekends in summer at the west edge of Temple Bar, is home to some of the most innovative young fashion and accessory designers in the country.

Docklands Market, held every Thursday from 10 to 3 in the area beside the IFSC, has an eclectic selection of food, fashion, and design. It's a nice place to hang out if you want to be near the water on a sunny day.

Meeting House Square Market, held Saturday mornings at the heart of Temple Bar, is a good place to buy homemade foodstuffs: breads, chocolate, and organic veggies. On Sunday it transforms into a craft and furniture bazaar spotlighting Irish and international artists and designers.

Moore Street, on the Northside behind the Ilac Center, is open Monday through Saturday from 9 to 6. Stalls, which line both sides of the street, sell fruits and vegetables; this is also a good place to buy shoes and boots. Moore Street vendors are known for their sharp wit, so expect the traditional Dublin repartee when you're shopping. African and Asian immigrant stores, dive restaurants, and exotic stalls have given a new vibrancy to the area.

Wolfe Tone Market fills Wolfe Tone Square (beside Jervis Shopping Center) every Saturday from 10 to 6. Artists and artisans operate their own stalls, offering everything from paintings and drawings to candles, glass, and textiles. There's a gourmet food market on the same spot every Friday from 11 to 3.

SPECIALTY SHOPS

ANTIQUES

Dublin is one of Europe's best cities in which to buy antiques, largely due to a long and proud tradition of restoration and high-quality craftsmanship. The Liberties, Dublin's oldest district, is, fittingly, the hub of the antiques trade, and is chockablock with shops and traders. Bachelor's Walk, along the quays, also has some decent shops. It's quite a seller's market, but bargains are still possible.

Antiques Fairs Ireland (⊠ *Hilton Hotel, Charlemont Pl., Southside* ☎ *01/453–7323*) takes place monthly, alternating between the Hilton Hotel in Dublin city center and Clontarf Castle, in south county Dublin.

Ha'penny Bridge Galleries (✉ *15 Bachelor's Walk, Northside* ☎*01/872–3950*) has four floors of curios, with a particularly large selection of bronzes, silver, and china.

O'Sullivan Antiques (✉ *43–44 Francis St., Dublin West* ☎*01/454–1143 or 01/453–9659*) specializes in 18th- and 19th-century furniture and has a high-profile clientele, including Mia Farrow and Liam Neeson. It even has a sister shop in New York.

BOOKS

You won't have any difficulty weighing down your suitcase with books. Ireland, after all, produced four Nobel literature laureates in just under 75 years. If you're at all interested in modern and contemporary literature, be sure to leave yourself time to browse through the bookstores, as you're likely to find books available here you can't find back home. Best of all, thanks to an enlightened national social policy, there's no tax on books, so if you only buy books, you don't have to worry about getting V.A.T. slips.

Books Upstairs (✉ *36 College Green, Southside* ☎*01/679–6687*) carries an excellent selection of special-interest books, including gay and feminist literature, psychology, and self-help books.

Cathach Books (✉ *10 Duke St., Southside* ☎*01/671–8676*) sells first editions of Irish literature and many other books of Irish interest, plus old maps of Dublin and Ireland.

Dublin Bookshop (✉ *24 Grafton St., Southside* ☎*01/677–5568*) is an esteemed, family-owned store that sells mass-market books.

Eason's/Hanna's (✉ *29 Nassau St., Southside* ☎*01/677–1255*) sells secondhand and mass-market paperbacks and hardcovers, and has a good selection of works on travel and Ireland.

Greene's (✉ *Clare St., Southside* ☎*01/676–2554*) carries an extensive range of secondhand volumes and new educational and mass-market books.

Hodges Figgis (✉ *56–58 Dawson St., Southeast Dublin* ☎*01/677–4754*), Dublin's leading independent bookstore, stocks 1½ million books on three floors. There's a pleasant café on the first floor.

Hughes & Hughes (✉ *St. Stephen's Green Centre, Southside* ☎*01/478–3060*) has strong travel and Irish-interest sections. There's also a store at Dublin Airport.

Stokes (✉ *George's Street Arcade, Southside* ☎*01/671–3584*) is a gem of an antique bookstore with a great used-book section.

Waterstone's (✉ *7 Dawson St., Southeast Dublin* ☎*01/679–1415*), a large two-story branch of the British chain, features a fine selection of Irish and international books.

CHINA, CRYSTAL, CERAMICS & JEWELRY

Ireland is *the* place to buy Waterford crystal, which is available in a wide selection of products, including relatively inexpensive items. Other lines are now gaining recognition, such as Cavan, Galway, and Tipperary crystal.

Angles (⊠ *Westbury Mall, Southside* ☎ *01/679–1964*) is chockablock with handmade, contemporary Irish jewelry by younger Irish designers. You can even get a piece made to order and sent to you at home.

Appleby's (⊠ *Johnson's Court, Southside* ☎ *01/679–9572*) is the best known of the several classy, old-style jewelry shops that line tiny Johnson's Court, a delightful little lane off busy Grafton Street.

Barry Doyle Design (⊠ *Georges Street Arcade, Southside* ☎ *01/671–2838*) is a true original with his Celtic modern jewelry. You can even watch him at work in his adjoining studio.

Blarney Woollen Mills (⊠ *21–23 Nassau St., Southside* ☎ *01/671–0068*) is one of the best places for Belleek china, Waterford and Galway crystal, and Irish linen.

Designyard (⊠ *Cows La., Temple Bar* ☎ *01/474–1011*) carries beautifully designed Irish and international tableware, lighting, small furniture, and jewelry.

House of Ireland (⊠ *37–38 Nassau St., Southside* ☎ *01/671–1111*) has an extensive selection of crystal, jewelry, tweeds, sweaters, and other upscale goods.

Kilkenny Shop (⊠ *5–6 Nassau St., Southside* ☎ *01/677–7066*) specializes in contemporary Irish-made ceramics, pottery, and silver jewelry, and regularly holds exhibits of exciting new work by Irish craftspeople.

McDowell (⊠ *3 Upper O'Connell St., Northside* ☎ *01/874–4961*), a jewelry shop popular with Dubliners, has been in business for more than 100 years.

Weir & Sons (⊠ *96 Grafton St., Southside* ☎ *01/677–9678*), Dublin's most prestigious jeweler, sells not only jewelry and watches, but also china, glass, lamps, silver, and leather.

CLOTHING STORES

A-Wear (⊠ *Grafton St., Southside* ☎ *01/872–4644*) has become something of a fashion institution for both men and women. Leading Irish designers, including John Rocha, supply A-Wear with a steady stream of exciting new looks.

BT2 (⊠ *Grafton St., Southside* ☎ *01/605–6666*) is swanky Brown Thomas's impressive attempt to woo a younger crowd. Most of the major labels are present, including DKNY and Paul Smith.

Costume (⊠ *10 Castel Market, Southside* ☎ *01/679–4188*) is a classy boutique where Dubliners with fashion sense and money like to shop for colorful, stylish clothes. Local designers include Leigh, Helen James, and Antonia Campbell-Hughes; Temperley and Preen are among the international designers featured.

Dolls (✉*32 Clarendon St., Southside* ☎*01/672–9004*), an independent boutique, likes to boast of its unusual designer pieces. Featured international designers include Karen Walker and Future Classics.

H&M (✉*ILAC Centre, Northside* ☎*01/872–7206*), the trendy Scandinavian clothes and accessory store, has opened in the ILAC centre. They even do their own cosmetics line.

Scarlet Row (✉*5 Scarlet Row, Temple Bar* ☎*01/672–9534*), opened by an ex-Donna Karan shoe designer and a Dublin art curator, is a high-concept shoe store, fashion outlet, and gallery—great for browsing and buying alike.

Smock (✉*West Essex St., Temple Bar* ☎*01/613–9000*) is a tiny designer shop with great, left-field taste. International labels include Pearson, Veronique, and A. F. Vandevoft. They also carry a beautiful line in fine jewelry.

Urban Outfitters (✉*4 Cecilia St., Temple Bar* ☎*01/670–6202*) is a U.S. chain shop that has become hugely popular with the locals. The music is almost as loud as the clothes, but this is a great place to shop with teenagers and young adults. Besides all the major street labels, they have a wide range of accessories.

MUSEUM STORES

National Gallery of Ireland Shop (✉*Merrion Sq. W, Southeast Dublin* ☎*01/678–5450*) has a terrific selection of books on Irish art, plus posters, postcards, note cards, and lots of lovely bibelots.

National Museum of Archaeology and History Shop (✉*Kildare St., Southeast Dublin* ☎*01/677–7444 Ext. 327*) carries jewelry based on ancient Celtic artifacts in the museum collection, contemporary Irish pottery, a large selection of books, and other gift items.

Trinity College Library Shop (✉*Old Library, Trinity College, Southside* ☎*01/608–2308*) sells Irish-theme books, *Book of Kells* souvenirs, clothing, jewelry, and lovely Irish-made items.

MUSIC

Celtic Note (✉*12 Nassau St., Southside* ☎*01/670–4157*) is aimed at the tourist market, with lots of compilations and greatest-hits formats.

Claddagh Records (✉*2 Cecilia St., Temple Bar* ☎*01/679–3664*) has a good selection of traditional and folk music.

Gael Linn (✉*26 Merrion Sq., Southside* ☎*01/676–7283*) specializes in traditional Irish music and Irish-language recordings; it's where the aficionados go.

HMV (✉*65 Grafton St., Southside* ☎*01/679–5334* ✉*18 Henry St., Northside* ☎*01/872–2095*) is one of the larger record shops in town.

McCullogh Piggott (✉ *25 Suffolk St., Southside* ☎*01/671–2410*) is the best place in town to buy instruments, sheet music, scores, and books about music.

Tower Records (✉*6–8 Wicklow St., Southside* ☎*01/671–3250*) is the best-stocked international chain.

SWEATERS & TWEEDS

Don't think Irish woolens are limited to Aran sweaters and tweed jackets. You can choose souvenirs from a wide selection of hats, gloves, scarves, blankets, and other goods here. If you're traveling outside of Dublin, you may want to wait to make purchases elsewhere, but if Dublin is it, you still have plenty of good shops from which to choose. The tweed sold in Dublin comes from two main sources: Donegal and Connemara. Labels inside the garments guarantee their authenticity. Kilkenny Shop and House of Ireland listed under China, Crystal, Ceramics and Jewelry above are also great places for all things woolen. The following are the other largest retailers of traditional Irish woolen goods in the city.

Avoca Handweavers (✉*11–13 Suffolk St., Southside* ☎*01/677–4215*) is a beautiful store with an eclectic collection of knitwear from contemporary Irish designers. The children's wear section on the second floor is a real joy. They also stock original ceramics.

Blarney Woollen Mills (✉*21–23 Nassau St., Southside* ☎*01/451–6111*) stocks a good selection of tweed, linen, and wool sweaters from their mills in County Cork, in all price ranges.

Cleo Ltd (✉*18 Kildare St., Southeast Dublin* ☎*01/676–1421*) sells hand-knit sweaters and accessories made only from natural fibers; it also carries its own designs.

Kevin and Howlin (✉*31 Nassau St., Southside* ☎*01/677–0257*) specializes in handwoven tweed men's jackets, suits, and hats, and also sells tweed fabric.

Monaghan's (✉*Royal Hibernian Way, 15–17 Grafton St., Southside* ☎*01/677–0823*) is a quality men's store that specializes in cashmere.

VINTAGE

Flip (✉*4 Upper Fownes St., Temple Bar* ☎*01/671–4299*), one of the original stores in Temple Bar, sells vintage and retro clothing from the '50s, '60s, and '70s.

Harlequin (✉*Castle Market, Southside* ☎*01/671-0202*) isn't cheap, but the owner–buyer has great taste in classic men's and women's wear.

Jenny Vander (✉*Drury St., Southside* ☎*01/677–0406*) is the most famous name in Irish vintage and retro clothing. Just browsing through her collection is a pleasure.

SIDE TRIPS: NORTH COUNTY DUBLIN

Dublin's northern suburbs remain largely residential, but there are a few places worth the trip, such as the architectural gem Marino Casino. As with most suburban areas, walking may not be the best way to get around. It's good, but not essential, to have a car. Buses and trains serve most of these areas—the only drawback is that to get from one suburb to another by public transportation, you have to backtrack through the city center. Even if you're traveling by car, visiting all these sights will take a full day, so plan your trip carefully before setting off.

Numbers in the text correspond to numbers in the margin and on the North County Dublin map.

GLASNEVIN

❶ *Drive from north city center by Lower Dorset St., as far as bridge over Royal Canal. Turn left, go up Whitworth Rd., by side of canal, for 1 km (½ mi); at its end, turn right onto Prospect Rd. and then left onto Finglas Rd., N2. You can also take Bus 40 or Bus 40A from Parnell St., next to Parnell Sq., in northern city center.*

Glasnevin Cemetery, on the right-hand side of the Finglas road, is the best-known burial ground in Dublin. It's the site of the graves of many distinguished Irish leaders, including Eamon De Valera, a founding father of modern Ireland and a former Irish *taoiseach* (prime minister) and president, and Michael Collins, the celebrated hero of the Irish War of Independence. Other notables interred here include the late-19th-century poet Gerard Manley Hopkins and Sir Roger Casement, an Irish rebel hanged for treason by the British in 1916. The large column to the right of the main entrance is the tomb of "The Liberator" Daniel O'Connell, perhaps Ireland's greatest historical figure, renowned for his nonviolent struggle for Catholic rights and emancipation, achieved in 1829. The cemetery is freely accessible 24 hours.

The **National Botanic Gardens,** on the northeastern flank of Glasnevin Cemetery and the south banks of the Tolka River, date from 1795 and have more than 20,000 varieties of plants, a rose garden, and a vegetable garden. The main attraction is the beautifully restored Curvilinear Range—400-foot-long greenhouses designed and built by a Dublin ironmaster, Richard Turner, between 1843 and 1869. The Great Palm House, with its striking double dome, was built in 1884 and houses orchids, palms, and tropical ferns. ⊠*Glasnevin Rd., North County Dublin* ☎*01/837–4388* ⊕*www.botanicgardens.ie* ☑*Free* ☉*Apr.–Sept., Mon.–Sat. 9–6, Sun. 11–6; Oct.–Mar., daily10–4:30.*

MARINO CASINO

❷ *Take Malahide Rd. from Dublin's north city center for 4 km (2½ mi). Or take Bus 20A or Bus 24 to Casino from Cathal Brugha St. in north city center.*

Fodor'sChoice
★

One of Dublin's most exquisite, yet also most underrated, architectural landmarks, the Marino Casino (the name means "little house by the sea," and the building overlooks Dublin Harbour) is a small-scale, Palladian-style Greek temple, built between 1762 and 1771 from a

2

North County Dublin

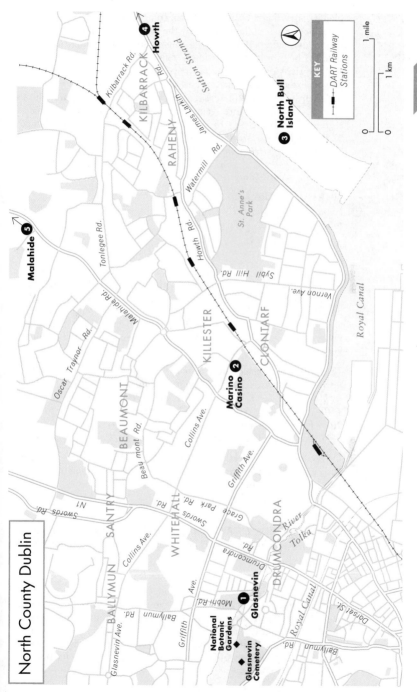

KEY

--|--|-- DART Railway Stations

0 1 km
0 1 mile

① Glasnevin
② Marino Casino
③ North Bull Island
④ Howth
⑤ Malahide

National Botanic Gardens
Glasnevin Cemetery

BALLYMUN
SANTRY
WHITEHALL
BEAUMONT
DRUMCONDRA
GLASNEVIN
KILLESTER
CLONTARF
RAHENY
KILBARRACK
Howth
Malahide

Swords Rd.
N1
Collins Ave.
Glasnevin Ave.
Ballymun Rd.
Griffith Ave.
Mobhi Rd.
Drumcondra Rd.
Swords Rd.
Grace Park Rd.
Griffith Ave.
Collins Ave.
Beaumont Rd.
Oscar Traynor Rd.
Tonlegee Rd.
Malahide Rd.
Howth Rd.
Sybil Hill Rd.
Vernon Ave.
Watermill Rd.
James Larkin Rd.
Sutton Strand
Kilbarrack Rd.

St. Anne's Park

Royal Canal
Royal Canal
River Tolka
Dorset St.

plan by Sir William Chambers. Often compared to the Petit Trianon at Versailles, it was commissioned by the great Irish grandee Lord Charlemont as a summerhouse. Inside, highlights are the china-closet boudoir, the huge golden sunset in the ceiling of the main drawing room, and the signs of the zodiac in the ceiling of the bijou library. When you realize that the structure has, in fact, 16 rooms—there are bedrooms upstairs—Sir William's sleight-of-hand is readily apparent: from its exterior, the structure seems to contain only one room. It makes a good stop on the way to Malahide, Howth, or North Bull Island. ⊠ *Malahide Rd., Marino, North County Dublin* ☎ *01/833–1618* ⊕ *www.heritageireland.ie* ✉ *€2.90* ⊙ *Feb., Mar., and Nov., Sun. and Thurs. noon–4; Apr., Sun. and Thurs. noon–5; May and Oct., daily 10–5; June–Sept., daily 10–6.*

NORTH BULL ISLAND

❸ *From Dublin's north city center, take Clontarf Rd. for 4 km (2½ mi) to causeway.*

A 5-km-long (3-mi-long) island created in the 19th century by the action of the tides, North Bull Island is one of Dublin's wilder places—it's a nature conservancy with vast beach and dunes. The island is linked to the mainland via a wooden causeway that leads to Bull Wall, a 1½-km (1-mi) walkway that stretches as far as the North Bull Lighthouse. The island is also accessible via a second, northerly causeway, which takes you to Dollymount Strand. (The two routes of entry don't meet at any point on the island.) You can reach this causeway from the mainland via James Larkin Road.

The small **visitor center** here largely explains the island's birdlife. ⊠ *Off northerly causeway, North County Dublin* ☎ *01/833–8341* ✉ *Free* ⊙ *Mar.–Oct., Mon.–Wed. 10:15–1 and 1:30–4, Thurs. 10:15–1 and 1:30–3:45, Fri. 10:15–1 and 1:30–2:30, weekends 10–1 and 1:30–5:30; Nov.–Feb., Mon.–Wed. 10:15–1 and 1:30–4, Thurs. 10:15–1 and 1:30–3:45, Fri. 10:15–1 and 1:30–2:30, weekends 10–1 and 1:30–4:30.*

On the mainland directly across from North Bull Island is **St. Anne's Park**, a public green with extensive rose gardens (including many prize hybrids) and woodland walks. ⊠ *James Larkin Rd. and Mt. Prospect Ave., North County Dublin.*

HOWTH

❹ *From Dublin, take DART train, or Bus 31B from Lower Abbey St. in city center. Or, by car, take Howth Rd. from north city center for 16 km (10 mi).*

A fishing village at the foot of a long peninsula, Howth (derived from the Norse *hoved*, meaning head; it rhymes with "both") was an island inhabited as long ago as 3250 BC. Between 1813 and 1833, Howth was the Irish terminus for the sea crossing to Holyhead in north Wales, but it was then superseded by the newly built harbor at Kingstown (now Dun Laoghaire). Today, its harbor, which supports a large fishing fleet, includes a marina. Both arms of the harbor pier form extensive walks.

2

Separated from Howth Harbour by a channel nearly 1½ km (1 mi) wide is **Ireland's Eye,** with an old stone church on the site of a 6th-century monastery, and an early-19th-century Martello tower. In calm summer weather, local boatmen make the crossing to the island from the East pier in Howth Harbour. Contact head boatman **Frank Doyle** (☎087/267–8211) for times and details.

At the King Sitric restaurant on the East Pier, a 2½-km (1½-mi) cliff walk begins, leading to the white **Baily Lighthouse,** built in 1814. In some places, the cliff path narrows and drops close to the water, but the views out over the Irish Sea are terrific. Some of the best views in the whole Dublin area await from the parking lot above the lighthouse, looking out over the entire bay as far south as Dun Laoghaire, Bray, and the north Wicklow coast. You can also see quite a bit of Dublin.

♺ Until 1959 a tram service ran from the railway station in Howth over Howth Summit and back down to the station. One of the open-top Hill of Howth trams that plied this route is now the star at the **National Transport Museum,** a short, 800-yard walk from Howth's DART station. Volunteers spent several years restoring the tram, which stands alongside other unusual vehicles, including horse-drawn bakery vans. ☎01/848–0831 or 01/847–5623 ⊕ *www.nationaltransportmuseum. org* ⊠€3 ☉ *June–Aug., Mon.–Sat. 10–5; Sept.–May, weekends 2–5.*

The **Howth Castle Gardens,** next door to the Transport Museum and accessible from the Deer Park Hotel, were laid out in the early 18th century. The many rare varieties in its fine rhododendron garden are in full flower April through June; there are also high beech hedges. The rambling castle, built in 1654 and considerably altered in the following centuries, is not open to the public, but you can access the ruins of a tall, square, 16th-century castle and a Neolithic dolmen. ⊠ *Deer Park Hotel, North County Dublin* ☎01/832–2624 ⊕ *www.deerpark-hotel. ie* ⊠ *Free* ☉ *Daily 8–dusk.*

$$$$ ✕**King Sitric.** Sitric was an 11th-century Norse king of Dublin who seemed
★ to be very fond of Howth. Joan and Aidan MacManus's well-known seafood restaurant down by the harbor attracts many contemporary visitors to the old town. It's in a Georgian house, with the yacht marina and port on one side and sea views from which you can watch the boats land the very fish that might be tomorrow's special. The upstairs seafood bar is great for informal lunches in summer. A house specialty is strips of monkfish tossed with a julienne of vegetables and topped with hollandaise sauce, but lobster, caught just yards away in Balscadden Bay, is the big treat—it's best at its simplest, in butter sauce. Crab is equally fresh, dressed with mayonnaise or Mornay sauce. Game and other meat dishes are also on offer, and Aidan is something of a collector when it comes to fine wines. ⊠ *East Pier, North County Dublin* ☎01/832–5235 ⊕ *www. kingsitric.ie* ⊟ *AE, DC, MC, V* ☉ *Closed Sun.*

$–$$ ✕**Wrights Findlater.** On Harbour Road right as you enter the village, this all-in-one bar, cocktail lounge, and Asian-fusion restaurant is causing quite a stir on the north coast. It's really about the harbor views, taken in from the many windows of the crisp modern dining rooms and from heated outdoor patios. The ground-floor bar serves a café-style menu and the top-floor cocktail lounge has to be one of Dublin's cooler spots to wait for a table. Sandwiched in between, the Lemongrass Restaurant presents Thai, Chinese, Vietnamese, and Indonesian dishes from an open kitchen—the *nasi goreng,* Indonesian rice served with prawn, chicken satay, and a fried egg is a standout. ⊠ *Wrights Findlater, Harbour Rd.* ☎ *01/832–4488* ⊕ *www.wrightsfindlaterhowth.com* ⌂ *Reservations essential* ⊟ *AE, DC, MC, V.*

MALAHIDE

❺ *By car, drive from north city center on R107 for 14½ km (9 mi). Or catch hourly train from Connolly Station. Or board Bus 42 to Malahide, which leaves every 15 minutes from Beresford Pl. behind Custom House.*

↻
Fodor'sChoice
★

Malahide is chiefly known for its glorious **Malahide Castle,** a picture-book castle occupied by the Talbot family from 1185 until 1976, when it was sold to the Dublin County Council. The great expanse of parkland around the castle has more than 5,000 different species of trees and shrubs, all clearly labeled. The castle itself combines styles and crosses centuries; the earliest section, the three-story tower house, dates from the 12th century. Hung with many family portraits, the medieval great hall is the only one in Ireland that is preserved in its original form. Authentic 18th-century pieces furnish the other rooms. Within the castle, the **Fry Model Railway Museum** houses rare, handmade models of the Irish railway and one of the world's largest miniature railway displays, which covers an area of 2,500 square feet. ⊠ *10 km (6 mi) north of Howth on Coast Rd., North County Dublin* ☎ *01/846–2184* ⊕ *www.malahidecastle.com* ⊇ *€7* ⊗ *Apr.–Sept., Mon.–Sat. 10–5, Sun. 11–6; Oct.–May, Mon.–Sat. 10–5, Sun. 11–5.*

↻
★

One of the greatest stately homes of Ireland, **Newbridge House,** in nearby Donabate, was built between 1740 and 1760 for Charles Cobbe, Archbishop of Dublin. A showpiece in the Georgian and Regency styles, the house is less a museum than a home because the Cobbe family still resides here, part of a novel scheme the municipal government allowed when they took over the house in 1985. The sober exterior and even more sober entrance hall—all Portland stone and Welsh slate—don't prepare you for the splendor of Newbridge's Red Drawing Room, perhaps Ireland's most sumptuous 18th-century salon. Cobbe's son, Thomas, and his wife, Lady Betty Beresford, sister of the marquess of Waterford, had amassed a great collection of paintings and needed a hall in which to show them off, so they built a back wing of the house to incorporate an enormous room built for entertaining and impressing others. That it does, thanks to its crimson walls, fluted Corinthian columns, dozens of old masters, and glamorous Rococo-style plaster ceiling designed by the Dublin stuccodore Richard Williams. Elsewhere in the house are fascinating family heirlooms: the kitchens still have their original utensils; crafts workshops and some examples of old-style transportation, such as coaches, are in the courtyard; and there is even a Museum of Curiosities, complete with the mummified ear of an Egyptian bull and relics of Lady Betty's medical practice (her chilblain plaster became famous). Some fine paintings are left, but the greatest were sold centuries ago in order to build proper houses for the estate servants. Beyond the house's walled garden are 366 acres of parkland and a restored 18th-century animal farm. Tara's Palace, a dollhouse that was made to raise funds for children's charities, is also here; it has 25 rooms, all fully furnished in miniature. The coffee shop is renowned for the quality and selection of its homemade goods. You can travel from Malahide to Donabate by train, which takes about 10 minutes. From the Donabate train station, it's a 15-minute walk to the Newbridge House grounds. ⊠*Donabate, 8 km (5 mi) north of Malahide, signposted from N1, North County Dublin* ☎*01/843–6534* ⊕*www.fingalcoco.ie* ⧠*€6.50* ☉*Apr.–Sept., Tues.–Sat. 10–1 and 2–5, Sun. 12–6; Oct.–Mar., weekends 12–5.*

WHERE TO EAT
$$–$$$$ ✕**Bon Appétit.** New owners have just completed a total renovation of this old Dublin classic, which now includes an informal café downstairs serving casual food. The more formal upstairs restaurant sees hotshot chef Oliver Dunne bring his exalted reputation for invention to bear on the contemporary French menu. There's the added bonus of the chilled-out piano bar downstairs where you can relax before or after your meal. ⊠*9 James's Terr., North County Dublin* ☎*01/845–0314* ⊕*www.bonappetit.ie* ⊟*AE, DC, MC, V* ☉*Closed Sun. No lunch Sat.*

DUBLIN ESSENTIALS

TRANSPORTATION

BY AIR

Dublin Airport, 10 km (6 mi) north of the city center, serves international and domestic flights. Three airlines have regularly scheduled flights from the United States to Dublin. Aer Lingus flies direct from New York, Boston, Los Angeles, San Francisco, Orlando, Baltimore, Washington, and Chicago to Dublin. Continental flies from New York (Newark Liberty International Airport) to Dublin. Delta flies from Atlanta to Dublin via New York.

There are daily services to Dublin from all major London airports. Flights to Dublin also leave from Birmingham, Bristol, East Midlands, Liverpool, Luton, Manchester, Leeds/Bradford, Newcastle, Edinburgh, and Glasgow.

Within Ireland, Aer Lingus operates flights from Dublin to Belfast, Cork, Derry, Kerry, Shannon, Galway, Knock in County Mayo, Donegal, and Sligo. Ryanair flies to Belfast, and Aer Arann flies to Cork, Kerry, Sligo, Knock, Galway, and Donegal. They also fly from London and Manchester to Waterford.

Carriers Aer Arann (☎*01/814–5240*). **Aer Lingus** (☎*01/844–4747*). **Air Wales** (☎*800/465–193*). **British Airways** (☎*800/626–747*). **BMI** (☎*01/283–8833*). **City Jet** (☎*01/870–0300*). **Continental** (☎*1890/925–252*). **Delta** (☎*01/844–4166 or 01/676–8080*). **Logan Air** (☎*800/626–747*). **Ryanair** (☎*01/844–4411*). **Thompsonfly** (☎*01/247–7723*).

Airport Information **Dublin Airport** (☎ *01/844–4900* ⊕ *www.dublin-airport. com*).

TRANSFERS Dublin Bus operates the Airlink shuttle service between Dublin Airport and the city center, with departures outside the arrivals gateway. Service runs from 5:45 AM to 11:30 PM, at intervals of about 10 minutes (after 8 PM buses run every 20 minutes), to as far as O'Connell Street and then Dublin's main bus station (Busaras), behind the Custom House on the Northside. Journey time from the airport to the city center is normally 30 minutes, but it may be longer in heavy traffic. The single fare is €5; pay the driver inside the bus or purchase a one-day bus pass for the same price. If you have time, you can save money by taking a regular bus for €2. Aircoach's comfortable coaches run from the airport to the city center 24 hours a day for €7 one way and €12 round-trip. The service stops at the major hotels. A taxi is a quicker alternative than the bus to get from the airport to Dublin center. A line of taxis waits by the arrivals gateway; the fare for the 30-minute journey to any of the main city-center hotels is about €18 to €20 plus tip (tips don't have to be large but they are increasingly expected). Ask about the fare before leaving the airport.

Contact **Aircoach** (☎ *01/844–7118* ⊕ *www.aircoach.ie*). **Busaras** (☎ *01/830– 2222*). **Dublin Bus** (☎ *01/873–4222* ⊕ *www.dublinbus.ie*).

BY BOAT & FERRY

Irish Ferries runs a regular high-speed car and passenger service into Dublin port from Holyhead in Wales. The crossing takes 1 hour and 50 minutes on the faster *Dublin Swift* and 3 hours and 15 minutes on the huge *Ulysses*. Stena Line has services to both Dublin and nearby Dun Laoghaire port from Holyhead (3½ hours) and a high-speed service, known as "HSS," which takes about 1 hour and 40 minutes. P & O sails from Dublin to Liverpool in a very slow 8 hours. Prices and departure times vary according to season, so call to confirm. In summer, reservations are strongly recommended; book online or through a travel agent. Dozens of taxis wait to take you into town from both ports, or you can take DART or a bus to the city center.

Boat & Ferry Lines **Irish Ferries** (⊠ *Merrion Row, Southside* ☎ *01/661–0511* ⊕ *www.irishferries.com*). **P & O** (⊠ *Terminal 3, Dublin Port, Southside* ☎ *01/407– 3434* ⊕ *www.poferries.com*). **Stena Line** (⊠ *Ferryport, Dun Laoghaire, South County Dublin* ☎ *01/204–7777* ⊕ *www.stenaline.ie*).

BY BUS

Busaras, just behind the Custom House on the Northside, is Dublin's main station for buses to and from the city. Bus Éireann is the main intercity bus company, with service throughout the country. Aircoach has direct bus connections to Cork and Belfast, and is usually a bit cheaper than Bus Éireann. In town, there's an extensive network of buses, most of which are green double-deckers. Some bus services run on cross-city routes, including the smaller "Imp" buses, but most buses start in the city center. Buses to the north of the city begin in the Lower

Abbey Street–Parnell Street area, while those to the west begin in Middle Abbey Street and in the Aston Quay area. Routes to the southern suburbs begin at Eden Quay and in the College Street area. Several buses link the DART stations, and another regular bus route connects the two main provincial railway stations, Connolly and Heuston. If the destination board indicates AN LÁR, that means that the bus is going to the city center. Museumlink is a shuttle service that links up the National Museum of Natural History, National Museum of Archaeology and History, and the National Museum of Decorative Arts and History. You can catch it outside any of the three museums.

FARES &
SCHEDULES
Intercity fares vary with the distance traveled. The Irish Rover Tourist pass, valid for all Bus Éireann services in the republic and for Ulsterbus services in Northern Ireland, costs €73 for three days' travel over eight consecutive days, and €165 for eight days' travel over 15 consecutive days. Timetables (€3.20) are available from Dublin Bus, staffed weekdays 9–5:30, Saturday 9–1. In the city, fares begin at €1 and are paid to the driver, who will accept inexact fares, but you'll have to go to the central office in Dublin to pick up your change as marked on your ticket. Change transactions and the city's heavy traffic can slow service considerably. Most bus lines run until 11:30 at night, but some late-night buses run Monday to Thursday until 2 AM and Friday to Saturday until 4:30 AM on all major routes; the fare is €4–€6.

Information **Aircoach** (☏ 01/844-7118 ⊕ www.aircoach.ie). **Busaras** (☏ 01/830-2222). **Bus Éireann** (☏ 01/873-4222 ⊕ www.buseireann.ie). **Dublin Bus** (✉ 59 Upper O'Connell St., Northside ☏ 01/873-4222 ⊕ www.dublinbus.ie).

BY CAR

Renting a car in Dublin is very expensive, with high rates and a 12½% local tax. Gasoline is also expensive by U.S. standards, at around €1 a liter. Peak-period car-rental rates begin at around €260 a week for the smallest stick models, like a Ford Fiesta. Dublin has many car-rental companies, and it pays to shop around and to avoid "cowboy" outfits without proper licenses. A dozen car-rental companies have desks at Dublin Airport; all the main national and international firms also have branches in the city center. Traffic in Ireland has increased exponentially in the last few years, and nowhere has the impact been felt more than in Dublin, where the city's complicated one-way streets are congested not only during the morning and evening rush hours but often during much of the day. If possible, avoid driving a car except to get in and out of the city (and be sure to ask your hotel or guesthouse for clear directions to get you out of town).

Agencies **Avis** (✉ 1 Hanover St. E, Southside ☏ 01/677-5204 ⊕ www.avis.ie ✉ Dublin Airport, North County Dublin ☏ 01/844-5204). **Budget** (✉ 151 Lower Drumcondra Rd., North County Dublin ☏ 01/837-9802 ⊕ www.budget.ie ✉ Dublin Airport, North County Dublin ☏ 01/844-5919). **Dan Dooley** (✉ 42-43 Westland Row, Southside ☏ 01/677-2723 ⊕ www.dan-dooley.ie ✉ Dublin Airport, North County Dublin ☏ 01/844-5156). **Hertz** (✉ Leeson St. Bridge, Southside ☏ 01/660-2255 ⊕ www.hertz.ie ✉ Dublin Airport, North County Dublin ☏ 01/844-5466).

Europcar Murray's Rent-a-Car (✉ *Baggot St. Bridge, Southside* ☎ *01/668–1777* ⊕ *www.europcar.ie* ✉ *Dublin Airport, North County Dublin* ☎ *01/844–4179).*

BY TAXI

There are taxi stands beside the central bus station, and at train stations, O'Connell Bridge, St. Stephen's Green, College Green, and near major hotels; the Dublin telephone directory has a complete list. The initial charge is €3.80, with an additional charge of about €1.50 per kilometer thereafter. The fare is displayed on a meter (make sure it's on). You may, instead, want to phone a taxi company and ask for a cab to meet you at your hotel, but this may cost up to €2 extra. Each extra passenger costs €1, but there is no charge for luggage. Many taxis run all night, but the demand, especially on weekends (and particularly near clubs on the Leeson Street strip and elsewhere, which stay open until 4 AM or later), can make for long lines at taxi stands. Hackney cabs, which also operate in the city, have neither roof signs nor meters and will sometimes respond to hotels' requests for a cab. Negotiate the fare before your journey begins. Although the taxi fleet in Dublin is large, the cabs are nonstandard and some cars are neither spacious nor in pristine condition. Cab Charge has a reliable track record. Metro is one of the city's biggest but also the busiest. VIP Taxis usually has a car available for a longer trip.

Taxi Companies **Cab Charge** (☎ *01/677–2222*). **Metro** (☎ *01/668–3333*). **VIP Taxis** (☎ *01/478–3333*).

BY TRAIN & TRAM

Connolly Station provides train service to and from the east coast, Belfast, the north (with stops in Malahide, Skerries, and Drogheda), the northwest, and some destinations to the south, such as Wicklow and Arklow. Heuston Station is the place for trains to and from the south and west; trains run from here to Kildare Town, west of Dublin, via Celbridge, Sallins, and Newbridge. Pearse Station is for Bray and connections via Dun Laoghaire to the Liverpool-Holyhead ferries. Contact the Irish Rail Travel Centre for information.

An electric railway system, the Dublin Area Rapid Transit (DART), connects Dublin with Howth to the north and Bray to the south on a fast, efficient line. There are 25 stations on the route, which is the best means of getting to seaside destinations, such as Howth, Blackrock, Dun Laoghaire, Dalkey, Killiney, and Bray.

The LUAS tram service runs two lines right into the heart of the city. One line carries the super-sleek silver trams from Tallaght in the southwest to the Abbey Street station, located north of the Liffey, and on down to the city center's Connolly Station. This line also takes you from Royal Hospital Killmainham and carries you across the Liffey, through Smithfield, and down to the Abbey Street hub. The other line runs from the Sandyford residential suburb in the south sector of the city north to St. Stephen's Green—this line is useful for ferrying the tourist between the city district of Ballsbridge to St. Stephen's Green in the city center. Together, these lines cross the city center north and south, and so the LUAS is ideal for short hops across those areas.

FARES &
SCHEDULES

DART service starts at 6:30 AM and runs until 11:30 PM; at peak periods, 8–9:30 AM and 5–7 PM, trains arrive every five minutes. At other times of the day, the intervals between trains are 15 to 25 minutes. Call ahead to check precise departure times (they do vary, especially on bank holidays). Tickets can be bought at stations, but it's also possible to buy weekly rail tickets, as well as weekly or monthly "rail-and-bus" tickets, from the Irish Rail Travel Centre. Individual fares begin at €1.40 and range up to €3.70. You'll pay a heavy penalty for traveling the DART without a ticket. LUAS trams run from 5:30 AM until 12:30 AM Monday to Saturday and 7 AM until 11:30 PM on Sunday. They come every 7 to 10 minutes at peak times and every 15 to 20 minutes after that. Fares begin at €1.40 and increase up to €2.10 according to the number of zones traveled.

Train Information **Irish Rail–Iarnod Éireann** (⊕ *www.irishrail.ie*). **Connolly Station** (⊠ *Amiens St., Northside*). **DART** (☎ *01/836–6222* ⊕ *www.irishrail.ie/dart*). **Heuston Station** (⊠ *End of Victoria Quay, Dublin West*). **Irish Rail Travel Centre** (⊠ *35 Lower Abbey St., Northside* ☎ *01/836–6222* ⊕ *www.irishrail.ie*). **LUAS** (☎ *800/300–604* ⊕ *www.luas.ie*). **Pearse Station** (⊠ *Westland Row, Southside*).

CONTACTS & RESOURCES

DUBLIN PASS

Like many tourist capitals around the world, Dublin now features a special pass to help travelers save on admission prices. In conjunction with Dublin Tourism, the Dublin Pass is issued for one, two, three, or six days, and allows free (or, rather, reduced, since the cards do cost something) admission to 30 sights, including the Guinness Brewery, the Dublin Zoo, the Dublin Writers Museum, and Christ Church Cathedral. Prices are €31 for one day; €49 for two days; €59 for three days; and €89 for six days; children's prices are much lower. You can buy your card online and have it waiting for you at one of Dublin's tourist information offices when you arrive. Another plus: you can jump to the head of any line at participating museums and sights.

Information **Dublin Tourism** (⊠ *Suffolk St., off Grafton St., Southside* ☎ *01/605–7700 in Dublin, 1850/230–330 in rest of Ireland* ⊕ *www.visitdublin.com/dublinpass*).

EMBASSIES

Embassies are open weekdays 9–1 and 2–5.

Contact **Australia** (⊠ *Fitzwilton House, Wilton Terr., Southside* ☎ *01/676–1517*). **Canada** (⊠ *65 St. Stephen's Green, Southside* ☎ *01/478–1988*). **United Kingdom** (⊠ *29 Merrion Rd., Southside* ☎ *01/205–3700*). **United States** (⊠ *42 Elgin Rd., Southside* ☎ *01/668–8777*).

EMERGENCIES

Call the Eastern Regional Health Authority for the names of doctors in the area. The Dublin Dental Hospital has emergency facilities and lists of dentists who provide emergency care. Hamilton Long, a Dublin pharmacy, is open Monday–Wednesday and Saturday 8:30–6, Thursday

8:30–8, and Friday 8:30–7. Temple Bar Pharmacy is open Monday–Wednesday, Friday, and Saturday 9–7, Thursday 9–8.

Doctors & Dentists **Dublin Dental Hospital** (✉ *20 Lincoln Pl., Southside* ☎ *01/662–0766* ⊕ *web1.dental.tcd.ie*). **Eastern Regional Health Authority** (☎ *01/679–0700* ⊕ *www.erha.ie*).

Emergency Services **Ambulance, fire, police (gardaí)** (☎ *999*).

Hospitals **Beaumont** (✉ *Beaumont Rd., North County Dublin* ☎ *01/837–7755* ⊕ *www.beaumont.ie*). **Mater** (✉ *Eccles St., Northside* ☎ *01/830–1122* ⊕ *www.mater.ie*). **St. James's** (✉ *1 James St., Dublin West* ☎ *01/453–7941* ⊕ *www.stjames.ie*). **St. Vincent's** (✉ *Elm Park, South County Dublin* ☎ *01/269–4533* ⊕ *www.stvincents.ie*).

Late-Night Pharmacies **Hamilton Long** (✉ *5 Upper O'Connell St., Northside* ☎ *01/874–8456*). **Temple Bar Pharmacy** (✉ *20 E. Essex St., Temple Bar* ☎ *01/670–9751*).

INTERNET CAFÉS

In the city center are a number of Internet cafés, which charge between €3 and €6 an hour. Some of the cheapest places are on Thomas Street, as it's not smack in the center of town. Central Cybercafe is one of the city's best, with top-notch computers and a good coffee bar.

Information **Central Cybercafe** (✉ *6 Grafton St., Southside* ☎ *01/677–8298* ⊕ *www.globalcafe.ie*). **Surf Centre One** (✉ *79a Talbot Street St., Northside* ☎ *01/855–2560* ⊕ *www.worldlink.ie/netcafe*).

SIGHTSEEING TOURS

BUS TOURS Dublin Bus has three- and four-hour "City Tours" of the city center that include Trinity College, the Royal Hospital Kilmainham, and Phoenix Park. The one-hour City Tour, with hourly departures, allows you to hop on and off at any of the main sights. Tickets are available from the driver or Dublin Bus. There's also a continuous guided open-top bus tour (€14), run by Dublin Bus, which allows you to hop on and off the bus as often as you wish and visit some 15 sights along its route. The company also conducts a north-city coastal tour, going to Howth, and a south-city tour, traveling as far as Enniskerry.

Gray Line Tours runs city-center tours that cover the same sights as the Dublin Bus itineraries. Bus Éireann organizes day tours out of Busaras, the main bus station, to country destinations such as Glendalough.

Information **Bus Éireann** (☎ *01/836–6111* ⊕ *www.buseireann.ie*). **Dublin Bus** (☎ *01/873–4222* ⊕ *www.dublinbus.ie*). **Gray Line Tours** (☎ *01/670–8822* ⊕ *www.grayline.com*).

CARRIAGE TOURS Horse-drawn-carriage tours are available around Dublin and in Phoenix Park. For tours of the park, contact the Department of the Arts, Culture and the Gaeltacht. Carriages can be hired at the Grafton Street corner of St. Stephen's Green, without prior reservations.

Information **Department of the Arts, Culture and the Gaeltacht** (☎ *01/661–3111*).

PUB & MUSICAL TOURS
Dublin Tourism has a booklet to its self-guided "Rock 'n Stroll" Trail, which covers 16 sights with associations to such performers as Bob Geldof, Christy Moore, Sinéad O'Connor, and U2. Most of the sights are in the city center and Temple Bar. The Traditional Musical Pub Crawl begins at Oliver St. John Gogarty and moves on to other famous Temple Bar pubs. Led by two professional musicians who perform songs and tell the story of Irish music, the tour is given April–October, daily at 7:30 PM, and from Thursday to Saturday the rest of the year; the cost is €12. The award-winning Viking Splash Tour is a big hit with kids. The amphibious ex–U.S. military vehicle takes your on a tour of the city center before launching onto the water down by the IFSC. Kids get a Viking helmet to wear and love terrifying native pedestrians with the "Viking Roar." An adult ticket is €16–€18.

Colm Quilligan arranges highly enjoyable evening tours of the literary pubs of Dublin, where "brain cells are replaced as quickly as they are drowned." The *Dublin Literary Pub Crawl* is a 122-page guide to those Dublin pubs with the greatest literary associations; it's widely available in the city's bookstores.

Information Colm Quilligan (☎ 01/454–0228 ⊕ www.dublinpubcrawl.com). **Music Bus** (☎ 01/475–3313). **Oliver St. John Gogarty** (✉ 57 Fleet St., Temple Bar ☎ 01/671–1822). **Traditional Musical Pub Crawl** (✉ Discover Dublin, 20 Lower Stephens St., Southside ☎ 01/478–0191 ⊕ www.discoverdublin.ie). **Viking Splash** (☎ 01/707–6000 ⊕ www.vikingsplashtours.com).

WALKING TOURS
Dublin Tourism has a new iWalk tour with a podcast audio guide narrated by well-known historian and artist Pat Liddy. Historical Walking Tours of Dublin, run by Trinity College history graduate students, are excellent two-hour introductions to the city. The Bord Fáilte–approved tours take place from May to September, starting at the front gate of Trinity College, daily at 11 AM and 3 PM, with an extra tour on weekends at noon; tours are also available October and April daily at 11 AM and November to March, Friday–Sunday at 11 AM. The cost is €12.

Dublin Footsteps conducts a Georgian/Literary Walking Tour that leaves from the Grafton Street branch of Bewley's Oriental Café June–September, Monday, Wednesday, Friday, and Saturday at 11; each tour lasts approximately two hours and costs €10. Trinity Tours organizes walks of the Trinity College campus on weekends from March 17 (St. Patrick's Day) through mid-May and from mid-May to September daily. The half-hour tour costs €10 and includes the *Book of Kells* exhibit; tours start at the college's main gate every 40 minutes from 10:15 AM. There are generally nine tours a day.

The 1916 Rebellion Tour is an exciting walk that outlines the key areas and events of the violent Dublin rebellion that began Ireland's march to independence. The guides are passionately political and the two-hour tour never flags. They meet at the International Bar on Wicklow Street and operate March through October, weekdays at 11 AM, Saturday 11:30 AM, and Sunday 1 PM. The cost is €12.

Information **Dublin Footsteps** (☎ 01/496–0641 ⊕ www.visitdublin.com). **Historical Walking Tours of Dublin** (☎ 01/878–0227 ⊕ www.historicalinsights.ie). **Trinity Tours** (☎ 01/608–2320 ⊕ www.tcd.ie/library/heritage/tours.php). **1916 Rebellion Tour** (☎ 086/858–3847 ⊕ www.1916rising.com).

VISITOR INFORMATION

Fáilte Ireland, the Irish Tourist Board, has its own visitor information offices in the entrance hall of its headquarters at Baggot Street Bridge; it's open weekdays 9:15–5:15. A suburban tourist office in Tallaght is open March–December, daily 9:30–5.

The main Dublin Tourism center is in the former (and still spectacular) St. Andrew's Church on Suffolk Street and is open July–September, Monday–Saturday 8:30–6, Sunday 11–5:30, and October–June, daily 9–6. On-site are many service counters, souvenir stands, and even a sandwich bar. The Dublin Airport branch is open daily 8 AM–10 PM; the branch at the Ferryport, Dun Laoghaire, is open daily 10–9.

The Temple Bar Information Centre produces the easy-to-use, annually updated *Temple Bar Guide*, which provides complete listings of the area's stores, pubs, restaurants, clubs, galleries, and other cultural venues.

Tourist Information **Fáilte Ireland** (✉ Baggot St. Bridge, Southside ☎ 01/602–4000 in Dublin, 1850/230–330 in rest of Ireland ✉ The Square, Tallaght ☎ 1850/230–330 ⊕ www.failteireland.ie). **Dublin Tourism** (✉ Suffolk St., off Grafton St., Southside ☎ 01/605–7700 in Dublin, 1850/230–330 in rest of Ireland ⊕ www.visitdublin.com). **Temple Bar Information Centre** (✉ 18 Eustace St., Temple Bar ☎ 01/671–5717).

Dublin Environs

Hiking in County Wicklow

WORD OF MOUTH

"Although Ireland is a relatively small country, those of us who 'visit' there will always leave feeling that we've left a great deal behind. So you would be well served to plan on seeing less but enjoying more. Just tell yourself that you'll return to Ireland someday and plan to s-l-o-w-l-y enjoy seeing some of the places you missed. There's certainly no law against planning a 3rd trip!"

—mkdiebold

WELCOME TO DUBLIN ENVIRONS

Old Lighthouses, Wicklow Head, County Wicklow

TOP REASONS TO GO

★ **Newgrange at Sunset:** Just standing amid these 5,000-year-old tombs (which pre-date the Pyramids), you'll wonder: how did they build them?

★ **A Day at the Races:** The Irish may like a drink, but they really love to gamble, as you'll discover in Kildare, center of the Irish bloodstock world.

★ **Georgian Country Houses:** Modesty never struck the rich Anglo-Irishman, whose propensity to flaunt his riches led to such over-the-top stately homes as Castletown, Russborough, and Powerscourt.

★ **Wicklow is for Walkers:** There's no better way to meet the locals and see the land than trekking out on the 132-km-long Wicklow Way, Ireland's most popular trail.

★ **Early Morning at Glendalough:** Before the tour buses arrive, channel the spirit of the 6th-century, isolation-seeking St. Kevin.

St Kevin's Church, Glendalough

1 **The Boyne Valley.** Set 48 km (30 mi) north of Dublin, this entire area is redolent with prehistoric and pagan sites. You don't have to be an Indiana Jones to be awed by the Hill of **Tara** or **Newgrange,** a Neolithic burial ground and solar observatory still evocative of the mysteries of pre-Celtic civilization.

Powerscourt Waterfall

2 County Wicklow. Set with dense woods and idyllic lakes, "the garden of Ireland" is a favorite day-out for Dubliners, thanks to sylvan estates like **Powerscourt** and **Glendalough,** a 6th-century monastic site so serene you may be tempted to renounce the profane world.

3 County Kildare & West Wicklow. After visiting stately **Castletown** and **Russborough**—two monuments to Ireland's Georgian age of elegance—check out Derby Day at the **Curragh** racecourse. The grinning bookmakers are just waiting to take your money.

CAVAN

N3

WESTMEATH

Kinnegad   N4

OFFALY

Cherryville

Athy

LAOIS

NORTHERN
IRELAND

ARMAGH

DOWN

Omeath

Carlingford Lough

MONAGHAN

N53

Dundalk

Inniskeen

N1

Dundalk Bay

N52

N2

Ardee

LOUTH

N52

N2

Kells

N3

1 Boyne Valley

Slane

N51

Drogheda

Newgrange

N51

Navan

N1

Irish Sea

Hill of Tara

N2

Trim

N3

DUBLIN

MEATH

Swords

Lambay Island

Drumleck Point

M1

KILDARE

M4

Dublin

Castletown

N7

N81

Russborough House

M11

Bray

3

N7

The Curragh

Naas

2

Powerscourt

Kildare

Kilcullen

N78

WICKLOW

Kilmacanoge

Wicklow Mountains

Ballinalea

Wicklow Way

Glendalough

Wicklow

Wicklow Head

0   10 mi

0   10 km

CARLOW

M11

Arklow

WEXFORD

GETTING ORIENTED

Dublin Environs includes three main regions: County Wicklow's coast and mountains, the Boyne Valley, and County Kildare. The Boyne Valley includes much of counties Meath and Louth to the north and east of Dublin. Kildare and Wicklow are to the southeast and south of the capital. Tour this small region, or opt for day-trips from Dublin, especially to the Wickow mountains, which rise up suddenly at the fringes of the city.

Malahide Castle, County Dublin

DUBLIN ENVIRONS PLANNER

Finding a Place to Stay

A lot of people opt to stay in Dublin and take day trips to the environs. If that's the case a hotel on the south side of the city or in South County Dublin might be a good idea if you're planning to spend time in Wicklow or East Kildare. For Meath and Louth a hotel on the north side or to the west of the city might work better. If don't want to "commute" from the city then the noted country-house hotels around Kildare and Wicklow are a great option. They are surprisingly good value for the unique, luxurious experience they offer. B&B's are another good option and though the ones in this region tend to be a little more expensive than other parts of Ireland, they also are a little classier and more stylish.

Getting Around

Driving distances to the nether reaches of this chapter from Dublin are less than two hours (in decent traffic), so the best option might be to base yourself in the city and make a couple of day trips into this region. For example, a trip to Newgrange, Tara, and the National Stud might take up one day. Then you can head into the Wicklow Mountains to Powerscourt House and then to Glendalough on another day. Country-house buffs can easily knock off Castletown and Russborough—two of the grandest in the land—in one afternoon. A car is handy, of course, and gives you flexibility to get off the beaten track and explore the numerous small towns and villages of Wicklow and west Kildare. But if you don't fancy driving on small country roads then there are numerous one-day and half-day bus tours from the city that take in the major sights.

The Big Two

Glendalough and Newgrange really are unique places, historically and indeed spiritually. They are not sights to be rushed through with a checklist of things to see. It's all about the atmosphere, the serenity, and the silence. So, in both places give yourself plenty of time.

They are also best enjoyed in relative tranquility, so try go as early in the morning as you can and beat the crowds. Strangely enough both places may in fact be at their best outside the summer months.

Newgrange was designed around the winter solstice, and seems to take on a special, ethereal feel at that time of year.

Glendalough can be breathtaking on a clear spring day when the flora and fauna assault the senses.

Pack for the possibility of bad weather in both places, and bring along some food as you don't want to be forced to track back to the visitor center to get a snack.

The Great Outdoors

Wicklow is Ireland's premier walking county, with the Wicklow Way trail the central attraction. Many of Ireland's best golf courses are also in the region, with the majestic K Club in Kildare topping the list as home of the 2006 Ryder Cup. Sailing and water sports are popular all along the coast north and south of the city, with Brittas Bay north of Arklow a favorite beach and Carlingford Loch east of Dundalk a center for water sports. Lessons and equipment are usually available at each location, for a price of course. The Boyne, Liffey, and many smaller rivers and lakes make the area perfect for course and salmon fishing. Tackle and boats are usually rentable nearby.

Guided Tours

Bus Éireann (☎01/836–6111 ⊕www.buseireann.ie/site/home) runs guided bus tours to many of the historic and scenic locations throughout the Dublin environs daily in summer. Visits include trips to Glendalough in Wicklow; Boyne Valley and Newgrange in County Louth; and the Hill of Tara, Trim, and Navan in County Meath. All tours depart from Busaras Station, Dublin; information is available by phone Monday–Saturday 8:30–7, Sunday 10–7. Gray Line Tours (☎01/670–8822 ⊕www.grayline.com), a privately owned touring company, also runs many guided bus tours throughout the Dublin environs between May and September. Their Grand Wicklow Tour lasts seven hours, as does their day trip to Newgrange and Mellifont Abbey. Prices start at €30. Wild Wicklow Tours (☎01/280–1899 ⊕www.wildwicklow.ie) uses small minibuses that can handle smaller groups and take you off the beaten track. Their full-day trips to Glendalough also take in Avoca Handweavers and a Dublin coastal drive. Prices start at €28. Railtours Ireland (☎01/856–0045 ⊕www.railtoursireland.com) has a half-day rail tour into the Wicklow Mountains. The train stops at Arklow and then a bus takes you through Avoca and on to Glendalough. The cost is €39.

How's the Weather?

While certainly not the wettest part of Ireland (the West gets that dubious distinction), the counties around Dublin do get their fair share of rain. June, July, August, and September tend to be the driest months, and the good news is that the rain in the region in summer is usually light and short-lived. Wicklow, with all its hills and valleys, seems to have an obscure micro-climate of its own, so don't rely too much on the weatherman to get it right.

Dining & Lodging Price Categories (In Euros)

	¢	$	$$	$$$	$$$$
RESTAURANTS	under €8	€8–€15	€15–€22	€22–€29	over €29
HOTELS	under €80	€80–€130	€130–€180	€180–€230	over €230

Restaurant prices are for a main course at dinner. Hotel prices are for a standard double room in high season.

Updated by
Anto Howard

LIKE AN OPEN-AIR MUSEUM LAYERED with legendary Celtic sites, grand gardens, and elegant Palladian country estates, the small counties immediately north, south, and west of Dublin—historically known as the Pale—seem expressly designed for the sightseer. Due to its location on the Irish Sea, facing Europe, the region has always been the first to attract conquerors, and the first over which they exercised the greatest influence. Traces of each new wave remain: the Celts chose Tara as the center of their kingdom; the Danes sailed the Rivers Boyne and Liffey to establish many of today's towns; and the region's great Protestant-built houses of the 18th century remind us that the Pale was the starting point and administrative center for the long, violent English colonization of the whole island.

The Dublin environs include three basic geographical regions: County Wicklow's coast and mountains, the Boyne Valley, and County Kildare. Lying tantalizingly close to the south of Dublin is the mountainous county of Wicklow, which contains some of the most *et-in-Arcadia-ego* scenery in the Emerald Isle. Here, the gently rounded Wicklow Mountains—to some, they are Ireland's finest—contain the evocative monastic settlement at Glendalough, many later abbeys and churches, and scores of the most beguiling attractions for the art lover: these are the great 18th-century estates of the Anglo-Irish aristocracy, whose reigning lords and ladies, prone to a certain sense of inferiority, were determined not to be outdone by the extravagant efforts of their English compatriots. The result was a string of spectacular stately home extravaganzas, such as Castletown, Powerscourt, and Russborough. Once you see their astonishingly elegant decoration, you may give thanks for the existence of vanity. A quick change of pace is nearby—an impressive eastern coastline that stretches from counties Wicklow to Louth, punctuated by delightful harbor towns and fishing villages. The coast is virtually unspoiled for its entire length.

North of Dublin lies the Boyne Valley, with its abundant ruins of Celtic Ireland extending from counties Meath to Louth. Some of the country's most evocative Neolithic ruins—including the famous passage graves at Newgrange—are nestled into this landscape, where layer upon layer of history reach back into earlier, unknowable ages. It was west of Drogheda—a fascinating town settled by the Vikings in the early 10th century—that the Tuatha De Danann, onetime residents of Ireland, went underground when defeated by invading Milesians and became, it's said, "the good people" (or fairies) of Irish legend. In pagan times this area was the home of Ireland's high kings, and the center of religious life. All roads led to Tara, the fabled Hill of Kings, the royal seat, and the place where the national assembly was held. Today, time seems to stand still—and you should, too, for it's almost sacrilegious to introduce a note of urgency here.

Southwest of Dublin are the flat pastoral plains of County Kildare; the plains stretch between the western Midlands and the foothills of the Dublin and Wicklow mountains—both names actually refer to the same mountain range, but each marks its county's claim to the land.

Kildare is the flattest part of Ireland, a natural playing field for breeding, training, and racing some of the world's premier Thoroughbreds.

Rapid, carnivorous expansion of the capital city in the last decade has seen its suburban limits spread deep into the once bucolic areas of Meath and Kildare, and the natives of these areas fear that their more rural way of life is under threat. Don't be surprised to hear Dublin accents starting to dominate in towns like Navan and Naas. But the new prosperity has meant the local young men and women no longer have to head off up to "the big smoke" of Dublin or even farther afield to find work, and the counties of the Pale are seeing their populations rise for the first time in decades.

EXPLORING DUBLIN ENVIRONS

This chapter is organized into three sections, each of which makes a reasonable day trip. Keep in mind that it's easy to lose an hour or so making detours, chatting with locals, and otherwise enjoying the unexpected. The itineraries above cover the area's highlights; if you have fewer than three days, use parts of each day's suggested itinerary to plan your excursion. A car is essential for visiting most sights, and don't plan on visiting both the north and south of Dublin during the same day. There are some points of interest accessible by public transport: bus tours from Dublin cover County Wicklow as far as Glendalough in the southwest and the Boyne Valley to the north; suburban bus services reach into the foothills of the Dublin Mountains; and Bus Éireann services take in the outlying towns. Some popular sights have direct connections to Dublin, including Enniskerry and Powerscourt Estate, which can be reached by taking the No. 44 bus from the Dublin quays area.

THE BOYNE VALLEY

For every wistful schoolboy in Ireland the River Boyne is a name that resonates with history and adventure. It was on the banks of that river in 1014 that the Celtic chieftain Brian Boru defeated the Danish in a decisive battle that returned the east of Ireland to native rule. It was also by this river that Protestant William of Orange defeated the Catholic armies of exiled James II of England, in 1690. In fact, this whole area, only 48 km (30 mi) north of cosmopolitan Dublin, is soaked in stories and legends that predate the pyramids. You can't throw a stick anywhere in the valley without hitting some trace of Irish history. The great prehistoric, pagan, and Celtic monuments of the wide arc of fertile land known as the Boyne Valley invariably evoke a sense of wonder. You don't have to be an archaeologist to be awed by Newgrange and Knowth—set beside the River Boyne—or the Hill of Tara, Mellifont Abbey, or the High Cross of Monasterboice. One way to approach exploring this area is to start at the town of Trim, the locale closest to Dublin, and work your way north. Keep in mind that Omeath and the scenic Cooley Peninsula at the end of this section are on the border

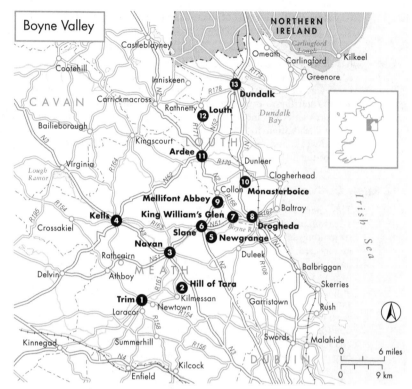

Boyne Valley

of Northern Ireland. *(If you make it this far north, consult Chapter 9, particularly the coverage of the Mountains of Mourne, which are just across Carlingford Lough.)*

TRIM

❶ *51 km (32 mi) northwest of Dublin via N3 to R154.*

The heritage town of Trim, on the River Boyne, contains some of the finest medieval ruins in Ireland. In 1359, on the instructions of King Edward III, the town was walled and its fortifications strengthened. In the 15th century several parliaments were held here. Oliver Cromwell massacred most of its inhabitants when he captured the town in 1649.

Trim Castle, the largest Anglo-Norman fortress in Ireland, dominates present-day Trim from its 2½-acre site, which slopes down to the river's placid waters. Built by Hugh de Lacy in 1173, the castle was soon destroyed, and then rebuilt from 1190 to 1220. The ruins include an enormous keep with 70-foot-high turrets flanked by rectangular towers. The outer castle wall is almost 500 yards long, and five D-shape towers survive. So impressive is the castle it was used as a medieval backdrop in Mel Gibson's movie *Braveheart*. The admission price includes a house tour. ⊠ *Trim* ☎ *046/943–8619* ⊕ *www.heritageire-*

DUBLIN ENVIRONS THROUGH THE AGES

You might think the counties that surround Dublin—Meath, Louth, Kildare, and Wicklow—suffer something of an inferiority complex in the shadow of the historic capital city on the Liffey. But the area historically known as the Pale can boast the oldest traces of civilization on the island of Ireland. Newgrange, the Neolithic burial chamber and solar observatory, dates from around 3200 BC and stands as a mysterious, enigmatic trace of a pre-Celtic civilization. The Celts, too, when they came, found a special resonance in this region and the Hill of Tara became the center of their spiritual and, to a lesser extent, political life. Next came the Normans, who quickly conquered the Pale and built great castles and walled towns to hold back the hordes of natives beyond. A long, gradual conquest of the rest of the island followed, but the aristocracy liked to remain near the political cauldron of Dublin. Thus, in the 18th-century Golden Age of the Irish nobility, they chose to build many of their great houses and ornate gardens in the counties surrounding the capital: the lavish Xanadus of Castletown, Russborough, and Powerscourt stand as monuments to their pride and prodigality. With the decline of the Irish gentry and the rise of the native farmer the land around Dublin became prized as some of the most fertile in the country. But now the bittersweet arrival of the Celtic Tiger's booming economy has seen rapid expansion of Dublin and a rude suburban intrusion into the once pastoral areas on its borders. But Kildare, Meath, Louth, and Wicklow have seen enough invasions come and go to know that history is a long tale whose outcome always surprises.

land.ie ✉*Keep and grounds €3.70, grounds only €1.60* ⊘*Easter–Sept., daily 10–6; Oct., daily 10–5:30, Nov.–Easter, weekends 10–5.*

Facing the river is the **Royal Mint,** a ruin that illustrates Trim's political importance in the Middle Ages. It produced coins with colorful names like "Irelands" and "Patricks" right up into the 15th century.

The **Yellow Steeple** overlooks Trim from a ridge situated opposite the castle. The structure was built in 1368 and is a remnant of the Augustinian abbey of St. Mary's, founded in the 13th century, which itself was the site of a great medieval pilgrimage to a statue of the Blessed Virgin. Much of the tower was deliberately destroyed in 1649 to prevent its falling into Cromwell's hands, and today only the striking, 125-foot-high east wall remains.

The Church of Ireland **St. Patrick's Cathedral** (⊠*Loman St.*) dates from early in the 19th century, but the square tower is from an earlier structure built in 1449.

In the old town hall, the "The Power and the Glory" audiovisual display of the **Visitor Center** tells the story of the arrival of the Normans and of medieval Trim. ⊠*Castle St.* ☎*046/943–7227* ⊕*www.meath tourism.ie* ✉*€3.20 for audiovisual show* ⊘*Mon.–Sat. 9:30–5:30, Sun. noon–5:30.*

If your ancestors are from County Meath, take advantage of the family-history tracing service at the **Meath Heritage and Genealogy Center.** ⊠*Castle St.* ☎*046/943–6633* ✉*Free* ☉*Mon.–Thurs. 9–1 and 1:30– 5, Fri. 9–2.*

At **Newtown,** 1¼ km (¾ mi) east of Trim on the banks of the River Boyne, are the ruins of what was once the largest cathedral in Ireland, built beginning in 1210 by Simon de Rochfort, the first Anglo-Norman bishop of Meath.

At **Laracor,** 3 km (2 mi) south of Trim on R158, a wall to the left of the rectory is where Jonathan Swift (1667–1745), the satirical writer, poet, and author of *Gulliver's Travels,* was rector from 1699 until 1714, when he was made dean of St. Patrick's Cathedral in Dublin. Nearby are the walls of the cottage where Esther Johnson, the "Stella" who inspired much of Swift's writings, once lived.

One of the most pleasant villages of south County Meath, **Summerhill,** 8 km (5 mi) southeast of Laracor along R158, has a large square and a village green with a 15th-century cross.

Cnoc an Linsigh, an attractive area south of Summerhill with forest walks and picnic sites, is ideal for a half day of meandering. Many of the lanes that crisscross this part of County Meath provide delightful driving between high hedgerows, and afford occasional views of the lush, pastoral countryside.

WHERE TO STAY & EAT

$–$$ ✕⊞**Castle Arch Hotel.** This newly refurbished hotel unashamedly hypes up the "castle" theme with its almost fairy-tale, lush decor in the guest rooms, not to mention the solid stone wall (complete with shooting window) that now adorns the bar–restaurant area. But behind all the hype there's a solid, reliable, small hotel with a great location right near the center of town and on the bank of the river. The bar has a good carvery and lively weekend entertainment, and the cozy restaurant ($–$$) plays it safe but sure with quality produce and typical Irish dishes like rack of lamb. ⊠*Trim, Co. Meath* ☎*046/943–1516* 🖷*046/943– 6002* ⊕*www.castlearchhotel.com* ↩*24 rooms* ♿*In-hotel: restaurant, bar, public Wi-Fi* ⊟*AE, MC, V* ¶◎*BP.*

¢   ⊞**Tigh Catháin.** The "House of O'Catháin" is a Tudor-style country cottage about 1 km (½ mi) outside of town on the Longwood road. Owner Marie Keane has artfully decorated the three large bedrooms in different color schemes echoing the natural colors of the region. But the real wonders here are the lovely gardens out back and in front, perfect for lounging around in the sun. Family rooms include a double and two single beds. ⊠*High St., Co. Meath* ☎*046/943–1996* ⊕*www. tighcathaintrim.com* ↩*3 rooms* ♿*In-hotel: public Wi-Fi* ¶◎*BP.*

CLOSE UP

Calling All Hike-a-holics

Whether you're a novice or veteran hiker, Wicklow's gentle, rolling hills are a terrific place to begin an Irish walking vacation. Devoted hikers come from all over the world to traverse the 137-km (85-mi) Wicklow Way (☎01/493–4059), the first long-distance trail to open in Ireland and one of the best. Wicklow is Ireland's little Alps, with bracing fresh air guaranteed among the blue skies and mountain heather and gorse. Much of the route lies above 1,600 feet and follows rough sheep tracks, forest firebreaks, and old bog roads (rain gear, windproof clothing, and sturdy footwear are essential). The trail starts in the outskirts of Dublin suburbs, in Marlay Park, just south of Dublin city center, then ascends into the Wicklow mountain foothills, before passing glens, farms, and historic sights like Rathgall,

home to the Kings of Leinster, and the Mill of Purgatory—a venerated "wardrobe" in Aghowle Church—before finishing up in Clonegal. Consider participating in one of the walking festivals held at Easter, in May, and in autumn. If your feet are less than bionic, you might opt for biking, another excellent way to see the area.

County Wicklow sponsors three annual walking festivals. The two-day Rathdrum Easter Walking Festival (☎0404/46262) includes hill walks of varying lengths over Easter weekend. The first weekend of May, the Wicklow Mountains May Walking Festival (☎0404/66058) is centered on Blessington. The Wicklow Mountains Autumn Walking Festival (☎0404/66058) is based in the Glenmalure area.

HILL OF TARA

❷ *8 km (5 mi) northeast of Trim, 40 km (25 mi) northwest off N3.*

In the legends and the popular imagination of the Irish this ancient site has taken on mythic proportions. As with much of the idealization of the Celtic past, it was the 19th-century revival led by Yeats and Lady Gregory that was responsible for the near-religious veneration of this Celtic site, set at the junction of the five ancient roads of Ireland, and known in popular folklore as the seat of the High Kings of Ireland. The 19th-century ballad by Thomas Moore, "The Harp That Once Through Tara's Halls," was also a major factor in the long over-romanticized view of Tara. Today, its ancestral banqueting hall and great buildings (one was the former palace of the Ard Rí, or High King) have all vanished but for a few columns. Still, the site is awe-inspiring. From the top of the Hill—it rises more than 300 feet above sea level—you can see across the flat central plain of Ireland, with the mountains of east Galway visible from nearly 160 km (100 mi) away. In the mid-19th century, the nationalist leader Daniel O'Connell staged a mass rally here that supposedly drew more than a million people—which would be nearly a third of Ireland's current population. On-site, first pay a call on the Interpretative Center housed in an old Church of Ireland church on the hillside. Here, you can learn the story of Tara and its legends. Without this background it will be difficult to identify many of the earthworks at Tara. Or just call upon your imagination to evoke the millennia-old spirit of the place and picture it in its prime, with the tribes congregating for some great pagan ceremony.

Systematic excavation by 20th-century archaeologists has led to the conclusion that the largest remains are those of an Iron Age fort that had multiple ring forts, some of which were ruined in the 19th century by religious zealots from England searching for the Ark of the Covenant here. The "Mound of the Hostages," a Neolithic passage grave, most likely gave the place its sacred air. During the hill's reign as a royal seat, which lasted to the 11th century, a great *feis* (national assembly) was held here every third year, during which laws were passed and tribal disputes settled. Tara's influence waned with the arrival of Christianity; the last king to live here was Malachy II, who died in 1022. But like with so many other prominent sites of the Irish pre-Christian era, Christianity remade Tara in its own image. Today a modern statue of St. Patrick stands here, as does a pillar stone that may have been the coronation stone (it was reputed to call out in approval when a king was crowned). In the graveyard of the adjacent Anglican church is a pillar with the worn image of a pagan god, and a Bronze Age stone standing on end. ⊠ *Hill of Tara* ☎ *046/902–5903* ⊕ *www.heritageireland.ie* ⊠ *€2* ⊗ *May–Oct., daily 10–6.*

WHERE TO STAY & EAT

$$$–$$$$
Fodor's Choice
★

✕⊞ **Bellinter House.** Surrounded by 12 acres on the banks of the Boyne, this splendid 1750 country house was once the home of the infamously wild, party-loving Briscoe clan (their hijinks once included a crazy dig for the Arc of the Covenant on the nearby Hill of Tara). The new owners have brought back the old glories of the place, and added a few modern twists: an infinity pool now graces the landscape, and contemporary lighting, handmade ash-wood furniture, and futuristic art installations mix easily with the drawing room's 18th-century decorative plasterwork.

> **FIRES OF FAITH**
>
> The Hill of Tara's decline was predicted one Easter Eve in the 5th century when, in accordance with the Druid religion, the lighting of fires was forbidden. Suddenly, on a hillside some miles away, flames were spotted. "If that fire is not quenched now," said a Druid leader, "it will burn forever and will consume Tara." The fire had been lit by St. Patrick at Slane, to celebrate the Christian rites of the Paschal.

While new rooms have been constructed in the old pavilion wings and the stables have been turned into cute, compact modern apartments, the four original massive bedrooms in the main house are the real Georgian gems of Bellinter. Their huge windows allow light to play across the wood-paneled walls and deep yellow rugs. The Eden restaurant ($$–$$$) offers similar high-class modern fare as its Dublin namesake, with the emphasis on top Irish produce served in daring and original combinations. Beautiful indoor and outdoor pools plus a large on-site spa with numerous treatments ensure maximum luxury. Be sure to book in advance—the Irish press has been loudly singing the praises of this place. ⊠ *Navan, Co. Meath* ☎ *046/903–0900* 🖨 *046/903–1367*

⊕*www.bellinterhouse.com* ⊅*34 rooms* ⅃*In-room: safe, VCR, dial-up. In-hotel: restaurant, room service, bar, spa, pools, public Wi-Fi, no elevator* ⊟*AE, MC, V* ⅃◎⅃*BP.*

NAVAN

❸ *10 km (6 mi) northwest of Hill of Tara on N3, 50 km (31 mi) north of Dublin on N3.*

Navan, at the crucial juncture of the Rivers Blackwater and Boyne, is a busy market and mining town with evidence of prehistoric settlements. It took off in the 12th century, when Hugh de Lacy, lord of Trim, had the place walled and fortified, making it a defensive stronghold of the English Pale in eastern Ireland. It's now the administrative center of Meath, increasingly part of the Dublin commuter belt.

At **St. Mary's Church,** built in 1839, you can find a late-18th-century wood carving of the Crucifixion, the work of a local artist, Edward Smyth, who at the time was the greatest sculptor Ireland had produced since the Middle Ages. On Friday, the **Fair Green,** beside the church, hosts a bustling outdoor market. ⊠*Trimgate St.* ⊡*Free* ⊗*Daily 8–8.*

The best views of town and the surrounding area are from the top of the **Motte of Navan,** a grassy mound said to be the tomb of Odhbha, the deserted wife of a Celtic king who, the story goes, died of a broken heart. It's more likely that the 50-foot-high mound is a natural formation. In the 12th century, D'Angulo, the Norman baron, adapted it into a motte and bailey (a type of medieval Norman castle), but there are no structural remains here from this period.

KELLS

❹ *16 km (10 mi) northwest of Navan on N3.*

In the 9th century, a group of monks from Iona in Scotland took refuge at Kells (Ceanannus Mór) after being expelled by the Danes. St. Columba had founded a monastery here 300 years earlier, and although some historians think it was indigenous monks who wrote and illustrated the *Book of Kells*—the Latin version of the four Gospels, and one of Ireland's greatest medieval treasures—most scholars now believe that the Scottish monks brought it with them. Reputed to have been fished out of a watery bog at Kells, the legendary manuscript was removed for safekeeping during the Cromwellian wars to Trinity College, Dublin, where it remains. A large exhibit is now devoted to it in the college's Old Library, where a few of the original pages at a time are on view.

A copy of the *Book of Kells* is on display in the Church of Ireland **St. Columba's** in Kells; it's open until 5 on weekdays and until 1 on Saturday. Four elaborately carved High Crosses stand in the church graveyard; you'll find the stump of a fifth in the marketplace—during the 1798 uprising against British rule it was used as a gallows.

Similar in appearance to St. Kevin's Church at Glendalough and Cormac's Chapel at Cashel, **St. Colmcille's House** is a small, two-story, 7th-century church measuring about 24 feet square and nearly 40 feet high, with a steeply pitched stone roof.

The nearly 100-foot-high **round tower,** adjacent to St. Colmcille's House, dates prior to 1076 and is in almost perfect condition. Its top story has five windows, each facing an ancient entrance into the medieval town.

LET THERE BE A LIGHT SHOW

A visit to Newgrange's passage grave during the winter solstice is considered to be a memorable experience. You'll have to get on the nine-year waiting list to reserve one of the 24 places available on each of the five mornings (December 19–23). And then pray that no clouds obscure the sun and ruin the light show the Bronze Age builders intended.

NEWGRANGE

❺

Fodor'sChoice
★

21 km (13 mi) east of Kells off N51, 28 km (17 mi) northwest of Dublin off N2.

Expect to see no less than one of the most spectacular prehistoric tombs in Europe when you come to Newgrange. Built in the 4th millennium BC—which makes it roughly 1,000 years older than Stonehenge—Newgrange was constructed with some 250,000 tons of stone, much of which came from the Wicklow Mountains, 80 km (50 mi) to the south. How the people who built this tumulus transported the stones to the spot remains a mystery. The mound above the tomb measures more than 330 feet across and reaches a height of 36 feet at the front. White quartz stone was used for the retaining wall, and egg-shape gray stones were studded at intervals. The passage grave may have been the world's earliest solar observatory. It was so carefully constructed that, for five days on and around the winter solstice, the rays of the rising sun still hit a roof box above the lintel at the entrance to the grave. The rays then shine for about 20 minutes down the main interior passageway to illuminate the burial chamber. The site was restored in 1962 after years of neglect and quarrying. The geometric designs on some stones at the center of the burial chamber continue to baffle experts.

The prehistoric sites of nearby Dowth and Knowth have been under excavation since 1962, and although Dowth is still closed to the public, **Knowth** is open at last. The great tumulus at Knowth is comparable in size and shape to Newgrange, standing at 40 feet and having a diameter of approximately 214 feet. Some 150 giant stones, many of them beautifully decorated, surrounded the mound. More than 1,600 boulders, each weighing from one to several tons, were used in the construction. The earliest tombs and carved stones date from the Stone Age (3000 BC), although the site was in use until the early 14th century. In the early Christian era (4th–8th centuries AD) it was the seat of the High Kings of Ireland. Much of the site is still under excavation, and you can often watch archaeologists at work here. Access to Newgrange and

Knowth is solely via **Brú na Bóinne** *(Palace of the Boyne)* , the Boyne Valley visitor center. Arrive early if possible, because Newgrange often sells out. The last tour leaves the visitor center one hour and 45 minutes before closing. ✉*Off N2, signposted from Slane, Donore* ☎*041/988–0300* ⊕*www.heritage ireland.ie* ✉*Newgrange and interpretive center €5.80, Knowth and interpretive center €4.50* ☺*Newgrange and Knowth daily,* Nov.–Feb., 9:30–5; Mar., Apr., and Oct., 9:30–5:30; May, 9–6:30; June–mid-Sept., 9–7; mid- to late-Sept., 9–6:30.

SLANE

❻ *2½ km (1½ mi) north of Newgrange, 46 km (29 mi) northwest of Dublin on N2.*

Slane Castle is the draw at this small, Georgian village, built in the 18th century around a crossroads on the north side of the River Boyne.

The 16th-century building known as the **Hermitage** was constructed on the site where St. Erc, a local man converted to Christianity by St. Patrick himself, led a hermit's existence. All that remains of his original monastery is the faint trace of the circular ditch, but the ruins of the later church includes a nave and a chancel with a tower in between.

The stately 18th-century **Slane Castle** is beautifully situated overlooking a natural amphitheater. In 1981 the castle's owner, Anglo-Irish Lord Henry Mountcharles, staged the first of what have been some of Ireland's largest outdoor rock concerts; REM's show holds the record for attendance, with 70,000. In 2001, after a decade of renovation following a devastating fire, the castle reopened to the public. The tour includes the main hall, with its delicate plasterwork and beautiful stained glass, the dazzling red, neo-Gothic ballroom completed in 1821 for the visit of King George IV, and other rooms. The stunning parklands were laid out by Capability Brown, the famous 18th-century landscape gardener. ☎*041/988–4400* ⊕*www.slanecastle.ie* ✉*€7* ☺*May–early Aug., Sun.–Thurs. noon–5.*

North of Slane town is the 500-foot-high **Slane Hill,** where St. Patrick proclaimed the arrival of Christianity in 433 by lighting the Paschal Fire. From the top, you have sweeping views of the Boyne Valley. On a clear day, the panorama stretches from Trim to Drogheda, a vista extending 40 km (25 mi).

A two-hour tour of farmer Willie Redhouse's fully functioning arable and livestock **Newgrange Farm** includes feeding the ducks, bottle-feeding the lambs, a tour of the aviaries with their exotic birds, and a straw maze for the kids. A blacksmith gives demonstrations of his ancient art, and there is a nice tractor-trailer ride around the farm. Every Sunday at

3 PM the "Sheep Derby" takes place, with teddy bears tied astride the animals in the place of jockeys. Visiting children are made "owners" of individual sheep for the duration of the race. The farm lies 3 km (2 mi) east of Slane on N51. ☎041/982–4119 ☞€7 ☉Easter–Aug., daily 10–5.

WHERE TO STAY & EAT

$-$$ ✕▦ **Conyngham Arms Hotel.** Although built in the mid-19th century, the Conyngham Arms, at the crossroads in Slane, maintains a village-inn look. Four-poster beds in the guest rooms let you imagine sleeping like the aristocracy. The Gamekeeper's Lodge Bistro ($$–$$$) serves simple but delightful fresh meat and fish dishes. Try the salmon in season. Quality bar and snack food is also available. ✉Co. Meath ☎041/988–4444 ☏041/982–4205 ⊕www.conynghamarms.com ⇱15 rooms ⚭In-room: no a/c. In-hotel: restaurant, bar ☰AE, MC, V ⎰BP, FAP, MAP.

KING WILLIAM'S GLEN

❼ On the northern bank of the River Boyne, King William's Glen is where a portion of King William of Orange's Protestant army hid before the Battle of the Boyne in 1690. They won by surprising the Catholic troops of James II, who were on the southern side, but many of the Protestant-Catholic conflicts in present-day Northern Ireland can be traced to the immediate aftermath of this battle. The site is marked with an orange-and-green sign; part of the site is also incorporated in the nearby, early-19th-century **Townley Hall Estate,** which has forest walks and a nature trail (the house is not open to the public).

DROGHEDA

❽ 6½ km (4 mi) east of King William's Glen on N51, 45 km (28 mi) north of Dublin on N1.

Drogheda (pronounced draw-hee-da) is one of the most enjoyable and historic towns on the east coast of Ireland—and a setting for one of the most tragic events in Irish history, the tragic seige and massacre wrought by Oliver Cromwell's English army. It was colonized in 911 by the Danish Vikings; two centuries later, the town was taken over by Hugh de Lacy, the Anglo-Norman lord of Trim, who was responsible for fortifying the towns along the River Boyne. At first, two separate towns existed, one on the northern bank, the other on the southern bank. In 1412, already heavily walled and fortified, Drogheda was unified, making it the largest English town in Ireland. Today, large 18th-century warehouses line the northern bank of the Boyne. The center of town, around West Street, is the historic heart of Drogheda.

Towering over the river is the long **railway viaduct.** Built around 1850 as part of the railway line from Dublin to Belfast, it's still used and is a splendid example of Victorian engineering. Its height above the river makes the viaduct Drogheda's most prominent landmark.

Bloody Cromwell!

In much of the English-speaking world Oliver Cromwell is regarded as something of a hero, a deeply religious self-made man, master general, and leader of the victorious parliamentary side in the English Civil Wars.

But in Ireland, Cromwell's name is usually followed by a spit and a curse. In 1649 Old Ironsides arrived in Ireland to subdue a Royalist and Catholic rebellion once and for all. His methods were simple: burn every building, and kill every person that stood in his way.

"To Hell or to Connaught" (the latter being the most westerly of Ireland's four provinces) was the dire choice he offered the native population as he drove them ever westward and off the more fertile lands of the east and south. When he approached the walled town of Drogheda, the gates were closed to him.

Led by the Anglo-Irish Sir Arthur Aston, the native Catholic population bravely defended their town against Cromwell's relentless siege, twice driving back the advancing army. On the third attempt the town fell, and the order went out that no mercy was to be shown.

It's estimated that up to 3,500 men, women, and children were slaughtered. One group hid in the steeple of St. Peter's Church, so Cromwell burned it down with them all inside. Sir Arthur was beaten to death with his own wooden leg.

While the massacre at Drogheda frightened many Irish towns into submission (and thereby prevented other battles), the bloody stain on Cromwell's reputation was permanent.

The bank building on the corner of West and Shop streets, called the **Tholsel,** is an 18th-century square granite edifice with a cupola.

The 13th-century **St. Laurence's Gate,** one of the two surviving entrances from Drogheda's original 11 gates in its town walls, has two four-story drum towers and is one of the most perfect examples in Ireland of a medieval town gate. **Butler's Gate,** near the Millmount Museum, predates St. Laurence's Gate by 50 years or more.

The Gothic-Revival Roman Catholic **St. Peter's Church** (⊠ *West St.*) houses the preserved head of St. Oliver Plunkett. Primate of all Ireland, he was martyred in 1681 at Tyburn in London; his head was pulled from the execution flames.

A severe, 18th-century church within an enclosed courtyard, the Anglican **St. Peter's** (⊠ *Fair St.*) is rarely open except for Sunday services. It's worth a peek for its setting and the fine views over the town from the churchyard.

Perhaps the main attraction in Drogheda lies across the river from the town center. The **Millmount Museum and Martello Tower,** off the Dublin road (N1) south of Drogheda, shares space in a renovated British Army barracks with crafts workshops, including a pottery- and picture-gallery and studio. It was on the hill at Millmount that the townsfolk made their last stand against the bloodthirsty Roundheads of Cromwell. Perhaps in defiance of Cromwell's attempt to obliterate the town from the map, the museum contains relics of eight centuries of Drogheda's commercial and industrial past, including painted banners of the old trade guilds, a circular willow-and-leather coracle (the traditional fishing boat on the River Boyne), and many instruments and utensils from domestic and factory use. Most moving are the mementos of the infamous 1649 massacre of 3,000 people by Cromwell. There are also geological and archeological displays. The exhibit inside the Martello Tower adjacent to the museum focuses on the military history of Drogheda. ☒ *Millmount* ☎ *041/983–3097* ⊕ *www.millmount.net* ☜ *Museum €4.50, tower €3* ☉ *Mon.–Sat. 10–5:30, Sun. 2:30–5.*

Across the Meath border in County Dublin, 18 km (11 mi) south of Drogheda, is **Ardgillan Demesne,** one of the prettiest parks along the coast. Its 194 acres consist of rolling pastures, mixed woodland, and gardens overlooking the Bay of Drogheda, with splendid views of the coastline. There's a top-class children's playground on-site as well as a beautiful rose garden and Victorian conservatory. The castle here, built in 1738 for a landowning family, rises two stories. Ground-floor rooms are decorated in Georgian and Victorian styles; first-floor rooms house a permanent display of 17th-century maps, and host an annual program of exhibitions. Guided tours are the only way to see the rest of the castle. ☒ *Balbriggan* ☎ *01/849–2212* ⊕ *www.fingalcoco.ie* ☜ *€6 for tour* ☉ *Apr.–June and Sept., Tues.–Sun. 11–6; Oct.–Mar., Tues.–Sun. 11–4:30; July and Aug., daily 11–dusk.*

WHERE TO STAY & EAT

¢–$ ✕ **Monk's.** This little café on the river is always full of locals looking for healthful food at a decent price. Monk's specializes in delicious, somewhat off-center sandwiches, including a wonderful goat-cheese bruschetta and a spicy Mexican chicken sandwich. The hot breakfasts are a treat, chunky French toast and fruit being the most popular dish. ☒ *North Quay* ☎ *041/984–5630* ▤ *MC, V.*

$$ ✕▥ **Boyne Valley Hotel and Country Club.** A 1-km (½-mi) drive leads to this 19th-century mansion on 16 acres that was once owned by a Drogheda brewing family. The newer wing of this owner-run hotel has double rooms, all with contemporary furnishings and bright color schemes full of pinks and pastels. The public spaces have been restored in period fashion, with Neoclassical pillars, intricate plasterwork, and crystal chandeliers. A large conservatory houses a bar and overlooks the grounds, while a spacious hall is decorated with antiques and comfy chairs. The Cellar Restaurant specializes in fresh fish. ☒ *Dublin Rd., Co. Louth* ☎ *041/983–7737* ☏ *041/983–9188* ⊕ *www.boyne-valley-hotel.ie* ⋑ *71 rooms, 1 suite* ⌂ *In room: Wi-Fi. In-hotel: restaurant, bar, golf course, tennis courts, pool, gym* ▤ *AE, DC, MC, V* ❍ *BP.*

EATING WELL IN DUBLIN ENVIRONS

The counties around Dublin are not an obvious place to go to find good food. They are often perceived as being caught between the exotic charms of city dining and the true, rustic fare of the wilder west and south coasts. And yes, there's a lot of mediocre, overcooked, overpriced food in the region. The increase in population and influx of Dubliners and immigrants has brought some finer, more daring establishments in its wake, including the French Pro-vençal delights of the Forge Gallery (just north of Slane) and the Scandinavian treats of Rolf's Bistro (in Ardee). But the real dining treasure here lies in the fact that the area is blessed with an abundance of old estates and country houses, which combine the most romantic and elegant of accommodations with some of the most exciting and mouth-watering dining rooms in Ireland. A deep respect for fresh, locally grown and raised produce and meats is a common theme, usually melded with a European outlook to the menu.

It's a tour of the best of Irish home cooking: from the seafood gems of Ballymascanlon House on the Cooley Peninsula, west to the hearty game dishes of Moyglare Manor, and south to the haute-Irish menu at Rathsallagh House. And somehow each house manages to mix the dazzlingly elegant surroundings and menu with an informal, family atmosphere that makes the Irish country house the great-value wonder that it is.

MELLIFONT ABBEY

⑨ *8 km (5 mi) east of Drogheda off R168.*

On the eastern bank of the River Mattock, which creates a natural border between Counties Meath and Louth, lie the remains of Mellifont Abbey, the first Cistercian monastery in Ireland. Founded in 1142 by St. Malachy, archbishop of Armagh, it was inspired by the formal structure surrounding a courtyard of St. Bernard of Clairvaux's monastery, which St. Malachy had visited. Among the substantial ruins are the two-story chapter house, built in 12th-century English-Norman style and once a daily meeting place for the monks; it now houses a collection of medieval glazed tiles. Four walls of the 13th-century octagonal lavabo, or washing place, still stand, as do some arches from the Romanesque cloister. At its peak Mellifont presided over almost 40 other Cistercian monasteries throughout Ireland, but all were suppressed by Henry VIII in 1539 after his break with the Catholic Church. Adjacent to the car park is a small **architectural museum** depicting the history of the abbey and the craftsmanship that went into its construction. ⊠*Near Collon* ☎*041/982–6459* ⊕*www.heritageireland.ie* ⊠*€2.10* ☉*May–Sept., daily 10–5.*

WHERE TO EAT

$$$–$$$$ ╳**Forge Gallery Restaurant.** For generations the local forge was the burning heart of any rural Irish community, and this well-established restaurant is still something of a beacon to locals and visitors for miles around. Warm rose and plum tones and antique furnishings decorate this two-story eatery in a converted forge, and an old fireplace fills the

place with a comforting warmth and light. The cuisine mixes French Provençal with a strong hint of traditional Irish cooking. Two popular specialties are roast duckling served on a bed of bok choy, with spring onion, soy, and ginger sauce, and tagine of mussels and scallops served with baby saffron potatoes. Make sure you try one of the seasonal homemade soups. Paintings by local artists hang in the reception area and are for sale. Reservations are essential on weekends. ⊠*North of Slane on N2, Collon* ☎*041/982–6272* ⊕*www.forgegalleryrestaurant. ie* ▤*AE, DC, MC, V* ⊙*No dinner Sun. No lunch Sat.*

MONASTERBOICE

❿ *8 km (5 mi) northeast of Mellifont Abbey on N1, 8 km (5 mi) north of Drogheda.*

Ireland has more carved-stone High Crosses than any other European country, and an outstanding collection is in the small, secluded village of Monasterboice, a former monastic settlement.

Dating to AD 923, the **Muireadach Cross** stands nearly 20 feet high and is considered to be the best-preserved example of a High Cross in Ireland. Its elaborate panels depict biblical scenes, including Cain slaying Abel, David and Goliath, and a centerpiece of the Last Judgment. (Figurative scenes are not a characteristic of earlier High Crosses, such as those found in Ahenny, County Clare.) The **West Cross** stands a couple of feet taller than Muiredach's, making it one of the tallest in Ireland. Its engravings are less impressive—many of them having been worn away by centuries of Irish wind and rain. From the adjacent, 110-foot-high **round tower,** the extent of the former monastic settlement at Monasterboice is apparent. The key to the tower door is kept at the nearby gate lodge.

ARDEE

⓫ *14½ km (9 mi) northwest of Monasterboice on N2.*

In this market town, formerly at the northern edge of the Pale (originally the Pale referred to the area of eastern Ireland ruled directly by the Normans), stand two 13th-century castles: Ardee Castle and Hatch's Castle. The town of Ardee (Baile Átha Fhirdia or Ferdia's Ford), interestingly, was named after the ford where the mythical folk hero Cuchulainn fought his foster brother Ferdia. There's a statue depicting this battle at the start of the riverside walk.

Ardee Castle (the one with square corners) was founded by Roger de Peppard in 1207, but much of the present building dates to the 15th century and later. The castle faces north—its objective to protect the Anglo-Irish Pale from the untamed Celtic tribes of Ulster. It was converted into a courthouse in the 19th century.

Hatch's Castle (with rounded corners) is a private residence and not open to the public. Built in the 13th century, it was given by Cromwell as a gift to the loyal Hatch family. If you look closely you can see it still flaunts two 18th-century cannons at its entrance.

St. Mary's Church of Ireland on Main Street incorporates part of a 13th-century Carmelite church burned by Edward the Bruce in 1316, including the holy water font. The current building was constructed in the 19th century.

WHERE TO EAT

$$-$$$ ✕**Rolf's Bistro.** When the husband-and-wife team of Paul and Berna-
★ dette Svender (Rolf is Paul's father's name) opened their new restaurant in Ardee they knew what they wanted: an informal atmosphere with high-quality food. They renovated an old house in the middle of town, retaining much of its cozy charm with the help of discreet lighting, old pine floors, and a luxurious antique sofa in the waiting area. The menu reflects chef Paul's Scandinavian background, with Swedish caviar and beef Lindstrom (minced meat with capers and beetroot), a popular starter and main course. The steamed mussels served with chili sauce and aioli bread are refreshingly spicy. ⌧ *52 Market St.* ☎*041/685–7949* ▤*MC, V* ☺*Closed Sun. No lunch.*

$–$$$ ✕**Carlito's.** Drinking a lazy aperitif before sitting down to eat is standard civilized behavior at this cozy Italian eatery in the small town of Dunleer, a few miles east of Ardee on the R170. The decor is nothing fancy, but the staff is sizeable and the commodious menu includes delicious homemade bread to go along with the real minestrone soup. The pizzas and pastas are streets ahead of your average joint, and the herb-crusted cod is a favorite main course. Save room for the killer tiramisu. ⌧*Main St., Dunleer* ☎*041/686–1366* ▤*MC, V* ☺*Closed Mon. No lunch.*

LOUTH

⑫ *11½ km (7 mi) north of Ardee on R171.*

Louth warrants a visit, if only for the splendidly preserved oratory here. St. Patrick, Ireland's patron saint, was reputed to have built his first church (which is no longer here) in this hilltop village in the 5th century. He also made St. Mochta (d. 534) the first bishop of Louth.

Standing at the center of the village is the excellently preserved **St. Mochta's House,** an oratory dating from the 11th century, whose steeply pitched stone roof can be reached by a stairway. The house is freely accessible—but watch out for cattle (and their droppings) in the surrounding field.

Nearby **Knockabbey Castle and Gardens** are perfect for a relaxing afternoon when the weather's good. Originally built in 1399, the castle was expanded by the Bellew family in 1650 and again in 1754, before suffering major damage in an IRA raid in 1923. But the real treat here is the recently restored historical water gardens, which originally date back as far as the 11th century. A stroll will take you through wildflower meadows, herbaceous borders, a Victorian flower garden, and a restored glasshouse. ⊠*Louth Village* ☎*01/677–8816* 🖅*House €6, gardens €6* ☉*May and Sept., weekends 10:30–5:30; June–Aug., Tues.–Sun. 10:30–5:30.*

DUNDALK

 14½ km (9 mi) east of Inniskeen, 80 km (50 mi) north of Dublin on N1.

Dundalk is a thriving, if uninspiring, frontier town—only 9½ km (6 mi) from the Northern Ireland border—with some fine historic buildings. It's the main town of County Louth (Ireland's smallest county), and it dates from the early Christian period, around the 7th century. In May the town hosts an avant-garde "fringe" drama and visual arts festival (with a nice schedule of children's events).

> ### UNWELCOME WAGON
>
> The area around Dundalk is closely connected with Cuchulainn (pronounced *coo*-chu-lain)—"a greater hero than Hercules or Achilles," as Frank McCourt, in *Angela's Ashes*, quotes his father. Cuchulainn, the warrior of the Irish epic *Táin Bó Cuailnge* (Cattle Raid of Cooley), heroically defended this area of ancient Ulster against invaders.

On Mill Street, the **bell tower** of a Franciscan monastery with Gothic windows dates from the 13th century.

The **St. Patrick's Cathedral** was built between 1835 and 1847, when the Gothic Revival was at its height. With its buttresses and mosaics lining the chancel and the side chapel walls, the cathedral was modeled on the 15th-century King's College Chapel at Cambridge, England. The fine exterior was built in Newry granite, and the high altar and pulpit are of carved Caen stone. ⊠*Town center* ☉*Daily 8–6.*

The Market House, the Town Hall, and the Courthouse are examples of the town's 19th-century heritage; the **Courthouse** is the most impressive of the three, built in the 1820s in a severe Greek Revival style, with Doric columns supporting the portico. It stands north of St. Patrick's Cathedral.

The **Dundalk County Museum** is dedicated to preserving the history of the dying local industries, such as beer brewing, cigarette manufacturing, shoe and boot making, and railway engineering. Other exhibits deal with the history of Louth from 7500 BC to the present. ⊠*Joycelyn St.* ☎*042/932–7056* ⊕*www.louthcoco.ie* 🖅*€3.80* ☉*June–Sept., Mon.–Sat. 10:30–5:30, Sun. 2–6; Oct.–May, Tues.–Sat. 10:30–5:30, Sun. 2–6.*

WHERE TO STAY & EAT

\$\$ ✕🖾 **Ballymascanlon House Hotel.** On 130 acres on the scenic Cooley Peninsula just north of Dundalk, you can find this converted Victorian mansion with a reputation for comfort and good cuisine. Reproduction period pieces fill the large guest rooms, which overlook either the spacious gardens or old stable yard. The restaurant (\$\$\$) serves a set menu of Irish and French cuisine; it specializes in fresh seafood, such as lobster in season. Vegetarian plates are also available. ⊠*Dundalk, Co. Louth* ☎*042/935–8200* 📠*042/937–1598* ⊕*www.ballymascan-lon.com* ⇆*90 rooms* ♿*In-hotel: restaurant, bars, golf course, tennis courts, pool, gym, public Wi-Fi* ☰*AE, DC, MC, V* ○|*BP.*

¢–$ 🏨**Balrobin House.** This Georgian house was the home of Sir Lionel Harty and his wife Lady Lucy, who in the late 19th century would wine and dine Ireland's elite in its lush surroundings. A marble fireplace, a walled garden, and antique gates are among the many original features of the house. The rooms maintain a period look with high, plasterwork ceilings and ornate furnishings. ⊠*Kilkerley, Co. Louth* ☎*042/937–7701* ⇆*4 rooms* ☰*MC, V* ○|*BP.*

COUNTY WICKLOW

Make your way to the fourth or fifth story of almost any building in Dublin that faces south and you can see off in the distance—amazingly, not *that* far off in the distance—the green, smooth hills of the Dublin and Wicklow mountains. On a clear day the mountains are even visible from some streets in and around the city center. If your idea of solace is green hills, and your visit to Ireland is otherwise limited to Dublin, County Wicklow—or Cill Mhantain (pronounced kill *wan*-tan), as it's known in Irish—should be on your itinerary. Not that the secret isn't out; rugged and mountainous with dark, wooded forests, central Wicklow, known as the "garden of Ireland," is a popular picnic area among Dubliners. It has some of Ireland's grandest 18th-century mansions, and cradles one of the country's earliest Christian retreats: Glendalough. Nestled in a valley of dense woods and placid lakes, Glendalough and environs can seem (at least during the off-season) practically untouched since their heyday 1,000 years ago. The granite mountains that have protected Glendalough all these years run into the sea along the east coast, which has several popular sandy beaches. Journey from Dublin down to Arklow, sticking to the east side of the Wicklow Mountains. A quick note about getting here: it takes stamina to extract yourself from the unmarked maze of the Dublin exurbs (your best bet is to take N11, which becomes M11, and then again N11). Once you've accomplished that feat, this gorgeous, mysterious terrain awaits.

BRAY

❶ *22 km (14 mi) south of Dublin on N11, 8 km (5 mi) east of Enniskerry on R755.*

One of Ireland's oldest seaside resorts, Bray is a trim, growing village known for its summer cottages and sand-and-shingle beach, which stretches for 2 km (1 mi). When the trains first arrived from Dublin in 1854, Bray became the number-one spot for urban vacationers and subsequently took on the appearance of an English oceanfront town. Some Dubliners still flock to the faded glory of Bray's boardwalk to push baby carriages and soak up the sun. It's the terminus of the DART

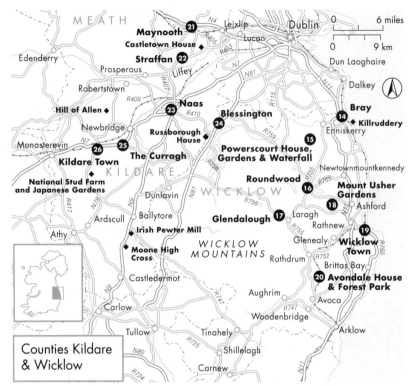

Counties Kildare
& Wicklow

train from Dublin, so it's easy to get here without a car. Uncrowded trails for hiking and mountain-biking crisscross the mountains bordering Bray to the south. One of the best is a well-marked path leading from the beach to the 10-foot-tall cross that crowns the spiny peak of Bray Head, a rocky outcrop that rises 791 feet from the sea. The semi-difficult, one-hour climb affords stunning views of Wicklow Town and Dublin Bay.

The **Heritage Centre,** opposite the Royal Hotel, in the old courthouse, houses on its lower level a re-created castle dungeon with a 1,000-years-of-Bray exhibition. Upstairs is a huge model railway and a display about modern Bray. ⊠ *Lower Main St.* ☎ *01/286–6796* 💶 *€4* ⊙ *June–Aug., weekdays 9–1 and 2–5, Sat. 10–3; Sept.–May, weekdays 9:30–1 and 2–4:30, Sat. 10–3.*

One Martello Terrace (☎ *01/286–8407*), at the harbor, is Bray's most famous address. James Joyce (1882–1941) lived here between 1887 and 1891 and used the house as the setting for the Christmas dinner in *A Portrait of the Artist as a Young Man.* Today the house is owned by an Irish Teachta Dála (member of Parliament, informally known as a "TD"). The phone number listed above rings at her constituency office; someone there should be able to help scholars and devotees arrange a visit. (Call on Thursday between 10 AM and 1 PM.) Although the residence has been renovated, the dining room portrayed in Joyce's novel maintains the spirit of his time.

National Sealife is an aquarium and museum dedicated to the creatures of the sea, with an emphasis on those that occupy the waters around Ireland. Besides massive sea tanks that contain all manner of swimming things, there's a major conservation project with captive breeding of sea horses. **FinZone** is an undersea adventure trail perfect for kids, including puzzles to solve. Touch-screen computers and video games give the whole thing a high-tech feel. In winter, call to confirm opening times before visiting. ⌧*Strand Rd.* ☎*01/286–6939* ⊕*www.sealifeeurope. com* ⌨*€10.50* ☉*May–Sept., daily 10–6; Oct.–Apr. weekdays 11–5, weekends 11–6.*

The 17th-century formal gardens at **Killruddery House** are precisely arranged, with fine beech hedges, Victorian statuary, and a parterre of lavender and roses. The Brabazon family, the earls of Meath, have lived here since 1618. In 1820 they hired William Morris to remodel the house as a revival Elizabethan mansion. The estate also has a Crystal Palace conservatory modeled on those at the botanic gardens in Dublin. ⌧*Off Bray–Greystones Rd., 3 km (2 mi) south of Bray, Killruddery* ☎*01/286–3405* ⊕*www.killruddery.com* ⌨*House and gardens €10, gardens only €6* ☉*Gardens Apr., weekends 1–5; May–Sept., daily 1–5; house May, June, and Sept., daily 1–5.*

WHERE TO EAT

$$–$$$$
Fodor'sChoice
★
✕**Hungry Monk.** The cloisters and refectory-style decor is definitely tongue in cheek at this upbeat, fun bistro in sleepy Greystones, an old-fashioned seaside resort a couple miles south of Bray. Owner Pat Keown is a great host and his laughter and love of good food and fine wine are catching. Dinner is served by candlelight and the menu specializes in uncluttered seafood dishes in summer and wild game on those cold winter nights. The "Seafood Symphony" is a particular favorite, as is the roast suckling pig. Sunday lunches are famous for the length of time they go on (often into the early evening) and for the lively atmosphere. ⌧*1 Church Rd., Greystones* ☎*01/287–5759* ⊕*www. thehungrymonk.ie* ⊟*AE, DC, MC, V* ☉*Closed Mon. and Tues. No lunch Wed.–Sat.*

¢–$
✕**Summerville Country Cooking.** This restaurant's ceilings are high, the space is airy and bright, and the food—ranging from shepherd's pie to vegetarian quiche—tastes absolutely delicious. In summer take advantage of the sun-drenched garden terrace. ⌧*1 Trafalgar Rd., Greystones* ☎*01/287–4228* ⊟*V.*

POWERSCOURT HOUSE, GARDENS & WATERFALL

⑮
☉ *25 km (16 mi) south of Dublin on R117, 22 km (14 mi) north of Glendalough on R755.*

Within the shadow of famous Sugar Loaf mountain, Enniskerry is one of the prettiest villages in Ireland. It's built around a sloping central triangular square with a backdrop of the wooded Wicklow Mountains. From Dublin you can get to Enniskerry directly by taking the No. 44 bus from the Dublin quays area. The main reason to visit the area around Enniskerry is the Powerscourt Estate.

They really had the life, those old aristocrats. At more than 14,000 acres, including stunning formal gardens and a 400-foot waterfall, **Powerscourt** must have been some

> **GENIUS IN A BOTTLE**
>
> Powerscourt's grand Victorian gardens were designed by an eccentric boozer, Daniel Robertson, who liked to be tooled around the gardens-in-progress in a wheelbarrow while taking nips from a bottle of sherry.

place to call home. The grounds were originally granted to Sir Richard Wingfield, the first viscount of Powerscourt, by King James I of England in 1609. Richard Castle (1690–1751), the architect of Russborough House, was hired to design the great house. His was an age not known for modesty, and he chose the grand Palladian style. The house took nine years to complete and was ready to move in 1740, truly one of the great houses of Ireland and, indeed, all of Britain. Unfortunately, you won't be able to see much of it. A terrible fire almost completely destroyed the house in 1974, cruelly on the eve of a huge party to celebrate the completion after a long period of restoration by the Slazenger family. A second period of renovation is currently under way and the original ballroom on the first floor—once "the grandest room in any Irish house," according to historian Desmond Guinness—is the only room that gives a sense of the place's former glory. It was based on Palladio's version of the "Egyptian Hall" designed by Vitruvius, architect to Augustus, emperor of Rome.

Powerscourt Gardens, considered among the finest in Europe, were laid out from 1745 to 1767 following the completion of the house—and were radically redesigned in the Victorian style, from 1843 to 1875, by Daniel Robertson. The Villa Butera in Sicily inspired him to set these gardens with sweeping terraces, antique sculptures, and a circular pond and fountain flanked by winged horses. There's a celebrated view of the Italianate patterned ramps, lawns, and pond across the beautiful, heavily wooded Dargle Valley, which stair-steps to the horizon and the noble profile of Sugar Loaf mountain. The grounds include many specimen trees (plants grown for exhibition), an avenue of monkey puzzle trees, a parterre of brightly colored summer flowers, and a Japanese garden. The kitchen gardens, with their modest rows of flowers, are a striking antidote to the classical formality of the main sections. A self-serve restaurant, crafts center, garden center, and a children's play area are also on the grounds. ⊠ *Enniskerry* ☎ *01/204–6000* ⊕ *www. powerscourt.ie* 🖾 *€9* ⊗ *Daily 9:30–5:30.*

One of the most inspiring sights to the writers and artists of the Romantic generation, the 400-foot **Powerscourt Waterfall,** 5 km (3 mi) south of the gardens, is the highest in the British Isles. ⊠ *Enniskerry* 🖾 *€5* ⊗ *Mar.–Apr. and Sept.–Oct., daily 10:30–5:30; May–Aug., daily 9:30–7; Nov.–Feb., daily 10:30–4.*

WHERE TO EAT

$ ✕ **Marc Michel.** To add on to his Organic Life shop in the nearby town of Kilpedder, the eponymous farmer set up this fantastic little café, which
★ sits inside a large greenhouse with adjoining deck in the middle of the land where he grows all the produce he uses. A 150-year-old Italian olive tree stands in the middle of the dining area and the food has that very Italian, casual but classy feel. A top-class wine list accompanies comfort dishes like the gorgeous homemade burger or the chicken-liver parfait with pear-and-date chutney. Deserts like the strawberry tart are always a highlight. The only negative is that it only opens for lunch. ⊠ *Tinna Park, Kilpedder* ☎ *01/201–1882* ▤ *MC, V* ⊙ *No dinner.*

$ ✕ **Poppies Country Cooking.** This cozy café—with a pine-panel ceiling, farmhouse furniture, and paintings of poppies on the walls—is a great place for breakfast, lunch, or late-afternoon tea. Expect potato cakes, shepherd's pie, lasagna, vegetarian quiche, house salads, and soup. But the most popular dishes are Poppies chicken (a casserolelike concoction) and homity pie (pot pie with potatoes, onion, garlic, and cream cheese). For dessert try the apple pie or the rhubarb crumble, which is so good that the Irish rugby team stops by for it after practice. ⊠ *The Square, Enniskerry* ☎ *01/282–8869* ⊕ *www.poppies.ie* ▤ *MC, V* ⊙ *No dinner Sat.–Thurs.*

ROUNDWOOD

⑯ *18 km (11 mi) south of Enniskerry on R755.*
★
At 800 feet above sea level, Roundwood is the highest village in Ireland. It's also surrounded by spectacular mountain scenery. The Sunday afternoon market in the village hall, where cakes, jams, and other homemade goods are sold, livens up what is otherwise a sleepy place. From the broad main street, by the Roundwood Inn, a minor road leads west for 8 km (5 mi) to two lakes, Lough Dan and Lough Tay, lying deep between forested mountains like Norwegian fjords.

WHERE TO EAT

$–$$$ ✕ **Roundwood Inn.** Travel back to the 17th century at this inn evocatively
★ furnished in a traditional style, with wooden floors, dark furniture, and diamond-shape windows. It's best known for its good, reasonably priced bar food—eaten at sturdy tables beside an open fire. The restaurant offers a combination of Continental and Irish cuisines, reflecting the traditions of the German proprietor, Jurgen Schwalm, and his Irish wife, Aine. The separate bar and lounge also serve an excellent menu that includes a succulent seafood platter of salmon, oysters, lobster, and shrimp. ⊠ *Main St., Roundwood village center* ☎ *01/281–8107* ⌁ *Reservations essential* ▤ *AE, MC, V* ⊙ *Closed Mon. and Tues. No dinner Sun.*

GLENDALOUGH

🔟 *9 km (6 mi) southeast of Roundwood via R755 and R756.*

FodorśChoice
★

Nestled in a lush, quiet valley deep in the rugged Wicklow Mountains, among two lakes, evergreen and deciduous trees, and acres of windswept heather, Gleann dá Loch ("Glen of Two Lakes") is one of Ireland's premier monastic sites. The hermit monks of early Christian Ireland were drawn to the Edenlike quality of some of the valleys in this area, and this evocative settlement remains to this day a sight to calm a troubled soul. Stand here in the early morning (before the crowds and the hordes of school-trippers arrive), and you can appreciate what drew the solitude-seeking St. Kevin to this spot. St. Kevin—or Coemghein, "fair begotten" in Irish (d. 618)—was a descendant of the royal house of Leinster who renounced the world and came here to live as a hermit before opening the monastery in 550. Glendalough then flourished as a monastic center until 1398, when English soldiers plundered the site, leaving the ruins that you see today. (The monastery survived earlier 9th- and 10th-century Viking attacks.) The visitor center is a good place to orient yourself and pick up a useful pamphlet. Many of the ruins are clumped together beyond the visitor center, but some of the oldest surround the Upper Lake, where signed paths direct you through spectacular scenery absent of crowds. Most ruins are open all day and are freely accessible.

Probably the oldest building on the site, presumed to date from St. Kevin's time, is the **Teampaill na Skellig** (Church of the Oratory), on the south shore of the Upper Lake. A little to the east is **St. Kevin's Bed,** a tiny cave in the rock face, about 30 feet above the level of the lake, where St. Kevin lived his hermit's existence. It's not easily accessible; you approach the cave by boat, but climbing the cliff to the cave can be dangerous. At the southeast corner of the Upper Lake is the 11th-century **Reefert Church,** with the ruins of a nave and a chancel. The saint also lived in the adjoining, ruined beehive hut with five crosses, which marked the original boundary of the monastery. You get a superb view of the valley from here.

The ruins by the edge of the Lower Lake are the most important of those at Glendalough. The **gateway,** beside the Glendalough Hotel, is the only surviving entrance to an ancient monastic site anywhere in Ireland. An extensive **graveyard** lies within, with hundreds of elaborately decorated crosses, as well as a perfectly preserved six-story **round tower.** Built in the 11th or 12th century, it stands 100 feet high, with an entrance 25 feet above ground level.

The largest building at Glendalough is the substantially intact 7th- to 9th-century **cathedral,** where you can find the nave (small for a large church, only 30 feet wide by 50 feet long), chancel, and ornamental oolite limestone window, which may have been imported from England. South of the cathedral is the 11-foot-high Celtic **St. Kevin's Cross.** Made of granite, it's the best-preserved such cross on the site. **St. Kevin's Church** is an early barrel-vaulted oratory with a high-pitched stone roof. ☎0404/45325 ⊕*www.heritageireland.ie* 💷€5.30 🕙 *Mid-*

Mar.–mid-Oct., daily 9:30–6; mid-Oct.–mid-Mar., daily 9:30–5; last admission 45 min before closing.

WHERE TO STAY

$ 🏠**Derrymore House** Located on six acres of woodland above the Lower Lake in Glendalough Valley, Derrymore is one of the most serene B&B's in Wicklow. Wild goats, foxes, and rabbits roam freely around nearby woods. The Kelleher family are avid traditional musicians and music can be heard regularly in their home.

> **CURVES AHEAD**
>
> Getting to hallowed Glendalough from Dublin is easy, thanks to the St. Kevin's bus service. If you're driving, consider taking the scenic route along R155, but be prepared for awesome, austere mountain-top passes. Don't take this route if you're in a hurry, and don't expect a lot of signage—just concentrate on the glorious views.

The bedrooms are big and comfortable, with Victorian beds and en suite bathrooms. The full Irish breakfast is the perfect way to start the day; they can provide a packed lunch for walkers. ⊠ *Co. Wicklow* 🕾*0404/45493* ⊕*homepage.eircom.net/~derrymore* 🛏*5 rooms* △ *In-room: no a/c. In hotel: no elevator* ⊟*MC, V* ⏴◯⏵*BP.*

MOUNT USHER GARDENS

⓲ Settled into more than 20 acres on the banks of the River Vartry, the ★ gardens here were first laid out in 1868 by textile magnate Edward Walpole. Succeeding generations of the Walpole family further planted and maintained the grounds, which today have more than 5,000 species. The "Robinsonian" (that is, informal) gardener has made the most of the riverside locale by planting eucalypti, azaleas, camellias, and rhododendrons. The river is visible from nearly every place in the gardens; miniature suspension bridges bounce and sway underfoot as you cross the river. Near the entrance, you'll find a cluster of crafts shops (including a pottery workshop) as well as a bookstore and self-service restaurant. The twin villages of Ashford and Rathnew are to the south and east, and Newtownmountkennedy is to the north. ⊠*Ashford* 🕾*0404/40205* ⊕*www.dublingardens.com* 🎟*€7* ⊘*Mid-Mar.–Oct., daily 10:30–6.*

WHERE TO STAY & EAT

$$–$$$$ ✕🏠**Tinakilly House.** All aboard who's going aboard! William and Bee ★ Power have restored beautifully this Victorian-Italianate mansion, built in the 1870s by Captain Robert Halpin. The lobby has mementos of Captain Halpin and his nautical exploits, including paintings and ship models; Victorian antiques fill the house. Some bedrooms have four-poster beds, sitting areas, and views of the Wicklow landscape, the Irish Sea, or the lovely gardens on the 7-acre grounds. In the dining room ($$$–$$$$), expect to be served French-influenced Irish cuisine, with fresh vegetables from the garden. Brown and fruit breads are baked daily. ⊠*Rathnew, Co. Wicklow* 🕾*0404/69274* 🖨*0404/67806* ⊕*www.tinakilly.ie* 🛏*52 rooms, 5 suites* △ *In-room:*

no a/c. In-hotel: restaurant, bar, tennis court, public Internet ▬*AE, DC, MC, V* ⍩I*BP.*

WICKLOW TOWN

⑲ *26 km (16 mi) east of Glendalough on R763, 51 km (32 mi) south of Dublin on N11.*

At the entrance to the attractive, tree-lined Main Street of Wicklow Town—its name, from the Danish *wyking alo*, means "Viking meadow"—sprawl the extensive ruins of a 13th-century Franciscan friary.

The **friary** was closed down during the 16th-century dissolution of the monasteries, but its ruins are a reminder of Wicklow's stormy past, which began with the unwelcome reception given to St. Patrick on his arrival in AD 432. Inquire at the nearby **priest's house** (⊠*Main St.* ☎*0404/67196*) to see the ruins. The streets of Wicklow ran with blood during the 1798 rebellion when Billy Byrne, member of a wealthy local Catholic family, led rebels from south and central Wicklow against the forces of the Crown. Byrne was eventually captured and executed at Gallow's Hill just outside town. There is a memorial to him in the middle of Market Square.

The old **Wicklow's Historic Gaol,** just above Market Square, has been converted into a museum and heritage center, where it's possible to trace your genealogical roots in the area. Computer displays and life-size models tell the gruesome history of the jail, from the 1798 rebellion to the late 19th century. ⊠*Market Sq.* ☎*0404/61599* ⊕*www.wicklowshistoricgaol.com* ⌑*€7.30* ⊙*Mid–Mar.–Oct., daily 10–5.*

The **harbor** is Wicklow Town's most appealing area. Take Harbour Road down to the pier; a bridge across the River Vartry leads to a second, smaller pier, at the northern end of the harbor. From this end, follow the shingle beach, which stretches for 5 km (3 mi); behind the beach is the broad lough, a lagoon noted for its wildfowl.

Immediately south of the harbor, perched on a promontory that has good views of the Wicklow coastline, is the ruin of the **Black Castle.** This structure was built in 1169 by Maurice Fitzgerald, an Anglo-Norman lord who arrived with the English invasion of Ireland. The ruins (freely accessible) extend over a large area; with some difficulty, you can climb down to the water's edge.

Between one bank of the River Vartry and the road to Dublin stands the Protestant **St. Lavinius Church,** which incorporates various unusual details: a Romanesque door, 12th-century stonework, fine pews, and an atmospheric graveyard. The church is topped off by a copper, onion-shape cupola, added as an afterthought in 1771. ⌑*Free* ⊙*Daily 10–6.*

WHERE TO STAY & EAT

$–$$ ✕**Rugantinos.** The heated deck overlooking the river is best spot to enjoy the hearty comfort food at this cozy little eatery on the South Quay. The spicy chicken wings in a Louisiana hot sauce are a specialty and the steaks are big and char-grilled to perfection. The early-bird menu (before 7:30 PM) is a big draw. ⊠*Schooner House, South Quay* ☎*0404/61900* ▤*AE, MC, V* ⊘*No lunch.*

$$$$ ▥**Wicklow Head Lighthouse.** This 95-foot-high stone tower—first built in 1781—once supported an eight-sided lantern, and has been renovated by the Irish Landmark Trust as a lodging. It sleeps four to six people in two delightfully quirky octagonal bedrooms and one double sofa bed in the sitting room. The kitchen–dining room at the top has stunning views out over the coast. Don't forget anything in the car; it's a long way down. You rent the entire lighthouse, and you must book for at least two nights. The old lighthouse is just south of town on Wicklow Head, right next to the new, automated one. ⊠*Wicklow Head, Co. Wicklow* ☎*01/670–4733* 🖷*01/670–4887* ⊕*www.irishlandmark.com* ⇘*2 rooms sleep up to 6 people* △*In-room: no a/c, kitchen, no TV. In-hotel: no elevator* ▤*MC, V.*

$$ ▥**Grand Hotel.** A traditional Irish town hotel, the Grand doesn't really deserve that adjective but has a great location in the center of Wicklow and is known for its small-town quality service and atmosphere. Guest rooms are big, if a little over-decorated, and most have large windows, which flood the rooms with light. Wynne's bar is well known for its lively traditional-music sessions and also serves up excellent pub grub. ⊠*Wicklow Town, Co. Wicklow* ☎*0404/67337* 🖷*0404/69607* ⊕*www.grandhotel.ie* ⇘*33 rooms* △*In-room: Wi-Fi. In-hotel: restaurant, bar* ▤*AE, MC, V* ⎮○⎮*BP.*

AVONDALE HOUSE & FOREST PARK

❷⓿ *17 km (10½ mi) southwest of Wicklow Town on R752.*

Outside the quaint village of Rathdrum, on the west bank of the Avondale River, is the 523-acre **Avondale Forest Park.** Part of a then-burgeoning movement to preserve and expand the Irish forest, it was, in 1904, the first forest in Ireland to be taken over by the state. There's a fine 5½-km (3½-mi) walk along the river, as well as pine and exotic-tree trails. **Avondale House,** on the grounds of the park, resonates with Irish history. The house was the birthplace and lifelong home of Charles Stewart Parnell (1846–91), the "Uncrowned King of Ireland," the country's leading politician of the 19th century and a wildly popular campaigner for democracy and land reform. Parnell's house, built in 1779, has been flawlessly restored—except for the reception and dining rooms on the ground floor, which are filled with Parnell memorabilia, including some of his love letters to Kitty O'Shea and political cartoons portraying Parnell's efforts to secure home rule for Ireland. ☎*0404/46111* ⊕*www.heritageireland.com* 🎫*€6* ⊘*May–Aug., daily 11–6; mid-Mar.–Apr., Sept., and Oct., Tues.–Sun. 11–6.*

COUNTY KILDARE TO WEST WICKLOW

Of all the artistic delights that beckon both north and south of Dublin, few impress as much as the imposing country estates of County Wicklow. Here, during the "glorious eighteenth," great Anglo-Irish estates were built by English "princes of Elegance and Prodigality." Only an hour or two from Dublin, these estates— Russborough, Powerscourt, and Castletown are but three of the most famous—were profoundly influenced by the country villas of the great Italian architect Andrea Palladio, who erected the estates of the Venetian aristocracy along the Brenta Canal, only a short distance from the city on the lagoon. As in other parts of Ireland, the ancestral homes of the dwindling members of the Anglo-Irish ascendancy dot the landscape in the Pale.

Horse racing is a passion in Ireland—just about every little town has at least one betting shop—and County Kildare is the country's horse capital. Nestled between the basins of the River Liffey to the north and the River Barrow to the east, its gently sloping hills and grass-filled plains are perfect for breeding and racing Thoroughbreds. For some visitors, the fabled National Stud Farm just outside Kildare Town provides a fascinating glimpse into the world of horse breeding. And don't forget the fabled Japanese Gardens, adjacent to the National Stud, which are among Europe's finest. You may want to pick up this leg from Glendalough—the spectacular drive across the Wicklow Gap, from Glendalough to Hollywood, makes for a glorious entrance into Kildare. *One last note: consult Chapter 4, the Southeast, if you make it as far south as Castledermot, because Carlow and environs are only 10 km (6 mi) farther south.*

MAYNOOTH

㉑ *21 km (13 mi) southwest of Dublin.*

A few minutes south of the tiny Georgian town of Maynooth is the hamlet of Celbridge, official address to Ireland's largest country house, **Castletown** *(see "Treasure Hunt: The Anglo-Irish Georgian House," in this chapter).* After touring this grand mansion, head slightly to the west to find Maynooth's **St. Patrick's College.** What was once a center for the training of Catholic priests is now one of Ireland's most important lay universities. The visitor center chronicles the college's history and that of the Catholic Church in Ireland. Stroll through the university gardens—the Path of Saints or the Path of Sinners. At the entrance to St. Patrick's College are the ruins of Maynooth Castle, the ancient seat of the Fitzgerald family. The Fitzgeralds' fortunes changed for the worse when they led the rebellion of 1536 (it failed). The castle keep, which dates from the 13th century, and the great hall are still in decent condition. Mrs. Saults at 9 Parson Street has the key. ☎*01/628–5222* ⊕*www.nuim.ie* ✉*Free* ☉*St. Patrick's May–Sept., Mon.–Sat. 11–5, Sun. 2–6; guided tours every hr.*

WHERE TO STAY & EAT

$$$$ ✕⊡**Moyglare Manor.** Owner Nora Devlin has exuberantly decorated this majestic Georgian manor house with her renowned antiques collection. Velvet chairs, oil paintings, and thickly draped windows furnish the drawing room, and the grand bedrooms have four-poster canopy beds, roomy wardrobes, marble fireplaces, and comfortable, chintz-covered armchairs. Lamp-shaded wall sconces add a romantic touch to the formal dining room, where a wonderful game-dominated, five-course set menu ($$$$) is served. The manor, which occupies 16 pastoral acres dotted with sheep and cows, is 29 km (18 mi) west of Dublin. ✉*Maynooth, Co. Kildare* ☎*01/628–6351* 🖷*01/628–5405* ⊕*www. moyglaremanor.ie* ⬅*17 rooms* ♿*In-hotel: restaurant, bars, no elevator, public Internet* ▭*AE, DC, MC, V* ☉|*BP, MAP.*

STRAFFAN

㉒ *5 km (3 mi) southwest of Castletown House on R403, 25½ km (16 mi) southwest of Dublin.*

Its attractive location on the banks of the River Liffey, its unique butterfly farm, and the Kildare Hotel and Country Club—where Arnold Palmer designed the K Club, one of Ireland's most renowned 18-hole golf courses—are what make Straffan so appealing.

The only one of its kind in Ireland, the **Straffan Butterfly Farm** has a tropical house with exotic plants, butterflies, and moths. Mounted and framed butterflies are for sale. ☎*01/627–1109* ⊕*www.straffanbutterflyfarm.com* ✉*€7* ☉*June–Aug., daily noon–5:30.*

The **Steam Museum** covers the history of Irish steam engines, handsome machines used both in industry and agriculture—churning butter, threshing corn. There's also a fun collection of model locomotives. Engineers are present on "live steam days" every Sunday and bank holiday. The adjoining Lodge Park Walled Garden is included in the price and is perfect for a leisurely summer stroll. ✉*Lodge Park* ☎*01/627–3155* ⊕*www.steam-museum.com* ✉*€7.50* ☉*June–Aug., Wed.–Sun. 2–6; May and Sept., by appointment only.*

WHERE TO STAY & EAT

$$$$ ✕⊡**Kildare Hotel and Country Club.** Manicured gardens and the renowned Fodor'sChoice Arnold Palmer–designed K Club golf course surround this mansard-★ roof country mansion. The spacious, comfortable guest rooms are each uniquely decorated with antiques, and all have large windows that overlook either the Liffey or the golf course. (The rooms in the old house are best.) The hotel also has a leasing agreement with several privately owned cottages on the property. Chef Michel Flamme serves an

unashamedly French menu—albeit with the hint of an Irish flavor—at the Byerly Turk Restaurant ($$$$, named after a famous racehorse). The K Club—for the full scoop, see the Irish Greens chapter—had the honor of hosting the biennial Ryder Cup golf tournament in 2006. ⊠ *K Club, Co. Kildare* ☎ *01/601–7200* 🖷 *01/601–7299* ⊕ *www.kclub.ie* ⤳ *69 rooms, 26 apartments* ⌂ *In-room: safe, Wi-Fi. In-hotel: 3 restaurants, room service, bars, golf courses, pool, spa, laundry service, public Internet* ⊟ *AE, DC, MC, V* ⦿ *BP, MAP.*

$$$–$$$$ ✕🖼 **Barberstown Castle.** With a 13th-century castle keep at one end, an
Fodor'sChoice Elizabethan central section, a large Georgian country house at the other,
★   and a whole new modern wing, Barberstown represents 750 years of Irish history. Ask for a room in one of the old sections where turf fires blaze in ornate fireplaces in the three sumptuously decorated lounges. Reproduction pieces fill the bedrooms, some of which have four-poster beds. The Georgian-style restaurant ($$$$) serves creatively prepared French food, also on tap for special parties in the banqueting room of the castle keep. ⊠ *Co. Kildare* ☎ *01/628–8157* 🖷 *01/627–7027* ⊕ *www.barberstowncastle.ie* ⤳ *59 rooms* ⌂ *In-room: Wi-Fi. In-hotel: restaurant, bar* ⊟ *AE, DC, MC, V* ⦿ *BP, MAP.*

NAAS

㉓   *13 km (8 mi) south of Straffan on R407, 30 km (19 mi) southwest of Dublin on N7.*

The seat of County Kildare and a thriving market town in the heartland of Irish Thoroughbred country, Naas (pronounced nace) is full of pubs with high stools where short men (trainee jockeys) discuss the merits of their various stables.

Naas has its own small racecourse, but **Punchestown Racecourse** (⊠ *3 km [2 mi] south of Naas on R411* ☎ *045/897–704*) has a wonderful setting amid rolling plains, with the Wicklow Mountains a spectacular backdrop. Horse races are held regularly here, but the most popular event is the Punchestown National Hunt Festival in April.

BLESSINGTON

㉔   *10 km (6 mi) southeast of Naas on R410, 23 km (14 mi) southwest of Dublin on N181.*

Just outside the small village of Blessington are two of the marvels of Ireland: fabulous, art-filled, 18th-century **Russborough House** *(see "Treasure Hunt: The Anglo-Irish Georgian House" in this chapter)* and its adjacent **Poulaphouca Reservoir.** Known locally as the Blessington Lakes, Poulaphouca (pronounced pool-a-*fook*-a) is a large, meandering, artificial lake minutes from Russborough House that provides Dublin's water supply. You can drive around the entire perimeter of the reservoir on minor roads; on its southern end lies Hollywood Glen, a particularly beautiful natural spot.

Continued on page 210

TREASURE HUNT
THE ANGLO-IRISH GEORGIAN HOUSE

For an upclose look at the Lifestyles of the Rich and Famous, 18th-century style, nothing beats a visit to the great treasure houses of Castletown and Russborough. Set just a half-hour south of Dublin and located only 20 miles apart, they offer a unique peek through the keyhole into the extravagant world of Ireland's "Princes of Elegance and Prodigality."

When the Palladian architectural craze swept across England, the Anglo-Irish---determined not to be outdone---set about building palaces in their own domain that would be the equal of anything in the mother country. Both Castletown House and Russborough House set new benchmarks in symmetry, elegance, and harmony for the Georgian style, which reigned supreme from 1714 to 1830, and was named after the four Georges who successively sat on the English throne. This style was greatly influenced by the Italian architect, Andrea Palladio, who promulgated his Neoclassical villa designs in his *Four Books of Architecture.*

Published in 1570, this treatise created Palladian wannabees overnight from England to Virginia (including Thomas Jefferson, whose Monticello is Palladian in spirit).

Although Castletown remains the largest private house in Ireland, and Russborough has the longest façade of any domicile in the country, Georgian groupies know that the real treasures lie inside: ceilings lavishly worked in Italianate stuccowork, priceless Old Master paintings, and an intimate look at the glory and grandeur of the Anglo-Irish lords.

Above: Castletown House and its impressive grounds.

CASTLETOWN: A GEORGIAN VERSAILLES

Reputedly the inspiration for a certain building at 1600 Pennsylvania Avenue, Castletown remains the finest example of an Irish Palladian–style house.

In 1722, William Conolly (1662–1729) decided to build himself a house befitting his new status as the speaker of the Irish House of Commons and Ireland's wealthiest man. On an estate 20 km (12 mi) southwest of Dublin, he began work on Castletown, designed in the latest Neoclassical fashion by the Florentine architect Alessandro Galilei. As it turns out, a young Irish designer and Palladian aficionado by the name of Sir Edward Lovett Pearce (1699–1733) was traveling in Italy, met Galilei, and soon signed on to oversee the completion of the house. Inspired by the use of outlying wings to frame a main building—the "winged device" used in Palladio's Venetian villas— Lovett Pearce added Castletown's striking colonnades and side pavillons in 1724. It is said that between them a staggering total of 365 windows were built into the overall design of the house—legend has it that a team of four servants were kept busy year-round keeping them all clean.

Conolly died before the interior of the house was completed, and work resumed in 1758 when his great nephew Thomas, and more importantly, his 15-year-old wife, Lady Louisa Lennox, took up residence there. Luckily, Louisa's passion for interior decoration led to the creation of some of Ireland's most stunning salons, including the Print Room and the Long Gallery. Little of the original furnishings remain today, but there is plenty of evidence of the ingenuity of Louisa and her artisans, chief among whom were the Lafranchini brothers, master crafstmen who created the famous wall plasterwork, considered masterpieces of their kind. Rescued in 1967 by Desmond Guinness of the brewing family, Castletown was deeded to the Irish state and remains the headquarters for the Irish Georgian Society.

Above: Castletown House inside and out.
Center: The family crest of William Conolly.

Castletown House:

- ✉ Celbridge
- ☎ 01/628-8252
- 🌐 www.heritageireland.ie
- 💶 € 3.70
- 🕐 Open Easter.–Sept., weekdays 10-6, weekends 1-6; Oct., weekdays 10-5, Sun. 1-5.

TREASURE HUNT: THE ANGLO-IRISH GEORGIAN HOUSE

The Entrance Hall

Studded with 17th-century hunting scenes painted by Paul de Vos, this soaring white-on-white entryway showcases one of Ireland's greatest staircases. Also extraordinary are the walls festooned with plasterwork sculpted by the Brothers Lafranchini, famous for their stuccoed swags, flora, and portraits.

The Long Gallery

Upstairs at the rear of the house, this massive room—almost 80 feet by 23 feet—is the most notable of the public rooms. Hued in a vibrant cobalt blue and topped by a coved ceiling covered with Italianate stuccowork and graced by three Venetian Murano glass chandeliers, it is a striking exercise in the antique Pompeian style.

The Print Room

Smaller but even more memorable is the Print Room, the only example in Ireland of this elegant fad. Fashionable young women loved to glue black-and-white prints—here, looking like oversize postage stamps in a giant album—onto salon walls. This was the 18th-century forerunner of today's teens covering their walls with posters of rock-star icons.

Above left: The Grand Staircase. Upper right: 18th-century Italian engravings decorate the Print Room. Bottom right: A marble statue within the Long Gallery. Far right: Mahagony bureau made for Lady Louisa, circa 1760.

WHAT A WAY TO GO

"I do not get any idea of the beauty of my house if I live in it... only if I can gaze upon the house from far off," proclaimed Lady Louisa in 1821 of her beloved Castletown. In her late seventies, she had a tent built on the front lawn so she could study the house at her leisure. After one evening on the lawn she promptly caught a chill and died.

5 Other Great Georgian Houses:

Newbridge, County Dublin
Emo Court, County Laois
Westport House, County Mayo
Florence Court, County Fermanagh
Castle Coole, County Fermanagh

RUSSBOROUGH: A TEMPLE TO ART

An Irish Xanadu, Russborough House pulls out all the stops to achieve Palladian perfection.

Another conspicuously grand house rising seemingly in the middle of nowhere—actually the western part of County Wicklow—Russborough was an extravagance paid for by the wages of beer. In 1741, a year after inheriting a vast fortune from his brewer father, Joseph Leeson commissioned architect Richard Castle to build him a home of palatial stature, and was rewarded with this slightly over-the-top house, whose monumental 700-foot-long façade one-upped every other great house in Ireland. Following Castle's death, the project was taken over and completed by his associate, Francis Bindon. Today, the house serves as a showcase for the celebrated collection of Old Master paintings of Sir Alfred Beit, a descendant of the De Beers diamond family, who had bought and majestically restored the property in 1952.

Princely Magnificence

The first sight of Russborough draws gasps from visitors: a mile-long, beech-lined avenue leads to a distant embankment on which sits the longest house frontage in Ireland. Constructed of silver-gray Wicklow granite, the façade encompasses a seven-bay central block, from either end of which radiate semi-circular loggias connecting the flanking wings—the finest example in Ireland of Palladio's "winged device."

The interiors are full of grand period rooms that were elegantly refurbished in the 1950s by their new, moneyed owner under the eye of the legendary 20th-century decorator, Lady Colefax. The Hall is centered around a massive black Kilkenny marble chimneypiece and has a ceiling modeled after one in the Irish Parliament. Four 18th-century Joseph Vernet marine landscapes—once missing but

A look at the 700-foot façade of Russborough House. Bottom left: The grand Saloon. Above right: The Hall. Opposite, top: Drawing Room. Opposite: Vermeer's *Lady Writing a Letter*.

found by Sir Alfred—once again grace the glorious stucco moldings created to frame them in the Drawing Room. The grandest room, the Saloon, is famed for its 18th-century stucco ceiling by the Lafranchini brothers; fine Old Masters hang on walls covered in 19th-century Genoese velvet. The views out the windows take in the foothills of the Wicklow Mountains and the famous Poulaphouca reservoir in front of the house.

VERMEER, DIAMONDS, AND GANGSTERS

If it can be said that beer paid for the house, then diamonds paid for the paintings. Russborough House is today as famed for its art collection—and the numerous attempts, some successful, to steal it—as for its architecture. Credit for this must go to Sir Alfred Beit (1903–1994), nephew of the cofounder of De Beers Diamonds. One evening in 1974 while Alfred was enjoying a quiet dinner with his wife, the door burst open and in marched Rose Dugdale, an English millionaire's daughter turned IRA stalwart. Her gang "liberated" 19 of the Beit masterpieces, including Vermeer's fabled *Lady Writing a Letter*, hopefully to bargain for the release of two IRA members jailed in London. Once the

paintings were recovered a week later, Sir Alfred decided to donate 17 works to the National Gallery of Ireland. Alas, a week before the handing-over ceremony in 1986, Sir Alfred and his wife were again settling down to dine when in marched Martin Cahill, a.k.a. "The General," Dublin's most notorious underworld boss (and subject of three major movies). He made off with the Vermeer and 16 other paintings. They didn't bring him much luck though, as he was subsequently shot to death in Dublin by the IRA for his Ulster affiliations. Seven years of secret negotiations resulted in the return of the paintings, which now sit safely (we hope) in the National Gallery.

Russborough House:

- ✉ Off N81, Blessington
- ☎ 045/865–239
- 🎫 € 6
- 🕐 Open May–Sept., daily 10:30–5; April and Oct., Sun. 10:30–5.

STUCCADORES

Sounds better than plasterworkers, no? Baroque exuberance reigns in the house's lavishly ornamented plasterwork ceilings executed by the celebrated *stuccadores*, the Brothers Lafranchini, who originally hailed from Switzerland and worked in other great houses in Ireland, including Castletown. Their decorative flair adorns the Music Room and Library, but even these pale compared to the plasterwork done by an unknown artisan in the Staircase Hall—an extravaganza of whipped-cream moldings, cornucopias, and Rococo scrolls: "the ravings of a maniac," according to one 19th-century critic, who guessed that only an Irishman would have had the blarney to pull it off.

On the western shore of the lakes, the small market town of **Blessington,** with its wide main street lined on both sides by tall trees and Georgian buildings, is one of the most charming villages in the area. It was founded in the late 17th century, and was a stop on the Dublin–Waterford mail-coach service in the mid-19th century. Until 1932, a steam train ran from here to Dublin.

Beyond the southern tip of the Poulaphouca Reservoir, 13 km (8 mi) south of Blessington on N81, look for a small sign for the **Piper's Stones,** a Bronze Age stone circle that was probably used in a ritual connected with worship of the sun. It's just a short walk from the road.

You can take in splendid views of the Blessington Lakes from the top of **Church Mountain,** which you reach via a vigorous walk through Woodenboley Wood, at the southern tip of Hollywood Glen. Follow the main forest track for about 20 minutes and then take the narrow path that heads up the side of the forest to the mountaintop for about another half hour.

WHERE TO STAY & EAT

$$$$ ✕🏠**Rathsallagh House.** At the end of a long drive that winds through
Fodor'sChoice   a golf course, and set in 530 acres of parkland, is Rathsallagh House,
★   which came into being when low-slung, ivy-covered Queen Anne stables were converted into a farmhouse in 1798. Enveloping couches and chairs, fresh flower arrangements, large windows, fireplaces, and lots of lamps furnish the two drawing rooms. Large rooms have enchanting, pastoral names like Buttercup and Over Arch and the Yellow Room, with its claw-foot bath set in an alcove. Try to get a room overlooking the walled garden, where the scent of wildflowers wafts in through the beautiful French doors. The cozy Eagle Lodge bungalow has three bedrooms and sleeps up to six people. The outstanding haute-Irish dinner menu ($$$$) changes daily. Specialties include roast tenderloin of veal with fondant potato morel and hazelnut jus. ⊠*Dunlavin, Co. Wicklow* ☎*045/403–112* 🖷*045/403–343* ⊕*www.rathsallagh.com* 🛏*31 rooms, 1 bungalow* ⚐*In-room: Wi-Fi (some). In-hotel: restaurant, bar, golf course, tennis court, no elevator* 🖃*AE, DC, MC, V* ⊧❑*BP, MAP.*

THE CURRAGH

㉕ *8 km (5 mi) southwest of Naas on M7, 25½ km (16 mi) west of Poulaphouca Reservoir.*

The broad plain of the Curragh, bisected by the main N7 road, is the biggest area of common land in Ireland, encompassing about 31 square km (12 square mi) and devoted mainly to grazing.

This is Ireland's major racing center, home of the **Curragh Racecourse** (⊠*N7* ☎*045/441–205* ⊕*www.curragh.ie*); the Irish Derby and other international horse races are run here.

KILDARE TOWN

26 *5 km (3 mi) west of the Curragh on M7, 51 km (32 mi) southwest of Dublin via N7 and M7.*

Horse breeding is the cornerstone of County Kildare's thriving economy, and Kildare Town is the place to come if you're crazy about horses.

Right off Kildare's main market square, the **Silken Thomas** (☎045/522–232) pub re-creates an old-world atmosphere with open fireplaces, dark wood, and leaded lights; it's a good place to stop for lunch before exploring the sights here.

The Church of Ireland **St. Brigid's Cathedral** is where the eponymous saint founded a religious settlement in the 5th century. The present cathedral, with its stocky tower, is a restored 13th-century structure. It was partially rebuilt around 1686, but restoration work wasn't completed for another 200 years. The stained-glass west window of the cathedral depicts three of Ireland's greatest saints: Brigid, Patrick, and Columba. In pre-Christian times druids gathered around a sacred oak that stood on the grounds and from which Kildare (*Cill Dara*), or the "Church of the Oak," gets its name. Also on the grounds is a restored fire pit reclaimed from the time of Brigid, when a fire was kept burning—by a chaste woman—in a female-only fire temple. Interestingly, Brigid started the place for women, but it was she who asked monks to move here as well. ⊠*Off Market Sq.* ☎*No phone* 🖃*€1.50* ⊗*Daily 10–6.*

The 108-foot-high **round tower,** in the graveyard of St. Brigid's Cathedral, is the second highest in Ireland (the highest is in Kilmacduagh in County Galway). It dates from the 12th century. Extraordinary views across much of the Midlands await you if you're energetic enough to climb the stairs to the top. ☎*045/521–229* 🖃*€3* ⊗*May–Sept., daily 10–1 and 2–5.*

If you're a horse aficionado, or even just curious, check out the **National Stud Farm,** a main center of Ireland's racing industry. The Stud was founded in 1900 by brewing heir Colonel William Hall-Walker, and transferred to the Irish state in 1945. It's here that breeding stallions are groomed, exercised, tested, and bred. Spring and early summer, when mares have foals, are the best times to visit. The **National Stud Horse Museum,** also on the grounds, recounts the history of horses in Ireland. Its most outstanding exhibit is the skeleton of Arkle, the Irish racehorse that won major victories in Ireland and England during the late 1960s. The museum also contains medieval evidence of horses, such as bones from 13th-century Dublin, and some early examples of equestrian equipment. ⊠*½ km (1 mi) south of Kildare Town* ☎*045/521–617* ⊕*www.irish-national-stud.ie* 🖃*€10, includes entry to Japanese Gardens* ⊗*Mid-Feb.–mid-Nov., daily 9:30–5, mid-Nov.–Dec., daily 10–5.*

★ Adjacent to the National Stud Farm, the **Japanese Gardens** were created between 1906 and 1910 by the Stud's founder, Colonel Hall-Walker, and laid out by a Japanese gardener, Tassa Eida, and his son Minoru. The gardens are recognized as among the finest Asian gardens in the world, although they're more of an East–West hybrid than authentically Japanese. The Scots pine trees, for instance, are an appropriate stand-in for traditional Japanese pines, which signify long life and happiness. The gardens symbolically chart the human progression from birth to death, although the focus is on the male journey. A series of landmarks runs along a meandering path: the Tunnel of Ignorance (No. 3) represents a child's lack of understanding; the Engagement and Marriage bridges

> **HORSEFEATHERS!**
>
> Besides being nutty about horses, Colonel Walker may just have been more than a little eccentric—a believer in astrology, he had charts drawn up for his foals. Those with unfavorable predictions were sold right away. He even built the stallion stalls with lantern roofs to allow the moon and stars to work their magic on the equine occupants.

(Nos. 8 and 9) span a small stream; and from the Hill of Ambition (No. 13), you can look back over your joys and sorrows. It ends with the Gateway to Eternity (No. 20), beyond which lies a Zen Buddhist meditation sand garden. This is a worthwhile destination any time of the year, though it's particularly glorious in spring and fall. ⊠ *About 2½ km (1½ mi) south of Kildare Town, clearly signposted off Market Sq.* ☏ *045/521–617* ⊕ *www.irish-national-stud.ie* 🎟 *€10, includes entry to National Stud* ☉ *Mid-Feb.–mid-Nov., daily 9:30–5, mid-Nov.–Dec., daily 10–5.*

WHERE TO STAY & EAT

$$$ ╳▥ **Keadeen Hotel.** The luxurious spa and health center are the big attraction at this family-owned hotel on 10 acres of award-winning, flower-filled gardens. Light is a constant theme in the spacious bedrooms with pastel color finishings and big windows overlooking the lawns below. Giant wall murals in the Derby Room restaurant ($$–$$$) are dedicated to the true heroes of Kildare, those famous race horses. Don't miss the chance to take a dip in the ancient Roman-style pool; it's a real miniature sea of tranquillity. ⊠ *Newbridge, Co. Kildare* ☏ *045/431–666* 🖷 *045/434–402* ⊕ *www.keadeenhotel.ie* ⤳ *75 rooms* ♨ *In–room: Wi-Fi. In-hotel: restaurant, bar, pool, gym* ▭ *AE, DC, MC, V* ⍾*BP, MAP.*

DUBLIN ENVIRONS ESSENTIALS

TRANSPORTATION

BY BUS

Bus services link Dublin with the main and smaller towns in the area. All buses for the region depart from Dublin's Busaras, the central bus station, at Store Street. For bus inquiries, contact Bus Éireann. You can reach Enniskerry and the Powerscourt Estate by taking Dublin Bus No. 44 from the Dublin quays area. The No. 45 and No. 45a head to Bray and the No. 84 goes to Greystones from near Merrion Square.

St. Kevin's, a private bus service, runs daily from Dublin (outside the Royal College of Surgeons on St. Stephen's Green) to Glendalough, stopping off at Bray, Kilmacanogue, Roundwood, and Laragh en route. Buses leave Dublin daily at 11:30 AM and 6 PM (7 PM on Sunday); buses leave Glendalough weekdays at 7:15 AM and 4:30 PM (9:45 AM and 4:30 PM on Saturday, 9:45 AM and 5:30 PM on Sunday). One-way fare is €11; a round-trip ticket costs €18.

Bus Information Bus Éireann (☎ *01/836–6111* ⊕ *www.buseireann.ie*). **Dublin Bus** (☎ *01/873–4222* ⊕ *www.dublinbus.ie*). **St. Kevin's** (☎ *01/281–8119* ⊕ *www. glendaloughbus.com*).

BY CAR

The easiest and best way to tour Dublin's environs is by car, because many sights are not served by public transportation, and what service there is, especially to outlying areas, is infrequent. *(If you need to rent a car, see Car Rental in Dublin Essentials in Chapter 1.)* To visit destinations in the Boyne Valley, follow N3, along the east side of Phoenix Park, out of the city and make Trim and Tara your first stops. Alternatively, leave Dublin via N1/M1 toward Belfast. Try to avoid the road during weekday rush hours (8 AM–10 AM and 5 PM–7 PM); stay on it as far as Drogheda and start touring from there.

To reach destinations in County Kildare, follow the quays along the south side of the River Liffey (they are one-way westbound) to St. John's Road West (N7); in a matter of minutes, you're heading for open countryside. Avoid traveling this route during the evening peak rush hours, especially on Friday, when Dubliners are themselves making their weekend getaways.

To reach destinations in County Wicklow, N11/M11 is the fastest and most clearly marked route. The two more scenic routes to Glendalough are R115 to R759 to R755, or R177 to R755.

BY TRAIN

Irish Rail (Iarnród Éireann) trains run the length of the east coast, from Dundalk to the north in County Louth to Arklow along the coast in County Wicklow. Trains make many stops along the way; there are stations in Drogheda, Dublin (the main stations are Connolly Station and Pearse Station), Bray, Greystones, Wicklow, and Rathdrum. From Heuston Station, the Arrow, a commuter train service, runs westward to Celbridge, Naas, Newbridge, and Kildare Town. Contact Irish Rail for schedule and fare information.

Train Information **Irish Rail–Iarnod Éireann** (⊕ *www.irishrail.ie*). **Connolly Station** (⊠ *Amiens St., Northside, Dublin*). **Heuston Station** (⊠ *Victoria Quay and St. John's Road W, Dublin West, Dublin*). **Irish Rail** (☏ *01/836–6222*). **Pearse Station** (⊠ *Westland Row, Southside, Dublin*).

CONTACTS & RESOURCES

EMERGENCIES
Contacts **Ambulance, fire, police** (☏ *999*).

VISITOR INFORMATION
For information on travel in the Dublin environs and for help in making lodging reservations, contact one of the following Tourist Information Offices (TIOs) year-round: Dublin Tourism and Bord Fáilte, Dundalk, Trim, or Wicklow Town. In summer, temporary TIOs are open throughout the environs, in towns such as Arklow in County Wicklow, Drogheda and Dundalk in County Louth, and Kildare Town in County Kildare. **East Coast Midlands Tourism** is the department of Bord Fáilte directly involved for the Dublin Environs area and their Web site—*www.eastcoastmidlands.ie*—is very useful.

Tourist Information **Drogheda** (⊠ *Bus Éireann Depot* ☏ *041/983–7070*). **Dublin Tourism** (⊠ *Suffolk St.* ☏ *01/605–7700 or 01/602–4129*). **Dundalk** (⊠ *Jocelyn St.* ☏ *042/933–5484*). **Kildare** (⊠ *Market House* ☏ *045/521–240*). **Trim** (⊠ *Old Town Hall, Castle St.* ☏ *046/943–7227*). **Wicklow Town** (⊠ *Rialto House, Fitzwilliam Sq.* ☏ *0404/69117*).

The Midlands

Athlon Town, County Westmeath

WORD OF MOUTH

"In Cavan, we remember seeing a group of men who were clearly on a meal break, who started playing the spoons and toe-tap dancing along to a traditional music tape. It was a moment we treasure. Cavan doesn't make all the tour books, but it stays in our memory as a grand place."

–Danna

WELCOME TO THE MIDLANDS

TOP REASONS TO GO

★ **Stately Clonmacnoise:** Atmospheric and still spirit-warm, this great early Christian monastery survived Viking, Norman, and English invaders over the centuries.

★ **Green Mansions:** "The biggest farm in the world," the Midlands is also home to stately homes and gardens, including fairy-tale Tullynally Castle and Birr Castle.

★ **Hiking the Slieve Bloom Mountains:** Dip in and out of the 20-mi Slieve Bloom Trail, ideal hiking country for those with a yen to rise above their surroundings.

★ **Bord na Mona Bog Rail Tour:** In a region where bogland reigns supreme, this rail tour on a narrow-gauge railway stops at turf banks and archaeological finds.

★ **The Treasure House of Emo:** A quintessential landmark of 18th-century Palladian elegance, Emo—the former home of the earl of Portarlington—has a spectacular rotunda inspired by Rome's Pantheon.

1 **The Eastern Midlands.** Just an hour from Dublin, this region is essentially rich farmland but is studded with even richer sights: grand homes like **Emo Court, Belvedere House,** and **Tullynally Castle;** once-a-time-fied villages such as **Abbeyleix;** and the historic treats of **Fore Abbey** and **Locke's Distillery.** Leaving the ancient kingdom of Leinster, you come to two counties of Ulster: Cavan and Monaghan. Beyond Cavan Town you enter the heart of the Northern Lakelands, dotted with hundreds of beautiful lakes.

2 **The Western Midlands.** One of the corners of "hidden Ireland," this region is unblighted by crowds. While some of the country's most distinctive boglands are here, cultural treasures also beckon: stately **Birr Castle** and **Strokestown House,** postcard-perfect **Terryglass,** and the great early Christian monastery of **Clonmacnoise,** burial place of the kings of Tara.

Clonmacnoise Historic Site, County Offaly

Birr Castle, County Offaly

NORTHERN IRELAND

Monaghan

N2
N12

Upper
Lough Erne

N54

Clones

N3

MONAGHAN

N2

Butler's Bridge

Cavan Town

LEITRIM

Bellananagh

N55

CAVAN

N3

LONGFORD

Longford

Edgeworthstown

◆ Tullynally Castle

MEATH

N4

**Fore
◆ Abbey**

WESTMEATH

Mullingar

N55

Moate

**Belvedere
House ◆**

N6

N62

N80

Tullamore

KILDARE

OFFALY

N52

N80

Portarlington

Emo Court ◆

N7

Portlaoise

Roscrea

N7

LAOIS

N7

Abbeyleix

N8

KILKENNY

| 0 | | 25 mi |
| 0 | | 25 km |

GETTING ORIENTED

Perfect for the relaxed visitor who values the subtle over the spectacular, the flat, fertile plain at the center of Ireland is full of relatively undiscovered historic towns, abbey ruins, and grand houses. While just two hours from the chaotic rush of Dublin, Cork or Galway, the region is carpeted with countryside perfect for bicycling: no wonder stressed-out Dubliners love to head here to chill out.

Whispering Door, Clonmacnoise, County Offaly

THE MIDLANDS PLANNER

Getting Around

The roads of the Midlands offer an easier intro to Irish driving than the hairpin bends of West Cork and Connemara. Because the area has a decent network of main arteries and off-the-beaten-track byroads, a car may deliver the best option for covering the widest itinerary of curiosity.

Happily, bus and train routes in the region have improved greatly over the past two decades. Public transport services are regular through the main towns—Athlone, Portarlington, Abbeyleix, Nenagh, and Longford. Of course, you may have to transfer—give time and attention to the appropriate timetables when planning your jaunts.

However, the freedom of your own wheels will bring ample rewards in transporting you to the area's many hidden lakes and villages. Don't be surprised to round a bend only to confront a herd of sheep idly grazing with little hurry about them—do what the locals do, slow to a stop and wait for an opening in the woolly mass to occur. The same goes for cows. Refrain from honking your horn on these occasions—it will only confirm your status as an impatient tourist and, besides, the cows won't take a bit of notice.

Finding a Place to Stay

The Irish B & B still reigns supreme in the Midlands—farmhouses and homes geared to paying guests offering a direct contact with local families and the lore of their area. Time was when these kinds of accommodations veered to the spartan—not anymore. Good beds, decent heating, en suite bathrooms, and the legendary Irish breakfast are now the norm; broadband, 32-inch TVs, and computer games courtesy of the landlady's kids are often part of the bargain.

Although B & Bs may not offer the same kind of privacy as hotels, they still work delightfully well as the ultimate way to meet genuine Irish folk—a bird's-eye view into working families and the organized chaos of a country household. As commercial progress has blossomed in the Midlands, so, too, have the options in hotels, country houses, and cottage rentals increased. Pretty much every town now has more than one decent hotel—most with health centers and spa facilities.

From June to early September, tourism gets into a serious stride, bolstered by the many Irish families using their holiday homes and getaway cottages in the region. Finding accommodation is never a major problem—except for those weekends when a town is holding an annual music festival.

Tourist offices generally cope bravely with these seasonal influxes and if you arrive without local knowledge or reservations, there's rarely a problem that can't be solved with a few phone calls. At a rock concert in Abbeyleix a few years ago, we heard that four travelers found temporary lodgings in a convent, but that's another story altogether...

Heading Out on the Water

Whether it's water sports, fishing, or nature-watching you seek, Ireland's heartland is full of waterborne opportunities for the visitor. The entire Midlands region is littered with thousands of loughs (the Irish term for lakes) and rivers as well as an extensive canal system. Historically, these waterways were the lifeblood of Ireland's commercial life. In the 18th century, the construction of the Royal and Grand canals allowed the transport of food, livestock, and, of course, Guinness brew, from Dublin to the west. The Shannon, flowing majestically through the center of the region, is the longest river in Ireland and Britain and one of Europe's great waterways. Along the course of the river lie two major lakes, Lough Ree (north of Athlone) and Lough Derg (north of Limerick city). The best way to see the Shannon is by river cruiser. These boats are for hire at riverside towns like Carrick-on-Shannon in County Leitrim and Ballina in County Offaly. These "self-drive" boats accommodate up to 12 people and allow amateur mariners to take a relaxing meander along the river, with opportunities for fishing, swimming, and "refueling stops" at pretty shoreside villages like Terryglass, County Tipperary, where cozy pubs and excellent restaurants are the order of the day.

Other activities, like waterskiing and canoeing, are also popular along the Shannon. You can also navigate the Shannon-Erne Waterway, a canal linking the majestic expanse of Upper and Lower Lough Erne in Northern Ireland to the Shannon. The link, created in 1994, is Europe's longest (750 km [466 mi]) navigable leisure waterway. Or if you just want to take in the riverscape at leisure, opt for a cruise on the *Viking*, which sets sail from Athlone. The northern Midlands are known as Ireland's Lakelands. The area is a paradise for anglers (note that fishing gear and tackle are usually rentable) and many boast of having an entire lake to themselves. The loughs of Cavan and Monaghan are also famed for their huge and rather fearsome pike fish.

Dining & Lodging Price Categories (In Euros)

	¢	$	$$	$$$	$$$$
RESTAURANTS	under €8	€8–€15	€15–€22	€22–€29	over €29
HOTELS	under €80	€80–€130	€130–€180	€180–€230	over €230

Restaurant prices are for a main course at dinner. Hotel prices are for a standard double room in high season.

How's the Weather?

C'mon, this is Ireland, after all—a rain mac or windbreaker should never be far from your side. Though, in fairness, it must be said that the legendary "soft" weather has become noticeably more clement; since 2000, Ireland has been recording more hours of sunshine.

The incremental increase in the number of sunny days each year has prompted many philosophical discussions in Irish pubs on whether that itty-bitty hole in the ozone is really such a bad thing…

Activities

Dotted with historical monuments like Clonmacnoise, Fore Abbey, and the Rock of Dunamase, as well as many fine ancient architectural gems like Emo Court and Carriglas Manor, you'll never be more than 16 km/10 mi from ancient history.

Like all of Ireland's regions during the summer months, the Midlands rocks with festivals, literary gatherings, and small-town fairs—check out the tourist boards for listings.

If you just want to wander where your nose takes you for a few days, the relatively quiet roads, unpopulated countryside, and tucked-away vistas around the Slieve Blooms will deliver many quiet rewards.

Updated by
John Daly

IRISH SCHOOL CHILDREN WERE ONCE taught to think of their country as a saucer, with mountains edging the rim and a dip in the middle. The dip is the Midlands—or the Lakelands, as it's sometimes referred to—and this often-overlooked region comprises nine counties: Cavan, Laois (pronounced leash), Westmeath, Longford, Offaly, Roscommon, Monaghan, Leitrim, and Tipperary. Ask people from other parts of Ireland what the purpose of the Midlands is and they will jest that the region exists simply to hold the rest of the country together.

Indeed, the Midlands is sometimes looked upon with disdain by the Irish people, a few of whom consider the area dull and mundane (the worst of offenses in Ireland). The perception is a bit true: the flat plains of the Midlands being the kind of terrain you rush through on the way to someplace else, and with no major city in the region (Dublin lies to the east, Galway and Limerick to the west, and Cork to the south), it remains a quiet and geographically unspectacular place. Night owls should probably keep going—the wildest thing in these parts is the wind.

But that is precisely why many travelers consider the Midlands a gem in the making. For when it comes to studying how Ireland gets on with its daily life, there are few better places. Here, a town's main hotel is usually one of its prime social centers and can be a good place from which to partake of local life. If you miss out witnessing a wedding reception, First Communion supper, or meeting of the Lion's Club, you can still get to know the locals simply by walking along a village's main street. Happily so, since there are plenty of folks who have nothing to do but be pleasant. Here, the pace of life is slower, every neighbor's face is familiar, and there are plenty of minor roads linking the more scenic areas—and if you're in no particular hurry, these are the ones to take. Spend enough time in the region and you might even get to recognize the difference between a Cavan twang and a Tipperary brogue.

The people and the slow pace of life here make the Midlands a throwback to the Ireland of 20 years ago—the hurry and bustle of modernity found elsewhere in the Celtic Tiger is still blessedly absent. Long the butt of jokes for their supposed frugality (like the one about the Cavan farmer who eats his dinner out of a drawer so he can hide it quickly should neighbors arrive unexpectedly), Midlanders have long met big-city ridicule with breezy nonchalance. Visitors, and the prosperity they bring to the local economy, are still prized in these flatland counties. The welcome is genuine, and the regional pride is abundantly evident once you get beyond those initial shy, self-deprecating shrugs.

The tourist sun also shines brightly on the region because of its notable cultural highlights. Among them are Clonmacnoise, Ireland's most important monastic ruins; historic towns with age-old industries, such as lace making and crystal making; the gorgeous gardens of Birr Castle; and some of Ireland's finest Anglo-Irish houses, including Strokestown Park House, Emo Court, and probably Ireland's most historically delightful hotel, Castle Leslie. As for scenic pleasures, this region of the country has its fair share of Ireland's 800 bodies of water. Speckling this lush countryside, many of these lakes were formed by glacial action some 10,000 years ago. Because of all the water, much of the landscape is blanket bog, a unique ecosystem that's worth exploring. The River Shannon, one of the longest rivers in Europe and the longest in the British Isles, bisects the Midlands from north to south, piercing a series of loughs (lakes): Lough Allen, Lough Ree, and Lough Derg. The Royal Canal and the Grand Canal cross the Midlands from east to west, ending in the Shannon north and south of Lough Ree.

These days, the Midlands is being "recolonized" by young couples unable to afford the high property prices in Dublin: Small towns in the region have expanded with new housing for city commuters who make daily two-hour round-trip journeys to work. In a region historically depopulated by emigration, the influx of new residents has reenergized many of the small towns. Eateries, farmers' markets, and renovated pubs are the order of the day as touches of big city cosmopolitanism take root. On weekends, Midland towns and villages are hives of activity as young families make their homes in this pastoral, and infinitely more affordable, region beyond the Pale. They reckon if Charlotte Brontë spent her honeymoon here and Anthony Trollope settled in one of the region's villages to write two of his novels, it's good enough for them.

EXPLORING THE MIDLANDS

This chapter is organized into two Midlands sections: eastern and western. The first can be easily covered in an extended visit to the Midlands region, as it starts in Abbeyleix, County Laois and charts a course almost due north to Northern Ireland. But not quite: the tour makes a loop to head back southward, linking up with the second tour. This includes sights west, which means they can be easily visited if you fly into Shannon and begin your explorations in the western half of the country.

THE EASTERN MIDLANDS

The eastern fringe of the Midlands is about an hour's drive from Dublin, and a visit to the area could easily be grafted onto a trip to the Dublin environs. In spite of its proximity to the capital, or perhaps because of it, this area is a bit removed from the regular tourist trail and is a source of constant surprises. Unspoiled Georgian villages, ruined castles, and quaint "towns-that-time-forgot" dot the landscape. There are also plenty of opportunities for hill walking, horseback riding, and other outdoor pursuits. Fans of stately homes are in for a treat, as Emo Court and Gardens, Charleville Forest Castle, Belvedere House Gardens, and Tullynally Castle await them.

The Eastern Midlands fan out from the central point of Mullingar. With richer farmland than is found in the northern area of the Midlands, the eastern region tends toward agriculture. But the Dublin commuter culture means that you're as likely to be delayed on a back road

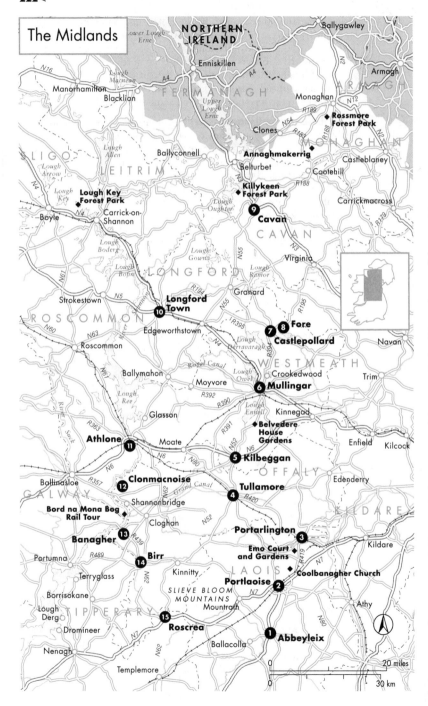

The Midlands

by a badly parked BMW as by a slow-moving tractor on its way home from the dairy.

ABBEYLEIX

❶ *99 km (61 mi) southwest of Dublin.*

> ### WRECKED RUGS
>
> The carpets for the ill-fated *Titanic* were woven at a now defunct carpet factory in Abbeyleix.

"One of the most pleasing villages in Leinster, with each cottage having a useful garden!" Thus spoke J. M. Brewer, a noted 19th-century writer, of Abbeyleix in 1826. Today it happily remains one of the most elegant small towns in Ireland, having retained its charming Georgian ambience and its broad main street, which is lined with well-appointed, stone-cut buildings and original shop fronts in the traditionally ornate Irish style. The entire tree-lined village was built in the 18th century, on the orders of the Viscount de Vesci, to house servants and tradesmen working on his nearby estate. Many town houses and vernacular buildings date from the 1850s, but more recent buildings, including the Market House, erected in 1906, and the Hibernian Bank, from 1900, contribute greatly to the town's tranquil and refined character.

★ Don't miss **Morrissey's Pub and Grocery Store,** which has been a working public house since 1775. One of Ireland's best-loved drinking emporiums, it has a dark, wood-panel interior furnished with antique bar fittings. Customers can warm themselves by an ancient potbelly stove. Until 2005 this award-winning establishment still functioned as a shop, and while it retains its stocks of groceries, they are no longer for sale. An evocative time capsule, it serves as a reminder of times when you could purchase a pound of butter, the newspaper, and cattle feed while enjoying the obligatory pint of Guinness. ✉ *Main St.* ☎ *0502/863–1281.*

The **Heritage House,** the former North Boys School, has fascinating informative displays on the de Vesci family and the history of Abbeyleix. The school was originally constructed for the education of Catholics (at the other end of the town you'll find the South School, built for Protestants). Also accessible through the Heritage House, ask to see the original Sexton's House (no extra charge), which boasts a stylish interior from the turn of the 19th century. ✉ *Top of town* ☎ *0502/863–1653* ⊕ *www.abbeyleixheritagetown.com* 🎫 *€3* 🕓 *Apr.–Sept., weekdays 9–5, weekends 1–5; Oct.–Mar. weekdays 9–5.*

Ballinakill, a pretty Georgian village about 5 km (3 mi) south of Abbeyleix, contains the **Heywood Gardens,** designed by the English architect Sir Edward Lutyens in the early 20th century within an existing 18th-century park. The Lutyenses' house burned down, but the gardens, with landscaping most likely attributable to the famed Gertrude Jeckyll, are worth a detour. Guided tours are available through this gardener's paradise where a formal lawn flanked by traditional herbaceous borders leads to a sunken Italian garden. ⊠ *Ballinakill* ☎ *0502/863–3563* ⊕ *www.heritageireland.ie* ⊠ *Free* ☉ *Daily 9–dusk.*

WHERE TO STAY & EAT

$$ ✕⊡ **Preston House.** This ivy-clad Georgian building on the main Cork–Dublin road was a schoolhouse until the 1960s. Now it's a popular lunch and coffee stop by day, renowned for good traditional home cooking. By night the restaurant ($$–$$$, closed Sun. and Mon.) takes on a more formal aspect. Owner Allison Dowling offers a menu featuring hearty, heartwarming dishes such as honey roast duck with plum and port sauce and sautéed venison with creamed potatoes and red currants. The spacious guest rooms, furnished with solid Victorian antiques, afford views of the long back gardens and fields beyond. ⊠ *Main St., Co. Laois* ☎ *0502/31432* ⇥ *4 rooms* ⬧ *In-room: no a/c. In-hotel: restaurant, no elevator, some pets allowed* ☰ *MC, V* ⭘ *BP.*

$ ⊡ **Foxrock Inn.** A friendly red setter by the name of Grouse greets new arrivals at this modest but friendly guesthouse in the picturesque heart of the County Laois countryside. The main attraction of this inn, set in the tiny village of Clough, is the genuinely warm welcome extended by its owners, Sean and Marian Hyland. The enthusiastic young couple can bring you up-to-date on the 200-year history of the inn and adjacent pub, advise you on hiking in the Slieve Bloom Mountains, and organize golf and angling packages. Traditional music on Tuesday nights in summer is a big local draw. Rooms are plain but clean and comfortable. Simple, home-cooked dinners and packed lunches are available. Clough is 8 km (5 mi) west of Abbeyleix (signposted off the R434 road to Borris-in-Ossary). ⊠ *Clough, Ballacolla, Co. Laois* ☎ *0502/873–8637* ⊕ *www.foxrockinn.com* ⇥ *5 rooms* ⬧ *In-room: no a/c, no phone, no TV. In-hotel: restaurant, public Internet, no elevator* ☰ *AE, V* ⭘ *BP.*

SHOPPING

The Rathdowney Designer Outlet (⊠ *Rathdowney* ☎ *0505/48900* ⊕ *www. rathdowneyoutlet.ie*) would not look out of place in the American Midwest and offers the usual mix of top labels at easy-on-the-pocket prices. The extraordinary thing about this huge indoor mall is its location. The investors behind the venture adopted a "build it and they will come" approach. It is (as the Irish would say) in the "back of beyond," on the outskirts of a sleepy country town in County Laois. It's perfect for the addicted label hunter and also has attractions—craft and produce sales, occasional circus shows, a kids' active-play center—for nonshoppers curious to experience a surreal slice of pure Americana in rural Ireland. To get here from Abbeyleix, follow R433 west for 19 km (12 mi).

PORTLAOISE

❷ *14 km (9 mi) north of Abbeyleix.*

Near the heart of County Laois, the rich farmland south and west of Portlaoise, an hour by train or car from Dublin, is one of Ireland's

One of the joys of an Irish vacation can be a splurge at a castle-hotel, especially if it is enjoyed at Dromoland, a jewel set in County Clare.

(above) Listen for ancient echoes on the windswept Aran Islands. (opposite page, top) Enjoy close encounters with wild ponies in County Limerick. (opposite page, bottom) The River Lee Foot Bridge in Cork City is a handsome landmark.

(top) Even if you order only an Evian, a visit to a Dublin pub—or two or three—is a must. (bottom) A cruise along the Connemara coast can take you to Inis Mór, one of the Aran Islands. (opposite page) Imagine yourself the squire of Castletown House, Celbridge.

(top) Muckross House in Killarney National Park now houses the Kerry Folklife Centre. (bottom left) Relentlessly picturesque Adare has some storybook cottages. (bottom right) Dublin is noted for its 18th-century Georgian doorways.

(top) The sunny colors of these houses in Cork brighten even the rainiest days. (bottom) Span the centuries within a few blocks of Dublin Castle.

Begorra! It's the Strawberry Festival in Enniscorthy, Wexford.

EATING WELL IN THE MIDLANDS

An old Irish joke concerns the tourist seeking sustenance in a country pub. "Toasted ham and cheese special" offers the barkeep as the total menu available to the famished visitor. "Wouldn't you have anything just a bit more exotic?" inquires the timid tourist. After a thoughtful pause, the barkeep replies: "Well, I suppose I could get the wife to take out the cheese."

Things have changed greatly in Ireland's food scene in tandem with EU membership and the more demanding customer. Those previously unheard words—tapas, latte, coriander, pesto, plus a whole lexicon of culinary adventure—have now become the norm across the country as a new breed of innkeeper responds to a changed cultural landscape.

The Midland town of Birr is known as the "belly button of Ireland" because of its central location, not because this region is known as a culinary hot spot. Nevertheless, the good news is that, as throughout Ireland, the economic boom that started in the 1990s has improved the standards and variety of the area's restaurants. Indeed, the Irish

Food Board (An Bord Bia) has been making efforts to promote the use of locally produced and seasonal produce through its Féile Bia program, so keep an eye out for eateries that have been awarded a Féile Bia certificate.

Happily, there are still restaurants that will pull you off the street, especially those offering beef—Mullingar, in the center of the Midlands, is the beef capital of Ireland. The more upmarket restaurants usually serve fish freshly caught in one of the innumerable lakes that dot the landscape. By and large, however, the mainstay of the Midlands culinary scene remains the traditional carvery—a buffet-style "meat and two veg" dinner. Those not worried about their waistline will also enjoy the traditional breakfast of the region. The "Full Irish" or "Ulster Fry," as it's known in the northern part of the region, is about as hearty as breakfasts come—the standard version consists of eggs, bacon, sausages, white and black puddings, and grilled tomato with a side order of Irish soda bread, and all washed down with a nice cup of tea. Not surprisingly, after all that, many travelers even skip lunch.

undiscovered gems. Golf, fishing, hiking, and horseback riding are traditional sports hereabouts, and the development of the Grand Canal for recreational purposes is adding to the area's attractions. Explore the pretty villages and romantic, ivy-covered ruins by car, or follow one of the many hiking trails.

Portlaoise's name is derived from the Irish for "Fort of Laois" and refers to the town's strife-filled history. In terms of its architecture, it's rather eclectic—it feels as if bits of other towns were picked up and dropped randomly onto the site. Once best known for having Ireland's highest-security prison, which housed the IRA's most notorious members during the 1970s and '80s and still looms over the town, Portlaoise is undergoing a renaissance. The main street, which once formed part of the main Dublin–Cork road, is now largely given over to pedestrians;

pubs and restaurants are beginning to flourish; and the thriving Dunamaise Arts Centre adds an extra dash of culture.

At the Tourist Information Office in Portlaoise you can pick up a map of the **Laois Heritage Trail** (⊕ *www. laoistourism.ie/HeritageTrail.asp*), a signposted, daylong drive on quiet back roads that takes in 13 heritage sites, ranging from Abbeyleix to Emo Court. The circular trail starts in Borris-in-Ossary on N7.

TRAVEL TIP
Staying in Portlaoise gives you a good base from which to explore the surrounding countryside and helps you to avoid the heavy traffic that can clog the main N7 Dublin road.

A dramatic 150-foot-high limestone outcrop, the famous **Rock of Dunamase** dominates the landscape east of Portlaoise. For this reason, it was used as a military stronghold. As far back as AD 140 its occupants kept watch against marauders, and it was fought over in turn by the Vikings, Normans, Irish, and English. Today it's crowned by the ruins of a 12th-century castle, once home to Diarmuid MacMurrough, king of Leinster, who precipitated the Norman invasion when he invited the famed and feared Norman leader Strongbow to Ireland to marry his daughter, whose dowry included the Rock. Some of the castle's thick walls still stand. The main reason for visiting the Rock today is to take the short walk to its summit to enjoy the view of the Slieve Bloom Mountains to the north and the Wicklow Mountains to the south. ⊠ *5 km (3 mi) east of Portlaoise on N80 Stradbally Rd..*

WHERE TO STAY & EAT

$$-$$$ ✕ **The Lemon Tree.** Although on Portlaoise's main street, this spot is its best-kept culinary secret. It combines an informal atmosphere with modern-but-cozy surroundings. Owner Kevin Hennessy used to be front-of-house supremo at swanky Dublin eatery Shanahan's on the Green, and has here managed to import the same style without the snobbery. Starters might include duck confit with hoisin sauce; many enjoy the prime Irish Angus sirloin for the main course. Lunch is available only to groups, by advance reservation. ⊠ *Main St.* ☎ *0502/866-2200* ⊕ *www.grellandelaney.com/lemontree* ▤ *AE, MC, V* ⊗ *No dinner Mon.*

$-$$ ✕ **Kingfisher.** In the town center, this is a particularly lively and stylish
★ spot. The high-ceiling room was once a banking hall, but now its softly lighted walls glow with warm terra-cotta tones, the perfect complement to the slightly spicy Punjabi cuisine. *Pappadams* (crunchy lentil-flour breads) and condiments appear on the table before you order, and the friendly staff in traditional dress can guide you expertly through the long menu. Dishes vary from mild and creamy *kormas* (curried meat dishes) to fresh cod with a mild blend of spices and lemon juice to chicken "cooked with angry green chilies." Last orders for dinner are taken as late as 11:30 PM, so this is definitely the place to go when your tummy rumbles late on a summer's eve. Check out their very snazzy

Web site. ✉ *Old AIB Bank, Main St.* ☎ *0502/62500* ⊕ *www.kingfish-errestaurant.com* ⊟ *AE, MC, V* ⊘ *No lunch Sat.–Tues.*

$ ⬚ **Ivyleigh House.** Owners Dinah and Jerry Campion say they like to
★ give their guests "the best of everything," and that maxim is certainly in
evidence the minute you step inside this elegant Georgian town house
next to the Portlaoise railway station. Open fires, antiques, and sumptuously cozy sofas await you in the beige-on-brown, wood-accented
sitting room. Upstairs, luxurious drapes grace the sash windows of
the spacious bedrooms, most of which are done in dramatic hues like
pink and emerald. A virtual avalanche of plump cushions scattered on
your antique bed reinforces the tone of rest and relaxation. Guests find
it hard to choose from all the goodies on the scrumptious breakfast
menu. The bread is home-baked, the food is locally produced, and
no one can resist the Cashel Blue cheese cakes with mushrooms and
tomatoes. Room TVs are available by request. ✉ *Bank Pl., Portlaoise,
Co. Laois* ☎ *0502/862–2081* ⎙ *0502/866–3343* ⊕ *www.ivyleigh.com*
⤳ *6 rooms* ⚘ *In-room: no a/c, no TV, dial-up. In-hotel: no-smoking
rooms, no elevator* ⊟ *MC, V* ⧉ *BP.*

NIGHTLIFE & THE ARTS

★ Also known as Turley's bar, the canal-side **Anchor Inn** (✉ *Grand Canal,
near Stradbally, Vicarstown* ☎ *0502/25454*), 10 km (6 mi) east of Portlaoise on N80, is popular for its lively Monday night traditional-music
sessions, which start around 9. Sessions take place more frequently
in summer. Fishing, boating, and canal-bank walks are all accessible from this location. The lively **Dunamaise Arts Centre** (✉ *Main St.*
☎ *0502/63355* ⊕ *www.dunamaise.ie*) has a 240-seat theater, an art
gallery, and a friendly coffeehouse (open daily 8:30–5:30). You may
catch a professional production on tour or a local amateur show. The
exhibition space displays the work, usually of a surprisingly high standard, of contemporary Irish artists. It's built into the back of the 18th-
century stone courthouse on Church Street in a space that used to be
the town jail.

SPORTS & THE OUTDOORS

The **Heritage Golf & Heritage Club** (✉ *Killenard* ☎ *0502/45500*), just off
the main Dublin-Cork road, is an 18-hole course. This parkland championship course was codesigned by Seve Ballesteros and features challenging doglegs, as well as five lakes and a number of streams, to keep
those fond of dodging water traps happy.

PORTARLINGTON

➌ *13 km (8 mi) northeast of Portlaoise.*

Built on the River Barrow in the late 17th century, Portarlington was
originally an English settlement. Later, a Huguenot colony developed
here, and French surnames are still common in the area. Some good
examples of Georgian architecture can be seen in the town.

A quintessential landmark of Irish Palladian elegance lies just 7 km
★ (4½ mi) south of Portarlington. **Emo Court and Gardens** is one of the

finest large-scale country houses near Dublin that is open to the public. Even if you elect to skip over much of the Midlands, try to tack on a visit to Emo, especially if you're in Kildare or Wicklow counties. To come upon the house from the main drive, an avenue lined with magisterial Wellingtonia trees, is to experience one of Ireland's great treasure-house views. Begun in 1790 by James Gandon, architect of the Custom House and the Four Courts in Dublin, Emo (the name derives from the Italian version of the original Irish name Imoe) is thought to be Gandon's only domestic work matching the grand scale of his Dublin civic buildings. Construction continued on and off for 70 years, as family money troubles followed the untimely death of Emo's original patron and owner, the first earl of Portarlington.

In 1996 Emo's English-born owner donated the house to the Irish nation. The ground-floor rooms have been beautifully restored and decorated and are prime examples of life on the grand scale. Among the highlights are the entrance hall, with trompe l'oeil paintings in the apses on each side, and the library, which has a carved Italian-marble mantel with putti frolicking among grapevines. But the showstopper, and one of the finest rooms in Ireland, is the domed rotunda—the work of one of Gandon's successors, the Irish architect William Caldbeck—inspired by the Roman Pantheon. Marble pilasters with gilded Corinthian capitals support the rotunda's blue-and-white coffered dome. Emo's 55 acres of grounds include a 20-acre lake, lawns planted with yew trees, a small garden (the Clocker) with Japanese maples, and a larger one (the Grapery) with rare trees and shrubs. ⊠ *Emo* 🕾 *0502/26573* ⊕ *www.heritageireland.ie* ⊠ *Gardens free, house €2.90* ☉ *Gardens daily 9–dusk, house mid-June–mid-Sept., Tues.–Sun. 10–5; last tour at 4:30.*

★ **Coolbanagher Church,** the familiar name for the exquisite Church of St. John the Evangelist, was, like Emo Court and Gardens, designed by James Gandon. On view inside are Gandon's original 1795 plans and an elaborately sculpted 15th-century font from an earlier church that stood nearby. Adjacent to the church is Gandon's mausoleum for Lord Portarlington, his patron at Emo. The church is open daily spring through autumn; at other times, ask around in the tiny village for a key, or at the rectory, a 10-minute drive away. ⊠ *8½ km (5 mi) south of Portarlington on R419* 🕾 *0502/24143 rectory* ⊠ *Free* ☉ *May–Oct., daily 9–6.*

WHERE TO STAY

$$ 🏠 **Roundwood House.** There's a dreamlike beauty to this place. As you
Fodor'sChoice   arrive, a dark tree-lined avenue suddenly opens up to reveal a dramati-
★   cally gorgeous Palladian villa. A flock of white geese and a collection of friendly dogs form the welcoming party to this chateauesque mansion, which is nestled on the slopes of the Slieve Bloom Mountains amid 18 acres of mature woodland and pasture. Antique family portraits of the builders, the Sharps—a prominent Quaker family whose wealth derived from the mid-1600s woolen industry—adorn the walls of the curio-filled drawing room. The bedrooms in the main house are elegant, airy, and painted in dramatic greens, yellows, and blues. If you prefer a cozier option, there are several rooms in the adjacent 17th-

century Old House, or on the grounds in the picturesque Coach House and Forge. Tiniest of all is the Cottage, a stone charmer whose original tenants may have been Hansel and Gretel, at least according to hosts Frank and Rosemarie Kennan, who often share your table at dinner. The house is 5 km (3 mi) from Mountrath on the scenic road to Kinnitty. ⊠*Mountrath, Co. Laois* ☎*0502/873–2120* 📠*0502/873–2711* ⊕*www.roundwoodhouse.com* ➪*10 rooms* ♿*In-room: no a/c, no phone, no TV. In-hotel: restaurant, no elevator, public Internet* ☱*AE, DC, MC, V* ❑*BP.*

¢ 🏨**Eskermore House.** In summer, a delightful display of rambling roses adorns the doorway of this charming farmhouse. The old-world quirks of these lovely lodgings also include a chiming grandfather clock and an organ in the sitting room for musically gifted guests (those without a talent for tickling the ivory are gently urged to refrain). Located 8 km (5 mi) north of Portarlington on R402, this is a good base for hiking in the Slieve Bloom Mountains. The guest rooms are simply but comfortably furnished and face south over a beech tree–lined avenue and semi-wild gardens. The sitting room has an open turf fire, a piano, and cable TV; room TVs are available on request. Host Ann Mooney will prepare a wholesome dinner with advance notice. ⊠*Mount Lucas, Edenderry, Co. Offaly* ☎*057/935–3079* ⊕*www.eskermore.com* ➪*3 rooms* ♿*In-room: no a/c, no phone. In-hotel: no elevator, public Internet, some pets allowed* ☱*MC, V* ❑*BP.*

TULLAMORE

❹ *27 km (17 mi) northwest of Portarlington.*

The county seat of Offaly, Tullamore is a bustling market town that has really begun to thrive since Ireland's "Celtic Tiger" boom took off in the mid-1990s. Its most famous native is Ireland's finance minister Brian Cowen and the people here share his down-to-earth approach to life. The town's historical success was based on its location on the Grand Canal, one of Ireland's most important trading links during the 18th and 19th centuries. One relic of its former splendor is found on the southwestern edge of town, where, if you take the road heading to Birr from the center of Tullamore, you'll find a storybook vision in splendid Tin Soldier Fortress style: **Charleville Forest Castle.** Perhaps the finest neo-Gothic, British-style 19th-century castle in Ireland, its Flag Tower and turrets rise above its domain of 30 acres of woodland walks and gardens. The Georgian–Gothic Revival house was built as a symbol of English might triumphing over French force (the French revolutionary forces, to be exact, who had become a little too cozy with the Irish locals). In fact, the floor plan is even modeled on the Union Jack. Commissioned by Baron Tullamore and dating from 1812, the castle is a rural example of the work of architect Francis Johnston, who was responsible for many of Dublin's stately Georgian buildings. The interiors are somewhat the worse for wear—most are gigantic chambers with a few sticks of furniture—but the William Morris–designed dining room still has its original stenciled wallpaper. Guided tours of the interior are available. Descended through the Bury family, fortunes depleted and without heirs, the castle became an orphan in the 1960s but has been slowly restored. The surrounding forest is said to have been the haunting grounds of the ancient Druids. ⊠*1½ km (1 mi) outside Tullamore on N52 to Birr* ☎*057/972–1279* ⊕*www.charlevillecastle.com* ✉*€16 for one adult or couple. Additional members of same party €6* ⊗ *May, weekends 2–5; June–Sept., Wed.–Sun. 2–5; Oct.–Apr., by appointment.*

WHERE TO STAY

$ 🏠**Annaharvey Farm.** A loving conversion of an old-world grain barn into an elegant accommodation has marked the past several years for innkeepers Lynda and Henry Deverell. Just 6 km (4 mi) outside of Tullamore town on the Portarlington road, this family farmhouse dedicated to all things equestrian contains pitch-pine floors, massive roof beams, and open fireplaces. Guest rooms are cozy and comfy and decorated with equestrian prints. It matters not a bit, however, if your interest doesn't run to things horsey—the area has all manner of walking, cycling, and golfing opportunities, and Clonmacnoise and Birr Castle are just a short drive away, making Annaharvey an ideal Midlands touring base. The inn bustles with Irish families and many young ladies leading their treasured ponies for canters around the open fields. Meals (available to guests only) are served in the Bistro; most of the produce is grown locally. ⊠*Tullamore, Co. Offaly* ☎*057/934–3544* 📠*057/934–3766* ⊕*www.annaharveyfarm.ie* 📞*7 rooms* ⚘*In-room: no a/c, dial-up. In-hotel: no elevator* 🟰*MC, V* ⊗*Closed Dec. and Jan.*

SPORTS & THE OUTDOORS

BOATING   Exploring the inland waterways by steering your own boat is a leisurely way to discover unspoiled scenery, hidden villages, and abundant wildlife of Ireland's interior. You can rent a river cruiser for a floating holiday from **Celtic Canal Cruisers Ltd** (⊠*24th Lock* ☎*057/932–1861*).

GOLF   **Esker Hills Golf & Country Club** (⊠*5 km [3 mi] north of Tullamore on N80* ☎*057/935–5999*) is a challenging 18-hole championship course with natural lakes and woodlands.

KILBEGGAN

❺ *11 km (7 mi) north of Tullamore.*

It's the whiskey (the Irish spell their traditional tipple with an "e") that brings most people to the unassuming little town of Kilbeggan. The town is the home of **Locke's Distillery,** which is the oldest pot-still distillery in the world and the last of its type in Ireland. This whiskey-lover's mecca was established in 1757 but was closed down as a functioning distillery in 1954. It has found new life as a museum of industrial archaeology illustrating the process of Irish pot-whiskey distillation and the social history of the workers. ☎*057/933–2134* ⊕*www.iol.ie/wmeathtc/lockes* ✉*€5.50* ⊗*Apr.–Oct., daily 9–6; Nov.–Mar., daily 10–4.*

MULLINGAR

6 *24 km (15 mi) northeast of Kilbeggan.*

The Irish are great ones for wrapping an insult up in a lyrical turn of phrase. Rather than describe a woman as overweight they'll say with a wink she's "beef to the ankle, like a Mullingar heifer." Of course, the phrase also illustrates Mullingar's role as Ireland's beef capital, a town surrounded by rich countryside where cattle trading has historically been one of the chief occupations. It's also County Westmeath's major town—a busy commercial and cattle-trading center on the Royal Canal, midway between two large, attractive lakes, Lough Owel and Lough Ennel. Buildings here date mostly from the 19th century. Although best used as a base to tour the surrounding countryside, Mullingar has some interesting sights.

BRIGHT ELIXIR

Kilbeggans know "Irish" is a straight pot-still whiskey, and it has a characteristic flavor that distinguishes it from Scotch, bourbon, or rye. Irish is not drunk until it has matured for at least seven years in wooden casks. It's best quaffed without a mixer, so try it straight or with water.

The town's largest structure is the Renaissance-style Catholic **Cathedral of Christ the King,** completed in 1939. Note the facade's finely carved stonework, and the mosaics of St. Patrick and St. Anne by the Russian artist Boris Anrep in the spacious interior. ✉ *Mary St.* ☎ *044/48338* ⊙ *Daily 9–5:30.*

Mullingar Bronze and Pewter Centre offers free tours of its workshop, where the 800-year-old craft of pewter making is still practiced. Sculptured bronze figures are also made here (by Genesis Fine Art). You can purchase everything from whiskey measures to baby gifts made from both pewter and bronze in the showroom. There's also a coffee shop on the premises. ✉ *Great Down, the Downs* ☎ *044/934–8791* ⊕ *www.mullingarpewter.com* ✉ *Free* ⊙ *Weekdays 9:30–5:30, Sat. 10–5:30.*

Belvedere House Gardens occupies a beautiful spot on the northeast shore of Lough Ennel. Access to this stately mid-18th-century hunting lodge with extensive gardens is through the servants' entrance—so you can see what life behind the scenes was like back then. Cries and whispers haunt this estate. Built in 1740 by architect Richard Cassels for Robert Rochfort, first earl of Belvedere, it became a byword for debauchery and dissipation, thanks to the hijinks of Rochfort's wife, the "very handsome" Mary Molesworth. After falling passionately in love with Rochfort's younger brother (and bearing him a child), she was locked up in another family house for decades. Robert regaled guests with the "scandal" while offering sumptuous dinners at this house under its great 18th-century plasterwork ceilings. He spent much of his family fortune dotting the gardens of the estate with "follies," including the Jealous Wall, a gigantic mock-castle ruin that served to cover up a view of the adjoining estate, owned by another brother, also hated. Today, the interiors are a quirky mix of Georgian stateliness and Victorian charm. The noted bow and Palladian windows have great parkland views sloping down to the lake and its islands. You can tour the 160 acres of the estate and woodland trails on the Belvedere tram. Also on the estate are a coffee shop, an animal sanctuary, and a children's play area. ✉ *4 km (2½ mi) south of Mullingar on N52* ☎ *044/934–9060* ⊕ *www.belvedere-house.ie* 🎫 *House and parkland €8.75, tram €2* ⊙ *Mar., Apr., and Sept., daily 10:30–6; May–Aug., daily 9:30–6; Oct.–Feb., daily 10:30–4:30.*

WHERE TO STAY & EAT

$$ ✕🏨 **Crookedwood House.** This former rectory has stunning views of
★   Lough Derravaragh, the magical lake where legend tells us the poor Children of Lir were forced to spend some 300 years after being turned into swans by their nasty stepmom. Legends aside, Crookedwood House has one of the premier restaurants in the Midlands. Chef–owner Noel Kenny has conjured up an exciting, German-inspired take on modern Irish cuisine ($$$–$$$$). Venison goulash, anyone? In winter try the Hunter's Plate, a selection of pheasant, wild duck, and pigeon. Also irresistible is the trio of salmon, sole, and scallops with lobster sauce. An unusual combination of honey-roasted pork steak and salmon is wrapped in phyllo pastry and baked with grapes. The restaurant's decor—rough white walls and oak beams—won't do too much for the digestive juices, but the guest rooms upstairs are tranquil and some are even accented with 19th-century-style pieces. The house is 13 km (8 mi) north of Mullingar on the R394 Castlepollard road. ✉ *Co. Westmeath* ☎ *044/72165* 🖷 *044/72166* ⊕ *www.crookedwood-house.com* 🛏 *18 rooms* ♿ *In-room: dial-up. In-hotel: restaurant, no elevator* ☰ *AE, MC, V* ⊙ *No dinner Sun. and Mon.* ⦿*BP.*

$ ✕🏨 **An Tintáin.** In the quiet backwater village of Multyfarnham, this
★   B&B is in one of the quaint cut-stone cottages along the main street, beside an old forge with a traditional horseshoe-shape entrance. An Tintáin means "The Hearth" and true to its name, there's a blazing fire and a cozy glow of hominess inside. The rooms are simply but comfortably furnished. To complete the family-friendly mood, children under five are actually welcomed. In the restaurant ($$–$$$, no dinner Monday or Tuesday, lunch only on Sunday), locals mingle with visitors and hearty fare is the order of the day, with the famous local beef being the star of the menu. The inn is 17 km (10 mi) north of Mullingar. ✉ *Main St., Multyfarnham, Co. Westmeath* ☎ *044/71411* 🖷 *044/71434* 🛏 *6 rooms* ♿ *In-room: dial-up. In-hotel: restaurant, no elevator* ☰ *AE, MC, V* ⦿*BP.*

SPORTS

GOLF   **Delvin Castle Golf Club** (✉ *Delvin* ☎ *044/966–4315*) is an 18-hole course in a mature parkland setting. It has beautiful views across north Westmeath.

Go for the Green

Few regions in Ireland equal the Midlands for pure greenness. It not only seems the entire area is planted with clover, but the green-thumbed will rejoice in the abundance of elegant gardens, many of them designed and planted 250 years ago.

Most of these green oases are found on the grounds of the famed stately homes that dot the region. Many of the Anglo-Irish gentry were enthusiastic botanists and went to great lengths to find rare plant specimens from far-flung parts of the world. The earls of Rosse have been planting exotic plants from as far away as South America since the 17th century in the demesne of their castle in Birr.

The adventurer-botanist archetype is very much alive in the person of Thomas Pakenham, the current earl of Longford, and author of *Meetings with Remarkable Trees*. He has traveled the globe searching for exotic plants.

The gardens in his home at Pakenham Hall in County Westmeath continue to evolve from their 18th-century origins. An "Oriental" garden added in the early 1990s features rare magnolias and lilies he collected as seed in China and other Asian countries.

Elsewhere, the gardeners at Strokestown House in County Roscommon have restored a 6-acre walled garden and now tend it with methods used in the 1700s. But you can visit modern gardens, too. The best example is Heywood Gardens in County Laois, which was completed in 1912. These formal gardens, featuring wonderful water terraces, were designed by the famous architect Sir Edwin Lutyens.

What typifies all the gardens in this part of Ireland is a lush serenity and the profusion of growth that is synonymous with the Irish landscape.

CASTLEPOLLARD

 21 km (13 mi) north of Mullingar.

Fodor's Choice
★

A pretty village of multihued 18th- and 19th-century houses laid out around a large, triangular green, Castlepollard is also home to **Tullynally Castle and Gardens,** the largest castle in Ireland that still functions as a family home. This is not just any family, but the Pakenhams, that famous Irish tribe that has given us Elizabeth Longford (whose biography of Queen Victoria is in most libraries) and Antonia Fraser, wife of Harold Pinter and best-selling biographer of Mary, Queen of Scots, among others. In fact, Tullynally—the name, literally translated, means "Hill of the Swans"—has been the home of 10 generations of this family, which also married into the earldom of Longford. Lady Fraser's brother Thomas, a historian, is the current earl but does not use the title. As a result of an 18th-century

BE IT EVER SO HUMBLE

Two wings designed by Sir Richard Morrison in 1840 joined the main block of Tullynally Castle to the stable court. They served dramatically different purposes: one was given over entirely to luxurious quarters for the dowager countess; the other housed 40 *indoor* servants.

"Gothicization," the former Georgian house was transformed into a faux-castle by architect Francis Johnston; the resulting 600 feet of battlements were not just for bluff, as the earls were foes of Catholic emancipation. Inside, the family has struggled to make the vast salons warm and cozy—a bit of a losing battle. The house really comes into its own as a stage set for the surrounding park—the gray-stone structure is so long and has so many towers it looks like a miniature town from a distance. The total circumference of the building's masonry adds up to nearly ½ km (¼ mi) and includes a motley agglomeration of towers, turrets, and crenellations that date from the first early fortified building (circa 1655) up through the mid-19th century, when additions in the Gothic Revival style went up one after another.

Today, more attention is given to the beautiful parkland, in part because Thomas Pakenham is a tree-hugger extraordinaire. He is the author of several books, his most famous being *Meetings with Remarkable Trees* (1996), an exceptional art book that includes many of his magnificent photographs. The estate's rolling parkland was laid out in 1760, much along the lines you see today, with fine rhododendrons, numerous trees, and two ornamental lakes. A garden walk through the grounds in front of the castle leads to a spacious flower garden, a pond, a grotto, and walled gardens. The kitchen garden here is one of the largest in Ireland, with a row of old Irish yew trees. Don't miss the forest path, which takes you around the perimeter of the parkland and affords excellent views of the romantic castle. ✉ *1½ km (1 mi) west of Castlepollard on the R395 road to Granard* ☎ *044/61159* ⊕ *www.tullynallycastle.com* 💷 *€5* ◷ *June–Aug., daily 2–6.*

FORE

⑧ *5 km (3 mi) east of Castlepollard.*

You've heard of the "seven wonders of the ancient world," but here in the heart of the Irish Midlands is a tiny village with seven wonders all to itself! According to Irish myth, this is the place where water runs uphill, where there's a tree that will not burn and water that will not boil, among other fantastical occurrences. The village is known not only for its legend, but also for its medieval church and the remains (supposedly the largest in Ireland) of a Benedictine abbey.

The spectacular remains of **Fore Abbey** dominate the simple village—its structure is massive and its imposing square towers and loophole windows make it resemble a castle rather than an abbey. Elsewhere in town, St. Fechin's Church, dating from the 10th century, has a massive, cross-inscribed lintel stone.

CAVAN

⑨ *36 km (22 mi) north of Fore, 114 km (71 mi) northwest of Dublin.*

Like all the larger towns of the region, Cavan is a growing and increasingly prosperous town, perhaps best known for its crystal factory.

There are two central streets: with its pubs and shops, Main Street is like many other streets in similar Irish towns. Farnham Street has Georgian houses, churches, and a courthouse.

Cavan Crystal is an up-and-coming rival to Waterford in the cut-lead-crystal line; the company offers guided factory tours and access to its factory shop. This is a good opportunity to watch skilled craftspeople at work if you can't make it to Waterford. A major building attached to the factory houses a visitor center, glass museum, restaurant, and coffee shop. ⊠*Dublin Rd.* ☎*049/433–1800* ⊕*www.cavancrystaldesign.com* 🖾*Free* ⊙*Guided tours weekdays at 9:30, 10:30, and 11:30.*

OFF THE BEATEN PATH

Killykeen Forest Park. This park is part of the beautiful, mazelike network of lakes called Lough Oughter. Within the park's 600 acres are a number of signposted walks and nature trails, stables offering horseback riding, and boats and bicycles for rent. Twenty-eight fully outfitted two- and three-bedroom cottages are available for weeklong, weekend, or midweek stays. Rates vary according to the season; call for details. ⊠*11 km (7 mi) north of Cavan* ☎*049/433–2541* 🖾*Free, parking €2.50* ⊙*Daily 9–5.*

4

WHERE TO STAY & EAT

$$–$$$ ✕**Pol O'D Restaurant.** Consisting of two rooms spread over two floors, this characterful restaurant of stripped pine and exposed stonework is a busy lunch and dinner place much favored by locals. Chef-owner Paul O'Dowd opts for contemporary Irish fare with a little adventure in dishes such as smoked duck salad, quail's egg salad, and a seafood medley with prawns and lemon sauce. Standard dishes reflecting traditional rural tastes include steak, lamb, and duck. Pristine starched tablecloths, simple candlelight, and local staff make Pol O'D an unexpected pleasure in an area not generally blessed with multiple options come dinnertime. Children are welcome, as is traditional music, which seems to happen on a spontaneous basis. ⊠*Main St., Ballyconnell,* ☎*049/95-6391* ⊟*AE, MC, V* ⊙*Closed Sun.*

$$–$$$ ✕▤**Cabra Castle.** A spectacular collection of mock-Gothic towers, tur-
★ rets, and crenellations, this hotel-castle stands sentinel amid a charming parkland of mature trees and pristine lawns. Cabra boasts rooms of all shapes and sizes from cozy attic rooms to elaborate, super-size suites. Rooms in the castle are recommended, but many of the bedrooms are in the adjoining courtyard area, in a carefully restored stone outbuilding overlooking a walled garden. The Victorian-Gothic theme of the main castle is carried through in the bar and the restaurant ($$–$$$, fixed-price Continental menu) with varying degrees of success. Don't miss the castle gallery, which has hand-painted ceilings and leaded-glass windows. ⊠*65 km (40 mi) south of Cavan, Kingscourt, Co. Cavan* ☎*042/966–7030* 🖶*042/966–7039* ⊕*www.cabracastle.com* 📞*80 rooms* ♿*In-room: no a/c. In-hotel: restaurant, bar, golf course, no elevator, some pets allowed* ⊟*AE, MC, V* ⏃⃠*BP.*

$ ✕▤**The Olde Post Inn.** In the village of Cloverhill, this lovingly restored
★ former post office (if you hadn't guessed from the name) has won a

clutch of awards and, as a result, is often booked solid. That magic formula of a genuine Irish welcome and fine food is what draws people here. Big open turf fires and cut stone walls provide the key to the warm feeling you get when you step inside. As for the guest bedrooms, they're done in a cheerful country-house style. In the restaurant ($$–$$$$), chef Gearóid Lynch gives a modern twist to some Irish classics, including fillet of beef served with colcannon (a traditional mash with cabbage and onion) and bacon and cabbage terrine. To get here, take the N53 to Cloverhill from Cavan Town. ⊠ *Cloverhill, Co. Cavan* ☎ *047/55555* 🖷 *047/55111* ⊕ *www.theoldepostinn.com* ⌂ *8 rooms* △ *In-room: no a/c. In-hotel: restaurant, no elevator* ☰ *MC, V* ⏷⭕ *BP.*

¢–$ ✕☒ **MacNean House & Bistro.** Nestled in the quietest of backwaters on

Fodor'sChoice the border with Northern Ireland, you would not expect the village of
★ Blacklion to have even the faintest whiff of glamour. You'd be wrong, for this town is home to Ireland's best known TV chef, Neven Maguire. Guests come from all over just to find out if the food ($$–$$$) tastes as good as it looks on the television and they are not disappointed. Maguire creates dishes to drool for—scallops wrapped in Parma ham and crab ravioli in a lobster cream sauce are two winners—and offers several inspired takes on traditional Irish dishes, such as a delicious lamb in an herb crust. Desserts are Maguire's specialty; try the hazelnut nougat glacé. The guest bedrooms are simply furnished in a modern Irish style and, given the remoteness of Blacklion, you might want to book a room when reserving a table to avoid a post-dinner, late-night drive. The 65-km (40-mi) detour makes sense if you are heading from Dublin northwest to Sligo or Donegal. ⊠ *Blacklion, Co. Cavan* ☎ *071/985–3022* 🖷 *071/985–3404* ⌂ *4 rooms* △ *In-room: no a/c, dial-up. In-hotel: restaurant, no elevator* ☰ *MC, V* ⏷⭕ *BP.*

LONGFORD TOWN

⑩ *37 km (23 mi) southwest of Cavan, 124 km (77 mi) northwest of Dublin.*

Longford, the seat of County Longford and a typical small market-town community, is rich in literary associations, though after Oliver Goldsmith, the names in the county's pantheon of writers may draw a blank from all but the most dedicated Irish literature enthusiasts. Longford Town provides a good base for exploring the largely untouristed countryside surrounding it. A day trip to the pretty heritage village of Ardagh (10 km [7 mi] southeast of Longford Town), with its quaint houses and village green, is a popular option.

Another lovely spot is Newtowncashel on the banks of Lough Ree, where you can visit **Bogwood Crafts,** a fascinating workshop run by sculptors Michael and Kevin Casey. The center displays sculptures and keepsakes made from bogwood, which is hewn from the 5,000-year-old trees submerged and ultimately preserved by the area's ancient peat-lands. To get there from Longford drive 14 km (9 mi) on the N63 to Lanesborough, then take the R392 for 2 km (1 mi) and follow signs for Turreen–Newtowncashel. ⊠ *Barley Harbour, Newtowncashel*

☎ *043/25297*   ⊕ *www.bogwood.
net* ☒ *Free* ⊙ *Mon.–Sat. 10–6.*

WHERE TO STAY & EAT

$–$$
Fodor'sChoice
★

✕ **The Purple Onion.** A perfect resting place for tired and hungry travelers on the road to the west of Longford Town, this pub and restaurant is on the main street of a tiny Shannon-side village. This place was origi-nally a standard public house with the obligatory low ceilings, nooks, crannies, and snugs, but under the patronage of Pauline Roe and Paul Dempsey it has been transformed into a gourmet's delight—a spe-cial "gastro pub," now abustle with locals, cruise-boat tourists, and food lovers from all over. Spe-cialties include a divine whiskey-flamed sirloin in a cream sauce, and potatoes and vegetables are abun-dant and even served (untypically, for an Irish pub) al dente. The huge servings of panfried mussels and crab claws in spicy garlic butter leave you blissfully sated. An upstairs gallery has work by some of the finest and best-known Irish artists, including Jack B. Yeats and Paul Henry, among 100 others. To get here from Longford Town drive 10 km (6 mi) west on the N5. ⊠ *Tarmonbarry* ☎ *043/59919* ⊕ *www.purpleonion. ie* ☱ *AE, MC, V.*

THE HOUSE THAT DARCY BUILT

Jane Austen—that most British of writers—is linked to Carrigglas Manor, a romantic Tudor-Gothic house near Longford. It was built in 1837 by Thomas Lefroy, who was at one point romantically involved with the novelist. Why they never married is a mystery, but it's believed that Austen based the character of Mr. Darcy in *Pride and Prejudice* on Mr. Lefroy. His descendants sold the house to golf resort developers in 2006, and as of this writing, plans were underway to incorporate the house into the project and rede-velop the grounds.

¢–$ ✕ **Keenans.** If you're in the market for some liquid refreshment, try this lovingly restored pub of yore next door to the Purple Onion. Inside, the fifth generation of Keenans still plies their trade and traditional music is on the menu Monday night. Keenans also serves excellent pub food. ⊠ *Tarmonbarry* ☎ *043/26052* ⊕ *www.keenans.ie* ☱ *AE, MC, V.*

$ ✕▦ **Viewmount House.** This sweet and exquisite Georgian home was
★ once owned by the earl of Longford and has been restored to its former charm by James and Beryl Kearney. The bedrooms are full of character and have impressive period wallpapers and antique mahogany ward-robes and beds. Breakfast is served in a vaulted room cheerily painted in robin's-egg blue. The 4 acres of grounds that surround the house are a gardener's paradise with an old orchard, a formal garden, and a Japa-nese garden replete with full-size pagoda. A courtyard restaurant ($$–$$$$) serves contemporary Irish and European delicacies. The house is 2 km (1 mi) outside Longford Town, just off the old Dublin road (R393). ⊠ *Dublin Rd., Co. Longford* ☎ *043/41919* ☏ *043/42906* ⊕ *www.viewmounthouse.com* ⬎ *5 rooms, 1 suite* ⸝ *In-room: no a/c, dial-up. In-hotel: no elevator* ☱ *AE, MC, V* ⊚ *BP.*

NIGHTLIFE & THE ARTS
The center of a thriving local arts scene is the **Backstage Theatre** (⊠ *Far-neyhoogan* ☎*043/47888* ⊕*www.backstage.ie*). In a country where many patriotic souls see the indigenous sports of Gaelic football and hurling as art forms, it's perhaps appropriate that the venue is on the grounds of the local Gaelic Athletic Association club, whose team has the intimidating title of the "Longford Slashers." Catch a local match before heading into the theater for a dose of drama, dance, classical music, or opera. The theater and club are located a mile outside Longford on the road to Athlone.

THE WESTERN MIDLANDS

This section covers the area's western fringe, picking up in the heart of the region, the town of Longford, skirting the hilly landscape of County Leitrim, dappled with lakes and beloved of anglers for its fish-filled waters. The area is the country's most sparsely populated, though it has a light sprinkling of villages (and is the home of one of Ireland's leading writers, John McGahern). Moving south through Roscommon, western Offaly, and the northern part of Tipperary, the scenery is generally low on spectacle but high on unspoiled, lush, and undulating countryside. The towns are small and undistinguished, except Birr and Strokestown, both designed to complement the "big houses" that share their names. This is one of the parts of the country where you're most likely to encounter the "hidden Ireland"—a place unblighted by the plastic leprechaun syndrome of the more touristy areas to the south and west. The historic highlight of this region is the ancient site of Clonmacnoise, an important monastery of early Christian Ireland. The route then takes you southward, to northern County Tipperary.

ATHLONE

🔟 *34 km (21 mi) southeast of Longford Town, 127 km (79 mi) west of Dublin, 121 km (75 mi) east of Limerick.*

The mighty Shannon flows majestically through the heart of Athlone, yet for years it seemed as if the town was happy to turn its back on one of Europe's great waterways. That trend has now been well and truly reversed and with it has come a real buzz of regeneration. The area around Athlone Castle has transformed into a veritable "Left Bank," and on both sides of the Shannon, new restaurants and stylishly modern architecture are beginning to spring up along streets lined with 200-year-old buildings. Once upon a time, tourists were few and far between in what was cuttingly termed the "dead center" of Ireland—but the renaissance has made Athlone an increasingly attractive destination.

Beside the River Shannon, at the southern end of Lough Ree, stands **Athlone Castle**, built in the 13th century. After their defeat at the Battle of the Boyne in 1691, the Irish retreated to Athlone and made the river their first line of defense. The castle, a fine example of a Norman

Goldsmith Country

All that glitters may not be Goldsmith but that hasn't prevented the Irish tourist board from promoting the Northern Lakelands to the burgeoning literary tourism market as "Goldsmith Country."

Yes, this is the region that gave birth to the writer Oliver Goldsmith (1730–74), celebrated for his farcical drama *She Stoops to Conquer* and his classic novel *The Vicar of Wakefield*. Goldsmith left his homeland as a teenager and returned rarely. However, he is thought to have drawn on memories of his native Longford for his most renowned poem, "The Deserted Village." At Goldsmith's childhood home in Lissoy in County Longford, only the bare walls of the family house remain standing. At Pallas, near Ballymahon in County Longford, his birthplace, there's a statue in his memory but little else. The plot

of *She Stoops to Conquer* involves a misunderstanding in which a traveler mistakes a private house for an inn. This actually happened to Goldsmith at Ardagh House, now a college, in the center of the village of Ardagh (just off N55) in County Longford. In the same play the character Tony Lumpkin sings a song about a pub called the Three Jolly Pigeons; today the pub of the same name, on the Ballymahon road (N55) north of Athlone, is the headquarters of the Oliver Goldsmith Summer School.

Every year on the first weekend in June, leading academics from around the world speak on Goldsmith at this pub and other venues, and there are readings by the best of Ireland's contemporary poets and evening traditional-music sessions in this tiny, atmospheric, traditional country pub. Call *0902/85162* for more information.

stronghold, houses a small museum of artifacts relating to Athlone's eventful past. The castle gatehouse also houses the town's tourist office. Admission includes access to an interpretive center depicting the siege of Athlone in 1691, the flora and fauna of the Shannon, and the life of the tenor John McCormack (1884–1945), an Athlone native and perhaps the finest lyric tenor Ireland has produced. ⊠*Town Bridge* ☎*090/647–2107* ⊠*€5.50* ☉*May–Sept., daily 10–5; Oct.–Apr. by appointment.*

WHERE TO STAY & EAT

$$–$$$ ✕**Le Château.** Owners Martina and Stephen Linehan have created a
★ wonderfully atmospheric restaurant in Athlone's old quarter. As in cooking, the raw ingredients are the key. They've transformed a former Presbyterian church into a lovely riverside bistro where, on summer evenings, light streams in through the original stained-glass windows and candles illuminate the nautically themed dining room at nightfall. Stephen Linehan's menu does not attempt to reinvent the wheel but emphasizes wonderfully fresh local produce. The dishes are mainly traditional favorites with an emphasis on locally reared beef and lamb. Seafood dishes like roast monkfish wrapped in bacon are also popular; there is also usually some vegetarian delight like a trio of golden Brie, garlic mushrooms, and Caesar salad. ⊠*St. Peter's Port, the Docks* ☎*090/649–4517* ⊟*AE, DC, MC, V.*

$$$–$$$$ ✕⊡**Wineport Lodge.** Once a wooden boathouse and now headquar-
★ ters of Lough Ree Yacht Club, this lakeside restaurant-with-rooms is
now billed as Ireland's first "wine hotel." Stylishly modern—all orange
cedarwood and plate-glass windows—and set against parkland groves
of trees, the striking light-filled wood-and-glass building seems like it
was airlifted from Sweden. Inside, guests make a beeline to the res-
taurant ($$$–$$$$), where chef Feargal O'Donnell draws praise for
his imaginative cooking and the way he matches food to the extensive
wine menu. Mouthwatering offerings like sauté of tiger prawns and
mango with coriander, lime, and pickled ginger or Clare Island organic
salmon orzo with leek stew are standard fare. Bar food ($) is also
available from 4 PM to 6 PM. The guest rooms are minimalist but filled
with stylish touches like leopard-skin prints. Once you've wined and
dined, treat yourself to one of the alluring spa treatments Bliss Dublin
provides for guests. Glasson lies 5 km (3 mi) north of Athlone on the
shores of Lough Ree. ⊠*Glasson, Co. Westmeath* ☎*090/643–9010*
🖷*090/648–5471* ⊕*www.wineport.ie* ↘*10 rooms* ⌂*In-room: Wi-Fi.
In-hotel: restaurant, bar, no elevator* ☐*AE, DC, MC, V* ⫯⊙*BP.*

SPORTS & THE OUTDOORS

BICYCLING   A combination of unfrequented back roads and lakeside scenery makes
this attractive biking country. Rent bikes from **M. R. Hardiman** (⊠*Irish-
town* ☎*090/647–8669*).

BOATING   A boat trip reveals the importance of Athlone's strategic location on the
River Shannon as well as the beauty of the region. *The Viking* (⊠*The
Strand* ☎*090/647–9277*) is a replica of a Viking longboat that travels
up the Shannon to nearby Lough Ree. The cost is €7.50; sailings take
place daily from July through September at 11, 2:30, and 4. A river
cruiser for a floating holiday can be rented by the week from **Athlone
Cruisers Ltd** (⊠*Jolly Mariner Marina* ☎*090/647–2892*).

GOLF   **Athlone Golf Club** (⊠*Hodson Bay* ☎*0902/92073*) is a lakeside 18-hole
parkland course. **Glasson Golf & Country Club** (⊠*Glasson* ☎*090/648–
5120*), an 18-hole parkland course, is bordered on three sides by Lough
Ree and the River Shannon. **Mount Temple Golf Club** (⊠*Campfield
Lodge, Moate* ☎*090/648–1841*) is an 18-hole parkland course 8 km
(5 mi) east of Athlone.

CLONMACNOISE

⓬   20 km (12 mi) south of Athlone, 93 km (58 mi) east of Galway.
★
Many ancient sites dot the River Shannon, but Clonmacnoise is early-
Christian Ireland's foremost monastic settlement and, like Chartres, a
royal site. The monastery was founded by St. Ciaran between 543 and
549 at a location that was not as remote as it now appears to be: near
the intersection of what were then two of Ireland's most vital routes—
the Shannon River, running north–south, and the Eiscir Riada, run-
ning east–west. Like Glendalough, Celtic Ireland's other great monastic
site, Clonmacnoise benefited from its isolation; surrounded by bog,
it's accessible only via one road or via the Shannon. Thanks to this

location, it almost survived everything thrown at it, including raids by feuding Irish tribes, Vikings, and Normans. But when the English garrison arrived from Athlone in 1552, they ruthlessly reduced the site to ruin. Still, with a little imagination, you can picture life here in medieval times, when the nobles of Europe sent their sons to be educated by the local monks.

The monastery was founded on an esker (natural gravel ridge) overlooking the Shannon and a marshy area known as the Callows, which today is protected habitat for the corncrake, a wading bird. Numerous buildings and ruins remain. The small **cathedral** dates as far back as the 10th century but has additions from the 15th century. It was the burial place of kings of Connaught and of Tara, and of Rory O'Conor, the last high king of Ireland, who was buried here in 1198. The two round towers include **O'Rourke's Tower,** which was struck by lightning and subsequently rebuilt in the 12th century. There are eight **smaller churches,** the littlest of which is thought to be the burial place of St. Ciaran. The only church of this group not built within the monastery walls is Nun's Church, about 1 km (½ mi) to the east. The High Crosses have been moved into the visitor center to protect them from the elements (copies stand in their original places); the best preserved of these is the Cross of the Scriptures, also known as Flann's Cross. Some of the treasures and manuscripts originating from Clonmacnoise are now housed in Dublin; most are at the National Museum, although the 12th-century *Book of the Dun Cow* is at the Royal Irish Academy Library.

Clonmacnoise has always been a prestigious burial place. Among the ancient stones are many other graves dating from the 17th to the mid-20th century, when a new graveyard was consecrated on adjoining land. The whole place is time-burnished, though in midsummer it can be difficult to avoid the throngs of tourists. ✉*Near Shannonbridge* ☎*090/574195* ⊕*www.heritageireland.ie* 🎫*€5.30* ⊗*Nov.–mid-Mar., daily 10–5:30; mid-Mar.–mid-May and mid-Sept.–Oct., daily 10–6; mid-May–early Sept. daily 9–7. Last admission 45 min before closing.*

BANAGHER

⓭ *31 km (19 mi) south of Clonmacnoise.*

"Well, that beats Banagher!" This small Shannon-side town is best known in Ireland because of this common phrase, which dates from the 19th century when the town was the very worst example of a "rotten borough"—a corrupt electoral area controlled by the local landed gentry. In short, if something "beats Banagher" it's either pretty bad or rather extraordinary. Nowadays, Banagher is a lively marina town that is a popular base for water-sports enthusiasts. Anthony Trollope (1815–82), who came to Ireland as a post office surveyor in 1841, lived here while he wrote his first book, *The Macdermots of Ballycloran.* Charlotte Brontë (1816–55) famously spent her honeymoon here.

Flynn's (✉*Main St.* ☎*0509/51312*), in the center of town, is worth visiting to appreciate its light and spacious Victorian-style design. The

Getting Bogged Down

Like the Eskimos with their 100 different words for snow, the natives of the Midlands retain a historic attachment to their vast boglands and will extol its virtues in great detail if prompted by a stranger.

In rural parts, turf, or peat, still accounts for much of the winter fuel supply and locals can always be counted upon to discuss in great detail the quality and consistency of this uniquely native resource.

"Grand year for the turf" will generally indicate a sunny August—key drying time when the "sods" are cut and allowed to dry along the banks. Conversely, "wicked bad turf" denotes a typically soft Irish summer with poor drying.

Along country lanes, the sight of reeks of cut turf is still commonplace. If you're tired of using the weather as a conversational ice-breaker, try turf as an alternative and virtually guaranteed discourse igniter.

No matter that from a distance an Irish peat bog looks like a flat, treeless piece of waterlogged land. A close-up view shows a much more exciting landscape.

Bogs support an extraordinary amount of wildlife, including larks and snipe, pale-blue dragonflies, and Greenland white-fronted geese. Amid the pools and lakes of the peat bog, amazing jewellike wildflowers thrive, from purple bell heather to yellow bog asphodel, all alongside grasses, lichens, and mosses.

As you pass through the small town of Shannonbridge, 10 km (6 mi) south of Clonmacnoise, on either side of the road are vast stretches of chocolate-brown boglands and isolated industrial plants for processing the area's natural resource.

Bord na Móna, the same government agency that makes commercial use of other boglands, has jurisdiction over the area.

To take a closer look at the bog, join the **Bord na Móna Bog Rail Tour** (⊠ *Near Shannonbridge, Uisce Dubh* ☎ *0905/74114* ⊕ *www.bnm.ie* 🎫 *€5.50* ⊙ *Tour Apr.–May and Sept., weekdays 10–5 on the hr; June–Aug., daily 10–5 on the hr*), which leaves from Uisce Dubh.A small green-and-yellow diesel locomotive pulls one coach across the bog while the driver provides commentary on a landscape unchanged for millennia.

There are more than 1,200 km (745 mi) of narrow-gauge bog railway, and the section on the tour, known as the Clonmacnoise and South Offaly Railway, is the only part accessible to the public.

lunch menu includes generously filled sandwiches, salad platters, a roast meat of the day, and chicken, fish, or burgers with chips.

If you happen to be in Banagher on a Thursday or a Sunday in summer, consider taking a two-hour **Shannon cruise** on *The River Queen,* an enclosed launch that seats 54 passengers and has a full bar on board. *Silver Line Cruisers Ltd.* ⊠ *The Marina* ☎ *057/915–1112* 🎫 *€10* ⊙ *Cruises June–mid-Sept., Thurs. at 3, Sun. at 2:30 and 4:30, weather permitting.*

Paddling a canoe is a nice alternative to a river cruise. **Shannon Adventure Canoeing and Camping Holidays** rents Canadian-class canoes, which allow you to explore the Shannon and other waterways on your own terms. ⊠ *The Marina* ☎*057/915–1411* ⊕*www.iol.ie/~advcanoe/index.html* ☉ *May–Oct., daily.*

BIRR

⑭ *12 km (7 mi) southeast of Banagher, 130 km (81 mi) west of Dublin.*

Beautifully reminiscent of an English county town with its tree-lined malls and well-preserved houses, the heritage town of Birr has roots that go back to the 6th century. Still, it's that mid-18th-century Georgian building boom that sets the tone.

4

Fodor'sChoice ★ All roads in Birr lead to the gates of **Birr Castle Demesne,** a gorgeous Gothic Revival castle (built around an earlier 17th-century castle that was damaged by fire in 1823) that is still the home of the earls of Rosse. It's not open to the public, but you can visit the surrounding 150 acres of gardens. The present earl and countess of Rosse continue the family tradition of making botanical expeditions all over the world for specimens of rare trees, plants, and shrubs. The formal gardens contain the tallest (32 feet) box hedges in the world and vine-sheltered hornbeam allées. In spring, check out the wonderful display of flowering magnolias, cherries, crab apples, and naturalized narcissi; in autumn, the maples, chestnuts, and weeping beeches blaze red and gold. The grounds are laid out around a lake and along the banks of two adjacent rivers, above one of which stands the castle. The grounds also contain **Ireland's Historic Science Centre,** an exhibition on astronomy, photography, botany, and engineering housed in the stable block. The giant (72-inch-long) reflecting telescope, built in 1845, remained the largest in the world for 75 years. Allow at least two hours to see everything. ⊠*Rosse Row* ☎*057/912–0336* ⊕*www.birrcastle.com* ⊡*Castle and grounds €9* ☉*Nov.–Mar., daily 10–4; Apr.–Oct., daily 9–6.*

WHERE TO STAY & EAT

$–$$ ✕**The Thatch Bar.** It's worth venturing 2 km (1 mi) south of Birr, just off the N62 Roscrea road, into this thatched country pub and restaurant, which offers a warm welcome and imaginative food. Inexpensive meals are available at the bar at lunchtime and early evening (until 7:30); in the evening, the restaurant offers a choice of a five-course dinner menu or an à la carte menu. Pigeon and rabbit terrines and sirloin steaks with mushrooms in garlic sauce vie for diners' attention with more exotic dishes like kangaroo and (locally farmed) ostrich. ⊠*Crinkle* ☎*0509/20682* ⊟*DC, MC, V* ☉*Closed Mon. Oct.–Apr. and Sun.–Tues. May–Sept.*

$$–$$$$ ✕▥ **Kinnitty Castle.** Venture over to the foot of the Slieve Bloom Mountains, 16 km (10 mi) east of Birr, to this exuberant, turreted, Gothic Revival edifice, rebuilt in 1927 of ashlar granite. Everything is on a grand scale and some of the guest bedrooms here will time-warp you back to the 17th century. Some, such as the O'Carroll Baronial rooms,

Fodor'sChoice ★

are outfitted with grand four-poster beds, blushing with red tartan throws. Or opt for the dazzler that is peaked with a wood-and-timber cathedral ceiling (even some bathrooms have wood beams here). Accommodations in the "new" wing (built in 1994) are smaller, while the Moneyguyneen Country House on the castle grounds has cheaper B&B rooms. The dining room has enormously tall windows and a dark wood floor. The Sli Dala is the hotel's main restaurant ($$–

$$$$), with a pre-fixe menu offering dishes like fillet of salmon in a champagne cream sauce, while the Monk's Kitchen restaurant offers more down-home fare. And for purest relaxation, there's a full-service spa offering massages, wraps, and beauty treatments. ⊠ *Kinnitty, Co. Offaly* ☎ *0509/37318* 🖷 *057/913–7284* ⊕ *www.kinnittycastle.com* ⟲ *48 rooms* ⟱ *In-room: no a/c, no TV, Wi-Fi. In-hotel: 2 restaurants, bar, tennis court, spa, no elevator* ☰ *AE, DC, MC, V* ⦿ *BP.*

$$ ✕🖭 **Dooly's.** This unpretentious country hotel began life as a coach house some 250 years ago and it has retained a charming old-style atmosphere. Floral patterns, open fires, and a relaxed welcome all form part of the decor. It's in Birr's central square, and a five-minute walk from the castle. The bustling bar and coffee shop are popular with locals. For a more formal dining experience you could try the Emmet Restaurant ($–$$), where fish dishes like baked sea bass in phyllo pastry and honey-glazed cod steak are specialties. ⊠ *Emmet Sq., Co. Offaly* ☎ *0509/20032* 🖷 *0509/21332* ⊕ *www.doolyshotel.com* ⟲ *18 rooms* ⟱ *In-room: no a/c, Wi-Fi. In-hotel: restaurant, bar, no elevator* ☰ *AE, DC, MC, V* ⦿ *BP.*

¢ ✕🖭 **The Maltings.** Sheltered beneath the eaves of Birr Castle on a river-
⟳ bank, this converted cut-stone storehouse is a good option for families and offers special rates for children. The spacious rooms have small windows, country pine furniture, and simple matching floral drapes and spreads. The cheerful, low-ceiling restaurant ($–$$) overlooks the river and serves reasonably priced plain Irish cooking. ⊠ *Castle St., Co. Offaly* ☎🖷 *0509/21345* ⟲ *13 rooms* ⟱ *In-room: no a/c, dial-up. In-hotel: restaurant, no elevator* ☰ *MC, V* ⦿ *BP.*

ROSCREA

⑮ *19 km (12 mi) south of Birr.*

Every corner you turn in this charming town will offer reminders of its rich and sometimes turbulent past. Ancient castles, towers, and churches dot the town's skyline, proof of a heritage that goes back to the 7th century. Roscrea is on the main N7 road between Dublin and Cork, making it ideal as a stopover en route to the south. The road cuts right through the remains of a monastery founded by St. Cronan. It also passes the west facade of a 12th-century Romanesque church that now forms an entrance gate to a modern Catholic church. Above the structure's rounded doorway is a hoodmold enclosing the figure of a bishop, probably St. Cronan.

In the very center of town is **Roscrea Castle,** a Norman fortress dating from 1314, given by King Richard II to the duke of Ormonde. Inside are vaulted rooms graced with tapestries and 16th-century furniture. A ticket to it also gains entry to the adjacent **Damer House,** a superb example of an early-18th-century town house on the grand scale. It was built in 1725 within the curtain walls of the castle, at a time when homes were often constructed beside or attached to the strongholds they replaced. The house has a plain, symmetrical facade and a magnificent carved-pine staircase inside; on display are exhibits about local history. To get here, start with your back to St. Cronan's monastery, turn left, and then turn right onto Castle Street. ⊠ *Castle St.* ☎ *0505/21850* ⊕ *www.heritageireland.ie* ⊡ *€3.70* ⊙ *May–Sept., daily 9:30–6; Oct.–Apr., weekends 10–5.*

WHERE TO STAY & EAT

$$$$ ✕ **Fiacrí Country House Restaurant.** In just a few years, this cozy farmhouse
★ restaurant has built up a legion of fans in spite of its remote location in the midst of the rolling Tipperary countryside. Chef Ailish Hennessy prepares modern country-house fare with an emphasis on locally produced meats. Meals are only served prix fixe but five courses are a fine value at €45. Specialties include panfried medallions of pork with caramelized apple, cider, and whole-grain mustard-cream sauce. Husband Enda does a charming turn overseeing the dining rooms, which also double as a cooking school. To get there take the Knock road off the Roscrea bypass; after 3 km (2 mi) turn right for Erril—the restaurant is signposted after 3 km (2 mi). ⊠ *Boulrea, Knock* ☎ *0505/43018* ⊕ *www.fiacrihouse.com* ⊟ *AE, MC, V* ⊙ *Closed Sun.–Tues.*

✕ **The Tower.** Gerard Coughlan's old-world bar in the town center is a reassuring connection to the familiar bric-a-brac of a bygone age, complemented with tumbling flower baskets adorning the entrance. A favorite of local farmers who tuck into good-size portions of such traditional staples as bacon and cabbage, steaks, and chicken, the restaurant also turns out lighter pasta dishes and salads. Filled with the banter of lunchtime regulars during the day, the restaurant is more subdued in the evening, when the lighting is low and a blazing fire warms the space. The menu offers a decent choice of standard Irish dishes in an old-fashioned atmosphere with simple round tables and attentive service. The basic but attractive bedrooms are all individually decorated with prints and paintings of local landscapes. The inn is near the town's 12th-century Round Tower and within walking distance of village center ⊠ *Church St., Co. Roscrea* ☎ *0505/21774* 🖷 *0505/22425* ⊕ *www.thetower.ie* ➯ *10 rooms* 🖭 *In-room: no a/c, dial-up. In-hotel: no elevator.* ⊟ *AE, DC, MC, V.*

SPORTS & THE OUTDOORS

Three marked trails—measuring 9 km (5½ mi), 3 km (2 mi), and 1½ km (1 mi)—run through the 450-acre, organic **Fairymount Farm** (⊠ *Ballingarry* ☎ *067/21139* ⊕ *www.fairymountfarm.com*), which has woodlands, horses, and sheep. Points of interest are explained in a booklet you can pick up here. The trails can also be followed on horseback (the farm's rangers can help you arrange this), and you can fish for pike or perch in the farm's 25-acre lake. Access to the farm costs €5.

MIDLANDS ESSENTIALS

TRANSPORTATION

If traveling extensively by public transportation, be sure to load up on information (the best taxi-for-hire companies, rail and bus schedules, etc.) upon arriving at the ticket counter or help desk of the bigger train and bus stations in the area, such as Mullingar and Cavan.

BY AIR

Dublin Airport is the principal international airport that serves the Midlands; car-rental facilities are available here. Sligo Airport has daily flights from Dublin on Aer Lingus.

Airport Information Aer Lingus (☎ *0818/365–000* ⊕ *www.dublin-airport.com*). **Dublin Airport** (☎ *01/814–1111*). **Sligo Airport** (☎ *071/916–8280* ⊕ *www. Sligoairport.com*).

BY BUS

Bus Éireann runs an express bus from Dublin to Mullingar in 1½ hours, with a round-trip fare of €17.10. Buses depart three times daily. A regular-speed bus, leaving twice daily, makes the trip in two hours. Express buses also make stops at Longford (2¼ hours), Boyle (3¼ hours), and Sligo (4¼ hours). There's also a daily bus from Mullingar to Athlone and an express service connecting Galway, Athlone, Longford, Cavan, Clones, Monaghan, and Sligo. Details of all bus services are available from the Bus Éireann depots listed below.

Bus Information Athlone Railway Station (☎ *090/648–4406*). **Bus Éireann** (☎ *01/836–6111 in Dublin* ⊕ *www.buseireann.ie*). **Cavan Bus Office** (☎ *049/433–1353*). **Longford Railway Station** (☎ *043/45208*). **Monaghan Bus Office** (☎ *047/82377*). **Sligo Railway Station** (☎ *071/916–0066*).

BY CAR

A car is necessary to really explore the region. Mullingar, Longford, and Boyle are on the main N4 route between Dublin and Sligo. It takes one hour to drive the 55 km (34 mi) from Dublin to Mullingar and two hours from Mullingar to Sligo (150 km [93 mi]). To get from Mullingar to southwestern Ireland, you can take N52 to Nenagh, where it meets N7, and follow that into Limerick. R390 from Mullingar leads you west to Athlone, where it connects with N6 to Galway. The 120-km (75-mi) drive takes about 2½ hours.

ROAD
CONDITIONS
Most of the winding roads in the Midlands are uncrowded, although you may encounter an occasional animal or agricultural machine crossing the road. In Mullingar, the cattle-trading town, roads can become badly congested.

Local Agencies **Gerry Mullin** (⊠ *North Rd., Monaghan* ☎ *047/81396*). **Griffiths Mullingar Ltd.** (⊠ *Harbour St., Mullingar* ☎ *044/48403*). **Longford Car & Van Rentals** (⊠ *Longford Town, Longford* ☎ *043/44099*).

BY TRAIN

A direct-rail service links Longford (via Mullingar) to Dublin (Connolly Station), with on average eight trains every day making the 1½-hour journey. It costs €31.50 one way and €34.50 round-trip. Contact Irish Rail for information. Trains from Mullingar, departing three times daily weekdays and Sunday, stop at Longford (35 minutes), Boyle (1¼ hours), and Sligo (2 hours). Portlaoise is served by a good commuter service and many of the intercity Dublin–Cork trains stop there. The intercity service to Galway City from Dublin Heuston serves Portarlington, Tullamore, and Athlone. Roscrea and Nenagh are served by a twice-daily train to Limerick City.

Train Information **Irish Rail** (☎ *01/836–6222* ⊕ *www.irishrail.ie*).

CONTACTS & RESOURCES

EMERGENCIES

The general emergency number in the area is 999. For medical service, contact the General Hospital in Mullingar

Emergency Services **Ambulance, fire, police** (☎ *999*). **General Hospital** (⊠ *Mullingar* ☎ *044/40221*). **Portlaoise Midland Regional Hospital** (⊠ *Portlaoise* ☎ *0502/21364*).

Pharmacy **Weir's Chemist** (⊠ *Market Sq., Mullingar* ☎ *044/48462*).

INTERNET CAFÉS

Even though much of Ireland has gone Wi-Fi over the past two years, in some of the more rural regions you'll need to rely on the local Internet café to catch up on messages from home. As well as good places to find a decent cup of java, they are generally quite cheap; expect to pay around €2 an hour.

Internet Cafés **Bishop Business Ventures** (⊠ *7a Mardyke St., Athlone* ☎ *090/647–7633*). **Ego Internet Cafe** (⊠ *Convent Building, Main St., Cavan* ☎ *049/437–3488*). **Escape Internet Café** (⊠ *4 Centenary Sq., Longford* ☎ *043/42864*). **Internet Café** (⊠ *17 Main St., Carrickmacross, Monaghan* ☎ *042/966–2737*).

TOUR OPTIONS

To plan a trip within any particular county or area, you're best off starting with the local tourist office. They will have a thorough list of the must-see attractions in their areas. Several of the region's larger travel agencies organize tours.

Tour Companies **Airboran Travel** (⊠ *4 Lismard Ct., Portlaoise* ☎ *0502/21226*). **Grenham Travel** (⊠ *1 Connaught St., Athlone* ☎ *090/649–2028*). **O'Hanrahan**

Travel (✉ *59 Dublin St., Monaghan* ☎ *047/81133*). **Trikon Travel** (✉ *Castle St., Roscommon* ☎ *090/662–6243*).

VISITOR INFORMATION

Five Midlands Tourist Information Offices (TIOs) are open all year: Carrick-on-Shannon, Cavan, Monaghan, Mullingar, and Portlaoise. The Mullingar TIO has information on Counties Westmeath, Offaly, Monaghan, Cavan, and Laois. Another five Midlands TIOs are open seasonally: Athlone (April–October), Birr (May–September), Clonmacnoise (April–October), Longford (June–September), and Tullamore (mid-June–mid-September).

Tourist Information **Athlone** (✉ *Church St., Co. Westmeath* ☎ *090/649–4630*). **Birr** (✉ *Rosse Row, Co. Offaly* ☎ *0509/20110*). **Cavan** (✉ *Farnham St., Co. Cavan* ☎ *049/433–1942* ⊕ *www.cavantourism.com*). **Clonmacnoise** (✉ *Near Clonmacnoise ruins, Co. Offaly* ☎ *0905/74134*). **Longford** (✉ *Main St., Co. Longford* ☎ *043/46566*). **Monaghan** (✉ *Market House, Co. Monaghan* ☎ *047/84786* ⊕ *www. monaghantourism.com*). **Mullingar** (✉ *Dublin Rd., Co. Westmeath* ☎ *044/48650* ⊕ *www.ecoast-midlands.travel.ie*). **Portlaoise** (✉ *James Fintan Lawlor Ave., Co. Laois* ☎ *0502/21178* ⊕ *www.laoistourism.ie*). **Tipperary** (✉ *Excel Centre, Co. Tipperary* ☎ *062/51457*). **Tullamore** (✉ *Bury Quay, Co. Offaly* ☎ *0506/52617*).

The Southeast

Farm in Tipperary

WORD OF MOUTH

"Cahir Castle is one of Ireland's best. There are many winding spiral staircases to explore and lots of nooks and crannies to see—but beware of the 'stumble steps' deliberately built into the castle."

—irisheyes

"The Rock of Cashel is a spectacular ruin and is one of the most important religious sites in Ireland. Its position overlooking the plains is quite amazing."

—wojazz3

www.fodors.com/forums

WELCOME TO THE SOUTHEAST

Saltee Islands, Kilmore, County Wexford

TOP REASONS TO GO

★ **Glittering Waterford:** Long before Kleenex and Xerox turned their brand names into the thing itself, the Waterford Crystal Factory set a standard for cut crystal that all the world knows by name.

★ **Kilkenny, Ireland's Medieval Capital:** With its famous 14th-century "witch" Petronilla, *Camelot*-worthy Black Abbey, and fairy-tale Kilkenny Castle, the city still conjures up the days of knights and damsels.

★ **Pretty-as-a-postcard Lismore:** Presided over by the storybook, neo-Baronial castle of the Dukes of Devonshire, this enchanting, thatched-roof village has attracted visitors ranging from Sir Walter Raleigh to Fred Astaire.

★ **Cashel of the Kings:** Ireland's "Rock of Ages," this 200-foot-tall rock bluff was the seat of the kings of Munster for seven centuries.

★ **Ireland in a Park:** Ranging over 9,000 years of history, with everything from re-creations of pre-Christian burial sites to a Norman castle, the Irish National Heritage Park remains one of Wexford's most popular sights.

1 Kilkenny City. Creativity is evident in every aspect of this town, from its medieval stonework to its array of modern and traditional craft and design found in galleries and studios as well as the many festivals and events held here year-round.

2 Southeast Inlands. Redolent of the Middle Ages, this once-upon-a-timefied region is home to some thrilling medieval sights, including Carlow Castle, Leighlinbridge's Black Castle, the tiny village of Old Leighlin, and Jerpoint Abbey, the most famous Cistercian ruins in Ireland.

3 Wexford. The warm welcome, the ancient Viking streets, and the tiny, atmospheric Theatre Royal add to the cultural pleasures as this proud town puts on its Sunday best for the Wexford Opera Festival, a weeklong binge of arias and charm held every October.

4 Southeast Coast. Combining the best of Ireland's climate with some wonderful sand-and-sea settings, this coastal headland is noted for quaint villages like Kilmore Quay and Ballyhack, the bustling and historic city of Waterford, and beachfront locations that attract Dubliners by the droves.

GETTING ORIENTED

Set around Tipperary—Ireland's largest inland county—the Southeast is a vast region that stretches near the town of Carlow near the border of County Wicklow in the north to Ardmore near the border of County Cork in the south. While main towns can be packed with camera-wielding tourists, you can easily escape the tour buses thanks to endless expanses of tranquil countryside.

Inside Saint Patrick's Rock of Cashel in County Tipperary

5 In & Around County Tipperary. The greatest group of monastic ruins in Ireland—the Rock of Cashel—lords it over miles of the idyllic region known as the Golden Vale along with some relentlessly romantic sights, like the 19th-century village of Lismore and Cahir's charming Swiss Cottage.

Parliament Street, Kilkenny City, County Kilkenny

THE SOUTHEAST PLANNER

Getting Around

The Southeast is well served with transportation infrastructure. Waterford Airport allows easy access to the United Kingdom, while Rosslare allows the option of ferry crossings to France and beyond. Train and bus services are plentiful, with Waterford, Kilkenny, and Wexford the main hubs for connections to Dublin and Cork. A car is the best option for covering ground quickly and easily. Unlike the Midlands, where the volume of traffic is generally mellow, roads in this Southeast corner can be busy during the summer months.

Finding a Place to Stay

Festivals, the good weather, and commerce make the Southeast one of Ireland's hottest corners, so plan way ahead for a stay in any of the main towns (and in many country manors, which usually have less than six bedrooms and fill up fast). As always, the local tourist offices can offer assistance if you arrive without reservations in a town packed with travelers. Assume that all hotel rooms reviewed in this chapter have air-conditioning, in-room phones, TVs, and private bathrooms, unless otherwise indicated.

Talk Radio

As you'll no doubt spend a good portion of your time behind the wheel during your travels, tune into Irish radio for another angle on the country. If you want to feel the true pulse of the nation, check out any of the RTE Radio 1's morning programs with well-known jocks like Pat Kenny, Joe Duffy, and Marian Finucane allowing the nation to give full vent to their spleens across the airwaves.

In a country still reeling from the clerical scandals and government corruption of the 1990s, the radio has become Ireland's modern confessional and a serious insight into what makes the Irish tick.

Eating Well in the Southeast

Other than its fabled strawberries, the Southeast is probably best known for its rich seafood, especially Wexford mussels, crab, and locally caught salmon. Kilmore Quay, noted for lobster and deep-sea fishing, hosts an annual Seafood Festival the second week of July. Many restaurants serve local lamb, beef, and game in season.

Food is usually prepared in a simple, country-house style, but be ready for some pleasant surprises, as there are a number of ambitious Irish chefs at work in the Southeast's restaurants and hotels. The best of the region's cuisine rests on modern interpretations of classic dishes.

One leading light in the area, chef Kevin Dundon at Dunbrody House, expounds a philosophy of understated but delicious food both in his cooking school and in his cookbook, *Full On Irish*. Informed by his culinary experience, dishes such as tea-smoked chicken and tarragon-glazed lamb exemplify Dundon's modern, international take on his Irish roots.

Another of the Southeast's prominent chefs, Jim Aherne of Kelly's hotel, still prepares the traditional dishes—Rosslare mackerel, Slaney salmon—that have shone for 30 years. But, a sign of the times: he has introduced more exotic fare, such as ostrich.

Passion on the High "C"s

Held in late October–early November, the two-week-long annual Wexford Opera Festival is the biggest social and artistic event in the entire Southeast. From mid-September until the final curtain comes down, Wexford becomes home to a colorful cast of international singers, designers, and musicians, as the town prepares for the annual staging of three grand opera productions at the tiny Theatre Royal. The festival has a huge international cachet, and the actual productions are expensive, full-dress affairs. The selection of operas runs toward the recherché and the choice is usually the envy of opera maestros around the world. In 2006 the operas presented two extraordinary rarities: Gaetano Donizetti's *Don Grigorio* and Conrad Susa's 1973 version of the Brothers Grimm, *Transformations*. Prices are €75–€95 a ticket, but the extensive fringe events and concerts are usually around €15, and sometimes far more fun. Best thing about the festival for nonopera buffs, though, is the excitement in the air: art exhibitions, street music, parades, and window-dressing contests are held every year, and local bars compete in a Singing Pubs competition. The bad news: nearly every single bed within a large radius of Wexford is booked during the festival weeks, and usually for months before the actual event kicks off.

Dining & Lodging Price Categories (In Euros)

	¢	$	$$	$$$	$$$$
RESTAU-RANTS	under €8	€8–€15	€15–€22	€22–€29	over €29
HOTELS	under €80	€80–€130	€130–€180	€180–€230	over €230

Restaurant prices are for a main course at dinner. Hotel prices are for a standard double room in high season.

Feeling Festive?

With practically every hamlet and village across the country glorying in its own festival or excuse for later pub opening, the Southeast delivers some of Ireland's most popular gatherings. Carlow's Eigse Arts festival is a 10-day celebration of visual arts in June. In August the Spraoi festival is a display of talented exuberance in Waterford City, using the city's extensive pedestrian areas; and Kilkenny's Arts Festival attracts many global premieres to its weeklong calendar in August. Check with the tourist boards for listings and dates of all events, big and small.

How's the Weather?

As well as having some of the richest land in the country, the Southeast is the envy of all Ireland for that most elusive element—sunshine.

The region is also the driest in Ireland, which is saying something in a country where seldom do more than three days pass without some rain.

Compared to an average of 80 inches on parts of the west coast, the Southeast gets as little as 40 inches of rainfall per year, varying from the finest light drizzle (a soft day, thank goodness!) to full-blown downpours.

Updated by
John Daly

THE IRISH LIKE TO LABEL their regions, and "Ireland's Sunny Southeast" is the tag they've applied to Counties Wexford, Carlow, Kilkenny, Tipperary, and Waterford. The moniker is by no means merely fanciful: the weather station on the coast at Rosslare reports that this region receives more hours of sunshine than any other part of the country. Little wonder the outdoors-loving Irish have made the Southeast's coast a popular warm-weather vacation destination. Receiving almost double the rays found anywhere else, the shore resorts buzz with activity from May to October. Thousands of families take their annual summer holidays here, where picnics and barbecues—often a rain-washed fantasy elsewhere in Ireland—are a golden reality.

The entire Southeast is rich with natural beauty—not the rugged and wild wonders found to the north and west, but a coast that alternates between long, sandy beaches and rocky bays backed by low cliffs, and an inland landscape of fertile river valleys and lush, undulating pastureland. The landscape of the region is diverse, the appeal universal: seaside fishing villages with thatched cottages, Tipperary's verdant, picturesque Golden Vale. Anglers appreciate the variety of fishing and scenery along the Barrow, Nore, and Suir rivers, and especially in the Blackwater Valley area.

The region doesn't lack for culture, either. History-rich Carlow Town, the cities of Kilkenny and Waterford, and Wexford Town have retained traces of their successive waves of invaders—Celt, Viking, and Norman. The most beautiful of these destinations is Kilkenny City, an important ecclesiastic and political center until the 17th century and now a lively market town. Its streets still hold remnants from medieval times—most notably St. Canice's Cathedral—and a magnificent 12th-century castle that received a sumptuous Victorian makeover. Wexford's narrow streets are built on one side of a wide estuary, giving it a delightful maritime air. Fans flock here for its Opera Festival, which draws top talent from around the world. Waterford, although less immediately attractive than Wexford, is also built at the confluence of two of the region's rivers, the Suir and the Barrow. It offers a rich selection of Viking and Norman remains, some attractive Georgian buildings, and the famed Waterford Glass Factory, which is open to visitors.

Deeper into the countryside, rustic charms beckon. The road between Rosslare and Ballyhack passes through quiet, atypical, flat countryside dotted with thatched cottages. Beyond Tramore, level, sandy beaches give way to rocky Helvick Head and the foothills of the Knockmealdown Mountains at Dungarvan. In the far southwest of County Waterford, near the Cork border, Ardmore presents early Christian ruins on an exposed headland, while in the wooded splendor of the Blackwater Valley, the tiny cathedral town of Lismore has a hauntingly beautiful fairy-tale castle.

EXPLORING THE SOUTHEAST

The Southeast is a large region, stretching from the town of Carlow near the border of County Wicklow in the north to Ardmore near the border of County Cork in the south. A car is not essential for getting around but it does help: you may find the frequency of public transport somewhat patchy once you leave the major towns and cities. The flow of summer visitor traffic has long been an economic lifeline for the Southeast, so main road networks have improved a great deal in recent years and travel between popular areas is fairly speedy. Apart from June, July, and August, when the Irish stream here for vacations, the region is relatively free of traffic, making it ideal for leisurely exploration. Wexford, Waterford, and Kilkenny have compact town centers easily explored on foot, and they make good touring bases.

KILKENNY CITY

Dubbed "Ireland's Medieval Capital" by its tourist board, and also called "the Oasis of Ireland" for its many pubs and watering holes, Kilkenny is one of the country's most alluring destinations. It demands to be explored by foot or bicycle, thanks to its easily circumnavigated town center, a 900-year-old Norman citadel that is now a lovely place of Georgian streets and Tudor stone houses. The city (population 20,000) is impressively preserved and attractively situated on the River Nore, which forms the moat of the magnificently restored Kilkenny Castle. In the 6th century, St. Canice (aka "the builder of churches") established a large monastic school here. The town's name reflects Canice's central role: Kil Cainneach means "Church of Canice." Kilkenny did not take on its medieval look for another 400 years, when the Anglo-Normans fortified the city with a castle, gates, and a brawny wall.

EXPLORING KILKENNY CITY

The city center is small, and despite the large number of historic sights and picturesque streets—in particular, Butter Slip and High Street—you can easily cover it in less than three hours. One of the most pleasant cities south of Dublin (and one of its most sports-minded—during June and July, practically the only topic of conversation is the fate of the city's team at the All-Ireland Hurling Championship), Kilkenny City has become in recent years something of a haven for artists and craft workers seeking an escape from Dublin. At such venues as the Kilkenny Design Centre, you can find an array of crafts, especially ceramics and sweaters, for sale. The city has more than 60 pubs, many of them on Parliament and High streets, which also support a lively music scene.

Many of the town's pubs and shops have old-fashioned, highly indi-vidualized, brightly painted facades, created as part of the town's 1980s revival of this Victorian tradition. So after taking in Kilkenny Castle and the Riverfront Canal Walk—an overgrown pathway that mean-ders along the castle grounds—mosey down High and Kieran streets. These parallel avenues, considered the historic center of Kilkenny, are connected by a series of horse cart–wide lanes and are fronted with some of the city's best-preserved pubs and Victorian flats. Be sure to look up over the existing modern storefronts to catch a glimpse of how the city looked in years past, as many of the buildings still have sec-ond-floor facades reflecting historic decorative styles. High and Kieran streets eventually merge into Parliament Street—the main commercial street—which stretches down to Irishtown.

Kilkenny holds a special place in the history of Anglo-Irish relations. The infamous 1366 Statutes of Kilkenny, intended to strengthen Eng-lish authority in Ireland by keeping the heirs of the Anglo-Norman invaders from assimilating into the Irish way of life, was an attempt at apartheid. Intermarriage became a crime punishable by death. Anglo-Norman settlers could lose their estates for speaking Irish, for giving their children Irish names, or for dressing in Irish clothing. The native Irish were forced to live outside the town walls in shantytowns. Ironi-cally, Irish and Anglo-Norman assimilation was already well under way by the time the statutes went into effect; perhaps if this intermingling had been allowed to evolve naturally, Anglo-Irish relations in the 20th century might have been more harmonious.

By the early 17th century, Irish Catholics began to chafe under such repression; they tried to bring about reforms with the Confederation of Kilkenny, which governed Ireland from 1642 to 1648, with Kilkenny as the capital. Pope Innocent X sent money and arms. Cromwell responded in 1650 by overrunning the town and sacking the cathedral, which he then used as a stable for his horses. This marked the end of Kilkenny's "Golden Age"; however, the succeeding centuries were not uneventful. In 1798 the city was placed under martial law due to a revolt by the United Irishmen; in 1904 King Edward VII paid a visit; and in 1923, at the height of Ireland's civil war, forces opposed to a government peace deal with the British briefly occupied Kilkenny Castle.

❶ In spite of Cromwell's defacements, **St. Canice's Cathedral** is still one of the finest cathedrals in Ireland; it's the country's second-largest medi-eval church, after St. Patrick's Cathedral in Dublin. The bulk of the 13th-century structure (restored in 1866) was built in the early-English style. Inside the massive walls is an exuberant Gothic interior, given a somber grandeur by the extensive use of a locally quarried black marble. Many of the memorials and tombstone effigies represent dis-tinguished descendants of the Normans, some depicted in full suits of armor. Look for a female effigy in the south aisle wearing the old Irish, or Kinsale, cloak; a 12th-century black-marble font at the southwest end of the nave; and St. Ciaran's Chair in the north transept, also made of black marble, with 13th-century sculptures on the arms. The big-gest attraction on the grounds is the 102-foot-high round tower, which

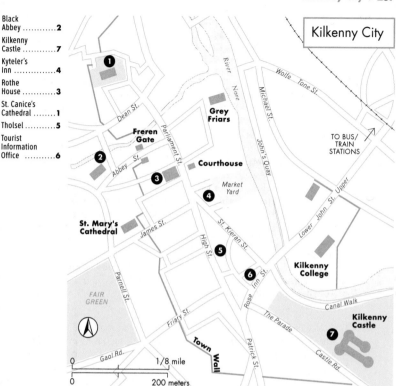

was built in 847 by King O'Carroll of Ossory and is all that remains of the monastic development reputedly begun in the 6th century, around which the town developed. If you have the energy, climb the tower's 167 steps for the tremendous 360-degree view from the top, as well as for the thrill of mounting 102 steps on makeshift wooden stairs. Next door is St. Canice's Library, containing some 3,000 16th- and 17th-century volumes. ✉*Dean St.* ☎*056/776–4971* ✆*Cathedral €4, tower €6* ⊗*Cathedral Easter–Sept., Mon.–Sat. 9–1 and 2–6, Sun. 2–6; Oct.–Easter, Mon.–Sat. 10–1 and 2–4, Sun. 2–4; tower access depends on weather.*

② With a stained-glass, carved-stone interior that seems right out of the
★ musical *Camelot,* the 13th-century **Black Abbey** is one of the most evocative and beautiful Irish medieval structures. Note the famous 1340 five-gabled Rosary Window, an entire wall agleam with ruby and sapphire glass, depicting the life of Christ. Home to a Dominican order of monks since 1225, the abbey was restored as a church by the order, whose black capes gave the abbey its name. Interestingly, it's also one of the few medieval churches still owned by the Roman Catholic Church, as most of the oldest churches in Ireland were built by the Normans and reverted to the Church of Ireland (Anglican) when the English turned to Protestantism. Nearby is the Black Freren Gate (14th century), the last

remaining gateway to the medieval city of yore. ⊠*South of St. Canice's Cathedral* ☎*056/772–1279* 🖃*Free* ⊙*Daily 9–1 and 2–6.*

❸ Set with splendidly sturdy stonework, **Rothe House** is one of the finest examples in Ireland of a Tudor-era merchant's house. There's a feeling of time travel as you step off the busy main street and into this medieval complex with its stone-wall courtyards, one of which houses a medieval well. Built by John Rothe between 1594 and 1610, it's owned by the Kilkenny Archaeological Society and houses a collection of Bronze Age artifacts, ogham stones (carved

with early Celtic symbols and messages), and period costumes. There's also a genealogical research facility that can help you trace your ancestry. ⊠*Parliament St.* ☎*056/772–2893* 🖃*€3* ⊙*Mar.–Oct., Mon.–Sat. 10:30–5, Sun. 3–5; Nov.–Feb., Mon.–Sat. 1–5.*

❹ **Kyteler's Inn,** the oldest in town, is notorious as the place where Dame Alice Le Kyteler, a member of a wealthy banking family and an alleged witch and "brothel keeper," was accused in 1324 of poisoning her four husbands. So, at least, said the enemies of this apparently very merry widow. The restaurant retains its medieval aura, thanks to its 14th-century stonework and exposed beams down in the cellar, built up around Kieran's Well, which predates the house itself. Food and drink in this popular pub are as simple and plentiful as they would have been in Dame Alice's day—but minus her extra ingredients *(see the Close Up box "From Stake to Steak" for more information).* ⊠*Kieran St.* ☎*056/772–1064.*

❺ The **Tholsel,** or town hall, which was built in 1761 on Parliament Street, stands near the site of the medieval Market Cross. With its distinctive clock tower and grand entrance portico, this limestone-marble building stands on the site of the execution of poor Petronilla, the "witch" burned at the stake in the 14th century in lieu of her mistress, Dame Alice Kyteler. The building itself burned down in 1985, but has since been completely rebuilt and now houses the city's municipal archives. Adjacent to the Tholsel is **Alice's Castle,** a town jail rather grandly fitted out in 18th-century architectural ornamentation.

❻ The **Tourist Information Office** (TIO) is housed in the Shee Alms House (off the east side of High Street). The building was erected in 1582 by Sir Richard Shee as a hospital for the poor and functioned as such until 1895. ⊠*Rose Inn St.* ☎*056/775–1500* ⊕*www.southeastireland.com* ⊙*Apr.–Oct., Mon.–Sat. 9–6; Nov.–Mar., Mon.–Sat. 9:15–5.*

From Stake to Steak

Kyteler's Inn is famous for having been owned by the notorious Dame Alice Kyteler, a beautiful enchantress from the Middle Ages who went through four wealthy husbands quicker than you can say "poison." Her behavior aroused suspicion in the superstitious Kilkenny farm folk, and she was charged with witchcraft and finally convicted of sacrificing animals to an evil demon she referred to as "Art."

The story picks up speed when the bishop of Ossory, Richard de Ledrede, paid a Lenten visit to the priory. Following an inquisition into a Kilkenny sect of heretics, Dame Le Kyteler and her former brother-in-law, one Roger Outlawe, were ordered to appear before the bishop to answer charges of witchcraft. Outlawe was supported by Arnold de Paor, lord of Kells, who arrested the bishop and had him imprisoned in Kilkenny Castle for 17

days. This, in turn, caused great scandal among the townsfolk and on his release the bishop managed to successfully prosecute the "heretics."

Dame Alice wound up being tossed into the dungeons of Kilkenny Castle, but thanks to her quick tongue—and the fact that her guards were beaten senseless (on order of Ireland's chancellor)—she managed to flee to England. The only problem is that she forgot to take her maid, Petronilla de Meath, who promptly became Ireland's first heretic to be burned at the stake in 1324.

Kyteler's Inn (⊠ *Kieran St.* ☎ *056/772–1064*) is now a popular pub-restaurant serving excellent bar food as well as traditional meals and good-quality steaks. Head down to the cellar for some pub grub and a chance to vent your hurrahs—or curses—at an effigy of Dame Alice.

❼ ★ A bewitching marriage of Gothic and Victorian styles, **Kilkenny Castle** dominates the south end of town. Amid rolling lawns beside the River Nore, the gray-stone castle stands on 50 acres of landscaped parkland (look for the garden shaped in the form of a gigantic Celtic cross). Its battlements, spired towers, and numerous chimneys conjure up fairy-tale images of knights and damsels. Built in 1172, Kilkenny Castle served for more than 500 years, beginning in 1391, as the seat of one of the more powerful clans in Irish history, the Butler family, members of which were later designated earls and dukes of Ormonde. Around 1820, William Robert, son of the first marquess of Ormonde, overhauled the castle to make it a wonderland in the Victorian Feudal Revival style. In 1859 John Pollen was called in to redo the most impressive part of the interior, the 150-foot-long, aptly named Long Gallery, a refined, airy hall. Its dazzling green walls are hung with a vast collection of family portraits and frayed tapestries, while above hangs a skylighted, marvelously decorated ceiling, replete with oak beams carved with Celtic lacework and brilliantly painted animal heads. The main staircase was also redone in the mid-1800s to become a showpiece of Ruskinian Gothic. In 1967 the sixth marquess of Ormonde handed over the building to the state for the rather pathetic sum of £75. A guided tour visits many of the salons, and the castle's Butler Gallery houses a superb collection of Irish modern art, including examples by Nathaniel Hone, Jack B. Yeats, Sir John Lavery, Louis Le Brocquy, and James Turrell. ✉ *The Parade* ☎ *056/772–1450* ⊕ *www.heritageireland.ie* 🎟 *Castle tour €5.30, grounds and Butler Gallery free* ⊘ *Apr. and May, daily 10:30–5; June–Sept., daily 9:30–7; Oct.–Mar., daily 10:30–12:45 and 2–5.*

$–$$$ ✕ **Ristorante Rinuccini.** A warm glow emanates from this excellent Italian restaurant as you descend the steps into its dining room in the basement of a Georgian town house. Owner-chef Antonio Cavaliere—who won Best Chef (National) in the Bushmills Irish Restaurant Awards 2003/2004—is intensely involved in preparing such luscious pasta dishes as tortellini stuffed with ricotta cheese and spinach, served in a Gorgonzola sauce. Other specialties, such as organic Irish veal, go particularly well with Antonio's garlic roasted potatoes—highly recommended as a side dish. A splendid all-Italian wine list complements the menu, and there's a host of delicious homemade desserts. This is one of the best Italian options in town. The restaurant accommodates overnight guests in the town house above. ✉ *1 the Parade, across from Kilkenny Castle* ☎ *056/776–1575* ⊕ *www.rinuccini.com* 🍴 *Reservations essential* ▤ *AE, DC, MC, V.*

$–$$ ✕ **Café Sol.** There's always a lively buzz about this small eatery, with its tropics-tinted decor and chirpy staff. Chef Liam O'Hanlon gives Continental flair to the best of local produce, famous Kilkenny beef, and fish bought daily off the quays at Dunmore East. The emphasis is on contemporary Mediterranean-influenced cuisine. During the day, light meals and sandwiches are on offer; at night, dining is more formal. ✉ *William St.* ☎ *056/776–4987* ▤ *MC, V* ⊘ *Closed Sun.*

$ ✕ **Chez Pierre.** A friendly spot, Pierre's serves nicely prepared meals for all times of the day. From breakfast to lunch it offers homemade cakes, sandwiches, and soups. But come evening, it plays true to its Gaelic name when chef Pierre Yves Schneider serves up bistro-style fare. The dishes are simple and fresh and are accompanied by a charming cast-iron skillet of roasted vegetables, ceremoniously placed on your candlelit table. ✉ *Parliament St.* ☎ *056/776–4655* ▤ *No credit cards* ⊘ *Closed Sun and Mon.*

$$$ ✕▦ **Langton's.** When it comes to restaurants and pubs, this is Kilkenny Central. A landmark since the 1940s, Langton's is a labyrinth of interconnected bars and eateries. Most of the seating areas, all with open fires, have different personalities—from the leather-upholstered gentlemen's club in the Horseshoe Bar to an attempt at Art Deco in the spacious dining room ($$–$$$). Up front is one of Ireland's most famous "eating pubs," often crammed with punters to the rafters of its low ceiling. For more tranquil environs, head out back, where you can chow down in a neo-Gothic garden framed by a stretch of the old city walls. The main restaurant has a great reputation and offers well-prepared traditional dishes, including (of course) Irish stew. In 2005, the Marble City Tea Rooms were opened, adjacent to the popular Marble City Bar. Upstairs, creams and browns decorate the Art Deco–style

guest rooms, which have king-size beds and bathrooms with chic massaging showerheads. ☒*69 John St., Co. Kilkenny* ☎*056/776–5133* 🖷*056/776–3693* ⊕*www.langtons.ie* ⟳*28 rooms, 2 suites* ⚫*In-room: no a/c (some), safe, Wi-Fi. In-hotel: restaurant, bar, public Wi-Fi* ⊟*AE, DC, MC, V* ⧄|*BP.*

$$ ✕▣ **Zuni Townhouse and Restaurant.** This popular hotel boasts the chi-chi gloss of a big-city boutique lodging but without the icy-cool reception you get in some fashionable joints. The clientele is mainly Dublin weekenders in search of Kilkenny's legendary nightlife and a good cross-section of local businesspeople. Relaxed and welcoming, room decor is minimalist, with walls painted in strong, modern colors. Zuni also has one of the city's leading nouvelle restaurants ($$–$$$), where the food, like the decor, is contemporary and light. The pervading signature here is the Asian influence, as seen in such dishes as spice-crusted cod, spiced duck breast, braised lamb shank, and teriyaki salmon. ☒*26 Patrick St., Co. Kilkenny* ☎*056/772–3999* 🖷*056/775–6400* ⊕*www. zuni.ie* ⟳*12 rooms, 1 suite* ⚫*In-room: no a/c. In-hotel: restaurant, bar, public Wi-Fi* ⊟*AE, DC, MC, V* ⧄|*BP.*

$$–$$$ ▣ **Butler House.** The closest you'll get to living in Kilkenny Castle during
★ your stay in the city, the dowager duchess of Ormonde's 18th-century former town house is still an integral part of the castle complex. It's a charming piece of Georgian grandeur with an ivy-covered, three-bay facade and walled garden. Inside, the reception salon has a magnificent plastered ceiling and marble fireplaces. Upstairs, any grande dame might look askance—a gradual renovation of the guest rooms is ongoing, so the decor ranges from muted 1970s minimalist to bright modern. The rooms vary in size, with some big as a house and others on the snug side. If you can, treat yourself to one of the huge, high-ceiling bedrooms overlooking the garden and castle. The only slight disadvantage (if you look at things that way) is that breakfast is not served on the premises; for your morning meal you must saunter through the walled rose garden to the adjoining Kilkenny Design Centre. ☒*16 Patrick St., Co. Kilkenny* ☎*056/776–5707* 🖷*056/776–5626* ⊕*www. butler.ie* ⟳*12 rooms, 1 suite* ⚫*In-room: no a/c, dial-up.* ⊟*AE, DC, MC, V* ⧄|*BP.*

NIGHTLIFE & THE ARTS

Every August, Kilkenny becomes the focus for Ireland's culture vultures when the **Kilkenny Arts Festival** (☎*056/776–3663* ⊕*www.kilkenny arts.ie*) takes over the city for about two weeks. The emphasis in the past was on classical music, but the program has grown increasingly populist. Street theater, elaborate parades, and even a rock concert (staged in the conveniently named Woodstock Desmesne) have lent the festival a more contemporary air and there's even speculation that it might soon eclipse Ireland's premier arts festival in Galway.

If you're craving a pint, you have a choice of pubs along Parliament and High streets. **John Cleere's** (☒*22 Parliament St.* ☎*056/776–2573*) is the best pub in town for a mix of live traditional music, poetry readings, and theatrical plays. The **Pumphouse** (☒*26 Parliament St.* ☎*056/776–*

3924) has traditional music during the week and live rock and pop on weekends. **Tynan's Bridge House** (✉ *2 Horseleap Slip* ☎ *056/21291*) is set on one of Kilkenny's famous "slips," and was first used as an exercise run for dray horses. Inside, you can guess that the pub is more than 200 years old from all the gas lamps, silver tankards, and historic teapots on display. The **Widow McGraths** (✉ *29 Parliament St.* ☎ *056/775–2520*) celebrates July 4 with a barbecue in its beer garden. It's also a good spot for live music.

The **Watergate Theatre** (✉ *Parliament St.* ☎ *056/776–1674* ⊕ *www. watergatekilkenny.com*) hosts opera, plays, concerts, comedy, and other entertainment at reasonable prices.

SPORTS & THE OUTDOORS

BICYCLING Bikes for exploring the quiet countryside around Kilkenny can be rented through **J. J. Wall** (✉ *88 Maudlin St.* ☎ *056/772–1236*).

GAELIC The 1366 Statutes of Kilkenny expressly forbade the ancient Irish game
FOOTBALL & of hurling. No matter: today, Kilkenny is considered one of the great
HURLING hurling counties. Like its neighbor and archenemy, Wexford, Kilkenny has a long history of success in hurling, and as the annual All-Ireland Hurling Championships draws to its final stages during June and July, interest in the county's team runs to fever pitch. Catch the home team at matches held at **Kilkenny GAA Grounds** (✉ *Nowlan Park* ☎ *056/777–0008* ⊕ *www.gaa.ie*).

SHOPPING

Kilkenny is a byword for attractive, original crafts that combine traditional arts with modern design elements.

You can see glass being blown at the **Jerpoint Glass Studio** (✉ *Stoneyford, (16 km/10 mi south of Kilkenny in the valley of the River Nore)* ☎ *056/772–4350*), where the glass is heavy, modern, uncut, and hand finished. The studio's factory shop is a good place to pick up a bargain. The town's leading outlet, the **Kilkenny Design Centre** (✉ *Kilkenny Castle* ☎ *056/772–2118*), in the old stable yard opposite the castle, sells ceramics, jewelry, sweaters, and handwoven textiles.

Murphy's Jewellers (✉ *85 High St.* ☎ *056/772–1127*) specializes in heraldic jewelry.

★ **Nicholas Mosse Pottery** (✉ *Bennettsbridge* ☎ *056/772–7505*) is the best-known name in Irish ceramics. Nicholas first set up his potter's wheel in an old flour mill in this quiet village (16 km/10 mi south of Kilkenny) in 1975. Since then, the business has boomed and the rustic floral-pattern pottery created here is instantly recognizable for its "spongeware" designs. A visit here allows you to see the pottery being made, and the adjoining factory shop often has good bargains.

Rudolf Heltzel (✉ *10 Patrick St.* ☎ *056/772–1497*) is known for its striking, modern designs of gold and silver jewelry.

Stoneware Jackson Pottery (✉ *Bennettsbridge* ☎ *056/772–7175*) makes distinctive, hand-thrown tableware and lamps.

Hurling: Fast & Furious

Get chatting with the locals in almost any pub across the Southeast, mention the sport of hurling, and an enthusiastic and often passionate conversation is bound to ensue. The region is the heartland of this ancient sport, whose followers have an almost religious obsession with the game.

Hurling is a kind of aerial field hockey with players wielding curved sticks. Its history comes from Ireland's Celtic ancestors, but it bears about the same relation to field hockey as ice hockey does to roller-skating. It's no accident that prowess on the hurling field is regarded as a supreme qualification for election to public office. A man who succeeds at hurling is eminently capable of dealing with anything that fate and the spite of other politicians can throw at him. Hurling is also an extremely skillful sport. A player must have excellent hand-eye coordination combined with an ability to run at high speeds while balancing a small golf-ball-size ball on his *camán* (hurling stick). Fans will also proudly tell you it's also the world's fastest team sport.

Ireland's other chief sporting pastimes, including soccer and hurling's cousin, Gaelic football, take a back seat in this part of the country. Stars like Kilkenny's D.J. Carey, rather than professional soccer players, are sporting icons for local kids. Counties Tipperary, Wexford, and Waterford are among the top teams in the region, but Kilkenny (nicknamed "The Cats") is currently the undisputed top team in the country. It has won three out of the last five All-Ireland hurling championships and is considered the best in the game.

There's an intense rivalry between the counties, especially between old foes Tipperary and Kilkenny. When it gets down to club level, passions run even higher. Almost every parish in the region has a hurling club, and a quick inquiry with locals will usually be enough to find out when the next game is on. Even for the uninitiated, hurling is a great spectator sport. Sporty types wishing to give it a go, be warned; it's fast, furious, and entails more than a hint of danger, as players flail the air to capture the bullet-fast *sliotar* (hurling ball).

The **Sweater Shop** (⌂*81 High St.* ☎*056/776–3405*) carries great sweaters.

SOUTHEAST INLANDS

North of Kilkenny City is a region notably rich in historical sights. Travel through the farmlands of the Barrow Valley to the small county seat of Carlow Town, with scenic detours to Leighlinbridge's picturesque castle and Old Leighlin's time-stained cathedral.

LEIGHLINBRIDGE

 14 km (9 mi) northeast of Kilkenny City on N10.

★ Shure, Ireland 'tis a land of sweet vistas, and one of the most romantic is found here on the east bank of Leighlinbridge: romantic, Norman-

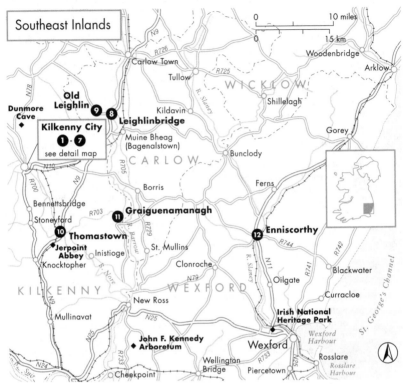

Southeast Inlands

era **Black Castle,** poetically mirrored in the waters of the River Barrow and framed by the bulk of a grandly medieval bridge. With five stone arches spanning the river since 1320, this is reputed to be one of the oldest functioning bridges in Europe and makes a magnificent repoussoir for the castle. Built in 1181 as one of the earliest Norman fortresses in Ireland, it has been the scene of countless battles and sieges. Its hulking, 400-year-old main tower still stands, all but daring you to set up your easel and canvas on the adjoining ageless towpath.

WHERE TO EAT & STAY

$$$

Fodor's Choice

★

✕▣ **Lord Bagenal Inn.** Old and new spectacularly collide at this noted hostelry. Its historic heart, a famous 19th-century pub, still nestles on the banks of the River Barrow in the heart of Leighlinbridge. Built in the early 1800s, its maze of nooks and fireplaces gives away its age in spite of renovations in 2003. A quaint walled garden replete with water accents adds to the charm, and there's even a small glassed-in playroom for children (open until 8 PM). These days, his Lordship also offers a perfect stopover for weary southbound travelers, thanks to a new, hypermodern wing built in the past few years. The showpiece is a vast, contempo-vibed restaurant, The Waterfront, where signature dishes include *crubeen* (pickled pigs' feet) braised in port and stuffed with truffles and sweetbreads; baked monkfish fillet wrapped in Serrano ham with a mango, mint, and tomato salsa; or fresh turbot with asparagus in beurre blanc. As for the nearly 40 guest rooms, they shimmer in modern style and the lobby and hallways are adorned with new Irish artworks. Niceties include an award-winning wine cellar and a pungent array of fine cigars on stock—although with Ireland's smoking ban now in full effect, you will be asked to enjoy your Cohiba outside. ✉ *Main St., Co. Carlow* ☎ *059/972–1668* ⊕ *www.lordbagenal.com* ⤶ *38 rooms* ⚐ *In-hotel: restaurant, public Wi-Fi* ☰ *DC, V.*

OLD LEIGHLIN

❾ *5¾ km (3 mi) west of Leighlinbridge, signposted to right off N9.*

Home to one of Ireland's undiscovered gems of late medieval architecture, the tiny village of Old Leighlin first found fame as the site of a monastery, founded in the 7th century by St. Laserian, that once accommodated 1,500 monks. It hosted the church synod in 630 at which the Celtic Church first accepted the Roman date for the celebration of Easter (the date was officially accepted at the Synod of Whitby in 664); this decision marked the beginning of a move away from old Brehon Law and the deliberalization of the Church. This old monastery was rebuilt in the 12th century as **St. Laserian's Cathedral.** Sitting among green fields, with a castellated tower and Irish-Gothic windows, it evokes a stirring sense of Wordsworthian forlornness. Enlarged in the 16th century, its interior is noted for its 11th-century font, a 200-year-old grand wind organ, and a fine wood vaulted ceiling. Guided tours are available. General admission is free but a donation of one euro is suggested. ☎ *059/972–1411* ⊕ *www.cashel.anglican.org/laserians.shtm* ⤳ *Free* ⊗ *July and Aug., weekdays 10–5.*

THOMASTOWN

❿ *14½ km (9 mi) south of Kilkenny on R700 and N9.*

Thomastown, originally the seat of the kings of Ossory (an ancient Irish kingdom), is a pretty, stone-built village on the River Nore. It takes its name from Thomas FitzAnthony of Leinster, who encircled the town with a wall in the 13th century. Fragments of this medieval wall remain, as do the partly ruined 13th-century church of St. Mary, and Mullins Castle, adjacent to the town bridge.

Fodor's Choice Landmarked by its rearing and massive 15th-century tower, **Jerpoint**
★ **Abbey,** near Thomastown, is one of the most notable Cistercian ruins in Ireland, dating from about 1160. The church, tombs, and the restored cloisters are must-sees for lovers of the Irish Romanesque. The vast cloister is decorated with affecting carvings of human figures and fantastical mythical creatures, including knights and knaves (one with a stomachache) and the assorted dragon or two. Dissolved in 1540, Jerpoint was taken over, as was so much around these parts, by the earls of Ormonde. The one part of the abbey that remains alive, so to speak, is its hallowed cemetery—the natives are still buried here. Guided tours of the impressive complex are available from mid-June to mid-Sep-

tember (last admission is 45 minutes before closing). ⊠ *2 km (1 mi) south of Thomastown on N9* ☎ *056/24623* ⊕ *www.heritageireland.ie* ☎ *€2.90* ⊙ *Mar.–May and Oct.–mid-Nov., daily 10–5; June–Sept., daily 9:30–6:30.*

WHERE TO STAY & EAT

$$$$
Fodor'sChoice
★

Mount Juliet. Once part of the nearby medieval Jerpoint Abbey estate, later owned by the earls of Carrick, and then famous as the seat of a horse-racing stud, Mount Juliet has long been an address of note in County Kilkenny. Today, this 1,500-acre kingdom is still lorded over by its three-story Georgian mansion, which the second earl of Carrick built along the banks of the River Nore and named in honor of his wife, Lady Juliana. Now a Conrad hotel (and voted one the world's top 100 hotels in the *Condé Nast Traveler* Readers' Choice Awards 2006, the only Irish property to feature in the prestigious "Best of the Best" list), this estate proffers the full princely treatment, thanks to a spa, famous golf course, and an array of restaurants that tempt one never to leave the grounds. Be sure to take a tour of the complex in the capable hands of estate manager Eamonn Houlihan, a mine of good cheer and information. The imposing mansion, whose elegant sash windows and mansard roof are creeper-covered in the best stately house manner, was subjected to full-blast renovation treatment in 1968. Begone, creaky floors and time-stained walls (and yesteryear's charm?); hello, large accommodations decorated with vibrant hues and fine fabrics, and suites with super-king-size beds and original fireplaces. Rooms are also available in a separate building, the Hunters Yard, plus there are modern two-room lodges, including the Rose Garden suites, each of which comes with two bedrooms, a kitchen, and very luxe decor. For many, the Jack Nicklaus–designed golf course—which has hosted the Irish Open on three occasions—is *the* reason to head here. More sedate types will enjoy a sherry in the Tetrarch Bar, a light lunch in Kendalls—a wood-trim casual bistro in the Yard complex—or fine Irish haute cuisine in the Lady Helen McAlmont Restaurant ($$$$), its tables adorned with crystal, silverware, and fine linen, and its windows with a grand vista over the Nore Valley. ⊠ *Thomastown, Co. Kilkenny* ☎ *056/777–3000* ☐ *056/777–3009* ⊕ *www.mountjuliet.com* ☞ *48 rooms, 11 lodges* ⟁ *In-room: no a/c. In-hotel: 2 restaurants, bars, golf course, tennis court, pool, spa, public Internet* ☰ *AE, DC, MC, V.*

$
★

Ballyduff House. This wonderfully picturesque house was used as a location in the nostalgic movie of Maeve Binchy's *Circle of Friends.* As this clematis-clad mansion comes into view at the top of a gently curving driveway you can understand why. Relaxation, long walks, and a warm welcome are the order of the day here. Three large, period bedrooms (one is a heavenly, superstylish vision in multiple hues of green) are decorated with Georgian furniture and ornate wallpaper and afford wonderful views of the river. You are welcome to walk around the gardens and participate in trout and salmon fishing. Mount Juliet

Golf Course is less than a five-minute drive away. ⊠ *Co. Kilkenny* 🏠056/775–8488 ⊕*www.ballyduffhouse.com* ⌂3 *rooms* ⌂*In-room: no a/c. In-hotel: public Internet, no elevator* ⊟*No credit cards* ⊙*Closed Nov.–Feb.* ⊙*BP.*

SPORTS & THE OUTDOORS

GOLF Visitors are welcome at the 18-hole **Mount Juliet Golf Course** (⊠*Mount Juliet Estate* 🏠056/772–4455), a championship parkland course. The course was designed by Jack Nicklaus and includes practice greens and a driving range.

GRAIGUENAMANAGH

⑪ *15 km (9 mi) northeast of Thomastown on R703.*

The village of Graiguenamanagh (pronounced graig-*na-manna*) sits on the banks of the River Barrow at the foot of Brandon Hill. This is good walking country; ask for directions to the summit of **Brandon Hill** (1,694 feet), a 7-km (4½-mi) hike.

In the 13th century the early-English-style church of **Duiske Abbey** was the largest Cistercian church in Ireland. The choir, the transept, and a section of the nave of the original abbey church are now part of a Catholic church. Purists will be disappointed by the modernization, carried out between 1974 and 1980, although medieval building techniques were used. 🏠059/972–4238 ⊙ *Weekdays 10–5.*

WHERE TO STAY & EAT

$ ✕▣ **Waterside.** A growing mecca for boating enthusiasts, anglers, and
★ those escaping the "big smoke," this wonderfully restored cut-stone corn mill certainly enjoys the perfect location, as it's perched on the banks of the River Barrow. This is an unpretentious and friendly accommodation. The mill's original pitch-pine beams have been retained in the guest rooms, which are simply and brightly decorated in reds and yellows. The restaurant ($$), which occupies the ground floor, also has exposed beams and decorated windows; it serves Continental cuisine and has a good wine list. Hill-walking trips, including transport and packed lunches, can be arranged for small groups. ⊠*The Quay, Co. Kilkenny* 🏠059/972–4246 🏠059/972–4733 ⊕*www.watersideguest-house.com* ⌂10 *rooms* ⌂*In-room: no a/c. In-hotel: restaurant* ⊟*AE, MC, V* ⊙*BP.*

ENNISCORTHY

⑫ *32 km (20 mi) east of Graiguenamanagh on R744.*

Enniscorthy, on the sloping banks of the River Slaney and on the main road between Dublin and Wexford, to the south of the popular resort of Gorey, is a thriving market town that is rich in history.

The town is dominated by **Enniscorthy Castle,** built in the first quarter of the 13th century by the Prendergast family. The imposing Norman castle was the site of fierce battles against Oliver Cromwell in the 17th century and during the Uprising of 1798. Its square-towered keep now houses the County Wexford Museum, which contains thousands of historic items, including military memorabilia from the 1798 and 1916 uprisings. ✉ *Castle Hill* ☎ *054/35926* 🎫 *€4.50* ⏲ *May–Sept., Mon.–Sat. 10–6, Sun. 2–5:30.*

The **National 1798 Center** tells the tale of the United Irishmen and the ill-fated 1798 rebellion. ✉ *Arnold's Cross* ☎ *054/37596* 🌐 *www.iol.ie/~98com* 🎫 *€6* ⏲ *Mid-Mar.–Nov., Mon.–Sat. 9:30–5, Sun. 11–5; Dec.–mid-Mar., weekdays 9:30–4, weekends 11–4.*

St. Aidan's Cathedral stands on a commanding site overlooking the Slaney. This Gothic Revival structure was built in the mid-19th century under the direction of Augustus Welby Pugin, architect of the Houses of Parliament in London. ✉ *Cathedral St.* ☎ *054/35777* 🎫 *Free* ⏲ *Daily 10–6.*

WHERE TO STAY & EAT

$$$ ✕ **Ballinkeele House.** Built in 1840, the ancestral home of the Maher family is beautifully maintained by the present generation. The house is on 350 acres of game-filled parkland with fine stands of mature trees, lakes, and ponds, and an atmosphere of complete tranquillity. Inside is a mix of antique ornaments, paintings, and furniture original to the house. Spacious bedrooms have pleasant views across the countryside. Bicycles are available for you to explore the surrounding countryside, or enjoy croquet on the lawn. One of Margaret's large breakfasts will set you up for a day of exploration; she is a keen cook and a member of Euro-Toques. At dinner ($$$$, guests only, Tues.–Sun.), she gives a touch of European flair to traditional dishes. Ballinkeele is 17 km (10 mi) from Wexford town center. ✉ *Ballymurn, Co. Wexford* ☎ *053/913–8105* 📠 *053/913–8468* 🌐 *www.ballinkeele.com* *5 rooms* *In-room: no phone, no TV. In-hotel: restaurant, bicycles, no-smoking rooms* 💳 *MC, V* ⏲ *Closed Dec.–Feb.* 🍽 *BP.*

$$–$$$ Fodor's Choice ★ ✕ **Kilmokea Country House.** A former Georgian rectory dating back to 1794, Kilmokea presides over seven acres of gardens blooming by the Barrow River. It recently earned an Irish Heritage Garden certificate—-a justifiable reward for 52 years of horticultural creation and dedication. The formal walled gardens were originally started in 1947 and contain over 130 different species to delight green-thumbers. Presiding over this domain are Mark and Emma Hewlett, who have managed to gild this lily with all manner of delights. Guest bedrooms are lavish with four-poster beds and great window views. A regular on Irish "best of" lists, the Peacock restaurant ($$$) has a noble menu that runs the gamut of duck leg confit to *Rims de Cabrito* (a Portuguese stew by chef Joe de Castro); the wine list is enormous and full of international gems. More casual meals are served in the Pink Tea Cup Cafe. The hotel's Patterdale Spa includes an indoor heated swimming pool, a sauna, a Jacuzzi, aromatherapy treatments, and a gym area, all set in a beautiful stone building with a sun terrace, an all-weather tennis court, and an adjacent croquet lawn. Kilmokea is located on the R733 south from New Ross to Ballyhack—look out for the sign-

post to Kilmokea Gardens. ✉ *Great Island, Campile, Co. Wexford* ☎ *051/388–109* 📠 *051/388–776* 🌐 *www.kilmokea.com* 6 *rooms* *In-room: no a/c, no elevator. In-hotel: restaurant, tennis court, pool, spa, public Wi-Fi* 💳 *MC, V.*

$ **Salville House.** Local legend has it that this fine Victorian farmhouse was once the home of a couple of "disreputable" ladies who danced at the Folies Bergères in Paris. Things are much more respectable nowadays: Gordon and Jane Parker have created a hilltop haven where food and relaxation are the order of the day. Gordon's inspired contemporary cuisine has a growing group of fans. Guests dine around a mahogany table and are invited to bring their own wine. The bedrooms are spacious, with plenty of books on the shelves and a great view of the River Slaney. In summer a grass tennis court in front of the house adds to its charm. To get there, look for the signpost, 2 km (1 mi) out of Enniscorthy on the Wexford road. ✉ *Wexford Rd., Co. Wexford* ☎ *054/35252* 📠 *054/35252* 🌐 *www.salvillehouse.com* 5 *rooms* *In-room: no a/c, no phone, no TV. In-hotel: tennis court, public Wi-Fi* *BP.*

5

SHOPPING

Carley's Bridge Pottery (✉ *Carley's Bridge* ☎ *054/33512*), established in 1654, specializes in large terra-cotta pots. **Kiltrea Bridge Pottery** (✉ *Kiltrea, Caime* ☎ *054/35107*) stocks garden pots, plant pots, and country kitchen crocks.

WEXFORD TOWN

Wexford's history goes back to prehistoric times, though you'll find scant traces of it now. Much more obvious are the Viking and Norman associations, evident in alleys as well as in the town walls, some of which are still standing. Today, this coastal town is most famed for its Wexford Opera Festival, usually held in October, which has been seducing the world with wonderful productions of rare opera for over fifty years. The warm and vivacious welcome, the narrow and ancient Viking streets, and the tiny, atmospheric Theatre Royal add to pleasure of this event and any visit to Wexford Town.

EXPLORING WEXFORD TOWN

From its appearance today, you would barely realize that Wexford is an ancient place, but in fact it was defined on maps by the Greek cartographer Ptolemy as long ago as the 2nd century AD. Its Irish name is Loch Garman, but the Vikings called it Waesfjord—the harbor of the mud flats—which became Wexford in English. Wexford became an English garrison town after it was taken by Oliver Cromwell in 1649.

The River Slaney empties into the sea at Wexford Town. The harbor has silted up since the days when Viking longboats docked here; nowadays only a few small trawlers fish from here. Wexford Town's compact center is on the south bank of the Slaney. Running parallel to the quays on the riverfront is the main street (the name changes several times), the major shopping street of the town, with a pleasant mix of old-fashioned bakeries, butcher shops, stylish boutiques, and a share of Wexford's many pubs. It can be explored on foot in an hour or two. Allow at least half a day in the area if you also intend to visit the Heritage Park at nearby Ferrycarrig, and a full day if you want to take in Johnstown Castle Gardens and its agricultural museum, or walk in the nature reserve at nearby Curracloe Beach. The town is at its best in late October and early November, when the presence of the Wexford Opera Festival creates a carnival atmosphere.

Rising above the town's rooftops are the graceful spires of two elegant examples of 19th-century Gothic architecture. These **twin churches** have identical exteriors, their foundation stones were laid on the same day, and their spires each reach a height of 230 feet. The **Church of the Assumption** is on Bride Street. The **Church of the Immaculate Conception** is on Rowe Street.

❸ The **Tourist Information Office** (*TIO* ✉ *Crescent Quay* ☎ *053/912–3111*) is a good place from which to start exploring Wexford Town on foot and to find out about guided walking tours organized by local historians.

❹ Standing in the center of Crescent Quay, a large bronze **statue of Commodore John Barry** (1745–1803) commemorates the man who came to be known as the father of the American Navy. Born in 1745 in nearby Ballysampson, Barry settled in Philadelphia at age 15, became a brilliant naval fighter during the War of Independence (thus avenging his Irish ancestors), and trained many young naval officers who went on to achieve fame.

❺ The **Franciscan Church** has a ceiling worth noting for its fine, locally crafted stuccowork. ✉ *School St.* ☎ *053/912–2758* 🎫 *Free* 🕐 *Daily 8:30–6:30.*

❻ The **Wexford Bull Ring** (✉ *Quay St., back toward quays*) was once the scene of bull baiting, a cruel medieval sport that was popular among the Norman nobility. Also in this arena, in 1649, Cromwell's soldiers massacred 300 panic-stricken townspeople who had gathered here to pray as the army stormed their town. The legacy of this heartless leader has remained a dark folk memory for centuries and is only now beginning to fade. A housing development at the old Cromwell's Fort is one of the ritzier addresses in town.

❼ The red sandstone **Westgate Tower** (✉ *Westgate*) was the largest of five fortified gateways in the Norman and Viking town walls, and it's the only one remaining. The early-13th-century tower has been sensitively restored. Keep an eye out as you wander this part of town for other preserved segments of the old town walls.

❽ The ruins of the 12th-century **Selskar Abbey** (✉ *Selskar St., south of Westgate Tower*) still stand. Here the first treaty between the Irish and the Normans was signed in 1169.

⑲ The **Wexford Wildfowl Reserve** is a nature-lover's paradise. Just a short walk across the bridge from the main part of town, it shelters one-third of the world's Greenland white-fronted geese. As many as 10,000 of them spend their winters on the mud flats, known locally as slobs, which also draw ducks, swans, and other waterfowl. Observation hides are provided for bird-watchers, and an audiovisual show and exhibitions are available at the visitor center. Lectures on the teeming birdlife of the reserve can be arranged on request. ⊠ *North Slob, Wexford Harbor* ☎ *053/912–3129* ⊠ *Free* ⊗ *Mid-Apr.–Sept., daily 9–6; Oct.–mid-Apr., daily 10–5.*

⑳ The **Irish National Heritage Park,** a 35-acre, open-air living history
⟳ museum beside the River Slaney, is one of Ireland's most successful
★ and enjoyable family attractions. In about 1½ hours, a guide takes you through 9,000 years of Irish history—from the first evidence of humans on this island, at around 7000 BC, to the Norman settlements of the mid-12th century. Full-scale replicas of typical dwelling places illustrate the changes in beliefs and lifestyles. Highlights of the tour include a prehistoric homestead, a *crannóg* (lake dwelling), an early Christian *rath* (fortified farmstead), a Christian monastery, a horizontal water mill, a Viking longhouse, and a Norman castle. There are also examples of pre-Christian burial sites and a stone circle. Most of the exhibits are "inhabited" by students in appropriate historic dress who will answer questions. The riverside site includes several nature trails. ⊠ *5 km (3 mi) north of Wexford Town on N11, Ferrycarrig* ☎ *053/910733* ⊕ *www.inhp.com* ⊠ *€7.50* ⊗ *Mar.–Oct., daily 9:30–6:30; Nov.–Feb., daily 9:30–5:30.*

Fodor'sChoice Only Walt Disney might have bettered the storybook look of the mas-
★ sive, Victorian-Gothic, gray-stone castle at **Johnstown Castle Gardens,** 5 mi (3 mi) southwest of Wexford following the N25 (direction Rosslare). A magical Gothic Revival extravaganza, this turreted, battlemented, and machicolated edifice, which bristles in silver-gray ashlar, was built for the Grogan-Morgan family between 1810 and 1855. Magnificent parklands—with splendid towering trees, lakes, and ornamental gardens—now frame the grand castle. Unfortunately, you can't tour the building (it houses a national agricultural college) other than its entrance hall, but the well-maintained grounds are open to the public. The centerpiece is the 5-acre lake, one side of which has a terrace, replete with statues, from which to take in the panorama of the mirrored castle. Because there's such a variety of trees framing the view—Japanese cedars, Atlantic blue cedars, golden Lawson cypresses—there's color through much of the calendar. Nearby are the Devil's Gate walled garden— a woodland garden set around the ruins of the medieval castle of Rathlannon—and the **National Museum of Agriculture and Rural Life.** The latter, housed in the quadrangular stable yards, shows what life was once like in rural Ireland. It also contains a 5,000-square-foot exhibition on the potato and the Great Famine (1845–49). ⊠ *Signposted just off N25, 6 km (4 mi) southwest of Wexford Town* ☎ *053/914–2888* ⊠ *Gardens May–Sept. €2, Oct.–Apr. free. Museum €5* ⊗ *Gardens daily 9:30–5:30. Museum Apr., May, and Sept.–Nov., weekdays*

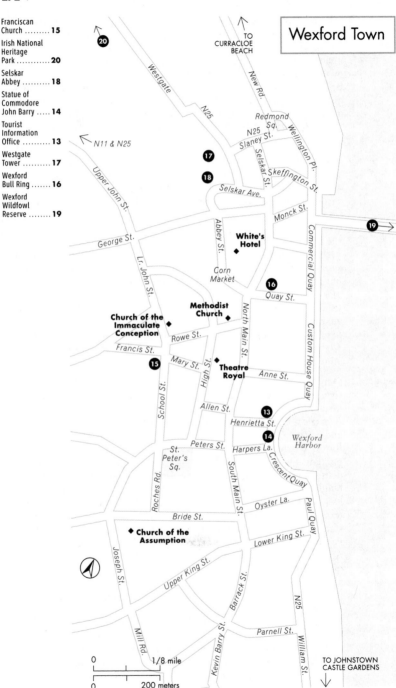

Wexford Town

THE SOUTHEAST THROUGH THE AGES

The Southeast's coastal and inland areas have long, interesting histories. The kings of Munster had their ceremonial center on the Rock of Cashel, a vast, cathedral-topped rock rising above the plain. Legend has it that St. Patrick converted the High King of Ireland to Christianity here. In the 7th century Cashel became an important monastic settlement and bishopric, and there were also thriving early Christian monasteries at Kilkenny, Ardmore, and Lismore.

But the quiet life of Christian Ireland was disrupted from the 9th century onward by a series of Viking invasions. Liking what they found here—a pleasant climate, rich, easily cultivated land, and a series of sheltered harbors—the Vikings stayed on, founding the towns of Wexford and Waterford. (Waterford's name comes from the Norse Vadrefjord, Wexford's from Waesfjord.)

But less than two centuries later, the Southeast was the location of the most significant turning point in Ireland's recorded history. In 1169 the Normans (who had conquered England a hundred years before) landed at Bannow Bay in County Wexford. It was the beginning of what Irish patriots commonly describe as "800 years of English oppression."

The English were invited into Ireland by the former king of Leinster, Dermot MacMurrough, who hoped to regain his crown with the help of the Norman earl, Richard FitzGilbert de Clare, famously known as "Strongbow." To seal their pact, Dermot's daughter Aoife married Strongbow. It was symbolic of the way that the Normans, once they had conquered the country, integrated into Irish life. It wasn't long before the Normans

were described as being "more Irish than the Irish themselves."

To this day, reminders of the Norman influence on Ireland remain strongest in the Southeast. Norman surnames are the most obvious indicator of the region's history, as names like Butler, Fitzgerald, Roche, and Fitzmaurice are all commonplace hereabouts. The architectural legacy of the Normans is also easy to spot in this part of Ireland.

The streetscapes of Kilkenny, Wexford, and Waterford cities owe their origins to the Normans. Travel the rural side roads of the region and it won't be long before you come across the ruins of a Norman castle, or "keep." Some are used to house animals or hay, while the best preserved are those that were integrated into later medieval or Georgian structures.

The Anglo-Normans and the Irish chieftains soon started to intermarry, but the process of integration came to a halt in 1366 with the Statutes of Kilkenny, based on English fears that if such intermingling continued they would lose whatever control over Ireland they had. The last great crisis was Oliver Cromwell's Irish campaign of 1650, which, in attempting to crush Catholic opposition to the English parliament, brought widespread woe.

5

9–12:30 and 1:30–5, weekends 2–5; June–Aug., weekdays 9–5, weekends 11–5; Dec.–Mar., weekdays 9–12:30 and 1:30–5.

WHERE TO STAY & EAT

$$–$$$ ✕**Heavens Above.** This cozy wood-panel loft restaurant has legions of fans—not least because of the unusual (for Ireland) wine policy. Owners John and Nuala Barron

also run the off-license next door and allow you to choose a bottle from their extensive range of more than 250 wines and beers, with no corkage charge to sully the taste of this sweet deal. The food has also been acclaimed, as you'll understand with your first bite of their Slaney salmon fillet paupiette with black pepper and lime butter or prawn tails served on homemade tagliatelle. ⊠ *112 S. Main St.* ☎ *053/911–273* ▤ *MC, V.*

$$–$$$ ✕**La Riva.** In summer the evening sun floods this quayside eatery with light, and the warm glow is reflected in the cooking—a colorful modern take on Mediterranean and Irish cuisine. Chef Warren Gillen sources organic and locally grown produce for his menu, which shows through in the delicately presented dishes. Expect to choose from entrées including spring lamb with shiitake mushrooms and spinach served with a warm red-wine-and-strawberry vinaigrette. The service is good, too—friendly without being over-attentive, giving you a chance to take in the pretty views of the harbor. ⊠ *Crescent Quay* ☎ *053/914–330* ▤ *MC, V.*

$$ ✕▦**Ferrycarrig.** A real favorite with families, this spot offers plenty of
☾ peace and tranquillity for parents thanks to its pleasant riverside location. All the bedrooms have wonderful views of the river, and some also have balconies. Tides restaurant ($$$–$$$$) overlooks its pleasant waterside location with a menu concentrating on seafood—scallops, salmon, and prawns prepared in simple lemon and butter sauces. For the kids there are a day-care facility and a swimming pool. There's also a well-equipped health center. The hotel is to be found 3 km (2 mi) from Wexford Town on the N11. ⊠ *Ferrycarrig Bridge, Co. Wexford* ☎ *053/912–0999* 🖶 *053/912–0982* ⊕ *www.griffingroup.ie* ☎ *102 rooms* ⌂ *In-room: no a/c. In-hotel: restaurant, bar, pool, gym, public Internet* ▤ *AE, DC, MC, V* ⦿ *BP.*

$ ▦**McMenamin's Town House.** From opera divas to Hollywood stars, they've all stayed at this cozy Victorian villa. It's become one of the lodgings of choice for the annual opera festival held in the town each autumn and is also popular as a last stopover for travelers heading for the Rosslare ferry to France. The bedrooms are spacious, warm, and immaculate, with large pieces of highly polished Victorian furniture and antique beds, including a mahogany half-tester. There are about eight choices at breakfast, including fresh fish of the day and hot porridge. Make sure you taste Kay and Seamus McMenamin's homemade whiskey marmalade. ⊠ *3 Auburn Terr., Redmond Rd., Co. Wex-*

ford 🖂📠*053/914–6442* ⊕*www.wexford-bedandbreakfast.com* ⇆*5 rooms* ⌂*In-room: no a/c, no phone. In-hotel: public Internet* ⊟*MC, V* ⊘*Closed last 2 wks of Dec.* ⫶⧄⫶*BP.*

¢ 🖼 **Darral House.** A handsome Georgian town house, Darral House offers a good base for exploring Wexford Town and is within a five-minute walk of the town center. Constructed at the turn of the 19th century, it was renovated in 2005; guest rooms are tastefully decorated in harmony with the history of the house. Run by Sean and Kathleen Nolan, it's well known for an excellent "Full Irish"—the classic Irish breakfast. 🖂*Spawell Rd., Co. Wexford* ☎*053/912–4264* 📠*053/912–4284* ⇆*4 rooms* ⌂*In-room: no a/c, no phone. In-hotel: parking (no fee), public Internet* ⊟*MC, V* ⫶⧄⫶*BP.*

NIGHTLIFE & THE ARTS

Touring companies and local productions can be seen in Wexford at the **Theatre Royal** (🖂*27 High St.* ☎*053/912–2400*). The **Wexford Opera Festival** (☎*053/912–2144 box office* ⊕*www.wexfordopera.com*), held during the last two weeks of October and the beginning of November, is the town's leading cultural event. The festival, which has been going strong since 1951, features seldom-performed operas sung by top talent from all over the world. Along with an ever-expanding offering of more populist fare performed in small venues and pubs, the festival supplies a feast of concerts and recitals that start at 11 AM and continue until midnight. For the full aria, *see* "Passion on the High C's" *in* the Planner at the front of this chapter.

As the saying goes, if you can find a street without at least one bar on it, you've left Wexford. **Centenary Stores** (🖂*Charlotte St.* ☎*053/912–4424*) is a Victorian-style pub. The adjoining nightclub makes it a popular place for the young crowd. Lunch is Monday through Saturday, and there's traditional music every Sunday morning. The **Sky and the Ground** (🖂*112 S. Main St.* ☎*053/912–1273*) is one of the best pubs in town and is a mecca for Irish music sessions, which pack in the crowds from Monday through Thursday. Dating to the 13th century, the **Thomas Moore Tavern** (🖂*Cornmarket* ☎*053/912–4348*) is Wexford's oldest pub, named after the renowned Irish poet whose parents lived here. The pub has its original medieval walls and fine old beams along the ceiling. It's the perfect place for a quiet drink by the fire. Light lunches and snacks are served on weekdays between noon and 3.

SPORTS

GAELIC FOOTBALL & HURLING You can watch Gaelic football and hurling at the **Wexford Park GAA** (🖂*Clonard Rd.* ☎*01/836–3222 GAA of Ireland in Dublin* ⊕*www.gaa.ie*).

SHOPPING

Barker's (🖂*36 S. Main St.* ☎*053/912–3159*) stocks Waterford crystal, local pottery, and crafts. **Martins Jewelers** (🖂*Lower Rowe St.* ☎*053/912–2635*) specializes in handmade Celtic jewelry. **Simone Walsh** (🖂*85 S. Main St.* ☎*053/912–3567*) features Irish art and design and original paintings. **Westgate Design** (🖂*22 N. Main St.* ☎*053/912–3787*) carries a good selection of Irish crafts, clothing, pottery, candles, and jewelry; there's also a restaurant here. **The Wool Shop** (✉ *39–41 S. Main St.* ☎ *053/912–2247*) is a good place to buy souvenirs, knitting yarn, and hand-loomed Aran sweaters.

WATERFORD & THE SOUTHEAST COAST

This journey takes you along mainly minor roads through the prettiest parts of the coast in counties Wexford and Waterford, pausing midway to explore Waterford City—home of the dazzling cut glass—on foot. Along the way expect to see long golden beaches, quaint fishing villages like Kilmore Quay and Ballyhack, some of the country's best nature reserves, and Tramore, Ireland's most unredeemable family waterside resort. If you're coming from the Continent or England, chances are you'll end up on a ferry bound for Rosslare Harbour, one of Ireland's busiest ferry ports.

ROSSLARE

㉑ *16 km (10 mi) southeast of Wexford Town on R470.*

Sometimes called Ireland's sunniest spot, the village of Rosslare is a seaside getaway with an attractive beach. Vacationers generally head here to hike, golf, sun, and swim. **Rosslare Harbor,** 8 km (5 mi) south of the village, is the terminus for car ferries from Fishguard and Pembroke in Wales (a four-hour trip) and from Cherbourg and Roscoff in France (a 22-hour trip). Indeed, taking the ferry is the only reason you should find yourself in this otherwise dull little town. The

> **TRAVEL TIP**
>
> Ferries to and from Rosslare frequently sell out, particularly in summer and any time the Irish soccer team is playing in a major tournament abroad. To be sure of getting a ticket on the boat of your choice, try to reserve your space in advance through the ferry companies' Cork or Dublin offices.

two ferry companies, Irish Ferries and Stena Sealink (contact information in Southeast Essentials, *below*), serving Rosslare Harbour have small information kiosks in the ultramodern terminal, which also has lockers, a sprawling waiting room, and a café. You can purchase ferry tickets at the terminal. Reservations are also a must if you're traveling by car because onboard parking space is at a premium. The **Rosslare Harbour rail depot** (☎ *053/57937* ⊕ *www.irishrail.ie*), adjacent to the ferry terminal, is served by frequent trains to Dublin's Connolly Station and Cork (change at Limerick Junction). Bus Éireann's Rosslare Harbour depot also adjoins the rail station.

WHERE TO STAY & EAT

$$ ✕🏨 **Kelly's.** Somewhat of a legend with Irish vacationers, this hotel has
★ become exceedingly popular. The reasons are numerous—a stunning beachfront location, second-to-none entertainment and leisure facilities, a child-friendly approach, and a reputation for excellent food being just a few. The guest rooms are comfort-laden havens decked out with rustic

The Southeast Coast

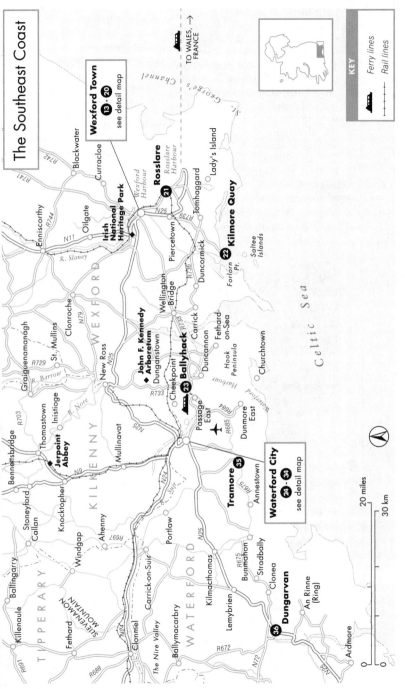

Blackwater

R742

R741

Enniscorthy

R744

Olgate

N11

R. Slaney

Curracloe

Wexford Town

13 · 20

see detail map

Irish National Heritage Park

Wexford Harbour

N25

Rosslare

Rosslare Harbour

21

St. George's Channel

TO WALES, FRANCE →

Lady's Island

Tomhaggard

Kilmore Quay

22

Piercetown

Duncormick

R736

R739

Forlorn Pt.

Saltee Islands

WEXFORD

Clonroche

R79

John F. Kennedy Arboretum

Dunganstown

Wellington Bridge

Carrick

Fethard on-Sea

Hook Peninsula

Churchtown

Celtic Sea

Graiguenamanagh

R729

St. Mullins

R. Barrow

New Ross

N25

Ballyhack

23

R733

Duncannon

Checkpoint

Passage East

R684

R685

Dunmore East

Waterford Harbour

Bennettsbridge

R703

Thomastown

Inistioge

R. Nore

Jerpoint Abbey

N9

KILKENNY

Mullinavat

N25

Stoneyford

Knocktopher

Callan

Ahenny

R697

Windgap

Portlaw

N24

Waterford City

24 · 34

see detail map

Tramore

35

Annestown

R675

Killenaule

Ballingarry

R691

Fethard

TIPPERARY

SLIEVENAMON MOUNTAIN

The Nire Valley

R688

Clonmel

N24

Carrick-on-Suir

R. Suir

Ballymacarbry

WATERFORD

Kilmacthomas

Lemybrien

R672

Bunmahon

Stradbally

R675

Clonea

Dungarvan

36

An Rinne (Ring)

N72

N25

Ardmore

20 miles

30 km

KEY

⛴ Ferry lines

---|--- Rail lines

5

furnishings. Waterford-glass chandeliers hang in the Beaches restaurant ($$), where the menu includes dishes like Wicklow venison with wild mushrooms and Madeira jus or roast crispy Barbary duck with sauce curaçao. You can also dine in La Marine ($$), a casual, bistro-style restaurant that does a fine job of cooking up Irish produce in Mediterranean style. The Sea-Spa incorporates a Seawater Vitality Pool, Bio Sauna, Mud Rooms, and seaweed baths among its many ecofriendly pleasures. Note that in July and August the hotel insists on a one-week minimum stay. ⊠ *Co. Wexford* ☎ *053/913–2114* 🖷 *053/913–2222* ⊕ *www.kellys.ie* ⤶ *106 rooms* ⚒ *In-hotel: 2 restau-rants, golf course, tennis courts, pools, gym, spa, bicycles, public Wi-Fi* ▭ *AE, MC, V* ⊘ *Closed Dec.–Feb.* †◎| *BP.*

> ## ROOKERY ON THE ROCKS
>
> The Saltee Islands, Ireland's largest bird sanctuary, make a fine day trip from Kilmore Quay. You can see kittiwakes, puffins, guillemots, cormorants, gulls, and petrels, especially in late spring and early summer, when several million seabirds nest among the dunes and rocky scarp on the southern of the two islands. From mid-May to mid-September, look for boats at the village waterfront or on the marina to take you to the islands, weather permitting.

NIGHTLIFE & THE ARTS

The Strand Bar (⊠ *Rosslare Harbor* ☎ *053/913–3110*), at the Hotel Rosslare, is a trendy spot with designer decor featuring stonework and fish tanks. It's popular for live music on weekends.

SPORTS

Rosslare Golf Club (⊠ *Rosslare Strand* ☎ *053/913–2203*) is a 27-hole championship links. A mixture of links and parkland can be found at the 27-hole **St. Helen's Bay** (⊠ *Kilrane* ☎ *053/913–3234*).

KILMORE QUAY

㉒ *22 km (14 mi) south of Rosslare on R739.*

Fodor's Choice
★

Noted for its fishing industry, this quiet, old-fashioned seaside village of thatched and whitewashed cottages is also popular with recreational anglers and bird-watchers. From the harbor there's a pleasant view to the east over the flat coast that stretches for miles.

Kehoe's Pub (⊠ *Kilmore Quay* ☎ *05391/29830*) is the hub of village activity; its collection of maritime artifacts is as interesting as that of many museums.

During two weeks in July (generally mid-month), the village hosts a lively **seafood festival** (☎ *053/912–9922 or 086/389–3278*) with a parade, seafood barbecues, and other events.

★ The **Kilmore Quay Maritime Museum** is onboard the lightship *Guillemot*. Built in 1923, this is the last Irish lightship to be preserved complete with cabins and engine room, and it contains models and artifacts relating to the maritime history of the area. ⊠ *Kilmore Quay* ☎ *053/912–1572* 🖭 *€5* ☉ *June–Aug., daily noon–6; Sept. and Apr., weekends noon–6.*

SLOW BOAT TO WATERFORD

The Knights Templars of St. John of Jerusalem were required to keep a boat at Ballyhack to transport injured knights to the King's Leper Hospital at Waterford.

WHERE TO STAY & EAT

$$–$$$$ ✕**Silver Fox.** A busy family-run seafood restaurant, this is considered one of the best in the area. Naturally, given its quayside location, seafood is the specialty here. Lemon sole gratin is a real favorite—a scrumptious fillet with a creamy sauce of fresh prawns, scallops, mushrooms, and onions, plus a sprinkling of cheese. Non-seafood options include chicken angelica stuffed with potatoes and leeks and wrapped in bacon with mushroom sauce. Simplicity and freshness define the food here. ⊠ *Kilmore Quay* ☎ *053/912–9888* ⌂ *Reservations essential* ☰ *AE, MC, V* ☉ *Closed mid-Jan.–mid-Feb. No lunch Mon.–Sat.*

$ 📺**Quay House.** A perfect base for those interested in boating or fishing, this guesthouse is a three-minute walk from the pier. The homey interior has Douglas fir pine floors throughout and country pine bedroom furniture. If you're the outdoors type you'll feel right at home: nearby are great waterside walks and boating options (a room for drying and storing diving and fishing equipment is available). ⊠ *Kilmore Quay, Co. Wexford* ☎ *053/912–9988* ⎙ *053/912–9808* ⊕ *www.quayhouse.net* ➪ *10 rooms* ⚬ *In-room: no a/c. In-hotel: restaurant* ☰ *MC, V* ⼟⏐*BP.*

SHOPPING

Country Crafts (⊠ *Kilmore Quay* ☎ *053/912–9885*), which overlooks the harbor of Kilmore Quay, sells Irish-made crafts, country-style furniture, and paintings by local artists.

BALLYHACK

㉓ *34 km (21 mi) west of Kilmore Quay.*

Fodor'sChoice
★

On the upper reaches of Waterford Harbor, this pretty village with a square castle keep, wooden buildings, thatched cottages, and a green, hilly background is admired by painters and photographers. A small car ferry makes the five-minute crossing to Passage East and Waterford.

The gray-stone keep of **Ballyhack Castle** dates from the 16th century. It was once owned by the Knights Templars of St. John of Jerusalem, who held the ferry rights by royal charter. The first two floors have been renovated and house local-history exhibits. Guided tours are available by appointment, and the last admission is 45 minutes before closing. ☎ *051/389–468* ⊕ *www.heritageireland.ie* 🖭 *€2.50* ☉ *Mid-June–mid-Sept., weekdays 10–1 and 2–6, weekends 10–6.*

Twelve kilometers (8 mi) to the north of Ballyhack lies the **John F. Kennedy Arboretum,** with more than 600 acres of forest, nature trails, and gardens, plus an ornamental lake. The grounds contain some 4,500 species of trees and shrubs, and serve as a resource center for botanists and foresters. Go to the top of the park to get fine panoramic views. The arboretum is clearly signposted from New Ross on R733, which follows the banks of the Barrow southward for about 5 km (3 mi). The cottage where the president's great-grandfather was born is in Dunganstown; Kennedy relatives still live in the house. About 2 km (1 mi) down the road at Slieve Coillte you can see the entrance to the arboretum. ⊠ *Dunganstown* ☎ *051/388–171* ⊕ *www.heritageireland. ie* ☎ *€2.90* ☺ *May–Aug., daily 10–8; Apr. and Sept., daily 10–6:30; Oct.–Mar., daily 10–5.*

WHERE TO STAY & EAT

$$$$

Fodor'sChoice

★

×▦ **Dunbrody Country House.** A rural jewel, this sprawling two-story 1830s Georgian manor house used to be the digs of the seventh marquess of Donegal, Dermot Chichester (who now lives nearby). Under the magic touch of current chatelains, Kevin and Catherine Dundon, the gardens are soul-restoring, the manse's public salons are a soigné symphony of mix-and-match tangerine-hue fabrics and stuffed armchairs, the views over the Barrow estuary remain grand, and the guest rooms charm with a judiciously luxe combination of period antiques and fine reproductions. Gourmands come here to stuff themselves cross-eyed in the ruby-red Harvest Room ($$$$), irresistibly drawn by master chef Kevin's Barbary duck in burnt-orange sauce, medallions of beef in Rhône wine jus, and a chocolate "selection of indulgences." (In fact, you may learn how to cook these delights yourself; Kevin runs a cooking school on the premises, with classes conveniently scheduled for weekends). After a dinner that is likely to be memorable sip-to-sup, sit back with a goblet of Irish mist in hand and catch a dramatic sunset fading over the Hook Peninsula. No need to rush the next morn: the famous breakfasts are served until 11:30. ⊠ *Arthurstown, New Ross, Co. Wexford* ☎ *051/389–600* 🖷 *051/389–601* ⊕ *www.dunbrodyhouse.com* ☞ *15 rooms, 7 suites* ☝ *In-room: no a/c, no elevator. In-hotel: restaurant, bar, public Wi-Fi* ⊟ *AE, DC, MC, V* ☉ *BP.*

WATERFORD CITY

10 km (6 mi) west of Ballyhack by ferry and road (R683), 62 km (39 mi) southwest of Wexford Town, 158 km (98 mi) southwest of Dublin.

The largest town in the Southeast and Ireland's oldest city, Waterford was founded by the Vikings in the 9th century and was taken over by Strongbow, the Norman invader, with much bloodshed in 1170. The city resisted Cromwell's 1649 attacks, but fell the following year. It did not prosper again until 1783, when George and William Penrose set out to create "plain and cut flint glass, useful and ornamental," and thereby set in motion a glass-manufacturing industry without equal.

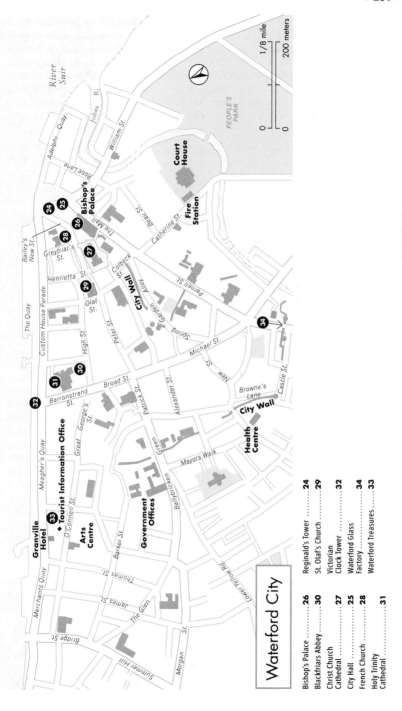

Waterford City

5

Waterford has better-preserved city walls than anywhere else in Ireland but Derry. Initially, the slightly run-down commercial center doesn't look promising. You need to park your car and proceed on foot to discover the heritage that the city has made admirable efforts since the mid-1990s to preserve, in particular the grand 18th-century Georgian buildings that Waterford architect John Roberts (1714–96) built, including the town's Protestant and Catholic cathedrals. The compact town center can be visited in a couple of hours. Allow at least another hour if you intend to take the Waterford crystal factory tour.

The **city quays**—at the corner of Custom House Parade and Peter Street—are a good place to begin a tour of Waterford City. (The TIO is also down here, at the Granary on Merchant's Quay.) The city quays stretch for nearly 2 km (1 mi) along the River Suir and were described in the 18th century as the best in Europe.

㉔ Reginald's Tower, a waterside circular tower on the east end of Waterford's quays, marks the apex of a triangle containing the old walled city of Waterford. Built by the Vikings for the city's defense in 1003, it has 80-foot-high, 10-foot-thick walls; an interior stairway leads to the top. The tower served in turn as the residence for a succession of Anglo-Norman kings (including Henry II, John, and Richard II), a mint for silver coins, a prison, and an arsenal. It's said that Strongbow's marriage to Eva, the daughter of Dermot MacMurrough, took place here in the late 12th century, thus uniting the Norman invaders with the native Irish. It has been restored to its original medieval appearance and furnished with appropriate 11th- to 15th-century artifacts. ⊠ *The Quay* ☏*051/304–220* ☞*€2.10* ☉ *Mid-Mar.–Sept., daily 10–6; Oct., daily 10–5; Nov.–mid-Mar., Wed. and Thurs. 10–5.*

㉕ One of Waterford's finer Georgian buildings, **City Hall,** on the Mall, dates from 1783 and was designed by John Roberts, a native of the city. Nearby are some good examples of domestic Georgian architecture—tall, well-proportioned houses with typically Irish semicircular fanlights above the doors. The arms of Waterford hang over City Hall's own entrance, which leads into a spacious foyer that originally was a town meeting place and merchants' exchange. The building contains two lovely theaters, an old Waterford dinner service, and an enormous 1802 Waterford glass chandelier, which hangs in the Council Chamber (a copy of the chandelier hangs in Independence Hall in Philadelphia). The Victorian horseshoe-shape Theatre Royal is the venue for the annual Festival of Light Opera in September. ⊠ *The Mall* ☏*051/309–900* ☞*Free* ☉ *Weekdays 9–5.*

㉖ The **Bishop's Palace** is among the most imposing of the remaining Georgian town houses. Only the foyer is open to the public. ⊠ *Alongside City Hall on the Mall* ☞*Free* ☉ *Weekdays 9–5.*

㉗
★ Lovers of Georgian decorative arts will want to visit the late-18th-century Church of Ireland **Christ Church Cathedral,** designed by local architect John Roberts and the only Neoclassical Georgian Cathedral in Ireland. Inside, all is cup-of-tea elegance—yellow walls, white-stucco trim in designs of florets and laurels, grand Corinthian columns—and you

can see why architectural historian Mark Girouard called this "the finest 18th-century ecclesiastical building in Ireland." It stands on the site of a great Norman Gothic cathedral. The then Bishop Cheneix, it's oft told, wouldn't consider knocking that great edifice down—never, that is, until it was arranged for a little stone vaulting to fall in his path. Medievalists will be sad, but those who prize Age-of-Enlightenment high style will rejoice. ⌧ *Henrietta St.* ☎ *051/858–958* ⊕ *www. christchurchwaterford.com* ⌧ *€3* ☉ *Easter–Sept., Mon.–Sat. 10–1 and 2–5; Sun. 11–1 and 2–5.*

> **ONE WAY OR ANOTHER**
>
> Although there are several theories about the origin of the phrase, some experts credit Cromwell with coining the expression "by hook or by crook." Planning two siege routes to Waterford—one via Hook Head, the other via Crooke Village on the estuary of the River Suir—Cromwell declared that he would take the city "by Hooke or by Crooke."

㉘ Roofless ruins are all that remain of **French Church** (⌧ *Greyfriar's St.*), a 13th-century Franciscan abbey. The church, also known as Greyfriars, was given to a group of Huguenot refugees (hence the "French") in 1695. A splendid east window remains amid the ruins. The key is available at Reginald's Tower.

㉙ **St. Olaf's Church** (⌧ *St. Olaf's St.*) was built, as the name implies, by the Vikings in the mid-11th century. All that remains of the old church is its original door, which has been incorporated into the wall of the existing building (a meeting hall).

㉚ The ruined tower of **Blackfriars Abbey** (⌧ *High St.*) belonged to a Dominican abbey founded in 1226 and returned to the crown in 1541 after the dissolution of the monasteries. It was used as a courthouse until Cromwellian forces destroyed it in the 17th century.

㉛ The Roman Catholic **Holy Trinity Cathedral** has a simple facade and a richly (some would say garishly) decorated interior with high, vaulted ceilings and ornate Corinthian pillars. It was designed in Neoclassical style by John Roberts, who also designed Christ Church Cathedral and City Hall. Surprisingly, it was built in the late 18th century—when Catholicism was barely tolerated—on land granted by the Protestant city fathers. ⌧ *Barronstrand St. between High St. and clock tower on quays* ☎ *051/875–166* ⊕ *www.waterford-cathedral.com* ⌧ *Free* ☉ *Daily 8:30–5:30.*

㉜ The **Victorian Clock Tower** (⌧ *Merchant's Quay*) was built in 1864 with public donations. Although it has no great architectural merit, it serves as a reminder of the days when Waterford was a thriving, bustling port.

㉝ **Waterford Treasures,** above the Southeast's main TIO, uses interactive audiovisual technology to guide you through 1,000 years in the history of Waterford. Entertaining and educational, the exhibition displays Waterford's rich inheritance of rare and beautiful artifacts—from the Charter Roll of 1372, a list of all charters granted to Waterford up to that time, written in Latin on vellum, to the sword of King Edward

FodorśChoice
★

Rolls-Royce of Crystal

Silica sand + potash + litharge = Waterford crystal: it reads like cold science, but something magical happens when the craftsmen of Waterford produce arguably the top crystal in the world (although France's Baccarat might have something to say about that).

When the Waterford Glass Factory opened in 1783, it provided English royalty and nobility with a regular supply of ornate handcrafted stemware, chandeliers, and decorative knickknacks. Since then Waterford crystal has graced the tables of heads of state the world over, and Waterford's earlier pieces have become priceless heirlooms.

The best Waterford glass was produced from the late 18th century to the early 19th century. This early work, examples of which can be found in museums and public buildings all over the country, is characterized by a unique, slightly opaque cast that is absent from the modern product.

Crystal glass is not cheap: each piece is individually fashioned by almost two-dozen pairs of hands before it passes final inspection and receives the discreet Waterford trademark.

If you're in Waterford, put a tour of the factory at the top of your itinerary. There you can see master craftspeople at work, fashioning the molten glass, blowing it into bulbous shapes, and then cutting and carving to give each piece those wonderful light-catching facets that cast multicolor reflections. You probably won't need any protective eye gear, but considering all the razzle-dazzle, sunglasses might come in handy.

IV to 18th-century crystal. A restaurant and a shop are also on the premises. ⊠ *The Granary, Merchant's Quay* ☎ *051/304–500* 💶 *€6* ☉ *Apr.–Sept., weekdays 9–5, Sat. 10–5, Sun. 11–5; Oct.–Mar., weekdays 10–5, Sun. 11–5.*

❸❹ The city's most popular attraction is the **Waterford Glass Factory**, about 2 km (1 mi) from the TIO, where the world-famous crystal is created. The factory opened in 1783, crafting elegant and ornate stemware, chandeliers, and other pieces. Over the years, its clientele and product line diversified, and today the United States is the biggest market. The tour of the factory takes you through the specialized crafts of blowing, cutting, and polishing glass—all carried out against a noisy background of glowing furnaces and ceaseless bustle. An extensive selection of crystal is on view (and for sale) in the showroom. Tours are offered on weekends (often booked solid weeks in advance during summer), but on weekdays you're allowed to go at a more relaxed pace, which is infinitely preferable. To reserve a place in a 60-minute tour, which includes an optional 18-minute audiovisual show, call the factory or the tourist office. To get here, take the N25 Waterford–Cork road south from the quay, or ask at the tourist office about the regular bus service. ⊠ *Cork Rd., Kilbarry* ☎ *051/358–398* ⊕ *www.waterfordvisitorcentre. com* 💶 *€9* ☉ *Tours daily 9–4; factory daily 8:15–6.*

If the weather is favorable, consider taking a **cruise** along Waterford's harbor and the wide, picturesque estuary of the River Suir. You can enjoy lunch, afternoon tea, or dinner aboard a luxury river cruiser or simply take in the sights. The boat departs from the quay opposite the TIO, where you can purchase tickets. ☎051/421–723 *Galley Cruises*

> **WATERFORD CITY LIMITS**
>
> Off Colbeck Street along Spring Garden Alley, you can see one of the remaining portions of the old city wall; there are sections all around the town center.

⊕*www.rivercruises.ie* ⊙*Cruises Apr.–Oct., daily at 12:30, 3, and 7, weather permitting.*

WHERE TO STAY & EAT

$$–$$$ ✕**Chez Ks Steak & Seafood Restaurant.** There's always a lively buzz about this fine American-style eatery—especially on weekends when the resident piano man plays a baby grand in the center of the restaurant. The mood is modern, with pieces of contemporary art adorning the walls, and grilled food is the specialty. After choosing from such house favorites as steak fillet with pepper sauce, and tempura of monkfish served with a pineapple-and-pear chutney, customize your meal with a choice of trimmings, sauces, and side dishes. You can watch your meal being prepared in the open kitchen—one of the first of its kind in the country. Another plus is the excellent service. ⊠*20–22 William St.* ☎*051/844–180* ≜*Reservations essential* ⊟*AE, DC, MC, V.*

$$–$$$
Fodor$Choice
★ ✕**Fitzpatricks Restaurant.** When he acquired the place in 2004, the new owner of the much-loved former O'Grady's Restaurant and Guesthouse had a tough act to follow, but somehow Billy Fitzpatrick has managed to pull it off. The restaurant is in a beautifully restored lodge house on the outskirts of the city, and though the interior has had a pleasing makeover, it has retained a subtly traditional ambience so as not to shock the regulars. The cuisine is firmly in the fine-dining camp with a Gallic flavor to the seafood-rich dishes on offer. ⊠*Cork Rd.* ☎*051/378–851* ⊟*DC, MC, V.*

$$–$$$ ✕**Goose's Barbecue & Wine House.** The rustic dining room complements the ranch-style cooking that's served at this unusual restaurant in the historic quarter of the city. Exposed brick, robust furniture, and bright walls make convivial surroundings for a meat-heavy menu. Specialties include "Boozy beef steaks"—a prime Irish cut marinated in soy sauce and stout—and the "sticky finger spare ribs" barbecued with hickory. Efficient table service, good desserts, and hearty food guarantee a satisfying night out. ⊠*19 Henrietta St.* ☎*051/858–426* ≜*Reservations essential* ⊟*MC, V* ⊙*Closed Sun. and Mon.*

$–$$
Fodor$Choice
★ ✕**The Wine Vault.** You'd never know it but underneath this modern building lies the cellar of an Elizabethan town house, thought to have been built by Peter Rice, the mayor of Waterford back in 1426. Famed for forging links between Waterford and the Spanish shrine of Santiago de Compostela, Rice was also a wealthy wine merchant and for centuries his fortified town house held stocks of Bordeaux, port, Madeira,

claret, and hock. Today, fittingly, you can sit down at the polished wooden tables of a restored bonded warehouse to enjoy the creations of chef Fergal Phelan, who likes to buy wines to match food. Expect to choose from dishes like roast skewered monkfish with vegetables and rice accompanied by an apricot, mango, and red currant salsa or braised duo of Waterford venison and beef sausages with thyme mash. On your way out, be sure to peruse the vintages, hailing from Australia to Alsace, on sale in the basement wineshop. ⊠*High St.* ☎*051/853-444* ⊕*www.waterfordwinevault.com* ⊟*AE, MC, V* ⊘*Closed Sun.*

$$$$

Fodor's Choice

★

╳▦ **Waterford Castle.** Not only does this fairy-tale castle come with an 800-year history, it sits in the middle of a 310-acre island, and allows lucky guests to be bed-and-boarded in the grandest Irish style. Back in Norman times, the Kfyeralds built a keep here and over the centuries— as their name became Fitzgeralds, "Kings of Ireland in all but name"— they expanded, adding two Elizabethan-style wings in the 17th century, fitting them out with rooftop gargoyles brought from Castle Irwell in Manchester. Today, the air of exclusivity lingers as the private ferry picks you up on the shores of the River Suir, and heightens with one step inside the Great Hall, a magnificent faux-baronial room in Portland stone and hung with medieval tapestries. Nearby is the Munster Dining Room ($$$$), whose luxe—oak paneling, darkened with age, and ancestral portraits spotlit in gilt frames—compliments one of the most stylish menus around. Most guest rooms are exquisitely done in real "country-house" style, some with canopied beds, chintz armchairs, and dark mahogany furniture. To top it all off, a prize-winning 18-hole golf course adjoins the castle. Obviously, the last great Fitzgerald to occupy the house, Mary Frances (whose son, Edward Fitzgerald, translated the *Rubaiyat of Omar Khayyam* into English) would be happy to see her former domain so lovingly cared for. ⊠*The Island, Ballinakill, Co. Waterford* ☎*051/878–203* 🖷*051/879–316* ⊕*www.waterfordcastle.com* ➷*14 rooms, 5 suites* ♿*In-room: no a/c. In-hotel: restaurant, golf course, tennis courts, public Wi-Fi* ⊟*AE, DC, MC, V.*

$–$$$

Fodor's Choice

★

╳▦ **Faithlegg House Hotel.** A gorgeous 18th-century mansion in mature woodlands has been converted into one of the Southeast's most popular getaway destinations for those who are out for both indulgence and relaxation. There's an acclaimed 18-hole golf course and a gym for healthy types. For those less inclined to such vigorous pursuits there's also the full gamut of pampering treatments available at the Estuary Club spa. Chef Eric Theze lends a French influence to the cuisine served in the hotel's restaurant, the Roseville Rooms ($$–$$$), which includes two of the house's original drawing rooms, replete with ornate stucco plasterwork ceilings. Self-catering accommodation is also available and good mid-week deals are usually available. To get here, take the Dunmore road out of Waterford for 3 mi (2 km), then follow the sign for Passage East and veer right under the railway bridge at Jack Meades' pub. ⊠*Faithlegg, Co. Waterford* ☎*051/382–000* 🖷*051/382–010* ⊕*www.faithlegg.com* ➷*68 rooms, 14 suites* ♿*In-room: no a/c. In-hotel: restaurant, golf course, tennis courts, pool, spa, public Wi-Fi* ⊟*AE, DC, MC, V* ❑*BP.*

$–$$$ 🖥 **Dooley's Hotel.** A friendly air pervades this unpretentious family-run hotel on the banks of the river Suir. Dooley's is also just a few minutes' walk from all the main attractions and is perfect for families. The rooms are simple, bright, and decorated in vibrant colors. The service is excellent and the traditional-style bar is popular with locals. The New Ship restaurant serves Continental dishes and has an early-bird menu. ✉*30 The Quay, Co. Waterford* ☎*051/873–531* 🖷*051/870–262* ⊕*www.dooleys-hotel.ie* ⬗*115 rooms* △*In-room: no a/c. In-hotel: restaurant, bar, public Wi-Fi* ▭*AE, DC, MC, V* ⑪*BP.*

$ 🖥 **Foxmount Farm & Country House.** For a pleasant change of pace, you can stay on a working dairy farm in the peaceful countryside. This elegant 17th-century creeper-clad country house on extensive grounds has an informal style, with welcoming log fires and intriguing antiques. It's about 5 km (3 mi) outside town on the road to the Passage East ferry. Your host, Margaret Kent, has been welcoming guests for 40 years and is renowned for her cooking. Sadly, she no longer provides dinners, but the breakfast remains legendary. Enjoy seasonal fruit and fresh farm produce accompanied by Margaret's home-baked bread. ✉*Passage East Rd., Co. Waterford* ☎*051/874–308* 🖷*051/854–906* ⊕*www.foxmountcountryhouse.com* ⬗*5 rooms* △*In-room: no a/c, no TV. In-hotel: restaurant, tennis court* ▭*No credit cards* ⊘*Closed Nov.–mid-Mar.* ⑪*BP.*

NIGHTLIFE & THE ARTS

The **Spraoi Festival** (☎*051/841–808* ⊕*www.spraoi.com*) is billed as the "biggest street carnival in Ireland"—with street theater, live music, and fireworks. This free outdoor festival, which appeals to children and adults alike, takes place annually during the August bank holiday, the first weekend of the month. The **Waterford International Festival of Light Opera** (☎*051/874–402* ⊕*www.waterfordfestival.com*), the only competitive event of its kind, is a great draw for amateur musical societies from Ireland and Great Britain. The festival runs for 17 nights every September at the **Theatre Royal** (✉*City Hall, The Mall* ☎*051/874–402*). The **Waterford Show** tells the story of Waterford's culture and heritage through music, song, and dance. The show begins at 9 PM on Tuesday, Thursday, and Saturday at City Hall from May through September. The admission cost of €11 includes a preshow drink and a glass of wine during the show. Book at Waterford Glass Factory or the **Waterford Tourist Information Office** (☎*051/875–788*).

You can see a wide selection of work by contemporary artists at the **Dyehouse Gallery and Waterford Pottery** (✉*Dyehouse La.* ☎*051/844–770* ⊕*www.dyehouse-gallery.com*), one of Ireland's only modern purpose-built galleries. The building is an attraction in itself and has won numerous awards for its architectural design. The **Forum** (✉*The Glen* ☎*051/871–111* ⊕*www.forumwaterford.com*) is a large entertainment venue that houses a 300-seat theater. Here you can watch local productions or those of traveling theater companies. Two music venues host big names as well as local acts performing all kinds of music. Culture buffs shouldn't miss the **Garter Lane Arts Centre** (✉*22A*

O'Connell St. (☎*051/855–038*), which hosts concerts, exhibits, and theater productions.

The five-screen **Waterford Cineplex** (✉*Patrick St.* ☎*051/874–595*) shows current releases.

Geoffs (✉*9 John St.* ☎*051/874–787*) is a dimly lighted pub frequented by a mixed crowd including students and locals. Big flagstones cover the floors, and seating is on old wooden benches. An outdoor area is available for those keen to avoid Ireland's smoking ban. A wide selection of food is served until 9, every day. Housed in an 800-year-old building, the **Old Ground** (✉*10 The Glen* ☎*051/852–283*) is a popular pub with locals. Lunch is served daily, and traditional-music sessions are held every Friday night. The circa-1700 **T & H Doolan's Bar** (✉*32 George's St.* ☎*051/872–764*), reputed to be one of the oldest pubs in Ireland, hosts traditional Irish music most summer nights and Monday through Wednesday year-round. Known to the natives as Meade's Under the Bridge, **Jack Meades** (✉*Cheekpoint Rd., Halfway House, Ballycanavan* ☎*051/873–187*) is snug under a time-stained stone bridge. In centuries past it was a stop on the coach road from Waterford to Passage East. There's a pub menu from May through September, and sing-along sessions are held throughout the year on the weekends. In winter the fireplaces roar, illuminating the wood beams and bric-a-brac. As in many pubs, the proprietors have created a patio area for the smoking fraternity, but this is an outdoor area with a difference—it also has a children's playground and a "minizoo" with a collection of cute farmyard animals.

SPORTS

GAELIC FOOTBALL
Watch Gaelic football and hurling at the **Waterford GAA Grounds** (✉*Walsh Park* ☎*01/836–3222 GAA in Dublin* ⊕*www.gaa.ie*).

GOLF
Faithlegg Golf Club (✉*Faithlegg House, Checkpoint* ☎*051/382–241*) is an 18-hole course set in mature landscape on the banks of the River Suir. **Waterford Castle Golf Club** (✉*The Island, Ballinakill* ☎*051/871–633*) is an 18-hole course that claims to be Ireland's only true island course.

SHOPPING

City Square Shopping Centre (✉*City Sq.* ☎*051/853–528*) has more than 40 shops, ranging from small Irish fashion boutiques to large international department stores. Fashion shows and other forms of entertainment take place on the stage area in the center of the mall.

Joseph Knox (✉*3 Barronstrand St.* ☎*051/875–307* ⊕*www.josephknox.com*) displays the best selection of crystal in Waterford City.

Kellys (✉*75–76 The Quay* ☎*051/873–557*) has excellent Irish souvenirs, including traditional musical instruments, dolls, Irish linen, jewelry, Waterford crystal, and CDs.

Even if you don't take the plant tour, pay a visit to the famed **Waterford Glass Factory** (✉*Cork Rd., Kilbarry* ☎*051/332–500* ⊕*www.waterfordvisitorcentre.com*). The showroom displays an extensive selection of Waterford crystal and Wedgwood china.

TRAMORE

35 **⏱** *11 km (7 mi) south of Waterford City on R675, 4 km (2½ mi) west of Dunmore East.*

Tramore's 5-km-long (3-mi-long) **beach** is a popular escape for families from Waterford and other parts of the Southeast, as the many vacation homes and camper parks indicate. This is Ireland's biggest seaside resort and a dream-come-true for young children, but it's not to everybody's taste. A 50-acre amusement park, a miniature railway, and vacation-home developments overshadow part of the seafront. (The upper half of town is more quiet and reserved.)

> **THREE'S A CHARM**
>
> At the western end of Tramore's beach, the sand gives way to rocky cliffs guarded by the Metal Man, a giant cast-iron figure that stands atop a great pillar. It's said that if a young woman hops on one foot around the base of the pillar three times, she will be married within a year. This custom, which is still observed in a lighthearted way, can be traced back to a stone that stood on the spot centuries ago and was used in ancient Celtic fertility rites.

WHERE TO EAT

$-$$ ✕ **Rockett's.** One mile beyond Tramore is Rockett's, part of The Metal Man pub—an unusual and tasty stop for thoroughly Irish refreshments. An old and welcoming place always packed with local farmers, truckers, and Southeast Willie Loman types, Rockett's specialty is thoroughly unpretentious—*crubeens* (pig's feet). You know what's in store for you by the open sink provided for rinsing your fingers. Long before roasted nuts and potato crisps arrived, every Irish pub served crubeens, but nowadays you have to look long and hard to find them. An Irish version of spare ribs with all their attendant oily, finger-licking goodness, crubeens will surely stave off hunger pangs for exhausted travelers. The menu also includes bacon and cabbage, colcannon, and decent Irish stew. ✉ *Westown* ☎ *051/381–496* ▭ *MC, V* ⊘ *Closed Mon.*

DUNGARVAN

36 *42 km (26 mi) southwest of Tramore on R675.*

With their covering of soft grasses, the lowlands of Wexford and eastern Waterford gradually give way to heath and moorland; the wetter climate of the hillier western Waterford countryside creates and maintains the bog. The mountains responsible for the change in climate rise up behind Dungarvan, the largest coastal town in County Waterford. This bustling fishing and resort spot sits at the mouth of River Colligan, which empties into Dungarvan Bay here. It's a popular base for climbers and hikers.

In **Ring (An Rinne)**, a Gaeltacht area on Dungarvan Bay, the Irish language is still in daily use—this is unusual in the south and east of the country. At Colaiste na Rinne, a language college, courses in Irish have been taught since 1909. ✉ *7 km (4¼ mi) southeast of Dungarvan, off N674F.*

WHERE TO STAY & EAT

$$ ✕ **The Tannery.** Clearly, out there in Knockmealdown, the mountain air
Fodor'sChoice   must do something to clear the brain and allow chefs to focus and
★   purify. Perhaps that's why this place is besieged on weekends, when Dubliners head here to taste the creations of culinary wizard Paul Flynn. He worked for almost a decade with London culinary legend Nico Ladenis and now wins raves from the likes of Sir Andrew Lloyd Webber. The dishes on offer may look slightly odd on the menu but they taste sensational on the palate. Check out crab crème brûlée with pickled cucumber and onion marmalade served with melba toast. Or if that doesn't tickle your taste buds opt for the homemade black pudding with risotto of parsley, pine nuts, and raisins or the roast rump of lamb with mild garlic crème and cocoa beans. Fanatical foodies who want to stay as close to the culinary action as possible can now overnight in the adjoining guesthouse, opened by the Flynns in 2005. Your waistline may never be the same again. ⊠*10 Quay St.* ☎*058/45420* ⊕*www.tannery.ie* ⊟*AE, DC, MC, V* ☉*Closed Mon. and 2 wks in Jan. No dinner Sun.*

$–$$ ▦ **The Gold Coast Golf Hotel.** Overlooking Dungarvan Bay, this hotel is
⟳   part of a family-run and family-friendly property that also includes self-catering holiday cottages (built around the hotel) and golf villas on the edge of a woodland course on a links setting. Hotel rooms are bright, comfortable, and spacious. Guests can use the facilities of the Gold Coast's sister hotel, the Clonea Strand, just 2½ km (1½ mi) away, which include a games room, a leisure complex, and Clonea's 3-km-long (2-mi-long) sandy beach. ⊠*Co. Waterford* ☎*058/42249 or 058/42416* ⊟*058/43378* ⊕*www.clonea.com* ⟿*37 rooms, 21 cottages, 10 villas* ⚘*In-hotel: restaurant, bar, golf course, tennis court, pool, gym, public Internet* ⊟*AE, DC, MC, V* ⑩*BP.*

NIGHTLIFE & THE ARTS

Several miles away from Dungarvan, a *ceilí* (Irish dance) is held nightly in summer at **Colaiste na Rinne** (⊠*Ring* ☎*058/46104*).

IN & AROUND COUNTY TIPPERARY

"It's a long way to Tipperary…" So run the words of that famed song sung all over the world since World War I. Actually, Tipperary is *not* so far to go, considering that, as Ireland's biggest inland county, it's within easy striking distance of Waterford and Cork. Moving in from the coastline, you can travel through some of Ireland's most lush pasturelands and to some of its most romantic sights, such as Lismore Castle. The Blackwater Valley is renowned for its beauty, peacefulness, and excellent fishing. Some of the finest racehorses in the world are raised in the fields of Tipperary, which is also the county where you can find the Rock of Cashel—the greatest group of monastic ruins in all Ireland.

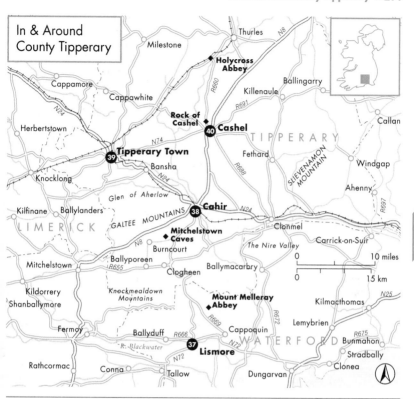

In & Around
County Tipperary

LISMORE

37 *20 km (13 mi) northwest of Dungarvan on N72.*

Fodor'sChoice
★

Popular with both anglers and romantics, the enchanting little town of Lismore is built on the banks of the Blackwater, a river famous for its trout and salmon. From the 7th to the 12th centuries it was an important monastic center, founded by St. Carthac (or Carthage), and it had one of the most renowned universities of its time. The village has two cathedrals; a Roman Catholic one from the late 19th century and the Church of Ireland St. Carthage's, which dates from 1633 and incorporates fragments of an earlier church. Glamour arrived in the form of the dukes of Devonshire, who built their Irish seat here (their main house is Chatsworth in England); in the 1940s, Fred Astaire, whose sister, Adele, had married Lord Charles Cavendish, younger son of the ninth duke, would bend the elbow at the town's Madden's Pub. There were darker interludes in the town's history: Lismore was hard hit by the Great Famine of 1845 and its Famine Graveyard bears poignant witness.

★ As you cross the bridge entering Lismore, take in the dramatic view of the magnificent **Lismore Castle**, a vast, turreted, gray-stone building atop a rock that overhangs River Blackwater. There has been a castle here since the 12th century, but the present structure, built by the sixth duke of Devonshire, dates from the mid-19th century. Today, the house remains the Irish estate of the current duke and duchess and is not open to the public (although you can call it your own for a very high rental fee). But the upper and lower gardens, which consist of woodland walks, including an unusual yew walk said to be more than 800 years old (Edmund Spencer is said to have written parts of *The Faerie Queen* there), are open during certain months of the year. Comprising 7 acres set with 17th-century defensive walls, the gardens have an impressive display of magnolias, camellias, and shrubs, and are adorned with examples of contemporary sculpture. ☎ *058/54424* ⊕ *www.lismorecastle.com* ⊠ *€6* ⊘ *Apr., May, Sept., and Oct., daily 1:45–4:45; June–Aug., daily 11–4:45.*

Almost the definitive example of an estate town, Lismore has in recent years taken the firm decision to project a pride of place linked with a deep sense of history. The **Lismore Heritage Center** in the former town courthouse lies at the core of the town, and its exhibits focus on the town's Celtic origins and its links to many famous people from Sir Walter Raleigh to Prince Charles to Fred Astaire. An award-winning video presentation on the history of the town from its monastic 7th century origins up to the present day is shown. ⊠ *The Old Courthouse* ☎ *058/54975* ⊕ *www.discoverlismore.com* ⊠ *€4* ⊘ *Apr.–Sept., weekdays 9:30–5:30, Sat. 10–5:30, Sun. noon–5:30.*

Mount Melleray Abbey was the first post-Reformation monastery, founded in 1832 by the Cistercian Order in what was then a barren mountainside wilderness. Over the years the order has transformed the site into more than 600 acres of fertile farmland. The monks maintain strict vows of silence, but you're welcome to join in services throughout the day and are permitted into most areas of the abbey. It's also possible to stay in the guest lodge by prior arrangement. If you're heading into the Knockmealdown Mountains from Lismore, you can easily stop on the way at the abbey for a visit. ⊠ *South of Vee Gap, signposted off R669, 13 km (8 mi) from Lismore, Cappoquin* ☎ *058/54404* ⊕ *www. cappoquin.org/abbey.shtml* ⊠ *Free* ⊘ *Daily 8:30–5:45.*

Leaving Lismore, heading east on N72 for 6½ km (4 mi) toward Cappoquin, a well-known coarse-angling center, you can pick up R669 north into the **Knockmealdown Mountains.** Your route is signposted as the Vee Gap road, the Vee Gap being its summit, from where you'll have superb views of the Tipperary plain, the Galtee Mountains in the northwest, and a peak called Slievenamon in the northeast. If the day is clear, you should be able to see the Rock of Cashel, ancient seat of the kings of Munster, some 32 km (20 mi) away. Just before you enter the Vee Gap, look for a 6-foot-high mound of stones on the left side of the road. It marks the grave of Colonel Grubb, a local landowner who liked the view so much that he arranged to be buried here standing up so that he could look out over the scene for all eternity.

WHERE TO STAY & EAT

$$–$$$$ ✕**Buggy's Glencairn Inn.** Ken and Cathleen Buggy's country pub oozes character and welcomes patrons from all over the world. Here, God is in the details, from the cozy fires to the good food, and especially the genuine sense of hospitality. Ken's mantra—"when we say fresh, we mean it"—comes through in preparations of organic fowl and meat, and fish direct from Helvic head. Pâté de campagne, smoked eel with horseradish sauce and salad, simple fish dishes cooked in butter and lemon, and pot-roasted guinea fowl issue from the kitchen, along with house-baked brown soda bread. Desserts may include fresh lime cake, homemade ice cream, and a farmhouse cheese selection that includes Durrus, Milleens, Carrigaline, Cashel Blue, and Dubliner. ⊠*Glencairn* ☎*058/56232* ⊕*www.glencairninn.com* ⊟*MC, V* ⊗*Closed Mon.*

$$–$$$ ✕🖼 **Richmond House.** It's been 300 years since the Earl of Cork and
★ Burlington built this handsome country house and it still retains its imposing aura of courtly elegance. Today, happily, owners Claire and Paul Deevy give it a relaxed and welcoming touch. The public rooms, with log fires and traditional rust-and-cream decor, are reminiscent of a classic country hotel, although one graced with silver plate, a tapestry, and a stuffed owl. The pièce de résistance here, however, is the restaurant ($$$$), where Paul and his small staff wow critics and diners alike. Famous for his warm asparagus wrapped in smoked salmon, he prides himself on using local game in season and fish from Helvic, Dunmore, and Ardmore, adding his personal flair. Triumphs include wild Blackwater salmon with Thai spices, a spring roll with smoked duck breast, and rabbit with black pudding. Reservations are essential for the restaurant. ⊠*Cappoquin, Co. Waterford* ☎*058/54278* 🖷*058/54988* ⊕*www.richmondhouse.net* ⇄*9 rooms* ♿*In-room: no a/c, no elevator. In-hotel: restaurant, bar* ⊟*AE, DC, MC, V* ⊗*Closed late Dec.–mid-Jan.* ⊙|*BP.*

CAHIR

38 *37 km (23 mi) north of Lismore, at crossroads of R668, N24, and N8.*

A pleasant Georgian square lies at the heart of this easygoing town, but **Cahir Castle** remains the unavoidable focal point. Perched on a rocky island on the River Suir, it's one of Ireland's largest and best-preserved castles, retaining its dramatic keep, tower, and much of its original defensive structure. An audiovisual show and guided tour are available upon request. ☎*052/41011* ⊕*www.heritageireland.ie* 🎟*€2.90* ⊗*Mid-Mar.–mid-June and mid-Sept.–mid-Oct., daily 9:30–5:30; mid-June–mid-Sept., daily 9–7; mid-Oct.–mid-Mar., daily 9:30–4:30; last admission 45 min before closing.*

Fodor's Choice If there's little storybook allure to the brute mass of Cahir Castle, fairy-
★ tale looks grace the first earl of Glengall's 1812 **Swiss Cottage,** a dreamy relic from the days when Romanticism conquered 19th-century Ireland. A mile south of town on a particularly picturesque stretch of the River Suir, this "cottage orné" was probably designed by John

Nash, one of the Regency period's most fashionable architects. Half thatched-roof cottage, half mansion, bordered by verandas constructed of branched trees, it was a veritable theater set that allowed the lordly couple to fantasize about being "simple folk" (down to the fact that secret doorways were constructed to allow servants to bring drinks and food without being noticed). Inside, some of the earliest Dufour wallpapers printed in Paris charm the eye. The Cottage is signposted from the R670 along the Cahir to Ardfinnan road, or you can hike from Cahir Castle on a footpath along the enchanting river. In peak season, crowds can be fierce. ☎052/41144 ⊕www.heritageireland.ie ☜€2.90 ⊙Mid-Mar.–mid-Apr., Tues.–Sun. 10–1 and 2–6; Mid-Apr.–mid-Oct., daily 10–6; mid-Oct.–mid-Nov., Tues.–Sun. 10–1 and 2–4:30.

WHERE TO STAY & EAT

$$$ – $$$$ ⚫ **The Old Convent.** A former convent run by the Sisters of Mercy dat-
★ ing back over 100 years, this prim and proper country house is situated in a spectacularly scenic location close to the Vee Gap in the Knockmealdown Mountains. A wonderfully tucked-away sanctuary, overlooking rolling fields, mountains, and the famous abundance of rhododendrons in spring months, this retreat has now been tastefully restored—in all senses of the word—by Christine and Dermot Gannon. Dermot's well-established credentials as one of Ireland's most innovative chefs are lovingly displayed in the restaurant (closed Mon.–Wed.), and his special skills in fusing Irish and Far Eastern tastes result in winners like wontons of fillet beef and foie gras; mozzarella popover with smoked salmon; and hot-buttered-rum baked brill with a crab, pea, and pistachio risotto, all offered on eight-course tasting menus. He also prides himself on artisanal foodstuffs, so you may well find yourself munching on Keating's Baylough Cheese, Mrs. Fryday's Lettuce, and Mrs. Houlihan's Meringues. Upstairs, Georgian-style marble tiles in the hallways, living rooms in restful shades of grey and fawn, chandeliers, and bold-hued accent pillows and original art works lend life to the Victorian manse. Bedrooms have antique furniture, silk curtains, and large bathrooms. Book in advance, as The Old Convent lies almost equidistant from Cahir and Lismore, attracting overnighters from both popular destinations. ⊠Mount Anglesby, Clogheen, Co. Tipperary ☎052/65565 ⊕www.theoldconvent.ie ⤴7 rooms ⚫In-room: no a/c, no elevator. In-hotel: restaurant ☐MC, V.

$ ⚫ **Bansha Castle.** Near the center of the heritage trail—with the Rock of Cashel, Holycross Abbey, and the medieval city of Kilkenny all nearby—this 18th-century stone house is a fine option. Venture into the heart of quiet, wooded country backed by the Glen of Aherlow and you'll enter the property's noted arboretum, which has outstanding examples of beech, oak, lime, and Norway spruce. Before long, a Norman-style round tower announces the house. Inside, large rooms, all with great views, are simply furnished with plain carpets and mahogany reproduction pieces, but walls are painted in strong, vibrant colors. The drawing room has marble fireplaces, polished wooden floors, and floral-patterned furniture. Locally grown, organic produce is used in the good home cooking. Dinner ($$, guests only) should be booked in advance. Outdoor activities, such as walking, golfing, salmon and trout fishing, and horseback riding, are nearby. Bansha is about 8 km (5 mi) from Cahir on the N24 Tipperary road. ⊠*Bansha, Co. Tipperary* ☎*062/54187* 🖷*062/54294* ♥*7 rooms* ♨*In-room: no a/c, no TV. In-hotel: restaurant* ▭*No credit cards* ◎*BP.*

TIPPERARY TOWN

39 *22 km (14 mi) northwest of Cahir on N24.*

Tipperary Town, a dairy-farming center at the head of a fertile plain known as the Golden Vale, is a good starting point for climbing and walking in the hills around the Glen of Aherlow. The small country town, on the River Ara, is also worth visiting in its own right. In New Tipperary, a neighborhood built by local tenants during Ireland's Land War (1890–91), buildings such as Dalton's Heritage House have been restored; you can visit the Heritage House by calling the offices of Clann na hEireann. You can also visit the old Butter Market on Dillon Street; the Churchwell at the junction of Church, Emmet, and Dillon streets; and the grave of the grandfather of Robert Emmett—one of the most famous Irish patriots—in the graveyard at St. Mary's Church. A statue of Charles Kickham, whose 19th-century novel *The Homes of Tipperary* chronicled the devastation of this county through forced emigration, has a place of honor in the center of town. Adjacent to Bridewell Jail on St. Michael's Street is St. Michael's Church, with its stained-glass window depicting a soldier killed during World War I.

The **headquarters of Clann na hEireann** (⊠*45 Main St.* ☎*062/33188*) researches the origins and history of surnames throughout Ireland and promotes clan gatherings.

CASHEL

40 *17 km (11 mi) northeast of Tipperary Town on N74.*

Cashel is a market town on the busy Cork–Dublin road, with a lengthy history as a center of royal and religious power. From roughly AD 370 until 1101, it was the seat of the kings of Munster, and it was probably at one time a center of Druidic worship. Here, according to legend, St. Patrick arrived in about AD 432 and baptized King Aengus, who became Ireland's first Christian ruler. One of the many legends associated with this event is that St. Patrick plucked a shamrock to explain the mystery of the Trinity, thus giving a new emblem to Christian Ireland.

Fodor'sChoice ★ The awe-inspiring, often mist-shrouded **Rock of Cashel** is one of Ireland's most visited sites. For complete information, *see* "Towering Glory: The Rock of Cashel" in this chapter.

In the same building as the town TIO, the **Cashel of the Kings Heritage Center** explains the historic relationship between the town and the Rock and includes a scale model of Cashel as it looked during the 1600s. ⊠*City Hall, Main St.* ☎*062/62511* ⊕*www.heritagetowns. com/cashel.html* 🖻*Free* ⊙*Daily 9:30–5:50.*

Continued on page 302

TOWERING GLORY: THE ROCK OF CASHEL

Haunt of St. Patrick, Ireland's "rock of ages" is a place where history, culture, and legend collide

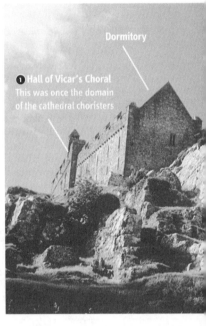

Dormitory

❶ Hall of Vicar's Choral
This was once the domain of the cathedral choristers

Seat of the Kings of Munster and the hallowed spot where St. Patrick first plucked a shamrock to explain the mystery of the Trinity, the Rock of Cashel is Ireland's greatest group of ecclesiastical ruins. Standing like an ominous beacon in the middle of a sloped, treeless valley, the Rock's titanic grandeur and majesty creates what one ancient scribe called "a fingerpost to Heaven."

Historians theorize the stupendous mass was born during the Ice Age. This being Ireland, however, fulsome myths abound: There are those who believe it was created when the Devil himself took a huge bite of the Slieve Bloom Mountains only to spit it out right in the middle of the Golden Vale. Today, the great limestone mass still rises 300 feet to command a panorama over all it surveys—fittingly, the name derives from the Irish *caiseal*, meaning stone fort, and this gives a good idea of the strategic importance of Cashel in days of yore.

For centuries, Cashel was known as the "city of the kings"—from the 5th century, the lords of Munster ruled over much of southern Ireland from here. In 1101, however, they handed Cashel over to the Christian fathers, and the rock soon became the center of the reform movement that reshaped the Irish Church. Along

the way, the church fathers embarked on a centuries-long building campaign that resulted in the magnificent group of chapels, round towers, and walls you see at Cashel today. View them from afar on the N8 highway and the complex looks so complete you're surprised upon arriving to discover guides in modern dress and not knights in medieval uniform.

■ TIP➔ The best approach to the rock is along the Bishop's Walk, a 10-minute hike that begins outside the drawing room of the Cashel Palace hotel on Main Street in the town of Cashel, just to the south of the rock.

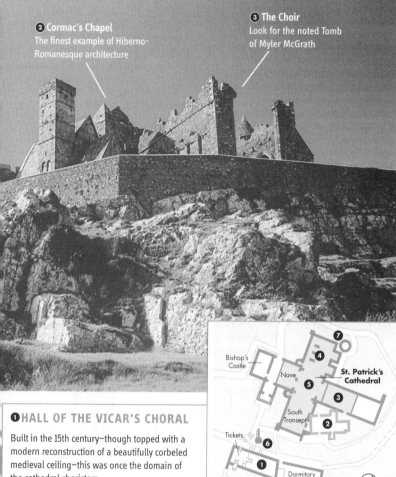

❷ Cormac's Chapel
The finest example of Hiberno-Romanesque architecture

❸ The Choir
Look for the noted Tomb of Myler McGrath

Bishop's Castle

Nave

St. Patrick's Cathedral

South Transept

Tickets

Dormitory

❶ HALL OF THE VICAR'S CHORAL

Built in the 15th century—though topped with a modern reconstruction of a beautifully corbeled medieval ceiling—this was once the domain of the cathedral choristers.

The Museum Located in the hall's undercroft, this collection includes the original St. Patrick's Cross and fast-forwards you to the present thanks to a striking audiovisual display on the Rock entitled the "Stronghold of the Faith."

❷ CORMAC'S CHAPEL

The real showpiece of Cashel is this chapel, built in 1127 by Cormac McCarthy, King of Desmond and Bishop of Cashel. A rare jewel in gleaming red sandstone, it is the finest example of Hiberno-Romanesque architecture. The entry archway carries a

tympanum featuring a centaur in a helmet with a bow and arrow aimed at a lion, perhaps a symbol of good over evil. Such work was rare in Irish architecture and points to possible European influence. Preserved within the chapel is a splendid but broken sarcophagus, once believed to be Cormac's final resting place. At the opposite end of the chapel is the nave, where you can look for wonderful medieval paintings now showing through old plasterwork.

ST. PATRICK'S CATHEDRAL

With thick walls that attest to its origin as a fortress, this now roofless cathedral is the largest building on the site. Built in 1169, it was dedicated on March 17th–St. Patrick's Day. On the theory that ancient churches were oriented to the sunrise on the feast day of their dedicated saint, the cathedral points east, a direction agreeing closely with March 17th. The original cathedral, constructed in a flamboyant variation on Irish Romanesque style, was destroyed by fire in 1495. In ❸ **The Choir**, look for the noted Tomb of Myler McGrath. Note the tombs in the ❹ **North Transept** whose carvings–of the apostles, other saints, and the Beasts of the Apocalypse–are remarkably detailed. The octagonal staircase turret that ascends the cathedral's central tower leads to a series of defensive passages built into the thick walls–

St. Patrick's Cathedral

from the top of the tower, you'll have wonderful views. At the center of the cathedral is the area known as ❺ **The Crossing**, a magnificently detailed arch where the four sections of the building come together.

COMING OF AGE

450 AD–St. Patrick comes to Cashel, bringing the advent of Christianity when King Aengus accepts baptism from Ireland's patron saint.

990–Cashel is fortified by King Brian Boru, the legendary figure who broke the stranglehold of the Danes at the Battle of Clontarf in 1014.

1101–King Murtagh O'Brien, grandson of Brian Boru, proclaims the royal fortress "for God, St. Patrick, and St. Ailbe," making Cashel center of the Irish Church.

1317–The arrival of the Scots: Edward Bruce, brother of Robert I, is inaugurated king of Ireland, and attends Mass on the Rock where he later holds a parliament.

1749–Protestant archbishop Price earns undying infamy by pulling down the roof of the cathedral to rebuild his own church.

King Brian Boru

❼ Round Tower

As the oldest building on the Rock, the Round Tower rises 92 feet.

❹ North Transe

❻ ST. PATRICK'S CROSS

Directly beyond the Rock's main entrance is this 7-foot-tall High Cross carved from one large block and resting upon what is said to have been the original coronation stone of the Munster kings. The cross was erected in the saint's honor to commemorate his famous visit to Cashel in 450. Upon both sides carved in high relief are two figures—the face of Christ crucified and a robed St. Patrick with his feet resting upon an ox head. Unique among High Crosses, this one has vertical supports on either side, perhaps allusions to the crosses of the good and bad thieves. A sort of early Irish bible class, these large stone crosses (which were sculpted from the 9th to the 12th centuries) were perfect teaching tools for a population that was largely illiterate. This cross is a faithfully rendered replica—the original now rests in the site museum.

❼ THE ROUND TOWER

As the oldest building on the Rock, the Round Tower rises 92 feet to command a panoramic view of the entire Vale of Tipperary. Dating back to 995, its construction followed the grim reality of the Viking invasions. A constant lookout was posted here to warn of any advancing armies and food was always provisioned in the tower so as to outlast any prolonged siege. Note the door 10 feet from the ground, allowing ladders to be pulled up to thwart attackers, some of whom attempted to chip the rock at the base, with little effect.

Central Tower   Bishop's Castle

❺ The Crossing   Nave

Northern View of the Rock

5

TOWERING GLORY: THE ROCK OF CASHEL

THE ST. PATRICK CONNECTION

Baptism, St. Paddy Style

Set in front of the Archbishop's Castle, the Rock of Cashel's famed 12th-century St. Patrick's Cross reputedly marks the spot where St. Patrick made a breakthrough in his conversion of Ireland by baptising King Aengus and his son in 450. During the baptism, Patrick accidentally stuck his crozier through Aengus's foot. Asked why he did not cry out, the king said he thought the pain was part of the initiation ceremony.

Enduring a crozier point in his foot without protest gives some notion of the bravery of King Aengus, a royal patron who played a crucial part in St. Patrick's mission. While no records exist, a close bond clearly grew between king and saint—the pair spoke for hours walking around Cashel's grounds. The young king provided the financial assistance for many of the churches St. Patrick founded over the 11 years he remained in Munster. Such acceptance by a king opened many doors that might otherwise have remained firmly shut for Patrick.

Properly known as St. Patrick's Rock, Cashel has many fabled associations with Ireland's patron saint.

Shamrocks & Snakes

Before converting King Aengus, St. Patrick picked a shamrock on the Rock of Cashel, and used it to explain the mystery of the Holy Trinity, three Gods in One, a central tenet of Christianity, to him. The other famous myth associated with St. Patrick is the banishment of the snakes from Ireland, who fled when St. Patrick rang his bell at the end of his 40-day fast on Croaghpatrick in County Mayo. Of course, the island of Ireland, being cut off from the European mainland, never had any snakes in the first place . . . but why ruin a good story?

But Who Was St. Patrick?

While many legends surround this saint, he was an actual historical figure—his writings, a Latin text dating from the 5th century AD, yield the few undoubted facts about him. Born into a wealthy family in Roman-occupied Britain, he was kidnapped as a young man by Irish marauders and enslaved for six years as a sheepherder on the slopes of Slemish in County Antrim. He escaped, and returned to Britain, but a vision called him back to Ireland to convert the people to Christianity. Arriving in 433, he defied the pagan priests of Tara by kindling the Easter fire on Slane but went on in a peaceful conversion of Ireland to Christianity—not a drop of blood was shed—until his death in AD 460.

St. Patrick's conversion of Ireland was characterized by clever diplomacy: his missionaries were careful to combine elements of then-current druidic ritual with new Christian practice. For example, the Irish Christian church popularized the Feast of all Saints, and arranged for it to be celebrated on November 1, the same day as the great Celtic harvest festival, Samhain. Today's Halloween evolved from this linking of Celtic and Christian holidays.

Clearly a skilled negotiator as well as missionary, St. Patrick wisely preserved the social structure of Ireland, converting the people tribe by tribe. He first attempted to establish the Roman system of dioceses and bishops, but—since Ireland had never been conquered by the Romans—this arrangement did not suit a society without large cities. Instead, the Celts preferred a religious institution introduced by the desert fathers: the monastery, an idea of a "family" of monks being easy to grasp in a tribal society where kinship ties were

The common phrase "land of milk and honey" is often attributed to St. Patrick. Upon his arrival at Cashel and viewing the rich lands of the Golden Vale, the saint was immediately taken by the fertile country all around him. To this day, much of Tipperary is still called "the best land in Ireland."

strong. Over 70 monasteries were founded in the 5th and 6th centuries, and by AD 700 abbots had replaced bishops as the leaders of the Catholic church.

In 457 St. Patrick retired to Saul, where he died. The only relic that can be tied to him is the famous 5th century iron bell in Dublin's National Museum. Even if it was not, as is traditionally believed, used by the saint, he carried one very like it, and used it to announce his approach.

St. Patrick stepping on a snake.

The **G.P.A. Bolton Library,** on the grounds of the St. John the Baptist Church of Ireland Cathedral, has a particularly fine collection of rare books, manuscripts, and maps, some of which date from the beginning of the age of printing in Europe. ⊠*John St.* ☎*062/61944* 🖻*€2* ⊙*Daily 10–4.*

WHERE TO STAY & EAT

$$–$$$$ ✕**Chez Hans.** It's rather fitting that this restaurant is in a converted
★ church, as it's become something of a foodies' shrine. Gourmands travel from Dublin and Cork to get their fix of chef Jason Matthia's cuisine, which is contemporary with a hint of nouvelle. He works wonders with fresh Irish ingredients, especially seafood. Their famous cassoulet of seafood—half a dozen varieties of fish and shellfish with a delicate chive velouté sauce—is legendary. Another specialty is diced lamb with ratatouille and couscous. The atmosphere is wonderful, too, with dark-wood decor and tapestries providing an elegant background for the white linen. ⊠*Rockside* ☎*062/61177* ⚠*Reservations essential* ▤*AE, DC, MC, V* ⊙*Closed Sun. and Mon. and late Jan.–early Feb. No lunch.*

$$$–$$$$ ✕▥**Cashel Palace.** Built in 1730 for archbishop Theophilus Bolton, this
Fodor's Choice grand house truly is a palace in every sense. It was designed by Sir
★ Edward Lovett Pearce, who also created the Old Parliament House in Dublin, and is gorgeously offset by a parkland replete with fountains and centuries-old trees. Inside, red-pine paneling, barley-sugar staircases, Corinthian columns, and a surfeit of cosseting antiques all create an air of Georgian *volupté*. Guest rooms on the second floor are cozier, though not small. The Bishop's Buttery restaurant ($$–$$$$) relies on game in season, local lamb and beef, and fresh fish creatively prepared, and also serves simple, light meals all day. Don't miss the lovely gardens at the rear of the house, where you can see the descendants of the original hop plants used by Richard Guinis to brew the first "Wine of Ireland." Guinis went on, with his son, Arthur, to found the Guinness Brewery in Dublin. ⊠*Main St., Co. Tipperary* ☎*062/62707* 🖷*062/61521* ⊕*www.cashel-palace.ie* ⊅*23 rooms* ⌂*In-room: no a/c. In-hotel: 2 restaurants, bar, public Wi-Fi* ▤*AE, DC, MC, V* ⎪◯⎪*BP.*

$$ ▥**Dundrum House Hotel.** Nestled beside the River Multeen, 12 km (7½ mi) outside busy Cashel, is this imposing, four-story 1730 Georgian house. Sixteen high-ceiling bedrooms take up the main house; the rest are in a three-story wing built during the house's previous incarnation as a convent. Opened as a hotel in 1981 by Austin and Mary Crowe, the renovation of the manor house was substantial and sensitive. Although highly renovated, many of the older rooms have accent pieces of early-Victorian furniture. A big plus: lovely views of the surrounding parkland. The old convent chapel, stained-glass windows intact, is now a cocktail bar. Elaborate plaster ceilings, attractive period furniture, and open fires make the spacious dining room and lounge inviting. The latest draw is a new, award-winning health and leisure club, along with an 18-hole championship golf course designed by Ryder Cup hero Philip Walton. ⊠*Dundrum, Co. Tipperary* ☎*062/71116* 🖷*062/71366* ⊕*www.dundrumhousehotel.com* ⊅*85 rooms* ⌂*In-room: no a/c. In-*

Voices of Ireland

URSULA SINNOTT; *Director, Wexford Opera Festival*

Wexford Opera is one of those festivals that everybody has always heard about. Held in October, it usually includes over forty daytime events as well as the eighteen evening performances of three major productions. Opera is the beating heart of the festival, and the Wexford company of artists are drawn from all over the world. It's a event that makes even the opera lovers of New York and Paris peagreen with envy.

"The success of the festival over the years is largely due to the overall Wexford experience, the relative uniqueness of coming here to find opera that is rarely performed anywhere else," notes Ms. Sinnott. "There is a constant sense of surprise among audiences here—an anticipation of 'what will this be like?' Moving along the narrow streets of the town from one event to the next, going in and out of shops where everybody is so well informed—little wonder the festival is so unique."

"It was originally founded through the efforts of a surgeon and a postman— and that all-encompassing ethos

continues to drive the event. We have a volunteer corps of 350 people that covers every strata of life: retired bank managers, police officers, doctors, unemployed people, farmers, shopkeepers. The running joke in the town is that volunteers can only 'retire' after 20 years service."

"Of course, we never rest on laurels—one week after this year's festival ends, the preparations for next year begin. Looking outward around the world and seeing what's happening is another factor in our success here—we've been so fortunate to have top class artistic directors over the years, some of which have been quite controversial, and all to the good of pushing the artistic envelope."

"Looking to the future, we are now in the second year of our Young Artists Development program. The other bright light in our future is the opening of our new theatre in 2008, still a venue where audiences will pass through the local neighborhoods to get to. This festival will never be above or away from the local people—it will always run through the town like a thread that binds us all together."

hotel: 2 restaurants, bars, golf course, pool, gym, public Wi-Fi ▭*AE, DC, MC, V* ⦿*BP.*

NIGHTLIFE & THE ARTS

You can enjoy folksinging, storytelling, and dancing from mid-June through September, Tuesday through Saturday, at the **Bru Boru Center** (☎*062/61122*) at the foot of the Rock of Cashel. Entertainment usually begins at 9 PM and costs €15, €40 with dinner.

SPORTS

GAELIC FOOTBALL & HURLING About 20 km (12 mi) north of Cashel, **Semple GAA Stadium** (✉*Thurles* ☎*0504/22702* ⦿*www.gaa.ie*) is where major hurling and Gaelic football championships in the Southeast take place, as well as many exciting minor contests.

SOUTHEAST ESSENTIALS

TRANSPORTATION

If traveling extensively by public transportation, be sure to load up on information (schedules, the best taxi-for-hire companies, etc.) upon arriving at the ticket counter or help desk of the bigger train and bus stations in the area, such as Kilkenny City, Wexford Town, and Waterford City.

BY AIR

Aer Arann flies once daily in both directions between Waterford City and London's Luton Airport. There are also flights three times per week to Manchester.

Carrier **Aer Arann** (☎ *1890/462–726* ⊕ *www.aerarann.ie*).

AIRPORT   Waterford Regional Airport is on the Waterford–Ballymacaw road in Killowen. Waterford City is less than 10 km (6 mi) from the airport. A hackney cab from the airport into Waterford City costs approximately €17.

Airport Information **Waterford Regional Airport** (☎ *051/875–589* ⊕ *www. flywaterford.com*).

BY BOAT & FERRY

The region's primary ferry terminal is just south of Wexford Town at Rosslare. Irish Ferries connects Rosslare to Pembroke, Wales, and France's Cherbourg and Roscoff. Stenaline sails directly between Rosslare Ferryport and Fishguard, Wales.

Boat & Ferry Information **Irish Ferries** (☎ *053/913–3158 or 0818/300–400* ⊕ *www.irishferries.com*). **Stenaline** (☎ *053/916–1590* ⊕ *www.stenaline.ie*).

BY BUS

Bus Éireann makes the Waterford–Dublin journey 10 times a day for about €11 one way and €16 round-trip. There are six buses daily between Waterford City and Limerick, and four between Waterford City and Rosslare. The Cork–Waterford bus runs 13 times a day. In Waterford City, the terminal is Waterford Bus Station.

Bus Information **Bus Éireann** (☎ *01/836–6111 in Dublin, 051/879–000 in Waterford* ⊕ *www.buseireann.ie*).

BY CAR

Waterford City, the regional capital, is easily accessible from all parts of Ireland. From Dublin, take N7 southwest, change to N9 in Naas, and continue along this highway through Carlow Town and Thomastown until it terminates in Waterford. N25 travels east–west through Waterford City, connecting it with Cork in the west and Wexford Town in the east. From Limerick and Tipperary Town, N24 stretches southeast until it, too, ends in Waterford City.

CAR RENTAL   The major car-rental companies have offices at Rosslare Ferryport, and in most large towns, rental information is available through the local tourism office. Typical car rental prices start at about €55 per day (€32 per day for seven days) with unlimited mileage, and they usually include insurance and all taxes.

Agencies **Budget** (⊠ *The Ferryport, Rosslare Harbor* ☎ *053/913–3318* ⊠ *Waterford Airport* ☎ *051/421–670*). **Hertz** (⊠ *The Ferryport, Rosslare Harbor* ☎ *053/913–3238*).

ROAD CONDITIONS For the most part, the main roads in the Southeast are of good quality and are free of congestion. Side roads are generally narrow and twisting, and you should keep an eye out for farm machinery and animals on country roads.

BY TRAIN

Waterford City is linked by Irish Rail service to Dublin. Trains run from Plunkett Station in Waterford City to Dublin four times daily, making stops at Thomastown, Kilkenny, Bagenalstown, and Carlow Town. The daily train between Waterford City and Limerick makes stops at Carrick-on-Suir, Clonmel, Cahir, and Tipperary Town. The train between Rosslare and Waterford City runs twice daily.

Train Information **Irish Rail** (☎ *01/836–6222 in Dublin, 051/873–401 in Waterford* ⊕ *www.irishrail.ie*).

CONTACTS & RESOURCES

EMERGENCIES

Emergency Services **Ambulance, fire, police** (☎ *112 or 999*).

Hospital **Waterford Regional Hospital** (⊠ *Ardkeen* ☎ *051/848–000*).

INTERNET CAFÉS

Even though much of Ireland has gone Wi-Fi over the past two years, in some of the more rural regions you'll need to rely on the local Internet café to catch up on messages from home. As well as good places to find a decent cup of java, they are generally quite cheap; expect to pay around €2 an hour.

Internet Access **Café Net** (⊠ *4 Lower Patrick St., Kilkenny City* ☎ *056/777–0051*). **I.O. Internet** (⊠ *5 Cornmarket, Wexford Town* ☎ *053/9123729*). **Voyager Internet Café** (⊠ *85 The Quay, Waterford City* ☎ *051/843–843*).

TOUR OPTIONS

Irish City Tours in Kilkenny operates open-top coach tours from the castle gate Easter through September, daily 10:30–5.

Burtchaell Tours in Waterford City leads a Waterford walk at noon and 2 PM daily from March through September. Tours depart from the Granville Hotel. Walking tours of Kilkenny are arranged by Tynan Tours from the Kilkenny TIO; tours take place daily April through October, and Tuesday through Saturday, November to March. Walking tours of historic Wexford Town can be prebooked for groups by contacting Wexford Town Walking Tours.

Bus Tour **Irish City Tours** (☎ *01/458–0054*).

Walking Tours **Burtchaell Tours** (☎*051/873–711*). **Tynan Tours** (☎*087/265–1745*). **Wexford Town Walking Tours** (☎*053/912–2663*).

VISITOR INFORMATION

Eight Tourist Information Offices (TIOs) in the Southeast are open all year. They are Carlow Town, Dungarvan, Enniscorthy, Gorey, Kilkenny, Lismore, Waterford City, and Wexford Town. Another five TIOs are open seasonally: Cahir (May–September); Cashel (April–September); Rosslare (April–September); Tipperary Town (May–October); Tramore (June–August).

Tourist Information **Cahir** (✉*Castle Car Park, Co. Tipperary* ☎*052/41453*). **Carlow Town** (✉*College St., Co. Carlow* ☎*059/913-1554*). **Cashel** (✉*Cashel Heritage Centre, Co. Tipperary* ☎*062/62511*). **Dungarvan** (✉*The Courthouse, Co. Waterford* ☎*058/41741*). **Enniscorthy** (✉*Wexford Museum, The Castle, Castle Hill, Co. Wexford* ☎*054/34699*). **Kilkenny** (✉*Shee Alms House, Rose Inn St., Co. Kilkenny* ☎*056/775-1500*). **Lismore** (✉*Heritage Centre, Co. Waterford* ☎*058/54975*). **Rosslare** (✉*Rosslare Ferry Terminal, Kilrane, Rosslare Harbor, Co. Wexford* ☎*053/913-3232*). **Tipperary Town** (✉*3 Mitchel St., Co. Tipperary* ☎*062/51457*). **Tramore** (✉*Town Centre, Co. Waterford* ☎*051/381-572*). **Waterford City** (✉*41 The Quay, Co. Waterford* ☎*051/875-823* ⊕*www.southeastireland.com*). **Wexford Town** (✉*Crescent Quay, Co. Wexford* ☎*053/912-3111*).

The Southwest

Gallarus Oratory on the Dingle Peninsula, County Kerry

WORD OF MOUTH

"I adore Cork—both the county and the city. The people are extremely friendly, the countryside is gorgeous, there are great places to eat, some decent clubs, excellent chippers for late-night snacking, and the Cork accent is absolutely delightful. Blarney, Kinsale, Clonakilty—what more can you ask for?"

—SAM

WELCOME TO
THE SOUTHWEST

TOP REASONS
TO GO

★ **Blarney Castle:** Visitors line up to kiss the Blarney Stone and acquire the gift of gab. This is an impressive 15th-century tower-house castle with unusual gardens, at their best in daffodil season— early to mid-March.

★ **Kinsale:** This picturesque port, long a favored haven of sailors, is famed for its fine dining in tiny front-parlor eateries. It's also a chic place to see and be seen—the Irish San Tropez.

★ **The Cork Coastline:** On the drive from Kinsale to Skibbereen you'll encounter friendly locals, charming little villages, unspoiled scenery, and excellent restaurants and pubs.

★ **The Gap of Dunloe:** A half-day tour lets you walk or ride horseback through the heart of Killarney's purple mountains and cross the glittering blue lake by rowboat.

★ **Skellig Michael:** The rocky, twin-peaked island, topped with a 7th-century monastery, looms offshore as you follow the Ring of Kerry.

Blarney Castle

Saint Patrick's Quay, Cork City

1 Cork City. Identifying Cork as Ireland's second-largest city is misleading—it has just one-tenth the population of Dublin, and its character is more along the lines of a college town (which it is) than a metropolis. That means lively pubs, quirky cafés, and lots of good music, trad and otherwise.

2 County Cork. South of Cork City, the resort town of **Kinsale** is the gateway to a rocky, attractive coastline containing **Roaring Water Bay** and the wide, magnificent **Bantry Bay.** To the north of the city, some of the best salmon fishing in the world is to be had on the peaceful **Blackwater River.**

6

GETTING ORIENTED

In the Southwest, five-star scenery is everywhere. This is Ireland's picture postcard country, from Kinsale on the south coast of County Cork, across Bantry Bay, inland to the mountains and lakes of Killarney, and out to Kerry's craggy western peninsulas. Brightly painted villages and small harbors encourage you to stop and linger—and when you do, you're rewarded with exceptional food, particularly in Kinsale and Kenmare, towns that vie for the title of Ireland's culinary capital. Off the western coast, the Skelligs rank as the region's most awesome sight, though it takes an often choppy boat ride to reach them.

3 County Kerry. The county's coast is formed by the **Iveragh Peninsula** (home to the Ring of Kerry), and **Corca Dhuibne (a.k.a. Dingle) Peninsula;** both are among the most beautiful places in Ireland. **Killarney's** blue lakes and sandstone mountains, inland from the peninsulas, have a unique and romantic splendor.

4 Shannon Estuary. Along the mouth of Ireland's greatest river is "castle country," an area dotted with ruined castles and abbeys, the result of Elizabeth I's 16th-century attempt to subdue the province of Munster. **Limerick City,** too, bears the scars of history, from a different confrontation with the English—the 1691 Siege of Limerick.

Dingle Peninsula

THE SOUTHWEST PLANNER

Getting Around

Scenery is the main attraction in the Southwest, and unless you're a biker or hiker, the best option for taking it in is to rent a car.

Once behind the wheel, plan to adopt the local pace—slow. Covering about 60 miles a day is ideal, with many stops along the way.

Speed is dictated to some degree by the roads: most are small, with one lane in each direction and plenty of bends and hills.

Without a car, your best bet is to base yourself in Cork or Killarney, both accessible by train from Dublin, and take organized day trips or use the local buses (where available) from there.

For the details about getting around, see "Transportation" in the Essentials section at the end of this chapter.

Making the Most of Your Time

If you're here for a short stay—three days or fewer—you'd do well to base yourself in **Killarney** and devote your time to exploring the surrounding area, then heading out to the **Ring of Kerry** or the **Dingle Peninsula.** With more time at your disposal, spend a day driving through **Kenmare** to **Glengarriff** on the famous tunnel road, and take a boat out to **Illnacullin** (Garnish Island). Other highlights are the drive from **Kinsale** to the **Mizen Head** along the coast of West Cork; elegant **Glin Castle** on the Shannon Estuary; **Adare,** one of Ireland's prettiest villages; and the magnificently restored **Bunratty Castle.** Though the scenery is the top draw in the Southwest, **Cork City** is good for a day or two of urban fun, topped off with a visit to nearby **Blarney Castle.**

Picking a Peninsula

Two of Ireland's most scenic destinations sit side by side on the map: the Iveragh Peninsula (also known as the Ring of Kerry, for its scenic drive), and the Dingle Peninsula (also known by its Irish name, Corca Dhuibne). If you like wild, rugged scenery, archaeological remains, and Irish music, Dingle is for you. The most scenic part of the peninsula is at its tip, to the west of An Daingean/Dingle Town. The town itself is a lively spot, with crafts shops, restaurants, and music bars. In contrast, the Ring of Kerry is a longer drive with more varied scenery, ranging from lush subtropical vegetation between Kenmare and Sneem, to rocky coves at Caherdaniel, and long sandy beaches near Glenbeigh. The scenery is punctuated by a series of small villages, all much quieter than Dingle.

What to Bring Home

Locally made ceramics, knitwear, and jewelry can be found in the region's crafts shops, but it's also worth stopping to investigate signposts on the road directing you to the studios of the craftspeople themselves. Between Youghal and Midleton you can follow a "crafts trail" known as **East Cork Creates** (☎021/463–4758) that runs past 15 studios.

Where to Eat & Where to Stay

The Southwest is a great place for good food. County Cork in particular has become Ireland's top foodie destination. Adventurous, well-traveled chefs make the most of the first-rate local specialties: succulent meats, fresh seafood, and farmhouse cheeses.

For another kind of dining experience, check out the medieval banquets at Bunratty and Knappogue castles, near Shannon—they're an undeniably touristy good time.

For accommodations, the Southwest has some of the great country houses, including Longueville House on the Blackwater River in County Cork, Adare Manor in County Limerick, the Park Hotel Kenmare, and the Sheen Falls Lodge, also in Kenmare.

At the other spectrum is the uniquely Irish experience of a farmhouse B&B, such as Ballymakeigh House, near Youghal, where you can watch the cows coming home as you breakfast.

In between is a range of excellent family-owned and -run traditional hotels, such as the Seaview in Ballylickey on Bantry Bay, The Butler Arms in Waterville, and the secluded Caragh Lodge near Killorglin.

Dining & Lodging Price Categories (In Euros)

	¢	$	$$	$$$	$$$$
RESTAURANTS	under €12	€12–€18	€18–€24	€24–€32	over €32
HOTELS	under €110	€110–€140	€140–€200	€200–€280	over €280

Restaurant prices are for a main course at dinner. Hotel prices are for a standard double room in high season.

How's the Weather?

The best times to visit the Southwest are mid-March to June, and September and October. In July and August it's the peak holiday period, meaning roads are more crowded, prices are higher, and the best places are booked in advance. March can be chilly, with daily temperatures in the 40s and 50s. The average high in June is 65°F, which is about as hot as it gets. May and June are the sunniest months. May and September the driest months. The further west you go, the more likely you'll get rain. From November to March daylight hours are short, the weather damp, and many places close.

Best Fests

Cork is known as Ireland's festival city, the longest-running being the **Cork Film Festival** in the second week in October, and the biggest the **Guinness Jazz Festival** on the last weekend in October.

The **West Cork Chamber Music Festival** brings internationally renowned musicians to perform in the intimate surroundings of the library of Bantry House for 10 days in late June.

People come back year after year to the **Kinsale Festival of Fine Food,** which creates a party atmosphere all over town for the first weekend in October.

Updated
by Alannah
Hopkin

CORK, KERRY, LIMERICK, AND CLARE—these southwest Ireland county names have an undeniable Irish lilt. Just as evocative is the scenery in each county: from Kinsale along the coast west to Mizen Head in the far southwest corner to the glorious mountains and lakes of Killarney. Thanks to its accomplished chefs and the bounty of farms, fields, lakes, and coast, County Cork has become a little paradise of fresh, rustic Irish cuisine. You can also find a mild climate, Irish-speaking areas, and Ireland's second- and third-largest cities—Cork and Limerick. But the most notable attractions are the miles and miles of pretty country lanes meandering through rich but sparsely populated farmland. To be in a hurry here is to be ill-mannered. It was probably a Kerryman who first remarked that when God made time, he made plenty of it.

As you look over the fuchsia-laden hedges that ring thriving dairy farms or stop at a wayside restaurant to sample seafood or locally raised meat, it's difficult to imagine that some 150 years ago this area was decimated by famine. Thousands perished in fields and workhouses, and thousands more took "coffin ships" from Cobh in Cork Harbor to the New World. Between 1845 and 1849 Ireland's population decreased by more than a million, or roughly 30% (according to the 1841 census, the Irish population was then 8,175,124). Many small Southwest villages were wiped out. The region was battered again during both the War for Independence and the Civil War that was fought with intensity in and around "Rebel Cork" between 1919 and 1921. Economic recovery didn't pick up until the late 1960s, and tourist development did not surge until the mid-'90s.

The Irish economic boom coincided with a marketing push to increase visitor numbers. The result has been a mixed blessing. The Southwest's main routes are no longer traffic-free, but the roads themselves are better. There's a greater choice of accommodations, with improved facilities, but many of the newer hotels and bed-and-breakfasts are bland. Even the traditional, warm Irish welcome is less ubiquitous, given the increased pace of everyday life. Furthermore, much of the development threatened the environment, although the Southwest is making a concerted effort to attract more visitors while keeping beaches and rivers clean and scenery unspoiled.

South of Cork City, the region's main business and shopping community, the resort town of Kinsale is the gateway to a rocky, attractive coastline containing Roaring Water Bay, with its main islands, and Bantry Bay, a magnificent natural harbor. The region's southwest coast is formed by three peninsulas: the Beara, the Iveragh, and the Dingle; the road known as the Ring of Kerry makes a complete circuit of the Iveragh Peninsula. Killarney's sparkling blue lakes and magnificent sandstone mountains, inland from the peninsulas, have a unique and romantic splendor, immortalized in the 19th century in the writings of William Thackeray and Sir Walter Scott. Around the Shannon Estuary you enter "castle country," an area rich with ruined castles and abbeys, the result of Elizabeth I's 16th-century attempt to subdue the old Irish province of Munster. Limerick City, too, bears the scars of history, from a different confrontation with the English—the Siege of Limerick, which took place in 1691. Its other "scars" of history—described so memorably in Frank McCourt's best-seller *Angela's Ashes*—lure travelers, who discover that modern Limerick is a compact, vibrant city, with lively riverfront bar, café, and arts scenes.

Although the southwest has several sumptuous country-house hotels, it's basically an easygoing, unpretentious region, where informality and simplicity prevail. As in the rest of Ireland, social life revolves around the pub, and a visit to any neighborhood favorite is the best way to find out what's going on. Local residents have not lost their natural curiosity about "strangers," as visitors are called. You will frequently be asked, "Are you enjoying your holiday?" "Yes," is not a good enough answer: What the locals are really after is your life story.

EXPLORING THE SOUTHWEST

This chapter starts in Cork City and makes a clockwise sweep. It ends on the northern fringe of the region, crossing over the border from County Kerry into County Limerick and then briefly dipping into the southeastern reaches of County Clare in the area immediately around Shannon Airport. (If you're flying into Shannon, you may want to start with that section of the chapter and work your way backward.)

6

CORK CITY

254 km (158 mi) south of Dublin, 105 km (65 mi) south of Limerick City.

The major metropolis of the south, Cork is Ireland's second-largest city—but you have to put this in perspective. It actually runs a distant second, with a population of 123,000, roughly one-tenth the size of Dublin. Cork is a spirited place, with a formidable pub culture, a lively traditional music scene, a respected and progressive university, attractive art galleries, and offbeat cafés. The city received a major boost in 2005 when it was named a Capital of Culture by the EU—the smallest city ever to receive the designation. The result was a burst in development; one of the lasting legacies is a striking but controversial redesign of the city center (Patrick Street and Grand Parade) by Barcelona-based architect Beth Gali.

In late summer and early autumn, the city hosts some of Ireland's premier festivals, including October's huge Cork Jazz Festival, which draws about 50,000 visitors from around the world, and the Cork Film Festival, also in October.

EXPLORING CORK CITY

"Cork is the loveliest city in the world. Anyone who does not agree with me either was not born there or is prejudiced." Whether Cork merits this accolade of native poet and writer Robert Gibbings, the city does have plenty to recommend it, including several noteworthy historic sites. They're spread out a bit, but still the best way to see the city is on foot. Patrick Street is the city center's main thoroughfare.

Outside the center city, Cork has several distinct neighborhoods, including Washington Village, Sunday's Well, Shandon, Tivoli, and Western Road.

You can tour the center of the city in a morning or an afternoon, depending on how much you plan to shop along the way. To really see everything, however, allow a full day, with a break for lunch at the Farmgate Café in the English Market. Also note that the Crawford Gallery and the English Market are closed on Sunday.

WHAT TO SEE

1 Bishop Lucey Park. This tiny green park in the heart of the city opened in 1985 in celebration of the 800th anniversary of Cork's Norman charter. During its excavation, workers unearthed portions of the city's original fortified walls, now preserved just inside the arched entrance. Sculptures by contemporary Cork artists are found throughout the park. ⊠ *Grand Parade, Washington Village* ☜ *Free.*

17 Cork City Gaol. This castlelike building contains an austere, 19th-century prison. Life-size figures occupy the cells, and sound effects illustrate the appalling conditions that prevailed here from the early 19th century through the founding of the Free State, after the 1916 Uprising. **The Radio Museum Experience** in the Governor's House tells the history of broadcasting in Cork, and features genuine artifacts from Cork's 1923 studio. ⊠ *Sunday's Well Rd., Sunday's Well* ☎ *021/430–5022* ⊕ *www.corkcitygaol.com* ☜ *€8* ⊗ *Nov.–Feb., daily 10–5; Mar.–Oct., daily 9:30–5.*

6 Cork Opera House. An unattractive concrete hulk that went up in 1965 to replace an ornate and much-loved opera house that was ruined in a fire. Later attempts to integrate the opera house with its neighbor, the Crawford Municipal Art Gallery, have, however, softened the grim facade. The piazza outside has sidewalk cafés and street performers. ⊠ *Lavitt's Quay, City Center South* ☎ *021/427–0022* ⊕ *www.corkoperahouse.ie.*

4 Cork Vision Centre. Located in the renovated St. Peter's Church, an 18th-century building in what was once the bustling heart of medieval Cork, this historical society provides an excellent introduction to the city's history and geography. The highlight is a detailed 1:500 scale model of the city, showing how it has changed over the ages. ⊠ *Washington St., Washington Village* ☎ *021/427–2706* ⊗ *Weekdays 9–5.*

3 Court House. A landmark in the very center of Cork, this magnificent classical building has an imposing Corinthian portico and is still used as the district's main courthouse. The exterior has been cleaned and fully restored and looks every bit as good as it did when it was built in 1835. ⊠ *Washington St., Washington Village* ☎ *021/427–2706* ⊕ *www.corkcorp.ie* ⊗ *Weekdays 9–5.*

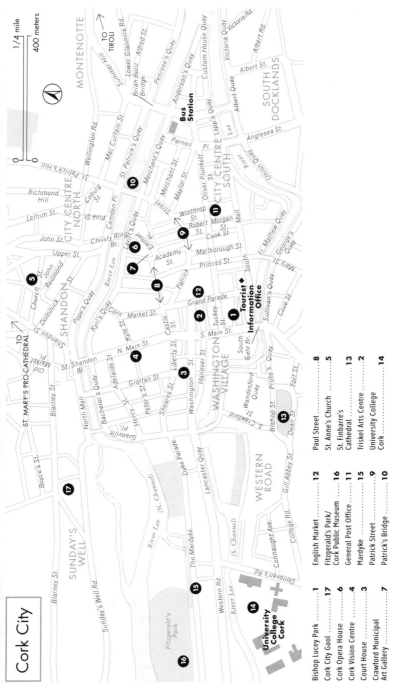

Cork City

1/4 mile

400 meters

Bishop Lucey Park **1**
Cork City Gaol **17**
Cork Opera House **6**
Cork Vision Centre **4**
Court House **3**
Crawford Municipal
Art Gallery **7**

English Market **12**
Fitzgerald's Park/
Cork Public Museum **16**
General Post Office **11**
Mardyke **15**
Patrick Street **9**
Patrick's Bridge **10**

Paul Street **8**
St. Anne's Church **5**
St. Finbarre's
Cathedral **13**
Triskel Arts Centre **2**
University College
Cork **14**

MONTENOTTE

TO TIVOLI →

Summer Hill

Lower Glanmire Rd.
Alfred St.

Brian Boru Bridge

Penrose's Quay

Anderson's Quay

Custom House Quay

Victoria Rd.

Victoria Quay

Albert Rd.

Albert St.

SOUTH DOCKLANDS

Albert Quay

Anglesea St.

Union Quay

Lapp's Quay

Parnell Pl.

Bus Station

St. Patrick's Quay

MacCurtain St.

Wellington Rd.

Richmond Hill

CITY CENTRE NORTH

Leitrim St.

John St.

Coburg St.

Camden Pl.

Pine St.

Christy Ring Br.

Emmet Pl.

Lavitt's Quay

Merchant's Quay

Merchant St.

Mayor St.

Oliver Plunkett St.

Winthrop St.

Robert St.

Morgan St.

Cook St.

Academy St.

Marlborough St.

Princes St.

Maylor St.

George's Quay

Ft. Mathew Quay

Mary St.

CITY CENTRE SOUTH

SHANDON

ST. MARY'S PRO-CATHEDRAL

Church St.

John Redmond

Dominick St.

Pope's Quay

Kyrl's Quay

River Lee

Upper St.

Academy St.

Patrick St.

Grand Parade

Market St.

Castle St.

Tuckey St.

S. Main St.

Sullivan's Quay

Cove St.

South Gate Br.

Tourist Information Office

WASHINGTON VILLAGE

N. Main St.

Liberty St.

Hanover St.

Washington St.

Grattan St.

Sheares St.

Peter St.

Henry St.

Bachelor's Quay

North Mall

Adelaide St.

St. Shandon Br.

Old Market Pl.

Shandon St.

Blarney St.

Grenville Pl.

Boyce's St.

SUNDAY'S WELL

Sunday's Well Rd.

Blarney St.

Fitzgerald's Park

River Lee (N. Channel)

The Mardyke

River Lee (S. Channel)

Dyke Parade

Lancaster Quay

WESTERN ROAD

Gill Abbey St.

College Rd.

Connaught Ave.

Western Rd.

Donovan's Rd.

University College Cork

Mardyke Walk

Crawford St.

Wandesford Quay

Proby's Quay

Bishop St.

Dean St.

Fort St.

St. Finbarre's

Gill Abbey

1 **2** **3** **4** **5** **6** **7** **8** **9** **10** **11** **12** **13** **14** **15** **16** **17**

6

7 Crawford Municipal Art Gallery. The
★ large redbrick building was built
in 1724 as the customs house and
is now home to Ireland's leading
provincial art gallery. An imaginative expansion has added an extra
10,000 square feet of gallery space
for visiting exhibitions and adventurous shows of modern Irish artists.
The permanent collection includes
landscape paintings depicting Cork

in the 18th and 19th centuries. Take special note of works by Irish painters William Leech (1881–1968), Daniel Maclise (1806–70), James Barry
(1741–1806), and Nathaniel Grogan (1740–1807). The café, run by the
Allen family of Ballymaloe, is a good place for a light lunch or a homemade sweet. ⊠*Emmet Pl., City Center South* ☎*021/427-3377* ⊕*www.
crawfordartgallery.com* ⊠*Free* ⊙ *Weekdays 9–5, Sat. 9–1.*

12 English Market. Food lovers: head for one of the misleadingly small entrances
★ to this large market in an elaborate, brick-and-cast-iron Victorian building. (Its official name is the Princes Street Market, and it's also known
locally as the Covered Market.) Among the 140 stalls, keep an eye out
for the Alternative Bread Co., which produces more than 40 varieties of
handmade bread every day. Iago, Sean Calder-Potts's deli, has fresh pasta,
lots of cheeses, and charcuterie. The Olive Stall sells olive oil, olive-oil
soap, and olives from Greece, Spain, France, and Italy. Kay O'Connell's
Fish Stall, in the legendary fresh-fish alley, purveys local smoked salmon.
O'Reilly's Tripe and Drisheen is the last existing retailer of a Cork specialty, tripe (cow's stomach), and *drisheen* (blood sausage). Upstairs is the
Farmgate, an excellent café. ⊠*Entrances on Grand Parade and Princes
St., City Center South* ⊕*www.corkcity.ie* ⊙*Mon.–Sat. 9–5:30.*

16 Fitzgerald's Park. This small, well-tended park is beside the River Lee's
♻ north channel in the west of the city. The park contains the **Cork Public
Museum,** a Georgian mansion that houses a well-planned exhibit about
Cork's history since ancient times, with a strong emphasis on the city's
Republican history. ⊠*Western Rd., Western Road* ☎*021/427-0679*
⊕*www.corkcity.ie* ⊠*Free* ⊙ *Museum weekdays 11–1 and 2:15-4,
weekends 3–5 (closed Sun., Oct.–Mar.).*

11 General Post Office. This Neoclassical building with an elegant colonnaded facade was once Cork's opera house. It dominates a street
otherwise occupied by boutiques, jewelry stores, and antiques shops.
⊠*Oliver Plunkett St., City Center South* ☎*021/427-2000* ⊙ *Weekdays 9–5:30, Sat. 9–5.*

**NEED A
BREAK?**

The friendly, old **Long Valley** (⊠ *Winthrop St., City Center South* ☎ *021/427-
2144*), popular with artists, writers, students, and eccentrics, serves tea, coffee, pints, and sandwiches. The dark, mismatched interior is like a time warp
taking you back to early-20th-century Cork. Some of the booths are built
from wood salvaged from wrecked ocean liners—ask to be told the story. The

Rebel Cork

Cork City received its first charter in 1185 from Prince John of Norman England, and it takes its name from the Irish word *corcaigh,* meaning "marshy place." The original 6th-century settlement was spread over 13 small islands in the River Lee. Major development occurred during the 17th and 18th centuries with the expansion of the butter trade, and many attractive Georgian-design buildings with wide bowfront windows were constructed during this time. As late as 1770, Cork's present-day main streets—Grand Parade, Patrick Street, and the South Mall—were submerged under the Lee. Around 1800, when the Lee was partially dammed, the river divided into two streams that now flow through the city, leaving the main business and commercial center on an island, not unlike Paris's Île de la Cité. As a result, the city features a number of bridges and quays, which, although initially confusing, add greatly to the port's unique character.

"Rebel Cork" emerged as a center of the Nationalist Fenian movement in the 19th century. The city suffered great damage during the War of Independence in 1919–21, when much of its center was burned down. Cork is now regaining some of its former glory as a result of sensitive commercial development and an ongoing program of inner-city renewal.

6

generously filled sandwiches, made to order from home-cooked meat and thickly cut bread, also seem to belong to another age.

⓯ Mardyke. This popular riverside walk links the city center with Fitzgerald's Park. Beside it is a field where cricket, very much a minority sport in Ireland, is played on summer weekends. ⊠ *Western Rd., Western Road.*

❾ Patrick Street. Extending from Grand Parade in the south to Patrick's Bridge in the north, Panna (as it's known locally) is Cork's main shopping thoroughfare. It has been designed as a pedestrian-priority area with wide walks and special street lights. A mainstream mix of department stores, boutiques, pharmacies, and bookshops line the way. If you look above some of the plate-glass storefronts, you can see examples of the bowfront Georgian windows that are emblematic of old Cork. The street saw some of the city's worst fighting during the War of Independence. ⊠ *City Center South.*

❿ Patrick's Bridge. From here you can look along the curve of Patrick Street and north across the River Lee to St. Patrick's Hill, with its tall Georgian houses. The hill is so steep that steps are cut into the pavement. Tall ships that served the butter trade used to load up beside the bridge at Merchant's Quay before heading downstream to the sea. The design of the large, redbrick shopping center on the site evokes the warehouses of old. ⊠ *Patrick St., City Center South* ⊕ *www.corkcity.ie.*

❽ Paul Street. A narrow street between the River Lee and Patrick Street and parallel to both, Paul Street is the backbone of the trendy shopping area that now occupies Cork's old French Quarter. The area was first settled by Huguenots fleeing religious persecution in France. Musicians and other street performers often entertain passersby in the Rory Gallagher Piazza, named for the rock guitarist (of the band Taste), whose family was from Cork. The shops here offer the best in modern Irish design—from local fashions to handblown glass—and antiques, particularly in the alley north of the piazza. ⊠ *City Center South.*

5 **St. Anne's Church.** The church's pepper-pot Shandon steeple, which has a four-sided clock and is topped with a golden, salmon-shape weather vane, is visible from throughout the city and is the chief reason why St. Anne's is so frequently visited. The Bells of Shandon were immortalized in an atrocious but popular 19th-century ballad of that name. Your reward for climbing the 120-foot-tall tower is the chance to ring the bells, with the assistance of sheet tune cards, out over Cork. Beside the church, Firkin Crane, Cork's 18th-century butter market, houses two small performing spaces. Adjacent is the Shandon Craft Market. ⊠ *Church St., Shandon* ⊕ *www.corkcity.ie* ☎ *€1.50 church, €2 church and bell tower* ⊙ *May–Oct., Mon.–Sat. 9:30–4:30; Nov.–Apr., Mon.– Sat. 10–3:30.*

13 **St. Finbarre's Cathedral.** This was once the entrance to medieval Cork. According to tradition, St. Finbarre established a monastery on this site around AD 650 and is credited as being the founder of Cork. The present, compact, three-spire Gothic cathedral, which was completed in 1879, belongs to the Church of Ireland and houses a 3,000-pipe organ. ⊠ *Bishop St., Washington Village* ☎ *021/496–3387* ⊕ *www.cathedral. cork.anglican.org* ☎ *€3* ⊙ *Oct.–Mar., Mon.–Sat. 10–12:45 and 2–5, Sun. 12:30–5; Apr.–Sept., Mon.–Sat. 9:30–5:30, Sun. 12:30–5.*

2 **Triskel Arts Centre.** An excellent place to get the pulse of artsy goings-on in town, Triskel Arts Centre occupies a converted pair of town houses, also home to a coffee shop and a small auditorium that hosts films and plays. Often on display are exhibitions devoted to contemporary art and crafts. ⊠ *Tobin St., Washington Village* ☎ *021/427–2022* ⊕ *www. triskelartscentre.com* ☎ *Free* ⊙ *Weekdays 11–6, Sat. 11–5.*

14 **University College Cork.** The Doric, porticoed gates of UCC stand about 2 ★ km (1 mi) from the center of the city. The college, which has a student body of roughly 10,000, is a constituent of the National University of Ireland. The main quadrangle is a fine example of 19th-century university architecture in the Tudor-Gothic style, reminiscent of many Oxford and Cambridge colleges. Several ancient ogham stones are on display in the North Quadrangle (near the Visitor Centre), and the renovated Crawford Observatory's 1860 telescope can be visited. The Honan Collegiate Chapel, east of the quadrangle, was built in 1916 and modeled on the 12th-century, Hiberno-Romanesque style, best exemplified by the remains of Cormac's Chapel at Cashel. The UCC chapel's stained-glass windows, as well as its collection of art and crafts, altar furnishings, and textiles in the Celtic Revival style, are noteworthy. Three large, modern buildings have been successfully integrated with the old, including the Boole Library, named for mathematician George Boole (1815–64), who was a professor at the college. Both indoors and out the campus is enhanced by works from the campus's outstanding collection of contemporary Irish art. The Lewis Glucksman Gallery, opened in late 2004, in a striking new building in a wooded gully beside the college's entrance gates. Besides displaying works from the college's collection, it hosts cutting-edge contemporary art exhibitions. ⊠ *Western Road* ☎ *021/490–1876* ⊕ *www.ucc.ie* ✉ *Free; Guided tours €4* ⊙ *Weekdays, Visitor Centre 9–5; Guided tours May, June, Sept., and Oct.: Mon., Wed., Fri., and Sat. at 3* PM; *call for hrs Easter wk, July, Aug., and mid-Dec.–mid-Jan.*

> **GRANDDAD OF THE COMPUTER**
>
> George Boole (1815–64), a University College professor, is one of the heroes of the computer age. Despite growing up in a working-class family with limited access to education, he developed into a mathematical genius, inventing Boolean algebra—the foundation upon which computer science was built.

OFF THE BEATEN PATH

St. Mary's Pro-Cathedral. It's worth hiking up to St. Mary's, which dates from 1808, only if you're interested in tracing your Cork ancestors. Its presbytery has records of births and marriages dating from 1784. ⊠ *Cathedral Walk, Shandon* ✉ *Free* ⊙ *Daily 9–6.*

6

WHERE TO STAY & EAT

$$$$ ✕ **Ivory Tower.** Seamus O'Connell, the adventurous owner-chef here, is famous in Ireland through his television series, *Soul Food.* He describes his approach as "trans-ethnic fusion." He has cooked in Mexico and Japan, so his accomplished menu has such brilliantly eclectic dishes as wild duck with vanilla, sherry, and jalapeños; pheasant tamale; and wild sea trout smoked to order over oak, with whiskey and scallion sauce. Imaginative presentation, including a surprise taster to set the mood, compensates for the bare wooden floors and somewhat stark decor of the first-floor corner dining room. Tuesday is sushi night. ⊠ *35 Princes St., Washington Village* ☎ *021/427–4665* ⊟ *AE, DC, MC, V* ⊙ *Closed Sun. and Mon. No lunch.*

$$$–$$$$ ✕ **Les Gourmandises.** With a Breton sommelier, Soizic, working the front of the house, and her U.K.-and-Dublin-trained Irish husband, Pat Kiely, in the kitchen, you can expect a genuinely interesting eating experience. The restaurant is small, but it has high ceilings and natural light pours in from an overhead skylight, brightening the quarry-tile floor and red-velvet chairs. Crisp white linen and fresh flowers are typical of Soizic's attention to detail. Pat's training with Marco Pierre White, John Burton Race, and Patrick Guilbaud shows in his mastery of robust modern French repertoire. Roasted fillet of cod is served with braised lentils and a thyme-and-balsamic dressing, while roast guinea fowl comes with buttered cabbage and Madeira sauce. Desserts include coffee crème brûlée with a Swiss meringue and chocolate madeleine. Good-value set menus are also available. ⊠ *17 Cook St., City Center South* ☎ *021/425–1959* ⊟ *MC, V* ⊙ *Closed Easter wk, last wk Aug., 1st wk Sept.*

EATING WELL IN THE SOUTHWEST

The Southwest, especially County Cork, rivals Dublin as Ireland's food-culture epicenter. Cork has astonishing resources: waters full of a wide array of fish, acre after acre of potato fields, cows galore, wild mushrooms and berries—not to mention inventive chefs who transform this bounty into feasts. In tiny Shanagarry, Darina Allen trains hundreds of chefs every year at the Ballymaloe Cookery School. Whether trained at home or abroad, area chefs put a premium on fresh, local (often organically grown) produce.

Mussels and scallops are farmed in the waters off the coast of Cork and Kerry, while the rivers teem with wild salmon. Small smokeries process salmon, trout, mussels, and mackerel over either oak or beech wood chips, with mouthwatering results. Most restaurants in the region bake their own bread daily, often producing both yeast breads and Irish soda bread, which uses buttermilk

or bicarbonate of soda in place of yeast. Kerry is famous for its delicately flavored mountain lamb, while local beef ensures a wide selection of tender steak cuts. Organic pork from heirloom breeds of pigs might remind you how tasty pork can be. And while in the Southwest, make a point of trying some local farmhouse cheeses; look out for Milleens, Coolea, Durrus, Coomkeen, Gubbeen, or the superb hard cheeses, Desmond and Gabriel, made by West Cork Natural Cheeses.

The smaller country restaurants ooze ambience, but service can be a little slow, especially in the peak season of July and August. The food is freshly prepared and usually worth waiting for, so meanwhile sample some of that home-baked bread, and maybe a glass of local stout or your usual aperitif, or maybe chat with the people at the next table to pass the time. It's all part of the Irish experience.

$$$–$$$$ ✕ **Star Anise.** What was once a small shop is now an intimate contemporary restaurant. Frosted windows and cleverly arranged plants insulate the warm terra-cotta–walled interior from the busy street outside. Well-designed contemporary cutlery, linen napkins, and large wine glasses bode well for a serious dining experience. Owner-chef Lambros Lambrou's menu is based on fresh local produce, and combines French expertise and Mediterranean flavors with the occasional Asian touch. Local lamb, for example, is wrapped in phyllo and slow cooked, while panfried fillet of wild sea bass is served with a basil ratatouille. The classic French desserts—tarte tatin, crème brûlée—are homemade and excellent. ⊠ *4 Bridge St., City Center North* ☎ *021/455–1635* ⊟ *AE, DC, MC, V* ☺ *Closed Sun. and Mon.*

$$–$$$$ ✕ **Jacobs on the Mall.** Mercy Fenton's imaginative cooking is one attraction; the other is the location—an erstwhile Victorian-style Turkish bath. The dining room has a high ceiling, an enormous skylight, cast-iron pillars, modern art, and a tall banquette room divider. Starters include duck liver parfait with plum chutney, and oysters with ginger-and-lime relish. For a main course, try seared John Dory with coconut rice or roast haunch of venison with celeriac and parsnip puree and beetroot confit. Look for such desserts as date-and-butterscotch

pudding with bourbon cream. ✉*30A South Mall, City Center South* ☎*021/425–1530* ▭*AE, DC, MC, V* ✆*Closed Sun.*

$$–$$$ ✗**Café Paradiso.** The Mediterranean-style food is so tasty that even
★ dedicated meat eaters forget that it's vegetarian. Australian owner-chef Denis Cotter, who has published two acclaimed cookbooks, garners raves for his risottos with seasonal vegetables, his *gougère-choux* (cheese-flavored pastries) with savory fillings, and his home-made desserts. The simple café-style dining room is busy and colorful, with enthusiastic young waiters who love to recite the daily specials. The food is creatively arranged on massive platters or bowls, which add a sense of occasion. The restaurant is midway between the court-house and the university. You can also stay the night here: there are three small but attractive rooms available for around €180 a night. ✉*16 Lancaster Quay, Western Road* ☎*021/427–7939* ▭*AE, MC, V* ✆*Closed Sun., Mon., and last 2 wks of Aug.*

$$–$$$ ✗**Fenn's Quay.** This tiny city-center restaurant, on the ground floor of a 250-year-old Georgian house, is always buzzing with a faithful local clientele—legal eagles from the nearby courthouse at lunch, theater- and moviegoers at dinner. The owners are also in the meat business; their baked ham is outstanding, and the char-grilled fillet steak with chunky chips has achieved legendary status: some regulars can't bring themselves to order anything else. But there are other good options: fish from the nearby market is given robust, unfussy treatment, and vegetarian options include a twice-baked goat cheese soufflé with apple and walnut salad. The ginger-and-toffee sticky pudding is a dessert specialty. Simple decor, with bright red café-style chairs and tan banquettes, gets a dose of character from striking modern paintings. ✉*Fenn's Quay, Sheares St., Washington Village* ☎*021/427–9527* ▭*AE, MC, V* ✆*Closed Sun.*

$$–$$$ ✗**Isaac's.** Cross Patrick's Bridge to the River Lee's north side and turn right to reach this large, atmospheric brasserie in a converted 18th-century warehouse. Modern art, jazz, high ceilings, and well-spaced tables covered in oilcloth set an eclectic tone. The East-meets-Mediter-ranean menu includes many tempting dishes, such as warm salads with Clonakilty black pudding, and king prawns in spicy tomato sauce. Reservations are advisable Friday and Saturday evenings. ✉*Mac-Curtain St., City Center North* ☎*021/450–3805* ▭*AE, DC, MC, V* ✆*No lunch Sun.*

$$–$$$ ✗**Jacques.** Hidden away on a tiny side street is one of Cork's favorite restaurants. Its windowless interior, with its warm terra-cotta walls and curved Art Deco–style bar, is carefully lighted to provide a calming ambience that makes you forget the world outside. Sisters Jacque and Eithne Barry have run the place for 25 years, and know their business. Food is always sourced locally, so it's as fresh as it comes. Eithne's cooking lets the flavor shine through, whether in a starter of fresh crab and baby spinach salad, or a main course of traditional roast duck with potato and apricot stuffing and red cabbage. For dessert try the fruited bread-and-butter pudding, or indulge in a chocolate and hazel-

nut torte. There's a special-value early dinner menu from 6 PM, and on Sunday a light menu is served from 4:30 PM. ⊠ *Phoenix St., off Oliver Plunkett St. near GPO, City Center South* ☎ *021/427–7387* ⊟ *AE, MC, V* ⊘ *Closed Sun.*

$–$$ ✕**Farmgate Café.** One of the best—and busiest—informal lunch spots in town is on a terraced gallery above the fountain at the Princes Street entrance to the covered English Market. One side of the gallery opens onto the market and is self-service; the other side is glassed in and has table service (reservations advised). Tripe and drisheen is one dish that is always on the menu; daily specials include less challenging but no less traditional dishes, such as corned beef with *colcannon* (potatoes and cabbage mashed with butter and seasonings) and loin of smoked bacon with *champ* (potatoes mashed with scallions or leeks). ⊠ *English Market, City Center South* ☎ *021/427–8134* ⊟ *DC, MC, V* ⊘ *Closed Sun. No dinner.*

¢–$$ ✕**Boqueria.** A gloomy old tavern on the street to the north of Patrick's Bridge has been transformed into an atmospheric tapas bar. The bar itself remains long and narrow, but skylights wipe out the gloom, and the walls are lined with attractive racks of Spanish wine. It's a popular breakfast spot, offering freshly squeezed orange and grapefruit juices, great coffee, and croissants, as well as a fine rendition of the traditional Irish fry. The tapas offerings cut loose from their Spanish roots to become showcases for artisanal Irish food: *queso raciones* is a plate of five Irish farmhouse cheeses and one Manchego, while four of the six elements in *charcuteria raciones* are made in west Cork. The results are enormously popular, so there's always a great buzz in the place. ⊠ *6 Bridge St., City Center North* ☎ *021/455–9049* ⊟ *MC, V* ⊘ *No lunch Sun.*

$$$$ ✕⌖**Hayfield Manor.** The Manor, a surprisingly soigné modern hom-
★ age to the country-house style, is beside the UCC campus, five minutes' drive from the city center. Ruddy with red brick and brightened by classy white-sash windows, its exterior hints at the comfy luxury within. Beyond a splendid, carved-wood double staircase, you can find the Drawing Room—a symphony of gilded silk, with white-marble fireplace, 19th-century chandelier, and chic armchairs—and the wood-panel library, which overlooks a walled patio and garden. Rooms are spacious and ever-so-elegantly furnished in a version of the Louis XV style. The Victorian-style bar serves lunch, and then bar food until 7 PM, when the Manor Room restaurant ($$$–$$$$) opens for dinner. ⊠ *College Rd., Western Road, Co. Cork* ☎ *021/431–5900* 🖷 *021/431–6839* ⊕ *www.hayfieldmanor.ie* 🖃 *88 rooms* ⌕ *In-room: Wi-Fi. In-hotel: restaurant, bar, pool, gym, public Wi-Fi* ⊟ *AE, DC, MC, V* ⊚| *BP.*

$$$ ✕⌖**The Ambassador.** It's not the fanciest hotel in Cork, nor the hippest,
★ but it has the most character and the best view—which you pay for by a steep 10-minute walk up from the town center. It's worth visiting the bar here just to enjoy the panoramic view of Cork City's docks, river, railway line, church steeples, and distant surrounding hills. An imposing redbrick and cut-limestone Victorian-era nursing home now

converted into a comfortable hotel (affiliated with the Best Western group), the Ambassador is near the army barracks in a hilly area made famous by Frank O'Connor's short stories, an area now favored by style-conscious academics and bohos. Architecture buffs may question some features, such as the modern, double-glaze windows, but overall the interior retains its Victorian charm and spaciousness. The Embassy Bar has dark-wood paneling and a large bay window overlooking the city, while the cocktail lounge, with book-filled shelves and chesterfields by an open fire, is a quieter venue. The Seasons restaurant is a spacious room with formal table linen and a sedate, old-fashioned air. Guest rooms are massive, with large bathrooms, patterned wallpapers, small sitting areas, and matching floral curtains and drapes. There are three floors of bedrooms and the higher you go, the better the view—some rooms even have splendid walk-out balconies at no extra charge. ⊠ *Military Hill, St. Luke's, City Center North, Co. Cork* ☎ *021/455–1996* 🖷 *021/455–1997* ⊕ *www.ambassadorhotel.ie* ➟ *58 rooms* ♿ *In-room: no a/c, dial-up, Wi-Fi (some). In-hotel: restaurant, bars, gym, public Wi-Fi* ⊟ *AE, DC, MC, V* ⋈ *BP.*

$$ ✕🖭 **Clarion.** Black-clad receptionists standing behind simple wooden desks at the far end of the vast, marble-floor lobby are the first indication that this place aspires to boutique-hotel chic. Occupying a corner block beside the River Lee, the Clarion is the first arrival of a huge docklands development. It's kitty-corner across the river from City Hall, and a short walk from shopping and dining. Rooms are built around a central, top-lighted atrium, and have views either of the river or the hotel's swanky main staircase. Decor is stark and hard-edged, with stylish pale-wood trim complemented by curtains and flooring in a khaki-olive theme. Kudos bar ($) spills out onto a riverside walkway and serves food from an open wok station until 8 nightly. The more formal restaurant Sinergie ($$–$$$) serves a light Mediterranean menu amid minimalist Japanese-inspired decor. ⊠ *Lapp's Quay, City Center South, Co. Cork* ☎ *021/422–4900* 🖷 *021/422–4901* ⊕ *www.clarionhotelcorkcity.com* ➟ *191 rooms* ♿ *In-room: dial-up, Wi-Fi (some). In-hotel: restaurant, bar, pool, gym, public Wi-Fi* ⊟ *AE, DC, MC, V* ⋈ *BP.*

$$ ✕🖭 **Hotel Isaac's.** A stylish renovation transformed an old, city-center warehouse into a busy restaurant and hotel complex. Rooms are bright and cheerful, with polished wood floors and rustic pine furniture. The restaurant and some of the rooms overlook a tiny courtyard garden with a waterfall cascading down one side. The dining room also operates as Greene's restaurant ($$–$$$$), where they serve seafood—king prawns with chili sauce, oysters poached in Guinness, brill, swordfish, and hake—as well as other intriguing concoctions, such as veal with apricot stuffing, Asian vegetables, and ginger soufflé. ⊠ *48 MacCurtain St., City Center North, Co. Cork* ☎ *021/450–0011* 🖷 *021/450–6355* ⊕ *www.isaacs.ie* ➟ *47 rooms* ♿ *In-room: Wi-Fi. In-hotel: restaurant, public Wi-Fi* ⊟ *AE, MC, V* ⋈ *BP.*

$$ ✕🖭 **Kingsley Hotel.** The riverside location is a boon, being close to open countryside yet a 10-minute walk from the city center. The Kingsley overlooks a rowing club on a pretty section of the River Lee, beside

the Lee Fields, a big meadow with paths that are popular with joggers. The lobby and lounge of this spanking-new establishment are paneled with dark wood and furnished with upright velvet armchairs, like an old-style gentlemen's club. Guest rooms have large bathrooms, super-king-size beds, mahogany furniture, workstations, and CD players. Otters ($$$–$$$$), the more formal restaurant, serves imaginative local seafood and seasonal game dishes; a lighter menu is served in the bar and library. The health center has a 20-meter pool and an outdoor hot tub. ⊠ *Victoria Cross, Western Road, Co. Cork* ☎ *021/480–0500* 🖷 *021/480–0527* ⊕ *www.kingsleyhotel.com* ⬳ *69 rooms* ⬭ *In-room: refrigerator (some), dial-up, Wi-Fi. In-hotel: restaurant, bar, pool, gym, public Wi-Fi* ☰ *AE, DC, MC, V* ⦿ *BP.*

$　✕⊡**Flemings.** On a hillside overlooking the river, this stately Georgian house is set in extensive grounds, which include a kitchen garden that supplies the restaurant. The grounds could be tidier, but owner-chef Michael Fleming is more interested in cooking. Classical French food is his forte, and is served, appropriately, in a dining room ($$–$$$$) decorated in the French Empire style with plush Louis XV–style chairs, gilt-framed portraits, and crystal chandeliers. Local ingredients are important; a starter of panfried foie gras is accompanied by black pudding from West Cork and glazed apple. Grilled monkfish from Michael's home town, Courtmacsherry, is served with a basil oil dressing and red wine sauce. The quiet, large guest rooms have high ceilings and elegant brocade fabrics. Ask about the special-value "dine and stay" package. ⊠ *Silver Grange House, Tivoli, Co. Cork* ☎ *021/482–1621* 🖷 *021/482–1178* ⬳ *4 rooms* ⬭ *In-room: no a/c. In-hotel: restaurant, bar, no elevator* ☰ *AE, DC, MC, V* ⦿ *BP.*

$$　⊡**Brookfield Hotel.** Next door to the campus of University College Cork, this reasonably priced hotel sits in 10 acres of private parkland with mature trees and is surrounded by blocks of redbrick, Georgian-style student accommodations, which double as a self-catering holiday village outside term time. This pleasant, quiet location, complete with secure car parking, is less than a mile from the city center. The hotel shares its main door with the pool and gym (a bonus in this price range), with a staircase leading up to reception, and three floors of guest rooms. Rooms are a bit boxy, with blond-wood desks, plain walls and carpets, patterned spreads, and dark-hue drapes, but are redeemed by the pretty views of green lawns and pine trees from the windows. ⊠ *Brookfield Holiday Village, College Rd., Western Road, Co. Cork* ☎ *021/480–4700* 🖷 *021/480–4793* ⊕ *www.brookfieldcork.ie* ⬳ *24 rooms* ⬭ *In-room: no a/c. In-hotel: restaurant, bar, tennis court, pool, gym, public Wi-Fi* ☰ *AE, DC, MC, V* ⊘ *Closed Dec. 23–Jan. 2.*

$$　⊡**Lancaster Lodge.** Free city-center parking, a great location next to the lively Jurys Hotel, and value are the main reasons to stay at this modern, four-story inn. Rooms look out over the car park or across a narrow, fast-flowing branch of the River Lee, to the main road, but to compensate, they're spacious and stylish, with pale-wood furniture and large bathrooms. A hearty breakfast from an extensive menu—served in your room or in the bright, contemporary dining room—is another

plus. ✉ *Lancaster Quay, Western Road, Co. Cork* ☎ *021/425–1125* 🖷 *021/425–1126* ⊕ *www.lancasterlodge.com* ➪ *37 rooms, 2 suites* ⚒ *In-room: no a/c, dial-up, Wi-Fi. In-hotel: restaurant, public Wi-Fi, parking (no fee)* ➡ *AE, DC, MC, V* ⊚ *BP.*

\$\$ ⬜ **Rochestown Park.** On seven lovely acres of mature gardens in the fashionable suburb of Douglas, 5 km (3 mi) south of the city, this stylish hotel was built around a Victorian manor house once used as a convent. The grounds help it to retain a peaceful, otherworldly air. Rooms are modern, with cotton spreads, wool carpets, and light-oak fixtures. There's good access to the city's four-lane ring road—and a distant view of same from some rooms, which is compensated for by a view of the river estuary beyond. The large health center specializes in thalassotherapy—seaweed wraps and baths. ✉ *Rochestown Rd., Douglas, Co. Cork* ☎ *021/489–0800* 🖷 *021/489–2178* ⊕ *www.rochestownpark.com* ➪ *160 rooms* ⚒ *In-room: Wi-Fi. In-hotel: restaurant, bar, pool, gym, public Wi-Fi* ➡ *AE, DC, MC, V* ⊚ *BP.*

NIGHTLIFE & THE ARTS

See the *Examiner* or the *Evening Echo* for details about movies, theater, and live music performances.

GALLERIES

The **Fenton Gallery** (✉ *Wandesford Quay, Washington Village* ☎ *021/431–5294* ⊕ *www.artireland.net*) shows work by important Irish artists. The **Lavit Gallery** (✉ *5 Father Mathew St., off South Mall, City Center South* ☎ *021/427–7749*) sells work by members of the Cork Arts Society and other Irish artists. The **Lewis Glucksman Gallery** (✉ *UCC Campus, Western Rd., corner of Donovan's Rd., Western Road* ☎ *021/490-1844* ⊕ *www.glucksman.org*), part of Cork's university, has won several awards for its striking modern architecture. Offbeat exhibits can be found at the **Triskel Arts Centre** (✉ *Tobin St. off S. Main St., Washington Village* ☎ *021/427–2022* ⊕ *www.triskelart.com*). The **Vangard Gallery** (✉ *Carey's La., Paul St., City Center South* ☎ *021/427–8718* ⊕ *www.vangardgallery.com*) exhibits leading contemporary Irish artists.

PERFORMING ARTS & FILM

Cork Opera House (✉ *Lavitt's Quay, City Center South* ☎ *021/427–0022* ⊕ *www.corkoperahouse.ie*) is the city's major hall for touring productions and variety acts. Smaller theatrical productions are staged at the **Everyman Palace** (✉ *MacCurtain St., City Center North* ☎ *021/450–1673*), which has an ornate Victorian interior.

The Kino (✉ *Washington St., Washington Village* ☎ *021/427–1571*) is Cork's only art-house cinema. Three films are usually showing, from 2 PM onward.

PUBS & NIGHTCLUBS

Traditional music sessions can happen anytime at **An Bodhrán** (✉ *42 Oliver Plunkett St., City Center South* ☎ *021/437–1392*). **The Bierhaus** (✉ *Pope's Quay, Shandon* ☎ *021/455–1648*) attracts a hip young crowd, and has over 30 beers to choose from, poker on Thursday, and live music every Friday. You can hear Cajun, folk, or Irish music from Sunday to Wednesday at the **Corner House** (⊠7 *Coburg St., City Center North* ☎021/450–0655). Night owls flock to **Half Moon** (⊠*Half Moon St., City Center South* ☎021/427–0022), the Cork Opera House's late-night music club. It showcases local, up-and-coming jazz and blues bands most weekends starting at 11 PM.

Loafers (⊠26 *Douglas St., South Docklands* ☎021/431–1612) is a friendly gay bar with a beer garden. **The Lobby** (⊠*Union Quay, South Docklands* ☎021/431–1113) has nightly music sessions: traditional and acoustic in the bar, folk and rock upstairs. **Long Valley** (⊠ *Winthrop St., South City Center* ☎021/427–2144) is a Cork institution, famous for its doorstep sandwiches (made with very thick slices of bread and lots of fillings) that are impossible to eat tidily, and its conversation, which is always lively. The bar at the **Metropole Hotel** (⊠*MacCurtain St., City Center North* ☎021/450–8122) is one of Cork's best jazz spots. **Redz Bar and Club** (⊠*Liberty St., Washington Village* ☎021/425–1855 ⊕*www.rebelbargroup.com*) has late-night live entertainment and DJs every night but Monday.

SHOPPING

DEPARTMENT STORES

Brown Thomas (⊠18 *Patrick St., City Center South* ☎021/427–6771), Ireland's high-end department store, carries items by Irish and international designers. The ground floor has an excellent cosmetics hall and a good selection of menswear and Irish crystal. Refuel at the coffee shop, which sells healthful open sandwiches and homemade soups. **Debenham's** (⊠*Patrick St., City Center South* ☎021/427–7727), Cork's largest department store and a branch of the U.K. chain, occupies a beautiful landmark building with a central glass dome. **Dunnes Stores** (⊠*Merchant's Quay, City Center South* ☎021/427–4200) began in Cork as a family-owned drapery store and became the place where all of Ireland buys its socks, underwear, and much more. The British retail giant **Marks & Spencer** (⊠6–8 *Patrick St., Merchant's Quay, City Center South* ☎021/427–5555) is as popular for its foods (great for picnics) and housewares as for its clothing basics. For inexpensive rain gear, T-shirts, underwear, and any other garments you forgot to pack, head for **Penney's** (⊠27 *Patrick St., City Center South* ☎021/427–1935).

MALLS

Mahon Point Shopping Centre (⊠*Mahon Point, South Link Rd.* ☎021/497–2800) is a massive out-of-town shopping center just south of the Lee Tunnel, with an emphasis on fashion. The **Merchant's Quay Shopping Centre** (⊠*Merchant's Quay, City Center South* ☎021/427–5466) is a large downtown mall.

SPECIALTY SHOPS

ANTIQUES **Gallery 44** (⊠*44A MacCurtain St., City Center North* ☎021/450–1319) stocks antique glass, porcelain, paintings, and prints. **Irene's** (⊠22 *Marlboro St., City Center South* ☎021/427–0642) sells antique jewelry. **Mills Antiques** (✉ *3 Paul's La., City Center South* ☎ *021/427–3528*) carries Irish, English, and European paintings, prints, silver, porcelain, and small furniture. **Victoria's** (✉ *2 Oliver Plunkett St., City Center South* ☎ *021/427–2752*) carries interesting jewelry and Victoriana.

BOOKS **Connolly's Bookshop** (✉ *Paul St. Piazza, City Center South* ☎ *021/427–5366*) has an extensive stock of new and secondhand books, with a good selection of Irish-interest titles. **Mainly Murder Bookstore** (✉ *2A Paul St., City Center South* ☎ *021/427–2413*) is a must for lovers of crime fiction. **Vibes & Scribes** (✉ *3 Bridge St., City Center North* ☎ *021/450–5370*) attracts a loyal following of avid readers, with three floors of new, secondhand, and discount books as well as CDs and videos. **Waterstones** (✉ *Patrick St., City Center South* ☎ *021/427–6522*) is the biggest bookshop in town, with a great choice of new fiction and nonfiction as well as a wide selection of locally published books.

CLOTHING **Cocoon** (✉ *6 Emmet Pl., City Center South* ☎ *021/427–3393*), a little shop in a hexagonal tower, has a ravishing selection of sexy Italian boots and shoes alongside unusual jewelry and accessories. Fashion lovers adore the evening and business attire at the **Dressing Room** (✉ *8 Emmet Pl., City Center South* ☎ *021/427–0117*), a tiny but tony boutique opposite the entrance to the Cork Opera House. **Monica John** (✉ *French Church St., City Center South* ☎ *021/427–1399*) sells locally designed high-fashion ladies' wear as well as some imported lines. **Quills** (✉ *107 Patrick St., City Center South* ☎ *021/427–1717*) has a good selection of Irish-made apparel for women and men. **Samui** (✉ *17 Drawbridge St., City Center South* ☎ *021/427–8080*) stocks dramatic—often quirky, but always flattering—clothes from Ireland, France, Germany, and the United Kingdom. For casual weatherproof clothing, try the **Tack Room** (✉ *Unit 3, Academy St., City Center South* ☎ *021/427–2704*).

JEWELRY **Designworks Ltd** (✉ *34 Grand Parade, City Center South* ☎ *021/427–9420*) has imaginative, modern jewelry. **IMB Design** (✉ *10a Paul St. shopping center, City Center South* ☎ *021/425–1800*) designs and sells contemporary jewelry in silver and gold.

MUSIC **HMV** (✉ *Patrick St.* ☎ *021/427–4433*) has a good selection of Irish traditional music in its classical and jazz sections. The best place for recordings of Irish music is **Living Tradition** (✉ *40 MacCurtain St., City Center North* ☎ *021/450–2040*). **Vibes & Scribes** (✉ *3 Bridge St., City Center North* ☎ *021/450–5370*) has a good selection of bargain and secondhand CDs, DVDs, and videotapes. Chart hits are the main business of the **Virgin Megastore** (✉ *Queen's Old Castle, City Center South* ☎ *021/427–9299*), but you can find some traditional Irish music for sale in the small classical and jazz sections.

SIDE TRIPS FROM CORK CITY

Blarney, northwest of Cork City on R617, and Cork Harbour, east of the city on N25 (follow signposts to Waterford), make perfect day trips. Blarney's attractions are Blarney Castle and the famous Blarney Stone.

Cork Harbour's draws include Fota Island, with an arboretum, a wildlife park, and Fota House—a renovated hunting lodge and estate—and the fishing port of Cobh.

BLARNEY

🔞 *10 km (6 mi) northwest of Cork City.*

"On Galway sands they kiss your hands, they kiss your lips at Carney, but by the Lee they drink strong tea, and kiss the stone at Blarney."

This famous rhyme celebrates one of Ireland's most noted icons—the Blarney Stone, which is the main reason most people journey to this small community built around a village green.

In the center of Blarney is **Blarney Castle,** or what remains of it: the ruined central keep is all that's left of this mid-15th-century stronghold. The castle contains the famed Blarney Stone; kissing the stone, it's said, endows the kisser with the fabled "gift of gab." It's 127 steep steps to the battlements. To kiss the stone, you must lie down on the battlements, hold on to a guardrail, and lean your head way back. It's good fun and not at all dangerous. Expect a line from mid-June to early September; while you wait, you can admire the views of the wooded River Lee valley and chuckle over how the word "blarney" came to mean what it does. As the story goes, Queen Elizabeth I wanted Cormac MacCarthy, Lord of Blarney, to will his castle to the crown, but he refused her requests with eloquent excuses and soothing compliments. Exhausted by his comments, the queen reportedly exclaimed, "This is all Blarney. What he says he rarely means."

You can take pleasant walks around the castle grounds; Rock Close contains oddly shaped limestone rocks landscaped in the 18th century and a grove of ancient yew trees that is said to have been the site of Druid worship. In early March there's a wonderful display of naturalized daffodils. ☎ *021/438-5252* ⊕ *www.blarneycastle.ie* ✉ *Blarney Castle: €8* ☉ *Blarney Castle: May and Sept., Mon.–Sat. 9–6:30, Sun. 9–5:30; June–Aug., Mon.–Sat. 9–7, Sun. 9–5:30; Oct.–Apr., Mon.–Sat. 9–sundown, Sun. 9–5:30.*

WHERE TO STAY & EAT

$–$$$ ✕ **Blair's Inn.** Surrounded by woods five minutes from Blarney, Blair's Inn—noted for its exuberant window-box displays—is the perfect retreat from Blarney's tour-bus crowds. This is a real "local," complete with genial owner-hosts, John and Anne, as well as a busy restaurant. In summer enjoy the beer garden; in winter, warm wood fires flicker in the cozy interior. Freshly prepared local produce is served in generous portions: best bets include Irish stew with lamb, carrots, and potatoes, as well as corned beef and a memorable gratin of prawns, crab, and salmon, served piping hot. There's live entertainment every Sunday at 9 PM as well as on Monday from May to October. ⊠*Cloghroe* ☎*021/438–1470* ▭*MC, V.*

¢–$ 🍴**Maranatha Country House.** This gray-stone Victorian manor surrounded by pretty gardens and 27 woodland acres makes an excellent base for exploring Blarney, Cork City, and even Killarney, 1½ hours away. The guest rooms in Olwen and Douglas Venn's impeccably run family home are individually decorated with antiques (Olwen has a passion for French inlaid furniture) and striking textiles. The Regal Suite has a four-poster bed swathed in pink, green, and white-sprigged fabric that matches the ruched drapes, as well as a sunken bath with a hot tub. Breakfast is served in the conservatory, which overlooks rolling lawns and majestic trees. To get here, drive through Blarney village on the R617 for 3 km (2 mi) to the village of Tower. ⊠*Tower, Co. Cork* ☎*021/438–5102* ⊕*www.maranathacountryhouse.com* ⇱*6 rooms* △*In-room: no a/c, no TV. In-hotel: no-smoking rooms, no elevator* ▭*MC, V* ⊗*Closed Dec.–Jan.* ⏺*BP.*

SHOPPING   Blarney has lots of crafts shops south and west of the village green, a two-minute walk from the castle. **Blarney Woolen Mills** (☎*021/438– 5280* ⊕*www.blarney.ie*) has the largest stock and the highest turnover of Blarney's crafts shops. It sells everything from Irish-made high fashion to Aran hand-knit items to leprechaun key rings.

CORK HARBOUR

⑲ *16 km (10 mi) east of Cork City.*

The 70-acre **Fota Island Wildlife Park** is 12 km (7 mi) east of Cork via N25, R624, and the main Cobh road. It's an important breeding center for cheetahs and wallabies, and also is home to monkeys, zebras, giraffes, ostriches, flamingos, emus, and kangaroos. ☎*021/481–2678* ⊕*www.fotawildlife.ie* 🎟*€12.50* ⊗*Mon.–Sat. 10–4:30, Sun. 11–4:30; last admission an hr before closing.*

Next to the Fota Island Wildlife Park is **Fota House,** the Smith-Barry ancestral estate: its name is derived from the Irish Fód te, which means "warm soil," a tribute to the unique tidal estuary microclimate here and the reason why one of Ireland's most exotic botanical gardens was established here. The original lodge house was built in the mid-18th century for the Smith-Barry family, which owned vast tracts of land in South Cork, including the whole of Fota Island. The next generation of the powerful family employed the renowned architects Richard and William Vitruvius Morrison to convert the structure into an impressive Regency–style house that has now been painstakingly restored. The symmetrical facade is relatively unadorned and stands in contrast to the resplendent Adamesque plasterwork of the formal reception rooms (somewhat denuded of furniture). The servants' quarters are almost as big as the house proper. Fota's glories continue in the gardens, which include an arboretum, a Victorian fernery, an Italian garden, an orangerie, and a special display of magnolias. You can relax over cake and scones in the tearoom after visiting the gift shop. ☎*021/481–5543* ⊕*www.fotahouse.com* 🎟*€5.50* ⊗*Apr.–Sept., Mon.–Sat. 10–5, Sun. 11—5; Oct.–Mar., daily 11–4.*

Many of the people who left Ireland on immigrant ships for the New World departed from **Cobh,** a pretty fishing port and seaside resort 24 km (15 mi) southeast of Cork City on R624. The **Queenstown Story at Cobh Heritage Center,** in the old Cobh railway station, re-creates the experience of the million emigrants who left from here between 1750 and the mid-20th century. It also tells the stories of great transatlantic liners, including the *Titanic,* whose last port of call was Cobh, and the *Lusitania,* which was sunk by a German submarine off this coast on May 7, 1915. Many of the *Lusitania's* 1,198 victims are buried in Cobh, which has a memorial to them on the local quay. ☎*021/481–3591* ⊕*www.cobhheritage.com* ✉*€6.60* ☉*Oct.–Apr., daily 9:30–5; May–Sept., daily 9:30–6.* The best view of Cobh is from **St. Colman's Cathedral,** an exuberant neo-Gothic granite church designed by the eminent British architect E.W. Pugin in 1869, and completed in 1919. Inside, granite niches portray scenes of the Roman Catholic Church's history in Ireland, beginning with the arrival of St. Patrick. ☎*021/481–3222* ✉*Free.*

ART GALLERIES   Philip Gray served as a diver in the Irish navy, and left to paint, which he does extremely well. The sea in all its guises is his subject. **The Philip Gray Gallery of Fine Art** (✉*Slipway Two, Cork Dockyard, Rushbrooke, Cobh* ☎*021/481–4170* ⊕*www.philipgray.com*) is on a slipway of a dockyard in Cork Harbour.

SPORTS & THE   Explore the sheltered, island-studded waters of Cork Harbour by rent-
OUTDOORS   ing a sailing dinghy from **International Sailing Center** (✉*Fort Lisle, Cobh* ☎*021/481–1237* ⊕*www.sailcork.com*).

EAST CORK & THE BLACKWATER VALLEY

Although most visitors to Cork head west out of the city for the coastal areas between Cork and Glengarriff, the east and the north of the county are also worth exploring. East Cork is popular with Irish tourists, who love the long sandy beaches here. North Cork's main attraction is the Blackwater River, which crosses the county from east to west. It's famous for its trout and salmon fishing and its scenery.

MIDLETON

20 *15 km (9 mi) northwest of Shanagarry on R629, 12 km (8 mi) east of Cork City on N25.*

Midleton is famous for its school, Midleton College, founded in 1696, and its distillery, founded in 1825 and modernized in 1975, which manufactures spirits—including Irish whiskey—for distribution worldwide. A pleasant market town set at the head of the Owenacurra estuary, near the northeast corner of Cork Harbour, it has many gray-stone buildings dating mainly from the early 19th century.

The **Jameson Heritage Centre** has tours of the Old Midleton Distillery, to show you how Irish whiskey—*uisce beatha* (pronounced ishka bah-hah), "the water of life"—was made in the old days. The old

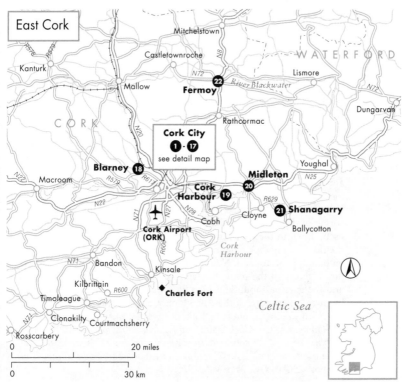

East Cork

stone buildings are excellent examples of 19th-century industrial architecture, the impressively large old waterwheel still operates, and the pot still—a copper dome that can hold 32,000 imperial gallons of whiskey—is the world's largest. Early in the tour, requests are made for a volunteer "whiskey taster," so be alert if this option appeals. Tours end with a complimentary glass of Jameson's Irish whiskey (or a soft drink). A gift shop and café are also on the premises. ☎021/461–3594 ⊕www.whiskeytours.ie ☎€9.75 ⊙Mar.–Oct., daily 9–4:30; Nov.–Feb., daily 10–4.

SHANAGARRY

㉑ *12 km (8 mi) southeast of Shanagarry on R629, 17 km (11 mi) southeast of Cork Harbour via N25 and R632.*

There are two reasons to come to Shanagarry, a farming village known chiefly for its Quaker connections: Ballymaloe House, one of Ireland's first country-house hotels, and Ballymaloe Cookery School and Gardens, a top destination for chefs-in-training.

The most famous Shanagarry Quaker was William Penn (1644–1718), the founder of the Pennsylvania colony, who grew up in **Shanagarry House,** still a private residence in the center of the village. The entry gates are across from Shanagarry Castle, now owned and being restored by the potter and entrepreneur Stephen Pearce. The house's most famous tenant since William Penn was Marlon Brando, who stayed here in the summer of 1995 while filming *Divine Rapture* in nearby Ballycotton.

WHERE TO STAY & EAT

$$$$

Fodor's Choice

★

✕ ▩ **Ballymaloe House.** Ballymaloe is world famous as the fountainhead of the New Irish Cuisine (for more information, see "A Taste of Ireland" in this chapter). Originally a farmhouse and family home, albeit on a gracious scale, Ballymaloe still functions partly as a working farm, one reason why the grounds—pleasant lawns, "which way home?" paths, and vegetable gardens—don't aspire to grandeur. Inside, past the doorway's demilune window, guests like to gather in the drawing room, a symphony of whites and beiges, with fine modern Irish paintings on the walls. A bigger dose of country charm can be found in some guest rooms (notably the ones cocooned in floral wallpapers). Nearly every corner of the Georgian manor (added on to a Norman tower house) is used, down to the charming "stable" bedrooms on the first floor and the tiny, ivy-covered gatekeeper's cottage—perhaps the cutest accommodation in all Ireland. Newer, more spacious rooms downstairs have direct access to the pool and tennis court, and to views of the river and the garden's abundant bird life. This arcadia has been overseen by three generations of the Allen family, and their loyal staff have the knack of making a guest feel like a cosseted member of the family. ⊠*Shanagarry, Co. Cork* ☎*021/465–2531* 🖷*021/465–2021* ⊕*www. ballymaloe.ie* ⇌*33 rooms* ♿*In-room: no a/c, no TV (some). In-hotel: restaurant, bar, golf course, tennis court, pool, some pets allowed, no elevator* ☰*AE, DC, MC, V* ⦿|*BP.*

$$

☾

✕ ▩ **Barnabrow House.** Owners John and Geraldine O'Brien stylishly combined the old and the new when they renovated the interior of this rambling 17th-century house. Specially made modern wood furniture from Africa sits beside Victorian antiques and against intensely colored walls. The results are romantic and relaxed and are helped by the stunning views across the countryside to Ballycotton Bay. The garden is lovely, and wildflowers are encouraged. The O'Briens pride themselves on the informal, relaxed atmosphere, which includes a cockerel that announces the break of day (you have been warned) and a child-friendly policy. Main-house rooms have high ceilings and canopy beds; courtyard rooms are cozier and have low, beamed ceilings. The Trinity Rooms restaurant ($$–$$$$), closed to nonguests Monday through Wednesday, resembles a medieval banqueting hall, with a high-beam ceiling and church windows, and is painted wine-red. It serves imaginative dishes made with local produce and meats, including fish from nearby Ballycotton. ⊠*Cloyne, Co. Cork* ☎🖷*021/465–2534* ⊕*www.barnabrowhouse.ie* ⇌*21 rooms* ♿*In-room: no a/c, no TV. In-hotel: restaurant, bar, no-smoking rooms, no elevator* ☰*DC, MC, V* ⦿|*BP.*

Continued on page 340

A TASTE OF IRELAND

Queen scallops with aubergine caviar

Great ingredients and innovative chefs are shaping West Cork into one of the most foodie-friendly places on the planet.

The next time you wander into a time-burnished 19th-century Irish pub bent on downing a platter of steak, bland potatoes, and mushy peas, don't be surprised if you end up with a main course of skewered John Dory in clonmel cider Sauce and a dessert of Cooleeney Camembert ganache with lavender jelly. Begorra—you've encountered the much-vaunted Irish food revolution! Since the mid-1990s, the New Irish Cuisine has changed the beige, boiled, and boring food of yore into a bounty of gourmet delights. Today, haute-hungry gourmands packing chubby wallets (and the cookbooks of Margaret Johnson and Noel Cullen) are all abuzz discovering emerging culinary wizards; artisanal producers of farmhouse cheeses; organic beef and smoked fish; and some of the best farmers' markets and provisioners around. Leading the charge of Ireland's food revolution are superstar chefs, and few have done more to transform the Irish kitchen than Myrtle Allen and her daughter-in-law, Darina Allen. The trip to bountiful Ireland begins with them.

Gubbeen Farmhouse

BALLYMALOE: A TRIP TO BOUNTIFUL

Bacon chop with Irish Whiskey sauce, Ballymaloe Cookery School

When Myrtle Allen opened a restaurant at her Georgian farm-estate, Ballymaloe (east of Cork City and pronounced Bah-lee-mal-oo), in 1964, she hadn't set out to change the way Ireland eats.

Moving to the historic Quaker stronghold of Shangarry in 1948, she and her husband, Ivan, began the restoration of an old Georgian farm estate. Before too long, their 400-acre cropland became the breeding ground for a new gastronomy as the couple reaped harvests of sea kale, parsnips, carrageen moss, rutabagas, gooseberries, globe artichokes, and other heritage veggies. Long before organic became a buzzword, Myrtle made freshness her mantra: eggs from her own hens, produce from her own garden, freshly landed fish from nearby Ballycotton. So, when she opened The Yeats Room at Ballymaloe in 1964, her refashioning of her great-grandparents food was embraced by a generation reared on frozen pizza. In no time, food critics were raving about Myrtle's everything-old-is-new-again-but-better take.

The Herb Garden at Ballymaloe

Myrtle Allen is now retired but chef Jason Fahey has a blanced touch that is is almost Quaker-like in its subtlety. Dinners here are the real thing: fresh-picked coriander from the greenhouse for the leg of lamb, the eggs in the Carageen Pudding—a custard mixed with Cork seaweed and bittersweet Irish-coffee sauce—the gift of hens with squatters' rights, and if the plaice weren't biting that day, it won't be on the menu. Under the hosts' celebrated collection of modern Irish paintings, diners can enjoy a kaleidoscope of specialties (selections change seasonally, weekly, and daily) be it a radish-leaf soup, a Ballymaloe cheddar cheese fondue, or a roast Ballycotton cod with Ulster champ. A final testimony to Myrtle's practice of supporting small-scale, local food purveyors is the adieu offering: the amazing cheese board, which conveys local artisanship at its best. Ballymaloe House has lovely overnight accomodations (⊕ www.ballymaloe.ie ⇨ review under Shanagarry), just one reason why many diners enjoy a leisurely repast at night.

NOW WE'RE COOKING

If Myrtle Allen is the Alice Waters of Ireland, Darina Allen is its Martha Stewart. Thanks to her eight television series, her bestselling cookbooks, and the happy status of being the daughter-in-law of Myrtle, Darina's celebrity in Ireland is about on a par with U2's. She arrived in 1963 to apprentice at Ballymaloe and promptly fell in love with Myrtle's son, Tim, and her culinary dream. So, in 1983, she and Tim opened the Ballymaloe Cookery School, setting up shop two miles east on the other side of Shanagarry village at Kinoith House. The ultimate spot for a don't-just-visit, stay-and-become-an-Irish-chef experience, the school offers everything from two-hour starter lessons to the famed 12-week Certificate Course (run three times a year for 58 students), which many Irish chefs regard as a rite of passage. Half-day courses can be combined with an indulgent stay at

Darina Allen

Ballymaloe House—choose from "Sushi Made Simple," "The Magic of Phyllo," or "Discovering Tapas." A new departure is the "forgotten skills" series, day-long courses on chicken keeping, beekeeping, and organic gardening. Evidence that history repeats itself: Darina's daughter-in-law, Rachel Allen, is now making her second TV series, and publishing her second cook book.

MENU BEST BETS

Goujons of Ballycotton Haddock with Tartare Sauce

John's Rosemary, Red Wine & Garden Leek Risotto

Gubbeen Ham Braised in Chablis & Cream Served with Peperonata & Chives

Roast East Cork Beef with Roast Garlic Mayonnaise, with Fondant Potato & Vegetable Pakorash

Ballymaloe Cheddar Cheese Fondue

Grilled Ballycotton Hake with Scallops & Lobster, Herb Relish & French Beans

THE BALLYMALOE COOKERY SCHOOL is in Kinoith, just outside Shanagarry (☎ 021/464-6785 ⊕ www.cookingisfun.ie). Classes range from afternoon demonstrations (€75) to half-day classes (€95) to 1, 2½, and 5 day courses to the full 12-week Certificate (€8,775). Students can stay in charming cottages on the grounds.

6

CORK CORNUCOPIA: THE FOOD ARTISANS

Compare a traditionally made butcher's sausage with the plastic-wrapped supermarket version, and you'll understand what all the fuss is about: flavor, texture, and general deliciousness.

You'll see why Ireland's new artisanal foodstuff makers, fed up with the formulaic, tasteless foods of big industry, have stepped in to pioneer the production of farmhouse cheeses, organic beef, and organic herb cultivation and fish smoking. They got a big boost with the 1998 founding of Slow Food Ireland (⊕ www.slowfoodireland.com), a loose collective of specialty producers and restaurateurs whose aim was to encourage careful food sourcing. West Cork has played an important role in the revival of Irish traditional foods, since incomers moving to the area seeking a change in lifestyle found that their small-business interests dovetailed with those of the traditional butchers, bakers, and farmers who had stayed put. These new artisans are now often listed on restaurant menus: Gubbeen Cheese, Ummera Smoked Salmon, Krawczyk's West Cork Salamis, Glenilen Dairy Products, and many others. Here are three of the best:

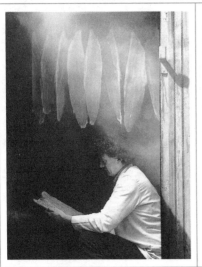

GUBBEEN FARMHOUSE PRODUCTS

Farmer Tom Ferguson tends a herd of prize cows, whose rich milk is made into creamy cheese by his wife Giana. The fresh-straw piggery allows its lucky pigs to have a view of Roaring Water Bay, one of the most scenic corners of Ireland. Tom and Giana's son, Fingal, runs the smokehouse (great smoked bacon, chorizo, and salamis), while daughter Clovisse grows organic vegetables and herbs. Products are sold at Neal's Yard in London and West Cork's Farmer's Markets. ⊠ *Gubbeen, Schull, near Skibbbereen, Co. Cork* ☎ *028/28231* ⊕ *www.gubbeen.com*

BELVELLY SMOKEHOUSE Frank Hederman smokes his eels, mackerel, salmon, trout, and mussels over beech rather than oak, giving them an unusually mild flavor. His smoked salmon is sold in London's Fortnum & Mason. The smokehouse is open for tastings, and his products can be bought at Cork City's English Market and Midleton Farmer's Market. ⊠ *Cobh* ☎ *021/481-1089* ⊕ *www.frankhederman.com*

MACROOM OATMEAL Since the early 1800s, Donal Creedon's porridge oats have been hand-roasted on the traditional cast-iron plate at Walton's Mills before being shelled and ground, giving them a distinctive smoky, nutty flavor. Great for breadmaking, the meal is sold at many food shops. ⊠ *Kanturk, Co. Cork* ☎ *026/41800* ⊕*macroomoatmealmills£eircom.net*

BLESSED ARE THE CHEESEMAKERS

Thirty years ago Irish cheese came in bright-orange blocks and tasted like salted plastic. Today, a thriving cheesemaking culture—a mix of native ingenuity and French, Swiss, German, and Dutch expertise—produces a wide range of artisanal farmhouse cheeses from the milk of goats and sheep, as well as from purebred cows. **Here are the best:**

Ardsallagh Goat's Cheese. A popular salad ingredient, this cheese can be bought from its maker, Jane Murphy, at the Midleton Farmer's Market.

Cashel Blue. The most famous Irish blue, this mild, creamy delight is made in Fethard, Co. Tipperary—it is as much used in cooking as on the cheese board.

Crozier Blue. Made from sheep's milk, this has a cult following.

Gabriel and Desmond. Using only summer-season raw milk from local herds grazed near the sea, these hard cheeses created by Americans Bill Hogan and Sean Ferry have a long maturation period, resulting in a piquant, aromatic bouquet.

Knockalara Sheep's Milk Cheese. Made by Wolfgang and Agnes Schiebitz, this is popular with chefs thanks to its soft, crumbly texture.

Milleens. This pungent, washed-rind winner is made from the milk of cows raised by Norman and Veronica Steele on their Beara Peninsula family farm.

FINDING THE FEAST

Long known as the "belly of Ireland," the West Cork region is celebrated for its rich fishing and even richer farming. These days, gourmets are busy rooting out the best Irish chorizo, sampling a new Durrus cheese and nutmeg pizza, or wolfing down Galway Bay oysters (heaven when served with Guinness!). Like a world-class picnic, this cook's tour is the tastiest recipe for a day trip through the region.

The best places to track down top temptations from Cork's gastronomic cornucopia are the area's food markets, often set in small villages and averaging only about a dozen stalls. Low overheads mean bargains for the buyers, who enjoy an amazing array of artisanal foodstuffs, from organic vegetables to sauces and relishes, Breton pancakes, handmade bread, home-cured ham, preserves, smoked salmon, and a great range of cheeses. And the markets' festive atmosphere (often livened up with a jazz trio or street performers) is complemented by the camaraderie of the stall-holders—this is often their main contact with the buying public. Darina Allen, with typical energy, can be found most Saturday mornings selling produce from her Ballymaloe Cookery School at a stall in Midleton. Check out the ever-changing market scene on its Web site (⊕ www.irelandmarkets.com) for up-to-date information. Here is a tip sheet:

COUNTY CORK

Bantry, Main Square, Friday 9 am to 1 pm. A traditional street market, with a strong presence of growers of organic plants and veggies.

Clonakilty, Thursday and Saturday, 10 am to 2 pm. Indoor market in MacCurtain Hall, with artisan food sold by its makers on Thursday and food and crafts sold by their makers on Saturday.

Kinsale, Market Square, Tuesday 10–1. Snack on a Breton crepe while stocking up on chutneys, smoked salmon, famhouse cheeses, fresh fish, and organic veg and fruit at this cute piazza market.

Midleton, Saturday 10 am–2 pm. One of the liveliest farmers' markets, it's held in a small car park, with buskers creating a festive vibe.

Schull, Sunday 11–3. At its best in summer and at Christmas, this foodie's market showcases superb products from local bakers, fish smokers and cheesemakers, and Gubbeen smoked pork products, all sold by their makers.

COUNTY KERRY

Kenmare, Wednesday 10 am–5 pm, closed Jan. and Feb. About 15 outdoor stalls offer local organic produce and a few exotic imports to an appreciative local clientele. Look out for Knockatee cheese from Tuosist down the road, Olivier's smoked trout from Killorglin, organic vegs, homemade pâtés, fresh fish, and French soaps and sweets.

Killarney, Parochial Hall, Country Market, Friday 11:30 am–1:30 pm. Famed for cakes, bread, savory tarts, jams, and farm-fresh eggs, the produce is all genuinely homemade, much of it from local farms, and sold at bargain prices.

Milltown, Old Church Market, Saturday 10 am–2pm. Organic producers converge on this church, on the main road (N70) between Killorglin and Castlemaine—specialist bakers, organic growers, a wheatgrass stall, and an herbalist are highlights.

OTHER FOODIE FAVES

THE ENGLISH MARKET Today, this famous city-center covered market is a thriving hub of artisanal butchers, fishmongers, and greengrocers. Organic fruits and vegs, top-quality meat and fresh fish, imported coffees and teas, locally made charcuterie, farmhouse cheeses—even a champagne from a local wine merchant, Bubble Brothers. ✉ *Grand Parade, Cork City* ⊕ *www.corkcity.ie*

THE LETTERCOLLUM SHOP Founders of the Lettercollum Kitchen Project, Con McLaughlin and Karen Austin are masters of the vegetarian and ethnic repertory (and also offer cooking classes). Their shop/bakery sells specialist breads, cooks' ingredients, sandwiches, and savory herb tarts. Pick up a picnic. ✉ *22 Connolly St., Clonakilty* ☎ *023/46251* ⊕ *www.lettercollum.ie*

URRU Once Ruth Healy took the Ballymaloe Certificate Cookery Course she left the corporate treadmill behind to open the ultimate cook's shop, which aims to bring urban chic to rural Ireland. Sip a latte while browsing among local artisanal foods, including homemade pâtés and patisserie, and a tempting range of cookbooks, cookwares, and chocolates. ✉ *The Mill, MacSwiney Quay, Bandon, Co. Cork* ☎ *023/54731* ⊕ *www.urru.ie*

6

A TASTE OF IRELAND

SHOPPING

The famous Irish ceramicist Stephen Pearce makes tableware and bowls in four signature styles that are available in many Irish crafts shops. He sells a wide selection at his own **Stephen Pearce Emporium** (⊠*Near Cloyne* ☎*021/464–6262*), where he also stocks an interesting range of Irish-made crafts.

FERMOY

㉒ *35 km (22 mi) north of Cork City on N8.*

An army town dating mainly from the mid-19th century, Fermoy is a major crossroads on the Dublin–Cork road (N8); the east–west road that passes through town (N72) is an attractive 98-km (61-mi) alternative route to Killarney. The bridge that spans the Blackwater is flanked by two weirs dating from 1689. From mid-April to early July you can watch salmon working their way back to their spawning grounds. A few miles upstream on the same river is Castlehyde, a fine Georgian house that is now the home of the lord of Irish dance, Michael Flatley. It's easy to see why he was so charmed by the quiet, lush country that surrounds this famous salmon river.

WHERE TO STAY & EAT

$$$ ╳🏨 **Ballyvolane House.** With Georgian splendor in the terra-cotta,
Fodor$Choice gilded, and black Italianate pillared hall, and Regency coziness non-
★ pareil in the daffodil yellow sitting room, Ballyvolane offers a setting as elegant as it is charming. Although this 1728 stone house looks imposing, life here unfolds with country-house informality. Expect to find old fishing gear and walking sticks lying about and the family dog greeting your return. The spacious bedrooms are beautifully decorated with a rich assortment of antiques and heirlooms, but also display an unpredictable sense of humor—the tub in Roland's Room, in full view of all on a wooden pedestal perched to give a garden view, always raises a smile. The guest rooms look out onto wonderful gardens, with a 100-acre dairy farm beyond. Dinner is served at a large table in the formal dining room ($$$$), with family silver set on white linens (both dinner and rooms must be booked at least 24 hours in advance). The village of Castlelyons is signposted off N8 in Rathcormac, just south of Fermoy. ⊠*Castlelyons, Co. Cork* ☎*025/36349* 🖷*025/36781* ⊕*www. ballyvolanehouse.ie* ⇝*6 rooms* ⚬*In-room: no a/c, no phone. In-hotel: restaurant, no elevator, no-smoking rooms* ⊟*AE, MC, V* ⫪⊙*BP.*

KINSALE TO GLENGARRIFF

The historic old port—and now booming seaside town—of Kinsale is the perfect place to begin the 136-km (85-mi) trip, via Bantry Bay and through a variety of seascapes, to the lush vegetation of Glengarriff. If you tackle this scenic West Cork coastal route nonstop, the drive takes less than two hours, but the whole point of this journey is to linger in places that tickle your fancy. Must-sees include the famed 18th-century manse of Bantry House and the romantic island gardens of Ilnacullin.

KINSALE

❷❸ *29 km (18 mi) southwest of Cork City on R600.*

Foodies flock to Kinsale, a picturesque port that pioneered the Irish small-town tradition of fine dining in unbelievably small restaurants. Back in the early '80s, Kinsale had a village-size population of 2,000 and at least a dozen top-grade restaurants, mostly run by enthusiastic owner-chefs. Things have leveled out since then—the town has grown, while the number of restaurants has remained nearly

the same, and most of the original chefs have moved on—but there is still a great buzz during the annual Autumn Flavours Festival; for more information, see ⊕*www.kinsalerestaurants.com.*

In the town center, at the tip of the wide, fjordlike harbor that opens out from the River Bandon, upscale shops and eateries with brightly painted facades line small streets. Kinsale has two yacht marinas, and skippers with deep-sea angling boats offer day charters. The Kinsale Yacht Club hosts racing and cruising events during the sailing season, which runs from March to October for hardy souls and from June to August for everyone else. This town is also where you can find Ireland's largest bareboat charter company.

The **Desmond Castle and the International Museum of Wine** are in a 15th-century fortified town house—originally a custom house—that has a dark history. It was used as a prison for French and American seamen in the 1700s, and was subsequently a jail and then a workhouse. Now it contains displays that tell the story of the wine trade and its importance to the Irish diaspora to France, America, Australia, and New Zealand. ⊠*Cork St.* ☎*021/477–4855* ⊕*www.heritageireland. ie* ⌹*€2.90* ☉*Mid–Apr.–mid–June, Tues.–Sun. 10–6; mid-June–mid-Oct., daily 10–6.*

Memorabilia from the wreck of the *Lusitania* are among the best artifacts in the **Kinsale Museum,** which is in a 17th-century, Dutch-style courthouse. The 1915 inquest into that ship's sinking took place in the courtroom, briefly making it the focus of the world's attention; it has been preserved as a memorial. Because the staff consists of volunteers, it's best to call to confirm opening times. ⊠*Old Courthouse, Market Pl.* ☎*021/477–2044* ⌹*€2.50* ☉*Mon.–Sat. 11–5, Sun. 3–5.*

★ The British built **Charles Fort** on the east side of the Bandon River estuary in the late 17th century, after their defeat of the Spanish and Irish forces. One of Europe's best-preserved "star forts" encloses some 12 cliff-top acres and is similar to Fort Ticonderoga in New York State. If the sun is shining, take the footpath signposted Scilly Walk; it winds along the harbor's edge under tall trees and then through the village of

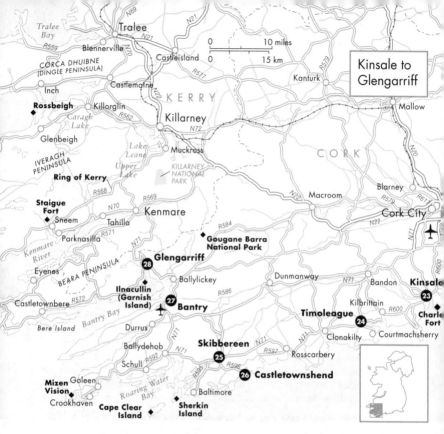

Summer Cove. ⊠ *3 km (2 mi) east of town* ☎ *021/477–2263* ⊕ *www. heritageireland.ie* ☞ *€3.70* ⊙ *Mid-Mar.–Oct., daily 10–6; Nov.–mid-Mar., weekends 10–5.*

The **Spaniard Inn** looks over the town and harbor from a hairpin bend on the road to Charles Fort. Inside, sawdust-covered floors and a big open fireplace make this onetime fishermen's bar a cozy spot in winter. In summer you can take a pint to the veranda and watch the world go by on land and sea. ⊠ *Scilly* ☎ *021/477–2436.*

WHERE TO STAY & EAT

$$–$$$$ ✕ **Man Friday.** Yes, the name refers to Kinsale's alleged connection with
★ the original Robinson Crusoe, Alexander Selkirk, for the town was reputedly his last port of call before shipwreck. Set about 1 km (½ mi) outside town, next to the Spaniard Inn, on a hilltop overlooking the harbor, the restaurant focuses on steaks and seafood, prepared in an unpretentious Continental style. A rustic downhill walkway leads to a series of interconnected rooms and a terrace where diners enjoy drinks in fine weather. The generous portions and the warm atmosphere make it the sort of place you'll want to revisit. ⊠ *Scilly* ☎ *021/477–2260* ⊟ *AE, DC, MC, V* ⊙ *Closed Sun. No lunch.*

A Battle Lost

Before Kinsale became the foodie capital of Ireland, it was chiefly famous for the Battle of Kinsale in 1601, when the Irish and the Spanish joined forces against the English—and lost. As generations of Irish school-children could tell you, the Battle of Kinsale was a turning point in Irish history. It precipitated an event known as "the Flight of the Earls" (the subject of Brian Friels' play *Making History*), in which the Irish aristocracy left for Europe, to seek help in furthering their cause from the Catholic king of Spain. The Irish earls never returned, leaving their lands to be colonized by the English settlers, who also filled the power vacuum created by their absence. The Spanish influence that can be traced back to this battle can be seen in Kinsale's older houses, which have slate roofs and unusual slate fronts. Because of its geographi-cal position (approximately 800 km [500 mi] of open sea due north of La Coruna) Kinsale continued to trade with Spain, and even today, Spanish trawlers regularly fish in the waters off the coast of County Cork. Kinsale went on to become an important fish-ing port as well as a British army and naval base.

$$–$$$ ✕ **The Bulman.** Kinsale has other pub-restaurants, but none with such ♻ an idyllic waterside location (kids love to play on the big stone quay here). In summer drinks are taken outside, either at tables or on the big stone quay, which looks back to the town and out to the unspoiled outer harbor. The lunch menu is served in the first-floor restaurant, and is drawn from a variety of cuisines, including Thai, Italian, and Continental. In the evening, the front tables have splendid views of the sun setting over the harbor. The menu includes steaks, tempura prawns, and local salmon. ✉*Summercove* ☎*021/477–2131* ▭*MC, V* ⊘*No lunch Sun.*

$$–$$$ ✕ **Crackpots.** A grocery was transformed into Carole Norman's "ceramic café," a simple but elegant eatery with warm yellow walls, an open fireplace, and cozy dining areas. The most popular tables are in the front "shop window" area. Behind the restaurant is Carole's pottery workshop; if you like your dinner plate, you can buy it. The eclectic menu has plenty of light dishes in the lower price range, with vegetarian dishes a strong point. Choices range from spinach and ricotta phyllo baked with red pepper sauce to Moroccan meatballs with couscous to Thai-style prawns with fragrant rice. There's always a steak option, too. ✉*3 Cork St.* ☎*021/477–2847* ▭*MC, V* ⊘*Closed Mon.–Wed. in Nov.–Mar.*

$$–$$$ ✕ **Jim Edwards.** One of Ireland's original bar-restaurants, this is a famous Kinsale institution known for its generous portions of local steak, lamb, and duck, and fresh seafood, all prepared under the careful eye of the owner and his wife, Paula. Choose from the daily specials in the busy bar, or have a more leisurely meal among the mahogany tables and dark-red decor of the somewhat baronial restaurant. With seafood this fresh, the preparation is kept simple: Kinsale oysters au naturel or crab claws tossed in garlic butter to start, followed by 10 ounces of prime fillet steak or medallions of monkfish (caught this morning) in a spring onion, ginger, and lime sauce. Fresh lobster from the tank is always available. The classic homemade desserts (profiteroles, crème brûlée) are substantial, and the Irish coffee is renowned. ⊠*Market Quay* ☎*021/477–2541* ⊟*AE, DC, MC, V.*

$$–$$$ ✕**Max's Wine Bar.** Low-beam ceilings and polished antique tables of different shapes and sizes lend this town house considerable charm. Lunches are light; it's a good place if you're keen on salads. At dinner, owner-chef Olivier Queva's classical French background is evident in his treatment of the daily catch and in his clever ways with such unusual cuts of meat as oxtail and trotters. The wine list is long and includes a good selection of French and New World wines, ranging in price from about €15 to €85. ⊠*Main St.* ☎*021/477–2443* ⊟*MC, V* ⊙*Closed Nov.–mid-Mar.*

$$ ✕**Fishy Fishy Café.** Originally a café in a fish shop, Fishy Fishy has
Fodor'sChoice moved up in the world, and now occupies sumptuous indoor-outdoor
★ premises in the town park. Previously an art gallery, the renovated quarters were remade by yacht designers and the eatery's nautical style, with classy wooden furniture and massive parasols, is modern and clean-lined. Chef Martin Shanahan and his wife, Marie, continue to operate no reservations, no credit cards, and no dinner policies, and still the crowds flock to stand in line for a table at peak times (1–2:30). Martin, who learned his craft in San Francisco, brings California pizzazz to his dishes. Look for langoustines with lemon, garlic, and sweet chili sauce; a fresh crab open sandwich; and seafood salad with a tangy herb dressing, all served by stylish young staff who give the impression they are thrilled to be part of the show. ⊠*Crowley's Quay* ☎*021/477– 0415* ⊴*Reservations not accepted* ⊟*No credit cards* ⊙*Closed Sun. Oct.–Mar. No dinner.*

$$$ ✕⊡**Blue Haven.** A restaurant, bar, and small hotel occupy this attractive, yellow-stucco, blue-trim town house, with its landmark wall clock and welcoming flags. Guest rooms in the main house, though small, are cheerful and have paintings by local artists; newer rooms have dark-oak furniture, antique canopy beds, and more spacious baths. All have double-glaze windows to mute the late night noise that can occur in this busy town. Inexpensive bar food is served until 9:30 PM in the lounge. Some nights a pianist entertains, and there's always a pleasant buzz, as the bar is a popular local haunt. The quiet, pastel-color restaurant ($$–$$$$) overlooks a garden and fountain, and is renowned for its seafood, which ranges from beer-battered fish-and-chips to grilled lobster. The menu also features simply prepared local steak and lamb, duck, chicken, and tempting vegetarian dishes. ⊠*3 Pearse St., Co. Cork* ☎*021/477–2209* ⊟*021/477–4268* ⊕*www.bluehaveninsale. com* ⊲*17 rooms* ⊴*In-room: no a/c. In-hotel: restaurant, bar, public Wi-Fi* ⊟*AE, DC, MC, V* ⊙*BP.*

$$$ ✕⊡**Trident.** The modern three-story building may lack old-world charm, but the waterfront location more than compensates. Built around three sides of a former dockyard on the very edge of Kinsale's magnificent harbor, the Trident features rooms that all showcase fabulous sea views. The hotel is adjacent to a working pier where rusty coasters tie up overnight, adding to the authentic harbor atmosphere and providing a conversation topic as you breakfast in the first-floor restaurant within feet of a ship's stern. The Wharf Tavern ($) and its bar food menu are popular with locals who range from stevedores to owners of the million-dollar yachts moored on the neighboring marina. ⊠ *World's End* ☎ *021/477-9300* ⊕ *www.tridenthotel.com* ⟳ *75 rooms* △ *In-room: no a/c, dial-up. In-hotel: restaurant, bar, gym* ⊟ *AE, DC, MC, V* ⊺⊙⏢*BP.*

$$ ✕⊞ **The White House.** One of Kinsale's oldest inns has maintained the tradition of a warm Irish welcome. Bedrooms vary in size, but all have fully tiled bathrooms and pastel color schemes. A wide-ranging menu is served both in the bar and in the adjacent Restaurant Antibes ($-$$$); the boiled bacon and cabbage—served with enormous potatoes—and the fish of the day are good bets, and vegetarians will enjoy the mushroom burger. Ask about the two- and three-day dinner-and-lodging specials. ⊠ *Pearse St. and Glen, Co. Cork* ☎ *021/477-2125* ⊜ *021/477-2045* ⊕ *www.whitehouse-kinsale.ie* ⟳ *10 rooms* △ *In-room: no a/c. In-hotel: restaurant, bar, no elevator* ⊟ *AE, DC, MC, V* ⊺⊙⏢*BP.*

$$$-$$$$ ⊞ **Perryville House.** Pretty in pink-and-white stone trim, offset by a
★ black wrought-iron veranda, and boasting a perch overlooking the inner harbor, Perryville House is in an adorable nook of town where homes often flower with hanging baskets and window boxes. The main salon hits all the right notes—emerald green walls, gilt-frame portrait, white fireplace—and one gets the impression of being in a private home. Front bedrooms have sea views, but rooms at the rear are quieter—key in July and August, when the town gets busy. All guest rooms are imaginatively furnished with Victorian antiques and have large beds and such extras as robes and fresh flowers. The lodging has a wine license, so you can buy by the glass or the bottle. ⊠ *Long Quay, Co. Cork* ☎ *021/477-2731* ⊜ *021/477-2298* ⊕ *www.perryvillehouse. com* ⟳ *27 rooms* △ *In-room: no a/c, Wi-Fi. In-hotel: no elevator, public Wi-Fi, no kids under 13, no-smoking rooms* ⊟ *AE, DC, MC, V* ⊙ *Closed Nov.–Mar.* ⊺⊙⏢*BP.*

$$ ⊞ **Friar's Lodge.** A large Georgian town house has been tastefully con-
★ verted into a cheerful guesthouse, with an array of facilities (but no bar or restaurant) that would do a hotel proud. The quiet residential location is only a short walk from the town center, and adjacent to the town's three churches, the bells of which merrily ring the hours. Guest rooms are large, pleasantly decorated in the Georgian style, with mustard-yellow spreads and drapes, wing armchairs, and good-size bathrooms. The warm welcome and friendly touring advice from owner-manager Maureen Tierney and her team, good parking facilities (in a town where spaces can be hard to find), and excellent value make this a popular venue with regular visitors (many of whom are golfers). ⊠ *Friar's St., Co. Cork* ☎ *021/477-7384* ⊕ *www.friars-lodge. com* ⟳ *18 rooms* △ *In room: no a/c, dial-up. In-hotel: public Wi-Fi* ⊟ *AE, MC, V* ⊙ *Closed Dec. 23–27* ⊺⊙⏢*BP.*

$$ ⌂**Innishannon House.** A pretty country house built in 1720 in the Petit Château style on the banks of the Bandon, Innishannon retains plenty of casual character. The bar and dining room are hung with contemporary Irish art, and have a busy local trade. Guest rooms vary greatly in shape and size—as do their windows—but have a variety of interesting antiques and strong color schemes. The hotel is surrounded by gardens and woods, with an attractive stretch of the Bandon River running through it, bordering the grounds. It's in a quiet rural location just off N7, about 6 km (4 mi) from Kinsale; it's quite perfect both as a retreat and as a base for touring the area. ⊠*Innishannon, Co. Cork* ☎*021/477–5121* 🖷*021/477–5609* ⊕*www.innishannon-hotel. ie* ⇄*12 rooms* ⚘*In-room: no a/c. In-hotel: restaurant, bar, no elevator* ☰*AE, DC, MC, V* ⏉*BP.*

NIGHTLIFE

The **Shanakee** (⊠*Market St.* ☎*021/477–4472*) is renowned for live music—both rock and Irish traditional. Check out the **Spaniard Inn** (⊠*Scilly* ☎*021/477–2436*) for rock and folk groups. There's a traditional Irish session on Wednesday from 10 PM year-round.

SPORTS & THE OUTDOORS

BICYCLING Rent a bike from **The Hire Shop** (⊠*18 Main St.* ☎*021/477–4884*) to explore the picturesque hinterland of Kinsale.

FISHING For deep-sea angling off the Old Head of Kinsale contact **Willem Van Dyk** (☎*021/477–8944*) who operates out of Castlepark Marina. **Kinsale Angling Co-op** (☎*021/477–4946*) is a popular option with various boats on offer sailing out of Castlepark Marina. For bareboat charters or skippered cruises—of a day or longer—contact **Sail Ireland Tours** (⊠*Trident Hotel, Kinsale, Co. Cork* ☎*021/477–2927* ⊕*www.sailireland.com*).

SHOPPING

Boland's Craft Shop (⊠*Pearse St.* ☎*021/477–2161*) sells some unusual items, including sweaters, designer rain gear, and linen shirts exclusive to this shop.

Giles Norman Photography Gallery (⊠*44 Main St.* ☎*021/477–4373*) sells black-and-white photographs of Irish scenes. **Granny's Bottom Drawer** (⊠*53 Main St.* ☎*021/477–4839*) has fine linen and lace in classic and contemporary styles.

The **Keane on Ceramics** (⊠*Pier Rd.* ☎*021/477–2085*) gallery represents the best of Ireland's ceramics artists.

You can spend quite a bit of time browsing through the excellent selection of Irish poetry and books on local history at the **Kinsale Bookshop** (⊠*8 Main St.* ☎*021/477–4244*).

Kinsale Crystal (⊠*Market St.* ☎*021/477–4463*) is a studio that sells 100% Irish, handblown, hand-cut crystal.

Hilary Hale (⊠*Rincurran Hall, Summercove* ☎*021/477–2010* ⊕*www. hilaryhale.com*) is a wood turner who uses storm-felled locally grown timber to make lamps, bowls, and platters. **The Trading House** (⊠*54*

Monks & Wine

A mid-13th-century Franciscan abbey at the water's edge is Timoleague's most striking monument. (Walk around the back to find the entrance gate.) The view of the sea framed by its ruined Gothic windows is an unmissable photo-op.

The abbey was built before the estuary silted up, and its main business was the importing of wine from Spain.

A tower and walls with Gothic-arch windows still stand, and you can trace the ground plan of the old friary—chapel, refectory, cloisters, and the extensive wine cellar.

It was sacked by the English in 1642 but, like many other ruins of its kind, was used as a burial place until the late 20th century, hence the modern gravestones.

Main St. ☎*021/477–7497*) has exclusive housewares from France, Spain, and Scandinavia alongside Irish and French antiques.

Victoria Murphy (✉*Market Quay* ☎*021/477–4317*) sells small antiques and antique jewelry.

6

TIMOLEAGUE

24 *19 km (12 mi) west of Kinsale on R600.*

The romantic silhouette of its ruined abbey dominates the view when you're approaching Timoleague, a village of multicolor houses on the Argideen River estuary. The town marks the eastern end of the Seven Heads Peninsula, which stretches around to Clonakilty.

You can glimpse **Courtmacsherry,** the postcard village of multicolor cottages, just across the water. It has a sandy beach that makes it a favorite for vacationers. To reach it follow the signposts from Timoleague.

Farther on you can find that many storefronts in **Clonakilty,** a small market town 9½ km (6 mi) west of Timoleague on R600/N71, have charmingly traditional, hand-painted signs and wooden facades. **Inchydoney,** 3 km (2 mi) outside Clonakilty, is one of the area's finest sandy beaches backed by sheltered sand dunes.

OFF THE
BEATEN
PATH

Birthplace of Michael Collins. The birthplace of Michael Collins (1890–1922) is signposted 9 km (6 mi) west of Timoleague off N71 (past the village of Lissavaird). You can see the ground plan of the simple homestead where the controversial founder of the modern Irish Army was born. There's also a bronze memorial (freely accessible), and another memorial in the nearest village, Woodfield, opposite the pub where Collins is said to have had his last drink on the day he was shot in an ambush.

WHERE TO STAY & EAT

$$–$$$ ✕ **Casino House.** Stop midway between Kinsale and Timoleague, on

Fodor'sChoice   coastal route R600, for a meal at this farmhouse, which has been

★   renovated in a cool, minimalist style and converted into a restaurant.
The two small but airy and well-lighted dining rooms—one blue and
one green—have private sitting rooms for pre-dinner drinks next to
an open fireplace, a treat that sets the tone of gentle pampering that
typifies the highly professional co-owner Kerrin Relja's hospitality.
Menu highlights from talented Croatian owner-chef Michael Relja
include garlic prawn salad, lobster risotto, a fine roast loin of lamb
served with Roman gnocchi, and, as one of the top seasonal desserts,
summer fruits with sabayon. ⊠ *Coolmaine, Kilbrittain* 📞 *023/49944*
🖃 *MC, V* ⊘ *Closed Wed. and mid-Jan.–mid-Mar. No dinner Sun. No
lunch Mon.–Sat.*

$$$$ 🏨 **Inchydoney Island Lodge & Spa.** With its dream location above a long
beach, this modern hotel is a refuge for overworked city folk. Although
the island is connected to the mainland by a causeway, it still feels
remote. Earth tones, plump sofas, and terrific natural light—reflected
off the Atlantic—are soothing. Public-area palettes continue in the guest
rooms, which have plush robes, soft slippers, and posh soaps. Although
staffers are pleasant, service can be laid-back. If this causes you stress,
unwind in the thalassotherapy spa, where treatments draw on the benefits of seawater, or head out on a golf, fishing, or horseback-riding
excursion. ⊠ *Inchydoney Island, 5 km (3 mi) south of Clonakilty, Co.
Cork* 📞 *023/33143* 🖷 *023/35229* ⊕ *www.inchydoneyisland.com* ➾ *67
rooms* ⌂ *In-room: safe, dial-up. In-hotel: restaurant, room service, bar,
pool, gym, beachfront, minibar* 🖃 *AE, DC, MC, V* ¶⊙|*BP.*

$ 🏨 **Kilbrogan House.** Bandon is a market town on the Bandon River,
midway between Kinsale and Clonakilty—it's a good, peaceful base
for touring that's off the beaten tourist trail. Kilbrogan House stands at
the highest point of town and has been the community's architectural
star since it was built in 1818. Owner Catherine FitzMaurice spent
12 years restoring it to its Georgian splendor. The ornate plasterwork
could easily grace a much larger country mansion, as could the elaborate flying staircase. Large windows afford garden views and bring
streams of sunlight into the spacious rooms, which are furnished with
well-selected antiques, original art, and handmade rugs over polished
wood floors. An open fireplace warms the breakfast rooms in colder
weather, and the geranium-filled conservatory glows with sun on clear
days. An evening meal can be provided on request. ⊠ *Kilbrogan Hill,
Bandon, Co. Cork* 📞 *023/44935* 🖷 *023/44935* ⊕ *www.kilbrogan.com*
➾ *5 rooms* ⌂ *In-room: no a/c. In-hotel: no elevator* 🖃 *AE, MC, V*
⊘ *Closed Jan.* ¶⊙|*BP.*

SHOPPING

Peter and Fran Wolsltenholme's hand-thrown and slab-made tableware
is eagerly collected, and sold only from their studio home and shop,
Courtmacsherry Ceramics (⊠ *Main St.* 📞 *023/46239*).

Delaney's (✉ *Delaney St. Clonakilty* ☎*023/48361*) is full of small antiques as well as antiquarian and secondhand books. **Edward Twomey** (✉*16 Pearse St., Clonakilty* ☎*023/33365*) is a traditional butcher's shop famed for its Clonakilty Black Pudding, a breakfast product that's prominently featured on the shop's nifty T-shirts—the

ultimate West Cork souvenirs. Assemble a superior picnic at the **Lettercollum Kitchen Shop** (✉*22 Connolly St., Clonakilty* ☎*023/36938*), a bakery and deli selling tasty breads and local organic produce. **Spiller's Lane Gallery** (✉*Spiller's La., Clonakilty* ☎*023/38416*), in a converted grain store at a pretty mews, sells Irish-made jewelry, cutlery, pottery, and paintings.

SKIBBEREEN

㉕ *35 km (22 mi) west of Timoleague.*

6

Skibbereen is the main market town in this neck of southwest Cork, and a good base for nearby sights. The Saturday country market and the plethora of pubs punctuated by bustling shops and coffeehouses keep the place jumping year-round.

A thoughtful renovation of a stone gasworks building has created an attractive, architecturally appropriate home for the **Skibbereen Heritage Center.** An elaborate audiovisual exhibit on the Great Famine presents dramatized firsthand accounts of what it was like to live in this community when it was hit hard by hunger. Other attractions include displays on area marine life, walking tours, access to local census information, and a varying schedule of special programs. ✉*Upper Bridge St.* ☎*028/40900* ⊕*www.skibbheritage.com* 🎫*€6* ☉*Mid-Mar.–late May and mid-Sept.–mid-Oct., Tues.–Sat. 10–6; mid-May–mid-Sept., daily 10–6; mid-Oct.–mid-Mar. by appointment.*

The **Mizen Vision Visitor Centre,** which occupies a lighthouse at the tip of the Mizen Head (follow the R591 through Goleen to the end of the road), is the Irish mainland's most southerly point. The lighthouse itself is on a rock at the tip of the headland; to reach it, you must cross a dramatic 99-step suspension footbridge. The lighthouse was completed in 1910; the Engine Room and Keepers' House have been restored by the local community. The exhilaration of massive Atlantic seas swirling 164 feet below the footbridge and the great coastal views guarantee a memorable outing. ✉*Harbour Rd., Goleen* ☎*028/35115* ⊕*www.mizenhead.ie* 🎫*€6* ☉*Mid-Mar.–May and Oct., daily 10:30–5; June–Sept., daily 10–6; Nov.–mid-Mar., weekends 11–4.*

$$$$　✕ **Island Cottage.** On Heir Island, this unlikely venture is a pilgrimage
★　　spot for food lovers, who praise the high standard of cooking and the
location. The five-course (no choices) set menu focuses on local produce, some of it picked in the wild on the island. Expect good, honest, unfussy food—the best of new Irish Traditional. The restaurant
is country-casual and tables seat 10, so be prepared to share. Cape
Clear turbot with sea spinach is typical; for dessert, try the terrine of
vanilla ice cream with meringue in blackberry sauce. The proprietors,
John Desmond and Ellmary Fenton, also operate "the world's smallest
cooking school" here. Advance booking is necessary for both the restaurant and the cooking classes; call for details about the four-minute
ferry ride to the island from Cunnamore, which is about 15 km (9 mi)
west of Skibbereen (follow signs on the road to Ballydehob). ✉ *Heir
Island* ☎ *028/38102* ⊕ *www.islandcottage.com* ⌂ *Reservations essential* ⊟ *No credit cards* ☉ *Closed mid-Sept.–mid-May and Mon. and
Tues. June–mid-Sept. No lunch.*

$$$–$$$$　✕ **Annie's.** A meal at this mildly eccentric cottage, in an offbeat vil-
lage 16 km (10 mi) west of Skibbereen, is a true West Cork experi-
ence. Annie Barrie and her chef husband, Dano, have been running the
place since the early '80s. When you arrive, chances are that Annie will
send you across the road to Levi's Pub, where you can wait for your
table, peruse the menu, and eventually give Annie your order. Dano's
simple, well-judged cooking lends the restaurant considerable magic.
Dishes are made from outstanding farmhouse cheeses, locally reared
cattle, and the freshest seafood. ✉ *Main St., Ballydehob* ☎ *028/37292*
⊟ *MC, V* ☉ *Closed Sun., Mon., and Nov. No lunch.*

$　✕▦ **Heron's Cove.** Although this B&B is only minutes by foot from
the main road and Goleen's village center, this harborside retreat is a
peaceable kingdom—expect to see herons outside your window. Sue
Hill's modern house, on the edge of a secluded inlet, is well run and
extremely civilized. The well-equipped guest rooms, furnished in part
with antiques, have excellent views from every window. In summer,
fresh local seafood stars on the menu ($$–$$$$), including John Dory
in a caper-butter sauce, and you can pick out a great wine to accom-
pany it from the racks along the wall. Off-season (November–March),
evening meals are prepared for guests only. ✉ *The Harbour, Goleen,
Co. Cork* ☎ *028/35225* ⊠ *028/35422* ⊕ *www.heronscove.com* ⇱ *5
rooms* ⌂ *In-room: no a/c. In-hotel: restaurant, no elevator, no-smoking
rooms* ⊟ *AE, DC, MC, V* ⊚ *BP.*

The **West Cork Arts Center** (✉ *North St., Skibbereen* ☎ *028/22090*) has
regular exhibits of work by local artists and an on-site crafts shop.

CASTLETOWNSHEND

26 *8 km (5 mi) southeast of Skibbereen.*

This town has an unusual number of large, gracious stone houses, most of them dating from the mid-18th century, when it was an important trading center. The main street runs steeply downhill to the 17th-century castle (built by the noted regional family of the Townshends) and the sea. The sleepy town awakens in July and August, when its sheltered harbor bustles. Sparkling views await from cliff-top St. Barrahane's Church, which has a medieval oak altarpiece and three stained-glass windows by early-20th-century Irish artist Harry Clarke.

WHERE TO EAT

$$–$$$$ ✕**Mary Ann's.** Writer Edna O'Brien calls this her favorite pub in the
★ world. Low-beamed, and one of Ireland's oldest, Mary Ann's attracts wealthy visitors from the United Kingdom and from other parts of Ireland, who mingle happily with the few locals left in the village in the front barroom, the quieter back room, or the large garden beyond. Energetic owner-manager Fergus O'Mahony is a brilliant host, and is always on the spot, supervising operations and contributing to the *craic* (lively conversation). Upstairs, the 32-seat restaurant nearly always buzzes, so reservations are a good idea. Try the trademark baked avocado stuffed with crab meat, the massively generous platter of Castlehaven Bay shellfish and seafood, or the succulent T-bone steak. ✉ *Main St.* ☎ *028/36146* ⊕ *www.maryannsbarrestaurant.com* ⊟ *MC,* *V* ☉ *Restaurant closed Nov.–Mar.; bar food available daily Apr.–Oct.,* *Tues.–Sun. in Nov.–Mar.*

BANTRY

27 *33 km (21 mi) northwest of Castletownshend, 25 km (16 mi) north-*
★ *west of Skibbereen on N71.*

As you enter Bantry—an unprepossessing town at the head of Bantry Bay (topped out with a large market square and long plaza, which attracts artisans, craftspeople, and musicians in summer)—on the right-hand side of the road you'll see the porticoed entrance to **Bantry House.** One of Ireland's most famed manors, it's noted for its picture-perfect perch: on a hillock above the south shore of Bantry Bay, it's surrounded by a series of stepped gardens and parterres that comprise "the stairway to the sky." Spreading out below the Georgian mansion lies the bay and, in the far distance, the spectacular range of the Caha Mountains—one of the great vistas of Ireland. Built in the early 1700s and altered and expanded later that century, the house was the ancestral seat of the White family. The house—now looking more than a bit worse for wear, according to readers—is largely the vision of Richard White, the second earl of Bantry, who traveled extensively through Europe and brought a lot of it back with him: fabulous Aubusson tapestries said to have been commissioned by Louis XV adorn the Rose Drawing Room, while state portraits of King George III and Queen

Charlotte glitter in floridly Rococo gilt frames in the hypertheatrical, Wedgwood-blue-and-gold dining room.

Outside, the drama continues in the stepped garden terraces, set with marble statues, framed by stone balustrades, and showcasing such delights as an embroidered parterre of dwarf box. Next to Bantry House is the **Bantry 1796 French Armada Center,** a small but worthwhile museum illustrating the abortive attempt by Irish Nationalist Wolfe Tone and his French ally General Hoche to land 14,000 troops in Bantry Bay to effect an uprising. The tearoom serves light lunches. In summer the house hosts concerts in the grand library room, notably the West Cork Chamber Music Festival (held during the first week of July). ⊠ *Bantry House is on right-hand side of N71 as you enter town from easterly Cork City direction* ☎ *027/50047* ⊕ *www.bantryhouse.ie* 🖃 *House, museum, and gardens €10; museum and gardens €5* ⊙ *Mar.–Oct., daily 10–6.*

WHERE TO STAY & EAT

$$$ ✕🍴 **Blair's Cove House.** In the converted stables of a Georgian mansion, gleaming silverware, pink tablecloths, and a large crystal chandelier are set off against stone walls and exposed beams. A covered, heated terrace overlooks a fountain and a rose-filled courtyard. The owners are French, and the cuisine ($$$$) is a mixture of French and Irish. Starters are displayed on a self-service buffet; a popular main course is steak or local lamb cooked on the open wood-fired grill. Stone outbuildings have been converted into well-equipped guest rooms furnished with country antiques and morning views of the still-blue waters of Dunmanus Bay (which are breathtaking). ⊠ *Blair's Cove, Durrus, Co. Cork* ☎ *027/61041* ⊕ *www.blairscove.ie* ⇖ *3 rooms* ⚴ *In-room: no a/c. In-hotel: no elevator, some pets allowed* ⊟ *DC, MC, V* ⊙ *Restaurant closed Sun. and Mon. and Nov.–mid-Mar. Guest rooms closed Nov.–mid-Mar.* ⦿| *BP.*

$$$ 🍴 **Sea View House.** Among private, wooded grounds overlooking
★   Bantry Bay, you'll find this large, three-story, 19th-century country house. Owner-manager Kathleen O'Sullivan keeps an eagle eye on what was, until 1980, her private home and today remains an oasis of calm, nestled in its own gardens well away from the main road. Antique furniture, plump sofas, polished brass, and ornate curtains provide comfort and elegance. Some bedrooms have sea views and small sofas in bay windows; others have views of the wooded gardens. In the dining room, polished tables are set with crocheted mats and linen napkins; service is friendly and informal. ⊠ *Ballylickey, Co. Cork* ☎ *027/50073* 🖷 *027/51555* ⊕ *www.seaviewhousehotel.com* ⇖ *25 rooms* ⚴ *In-room: no a/c. In-hotel: restaurant, bar, no elevator* ⊟ *AE, DC, MC, V* ⊙ *Closed mid-Nov.–mid-Mar.* ⦿| *BP.*

SHOPPING

Manning's Emporium (⊠ *Ballylickey* ☎ *027/51049*) is a showcase for locally made farmhouse cheeses, pâtés, and salamis—an excellent place to put together a picnic or just to browse.

GLENGARRIFF

 14 km (8 mi) northwest of Bantry on N71, 21 km (13 mi) south of Kenmare.

One of the jewels of Bantry Bay is Glengarriff, the "rugged glen" much loved by Thackeray and Sir Walter Scott. The descent into wooded, sheltered Glengarriff reveals yet another landscape: thanks to the Gulf Stream, it's mild enough down here for subtropical plants to thrive. Trails along the shore are covered with rhododendrons and offer beautiful views of the nearby inlets, loughs, and lounging seals. You're very much on the beaten path, however, with crafts shops, tour buses, and boatmen soliciting your business by the roadside. Many are heading this way because of that Irish Eden, Ilnacullin. Set on Garnish Island, **Ilnacullin,** about 10 minutes offshore from Glengariff and beyond islets populated by comical-looking basking seals, you can find one of the country's horticultural wonders. In 1910 a Belfast businessman, John Annan Bryce, purchased this rocky isle, and, with the help of famed English architect Howard Peto and Scottish plantsman Murdo Mackenzie, transformed it into a botanical Disneyland. The main showpiece is a wisteria-covered "Casita"—a rather strange-looking half-shed, half-mansion Peto cooked up—which is over a sunken Italian garden. A touch of Japan is supplied by the bonsai specimens lining the terrace. In fact, Ilnacullin has a little bit of everything, from a Grecian temple to a Martello tower (from which the British watched for attempted landings by Napoleonic forces) to a Happy Valley, all bedded with extraordinary shrubs, trees, and many unusual subtropical flowers. You get to Ilnacullin by taking a Blue Pool ferry, which departs for the island from Glengarriff. George Bernard Shaw found Ilnacullin peaceful enough to allow him to begin his *St. Joan* here; maybe you'll find Garnish inspiring, too. ☎027/63040 ⊕*www.heritageireland.ie* ✉*Gardens €3.70, boat ride €10 round-trip* ۞*July and Aug., Mon.–Sat. 9:30–6:30, Sun. 11–7; Apr.–June and Sept., Mon.–Sat. 10–6:30, Sun. 1–7; Mar. and Oct., Mon.–Sat. 10–4:30, Sun. 1–5.*

Glengarriff is the gateway to the **Ring of Beara,** a 137-km (85-mi) scenic drive that circles the Beara Peninsula on R572. The least famous of the southwest's three peninsulas is also the least frequented—and, some would say, the most ruggedly beautiful. One of the main attractions is the Beara Way, a 196-km (120-mi) marked walking route that takes one to many prehistoric archaeological sites. Dursey Island, at the peninsula's tip, is a bird-watcher's paradise that you reach by cable car. From Dursey Island, head for tiny Allihies, the former site of a huge copper mine, now the home of several leading Irish artists, some of whom invite studio visits—watch for signs. This is also great hiking country—known for some of the most scenic stretches of the Beara Way. Continue along a breathtaking coastal road to Eyeries—a village overlooking Coulagh Bay—and then up the south side of the Kenmare River to Kenmare.

If you have time left over after exploring the Ring of Beara, you might want to backtrack to R584 and visit **Gougane Barra Forest Park** (⊕*www.*

coillte.ie), where the hermit St. Finbarre had his mountain retreat. It's the source of the River Lee, and it has nature trails.

THE RING OF KERRY

Along the perimeter of the Iveragh Peninsula, the dramatic Ring of Kerry is probably Ireland's single most popular tourist route. Stunning mountain and coastal views are around almost every turn. The only drawback: on a sunny day, it seems like half the nation's visitors are traveling along this two-lane road, packed into buses, riding bikes, or backpacking. The route is narrow and curvy, and the local sheep think nothing of using it for a nap; take it slowly. Tour buses tend to start in Killarney and ply the Ring counterclockwise, so consider jumping ahead and starting in Killorglin or following the route clockwise, starting in Kenmare (although this means you risk meeting tour buses head-on on narrow roads). Either way, bear in mind that most of the buses leave Killarney between 9 and 10 AM. The trip covers 176 km (110 mi) on N70 (and briefly R562) if you start and finish in Killarney; the journey will be 40 km (25 mi) shorter if you only venture between Kenmare and Killorglin. Because rain blocks views across the water to the Beara Peninsula in the east and the Dingle Peninsula in the west, hope for sunshine. It makes all the difference.

KENMARE

㉙ *21 km (13 mi) north of Glengarriff on N71, 34 km (21 mi) south of Killarney.*

A lively touring base, this market town is set at the head of the sheltered Kenmare River estuary. It's currently a matter of lively debate as to whether Kenmare has displaced Kinsale as the culinary capital of Ireland. Kenmare offers an amazing number of stylish little restaurants for a town its size, and also boasts two of Ireland's most highly reputed hotels, the Park and the Sheen Falls. The shopping is pretty good, too, with Irish high fashion, crafts, and original art vying for your attention. The town was founded in 1670 by Sir William Petty (Oliver Cromwell's surveyor general, a multitasking entrepreneur), and most of its buildings date from the 19th century, when it was part of the enormous Lansdowne Estate—itself assembled by Petty.

The **Kenmare Heritage Centre** explains the town's history and can outline a walking route to Kenmare's places of interest. ⊠ *The Sq.* ☎ *064/41233* 🎟 *Free* ☉ *Easter–Sept., Mon.–Sat. 9:30–5:30.*

WHERE TO STAY & EAT

$$–$$$ ✕ **Lime Tree.** An open fire, stone walls, and a minstrel's gallery on a large balcony above the main room lend considerable character to this restaurant in a former schoolhouse. Try one of the imaginative vegetarian options—deep-fried eggplant with slow-roasted tomatoes—or go for Kerry lamb oven roasted with honey-mint jus. Leave room for a warm

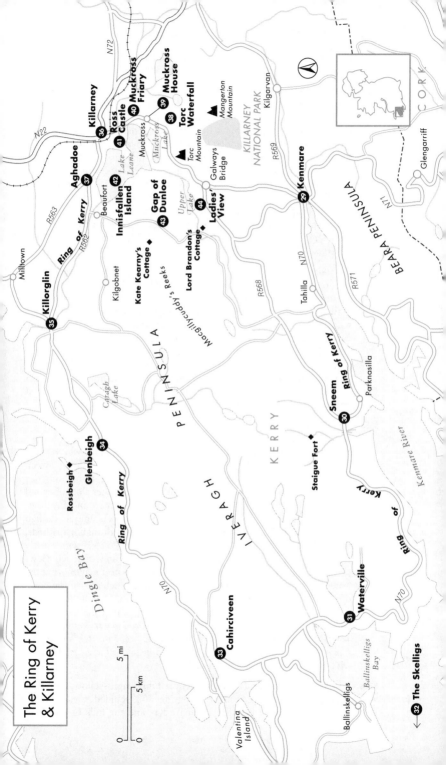

dessert, such as blackberry and pear fruit crumble. ⊠*Shelburne St.* ☎*064/41225* ☰*MC, V* ⊘*Closed Nov.–Mar.*

$$–$$$ ✕**Mulcahy's.** Should you be struck by a yen for sushi in deepest Kerry, you can satisfy it here. Owner-chef Bruce Mulcahy studied sushi making in Japan, and learned about fusion food in Thailand. He offers an unusual menu that combines fresh local ingredients traditionally prepared, with exotic specialties for the more adventurous palate. Try a parcel of braised Kerry lamb shank with parsnip puree, or choose from house specialties, the sushi and sashimi. For dessert, try the lemon tart with amaretto cream. The 6-course tasting menu ($$$) is a real treat. The light-filled room, on the main street, previously a pub, has stylish contemporary place settings, with a selection of homemade breads on a bamboo tray. All produce is certified organic, and there is a vegetarian dish of the day. ⊠*36 Henry St.* ☎*064/42383* ☰*AE, DC, MC, V* ⊘*No lunch Mon.–Sat.*

$$–$$$ ✕**Packies.** Owner Maura O'Connell Foley established Kenmare's original first-class restaurant, the Lime Tree, but has since opted for a quieter life at this smaller, cozier venue. She's passed her chef's toque to Martin Hallissey, who continues her practice of using local organic produce whenever possible. Stone walls, fireplace, and floors are warmed up by colorful local paintings, and the buzz of expectation among the closely packed diners. The contemporary Irish menu may feature crab cakes with tartar sauce, or rack of lamb with rosemary-and-garlic gravy. Leave room for desserts, which include homemade praline ice cream and a memorable sticky toffee pudding. ⊠*Henry St.* ☎*064/41508* ☰*AE, MC, V* ⊘*Closed Sun. and mid-Jan.–Feb. No lunch.*

$$$$ ✕🏨 **Park Hotel.** One of Ireland's premier country-house hotels, this 1897
Fodor'sChoice stolid and vast stone château has spectacular views of the Caha Moun-
★ tains. No one can fault its setting: an 11-acre parkland, where every tree seems manicured and where magnificent terraced lawns sweep down to the bay. A welcoming fire is always burning in the lobby—a cute and traditional setting, replete with tall grandfather clock. Beyond lies a drawing room aglow with ivory flocked wallpapers and any number of comfy chairs. Each of the spacious bedrooms is unique, though most have late-Victorian pieces; suites have walnut or mahogany beds, wardrobes, and chests of drawers. The restaurant ($$$$) serves justly famed modern Irish cuisine in an elegant dining room with lovely views of rolling lawns. The deluxe spa, on a wooded knoll neighboring the hotel, has individualized "Lifestyle" programs, which incorporate outdoor activities, including tai chi, meditation walks, mountain biking, golf, horseback riding, and walks on the Kerry Way. ⊠*Shelburne Rd., Co. Kerry* ☎*064/41200* 🖷*064/41402* ⊕*www.parkkenmare.com* ⇥*35 rooms, 9 suites* ⌂*In-room: no a/c, dial-up. In-hotel: restaurant, bar, golf course, tennis court, pool, spa, some pets allowed* ☰*AE, DC, MC, V* ⊘*Closed Nov. 26–Dec. 23* ⫣*BP.*

$$$$ ✕🏨 **Sheen Falls Lodge.** The magnificence of this bright-yellow, slate-roof
Fodor'sChoice stone manor is matched only by its setting: 300 secluded acres of lawns,
★ gardens, and forest between Kenmare Bay and the falls of the River

Sheen. La Cascade restaurant ($$$$), which overlooks the falls, headlines modern Irish cuisine, while Oscar's Bistro ($–$$$) serves Mediterranean fare. The public salons are painted in warm, terra-cotta tones, and the mahogany-panel library has more than 1,000 books, mainly on Ireland. Guest rooms—all modern-traditional, in bright yellows and tranquil beiges—have bay or river views. You can hire one of the hotel's vintage cars, which include a Bentley and a Rolls, for picnics, trips into town, and other excursions. ⌂*Sheen Falls, Co. Kerry* ☎*064/41600* ⎙*064/41386* ⊕*www.sheenfallslodge.ie* ⇆*55 rooms, 11 suites* ⚿*In-hotel: 2 restaurants, bars, tennis court, pool, gym, spa* ▭*AE, DC, MC, V* ☾*Closed Jan.* ⍩|*BP.*

$$ ▥ **Sallyport House.** Across the bridge on the way into Kenmare, this 1932 family home has been enlarged to serve as a comfortable B&B. The spotless rooms, all with harbor or mountain views, are furnished with a variety of Victorian and Edwardian antiques. Owner Janey Arthur has placed family heirlooms everywhere; if you're interested in old Irish furniture, ask for a tour. A varied breakfast menu—which might include apples from Sallyport's own orchard—is served in a sunny room overlooking the garden. ⌂*Glengarriff Rd., Co. Kerry* ☎*064/42066* ⎙*064/42067* ⊕*www.sallyporthouse.com* ⇆*5 rooms* ⚿*In-room: no a/c. In-hotel: no elevator, no kids under 13* ▭*No credit cards* ☾*Closed Nov.–Mar.* ⍩|*BP.*

$ ▥ **Sea Shore Farm.** Mary Patricia O'Sullivan offers a warm but professional welcome to her spacious farmhouse on Kenmare Bay. In fair weather there are views across the sea to the hills on the Beara Peninsula, and although the place is very close to Kenmare, you can walk across her farmland to the deserted seashore and view its plentiful wildlife. You can also walk—or run—the mile into town along a scenic back road. Rooms are furnished with ornate heirlooms and have good-size bathrooms and placid views. Breakfast includes a choice of pancakes, kippers, or smoked salmon as well as the usual fry. ⌂*Tubrid, Co. Kerry* ☎⎙*064/41270* ⊕*www.seashorekenmare.com* ⇆*6 rooms* ⚿*In-room: no a/c. In-hotel: no-smoking rooms, no elevator* ▭*MC, V* ☾*Closed Nov.–Feb.* ⍩|*BP.*

SPORTS & THE OUTDOORS

☿ **Seafari** (⌂*Kenmare Pier* ☎*064/42059* ⊕*www.seafariireland.com*) has two-hour, fun, ecotours with seal-watching cruises, with complimentary tea and coffee for adults, and lollipops for the kids. Cruises cost €20 per adult, with special family rates.

SHOPPING

Avoca Handweavers (⌂*Moll's Gap, on N71 road to Killarney* ☎*064/34720*) sells wool clothing and mohair rugs and throws in remarkable palettes and a variety of weaves. **Black Abbey Crafts** (⌂*28 Main St.* ☎*064/42115*) specializes in fine Irish-made crafts. **Brenmar Jon** (⌂*25 Henry St.* ☎*064/41138*) sells sophisticated knitwear. **Cleo's** (⌂*2 Shelbourne St.* ☎*064/41410*) stocks Irish-made woolens and linens that have striking designs, often drawn from Ireland's past.

Kenmare Art Gallery (⊠ *Bridge St.* ☎ *064/42999* ⊕ *www.kenmareart-gallery.com*) has a good selection of works by contemporary artists, all of whom live locally but show internationally. **Noel & Holland** (⊠ *3 Bridge St.* ☎ *064/42464*) stocks secondhand books, including Irish-interest and children's titles. At **PFK** (⊠ *18 Henry St.* ☎ *064/42590*), Paul Kelly makes striking, modern jewelry in gold and silver.

SNEEM

③⓪ *27 km (17 mi) southwest of Kenmare on N70.*

The pretty village of Sneem (from the Irish for "knot") is settled around an English-style green on the Ardsheelaun River estuary, and its streets are filled with houses washed in different colors. Beside the parish church are the "pyramids," as they're known locally. These 12-foot-tall, traditional stone structures with stained-glass insets look as though they've been here forever. In fact, the sculpture park was completed in 1990 to the design of the Kerry-born artist James Scanlon, who has won international awards for his work in stained glass.

The approximately 2,500-year-old, stone **Staigue Fort,** signposted 4 km (2 mi) inland at Castlecove, is almost circular and about 75 feet in diameter with a single south-side entrance. From the Iron Age (from 500 BC to the 5th century AD) and early Christian times (6th century AD), such "forts" were, in fact, the fortified homesteads for several families of one clan and their cattle. The walls at Staigue Fort are almost 13 feet wide at the base and 7 feet wide at the top; they still stand 18 feet high on the north and west sides. Within them, stairs lead to narrow platforms on which the lookouts stood. (Private land must be crossed to reach the fort, and a "compensation for trespass" of €1 is often requested by the landowner.)

WHERE TO STAY

$$$$ 🏨 **Parknasilla Great Southern.** "Parknasilla": for many travelers in decades past, this word alone conjured up an Irish Xanadu—a towering, awe-inspiring, faux-baronial pile, stunningly set by the waters of the Kerry coast, with the sort of grand, slightly stuffy, early-20th-century sensibility that welcomed visitors with a porter in a frock coat and striped gray pants. So it's little wonder everyone from Charles de Gaulle to Princess Grace headed here; George Bernard Shaw found it so accommodating he wrote much of *Saint Joan* here. The hotel is under new ownership, and a renovation program is underway during the winter to upgrade all rooms and facilities. Continental cuisine is served in the Pygmalion restaurant, and you can down your sherry in the Doolittle Bar. There are some great ways to relax here, ranging from a hot tub perched over the lake and a golf course set around the ruins of Derryquin Castle. The sheltered coastal location—3 km (2 mi) south of Sneem—and excellent sporting facilities make this hotel an ideal retreat and an incomparable little world in County Kerry. ⊠ *Parknasilla, Co. Kerry* ☎ *064/45122* 🖷 *064/45323* ⟿ *84 rooms* ♿ *In-room: no a/c. In-hotel: restaurant, bar, golf course, tennis court, pool* ⊟ *AE, DC, MC, V* ⊘ *Closed Oct.–mid-July* ⟦◯⟧ *BP.*

Continued on page 366

GETTING OUTSIDE:
THE RING OF KERRY

When you travel Ireland's most popular scenic route, leaving your car behind makes all the difference.

The Ring of Kerry is one of Europe's great drives. The common wisdom, though, is that it suffers from its own popularity: tour buses dominate the road from sunup to sundown. There's more than a grain of truth to this reputation, but that doesn't mean you should scratch the Ring from your itinerary. Instead, plan to turn off the main road and get out of your car. You'll make a blissful discovery: the Iveragh Peninsula—one of the most beautiful locations in all of Ireland—remains largely unspoiled. It's full of fabulous places to hike, bike, and boat—and best of all, there are views the tour-bus passengers can only dream of.

Top: Looking from the island of Skellig Michael to Little Skellig Below left: Biking the Ring of Kerry Below right: On horseback at Rossbeigh Strand

AROUND THE RING BY FOOT & BY BIKE

HIKING THE RING

Option number one for getting outdoors around the Ring of Kerry is to go by foot. There are appealing walking options for every degree of fitness and experience, from gentle, paved paths to an ascent up Ireland's tallest mountain.

The Kerry Way

The main hiking route across the peninsula is the Kerry Way, a spectacular 133-mile footpath that's easily broken down into day-trip-size segments. The path winds from **Killarney** through the foothills of the **MacGillicuddy's Reeks** and the **Black Valley** to **Glencar** and **Glenbeigh**, from where it parallels the Ring through **Cahirciveen, Waterville, Caherdaniel,** and **Sneem,** before ending in **Kenmare**. The route, indicated by way markers, follows grassy old paths and unpaved drovers' roads situated at higher elevations than the Ring—meaning better, and more tranquil, views.

Hiking the entire Kerry Way can take from 10 to 12 days. Numerous outfitters organize both guided and unguided tours. For a great day trip, hike the 10 km (6 mi) section from **Waterville** to **Caherdaniel,** which has great views of small islands and rocky coves. In the **Glencar** area near

Blackstones Bridge, a series of shorter signposted walks, from 3 km (2 mi) upward, put you in the shadow of **Carrauntuohill,** Ireland's highest mountain.

> ### HIKING RESOURCES
>
> A copy of the **Kerry Way Map Guide,** available from Cork Kerry Tourism, is invaluable. For organized tours of the Way, try **Activity Ireland,** based in Caherdaniel (☎ 66/9475277 ⊕ www. activity-ireland.com). Climbers should check out the website of the **Mountaineering Council of Ireland,** ⊕ www.mountaineering.ie.

Taking It Easy: Three Gentle Strolls

🚶 **Muckross Park** in Killarney is a car-free zone with four signposted nature trails. Try the 4 km (2½ mi) Arthur Young's Walk through old yew and oak woods frequented by sika deer. You can also take an open boat from Ross Castle to the head of the **Upper Lake,** then walk back along the lakeside to Muckross House—about 10 km (6 mi).

🚶 The trails in **Derrynane National Park,** a 320-acre estate, run through mature woodland, bordering on rocky outcrops that lead to wide sandy beaches and dunes. At low tide, you can walk to **Abbey Island** offshore.

🚶 Even in high summer, **Valentia Island** is a peaceful spot for walking, with little traffic. Walk the road from **Knightstown** through the subtropical vegetation of the Knight of Kerry's estate, to the historic **Slate Quarry** (3 km/2 mi), 900 ft above the sea, with views of the Skelligs offshore.

CYCLING THE RING

The Ring of Kerry Cycle Route follows the main road for about a third of its 134 miles, but the rest is on deserted roads, including a long, scenic loop through Ballinskelligs, Portmagee, and Valentia Island. There are significant climbs and strong winds along the way, so good fitness is a prerequisite.

Easy Rides

From **Killarney,** the N71 road past **Muckross Park** and the **Upper Lake** takes you through ancient woodlands to **Ladies' View** (about 12 km/7.5 mi). From here you have one of the area's best panoramas, with the sparkling blue lakes backed by purple mountains. The scene will be in front of you as you make the ride back.

From **Glenbeigh,** escape the traffic by riding inland to peaceful **Caragh Lake** through a bog and mountain landscape that's rich in wildlife. You might spot a herd of long-bearded wild goats, or a peregrine falcon hovering above its prey. The full circuit of the lake, returning to Glenbeigh, is about 35 km (22 mi).

BIKING RESOURCES

You can rent bikes and get route information at **O'Sullivan's Cycles** (064/31282) in Killarney. Along the Ring at Glenbeigh, bikes are for rent at **Glenross Caravan & Camping Park** (066/976-8451 www.killarneycamping.com/glenross.html).

For an organized tour, contact **Irish Cycling Safaris** (www.cyclingsafaris.com), which has trips along quiet back roads with local guides and support vans to carry luggage.

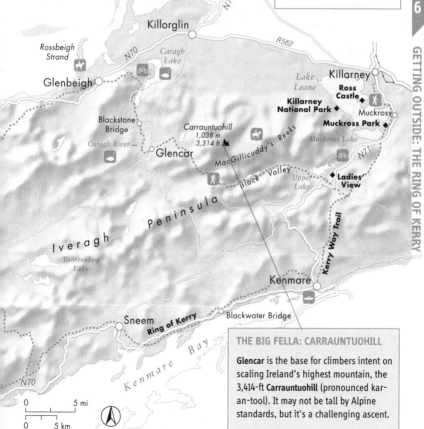

THE BIG FELLA: CARRAUNTUOHILL

Glencar is the base for climbers intent on scaling Ireland's highest mountain, the 3,414-ft **Carrauntuohill** (pronounced kar-an-tool). It may not be tall by Alpine standards, but it's a challenging ascent.

TESTING THE WATERS

Boating around the Ring . . .

Kenmare Bay is the best spot for boating expeditions. **Kenmare Angling** (⊕ www.kenmareanglingandsightseeing. com) offers customized tours, on which you can see castles, seals, dolphins, and salmon farms. Boats can take up to 10 people, and cost €300 for a full day, €200 for a half day. **Seafari** (⊕ www. seafariireland.com) at Kenmare Pier has a two-hour econature and seal watching cruise and also is an outfitter for kayaking, sailing, and wind-surfing. The **Cappanalea Outdoor Education Centre** (⊕ www. cappanalea.ie), 7 mi west of Killorglin, near Caragh Lake, offers windsurfing, canoeing, rock climbing and guided hikes.

. . . and Fishing

There's good fishing here, both inland and at sea. **Portmagee** and **Waterville** are the main deepsea angling centers; outings are generally from small open boats carrying up to 10 rods and run about €30 per person per day. Wreck and reef fishing promises pollock, ling, cod, conger, monkfish, and shark. Inshore there are bass, turbot, dogfish, flounder, and tope.

The **Caragh Lake** and the rivers **Laune, Inny, Roughty,** and **Caragh** are all excellent for wild salmon—and all are beautiful wilderness locations. **Lough Currane** near Waterville is one of the great sea trout fisheries. The season runs from March to September, and fishing permits are available locally from hotels. You'll find tackle shops in Killarney and Waterville. For detailed information before you go, check out the Web site of the South Western Regional Fisheries Board (⊕ www.swrfb.com).

. . . and Swimming

Swimming off the beaches around the coast is confined to July and August, when the water temperatures reach 55 to 60 degrees. There are dive centers at Caherdaniel, Kenmare, and Valentia Island; ⊕ www.scuba.ie is a good information resource.

Top Left: St Finian's Bay Right: Derrynane Bay
Bottom: Arriving by boat at Skellig Michael

THE TWIN PEAKS OF YOUR TRIP

The distinctive conical **Skellig Rocks** hover offshore at the western end of the Iveragh Peninsula, surrounded by swirling blue sea. They're a haunting presence that seems to follow along as you travel the mainland from Valentia to Waterville and Caherdaniel.

A venture out to the twin peaks of **Skellig Michael** (shown above, also known as Great Skellig) is a truly awesome experience. Boats leave from Waterville, Ballinskelligs, and Portmagee for a white-knuckle ride lasting about 45 minutes. Along the way you pass Michael's companion, **Little Skellig**, where people aren't allowed but gannets flourish.

Skellig Michael rises steeply for 700 feet; you reach the summit by climbing 600 steps cut into the rockface. Once there, you find, amazingly, the remains of a monastery, occupied by hermit monks from the 7th to 12th century. Looking back to the mainland and out at the wild expanse of open sea, you get an inkling of the monks' isolation from all things worldly. A visit to Skellig Michael may not be the most comfortable outing of you trip, but it will probably be the most memorable.

Birds of the Skelligs

The Ring of Kerry is one of the best places in Europe for observing seabirds, and the Skelligs are a particular treasure for birders. The **gannet** (below) with a wing span of 2 yards, is Ireland's largest seabird, and up to 22,000 nesting pairs reside on Little Skellig, where they dive for food from heights of up to 120 feet.

If you are lucky enough to get out to Skellig Michael in May, you'll be warned to watch out for comical-looking **puffins** (left) nesting in burrows underfoot.

THE RING ON HORSEBACK

Horses hold a special place in the hearts of the Irish. Horsemanship and breeding are sources of national pride—it's an oft-quoted fact that the Duke of Wellington rode an Irish horse at the Battle of Waterloo, while Napoleon's horse came from County Wexford. All over the country you'll find horses grazing in the fields, being ridden down country lanes, and galloping along beaches. If you share the Irish passion for all things equine, there's no better way to see the Ring than from the back of a horse.

You can gallop along the 3 mile stretch of **Rossbeigh Strand**, or take a trek around quiet country roads, on a horse from **Burke's Horse Trekking Center** in Glenbeigh (☎ 087/237–9110). They've been in the business for years and use mainly quiet-colored cobs (black and white all-rounders). Hats and boots are included in the price, which ranges from €20 to €30.

The six-day **Reeks Trail** riding led by **Killarney Riding Stables** (☎ 064/31–686 ⊕ www.killarney-reeks-trail.com) takes you through the mountains and woodland of MacGillicuddy's Reeks. The stables also book half- and full-day rides.

Near **Cahirciveen**, the **Final Furlong Farmhouse B & B** has a riding stable and a gorgeous location overlooking the sea. Ride as little or as much as you like during your stay, in small groups supervised by members of the proprietors, the O'Sullivan family. Contact Kathleen O'Sullivan (☎ 066/947 –3300 ✉ final-furlong@eircom.net).

Top: Horse Racing in Rossbeigh Strand
Above Left: Gap of Dunloe. Right: Lakes of Killarney

THE WET AND MILD RING...

Rossdohan Pier, Sneem

... Courtesy of the Gulf Stream

The warm waters flowing from the Gulf of Mexico across the Atlantic, known as the Gulf Stream, give Ireland a mild climate, and the effects are particularly felt along the Ring of Kerry. The area is frost-free year round, with temperatures averaging 45 degrees Fahrenheit in winter and 60 in summer. But rain is a constant threat, brought in from the Atlantic by the prevailing southwesterly winds. Console yourself with this though: it may be wet, but it is never freezing.

Don't bother touring the Ring in heavy sea mist: you won't see a thing. But don't let other forms of rain deter you. Part of the attraction of the Ring is the interplay of light with sea, mountain, and distant horizons. Rain often enhances the view, and can give delightful effects. The sun is often shining before the rain has finished, so rainbows abound. Any weather, good or bad, seldom lasts more than half a day: if it's wet in the morning, it will probably be sunny in the afternoon, and vice versa.

Sock It to Me

Bring a rain jacket and a warm fleece or sweater: sea winds can be chilly. Above all, wear sensible footwear. If you're venturing off-road, even in summer, you will be glad of strong, waterproof shoes. And bring plenty of socks. There's nothing more miserable than wet feet!

Land of Exotic Palms

With no frost, Killarney and the Iveragh Peninsula are havens for subtropical vegetation. The New Zealand fern tree and the banana tree thrive. The "palm trees" you see here are usually yuccas that have been allowed to grow tall. Flax also grows to enormous size, and is often used as a shelter belt. The leaves of the gunnera can grow to the size of a compact car—look for them in Muckross Park. The lakes of Killarney are surrounded by luxuriant woods of oak, arbutus, birch, holly and mountain ash, with undergrowth of ferns, saxifrages, and mosses. Rhododendron and azaleas thrive on pockets of acid soil, and are at their best from mid-April to May.

THE ICE AGE COMETH, AND GOETH

Some 60 million years ago, the great rias, or drowned rivers, that became the bays of Bantry, Kenmare, and Dingle were formed. The sea penetrated far inland, forming the peninsulas of Beara, Iveragh, and Dingle. A million years ago, these lands were gripped by the Ice Age. When the ice receded, some 10,000 years ago, it left corries (or glacial hollows) gouged out of the mountains, great rocks scattered on the landscape (giving rise to legends of giants throwing stones), and outcrops of ice-smoothed sandstone.

Valentia Island

6

GETTING OUTSIDE: THE RING OF KERRY

$$ 🏠**Tahilla Cove Country House.** An idyllic location—with its own stone
★ jetty in a sheltered private cove—gives this place its particular charm.
The house itself is modern and much added to over the years, and has
the appeal of a modest but comfortable private home. No doubt it
won't be difficult to enjoy the plump chintz armchairs and open log
fire in the large sitting room, or to laze on the terrace overlooking 14
acres of subtropical gardens and the cove. Rooms vary in size and are
comfortably furnished, and all but two have sea views. ⊠ *Tahilla Cove,
Co. Kerry* ☎ *064/45204* 🖨 *064/45104* ⊕ *www.tahillacove.com* ➣ *9
rooms* △ *In-room: no a/c. In-hotel: restaurant, bar, no elevator, some
pets allowed* ☰ *AE, DC, MC, V* ⊘ *Closed mid-Oct.–mid-Mar* ⏺️ *BP.*

EN
ROUTE

Derrynane House was the home of Daniel O'Connell (1775–1847), "The
Liberator," who campaigned for Catholic Emancipation (the granting of full
rights of citizenship to Catholics), which became a reality in 1828. The house,
with its lovely garden and 320-acre estate, now forms Derrynane Nation-
al Park. The south and east wings of the house (which O'Connell himself
remodeled) are open to visitors and contain much of the furniture and other
items associated with O'Connell. ⊠ *Near Caherdaniel, 30 km (18 mi) west of
Sneem off N70* ☎ *066/947–5113* 🎫 *€2.90* ⊘ *Nov.–Mar., weekends 1–5; Apr.
and Oct., Tues.–Sun. 1–5; May–Sept., Mon.–Sat. 9–6, Sun. 11–7.*

WATERVILLE

③¹ *35 km (22 mi) west of Sneem.*

Waterville is famous for its sportfishing, its 18-hole championship
golf course (adopted as a warm-up spot for the British Open by Tiger
Woods, who was a big hit with the locals), and for the fact that Charlie
Chaplin and Charles de Gaulle spent summers here. Besides all that, the
village, like many others on the Ring of Kerry, has a few restaurants
and pubs, but little else. There's excellent salmon and trout fishing at
nearby Lough Currane.

Outside Waterville and 1 km (½ mi) before Ballinskelligs, an Irish-
speaking fishing village, is the **Cill Rialaig,** an artistic retreat. Here, a
cluster of derelict stone cottages in a deserted village were given new
life as artists' studios. Cill Rialaig attracts both Irish and international
artists for residencies, and their work, and ceramics, metalwork, jew-
elry, and other handmade crafts, are exhibited and sold at the attrac-
tively designed, beehive-shape store. There's also a coffee shop. ⊠ *R566*
☎ *066/947–9277* 🎫 *Free* ⊘ *Daily 11–5.*

WHERE TO STAY

$$$ 🏠**Butler Arms.** Charlie Chaplin loved it here. The rambling building—
♻ with white, castellated corner towers—is a familiar landmark on the
Ring. It has been in the same family for four generations, and the clientele returns year after year for the excellent fishing and golf facilities
nearby and the proximity of long, sandy, windswept beaches. Many
regulars like the smallish rooms in the old part of the hotel, which are

neither smart nor chic. More-spacious rooms, with streamlined decor and sensational sea views, can be had in a newer wing, and there are 12 junior suites. The rambling old lounges with open turf fires are comfortable places to relax and read or converse. ⊠ *Waterville, Co. Kerry* ☎ *066/947–4144* 🖷 *066/947–4520* ⊕ *www.butlerarms.com* 🛏 *40 rooms* ♿ *In-room: no a/c, dial-up. In-hotel: restaurant, tennis court, public Wi-Fi* ▤ *AE, DC, MC, V* ⊗ *Closed Nov.–Mar.* ⏐⊙⏐*BP.*

NIGHTLIFE
Head to the **Inny Tavern** (⊠ *Inny Bridge, Waterville* ☎ *066/947–4512*) for live Irish music.

SPORTS
Famously adopted by Tiger Woods to practice his swings for the British Open, the **Waterville Golf Links** (⊠ *Co. Kerry* ☎ *066/947–4102*), an 18-hole course, remains one of the toughest and most scenic in Ireland or Britain.

THE SKELLIGS

③② *21 km (13 mi) northwest of Waterville.*

Fodor'sChoice
★
In the far northwestern corner of the Ring of Kerry, across Portmagee Channel, lies Valentia Island, which is reachable by a bridge erected in 1971. Visible from Valentia, and on a clear day from other points along the coast are the **Skelligs,** one of the most spectacular sights in Ireland. Sculpted as if by the hand of God, the islands of Little Skellig, Great Skellig, and the Washerwoman's Rock are distinctively cone-shape, surrounded by blue swirling seas. The largest island, the Great Skellig, or Skellig Michael, distinguished by its twin peaks, rises 700 feet from the Atlantic. It has the remains of a settlement of early Christian monks, reached by climbing 600 increasingly precipitous steps. In spite of a thousand years of battering by Atlantic storms, the church, oratory, and beehive-shape living cells are surprisingly well preserved.

To visit the Skelligs, you can take a half-day trip in an open boat—perfect for adventurers who pack plenty of Dramamine. The entire visit takes three to four hours, with 1½ hours on the Skellig Michael, where visitors are supervised by resident guides, and the remaining time in transit (the duration varies depending on the weather and tides). During the journey you'll pass Little Skellig, the breeding ground of more than 22,000 pairs of gannets. Puffin Island, to the north, has a large population of shearwaters and storm petrel. Puffins nest in sand burrows on the Great Skellig in the month of May. But the masterpiece is the phenomenal Skellig Michael, home to that amazing 7th–12th-century village of monastic beehive dwellings, and offering vertigo-inducing views. Note that the waters are choppy at the best of times, and trips are made when the weather permits. Even in fine weather, it can be a rough, white-knuckle ride as you cross the swell of the open sea, lasting at least 45 minutes, and is not suitable for small children. One worthy outfitter is **Pat Joe Murphy** (⊠ *Portmagee* ☎ *066/947–7156* 💶 *€30* ⊙ *Cruises daily at 10 AM, weather permitting, May–Aug.*).

6

Where the bridge joins Valentia Island, **Skellig Experience** (✉ *Valentia Island* ☎*066/947–6306* ⊕*www.skelligexperience.com* ☞*€5* ⊘*Apr.–June and Sept., daily 9:30–5; July and Aug., daily 9:30–7; Oct.–Nov., daily 10–6*) offers an alternative for the less adventurous traveler. This center contains exhibits on local birdlife, the history of the lighthouse and keepers, and the life and work of the early Christian monks. There's also a 15-minute audiovisual show that allows you to "tour" the Skelligs without leaving dry land. But if you're up for it, don't miss the boat ride out to the rocks; Skellig Michael is something you won't soon forget.

WHERE TO STAY

¢   ⛱ **Shealane Country House.** Cows graze in the adjoining field, and the
★   breakfast room at this easily reached island retreat overlooks the ocean and the mainland hills. The large, modern detached house is on Valentia Island, beside the bridge to the mainland. The Skellig Experience Visitor Centre is across the road, and a brisk five-minute walk across the bridge leads you to Port Magee and should sharpen your appetite for hearty bar food. Alternatively, you can drive 10 minutes north on the island to Knightstown, which offers additional modest dining options. Host Mary Lane is native to the area and can organize boat trips to the Skelligs, as well as fishing, horseback riding, and golf excursions; she can also recommend local bars for live music. Her home is a delight, with bright airy rooms, polished pine floors, and large traditional wooden windows framing the peaceful views guests often dream about long after leaving. ✉*Corha-Mor, Valentia Island* ☎*066/947–6354* ✍ marylane@eircom. net ⇋*5 rooms* ⚐*In-room: no a/c, no phone, no TV. In-hotel: no elevator* ⊘*Closed Nov.–Feb.* ⫶⊙⫶*BP.*

CAHIRCIVEEN

㉝ *18 km (11 mi) north of Waterville on N70.*

Cahirciveen (pronounced cah-her-sigh-*veen*), at the foot of Bentee Mountain, is the gateway to the western side of the Ring of Kerry and the main market town for southern Kerry. Following the tradition in this part of the world, the modest, terraced houses are each painted in different colors (sometimes two or three)—the brighter the better.

The **O'Connell Memorial Church,** a large, elaborate, neo-Gothic structure that dominates the main street, was built in 1888 of Newry granite and black limestone to honor the local hero Daniel O'Connell. It's the only church in Ireland named after a layman.

The **Cahirciveen Heritage Centre** is in the converted former barracks of the Royal Irish Constabulary, an imposing, castlelike structure built after the Fenian Rising of 1867 to suppress further revolts. The center has well-designed displays depicting scenes from times of famine in the locality, the life of Daniel O'Connell, and the restoration of this fine building from a blackened ruin. ✉*Barracks* ☎*066/947–2777* ☞*€3.50* ⊙*June–Sept., Mon.–Sat. 10–6, Sun. 2–6; Mar.–May and Oct., weekdays 9:30–5:30.*

GLENBEIGH

34 *27 km (17 mi) northeast of Cahirciveen on N70.*

The road from Cahirciveen to Glenbeigh is one of the Ring's highlights. To the north is Dingle Bay and the jagged peaks of the Dingle Peninsula, which will, in all probability, be shrouded in mist. If they aren't, the gods have indeed blessed your journey. The road runs close to the water here, and beyond the small village of Kells it climbs high above the bay, hugging the steep side of Drung Hill before descending to Glenbeigh. Note how different the stark character of this stretch of the Ring is from the gentle, woody Kenmare Bay side.

On a boggy plateau by the sea, the block-long town of Glenbeigh is a popular holiday base—there's excellent hiking in the Glenbeigh Horseshoe, as the surrounding mountains are known, and exceptionally good trout fishing in Lough Coomasaharn. The area south of Glenbeigh and west of Carrantouhill Mountain, around the shores of the Caragh River and the village of Glencar, is known as the Kerry Highlands. The scenery is wild and rough but strangely appealing. A series of circular walks have been signposted, and parts of the Kerry Way pass through here. The area attracts serious climbers who intend to scale Carrantouhill, Ireland's highest peak (3,408 feet).

Worth a quick look, the **Kerry Bog Village Museum** is a cluster of reconstructed, fully furnished cottages that vividly portray the daily life of the region's working class in the early 1800s. ⊠ *Beside Red Fox Bar* ☎ *066/976–9184* ⊡ *€4* ⊘ *Mar.–Nov., daily 8:30–7; Jan. and Feb. by request.*

A signpost to the right outside Glenbeigh points to **Caragh Lake,** a tempting excursion south to a beautiful expanse of water set among gorse- and heather-covered hills and majestic mountains. The road hugs the shoreline much of the way.

North of Glenbeigh, the beach at **Rossbeigh** consists of about 3 km (2 mi) of soft, sandy coast backed by high dunes. It faces Inch Strand, a similar formation across the water on the Dingle Peninsula.

WHERE TO STAY & EAT

$$–$$$

Fodor'sChoice

★

✕🏠 **Carrig Country House.** A rambling two-story Victorian house covered in flowering creepers, and set on four acres of lush gardens running down to a secluded lakeshore—this comes pretty close to most people's dream rural retreat. The atmosphere is more grand country house than hotel, with turf fires in the reception rooms encouraging guests to linger in an armchair with a book. Guest rooms are lavishly decorated with period antiques ranging from cozy cottage-style to ornate Victoriana, with spoon-backed chairs and mahogany writing desks; some have private patios. As well as enjoying views over the gardens (which have 950 species of plants) to the peaceful waters of the lake and the surrounding mountains, you can also *hear* the lake water lapping the shore from most rooms. Boating and fishing facilities are available. Your friendly hosts Frank and Mary Slattery were restaurateurs, and their kitchen maintains a tempting menu of local meat, duck, and seafood, served with homegrown vegetables. The dining room ($$–$$$$) is partly in a conservatory extension, and has William Morris wallpaper and elegant, high-backed Edwardian chairs. Finish up a lovely repast with classic desserts: chocolate and orange mousse, iced-coffee parfait, or peach, nectarine, and rosemary crème brûlée—all made on the premises. ⊠ *Caragh Lake, Killorglin, Co. Kerry* ☎ *066/976–9100* 🖷 *066/976–9166* ⊕ *www.carrighouse.com* ⇨ *17 rooms* ⟡ *In-room: no a/c, no TV. In-hotel: restaurant, bar, no elevator, public Internet* ▭ *MC, V* ⊗ *Closed Dec.–Feb. No lunch* ⟨◉⟩ *BP.*

$$$ ⛨**Ard na Sidhe.** "Sidhe" (pronounced *sheen*) means "Hill of the Fairies," and this secluded, gabled Edwardian mansion certainly looks like it belongs in a fairy tale. Its courtly, ivy-covered stone walls are punctuated by casement windows set in gorgeous stone mullions, while the neatly manicured lakeside gardens contrast with the surrounding wilderness. The storybook mansion, built by Lady Gordon in 1913, has attractive, large rooms furnished with coordinated carpets and spreads, and floral drapes on bay windows; rooms in the main building are the nicest. Antiques and fireplaces dot the traditionally furnished lobby and lounges, but most of the furnishings are reproduction quality. Still, the setting and the house itself are incomparable, and guests have the use of the pools and gyms at two sister hotels in Killarney. Boating and fishing facilities are also offered. ⊠ *Caragh Lake, Co. Kerry* ☎ *066/976–9105* 🖷 *066/976–9282* ⊕ *www.killarneyhotels.ie* ⇨ *18 rooms* ⟡ *In-room: no a/c, no TV. In-hotel: restaurant, bar, no elevator* ▭ *AE, DC, MC, V* ⊗ *Closed Oct.–Apr.* ⟨◉⟩ *BP.*

$ ⛨**Blackstones House.** Padraig and Breda Breen's farmhouse is a ram-
☾ bling old building on Caragh River in Lickeen Wood, where a gentle stretch of rapids leads to a salmon pool. With four golf courses within 20 minutes' drive, and fishing and hiking on the doorstep, the conversion to guesthouse was a good move. All rooms have river views and are simply furnished with country-pine bedsteads and pink, blue, and yellow floral drapes and spreads against plain walls and carpets. Breda provides a simple evening meal on request. ⊠ *Glencar, Co. Kerry* ☎ *066/976–0164* 🖷 *066/976–0269* ⊕ *www.glencar-blackstones.com* ⇨ *9 rooms* ⟡ *In-room: no a/c, no phone, no TV (some). In-hotel: restaurant, no elevator* ▭ *MC, V* ⊗ *Closed Nov.–Mar.* ⟨◉⟩ *BP.*

$ ⛨**Glencar House.** A hunting lodge on the Caragh River, built in 1670 by the earl of Lansdowne, is now an unpretentious guesthouse. Huge elk antlers hang over the fireplace and taxidermy greets you at every turn. The large rooms have country-pine furniture and breathtaking views of Killarney's famous mountains, MacGillicuddy's Reeks. The house is a 20-minute drive from Killarney, Waterville, and Kenmare, and is a popular base for golfers. (From Killarney, turn off the N72 Killorglin road for Beaufort, and follow signs for Glencar.) When asked if the hotel had installed air-conditioning, the concierge replied, "No, we have real air!" ⊠ *Glencar, Co. Kerry* ☎ *066/976–0102* 🖷 *066/976–0167* ⊕ *www.glencarhouse.com* ⇨ *20 rooms* ⟡ *In-room: no a/c. In-hotel: restaurant, bar, tennis court, no elevator* ▭ *AE, MC, V* ⊗ *Closed mid-Oct.–mid-Mar.* ⟨◉⟩ *BP.*

KILLORGLIN

③⑤ *14 km (9 mi) east of Glenbeigh, 22 km (14 mi) west of Killarney.*

The hilltop town of Killorglin is the scene of the Puck Fair, three days of merrymaking during the second weekend in August. A large billy goat with beribboned horns, installed on a high pedestal, presides over the fair. The origins of the tradition of King Puck are lost in time. Though some horse, sheep, and cattle dealing still occurs at the fair, the main attractions these days are free outdoor concerts and extended drinking hours. The crowd is predominantly young and invariably noisy, so avoid Killorglin at fair time if you've come for peace and quiet. On the other hand, if you intend to join in the festivities, be sure to book accommodations well in advance.

WHERE TO EAT

$$$–$$$$ ✕**Nick's Seafood and Steak.** Owner Nick Foley comes from the family that established Killarney's famous eatery, Foley's, and has made a name for himself as a chef. The old stone town house has a bar-cum-dining room at street level and a quieter dining room on the floor above. Foley is known for his generous portions, his wide choice of local seafood, and his steaks. Nick's is famous for its generous seafood plate, served with an individual sauce for each item. In winter sample the haunch of Kerry venison in red-wine and juniper sauce. ⊠*Lower Bridge St.* ☎*066/976–1219* ▤*MC, V* ☉*Closed Nov. and Mon. and Tues. Dec.–Easter.*

IN & AROUND KILLARNEY

One of southwest Ireland's most attractive locales, Killarney is also the most heavily visited town in the region (its proximity to the Ring of Kerry and to Shannon Airport helps to ensure this). Light rain is typical of the area, but because of the topography, it seldom lasts long. And the clouds' approach over the lakes and the subsequent showers can actually add to the spectacle of the scenery. The rain is often followed within minutes by brilliant sunshine and, yes, even a rainbow.

EXPLORING KILLARNEY & ENVIRONS

Killarney: 87 km (54 mi) west of Cork City on N22, 19 km (12 mi) southeast of Killorglin, 24 km (15 mi) north of Glengarriff.

With its glacial landscape enhanced by subtropical vegetation, Killarney's views are legendary. Yes, the lakes really are sapphire-blue (at least when the sun is out), and seen from a distance, the MacGillicuddy Reeks really are purple. Add a scattering of large gray rocks (large, as in big as a car), and acres of lush green flowering shrubs and trees, and you're starting to get the picture.

Much of the area is part of Killarney National Park, which has more than 24,000 acres and is famous for such native habitats and species as oak holly woods, yew woods, and red deer. Signposted self-guiding

A Romantic Past

Such great writers as Sir Walter Scott and William Thackeray struggled to find the superlatives to describe Killarney's heather-clad peaks, subtropical vegetation, and deep-blue waters dotted with wooded isles. Indeed the lakes and the mountains have left a lasting impression on a long stream of people, beginning in the 18th century with the English travelers Arthur Young and Bishop Berkeley. Visitors in search of the natural beauty so beloved by the Romantic movement began to flock to the Southwest. By the mid-19th century, Killarney's scenery was considered as exhilarating and awe-inspiring as anything in Switzerland. The influx of affluent visitors that followed the 1854 arrival of the railway transformed the lives of Kerry's impoverished natives and set in motion the commercialization that continues today.

trails within the park introduce these habitats. At the park's heart is Muckross Demesne; the entrance is 4 km (2½ mi) from Killarney on N71. The National Park Visitor Centre is at Muckross House. Cars aren't allowed in Muckross Demesne; you can either walk, rent a bicycle, or take a traditional jaunting car—that is, a pony and a cart.

The air here smells of damp woods and heather moors. The red fruits of the Mediterranean strawberry tree (*Arbutus unedo*) are at their height in October and November, which is also about the time when the bracken turns rust-color, contrasting with the evergreens. In late April and early May, the purple flowers of the rhododendron *ponticum* put on a spectacular display.

36 You may want to limit time spent in **Killarney** itself if discos, Irish cabarets, and singing pubs—the last a local specialty with a strong Irish-American flavor—aren't your thing. The nightlife is at its liveliest from May to September; the Irish and Europeans pack the town in July and August. Peak season for Americans follows in September and October. At other times, particularly from November to mid-March, when many of the hotels are closed, the town is quiet to the point of being eerie. Given the choice, go to Killarney in April, May, or early October.

37 **Aghadoe** (⊠ *5 km [3 mi] west of Killarney on R562 Beaufort–Killorglin Rd.*) is an outstanding place to get a feel for what Killarney is all about: lake and mountain scenery. Stand beside Aghadoe's 12th-century ruined church and round tower, and watch the shadows creep gloriously across Lower Lake, with Innisfallen Island in the distance and the Gap of Dunloe to the west.

38 You reach **Torc Waterfall** (⊠ *Killarney National Park, N71 [Muckross Rd.], 8 km [5 mi] south of Killarney*) by a footpath that begins in the parking lot outside the gates of the Muckross Demesne. After your first view of the roaring cascade, which will appear after about 10 minutes' walk, it's worth the climb up a long flight of stone steps to the second, less-frequented clearing.

39 **Muckross House,** the famous 19th-century, Elizabethan-style manor, now houses the Kerry Folklife Centre, where bookbinders, potters, and weavers demonstrate their crafts. Upstairs, elegantly furnished rooms portray the lifestyle of the landed gentry in the 1800s; downstairs in the basement you can experience the conditions of servants employed in the house. Inside you'll also find the Killarney National Park Visitor Centre. The informal grounds are noted for their rhododendrons and azaleas, the water garden, and the outstanding limestone rock garden.

In the park beside the house, the Muckross Traditional Farms comprise reconstructed farm buildings and outbuildings, a blacksmith's forge, a carpenter's workshop, and a selection of farm animals. It's a reminder of the way things were done on the farm before electricity and the mechanization of farming. Meet and chat with the farmers and their wives as they go about their work. The visitor center has a shop and a restaurant. ✉*Killarney National Park, Muckross Demesne, Muckross Rd. (N71), 6½ km (4 mi) south of Killarney* ☎*064/31440* ⊕*www.heritageireland. ie* ✉*Visitor center free, farms or house €5.75, farms and house €8.65* ⊙*House Sept.–June, daily 9–5:30. Visitor center Nov.–mid-Mar., daily 9–5.30; mid-Mar.–June, Sept., and Oct., daily 9–6; July and Aug., daily 9–7. Farms mid-Mar.–Apr., weekends 2–6; May, daily 1–6; June–Sept., daily 10–7; Oct., daily 2–6.*

40 The 15th-century Franciscan **Muckross Friary** is amazingly complete, although roofless. The monks were driven out by Oliver Cromwell's army in 1652. An ancient yew tree rises above the cloisters and breaks out over the abbey walls. Three flights of stone steps allow access to the upper floors and living quarters, where you can visit the cloisters and what was once the dormitory, kitchen, and refectory. ✉*Killarney National Park, Muckross Demesne, Muckross Rd. (N71), 4 km (2½ mi) south of Killarney* ✉*Free* ⊙*Mid-June–early Sept., daily 10–5.*

41 **Ross Castle,** a fully restored 14th-century stronghold, was the last place in the province of Munster to fall to Oliver Cromwell's forces in 1652. A later dwelling has 16th- and 17th-century furniture. ✉*Knockreer Estate, off Muckross Rd. (N71), 2 km (1 mi) south of Killarney* ☎*064/35851* ✉*€5.30* ⊙*Apr. and Oct., daily 10–5; May and Sept., daily 9–6; June–Aug., daily 9–6:30.*

42 The romantic ruins on **Innisfallen Island** date from the 6th or 7th century. Between 950 and 1350 the *Annals of Innisfallen* were compiled here by monks. (The book survives in the Bodleian Library in Oxford.) To get to the island, which is on Lough Leane, you can rent a rowboat at Ross Castle (€4 per hour), or you can join a cruise (€8) in a covered, heated launch.

43 ⏱ ★ Massive, glacial rocks form the side of the **Gap of Dunloe,** a narrow mountain pass that stretches for 6½ km (4 mi) between MacGillicuddy's Reeks and the Purple Mountains. The rocks create strange echoes: give a shout to test it out. Five small lakes are strung out beside the road. Cars are banned from the gap, but in summer the first 3 km (2 mi) are busy with horse and foot

TRIP TIP

While the immediate region of Killarney has a vast array of accommodations, visitors should consider staying in hotels in Glenbeigh (less than 20 minutes' drive away) if they really want to savor the region's peace and quiet.

traffic, much of which turns back at the halfway point.

At the entrance to the Gap of Dunloe, **Kate Kearney's Cottage** (⊠ *19 km [12 mi] west of Killarney* ☎ *064/44116*) is a good place to rent a jaunting car or pony. Kate was a famous beauty who sold illegal *poteen* (moonshine) from her home, contributing greatly, one suspects, to travelers' enthusiasm for the scenery. Appropriately enough, Kearney's is now a pub and a good place to pause for an Irish coffee. The gap's southern end is marked by **Lord Brandon's Cottage,** a tea shop serving soup and sandwiches. From here, a path leads to the edge of Upper Lake, where you can journey onward by rowboat. It's an old tradition for the boatman to carry a bugle and illustrate the echoes. The boat passes under Brickeen Bridge and into Middle Lake, where 30 islands are steeped in legends, many of which your boatman is likely to recount. Look out for caves on the left-hand side on this narrow stretch of water. ⊠ *7 km (4½ mi) west of Killarney* ☉ *Easter–Sept., 10* AM*–dusk.*

44 ★ If the weather is fine, head southwest 19 km (12 mi) out of Killarney on N71 to **Ladies' View,** a famed panorama of the three lakes and the surrounding mountains. The name goes back to 1905, when Queen Victoria was a guest at Muckross House. Upon seeing the view, her ladies-in-waiting were said to have been dumbfounded by its beauty.

WHERE TO STAY & EAT

$$$–$$$$ ✕**Gaby's Seafood.** Expect the best seafood in Killarney from Belgian owner-chef Gert Maes. Inside the rustic exterior is a little bar beside an open fire; steps lead up to the main dining area. Try the seafood platter (seven or eight kinds of fish in a cream-and-wine sauce) or lobster Gaby (shelled, simmered in a cream-and-cognac sauce, and served back in the shell). ⊠ *27 High St.* ☎ *064/32519* ▭ *AE, DC, MC, V* ☉ *Closed Sun. and mid-Feb.–mid-Mar. No lunch.*

$$–$$$ ★ ✕**Treyvaud's.** Step behind the Victorian arched facade here and you'll discover a buzzing contemporary restaurant, masterminded by a pair of brothers, chefs Paul and Mark Treyvaud. The decor is simple: pin floorboards, wood-beamed ceiling, lines of red-backed chairs, and plain wooden tabletops. The food takes center stage, as it should, since Killarney's restaurants have a long tradition of providing hearty fare for visitors who have worked up a keen appetite hiking the surrounding hills. Start with the shredded duck confit with cream cheese and beetroot carpaccio or homemade smoked haddock fish cakes with gar-

lic aioli. Few will want to miss the beef-and-Guinness pie with mashed potatoes, renowned for its flavor. More adventurous diners might care to try panfried ostrich fillet with caramelized shallots and red-wine jus (the bird is farmed in Waterford). In winter Treyvaud's is famous for its wide selection of game, including rabbit, wild boar, pheasant, and quail. With a seafood plate featuring Dover sole, tiger prawns, and crab claws, this is a restaurant determined to satisfy the hungriest hiker. ⊠ *62 High St.* ☎ *064/33062* ☰ *AE, DC, MC, V* ⊗ *Closed Mon. and Tues. April–Oct.*

$ ✗ **Panis Angelicus.** Daylight streams in through the large plate-glass shop windows of this stylish, contemporary café, and mellow jazz plays softly in the background. Add black-tile floors, original art on dark-red walls, and the smell of freshly ground coffee, and you have the ideal place to take a break. There are home-baked breads and cakes as well as a good selection of sandwiches, and the hot Irish potato cake with garlic butter and green salad is delicious. Dinner menus feature pasta specials, seafood salad, and other light bites. ⊠ *15 New St.* ☎ *064/39648* ☰ *MC, V* ⊗ *No dinner Oct.–Apr.*

$$$$ ✗⊞ **Aghadoe Heights.** Once inside this large, modern hotel you'll soon
★ forget its blocklike external appearance, as the entrancing panorama of Killarney's lakes spread out before you takes its hold. It's hard to take your eyes off the view, as the famously changeable Killarney weather scuds across the skies (sunsets are not to be missed). As for the interior, standard international-hotel decor is enlivened by an impressive collection of original Irish art. Guest rooms are spacious, with all the luxury touches you would expect, including fruit bowl, sitting area, crisp white bed linen, and fluffy robes, plus a booklet on hiking trails that start right outside the hotel's door. The staff, many of whom are local, are unfailingly helpful. The Lakeside Restaurant ($$$$) has views over the lakes from the outside tables; the more intimate indoor dining areas are made cozy with wood paneling. Executive chef Robin Suter supervises a seasonal menu described as "eclectic European," which might feature confit belly of pork and milk-fed veal with peach sauce or sea trout with rock-salt beans and sauce verte. The Spa at Aghadoe offers a full range of treatments, or you can simply relax in the Thermal Suite, where the mild heat should ease any post-golfing or post-hiking aches and pains. ⊠ *Aghadoe Heights, 4 km (2½ mi) outside Killarney, on Tralee side, signposted off N22, Co. Kerry* ☎ *064/31766* ☎ *064/31345* ⊕ *www.aghadoeheights.com* ➥ *71 rooms, 3 suites* ⊘ *In-room: refrigerator, dial-up, Wi-Fi (some). In-hotel: restaurant, bar, tennis court, pool, gym, spa, public Wi-Fi* ☰ *AE, DC, MC, V* ⫟O⫟*BP.*

$$$$ ✗⊞ **Cahernane House.** Get a glimpse of the Killarney that attracted discerning 19th-century visitors at this imposing grey-stone house, which stands at the end of a long private avenue with trees that meet overhead to form a tunnel. Clearly, if you need a refuge from the touristy buzz of Killarney town, this is the place. Formerly the residence of the earls of Pembroke, the estate borders on the national park, and the current house dates from 1877. It oozes baronial grandeur, with a flight of stone steps leading up to its tall front door. A crackling log fire awaits

6

you in the drawing room, which, like all the reception rooms, features highly polished mahogany furniture and wall paneling. It's worth paying extra for a room in the original house—they are large with high ceilings, and have a genuine sense of history, with fine Victorian antique furniture. The newer rooms have private garden access, peaceful parkland views, and large bathrooms with marble tiling. The Herbert Room ($$$$) is a well-reputed formal restaurant serving classic French cuisine, but many prefer the more relaxed Cellar Bar, which serves a hearty bistro-style menu ($) under low-vaulted stone ceilings. ⊠ *Muckross Rd., Co. Kerry* ☎ *064/31895* 🖷 *064/34340* ⊕ *www.cahernane.com* 🛏 *36 rooms, 2 suites* ⚘ *In-room: no a/c, dial-up. In-hotel: no-smoking rooms* ☐ *MC, V* ⧓ *BP.*

$$ ✕⊞ **Foley's Townhouse and Restaurant.** Rooms in this 19th-century row of interconnected town houses have Victorian antiques and rustic, pine furniture. Windows are double-glazed, so the rooms are quieter than you would expect for a hotel right in the center of Killarney. In the restaurant ($$–$$$$) chef-owner Carol Hartnett makes use of local ingredients, including superior Irish cream and butter. Roulade of trout stuffed with prawn mousse and grilled T-bone steak with garlic butter are typical dishes. The wine list has more than 300 selections, and a pianist entertains in summer. ⊠ *23 High St., Co. Kerry* ☎ *064/31217* 🖷 *064/34683* ⊕ *www.foleystownhouse.com* 🛏 *28 rooms* ⚘ *In-room: no a/c, dial-up. In-hotel: restaurant* ☐ *AE, DC, MC, V* ⊙ *Closed Dec.* ⧓ *BP.*

$ ✕⊞ **Mills Inn.** If you wince at tour-bus crowds, consider this coaching inn in Ballyvourney, a village 15 minutes outside Killarney and on the main Cork–Killarney road. The inn is beside the rapid-flowing River Sullane, and its grounds have old castle ruins as well as a stable yard and gardens. Its bar, established in 1755, is popular with Irish-speaking locals and has traditional Irish music every night from Thursday to Sunday. Rooms are well insulated from bar and traffic noise and have mahogany four-poster beds and a cream-and-gold color scheme. The award-winning restaurant and bar (both $$–$$$) serve generous portions of local meat and seafood from the same menu (it's quieter in the restaurant, but you may need to reserve). Typical daily specials include panfried sea bass on a crab risotto or lamb en croute with wild mushrooms. ⊠ *Ballyvourney, Macroom, Co. Cork* ☎ *026/45237* 🖷 *026/45454* ⊕ *www.millsinn.ie* 🛏 *14 rooms* ⚘ *In-room: no a/c. In-hotel: restaurant, bar, no elevator* ☐ *MC, V* ⧓ *BP.*

$$ ⊞ **Europe.** A secluded lakeside location (a five-minute drive from Killarney) and a luxurious but unfussy style give this large, modern, five-story hotel the edge over its competitors. Most bedrooms have solid-pine details, a lake view, and a private balcony. The spacious lounges and lobbies have picture windows overlooking the lake and mountains, an imaginative display of old carved timber, and antiques. The sports facilities, including an Olympic-size pool, are among the area's most up-to-date. ⊠ *Killorglin Rd., Fossa, Co. Kerry* ☎ *064/31900* 🖷 *064/32118* ⊕ *www.killarneyhotels.ie* 🛏 *205 rooms* ⚘ *In-room: refrigerator, dial-up. In-hotel: 2 restaurants, bars, tennis court, pool, gym, public Wi-Fi* ☐ *AE, DC, MC, V* ⧓ *BP* ⊙ *Closed Jan.–Mar.*

$$ ⊡**Earls Court House.** In a quiet suburb within walking distance of
★ Killarney's center, this spacious guesthouse is furnished with interesting
antiques collected by Emer Moynihan, who likes to greet her guests by
offering home-baked goods in front of the open fire. The front lounge
is a popular meeting place, where you can peruse the menus of local
restaurants, read up on Kerry's attractions, or go online. Bedrooms are
spacious, with large bathrooms, a mix of antique and reproduction Vic-
torian furniture, and unfussy decor with plain walls and dark colors.
Older rooms have balconies, others feature four-poster beds, and some
have Jacuzzi baths. Breakfast is served in a large, cheerful room; menu
choices include pancakes and kippers. The house has a wine license.
⊠*Woodlawn Junction, Muckross Rd., N71, Co. Kerry* ☎*064/34009*
🖷*064/34366* ⊕*www.killarney-earlscourt.ie* ⨼*24 rooms* ☒*In-room:
no a/c, dial-up. In-hotel: restaurant, public Wi-Fi* ⊟*MC, V* ☉*Closed
Dec. and Jan.* ⦅O⦆*BP.*

$ ⊡**Lime Court.** On the Muckross Road between Killarney and the
national park—yet only a five-minute walk from the town center and
the railway station—this modern guesthouse offers simple, no-frills
accommodation. Rooms are in an extension at the back and away
from the road. Antiques and large potted plants decorate the reception
area; a baby grand piano anchors the spacious lounge. Although guest
rooms are plain, they're comfortable and light; all have small sitting
areas. There are four pubs nearby, all offering Irish music and good
food. ⊠*Muckross Rd., N71, Co. Kerry* ☎*064/34547* 🖷*064/34121*
⊕*www.hoztel.com* ⨼*22 rooms* ☒*In-room: no a/c. In-hotel: no eleva-
tor* ⊟*MC, V* ⦅O⦆*BP.*

NIGHTLIFE & THE ARTS

Bars where a professional leads the songs and encourages audience par-
ticipation and solos are popular in Killarney—try the **Laurels** (⊠*Main
St.* ☎*064/31149*). **Buckley's Bar** (⊠*College St.* ☎*064/31037*) in the
Arbutus Hotel has traditional Irish entertainment nightly from June to
September. **Gleneagles** (⊠*Muckross Rd.* ☎*064/31870*) is the place for
big-name cabaret—from Sharon Shannon to the Wolfe Tones. It also
has a late-night disco. **McSorleys Nite Club** (⊠*College St.* ☎*064/39770*)
is a lively late-night venue for the over-25s.

SPORTS & THE OUTDOORS

BICYCLING A bicycle is the perfect way to enjoy Killarney's mild air, whether within
the confines of Muckross Park or farther afield in the Kerry Highlands.
Rent by the day or week from **O'Sullivan's Cycles** (⊠*Bishop's La., off
New St.* ☎*064/31282*).

FISHING Salmon and brown trout populate Killarney's lakes and rivers. **O'Neill's**
(⊠*Plunkett St.* ☎*064/31970*) provides fishing tackle, bait, and licenses.

GOLF **Beaufort Golf Course** (⊠*Churchtown, Beaufort* ☎*064/44440*) has an
18-hole course surrounded by magnificent scenery, and unlike most
other Irish golf clubs, it has buggy-, trolley-, and club-rental facilities.
For many, the three courses at the legendary **Killarney Golf and Fishing
Club** (⊠*Mahony's Point* ☎*064/31034*) are the chief reason for com-
ing to Killarney.

HIKING   The **Kerry Way,** a long-distance walking route, passes through the Killarney National Park on its way to Glenbeigh. You can get a detailed leaflet about the route from the tourist information office. For the less adventurous, four safe and well-signposted nature trails of varying lengths are in the national park. Try the 4-km (2½-mi) Arthur Young's Walk, which passes through old yew and oak woods frequented by Sika deer. You can reach the **Mangerton walking trail,** a small tarred road leading to a scenic trail that circles Mangerton Lake, by turning left off N71 midway between Muckross Friary and Muckross House (follow the signposts). The summit of **Mangerton Mountain** (2,756 feet) can be reached on foot in about two hours—less if you rent a pony. It's perfect if you want a fine, long hike with good views of woodland scenery. **Torc Mountain** (1,764 feet) can be reached off Route N71; it's a satisfying 1½-hour climb, with lake views. Don't attempt mountain climbing in the area in misty weather; visibility can quickly drop to zero.

SHOPPING

Bricín Craft Shop (⊠26 High St. ☎064/34902) has interesting handicrafts, including candles, ceramics, and woolens. Visit the **Frank Lewis Gallery** (⊠6 Bridewell La., beside General Post Office ☎064/34843) for original paintings and sculptures. If you have Irish roots, you can learn all about your name and buy an item with its heraldic crest—from key rings to crystal to sweaters—at **House of Names** (⊠Kenmare Pl. ☎064/36320). **The Kilkenny Shop** (⊠3 New St. ☎064/35406) stocks contemporary Irish pottery, ironwork, woodwork, crystal, and jewelry.

The **Killarney Bookshop** (⊠32 Main St. ☎064/34108) has local-interest books as well as fiction, biography, and travel titles. Bargain hunters should head for **Killarney Outlet Centre** (⊠Fair Hill ☎064/36744 ⊕www.killarneyoutletcentre.com) adjacent to the Great Southern Hotel and the Railway Station. The Nike Factory Store and Blarney Woolen Mills are the anchor tenants of this discount shopping center. **MacBee's** (⊠New St. ☎064/33622) is a modern boutique stocking the best of Irish high fashion. **Quills Woolen Market** (⊠Market Cross ☎064/32277) has the town's biggest selection of Irish knitwear. It also carries tweeds, linens, and Celtic jewelry.

CORCA DHUIBNE: THE DINGLE PENINSULA

The brazenly scenic Dingle Peninsula stretches for some 48 km (30 mi) between Tralee (pronounced tra-*lee*) in the east and Ceann Sleibne (Slea Head) in the west. Often referred to by its Irish name, Corca Dhuibne (pronounced *corca-guiney*), the peninsula is made up of rugged mountains, seaside cliffs, and softly molded glacial valleys and lakes. Long sandy beaches and Atlantic-pounded cliffs unravel along the coast. Drystone walls enclose small, irregular fields, and exceptional prehistoric and early Christian remains dot the countryside. As you drive over its mountain passes, looking out past prehistoric remains to the wild Atlantic sea, Dingle can be a magical destination that makes you feel like you're living in an ancient legend. Unfortunately, Dingle is notorious for its heavy rainfall and impenetrable sea mists, which can strike

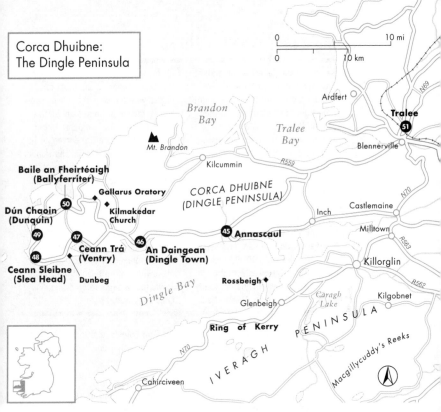

Corca Dhuibne:
The Dingle Peninsula

at any time of year. If they do, sit them out in An Daingean (Dingle Town) and enjoy the friendly bars, cafés, and crafts shops. West of Annascaul, the peninsula is Irish-speaking: English is considered a second language. A good Irish–English map can prove handy.

You can cover the peninsula in a long day trip of about 160 km (99 mi). If mist or continuous rain is forecast, postpone your trip until visibility improves. From Killarney, Killorglin, or Tralee, head for Castlemaine, and take the coast road (R561 and R559) to Dingle Town. You'll pass through the sheltered seaside resort of Inch, 19 km (12 mi) west of Castlemaine and 45 km (28 mi) northwest of Killarney, where the head of Dingle Bay is cut off by two sand spits that enclose Castlemaine Harbour. Inch has a 6½-km (4-mi) beach backed by dunes that are home to a large colony of natterjack toads.

ANNASCAUL

45 *7 km (4½ mi) west of Inch.*

An important livestock center until the 1930s, this village near the junction of the Castlemaine and Tralee roads has a wide road, as cattle trading was once carried out in the streets. The town also has many pubs.

CLOSE UP

Dingle by Any Other Name

Residents of Dingle, especially those involved in the tourist business, are fighting a battle with the government for the right to continue to call their town and their peninsula by the name of Dingle. The problem arises because the western part of Dingle Peninsula—known in Irish as Corca Dhuibne (pronounced *corca-guiney*) and its main town, Dingle (An Daingean in Irish)—is officially an Irish-speaking area, part of the Kerry Gaeltacht. The Official Languages Act 2003 was introduced to strengthen the rights of Ireland's 90,000 Irish speakers to do business with the state in their native tongue—officially Ireland's first language. A side effect of this act was the necessity, under the new law, for all signposts for places where Irish is the official spoken language, to be in Irish. So the name Dingle has disappeared from all signposts by official decree, to be replaced by An Daingean. The traders of Dingle claim that the name of their town is equivalent to an internationally recognized brand name, and are demanding that an exception be made in their case. The compromise suggested by the traders of Dingle, Dingle Daingean Uí Chúis, has yet to be approved by the government. Meanwhile, when heading for Dingle Town, follow signs to An Daingean. Only in Ireland.

Photographers will be tempted to snap **Dan Foley's** (☎ *066/915–7252*) flamboyantly painted pub. Wander in for a pint; the legendary Dan Foley, who was a magician, a farmer, and an expert on local history, is no longer with us, but tales about him are still told in Annascaul.

The South Pole Inn (☎ *066/915–7388*) was built by local hero Tom Crean (1877–1938). Crean enlisted in the English navy at the age of 15, and served on three expeditions to Antarctica—the *Discovery* (1901–04) and the *Terra Nova* (1910–13), both under the command of Captain Robert Falcon Scott, and the *Endurance* (1914–16), where he was second officer to Ernest Shackleton. Crean himself failed to reach the South Pole on any of these expeditions, and named his pub so that in his retirement he could go to work at the South Pole every day. Memorabilia at the pub will fill in the details of Crean's Antarctic adventures. Crean was famed for his amazing strength and resilience. He walked 35 mi through an Antarctic blizzard to bring help to his colleagues, with only two bars of chocolate and three biscuits for sustenance. For this he received the Albert Medal for Bravery. On another occasion he survived a 15-day journey across 800 mi of ocean in an open boat. The pub is the headquarters of the Tom Crean Society, which hosts occasional lectures and festivals and has been addressed by Sir Edmund Hillary and the grandsons of both Scott and Shackleton.

AN DAINGEAN (DINGLE TOWN)

46 *18 km (11 mi) west of Annascaul, 67 km (42 mi) west of Killarney, 45 km (28 mi) west of Killorglin on R561.*

Backed by mountains and facing a sheltered harbor, An Daingean, the chief town of its eponymous peninsula, has a year-round population of 1,400 that more than doubles in summer. Although many expect Dingle (to use its English name) to be a quaint and undeveloped Gaeltacht village, it has many crafts shops, seafood restaurants, and pubs. Still, you can explore its main thoroughfares—the Mall, Main and Strand streets, and the

Wood—in less than an hour. Celebrity hawks, take note: off-season Dingle is favored as a hideaway by the likes of Julia Roberts, Paul Simon, and Dolly Parton. These and others have their visits commemorated on Green Street's "path of stars."

6

An Daingean's pubs are well known for their music, but among them **O'Flaherty's** (⊠ *Bridge St., at entrance to town* ☎ *066/915–1983*), a simple, stone-floor bar, is something special and a hot spot for traditional musicians. Spontaneous sessions occur most nights in July and August, less frequently at other times. Even without music, this pub is a good place to compare notes with fellow travelers.

Since 1985, An Daingean's central attraction, apart from its music scene, has been a winsome bottle-nosed dolphin who has taken up residence in the harbor. The Dingle dolphin, or **Fungie,** as he has been named, will play for hours with swimmers (a wet suit is essential) and scuba divers, and he follows local boats in and out of the harbor. It's impossible to predict whether he will stay, but boatmen have become so confident of a sighting that they offer trippers their money back if Fungie does not appear. Boat trips (€8) leave the pier hourly in July and August between 11 and 6, weather permitting. At other times, call **Brosnan's Wet Suit Hire** (☎ *066/915–1967*), who can arrange a swim with the dolphin.

WHERE TO STAY & EAT

$$$–$$$$ ✕**Fenton's.** Step beyond the yellow door of this town house to find a cozy, cottage-style restaurant with quarry-tile floors, a stone fireplace, and local art (for sale) on the soft-blue walls. Rush-seat ladder-back chairs are drawn up to wood-top candlelighted tables. The bistro-style menu is unfussy, allowing for quick turnovers during Dingle's hectic high season. Some dishes, such as the *moules mariniers* (steamed mussels), are available in starter or main-course portions. Lamb and beef come from the Fenton family farm. Sirloin steak may be served with caramelized onions and a red-wine sauce, or try local black sole on the bone with fresh herb butter. ⊠ *Green St.* ☎ *066/915–2172* ⊟ *AE, DC, MC, V* ☉ *Closed Mon. and mid-Nov.–Easter.*

$$-$$$ ╳ **Chart House.** Host Jim McCarthy is often found in the early evening
★ leaning over the red half-door of the low, cabinlike stone building. The
exterior gives little hint of the spacious, cleverly lighted dining room
within, nor of the beautiful pair of windows at the back that frame
lovely views of Dingle Harbor's trawler fleet. Nautical artifacts, including an antique compass, complement the rusty-red walls and matching tablecloths. Have a drink at the smart little bar while studying the
night's menu. The atmosphere is pleasantly informal, but both food
and service are polished and professional. The signature starter is a
phyllo parcel of Annascaul black pudding with chutney. Move on to
roast cod fillet with a basil mash, or roast guinea fowl, served with
a simple but perfectly judged port-wine jus. Finish the meal with a
selection of Irish cheeses, served with a glass of port, or a homemade
apple and clove tartlet with ginger-nut crumble and a glass of calva-
dos. ⊠ *The Mall* ☎ *066/915–2255* ▤ *MC, V* ⊗ *Closed Jan.–mid-Feb.
Phone to confirm hrs Oct.–May. No lunch.*

$$-$$$ ╳ **Out of the Blue.** Every fishing port should have a simple waterfront
bistro like this one, serving the best seafood (owner Tim Mason won't
open his tiny restaurant if there's no fresh-caught seafood available,
which is almost never). Lobster, scallops, and crayfish are specialties,
but also expect turbot, black sole, plaice, brill, monkfish, and even
the humble pollack on the daily blackboard menu. Breton chef Eric
Maillard puts modern twist on seafood classics, perhaps sole on the
bone with almond cream, or John Dory with a pepper sauce and garlic
eggplant. There's a short but well-chosen wine list, and a basic dessert
selection. ⊠ *Waterside, beside pier* ☎ *066/915–0811* ⌂ *Reservations
essential* ▤ *MC, V* ⊗ *Closed Wed.*

$$$$ ╳▦ **Dingle Skellig.** Rambling and modern as this building may be, its
center is occupied by a beehivelike shape that's intended to echo local
clocháns (prehistoric beehive huts). The octagonal reception area has
wood cladding, contemporary stained-glass doors, and original paintings. Modern, pale-wood furniture and bold fabrics adorn the spacious
rooms, which are in separate wings, most of which have sea views. The
Peninsula Spa features an outdoor hot tub with stunning bay views.
The bar is a busy local meeting place where anything can—and does—
happen. Floor-to-ceiling windows in the Coastguard restaurant look
out over Dingle Bay. As you'd expect, the specialty is seafood. ⊠ *Co.
Kerry* ☎ *066/915–0200* 🖷 *066/915–1501* ⊕ *www.dingleskellig.com*
⤶ *110 rooms* ⌂ *In-hotel: restaurant, bar, pool, gym, spa* ▤ *AE, DC,
MC, V* ⏀ *BP.*

$$$$ ▦ **Emlagh House.** You'll be right on the waters' edge in this spacious,
yellow, mansard-roof family home. Although most accommodations in
An Daingean are cottagelike, the Kavanagh family chose the grander
Georgian style: Emlagh looks like a historic mansion but actually dates
from the late 20th century. The marble-floor lobby, with its exquisite
mahogany side table and large vase of fresh flowers, sets a tone of quiet,
unostentatious luxury. Relax on the goose-down–filled velvet sofas in
front of the drawing room's open fire while sipping a drink from the
honor bar. Bedrooms are large, with sitting areas in the bay windows.

Each one is color-themed to a local wildflower, with plush carpets, Regency-stripe drapes, and Victorian antiques. There are more than 185 pieces of original Irish art in the house from the family's private collection. For rainy days, there's a piano in the drawing room, history books and Internet access in the library, and CD players in the bedrooms. It's a short, water's edge walk into town to sample Dingle's famous seafood. ⊠*An Daingean Harbour, Co. Kerry* ☎*066/915–2345* 🖷*066/915–2369* ⊕*www.emlaghhouse.com* ⟳*10 rooms* ⚒*In-room: dial-up, Wi-Fi (some). In-house: no elevator, public Wi-Fi* ⊟*AE, DC, MC, V* ⊗*Closed Nov.–mid-Mar.* ❑*BP.*

$$ ⬚**Greenmount House.** Wonderful views of the town and harbor await at this modern B&B, a short walk uphill from the town center (turn right at the traffic circle at the entrance to An Daingean and right again when you come to the first T-junction). It looks just like many modern bungalows, but the interior has been cleverly redesigned by a local architect, with bright color schemes enlivening the traditional chintzy look. There are six suites in a connecting wing, each with a sitting room and balcony. Rooms in the original house, though smaller, are impeccable and comfortable, with pine beds and floral fabrics. Mary Curran is known for her baking, so an outstanding breakfast is served in the conservatory, which connects the two buildings. ⊠*Upper John St., Co. Kerry* ☎*066/915–1414* 🖷*066/915–1974* ⊕*www.greenmount-house. com* ⟳*9 rooms* ⚒*In-room: no a/c, dial-up. In-hotel: public Wi-Fi, no elevator* ⊟*MC, V* ⊗*Closed Dec.* ❑*BP.*

$$ ⬚**Pax House.** You can stand on the outdoor terrace of this modern bungalow and watch the boats return with their catch while the sun sets slowly in the west. Rooms are simple but well equipped. Breakfast is a generous affair, with fresh seafood on the menu and a selection of Irish cheeses on the buffet. Pax House is 1 km (½ mi) from the town center. ⊠*Upper John St., Co. Kerry* ☎*066/915–1518* 🖷*066/915–2461* ⊕*www.pax-house.com* ⟳*12 rooms* ⚒*In-room: no a/c. In-hotel: no elevator* ⊟*MC, V* ⊗*Closed Dec.–Feb.* ❑*BP.*

$ ⬚**Alpine House.** The landmark Alpine is neither spanking-new nor old-world. One of An Daingean's original guesthouses—dating from 1963—is a plain, family-run, three-story establishment located in spacious grounds on the edge of town that has many admirers; book well in advance. Pine pieces furnish bright, cheerful, well-equipped rooms. The location, at the entrance to town with views over Dingle Bay, is superb: it's quiet, yet the harbor, pubs, and restaurants are only a two-minute walk away. ⊠*Mail Rd., Co. Kerry* ☎*066/915–1250* 🖷*066/915–1966* ⊕*www.alpineguesthouse.com* ⟳*10 rooms* ⚒*In-room: no a/c. In-hotel: no-smoking rooms, no elevator* ⊟*AE, MC, V* ❑*BP.*

NIGHTLIFE

Nearly every bar on the Corca Dhuibne (Dingle Peninsula), particularly in the town of An Daingean, offers live music nightly in July and August. **O'Flaherty's** (⊠*Bridge St., at entrance to town* ☎*066/915–1983*) is a gathering place for traditional musicians—you can hear impromptu music sessions most nights in July and August. For sing-along and dancing, try **Máire de Barra** (⊠*The Pier Head* ☎*066/912–1215*).

THE OUTDOORS

You're likely to remember a bike ride around Slea Head for a long time. You can rent bicycles at **Dingle Bicycle Hire** (⊠*The Tracks* ☎*066/915–2166*).

SHOPPING

Don't miss An Daingean's café-bookshop, **An Cafe Liteartha** (⊠*Bothar An Dadhgaide* ☎*066/915–2204*), which locals insist is one of the world's first (it has been here since the 1970s). Regardless, you can find friendly conversation as well as new and secondhand books. You can watch **Brian de Staic** (⊠*Green St.* ☎*066/915–1298*) and his team make modern, Celtic-inspired jewelry in his studio, which is also a shop. **Greenlane Gallery** (⊠*Holy Ground* ☎*066/915–2018*) has shows of contemporary Irish art with an emphasis on local landscapes. **Leác a Ré** (⊠*Strand St.* ☎*066/915–1138*) sells handmade Irish crafts. One of Ireland's more unusual culinary success stories is **Murphys Ice Cream** (⊠*Strand St.* ☎*066/915–2644*), which has won international awards. Find out why at this flagship parlor. Lisbeth Mulcahy at the **Weaver's Shop** (⊠*Green St.* ☎*066/915–1688*) sells outstanding handwoven, vegetable-dyed woolen wraps, mufflers, and fabric for making skirts.

CEANN TRÁ (VENTRY)

47 *8 km (5 mi) west of An Daingean (Dingle Town) on R561.*

The next town after An Daingean along the coast, Ceann Trá has a small outcrop of pubs and small grocery stores (useful, since west of Dingle Town you'll find few shops of any kind), and a long sandy beach with safe swimming and ponies for rent. Between Ventry and Dún Chaoin (Dunquin) are several interesting archaeological sites on the spectacular cliff-top road along Ceann Sleibne (Slea Head).

Continuing west along the coast road beyond **Dunbeg,** you can see signs for PREHISTORIC BEEHIVE HUTS, called clocháns (pronounced cluck-*awns*) in Irish. Built of drystone on the southern slopes of Mt. Eagle, these cells were used by hermit monks in the early Christian period; some 414 exist between Ceann Sliebne and Dún Chaoin. Some local farmers, on whose land these monuments stand, charge a "trespass fee" of €1 to €2.

CEANN SLEIBNE (SLEA HEAD)

48 *16 km (10 mi) west of An Daingean (Dingle Town) on R561, 8 km (5 mi) west of Ceann Trá.*

From the top of the towering cliffs of Ceann Sleibne at the southwest extremity of the Dingle Peninsula, the view of the Blasket Islands and the Atlantic Ocean is guaranteed to stop you in your tracks. Alas, Slea Head—to use its English name—has become so popular that tour buses, barely able to negotiate the narrow road, are causing traffic jams, particularly in July and August. Coumenole, the long sandy strand below, looks beautiful and sheltered, but swimming here is dangerous. This treacherous stretch of coast has claimed many lives in shipwrecks—most recently in 1982, when a large cargo boat, the *Ranga,* foundered on the rocks and sank. In 1588 four ships of the Spanish Armada were driven through the Blasket Sound; two made it to shelter, and two sank. One of these, the *Santa Maria de la Rosa,* is being excavated by divers in summer.

The largest of the **An Bhlaskaoid Mhóir (Blasket Islands)** visible from Ceann Sleibne, the Great Blasket was inhabited until 1953. The Blasket islanders were great storytellers and were encouraged by Irish linguists to write their memoirs. *The Islandman,* by Tomás O Crohán, gives a vivid picture of a hard way of life. "Their likes will not be seen again," O Crohán poignantly observed. The Blasket Centre explains the heritage of these islanders and celebrates their use of the Irish language with videos and exhibitions. ⊠ *Dún Chaoin (Dunquin)* ☎ *066/915–6444* ⊕ *www.heritageireland.ie* ⊠ *€3.70* ☉ *Easter–June and Sept. and Oct., daily 10–6; July and Aug., daily 10–7.*

Fodor's Choice ★

DÚN CHAOIN (DUNQUIN)

49 *13 km (8 mi) west of Ceann Trá on R559, 5 km (3 mi) north of Ceann Sleibne (Slea Head).*

Once the mainland harbor for the Blasket islanders, Dún Chaoin is at the center of the Gaeltacht, and attracts many students of Irish language and folklore. David Lean shot *Ryan's Daughter* hereabouts in 1969. The movie gave the area its first major boost in tourism, though it was lambasted by critics—"Gush made respectable by millions of dollars tastefully wasted," lamented Pauline Kael—sending Lean into a dry spell he didn't come out of until 1984's *A Passage to India.*

Kruger's Pub (☎ *066/915–6127*), Dunquin's social center, has long been frequented by artists and writers, including Brendan Behan; it's also the only eatery for miles.

Dún Chaoin's **pier** (signposted from main road) is surrounded by cliffs of colored Silurian rock, more than 400 million years old and rich in fossils. Down at the pier you can see *curraghs* (open fishing boats traditionally made of animal hide stretched over wooden laths and tarred) stored upside down, usually covered in canvas. Three or four men walk the curraghs out to the sea, holding them over their heads. Similar boats are used in the Aran Islands, and when properly handled they're extraordinarily seaworthy.

In good weather **Blasket Island Ferry** (⊠ *Dún Chaoin Pier* ☎ *066/915–4864* ⊕ *www.blasketislands.ie*) vessels bring you from Dún Chaoin Pier to Great Blasket Island, a 20-minute trip. Landing is by transfer to rubber dinghy, and the island is steep and rocky, so you need to be fit and agile. (At the time of this writing, the Irish government is in the process of buying the island for the nation. By 2008 a new pier might be in place on the island. Then again, it might not. Check with Dingle TIO near your travel date.) Still, the unique experience offered by the

The Silence Strikes You at Once

The Great Blasket, which measures roughly 2 mi by a half mile, has no traffic, no pub, no hotel, and no electricity. Yet this island—centerpiece of the An Bhlaskaoid Mhóir (Blasket Islands)—is one of the most memorable places in Ireland to visit.

These days it takes only 20 minutes from Dún Chaoin (Dunquin) Pier to make the 2-mi crossing of the Blasket Sound, but even on a calm day the swell can be considerable. In summer the island is inaccessible on about one day in five; in winter, the island can be cut off for weeks. Until 1954 a small community of hardy fisherfolk and subsistence farmers eked out a living here.

Today, visitors are usually attracted by the literary heritage of the island—the Irish-language writings of Tomás O Criomhthain, Muiris Ó Suilleabhain, and Peig Sayers—but what makes people return is something else: a rare quality of light and an intense peace and quiet in beautiful, unspoiled surroundings.

The inadequacy of the existing piers limits visitors to the island to a maximum of about 400 per day, a figure that is reached only rarely, with the average under 200. Most visitors stay for three or four hours, walking, sketching, or taking photographs.

The silence strikes you at once. The sea birds, stone chats, and swallows sound louder than on the mainland; sheep graze silently on the steep hillside.

The simple domestic ruins are very touching; you do not need to know the history to work out what happened to their owners (most departed for other locales, with many settling in Springfield, Massachusetts).

When the last boat of day-trippers leaves, the foreshore teems with rabbits, and seals bask on the white strand. At the time of this writing, camping is permitted, but it may well be banned in the near future. You can book a bed in the small hostel and self-cater, or eat an evening meal in the island café before sitting outside to watch the stars.

Many visitors, including John Millington Synge, have warned that there's something addictive about the Great Blasket. "I have a jealousy for that Island," he wrote after his 1907 sojourn, "...like the jealousy of men in love."

The **Blasket Island Ferry** (☎ 066/915–4864 or 087/231–6131) makes the 20-minute crossing from Dún Chaoin Pier to the island daily from May to September, weather permitting, costing €20 round-trip. **Peig Sayers ferry** (☎ 066/915–1344) sails from An Daingean (Dingle Town) to the island and takes about 30 minutes, costing €30 for a round-trip ticket.

As for accommodations on the island, the only option is a sporadically open **Hostel** (☎ 066/915–1344). If it's open, a bed will cost you around €20. Before you go, get a copy of Maurice O'Sullivan's *Twenty Years a-Growing*, which gives a fascinating account of a simple way of life that has only recently disappeared on the Blaskets.

deserted village and old cliff paths of the island makes it well worth the effort. The cost of the boat ride is €20 round-trip. Boats run from 10 to 4, weather permitting, between Easter and September.

EN ROUTE

Clogher Strand, a dramatic, windswept stretch of rocks and sand, is not a safe spot to swim, but it's a good place to watch the ocean dramatically pound the rocks when a storm is approaching or a gale is blowing.

Overlooking the beach is **Louis Mulcahy's pottery studio.** One of Ireland's leading ceramic artists, Mulcahy produces large pots and urns that are both decorative and functional. You can watch the work in progress and buy items at workshop prices. ⊠ *Clogher Strand* ☎ *066/915–6229* ☉ *Daily 9:30–6.*

BAILE AN FHEIRTÉAIGH (BALLYFERRITER)

50 *5 km (3 mi) northeast of Dún Chaoin (Dunquin), 14 km (9 mi) west of An Daingean (Dingle Town) on R559.*

Like the other towns at this end of the Dingle Peninsula, Baile an Fheirtéaigh is a Gaeltacht village and mainly a spot for vacationers with RVs, many of them German or Dutch. The area around here is great for walking. A top sight in Ballyferriter itself is one of Ireland's best-preserved early Christian churches, **Gallarus Oratory.** It dates from the 7th or 8th century and ingeniously makes use of corbeling—successive levels of stone projecting inward from both side walls until they meet at the top to form an unmortared roof. The structure is still watertight after more than 1,000 years. ⊠ *8 km (5 mi) northeast of Baile an Fheirtéaigh on R559* ⌨ *€2.50.*

Kilmalkedar Church is one of the finest surviving examples of Romanesque architecture. Although the Christian settlement dates from the 7th century, the present structure was built in the 12th century. Native builders integrated foreign influences with their own traditions, keeping the blank arcades and round-headed windows but using stone roofs, sloping doorway jambs, and weirdly sculpted heads. Ogham stones and other interestingly carved, possibly pre-Christian stones are on display in the churchyard. ⊠ *8 km (5 mi) northeast of Baile an Fheirtéaigh on R559* ⌨ *Free.*

OFF THE BEATEN PATH

Connor Pass. This mountain route, which passes from south to north over the center of the peninsula, offers magnificent views of Brandon Bay, Tralee Bay, and the beaches of North Kerry. The road is narrow, and the drops on the hairpin bends are precipitous. Be sure to nominate a confident driver who isn't scared of heights—such a soul is especially important in misty weather. It was from Brandon Bay that Brendan the Navigator (AD 487–577) is believed to have set off on his voyages in a specially constructed curragh. On his third trip he may have reached Newfoundland or Labrador, then Florida. Brendan was an inspiration to many voyagers, including Christopher Columbus.

6

The summit of Mt. Brandon (3,127 feet) is on the left as you cross the Connor Pass (from south to north). It's accessible only to hikers. Don't attempt the climb in misty weather. The easiest way to make the trek is to follow the old pilgrims' path, Saint's Road; it starts at Kilmalkedar Church and rises to the summit from Ballybrack, which is the end of the road for cars. At the summit you reach the ruins of an early Christian settlement. You can also approach the top from a path that starts just beyond Cloghane (signposted left on descending the Connor Pass); the latter climb is longer and more strenuous.

TRALEE

⑤ *5 km (3 mi) northeast of Blennerville, 50 km (31 mi) northeast of An Daingean (Dingle Town) on R559.*

County Kerry's capital and its largest town, Tralee (population 21,000) has long been associated with the popular Irish song "The Rose of Tralee," the inspiration for the annual Rose of Tralee International Festival. The last week of August, Irish communities worldwide send young women to join native Irish competitors; one of them is chosen as the Rose of Tralee. Visitors, musicians, and entertainers pack the town then. A two-day horse-race meeting—with seven races a day—runs at the same time, which contributes to the crowds. Tralee is also the home of Siamsa Tíre—the National Folk Theatre of Ireland—which stages dances and plays based on Irish folklore.

Kerry County Museum, Tralee's major cultural attraction, traces the history of Kerry's people since 5000 BC, using dioramas and an entertaining audiovisual show. You can also walk through a life-size reconstruction of a Tralee street in the Middle Ages. ⊠ *Ashe Memorial Hall, Denny St.* ☎ *066/712-7777* ⊕ *www.kerrymuseum.ie* 🎟 *€8* ⊗ *Jan.–Mar., Tues.– Fri. 10–4:30; Apr. and May, Tues.–Sat. 9:30–5:30; June–Aug., daily 9:30–5:30; Sept.–Dec., Tues.–Sat. 9:30–5.*

WHERE TO STAY & EAT

$$–$$$ ✕ **Restaurant David Norris.** A modest terrace of modern buildings on the edge of the town park is home to this pleasant first-floor restaurant. You're greeted in a small reception area with sofa and stool, and offered a drink at the small bar while you peruse the owner-chef's menu of the day. Pale wood furniture in a crisp Art Deco style is complemented by a dusky pink-and-cream decor, with linen cloths and fresh flowers on the well-spaced tables. The menu is built around seasonal local produce, and everything is made on the premises, including bread, pasta, and ice cream. Roast fillet of Kerry beef may be served with black pepper mash, fried mushrooms, and caramelized onions and garlic. Seafood is always well represented, and there's always a vegetarian option. For extra value for money, try the "early-bird menu" served until 7:30. ⊠ *Ivy House, Ivy Terr.* ☎ *066/718-5654* ⊟ *AE, MC, V* ⊗ *Closed Sun., Mon., and 1 wk in Nov. and 2 wks in late Jan.–early Feb. No lunch.*

$$–$$$ ✕⊡**Meadowlands.** In a quiet suburb on the road to Listowel, 10 minutes' walk from Tralee's city center, this lively luxury hotel is turreted in the French château style and done up in exuberant, sumptuously stylish decors. Touches of nouvelle country-house style are everywhere, from the grand barrel-vaulted reception area to the two-story bar, which has a balcony library. A light bar menu is offered here, but for the full treatment, repair to the restaurant, a cozy bedazzlement of stonework, timber beams, and stone pillars. The hotel's owner runs a fleet of fishing boats in Dingle, so seafood is a major draw, with seared west coast scallops in a lime-and-butter sauce served with panfried Annascaul black pudding, or a kilo of steamed Atlantic mussels being two top choices. Large and exceptionally comfortable in an unfussy way, with darkwood, Victorian-style furniture and plaster cornices on the ceiling, the guest rooms are decorated in sumptuous hues or tranquil beiges. The hotel is popular with golfers, who generally find the small extra fee for upgrading to an even larger room with two double beds well worth it. A festive, friendly, and stylish place, Meadowlands turns up the charm on weekends, when the bar hosts live music. ⊠*Oakpark, Co. Kerry* ☎*066/718–0444* 🖷*066/718–0694* ⊕*www.meadowlands-hotel.com* 🛏*58 rooms* &*In-hotel: restaurant, bar* ⊟*AE, DC, MC, V* ✵|*BP.*

$$$ ⊡**Abbeygate.** Built on the site of Tralee's old marketplace, in a quiet spot behind the main shopping street, Abbeygate is an attractive modern hotel. Rooms have country-style wood furniture and large, tiled bathrooms. The Old Market Place Pub, a rambling, imaginatively designed bar, seats 500 people and is built in the traditional style, with wooden floors and open fireplaces. There's bar food at lunch and music and dancing nightly from June to September and at least three nights a week at other times. ⊠*Maine St., Co. Kerry* ☎*066/712–9888* 🖷*066/712–9821* ⊕*www.abbeygate-hotel.com* 🛏*100 rooms* &*In-room: no a/c. In-hotel: restaurant, bars, Wi-Fi* ⊟*AE, DC, MC, V* ✵|*BP.*

NIGHTLIFE & THE ARTS

Ballad sessions are more popular here than traditional Irish music. **Horan's Hotel** (⊠*Clash St.* ☎*066/712–1933*) has dance music and cabaret acts nightly during July and August and on weekends only during the off-season. Try to catch the **National Folk Theater of Ireland** *(Siamsa Tíre)* (⊠*Godfrey Pl.* ☎*066/712–3055* ☉*Shows July and Aug., Mon.–Sat. at 8:30* PM*; May, June, and Sept., Tues. and Thurs. at 8:30* PM). Language is no barrier to this colorful entertainment, which re-creates traditional rural life through music, mime, and dance.

SPORTS & THE OUTDOORS

BICYCLING You can rent bicycles from **Tralee Bicycle Supplies** (⊠*Strand St.* ☎*066/712–2018*).

GOLF Tralee is the heart of great golfing country. The **Ballybunion Golf Club** (*Old Course* ⊠*Ballybunion* ☎*068/27146*) is universally regarded as one of golf's holiest grounds. The **Tralee Golf Club** (⊠ *West Barrow, Ardfert* ☎*066/713–6379*) is a seaside links, designed by Arnold Palmer, with cliffs, craters, and dunes.

NORTH KERRY & SHANNONSIDE

Until several decades ago, Shannon meant little more to most people—if it meant anything at all—than the name of the longest river in Ireland and Great Britain, running for 273 km (170 mi) from County Cavan to Limerick City in County Clare. But mention Shannon nowadays and people think immediately of the airport, which has become western Ireland's principal gateway. In turn, what also comes to mind are many of the glorious sights of North Kerry and Shannonside: a slew of castles, including Bunratty, Glin, and Knappogue; Adare, sometimes called "Ireland's Prettiest Village," and the neighboring Adare Manor, a grand country-house hotel; and Limerick City, which attracts visitors tracing the memories so movingly captured in Frank McCourt's international best-seller *Angela's Ashes*. You could begin a tour of the area in Listowel, in northwest County Kerry, and then jump across the Kerry–Limerick border to Glin, on the south side of the Shannon River estuary. Limerick City and those parts of County Clare on the north side of the Shannon round out the tour.

LISTOWEL

52 *27 km (16 mi) northeast of Tralee on N69.*

The small, sleepy market town of Listowel comes alive for its annual horse-racing festival during the third week of September. Writers' Week in June attracts international names for a more restrained but still festive event. You reach the town from the west by driving along a plain at the base of Stack's Mountain.

WHERE TO STAY & EAT

$ ✕⬚ **Allo's Bar and Bistro.** Just off Listowel's main square, this cheerful, welcoming bar, which dates from 1859, serves the best local foods. Chef Armel Whyte and his partner, Helen Mullane, are known for their lively combinations of traditional and contemporary Irish cooking ($–$$$). The spacious bedrooms are furnished with Baroque-style mirrors, designer lamp shades, cherubs, and oil paintings, and have four-poster beds and large, Connemara-marble bathrooms. If you like Irish whiskey, Armel will be pleased to introduce you to his collection; be warned, one vintage malt costs €60 a shot. ⊠*41 Church St.* 🕾🕾*068/22880* ⏎*3 rooms* ⎔*In-room: no a/c. In-hotel: restaurant, bar, no elevator* ⊟*AE, MC, V* ⊙*Bar and bistro closed Sun. and Mon.*

GLIN

53 *6½ km (4 mi) east of Tarbert on N69, 51 km (32 mi) north of Tralee*
Fodor'sChoice *on N69.*
★
If you're into Irish decorative arts of the 17th and 18th centuries, you'll want to make a beeline for **Glin Castle**, a fantastical neo-Gothic crenellated structure, set on the banks of the Shannon, which has been home to the FitzGerald family for centuries. The rich, red dining room is set with baronial Jacobean-style furniture, the Morning Room is lined

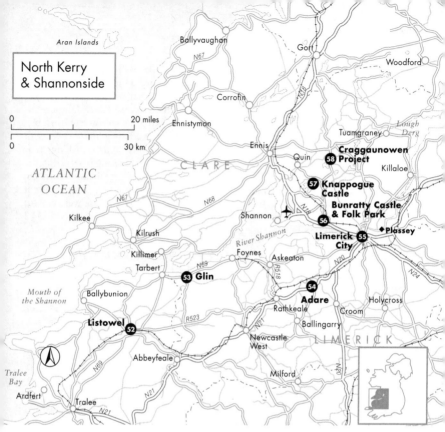

ATLANTIC
OCEAN

*Mouth of
the Shannon*

*Tralee
Bay*

with family curios, and the main Hall is set with Corinthian columns
and a dazzling Dublin-style Georgian plaster ceiling. Everywhere you
look are exceptional antiques, most with the vibrant, virile Irish touch.
It wasn't always so. The family has seen more than its fair share of
decapitations, bankruptcies, and other hair-raising tales (one knight
was tied to a cannon by Cromwell's forces and threatened with being
blown apart; another was drawn and quartered during the Middle
Ages). The family was, in fact, of English origin but became "more
Irish than Irish" by marrying into the Gaelic chieftainry families. Their
latest house was built in 1785, then largely expanded between 1820
and 1836 into a full-fledged Irish Gothic mansion by the 25th knight,
who added castellations and pepper-pot towers, which look like gigantic chess pieces. Inside, many marvel at the splendid "flying" staircase,
the full-length family portraits, the equine paintings of Lady Rachel
FitzGerald, and the famous mahogany furniture. Outside, clipped yews,
walled gardens, an "antique" temple, and a neo-Gothic henhouse cast
their own spell. ☎068/34173 ⊕*www.glincastle.com* ✉€8 ☉*May
and June, daily 10–noon and 2–4; other times by appointment.*

WHERE TO STAY & EAT

$$$$ ✕🏨 **Glin Castle.** Experience top-of-the-scale Irish castle living at the knight of Glin's imposing ancestral home, which has been in the FitzGerald family for 700 years (for information on its history, see our sight write-up). The palatial rooms showcase Glin's famous collection of 18th-century Irish furniture, and are superbly comfortable. The guest rooms are magnificent exercises in country-house style, with four-poster beds, vintage china–adorned walls, and furnishings that are the height of historic Irish chic. Traditional cuisine is served in the red dining room ($$$$), beneath portraits of FitzGerald ancestors. On the menu you'll find locally raised meat and poultry, freshly caught fish, and produce from the walled garden. Nonguests are welcome for dinner but must reserve in advance. ✉ *Co. Limerick* ☎ *068/34112* 📠 *068/34364* 🌐 *www.glincastle.com* *15 rooms* *In-room: no a/c. In-hotel: restaurant, tennis court, no elevator, no kids under 10, some pets allowed* 💳 *AE, DC, MC, V* ⏲ *Closed Dec.–Feb.* 🍴 *BP.*

ADARE

54 Fodor's Choice ★ *19 km (12 mi) southwest of Limerick City on N21, 82 km (51 mi) northeast of Tralee on N21, 40 km (25 mi) east of Glin.*

A once-upon-a-timefied spot with several thatched cottages amid wooded surroundings on the banks of the River Maigue, Adare is famed as one of Ireland's prettiest villages. Perhaps it's more correct to say it's actually one of England's: the place was given a beauty makeover by a rich Anglo lord, the third earl of Dunraven, in the 1820s and 1830s, in an effort to create the "perfect rustic village." Few local feathers were ruffled since he won goodwill by restoring many villagers' houses. Playing into the mid-19th century vogue for romantic rusticity, the earl "picturesquely" restored many of the town's historic sights, including the remains of two 13th-century abbeys, a 15th-century friary, and the keep of the 13th-century **Desmond Castle** (now the centerpiece of a private golf course). Adjacent to the Adare Heritage Centre you'll find the **Trinitarian Priory,** founded in 1230 and now a convent. From the main bridge (where you can best view the castle), head to the **Augustinian Priory** and its gracious cloister. The most fetching time-burnished allure is provided by Adare's stone-built, thatched-roof cottages, often adorned with colorful, flower-filled window boxes and built for the earl's estate tenants. Some now house boutiques selling Irish crafts and antiques, along with a fine restaurant called The Wild Geese. Adare Manor, an imposing Tudor–Gothic Revival mansion, which was once the grand house of the Dunraven peerage, is now a celebrated hotel; on its grounds you can view two 12th-century ruins, the **St. Nicholas Chapel** and the **Chantry Chapel.**

Adare Heritage Centre has an exhibition of the town's history since 1223, with a 15-minute audiovisual display. There are also a restaurant and three retail outlets: one sells sweaters, another crafts, and the third heraldry items. Guided walking tours of the village (€5) are offered from July to September. ✉ *Main St.* ☎ *061/396–666* 🌐 *www.adarevillage.*

com ⊠*Heritage center free, exhibition €5* ⊙*Daily 9–6. Historical exhibition: Mar.–June, daily 9–5; July–Sept., daily 9–5:30; Oct.–Dec., weekdays 9–5, weekends 9:30–5:30; Jan. and Feb., weekdays 10–4, weekends 10–5.*

WHERE TO STAY & EAT

$$$$ ✕ **The Wild Geese.** There's a charming, old-world atmosphere in the
★ series of small dining rooms in this low-ceiling thatched cottage, one of the prettiest in a village famed for its fairy-tale looks. Co-owner and chef David Foley uses the best local produce to create imaginative and seriously good dishes. Try roast rack of lamb with tempura vegetables or roast breast of duck with an onion tartlet and mushroom-flavor rice. Lobster—grilled with snow peas and shallots and topped with a chive mayonnaise—is a popular summer option. The house dessert platter for two lets you sample all desserts, including the fantastic homemade ice cream. The restaurant is opposite the Dunraven Arms. ⊠*Rose Cottage* ☎*061/396–451* ⊟*AE, DC, MC, V* ⊙*Closed Mon. May–Sept.; Sun. and Mon. Oct.–Apr., and 3 wks in Jan.*

$$$$ ✕⊞ **Dunraven Arms.** Adare's landmark coach-stop inn, established in 1792, makes a popular first port of call if you're arriving at Shannon Airport, 40 km (25 mi) northwest—Charles Lindbergh, in fact, stayed in Room 6 while he advised on the airport's design. He might still cotton to the tranquil, antiques-adorned place, even though it is somewhat over-restored and generic. Paintings and prints of horseback riders decorate the pale-yellow walls of the cozy bar and lounges; the county hunt still meets here regularly, continuing a centuries-old tradition. The comfortable bedrooms (and there are lots of them) are tastefully furnished with antiques, and have large, luxurious bathrooms. Junior suites in the newer wing have antique four-poster beds. The elegant Maigue restaurant ($$$–$$$$) specializes in modern Irish cuisine; in winter local game, including pheasant, is a popular option. You can dine informally in the bright, airy bar overlooking the rose garden. Service is impeccable, yet the staff also manages to find time to have a friendly chat, knowing the difference this can make. ⊠*Main St., Co. Limerick* ☎*061/396–633* 🖷*061/396–541* ⊕*www.dunravenhotel.com* ➹*76 rooms, 20 suites* ⚹*In-room: no a/c, dial-up. In-hotel: restaurant, bar, pool, gym, public Wi-Fi, no elevator* ⊟*AE, DC, MC, V* ⌾*BP.*

$$ ✕⊞ **Fitzgeralds Woodlands House Hotel and Spa.** In the energetic, capable hands of the Fitzgerald family, what was once a small B&B has evolved into a thriving modern hotel. It's on 44 acres of landscaped grounds at the Limerick side of the village. Rooms are spacious, individually decorated in various modern styles, and well maintained. Expect to see locals in Timmy Mac's bar. The Brennan Room ($$) serves a traditional Irish set menu: lamb, pork, and beef. More adventurous cooking takes place in the bistro-style restaurant in Timmy Mac's ($), which serves locally grown organic food. ⊠*Knockanes, Co. Limerick* ☎*061/605–100* 🖷*061/396–073* ⊕*www.woodlands-hotel.ie* ➹*84 rooms, 8 suites* ⚹*In-room: no a/c, dial-up. In-hotel: 2 restaurants, bar, pool, gym, spa, no elevator, public Wi-Fi* ⊟*AE, DC, MC, V* ⌾*BP.*

$$ ✕⚏ **Mustard Seed at Echo Lodge.** Dan Mullane's spacious Victorian country-house hotel and restaurant ($$$$) has flamboyantly decorated, themed guest rooms—black-and-white, carnival, Chinese, and so on—and commands a view over the countryside. Chef Tony Schwartz uses only the best local produce, plus herbs and vegetables from his organic garden. Shark is an unusual seafood option in summer; more typical is the honey-glazed lamb shank with a cassoulet of beans and homegrown baby vegetables. His basil-flavored potato cakes are renowned. Fruits from the garden are used in such desserts as hot, crunchy apple-and-black-currant crumble with calvados, cream, and caramel sauce. The hotel is 13 km (8 mi) southwest of Adare in Ballingarry. ⊠*Ballingarry, Co. Limerick* ☎*069/68508* ⎙*069/68511* ⊕*www.mustardseed.ie* ⇋*14 rooms, 3 suites* ⚘*In-room: no a/c. In-hotel: restaurant, bar, no elevator* ⊟*AE, MC, V* ☉*Closed 2 wks in Feb.* �📋*BP.*

$$$$ ⚏ **Adare Manor.** Play king or queen for a day at this spectacular (and, interestingly, American-owned) Victorian Gothic mansion, once the abode of the earls of Dunraven. The castellated mansion is enormous and set amid French-style gardens. Inside is a wonderland of vast stone arches and heavy wood carvings. Center stage is taken by the decorated ceiling in the baronial central hall and the 36-foot-high, 100-foot-long Minstrels' Gallery, wainscoted in oak. As for decor, a period air is retained but several of the color schemes are as bright as today and, thus, much of the time-burnished ambience is lost. The eight "staterooms" in the original house are the most sumptuous, with huge marble bathrooms and stone-mullioned windows. Most rooms have super-king-size beds; all have heavy drapes and carpets and overlook the 840 acres of grounds. Adare's golf course, designed by Robert Trent Jones Sr., is one of Ireland's best. (Note that breakfast is a hefty €23 extra here; plan accordingly.) ⊠*Co. Limerick* ☎*061/396–566* ⎙*061/396–124* ⊕*www.adaremanor.ie* ⇋*63 rooms* ⚘*In-room: no a/c, In-hotel: restaurant, bars, golf course, pool, public Wi-Fi* ⊟*AE, DC, MC, V.*

SPORTS

GOLF   **Adare Manor Golf Course** (☎*061/396–204*) is an 18-hole parkland course.

SHOPPING

Adare Gallery (⊠*Main St.* ☎*061/396–898*) sells Irish-made jewelry, porcelain, and woodwork, as well as original paintings. **Carol's Antiques** (⊠*Main St.* ☎*061/396–977*) has antique furniture, silver, china, and art objects from one of Adare's tiny cottages. At **George Stacpoole** (⊠*Main St.* ☎*061/396–409*) you can find antiques and books.

LIMERICK CITY

❺❺ *19 km (12 mi) northeast of Adare, 198 km (123 mi) southwest of Dublin.*

Before you ask, there's *no* direct connection between Limerick City and the facetious five-line verse form known as a limerick, which was first popularized by the English writer Edward Lear in his 1846 *Book of Nonsense.* The city, at the head of the Shannon estuary and at the intersection of a number of major crossroads, is an industrial port and the republic's third-largest city (population 75,000). If you fly into or out of Shannon Airport, and have a few hours to spare, do take a look around. The area around the cathedral and the castle is dominated by mid-18th-century buildings with fine Georgian proportions. What's more, the city has undergone considerable revitalization since the days recounted in Frank McCourt's childhood memoir, *Angela's Ashes.* Limerick is trying hard to counter a reputation for gang warfare, confined primarily to its less privileged outer suburbs. You need have no fear of violence in the city center: it still has the aura of a ghost town once the workers have gone home at the end of the day, in spite of the large sums of money spent recently on revitalizing Limerick's quays. It doesn't help that the things for which Limerick is famous—rugby football, lace, and (Catholic) religious devotion—are all so uncool.

In the Old Customs House on the banks of the Shannon in the city center, the **Hunt Museum** has the finest collection of Celtic and medieval treasures outside the National Museum in Dublin. Ancient Irish metalwork, European objets d'art, and a selection of 20th-century European and Irish paintings—including works by Jack B. Yeats—are on view. A café overlooks the river. ⊠ *Rutland St.* ☎ *061/312–833* ⊕ *www.huntmuseum.com* ☞ €7.50 ⊗ *Mon.–Sat. 10–5, Sun. 2–5.*

Limerick is a predominantly Catholic city, but the Protestant **St. Mary's Cathedral** is the city's oldest religious building. Once a 12th-century palace—pilasters and a rounded Romanesque entrance were part of the original structure—it dates mostly from the 15th century (the black-oak carvings on misericords in the choir stalls are from this period). ⊠ *Bridge St.* ☎ *061/416–238* ⊗ *Daily 9–5.*

☼ First built by the Normans in the early 1200s, **King John's Castle** still bears traces on its north side of a 1691 bombardment. If you climb the drum towers (the oldest section), you'll have a good view of the town and the Shannon. Inside, a 22-minute audiovisual show illustrates the history of Limerick and Ireland; an archaeology center has three excavated, pre-Norman houses; and two exhibition centers display scale models of Limerick from its founding in AD 922. ⊠ *Castle St.* ☎ *061/411–201* ☞ €8.35 ⊗ *Daily 9:30–5.*

☼ The **Georgian House and Garden** will show you how people lived in Limerick's 18th-century heyday. A tall, narrow row house has been meticulously restored and filled with furnishings from the period, and the garden has been planted in a manner true to the time. The coach house at the rear of the house gives on to a Limerick lane and contains displays relating to the filming of *Angela's Ashes,* including a life-size reconstruction of the McCourt family home. ⊠ *Tontine Buildings, 2 Pery Sq.* ☎ *061/314–130* ⊕ *www.limerickcivictrust.ie/georgian* ☞ €6 ⊗ *Weekdays 10–4, weekends by appointment.*

On **O'Connell Street** you can find the main shopping area, which mainly consists of modest chain stores. However, the street lies one block inland

Guardian of the Shannon

Limerick was founded by Vikings who sailed up the Shannon in the year 922 and established a colony on an island in the estuary between the Rivers Shannon and Abbey, now known as King's Island. In 1194, after the death of Dónal Mór O'Brien, King of Munster, the Normans appropriated Limerick, and Richard I granted its charter in 1197. The great castle of King John and the cathedral of St. Mary's, both on King's Island, date from this period. Later a wall was built around this city, known as Englishtown, to divide it from Irishtown across the Abbey River. In the 18th-century the walls came down, the slums of Irishtown were cleared, and in its place stand the elegant Georgian buildings of Limerick's old town center.

Because of its strategic position at the crossing of the Shannon, the river that divides the old Irish province of Munster from the province of Connaught in the west, the taking of Limerick was a key feature in the wars of the 16th and 17th centuries. In 1691, after the Battle of the Boyne, the Irish retreated to the walled city, where they were besieged by William of Orange, who made three unsuccessful attempts to storm the city but then raised the siege and marched away. A year later, another of William's armies overtook Limerick for two months, and the Irish opened negotiations. The resulting Treaty of Limerick—which guaranteed religious tolerance—was never ratified, and 11,000 men of the Limerick garrison joined the French Army rather than fight in a Protestant "Irish" army. The stone on which the Treaty was signed can still be seen on Thomond Bridge.

from (east of) the Arthur's Quay Shopping Centre, a mall, which, along with the futuristic tourist information center, is one of the first fruits of a civic campaign to develop the Shannonside quays.

Cruises Street, an inviting pedestrian thoroughfare, has chic shops and occasional street entertainers. It's on the opposite side of O'Connell Street from the Arthur's Quay Shopping Centre.

Plassey, 5–10 minutes from Limerick on the ring road (signposted Dublin N7), is the setting for the University of Limerick, which has a small, but very attractive, campus notable for its rolling lawns and several striking architectural features.

WHERE TO STAY & EAT

$$$ ✕ **Brulées Restaurant.** The dining rooms in this redbrick Georgian town house, on a corner one block from the River Shannon, are elegantly furnished in a simple, classical style. Chef and co-owner Teresa Murphy uses only the finest local ingredients, and gives a contemporary touch to Irish fare. Try the beef fillet with black-pudding mash or the grilled liver and bacon with grain mustard and mushroom cream. And, yes, the menu does include a classic crème brûlée among the tempting desserts, served with a crunchy brandy snap. ⊠ *8 Lower Mallow St.* ☎ *061/319–931* ⊟ *AE, DC, MC, V* ⊘ *Closed Sun. No lunch Mon. and Sat.*

$$-$$$ ✕**Freddy's Bistro.** On a quiet lane between busy O'Connell and Henry streets, this informal two-story restaurant fills a charming 18th-century coach house. Old brick walls are complemented by a warm color scheme that glows in candlelight. Steak with brandy, bacon, and mushroom sauce, and monkfish with basil-and-lemon pesto are popular main courses. For dessert try the hot, sticky toffee pudding. ⊠*Theatre La., off Lower Glentworth St.* ☎*061/418–749* ▭*MC, V* ⊘*Closed Sun. and Mon. No lunch.*

$–$$ ✕**Green Onion Café.** The Irish-French chef team of Marie Munnelly and Geoff Gloux produces a witty, stylish menu at this hip eatery across from the Hunt Museum. The large room, which used to comprise the town hall, is split into two levels, which are, in turn, divided into intimate spaces through a judicious use of booths. Typical dishes include smoked Irish cheese (Gubbeen) and spinach tartlet, pork fillet coated in pistachio nuts with herb butter, jerk chicken with jalapeño salsa, and salmon with basil beurre blanc. For dessert, try the prune-and-toffee pudding with roasted nutty butterscotch. ⊠*Old Town Hall Bldg., Rutland St.* ☎*061/400–710* ▭*AE, DC, MC, V* ⊘*Closed Sun. and Mon.*

¢–$ ✕**Mortell's.** For fish-and-chips, this is *the* place. It's a simple café, but it serves only the freshest local seafood. You can also get full Irish breakfasts and baked goods. Mortell's has been in the family for more than 40 years, and everything, from the doughnuts to the brown bread to the mayo, is made on the premises. It's in the main shopping area. ⊠*49 Roches St.* ☎*061/415–457* ▭*AE, DC, MC, V* ⊘*Closed Sun. No dinner.*

$$$$ ✕🏨**Castletroy Park.** This large, redbrick-and-stone hotel, which grandly crowns a hill on the outskirts of town, is close to the university campus, and has splendid views of the Clate hills. The lobby, with its polished woods and Asian rugs, leads to a conservatory-cum-coffee shop overlooking an Italian-style courtyard. Guest rooms, scented with potpourri, have solid wood furniture, muted floral drapes and spreads, and rag-rolled walls. The fitness center is one of the best in the region. You can mix with the locals in the Merry Pedlar Pub and Bistro ($) or enjoy a formal meal in MacLaughlin's restaurant ($$–$$$). ⊠*Dublin Rd., Co. Limerick* ☎*061/335–566* 🖷*061/331–117* ⊕*www.castletroy-park.ie* ➠*101 rooms, 6 suites* ⚒*In-room: dial-up. In-hotel: 2 restaurants, bar, pool, gym, public Wi-Fi* ▭*AE, DC, MC, V* ⫶◯⫶*BP.*

$$$$ ✕🏨**Clarion Hotel.** Limerick's tallest building, this dramatic, 17-story, boat-shape structure towers over the rest of the city, and is the focal point of Limerick's dock redevelopment. The interior is a bold statement in modern design—from the cutlery to the carpets—with simple geometric lines and earthy color schemes. Rooms are spacious and restful with bold color schemes and white Egyptian-cotton comforters, large windows, and views of the twinkling cityscape upriver or the wide estuary downriver. The Kudos bar ($) offers Thai food, and the boldly minimalist, waterside Sinergie ($–$$) restaurant serves imaginative Continental cuisine. ⊠*Steamboat Quay, Co. Limerick* ☎*061/444–100* 🖷*061/444–101* ⊕*www.clarionhotellimerick.com* ➠*158 rooms*

⛵ *In-room: dial-up. In-hotel: restaurant, bar, pool, gym, public Wi-Fi* ▤*AE, DC, MC, V* ⦿|*BP.*

$ 🖵**Jurys Inn.** Clean, airy, and in good shape (unlike some of Limerick's other inner-city lodgings), this big, well-run hotel is part of the Jurys budget chain. Rooms are good sized and have light-wood furnishings. The hotel overlooks an urban stretch of the Shannon being converted from industrial to leisure use and is a short step from the main shopping and business district. ⊠*Lower Mallow St., Mount Kennett Pl., Co. Limerick* ☎*061/207–000* 🖷*061/400–966* ⊕*www.jurysdoyle. com* ⇴*151 rooms* ⛵*In-room: no a/c, dial-up. In-hotel: restaurant, bar, public Wi-Fi* ▤*AE, DC, MC, V* ⦿|*BP.*

$ 🖵**Sarsfield Bridge Hotel.** This modern budget accommodation has a great location beside the Sarsfield Bridge, midway between old Limerick and the shopping area. The popular, ground-floor Pier One bar-restaurant has leather sofas overlooking the river. Rooms above are built in a square around an enclosed courtyard; those on the inside have no views but are truly quiet. Red-velvet armchairs are the only touches of luxury in otherwise plain, small rooms, but overall, the hotel offers good value. ⊠*Sarsfield Bridge, Co. Limerick* ☎*061/317–179* 🖷*061/317–182* ⊕*www.tsbh.ie* ⇴*55 rooms* ⛵*In-room: no a/c. In-hotel: restaurant* ▤*AE, MC, V* ⦿|*BP.*

NIGHTLIFE & THE ARTS

ART GALLERIES The **Belltable Arts Center** (⊠*69 O'Connell St.* ☎*061/319–866*) has exhibition space and a small auditorium for touring productions. The **Limerick City Gallery** (⊠*Pery Sq.* ☎*061/310–633*) owns a small permanent collection of Irish art and mounts exhibits of contemporary art.

PUBS, **Dolan's Pub** (⊠*3–4 Dock Rd.* ☎*061/314–483*) is a lively waterfront CABARET & spot with traditional Irish music every night, and dancing classes from DISCOS September to May. Dolan's Warehouse, under the same management and in the same location, is a live-music venue with top national and international acts. **Hogan's** (⊠*20–24 Old Clare St.* ☎*061/411–279*) has a traditional music session every Monday, Wednesday, and Saturday. The riverside **Locke's Bar** (⊠*3 George's Quay* ☎*061/413–733*) is one of Limerick's oldest bars, dating from 1724, and has Irish music Sunday, Monday, and Tuesday nights. It's also a great place for outdoor drinking in summer. There's traditional music at **Nancy Blake's Pub** (⊠*19 Denmark St.* ☎*061/416–443*) year-round Sunday–Wednesday from 9 PM. **William G. South's Pub** (⊠*The Crescent* ☎*061/318–850*) is an old-fashioned pub that's typical of the age of Frank McCourt's *Angela's Ashes*. There's no music, but do drop by for lunchtime bar food (Mon.–Sat. 12:30–3) or a drink.

SHOPPING

DEPARTMENT Limerick has a branch of **Brown Thomas** (⊠*O'Connell St.* ☎*061/417–* STORES *222*), Ireland's upscale department store. **Debenham's** (⊠*O'Connell St.* ☎*061/415–622*) is a large, mid-range department store. **Dunnes Stores** (⊠*130 Sarsfield St.* ☎*061/412–666*) is, perhaps, Ireland's favorite department store chain. **Penneys** (⊠*137 O'Connell St.* ☎*061/227–244*) sells inexpensive clothing; it's a great place for low-price rain gear.

MALLS The shops in **Arthur's Quay Shopping Centre** (⊠*Arthur's Quay* ☎*061/419–888*) mainly sell clothing and accessories. The **Crescent Shopping Center** (⊠*Dooradoyle* ☎*061/228–560*), Limerick's biggest, swankiest mall, with branches of most High Street fashion chains, is a five-minute bus or car ride from the city center.

SPECIALTY The **Celtic Bookshop** (⊠*2 Rutland St.* ☎*061/401–155*) specializes in
SHOPS books of Irish interest. **Davern & Bell** (⊠*22 Thomas St.* ☎*061/481–967*) is a gallery of contemporary Irish crafts, mainly ceramics. **Deoidín** (⊠*6 Sarsfield St.* ☎*061/318–011*) has an interesting selection of crafts, jewelry, and gifts. **Lane Antiques** (⊠*45 Catherine St.* ☎*061/339–307*) sells collectibles, antiquarian books, prints, and paintings.

BUNRATTY CASTLE & FOLK PARK

56 🕐 *18 km (10 mi) west of Limerick City on N18 road to Shannon Airport.*
★

Bunratty Castle and Folk Park are two of those rare attractions that appeal to all ages and manage to be both educational and fun. Built in 1460, the castle—a stolid, massive affair with four square keep towers—has been fully restored and decorated with 15th- to 17th-century furniture and furnishings. It gives wonderful insight into the life of those times. As you pass under the walls of Bunratty, look for the three "murder holes" that allowed defenders to pour boiling oil on attackers below.

The castle is the site of medieval banquets, which are held nightly at 5:45 and 8:45; the cost is €51.95. You're welcomed by Irish colleens in 15th-century dress, who bear the traditional bread of friendship. Then you're led off to a reception, where you'll quaff mead made from fermented honey, apple juice, clover, and heather. Before sitting down at long tables in the candlelighted great hall, you can don a bib. You'll need it, because you eat the four-course meal medieval-style—with your fingers. Serving "wenches" take time out to sing a few ballads or pluck harp strings. The banquets may not be authentic, but they're fun; they're also popular, so book as far in advance as possible.

On the castle grounds the quaint Bunratty Folk Park re-creates a 19th-century village street and has examples of traditional rural housing. Exhibits include a working blacksmith's forge; demonstrations of flour milling, bread making, candle making, thatching, and other skills; and a variety of farm animals. An adjacent museum of agricultural machinery can't compete with the furry and feathered live exhibits. If you can't get a reservation for the medieval banquet at the castle, a *ceilí* (known as the Traditional Irish Night; held nightly May to September at 5:45 and 9 for €43.25) at the folk park is the next best thing. The program features traditional Irish dance and song and a meal of Irish stew, soda bread, and apple pie. No visit to Bunratty is complete without a drink in **Durty Nelly's** (☎*061/364–072*), an old-world (but touristy) pub beside the folk park entrance. Its fanciful decor has inspired imitations around the world. ☎*061/361–511* ⊕*www.shannonheritage.com* 🎟️*€14* 🕐*Sept.–May, daily 9:30–5:30, last entry 4:15; June–Aug., daily 9:30–7, last entry 6.*

6

KNAPPOGUE CASTLE

57 *21 km (13 mi) north of Bunratty.*

With a name that means "hill of the kiss," Knappogue is one of Ireland's most beautiful medieval tower-house castles. A 15th-century MacNamara stronghold, Knappogue Castle was renovated in the Victorian era and fitted with storybook details. Restored by a wealthy American family, the castle has now been retro-ed in 15th-century style. By day you can enjoy a castle tour, including the walled garden, which looks like something out of a medieval Book of Hours. In the evenings it hosts fun and fabulous "medieval-style" banquets (€49.95). You're first greeted at the main door by the Ladies of the castle who escort you to the Dalcassian Hall, where you enjoy a goblet of mead (honey wine), listen to Harp and Fiddle, then proceed to the banqueting hall for a four-course meal, great Irish choral music, and a theatrical set-piece in which the Butler and the Earl argue the virtues of Gallantry. As an added allure, the castle looks spectacular when floodlit. Who can resist? ⊠ *5 km (3 mi) southeast of Quin on R649* ☎ *061/368–103* ⊕ *www.shannonheritage.com* ⊠ *€7* ⊘ *May–Sept., daily 9:30–4:30.*

CRAGGAUNOWEN PROJECT

58 *6 km (4 mi) northeast of Knappogue Castle.*

It's a strange experience to walk across the little wooden bridge above reeds rippling in the lake into Ireland's Celtic past as a jumbo jet passes overhead on its way into Shannon Airport—1,500 years of history compressed into an instant. But if you love all things Celtic, you'll have to visit the **Craggaunowen Project.** The romantic centerpiece is Craggaunowen Castle, a 16th-century tower house restored with furnishings from the period. Huddling beneath its battlements are two replicas of early-Celtic-style dwellings. On an island in the lake, reached by a narrow footbridge, is a clay-and-wattle *crannóg,* a fortified lake dwelling; it resembles what might have been built in the 6th or 7th century, when Celtic influence still predominated in Ireland. The reconstruction of a small ring fort shows how an ordinary soldier would have lived in the 5th or 6th century, at the time Christianity was being established here. Characters from the past explain their Iron Age (500 BC–AD 450) lifestyle; show you around their small holding, stocked with animals; and demonstrate crafts skills from bygone ages. ⊠ *Signposted off road to Sixmilebridge about 10 km (6 mi) east of Quin, Kilmurry, Sixmilebridge* ☎ *061/360–788* ⊕ *www.shannonheritage.com* ⊠ *€8.50* ⊘ *May–Oct., daily 10–6.*

THE SOUTHWEST ESSENTIALS

TRANSPORTATION

BY AIR

The southwest has two international airports: Cork (ORK) on the southwest coast, and Shannon (SNN) in the west. Cork Airport, 5 km (3 mi) south of Cork City on the Kinsale road, has direct flights daily to Dublin, London (Heathrow, Gatwick and Stansted), Manchester, East Midlands, Paris, and Brussels, and direct flights to many other European cities.

Shannon Airport, 26 km (16 mi) west of Limerick City, is the point of arrival for many transatlantic flights, including direct flights from Atlanta, Chicago, Philadelphia, Toronto (summer only), and New York City (from both JFK and Newark); it also has regular flights from the United Kingdom and many European cities. Kerry County Airport (KIR) at Farranfore, 16 km (10 mi) from Killarney, has daily flights from London (Stansted), Liverpool, and Frankfurt (Hahn) operated by Ryanair, and a regular service to Dublin and Manchester operated by Aer Arran.

Airport Information Cork Airport (☎ *021/431–3131* ⊕ *www.corkairport.com*). **Kerry County Airport** (☎ *066/976–4644* ⊕ *www.kerryairport.ie*). **Shannon Airport** (☎ *061/471–444* ⊕ *www.shannonairport.com*).

TRANSFERS Bus service runs between Cork Airport and the Cork City Bus Terminal every 30 minutes, on the hour and the half hour. The ride takes about 10 minutes and costs about €3. Bus Éireann runs a regular bus service from Shannon Airport to Limerick City between 8 AM and midnight. The ride takes about 40 minutes and costs €5.

All buses running from Cork to Galway are now routed via Shannon Airport, giving direct connections to those cities. For buses to Dublin, Waterford, Tralee, and Killarney, change at Limerick.

You can find taxis outside the main terminal building at Shannon and Cork airports. The ride from Shannon Airport to Limerick City costs about €35; from Cork Airport to Cork City costs about €12.

Shuttles Bus Éireann (☎ *061/474–311* ⊕ *www.buseireann.ie*). **Cork City Bus Terminal** (✉ *Parnell Pl.* ☎ *021/450–6066*).

BY BUS

Bus Éireann operates express services from Dublin to Limerick City, Cork City, and Tralee. Most towns in the region are served by the provincial Bus Éireann network. The main bus terminals in the region are at Cork, Limerick, and Tralee. The U.K. bus company National Express jointly with Bus Eireann run services from most U.K. cities to most Irish cities. The journey from London to Cork via Rosslare is by bus and ferry, and, at about 14 hours, arduous.

FARES & SCHEDULES The provincial bus service, cheaper and more flexible than the train, covers all the region's main centers. Express services are available between Cork City and Limerick City (seven times a day); Cork, Killarney, and Tralee (seven times a day); and Killarney, Tralee, Limerick, and Shannon.

If you plan to travel extensively by bus, a copy of the Bus Éireann timetable (€2 from bus terminals) is essential. It's possible to tour the region by bus, but you need careful timing. Buses tend to stop running in the early evening, which is fine if you want to stay overnight and leave the next morning, but rules out many day trips—unless you want to spend most of the day on the bus. As a general rule, the smaller the town, and the more remote, the less frequent its bus service. For example, Kinsale, a well-developed resort 29 km (18 mi) from Cork, is served by at least seven buses a day, both arriving and departing, while some of the smaller villages on the remote Corca Dhuibne (Dingle Peninsula) have bus service only one day a week in winter. Bus Éireann runs a regular bus service around the Ring of Kerry between mid-June and mid-September, but there are only two buses a day, leaving Killarney at 8:45 AM or 1:45 PM. The trip takes more than four hours. Consult with hotel concierges, tourist board staffers, or the bus line Web site for the full scoop on bus schedules.

Bus Information Bus Éireann (☎ *01/836–6111 in Dublin, 061/313–333 in Limerick, 021/450–8188 in Cork, 066/712–3566 in Tralee* ⊕ *www.buseireann.ie*). **Cork Bus Station** (⊠ *Parnell Pl.* ☎ *021/450–8188*). **Limerick Bus Station** (⊠ *Colbert Station* ☎ *061/313–333*). **National Express** (⊠ *London, U.K.* ☎ *087/058–08080 drop the initial zero and add prefix 00–44 if dialing from Ireland*). **Tralee Bus Station** (⊠ *Casement Station* ☎ *066/712–3566*).

BY CAR

The main driving route from Dublin is N7, which goes 192 km (120 mi) directly to Limerick City; from Dublin, you can also pick up N8 in Portlaoise and drive the 257 km (160 mi) to Cork City. The journey time between Dublin and Limerick runs just under three hours; between Dublin and Cork it takes about three hours. From Rosslare Harbour by car, take N25 208 km (129 mi) to Cork; allow 3½ hours for the journey. You can pick up N24 in Waterford for the 211-km (131-mi) drive to Limerick City, which also takes about 3½ hours.

A car is the ideal way to explore this region, packed as it is with scenic routes, attractive but remote towns, and a host of out-of-the-way restaurants and hotels that deserve a detour. That said, the Celtic Tiger is not all gain; increased prosperity has led to an enormous growth in car ownership. Road upgrading has not kept up with the increased usage, and the result is our old friend, the peak-hour traffic jam. This is especially bad in the mornings between 8 AM and 9 AM on all major roads around Cork City, Limerick, and even Killarney. The evening rush hour has a wider spread, and can build up anytime between 4 PM and 6 PM.

Cork, Kinsale, Killarney, Tralee, and Limerick all have strict parking bylaws. Kinsale, Killarney, and Tralee are all amply provided with ground-level car parks: follow the blue "P" signs. In Cork and Limerick it's advisable to use a multistory car park, as on-street parking can be hard to find. If you do get lucky, you'll have to become familiar with "disk" parking regulations, which involve buying a ticket (or disk) for around €2 an hour from a machine or a shop and displaying it. In Cork and Limerick car clampers are active, especially during peak traffic times.

Rental Agencies **Alamo** (✉ Cork Airport ☎ 021/431-8623 ⊕ www.alamo. com). **Avis** (✉ Cork Airport ☎ 1890/405-060 ✉ Killarney ☎ 1890/405-060 ✉ Shannon Airport ☎ 1890/405-060 ⊕ www.avis.com). **Budget** (✉ Cork Airport ☎ 021/431-4000 ✉ Killarney ☎ 064/34341 ✉ Shannon Airport ☎ 061/471-361 ⊕ www.budget.ie). **Dan Dooley** (✉ Cork Airport ☎ 021/432-1099 ✉ Shannon Airport ☎ 061/471-098 ⊕ www.dan-dooley.ie). **Enterprise** (✉ Cork Airport ☎ 021/497-7031 ⊕ www.enterprise.com). **Europcar** (✉ Cork Airport ☎ 1850/403-803 ✉ Shannon Airport ☎ 1850/403-803 ⊕ www.europcar.ie). **Hertz** (✉ Cork Airport ☎ 021/496-5849 ✉ Kerry Airport ☎ 066/976-3270 ✉ Shannon Airport ☎ 061/471-369 ⊕ www.hertz.ie). **Irish Car Rentals** (✉ Shannon Airport ☎ 061/328-328, 021/431-8644 Cork ✉ Ennis Rd., Limerick ☎ 061/206-088 ⊕ www.irishcarrentals.ie).

BY TAXI

There are taxi stands at Cork Airport, Cork Railway Station, and on Patrick Street. It costs €3.10 to hire a taxi on the street (€4.20 by night, €5 on Sunday and bank holidays); add €1.50 to book one by phone, and €1.80 per kilometer or part of a mile. For journeys outside the 6-km city limit, the average price is €2 per kilometer, and the price should be agreed before setting off.

Taxis will also be found at railway stations in Tralee, Killarney, Limerick, and at Shannon and Kerry airports.

Taxi Companies **Cork Taxi Co Op** (☎ 021/477-2222 ⊕ corktaxicoop.ie). **Killarney Cabs** (☎ 064/34888). **Tralee Radio Cabs** (☎ 066/721-5451). **Speedi Taxis Limerick** (☎ 061/314-444).

BY TRAIN

From Dublin Heuston Station the region is served by three direct rail links, to Limerick City, Tralee (via Killarney), and Cork City. Journey time from Dublin to Limerick is 2½ hours; to Cork, 2¾ hours; to Tralee, 3¾ hours.

The rail network, which covers only the inner ring of the region, is mainly useful for moving from one touring base to another. On the Dublin-Cork line there is an hourly service in each direction between 7 AM and 9 PM, and nine trains a day from Dublin to Tralee (most of which involve one change at Mallow). A major upgrade of the Dublin-Cork line is due in 2007, with promises of hourly service in each direction. There are currently four trains a day from Cork to Tralee, but this too is scheduled to improve in 2008. The journey from Cork to Tralee takes about 2 hours; from Cork to Limerick, about 1¼ hours; from Limerick to Tralee, about 3 hours.

A suburban rail service runs up to four times hourly from Kent Station and has stops at Fota Island and Cobh and offers better Cork Harbour views than the road.

Train Information **Irish Rail–Iarnod Éireann** (⊕ *www.irishrail.ie*). **Dublin Heuston Station** (☎ *01/836–6222*). **Inquiries** (☎ *061/315–555 in Limerick, 021/450–6766 in Cork, 066/712–3522 in Tralee*). **Kent Station** (☎ *021/450–6766 for timetable*).

CONTACTS & RESOURCES

EMERGENCIES

Contacts **Ambulance, fire, police** (☎ *999*). **Health Service Executive West** (✉ *31–33 Catherine St., Limerick* ☎ *061/316–655*). **Health Service Executive Cork and Kerry** (✉ *Dennehy's Cross, Cork City* ☎ *021/454–5011*).

Pharmacies **Phelan's** (✉ *9 Patrick St., Cork City* ☎ *021/427–2511*). **P. O'Donoghue** (✉ *Main St., Killarney* ☎ *064/31813*). **Roberts** (✉ *105 O'Connell St., Limerick City* ☎ *061/414–414*).

TOURS

BUS TOURS Bus Éireann, part of the state-run public-transport network, offers a range of daylong and half-day guided tours from June to September. You can book them at the bus stations in Cork or Limerick or at any tourist office. A full-day tour costs about €30, half-day €15. Bus Éireann also offers open-top bus tours of Cork City on Tuesday and Saturday in July and August for €6.

Dero's Tours and Corcoran's Tours organize full-day and half-day trips by coach or taxi around Killarney and the Ring of Kerry.

Keating Coaches offer day trips and half-day tours of the Shannon region from Limerick City. Themes include "castles and gardens," "waterways, highways, and byways," and "flying boats, monks, and dolphins."

Fees & Schedules **Bus Éireann** (☎ *01/836–6111 in Dublin, 061/313–333 in Limerick, 021/450–8188 in Cork, 066/712–3566 in Tralee* ⊕ *www.buseireann. ie*). **Corcoran's Tours** (✉ *10 College St., Killarney* ☎ *064/36666*). **Dero's Tours** (✉ *22 Main St., Killarney* ☎ *064/31251* ⊕ *www.derostours.com*). **Keating Coaches** (✉ *Ballingarry, Co. Limerick* ☎ *069/68201* ⊕ *www.limericktours.com*).

SPECIAL-INTEREST TOURS Gerry Coughlan of Arrangements Unlimited can prearrange special-interest group tours of the region. Half-day and full-day tours are individually planned for groups of 10 or more to satisfy each visitor's needs. Country House Tours organizes self-driven or chauffeur-driven group tours with accommodations in private country houses and castles. It also conducts special-interest tours, including gardens, architecture, ghosts, and golf, while Killorglin-based Go Ireland offers comprehensive packages for walking, cycling, fishing, golfing, and equestrian holidays on the ring of Kerry and the Dingle Peninsula with experienced local guides.

Destination Killarney is the foremost Killarney tour operator. Besides offering full-day and half-day tours of Killarney and Kerry by coach or taxi, the group will prearrange your visit, lining up accommodations, entertainment, special-interest tours, and sporting activities in one package. A full-day (10:30–5) tour costs from €16 to €20 per person, excluding lunch and refreshments. The Killarney Local Circuit tour is an excellent half-day (10:30–12:30) orientation. The memorable Gap of Dunloe tour at €20 includes a coach and boat trip. Add €15 for a horseback ride through the gap. More conventional day trips can also be made to the Ring of Kerry, the Loo Valley, and Glengarriff; the city of Cork and Blarney Castle; An Daingean (Dingle) and Ceann Sleibne (Slea Head); and Caragh Lake and Rossbeigh.

Jaunting cars (pony and cart) that carry up to four people can be rented at a stand outside the Killarney tourist office. They can also be found at the entrance to Muckross Estate and at the Gap of Dunloe. A ride costs between €16 and €32, negotiable with the driver, depending on duration (one to two hours) and route. Tangney Tours is the leading jaunting-car company and will also organize tours by coach or water bus, as well as entertainment.

Fees & Schedules **Arrangements Unlimited** (✉ *1 Woolhara Park, Douglas, Cork City, Co. Cork* ☎ *021/429–3873* ⊕ *www.arrangements.ie*). **Country House Tours** (✉ *71 Waterloo Rd., Dublin 4* ☎ *01/668–6463* 🖶 *01/668–6578* ⊕ *www. tourismresources.ie*). **Destination Killarney** (✉ *Scott's Gardens, Killarney, Co. Kerry* ☎🖶 *064/32638* ⊕ *www.gleneaglehotel.com*). **Shannon Castle Tours** (✉ *Bunratty Folk Park, Bunratty, Co. Clare* ☎ *061/360–788* ⊕ *www.shannonheritage.com*). **Tangney Tours** (✉ *Kinvara House, Muckross Rd., Killarney, Co. Kerry* ☎ *064/33358*).

6

WALKING TOURS SouthWest Walks Ireland has a variety of packages for all levels of walkers along the coast of West Cork, around the Sheep's Head and Beara Peninsula in Bantry Bay, as well as in Kerry. Trips include accommodation, baggage transfer, and evening meals for self-guided or escorted groups. Activity Ireland organizes customized walking and climbing tours on the Ring of Kerry. Go Ireland specializes in active vacations, included walking and cycling excursions along the Kerry Way or the Dingle Peninsula. Michael Martin's Titanic Trail, a 90-minute guided walking tour of Cobh takes its name from the *Titanic,* but in fact covers the whole of Cobh's fascinating history, from coffin ships to ocean liners via naval fire power and tall ships. Trips are daily at 11 AM starting from outside the Commodore Hotel; the cost is €7.50. Martin can also customize a walk or tour by minibus.

Richard Clancy, an expert on the legends and history of Killarney, offers a two-hour guided walk in Killarney National Park daily at 11 AM (other times by arrangement). Trips leave from the Shell gas station on Lower New Street. The cost is €8. Limerick City Tours provides inexpensive walking tours of Limerick from June to September (and by arrangement other months). St. Mary's Action Centre has walking tours of Limerick's historic centers and of locations highlighted in Frank McCourt's *Angela's Ashes*. They're conducted daily at 11 and 2:30.

Information **Activity Ireland** (✉ *Caherdaniel, Co. Kerry* ☎ *066/947–5277* ⊕ *www.activity-ireland.com*). **Go Ireland** (✉ *Killorglin* ☎ *066/976–2094* ⊕ *www. goactivities.com*). **Limerick City Tours** (✉ *Noel Curtin, Rhebogue* ☎ *061/311–935*). **Richard Clancy** (☎ *064/33471* ⊕ *www.killarneyguidedwalks.com*). **St. Mary's Action Centre** (✉ *44 Nicholas St., Limerick* ☎ *061/318–106* ⊕ *www.iol.ie/~smidp*). **SouthWest Walks Ireland** (✉ *6 Church St., Tralee* ☎ *066/712–8733* ⊕ *www. southwestwalksireland.com*). **Titanic Trail** (✉ *Cobh* ☎ *021/481–5211* ⊕ *www. titanic-trail.com*).

VISITOR INFORMATION

Bord Fáilte provides a free information service; its tourist information offices (TIOs) also sell a selection of tourist literature. For a small fee it will book accommodations anywhere in Ireland.

Seasonal TIOs in Bantry, Cahirciveen, and Clonakilty are open from May to October; offices in An Daingean (Dingle Town) and Kinsale are open from March to November; the TIO in Kenmare is open April to October, and the one in Youghal is open May to mid-September. All of the seasonal TIOs are generally open Monday–Saturday 9–6; in July and August they are also open Sunday 9–6. Year-round TIOs can be found in An Daingean, Blarney, Clonakilty, Cork City, Killarney, Limerick, Shannon, Skibbereen, and Tralee and are open Monday–Saturday 9–6; in July and August TIOs are also open Sunday 9–6.

Tourist Information Adare (✉ *Heritage Centre* ☎ *061–396–255* ⊕ *www.shannonregiontourism.ie*).**An Daingean (Dingle Town)** (✉ *The Quay, Co. Kerry* ☎ *066/915–1188*). **Bantry** (✉ *Co. Cork* ☎ *027/50229* ⊕ *www.corkkerry.ie*). **Blarney** (✉ *Co. Cork* ☎ *021/438–1624* ⊕ *www.corkkerry.ie*). **Cahirciveen** (✉ *The Old Barracks, Co. Kerry* ☎ *066/947–2589* ⊕ *www.corkkerry.ie*). **Clonakilty** (✉ *Co. Cork* ☎ *023/33226* ⊕ *www.corkkerry.ie*). **Cork City** (✉ *Grand Parade, Co. Cork* ☎ *021/425–5100* 🖷 *021/425–5199* ⊕ *www.corkkerry.ie*). **Kenmare** (✉ *Co. Kerry* ☎ *064/41233*). **Killarney** (✉ *Aras Fáilte, Beech Rd., Co. Kerry* ☎ *064/31633* 🖷 *064/34506* ⊕ *www.corkkerry.ie*). **Kinsale** (✉ *Pier Rd., Co. Cork* ☎ *021/477–2234* 🖷 *021/477–4438*). **Limerick** (✉ *Arthur's Quay, Co. Limerick* ☎ *061/317–522* ⊕ *www.visitlimerick.com*). **Skibbereen** (✉ *North St., Co. Cork* ☎ *028/21766*). **Tralee** (✉ *Ashe Memorial Hall, Denny St., Co. Kerry* ☎ *066/712–1288* ⊕ *www.corkkerry.ie*).

The West

Gallarus Oratory on the Dingle Peninsula, County Kerry

WORD OF MOUTH

"The Aran Islands are everything you imagine Ireland to be: green, rolling land, quaint village life, and much hospitality."

—abuster

"Connemara is hauntingly beautiful. No one has been able to describe it to me. They just look at me, dreamy-eyed, and say 'Ah, Connemara.' I'm going there on my next trip and I'm going to translate Connemara into poetry, so I can take a piece home with me."

—Melissa5

WELCOME TO THE WEST

TOP REASONS TO GO

★ **Ancient Aran:** Spend at least one night on one of the Oileáin Arainn (Aran Islands), three outposts of Gaelic civilization, which still have a strong whiff of the "old ways"—and not just the whiff of turf smoke.

★ **Foot-tapping in Doolin and Ennis:** Tap your foot in time to "trad" Irish music and sip your pint as you while away an afternoon—and maybe an evening as well—in one of Doolin's or Ennis's noted music bars.

★ **High-style Galway:** A university town and booming, buzzing hive of activity, with great theaters, bars, nightlife, shopping and restaurants, Galway is the city that loves to celebrate and, as one of Europe's fastest growing townships, has much to offer.

★ **The Mighty Cliffs of Moher:** Rising straight out of the sea to a height of 700 feet, these cliffs—standing in silence as they look out over the wild Atlantic—give you a new understanding of the word "awesome."

Ashleram Bay, Achill Island, County Mayo

1 Connemara & County Mayo. Gorgeous **Clifden** would be considered just a village elsewhere, but out here in rugged, sparsely populated Connemara, set between Galway City and the coast, it's a booming metropolis. Opt for **Cong**—famed setting of *The Quiet Man*—or Georgian-flavored **Westport** as other bases for exploring the glacial lakes and silent mountains of this beautiful wilderness area.

Cottage, Inis Mor, Aran Islands
County Galway

2 County Clare & the Aran Islands. Set with postcard-perfect villages like **Doolin, Kinvara,** and **Lisdoonvarna,** the lunar landscape of the **Burren,** and the towering **Cliffs of Moher,** County Clare is pure tourist gold. An hour or less on a ferry away are the ageless **Aran Islands**—once famed for their isolation, they are now disturbed a bit by 200,000-plus curious annual visitors.

GETTING ORIENTED

With the most westerly seaboard in Europe, this region remains a place apart—the most Irish part of Ireland. The "west" here refers to the counties west of the River Shannon. Rich in Nature's magnificence—the Burren and the Cliffs of Moher—they are also home to sophisticated outposts like Galway City and Westport. Last outpost before America: the Aran Islands, which do constant battle with the Atlantic.

7

ROSCOMMON

WESTMEATH

GALWAY

Loughrea

Gort

Laough Derg

TIPPERARY

LIMERICK

Cliffs of Moher, County Clare

3 Galway City. Easily the liveliest city in Ireland after Dublin, you've got to get your fill of its buzz when visiting, best done by checking out its eyepopping "g" hotel, stylish new boutiques and craft shops, and dazzling weekend festivals.

Galway City, County Galway

THE WEST PLANNER

Getting Around

Public transport is not a strong point in the West. Trains arrive from Dublin on separate lines to Ennis, Galway, and Ballina via Westport, but do not run between these towns.

The bus network is more flexible, but there are not many services a day, and you will need to do some serious planning to get around.

Both the Burren and Connemara can be explored on guided day trips from Galway City. But to do full justice to the region, you really need a car—and a good map.

How's the Weather?

It will most likely rain, but the locals just call it "soft" weather. Average rainfall in the rest of Ireland is between 31 inches and 47 inches, but here on the west coast, it can exceed 79 inches. It is said to rain in the west on at least 300 of the 365 days in the year.

Take comfort from the thought that it may be damp, but it is never really cold, with a mean daily temperature around 6° Celsius in January and February, the coldest months.

In the warmest months, July and August, average temperatures are around 15°C (60°F).

Traveling to the Aran Islands

The spell of the Aran Islands is such that many travelers can't resist their siren call and make for the first ferry leaving from Doolin. However, locals will tell you that it may be best to wait until you are in Galway City before you make arrangements to travel to the famed Oileáin Arainn (Aran Islands). That way you can postpone your trip if the weather looks bad, and shop around for the best deals from the various ferry firms.

You can do a day trip, leaving the city at 9:30 or noon and returning by 6:30, but staying overnight is more rewarding. Everyone wants to go to the islands, and it is made as easy as possible to organize by the various transport companies. They are all genuine and licensed: no one is going to rip you off. Book at the Tourist Information Office in Forster Place, where the ferry companies and Aer Arran have concessions.

The standard ferry deal is €25 round-trip and €6 for bus transfer to the ferry port at Rossaveal. Look out for money-saving offers that may include B & B accommodation, free transfers to Rossaveal, or Connemara airport (both 40 minutes away), bicycle hire on the islands, or a ferry-out, flight-back plan.

There are three different ferry operators, and tickets are not transferable, so check the return sailing times of your operator when you get on board.

If you opt for the five-minute flight, for safety reasons, you (yes, you, not your bags!) will be weighed at check-in, and allocated an appropriate seat. *For more information, see By Boat & Ferry in The West Essentials section at the end of this chapter.*

When Ireland Celebrates

For both visitors and locals, festivals provide both free entertainment and a chance to meet people from all backgrounds who share a common interest.

Some festivals are traditional events, now tarted up with entertaining side shows: Kinvara's Criuinniú na mBád on the third Thursday in August centers around turf-laden "hookers" (heavy wooden sailing boats) racing across Galway Bay, while on the third weekend in August the Connemara Pony Show in Clifden attracts a nationwide equine entry, and creates a terrific buzz.

The Fleadh Nua in Ennis in late May is one of the country's biggest traditional music festivals, and a great place to make friends. There is plenty of free entertainment there, and also at the Lisdoonvarna Matchmaking Festival held in late September, an outing which may well change your life—stranger things have happened!

In contrast, the Galway Arts Festival, in the middle two weeks of July, hosts an international array of the best of contemporary theater, film, rock, jazz, traditional music, poetry readings, comedy acts, visual arts exhibitions, and an open-air parade by the street theater company Macnas, one of several local troupes to gain international recognition.

This is followed immediately by the Galway Races, the "only place" for Irish socialites to be seen in late July. These Thoroughbred horse races now feature a new sport: the game of Spot the Celebrity (usually arriving by helicopter).

Both Galway and neighboring Clarinbridge have Oyster Festivals in September, celebrating the local product with oyster-opening competitions and lots of free entertainment.

Dining & Lodging Price Categories (In Euros)

	¢	$	$$	$$$	$$$$
RESTAURANTS	under €10	€10–€15	€15–€22	€22–€29	Over €29
HOTELS	under €80	€80–€130	€130–€180	€180–€230	Over €230

Restaurant prices are for a main course at dinner. Hotel prices are for a standard double room in high season.

Finding a Place to Stay

Some of Ireland's finest country-house and castle hotels are in the West. Ashford and Dromoland castles provide a standard of luxury that you should experience at least once, if you can stretch your budget.

Star country house destinations include antique-filled Enniscoe House and Zetland Country House. Try to sample some of the smaller B & Bs as well: the home cooking at Kilmurvey House on the Aran Islands is renowned.

Other memorable destinations include the cliff-top Moy House, picture-perfect Gregan's Castle in the Burren, the gracious creeper-clad Newport House in Mayo, and the stunning Renvyle House in scenic Connemara.

One of the great attractions of the West's hotels and guesthouses is their restful environment: many lodgings sit in the middle of a private estate beside a lake or river, overlooking the sea or a hilly valley.

Most of the moderately priced hotels are relatively new, and thus more modern than charming, but these newer hotels often have facilities—tennis courts and indoor pools—that are scarce at B & Bs and older hotels. Assume that all hotel rooms in this chapter have air-conditioning, in-room phones, TVs and private bathrooms, unless otherwise indicated.

Updated
by Alannah
Hopkin

THE MOST WESTERLY SEABOARD IN Europe, Ireland's West is richly endowed by nature: the majestic Cliffs of Moher; the rocky expanse of the Burren (whose gray rocks hide a profusion of wild plants); Connemara's combination of rugged coastline, mountains, moorland, and lakes; and the famous Oileáin Árainn (Aran Islands), which do constant battle with the fury of the Atlantic. But the West also abounds in characterful small country towns and villages, such as Kinvara, Ballyvaughan, Clifden, and Westport, rife with good restaurants and pubs, and Galway, the city that loves to celebrate.

The West refers to the region that lies west of the River Shannon; most of this area falls within the old Irish province of Connaught. This region faces its nearest North American neighbors across 3,200 km (2,000 mi) of the Atlantic Ocean: next parish, New York, as they say in the West.

Towns as communities were unknown in pre-Christian Irish society, and even today, more than 150 years after the famine, many residents still live on isolated small farms rather than in towns and villages. Especially during the wet, wintry months, you can still walk out of your country house, hotel, or bed-and-breakfast in the morning and smell turf fires burning nearby.

Today, the West is, for many, the most typically Irish part of the country. Particularly in western County Galway, the region has the highest concentration of Gaeltacht (Irish-speaking) communities in all Ireland, with roughly 40,000 native Irish speakers making their homes here. The country's first Irish-language TV station broadcasts from the tiny village of An Spidéal (Spiddle), on the north shore of Galway Bay in the heart of the Gaeltacht. Throughout this area, you'll see plenty of signs printed in Irish only. Who would suspect that Gaillimh is Irish for Galway? But wherever you go in the West, you'll not only see, but more importantly *hear,* the most vital way in which traditional Irish culture survives here: musicians play in pubs all over the West, and they are acknowledged to be the best in the Republic.

A major factor in the region's economic development has been the lure of its spectacular scenery to visitors. So far, the development that typically comes with the cultivation of tourism has been mercifully low-key in the West. The Irish people are well aware of what a jewel they have in the largely unspoiled wilderness, grazed by sheep and herds of wild ponies, that is Connemara. The 5,000-acre Connemara National Park is the result of a successful lobby for landscape preservation. Peatlands, or bogs as they are called around here, are at last being valued for their unique botanical character. Ireland's last remaining peat-burning electricity-generating station—at Bellacorick in County Mayo—has closed. Galway City's suburbs have spread in all directions, and throughout the region the landscape is marked by newly built bungalows and houses. With increasing prosperity, the West of Ireland is undoubtedly losing some of its old-style visual charm. But while this is regrettable in terms of unspoiled views, for the people who live in the area, it is a boon.

THE WEST THROUGH THE AGES

Although Ireland's East, Southwest, and the North were influenced by either Norman, Scots, or English settlers, the West largely escaped systematic resettlement and, with the exception of the walled town of Galway, remained purely Irish in language, social organization, and general outlook far longer than the rest of the country. The land in the West, predominantly mountains and bogs, did not immediately tempt the conquering barons. Oliver Cromwell was among those who found the place thoroughly unattractive, and he gave the Irish chieftains who would not conform to English rule the choice of going "to Hell or Connaught."

It wasn't until the late 18th century, when better transport improved communications, that the West began to experience the so-called foreign influences that had already Europeanized the rest of the country.

The West was, in effect, propelled from the 16th century into the 19th. Virtually every significant building in the region dates either from before the 17th century or from the late 18th century onward. As in the southwest, the population of the West was decimated by the Great Famine (1845–49) and by the waves of emigration that persisted until the 1950s.

It's nothing new that the West's greatest virtue for visitors—apart from its glorious scenery and the vibrant capital city of Galway—is its people. No matter how many times you get out of the car for a photo op (and you should expect to *fly* through megabytes of memory here), the stories that you'll most likely tell when you show your friends and family those pictures are going to be about the *seisún*, or sessions (informal performances of traditional music) you stumbled upon in a small pub; the tiny, far-from-the-madding-crowd lake in Connemara that you made your own; and the great *craic* ("crack," or good conversation and fun) you're likely to discover wherever you go.

EXPLORING THE WEST

This chapter is organized into four parts, covering the territory from south to north. The first section, the Burren and Beyond—West Clare to South Galway—picks up minutes from Shannon Airport and is not far from Ennis, the gateway to coastal County Clare. The second section takes you through the best of buzzing, bustling Galway City, and the third takes you out to the three Oileáin Árainn (Aran Islands), standing guard at the mouth of Galway Bay. The fourth section, covering Connemara and County Mayo, brings you north of Galway Bay and west of Galway City into fabled Connemara, and its spectacularly situated "capital," Clifden. Beyond lie the highlights of County Mayo: monumental Croagh Patrick, the pretty town of Westport, the Museum of Country Life in Turlough, and Ballina. Allow at least four days for exploring the region, six days if you include a visit to the Aran Islands. Although distances between sights are not great, you may want to take scenic—meaning slower—national secondary routes. Covering 80 km to 112 km (50 mi to 70 mi) per day on these roads is a comfortable target.

COUNTY CLARE: THE BURREN & BEYOND

County Clare claims two of Ireland's unique natural sights: the awesome Cliffs of Moher and the stark, mournful landscape of the Burren, which hugs the coast from Black Head in the north to Doolin and the Cliffs of Moher in the south. Yet western County Clare (West Clare for short) is widely beloved among native Irish for a natural phenomenon significantly less unique than these: its sandy beaches. Though just another Irish beach town to some, Kilkee, to name just one, is a favorite summer getaway. So whether you're looking for inimitable scenery or just a lovely beach to plunk down on to relax in the sun (if you're lucky!) for a few hours, you can find it in West Clare.

This journey begins at Newmarket-on-Fergus, within minutes of Shannon Airport, a good jumping-off point for a trip through the West if you've just arrived in Ireland and are planning to head for Galway. This route also follows directly from the end of Chapter 5, which concludes 10 km (6 mi) down the road, at Bunratty Castle and Folk Park (and the Knappogue Castle and Craggaunowen Project, also nearby), so be sure to take a moment to glance at those sights to decide whether to include them as you get under way. The Shannon region is also the connecting link between County Limerick (and other points in the southwest) and Galway City. If you're approaching it from the southwest and you're not going into Limerick City, it makes sense to begin exploring the region from Killimer, reached via the ferry from Tarbert.

NEWMARKET-ON-FERGUS

❶ *13 km (8 mi) north of Shannon Airport on N18.*

A small town in County Clare, Newmarket-on-Fergus is chiefly remarkable as the village nearest the famed hotel of Dromoland Castle, formerly the home of Lord Inchiquin, chief of the O'Brien clan.

WHERE TO STAY & EAT

$$$$ ✕🏨 **Dromoland Castle.** This massive, turreted, neo-Gothic castle—the
Fodor'sChoice   ancestral home of the O'Briens, descendants of Brian Boru, High King
★   of Ireland—certainly looks the part. Dating from the 19th century (it replaced the 16th-century original) and now one of Ireland's grandest and best loved hotels, it bristles with towers and crenellations that rise up over the forest and a picture-perfect lake, looking like a storybook illustration from King Arthur and his knights. Inside, Dromoland really sets out to give you the full country-house treatment: oak paneling, ancestral portraits, plushly carpeted rooms, crystal chandeliers, Irish-Georgian antiques—all the creature comforts any highborn duke would want. But the cordiality of the long-serving staff, and the pervading aroma of wood smoke help to create an easygoing, relaxing ambience. Bedrooms (suites, in fact) in the main wing are the largest and most elaborate, with massive four-poster beds, tall, draped windows, custom fabrics, and genuine Hepplewhite armoires. Rooms in the discreetly added newer wings are more hotel-like, with Regency-style furniture, but all have luxurious bathrooms. The neo-

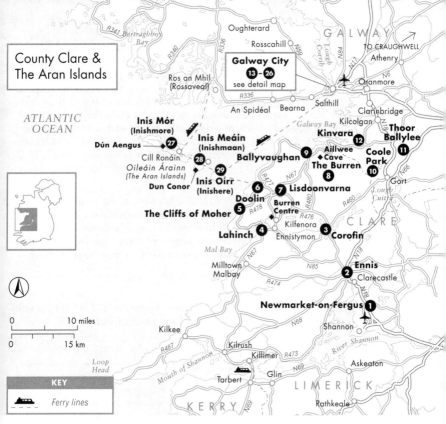

County Clare &
The Aran Islands

ATLANTIC
OCEAN

KEY

Ferry lines

Gothic, oak-wainscoted Earl of Thomond Restaurant is magnificent, with beautifully presented tables decked with crystal and Irish linen, a harpist providing gentle background music, period wallpapers, Japanese vases, and spectacular chandeliers. Classic French cuisine is served with appropriate ceremony—perhaps poached lobster with steamed greens for the main course, or roast Clare lamb with salsa vert. The Green Room Bar and the Fig Tree restaurant offer more casual dining. For activities, the estate offers a full golf course, golf academy, tennis, fishing, a spa, and those idyllic woodlands and gardens—perfect for jogging, cycling, or a blissful stroll. ⊠*5 km (3 mi) west of Newmarket-on-Fergus, signposted from N18, Co. Clare* ☎*061/368–144* 🖷*061/363–355* ⊕*www.dromoland.ie* 🛏*100 rooms* ⌂*In-room: no a/c. In-hotel: 2 restaurants, bar, golf course, tennis courts, pool, spa, bicycles, public Wi-Fi* ⊟*AE, DC, MC, V* ⊚*EP.*

\$ ✕🏨 **Hunter's Lodge.** A good first or last stop for those arriving at Shannon, this unpretentious village pub with rooms is only 12 km (7 mi) from the airport. The village itself is still basking in the pleasure of no longer being on the main road, since it was bypassed by a new highway in 2003. The resulting cheerful little community will suit those who like to get to know "the real people" when arriving in a new country. Downstairs is a plush, upmarket version of an Irish pub, with dark-mahogany furniture and brass trim in the bar, where locals congregate around a roaring open fire. Select pieces of old oak furniture dot the attractive, well-equipped guest rooms, and scatter rugs decorate the timber floors. The restaurant ($–$$$), known for its cheerful service, has an uncomplicated menu of old familiars like sirloin steak in pepper sauce, burgers béarnaise, pasta Alfredo, and—the most popular of all—salmon *en croute* (wrapped in pastry with a seafood sauce). ⊠ *The Square, Co. Clare* ☎ *061/368–577* 🖷 *061/368–057* �5 *6 rooms* ⟐ *In-room: no a/c. In-hotel: restaurant, bar, no elevator* ⊟ *AE, DC, MC, V* ⟐ *BP.*

SPORTS & THE OUTDOORS

Dromoland Golf Course (☎ *061/368–144*) is one of the most scenic in the country, set in a 700-acre estate of rich woodland on the grounds of Dromoland Castle. The 18-hole, par-71 course has a natural lake that leaves little room for error on a number of holes. Improvers take note: a state-of-the-art golf academy can help you to improve your swing.

ENNIS

❷ *9½ km (6 mi) north of Newmarket-on-Fergus on N18, 37 km (23 mi) northwest of Limerick, 142 km (88 mi) north of Tralee.*

A major crossroads and a convenient stop between the West and the Southwest, Ennis is the main town of County Clare. The pleasant market town has an attractively renovated, pedestrian-friendly center, bisected by the fast-flowing River Fergus. Ennis has always fostered the traditional arts, especially fiddle-playing and step-dancing (a kind of square dance).

> SPICY IRISH STEW
>
> These days the Ennis town center has a pleasantly multicultural ambience, as many emigrants arriving at Shannon Airport from faraway locations—including Brazil and West Africa—have settled here.

The **Fleadh Nua** (pronounced fla-*nooa*) festival at the end of May attracts both performers and students of Irish music and serves as the venue for the National Dancing Championships.

WHERE TO STAY & EAT

$$ ✕🏠 **Lynch West County.** You will meet both leisure and business travelers from all walks of life at this popular stopping point on the Limerick–Galway road (N18), a lively, modern hostelry affiliated with Best Western. It's a five-minute walk from Ennis's town center. Rooms are ample—most overlook the car park but are at least quiet. Service is helpful and friendly, despite the hotel's relatively large size. In July and August there's nightly Irish cabaret-style entertainment in the large bar, Boru's Porterhouse, which also serves bar food. The County Grill is a more intimate venue ($$–$$$) serving an à la carte menu of traditional Irish fare, while the Pine Room ($) offers a good-value four-course set menu. ⊠ *Clare Rd., Co. Clare* ☎ *065/682–3000* 🖷 *065/682–3759* ⊕ *www.lynchotels.com* �5 *152 rooms* ⟐ *In-room:*

CLOSE UP

Local Heroes

The Member of Parliament (or Dáil Éireann as it became known after independence) for Ennis has twice been a national leader at a time of great significance for Irish democracy, and each is commemorated by a town statue.

On a tall limestone column above a massive pediment in Ennis's town center stands a **statue of Daniel O'Connell** (1775–1847), "The Liberator," a member of Parliament for County Clare between 1828 and 1831 who was instrumental in bringing about Catholic Emancipation. Outside the courthouse (in the town park, beside the River Fergus, on the west side of Ennis) stands a larger-than-life bronze **statue of Eamon De Valera** (1882–1975), who successfully contested the election here in 1917, thus launching a long political career.

He was the dominant figure in Irish politics during the 20th century, serving as prime minister for most of the years from 1937 until 1959, when he resigned as leader of Fianna Fáil, the party he founded, and went on to serve as president of Ireland until 1973.

Although De Valera was born in the United States, his maternal forebears were from County Clare.

no a/c, Wi-Fi (some). In-hotel: 3 restaurants, bar, pool, gym, no elevator, public Wi-Fi ☰*AE, DC, MC, V* ⍥|*BP.*

$$ ☖**Temple Gate.** Before its conversion, this lodging was a Gothic-style convent, and remnants of its previous existence (including the chapel, which is now a banquet hall) give character to this bright, modern hotel in the town center. Coordinated drapes and bedspreads in warm, earthy colors decorate the compact, well-equipped rooms, which have unusual views of pretty corners of Ennis's historic center. Preacher's Pub is popular with locals, while the guest lounge is a country house–style library. The entrance is via a cobblestone courtyard adorned with Victorian street lamps. ⊠*The Square, Co. Clare* ☎*065/682–3300* ☐*065/692–3322* ⊕*www.templegatehotel.com* ⬐*70 rooms* ⚷*In-room: no a/c, Ethernet. In-hotel: restaurant, bar, no elevator, public Wi-Fi* ☰*AE, DC, MC, V* ⍥|*BP.*

NIGHTLIFE & THE ARTS

Glór–Irish Music Centre (⊠*Friar's Walk* ☎*065/684–3103* ⊕*www.glor.ie*) is Ennis's venue for large concerts, hosting competitions of Irish music, song, and dance, and big-name touring acts on the Irish music scene, including Mary Black, Paul Brady, and Aslan. There's also a crafts gallery and coffee shop, and free parking.

Although Ennis is not as fashionable as, say, Galway, it's one of the West's traditional-music hot spots. You're likely to hear sessions at the following pubs, but keep in mind that sessions don't necessarily take place every night and that the scene is constantly changing. Phone ahead to check whether a session is happening.

Cruise's (⊠*Abbey St.* ☎*065/684–1800*). **Fawl's** (⊠*The Railway Bar, 69 O'Connell St.* ☎*065/682–4463*). **Kerins'** (⊠*Lifford* ☎*065/682–*

0582). **Knox's** (⊠*Abbey St.* ☎*065/682–9264).* **Poet's Corner Bar** (⊠*Old Ground Hotel, Main St.* ☎*065/682–8155).* **Preachers Pub** (⊠*Temple Gate Hotel, the Square* ☎*065/682–3300).*

SPORTS & THE OUTDOORS

BICYCLING You can follow the scenic Burren Cycleway (69 km [43 mi]) to the famous Cliffs of Moher on a bike rented from **Tierney Cycles & Fishing** (⊠*17 Abbey St.* ☎*065/682–9433).*

SHOPPING

Stop in at the **Antique Loft** (⊠*Clarecastle* ☎*065/684–1969)* for collectibles and pine and mahogany antiques. The **Belleek Shop** (⊠*36 Abbey St.* ☎*065/682–9607)* carries Belleek china, Waterford crystal, and Donegal Parian china, as well as Lladró, Hummel, and other collectible china. **Carraig Donn** (⊠*29 O'Connell St.* ☎*065/682–8188)* sells its own line of knitwear. The long-established **Ennis Bookshop** (⊠*13 Abbey St.* ☎*065/682–9000* ⊕*www.ennisbookshop.ie)* carries a big range of local history and Irish-interest titles. **The Rock Shop** (⊠*2 O'Connell St.* ☎*065/682–2636)* displays polished gemstones, fossils, and other rocks alongside jewelry and small sculptures in stone and marble.

COROFIN

❸ *14 km (10 mi) northwest of Ennis via N18.*

Corofin? It's not a town but a tiny village of perhaps 200 people, just a line of houses and some lovely, unspoiled country pubs—but perhaps that is all you're looking for today. Corofin's **Clare Heritage and Genealogical Center** has a genealogical service and advice for do-it-yourselfers researching their Irish roots. Displays on west-Ireland 19th-century history cover culture, traditions, emigration, and famine. ⊠*Church St.* ☎*065/683–7955* ⊕*www.clareroots.com* 🏷€4 ☉*Apr.–Oct., weekdays 9:30–5:30; Nov.–Mar. by appointment.*

A 15th-century castle on the edge of Corofin houses the **Clare Archaeology Centre**, which has an exhibition on the antiquities of the Burren. Twenty-five monuments stand within a 1½-km (1-mi) radius of the castle; these date from the Bronze Age to the 19th century, and all are described at the center. ⊠*Dysert O'Dea Castle* ☎*065/683–7794* 🏷€4 ☉*May–Sept., daily 10–6.*

LAHINCH

❹ *30 km (18 mi) west of Ennis on N85.*

Lahinch, a busy resort village beside a long, sandy beach backed by dunes, is best known for its links golf courses and—believe it or not—its surfing. In 1972 the European Surfing Finals were held here, putting Lahinch on the world surfing map, where it has stayed ever since. But the center ring here is occupied by golf—with three world-class courses and a dazzling bay-view backdrop, Lahinch is often called the "St. Andrews of Ireland."

EATING WELL IN THE WEST

Because the West has a brief high season—from mid-June to early September—and a quiet off-season, it doesn't have as broad a choice of small, owner-operated restaurants as do other parts of Ireland. Often the best place to eat is a hotel—Sheedy's Restaurant and Country Inn in Lisdoonvarna, for example, which has one of the best chefs in County Clare, or Rosleague Manor in Letterfrack. The dominant style of cuisine in the West is an unfussy, traditional approach that allows the natural flavors of fresh local delights—locally reared lamb and beef, and freshly landed seafood—to shine through. Look out for wild salmon or sea trout, fresh from one of the region's fast-flowing rivers, and Connemara mountain lamb, which has a particular flavor from grazing on mountain herbs and grass: these three regional delicacies are well worth the premium. Most of the chefs working in the region have traveled widely, and on many menus you will find a whiff of Asia—Thailand especially—along with the expected classic French repertoire. A handful of restaurants, including Kirwan's Lane Creative

Cuisine and K.C. Blake's in Galway, showcase adventurous contemporary Irish cooking with a bold fusion element. But many of the best things to eat in these parts are extremely simple, which makes a bar-food lunch a tempting option. It's hard to beat a platter of freshly sliced smoked salmon with half a lemon squeezed over it, home-baked brown bread with butter, and a glass of dry white wine. Oysters, too, (the local one is the European oyster, *ostrea edulis*) are often ordered in their shells and slipped directly into the mouth, followed by a bite of soda bread and butter and a sip of black stout; a combination made in heaven, many say. Galway oysters are in season from September to April. Fans say they taste of the sea, but not everyone likes the rubbery texture—the good news is each oyster contains only seven calories. Home-baked brown bread, whether soda (made with buttermilk) or yeast, is one of the great pleasures of the region, and another is the home baking—porter cake, fruit scones, breakfast muffins—which is on offer at many of the region's B&Bs and inns.

WHERE TO STAY & EAT

$ ✕⌂ **Berry Lodge.** Just south of Milltown Malbay, 8 km (5 mi) south of Lahinch (near the turn-off for Spanish Point) and way out in the country but within view of the sea, this is a good choice for people who relish peace and quiet, birdsong, and simple home comforts. The traditional white, two-story, slate-roof house dates from 1775 and has been in Rita Meade's family for three generations. At an age when most of us would be putting our feet up, Rita not only runs the guesthouse and restaurant but hosts a popular local radio show on cooking. The country-pine pieces in her crisply clean rooms are genuine antiques, beds are covered in patchwork quilts, and the sprigged curtains have pretty tiebacks. Floors are genuine old pine, fireplaces are original, and the rooms are dotted with local craft work. The restaurant ($–$$) occupies a large room with a sofa and armchairs at one end, and a tall dresser laden with family treasures (reservations essential; call to confirm restaurant is open from September to June—otherwise open daily July and August). Cooking is simple and unfussy, the fresh local ingredients first-rate. A typical main course might be slow-roasted spiced duckling with red onion marmalade and a Guinness, honey, and orange sauce. ⊠ *Annagh, Milltown Malbay, Co. Clare* ☎ *065/708-7022* 🖷 *065/708–7011* ⊕ *www. berrylodge.com* 🛏 *5 rooms* ⼊ *In-room: no a/c, no phone. In-hotel: no elevator* ☐ *MC, V* ⊗ *Closed Jan.–mid-Feb.* ⏐◎⏐ *BP.*

> **GNARLY, DUDE**
>
> Tom and Rosemary Buckley's Lahinch Surf Shop (☎065/708–1543) in The Promenade is the main center for County Clare surfers. Contact their Web site, ⊕www.lahinchsurfshop.com, for today's surf report.

$$$$
Fodor's Choice
★
🏠 **Moy House.** Built for Sir Augustine Fitzgerald, this enchanting, 18th-century Italianate-style lodge sits amid 15 private acres on an exhilarating, Wuthering Heights–like windswept cliff top that's a three-minute drive from Lahinch. It's a world away from the bustling seaside resort—a peaceful haven, where you are made to feel like you're a guest in a privately owned country house. The decor is most alluring, with period velvet sofas, marble fireplaces, and gilt-framed paintings. Upstairs, brocade curtains and Oriental rugs complement the guest rooms' Georgian and Victorian polished-mahogany antiques. Some rooms have open fires, some have freestanding cast-iron bathtubs, six have stunning sea views, and two overlook the pretty, sheltered garden. Once you settle in, enjoy a drink at the "honesty bar" in the elegant drawing room (help yourself, and write it down), one of many touches that make the place so relaxing. In bad weather, curl up with a book in the peaceful library on the lower floor. Guests are given the run of the kitchen should they need to rustle up a snack in the night. The cozy dining room (guests only) serves an imaginative four-course dinner (€50) of contemporary cuisine. The real dessert is the vista from the veranda over Lahinch Bay. ⊠ *Milltown Malbay Rd., Lahinch, Co. Clare* ☎ *065/708–2800* 🖷 *065/708–2500* ⊕ *www.moyhouse.com* 🛏 *9 rooms* ⼊ *In-room: no a/c. In-hotel: restaurant, no elevator, public Internet* ☐ *AE, MC, V* ⏐◎⏐ *BP.*

$$
🏠 **The Greenbrier Inn.** A well-designed modern building, this inn was designed as a guesthouse and both the guest rooms and the large lounge–dining room overlook Lahinch's famous golf links, Liscannor Bay, and the Atlantic Ocean. Set 250 yards from the beach, with ample parking, this is a practical, good-value choice for golfers and for those who like things traditional-modern and uncomplicated. The location and the views are the strong points here. Rooms are a good size, and have double-glazed windows with great views; some have small balconies. ⊠ *Ennistymon Rd., Co. Clare* ☎ *065/708–1242* 🖷 *065/708–1247* ⊕ *www.greenbrierinn.com* 🛏 *14 rooms* ☐ *MC, V* ⊗ *Closed Nov. 20–early Mar.* ⏐◎⏐ *BP.*

NIGHTLIFE & THE ARTS

For traditional music try the **19th Bar** (⊠*Main St.* ☎*065/708–1440*). **O'Looney's** (⊠*The Promenade* ☎*065/708–1414*) is known as Lahinch's surfers' pub; there's music every night in summer and on Saturday nights in winter.

SPORTS & THE OUTDOORS

Doonbeg Golf Club (⊠*On main N67 between Lahinch and Kilkee, Doonbeg* ☎*065/905–5246* ⊕*www.doonbeggolfclub.com*), an 18-hole links course designed by Greg Norman, winds along 2½ km (1½ mi) of crescent-shape beach; the ocean is visible from almost every hole. The 6,613-yard, 18-hole championship course at **Lahinch Golf Club** (⊠*The Seafront* ☎*065/708–1003*), which opened in 1892, has challenging links that follow the natural contours of the dunes. The 18-hole **Castle Course** (⊠*The Seafront* ☎*065/708–1003*) is ideal for a carefree round of seaside golf, with shorter holes than the championship course at Lahinch Golf Club.

SEA FOR YOURSELF
The Cliffs of Moher are so popular that you may find this "escape to nature" packed with visitors. To get a new perspective, why not explore one of the sightseeing boat cruises that sail up and down the coast along the Cliffs? A sea voyage under the command of Captain P.J. Garrihy of Cliffs of Moher Cruises (⊠*Doolin Pier* ☎*065/708–6060* ⊕*www.cliffs-of-moher-cruises. com; A*€*25 for 1½ hrs*) allows you to view the Cliffs of Moher from beneath, and get a better view of more than 20 species of seabirds that nest on its ledges. April through October there are six sailings per day, starting at 10 am. By advance request, you can take a sunrise or sunset cruise.

SHOPPING

The small **Design Lodge** (⊠*Main St.* ☎*065/708–1744*) specializes in ladies' fashions and carries several Irish labels.

THE CLIFFS OF MOHER

⑤ *10 km (6 mi) northwest of Lahinch on R478.*

★ One of Ireland's most breathtaking natural sights, the majestic Cliffs of Moher rise vertically out of the sea in a wall that stretches over a long, 8-km (5-mi) swath and in places reaches a height of 710 feet. Stratified deposits of five different rock layers are visible in the cliff face. This was considered a venerated place in the Celtic era and was a favorite hunting retreat of Brian Boru, the High King of Ireland. Numerous seabirds, including a large colony of puffins, make their homes in the shelves of rock on the cliffs. On a clear day you can see the Aran Islands and the mountains of Connemara to the north, as well as the lighthouse on Loop Head and the mountains of Kerry to the south. Built in 1835 by Cornelius O'Brien—of Bunratty Castle fame and a descendant of the Kings of Thomond—**O'Brien's Tower** is a defiant, broody sentinel on the cliffs' highest point, built to encourage tourism (yes, there were tourists even back then). Cornelius also erected here a wall of Liscannor flagstones (noted for their imprints of prehistoric eels). His tower

7

CLOSE UP

The Great Outdoors

While the West's rugged scenery has always been popular with outdoor types, the biggest growth area in recent years has been in provision of facilities for walkers and hikers. The last decade has seen the completion of various "way-marked" (signposted) walking routes. Better, there are also several new tour operators specializing in customized walking holidays, providing accommodation and a guide, or annotated walking maps (see Tour Options in Essentials at end of this chapter). If you like challenging hills and relatively rough terrain, the West is excellent hiking country. The unusual, almost lunar landscape of the Burren in County Clare is less demanding than the terrain in Connemara. Here, and in the area north of Connemara in south County Mayo, the countryside is sparsely populated and subject to sudden changes in weather, usually a shower of rain. There are four signposted trails in the area, but it's always advisable to buy a good map locally before setting out. The **Burren Way** runs from Lahinch

to Ballyvaughan on the shores of Galway Bay, a distance of 35 km (22 mi). The most spectacular part of the trail runs along the top of the Cliffs of Moher from Doolin to the coast near Lisdoonvarna, a distance of about 5 km (3 mi). The trails continue through the heart of the Burren's gray, rocky limestone landscape, with ever-changing views offshore of the Aran Islands and Galway Bay. The **Western Way's County Galway section** extends from Oughterard on Lough Corrib through the mountains of Connemara to Leenane on Killary Harbour, a distance of 50 km (30 mi). Its 177-km (110-mi) County Mayo section, known as the Western Way (Mayo), continues past Killary Harbor to Westport on Clew Bay to the Ox Mountains east of Ballina; this trail includes some of the finest mountain and coastal scenery in Ireland. A new, 224-km (140-mi) hiking route, *slí Chonamara*, through Irish-speaking Connemara, stretches along the shores of Galway Bay from An Spidéal to Carraroe, Carna, Letterfrack, and Recess.

is near the village of Liscannor. The glass-dome, subterranean visitor center, **Atlantic Edge,** is built into the cliff face and is a good refuge from passing rain squalls. Its interior imitates the limestone caves of County Clare and has elevated viewing platforms, a gift shop, and tearoom. ☎065/708–6141 ⊕*www.cliffsofmoher.ie* ✉*€24* ♥*Cliffs daily 24 hrs; visitor center daily Nov.–Feb., daily 9–5:30; Mar., Apr., and Oct., daily 9–6; May–Sept., daily 8:30 AM–9 PM. O'Brien's Tower May–Sept., daily 9:30–5:30, weather permitting.*

DOOLIN

❻ *6 km (4 mi) north of the Cliffs of Moher on R479.*

With houses shimmering in pink and lime, nestled along verdant ridges, and surrounded by farms, Doolin holds claims to a few of the most postcard-perfect spots in Ireland. Beyond charm, however, this tiny village, which seems to consist almost entirely of B&Bs, hostels, pubs, and restaurants, is widely reputed to have three of the best pubs for traditional music in Ireland. With the worldwide surge of interest in

Irish music during the last decade, the village has become more of a magnet for European musicians than it is for young, or even established, Irish artists.

But popularity brings its own price: when every other person is toting a videocam at a packed evening session, the magic can disappear quickly.

Doolin Ferries (☎065/707–4455 ⊕*www.doolinferries.com*) makes the 30-minute trip from Doolin Pier to Inis Oirr (Inisheer), the smallest of the Aran Islands, from spring until early fall (weather permitting). There are at least three round-trip sailings a day, and up to eight in July and August, but inquire on the day you plan to embark, as schedules vary according to weather and demand. Sometimes more than one ferry company operates out of Doolin; your return ticket will only be valid with the company that took you out, so when boarding the outbound ferry, be sure to check the return schedule. Sightseeing cruise lines heading up and down the Cliffs of Moher coast also leave and return from Doolin Pier, 1½ km. (1 mi) outside the village.

WHERE TO STAY & EAT

$$$ ✕🖼 **Ballinalacken Castle.** One hundred acres of wildflower meadows sur-
★ round this restored, low-slung Victorian lodge, which was built alongside the 16th-century ruins of an O'Brien castle (hence its somewhat bogus name). It's one of the most memorably sited of Ireland's coastal inns, with panoramic views of the Atlantic, the Aran Islands, and distant Connemara. The sense of spaciousness is exhilarating, and manager Marian Sheedy reports that many guests regularly oversleep due to the quietness. The public rooms display a mix of comfy old armchairs and antique, baronial-style Irish oak, amid floral wallpaper and rampant pots of aspidistra. Guest rooms in the older house have massive four-poster beds, marble fireplaces, and high ceilings. Some large, sunny rooms have bay windows to frame that stunning view; nice but plainer rooms in the new wing, with antique-style decor, are equally sought after. Chef Frank Sheedy, who has cooked in some of Ireland's best restaurants, serves an imaginative and sophisticated Continental menu ($$$$)—you'll want to finish off your feast of roast loin of Burren lamb with a platter of Cashel blue, Cooney, and smoked Gubbeen cheeses. Book in advance or you may not get a table. Ballinalacken is about 1 km (½ mi) outside Doolin on the Lisdoonvarna road. ⊠*Coast Rd., Co. Clare* ☎065/707–4025 🖷065/707–4025 ⊕*www.ballinalackencastle. com* ➵*10 rooms, 2 suites* ⚫*In-room: no a/c. In-hotel: restaurant, bar, no elevator* ⊟*AE, DC, MC, V* ☉*Closed Nov.–mid-Apr.* ⊺⊜*BP.*

$$ ✕🖼 **Aran View House.** This extensively modernized 1736 house on 100 acres of farmland offers magnificent views in nearly every direction: the Aran Islands to the west, the Cliffs of Moher to the south, and the gray limestone rocks of the Burren to the north. The interior is decorated with antique touches, such as four-poster beds and Georgian reproduction furniture. You can savor the view from the restaurant's bay windows while enjoying Continental cuisine ($$–$$$), featuring top seafood, with an atmosphere nicely enhanced by Regency chairs and dusky pink napery. It's on the coast road in the Fanore direction,

about a 10-minute walk north from Doolin village. ⊠*Coast Rd., Co. Clare* ☎*065/707–4061* 🖷*065/707–4540* ⊕*www.aranview.com* ➪*19 rooms* ☖*In-room: no a/c. In-hotel: restaurant, bar, no elevator* ⊟*AE, DC, MC, V* ☽*Closed Nov.–mid-Apr.* ⦿|*BP.*

$ ✕🏠 **Cullinan's Seafood Restaurant and Guesthouse.** The small restaurant ($$–$$$) here, in the back of a modest traditional farmhouse, is famed for its fresh, simply prepared seafood, but vegetarian and meat dishes are also served. Local ingredients—Inagh goat cheese, Burren smoked salmon, Doolin crabmeat, and Aran scallops—form the basis of a light, imaginative menu. A €25 early-bird set menu is served from 6 to 7. The floor-to-ceiling windows on two sides of the restaurant overlook the Aille River. The cottage-style rooms have simple pine furniture, fresh cotton comforters, pleasant country views, and room TVs on request. ⊠*Coast Rd., Co. Clare* ☎*065/707–4183* 🖷*065/707–4239* ⊕*www. cullinansdoolin.com* ➪*8 rooms* ☖*In-room: no a/c, no TV, dial-up. In-hotel: restaurant, no elevator* ⊟*MC, V* ☽*Guesthouse closed mid-Dec.–mid-Feb.; restaurant closed Oct.–Easter* ⦿|*BP.*

NIGHTLIFE & THE ARTS

Famous for their traditional-music sessions, Doolin's three pubs are designed to hold big crowds, which means you should expect minimal comfort: hard benches or bar stools if you're lucky, and spit-and-sawdust flooring. The theory is that the music will be so good, you won't notice anything else. However, interesting music-related memorabilia hang on the walls, and O'Connors and McGann's serve simple bar food from midday until 9 (Irish stew is a good bet). As you might imagine, the word is out about Doolin's "trad" scene—some nights the pubs overflow with crowds (and the videocams can get really annoying).

Gus O'Connor's (⊠*Fisher St.* ☎*065/707–4168*) sits midway between the village center and the pier and has tables outside near a stream. **McDermott's** (⊠*Lisdoonvarna Rd.* ☎*065/707–4700*) is popular with locals. Autumn through spring it's sometimes closed during the daytime. **McGann's** (⊠*Lisdoonvarna Rd.* ☎*065/707–4133*), across the road from McDermott's, is the smallest of Doolin's three famous pubs and has been run by the same family for 70 years.

SPORTS & THE OUTDOORS

You can book a self-guided cycle tour of the Burren through **Irish Cycle Hire** (⊠*Enterprise Centre, Aredee, Co, Louth* ☎*041/685–3772* ⊕*www.irishcylehire.com*), which rents bikes and provides luggage transfers.

SHOPPING

★ **Doolin Crafts Gallery** (⊠*Coast Rd.* ☎*065/707–4309*), beside the cemetery and the church, carries a diverse range of unusual Irish-made goods, including jewelry, sweaters, scarves, pottery, and leatherwork, from local craftspeople, reflecting the cosmopolitan background of the Irish-Dutch owners. Don't miss the 1-acre garden, which has more than 600 plants from all over the world. The garden and the Flagship Restaurant, which serves only home-cooked food and mounts art exhibits, are open daily from Easter through September.

LISDOONVARNA

❼ *5 km (3 mi) east of Doolin on R478.*

One of only three spa towns in Ireland (the others are Enniscrone, in western County Sligo, and Ballybunion, in County Kerry), Lisdoonvarna has several sulfurous and iron-bearing springs with radioactive properties, all containing iodine. In the late 19th century the town grew to accommodate visitors who wanted to "take the waters"; today, a major refurbishment of the Victorian spa complex was recently completed. The modest buildings reflect a mishmash of mock architectural styles: Scottish baronial, Swiss chalet, Spanish hacienda, and American motel. Depending on your taste, it's either lovably kitschy or just plain tacky. It's a popular weekend spot for Dubliners and other Irish vacationers, who stay at the big hotels (not the one reviewed below) and many of these roustabouts like to party well into the night.

If you're curious about health cures, the **Lisdoonvarna Spa Wells** is worth a visit. Iron and magnesia elements make the drinking water taste terrible (as does most spa water), but the bathing water is pleasant, if enervating. Electric sulfur baths, massage, wax baths, a sauna, and a solarium are available at the spa complex, which is on the edge of town in an attractive parkland setting. ⊠ *Town Park* ☎ *065/707–4023* ☎ *Complex free, sulfur baths €6.50, book in advance* ☉ *Early June– early Oct., daily 10–6.*

WHERE TO STAY & EAT

$$$ ✕🏠 **Sheedy's Restaurant and Country Inn.** A 17th-century farmhouse just a
★ short walk from the town center and the spa wells has been converted into this small, friendly hotel. It's been in the hands of the Sheedy family since 1855. Proprietor John Sheedy, who was chef de cuisine at Ashford Castle until moving back home, makes creative use of local produce in contemporary French-Irish fare ($$–$$$), and has turned Sheedy's into a much-lauded gastronomic destination. The green-gray dining room with plain, candlelighted tables provides a suitably sophisticated background for John's unusual and confident cooking. Try his fresh prawn soup, or a starter of warm salad of roasted monkfish with smoked bacon, mushrooms, and champagne dressing. His menu also features classic dishes like slow-roasted crispy duck with potato stuffing and apple sauce. The guest rooms are spacious and well-designed, with hip touches like power showers and CD players. All have relax-

ing views of the surrounding hilly countryside. ⊠*Spa Rd., Co. Clare* ☎*065/707–4026* 🖷*065/707–4555* ⊕*www.sheedys.com* ⤺*11 rooms* ♨*In-room: no a/c. In-hotel: restaurant, bar, no elevator* ▤*MC, V* ☉*Closed Oct.–mid-Mar.* ⍑*BP.*

NIGHTLIFE & THE ARTS

Country music and ballad singing are popular in the bars of Lisdoonvarna. For traditional music try the **Roadside Tavern** (⊠*Doolin Rd.* ☎*065/707–4084*).

SHOPPING

To see an audiovisual presentation on the technique of smoking Atlantic salmon, plus live demonstrations of the oak-smoking process, visit the **Burren Smokehouse Ltd** (⊠*Ballyvaughan Rd.* ☎*065/707–4432* ⊕*www. currensmokehouse.ie*). Neatly packaged whole sides of salmon, organic treats, and unusual crafts are for sale.

THE BURREN

❽ *Extending throughout western County Clare from Cliffs of Moher in*
★ *south to Black Head in north, and as far southeast as Corofin.*

As you travel north toward Ballyvaughan, the landscape becomes rockier and stranger. Instead of the seemingly ubiquitous Irish green, gray becomes the prevailing color. You're now in the heart of the Burren, a 300-square-km (116-square-mi) expanse that is one of Ireland's strangest landscapes. The Burren is aptly named: it's an Anglicization of the Irish word *bhoireann* (a rocky place). Stretching off in all directions, as far as the eye can see, are vast, irregular slabs of fissured limestone, known as karst, with deep cracks between them. From a distance, it looks like a lunar landscape, so dry that nothing could possibly grow on it. But in spring (especially from mid-May to mid-June), the Burren becomes a wild rock garden, as an astonishing variety of wildflowers blooms in the cracks between the rocks, among them at least 23 native species of orchid. The Burren also supports an incredible diversity of wildlife, including frogs, newts, lizards, badgers, stoats, sparrow hawks, kestrels, and dozens of other birds and animals. The wildflowers and other plants are given life from the spectacular caves, streams, and potholes that lie beneath the rough, scarred pavements. With the advent of spring, *turloughs* (seasonal lakes that disappear in dry weather) appear on the plateau's surface. Botanists are particularly intrigued by the cohabitation of Arctic and Mediterranean plants, many so tiny (and so rare, so please do not pick any) you can't see them from your car window; make a point of exploring some of this rocky terrain on foot. Numerous signposted walks run through both coastal and inland areas. For a private guided tour, contact **Mary Angela Keane** (☎*065/707–4003* ⊠€*35 per hour*), or Shane Connolly of **Burren Hill Walks** (☎*065/707–7168* ⊠€*15 per person*). May and June are peak months for flora, but a tour is worthwhile at any time of year.

The tiny **Burren Centre** has a modest audiovisual display and other exhibits that explain the Burren's geology, flora, and archaeology. Also here are a café and a crafts shop with good maps and locally published guides. ⊠*8 km (5 mi) southeast of Lisdoonvarna on R476, Kilfenora* ☎*065/708–8030* ⊕*www.theburrencentre.ie* ⊡*€5.75* ⊘*Mid-Mar.– May, Sept., and Oct., daily 10–5; June–Aug., daily 9:30–6.*

Beside the Burren Centre in Kilfenora, the ruins of a small 12th-century church, once the **Cathedral of St. Fachtna,** have been partially restored as a parish church. There are some interesting carvings in the roofless choir, including an unusual, life-size human skeleton. In a field about 165 feet west of the ruins is an elaborately sculpted high cross that is worth examining, though parts of it are badly weathered.

NIGHTLIFE & THE ARTS

Vaughan's Pub (⊠*Main St., Kilfenora* ☎*065/708–8004*) is known for its traditional-music sessions.

BALLYVAUGHAN

❾ *16 km (10 mi) north of Lisdoonvarna on N67.*

A pretty little waterside village and a good base for exploring the Burren, Ballyvaughan attracts walkers and artists who enjoy the views of Galway Bay and access to the Burren.

Aillwee Cave is the only such chamber in the region accessible to those who aren't spelunkers. This vast 2-million-year-old cave is illuminated for about 3,300 feet and contains an underground river and waterfall. Above ground, there are a big crafts shop, and cheese- and honey-making demonstrations. ⊠*5 km (3 mi) south of Ballyvaughan on R480* ☎*065/707–7036* ⊕*www.aillweecave.ie* ⊡*€12* ⊘*Sept.—June, daily 9:30–6, last tour at 5:30; July and Aug., daily 10–7, last tour at 6:30; phone in advance in Dec.*

WHERE TO STAY & EAT

$$$ ✕⊡**Gregan's Castle Hotel.** Sharon Stone, Gabriel Byrne, and Edna
★ O'Brien have all been guests at this quiet, picturesque, creeper-covered and highly romantic Victorian country house, set at the base of the aptly named Corkscrew Hill (on N67, mid-way between Ballyvaughan and Lisdoonvarna). The Haden family obviously knows a thing or two about hospitality. They certainly know how to decorate in the loveliest fashion—the Corkscrew Bar is a cozy corner hung with copper pots, the guest bedrooms are lined with wallpaper patterns based on William Morris designs and stocked with Georgian and Victorian antiques, while the dining room allures in brilliant red. The house is surrounded by gardens and overlooks Galway Bay and the gray mountains of the Burren. The spacious ground-floor rooms have private patio gardens but lack the splendid views of the rooms upstairs. Ask about special deals for three-day stays. The restaurant ($$$–$$$$; jacket and tie required) serves updated French cuisine. ⊠*Base of Corkscrew Hill, Co. Clare* ☎*065/707–7005* 🖷*065/707– 7111* ⊕*www.gregans.ie* 🛏*18 rooms, 4 suites* ⚘*In-room: no a/c, no TV. In-hotel: restaurant, bar, no elevator, bicycles, public Wi-Fi* ⊟*AE, MC, V* ⊘*Closed Nov.–Mar.* ⍓*BP.*

7

$$ ✕⊞ **Hyland's Burren Hotel.** A turf fire greets you in the lobby of the hotel, a cheerful, welcoming spot with a reputation for friendliness and good entertainment. This unpretentious yellow-and-red coaching inn, in the heart of the Burren, dates from the early 18th century, and has been much expanded. Rooms vary in size and shape, but all have pine furniture and color-coordinated drapes and spreads. Ask for a room overlooking the Burren. The restaurant ($$–$$$), cheerfully furnished with country pine and red tablecloths, specializes in simply prepared local produce. The bar hosts live music most nights from June to mid-September, and Irish storytelling once a week. Ask about special weekend rates. ⊠ *Main St., Co. Clare* ☎ *065/707–7037* 🖨 *065/707–7131* ⊕ *www.hylandsburren.com* 🛏 *30 rooms* ♿ *In-room: no a/c. In-hotel: restaurant, bar, no elevator* ⊟ *AE, DC, MC, V* ⦿*BP.*

$ ⊞ **Drumcreehy House.** The pretty gabled facade with dormer windows is traditional in style, but, in fact, Bernadette Moloney and her German husband, Armin Grefkes, designed and built this house specifically as a B&B. It's just across the road from the sea, about 2 km (1 mi) north of the village, just beyond the Whitethorn Craft Shop. The interior has character and style, thanks to a mix of imposing 19th-century German antiques, stripped-pine floors, and comfortable sofas and armchairs. Rooms are spacious and airy, with small sitting areas overlooking the peaceful countryside. Each room is individually styled on a wildflower theme, with plain walls, color-coordinated quilts and curtains, brass bedsteads, and attractive small antiques. A light, bar-food–style menu is served in the lounge, where you can also take a glass of wine; from April to October you can reserve for a more formal evening meal. The breakfast menu offers an unusually wide choice, including French toast, kippers, or creamed mushrooms on toast. Your hosts are knowledgeable and enthusiastic about the area, and have a good supply of books and maps. ☎ *065/707–7377* 🖨 *065/707–7379* ⊕ *www.drumcreehyhouse.com* 🛏 *12 rooms* ♿ *In-room: no a/c. In-hotel: No elevator, public Wi-Fi* ⊟ *MC, V* ⦿*BP.*

NIGHTLIFE & THE ARTS

Fodor'sChoice ★ The friendly **Monk's Pub** (⊠ *Main St.* ☎ *065/707–7059*), near the waterfront, hosts great sessions of traditional and folk music. The bar food is excellent.

COOLE PARK

❿ *24 km (15 mi) northeast of Corofin on N18.*

Coole Park, north of the little town of Gort, was once the home of Lady Augusta Gregory (1859–1932), patron of W. B. Yeats and cofounder with the poet of Dublin's Abbey Theatre. Yeats visited here often, as did almost all the other writers who contributed to the Irish literary revival in the first half of the 20th century, including George Bernard Shaw (1856–1950) and Sean O'Casey (1880–1964). Douglas Hyde (1860–1949), the first president of Ireland, was also a visitor. The house fell derelict after Lady Gregory's death and was demolished in 1941; the grounds are now a national forest and wildlife park. Picnic tables make this a lovely alfresco lunch spot. The only reminder of its literary past is the Autograph Tree, a copper beech on which many of Lady Gregory's famous guests carved their initials. There's also a visitor center with displays on Lady Gregory and Yeats. ⊠ *Galway Rd.* ☎ *091/631–804* ⌕ *Park free, visitor center €3* ⊙ *Park daily 10–dusk; visitor center Apr.–mid-June, Tues.–Sun. 10–5; mid-June–Aug., daily 9:30–6:30; Sept., daily 10–5.*

THOOR BALLYLEE

⓫ *5 km (3 mi) north of Coole Park, signposted from N66.*

Thoor Ballylee is a sight Yeats fans won't want to miss. (It's one of the few major Yeats-related sights in the West that's not in County Sligo.) In his fifties and newly married, Yeats bought this 14th-century Norman "thoor," or tower, as a ruin in 1916 for the equivalent of about €45 in today's funds. The tower stands beside a whitewashed, thatched-roof cottage with a tranquil stream running alongside it. Its proximity to Lady Gregory's house at Coole Park made this a desirable location, though it required significant work on Yeats's part to make the ruin livable. He stayed here intermittently until 1929 and penned some of his more mystical works here, including *The Tower* and *The Winding Stair.* It's now fully restored and some rooms showcase the poet's original furnishings. The audiovisual display is a useful introduction to Yeats and his times. High up the tower's parapet you can get some great views of Coole's Seven Woods. ⊠ *N66, 2 km (3 mi) north of Gort* ☎ *091/631–436* ⊕ *www.irelandwest.ie* ⌕ *€6* ⊙ *June–Sept., Mon.–Sat. 9:30–5.*

KINVARA

⓬ *13½ km (8 mi) east of Ballyvaughan, 15 km (9 mi) northwest of Gort*
★ *on N67, 25 km (15½ mi) south of Galway City.*

The picture-perfect village of Kinvara is a growing holiday base, thanks to its gorgeous bay-side locale, great walking and sea angling, and numerous pubs. It's well worth a visit, whether you're coming from Ballyvaughan or Gort. Kinvara is best known for its longstanding early August sailing event, Cruinniú na mBád (Festival of the Gathering of the Boats), in which traditional brown-sailed Galway hookers laden with turf race across the bay. Hookers were used until the early part of this century to carry turf, provisions, and cattle across Galway Bay and out to the Aran Islands. A sculpture in Galway's Eyre Square honors their local significance.

★ On a rock north of Kinvara Bay, the 16th-century **Dunguaire Castle** spectacularly commands all the approaches to Galway Bay. It's said to stand on the site of a 7th-century castle built by the King of Connaught. Built in 1520 by the O'Hynes clan, the tiny, storybook castle takes its name from the fabled king of Connaught, Guaire. In 1929 it was purchased by Oliver St. John Gogarty, the noted surgeon, man of letters, and model for Buck Mulligan, a character in James Joyce's *Ulysses.*

To his outpost came many of the leading figures of the 19th-century Celtic revival in Irish literature. Today Dunguaire is used for a Middle Ages–style banquet that honors local writers and others with ties to the West, including Lady Gregory, W. B. Yeats, Sean O'Casey, and Pádraic O'Conaire. ⊠ *West Village* ☎ *091/637–108* ⊕ *www.shannonheritage. com* ⊡ *Castle €5.95, banquet €51* ⊘ *Mid-Apr.–Oct., daily 9:30–5; banquet at 5:30 and 8:30.*

WHERE TO STAY & EAT

$–$$$ ✕ **Moran's Oyster Cottage.** Signposted off the main road on the south
★   side of Clarinbridge, this waterside thatched cottage, the home of the Moran family since 1760, houses at its rear a simply furnished restaurant that serves only seafood: Gigas oysters, chowder, smoked salmon, seafood cocktail, lobster with boiled potatoes and garlic butter, and fresh crab salad. It's *the* place to sample the local oysters, grown on a nearby bed owned by the Moran family, who have had the pub for six generations. Hope for good weather, so that you can eat outside overlooking the weir and watch the swans float by. The front bar has been preserved in the "old style," which means it's small and cramped, but very interesting if you want to get an idea of what most pubs around here were like 50 years ago. ⊠ *The Weir, Kilcolgan* ☎ *091/796–113* ⊟ *AE, MC, V.*

$$ ✕🏨 **Merriman Inn.** Don't let its traditional looks deceive you: this white-washed, thatched inn on the shores of Galway Bay is, in fact, a mid-size hotel, decorated with locally made, well-designed furniture, and original crafts, paintings, and sculpture. Guest rooms are medium-size with smallish, cottage-style windows at head height, and modern pine furniture; small paintings of local scenes provide the principal color. If you're lucky you could get a room with a breathtaking view of Galway Bay; less than half have one, so if it matters, ask when booking. The Quilty Room is a large, airy restaurant ($$–$$$) hung with interesting landscape and still-life paintings by an artist named Quilty. Its menu is French influenced—try the outstanding tournedos of salmon pan-seared with a confit of fennel and a sharp, spicy jus. ⊠ *Main St., Co. Galway* ☎ *091/638–222* 🖷 *091/637–686* ⊕ *www.merrimanhotel. com* ⇆ *32 rooms* ⚭ *In-room: no a/c, dial-up. In-hotel: restaurant, bar* ⊟ *AE, DC, MC, V* ⊘ *Closed Jan.–mid-Mar.* ¶◎¶ *BP.*

¢ 🏨 **Burren View Farm.** A million-dollar view awaits you at this modest, yellow, two-story B&B on the edge of Galway Bay, 5 km (3 mi) west of Kinvara. Set on a working sheep and cattle farm, it's relatively isolated amid stone-walled fields dotted with sheep. The breakfast room, sun lounge, and front bedrooms look out across a wide sea inlet to the gray expanse of the Burren. Rooms are plain and homey but clean and well maintained. Wholesome evening meals, Irish or Continental-style, are cooked on request, and food is also served in the local pub, a five-minute walk away. ⊠ *Doorus, Co. Galway* ☎ *091/637–142* ⊕ *www. kinvara.com* ⇆ *5 rooms, 3 with bath* ⚭ *In-room: no a/c, no phone, no TV. In hotel: restaurant, tennis, fishing, no elevator* ⊘ *Closed Nov.– Apr.* ¶◎¶ *BP.*

NIGHTLIFE & THE ARTS

The first weekend in May, Kinvara hosts the annual **Cuckoo Fleadh** (✉ *Main St.* ☎*091/637–145*), a traditional-music festival. Traditional music is played most nights at the **Winkles Hotel bar** (✉*The Square* ☎*91/637–137*), where Sharon Shannon got her start in the music business.

GALWAY CITY

Galway is often said to be a state of mind as much as it is a specific place. The largest city in the West today and the ancient capital of the province of Connaught, Galway, with a current population of 72,400, is also one of the fastest-growing cities in Europe. It's an astonishing fact, and you have to wonder where this city can possibly grow. For despite Galway's size, its commercially busy ring road, and its ever-spreading suburbs, its heart is *tiny*—a warren of streets so compact that if you spend more than a few hours here, you'll soon be strolling along with the sort of easy familiarity you'd feel in any small town.

For many Irish people, Galway is a favorite weekend getaway: known as the city of festivals, it's the liveliest place in the Republic. It's also a university town: University College Galway (or UCG as it's locally known) is a center for Gaelic culture (Galway marks the eastern gateway to the West's large Gaeltacht). A fair share of UCG's 9,000 students pursue their studies in the Irish language. Galway is, in fact, permeated by youth culture. On festival weekends, you'll see as many pierced and tattooed teenagers and twentysomethings here as you'd find at a rock concert. (If you're looking for the quiet, quaint side of Ireland depicted on travel posters, have a quick look at Galway and push on to Clifden or Westport, where you can still savor the atmosphere of a small old-world town.) But its students aren't its only avant-garde, as Galway has long attracted writers, artists, and musicians. The latter whip up brand-new jigs while also keeping the traditional-music pubs lively year-round. And the city's two small but internationally acclaimed theater companies draw a steady stream of theater people.

Although you're not conscious of it when you're in the center of town, Galway is spectacularly situated, on the north shore of Galway Bay, where the River Corrib flows from Lough Corrib to the sea. The seaside suburb of Salthill, on the south-facing shore of Galway Bay, has spectacular vistas across the vividly blue bay to Black Head on the opposite shore.

Galway's growth and popularity mean that at its busiest moments, its narrow, one-way streets are jam-packed with pedestrians, while cars are gridlocked. If there's a city in Ireland that never sleeps, this must be it. In fact, if you want to be guaranteed a quiet night's sleep, ask either for a room in the back of your center-city hotel or simply stay outside of town.

7

City of the Tribes

Galway's founders were Anglo-Normans who arrived in the mid-13th century and fortified their settlement against "the native Irish," as local chieftains were called.

Galway became known as "the City of the Tribes" because of the dominant role in public and commercial life of the 14 families that founded it.

Their names are still common in Galway and elsewhere in Ireland: Athy,

Blake, Bodkin, Browne, D'Arcy, Dean, Font, French, Kirwan, Joyce, Lynch, Morris, Martin, and Skerret.

The city's medieval heritage, a fusion of Gaelic and Norman influences, is apparent in the intimate two- and three-story stone buildings, the winding streets, the narrow passageways, and the cobblestones underfoot.

EXPLORING GALWAY CITY

Most of the city's sights, aside from the cathedral and the university campus, can be found in a narrow sector of the medieval town center that runs in a southwesterly direction from Eyre Square to the River Corrib. Eyre Square is easily recognizable, as it's the only open space in central Galway. It only takes five minutes to walk straight down Galway's main shopping street, the continuation of the north side of Eyre Square, to the River Corrib, where it ends (note that the name of this street changes several times). Not only is the city center compact, it's also largely pedestrian-friendly, so the best way to explore it is on foot. Even the farthest point, the university campus, is less than a 15-minute walk from Eyre Square. A walk (or drive, for that matter) to Galway's seaside suburb, Salthill, 3 km (2 mi) west of Galway, with its long seaside promenade, is a favorite local occupation, traditionally undertaken on a Sunday afternoon.

WHAT TO SEE

㉓ Cathedral of Our Lady Assumed into Heaven and St. Nicholas. On Nun's Island, which forms the west bank of the River Corrib beside the Salmon Weir Bridge, stands Galway's largest Catholic church, dedicated by Cardinal Cushing of Boston in 1965. The cathedral was built on the site of the old Galway jail; a white cross embedded in the pavement of the adjacent parking lot marks the site of the cemetery that stood beside the prison. ✉*Free* ☉*Freely accessible.*

㉕ Claddagh. On the west bank of the Corrib estuary, this district was once an Irish-speaking fishing village outside the walls of the old town. The name is an Anglicization of the Irish *cladach,* which means "marshy ground." It retained a strong, separate identity until the 1930s, when its traditional thatched cottages were replaced by a conventional housing plan and its unique character and traditions were largely lost. One thing has survived: the Claddagh ring, composed of two hands clasped around a heart with a crown above it (symbolizing love, friendship, and loyalty), is still used by many Irish people as a wedding ring. Reproductions in gold or silver are favorite Galway souvenirs.

⑰ **Collegiate Church of St. Nicholas.** Built by the Anglo-Normans in 1320 and enlarged in 1486 and again in the 16th century, the church contains many fine carvings and gargoyles dating from the late Middle Ages, and it's one of the best-preserved medieval churches in Ireland. Legend has it that Columbus prayed

TRAVEL TIP

If you have postcards to mail, you may want to stop at the General Post Office at the start of your walking tour. It's on the left side of Eglinton Street, the first right off Williamsgate Street as you head toward the river from Eyre Square.

here on his last stop before setting off on his voyage to the New World. On Saturday mornings, a street market, held in the pedestrian way beside the church, attracts two dozen or so vendors and hundreds of shoppers. ⊠ *Lombard St., Center* 🖼 *Free* ☉ *Daily 8–dusk.*

⑬ **Eyre Square.** The largest open space in central Galway and the heart of the city, on the east side of the River Corrib, Eyre Square incorporates a sculpture garden and children's play area on its east side, while its west side is bound by a heavily traveled road. A controversial renovation saw the removal of several well-loved landmarks, including most of the trees in the square (they were diseased). They were replaced by 95 new trees that will take time to mature. In the center is **Kennedy Park,** a patch of lawn named in honor of John F. Kennedy, who spoke here when he visited the city in June 1963. At the north end of the park, a 20-foot-high steel sculpture standing in the pool of a fountain represents the brown sails seen on Galway hookers, the area's traditional sailing boats. Now the entrance to Kennedy Park, the **Browne Doorway** was taken in 1905 from the Browne family's town house on Upper Abbeygate Street; it has the 17th-century coats of arms of both the Browne and Lynch families (two of Galway's 14 founding families), called a "marriage stone" because when the families were joined in marriage their coats of arms were, too. Keep an eye out for similar if less elaborate Browne doorways as you walk around the old part of town.

㉑ **Galway City Museum.** The city's civic museum, housed in a modern building behind the Spanish Arch, contains materials relating to local history: old photographs, antiquities (the oldest is a stone ax head carbon-dated to 3500 BC), and other historical gewgaws. ⊠ *Fishmarket, Spanish Arch* 🕾 *091/567–641* 🖼 *€2* ☉ *Daily 10–5.*

⑯ **Lynch Memorial Window.** Embedded in a stone wall above a built-up Gothic doorway off Market Street, the window marks the spot where, according to legend, James Lynch FitzStephen, mayor of Galway in the early 16th century, condemned his son to death after the young man confessed to murdering a Spanish sailor who had romanced his girlfriend. When no one could be found to carry out the execution, Judge Lynch hanged his son himself, ensuring that justice prevailed, before retiring into seclusion. ⊠ *Market St., Center.*

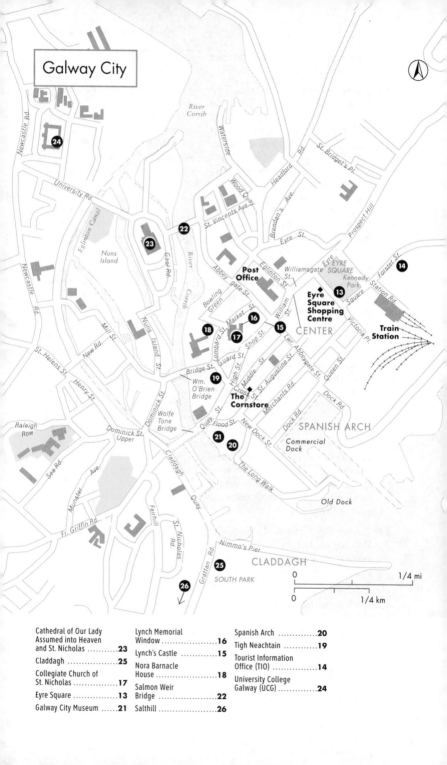

Galway City

River Corrib

Newcastle Rd.

University Rd.

Eglinton Canal

Nuns Island

Newcastle Rd.

Mill St.

New Rd.

St. Helens St.

Henry St.

Raleigh Row

Sea Rd.

Munster Ave.

Fr. Griffin Rd.

Fairhill

Dominick St. Upper

Wolfe Tone Bridge

Dominick St.

Claddagh Quay

St. Nicholas Rd.

Grattan Rd.

Nimmo's Pier

SOUTH PARK

CLADDAGH

Waterside

Wood Quay

St. Vincents Ave.

Gael Rd.

River Corrib

Nuns Island St.

Abbeygate St.

Bowling Green

Market St.

Lombard St.

Bridge St.

Wm. O'Brien Bridge

High St.

Guard St.

Cross St.

Middle St.

Quay St.

Flood St.

New Dock St.

The Long Walk

Headford Rd.

Brendan's Ave.

Eyre St.

Williamsgate St.

Eglinton St.

William St.

Shop St.

St. Augustine St.

Merchants Rd.

EYRE SQUARE

Kennedy Park

Eyre Square

Lwr. Abbeygate St.

Victoria Pl.

Queen St.

Dock Rd.

Dock Rd.

SPANISH ARCH

Commercial Dock

Old Dock

St. Bridget's Pl.

Prospect Hill

Forster St.

Station Rd.

Train Station

Post Office

Eyre Square Shopping Centre

The Cornstore

CENTER

24

23

22

13

14

15

16

17

18

19

20

21

25

26

0 ···················· 1/4 mi

0 ···················· 1/4 km

Designer Galway (How to Get the Look): A Walk

There's no question about it: they have a different look in Galway. People have always dressed differently, because they dress for the Galway weather, which can be wet and windy at any time of year. But ever since Galway was transformed by Ireland's "Celtic Tiger" economic boom, they have also dressed—and decorated—with a real sense of style. Want proof? Just join the locals on the following walk.

Pick up a free map of Galway from the swanky new **Tourist Information Office** on Forster Place. Turn left out the front door to reach the **Great Southern Hotel,** a monumental 19th-century grande dame in cut stone (its lobby is just the place for "scene-iors" to take their coffee or tea). Turn left beyond the hotel and right into Merchants Road to find the lively **Bold Art Gallery.** Then turn left into **Flood Street,** the heart of medieval Galway, a tiny area where all the cutest shops are jam-packed together, including **Cobwebs,** abrim with offbeat antique jewelry, old binoculars, and bronze model airplanes. For a feel of the essential Galway, cross the road to the banks of the **River Corrib** and walk to your left to the **Spanish Arch.** When natives feel homesick, this is the view they think of: white water breaking on the dark surface of the swift-flowing Corrib, the fishing boats of the Claddagh, and as many as a hundred swans floating by.

Staying on this side of the Corrib, cross over the bridge and take the riverside footpath past the contempo Jurys Inn and some old warehouses. Turn left over O'Brien's Bridge for the historic **Bridge Mills,** now outfitted

with a designer swap shop, a fun haberdashery, and **Tús Craft Design.** Continue along Bridge Street, turning right into Cross Street and right into Kirwan's Lane. Here, **Design Concourse Ireland/Judy Greene Pottery** has locally made turned-wood objects, basketware, and perfumery. Medieval Kirwan's Lane leads you on to Quay Street and **Twice as Nice,** a vintage and antique clothing boutique with old Irish linen. Continue up High Street to **Faller's Sweaters and Tweeds,** just the place to buy an Aran sweater, and **The Kilkenny Shop,** Galway's largest emporium of Irish-designed products, with a dazzling selection of chic John Rocha crystal, Newbridge Silver, and Nicholas Mosse pottery. Across High Street, **Kenny's Gallery,** run by Tom Kenny, shows mainly artists working in the area. Farther up on the right, **Maille** has some great mohair wraps and *the* essential Galway fashion item, a Jack Murphy raincoat. Choose between a short version or a caped version (for those really wet days)—top one off with a rainproof Stetson with a feather in it and you'll pass for a local. High Street leads into William Street, where you'll find **The Treasure Chest,** a three-story shop selling upmarket Irish goods. Its exterior, painted in Wedgwood blue with white swags, just like the famous china, is a favorite with photographers. **Brown Thomas,** on William at the corner of Eglinton, has long been Galway's most upscale department store. A few steps up Williamsgate Street brings us back to Eyre Square and your starting point at the TIO.

⓯ Lynch's Castle. Now a branch of the Allied Irish Banks, this is the finest remaining example in Galway of a 16th-century fortified house—fortified because neighboring Irish tribes persistently raided the village, whose commercial life excluded them. The decorative details on its stone lintels are of a type usually found only in southern Spain. Like the Spanish Arch, it serves as a reminder of the close trading links that once existed between Galway and Spain. ⊠*Shop St., Center.*

⓲ Nora Barnacle House. On June 16, 1904, James Joyce (1882–1941) had his first date with Nora Barnacle, who would later become his wife. He subsequently chose to set *Ulysses* on this day, now known universally as Bloomsday—"a recognition of the determining effect upon his life of his attachment to her," as Joyce's biographer Richard Ellman has said. Nora, the daughter of a poor baker, was born here. Today it has a modest collection of photographs, letters, and memorabilia, and a small gift shop. ⊠*4 Bowling Green, Center* ☎*091/564–743* ⊠*€2.50* ☉*Mid-May–Aug., Mon.–Sat. 10–5; mid-Sept.–mid-May by appointment.*

㉒ Salmon Weir Bridge. The bridge itself is nothing special, but in season—from mid-April to early July—shoals of salmon are visible from its deck as they lie in the clear river water before making their way upstream to the spawning grounds of Lough Corrib. ⊠*West end of St. Vincent's Ave., Center.*
★

㉖ Salthill. A lively, hugely popular seaside resort, Salthill is beloved for its seaside promenade—the traditional place "to sit and watch the moon rise over Claddagh, and see the sun go down on Galway Bay," as Bing Crosby used to croon in the most famous song about the city. The main attraction of the village, set 3 km (2 mi) west of Galway, is the long sandy beach along the edge of Galway Bay and the promenade above it. The building of big new hotels along the seafront has nevertheless left plenty of room for the traditional amusement arcades (full of slot machines), seasonal cafés, and a fairground.

⓴ Spanish Arch. Built in 1584 to protect the quays where Spanish ships unloaded cargoes of wines and brandies, the arch now stands in the parking lot opposite Jurys Galway Inn. It's easily (and often) mistaken for a pile of weathered stones, yet it's another reminder of Galway's—and Ireland's—past links with Spain. ⊠*The Long Walk, Spanish Arch.*

⓳ Tigh Neachtain *(Naughton's Pub).* You can hear traditional music every night at this popular pub, which stands at a busy little crossroads in the heart of the old town. Grab a spot at one of its old-fashioned partitioned snugs at lunchtime for an inexpensive selection of imaginative bar food. It's a good place to mingle with local actors, writers, artists, musicians, and students, although it can become sardine-can crowded. ⊠*17 Cross St., Spanish Arch* ☎*091/566–172.*

FodorsChoice
★

⓮ Tourist Information Office *(TIO).* Just off Eyre Square, east of the bus and train station and the Great Southern Hotel, this is the place to make reservations for events around town and find out about the latest happenings. You can also book tickets to the Aran Islands

The Galway Saturday Market

Locals get up very early on Saturday in Galway in order to get the pick of the goods on offer at the Saturday food market. About 90 colorful stall-holders, many of whom follow an alternative lifestyle, set out their wares in the area behind the Collegiate Church of St. Nicholas in the city center. Take your pick of the Mediterranean goods on offer at the Real Olive Company, or sample some Aran Smoked Salmon, or treat yourself to an outdoor lunch at the Madras Curry Stall, or sushi from the Japanese-run Da Kappa-ya Sushi, followed by dessert from Yummy Crêpes. Organic vegetable sellers, plant sellers, herbalists, cheese mongers, and bakers are joined by hat sellers, wood carvers, and knitwear stalls, while a selection of Galway's famously wacky buskers entertain with music, juggling, and dance. Who could resist?

here. ⊠ *Forster Pl., Center* ☎ *091/537–700* ⊕ *www.irelandwest.ie* ⊗ *Weekdays 9–6, Sat. 9–1.*

㉔ **University College Galway** *(UCG).* Opened in 1846 to promote the development of local industry and agriculture, the UCG today is a center for Irish-language and Celtic studies. The Tudor Gothic–style quadrangle, completed in 1848, is worth a visit, though much of the rest of the campus is architecturally undistinguished. The library here has an important archive of Celtic-language materials, and in July and August the university hosts courses in Irish studies for overseas students. The campus is across the River Corrib, in the northwestern corner of the city. ⊠ *Newcastle Rd., University.*

WHERE TO STAY & EAT

Note: During peak events, such as the Galway Festival Race Week, hotel rates in Galway do shoot up.

$$–$$$ ✕ **Kirwan's Lane Creative Cuisine.** Look for Mike O'Grady's stylish modern restaurant in a revamped alley at the river end of Quay Street. Blue-stained wooden tables, narrow floor-to-ceiling windows, and a quarry-tile floor set the stage for an informal, bistro-style menu. Fresh prawn cocktail is served with sauce Marie-Rose and a passion-fruit mayonnaise; confit of duck leg comes with braised red cabbage, star anise, and balsamic oil. Main courses have similarly unpredictable twists—rack of lamb is accompanied by sweet potato mash, basil oil, and apricots, and monkfish tails are dressed with a simple lemon and coriander dressing. ⊠ *Kirwan's La., Spanish Arch* ☎ *091/568–266* ▤ *AE, DC, MC, V* ⊗ *Closed Sun.*

$$–$$$ ✕ **Malt House.** Hidden away in a flower-filled courtyard off High Street in the center of old Galway, Barry and Therese Cunningham's cozy pub-restaurant has long been popular with locals and visitors. In a city where the dining scene is trend-driven and youth-oriented, this is an oasis of calm and tradition, where nothing ever changes much, and you wouldn't want it to—just like your favorite armchair. You can either eat in the bar itself or just off the bar in the restaurant, a square room with beamed ceilings, rough-cast walls and appointments in the Galway team colors–white and maroon. Try the five-course seafood sampler menu, or choose à la carte. Fresh prawns panfried in garlic butter are popular; the sirloin steak with green-peppercorn sauce and the rack of lamb with a parsley crust should please landlubbers. ⊠*Old Malte Arcade, High St., Center* ☎*091/563–993* ⊟*AE, DC, MC, V* ⊘*Closed Sun.*

¢–$$$ ✕**McDonagh's Seafood House.** This longtime Galway landmark is partly
★ a fish-and-chips bar and partly a "real" fish restaurant. If you haven't yet tried fish-and-chips, this is the place to start: cod, whiting, mackerel, haddock, or hake is deep-fried in a light batter while you watch. The fish is served with a heap of freshly cooked chips (french fries). Or go for the more sophisticated (and expensive) Seafood Bar menu: Galway oysters au naturel, perhaps, or a bowl of mussels steamed in wine and garlic, followed by flame-grilled black sole. The McDonaghs are one of Galway's most entrepreneurial families, in charge of several hotels in addition to this spot. ⊠*22 Quay St., Spanish Arch* ☎*091/565–001* ⊟*DC, MC, V* ⊘*No lunch Sun. Oct.–Apr.*

$$ ✕**Nimmo's.** Good food and a great ambience—due partly to the friendly, enthusiastic staff—makes this bustling bistro one of Galway's most popular restaurants. The central location in an old stone building overlooking the Corrib River adds to the pleasure. The long, spacious, second-floor room has original paintings on the walls and well-spaced tables set with white linen. The menu is short but well balanced, and while presentation is flamboyant, the food also tastes good. Try the salmon and chive terrine wrapped in smoked almonds, or rack of lamb with roasted red peppers and spring onion–mashed potatoes. There's a separate wine bar downstairs. ⊠*The Long Walk, Spanish Arch* ☎*091/561–114* ⊟*AE, DC, MC, V* ⊘*Closed Mon. No lunch Tues.,, Wed., and mid-Sept.–May.*

$–$$ ✕**K.C. Blake's.** K.C. stands for Casey, as in owner-chef John Casey, a larger-than-life character, who turned a medieval stone town house once associated with the Blake family—one of the families that founded Galway—into an ultramodern eatery. The hard-edge, minimalist decor, which features sleek black walls, provides a strong contrast with the old stone building. Dishes range from traditional beef-and-Guinness stew to funky starter combinations like black pudding croquettes with pear and cranberry sauce. ⊠*10 Quay St., Spanish Arch* ☎*091/561–826* ⊟*AE, MC, V.*

$$$$ ✕▦**Glenlo Abbey.** With distant views of Lough Corrib and a golf course on its 138-acre estate, Glenlo Abbey is a rural hideaway just 5 km (2½ mi) from Galway. Built as a private home in 1740, it takes its name from the vast church built next door for the owner's ailing wife, who died before it was consecrated. Today, the church is used as a conference center and banquet room. The Abbey's lobby resembles a gentlemen's club, with parquet floors, chesterfields, and leather-bound books. Upstairs, official

Voices of Ireland

TOM KENNY
Owner, The Kenny Gallery

Tom Kenny grew up in old Galway, a run-down city where nothing much happened. As a member of the legendary family behind the city's old landmark, Kenny's Bookshop, he has experienced the boom years firsthand. Founded by his mother in the 1940's, Kenny's had become world-famous by the 1980's. Continuing their trend of moving with the times, in 2006 Kenny's Bookshop closed its retail premises, but continues to trade online (⊕*www.kennys.ie*), employing three generations of the family. Today, Tom Kenny, runs an art gallery in the former shop: The Kenny Gallery High St. ☎091/334-760 ⊕www.thekennygallery.ie). "It was a great help that in 1984 Galway celebrated a Quincentennial," he recalls. "We were 500 years a city. It was like a year-long birthday bash, but more importantly, a whole new sense of civic pride was generated, a new sense of duchas (heritage) and our history. At the same time, curiously, it was forward-looking and since then, the city center has

been transformed. Up until then, it had been like a mouthful of bad teeth, with streets that were run-down, derelict, decaying—a terrible relic from the years of poverty in the mid-20th century and the effects of emigration. That's changed utterly. Galway is now known as a city of young people, because the prosperity allows them to stay here.

When we opened our gallery in the 1960s, there wasn't one full-time professional artist working in County Galway. Artists, yes, but they needed day jobs. Today, there's an army of artists. And an army of art troupes and festivals: the Druid Theater Company, the Mánas street theater, the Galway Arts Festival, the Cúirt literary festival, the festivals devoted to film, children's arts, traditional music, and comedy. Galway has become an attractive place to live for people with young children, and when the children grow up, they don't want to leave. And for those of us who are not so young anymore, all the artistic activity keeps us young."

and correct Georgian-style furniture, brass lamps, and king-size beds fill the spacious bedrooms. Warming everything up, happily, is the genuinely friendly service. The delightfully unstuffy atmosphere is best seen in the Pullman Restaurant ($$$–$$$$), Glenlo's most popular feature. This is set in two *Orient Express* carriages installed on the grounds (and used in the famous Agatha Christie film of that name), offering a fun dining experience, complete with background click-clacks and train whistles. For more formal surroundings, repair to the classical River Room restaurant. Chandeliers hang from high, stucco ceilings and tall windows framed by peach-color curtains overlook the river. The food, beautifully served, includes delights like marinated venison on a bed of braised red cabbage. ⊠*Bushy Park, Co. Galway* ☎*091/526–666* ☏*091/527–800* ⊕*www.glenlo.com* ↻*38 rooms, 6 suites* ⚇*In-room: Wi-Fi. In-hotel: 2 restaurants, bar, golf course* ☱*AE, DC, MC, V* ⬡*EP.*

$$$$
Fodor'sChoice
★
✕☒**Radisson SAS.** The striking contemporary design of the Radisson has revived a run-down area a stone's throw from Eyre Square and overlooking a landlocked inflow of Galway Bay, Lough Atalia. Against

several newcomers, the hotel has successfully defended its reputation as Galway's hippest hotel. Potted 20-foot bamboo sways at the entrance, while four palm trees grow in the spacious reception area. Two glass-wall elevators divide the lobby from the bar and waft you upstairs while delivering breathtaking views of Galway Bay. Rooms are spacious, with fully tiled bathrooms, restful, unfussy color schemes, Scandinavian-design contemporary furniture, and comfortable sitting areas. Double-glazing and altitude (starting on the third story) insulate the rooms from noise even on the loudest Galway night. The Atrium lounge and bar, its triple-height windows framing views of the water, is a popular lunch spot and buzzes with life from early to late. A pianist entertains on weekends, and in summer the large terrace with its views of the sea and the distant hills is a lively spot. Also overlooking the Lough, the spacious blue-and-white Marinas Restaurant ($$–$$$$) offers a wide selection of local seafood, as well as a good choice of international dishes. ⊠*Lough Atalia Rd., Center, Co. Galway* ☎*091/538–300* 🖷*091/538–380* ⊕*www.radissonhotelgalway.com* ☜*217 rooms* ♿*In-room: refrigerator, Ethernet, some Wi-Fi. In-hotel: restaurant, bars, pool, spa, parking (fee), public Wi-Fi* ⊟*AE, DC, MC, V* ⽬*BP.*

$$$$ ✕🖻 **St. Cleran's.** Once home to film director John Huston, this gray-
★   stone, veddy, veddy proper Georgian mansion has been dramatically restored by noted entertainer Merv Griffin (who passed away in August 2007) into a super-luxe inn. Subtle it is not, and some people are overwhelmed by the deep-pile carpets and ubiquitous crystal chandeliers; others find the furnishings delightful and revel in all the top-quality antiques. You can also expect superb views of the rolling countryside, and excellent opportunities for country sports. The elegant, formal restaurant ($$$$, reservations essential) has a highly renowned Japanese chef, who cooks mainly in the classic French style with just the odd Japanese touch—tempura of tiger prawns with wasabi mayonnaise may be featured alongside a French classic like honey-roasted duck breast with orange-Cointreau sauce. It's 35 km (22 mi) east of Galway on the N6 Dublin road. ⊠*Craughwell, Loughrea, Co. Galway* ☎*091/846–555* 🖷*091/846–752* ⊕*www.stclerans.com* ☜*12 rooms* ♿*In-room: no a/c, Wi-Fi. In-hotel: restaurant, bar, no elevator, public Wi-Fi* ⊟*AE, MC, V* ⽬*BP.*

$$ ✕🖻 **Huntsman Inn.** Situated 1 km (½ mi) from Eyre Square, across the road from the exotic "g" hotel and a stone's throw from Lough Atalia, this pub with rooms makes an excellent base for touring Galway by car. There's ample free parking, and it's away from Galway's frequent inner-city gridlock—leave the car here, and explore on foot. A row of attractive old houses alternating stone facing with traditional wooden pub windows and floral window boxes has been converted into one building, with three large bar areas taking up most of the ground floor. The rooms, on the floor above, are smallish but comfortable, with unfussy, contemporary furniture, generous proportioned bathrooms, and good sound insulation. The pub ($$) serves hearty, bistro-style fare, freshly prepared to order, and is enormously popular with locals—always a

sign of good value. You can dine in the bars or a large, modern restaurant. Here's a chance to sample traditional fish-and-chips, or honeybaked lamb shank with parsley sauce, another Irish favorite. ✉*164 College Rd., Co. Galway* ☎*091/562–849* ⊕*www.huntsmaninn.com* ⇌*12 rooms* ⏶*In-room: Wi-Fi. In-hotel: restaurant, bar, Wi-Fi, parking (no fee)* ▭*MC, V.*

$$$$ 🖭**the g.** "G" is for glamour—or good grief, depending on your taste—at this flamboyant player at the top end of Galway's hotel scene. The g opened in 2006 in a retail and leisure complex beside a busy roundabout, about 15 minutes' walk from Eyre Square—it's an oddly unhip location for a style icon. The architects worked with superstar hat designer Philip Treacy, a native of Galway, to create an interior that is every bit as extreme as Treacy's hats. The reception area is in black glass and marble, lighted by a tank of sedately bobbing, Connemarabred seahorses. Yes, seahorses. Black-and-white op-art whorls feature on the aptly named Vertigo carpet in the vivid Pink Room, where afternoon tea (€45 for two) is popular with the ladies. There are also a self-consciously stylish bar and a more serene, silvery salon. Dimly lighted corridors with pink carpet lead to rooms where the decor is thankfully more restrained. Massive, extremely comfortable beds are dressed in white linen, and graceful custom-made furniture with an art deco air is upholstered in soothing gray and *eau de nil* upholstery. Mirrors are everywhere, and windows look onto pebbled areas with greenery that distract from the mundane views. Sea-shell–theme bathrooms are luxurious havens of marble and fine porcelain. Perched on scallop-shape purple velvet banquettes or jelly-tot–bright chairs in the ordinary but expensive Restaurant at the g, you can order from an Italian menu. The ESPA spa takes pampering to serious extremes. ✉*Wellpark, Co. Galway* ☎*091/865–200* 🖷*091/865–203* ⊕*www.monogramhotels.ie* ⇌*98 rooms* ⏶*In-room: refrigerator, Wi-Fi. In-hotel: restaurant, bars, public Internet, pool, gym* ▭*AE, DC, MC, V* ⏏*BP.*

$$$ 🖭**Grand Hotel Meyrick.** Built in 1845 right on Eyre Square to coincide with the arrival of the railway, and known formerly as the Galway Great Southern, this is still a popular lodging. Tastefully muted, color-coordinated schemes and Victorian-style tables and chairs decorate the guest rooms. The deluxe rooms in the original building have tall ceilings and windows and are particularly elegant, though those at the front directly above the bar can be noisy late into the night. Rooms in the back, on the fifth floor, have views of the docks and Galway Bay. The rooftop spa includes an open-air hot tub. French-Irish cuisine is served at the formal, pleasantly old-fashioned Oyster Room. ✉*Eyre Sq., Center, Co. Galway* ☎*091/564–041* 🖷*091/566–704* ⊕*www. greatsouthernhotels.com* ⇌*96 rooms, 3 suites* ⏶*In-room: no a/c, Ethernet, some Wi-Fi. In-hotel: restaurant, bars, spa, public Wi-Fi* ▭*AE, DC, MC, V* ⏏*BP.*

$$ 🖭**Killeen House.** Proper tea—served to you on the finest china—will welcome you here as you ease into a high-back armchair in Catherine Doyle's impeccable drawing room. Her peaceful country home is only 7 km (4 mi) from the city, but it could be in another world.

In fact, you can walk through the immaculately kept garden and on for 10 minutes to the shore of Lough Corrib, which can be seen from some of the rooms. These are spacious and furnished with highly polished antiques, each on a different theme—Victorian, Edwardian, or Regency. The large beds are made up with crisp white bed linen, the furniture is in dark woods, and curtains and handwoven rugs are in calming neutral shades. The location, on the N59 Clifden road, makes this a fine location for both exploring the Connemara countryside by day and enjoying the considerable buzz of Galway City by night. ⊠*Killeen, Bushypark, Co. Galway* ☎*091/524–179* 🖷*091/528–065* ⊕*www.killeenhousegalway.com* ⇆*5 rooms* ⌂*In-room: no a/c. In-hotel: restaurant, no elevator, parking (no fee)* ⊟*MC, V* ⊘*Closed Christmas wk* ⊺⊙⊺*BP.*

¢–$$　🎫**Jurys Inn Galway.** Expect good-quality budget accomodations at this four-story hotel set beside the historic Spanish Arch and the river. Each room is big enough for three adults, or two adults and two children, and the rates are the same regardless of how many guests stay in each unit. The light, airy rooms have modern pine fittings, plain carpets and walls, double-glaze windows, and fully equipped bathrooms. Those overlooking the river are quieter than those in front. The atmosphere runs toward anonymous international, but the inn is central—at the foot of Galway's busy Quay Street, right on the bank of the Corrib— and the level of comfort is high for the price (note that rates shoot up at peak times, such as during the Galway Races). ⊠*Quay St., Spanish Arch, Co. Galway* ☎*091/566–444* 🖷*091/568–415* ⊕*www.jurysinn. com* ⇆*130 rooms* ⌂*In-room: no a/c, Wi-Fi. In-hotel: restaurant, bar, public Internet, parking (fee)* ⊟*AE, DC, MC, V.*

$　🎫**Adare Guest House.** A five-minute walk from the city center, this family-run guesthouse, managed by the son of the original owners, makes a handy base for exploring Galway. There's ample space to park your car, and there's none of the nighttime noise of the city center. Rooms are relatively spacious for the price, extremely well equipped, and plainly decorated in browns and creams. The multichoice breakfast is served in a sunny room, with country-pine furniture and floors, that overlooks a flower-filled patio. ⊠*9 Father Griffin Pl., Spanish Arch, Co. Galway* ☎*091/582–638* 🖷*091/583–693* ⊕*www.adarebedandbreakfast.com* ⇆*11 rooms* ⌂*In-room: no a/c. In-hotel: restaurant, elevator, parking (no fee)* ⊟*AE, MC, V* ⊺⊙⊺*BP.*

NIGHTLIFE & THE ARTS

Because of its small size and concentration of pubs and restaurants, Galway can seem even livelier at 11 PM than it does at 11 AM. On weekends, when there are lots of students and other revelers in town, Eyre Square and environs can be rowdy after pub-closing time. On the plus side, if you've been staying out in the country and you're ready for a little nightlife, you're certain to find plenty of it here.

CLUBS & PUBS

The best spot for traditional music is the area between Eyre Square and the Spanish Arch. There's a big post-nightclub (open until 1 or 2) scene here—there are some clubs in town, but most everyone heads to Salthill, the small suburban community 3 km (2 mi) west of Galway. The main road, Upper Salthill, is lined with clubs.

CLUBS **Cuba** (⊠*Eyre Sq., Center* ☎*091/565–991*), in the heart of Galway City, with three floors, draws diners and salsa lovers for Cuban cocktails and cigars to the beat of Latin music from DJs and live bands. Busy with students from the university, **GPO** (⊠*Eglinton St., Center* ☎*091/563–073*) is perhaps the most popular dance club in the city center. **McSwiggan's** (⊠*3 Eyre St., Wood Quay, Center* ☎*091/568–917*) is a huge Galway City place, with everything from church pews to ancient carriage lamps contributing to its eclectic character.

For late-night sounds heard from the comfort of your own table, try **Sally Longs** (⊠*Upper Abbeygate St., Center* ☎*091/565–756*), Galway's hard rock pub, much loved by bikers. **Warwick** (⊠*O'Connor's Warwick Hotel, Lower Salthill, Salthill* ☎*091/521–244*) has a DJ on Friday nights and a band on Saturday, both playing rock and pop oldies. Admission is €4 to €10.

Tigh Neachtain (⊠*17 Cross St., Spanish Arch* ☎*091/568–820*) is *the* place for traditional music in Galway City, and each visit will be an experience.

Aras na Gael (⊠*45 Lower Dominick St., Spanish Arch* ☎*091/526–509*) is one of the few pubs in the city center where Irish is spoken. Master of the tin whistle Seán Ryan plays every Sunday at **Crane's** (⊠*2 Sea Rd.* ☎*091/587–419*). You can usually find a session after about 9 PM at **King's Head** (⊠*15 High St., Center* ☎*091/566–630*). **Monroe's** (⊠*20 Dominick St., Center* ☎*091/583–397*) is a large, sociable pub with traditional music nightly and set dancing on Tuesdays. **Paddy's** (⊠*Prospect Hill, Center* ☎*091/567–843*) is a good place for a pint near the bus and train station. **Roisin Dubh** (⊠*Dominick St., Spanish Arch* ☎*091/586–540*) is a serious venue for emerging rock and traditional bands—it often showcases big, if still-struggling, talents. **Taaffe's** (⊠*19 Shop St., Center* ☎*091/564–066*), in the midst of the shopping district, is very busy on afternoons. Up-and-coming young musicians play at the cozy **Tigh Coili Bar** (⊠*Mainguard St., Center* ☎*091/561–294*) in traditional sessions daily at 5:30 and 10 PM.

THEATER

An Taibhdhearc (⊠*Middle St., Center* ☎*091/562–024* ⊕*www.antaibhdearc.com*), pronounced "on *tie*-vark," was founded in 1928 by Hilton Edwards and Micháel Macliammóir as the national Irish-language theater. It continues to produce first-class shows, mainly of Irish works in both the English and the Irish languages and hosts touring productions.

The **Druid Theatre Company** (⊠*Chapel La., Center* ☎*091/568–617* ⊕*www.druidtheatre.com*) is esteemed for its adventurous and accom-

Continued on page 452

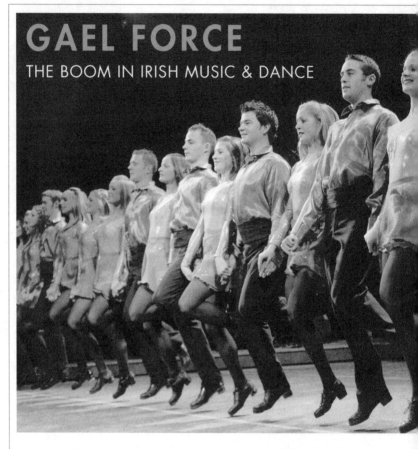

GAEL FORCE
THE BOOM IN IRISH MUSIC & DANCE

Traditional Irish music and dance has taken the world by storm—but you need to journey to the West of Ireland to really get in step.

Folkloric music and dance may have faded in countries around the globe but don't tell that to the thousands of young Irish who are learning to play hornpipes and concertinas, sing the old shanties, and dance the old jigs. Once languishing, these "old-fashioned" arts have taken on a modern chic here at home and the reason why can be summed up in one word: Riverdance.

When this eye-popping spectacular first "tapped" its way into the Irish psyche in 1995 by jazzing up traditional step dancing and moving it from the local parish hall to the stages of Dublin's Point Theatre, it immediately sent its audiences reeling—in more ways than one. The first troupe to introduce the Irish jig to world theaters, it has since performed before 18 million people and, having taken in more than $1 billion at the box office, has danced all the way to the bank. Hand in hand with the fiddle-fueled rise of traditional Irish music—the wistful drone of an Irish tin whistle helped make 1997's *Titanic* the best-selling film soundtrack

Riverdance Irish Dance Troupe

HARPING ON

Ireland is the only country to have a musical instrument as its national emblem. The harp appears on *garda* (police) caps, Irish Euro coins, and government stationery. The original Irish harp was a small, triangular instrument designed to be held on the knee (not the large version of today's concert halls). The harp was first used as a logo for Guinness stout in 1850. The Guinness harp faces right, while the national emblem faces left.

7

GAEL FORCE

of all time—Riverdance has resulted in the spectacular rebirth of old Gaelic culture over the past decade. And today, the world has fallen in step—literally. Riverdance's most fervent audiences are now found in far-off lands like Japan and Estonia; there's practically an Irish Step Dancing *Feis* (Irish for festival) every week somewhere in the U.S., and the sensational success of Celtic Woman—their Eire-savvy fusion of new-age pop, Celtic music, and classical crossover has catapulted their CDs to the top of the charts—are all signs that the tree of Irish music has deep roots around the globe.

What acccounts for its enormous crossover success? Does it appeal because it offers a return to a simpler time? Or allows us to enjoy a dazzling slice of national culture in an age that has grown blandly homogeneous? Or is it because songs such as "Oh, Danny Boy, the Pipes, the Pipes Are Calling" offer deep and universal resonances of love and loss, distance and memory? Whatever the answer, you'll find that Ireland's "trad" musicians and dancers are seeking to bring Gaelic culture into the realm of world music—or could it be the other way round?

COME AND MEET THOSE DANCING FEET

Ireland was swept off its feet, and its collective feet onto the boards, by the spectacular success of Riverdance. Thanks to that phenonemon, the thunderous dancing, stomping, clacking feet of today's Irish youth have once again taken up the trigger-quick step dances of old and the traditional music of the past.

Before Riverdance, Irish dancing was something schoolchildren performed chiefly for competitions, and sometimes on civic occasions, with their arms rigidly held by their sides (only the legs would move—a holdover from religious teachings that felt that dancing was sinful), and an expression of grave concentration on their faces. Today, it's a big thing for young people and also, due to those glitzy costumes and contests, a very expensive hobby.

Riverdance was a conscious attempt to project a more modern image of Ireland, and central to its roaring success were two American step dancers, Michael Flatley and Jean Butler. Their dazzling innovations reflected their origin in the more flexible American step dance competition world. Before Riverdance, the only options for prize-winning Irish step-dancers

were to teach or to retire—now hundreds of dancers are employed worldwide in touring shows inspired by Riverdance, such as Flatley's Celtic Tiger and Butler's Dancing on Dangerous Ground.

Set Dancing

Set dancing is also the name given to social dancing in which four couples face one another in a square in dances based on the French cotillion and the quadrilles. Set dancing has enjoyed a huge revival in recent years and nearly every town in Ireland once again has dancing at least one evening a week. Set dancing's successful revival is often attributed to the Willie Clancy Summer School in Co. Clare. Set dancing is fast and exhilarating and great social fun, so no wonder it caught on a second time.

Riverdance

STEPS & SETS

Ireland has a long tradition of solo dancing, first introduced by the jigs, reels, and hornpipes that traveling dancing masters taught in the 18th century. Some are performed in hard shoes, with the dancer beating out rhythms on the floor to complement the music, while others are danced with soft shoes to emphasize their graceful, airborne nature. In both cases, the main interest of the dance is in the foot and lower leg. Some solo dances have specific patterns of steps and are only danced to one tune and are known as "set dances"—in some places, set dances are known as table dances because the dancer often jumped up on the table to display his or her skills.

The main interest of the dance is in the foot and lower leg

FANCY FOOTWORK

Because there were no accompanying drums, the sound of the feet on wooden floors has always been an important element in Irish dancing. When dancing really took off in the 18th century, many cabins only had earth floors, so the custom was to remove the top half of the half-door, and dance on that. Dancing masters used to display their prowess on fair days by dancing on soapy barrel lids, so they developed the ability to vary their steps in a confined space. From this came the tradition of dancing solos on one spot.

JUST FOLLOW THE SOUND OF THE MUSIC...

If you're interested in "Trad" music, the beat of a bodhrán or the tap of a shoe will likely lead you to Galway and County Clare's great folk *fleadhs* (festivals) and pub *seisiuns* (sessions).

THE BIGGEST FLEADH

The biggest festival of all is a three-day event called the All-Ireland finals at Fleadh Cheoil na hÉireann (pronounced flah-kwoil–"festival of music"). The 2007 event was held in Tullamore, County Offaly, August 29–26, and was attended by nearly 11,000 musicians and 250,000 visitors, many of them second-generation Irish from overseas. This noncommercial festival of traditional music takes over a whole town, whose pubs become centers for casual music making. The All-Ireland rotates to different towns every year, much to the delight of the pub owners in the chosen town (⊕ www.fleadh2007.com).

THE ENNIS BLOW-OUT

During the last week in May, the pleasant county town of Ennis hosts the **Fleadh Nua** (⊕ http://fleadhnua.com/), a massive eight-day-long celebration of dancing and song, with concerts, workshops, competitions, and *céilis*. Many of the events are open-air and free, and there is a great festive buzz. Ennis is home to a growing cadre of musicians: the Custys, Siobhán and Tommy Peoples, flute player Kevin Crawford, and accordion whiz kid Murty Ryan. Check out **Knox's Pub** (⊠ Abbey St. ☎ 065/682-9264) and **Cruise's Bar** (⊠ Abbey St. ☎ 065/684-1800) for lively evening sessions.

TOE-TAPPING IN MILTOWN

Held during the first week in July, the **Willie Clancy Summer School** (⊕ http://www.setdancingnews.net/wcss) is Ireland's biggest traditional music summer school. Classes, lectures, and recitals attract around 1,500 students from 42 countries to this tiny village on the west coast of Clare near Spanish Point. Set dancing is a big draw here, and a surefire way to make friends.

CEOL AGUS RINCE

Ceol (pronounced coil) is the Irish for music. And what always goes with the Irish for music? *Rince* (pronounced rincha), the Irish for dance: Music and Dance: you often see *Ceol agus Rince* on a poster advertising a traditional session or a céili.

Traditional Folk Music, Sligo, Co. Sligo, Ireland

Members of Kila mid-performance

DARLIN' DOOLIN

Doolin, County Clare, is little more than a dot on the map on the west coast of Clare (and to confuse things some maps have it down as "Roadford"). To traditional musicians its three main pubs—**O'Connor's** (⊠ Fisher St. ☎ 065/707-4168 ⊕ www.oconnorspubdoolin.com), **McDermott's** (⊠ Lisdoonvarna Rd. ☎ 065/707-4700 ⊕ www.mcdermottspubdoolin.com), and **McGann's** (⊠ Lidoonvarna Rd. ☎ 065/707-4133 ⊕ *www.esatclear.ie/mcgannsdoolin*) are an irresistible magnet, as is the village's legendary charm. Some young musicians camp here all summer to learn from old masters.

CUCKOOS AND WINKLES

Kinvara, County Galway, is a pretty waterside village with an especially strong traditional music tradition. During the first weekend in May Kinvara hosts the annual **Cuckoo Fleadh** (⊠ Main St. ☎ 091/637-145), a traditional music festival. Resident musicians like De Danann alumni Jackie Daly and Charlie Piggott play regularly at the town's **Winkles Hotel** (⊠ The Square ☎ 091/637-137). Back in 1989, a young accordion player got together with her friends for a casual recording session. The resulting album, *Sharon Shannon*, became the most successful Trad-music recording ever released.

GIGGING IN GALWAY

Galway is the heart of Trad—the city and its environs have nurtured some of the most durable names in Irish music: Dé Danann, Arcady, singers Dolores and Seán Keane, and the mercurial accordion genius, Mairtin O'Connor. Seán Ryan, master of the tin whistle,

has been playing every Sunday at **Crane's** (⊠ 2 Sea Rd. ☎ 091/587-419) since the 1980s. **Tigh Coili** (⊠ Mainguard St. ☎ 091/561-294) has traditional Irish music sessions every day at 5:30 and 10 PM. **Monroe's Tavern** (⊠ Dominick St. ☎ 091/583-397) has traditional music every night from 9:30 PM, and invites you to join the locals in set dancing. There is also plenty of music to be found at old favorites in the city center like **Tigh Neachtain** (⊠ 17 Cross St. ☎ 091/568-820), **Taaffe's** (⊠ 19 Shop St. ☎ 091/564-066), and **Aras na Gael** (⊠ 45 Lower Dominick St. ☎ 091/526-509). **The Bard's Den** (⊠ Main St. ☎ 091/41042) in Letterfrack, Co. Galway, is noted for its Trad sessions. **Molloy's Bar** (⊠ Bridge St. ☎ 098/26655) in Westport, Co. Mayo, is owned by Matt Molloy, flute player of the Chieftains, and is renowned for its great sessions.

■ TIP→ For details, log on to www. comhaltas.com or get a copy of the "trad" bible, *Walton's Guide to Irish Music* (www.waltonmusic.com). All together now: "Too-ra-loo-ra-loo-ra, Too-ra-loo-ra-li!"

GOOD BEHAVIOR

If you happen on a pub session there are a few ground rules. Don't talk during the solo, and don't stare at the singer; most people look at the floor. Buy the musicians a drink if it's a small session, and if at all possible, have a party piece to contribute yourself. If you can't sing or play, recite a poem or tell a joke, even a short one. It's the gesture that counts.

FIDDLING AROUND

Irish Traditional music is very much the music of the people, played on relatively simple, portable instruments: fiddle, flute, tin whistle, accordion, handheld drum, and, recent additions, guitar or banjo.

UILLEANN PIPES

The uilleann (pronounced "illun") pipes, literally "elbow" pipes, are a quieter indoor version of bagpipes. The player sits while playing with a bag under one arm, the bellows under the other, and the "chanter," which plays the melody, on the thigh. A temperamental instrument, it can be heartrenderingly beautiful in the hands of a master like Liam O'Flynn or Paddy Keenan of the Bothy Band.

FIDDLE

The classical violin all but in name, this is the most popular instrument in Trad music for its singing, swooping versatility, its portability, and its relative affordability. Local fiddle styles still persist, especially in Donegal, Sligo, and the Sliabh Luachra region of Cork and Kerry and virtuosos such as Frankie Gavin of Dé Dannan, Martin Hayes, Tommy Peoples, and Liz Doherty are famed for their rhythm, color, and ornamentation.

SQUEEZE-BOXES & ACCORDIONS

Squeeze-box is a generic term for a variety of melodeons, accordions, and concertinas. The concertina is a small, hexagonal-shaped button-key instrument. The simplest accordion is the one-row button accordion, usually called a melodeon. Styles of playing can vary enormously. Sharon Shannon is rooted in the highly rhythmic East Clare style but can veer into swing and Cajun styles as she plays her wildly energetic dance music.

FLUTES & WHISTLE

The tin whistle is the ideal beginner's instrument, but be sure to buy one in the key of D. It is still called the penny whistle because it costs so little to buy. But the flute used in Irish music is usually a simple wooden flute—hear it at its best in the hands of Matt Molloy and Paddy Moloney of the Chieftains, Mary Bergin, and Gavin Whelan.

BODHRÁN

The Bodhrán (pronounced "bow-rawn") is a simple goat's skin drum played with the back of the hand or a small wooden stick. When played well, by Mel Mercier, John Joe Kelly, or Tommy Hayes, it makes an exciting addition to the running rhythms of Trad music. They make it look easy, but in the hands of an untrained amateur, a badly played bodhrán can wreck a session.

HAPPY LISTENING!

Traditional Irish pub music

SEÁN Ó RIADA The father of "modern" Trad music, this composer and visionary Irish language enthusiast (1931–71)—noted for his film score *Mise Éire* and his Irish language *Mass Cúil Aodha*—established the prototype traditional Irish group, Ceoltóiríc Chualann, in 1963, who evolved into the Chieftains.

THE CHIEFTAINS If you've seen a poster of Irish musicians wearing unhip cardigans, baggy trousers, and bad haircuts, it was probably the Chieftains, who went professional in 1975. Outstanding musicians, they include uilleann-piper Paddy Moloney, flute player Matt Molloy, harper Derek Bell (recently deceased), and Seán Keane and Martin Fay (fiddlers). Any of their famous 35 albums are worth owning.

PLANXTY The word *planxty* means a lively tune (without words) written to honor a patron, but it is now forever associated with a "super-group" formed in 1972 by singer Christy Moore, with Dónal Lunny, Andy Irvine, and Liam O'Flynn. Their haunting debut album, *Planxty* (1972), is a must. Reincarnated in the later '70s as The Bothy Band, their 1975 debut album remains a classic.

DÉ DANNAN This famed group grew from regular sessions in Hughe's bar in Spiddal, Co. Galway, in 1974. Brilliant fiddle and flute player Frankie Gavin, bouzouki whiz Alec Finn, banjo master Carlie Piggot, and Johnny "Ringo" McDonagh on bodhrán were joined by singers Dolores Keane, Mary Black, and Maura O'Connell (all now solo artists). *Dé Dannan* (1975) and *Mist-Covered Mountain* (1980) are their timeless evocations of the West of Ireland.

ALTAN Donegal-born husband-and-wife duo, Frankie Kennedy on flute and Máiréead Mhaonaight (fiddle and vocals), showcase the special Donegal way with fiddle and flute.

ANÚNA This vocal and instrumental ensemble, founded in the 1990s, represents the mystical, spiritual aspect of Celtic music, and is widely known through performances with the original Riverdance production. *Anúna* (1993), their first album, is still their best.

KILA Touted by the under-30s to be the future of Irish music, you can discern African percussion, Andean flute, and Eastern European folk music among the influences on their debut album, *Tóg É Go Bog É*—roughly translated as "The Living is Easy."

Altan

plished productions, mainly of 20th-century Irish and European plays. The players perform at the Royal Court's small stage in London. When they're home, they usually appear at the Town Hall, and they host many productions during the Galway Arts Festival in late July.

Macnas (⊠ *Fisheries Field, Salmon Weir Bridge, Center* ☎ *091/561–462* ⊕ *www.macnas.com*) is an internationally renowned, Galway-based troupe of performance artists who have raised street theater to new levels. Their participation in the Galway Arts Festival's annual parade is always much anticipated.

VISUAL ARTS & GALLERIES

Bold (⊠ *Merchants Rd. and Augustien St., Center* ☎ *091/539–900* ⊕ *www.boldartgallery.com*) shows work by big name and up-and-coming Irish artists.

Kenny's Gallery (⊠ *High St., Center* ☎ *091/534–760* ⊕ *www.kennys. ie*) specializes in artists who paint scenes of Galway and Connemara. Reflecting a passion for modern Irish art, **Norman Villa Gallery** (⊠ *86 Lower Salthill, Salthill* ☎ *091/521–131* ⊕ *www.normanvillagallery. com*) shows work in the gallery owner's home. The art gallery at **University College Galway** (⊠ *Newcastle Rd., University* ☎ *091/524–411*) has a number of exhibits each year.

SPORTS & THE OUTDOORS

BICYCLING

Set off to explore the Galway area, especially its coast, by renting a bike from **Mountain Trail Bike Shop** (⊠ *The Cornstore, Middle St., Center* ☎ *091/569–888*).

FISHING

Galway City is the gateway to Connemara, and Connemara is the place to fish. You can get fishing licenses, tackle, and bait, and arrange to hire a traditional fly-fishing guide or book a sea-angling trip at **Freeny's Sports** (⊠ *19–23 High St., Center* ☎ *091/562–609*). **Murt's** (⊠ *7 Daly's Pl., Woodquay* ☎ *091/561–018*) can handle your fishing needs.

GOLF

Galway Bay Golf and Country Club (⊠ *Renville, Oranmore* ☎ *091/790–500*) is an 18-hole parkland course, designed by Christy O'Connor Jr., on the shores of Galway Bay. The **Galway Golf Club** (⊠ *Blackrock, Salthill* ☎ *091/522–033*) is an 18-hole course with excellent views of Galway Bay, the Burren, and the Aran Islands. Some of the fairways run close to the ocean.

RIVER CRUISING

A **Corrib Cruise** (☎091/592–447 ⊕*www.corribprincess.ie*) from Wood Quay, behind the Town Hall Theatre at the Rowing Club, is a lovely way to spend a fine afternoon; it lasts 1½ hours and travels 8 km (5 mi) up the River Corrib and about 6 km (4 mi) around Lough Corrib. There's a bar on board, tea and coffee, and a commentary. The trip costs €14, and boats depart daily at 2:30 and 4:30 from May through September, with an additional departure at 12:30 July through August. You can also rent the boat for an evening.

CLOTHES MAKE THE MAN

The grease in the wool of a hand-knit, heirloom-quality Aran sweater will make it feel very stiff for the first few months—or even years. Locals of all ages wear the traditional sweaters in Galway and on the Aran islands, but in other parts of Ireland the assumption is usually that anyone wearing an Aran is a visitor.

SHOPPING

ANTIQUES

Connaught Antiques (⊠*9 Eyre Sq., Center* ☎*091/567–840* ⊕*www.connaughtantiques.com*) stocks a wonderful selection of Irish, English, and French antiques, clocks, and *objets d'art,* mainly from the 18th and 19th centuries.

BOOKS

Charlie Byrne's Bookshop (⊠*Middle St., Center* ☎*091/561–766*) sells a large, varied selection of used books and remainders. **Hughes and Hughes** (⊠*Galway Shopping Centre, Headford Rd.,* ☎*091/563–903*) is the biggest bookshop in Galway.

CLOTHING

Faller's Sweater Shop (⊠*25 High St., Center* ☎*091/564–833* ⊠*35 Eyre Sq., Center* ☎*091/561–255*) has the choicest selection of Irish-made sweaters, competitively priced. **O'Máille's** (⊠*16 High St., Center* ☎*091/562–696*) carries Aran sweaters, handwoven tweeds, and classically tailored clothing.

CRAFTS & GIFTS

★ Don't miss **Design Concourse Ireland** (⊠*Kirwan's La., Center* ☎*091/566–927*), a spectacular one-stop shop for the best in Irish handcrafted design. Ceramics, small pieces of furniture, contemporary basketware, handmade jewelry, wood turnings, handblown glass—in fact just about anything for the home that can be handmade—will be found in this two-story treasure trove.

Galway Irish Crystal (⊠*Dublin Rd., Merlin Park* ☎*091/757–311* ⊕*www.galwaycrystal.ie*), a factory outlet on the city's ring road, has hand-cut Irish glass, an informative heritage center on Galway lore, a crystal workshop you can visit, and a restaurant with a view of Galway Bay.

The **Kilkenny Shop** (⌧*6 High St., Center* ☎*091/566–110*) is synonymous with good modern design in Ireland. This shop stocks the best ceramics, crystal, leatherware, clothing, and other craft items from around the country.

Meadows & Byrne (⌧*Castle St., Center* ☎*091/567–776*) sells the best in modern household items.

Browse in **Tempo** (⌧*9 Cross St., Center* ☎*091/562–282*), which has a good selection of decorative pieces, gifts, and antique furniture.

Browse in **Treasure Chest** (⌧ *William St., Center* ☎*091/563–862*) for china, crystal, gifts, and classic clothing.

> ### THE WEARING OF THE GREEN
>
> Stands of Scotch pine, Norwegian spruce, Douglas fir, and Japanese Sitka grow in Connemara's valleys and up hillsides—the result of a concerted national project that has thus far reforested 9% of Ireland.

FOOD

Sheridan's Cheesemongers (⌧*16 Churchyard St.* ☎*091/564–829* ⊕*www.sheridanscheesemongers.com*) is run by Seamus and Kevin Sheridan. Together, they know all of Ireland's artisan cheese makers personally and stock the widest possible range of delectable cheeses, complemented by charcuterie (mainly Italian). The wineshop upstairs will complete your picnic.

JEWELRY

Phyllis MacNamara's cute two-story boutique, **Cobwebs** (⌧*7 Quay St., Spanish Arch* ☎*091/564–388* ⊕*www.cobwebs.ie*) is filled with an irresistible selection of antique jewelry (real and costume) and collectibles for men and women, all with a witty twist. Dating from 1750, **Thomas Dillon's** (⌧*1 Quay St., Spanish Arch* ☎*091/566–365* ⊕*www.claddaghring.ie*) claims to be the original maker of Galway's famous Claddagh ring. In the back of the shop there's a small but interesting display of antique Claddagh rings and old Galway memorabilia.

MALLS

The spacious indoor **Galway Shopping Centre** (⌧*Headford Rd.*) is a mall with more than 60 outlets, 10 minutes' walk from Eyre Square with ample car parking. On the southwest side of Eyre Square and imaginatively designed to incorporate parts of the old town walls, the **Eyre Square Shopping Centre** is a good spot to pick up moderately priced clothing and household goods.

MUSIC

Back2Music (⌧*30 Upper Abbeygate St., Center* ☎*091/565–272*) specializes in traditional Irish musical instruments, including the handheld drum, the *bodhrán* (pronounced bau-*rawn*). **Mulligan** (⌧*5 Middle St. Ct., Center* ☎*091/564–961*) carries thousands of CDs, records, and cassettes, with a large collection of traditional Irish music. **P. Powell and Sons** (⌧*The Four Corners, William St., Center* ☎*091/562–295*) sells traditional Irish musical instruments and CDs, and has a knowledgeable staff.

VINTAGE GOODS

Twice as Nice (✉ *5 Quay St., Spanish Arch* ☎ *091/566–332*) sells a mix of new and vintage men's and women's clothing, linens, lace, and jewelry at reasonable prices.

THE OILEÁIN ÁRAINN (ARAN ISLANDS)

No one knows for certain when the Aran Islands—Inis Mór (Inishmore), Inis Meáin (Inishmaan), and Inis Oirr (Inisheer)—were first inhabited, but judging from the number of Bronze Age and Iron Age forts found here (especially on Inis Mór), 3000 BC is a safe guess. Why wandering nomads in deerskin jerkins would be attracted to these barren islets remains a greater mystery, not the least because fresh water and farmable land were (and still are) scarce commodities. Remote western outposts of the ancient province of Connaught (though they are not the country's westernmost points; that honor belongs to the Blasket Islands), these three islands were once as barren as the limestone pavements of the Burren, of which they are a continuation. Today, the land is parceled into small, human-made fields surrounded by stone walls: centuries of erosion, generations of backbreaking labor, sheep, horses, and their attendant tons of manure have finally transformed this rocky wasteland into reasonably productive cropland.

> ### ISLAND NIGHTS
>
> To appreciate the fierce loneliness of the Aran islands you must spend the night on one. Because all the islands, especially Inishmore, crawl with day-trippers, it's difficult to let their rugged beauty sink into your soul until 10 PM, when the sky is dark and the pubs fill with the acrid smell of peat smoke and Guinness. Once the day-trippers clear out, the islands' stunningly fierce and brooding beauty is disturbed only by the "baa" of the sheep and the incessant rush of the wind.

7

While traditional Irish culture fights a rear-guard battle on the mainland, the islanders continue to preserve as best as they can a culture going back generations. Still, the Irish-speaking inhabitants enjoy a daily air service to Galway (subsidized by the government), motorized curraghs, satellite TV, and all the usual modern home conveniences. Yet they have retained a distinctness from mainlanders, preferring simple home decor, very plain food, and tightly knit communities, like the hardy fishing and farming folk from whom they are descended. Crime is virtually unknown in these parts; at your B&B, you'll likely find no locks on the guest-room doors, and the front-door latch will be left open. Many islanders have sampled life in Dublin or cities abroad but have returned to raise families, keeping the population stable at around 1,500. Tourists now flock here, to see the ancient sights and savor the spectacular views: the uninterrupted expanse of the Atlantic on the western horizon; the Connemara coast and its Twelve Bens to the northeast; and County Clare's Burren and the Cliffs of Moher to the southeast.

Aran Rediscovered

During the 1800s, the islands, wracked by famine and mass emigration, were virtually forgotten by mainland Ireland. At the turn of the 20th century, however, the books of J.M. Synge (1871–1909)—who learned Irish on Inishmaan and wrote about its people in his famous play *Riders to the Sea*— prompted Gaelic revivalists to study and document this isolated bastion of Irish culture. To this day, Synge's travel book *The Aran Islands*, first published in 1907, and reissued by Penguin with a brilliant introduction by artist and map maker Tim Robinson in 1992, remains the best book ever written about the islands. Liam O'Flaherty became one of the most famous sons of Inishmore through his novels, such as *Famine*. And in 1934, American director Robert Flaherty filmed his classic documentary *Man of Aran* on Inishmore, recording the islanders' dramatic battles with sea and storm, and bringing the islands into the world spotlight. The film is shown in the *Ionad Árainn* (Aran Heritage Center) in Cill Rónáin (Kilronan) on Inishmore daily during July, August, and early September. Flaherty, incidentally, continues to be a common surname on the islands; it is hard to visit the islands *without* meeting a Flaherty.

There's a small hotel on Inisheer, and two others on Inishmore, but there's no shortage of guesthouses and B&Bs, mostly in simple family homes. The best way to book is through the Galway City TIO. Each island has at least one wine-licensed restaurant serving plain home cooking. Most B&Bs will provide a packed lunch and an evening meal (called high tea) on request.

INIS MÓR (INISHMORE)

 ★ *31 km (18 mi) Southwest of Salthill docks, 5km (3 mi) northwest of Doolin docks, 48 km (30 mi) west of Galway Docks.*

With a population of 900, Inis Mór is the largest of the islands and the closest to the Connemara coast. It's also the most commercialized, its appeal slightly diminished by road traffic. In summer, ferries arriving at Cill Rónáin (Kilronan), Inis Mór's main village and port, are met by minibuses and pony-and-cart drivers, all eager to show visi-

> **TRAVEL TIP**
>
> You can rent bicycles from May through October for €12 per day from Aran Bike Hire (☎ 099/61132), at the ferry landing at Inis Mór (Inishmore) Pier.

tors "the sights." More than 8 km (5 mi) long and about 3 km (2 mi) wide at most points, with an area of 7,640 acres, the island is just a little too large to explore comfortably on foot in a day. The best way to see it is really by bicycle; bring your own or rent one from one of the vendors operating near the quay.

The **Ionad Árainn (Aran Heritage Centre)** explains the history and culture of the islanders, who for many years lived in virtual isolation from the mainland. ⊠*Cill Ronáin (Kilronan)* ☎*099/61355* ⊕*www. visitaranislands.com* ☎€3 ☽*Apr., May, Sept., and Oct., daily 11–5; June–Aug. daily 10–7; Nov.–Mar., by appointment.*

Even if you only have a few hours to explore Inis Mór, rent a bike (next to the pier) and head straight for **Dún Aengus,** one of the finest prehistoric monuments in Europe, dating from about 2000 BC. Spectacularly set on the edge of a 300-foot-tall cliff overlooking a sheer drop, the

WORD OF MOUTH

"In my opinion, the visit to Dún Aengus made the trip to Ireland worthwhile. It is a stunningly beautiful fort situated on cliffs that drop off dramatically into the Atlantic Ocean. The views are exhilarating. I can't begin to imagine how beautiful it would be on a sunny day?"

—Desiderado

fort has defenses consisting of three rows of concentric circles. Whom the builders were defending themselves against is a matter of conjecture. From the innermost rampart there's a great view of the island and the Connemara coast. In order to protect this fragile monument from erosion, you should approach it only through the visitor center, which gives access to a 1-km (½-mi) uphill walk over uneven terrain—wear sturdy footwear. ⊠*7 km (4 mi) west of Cill Ronáin (Kilronan), Kilmurvey* ☎*099/61010* ⊕*www.heritageireland.ie* ☎€2 ☽*Mar.–Oct., daily 10–6; Nov.–Feb., daily 10–4.*

WHERE TO STAY & EAT

$-$$$ ✕▣**Kilmurvey House.** This rambling 200-year-old stone farmhouse is the
★ first choice of many visitors to the island. It's at the foot of Dún Aengus fort, a three-minute walk from the beach, and about 6½ km (4 mi) from the quay and the airport (accessible by minibus). The old stone house has been cleverly extended to provide extra guest rooms. The neatly kept front garden leads to a large, high-ceiling hall and wide stairs, giving a pleasant sense of space. The walls are hung with portraits of the house's previous owners, the warrior clan of O'Flahertys—one of whom was Oscar Wilde's godfather—and whose descendants include the famed writers Liam and Robert. Rooms are spacious and comfortable, with wonderful sea views. Dinners ($) are cooked about five nights a week by the warm, chatty owner, Treasa Joyce, and are not to be missed. Vegetables and herbs come from the back garden, the floury potatoes are island grown, and wild Atlantic salmon is a popular main course. ⊠*Cill Ronáin (Kilronan), Co. Galway* ☎*099/61218* 🖷*099/61397* ⊕*www. kilmurveyhouse.com* ⊅*12 rooms* ⚷*In-room: no a/c, no TV, dial-up. In-hotel: restaurant, no elevator* ▤*MC, V* ☽*Closed Nov.–Mar.* ⏱*BP.*

$ ▣**Ard Einne Guesthouse.** Almost every window at this B&B on Inishmore looks out to the sea, making it the perfect place to de-stress. The rambling 80-year-old house, with its distinctive dormer windows, is close to both the beach and the town; many guests base themselves here for two or three nights, to make a thorough exploration of the island. The public rooms and guest rooms are relaxed, with modern decor including light-color linens and walls paneled with blond wood. Simple evening meals ($) are prepared by your host, Clodagh Ní Ghoill, who will discuss the four-course set menu in advance. ⊠*Cill Ronáin (Kilronan), Co. Galway* ☎*099/61126* 🖷*099/61388* ⊕*www.ardeinne.com* ⤳*14 rooms* ⌂*In-room: no a/c, no phone, no TV. In-hotel: restaurant, no elevator* ▤*MC, V* ⊘*Closed Nov.–Jan.* ⫿◎⫿*BP.*

NIGHTLIFE

The place to go for traditional music is the **American Bar** (⊠*Cill Ronáin* ☎*099/61130*). **Joe Mac's** (⊠*Cill Ronáin* ☎*099/61248*), right off the pier, is a good place for a pint while waiting for the ferry home. **Joe Watty's** (⊠*Main Rd., Cill Ronáin* ☎*099/61155*) is a good bet for traditional music virtually every night in summer.

INIS MEÁIN (INISHMAAN)

㉘ *3 km (2 mi) east of Inis Mór (Inishmore).*

The middle island in both size and location, Inis Meáin has a population of about 300 and can be comfortably explored on foot. In fact, you have no alternative if you want to reach the island's major antiquities: **Dun Conor (Conor Fort)**, a smaller version of Dún Aengus; the ruins of two **early-Christian churches;** and a chamber tomb known as the **Bed of Diarmuid and Grainne,** dating from about 2000 BC. You can also take wonderful cliff walks above secluded coves. It's on Inishmaan that the traditional Aran lifestyle is most evident. Most islanders still don hand-knitted Aran sweaters, though nowadays they wear them with jeans and sneakers.

SHOPPING

Inis Meáin Knitting (⊠*Carrown Lisheen* ☎*099/73009*) is a young company producing quality knitwear in luxury fibers for the international market—including Liberty of London, Barneys New York, and Bergdorf Goodman—while providing much-needed local employment. The factory showroom has an extensive selection of garments at discount prices. To get here from the pier, walk five minutes due west.

INIS OIRR (INISHEER)

㉙ *4 km (2½ mi) east of Inis Meáin (Inishmaan), 8 km (5 mi) northwest of Doolin docks.*

The smallest and flattest of the islands, Inis Oirr can be explored on foot in an afternoon, though if the weather is fine you may be tempted to linger on the long, sandy beach between the quay and

> **EXTRA CREDIT**
>
> In summer Inis Oirr's population of 300 is augmented by high school students from all over Ireland attending the Gaeltacht, or Irish-language, school.

the airfield. Only one stretch of road, about 500 yards long, links the airfield and the sole village. "The back of the island," as Inis Oirr's uninhabited side facing the Atlantic is called, has no beaches, but people swim off the rocks.

It's worth making a circuit of the island to get a sense of its utter tranquillity. A maze of footpaths runs between the high stone walls that divide the fields, which are so small that they can support only one cow each, or two to three sheep. Those that are not cultivated or grazed turn into natural wildflower meadows between June and August, overrun with harebells, scabious, red clover, oxeye daisies, saxifrage, and tall grasses. It seems almost a crime to walk here—but how can you resist taking a rest in the corner of a sweet-smelling meadow on a sunny afternoon, sheltered by high stone walls with no sound but the larks above and the wind as it sifts through the stones?

The **Church of Kevin,** signposted to the southeast of the quay, is a small, early-Christian church that gets buried in sand by storms every winter. Each year the islanders dig it out of the sand for the celebration of St. Kevin's Day on June 14.

A pleasant walk through the village takes you up to **O'Brien's Castle,** a ruined 15th-century tower on top of a rocky hill—the only hill on the island.

WHERE TO STAY & EAT

$ ✕⊡ **Hotel Inisheer.** A pleasant, modern low-rise in the middle of the island's only village, a few minutes' walk from the quay and the airstrip, this simple, whitewashed building with a slate roof and half-slated walls has bright, plainly furnished rooms. The restaurant (open to nonguests) is the best bet on the island, although some of the food is imported frozen. The social life of the island centers on "the hotel," as it is called, and there are nightly sessions of traditional music. ⊠ *Lurgan Village, Co. Galway* ☎ *099/75020* 🖷 *099/75099* 🛏 *27 rooms* ⚬ *In-room: no a/c, no phone, no TV. In-hotel: restaurant, bar, no elevator* 🖃 *AE, DC, MC, V* ⊘ *Closed Oct.–Mar.* ℺ *BP.*

CONNEMARA & COUNTY MAYO

Bordered by the long expanse of Lough Corrib on the east and the jagged coast of the Atlantic on the west is the rugged, desolate region of western County Galway known as Connemara. Like the American West, it's an area of spectacular, almost myth-making geography—of glacial lakes; gorgeous, silent mountains; lonely roads; and hushed, uninhabited boglands. The Twelve Bens, "the central glory of Connemara," as author Brendan Lehane has called them, together with the Maamturk Mountains to their north, lord proudly over the area's sepia boglands. In the midst of this wilderness there are few people, since Connemara's population is sparse even by Irish standards. Especially in the off-season, you're far more likely to come across sheep strolling its roads than another car.

Two main routes—one inland, the other coastal—lead through Connemara. To take the inland route described below, leave Galway City on the well-signposted outer-ring road and follow signs for N59—Moycullen, Oughterard, and Clifden. If you choose to go the coastal route, you can travel due west from Galway City to Ros an Mhil (Rossaveal) on R336

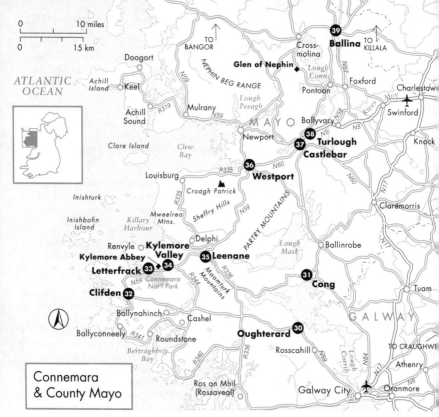

through Salthill, Bearna, and An Spidéal—all in the heart of the West's strong Gaeltacht, home to roughly 40,000 Irish speakers (note that most place signage hereabouts will be in Irish, so a map with both English and Irish names will prove handy). You can continue north on R336 from Ros an Mhil (Rossaveal) to Maam Cross and then head for coastal points west, or pick up R340 and putter along the coast.

OUGHTERARD

③⓪ *27 km (17 mi) northwest of Galway City on N59.*

Bustling Oughterard (pronounced *ook*-ter-ard) is the main village on the western shores of Lough Corrib and one of Ireland's leading angling resorts. The prettiest part of the village is on the far (Clifden) side, beyond the busy commercial center, beside a wooded section of the River Corrib. The lough is signposted to the right in the village center, less than 1½ km (1 mi) up the road. From mid-June to early September, local boatmen offer trips on the lough, which has several islands. It's also possible to take a boat trip to the village of Cong, at the north shore of the lough. Midway between Oughterard and Cong, Inchagoill Island (the Island of the Stranger), a popular destination for a half-day trip, has several early-Christian church remains. The cost of boat rides is negotiable; expect to pay about €10 per person.

WHERE TO STAY & EAT

$$$ ✕⚏ **Ross Lake House.** Well off the beaten path, this surprisingly stylish
★ country hideaway sits near a stream and is surrounded by 5 acres of colorful gardens. Built by James Edward Jackson, land agent for Lord Iveagh at Ashford Castle, the white-trim Georgian house, managed by the enthusiastic Henry and Elaine Reid, has a suavely furnished interior, with 19th-century antiques and welcoming open fires. Guest rooms in the converted stables are simpler and a little smaller than those in the house, but all have peaceful garden views. A table d'hôte dinner menu ($$–$$$), set in a salon with Regency-stripe wallpapers, offers good-quality, plain country-house cooking featuring local delicacies, including the much-sought after Connemara mountain lamb. The house is 5 km (3 mi) from Oughterard. ⊠ *Rosscahill, Co. Galway* ☎☎*091/550–109* ⊕*www.rosslakehotel.com* ⇨*13 rooms* ⏶*In-room: no a/c. In-hotel: restaurant, bar, no elevator, tennis court* ▭*AE, DC, MC, V* ☺*Closed Nov.–mid-Mar.* ⏶⏶*BP.*

NIGHTLIFE

For good traditional music try **Flaherty's** (⊠*Main St.* ☎*091/552–194*).

EN ROUTE As you continue northwest from Oughterard on N59, you'll soon pass a string of small lakes on your left; their shining blue waters reflecting the blue sky are a typical Connemara sight on a sunny day. About 16 km (10 mi) northwest of Oughterard, the continuation of the coast road (R336) meets N59 at Maam Cross in the shadow of Leckavrea Mountain. Once an important meeting place for the people of north and south Connemara, it's still the location of a large monthly cattle fair. Walkers will find wonderful views of Connemara by heading for any of the local peaks visible from the road. Beyond Maam Cross, some of the best scenery in Connemara awaits on the road to Recess, 16 km (10 mi) west of Maam Cross on N59. At many points on this drive, a short walk away from either side of the main road will lead you to the shores of one of the area's many small loughs. Stop and linger if the sun is out—even intermittently—for the light filtering through the clouds gives splendor to the distant, dark-gray mountains and creates patterns on the brown-green moorland below. In June and July, it stays light until 11 PM or so, and it's worth taking a late-evening stroll to see the sun's reluctance to set.

In Recess, **Joyce's** (☎*095/34604*) is a crafts shop owned by a family that is famed for its traditional Connemara tweeds. The emporium has a good selection of tweed, and also carries an enticing selection of contemporary ceramics, handwoven shawls, books of Irish interest, original paintings, and small sculptures.

7

CONG

31

23 km (14 mi) northeast of Maam Cross on N59.

On a narrow isthmus between Lough Corrib and Lough Mask on the County Mayo border, the pretty, old-fashioned village of Cong, near Maam Cross, is dotted with ivy-covered thatched cottages, dilapidated farmhouses, and one immensely posh hotel, Ashford Castle.

Cong is surrounded by many stone circles and burial mounds, but its most notable ruins are those of the **Augustine Abbey** (⊠ *Abbey St.*), dating from the early 13th century and still exhibiting some finely carved details. It can be seen overlooking a river near fabulous Ashford Castle, now a hotel.

Cong's 15 minutes of fame came in 1952, when John Ford filmed *The Quiet Man,* one of his most popular films, here; John Wayne plays a prizefighter who goes home to Ireland to court the fiery Maureen O'Hara. (Film critic Pauline Kael called the movie "fearfully Irish and green and hearty.") The **Quiet Man Heritage Cottage,** in the village center, is an exact replica of the cottage used in the film, with reproductions of the furniture and costumes, a few original artifacts, and pictures of actors Barry Fitzgerald and Maureen O'Hara on location. For much of the year, Margaret and Gerry Collins host "Quiet Man" tours, originating at the cottage and exploring such Cong village sites as the river fight scene, the "hats in the air" scene, and Pat Cohan's Bar. ⊠ *Cong Village Center* ☎ *094/954–6089* ⊕ *www.quietman-cong.com* ⊠ *€4* ⊙ *Mar.–Nov., daily 10–6.*

WHERE TO STAY

$$$$
★

Ashford Castle. Nearly bigger than the neighboring village of Cong, this famed mock-Gothic baronial showpiece was built in 1870 for the Guinness family and has been wowing visitors ever since—that is, if your guest list runs to Prince Rainier, John Travolta, and Jack Nicholson. Massive, flamboyantly turreted, built of stone with towers and bridges, crenellations and mullioned windows, Ashford is the very picture of a romantic Irish castle. As a world apart from the normal hubbub of Irish life, it remains strong on luxury, charm, and good service, but—some pundits would say—light on authenticity as time-stained charm has given way to too many creature comforts. Inside, large paintings in gilt frames hang from the castle's carved stone walls above polished wood paneling, illuminated by crystal chandeliers. Deluxe rooms have generous sitting areas, heavily carved antique furniture, open fireplaces and extra-large bathrooms. Standard bedrooms in the discreetly added new wing are smaller, with marble bathroom fittings and Victorian-style antiques, have ample amenities but lack the scale and baronial flamboyance of the rest of the castle. The suites in the original castle building are vast, with double-height windows, furnished with Georgian antiques, and blissfully comfortable. The Prince of Wales Cocktail Bar (named for the one who visited in the 1890s) is the venue for elegant predinner drinks. The cuisine, by distinguished Swiss chef Stefan Matz, is stylish and unfussy, showcasing fresh local ingredients. The hotel makes the most of its superb location at the head of Lough Corrib and the surrounding formal lawns and gardens are possibly the most neatly manicured outdoor space in Ireland. Accordingly, fly-fishing is a popular outdoor sport, and the river bank has recently been landscaped to facilitate anglers—typical of the no-expense-spared Ashford approach—while there has also been massive investment in the hotel's spa facilities. ⊠*Co. Mayo* ☎*094/954–6003* 🖷*094/954–6260* ⊕*www.ashford.ie* 🖙*72 rooms, 11 suites* ⚷*In-room: no a/c, Ethernet, Wi-Fi. In-hotel: 2 restaurants, bars, golf course, tennis courts, gym, bicycles* ▱*AE, DC, MC, V* ⦿*EP.*

CLIFDEN

32 46 km (29 mi) southwest of Cong on N59, 79 km (49 mi) northwest
★ of Galway City on N59.

With roughly 1,100 residents, Clifden would be called a village by most, but in these parts it's looked on as something of a metropolis. It's far and away the prettiest town in Connemara, as well as its unrivaled "capital." Clifden's first attraction is its location—perched high above Clifden Bay on a forested plateau, its back to the spectacular Twelve Ben Mountains. The tapering

> **TRAVEL TIP**
>
> Clifden's popularity necessitates a chaotic one-way traffic system, and loud techno music blasts out of certain bars. If you're over 25 and value your peace and quiet, you'd best choose a base outside town.

spires of the town's two churches add to its alpine feel. A selection of small restaurants, lively bars with music most summer nights, pleasant accommodations, and excellent walks make the town a popular base. It's quiet out of season, but in July and August crowds flock here, especially for August's world-famous Connemara Pony Show.

A 2-km (1-mi) walk along the beach road through the grounds of the ruined **Clifden Castle** is the best way to explore the seashore. The castle was built in 1815 by John D'Arcy, the town's founder, who laid out the town's wide main street on a long ridge with a parallel street below it. D'Arcy was High Sheriff of Galway, and his greatest wish was to establish a center of law and order in what he saw as the lawless wilderness of Connemara. Before the founding of Clifden, the interior of Connemara was largely uninhabited, with most of its population clinging to the seashore.

Take the aptly named **Sky Road** to really appreciate Clifden's breathtaking scenery. Signposted at the west end of town, this high, narrow circuit of about 5 km (3 mi) heads west to Kingstown, skirting Clifden Bay's precipitous shores.

WHERE TO STAY & EAT

¢–$$ ✕**Mitchell's Seafood.** A town-center shop has been cleverly converted into a stylish, two-story eatery. On the first floor, beyond the plate-glass windows, there's a welcoming open fire, and you can eat at the bar or at one of the polished wood tables. Exposed stone walls and wooden floors are alluring accents on the quieter second level. Braised whole sea bass with fennel butter typifies the simple treatment given to seafood. The all-day menu also features lighter options like homemade spicy fish cakes and fresh crab salad. There are several meat options, including traditional Irish stew of Connemara lamb and fresh vegetables. ⊠*Market St.* ☎*095/21867* ☐*MC, V* ☉*Closed Nov.–Feb.*

$$$ ✕⊡ **Rock Glen Manor House.** You will probably be "greeted" by a pair of
★ braying donkeys who graze beside the driveway. Enter this realm and you can see riding boots and tennis rackets in the hall—clearly, Peadar Nevin's beautifully converted 1815 shooting lodge feels more like a private home than a top-class hotel. A turf fire warms the large, sumptuous drawing room—an eye-knocking symphony in red, chicly fitted out with houndstooth-check armchairs and gilt-frame mirrors (plus a lovely array of magazines, books, and board games). Fluffy mohair or chintz spreads cover the beds in the sweetly furnished guest rooms. In the Victorian-style restaurant ($$$), you can expect such winners as roasted rack of lamb with an herb crust and duxelles. To get here from Clifden, cross the bridge at the west end of town and walk less than 1 km (½ mi) down the R341 Roundstone road. ⊠*Co. Galway* ☎*095/21035* ☐*095/21737* ⊕*www.rockglenhotel.com* ⤶*27 rooms* ⏚*In-room: no a/c. In-hotel: restaurant, bar, no elevator, tennis court* ☐*AE, MC, V* ☉*Closed Jan. and Feb. No lunch* ⊠*BP.*

$$$ ⊡ **Abbeyglen Castle Hotel.** Creeper covered, as if under a Sleeping Beauty spell, gorgeous Abbeyglen sits framed by towering trees at the foot of the glorious Twelve Bens Mountains. If time hasn't completely stopped here, it has certainly slowed down—but that's just the way the relaxed guests want it. Surrounded by gardens with waterfalls and streams, the Victorian castle-manor was built in 1832 by John D'Arcy, the founder of Clifden and builder of Clifden Castle. Inside, each guest room is uniquely decorated with heavy, ornate, dark-wood furniture and rich colors befitting a castle. Although it's in a very quiet and seemingly secluded location, the hotel becomes busy during complimentary afternoon tea, and has a busy nightlife scene, with live traditional music in its bar and big-name touring acts in its function room. This makes it a particularly popular weekend destination with Irish city-dwellers. ⊠*Sky Rd., Co. Galway* ☎*095/22832* ☐*095/21797* ⊕*www.abbeyglen.ie* ⤶*48 rooms* ⏚*In-room: no a/c. In-hotel: restaurant, bar, tennis court, pool* ☐*AE, DC, MC, V* ☉*Closed Jan.* ⊠*BP.*

$$ ⊡ **Quay House.** A roaring turf fire in the sitting room greets you at this three-story Georgian house, Clifden's oldest building (1820). It's a short walk from the busy town center, and an oasis of calm beside the harbor quay. Guest rooms are unusually spacious, and those in the main house are imaginatively decorated with deep-color walls and period accents; all but one have sea views. There's also a new wing with seven studio rooms with balconies overlooking the harbor. Proprietors Julia and Patrick Foyle have tucked in homey touches, such as books and model boats. ⊠*The Quay, Connemara, Co. Galway* ☎*095/21369* ☐*095/21608* ⊕*www.thequayhouse.com* ⤶*20 rooms* ⏚*In-room: no*

a/c, kitchen (some). In-hotel: no elevator ▭MC, V ☉ *Closed Nov.– mid-Mar., except by arrangement.*

¢ 🏨**Dun Rí.** An old town house in the lower, quieter part of Clifden has been extended and converted into a comfortable guesthouse with private parking. The town's bars and restaurants are only two minutes' walk away, yet there can be sheep grazing on a vacant lot across the road. Rooms are a good size, with hotel-like features including adjustable radiators, swagged floral curtains and efficient showers. Help yourself to tea and coffee in the residents' lounge, a good place to compare notes with fellow travelers. The breakfast room has pine floor and white damask cloths, and the toast is accompanied by butterballs (shaped by butter pats, once ubiquitous in country hotels, now seldom seen) and homemade jam. ⊠*Hulk St., Co. Galway* ☎*095/21625* 🖷*095/21635* ⊕*www.connemara.net/dun-ri* 🛏*13 rooms* ⌂*In-room: no a/c. In-hotel: bar, no elevator* ▭MC, V ⊧*BP.*

NIGHTLIFE

Abbeyglen Castle Hotel (⊠*Sky Rd.* ☎*095/21201*) hosts musical sessions in the bar most nights from June to September and occasional visits by big-name acts.

SPORTS & THE OUTDOORS

BICYCLING   Explore Connemara by renting a bike from **John Mannion & Son** (⊠*Railway View* ☎*095/21160*).

GOLF   On a dramatic stretch of Atlantic coastline, the 18-hole course at the **Connemara Golf Club** (⊠*South of Clifden, Ballyconneely* ☎*095/23502*) measures 7,174 yards.

SHOPPING

The Connemara Hamper (⊠*Market St.* ☎*095/21054*), a small but well-stocked specialty food shop, is an ideal place to pick up picnic fare, with its excellent Irish farmhouse cheeses, pâtés, smoked Connemara salmon, and Irish handmade chocolates. **Millar's Connemara Tweeds** (⊠*Main St.* ☎*095/21038*), an arts-and-crafts gallery, carries a good selection of traditional tweeds and hand knits. The **Station House Courtyard** (⊠*Old Railway Station, Bridge St.* ☎*095/21699*) is a cobbled courtyard with crafts studios and designer-wear outlets.

LETTERFRACK

❸❸ *14 km (9 mi) north of Clifden on N59.*

The 5,000-acre **Connemara National Park** lies southeast of the village of Letterfrack. Its visitor center covers the area's history and ecology, particularly the origins and growth of peat—and presents the depressing statistic that more than 80% of Ireland's peat, 5,000 years in the making, has been destroyed in the last 90 years. You can also get details on the many excellent walks and beaches in the area. The misleadingly named "park" is, in fact, just rocky or wooded wilderness territory, albeit with some helpful trails marked out to aid your exploration. It includes part of the famous **Twelve Bens** mountain range, which are for experienced hill walkers only. An easier hike is the spectacular **Pollrark River Gorge** and **Glanmore Valley**. Ask for advice on a hike suited to your abilities and interests at the visitor center. ☎*095/41054* ✉*Park free, visitor center €2.50* ☉*Park freely accessible; visitor center Apr., May, and Sept.–mid-Oct., daily 10–5:30; June, daily 10–6:30; July and Aug., daily 9:30–6:30.*

WHERE TO STAY & EAT

$$$ ✕🏨 **Renvyle House.** A lake at its front door, the Atlantic Ocean at its
★ back door, and the mountains of Connemara as a backdrop form the enthralling setting for this hotel 8 km (5 mi) north of Letterfrack. Once the legendary retreat of that noted Irish man of letters, Oliver St. John Gogarty of Dublin (on whom James Joyce modeled Buck Mulligan in *Ulysses*)—and, as such, a focal point for the Irish literary renaissance of the early 20th century—-Renvyle is rustic and informal; it has exposed beams and brickwork, and numerous open turf fires. The main salon, called the Long Room, is one of the most eminently civilized rooms in Ireland—all tranquil beige, endless chairs, and pretty pictures. The comfortable guest rooms, elegantly decorated in a floral style, all have breathtaking views. The softly lighted restaurant's table d'hôte menu is based on traditional Irish fare ($$$$). ✉*Renvyle, Co. Galway* ☎*095/43511* 🖶*095/43515* ⊕*www.renvyle.com* ⬥*68 rooms* ⚫*In-room: no a/c, Wi-Fi. In-hotel: restaurant, bar, no elevator, golf course, tennis courts, pool* ☰*AE, DC, MC, V* ☉*Closed early Jan.–mid-Feb.* ⦿*BP.*

$$$ ✕🏨 **Rosleague Manor.** This pink, creeper-clad, two-story Georgian house
★ occupies 30 lovely acres overlooking an eye-knocking view: a gorgeous lawn backdropped by Ballinakill Bay and the dreamy mountains of Connemara. Inside, the clutter of walking sticks and shooting sticks beneath the grandfather clock in the hall sets the informal, country-house tone. Well-used antiques, four-poster or large brass bedsteads, and drapes that match the William Morris wallpaper decorate the solidly comfortable and impeccably kept bedrooms. The best rooms are at the front on the first floor, overlooking the bay. At dinner in the superb restaurant ($$$$), baked monkfish with crispy capers and balsamic vinegar is one of the tastiest entrées. ✉*Rosleague Bay, Co. Galway* ☎*095/41101* 🖶*095/41168* ⊕*www.rosleague.com* ⬥*20 rooms* ⚫*In-room: no a/c, Wi-Fi In-hotel: restaurant, bar, no elevator, tennis court* ☰*AE, MC, V* ☉*Closed mid-Nov.–mid-Mar.* ⦿*BP.*

NIGHTLIFE

For traditional music, try the **Bards' Den** (✉*Main St.* ☎*095/41042*).

SHOPPING

Connemara Handcrafts (✉*Village center* ☎*095/41058*), on the N59, carries an extensive selection of crafts and women's fashions made by the stellar Avoca Handweavers; there's also a quaint coffee shop.

KYLEMORE VALLEY

34 *Runs for 6½ km (4 mi) between Letterfrack and intersection of N59 and R344.*

One of the more conventionally beautiful stretches of road in Connemara passes through Kylemore Valley, which is between the Twelve Bens to the south and the naturally forested Dorruagh Mountains to the north. Kylemore (the name is derived from Coill Mór, Irish for "big wood") looks "as though some colossal giant had slashed it out with a couple of strokes from his mammoth sword," as artist and author John FitzMaurice Mills has written.

Fodor's Choice ★ **Kylemore Abbey,** one of the most photographed castles in all of Ireland, is visible across a reedy lake with a backdrop of wooded hillside. The vast Gothic Revival, turreted, gray-stone castle was built as a private home between 1861 and 1868 by Mitchell Henry, a member of Parliament for County Galway, and his wife, Margaret, who had fallen in love with the spot during a carriage ride while on their honeymoon. The Henrys spared no expense—the final bill for their house is said to have come to £1.5 million—and employed mostly local laborers, thereby abetting the famine relief effort (this area was among the worst hit in all of Ireland). Adjacent to the house is a spectacular neo-Gothic church, which, sadly, became the burial place for Margaret, who died after contracting "Nile fever" on a trip to Egypt. In 1920, nuns from the Irish Abbey of the Nuns of St. Benedict, who fled their abbey in Belgium during World War I, eventually sought refuge in Kylemore, which had been through a number of owners and decades of decline after the Henrys died. Still in residence, the Benedictine nuns run a girls' boarding school here. Three reception rooms and the main hall are open to the public, as are a crafts center and cafeteria. There's also a 6-acre walled Victorian garden; a shuttle bus from the abbey departs every 15 minutes during opening hours for the garden. An exhibition and video explaining the history of the house can be viewed year-round at the abbey, and the grounds are freely accessible most of the year. Ask at the excellent crafts shop for directions to the **Gothic Chapel** (a five-minute walk from the abbey), a tiny replica of Norwich Cathedral built by the Henrys. (Norwich was built by the English Benedictines, in a felicitous anticipation of Kylemore's fate.) ⊠ *About ¾ km (½ mi) back from Kylemore Valley Rd.* ☎ *095/41146* ⊕ *www.kylemoreabbey.com* ☜ *€12, including shuttle bus to garden* ⊙ *Crafts shop, grounds, and cafeteria daily 10–6; exhibition and garden mid-Mar.–Nov., daily 9–5:30.*

Fodor's Choice ★ Beyond Kylemore, N59 travels for some miles along **Killary Harbour,** a narrow fjord (the only one in Ireland) that runs for 16 km (10 mi) between County Mayo's Mweelrea Mountains to the north and County Galway's Dorruagh Mountains to the south. The dark, deep water of the fjord reflects the magnificent steep-sided hills that border it, creating a haunting scene of natural grandeur. The harbor has an extremely safe anchorage, 13 fathoms (78 feet) deep for almost its entire length and sheltered from storms by mountain walls. The rafts floating in Killary Harbour belong to fish-farming consortia that artificially raise

7

salmon and trout in cages beneath the water. This is a matter of some controversy all over the West. Although some people welcome the employment opportunities, others bemoan the visual blight of the rafts. From April through October **Killary Cruises** (✉ *Nancy's Point, 2 km [1 mi] west of Leenane on N59 Clifden Rd.* ☎ *091/566–736* ⊕ *www.killarycruises.com*) runs 1½-hour trips around Killary Harbour in an enclosed catamaran launch with seating for 150 passengers, plus a bar and restaurant.

LEENANE

㉟ *18 km (11 mi) east of Letterfrack on N59.*

Nestled idyllically at the foot of the Maamturk Mountains and overlooking the tranquil waters of Killary Harbour, Leenane is a tiny village noted for its role as the setting for the film *The Field*, which starred Richard Harris.

The **Sheep and Wool Centre,** in the center of Leenane, focuses on the traditional industry of North Connemara and West Mayo. More than 20 breeds of sheep graze around the house, and there are demonstrations of carding, spinning, weaving, and the dyeing of wool with natural plant dyes. ☎ *095/42323* ⊕ *www.sheepandwoolcentre.com* ✉ *€3* ⊙ *Apr.–June, Sept., and Oct., daily 9:30–7; July and Aug., daily 9–7.*

EN ROUTE

You have two options for traveling onward to Westport. The first is to take the direct route on N59. The second is to detour through the **Doolough Valley** between the Mweelrea Mountains (to the west) and the Sheeffry Hills (to the east) and on to Westport via Louisburgh (on the southern shore of Clew Bay). The latter route adds about 24 km (15 mi) to the trip, but devotees of this part of the West claim that it will take you through the region's most impressive, unspoiled stretch of scenery. If you opt for the longer route, turn left onto R335 1½ km (1 mi) beyond Leenane. Just after this turn, you can hear the powerful rush of the Aasleagh Falls. You can park over the bridge, stroll along the river's shore, and soak in the splendor of the surrounding mountains.

Look out as you travel north for the great bulk of 2,500-foot-high **Croagh Patrick**; its size and conical shape make it one of the West's most distinctive landmarks. On clear days a small white building is visible at its summit (it stands on a ½-acre plateau), as is the wide path that ascends to it. The latter is the Pilgrim's Path. Each year about 25,000 people, many of them barefoot, follow the path to pray to St. Patrick in the oratory on its peak. St. Patrick spent the 40 days and nights of

Lent here in 441, during the period in which he was converting Ireland to Christianity. The traditional date for the pilgrimage is the last Sunday in July; in the past, the walk was made at night, with pilgrims carrying burning torches, but that practice has been discontinued. The climb involves a gentle uphill slope, but you need to be fit and agile to complete the last half hour, over scree (small loose rocks with no trail). This is why most climbers carry a stick or staff (traditionally made of ash, and called an ash plant), which helps you to stop sliding backward. These can sometimes be bought in the parking area. The hike can be made in about three hours (round-trip) on any fine day and is well worth the effort for the magnificent views of the islands of Clew Bay, the Sheeffry Hills to the south (with the Bens visible behind them), and the peaks of Mayo to the north. The climb starts at Murrisk, a village about 8 km (5 mi) before Westport on the R335 Louisburgh road.

WESTPORT

36 *32 km (20 mi) north of Leenane on R335.*

★ By far the most attractive town in County Mayo, Westport is on an inlet of Clew Bay, a wide expanse of sea dotted with islands and framed by mountain ranges. It's one of the most gentrified and Anglo-Irish heritage towns in Ireland, its Georgian origins clearly defined by the broad streets skirting the gently flowing river and, particularly, by the lime-fringe central avenue called the Mall. Built as an O'Malley stronghold, the entire town received a face-lift when the Brownes, who came from Sussex in the reign of Elizabeth I, constructed Westport House and much of the modern town, which was laid out by architect James Wyatt when he was employed to finish the grand estate of Westport House.

Today Westport's streets radiate from its central **Octagon,** where an old-fashioned farmers' market is held on Thursday mornings; look for work clothes, harnesses, tools, and children's toys for sale. Traditional shops—of ironmongers, drapers, and the like—dot the streets that lead to the Octagon, while a riverside mall is lined with tall lime trees. At Westport's Quay, about 2 km (1 mi) outside town, a large warehouse has been attractively restored as holiday apartments, and there are some good bars and decent restaurants.

The showpiece of the town remains **Westport House and Country Park,** a stately home built on the site of an earlier castle (believed to have been the home of the 16th-century warrior queen, Grace O'Malley) and most famed for its setting right on the shores of a beautiful lake. The house was begun in 1730 to the designs of Richard Castle, added to in 1778, and completed in 1788 by architect James Wyatt for the Marquess of Sligo of the Browne family. The rectangular, three-story house is furnished with late-Georgian and Victorian pieces. Family portraits by Opie and Reynolds, a huge collection of old Irish silver and old Waterford glass, plus an opulent group of paintings—including *The Holy Family* by Rubens—are on display. A word of caution: Westport isn't your usual staid country house. The old dungeons now house video games and the grounds have given way to a small amusement park for children and a children's zoo. In fact, the lake is now littered with swan-shaped "pedaloes," boats that may be fun for families but help destroy the perfect Georgian grace of the setting. If these elements don't sound like a draw, arrive early when it's less likely to be busy. The Farmyard area has garden-plant sales, an indoor soft-play area, a gift shop, and a coffee shop. ⊠ *Off N59 south of Westport turnoff, clearly signposted from Octagon* ☎ *098/25430* ⊕ *www.westporthouse.ie* ☜ *House €11.50; attractions €20, family day-ticket for all attractions €68* ☉ *House and gardens, Mar. and Oct., weekends 11:30–5:30; Apr.–Sept., daily 11:30–5:30. Attractions, Easter wk., July, and Aug., daily 11:30–5:30; May, Sun. and holidays 11:30–5:30; June, Thurs.–Sun. 11:30–5:30.*

Clew Bay is said to have 365 islands, one for every day of the year. The biggest and most interesting to visit is **Clare Island**, at the mouth of the bay. In fine weather the rocky, hilly island, which is 8 km (5 mi) long and 5 km (3 mi) wide, affords beautiful views south toward Connemara, east across Clew Bay, and north to Achill Island. About 150 people live on the island today, but before the 1845–47 famine it had a population of about 1,700. A 15th-century tower overlooking the harbor was once the stronghold of Granuaile, the pirate queen, who ruled the area until her death in 1603. She is buried on the island, in its 12th-century Cistercian abbey. Today most visitors seek out the island for its unusual peace and quiet, golden beaches, and unspoiled landscape. Ferries depart from Roonagh Pier, near Louisburgh, a scenic 19-km (12-mi) drive from Westport on R335 past several long sandy beaches. The crossing takes about 15 minutes. Dolphins often accompany the boats on the trip, and there are large populations of seals under the island's cliffs. Bird-watchers, hikers, cyclists, and sea anglers may want to stay for longer than a day trip; inquire at the Westport TIO or call the **Clare Island Development Office** (☎ *098/25087*) for information about accommodations on the island. ☎ *098/25045 O'Malley's Ferries, 098/25212 Pirate Queen boat* ☜ *Ferry €16 round-trip* ☉ *Sailings usually twice daily, May–mid-Sept., weather permitting.*

WHERE TO STAY & EAT

$$–$$$
★
✕ **Quay Cottage.** Fishing nets, glass floats, lobster pots, and greenery hang from the high-pitched, exposed-beam roof of this tiny waterside cottage at the entrance to Westport House. It's an informal wine bar and a shellfish restaurant. Rush-seat chairs, scrubbed pine tables, and an open fire in the evenings add to the comfortable, none-too-formal atmosphere. Try the chowder special (a thick vegetable and mussel soup), garlic-butter crab claws, or a half-pound steak fillet, and be sure to sample the homemade brown bread and ice cream. ⊠ *The Quay* ☎ *098/26412* ▤ *AE, MC, V* ☉ *Closed Jan. and Sun.–Mon. Nov.–Easter.*

$$$$
✕▯ **Newport House.** This handsome, riverside Georgian house dominates the village of Newport, 12 km (7 mi) north of Westport on N59. Kieran and Thelma Thompson's grand and elegant private home has spacious public rooms furnished with gilt-frame family portraits, Regency mirrors and chairs, handwoven Donegal carpeting, and crys-

tal chandeliers. A sweeping staircase leads to the bedrooms, which are decorated with pretty chintz drapes and a mix of Victorian antiques and old furniture. Most bedrooms have sitting areas and good views of the gardens. Home-smoked salmon and fresh local seafood are specialties on the traditional four-course set dinner menu; the ice cream is also homemade. ⊠*Newport, Co. Mayo* ☎*098/41222* 🖷*098/41613* ⊕*www.newporthouse.ie* 🛏*19 rooms* &*In-room: no a/c, no TV, dial-up. In-hotel: restaurant, bar, no elevator* ⊟*AE, MC, V* ⊘*Closed mid-Oct.–mid-Mar.* ⊺⊙⏐*BP.*

$$ 🏨**Westport Woods.** Midway between the town and the busy quay area, this imaginatively designed modern hotel (Swiss chalet-style wooden structure with plenty of large windows) occupies a quiet, wooded location. Some rooms overlook the lake, and all are spacious and color-coordinated with plain carpets and walls. It's a popular holiday destination for families aiming to spend time on Clew Bay's sandy beaches, or visit the Westport House amusement park next door. There are kids' clubs for various age groups between 3 and 15, daily from 10:30 to noon and 6:30 to 10 PM. The beach and woodland rides on the hotel's own trekking ponies come highly recommended, as do the spa treatments. ⊠*Quay Rd., Co. Mayo* ☎*098/25811* ⊕*www.westportwoodshotel. com* 🛏*111 rooms* &*In-room: no a/c, Wi-Fi. In-hotel: restaurant, bar, gym, spa, pool, tennis court, horseback riding, public Wi-Fi, some pets allowed* ⊺⊙⏐*BP.*

NIGHTLIFE

A good spot to try for traditional music and good pub grub is the **Towers Pub and Restaurant** (⊠*The Quay* ☎*098/26534*). In summer there are outdoor tables set up here beside the bay. In Westport's town center try **Matt Molloy's** (⊠*Bridge St.* ☎*098/26655*); Matt Malloy is not only the owner but also a member of the musical group the Chieftains. Traditional music is, naturally, the main attraction.

SPORTS & THE OUTDOORS

BICYCLING Enjoy the spectacular scenery of Clew Bay at a leisurely pace on a rented bike from **J. P. Breheny & Sons** (⊠*Castlebar St.* ☎*098/25020*).

GOLF The Fred Hawtree–designed **Westport Golf Club** (⊠*Carrowholly* ☎*098/28262*), beneath Croagh Patrick, overlooks Clew Bay. The 18-hole course has twice been the venue for the Irish Amateur Championship.

SHOPPING

Carraig Donn (⊠*Bridge St.* ☎*098/26287*) carries its own line of knitwear and a good selection of crystal, jewelry, and ceramics. **McCormack's** (⊠*Bridge St.* ☎*098/25619*) has a traditional butcher shop downstairs, but upstairs it's an attractive gallery and café with work by local artists for sale. **O'Reilly/Turpin** (⊠*Bridge St.* ☎*098/28151*) sells the best of contemporary Irish design in knitwear, ceramics, and other decorative items. **Satch Kiely** (⊠*Westport Quay* ☎*098/25775*) carries fine antique furniture and decorative pieces. **Treasure Trove** (⊠*Bridge St.* ☎*098/25118*) has a good stock of antiques and curios, including linen and local memorabilia. **Westport Crystal** (⌂ *The Quay* ☎ *098/27780*) is a factory outlet that sells exclusive stemware and giftware.

CASTLEBAR

③⑦ *18 km (11 mi) east of Westport on N5.*

The administrative capital of Mayo, Castlebar is a tidy little town with an attractive, tree-bordered green. Hatred of landlords ran high in the area, due to the ruthless, battering-ram evictions ordered by the earl of Lucan during the mid-19th-century famine. The disappearance in the 1960s of his high-living successor, the seventh earl, after the violent death in London of his children's nanny, is said to have given the few tenants who remain a perfect pretext for withholding their rents.

In 1879 Michael Davitt founded the Land League, which fought for land reform, in the **Imperial Hotel** (⌂ *The Green* ☎ *094/902–1961*); it's worth a visit to take in the splendor of the decor in the Gothic-style dining room, which was used for many historic meetings in the 19th century.

At the **Linen Hall Arts Centre** (⌂ *Linenhall St.* ☎ *094/902–3733*), exhibitions and performances are often scheduled.

TURLOUGH

③⑧ *6½ km (4 mi) east of Castlebar on N5.*

Before the opening of the Museum of Country Life, Turlough was chiefly visited for its round tower (freely accessible), which marks the site of an early monastery, traditionally associated with St. Patrick, and the nearby ruins of a 17th-century church. Nowadays, it's one of many Irish villages whose empty streets bear witness to dramatic changes in the rural way of life. Once a thriving hub, with a village school, two pubs, and a busy shop, Turlough now has a population of about 300, one pub with a small shop attached, and no school. Rather than working on the land, most of the locals commute to jobs in nearby Castlebar.

☾ To understand the forces that have led to such dramatic changes in
Fodor'sChoice Turlough, pay a visit to the **Museum of Country Life,** which focuses on
★ rural Ireland between 1860 and 1960—a way of life that remained unchanged for many years, then suddenly came to an end within living memory. At this highly acclaimed museum, the only branch of the National Museum of Ireland outside Dublin, you're invited to imagine yourself back in a vanished world, before the internal combustion engine, rural electrification, indoor plumbing, television, and increased education transformed people's lives and expectations. For many, this is a journey into a strange place, where water had to be carried from a well, turf had to be brought home from the bog, fires had to be lighted daily for heat and cooking, and clothes had to be made painstakingly by hand in the long winter evenings. Among the displayed items are authentic furniture and utensils; hunting, fishing, and agri-

cultural implements; clothing; and objects relating to games, pastimes, religion, and education.

The museum experience starts in Turlough Park House, built in the High Victorian Gothic style in 1865 and set in pretty lakeside gardens. Just three rooms have been restored to illustrate the way the landowners lived. A sensational modern four-story, curved building houses the main exhibit. Cleverly placed windows allow panoramic views of the surrounding park and the distant round tower, allowing you to reflect on the reality beyond the museum's walls. Temporary exhibitions, such as one called "Romanticism and Reality," help illustrate the divide between the dreamy image of old rural life and its actual hardships. The shop sells museum-branded and handcrafted gift items as well as a good selection of books on related topics. A café with indoor and outdoor tables is in the stable yard, and you can take scenic lakeside walks in the park. Crafts demonstrations and workshops take place on Wednesday and Sunday afternoons. ⊠ *Turlough Park* ☎ *01/648–6453 in Dublin* ⊕ *www.museum.ie* ⊠ *Free* ⊙ *Tues.–Sat. 10–5, Sun. 2–5.*

EN ROUTE As you travel from Turlough northeast to Ballina, you have a choice of two routes. The longer and more scenic is via the tiny, wooded village of Pontoon, skirting the western shore of Lough Conn and passing through the rough bogland of the Glen of Nephin, beneath the dramatic heather-clad slopes of Nephin Mountain (2,653 feet). The shorter route follows N5 and N58 to Foxford, a pretty village with several crafts and antiques shops.

A good place for a break is the **Foxford Woolen Mills Visitor Center,** where you can explore the crafts shop and grab a bite at the restaurant. The "Foxford Experience" tells the story of the wool mill, famous for its tweeds and blankets, from the time of the famine in the mid-19th century—when it was founded by the Sisters of Charity to combat poverty—to the present day. ⊠ *Lower Main St., Foxford* ☎ *094/925–6756* ⊠ *€8* ⊙ *Nov.–Apr., Mon.–Sat. 10–6, Sun. 2–6; May–Oct., Mon.–Sat. 10–6, Sun. noon–6; tour every 20 min.*

BALLINA

39 *34 km (22 mi) northeast of Turlough.*

Ballina's chief attraction is fishing for salmon and trout in the River Moy and nearby Lough Conn. With a population of 7,500, this is the largest town in County Mayo. To some eyes, Ballina's town center may appear run-down, but its unspoiled, old-fashioned shops and pubs contain many treasures. Try the bar food (Mon.–Sat. 11 AM–6 PM) at **Gaughan's** (⊠ *O'Rahilly St.* ☎ *096/21151*), where the classic wooden interior dates from the mid-19th century.

WHERE TO STAY & EAT

$$$
Fodor'sChoice
★

╳▥ **Enniscoe House.** Magnificent and magical, this pink, square Georgian mansion is dramatically sited on the shores of Lough Conn under towering Mt. Nephin. However, there's nothing intimidating about its interior, even though its well-worn grandeur is steeped in history. Susan

Kellett is a descendant of the original family who arrived here in the 1660s, and will give you the story behind the many ancestral portraits staring at you from the calico-flocked library walls. Your jaw may drop at the sight of the magisterial main salon—a vast room done in stately house ivories and beiges, swathed in period wallpapers and draperies, set with 18th-century breakfronts, gilded French side tables, Chippendale mahogany chairs, gilt-frame paintings, and enough cozy corners to please even a Jane Austen. A maze of quirky corridors and staircases leads to the guest rooms, which are both charming and characterful, with candy-stripe wallpapers, floral drapes on tall sash windows, and massive beds (some four-posters are so high you need a step ladder to get in). The beauty continues outside, as the demesne's 150 acres are crisscrossed with walks and have more than 3 km (2 mi) of peaceful lakeshore. All paths lead to the five acres of Victorian gardens (historic farm buildings here now house a Mayo genealogy center, an antiques shop, and a tearoom). Meals ($$$$; reservations essential) include fruits and vegetables grown in the organic garden. The house lies 4½ km (3 mi) south of Crossmolina and 20 km (12½ mi) west of Ballina. ⊠*Castlehill, near Crossmolina, Co. Mayo* ☎*096/31112* 🖷*096/31773* ⊕*www.enniscoe.com* ➷*6 rooms* ♨*In-room: no a/c, no TV. In-hotel: restaurant, no elevator, some pets allowed* ⊟*MC, V* ☾*Closed Nov.–Mar.* �†⊙†*BP.*

SPORTS & THE OUTDOORS

GOLF **Ballina Golf Club** (⊠*Bonniconlon Rd.* ☎*096/21718*) is an 18-hole parkland course, built in 1924, 1½ km (1 mi) from the town center; you can rent golf clubs here. The 18-hole **Carne Golf Links** (⊠*Belmullet* ☎*097/82292*), at Belmullet Golf Club, 72 km (45 mi) west of Ballina, is one of Ireland's renowned links courses.

SHOPPING

McGrath's Food and Delicatessen (⊠*O'Rahilly St.* ☎*096/21198*) is an old-fashioned grocery, handy for picnic ingredients.

THE WEST ESSENTIALS

TRANSPORTATION

If you're traveling extensively by public transportation, be sure to load up on information (the best taxi-for-call companies, rail and bus schedules, etc.) upon arriving at the ticket counter or help desk of the bigger train and bus stations in the area, such as Galway City and Westport.

BY AIR

Aer Arann has five flights a day from London's Luton Airport and five a day from Dublin to Galway Airport (GWY). Aer Arann also flies to Cardiff, Edinburgh, Manchester, Leeds, Lorient, and Liverpool from Galway. Ryanair flies to Knock daily from London's Stansted Airport and from London's Luton Airport; flying time is 80 minutes. BmiBaby has several flights to Knock from Manchester daily.

Aer Arann flies hourly in July and August to the Oileáin Árainn (Aran Islands) from Connemara Airport in Inverin. Off-peak there are half a dozen flights a day, fewer in December and January. The flights call at all three Aran Islands. The journey takes about six minutes and costs about €45 round-trip. The airline will book a B&B for you when you book your flight. Ask about other special offers, including scenic routes, at the time of booking.

Carriers Aer Arann (☎ *091/593–034* ⊕ *www.aerarann.ie*). **Aer Lingus** (☎ *0818/365–022* ⊕ *www.aerlingus.com*). **BmiBaby** (☎ *1890/340122* ⊕ *www.bmibaby.com*). **Ryanair** (☎ *0818/303–030* ⊕ *www.ryanair.com*).

AIRPORTS

The West's most convenient international airport is Shannon, 25 km (16 mi) east of Ennis *(see Chapter 6, The Southwest)*. Galway Airport, near Galway City, is used mainly for internal flights, with steadily increasing U.K. traffic. Knock International Airport, at Charlestown—near Knock, in County Mayo—has direct daily service to London's Stansted, Luton, and Gatwick, and to Manchester and Birmingham. A small airport for internal traffic only is at Knockrowen, Castlebar, in County Mayo. Flying time from Dublin is 25 to 30 minutes to all airports. No scheduled flights run from the United States to Galway or Knock; use Shannon Airport. Connemara Airport at Inverin, which is 29 km (18 mi) west of Galway on R336, services the Aran Islands.

7

Airport Information Connemara Airport (☎ *091/593–034*). **Galway Airport** (☎ *091/752–874* ⊕ *www.galwayairport.com*). **Knock International Airport** (☎ *094/936-7222* ⊕ *www.knockairport.com*). **Shannon Airport** (☎ *061/471–444* ⊕ *www.shannonairport.com*).

TRANSFERS From Shannon Airport you can pick up a rental car to drive into the West, or you can take a bus to Limerick, from which there are bus connections into the West. Galway Airport is 6½ km (4 mi) from Galway City. No regular bus service is available from the airport to Galway, but most flight arrivals are taken to Galway Rail Station in the city center by an airline courtesy coach. Inquire when you book. A taxi from the airport to the city center costs about €15. If you're flying to Knock International Airport, you can pick up your rental car at the airport. Otherwise, inquire at the time of booking about transport to your final destination. There's a bus link to Charlestown where you can connect with Bus Éireann's national network. Connemara Airport is 27 km from Galway City, and is accessible by shuttle bus.

BY BOAT & FERRY

The Tarbert–Killimer Ferry leaves every hour on the half hour and takes 20 minutes to cross the Shannon Estuary from North County Kerry to West County Clare; this saves you a 137 km (85 mi) drive through Limerick City. The ferry runs every day of the year except Christmas and costs €15 one way, €25 round-trip. (Ferries return from Killimer every hour on the hour.)

There are several options for traveling to the Oileáin Árainn (Aran Islands). Island Ferries runs a boat to the islands from Ros an Mhil

(Rossaveal), 32 km (20 mi) west of Galway City, which makes the crossing in 20 minutes and costs about €28 round-trip (or, weather permitting, you can opt for a boat that takes an hour, costing about €20), including the shuttle bus from Galway; they also offer a ferry route between Doolin and the Aran Islands. Note they offer a handy ticket office in the TIO (Travel Information Office) in Galway City. If you're heading for Inis Oírr (Inisheer), the smallest island, the shortest crossing is from Doolin in County Clare on Aran Doolin Ferries. Aran Doolin Ferries offers service from Doolin Pier, with up to 12 sailings daily, from June through the end of September. The crossing takes about 20 minutes and costs €20 round-trip. Aran Direct goes from Doolin and Rossaveal and does interisland hops. Bicycles are transported free off-season, but there may be a charge in July and August: inquire when booking. There's lively competition between the ferry companies, so shop around for the best deal. Discounts are available for families, students, and groups of four or more. If you want to stay a night or two on the islands, ask about accommodations when booking your ferry, as there are some very good deals.

For travel between the Aran Islands, frequent interisland ferries (run by Island Ferries and Aran Direct) are available in summer, but tickets are nontransferable, so ask the captain of your ferry about the interisland schedule if you plan to visit more than one island; otherwise, your trip can become expensive. You can purchase ferry tickets on the island or at the TIO in Galway.

Boat & Ferry Information **Island Ferries** (⊠ *Travel Information Office, Forster St., Eyre Sq., Galway City* ☎ *091/568–903 or 091/537–700* ⊕ *www.aranisland-ferries.com*). **Aran Doolin Ferries** (⊠ *Doolin Pier, Co. Clare* ☎ *065/707–4455* ⊕ *www.doolinferries.com*). **Aran Direct** (⊠ *Victoria Place, and 29 Forster St., Galway City* ☎ *091/506–786* ⊕ *www.arandirect.com*). **Tarbert–Killimer Ferry** (☎ *065/905–3124* ⊕ *www.shannonferries.com*).

BY BUS

Bus Éireann runs several expressway buses into the region from Dublin, Cork City, and Limerick City to Ennis, Galway City, Westport, and Ballina, the principal depots in the region. Expect bus rides to last about one hour longer than the time it would take you to travel the distance by car. In July and August, the provincial bus service is augmented by daily services to most resort towns. Outside these months, many coastal towns receive only one or two buses per week. Bus routes are often slow and circuitous, and service can be erratic. A copy of the Bus Éireann timetable (€2 from any station) is essential. Citylink operates frequent buses, with up to 17 departures daily, between Galway City and Dublin and Dublin Airport. The trip costs €19 one way. Citylink also makes five daily trips in each direction between Shannon Airport and Galway City, costing €16 one way.

Bus Depots **Ballina Station** (☎ *096/71800*). **Ennis Station** (☎ *065/682–4177*). **Galway City Station** (*Ceannt Station* ☎ *091/562–000*). **Westport Station** (☎ *098/25711*).

Bus Lines Bus Éireann (☎ *01/836–6111 in Dublin, 061/313–333 in Limerick, 021/508–188 in Cork* ⊕ *www.buseireann.ie*). **Citylink** (✉ *Unit 1, Forster Ct., Galway City* ☎ *091/564–163* ⊕ *www.citylink.ie*).

BY CAR

A car is the best means of traveling within the West. The 219-km (136-mi) Dublin–Galway trip takes about three hours. From Cork City take N20 through Mallow and N21 to Limerick City, picking up the N18 Ennis–Galway road in Limerick. The 209-km (130-mi) drive from Cork to Galway takes about three hours. From Killarney the shortest and most pleasant route to cover the 193 km (120 mi) to Galway (three hours) is to take N22 to Tralee, then N69 through Listowel to Tarbert and the ferry across the Shannon Estuary to Killimer in County Clare. From there, join N68 in Kilrush, and then pick up N18 in Ennis.

ROAD CONDITIONS
The West has good, wide main roads (National Primary Routes) and better-than-average local roads (National Secondary Routes), both known as "N" routes. If you stray off the beaten track on the smaller Regional ("R") or unnumbered routes, particularly in Connemara and County Mayo, you may encounter some hazardous mountain roads. Narrow, steep, and twisty, they are also frequented by untended sheep, cows, and ponies grazing "the long acre" (as the strip of grass beside the road is called) or simply straying in search of greener pastures. If you find a sheep in your path, just sound the horn, and it should scramble away. A good maxim for these roads is: "you never know what's around the next corner." Bear this in mind, and adjust your speed accordingly. Hikers and cyclists constitute an additional hazard on narrow roads.

Within the Connemara Irish-speaking area, signs are in Irish only. The main signs to recognize are Gaillimh (Galway), Ros an Mhil (Rossaveal), An Teach Doite (Maam Cross), and Sraith Salach (Recess).

TAXIS
Within Galway City taxis operate on the meter. Outside the city, agree on the fare in advance. Sample fares include Galway to Moycullen €20, to Salthill €12; Shannon Airport to Galway City €140; Knock Airport to Galway City €120.

Galway Taxis (☎ *091/561–111* ⊕ *www.galwaytaxi.com*). **Big O Taxis** (☎ *091/585–858* ⊕ *www.bigotaxis.com*).

BY TRAIN

The region's main rail stations are in Galway City, Westport, and Ballina. For County Clare, travel from Cork City, Killarney, or Dublin's Heuston Station to Limerick City and continue the journey by bus. Trains for Galway, Westport, and Ballina leave from Dublin's Heuston Station. The journey time to Galway is 3 hours; to Ballina, 3¾ hours; and to Westport, 3½ hours.

Rail service within the region is limited. The major destinations of Galway City and Westport/Ballina are on different branch lines. Connections can only be made between Galway and the other two cities by traveling inland for about an hour to Athlone.

7

Train Information **Irish Rail–Iarnod Éireann** (⊕ *www.irishrail.ie/home*). **Ballina Station** (☎ *096/71818*). **Galway Station** (☎ *091/564–222*). **Heuston Station** (☎ *01/836–6222*). **Limerick City Station** (☎ *061/315–555*). **Westport Station** (☎ *098/25253*).

TRANSPORTATION AROUND THE WEST

A car is helpful in the West, especially from September through June. Although the main cities of the area are easily reached from the rest of Ireland by rail or bus, transport within the region can be sparse. If a rental car is out of the question, one option is to make Galway your base and take day tours (available mid-June through September) west to Connemara and south to the Burren, and a day or overnight trip to the Aran Islands. Of course, it *is* possible to explore the region by local and intercity bus services, but have no illusions that buses run every hour.

CONTACTS & RESOURCES

CAR RENTAL

If you haven't already booked a rental car at Shannon Airport, try the following rental agencies.

Agencies **Avis** (⊠ *Galway Airport* ☎ *091/786–440*). **Avis** (⊠ *Knock International Airport, Charlestown* ☎ *094/936–7707*). **Budget** (⊠ *Eyre Sq., Galway City* ☎ *091/566–376*). **Budget** (⊠ *Knock International Airport, Charlestown* ☎ *090/662–4668*). **Casey's Auto Rentals** (⊠ *Breaffy Rd., Castlebar* ☎ *094/904–8620*). **Casey's Auto Rentals** (⊠ *Knock international Airport, Charlestown* ☎ *094/902–1411*). **Euro Mobil** (⊠ *Tuam Rd., Galway City* ☎ *091/753–037*). **Hertz Rent A Car** (⊠ *Galway Airport* ☎ *091/752–502*). **Hertz Rent A Car** (⊠ *Knock International Airport, Charlestown* ☎ *094/936–7333*).**National Car Rental** (⊠ *Knock International Airport, Charlestown* ☎ *094/936–7252*).

EMERGENCIES

For a doctor or dentist in County Clare, contact the Mid-Western Health Board (in County Limerick); in Counties Galway and Mayo, contact the Western Health Board.

Doctors & Dentists **Health Service Executive (Mid-Western)** (⊠ *Catherine St., Limerick* ☎ *061/316–655*). **Health Service Executive (Western)** (⊠ *Merlin Park, Galway City* ☎ *091/751–131*).

Emergency Services **Ambulance, fire, police** (☎ *999*).

Pharmacies **Matt O'Flaherty** (⊠ *39 Eyre Sq., Galway City* ☎ *091/563–526*). **O'Donnell's** (⊠ *Bridge St., Westport* ☎ *098/25163*).

INTERNET, MAIL & SHIPPING

Most hotels in the West now offer some form of Internet access. The Internet cafés below also offer printing, photocopying, faxing, and money transfers. Post offices generally open weekdays 9–5:30 and Saturday 9–1. Smaller branches may close between 1 PM and 2 PM.

Internet Cafés **Kinlay House** (⊠ *Merchants Rd., Eyre Sq., Galway City* ☎ *091/565–244*). **Net@access** (⊠ *Olde Malt Arcade, Galway City* ☎ *091/535–470*).

Post Offices Ennis GPO (⊠ *Bank Place, Ennis* ☎ *065/682–1054*). **Galway City GPO** (⊠ *3 Eglinton St., Galway City* ☎ *091/563–768*). **Westport GPO** (⊠ *The Mall, Westport* ☎ *098/25219*).

TOUR OPTIONS

Galway City's TIO (Travel Information Office) has details of walking tours of Galway, which are organized by request. All TIOs in the West provide lists of suggested cycle tours.

The only full- and half-day guided bus tours in the region start from Galway. Bus Éireann coordinates two full-day tours, one covering Connemara and the other the Burren (each €20). Tours run from early June to mid-October only, with the widest choice available between mid-July and mid-August. Book in advance at the Galway City TIO, Ceannt Railway Station on Eyre Square, or the Salthill TIO, which also serve as departure points.

Lally Tours runs a day tour through Connemara and County Mayo and another to the Burren. It also operates a vintage double-decker bus, departing from Eyre Square, which runs hourly tours of Galway City from 10:30 AM until 4:30 PM from mid-March to October; tickets cost €12.

O'Neachtain Day Tours operates full-day tours of Connemara and the Burren. Tickets, €25 each, can be purchased from the Galway City TIO; tours depart across the street.

Healy Tours offers historical sightseeing tours with professional guides, including Kylemore Abbey and Connemara or the Cliffs of Moher and the Burren. Tickets, €25 each, can be purchased from the Galway and Salthill Tourist Information Offices or on the tour bus.

The Connemara Walking Centre in Clifden, run by leading archeologist Michael Gibbons, organizes everything from daylong mountain treks to weeklong holidays.

Also based in Clifden, Connemara Safari Walking Holidays offers five- and seven-day residential walking holidays starting in either Clifden or Westport. They specialize in "island-hopping" and will take you to remote islands for some unforgettable walks.

Killary Tours provides self-guided walking tours around the west coast of Ireland, with carefully chosen accommodations, comprehensive route notes, transfers to the start and finish of your walks, and plenty of friendly advice.

Croagh Patrick Walking Holidays runs weeklong walking holidays between April and September, based in B&B accommodations in the countryside near Westport on Clew Bay. Prices include pickup from Shannon Airport, all transfers to and from walks, and the services of an experienced guide. Contact Gerry Greensmyth in Belclare, Westport, County Mayo.

Tours Bus Éireann (☎ *091/562–000*). **Ceannt Railway Station** (☎ *091/562–000*). **Connemara Safari Walking Holidays** (⊠ *Sky Rd., Clifden, Co. Galway* ☎ *095/21071* ⊕ *www.walkingconnemara.com*). **Connemara Walking Centre** (⊠ *Island House,*

Market St., Clifden, Co. Galway ☎ *095/21492* ⊕ *www.walkingireland.com).***Croagh Patrick Walking Holidays** (✉ *Belclare, Westport, Co. Mayo* ☎ *098/26090* ⊕ *www. walkingguideireland.com).* **Healy Tours** (☎ *091/770–066* ⊕ *www.healytours.ie).* **Killary Tours** (☎ *095/42276* ⊕ *www.killary.com).* **Lally Tours** (☎ *091/562–905* ⊕ *www.lallytours.com).* **O'Neachtain Day Tours** (☎ *091/553–188* ⊕ *www. oneachtaintours.com).* **Salthill TIO** (☎ *091/520–500).*

VISITOR INFORMATION

Bord Fáilte provides free information service, tourist literature, and an accommodations booking service at its TIOs (Travel Information Offices). The following offices are open all year, generally weekdays 9–6, daily during the high season: Aran Islands (Inis Mór), Ennis, Galway City, Oughterard, and Westport.

Other TIOs, which operate seasonally, generally weekdays 9–6 and Saturday 9–1, are open as follows: Achill (June–August), Ballina (April–October), Castlebar (May–mid-September), Clifden (March–October), Cliffs of Moher (April–October), Kilkee (May–August), Kilrush (June–August), Salthill (May–September), Thoor Ballylee (April–mid-October).

Tourist Information The areas covered in this chapter come under two different regional headquarters of tourism: Shannon ⊕ *www.shannonregiontourism.ie* and West of Ireland ⊕ *www.irelandwest.ie.* The following come under Shannon: Cliffs of Moher, Ennis, and Kilrush. All the rest are Ireland West. **Oileáin Árainn (Aran Islands)–Inis Mór (Inishmore)** (✉ *Co. Galway* ☎ *099/61263).* **Ballina** (✉ *Cathedral Rd., Co. Mayo* ☎ *096/70848).* **Clifden** (✉ *Galway Rd., Co. Galway* ☎ *095/21163).* **Cliffs of Moher** (✉ *Co. Clare* ☎ *065/708–1171).* **Ennis** (✉ *Arthur's Row, Town Center, Co. Clare* ☎ *065/682–8308* ⊕ *www.ennis.ie).* **Galway City** (✉ *Forster St., Eyre Sq., Co. Galway* ☎ *091/537–700* ⊕ *www.irelandwest.ie).* **Oughterard** (✉ *Main St., Co. Galway* ☎ *091/552–808).* **Salthill** (✉ *The Promenade, Co. Galway* ☎ *091/520–500).* **Thoor Ballylee** (✉ *Near Gort, Co. Clare* ☎ *091/631–436).* **Westport** (✉ *The Mall, Co. Mayo* ☎ *098/25711).*

The Northwest

Ramelton harbor, County Donegal

8

WORD OF MOUTH

"County Sligo is chock-full of sightseeing possibilities and is one of Ireland's most underrated, underexplored regions. Just outside Sligo town is Drumcliff, the final resting place of W. B. Yeats. His gravesite is in a churchyard in the shadow of the great Ben Bulben, a flat-topped peak that is one of the most memorable sights in all Ireland. Drumcliff also features a fine 10th-century High Cross and a Round Tower."

—DavidD

WELCOME TO THE NORTHWEST

TOP REASONS TO GO

★ **Gaeltacht Country:** Venture to the seaside village of Ard an Ratha to listen to the seductive rhythms of locals conversing in full Irish (Gaelic) flight. Don't worry: everyone has English at the ready for lost visitors.

★ **The Yeats Trail:** From Sligo Town's museums head out to the majestic Ben Bulben peak to follow in the footsteps of the famous brother duo, W. B. Yeats, the great poet, and Jack B. Yeats, one of Ireland's finest 20th-century painters.

★ **Garbo's Shangri-la:** The legendary screen actress was just one of the many notables who enjoyed a stay at Glenveagh Castle.

★ **Hiking the Slieve League cliffs:** To truly humble yourself before ocean, cliff, and sky, hike these fabled headlands, the highest sea cliffs in Europe. The views will set your heart racing and the Atlantic sea winds are sure to blow away the cobwebs.

Greencastle Fishing Port, Inishowen Head, County Donegal

1 **Yeats Country:** What the poet William Butler Yeats would say about his native **Sligo Town**—a once picturesque spot now overrun with modern shopping malls—can only be imagined but it makes a great jumping-off point for exploring Yeats Country: the lake isle at **Innisfree,** the cairn-crowned **Knocknarea** (a peak often painted by brother Jack), and **Drumcliff,** where W. B. lies buried under the shadow of Ben Bulben.

Hiking in Sligo

Gleann Cholm Cille, County Donegal

2 **Around Donegal Bay: Donegal Town,** with its fine medieval castle and abbey, is the gateway to County Donegal, regarded by many as the runner-up to Kerry as Ireland's most scenic region. This is the ever-shrinking heart of the Donegal Gaeltacht (Irish-speaking region), where the moody hamlet of **Gleann Cholm Cille** and the majestic Slieve League mountains beckon, as does the Belleek china of **Ballyshannon.**

Donegal Castle

3 **Northern Donegal:** The is the far Northwest, Ireland's back-of-the-beyond. The gateway town is **Letterkenny,** presided over by the 212-foot-high spire of St. Eunan's Cathedral. Westward lies **Glenveagh National Park,** where you'll find the storybook lair and gardens of Glenveagh Castle.

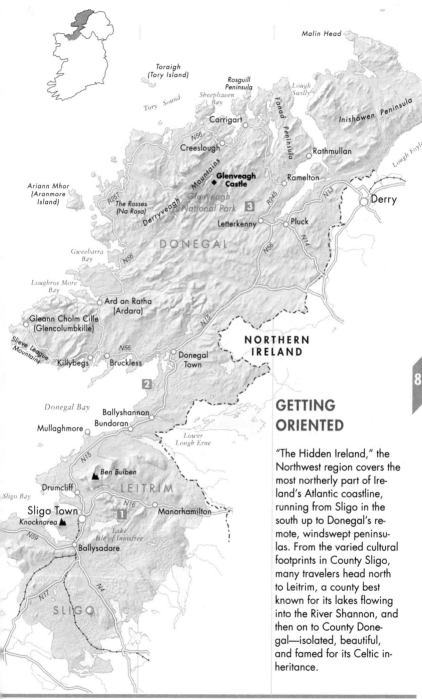

Malin Head

Toraigh
(Tory Island)

Rosguill
Peninsula

Sheephaven
Bay

Tory Sound

Lough
Swilly

Fanad Peninsula

Inishowen Peninsula

Carrigart

N56

Creeslough

Rathmullan

Lough Foyle

Ariann Mhor
(Aranmore
Island)

Mountains

**Glenveagh
Castle**

Ramelton

R257

The Rosses
(Na Rosa)

Glenveagh
National Park

Derryveagh

3

R245

Derry

Letterkenny

Pluck

N13

N14

DONEGAL

Gweebarra
Bay

N56

N56

Loughros More
Bay

Ard an Ratha
(Ardara)

N15

Gleann Cholm Cille
(Glencolumbkille)

**NORTHERN
IRELAND**

Slieve League
Mountains

N56

Killybegs

Bruckless

Donegal
Town

8

2

Donegal Bay

Ballyshannon

Mullaghmore

Bundoran

Lower
Lough Erne

N15

Ben Bulben

LEITRIM

Drumcliff

Sligo Bay

N16

Sligo Town

Knocknarea

Manorhamilton

1

Lake
Isle of Innisfree

N59

Ballysadare

N17

N4

SLIGO

GETTING
ORIENTED

"The Hidden Ireland," the
Northwest region covers the
most northerly part of Ireland's Atlantic coastline,
running from Sligo in the
south up to Donegal's re-
mote, windswept peninsu-
las. From the varied cultural
footprints in County Sligo,
many travelers head north
to Leitrim, a county best
known for its lakes flowing
into the River Shannon, and
then on to County Done-
gal—isolated, beautiful,
and famed for its Celtic inheritance.

THE NORTHWEST PLANNER

Finding a Place to Stay

True, it's the farthest-flung corner of Ireland, but thanks to the area's popularity, good bed-and-breakfasts and small hotels are abundant.

In the two major towns—Sligo Town and Donegal Town—and the small coastal resorts in between, many traditional provincial hotels have been modernized (albeit not always elegantly). Yet most manage to retain some of the charm that comes with older buildings and personalized service.

Away from these areas, your best overnight choice is usually a modest guesthouse that includes bed, breakfast, and an evening meal, though you can also find first-class country-house hotels with a gracious professionalism comparable to properties elsewhere in Ireland.

Consider staying in an Irish-speaking home to get to know members of the area's Gael-tacht population; the local Tourist Information Office (TIO) can be helpful in making a booking with an Irish-speaking family.

Assume that all hotel rooms reviewed in this chapter have air-conditioning, in-room phones and TVs, and private bathrooms unless otherwise noted.

Making the Most of Your Time

In all honesty, there is only one way to fully explore the rural Northwest of Ireland and that's by car. Once here, you can always rent a car at Knock airport or Sligo Town. But if coming from Dublin, many opt to rent from one of the bigger companies at the larger airports.

If arriving from Northern Ireland, there are rental agencies aplenty in Derry or Belfast, but be sure to tell your agency if you are planning to cross the border.

Cars are invariably compact—no SUVs—and stick shift is the norm (you will have to specially request an automatic). The roads between the larger towns are fairly well maintained and signposted, but go slightly off the beaten track and conditions can vary from bad to dirt track.

As long as you're not in a mad rush, this can add to the delight of your journey. This is rural Ireland and if the scenery doesn't make this blissfully clear, then the suspension on your rented car certainly will!

Getting Around by Public Transportation

Getting around on bus is easy enough if you plan to only visit the larger towns. Ireland's principal bus company is Bus Éireann.

The routes are regular and reliable and you'll find route planners and schedules on www.buseireann.ie. There are also several privately run local bus companies operating in the Northwest, including McGeehans.

As for train travel, Sligo Town is the northernmost direct rail link to Dublin. From Dublin, three trains a day make the three-hour-and-20-minute journey (prices vary and can be higher on weekends).

If you want to get to Sligo Town by rail from other provincial towns, you're forced to make some inconvenient connections and take roundabout routes. Sadly, the rest of the region has no railway services.

Do You Read Irish?

County Donegal was part of the ancient kingdom of Ulster not conquered by the English until the 17th century.

When the English withdrew in the 1920s, they had still not eradicated rural Donegal's Celtic inheritance.

It thus shouldn't come as a surprise that is contains Ireland's largest Gaeltacht (Irish-speaking) area.

Driving in this part of the country, you may either be frustrated or amused when you come to a crossroads whose signposts show only the Irish place-names, often so unlike the English versions as to be completely incomprehensible.

To make things more confusing, some shop and hotel owners have opted to go with English, not Irish, variant for their establishments' names.

All is not lost, however, as maps—and this chapter—generally give both the Irish and English names. And locals are usually more than happy to help out with directions (in English)—often with a colorful yarn thrown in.

How's the Weather?

When it rains, it really pours. Forget about the winter months, when inclement weather and a heavy fog swing in from the Atlantic and settle in until spring, masking much of the beautiful scenery. But in all seasons remember to pack a warm and waterproof coat (especially if you're headed to the coast) and bring a good pair of walking shoes. It's not all doom and gloom: the weather can be glorious in the summer months—just don't bet your house on it.

Feiles & Festivals

In the northwest, each village tends to have its own *féile* (festival) during the summer months and it's often worth making the effort to attend. Music festivals are tops, from the traditional Irish Sligo Feis Ceoil in mid-April to the country-and-western Bundoran Music Festival in June, and the jazz and blues weekend feile in Gortahork, Donegal, in April. But being an Irish-speaking stronghold, the emphasis is on Irish traditional music. Every summer weekend you are guaranteed a bit of "craic" (fun) with lively sessions in most pubs. Sligo Town, Ard an Ratha (Ardara), and Letterkenny are all hot spots. There are village festivals dedicated to hill-walking, fishing, poetry, art, and food—few can resist the Mullaghmore Lobster Festival in August.

Dining & Lodging Price Categories (In Euros)

	¢	$	$$	$$$	$$$$
RESTAURANTS	under €8	€8–€15	€15–€22	€22–€29	over €29
HOTELS	under €80	€80–€130	€130–€180	€180–€230	over €230

Restaurant prices are for a main course at dinner. Hotel prices are for a standard double room in high season.

8

Updated by
John Daly

GLANCE AT A MAP OF Ireland that has scenic roads printed in green and chances are your eye will be drawn to the far-flung peninsulas of Northwest Ireland. At virtually every bend in the roads weaving through counties Donegal, Leitrim, and Sligo, there will be something to justify all those green markings. On an island with no shortage of majestic scenery, the Northwest claims its full share. Cool, clean waters from the roaring Atlantic have carved the terrain into long peninsulas—creating a raw, sensual landscape that makes it seem as if the earth is still under construction.

But what you see *this moment* may not be what you will see an hour hence. Clouds and rain linger over mountains, glens, cliffs, beaches, and bogs, to be chased minutes later by sunshine and rainbows. The air, light, and colors of the countryside change as though viewed under a kaleidoscope. Skies brighten, then darken, calling forth a spectrum of subtle reds and purples from fields of unkempt gorse and heather, and then just as quickly paint the grassy meadows greener than any green you've ever seen. The writer William Butler Yeats and his brother Jack Butler Yeats, a painter, immortalized this splendidly lush and rugged countryside in their work.

Northwest Ireland covers the most northerly part of Ireland's Atlantic coastline, running from Sligo in the south along Donegal's remote, windswept peninsulas to Malin Head in the far north. These maritime landscapes are said to have given their colors to the most famous local product, handwoven tweed, which reflects the browns of the peaty heathland and the purples of the heather. Donegal, a sparsely populated rural county of small farms and fishing boats, shares its inland border with Northern Ireland; the border is partly formed by the River Foyle. Inland from Sligo is Leitrim, a county best known for its numerous lakes and loughs, some of which join up with the River Shannon, on the easterly border of this region.

The area is overwhelmingly rural and underpopulated. That's not to say there isn't a bit of action here. Sligo Town, for instance, has gone through a major renaissance. On a typical weekday, the little winding streets are as busy as those of Galway, and when it comes to stylish restaurants and trendy people, it seems to be giving Dublin's Temple Bar a run for its money—an amazing feat for a town of only 19,000. Sligo Town pulses not only in the present but also with the charge of history, for it was the childhood home of W. B. and Jack B. Yeats, the place that, more than any other, gave rise to their particular geniuses—or, as Jack B. put it: "Sligo was my school and the sky above it."

There are more bright lights in Letterkenny, which has to its credit the longest main street of any town in Ireland. Glenveagh National Park exemplifies the surprising alliance between nature and culture in this part of Ireland. Here, perched on the edge of a glorious lake in the midst of 24,000 acres of thrilling wilderness, sits a fairy-tale castle, restored by the great American art connoisseur, Henry McIlhenny. Elsewhere, a few places are blighted by careless development—Bundoran, a beach resort full of so-called "Irish gift shops" and "amusement arcades," is one of the places to pass through rather than visit—but on the whole, Northwest Ireland remains big enough, untamed enough, and grand enough to make for an enticing visit.

EXPLORING THE NORTHWEST

This chapter outlines three autonomous routes through Northwest Ireland. These routes can easily be linked if you want to poke around the area over five or so days. The first journey begins in Sligo Town and covers its immediate environs—all the major sights, many of which have strong associations with the Yeatses, are within a roughly 24-km (15-mi) radius. The second trip skirts the entirety of Donegal Bay, from Mullaghmore in the south to Gleann Cholm Cille (Glencolumbkille) to the far north and west, before heading inland as far as Ard an Ratha (Ardara). The last route begins at the other end of Donegal, in Letterkenny, and travels to magical Glenveagh National Park. If you decide to explore this chapter from back to front (which makes sense if you're arriving from Northern Ireland), pick it up in Letterkenny.

TIMING

Although hotels are often fully booked in July and August—when the weather may be warm enough for hardy swimmers to take to the sea—the area is empty of tourists between November and February, and with good reason—wintry gales bring cold rain lashing in from the Atlantic, shrouding the wild, lonely scenery that is northwest Ireland's greatest asset. Because so many of the area's hotels are seasonal, choices in winter are limited. The best months to visit are April through June, September, and October.

8

YEATS COUNTRY: SLIGO TO DRUMCLIFF

Just as James Joyce made Dublin his own through his novels and stories, Sligo and environs are bound to the work of W.B. Yeats (1865–1939), Ireland's first of four Nobel laureates, and to the work of his brother Jack B. (1871–1957), one of Ireland's most important 20th-century painters, whose expressionistic landscapes and portraits are as emotionally fraught as his brother's poems are lyrical and plangent. The brothers intimately knew and eloquently celebrated in their art not only Sligo Town itself but the surrounding countryside, with its lakes, farms, woodland, and dramatic mountains that rise up not far from the center of town. On this route, you will often see glimpses of Ben Bulben Mountain, which looms over the western end of the Dartry range. The areas covered here are the most accessible parts of Northwest Ireland, easily reached from Galway.

Yeats Country & Donegal Bay

Na Gleannta

Kilrean

BLUE STACK MOUNTAINS

18 Ard an Ratha (Ardara)

Glengesh Pass

D O N E G A L

17 Gleann Cholm Cille (Glencolumbkille)

Malin More

SLIEVE LEAGUE MOUNTAINS

An Charraig (Carrick)

TO LOUGH ESKE

Donegal Town 15

Killybegs 16

Bruckless

Teileann

Cill Chaitaigh

Dunkineely

Mac Swyne's Bay

Inver Bay

Laghy

TO LOUGH DERG

Ballintra

St. John's Point

Rossnowlagh

Donegal Bay

Ballintra

Ballyshannon 14

TO LOUGH ERNE

Belleek

NORTHERN IRELAND

Bundoran 13

Lough Melvin

Mullaghmore 12

Cliffony

Kinlough

Garrison

Grange

Creevykeel

Glenade

Carney

BEN BULBEN

Glenade

Drumcliff 11

Drumcliff Bay

Glencar Lough

Rathcormack

N16

Sligo Bay

Rosses Point 10

Cregg

Sligo Town
1 · 7
see detail map

Manorhamilton

Strandhill

R292

R286

Parke's Castle

Knocknarea

Lough Gill 8 **9**

Creevelea Abbey

L E I T R I M

TO BALLINA

Carrowmore

Lake Isle of Innisfree

Killarga

Beltra

Dromahair

Templeboy *N59*

Colooney

Ballygawley

Drumkeeran

Ropefield

S L I G O

Drumfin

Riverstown

0 ___ 6 miles
0 ___ 9 km

TO GALWAY

Ballymote
TO CARRICK-ON-SHANNON

Lough Arrow

SLIGO TOWN

★ *60 km (37 mi) northeast of Ballina, 138 km (86 mi) northeast of Galway, 217 km (135 mi) northwest of Dublin.*

Sligo, the only sizable town in the whole of Northwest Ireland, is the best place to begin a tour of Yeats Country. It retains all the charm of smaller, sleepier villages, even though it's in the throes of an economic boom. Europe's largest videotape factory is just outside of town and Sligo is the center of Ireland's plastics industry. Since the early 2000s, the streets have

> ### LOUD AND CLEAR
>
> Legend has it that when the soldiers of Sir Frederick Hamilton sacked Sligo in 1642, they flung the silver bell of the abbey into the depths of Lough Gill; today it's said that only the "pure" can hear it ring.

been ringing with the bite of buzz saws, as apartments, shopping malls, and cinema complexes have been erected behind tasteful, traditional facades. By day Sligo is as lively and crowded as its considerably larger neighbor to the southwest, Galway, with locals, students from the town's college, and tourists bustling past its historic buildings and along its narrow sidewalks and winding streets, and crowding its one-of-a-kind shops, restaurants, and traditional pubs. More than any other town in Northwest Ireland, the Sligo of today has an energy that would surprise anyone who hasn't been there in the past few years.

Squeezed onto a patch of land between Sligo Bay and Lough Gill, the town is clustered on the south shore between two bridges that span the River Garavogue, just east of where the river opens into the bay. Thanks to the pedestrian zone along the south shore of the river (between the two bridges), you can enjoy vistas of the river while right in the center of town. All along High Street and Church and Charles streets, Sligo has churches of almost every denomination. Presbyterians, Methodists, and even Plymouth Brethren are represented, as are Anglicans (Church of Ireland) and, of course, Roman Catholics. According to the Irish writer Sean O'Faolain, "The best Protestant stock in all Ireland is in Sligo." The Yeats family was part of that stock.

Sligo was often a battleground in its earlier days. It was attacked by Viking invaders in 807; later, it was invaded by a succession of rival Irish and Anglo-Norman conquerors. In 1642 the British soldiers of Sir Frederick Hamilton fell upon Sligo, killing every visible inhabitant, burning the town, and destroying the interior of the beautiful medieval abbey. Between 1845 and 1849, more than a million inhabitants of Sligo county died in the potato famine or fled to escape it—an event poignantly captured in a letter written in 1850 by a local father, Owen Larkin, to his son in America. Its words are inscribed on a brass plaque down by the river: "I am now I may say alone in the world all my brothers and sisters are dead and children but yourself. We are all ejected out of Lord Ardilaun's ground, the times was so bad and all Ireland in such a state of poverty that no person could pay rent. My only hope now rests with you, as I am without one shilling and I must

EATING WELL IN NORTHWEST IRELAND

Although Northwest Ireland has not been considered a noted gastronomic center, many visitors make their journeys memorable by stopping off en route at a local pub to enjoy steaming-hot soups, stews, and hot meat platters in front of a raging turf fires. In the last few years, Sligo Town has become host to a number of food-related shops worth visiting, and this being farming country, the region has a number of top-notch farmers' markets, usually held during the March to October growing season (great for picnic fixings).

Newcomers are serving up well-above-average food in memorable settings, though the majority of restaurants still serve plain and simple fare, such as traditional Irish lamb stew or bacon and cabbage served with generous helpings of potatoes (often prepared in at least two ways on the same plate), washed down with creamy, lip-smacking pints of Guinness. You're likely to find the finest food at the higher-quality country houses—Donegal mountain spring lamb, Glen Bay lobster and crab, Donegal Bay oysters and mussels, Lough Swilly wild salmon, and Guinness cakes—where chefs elegantly specialize in a hybrid Irish-French haute cuisine.

Generally, restaurants in towns stay open year-round, as they do not have to rely solely on the tourist trade. But eateries in remote villages will often close for an extended period during the winter months, usually from November to mid-March. It does tend to vary, but check with the tourist office to avoid disappointment.

either beg or go to the poorhouse." Stand there a moment by the river, then turn again to the bustling heart of Sligo, and marvel at humanity's capacity to rise above adversity.

❶ Picturesquely set atop the stone Hyde Bridge, the **Yeats Memorial Building** makes for a suitably imposing address for the Yeats Society, Sligo Art Gallery, and the Tourist Information Centre. The Sligo Arts Gallery lends itself well to the host of rotating exhibitions of contemporary art. In addition, the Yeats International Summer School is conducted here every August. Across the street is Rohan Gillespie's photo-worthy sculpture of the poet, draped in a flowing coat overlaid with excerpts from his work. It was unveiled in 1989 by Michael Yeats, W. B.'s son, in commemoration of the 50th anniversary of his father's death. ⊠*Hyde Bridge* ☎*071/914–5847 gallery, 074/914–2693 summer school* ⊕*www.sligoartgallery.com* 🎫*Free* ⊙*Mon.–Sat. 10–5:30.*

❷ Housed in a beautifully renovated school, built in 1862, the **Model Arts Centre and Niland Gallery,** is one of Ireland's premier arts venues with an extensive calendar devoted to the visual and performing arts. The main attraction is one of Ireland's largest collections of works by 20th-century artists from Ireland and abroad. The gallery displays works by Jack B. Yeats, who said, "I never did a painting without putting a thought of Sligo in it." (Beckett wrote that Yeats painted "desperately immediate images.") Paintings by John Yeats (father of Jack B. and

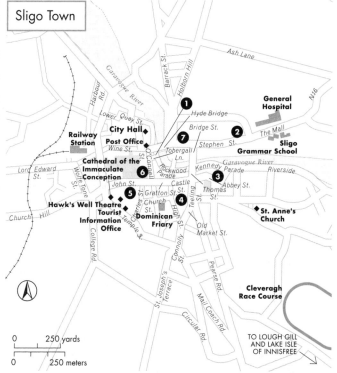

Sligo Town

0 ——— 250 yards

0 ——— 250 meters

TO LOUGH GILL AND LAKE ISLE OF INNISFREE

8

W. B.), who had a considerable reputation as a portraitist, also hang here, as do portraits by Sean Keating and Paul Henry. The center has performance and workshop spaces and hosts literature, music, and film programs. There's also the Atrium café. ⊠ *The Mall* ☎ *071/914–1405* ⊕ *www.modelart.ie* ☒ *Free* ⊙ *Tues.–Sat. 10–5:30, Sun. 11–4, and during performances.*

❸ A massive stone complex that is still redolent of "auld grandeur" and famed for its medieval tomb sculptures, **Sligo Abbey** is the town's only existing relic of the Middle Ages. Maurice FitzGerald erected the structure for the Dominicans in 1253. After a fire in 1414, it was extensively rebuilt, only to be destroyed again by Cromwell's Puritans under the command of Sir Frederick Hamilton, in 1642. Today the abbey consists of a ruined nave, aisle, transept, and tower. Some fine stonework remains, especially in the 15th-century cloisters. The visitor center is the base for guided tours, which are included with admission. The site is accessible to the disabled, though some parts of the grounds are quite rocky. ⊠ *Abbey St.* ☎ *071/914–6406* ⊕ *www.heritageireland.ie* ☒ *€2.10* ⊙ *Apr.–Oct., daily 10–6; Nov.–Jan., Fri.–Sun. 9:30–4:30.*

❹ The **Courthouse,** built in 1878 in the Victorian Gothic style, has a flamboyant, turreted sandstone exterior. After it was built, it became a symbol of English power. The Courthouse takes its inspiration from the much larger Law Courts in London. Unfortunately, the structure is not open to tourists. Just north of the Courthouse on the east side of Teeling Street, look for the window designating the law firm Argue and Phibbs, one of Sligo's most popular photo-ops. ⊠*Teeling St.* ☎*No phone* ۞*Closed to public.*

⑤ Designed in 1730 by Richard Castle, who designed Powerscourt and Russborough houses in County Wicklow, little **St. John's Cathedral** *(Church of Ireland)* has a handsome square tower and fortifications. In the north transept is a memorial to Susan Mary Yeats, mother of W. B. and Jack B. Next door is the larger and newer Roman Catholic Cathedral of the Immaculate Conception (with an entrance on Temple Street), consecrated in 1874. ⊠*John St.* ☎*No phone.*

⑥ Sligo's most famous pub, **Hargadon's**, is a dark, old-style public house with cozy, private, wood-panel snugs (cubicles); stone-and-wood floors; rust-red interior walls; and a handsome golden-oak and green-painted facade. The pub has been operated by the Hargadon family since 1908; before that it was owned by a local member of the British parliament, who was more interested in debating with his peers in London than pulling pints in Sligo. Hargadon's is justly famous for its bowls of stew and pints of creamy Guinness. ⊠*4 O'Connell St.* ☎*071/917–0933.*

⑦ The showpiece of the **Sligo County Museum** is its Yeats Hall, which houses a comprehensive collection of W. B. Yeats's writings from 1889 to 1936, various editions of his plays and prose, the Nobel Prize medal awarded to him in 1923, and the Irish tricolor (flag) that draped his coffin when he was buried at nearby Drumcliff. The penmanship is dreadful, but Yeats's letters to James Stephens and Oliver St. John Gogarty offer insight into Yeats's obsessive love for Sligo. The museum also has small sections on local society, history, and archaeology. Some artwork by Jack B. Yeats is hung in the adjoining church. ⊠*Stephen St.* ☎*071/914–1623* 🖭*Free* ۞*June–Sept., Tues.–Sat. 10–noon and 2–4:50; Oct.–May, Tues.–Sat. 2–4:50.*

WHERE TO STAY & EAT

$–$$ ✕**Bistro Bianconi.** With blond-wood furniture and white-tile floors, Bianconi lives up to its name in the dining room's design, but it serves Italian food that's full of color. Peruse the long list of fancy pizzas that are baked in a wood-burning oven. Cannelloni and ravioli are also popular. ⊠*44 O'Connell St.* ☎*071/914–1744* ⊕*www.bistrobianconi. ie* ▤*MC, V* ۞*Closed Sun.*

$$$$ ✕🏨**Cromleach Lodge.** Comfort is paramount at this small hotel with fantastic views out over Lough Arrow. Plate-glass windows pepper the modern building, the low-slung dimensions of which are topped off with a faux-mansard roof. Inside, things are considerably more comfy

and stylish: reception areas are dotted with antiques and fine wallpapers, while spacious guest bedrooms are decorated in pastel shades. The restaurant ($$–$$$; reservations required) is notable; Chef Moira Tighe is a former recipient of the Irish Chef of the Year award (and her staff offers a series of cooking lesson "holidays" in February). Two fetching entrées are fillet of turbot on a julienne of fennel with Pernod cream, and warm salad of marinated lamb fillet with organic lentils. Also delicious is the restaurant's panoramic vista. Staff members lead walks ranging from 20 minutes to two hours long. *⊠27 km (17 mi) east of Sligo, 8 km (5 mi) east of Ballymote; off N4 at Castlebaldwin, Lough Arrow, Co. Sligo ☎071/916–5155 ⊟071/916–5455 ⊕www. cromleach.com ♺11 rooms ⚬In-room: no a/c, Wi-Fi. In-hotel: restaurant, bar, no elevator ⊟AE, DC, MC, V ⎟⊙⎟BP, MAP.*

$$–$$$ ✕⌂ **Markree Castle.** One of the most beautiful fortress fronts in Ireland
Fodor'sChoice   greets you on arrival at Markree, Sligo's oldest inhabited castle and the
★   home of the Cooper family for 350 years. Today, Charles and Mary Cooper preside over this lush and lavish 1,000-acre estate. Renovated in 1802, the castle was given the full storybook treatment, complete with a vast, oak-panel entry hall and skylight atrium. Atop the grand staircase is a glorious stained-glass window depicting the Cooper family tree (their roots are essentially English—having arrived with the bloody troops of Cromwell—but they were also related to the great Irish clan of the O'Briens). Upstairs, guest bedrooms are super-spacious, many adorned with cozy-sumptuous pieces of 19th century–style furniture; bathrooms are modern. Chandeliered and gilt-limned, the restaurant dining room has ornate Louis XIV plasterwork—ask about the three-course pre-fixe menu (€38) that's occasionally served—and serves food good enough to draw in families for Sunday brunch. *⊠11 km (7 mi) south of Sligo Town, off N4, Collooney, Co. Sligo ☎071/916–7800 ⊟071/916–7840 ⊕www.markreecastle.ie ♺30 rooms ⚬In-room: no a/c, Wi-Fi. In-hotel: restaurant, bar, no elevator ⊟AE, MC, V ⎟⊙⎟BP, MAP.*

$$ ✕⌂ **Temple House.** Off the beaten path on more than 1,000 acres, this vast Georgian mansion and working organic farm has been in owners Sandy and Deb Perceval's family since 1665. Their son Roderick manages the estate. Georgian and Victorian furniture—mahogany tables and original rugs—adorn the bedrooms. Outside, formal terraced gardens and a lake beckon. Deb prepares the prix-fixe evening meal ($$$$; book by noon) using the farm's own produce. Typical entrées include herbed leg of lamb with roast potatoes and tomato fondue with glazed carrots. High tea is served for children at 6:30 PM; they are not allowed at dinner. *⊠19 km (12 mi) south of Sligo, off N17, Ballymote, Co. Sligo ☎071/918–3329 ⊟071/918–3808 ⊕www.templehouse.ie ♺6 rooms ⚬In-room: no a/c, no phone, no TV, Wi-Fi. In-hotel: restaurant, no elevator ⊟AE, MC, V ⊙Closed Dec.–Mar. ⎟⊙⎟BP.*

$ ✕⌂ **Glebe House.** Dorothy and Jeremy Bird run a Georgian guesthouse
★   and a restaurant ($$$$) with an emphasis on local produce. You might choose from roast rack of Sligo lamb in an herb crust or wild Owenmore salmon with an herb hollandaise from the prix-fixe menu. Indulge

in pink grapefruit-and-gin sorbet or chocolate-and-Amaretto mousse for dessert. It's a relaxed place, with simple but pleasant guest rooms. ⊠*12 km (7 mi) south of Sligo Town, Coolaney Rd., off N4 at 2nd roundabout, Collooney, Co. Sligo* ☎*071/916–7787* ⇋*4 rooms, 1 with bath* ⌂*In-room: no a/c, no TV, Wi-Fi. In-hotel: restaurant, no elevator* ⊟*MC, V* ⦿*BP, MAP.*

$$$ ⊞**Coopershill.** Seven generations of the O'Hara family have lived in
★   this three-story Georgian farmhouse since it was built in 1774. Beyond the elegant, symmetrical stone facade, with its central Palladian window, an appealing mix of antique bureaus, marble busts, mounted deer heads, and 19th-century paintings fill the large reception rooms—especially the main emerald-hued salon. Spacious, beautifully furnished guest rooms have floral wallpaper and most have four-poster or canopy beds. Dine by candlelight on meals made with fresh Irish ingredients, accompanied by a wide choice of wines, served from a grand sideboard set with family silver and crystal. Nonguests are welcome to dine only when the lodging is not full. ⊠*Off N4, 17 km (11 mi) southeast of Sligo, Riverstown, Co. Sligo* ☎*071/916–5108* 🖷*071/916–5466* ⊕*www.coopershill.com* ⇋*8 rooms* ⌂*In-room: no a/c, no TV, Wi-Fi. In-hotel: restaurant, tennis court, no elevator* ⊟*AE, DC, MC, V* ⊙*Closed Nov.–Mar.* ⦿*BP.*

$ ⊞**Sligo Park Hotel.** Expect a modern establishment designed for a contemporary traveler: a first-rate fitness center, dancing and piano entertainment some evenings, and a good restaurant. It's a reasonable base of operations for touring Yeats Country. The staff is quite friendly. ⊠*Pearse Rd., off N4, Co. Sligo* ☎*071/916–0291* 🖷*071/916–9556* ⊕*www.leehotels.com* ⇋*110 rooms* ⌂*In-room: no a/c, Wi-Fi. In-hotel: restaurant, bar, tennis court, pool, gym, no elevator* ⊟*AE, MC, V* ⦿*BP, MAP.*

NIGHTLIFE & THE ARTS

A few miles south of town is a popular spot with the locals, the **Thatch pub** (⊠*Thatch, Ballysadare* ☎*071/916–7288*), which has traditional music sessions from Thursday to Sunday.

A sizable dance floor at **Toffs** (⊠*Kennedy Parade* ☎*071/916–1250*) teems with Sligo's younger set moving to a mix of contemporary dance music and older favorites. It stays open later than most places.

THEATER   With a jam-packed calendar year-round, **Hawk's Well Theatre** (⊠*Temple St.* ☎*071/916–1526* ⊕*www.hawkswell.com*) hosts amateur and professional companies from all over Ireland (and occasionally from Britain) in an eclectic mix of shows. Shows run €15–€25; the box office is open weekdays 10–6 and Saturday 2–6.

SPORTS & THE OUTDOORS

For riding in the countryside around Sligo, contact the **Sligo Riding Centre** (⊠*3 km [2 mi] from Sligo Town, Carramore* ☎*087/0230–4828* ⊕*www.irelandonhorseback.com*).

SHOPPING

Sligo Town has Northwest Ireland's most thriving shopping scene, with lots of food-related, crafts, and hand-knits shops.

In addition to stylish sweaters, **Carraig Donn** (⊠*41 O'Connell St.* ☎*071/914–4158*) carries pottery, glassware, linens, and Aran knits for children.

The **Cat & the Moon** (⊠*4 Castle St.* ☎*071/914–3686*) specializes in eclectic and stylish Irish-made crafts, jewelry, pottery, ironwork, and scarves.

The upscale deli **Cosgrove and Son** (⊠*32 Market St.* ☎*071/914–2809*) sells everything from Parma ham to carrageen moss boiled in milk (a local cure for upset stomachs). Stock up here for a picnic.

Cross Sections (⊠*2 Grattan St.* ☎*071/914–2265*) sells lovely tableware, glassware, and kitchenware.

Tír na nóg (⊠*Grattan St.* ☎*071/916–2752*), Irish for "Land of the Ever-young," sells organic foods, including local cheeses and honeys, and other health-oriented items. A sister store across the street sells cards and posters.

LOUGH GILL

❽ *1½ km (1 mi) east of Sligo Town on R286.*
★

Lough Gill means simply "Lake Beauty." In fine weather the beautiful river-fed lough and its surroundings are serenity itself: sunlight on the meadows all around, lough-side cottages, the gentle sound of water, salmon leaping, a yacht sailing by. To get to the lake from Sligo Town, take Stephen Street, which turns into N16 (signposted to Manorhamilton and Enniskillen). Turn right almost at once onto R286. Within minutes you can see gorgeous views of the lake so adored by the young W. B. Yeats.

In the 17th century an English Planter (a Protestant colonist settling on Irish lands confiscated from Catholic owners) built the fortified house of **Parke's Castle** on the eastern shore of Lough Gill. He needed the strong fortifications to defend himself against a hostile populace. His relations with the people were made worse by the fact that he obtained his building materials mainly by dismantling a historic fortress on the site that had belonged to the clan leaders the O'Rourkes of Breffni (once the name of the district). The entrance fee includes a short video show on the castle and local history, and a guided tour. In summer, boat tours of the lough leave from here. There's also a snack bar. ⊠*R288, Fivemile Bourne* ☎*071/916–4149, 087/270–4032 for appointment* ⊕*www.heritageireland.ie* ☐*€2.90* ⊙*Daily, May–Oct., 10–6, last admission at 5:15; Nov.–Apr., by appointment.*

A few minutes' walk along a footpath south of Parke's Castle lie the handsome ruins of **Creevelea Abbey.** In fact not an abbey but a friary, Creevelea was founded for the Franciscans in 1508 by a later generation of O'Rourkes. It was the last Franciscan community to be founded before the suppression of the monasteries by England's King Henry VIII. Like many other decrepit abbeys, the place still holds religious significance for the locals, who revere it. One curiosity here is the especially large south transept; notice, too, its endearing little cloisters, with well-executed carvings on the pillars of St. Francis of Assisi. ⊠ *R288, Dromahair.*

WHERE TO STAY & EAT

¢ ✕⊞ **Stanford Village Inn.** This stone-front inn is one of the few stops for sustenance near Lough Gill. A hearty meal of traditional, homey food ($–$$), an open fire, and, if your timing is good, an impromptu session of traditional Irish music await you. It has six newly refurbished country rooms. ⊠ *7 km (5 mi) from Parke's Castle, 19 km (12 mi) from Sligo Town, off R288, Dromahair, Co. Leitrim* ☎ *071/916–4140* ☐ *071/916–4770* ♻ *6 rooms* ☖ *In-room: no a/c, dial-up. In-hotel: restaurant, bar, no elevator* ☐ *MC, V* ☖ *BP.*

LAKE ISLE OF INNISFREE

❾ *15 km (9 mi) south of Sligo Town via Dromahair on N4 and R287.*

In 1890 W. B. Yeats was walking through the West End of London when, seeing in a shop window a ball dancing on a jet of water, he was suddenly overcome with nostalgia for the lakes of his Sligo home. It was the moment, and the feeling, that shaped itself into his most famous poem, "The Lake Isle of Innisfree":

I will arise and go now, and go to Innisfree,
And a small cabin build there, of clay and wattles made:
Nine bean-rows will I have there, a hive for the honey-bee,
And live alone in the bee-loud glade.
And I shall have some peace there, for peace comes dropping slow.

Though there's nothing visually exceptional about Innisfree (pronounced *innish*-free), the "Lake Isle" is a must-see if you're a W. B. Yeats fan. To reach Innisfree from Dromahair, take R287, the minor road that heads back along the south side of Lough Gill, toward Sligo Town. Turn right at a small crossroads, after 4 or 5 km (2 or 3 mi), where signposts point to Innisfree. A little road leads another couple of miles down to the lakeside, where you can see the island just offshore.

ROSSES POINT

❿ *8 km (5 mi) northwest of Sligo Town on R291.*

It's obvious why W. B. and Jack B. Yeats often stayed at Rosses Point during their summer vacations: glorious pink-and-gold summer sunsets over a seemingly endless stretch of sandy beach. Coney Island lies just off Rosses Point. Local lore has it that the captain of the ship *Arathusa* christened Brooklyn's Coney Island after this one, but there's probably more legend than truth to this, as it's widely agreed that New York's

Continued on page 501

A PIECE OF
THE SHAMROCK

Prepping dishes for Spongeware patterns

With its Belleek porcelains and Waterford crystals, Ireland has always
been a treasured island for shoppers. Today, its traditional crafts—
centuries old yet very much alive—are enjoying a revival of the fittest.

Remember all those traditional leprechaun figurines with "Made in China" stickers on their bottoms? Fifteen years ago, Aunt Maud was probably resigned to buying one when she wanted to bring a bit of the Emerald Isle home with her. Today, however, Irish traditional crafts are flourishing as never before. In a land where many villages are still redolent of a preindustrial age, "trad" culture has become commerce—big commerce. Claddagh friendship rings, spongeware pottery, heirloom Aran sweaters, Belleek china wedding plates, Carrickmacross lace, and Waterford crystal (so finely cut you'll need to don antibrilliance eye goggles) are all objects endowed with vibrant personality. If Ireland has never been a country of great artists it has always been one of great *artistry*.

From north to south, an army of indulgent shoppers tour the country joking "Veni, vidi, Visa—I came, I saw, I charged." While the entire country is blooming with craftsworkers, the Northwest region offers some seventh-level shopping, thanks to hand-knit Aran sweaters, fine Parian china, and handwoven tweeds. Those who want to make browsing—and buying—easy will find the famous multidealer town cooperatives (such as Midleton's Courtyard Crafts or Doolin's Celtic Waves) as tempting as boxes of Godiva chocolates. But, in general, the more interesting craftspeople are found outside the main cities, and intrepid consumers should head for smaller towns where overheads are lower (and the scenery is better). Don't buy the first blackthorn walking stick you see. Take a good look around and visit any number of crafts shops—it's part of the fun and you'll probably end up with a bogwood paperweight and basketweave china tureen as well!

Above: Claddagh ring.
Below: Louis Mulcahey at work on his pottery.
Dingle Peninsula, Southwest Ireland

CHERISHED COLLECTIBLES

WATERFORD CRYSTAL

Founded in 1783, Waterford crystal is noted for its sparkle, clarity, and heft. Thicker glass means that each piece can be wedge-cut on a diamond wheel to dramatic effect (as you can see during the famous factory tour held at the Waterford factory in Southeast Ireland). Waterford artisans apprentice for *eight* years.

BELLEEK CHINA

China has been made in Belleek, a village just on the border with County Fermanagh, Northern Ireland, since 1857. This local product is a fine-bone china with a delicate green or yellow-on-white design. Americans love it.

TRADITIONAL LACEMAKING

Traditional Irish crochet and lace-making use a fine cotton and date back to the 1840s when they originated in the cottage homes and lace schools of Carrickmacross.

SPONGEWARE POTTERY

One of Ireland's most beautiful collectibles, Irish Spongeware first appeared in 18th-century potteries. With the use of a cut sponge, patterns and images—often "rural" in flavor, like plants and sheep—are applied to the lovely cream-colored surface.

CLADDAGH RINGS

Born in the Claddagh area of Galway during the 17th century, the Claddagh ring incorporates three symbols: a heart (for love), a pair of hands (for friendship), and a crown (for loyalty). Worn on the right hand, with crown and heart facing out, it symbolizes the wearer is still "free"; worn on the left, with symbols tucked under, indicates marriage.

ARAN: FROM FLEECE TO FASHION

Made of plain, undyed wool and knit with distinctive crisscross patterns, sometime referred to as *bainin* sweaters or "ganseys," the Aran sweater is a combination of folklore and fashion.

Since harsh weather made warmth and protection vital out in the Atlantic Ocean, the women of Aran long ago discovered the solution to this problem in this strong, comfortable, hand-knit sweater. Indeed, these Arans can hold 30 percent of their weight in water before they even start to feel wet. The reason? Traditionally, the wool used was unwashed and retained its water-repellent natural sheep's lanolin.

Not so long ago, these pullovers were worn by every County Donegal fisherman, usually made to a design belonging exclusively to his own family. It's said that a native can tell which family the knitter belongs to from the patterns used in a genuine Aran sweater. Often the patterns used religious symbols and folk motifs, such as the Tree of Life, the Honeycomb (standing for thrift and thought to be lucky), the SeaHorse, the Blackberry—all are patterns in the almost sculptured, deeply knitted work that characterizes the Aran method. Their famous basket stitch represents the fisherman's basket, a hope for a *curragh* (fisherboat) heavy with catch. A colorful belt called a *crios* (pronounced "criss") is handcrafted in many traditional designs by the Aran women and makes a useful accessory.

Most of the Aran sweaters you'll see throughout Ireland are made far north of the islands themselves, in County Donegal, an area most associated with high-quality, handwoven textiles. The best are painstakingly knitted by hand, a process that can take weeks. As a result, prices are not cheap, and if you think you've found a bargain, check the label before buying—it's more likely a factory copy. Still, the less expensive, lighter-weight, hand-loomed sweaters (knitted on a mechanical loom, not with needles) are less than half the price, and more practical for most lifestyles. But the real McCoy is still coveted: some of the finest examples woven by Inis Meáin are sold at luxury stores like Bergdorf Goodman and Wilkes Bashford. And young Irish designers like Liadain De Buitlear (⊕ www.liadainbuitlear.com) are giving the traditional Aran a newer-than-now spin, highly popular in Dublin boutiques.

Above Left: A large selection of styles and sizes
Above right: A closer look at the knitting

The Sporting Life

Along the rugged coasts of Sligo and Donegal, beaches come in all shapes and sizes. Chief among them is Strandhill, a few miles outside Sligo Town; it's a particularly delightful stretch of fine sand and rolling waves, perfect for surfers. Donegal's seaside resorts, like the family-oriented Bundoran on the west coast and Buncrana in northern Donegal, can get very crowded in summer, and are packed full of amusement arcades. But there are quieter alternatives, like Rossnowlagh (meaning "heavenly cove"), in Donegal Bay, with its pristine shoreline. Water sports from windsurfing to sailing are rife in both counties and fishing enthusiasts will be in their element, with excellent fishing for salmon and sea, brown, and rainbow trout in countless lakes, rivers, and streams. The Atlantic coast offers unrestricted shore angling. The numerous headlands of the north Donegal coast are perfect settings for invigorating walks, with the fresh Atlantic sea air sure to blow away the cobwebs. See if you can get as far as Malin Head, the most northerly tip of Ireland. The Slieve League cliffs are the highest sea cliffs in Europe, and the view from the top will set your heart racing. Inland, the Blue Stack Mountains in Donegal offer wonderful views of the surrounding area, looming above Sligo Town, with the serene mass of Ben Bulben seeming to glow in the sunset. Both counties are justly famous for their loughs (lakes), from beautiful, gentle Lough Gill, with its tiny island of Innisfree, immortalized in a poem by W.B. Yeats, to the pilgrims' favorite Lough Derg, with its shrines to St. Patrick.

Coney Island was named after the Dutch word *konijn* (wild rabbits, which abounded there during the 17th century).

8

The popular **County Sligo Golf Club** (✉ *Rosses Point* ☎ *071/917–7134* ⊕ *www.countysligogolfclub.ie*) is one of Ireland's grand old venues; it's more than a century old, and has hosted most of the country's major championships. Established in 1894 on land leased from Henry Middleton, an uncle of the famous Yeats brothers, the course offers magnificent views of the sea and Ben Bulben.

The **Sligo Yacht Club** (✉ *Rosses Point* ☎ *071/917–7168* ⊕ *www.sligo yachtclub.org*), with a fleet of some 25 boats, has sailing and social programs, and regularly hosts races.

DRUMCLIFF

⑪ *15 km (9 mi) northeast of Rosses Point, 7 km (4½ mi) north of Sligo Town on N15.*

W.B. Yeats lies buried with his wife, Georgie, in an unpretentious grave in the cemetery of Drumcliff's simple Protestant church, where his grandfather was rector for many years. W.B. died on the French Riviera in 1939; it took almost a decade for his body to be brought back to the place that more than any other might be called his soul-land. In the poem "Under Ben Bulben," he spelled out not only where he was to be buried but also what should be written on the tombstone: "Cast a cold eye/On life, on death./Horseman, pass by!" It is easy to see why the majestic Ben Bulben (1,730 feet), with its sawed-off peak (not unlike Yosemite's Half-Dome), made such an impression on the poet: the mountain gazes calmly down upon the small church, as it does on all of the surrounding landscape—and at the same time stands as a sentinel facing the mighty Atlantic.

Drumcliff is where St. Columba, a recluse and missionary who established Christian churches and religious communities in Northwest Ireland, is thought to have founded a monastic settlement around AD 575. The monastery that he founded before sailing off to the Scottish isle of Iona flourished for many centuries, but all that is left of it now is the base of a round tower and a carved high cross (both across N15 from the church) dating from around AD 1000, with scenes from the Old and New Testaments, including Adam and Eve with the serpent, and Cain slaying Abel.

Drumcliff Craft Shop is a good place to buy local crafts, books of W. B.'s poetry, and books about the poet's life. You can also get a snack here. ⊠*Next to Protestant church* ☎*071/914–4956* ☺*Mon.–Sat. 9:30–6, Sun. noon–6.*

> ### HILLTOP DOINGS
>
> The massive flat-domed plateau of Ben Bulben dominates the surrounding bogland. Dating to 574 when St. Columcille founded a monastery on its peak (these fellows were seriously into inaccessibility), it became a major religious destination until Oliver Cromwell extinguished it. The 1,729-foot climb has superb views, but remember it is always windy on top and frequently soggy underfoot.

AROUND DONEGAL BAY

As you drive north to Donegal Town, the glens of the Dartry Mountains (to which Ben Bulben belongs) gloriously roll by to the east. Look across coastal fields for views of the waters of Donegal Bay to the west. In the distant horizon the Donegal hills beckon. This stretch, dotted with numerous prehistoric sites, has become Northwest Ireland's most popular vacation area. There are a few small and unremarkable seashore resorts, and in some places you may find examples of haphazard and fairly tasteless construction that detracts from the scenery. In between these minor resort developments, wide-open spaces are free of traffic. The most intriguing area lies on the north side of the bay—all that rocky indented coastline due west of Donegal Town. Here you enter the heart of away-from-it-all: County Donegal.

MULLAGHMORE

⑫ *37 km (24 mi) north of Sligo Town off N15.*

In July and August, the picturesque, sleepy fishing village of Mullaghmore becomes congested with tourists. Its main attractions: a 3-

km-long (2-mi-long) sandy beach; and the turreted, fairy-tale Classie Bawn—the late Lord Louis Mountbatten's home (he, his grandson, and a local boy were killed when the IRA blew up his boat in the bay in 1979). A short drive along the headland is punctuated by unobstructed views beyond the rocky coastline out over Donegal Bay. When the weather is fair, you can see all the way across to St. John's Point and Drumanoo Head in Donegal.

Creevykeel is one of Ireland's best megalithic court-tombs. There's a burial area and an enclosed open-air court where rituals were performed around 3000 BC. Bronze artifacts found here are now in the National Museum in Dublin. The site (signposted from N15) lies off the road, just beyond the edge of the village of Cliffony. ⊠ *3 km (2 mi) southeast of Mullaghmore off N15.*

WHERE TO STAY & EAT

$ ✕🖻 **Beach Hotel.** If there's a chill in the air, you can warm up at the roaring fires in the restaurant and residents' lounge of this large harborside Victorian hotel. The exterior of the simple, three-story building wears a dashing coat of red. Inside, nautical accents tout the history of the bay (it seems three galleons of the Spanish Armada went aground here in September 1588). Enjoy wonderful views of the pier and the bay from the hotel bars, or tuck into the de'Cuellar Restaurant's acclaimed seafood menu ($–$$$). Try the favorites: hot crab claws, lobster, and the house seafood platter. Save room for the homemade apple-and-rhubarb crumble. ⊠ *The Harbour, Co. Sligo* ☎ *071/916–6103* 🖨 *071/916–6448* ⊕ *www.beachhotelmullaghmore.com* ⇆ *28 rooms* △ *In-room: no a/c, Wi-Fi. In-hotel: restaurant, bars, pool, gym* ⊟ *AE, MC, V* ⊠*BP, MAP.*

BUNDORAN

⓭ *17 km (11 mi) northeast of Mullaghmore, 35 km (22 mi) northeast of Sligo Town on N15.*

Resting on the south coast of County Donegal, Bundoran is one of Ireland's most popular seaside resorts, a favorite haunt of the Irish from both the north and the south. To avoid souvenir shops and amusement arcades, head north of the center to the handsome beach at **Tullan Strand,** washed by good surfing waves. Between the main beach and Tullan, the Atlantic has sculpted cliff-side rock formations that the locals have christened with whimsical names such as the Fairy Bridges, the Wishing Chair, and the Puffing Hole (which blows wind and water from the waves pounding below).

WHERE TO EAT

$–$$ ✕ **Brennans.** An absence of TVs and the welcoming hum of conversation mark this atmospheric and unspoiled relic of old-fashioned pub culture, which existed back before watching televised sports had become a seemingly round-the-clock pastime. Painstakingly preserved, Brennans, with all its wonderful 20th-century alehouse nostalgia, is a solid and honest example of that apt if overused description, "good food and fine company." It's a place where locals, holidaymakers, and surfers congregate to create a vibe that'll entice you to stay for that second pint. This is fairly standard pub fare—the point here is people-watching and conversation. ⊠ *Main St.* ☎*071/985–1810* ⊟*No credit cards.*

BALLYSHANNON

⓮ *6 km (4 mi) north of Bundoran, 42 km (26 mi) northeast of Sligo Town on N15.*

The former garrison town of Ballyshannon rises gently from the banks of the River Erne and has good views of Donegal Bay and the surrounding mountains. Come in early August, when this quiet village springs to life with a grand festival of folk and traditional music. The town is a hodgepodge of shops, arcades, and hotels. Its triangular central area has several bars and places to grab a snack. The town was also the birthplace of the prolific poet William Allingham.

A few kilometers down the road are several factories where, for generations, master craftsmen have made eggshell-thin Irish porcelain. It's said that if a newlywed couple receives a piece of this china, their marriage will be blessed with everlasting happiness.

The name Belleek has become synonymous with much of Ireland's delicate ivory porcelain figurines and woven china baskets (sometimes painted with shamrocks). **Belleek Pottery Ltd.** is the best known of the producers, in operation since 1857. The main factories are just down the road from Ballyshannon in Northern Ireland (which is why their prices are quoted in pounds sterling, not euros). Watch the introductory film, take the 30-minute tour, stop by for refreshment in the tearoom, or just head to the on-site shop. A cup-and-saucer set starts at £16, a typical basket £69, and prices head skyward from there. The factory-museum-store is near the border with Northern Ireland. Company products can also be found in the shops of Donegal and Sligo. ⊠*6 km (4 mi) east of Ballyshannon, Belleek, Northern Ireland* ☎*028/6865–9300 in Northern Ireland* ⊕*www.belleek.ie* ⊠*£4* ☾*Apr.–June, Sept., and Oct., weekdays 9–6, Sat. 10–6, Sun. 2–6; July and Aug., weekdays 9–8, Sat. 10–6, Sun. 11–6; Nov.–Mar., weekdays 9–5:30.*

The fourth generation (since 1866) of the Daly family handcrafts and paints the elaborate floral and basket-weave designs at **Celtic Weave China.** Because it's a small, personal operation, they can make a single piece of china to your specifications. Prices start at €7, and most pieces cost less than €125. ⊠*R230, 5 km (3 mi) east of Ballyshannon, Cloghore* ☎*071/985–1844* ⊕*www.celticweavechina.ie* ⊠*Free* ☾*Weekdays 8–6, Sat. 9–5.*

OFF THE BEATEN PATH

Lough Derg. From Whitsunday to the Feast of the Assumption (June to mid-August), tens of thousands beat a path to the celebrated lake of Lough Derg, ringed by heather-clad slopes. In the center of the lough, Station Island—known as St. Patrick's Purgatory (the saint is said to have fasted here for 40 days and nights)—is one of Ireland's most popular pilgrimage sites. It's also the most rigorous and austere of such sites in the country. Pilgrims stay on the island for three days without sleeping, and ingest only black tea and dry toast. They walk barefoot around the island, on its flinty stones, to pray at a succession of shrines. The pilgrimage has been followed since time immemorial; during the Middle Ages, devotees from foreign lands flocked here. Nonpilgrims may not visit the island from June to mid-August. To find out how to become a pilgrim, write to the Reverend Prior. To reach the shores of Lough Derg, turn off the main N15 Sligo–Donegal road in the village of Laghy onto the minor R232 Pettigo road, which hauls itself over the Black Gap and descends sharply into the border village of Pettigo, about 21 km (13 mi) from N15. From here, take the Lough Derg access road for 8 km (5 mi). During pilgrim season, buses connect Pettigo with Donegal, Laghey, and Ballybofey. ✉ *Lough Derg Visitor Centre, Main St., Pettigo* ☎ *072/61546.*

NIGHTLIFE

The biggest and most popular pub, **Seán Óg's** (✉ *Market St.* ☎ *071/985–8964*), has live music on Friday, Saturday, and Sunday evenings.

DONEGAL TOWN

⑮ *21 km (13 mi) north of Ballyshannon, 66 km (41 mi) northeast of Sligo Town on N15.*

The town of Donegal was previously known in Irish as Dun na nGall, "Fort of the Foreigners." The foreigners were Vikings, who set up camp here in the 9th century to facilitate their pillaging and looting. They were driven out by the powerful O'Donnell clan (originally Cinel Conail), who made it the capital of Tyrconail, their extensive Ulster territories. Donegal was rebuilt in the early 17th century, during the Plantation period, when Protestant colonists were planted on Irish property confiscated from its Catholic owners. The **Diamond,** like that of many other Irish villages, dates from this period. Once a marketplace, it has a 20-foot-tall obelisk monument (1937), which honors the town monks who, before driven out by the English in the 17th century, took the time to copy down a series of Old Irish legends in what they called *The Annals of the Four Masters.*

With a population of about 3,000, Donegal is Northwest Ireland's largest small village—marking the entry into the back-of-the-beyond of the wilds of County Donegal. The town is centered on the triangular Diamond, where three roads converge (N56 to the west, N15 to the south and the northeast) and the mouth of the River Eske pours gently into Donegal Bay. You should have your bearings in five minutes, and seeing the historical sights takes less than an hour; if you stick around any longer, it'll probably be to do some shopping—arguably Donegal's top attraction.

Picturesque **Donegal Castle** was built by clan leader Hugh O'Donnell in the 1470s. More than a century later, this structure was the home of his descendant Hugh Roe O'Donnell, who faced the might of the invading English and was the last clan chief of Tyrconail. In 1602 he died on a trip to Spain while trying to rally reinforcements from his allies. In 1610 its new English owner, Sir Basil Brooke, reconstructed the little castle, adding the fine Jacobean fortified mansion with towers and turrets that can still be seen. Inside there are only a few rooms to see, including the garderobe (the restroom) and a great hall with an exceptional vaulted wood-beam roof. Also of note is the gargantuan sandstone fireplace nicely wrought with minute details. The small, enclosed grounds are pleasant. ⊠ *Tirchonaill St., near north corner of Diamond* ☎ *074/972–2405* 🎫 *€4* ☉ *Apr.–Oct., daily 10–6; Nov.–Mar., Fri.–Sun., 10–4.*

The ruins of the **Franciscan Abbey,** founded in 1474 by Hugh O'Donnell, are a five-minute walk south of town at a spectacular site perched above the Eske River, where it begins to open up into Donegal Bay. The complex was burned to the ground in 1593, razed by the English in 1601, and ransacked again in 1607; the ruins include the choir, south transept, and two sides of the cloisters, between which lie hundreds of graves dating to the 18th century. The abbey was probably where *The Annals of the Four Masters,* which chronicles the whole of Celtic history and mythology of Ireland from earliest times up to the year 1618, was written from 1632 to 1636. The Four Masters were monks who believed (correctly, as it turned out) that Celtic culture was doomed by the English conquest, and they wanted to preserve as much of it as they could. At the National Library in Dublin, you can see copies of the monks' work; the original is kept under lock and key. ⊠ *Off N15, behind Hyland Central Hotel* 🎫 *Free* ☉ *Freely accessible.*

WHERE TO STAY & EAT

¢–$ ✕ **Blueberry Tea Room.** Proprietors Brian and Ruperta Gallagher serve
★ breakfast, lunch, afternoon tea, and a light evening meal—always using homegrown herbs. Daily specials—Irish lamb stew, pasta dishes, and quiche—are served from 8 AM to 8 PM. Soups, sandwiches, salads, and fruit are on the regular menu, along with homemade desserts, breads, scones, and jams. Upstairs is an Internet café. It's across the street from Donegal Castle. ⊠ *Castle St.* ☎ *074/972–2933* ▭ V ☉ *Closed Sun.*

$$$$ ✕🏨 **Harvey's Point.** Set in a remote and breathtaking location on the
★ shores of Lough Eske at the foot of the Blue Stack Mountains, Harvey's Point offers a spirit-lifting setting. The drive to the hotel is awe-inspiring in itself—no other man-made structure blights the perfect landscape for miles, and your surprise is complete when the elegant edifice looms up along the shores of the lake. Reception areas gleam with cherrywood and polished stone and flaunt great views. A major extension, with 42 additional guest rooms, was completed in 2005, with huge suites and bathrooms the size of most Irish hotel rooms. The Irish-with-a-French-flair restaurant ($$$$) serves a four-course dinner—a great option is the roast Donegal lamb with crispy sweetbreads. Even if your itinerary prevents you from overnighting, it is well worth dropping in for the Sunday carvery lunch, famous with the locals. ⊠ *6 km (4 mi) northwest of Donegal Town, off N15, Lough Eske, Co. Donegal*

☎074/972–2208 ☏074/972–2352 ⇆*75 rooms* ☖*In-room: no a/c, Wi-Fi. In-hotel: restaurant, bar, bicycles* ▤*AE, DC, MC, V* ⍾*MAP.*

$$$$

Fodor'sChoice

★

✕🔲 **St. Ernan's House.** A most sweetly situated country house, St. Ernan's occupies its own tiny wooded tidal island in Donegal Bay. A nephew of the duke of Wellington built the two-story house in 1826, and it is outfitted with a lordly veranda, white stone trim, and a facade that glows in lilac hues. Today, this forgetaway remains a relaxed, serene lodging, thanks to owners Brian and Carmel O'Dowd. The entry salon is nearly baronial in taste, thanks to its aged, wood panels and elegant fireplace. Guest rooms are neatly refurbished; most of the furnishings are standard-issue antique or traditional, with a chair or sofa stylishly done up in plaid ticking. All fades into insignificance when you drink in the bay views. Dinner is served in the intimate dining room ($$$$) and may include fresh homemade tagliatelle with smoked salmon, followed by crispy breast of duckling or wild salmon. ✉*3 km (2 mi) south of Donegal Town, off R267, St. Ernan's, Donegal, Co. Donegal* ☎*074/972–1065* ☏*074/972–2098* ⊕*www.sainternans.com* ⇆*10 rooms, 2 suites* ☖*In-room: no a/c, Wi-Fi. In-hotel: restaurant, no elevator* ▤*MC, V* ⊗*Closed Nov.–mid-Apr.* ⍾*BP.*

$ 🔳 **Central Hotel.** With its bright white shutters and boldly red facade, this pretty-as-an-Irish-picture inn sits smack on Donegal's central square. While family-run, it is affiliated with the big Irish firm of White's Hotels. Huge picture windows in the back reveal lovely views of Donegal Bay. The efficient staff serves good, filling food in the Captain's Cove restaurant and there's an adjacent and cheaper Carvery. ✉*The Diamond, Co. Donegal* ☎*074/972–1027* ☏*074/972–2295* ⊕*www.whites-hotelsireland.com* ⇆*112 rooms* ☖*In-room: no a/c, Wi-Fi. In-hotel: 2 restaurants, bar, pool, gym, no-smoking rooms* ▤*AE, DC, MC, V* ⍾*BP, MAP.*

8

NIGHTLIFE

The **Abbey Hotel** (✉*The Diamond* ☎*074/972–1014*) has music every night in July and August and a disco every Saturday and Sunday night throughout the year. In summer, people pack **McGroarty's Bar** (✉*The Diamond* ☎*074/972–1049*) to hear traditional music Thursday nights and contemporary music on weekends. It's also a good place to stop for a casual bite to eat.

SPORTS & THE OUTDOORS

Donegal Golf Club (✉*8 km [5 mi] from Donegal Town, Murvagh, Laghy, Co. Donegal* ☎*074/973–4054* ⊕*www.donegalgolfclub.ie*) is one of Ireland's great 18-hole championship courses.

SHOPPING

Long the principal marketplace for the region's wool products, Donegal Town has several smaller shops with local hand weaving, knits, and crafts. **Browse a While** (✉*Main St.* ☎*074/912–2783*) is a good place to stop if you're in the mood for some light reading. The shop is stocked with tons of magazines and a small selection of pulp fiction. Explore **Donegal Craft Village** (✉*N15, 1½ km [1 mi] south of town* ☎*No phone*), a complex of workshops where you can buy pottery, handwoven goods, jewelry, and ceramics from young, local craftspeople. You can even watch the items being made Monday to Saturday 9–6, and Sunday 11–6.

The main hand-weaving store in town, **Magee's** (⊠ *The Diamond* ☎ *074/972–2660*) carries renowned private-label tweeds for both men and women (jackets, hats, scarves, suits, and more), as well as pottery, linen, and crystal. **Simple Simon's** (⊠ *The Diamond* ☎ *074/972–2687*), the only fresh food shop here, sells organic vegetables, essential oils, and other whole-earth items, as well as breads and cakes from the kitchen on the premises. They also stock a lot of local Irish cheeses.

EN ROUTE

As you travel west on N56, which runs slightly inland from a magnificent shoreline of rocky inlets with great sea views, it's worthwhile to turn off the road from time to time to catch a better view of the coast. About 6 km (4 mi) out of Donegal Town, N56 skirts Mountcharles, a bleak hillside village that looks back across the bay.

KILLYBEGS

⑯ *28 km (17 mi) west of Donegal Town.*

Trawlers from Spain and France are moored in the harbor at Killybegs, one of Ireland's busiest fishing ports. Though it's one of the most industrialized places along this coast, it's not without some charm, thanks to its waterfront location. Killybegs once served as a center for the manufacture of Donegal hand-tufted carpets, examples of which are in the White House and the Vatican.

Killybegs Carpets (⊠ *Kilcar Rd.* ☎ *074/973–1688*) has a factory on the outskirts of the village, and produces high-quality hand-knotted and hand-tufted carpets to order: a square meter costs around €2,000. Visitors are welcome to commission a piece, but examples of the carpets are not sold off the peg.

EN ROUTE

The narrows, climbs, and twists of R263 afford terrific views of Donegal Bay before descending into pretty Cill Chartaigh (Kilcar), a traditional center of tweed making. Signposted by its Irish name, the next village, An Charraig (Carrick), clings to the foot of the **Slieve League Mountains**, whose dramatic, color-streaked ocean cliffs are, at 2,000 feet, the highest in Ireland and among the most spectacular. Slieve League (Sliah Liec, or Mountain of the Pillars) is a ragged, razor-backed rise bordered by the River Glen. To see the cliffs, take the little road to the Irish-speaking village of Teileann, 1½ km (1 mi) south from Carrick. Then take the narrow lane (signposted to the Bunglass Cliffs) that climbs steeply to the top of the cliffs. The mountain looks deceptively climbable from the back (the inaccessible point borders the Atlantic), but once the fog rolls in, the footing can be perilous. If you want to take in this thrilling perspective—presuming you're hardy and careful— walk along the difficult coastal path from Teileann.

WHERE TO STAY & EAT

$ ✕⏚ **Bay View Hotel.** Across from Killybegs's harbor, the Bay View is the town's most bustling spot. The hotel lobby, done in light wood, offers a modern take on classic designs, and the functional but very pleasant bedrooms are decorated in pale colors; many rooms offer bay-side views. The Irish set menu ($$$$) changes daily, with Bruckless mussels in a white wine and garlic sauce and braised young duckling served with market vegetables and an orange and cherry coulis as potential options. The hotel is well placed for seeing the glorious north shore of Donegal Bay. Special rates include golf greens fees for Portnoo (outside Ard an Ratha) and Murvagh (outside Donegal). ⊠ *Main St., Co. Donegal* ☎ *074/973–1950* 🖷 *074/973–1856* ⊕ *www.bayviewhotel.ie* 🛏️ *40 rooms* ⚲ *In-room: no a/c, Wi-Fi. In-hotel: restaurant, bar, pool, gym* 🖃 *AE, MC, V* ⏚ *BP, MAP.*

SHOPPING

The **Harbour Store** (⊠ *Main St.* ☎ *074/973–2122*), right on the wharf, has plenty to make both fisherfolk and landlubbers happy, including boots and rain gear, competitively priced sweaters, and unusual bright-yellow or orange fiberglass-covered gloves (made in Taiwan).

GLEANN CHOLM CILLE (GLENCOLUMBKILLE)

17 *27 km (17 mi) west of Killybegs on R263, 54 km (27 mi) west of Donegal Town.*

"The Back of Beyond," at the far end of a stretch of barren moorland, the tiny hamlet of Gleann Cholm Cille clings dramatically to the rock-bound harbor of Glen Bay. Known alternatively as Glencolumbkille (pronounced glen-colm-*kill*), it remains the heart of County Donegal's shrinking Gaeltacht region and retains a strong rural Irish flavor, as do its pubs and brightly painted row houses. The name means St. Columba's Glen; the legend goes that St. Columba, the Christian missionary, lived here during the 6th century with a group of followers before many of them moved on to find greater glory by settling Scotland's Isle of Iona. Some 40 prehistoric cairns, scattered around the village, have become connected locally with the St. Columba myths.

The **House of St. Columba,** on the cliff top rising north of the village, is a small oratory said to have been used by the saint himself. Inside, stone constructions are thought to have been his bed and chair. Every year on June 9, starting at midnight, local people make a 3-km (2-mi) barefoot procession called "An Turas" (the journey) around 15 medieval crosses and ancient cairns, collectively called the stations of the cross.

★ Walk through the beachfront **Folk Village Museum** to explore rural life. This *clachan,* or tiny village, comprises a mere six cottages, all of which are whitewashed, thatched-roofed, and extremely modest in appearance. Three showcase particular years in Irish culture: 1720, 1820, and 1920; pride of place goes to the 1881 schoolhouse and the recreated *sheebeen* (pub). The complex was built after local priest Father McDyer started a cooperative to help combat rural depopulation. You'll also find an interpretive center, nature walk, tea shop (don't dare miss out on the Guinness cakes), and crafts shop selling local handmade products, including, intriguingly, wines made from fuchsias, bluebells, heather, and seaweed. In summer, the museum hosts traditional music evenings. Three small cottages, with bare-earth floors, represent the very basic living conditions of the 1720s, 1820s, and 1920s. ✉*Near beach* ☎*074/973–0017* ⊕*www.glenfolkvillage.com* ✉*€3* ☉*Easter–Sept., Mon.–Sat. 10–6, Sun. noon–6.*

Cliffs surrounding Glean Cholm Cille rise up to more than 700 feet, including Glen Head; many cliffs are studded with ancient hermit cells. Also of note is a squat Martello Tower, built by the British in 1804 to protect against an anticipated French invasion that never happened. Another good walk is the 8-km (5-mi) trek to Malinbeg, reached by the coast road running past Doon Point. Look for the ruins of no less than five burial cairns, a ring fort, a second Martello tower, and one of the best beaches in Ireland, famed for its calm waters, dramatic scenery, and lovely golden sand.

ARD AN RATHA (ARDARA)

⑱ *28 km (17 mi) northeast of Gleann Cholm Cille, 40 km (25 mi) north-*
★ *west of Donegal Town on N56.*

At the head of a lovely ocean inlet, the unpretentious, old-fashioned hamlet of Ard an Ratha (Ardara) is built around the L-shape intersection of its two main streets. (If you come from Gleann Cholm Cille, expect a scenic drive full of hairpin curves and steep hills as you cross over Glengesh Pass.) For centuries, great cloth fairs were held on the first of every month; cottage workers in the surrounding countryside still provide Ard an Ratha (and County Donegal) with high-quality, handwoven cloths and hand knits.

WHERE TO STAY & EAT

$$–$$$ ✕**Nesbitt Arms Hotel.** Offering both casual pub grub and more substantial fare, this old-fashioned inn gets understandably busy in summer. Decor harks back to the days when Ard an Ratha was Donegal's foremost weaving and wool center, which explains the wooden loom in the corner of the dining room. And what about the weaver depicted on the menu? He's the grandfather of the owner, Marie Gallagher, who, along with her husband, recently took over the operation. If you want a quick bite, check out the daily specials in the bar—the beef and Guinness pie is particularly tasty. Upstairs in the dining room, standout dishes include a smoked salmon-and-dill terrine starter, followed by crispy baked duck with black-cherry-and-orange sauce. The hotel also rents simple rooms. ✉*Main St.* ☎*074/954–1103* ⊕*www.nesbittarms.com* ▭*MC, V.*

Dream-Weavers

Most of the Aran sweaters you'll see throughout Ireland are made in County Donegal, the area most associated with high-quality, handwoven tweeds and hand-knit items. Made of plain, undyed wool and knit with distinctive crisscross patterns, Aran sweaters are durable, soft, often weatherproof, and can be astonishingly warm. They once provided essential protection against the wild, stormy Atlantic Ocean. Indeed, these Arans can hold 30% of their weight in water before they even start to feel wet.

Not so long ago, these pullovers were worn by every County Donegal fisherman, usually made to a design belonging exclusively to his own family. It's said that a native can tell which family the knitter belongs to from the patterns used in a genuine Aran sweater. Produced for centuries in the fishing communities of north and west Ireland, they are painstakingly knitted by hand, a process that

can take weeks. As a result, prices are not cheap, and if you think you've found a bargain, check the label before buying—it's more likely a factory copy.

When it comes to Donegal tweed, weavers—inspired by the soft greens, red rusts, and dove grays of the famed Donegal landscape—have been producing it for centuries. In long-gone days, crofters' wives concocted the dyes to give Donegal tweed its distinctive flecks, and their husbands wove the cloth into tweed. Traditional Donegal tweed was a salt-and-pepper mix, but gradually, weavers began adding dyes distilled from yellow gorse, purple blackberries, orange lichen, and green moss. Today most tweed comes from factories. However, there are still about 25 local craftsmen working from their cottages. Chic fashion designers like Armani, Ralph Lauren, and Burberry all use handwoven Donegal tweed—obviously, more fashionable than ever.

$ ✕⊞ **Woodhill House.** The cream-color exterior of John and Nancy ★ Yates's spacious manor house is Victorian, but parts of the interior and the coach house date from the 17th century; there's even a small agricultural museum. High ceilings, marble fireplaces, and stained glass are part of the public spaces. Bedrooms have superb views of the Donegal highlands. The 40-seat restaurant ($$$$) uses local ingredients in dishes on its French-Irish pre-fixe menus, which include roast duckling with cherry-and-orange sauce, rack of lamb with herbs picked from the 18th-century walled garden, and elaborate homemade desserts. Frequent Irish folk music sessions take place in the bar. At the time of this writing, work continued on a new wing with six guest rooms overlooking the gardens. ⊠*Just outside Ard an Ratha, Donegal Rd., Co. Donegal* ☎*074/954–1112* ⊟*074/954–1516* ⊕*www.woodhillhouse. com* ➲*9 rooms* ♿*In-room: no a/c, Wi-Fi. In-hotel: restaurant, bar, no elevator* ⊟*AE, DC, MC, V* ⊘*Closed Christmas wk* ⫿⊘⫿*BP.*

¢–$ ⊞ **Green Gate.** For an alternative to country estates and village hotels, Fodor'sChoice try Frenchman Paul Chatenoud's remote cottage B&B overlooking Ard ★ an Ratha, the Atlantic, and spectacular Donegal scenery—it's one of Ireland's most beautiful little guesthouses. The four spare rooms are in a converted stone outbuilding with a thatched roof. Chatenoud, as charming as his hideaway, eagerly directs you to Donegal's best-kept secrets. To reach the hotel from Ard an Ratha, follow the sign for Donegal and turn right after 200 yards. ⊠*Ardvally, Co. Donegal* ☎*074/954–1546* ⊕*http://thegreengate.eu* ⇱*4 rooms* ⏃*In-room: no a/c, no phone, no TV. In hotel: public Internet, no elevator* ⊟*No credit cards* ⎮⊘⎮*BP.*

NIGHTLIFE

For a small, old-fashioned village, Ard an Ratha has a surprising number of pubs, many of which have traditional music in the evenings. The **Central Bar** (⊠*Main St.* ☎*074/954–1311*) has music almost every night in July and August and on weekends the rest of the year. One of the smallest bars in the Republic, **Nancy's Pub** (⊠*Front St.* ☎*074/954–1187*) makes you wonder if you've wandered into the owner's sitting room, but it occasionally finds space for a folk group.

SHOPPING

Many handwoven and locally made knitwear items are on sale in Ard an Ratha. Some stores commission goods directly from knitters, and prices are about as low as anywhere. Handsome, chunky Aran hand-knit sweaters (€80–€130), cardigans (similar prices), and scarves (€25) are all widely available. Stores such as **Campbells Tweed Shop** (⊠*Front St.* ☎*074/954–1128*) carry ready-to-wear tweeds—sports jackets can run up to €120. **C. Bonner & Son** (⊠*Front St.* ☎*074/954–1303*) stocks factory knitwear from €30 to €120, as well as pottery, tweeds, jewelry, and gifts. There's also a good selection of hand-knit Aran sweaters and cardigans available. **E. Doherty (Ardara) Ltd** (⊠*Front St.* ☎*074/954–1304*) sells handwoven tweeds, from scarves for €25 to capes for €195, as well as traditional Irish products, such as glassware and linen, from Ard an Ratha and other parts of the country. At **John Molloy** (⊠*Main St.* ☎*074/954–1133*) you will find a factory shop offering high-quality, handwoven Donegal tweed, and hand-knit Aran sweaters.

NORTHERN DONEGAL

Traveling on northern County Donegal's country roads, you've escaped at last from the world's hurry and hassle. There's almost nothing up here but scenery, and plenty of it: broad, island-studded loughs of deep, dark tranquillity; unkempt, windswept, sheep-grazed grasses on mountain slopes; ribbons of luminous greenery following sparkling streams; and the mellow hues of wide boglands, all under shifting and changing cloudscapes. This trip begins in Letterkenny, the largest town in the county (population 6,500), and makes a beeline to the Irish Xanadu of Henry P. McIlhenny's Glenveagh Castle. Just one word of warning—don't be surprised if you find a sheep standing in the middle of a mountain road looking as though you, rather than it, are in the wrong place.

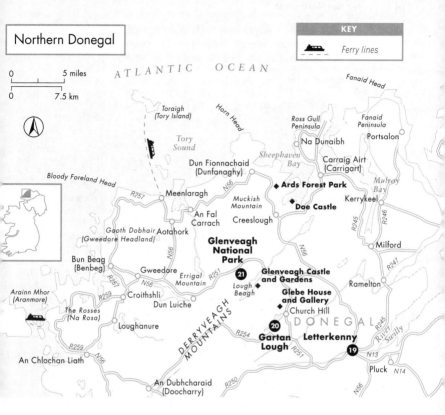

Northern Donegal

ATLANTIC OCEAN

0   5 miles
0   7.5 km

Fanaid Head

Toraigh
(Tory Island)

Horn Head

Ross Gull
Peninsula

Fanaid
Peninsula

Portsalon

Na Dunaibh

Tory
Sound

Sheephaven
Bay

Carraig Airt
(Carrigart)

Dun Fionnachaid
(Dunfanaghy)

Mulroy
Bay

Bloody Foreland Head

R257

Meenlaragh

◆ Ards Forest Park

Kerrykeel

An Fal
Carrach

Muckish
Mountain

Creeslough

● Doe Castle

N56

Milford

Gaoth Dobhair
(Gweedore Headland)

Aotahork

Glenveagh
National
Park

N56

Bun Beag
(Benbeg)

R257

Gweedore

Errigal
Mountain

R251

(21)

Lough
Beagh

Glenveagh Castle
and Gardens

Ramelton

Arainn Mhor
(Aranmore)

R259

Croithshli

N56

Dun Luiche

Glebe House
and Gallery

◆ Church Hill

R245

R246

R247

The Rosses
(Na Rosa)

Loughanure

DERRYVEAGH
MOUNTAINS

DONEGAL

River Swilly

R254

(20)

Gartan
Lough

R251

Letterkenny

R259

An Chlochan Liath

N56

(19)

Pluck   N14

An Dubhcharaid
(Doocharry)

R250

N56

N13

LETTERKENNY

(19) *55 km (34 mi) northeast of Ard an Ratha, 51 km (32 mi) northeast of Donegal Town, 35 km (21 mi) west of Derry.*

One of the fastest-growing towns in all of Ireland, Letterkenny, like Donegal to the south, is at the gateway to the far northwest; you're likely to come through here if you're driving west out of Northern Ireland. Letterkenny's claim to fame has been that it has the longest main street in the whole country. None of Letterkenny's shops or pubs are particularly special, but lots of locals bustling around make it an interesting place to get a feel for what it's like to live in a modest-size Irish town.

The 212-foot-high spire of **St. Eunan's Cathedral** (⊠ *Convent Rd.* ☎ *No phone*) dominates the town, especially when illuminated at night. This striking, ornate neo-Gothic structure was finally finished in 1901, and is the only cathedral in the county. Designed by William Hague of Dublin and built of white Donegal sandstone, the exterior of the building is said to be in perfect classical-rule proportion. Inside, the intricate decorative ceilings and ceramic floor mosaics are the work of an Italian artist, Signor Amici of Rome. The main and side altars are carved from the finest Italian marble, while the great nave arch depicts the lives of St. Eunan and St. Columba in meticulous detail.

$$–$$$ ×⬚ **Mount Errigal Hotel.** One of County Donegal's smartest and most modern hotels (although not at all posh), Mount Errigal Hotel appeals to both business and family travelers. Service is friendly and professional. The clean and comfortable bedrooms are efficiently arranged with light-color wood furnishings. The Strawberry Garden ($$), the hotel's popular and softly lighted restaurant, serves contemporary Irish food, while its dazzling Café Renaissance's steel chandeliers, moderne seating, and wood-panel accents will light up any design aficionado's eyes. The bar buzzes with locals seeking a relaxed night out, and folk music, jazz, and dancing are frequently scheduled on weekends. ✉*Ballyraine, Co. Donegal* ☎*074/912–2700* 🖨*074/912–5085* ⊕*www. mounterrigal.com* ↩*140 rooms, 2 suites* ♿*In-room: no a/c, Wi-Fi. In-hotel: restaurant, bars, pool, gym* ⊟*AE, DC, MC, V* ⏱*BP, MAP.*

$$ ⬚ **Ardeen House.** Overlooking Lough Swilly and the River Lennon and set at the edge of Ramelton, Ardeen House makes an ideal base for exploring the region, especially Glenveagh National Park. Built in 1945, it was the home of Catherine Black, who had been the private nurse to King George V at Buckingham Palace in the 1930s (her autobiography, King's Nurse, Beggar's Nurse, tells her story). The house has a Victorian feel, with its well-chosen antiques, fireplaces ablaze, and regal and relaxing gardens. Current proprietor Anne Campbell's breakfasts and afternoon teas are reason enough to stay here—add in her genuinely welcoming spirit, and you should feel right at home. The five attractively decorated bedrooms afford views over the Donegal hills. ✉*Ramelton, Co. Donegal* ☎*074/975–1243* 🖨*074/915–1243* ⊕*www.ardeenhouse.com* ↩*5 rooms* ♿*In-room: no a/c, dial-up. In-hotel: no elevator* ⊟*MC, V* ⏱*Closed Oct.–Mar.* ⏱*BP.*

GARTAN LOUGH

㉕ *21 km (13 mi) northwest of Letterkenny on R251.*

Gartan Lough and the surrounding mountainous country are astonishingly beautiful. St. Columba was supposedly born here in AD 521, and the legendary event is marked by a huge cross at the beginning of a footpath into Glenveagh National Park. (Close to Church Hill village, Gartan Lough is technically within the national park and is administered partly by the park authorities.)

On the northwest shore of Gartan Lough just off R251 is **Glebe House and Gallery,** a sweetly elegant redbrick Regency manor with 25 acres of gardens. For 30 years, Glebe House was the home of the distinguished landscape and portrait artist Derek Hill, who furnished the house in a mix of styles with art from around the world; in 1981 he gave the house and its contents, including his outstanding art collection, to the nation. Highlights include paintings by Renoir and Bonnard, lithographs by

Kokoschka, ceramics and etchings by Picasso, and the paintings *Whippet Racing* and *The Ferry, Early Morning* by Jack B. Yeats, as well as Donegal folk art produced by the Toraigh Islanders. The decoration and furnishings of the house, including original William Morris wallpaper, are also worth a look. ✉ *Church Hill* ☎ *074/913–7071* 🎫 *€2.75* ☾ *Sat.–Thurs. 11–6:30.*

At the **Colmcille Heritage Centre** you can learn more about St. Columba and his times. The exhibition and interpretation center has medieval manuscripts, stained glass, and displays tracing the decline of the Celtic religion and the rise of Irish Christianity. Audiovisual displays and interactive computer presentations enhance the historical journey. The staff can show you walks in the area. ✉ *R254, Church Hill* ☎ *074/913–7306* 🎫 *€3* ☾ *May–Sept., Mon.–Sat. 10:30–6:30, Sun. 1–6:30.*

> ## THE GOOD EARTH
>
> Near Gartan Lough are other dubious "relics" of St. Columba, which are popularly believed to possess magical powers: the Natal Stone, where the saint is thought to have first opened his eyes, and the Stone of Loneliness, where he is said to have slept. The superstitions do rub off—in the First World War, soldiers carried pocketfuls of Gartan soil to the trenches as a protective relic.

GLENVEAGH NATIONAL PARK

㉑ *21 km (13 mi) northwest of Letterkenny on R251.*

Fodor's Choice
★

Bordered by the Derryveagh Mountains (Derryveagh means "forest of oak and birch"), Glenveagh National Park encompasses 24,000 acres of wilderness—mountain, moorland, lakes, and woods—that has been called the largest and most dramatic tract in the wildest part of Donegal. Within its borders, a thick carpet of russet-color heath and dense woodland rolls down the Derryveagh slopes into the broad open valley of the River Veagh (or Owenbeagh), which opens out into Glenveagh's spine: long and narrow, dark and clear Lough Beagh.

The lands of Glenveagh (pronounced glen-*vay*) have long been recognized as a remote and beautiful region. Between 1857 and 1859, John George Adair, a ruthless gentleman farmer, assembled the estate that now makes up the park. In 1861 he evicted the estate's hundreds of poor tenants without compensation and destroyed their cottages. Nine years later Adair began to build **Glenveagh Castle** on the eastern shore of Lough Veagh, but he soon departed for Texas. He died in 1885 without returning to Ireland, but his widow, Cornelia, moved back to make Glenveagh her home. She created four gardens, covering 27 acres; planted luxuriant rhododendrons; and began the job of making this turret-and-battlement–laden 19th-century folly livable. At the end of a dramatic 2-mi-long entryway, perched over the lake waters, this is a true fairy-tale castle. Like a dollhouse Balmoral, its castellated, rectangular keep, battlemented ramparts, and a Round Tower enchantingly conjure up all the Victorian fantasies of a medieval redoubt.

8

The gardens and castle as they appear today are almost entirely an American invention, the product of the loving attentions of Glenveagh's last owners, including Mr. Kingsley Porter, a venerated professor of medieval art history at Harvard. He, then, passed the property over to U.S. millionaire Henry P. McIlhenny, who bought the estate in 1937 and, beginning in 1947, lived here for part of every year for almost 40 years. An avid art collector and philanthropist (his collection of Degas, Toulouse-Lautrec, and Ingres masterworks now resides at the Philadelphia Museum of Art), McIlhenny decorated every inch of the house himself in faux-baronial fashion and entertained the beau monde (Greta Garbo once slept in the Pink Room) lavishly. The house has been maintained just as it was on his last occupancy in 1983; later that year, he made a gift of the house to the nation. He had sold the government the surrounding land in 1975, which it opened to the public in 1984 as Ireland's third national park.

Beyond the castle, footpaths lead into more remote sections of the park, including the **Derrylahan Nature Trail,** a 1½-km (1-mi) signposted trail where you may suddenly catch sight of a soaring falcon or chance upon a shy red deer. The park is the home of one of Ireland's two largest herds; the other is at Killarney. Guided walks are held from May through October. The visitor center at the park's entrance has a permanent exhibition on the local way of life and on the influence of climate on the park's flora and fauna. Skip the sleep-inducing audiovisual and instead have a bite to eat in the cafeteria, or enjoy your own picnic on the extensive estate grounds, which are free for walkers. A bus runs from the visitor center to the castle. ✉ *R251, Church Hill* ☎ *074/913–7090* ⊕ *www.heritageireland.ie* 🚌 *Shuttle bus €2 roundtrip, castle tour €3* ☉ *Feb.–Nov., daily 10–6:30.*

NORTHWEST ESSENTIALS

TRANSPORTATION

If traveling extensively by public transportation, be sure to load up on information (the best taxi-for-hire companies, rail and bus schedules, etc.) upon arriving at the ticket counter or help desk of the bigger train and bus stations in the area, such as Sligo Town and Letterkenny.

BY AIR

The principal international air-arrival point to Northwest Ireland is the tiny airport at Charlestown, Knock International Airport, 55 km (34 mi) south of Sligo Town. City of Derry Airport, a few miles over the border, receives flights from Manchester and Glasgow. City of Derry (also called Eglinton) is a particularly convenient airport for reaching northern County Donegal. Donegal Airport, in Carrickfinn, is not far from An Chlochan Liath (Dungloe) and typically receives flights from Dublin. Sligo Airport at Strandhill, 8 km (5 mi) west of Sligo Town, is the other area airport.

Airport Information City of Derry Airport (☎028/7181–0784). **Donegal Airport** (☎074/954–8232). **Knock International Airport** (☎094/936–7222). **Sligo Airport** (☎071/916–8280 or 071/916–8318).

CARRIERS Aer Arann has flights from Knock International daily to Dublin and four times a week to Liverpool. It also flies twice daily between Sligo and Dublin. BmiBaby flies from Knock to Manchester daily and to Birmingham six days a week. Ryanair has daily flights to Knock Airport from London Stansted and London Gatwick, and also serves City of Derry Airport daily from London and Dublin. Aer Lingus has flights to Derry from Dublin. British Airways Express flies to City of Derry Airport from Manchester, Glasgow, and Dublin. At this writing, a new carrier, flyglobespan, had just announced weekly services between Knock and New York and Boston.

Airlines & Contacts Aer Arann (☎081/821–0210 or 0800/587–2324 ⊕www. aerarann.ie). **British Airways City Express** (☎0870/850–9850 ⊕www.british airways.com). **British Midland Airways (BmiBaby)** (☎0870/607–0555 ⊕www. bmibaby.com). **Ryanair** (☎0818/830–3030 ⊕www.ryanair.com).

TRANSFERS If you aren't driving, Knock Airport becomes less attractive; there are no easy public transportation links, except the once-a-day (in season) local bus to Charlestown, 11 km (7 mi) away. Nor can you rely on catching a bus at the smaller airports, except at Sligo Airport, where buses run from Sligo Town to meet all flights.

You can get taxis—both cars and minibuses—right outside Knock Airport. The average rate is around €1.50 per kilometer. If you're not flying into Knock, you may have to phone a taxi company. Phone numbers of taxi companies are available from airport information desks and are also displayed beside pay phones inside the airport terminals.

8

Taxi Companies **Castle Cabs** (☎087/638–8588 or 087/252–7407). **OK Cabs** (☎087/639–6666). **Tom Cronnolly** (☎087/244–0597).

BY BUS

Bus Éireann can get you from Dublin to Sligo Town in four hours for €15.80 one way, €23.90 round-trip. Four buses a day from Dublin are available. Another bus route, six times a day from Dublin (five on Sunday), goes to Letterkenny, in the heart of County Donegal, in 4¼ hours, via a short trip across the Northern Ireland border; it's €16 one way, €26 round-trip. Other Bus Éireann services connect Sligo Town to towns all over Ireland. Bus Éireann also operates out of Sligo Town and Letterkenny to destinations all over the region, as well as to other parts of Ireland. From Sligo Town, you can reach almost any point in the region for less than €16. McGeehans is one of several local bus companies linking towns and villages in Northwest Ireland.

Bus Information **Bus Éireann** (☎01/836–6111 in Dublin, 071/916–0066 in Sligo Town, 074/912–1309 in Letterkenny). **McGeehans** (☎074/954–6150).

BY CAR

Sligo, the largest town in Northwest Ireland, is relatively accessible on the main routes. The N4 travels the 224 km (140 mi) directly from Dublin to Sligo. Allow at least four hours for this journey. The N15 continues from Sligo Town to Donegal Town and proceeds from Donegal Town to Derry City, just over the border in Northern Ireland. The fastest approach for anyone driving up from the west and the southwest is on N17, connecting Sligo to Galway, though the landscape is undistinguished.

CAR RENTAL   You can rent a car in Sligo Town from Hertz. Murray's Europcar rents cars from Knock Airport. A medium-size four-door costs around €65 per day with unlimited mileage (inclusive of insurance and taxes) or around €250 per week. If you're planning to tour mostly northern County Donegal, you may find it more convenient to rent a car in Derry from Ford. If you're planning to drive a rental car across the border to Northern Ireland, inform the company in advance and check the insurance policy.

Agencies **Avis** (☎071/912–8004) operates out of Sligo Airport. **Hertz** (☎071/914–4068). **Ford** (☎028/7181–2222). **Murray's Europcar** (☎094/936–7221 at Knock Airport, 01/614–2800 reservations).

ROAD   Roads are not congested, but in some places they are in a poor state
CONDITIONS   of repair (French bus drivers refused to take their buses into County Donegal some summers back, as a gesture of protest about the state of the roads). In the Irish-speaking areas, signposts are written only in the Irish (Gaelic) language, which can be confusing. Make sure that your map lists both English and Irish place names.

BY TRAIN

Sligo Town is the northernmost direct rail link to Dublin. From Dublin, three trains a day make the journey (3 hours and 20 minutes) for €24 one way, €33 round-trip (prices are a bit higher on weekends). If you want to get to Sligo Town by rail from other provincial towns, you must make some inconvenient connections and take roundabout routes. The rest of the region has no railway services.

Train Information **Irish Rail** (☎ *01/836–6222* ⊕ *www.irishrail.ie*).

CONTACTS & RESOURCES

EMERGENCIES

Contacts **Ambulance, fire, police** (☎ *999*). **Letterkenny General Hospital** (✉ *High Rd., Letterkenny, Co. Donegal* ☎ *074/912–5888*). **Sligo General Hospital** (✉ *The Mall, Sligo Town, Co. Sligo* ☎ *071/917–1111*).

INTERNET, MAIL & SHIPPING

Most hotels will allow guests to use their Internet facilities, but cyber-cafés are thin on the ground in this part of rural Ireland. There's one in Sligo Town, called the Cygo Internet Café and it costs about €3.50 per hour.

Mail service in the Northwest of Ireland is reliable and efficient. The two main post offices in Donegal Town and Sligo Town are open weekdays 9 to 5:30, Saturday 9 to 1, and closed Sunday and public holidays. Look for the green signs that say "An Post." In rural villages, the opening hours are generally the same but most post offices will close for lunch from 1 to 2.

Internet cafés **Cygo Internet Café** (✉ *19 O'Connell St.* ☎ *071/914–0082*).

Post offices **Donegal Town post office** (✉ *Tirconaill St.* ☎ *074/972–1024*). **Sligo Town post office** (✉ *Lower Knox St.* ☎ *071/915–9273*).

TOUR OPTIONS

Bus Éireann has budget-priced, guided, one-day bus tours of the Donegal Highlands and to Glenveagh National Park; they start from Bundoran, Sligo Town, Ballyshannon, and Donegal Town. For a friendly, relaxed minibus tour of the area in July and August, call John Houze. He's a knowledgeable guide who leads popular tours (€14 each) to the Lake Isle of Innisfree, the Holy Well, and Parke's Castle; and north of Sligo Town to W. B. Yeats's grave and Glencar Lake and waterfall.

Walking tours of Sligo Town may be arranged in advance for groups, and last about 1½ hours. Depending on the number of people, the charge is approximately €4.

Bus Tours **Bus Éireann** (☎ *01/836–6111* ⊕ *www.buseireann.ie*). **John Houze** (☎ *071/914–2747 or 086/193–5045*).

Walking Tours **Sligo Path Guided Walking Tours** (☎ *071/915–0920*).

8

The Tourist Information Office (TIO) in Sligo Town provides a walking map of Sligo, information about bus tours of Yeats Country, and details of boat tours of Lough Gill. It's also the main visitor information center for Northwest Ireland. Open hours are September to mid-March, weekdays 9–5; mid-March to August, weekdays 9–6, Saturday 10–2, and Sunday 11–3. If you're traveling in County Donegal in the north, try the TIO at Letterkenny, about 1½ km (1 mi) south of town. It's open September to May, weekdays 9–5; June to August, Monday–Saturday 9–6 and Sunday noon–3. The offices at Bundoran and An Chlochan Liath (Dungloe) are open only in summer (usually the first week in June to the second week in September).

Tourist Information **Bundoran TIO** (⊠ *Main St., Bundoran, Co. Donegal* ☎ *071/984–1350* ⊕ *www.countydonegal.com*). **Co. Donegal TIO** (⊠ *N13, Derry Rd., Letterkenny, Co. Donegal* ☎ *074/912–1160* ⊕ *www.irelandnorthwest.ie*). **Co. Sligo TIO** (⊠ *Temple and Charles Sts., Sligo Town, Co. Donegal* ☎ *071/916–1201* ⊕ *www.sligotown.net*) is a good unofficial guide to Sligo town. **Donegal Town TIO** (⊠ *Quay St., Donegal Town, Co. Donegal* ☎ *074/972–1148* ⊕ *www.donegaltown. ie*). **Dungloe TIO** (⊠ *Village Center, An Chlochan Liath (Dungloe), Co. Donegal* ☎ *074/952–1297* ⊕ *www.countydonegal.com*).

Northern Ireland

Giant's Causeway

WORD OF MOUTH

"Tyrone's Ulster-American Folk Park is history brought to life in a format perfect for vacation time. You get to walk into cottages where the poorest families dined on potatoes around an open fire. Then the tour takes you to the boat yards where you sit in a typical 'coffin-ship,' which brought hundreds of thousands of Irish to the U.S. during the famine. The sound effects are amazing. I have grown up with this story, yet I found myself close to tears."

—AnnaG

WELCOME TO NORTHERN IRELAND

Giant's Causeway, Ireland's first World Heritage Site: over 40,000 stone columns.

Town center, Belfast.

TOP REASONS TO GO

★ **Belfast, Gateway City:** As the locals put it, "despite what you've probably heard, Belfast is not what you expect"—so get ready to love this bustling city that bristles with Victorian shop fronts and hip restaurants.

★ **The Giant's Causeway:** This spectacular remnant of Ireland's volcanic period will steal you away from your 21st-century existence and transport you to a time when the giant Finn Mc-Cool roamed the land.

★ **Nine Glens of Antrim:** Fabled haunt of "the wee folk," the glacier-carved valleys have a beauty that has become synonymous with Irishness. Don't miss Glenariff, dubbed "Little Switzerland" by Thackeray.

★ **Ulster-American Folk Park:** A tale of two countries joined by a common people is told at this impresive open-air museum, which recreates a 19th-century Tyrone village and boasts the Centre for Migration Studies.

1 **The Giant's Causeway Coast.** North of the famously beautiful **Glens of Antrim**—still considered "gentle" (supernatural) in spirit— this continues up to Northern Ireland's premier attraction, the **Giant's Causeway.** Farther along the North Antrim coast is **Bushmills**, the oldest distillery in the world; **Dunluce Castle**, spectacularly perched over its "Mermaid's Cave"; and the heart-stopping **Carrick-a-Rede** rope bridge.

2 **Derry.** A walk through Ireland's only walled city provides a unique way to view the layout of the 17th-century inner town, particularly noticeable in the streets and alleys that fan outward from the Diamond, where fine examples of Georgian and Victorian architecture rub shoulders with old-style pubs and museums.

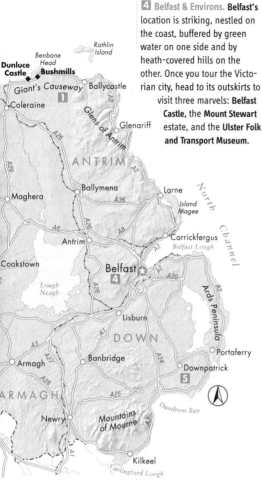

4 Belfast & Environs. **Belfast's** location is striking, nestled on the coast, buffered by green water on one side and by heath-covered hills on the other. Once you tour the Victorian city, head to its outskirts to visit three marvels: **Belfast Castle,** the **Mount Stewart** estate, and the **Ulster Folk and Transport Museum.**

GETTING ORIENTED

With peace—precious peace—abiding, Northern Ireland can finally go about the business of charming visitors full-time. North of the vibrant Victorian city of Belfast, they'll find the ageless wonders of the Causeway Coast while south of the inspiring skyline of Derry lies the Border Counties, where tiny "Ulster" towns dot the scenic landscapes around the Lakes of Fermanagh and Mountains of Mourne.

9

3 The Western Border Counties. The Fermanagh Lakeland is an intricate patchwork quilt of undulating hillsides and some of the most uncongested lakes in Europe. A paradise of open horizons and opportunities for those who love the outdoor life, it is also home to stately homes like **Florence Court** and **Castle Coole,** the **Ulster-American Folk Park,** and the famous porcelain town of **Belleek.**

5 The Eastern Border Counties. South of Belfast past the Ards Peninsula is St. Patrick Country: **Downpatrick,** reputed to be the burial place of the saint; **Armagh's** two St. Patrick cathedrals; and the seaside **Mountains of Mourne.**

Carrick-a-Rede Rope Bridge, Co. Antrim, Northern Ireland

NORTHERN IRELAND PLANNER

Talking About It

While "The Troubles" are now hopefully a thing of the past, Northern Ireland is a political entity that draws its mandate from religion and history—a country where God and politics are tightly interwoven and where ancient quarrels can sometimes still affect the tone of everyday life. So if you find yourself in a pub, it often helps to play a little dumb about facts and events, as the residents seem to be even more willing to explain the history to visitors with no preconceived notions of how things should be. Take any questions of politics gently at first, smell the air of the company you're in, then play the gee-this-is-all-new-to-me card, and things should roll along fine. And certainly stay away from any deep political discussion after four pints of beer!

Making the Most of Your Time

Though Northern Ireland may not look that big on paper, tackling a fair share of its many attractions in less than a week isn't possible without exhausting yourself in the process. If your time is limited, choose the eastern half (Belfast, the Antrim Coast, and the Mountains of Mourne) or the western half (Derry and the Border Counties). The cities are small enough to tackle in a day or two. But remember that the rural wonders—the Antrim Coast, the Fermanagh lakes, the Mountains of Mourne—cast their spell easily. You may head out to enjoy them for a day trip and find yourself wishing that you'd factored in more time to explore the endless string of postcard-worthy villages, emerald-green glens, and rugged mountains. And although distances are not great, neither are the roads—you'll spend most of your time traveling smaller roads, not major express highways.

Getting Around

Northern Ireland is small—about half the size of Delaware and less than one-fifth the size of the Republic of Ireland, its neighbor to the south. And because it's so small, one option is to simply base yourself in the two main cities, Belfast and Derry, and make day trips out. However, one of the real glories of Ulster is its endless supply of spectacular rural scenery, so much so that you may find yourself ho-humming at your umpteenth view of emerald green glens. The good news is that bus travel is both quick and fairly priced. The extensive network of the state-owned Ulsterbus (⊕ www.ulsterbus.co.uk) means it's easy to reach many towns. The bad news is that Northern Irish Railways (NIR) is sorely limited, with only three main routes: Belfast–Derry, Belfast–Bangor; and Belfast–Dublin. In the past decade, however, more runs have been scheduled, along with an official merger of the national bus and train system, now officially dubbed Translink (⊕ www.translink.co.uk). That noted, in many areas, including the wildly popular Causeway Coast, you'll definitely end up on such bus routes as the Causeway Coast Express if you don't drive a car.

Finding a Place to Stay

Major hotel chains based both in the republic and abroad have invested in Northern Ireland's cities. In Belfast's environs you can also choose from the humblest terraced town houses or farm cottages to the grandest country houses. Dining rooms of country-house lodgings frequently match the standard of top-quality restaurants. All accommodations in the province are inspected and categorized by the Northern Ireland Tourist Board Information Centre, which publishes hostelry names, addresses, and ratings in the free guidebooks *Hotel and Guest House Guide* and *Bed & Breakfast Guide,* also available online. Hundreds of excellent-value specials—single nights to weekend deals, the most intimate bed-and-breakfasts to Belfast's finest hotels—become available in the low season, October to March. Assume that all hotel rooms reviewed in this chapter have air-conditioning, in-room phones and TVs, and private bathrooms unless otherwise indicated.

How's the Weather?

If the weather is good—and most of the year it isn't—touring Northern Ireland can be a real pleasure. But the place is so green for a reason: lots of rain, which means you should certainly pack your Burberry. Because you're on the coast, even on bright summer days you can feel the chill from the sea, so it's best to travel layered-up and, depending on the meteorological situation, peel back a sweater or two. Needless to say, the weather is a little friendlier to tourists May to September.

Feeling Festive in Belfast?

Northern Ireland is a great place for festivals and almost every town has its own theme festival of some sort. The Belfast Festival at Queen's University is one of the biggest with a packed program of arts, music, and literature held in October. Belfast's Cathedral Arts Quarter Festival, held late April–early May, uses established, new, and unusual venues throughout the oldest part of the city center for two weeks of music, theater, and visual arts. Feile an Phobail, the West Belfast Festival, held in early August, is a 10-day schedule of events with a political and international theme. Hillsborough International Oyster Festival, held in September, is three days of good food and entertainment—the highlight is, of course, an oyster-eating competition. For a rundown on many other festivals, contact the Northern Ireland Tourist Board.

Pounds, not Euros

Northern Ireland uses British currency. Euros are rarely accepted. You may sometimes be given bank notes, drawn on Ulster banks. Be sure not to get stuck with a lot of these when you leave, because they're accepted with reluctance, if at all, in the rest of the United Kingdom and will be difficult to change at banks back home.

Dining & Lodging Price Categories (In Euros)

	¢	$	$$	$$$	$$$$
RESTAU-RANTS	under €7	€7–€13	€13–€18	€18–€22	over €22
HOTELS	under €50	€50–€80	€80–€115	€115–€160	over €160

Restaurant prices are for a main course at dinner. Hotel prices are for a standard double room in high season.

Updated by
John Daly

LEGEND HAS IT THAT A millennium ago a seafaring chieftain caught sight of the green shores of Northern Ireland, and offered the land to whichever of his two sons would be first to lay a hand upon it. As the two rivals rowed toward shore in separate boats, one began to draw ahead, whereupon the other drew his sword, cut off his own hand, and hurled it onto the beach—and so, by blood and sacrifice, gained the province. To this day the coat of arms of Northern Ireland bears the severed limb: the celebrated "Red Hand of Ulster."

From this ancient bardic tale to the recent Troubles—lasting from 1969 to 1994—Northern Ireland has had a long and often ferocious history. But all such thoughts vanish in the face of the country's natural beauty, magnificent stately houses, and the warm hospitality of its people. The Six Counties, or Ulster (as Northern Ireland is often called), cover less than 14,245 square km (5,500 square mi). These boundaries contain some of the most unspoiled scenery you could ever hope to find on this earth: the granite Mountains of Mourne; the Giant's Causeway, made of extraordinary volcanic rock; more than 320 km (200 mi) of coastline beaches and hidden coves; and rivers and leaf-sheltered lakes, including Europe's largest freshwater lake, Lough Neagh, that provide fabled fishing grounds. Ancient castles and Palladian-perfect 18th-century houses are as numerous here as almost anywhere else in Europe, and each has its own tale of heroic feats, dastardly deeds, and lovelorn ghosts. Northern Ireland not only houses this heritage within its native stone, but has also given the world perhaps an even greater legacy: its roster of celebrated descendants. Nearly one in six of the more than 4.5 million Irish who journeyed across the Atlantic in search of fortune in the New World came from Ulster, and of this group (and from their family stock), more than a few left their mark in America: Davy Crockett, President Andrew Jackson, General Ulysses S. Grant, President Woodrow Wilson, General Stonewall Jackson, financier Thomas Mellon, merchant J. Paul Getty, writers Edgar Allan Poe and Mark Twain, and astronaut Neil Armstrong.

Present-day Northern Ireland, a province under the rule of the United Kingdom, includes six of the old Ulster's nine counties and retains its sense of separation, both in the vernacular of the landscape and, some would say, in the character of the people. The hardheaded and industrious Scots-Presbyterians, imported to make Ulster a bulwark against Ireland's Catholicism, have had a profound and ineradicable effect on the place. The north has more factories, neater-looking farms, better roads, and—in its cities—more fine, two-story redbrick houses typical of those found in the republic. For all that, the border between north and south is of little consequence if you're just here to see the country.

On the political front, peace reigns in Northern Ireland today. There are no checkpoints anymore—not security-related ones anyway. As far as border issues go (with the Republic of Ireland to the south), the border is there in name only. No one is stopped or questioned, no passports are checked, and there isn't even a sign announcing you are passing into the republic. Visitors—even ones with English accents—are not hassled in any way, and Americans are more than warmly welcomed. Further progress was made toward peace in the summer of 2005 with the IRA's announcement that they were disbanding, and decommissioning their weapons—a historic move.

Only the direst political commentators predict a return to the dark days of conflict. Instead, the "peace dividend" has led to massive investment in places like Belfast, Derry, and Newry. Every year, Derry gets dolled up for its annual Halloween fancy-dress party and Northern Ireland's vivacious spirit truly takes center stage. Everyone realizes that the more tourists that are welcomed, the further the "normalization" process for these embattled people proceeds. As usual, many visitors arrive to view Belfast's "Peace Walls"—built to keep two warring communities apart—but their painted images have changed and are now less of war and more of hope and history. No longer are the Republican heartlands of the Falls and the loyalist Shankill no-go areas, but are now touted as places to witness firsthand human triumph over adversity. Naysayers may remind you that Belfast is no utopia and there is still a way to go, but just come during Feile an Phobail (the West Belfast Festival held in August) and you'll see just how heartedly the city celebrates Northern Ireland's newfound peace.

EXPLORING NORTHERN IRELAND

The city of Belfast is Northern Ireland's main gateway. A naturally lively, friendly city, Belfast has plenty of distinguished hotels and restaurants, fascinating museums, Victorian architecture, and strong maritime connections. It's testimony to the spirit of Belfast that the long years of sectarian violence have not dimmed its vibrancy. Northern Ireland's second city, Derry, is also looking to the future and has an appealing personality of its own. Rows of beautiful Georgian houses are being restored and museums and crafts shops have opened in the small city center, still enclosed by its medieval walls and one of Europe's best-preserved examples of a fortified town.

Along the shores of Northern Ireland's coasts and lakes, green, gentle slopes descend majestically into hazy, dark-blue water against a background of more slopes, more water, and huge, cloud-scattered skies. The Antrim Coast is among the most scenic in all of Ireland: Dunluce Castle, the Giant's Causeway, and the small towns along the excellent roads traversing the east coast give the traveler a choice of rewarding stops. Enniskillen, in County Fermanagh, is bright and bustling, and the surrounding Lough Erne has magnificent lake views, as well as one of Ireland's famous round towers, on Devenish Island. On the other side of Enniskillen stand Castle Coole and Florence Court, two exquisitely graceful mansions built for members of the 18th-century Anglo-Irish nobility. And many will say you'll never forgive yourself if you don't discover the pretty scenery and slow pace of life that is County Down where the beautiful and dark Mountains of Mourne do indeed—just as the song says—sweep down to the sea.

BELFAST

The city of Belfast was a great Victorian success story, an industrial boom town whose prosperity was built on trade—especially linen and shipbuilding. Famously (or infamously), the *Titanic* was built here, giving Belfast, for a time, the nickname "Titanic Town." The key word here, of course, is *was*—linen is no longer a major industry, and shipbuilding is greatly diminished. For two decades, news about Belfast meant news about the Troubles—until the 1994 cease-fire. Since then, Northern Ireland's capital city has benefited from major hotel investment, gentrified quaysides (or strands), a heralded performing arts center, and strenuous efforts on the part of the tourist board to claim a share of the visitors pouring into the Emerald Isle. Although the 1996 bombing of offices at the Canary Wharf in London disrupted the 1994 peace agreement, cease-fire was officially reestablished on July 20, 1997, and this embattled city began its quest for a newfound identity.

Magnificent Victorian structures still line the streets of the city center, but instead of housing linen mills or cigarette factories, they are home to chic new hotels and fashionable bars. Smart restaurants abound, and the people of Belfast, who for years would not venture out of their districts, appear to be making up for lost time. Each area of the city has changed considerably in the new peaceful era, but perhaps none more than the docklands around the Harland and Wolff shipyards, whose historic and enormous cranes, known to the locals as Samson and Goliath, still dominate the city's skyline. New developments—dubbed Laganside and the Titanic Quarter—are springing up all around the now-deserted shipyards, from luxury hotels to modern office blocks. And in the center of the city, Victoria Square is a gigantic new shopping and residential complex, replete with geodesic dome, floors of glossy shops, and renovated Victorian row houses. In the west of the city, the physical scars of the Troubles are still evident, from the *peace line* that divides Catholic and Protestant West Belfast to the murals on every gable wall. Visitors are discovering that it's safe to venture beyond the city center; indeed, backpackers are becoming a regular sight on the Falls Road, and taxi tours of these once troubled areas are more popular than ever.

Before English and Scottish settlers arrived in the 1600s, Belfast was a tiny village called Béal Feirste ("sandbank ford") belonging to Ulster's ancient O'Neill clan. With the advent of the Plantation period (when settlers arrived in the 1600s), Sir Arthur Chichester, from Devon in southwest England, received the city from the English crown, and his son was made Earl of Donegall. Huguenots fleeing persecution from France settled near here, bringing their valuable linen-work skills. In the 18th century Belfast underwent a phenomenal expansion—its population doubled in size every 10 years, despite an ever present sectarian divide. Although the Anglican gentry despised the Presbyterian artisans—who, in turn, distrusted the native Catholics—Belfast's growth continued at a dizzying speed. Having laid the foundation stone of the city's university in 1845, Queen Victoria returned to Belfast in 1849 (she is recalled in the names of buildings, streets, bars, monu-

Albert Memorial
Clock Tower **9**

Botanic
Gardens **14**

City Hall **4**

Crown Liquor
Saloon **3**

Custom
House **11**

Europa Hotel **1**

Grand Opera
House **2**

Lagan Lookout
Visitor Centre ..**10**

Linen Hall
Library **7**

Queen's
University **13**

St. Anne's
Cathedral **8**

St. Malachy's
Church **5**

Ulster Hall **6**

Ulster
Museum **15**

Union
Theological
College **12**

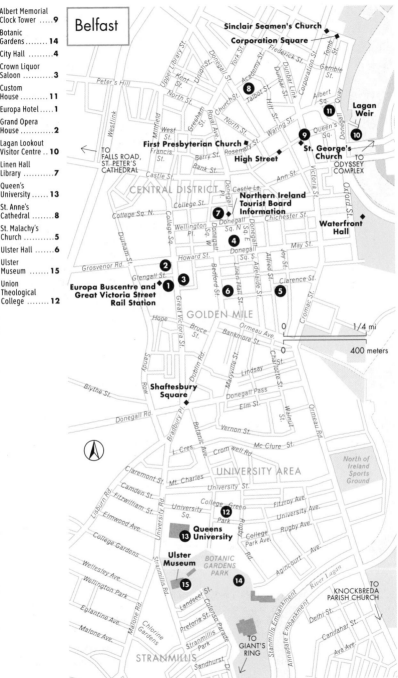

Belfast

NORTHERN IRELAND THROUGH THE AGES

Ireland's ancient history truly began in the north, when settlers came to the banks of the River Bann 9,000 years ago.

Five thousand years later Bronze Age settlers built the great stone circles idiomatic to Counties Down and Tyrone, and later the Iron Age brought the Celts.

St. Patrick, the son of a Roman official who was forced into slavery in County Antrim, returned to spread Christianity in the 5th century.

Starting with the first Norman incursions in the 12th century, however, the English made greater and greater inroads into Ireland, endeavoring to subdue what they believed was a potential enemy.

Ulster proved the hardest to conquer, but in 1607, in the great exodus known as the Flight of the Earls, many of Ulster's beaten-down Irish nobility fled to France and Spain, never to return to their homeland.

Their abandoned lands were distributed by the English to "the Planters"—staunch Protestants from England and Scotland.

After three centuries of smoldering tensions and religious strife, 1916 saw the Easter Uprising and then, in the parliamentary elections of 1918, an overwhelming Nationalist vote across Ireland for Sinn Féin ("Ourselves Alone"), the party that believed in independence for all of Ireland.

In the five northeastern counties of Ulster, however, only seven seats went to the Nationalists, and 22 to the Unionists, whose objective was to remain an integral part of the United Kingdom.

At 2:10 AM on December 6, 1921, in the British prime minister's residence at 10 Downing Street, Michael Collins—the Republican leader and controversial hero—signed the Anglo-Irish Treaty.

This designated a six-county North to remain in British hands in exchange for complete independence, as the Irish Free State, for Ireland's 26 counties.

Fast-forward to 1968, when, in the spirit of student uprisings occurring in Paris and Washington, and after 40 years of living with an apparently permanent and sectarian Unionist majority, students in Belfast's Queen's University launched a civil rights protest, claiming equal rights in jobs, housing, and opportunity.

The brutality with which these marches were suppressed, triggering riots and counter-riots, led to worldwide revulsion.

The Irish Republican Army (IRA), which had been dormant for decades, took over what was left of the shattered civil rights movement, which once had a smattering of Protestant students among its ranks.

Armed British troops, who had at first been welcomed in the Catholic ghettos as protectors from Protestant paramilitaries, now found themselves shunned by both sides. Britain imposed Direct Rule.

January 30, 1972, came to be known as Bloody Sunday, when British paratroopers opened fire on people participating in a nonviolent protest in Derry against the British policy of internment without trial.

When the smoke cleared, 13 people, all Catholic and unarmed, had been killed. Many rallied in support of the victims, who were accused by the British Army of handling weapons.

In an event known as the Bloody Sunday Justice Campaign, the supporters attained some success when the British government finally admitted the victims were "innocent."

Derry is filled with murals and memorials that serve as constant reminders of the struggle for justice, including one monument carved with the inscription, "Their epitaph is the continuing struggle for democracy."

Decades of guerrilla conflict ensued between the IRA, the UDA/UVF (Protestant/Loyalist paramilitaries), and the British government and continued in a mix of lulls and terrors—apart from the IRA's annual Christmas "truce"—until the summer of 1994, when the "Provos," as they are colloquially known, called for an ongoing cease-fire, confirmed in July 1997.

After two years of intensive and complex talks, an agreement was finally reached between Northern Ireland's political parties in April 1998.

The Good Friday Agreement (so called because it was secured on the Friday before Easter Sunday), also known as the Belfast Agreement, gave the province limited powers and its own parliament.

Put to the people of both the north and south of Ireland in separate referenda, it was endorsed by an overwhelming majority and elections to the parliament were held in June 1998.

But a mere two months later, the province's fragile peace was shattered when a massive car bomb exploded in the quiet market town of Omagh, County Tyrone.

On August 15, dissident Republicans—a minority within the movement who were, and still are, opposed to the Good Friday Agreement—succeeded in killing 31 people, including unborn twins. It was the single worst atrocity in the history of the Troubles.

Despite this appalling act, the peace process continued and Unionists eventually entered government proceedings with Sinn Féin at the end of 1999.

Since then, the assembly—the first democratically elected in the history of Northern Ireland—has been suspended three times.

Political parties are divided into pro-agreement and anti-agreement camps and when fresh elections to the assembly were held in November 2003, it was the anti-agreement Democratic Unionist Party that profited.

Despite these numerous setbacks, Northern Ireland is today enjoying the longest period of peace and stability in its history.

In September 2005, the IRA decommissioned all of its weapons. After the St. Andrews Agreement of October 2006, and the subsequent March 2007 elections, the Democractic Unionist Party and Sinn Fein joined forces to form a government in May 2007. The same year, the British Army withdrew their patrols for the first time in 38 years.

9

A GOOD WALK: VICTORIAN BELFAST

Most of Belfast's landmarks were built during the reign of Queen Victoria. Three decades ago, many of them were considered unappealing—"Victorian Grisly" was the epithet used by more than one critic—but today they are marvelous remnants of an age that considered show, pomp, and circumstance paramount.

Fire up your time machine by starting out in the heart of the city and the focal point of the downtown area: huge Donegall Square, still dominated by the columned and domed ❹City Hall, built between 1898 and 1906.

Fashioned of Portland stone and modeled after London's St. Paul's Cathedral, the structure is topped by a 173-foot-high dome. Edwardian-style stained glass, ornate plasterwork, and a mural by Belfast artist John Luke gleam forth from all corners of the three main reception rooms.

Facing City Hall is the ❼Linen Hall Library, which reposes in an old linen warehouse designed in a noble Late Victorian–Early Edwardian way. Scholars love its Robert Burns collection, journalists its vast repository of documents on The Troubles.

Head up Wellington Place to Great Victoria Street. Here on the strip known as "the Golden Mile" you'll see the ❷Grand Opera House, housed in a wonderful Victorian gingerbread building built in 1894 with plenty of fanciful turrets and curlicues.

The interior (guided tours offered) is a red-and-gilt extravaganza of brass rails, gilded balconies, stucco elephants, and exotic motifs.

Just across the street is that Victorian showstopper: the ❸Crown Liquor Saloon, now owned by the National Trust and entirely lighted by gas lamps. The place positively oozes history, with carved wood, stained glass, and the Distiller's Mirror.

Stroll down Howard Street and make a right turn on Bedford one block to ❻Ulster Hall, another 19th-century theater. Its Mulholland organ is a Victorian monument as is the 1903 painted ceiling; the theater interior can be viewed during the day.

Two blocks to the west is Alfred Street, presided over by ❺St. Malachy's Church, a 19th-century edifice with a famed fan-work ceiling inspired by that of Westminster Abbey.

Head north to Victoria Street and continue six or so blocks until reaching the ❾Albert Memorial Clock Tower, Belfast's very own leaning tower, named for Queen Victoria's beloved consort.

The reason for the lean is that it was originally built on what was one of the banks of the Farset River (happily, the clock is now stabilized).

Walk one block north to Waring Street, then up Hill Street, and left on Talbot to Lower Donegall Street to find ❽St. Anne's Cathedral, a Victorian-era essay in Irish Romanesque.

You're now smack-dab in the Cathedral Quarter, dominated with small art galleries and interesting bars, so head off to the John Hewitt pub on Donegall—named after the poet, it's a place where the world is often put to rights.

ments, and other places around the city), and in the same year, the university opened under the name Queen's College. Nearly 40 years later, in 1888, Victoria granted Belfast its city charter. Today its population is nearly 300,000—one-quarter of Northern Ireland's citizens.

Belfast is a fairly compact city, 167 km (104 mi) north of Dublin. The city center is made up of three roughly contiguous areas that are easy to navigate on foot; from the south end to the north it is about an hour's leisurely walk.

GOLDEN MILE

This arrowhead-shape area extending from Howard Street in the north to Shaftesbury Square at the southern tip, and bordered on the west by Great Victoria Street and on the east by Bedford Street and Dublin Road, is a great area from which to begin an exploration of Belfast. Although it doesn't glow quite the way the name suggests, bustling Golden Mile and its immediate environs harbor some of Belfast's most noteworthy historic buildings. In addition, the area is filled with hotels and major civic and office buildings, as well as some restaurants, cafés, and shops. Even if you don't end up staying here, you're likely to pass through it often.

WHAT TO SEE

④ City Hall. Massive, exuberant, Renaissance Revival City Hall domi-
★ nates Donegall Square. Built between 1898 and 1906 and modeled on St. Paul's Cathedral in London, it was designed by Brumwell Thomas, who was knighted but had to sue to get his fee. It was from a specially built platform on its front steps that American President Bill Clinton made an emotional address to the people during his historic 1995 visit. Before you enter, take a stroll around Donegall Square, to see statues of Queen Victoria; a monument commemorating the *Titanic*, which was built in Belfast; and a column honoring the U.S. Expeditionary Force, which landed in the city on January 26, 1942—the first contingent of the U.S. Army to land in Europe during World War II. Enter under the porte cochere at the front of the building. From the entrance hall (the base of which is a whispering gallery), the view up to the heights of the 173-foot-high Great Dome is a feast for the eyes. With its complicated series of arches and openings, stained-glass windows, Italian-marble inlays, decorative plasterwork, and paintings, this is Belfast's most ornate public space—homage to the might of the British Empire. The guided tour gives access to the Council Chamber, Great Hall, and Reception Room, all upstairs. Your guide should have plenty of juicy stories to tell about past events in the Chamber, once dubbed the "bear pit," as Unionist and Nationalist elected councillors verbally battled it out while civil unrest raged in the streets. ⊠*Donegall Sq., Central District* ☎*028/9032–0202* ⊕*www.belfast-city.gov.uk* ☒*Free* ⊗*Mon.–Thurs. 9–5, Fri. 9–4.30; guided tours June–Sept., weekdays at 11, 2, and 3, Sat. at 2:30; Oct.–May, weekdays at 11 and 2:30, Sat. at 2:30.*

9

❸ **Crown Liquor Saloon.** Opposite the Europa Hotel on Great Victoria Street

Fodor's Choice and now owned by the National Trust (the United Kingdom's official
★ conservation organization), the Crown is one of Belfast's glories. Built
in 1894, the bar has richly carved woodwork around cozy snugs (cubicles), leather seats, color tile work, and an abundance of mirrors. It
has been immaculately preserved—it is still lighted by gas—apart from
some of the stained-glass windows that were blown out by an IRA
bomb after having survived almost a century. They claim to serve the
perfect pint of Guinness—so no need to ask what anyone's drinking—
and a great plateful of oysters. When you settle down in your snug,
note the little gunmetal plates used by the Victorians for lighting their
matches. ⊠ *46 Great Victoria St., Golden Mile* ☎ *028/9027–9901*
⊙ *Mon.–Sat. 11:30 AM–midnight, Sun. 11:30–10.*

❶ **Europa Hotel.** A landmark in Belfast, the Europa is a monument to the
resilience of the city in the face of the Troubles. The most bombed hotel
in western Europe, it was targeted 11 times by the IRA starting in the
early 1970s and was refurbished every time; today it shows no signs
of its explosive history. Indeed, even with this track record, President
Bill Clinton and his wife Hillary chose the hotel for an overnight visit
during their 1995 visit—for 24 hours the phones were answered with
"White House Belfast, can I help you?" The president's room is now
called the Clinton Suite and contains memorabilia from the presidential stay. The Europa is owned by affable Ulster millionaire and hotel
magnate Billy Hastings. ⊠ *Great Victoria St. at Glengall St., Golden
Mile* ☎ *028/9027–1066* ⊕ *www.hastingshotels.com.*

❷ **Grand Opera House.** The Grand Opera House exemplifies the Victori-
★ ans' fascination with ornamentation, opulent gilt moldings, and intricate
plasterwork. The renowned theater architect Frank Matcham beautifully designed the building in 1894. In the past five years, the theater has
undergone a massive extension program that has almost doubled its size,
thanks to a brand new foyer bar, café, and party room. Contemporary
Irish artist Cherith McKinstry's exquisite angel-and-cherub–laden fresco
floats over the auditorium ceiling. You can take a tour of the opera
house, but by far the best way to see and enjoy the place is to attend a
show. The theater regularly hosts musicals, operas, plays, and concerts.
⊠ *Great Victoria St., Central District* ☎ *028/9024–1919* ⊕ *www.goh.
co.uk* ⊠ *£5* ⊙ *Tours Sat., hrs vary, so phone ahead.*

❺ **St. Malachy's Church.** Just inside the doors to St. Malachy's Cathedral
is a memorial to its chief benefactor, Captain Thomas Griffiths. The
church, designed by Thomas Jackson, was built in 1844, and its interior is well worth a viewing. Pay particular attention to its fan-vaulted
ceiling. Although many of the original fixtures and fittings have suc-
cumbed to the ravages of time, this swirling masterpiece of plasterwork
survives intact. Inspiration for the design was taken from the chapel
of Henry VII at Westminster Abbey in London. Note the 150-year-old
church organ. ⊠ *Alfred St., Golden Mile* ☎ *028/9032–1713* ⊠ *Free.*

❻ **Ulster Hall.** The home of the Ulster Orchestra, and host to occasional
rock concerts (one of the most famous was marked by Led Zeppelin's

stage debut of the song "Stairway to Heaven" in March 1971), Ulster Hall was built as a ballroom in 1862. The hall was the venue for the political rallying of Nationalist politicians, among them Charles Stewart Parnell (1846–91) and Patrick Henry Pearse (1879–1916), before the Irish Republic was formed in 1921. There's also a splendid Mulholland Organ, a Victorian instrument of considerable size. The facility closed for a major refurbishment in spring 2007, and as of this writing, it was not certain when it would reopen, so call ahead. When the Ulster Hall is open, there's no charge for looking around when shows are not going on. ⊠ *Bedford St., Golden Mile* ☎ *028/9032–3900* ⊕ *www. ulsterhall.co.uk.*

CENTRAL DISTRICT

Belfast's Central District, immediately north of the Golden Mile, extends from Donegall Square north to St. Anne's Cathedral. It's not geographically the center of the city, but it's the old heart of Belfast. Shoppers note: it also has the highest concentration of retail outlets in town. It's a frenetic place—the equivalent of Dublin's Grafton and Henry streets in one—where both locals and visitors shop. Cafés, pubs, offices, and stores of all kinds, from department stores to the Gap and Waterstone's (there's even a Disney store), occupy the redbrick and white-Portland-stone and modern buildings that line its narrow streets. Many of the streets are pedestrian-only, so it's a good place to take a leisurely stroll, browse, and see some sights to boot. It's easy to get waylaid shopping and investigating sights along the river when taking this walk, so give yourself at least two hours to cover the area comfortably.

WHAT TO SEE

❾ Albert Memorial Clock Tower. Tilting a little to one side, not unlike Pisa's more notorious leaning landmark, is the clock tower that was named for Queen Victoria's husband, Prince Albert. The once-dilapidated square on which it stands has undergone a face-lift and a recent restoration has brought the clock itself back to its original glory. The tower itself is not open to the public. ⊠ *Victoria Sq., Central District.*

⓫ Custom House. The 19th-century architect Charles Lanyon designed the Custom House. This building, along with many others in Belfast, including the main building of Queen's University and the unusual Sinclair Seaman's Church, bear the hallmarks of his skill. It's not open to the public, but it's worth circling the house to view the lofty pediment of Britannia, Mercury, and Neptune on the front, carved by acclaimed stonemason Thomas Fitzpatrick. Custom House Square has recently been refurbished for use for open-air concerts and performances during the autumn festival season. ⊠ *Donegall Quay, Central District.*

★ High Street. Off High Street, especially down to Ann Street (parallel to the south), run narrow lanes and alleyways called entries. Though mostly cleaned up and turned into chic shopping lanes, they still hang on to something of their raffish character, and have distinctive pubs with little-altered Victorian interiors. Among the most notable are the Morning Star (Pottinger's Entry off High Street), with its large windows

Churches Around the City

Belfast has so many churches you could visit a different one nearly every day of the year and still not make it to all of them.

The oldest house of worship is the Church of Ireland **Knockbreda Parish Church** (✉ Church Rd. off A24, Belfast ☎ 028/9064–5372). This dark structure was built in 1737 by Richard Cassels, who designed many of Ireland's finest mansions. It quickly became *the* place to be buried—witness the vast 18th-century tombs in the churchyard.

The **First Presbyterian Church** (✉ Rosemary St., Central District, Belfast) dates from 1783 and has an interesting elliptical interior. It also hosts lunchtime concerts.

The Church of Ireland's **St. George's** (✉ High St., Central District, Belfast ☎ 028/9023–1275), built in 1816, has a tremendous Georgian portico and pretty box pews.

By the riverfront is one of the most appealing churches, Presbyterian **Sinclair Seamen's Church** (✉ Corporation Sq. off Donegall Quay, Central District, Belfast ☎ 028/9071–5997). Designed by Charles Lanyon, the architect of Queen's University, it has served the seafaring community since 1857. The pulpit is shaped like a ship's prow; the bell is from HMS *Hood*, sunk in 1916; and even the collection plates are shaped like lifeboats.

The elegant neo-Gothic "twin spires" of **St. Peter's Cathedral** (✉ St. Peters Sq., Belfast ☎ 028/9032–7573), dominates the skyline of West Belfast. Finding this Roman Catholic cathedral is difficult, but worth the effort. Built in 1866, when the Catholic population was rapidly increasing, St. Peter's acted as a focal point for the community.

and fine curving bar; White's Tavern (entry off High Street), Belfast's oldest pub, founded in 1630, which, although considerably updated, is still warm and comfortable, with plush seats and a big, open fire; Magennis's Whiskey Café (on May Street), in splendid counterpoint to the Waterfront Hall's space-age style; and McHugh's (in Queen's Square), in what is reckoned to be the city's oldest extant building, dating from 1710.

Lagan Boat Company. Take a guided 75-minute river tour that departs from the dock by the Lagan Lookout Visitor Centre and travels down to Stranmillis and back, with running commentary on the colorful history of the city. A one-hour Titanic tour takes in the shipyard where the famous liner was built as well as harbor sights related to the ship. The Lagan Boat tours are offered Tuesday through Thursday, March through October, and the Titanic tours are offered Friday through Monday, March through October, and then weekends November and December. ✉ 48 St. John's Close, at Laganbank Rd., Central District ☎ 028/9033–0844 ⊕ www.laganboatcompany.com ✆ Tours £8.

⑩ Lagan Lookout Visitor Centre. At the edge of Lagan Weir, the center delves into the history of the River Lagan and the weir by means of interactive exhibits. It's a good way for children to learn about the river's history and surroundings. At night, the exterior of the building is flooded with blue light, adding to the feel that the riverside developments in Belfast have been inspired by the Southbank in London. The famous shipyard cranes, Samson and Goliath, are visible beyond. ✉*Lagan Weir, Donegall Quay, Central District* ☎*028/9031–5444* ⊕*www. laganside.com* ✆*£2* ⊙*Apr.–Sept., weekdays 11–5, Sat. noon–5, Sun. 2–5; Oct.–Mar., Tues.–Fri. 11–3:30, Sat. 1–4:30, Sun. 2–4:30.*

> **TUNNEL OF TREASURES**
>
> The emergence of public commissioned art along the River Lagan has prompted the Lagan Lookout Visitor Centre to run special "art trails," lasting from one hour to two-and-a-half hours. Times vary and details are available on the Web site. During the Cathedral Quarter Arts Festival in late April and May, exhibitions take place in the Lagan Weir tunnel, which is transformed into a unique gallery.

❼ Linen Hall Library. This gray building on Donegall Square's northwest corner is in fact a comfortable private library, founded in 1788 and designed by Charles Lanyon. The library has an unparalleled collection of 80,000 documents relating to the Troubles. One early librarian, Thomas Russell, was hanged in 1803 for supporting an Irish uprising. On the walls are paintings and prints depicting Belfast views and landmarks. Much of this artwork is for sale. It's an ideal hideaway for relaxing with a newspaper and enjoying the library's café. ✉*17 Donegall Sq. N, Central District* ☎*028/9032–1707* ⊕*www.linenhall.com* ✆*Free* ⊙*Weekdays 9:30–5:30, Sat. 9:30–1.*

❽ St. Anne's Cathedral. A somber heaviness—a hallmark of the Irish neo-Romanesque style—marks this large edifice, which is basilican in plan and was built at the turn of the 20th century. Lord Carson (1854–1935), who was largely responsible for keeping the six counties inside the United Kingdom, is buried here beneath a suitably austere gray slab. New landscaping around the Anglican cathedral provides a perch to rest your feet in good weather. The guides on duty show you around for no charge. ✉*Donegall St., Central District* ☎*028/9032–8332* ⊕*www.belfastcathedral.com* ✆*Free* ⊙*Daily 10–4.*

NEED A BREAK?
At the start of Royal Avenue, turn left onto Bank Street to find Kelly's Cellars (✉*30–32 Bank St., Central District* ☎*028/9024–6058*), a circa-1720 pub with loads of character. Try the two specialties: Ulster fry or champ and sausages. Two centuries ago, Kelly's Cellars was the regular meeting place of a militant Nationalist group, the Society of United Irishmen, whose leader, Wolfe Tone (who was a Protestant), is remembered as the founder of Irish Republicanism. Traditional music and plenty of local banter make the pub particularly lively on weekends.

☾ W5: Whowhatwherewhywhen. Part of the Odyssey complex in Belfast's docks, this science discovery center takes a high-tech, hands-on approach to interpreting science, engineering, and technology for adults and children. Video displays and flashing lights provide a modern feel, and you can do everything from explore the weather to build bridges

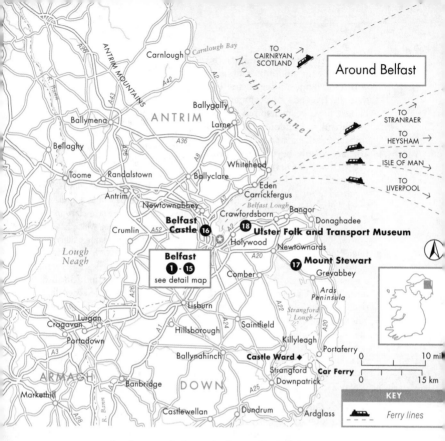

and robots. ⊠ *2 Queen's Quay, Central District* ☎ *028/9046–7700*
⊕ *www.w5online.co.uk* ⊡ *£6* ⊗ *Mon.–Sat. 10–6, Sun. noon–6; last
admission at 5.*

UNIVERSITY AREA

At Belfast's southern end, the part of the city around Queen's University is dotted with parks, botanical gardens, and leafy streets with fine, intact, two- and three-story 19th-century buildings. The area evokes an older, more leisurely pace of life. The many pubs and excellent restaurants make this area the hub of the city's nightlife. However, remember that Belfast is a student town and this is the main university area—the pace of life here can be fast (and sometimes a little furious) during school-term weekends.

WHAT TO SEE

⓮ Botanic Gardens. In the Victorian heyday, it was not unusual to find
★ 10,000 of Belfast's citizens strolling about here on a Saturday afternoon. These gardens are a glorious haven of grass, trees, flowers, curving walks, and wrought-iron benches, all laid out in 1827 on land that slopes down to the River Lagan. The curved-iron and glass Palm House is a conservatory marvel designed in 1839 by Charles Lanyon. The

Tropical Ravine House, though not architecturally distinguished, has an outstanding collection of tropical flora, in addition to some indigenous plants (it was famously said that it once held more Killarney ferns than could be found in Killarney itself). Once known as "the Glen," the Ravine House is unusually and exotically built over a faux-ravine that you walk around. ⊠ *Stranmillis Rd., University Area* ☎ *028/9032–4902* ⊠ *Free* ⊙ *Gardens daily dawn–dusk; Palm House and Tropical Ravine House Apr.–Aug., weekdays 10–5, weekends 1–5; Sept.–Mar., weekdays 10–4, weekends 2–4.*

⑬ **Queen's University.** Dominating University Road is Queen's University. The main buildings, modeled on Oxford's Magdalen College and designed by the ubiquitous Charles Lanyon, were built in 1849 in the Tudor Revival style. The long, handsome redbrick-and-sandstone facade of the main building features large lead-glass windows, and is topped with three square towers and crenellations galore. University Square, really a terrace, is from the same era. The Seamus Heaney Library is named after the Ulster-born 1997 Nobel Prize–winning poet. The Queen's Visitors Centre hosts a regular program of exhibitions and serves as an information point for visitors and tourists, as well as offering a varied selection of souvenirs and gifts. Guided tours can be arranged by prior reservation. ⊠ *University Rd., University Area* ☎ *028/9033–5252* ⊕ *www.qub.ac.uk* ⊙ *Visitor Center, May–Sept., Mon.–Sat. 10–4; Oct.–Apr., weekdays 10–4.*

Stranmillis. Once its own village, Stranmillis is now an off-campus quarter—an appealing neighborhood with tree-lined residential streets and a wide choice of ethnic eateries. You can get here via Stranmillis Road (near the Ulster Museum). The "Little Paris" stretch of shops and cafés extends down to the riverside towpath along the Lagan. Malone Road joins the river farther south, close to the out-of-town Giant's Ring (off Ballyleeson Road), a large, Neolithic earthwork focused on a dolmen. To get this far, unless you're a vigorous walker (it's possible to come all the way on the Lagan towpath), you may be happier driving or taking a bus. Ulsterbus 13 passes close to the site, and on the return journey it will take you back to Donegall Square.

⑮ **Ulster Museum.** Set in a grandly impressive marble edifice at the southwest corner of the Botanic Gardens, the Ulster Museum is currently undergoing a major renovation and will probably be shuttered until 2009. The museum's forte is the history and prehistory of Ireland, in particular Northern Ireland, with exhibitions colorfully tracing the rise of Belfast's crafts, trade, and industry; the Nationalist movement; a large natural history section, with its famed skeleton of the extinct Irish giant deer; a trove of jewelry and gold ornaments—as well as a cannon and other armaments—recovered from the Spanish Armada vessel *Girona* and two sister galleons sunk off the Antrim coast in 1588; and a considerable collection of 19th- and 20th-century art. ⊠ *Stranmillis Rd., University Area* ☎ *028/9038–3000* ⊕ *www.ulstermuseum.org.uk* ⊙ *Closed for renovations fall 2006–09.*

⓬ Union Theological College. Like Queen's University on the opposite side of the street, the Union Theological College, with its colonnaded, Doric facade, owes the charm of its appearance to architect Charles Lanyon. The building's other claim to fame is that, before the completion of the parliament buildings at Stormont, Northern Ireland's House of Commons was convened in its library, and the college's chapel played host to the Senate. The college completed a major renovation in 2007 and is once again offering tours to visitors. ⊠ *108 Botanic Ave., University Area* ☎ *028/9020–5080* ⊕ *www.union.ac.uk* ☒ *Free.*

BELFAST ENVIRONS

The four sights below are closer to Belfast than to other areas covered in this chapter. However, none of the sights along the Ards Peninsula and the north coast are more than a few hours' drive from Belfast—perfect for day trips.

WHAT TO SEE

⓰ Belfast Castle. In 1934 this spectacularly baronial castle, built for the
★ Marquis of Donegall in 1865, was passed to Belfast Corporation. Although the castle functions primarily as a restaurant, it also houses the Cave Hill Heritage Centre, which provides information about the castle's history and its natural surroundings in Cave Hill Country Park. Guided tours (by reservation) of the reception rooms built by the Earls of Shaftesbury are sometimes offered on weekends in May and June. The best reason to visit is to take a stroll in the lovely ornamental gardens and then make the ascent to McArt's Fort. This promontory, at the top of sheer cliffs 1,200 feet above the city, affords an excellent view across Belfast. Take the path uphill from the parking lot, turn right at the next intersection of pathways, and then keep left as you journey up the sometimes steep hill to the fort. ⊠ *4 km (2½ mi) north of Belfast on Antrim Rd.* ☎ *028/9077–6925* ⊕ *www.belfastcastle.co.uk/* ☒ *Free* ⊙ *Visitor center daily 9–6.*

☺ Belfast Zoo. Great strides have been taken to make this place a more friendly and less repressive environment for the animals. But note that it's on the steep side of Cave Hill and getting around the zoo involves a strenuous uphill walk for even the most energetic (not ideal for anyone with mobility problems)—a stroller would be advisable for small children. The zoo is noted for its children's farm and underwater views of the resident penguins and sea lions. It's near Belfast Castle—just hop on a pink metrobus (Numbers 1A, 1B, 1C, or 1D) at Donegall Square West, by City Hall. ⊠ *Antrim Rd.* ☎ *028/9077–6277* ⊕ *www.belfastzoo.co.uk* ☒ *£7.80* ⊙ *Apr.–Sept., daily 10–5; Oct.–Mar., daily 10–2:30.*

⓱ Mount Stewart. The grandest stately house near Belfast, this was the
★ country estate of the Marquesses of Londonderry, whose fame, or infamy, became known around the world thanks to the historical role played by the 2nd Marquess. Known as Castlereagh, this Secretary of Ireland put down the Rising of 1798, helped forge the Act of Union, and killed himself by cutting his own throat. Mount Stewart was con-

Belfast's Wall Murals

In Northern Ireland they say the Protestants make the money and the Catholics make the art, and as with all clichés, there is some truth in it. It's a truth that will become clear as you look up at the gable walls of blue-collar areas of Belfast on which the two communities—Catholic and Protestant—have expressed themselves in colorful murals that have given rise to one of the more quirky tours of the city.

Although the wildly romantic Catholic murals often aspire to the levels of Sistine Chapel–lite, those in Protestant areas (like the tough, no-nonsense Shankill and the Newtownards Road) are more workmanlike efforts that sometimes resemble war comics without the humor. It was not always this way.

In Protestant areas, murals were once painted by skilled coachbuilders to mark the July 12 celebrations of the defeat of the Catholic King James by King William at the Battle of the Boyne. As such, they typically depicted William resplendent in freshly laundered scarlet tunic and plumed cap, sitting on a white stallion that has mastered the art of walking on water. On the banks of the Boyne sits a mildly disheveled James, the expression on his face making him look as if he has just eaten an overdose of anchovies. Other popular themes in Protestant areas are the Red Hand of Ulster, symbolizing the founding of the province, and, on Carnmore Street, the 13 Protestant apprentice boys shutting the gates of Derry against King James in 1688, leading to the famous siege.

More recently, though, Protestant murals have taken on a grimmer air, and typical subjects include walleyed paramilitaries perpetually standing firm against increasing liberalism, nationalism, and all the other isms that Protestants see eroding their stern, Bible-driven way of life. Nationalist murals, on the other hand, first sprang up in areas like the Falls Road in 1981, when IRA inmates of the Maze prison began a hunger strike in an unsuccessful bid to be recognized by the British government as political prisoners rather than common criminals. Ten died, and the face of the most famous, Bobby Sands, looks down now from a gable wall on the Falls Road alongside the words: "Our revenge will be the laughter of our children."

Since then, themes of freedom from oppression and a rising Nationalist confidence have expressed themselves in murals that romantically and surreally mix and match images from the *Book of Kells,* the Celtic Mist mock-heroic posters of Irish artist Jim Fitzpatrick, assorted phoenixes rising from ashes, and revolutionaries clad in splendidly idiosyncratic sombreros and bandannas from ideological battle-grounds in Mexico and South America. Irish words and phrases that you will see springing up regularly include the much-used slogan "Tiocfaidh ár lá" (pronounced *chuck*y ohr *law* and meaning "Our day will come") and the simple cry "Saoirse" (pronounced *seer*-she), meaning "Freedom."

The murals in both Protestant and Catholic areas are safe to view in daylight and outside the sensitive week of the July 12 marches by Protestant Orangemen. However, the most sensible way to view them would be to take a guided tour with Citybus.

9

structed in two stages where an earlier house had stood: George Dance designed the west facade (1804–05), and William Vitruvius Morrison designed the Neoclassical main part of the building (1845–49), complete with awe-inspiring Grecian portico facade. The 7th Marchioness, Edith, managed to wave her wand over the interior—after a fashion: Chinese vases, Louis-Philippe tables, and Spanish oak chairs do their worst to clutter up the rooms here. Still, the house does have some noted 18th-century interiors, including the Central Hall and the grand staircase hung with one of George Stubbs's most famous portraits, that of the celebrated racehorse Hambletonian, after he won one of

> ## THE GREENING OF BELFAST
>
> It was due to Edith, the 7th Marchioness of Londonderry, that Mount Stewart was transformed into a garden showplace in the 1920s. Taking advantage of the salubrious microclimate of the Ards Peninsula, she created, in short order, a Shamrock Garden, Dodo Garden (note the stone figures that honor her close circle of friends—the "Warlock" is Winston Churchill), and Lady Mairi's Garden, complete with a "Mary, Mary, Quite Contrary" statue surrounded with silverbells and cockleshells.

the most prominent contests of the 18th century—this is perhaps the greatest in situ setting for a painting in Ireland. On the grounds, don't miss the octagonal Temple of the Winds—a copy of a similar structure in Athens—and there's a remarkable bathhouse and pool at the end of the wooded peninsula just before the entrance to the grounds. Opening times often change here—it's prudent to phone ahead or log on to the Web site for the complete schedule. ⊠*Portaferry Rd., Newtownards* ☏*028/4278–8387* ⊕*www.nationaltrust.org.uk* ☏*£6.50* ⊙*Gardens Apr. and Oct., daily 10–6; May–Sept., daily 10–8; Nov.–Mar., daily 10–4; house by guided tour Mar.–June and Oct., weekends noon–6; July and Aug., daily noon–6; Sept., Wed.–Mon. noon–6.*

NEED A BREAK?　Reputed to be the oldest pub in Ireland, Grace Neill's (⊠*33 High St., 22 km [13 mi] from Mount Stewart, Donaghadee* ☏*028/9188–4595*) served its first pint in 1611 and has hosted such luminaries as Peter the Great, Franz Liszt, and John Keats. Behind the original pub, a cubby under the stairs with bar stools, is a larger bar where you can try a simple peppered beef sandwich with a pint of Guinness. Saturday sees jazz, and on Sunday afternoons, there's other music.

⑱ **Ulster Folk and Transport Museum.** Devoted to the province's social history, the excellent Ulster Folk and Transport Museum vividly brings Northern Ireland's past to life. First, the Folk Museum invites you to visit Ballycultra—a typical Ulster town of the early 1900s—which comes alive thanks to costumed guides who practice such regional skills as lace making, sampler-making, spinning, weaving, wood turning, forgework, printing, open-hearth cooking, carpentry, basket making, and needlework. The setting is evocative: a score of reconstructed buildings moved here from around the region, including a traditional

Fodor's Choice
★

weaver's dwelling, terraces of Victorian town houses, an 18th-century country church, a village flax mill, a farmhouse, and a rural school. Across the main road (by footbridge) is the beautifully designed Transport Museum, where exhibits include locally built airplanes and motorcycles; the iconoclastic car produced by former General Motors whiz kid John De Lorean in his Belfast factory in 1982; and a moving section on the *Titanic,* the Belfast-built luxury liner that sank on her first voyage, in 1912, killing 1,500 of the passengers and crew. A miniature railway runs on Saturday in July and August. The museum is on the 70 acres of Cultra Manor, encircled by a larger park and recreation area. ⊠*163 Bangor Rd., 16 km (10 mi) northeast of Belfast on A2, Cultra* ☎*028/9042–8428* ⊕*www.uftm.org.uk* ☏*£7* ⊗*Mar.–June, weekdays 10–5, Sat. 10–6, Sun. 11–6; July–Sept., Mon.–Sat. 10–6, Sun. 11–6; Oct.–Feb., weekdays 10–4, Sat. 10–5, Sun. 11–5.*

WHERE TO EAT

$$$$ ✕**The Great Room.** Inside the swank and lavish Merchant Hotel, beneath the grand dome of this former bank's great hall, you'll find the perfect setting for a memorable dinner of adventurous European fare. Exceptional offerings from the kitchen include suckling pig and sautéed langoustines with baby bok choy and ginger dressing, and duck–and–foie gras terrine with sauternes jelly, toasted brioche, and fig puree. Apple crumble with lavender ice cream is a fair sample of what you'll discover on the unusual dessert trolley. First-class service in truly opulent surroundings makes this restaurant worth a detour. ⊠*35 Waring St., Central District* ☎*028/9024–4888* ⊕*www.themerchanthotel.com* ⊟*AE, MC, V.*

$$$–$$$$ ✕**Restaurant Michael Deane.** Armed with a Michelin star, a sharp tongue
Fodor's Choice (usually aimed at rival chefs), and a fabulous way with confit of quail,
★ Michael Deane has become one of Ireland's most buzz-worthy chefs. Journalists like him because of his acerbic sound bites; gourmands love him when they bite into his foie gras and pigeon terrine. In one of Belfast's Victorian districts, this is fine dining at its local best. The setting is lavish, although some carp that all the garden treillage, tartan rugs, marble trim, and upholstered taffeta have seen better days. The centerpiece is the actual kitchen where Belfast's power brokers (who usually opt for the Menu Prestige at £65 for nine courses) see their dishes delivered under the watchful gaze of head chef Derek Creagh. Deane's tastes are eclectic—he has worked in Bangkok, and the influence of Thai cooking is revealed in his especially subtle way with spices. Squab is a specialty, served as a kedgeree with cucumber and quail eggs for a starter. As a main dish, he serves French squab with local rabbit, roast potato, and parsnip with Madeira. Ravioli of lobster, seared scallops and Clonakilty black pudding, or the slow-roast Mount Stewart pheasant are all winners. If you can't fit into this intimately scaled room (only 30 seats, so book early), you can settle for the Brasserie found on the ground floor, where the prices are much gentler and the setting much livelier. ⊠*36–40 Howard St., Golden Mile* ☎*028/9033–1134 restau-*

9

rant, 028/9056–0000 brasserie ⊕*www.michaeldeane.co.uk* ⊟*AE, MC, V* ⊘ *Restaurant closed Sun.–Tues., brasserie closed Sun.*

$$–$$$ ✕**Aldens.** East Belfast was a gastronomic wilderness until this cool mod-
★ ernist restaurant opened with chef Cath Gradwell at the helm. Now
city-center folk regularly make the pilgrimage to take advantage of an
opulent menu and wine list at comparably reasonable prices. The set dinner menus Monday to Thursday are particularly good value—£22 for
three courses. Lunch is an informal affair—traditional pork and leek sausages with mash-and-onion gravy—but dinner tarts up with such tasty
treats as roast poussin with tabbouleh and broad beans or the grilled
quail with wild cranberry compote and baked polenta. With its great
atmosphere, gentle prices, perpetually friendly staff, and fine food, it's
little wonder that Aldens has scooped several top awards in recent years,
including the prestigious Bridgestone accolade. This is a good time-out if
visiting the Parliament buildings at Stormont Castle. ⊠*229 Upper Newtownards Rd., East Belfast* ☎*028/9065–0079* ⊕*www.aldensrestaurant.
com* ⊟*AE, DC, MC, V* ⊘ *Closed Sun. No lunch Sat.*

$$–$$$ ✕**Cayenne.** One of Belfast's most exciting restaurants, Cayenne
★ explodes with culinary fireworks. To wit, the duck and shiitake pot
stickers with sesame ginger sauce or the salt 'n' chili squid with chili
jam and aioli—and let's not forget the hot banana strudel. These
are just a few of the creations of celebrity TV chefs Paul and Jeanne
Rankin. They travel widely and have several other restaurants, but
happily mastermind this Golden Mile spot. The cutting-edge fusion
cuisine, always with that Asian twist, comes up winners with such
other dishes as coconut-crusted cod, breast of duck with wild rice pancakes, and Donegal wild salmon with hazelnut beurre blanc. A favorite
with theatergoers, Cayenne accepts orders until 11:15 on Friday and
Saturday evenings. ⊠*Shaftesbury Sq. at Great Victoria St., Golden
Mile* ☎*028/9033–1532* ⊕*www.rankingroup.co.uk* ⊟*AE, DC, MC,
V* ⊘ *No lunch weekends.*

$–$$$ ✕**Red Panda.** It comes as a surprise to visitors to learn that Belfast
has a large Chinese community, a sizable portion of whom seems
to favor this bustling spot (making reservations always a good way
to go). Both venues—Belfast city center and the one in the Odyssey
Arena complex—are large, spacious, and modern with plenty going
on to tempt the taste buds. A five-course set dinner can include such
delights as crispy aromatic duck pancakes or sizzling king prawns with
ginger. More adventurous diners will want to spring for the stir-fried
squid with Chinese bok choy. ⊠*60 Great Victoria St., Central District*
☎*028/9080–8700* ⊠*Odyssey Arena 2, Queen's Quay* ☎*028/9046–
6644* ⊕*www.theredpanda.co.uk* ⊟*AE, DC, MC, V* ⊘ *No lunch
weekends or dinner Sun.*

$–$$ ✕**Ginger.** Chef–owner Simon McCance's Asian-influenced Irish classics
attract foodies to this tiny gem just off Great Victoria Street. A short
but perfectly balanced menu emphasizes locally sourced seafood and
lean meats. Highlights include the lip-smacking roast hoisin duck salad,
and fresh peppered swordfish in a creamy bacon and mussel sauce. The
wine list is one of the most reasonably priced in Belfast and boasts a
mouthwatering Sancerre, exclusive to Ginger. Next door, Ginger Café

provides lunchtime sustenance for office workers in the form of fresh salads and tasty sandwiches. One drawback is the lack of a no-smoking area, although pipes and cigars are banned. ⊠*7–8 Hope St., Golden Mile* ☎*028/9024–4421* ☐*MC, V* ⊘*Closed Sun. and Mon.*

$–$$ ✕**Nick's Warehouse.** Nick Price has created one of Belfast's most relaxing watering holes in this cool, cozy wine bar with adjacent restaurant. At the busy bar you can get tasty casseroles, and warm salads with a choice of nut oils. In the slightly more formal restaurant, top bets include duck with red cabbage and apple compote, and halibut with langoustine and sweet peppers. Finish off your meal with a sampling of cheeses. The wine and imported beer lists are impressive. Nick's is on a narrow, cobbled street in an increasingly fashionable area. ⊠*35 Hill St., Central District* ☎*028/9043–9690* ⚖*Reservations essential* ☐*AE, MC, V* ⊘*Closed Sun. No lunch Sat. No dinner Mon.*

$–$$ ✕**Raj Put.** You won't leave this Indian restaurant feeling as if you've been kissing a flame-thrower: in even the hottest dishes, nuanced flavors shine through. Aromatic spices, nuts, and herbs mingle in the piquant chicken masala. For side dishes, favorites include a tasty *saag aloo* (spicy potatoes and spinach). Wash it all down with cold Indian lager. You can sit in or take away. ⊠*461 Lisburn Rd., University Area* ☎*028/9066–2168* ☐*AE, MC, V.*

$–$$ ✕**Zen.** Entrepreneur Eddie Fung has miraculously transformed a red-brick 19th-century Belfast mill into an Asian oasis housing the city's finest Japanese restaurant. Upstairs you traverse a 30-foot-long mirrored catwalk with a glass walkway to get to the seating area. Choose between wooden booths, or, if you're prepared to hunker down on the floor, Japanese-style, opt for the traditional dining area. Downstairs, handpick your meal at the sushi bar, or choose a discreet table for two under the serene gaze of (reputedly) Ireland's largest Buddha. Zen has a reputation for authentic fresh sushi and sashimi. Purists may be bemused at the deep-fried prawns but everyone declares them delicious. ⊠*Behind City Hall, 55–59 Adelaide St., Central District* ☎*028/9023–2244* ☐*AE, MC, V* ⊘*No lunch Sat.*

$ ✕**Whitefort Inn.** Situated beside Casment Park—home ground of the Antrim Gaelic Athletic Club—this lively and impressive bar-restaurant is just the place to catch your breath after taking a black-taxi tour of the nearby political murals. It's been described by one local newspaper as looking more like a Las Vegas hotel foyer than a West Belfast bar, but the opulent decor is at least a sign of the sheer level of investment in this area since the peace process. Stop off for a meal in the upstairs Copper One restaurant or just to enjoy a quick "half" in the downstairs bar. ⊠*Andersonstown Rd., West Belfast* ☎*028/9060–2210* ☐*MC, V.*

¢–$ ✕**The Morning Star.** Halfway down a narrow lane is the 19th-century Morning Star, one of the city's most historic pubs, first built as a coaching stop for the Belfast to Dublin post. There's a traditional bar downstairs and a cozy velvet and wood-panel restaurant upstairs. Head chef Seamus McAlister, far from resting on the pub's laurels, is constantly experimenting—he's known for his quirky takes on fresh local ingredients. You might find venison and game in winter, lamb in spring, and grilled haddock with dark rum or roast Antrim pork in summer. Also

9

notable is the steak menu; you'd be hard-pressed to find a larger assortment of aged-beef cuts. Sizzling steaks arrive at the table in red-hot cast-iron skillets and are served with a flourish by the friendly staff. ⊠ *17–19 Pottinger's Entry, Central District* ☎ *028/9023–5986* ▭ *MC, V* ⊘ *Closed Sun.*

¢–$ ✕ **The Northern Whig.** Housed in an elegant former newspaper building, the Northern Whig is spacious and stylish. Three 30-foot-high statues of Soviet heroes that once topped Communist Party headquarters in Prague dominate the wood-and-leather interior. In the evenings, one wall slides away so you can watch classic movies, a jazz band, or a DJ playing laid-back blues, soul, or retro music. The food is brasserie-style—not astonishing, but good. It's the environment, the thoughtful wine list, and the cocktail bar—which specializes in rare vodkas—that are the main draws. ⊠ *2 Bridge St., Central District* ☎ *028/9050–9888* ⊕ *www.thenorthernwhig.com* ▭ *MC, V.*

> **CARBING UP**
>
> When it comes to food, Northern Ireland is most famed (or notorious) for its Ulster Fry, a fried-up, carbohydrate blowout of a breakfast that is a cardiologist's nightmare. Sausage, bacon, eggs, black pudding, fried soda bread, and potato bread (perhaps a grilled tomato or fried mushrooms) all make a meal that sounds as dangerous to your health as bungee jumping without a rope. After a night on the Guinness, however, you'll understand why this breakfast is so popular: it makes a great cure for a hangover.

¢ ✕ **Deane's Deli.** Half take-out deli, half comfort-food eaterie, this is ★ another great addition to the Michael Deane kingdom. Close to historic Ulster Hall, this is an all-day affair and, at that, you'll rarely find an empty seat—try the old-fashioned beer-battered fish-and-chips or one of the ever-changing daily specials. Next door is the gourmet deli, where the shelves groan with homemade cheeses, breads, chocolates, and chutneys, many of them from the local farmers' market. They make great take-away sandwiches. ⊠ *44 Bedford St., Central District* ☎ *028/9024–8800* ▭ *AE, MC, V* ⊘ *Closed Sun.*

¢ ✕ **Long's.** Long's has been serving fish-and-chips in its tiny, completely ★ basic Athol Street premises for more than 85 years. Garbage collectors, millionaires, and every sector in between flocks here for the secret-batter-recipe fish, served with chips, bread, butter, and a mug of tea. ⊠ *39 Athol St., Golden Mile* ☎ *028/9032–1848* ▭ *No credit cards* ⊘ *Closed Sun.*

WHERE TO STAY

CENTRAL DISTRICT

$$$ ▦ **Malmaison.** The renaissance of Belfast's industrial Laganside dis-★ trict was spearheaded in part by the spiffy renovation of the historic former McCausland Hotel. The stunning 19th-century former grain warehouse has been transformed with low lighting, bold black-wood paneling, and velvet drapes, creating a modern Gothic feel. The bar—dubbed "Dracula's living room" by one wag—continues the moody

but luxurious look, with red crushed velvet chairs and dark suede sofas. Oversize purple *Alice in Wonderland*–style furniture adds to the slightly surreal aesthetic. Swish bedrooms contain flat-screen TVs and DVD players, and comfortable beds with Irish linens in muted colors. In the restaurant, helmed by inspired chef Alexander Plumb, specialties include steak hand-chosen from the Duke of Buccleuch's estate in the Scottish Highlands and aged for a minimum of 21 days. Situated on the edge of blossoming Laganside, the hotel is five minutes' walk from the heart of Belfast. ⊠*34–38 Victoria St., Central District, BT1 3GH* ☎*028/9022–0200* ⊟*028/9022–0220* ⊕*www.malmaison.com* ☜*62 rooms, 2 suites* ⌂*In-room: DVD, Wi-Fi. In-hotel: restaurant, bar* ⊟*AE, MC, V.*

$$–$$$ ⊞**Belfast Hilton.** This riverside hotel should be able to cater to your every whim with its excellent business and leisure facilities. Earthy colors and bold stripes decorate the beds and windows. Ask for a suite or room with a view of the river. The restaurant serves contemporary cuisine and it has good views of the river and the city. The hotel is beside Waterfront Hall, in an area undergoing an urban rejuvenation. ⊠*4 Lanyon Pl., Central District, BT1 3LP* ☎*028/9027–7000* ⊟*028/9027–7277* ⊕*www.hilton.co.uk* ☜*181 rooms, 14 suites* ⌂*In-room: refrigerator, dial-up. In-hotel: restaurant, bar, pool, no-smoking rooms* ⊟*AE, DC, MC, V* ⎮⎾⎮*BP.*

GOLDEN MILE

$$$–$$$$ ⊞**TENsq.** You don't get much more downtown or contemporary than
★ this fashionable boutique hotel right behind City Hall. The neoclassical facade of this former post office hides a serene interior that houses a fashionable bar and also the Grill Room, which serves lunch and evening meals. The bedrooms are minimalist-Asian in style—with big, low-lying beds topped with white duvets, soft armchairs to sink into, and fresh flowers brought daily. There's Wi-Fi in all rooms, and a common DVD and CD library. ⊠*10 Donegall Sq. S, Golden Mile, BT1 5JD* ☎*028/9024–1001* ⊟*028/9024–3210* ⊕*www.ten-sq.com* ☜*23 rooms* ⌂*In-room: Wi-Fi. In-hotel: restaurant, bars, concierge, parking (no fee)* ⊟*AE, MC, V* ⎮⎾⎮*BP, MAP.*

$$–$$$ ⊞**Holiday Inn Belfast.** Expect outstanding facilities at a reasonable price. Furnishings are modernist blond wood and leather, and rooms are best described as Japan-meets-Sweden: they have strong, simple colors and sliding wooden screens (a lovely touch) instead of curtains. The hotel is superbly located, only a 10-minute walk to the city center and five minutes to the Golden Mile. ⊠*22 Ormeau Ave., Golden Mile BT2 8HS* ☎*870/0400–9005* ⊟*028/9062–6546* ⊕*www.holiday-inn.co.uk* ☜*170 rooms* ⌂*In-room: no a/c, Wi-Fi. In-hotel: restaurant, bar, pool, gym* ⊟*AE, DC, MC, V* ⎮⎾⎮*BP, MAP.*

$–$$ ⊞**Jurys Inn Belfast.** The first Jurys north of the border brings the chain's flat-rate formula—a single price for up to three adults or two adults and two children—to the Golden Mile. Once you get past the forbidding warehouselike exterior, a spacious, marble-tile foyer with warm green and salmon hues awaits. Room decor is pretty standard. Some rooms overlook College Square, the cricket lawn of the 1814 Royal Belfast Academical Institution. The Arches restaurant serves well-prepared hotel food. Tartan fabrics and dark wood decorate the Inn Pub, which serves pub grub all day. ⊠*Fisherwick Pl. at Great Victoria St., Golden Mile, BT2 7AP* ☎*028/9053–3500* 📠*028/9053–3511* ⊕*www. jurysdoyle.com* ⤶*190 rooms* ♿*In-room: no a/c, Wi-Fi. In-hotel: restaurant, bar, no-smoking rooms* ⊟*AE, DC, MC, V* ⦿*CP.*

$ 🏠**Benedict's of Belfast.** Friendly, lively, and convenient, Benedict's stands out on Shaftsbury Square. Rooms on the second floor are bright and colorful, and have wooden floors; rooms on the third floor are darker, with an Asian influence—dark wood and light walls, simple but comfortable. If you don't feel like straying too far from your home base for some nightlife, Benedict's has a buzzing bar and restaurant serving finely done Continental food. They have a "beat the clock" promotion on their menu: a rib-eye steak with champ potatoes and brandy sauce, for instance, is usually £14, but order it up 5:30–7:30 PM and it's only £5.50. ⊠*7–21 Bradbury Pl., Golden Mile, BT7 1RQ* ☎*028/9059–1999* 📠*028/9059– 1990* ⊕*www.benedictshotel.co.uk* ⤶*32 rooms* ♿*In-room: no a/c, Wi-Fi. In-hotel: restaurant, bar* ⊟*AE, MC, V* ⦿*BP.*

OUTSIDE THE CITY CENTER

$–$$ ✕🏠**The Old Inn.** Set in the village of Crawfordsburn, this 1614 coach
★   inn, reputedly Ireland's oldest, certainly looks the part: it's pure 17th-century England, with a sculpted thatch roof, half doors, and leaded-glass windows. As it was near one of the leading cross-channel ports linking Ireland and England, the coach always stopped here, often bearing visitors with names like Swift, Tennyson, Thackeray, Dickens, and Trollope. More recently, C. S. Lewis and his wife, Joy, "booked" the inn to enjoy a belated honeymoon. You can see why: some of the finest bedrooms have 17th-century-style woodwork, sitting rooms, and faux-Jacobean beds, while public salons offer beam ceilings, roaring log fires, and lots of Ulster "craic" (chat). Repair to the grand 1614 restaurant to tuck into a Finnebrogue venison with sweet potato puree, red-onion marmalade and thyme beurre blanc, and also savor the delicious setting of flocked curtains, English wood panels, sculpted portrait medallions, and a soaring coved ceiling. "Pub Fayre" is offered at the Churn Bistro, where the menu is solidly Irish, the staff jovial, and the locals inquisitive. Over the centuries, large portions of the inn were rebuilt, and the East Wing is a completely modern take on Irish Georgian style. ⊠*16 km (10 mi) east of Belfast on A2, 15 Main St., Crawfordsburn, Co. Down BT19 1JH* ☎*028/9185–3255* 📠*028/9185–2775* ⊕*www. theoldinn.com* ⤶*32 rooms* ♿*In-room: no a/c, Wi-Fi. In-hotel: restaurant, bars* ⊟*AE, MC, V* ⦿*BP.*

$$$$ 🏠**Culloden Hotel.** Built in 1876 by the very rich William Robinson and
★   christened in honor of his wife's famed family, this imposingly grand vision in Belfast stone presides over the forested slopes of the Holywood hills and the busy waters of Belfast Lough. Topped off with a storybook turret and crenellated tower, the Scottish Baronial mansion was greatly enlarged in the early 20th century when it was given as a residence to the Bishops of Down, then transformed in the 1960s into a hotel (today, the flagship of the luxe Hastings chain). Inside, neoclassical salons warmed by lime-green walls, gilded coffered ceilings, 19th-century paintings, stained-glass accents, and overstuffed Louis

XV–style chairs make you feel like you're a member of the Robinson family. Antiques and silk-and-velvet fabrics grace guest rooms both in the original section and in a newer wing; all rooms have fine views. At mealtime choose from the posh Mitre restaurant—transformed from the former refectory and now a pleasant room of paneled walls, green-fabric booths, and presided over by a statue of St. Pat—and the Cultra Inn, which serves snacks and full meals. The hotel is close to both the village of Holywood (temptingly filled with boutiques) and the Ulster Folk and Transport Museum. Chances are, however, that you won't want to leave Culloden's lovely 12 acres of grounds. Even those tempted by a quick walk to the nearby Royal Belfast Golf Club may not be able to forgo another afternoon spent at the hotel's Elysium Spa, a glamorous Beverly Hills–type affair. ⊠ *8 km (5 mi) east of Belfast on A2, 142 Bangor Rd., Holywood, Co. Down BT18 0EX* ☎*028/9042–1066* 🖷*028/9042–6777* ⊕*www.hastingshotels.com* ⤙*79 rooms, 10 suites* ⟳*In-room: no a/c, Wi-Fi. In-hotel: 2 restaurants, bar, tennis court, pool, spa, laundry service, no-smoking rooms* ▤*AE, DC, MC, V* ⍾*BP, MAP.*

$$ 🛈**Rayanne House.** Famous both for its food and for its hospitality, this country house run by the devoted Bernadette McClelland is in leafy Holywood, 10 km (6 mi) from Belfast city center. Rooms are airy, each with individual country furnishings and garden views. Breakfast includes an Irish grill and such specialties as prune soufflé on a puree of green figs, and hot Rayanne baked cereal (laced with spices, fruit, whis-key, honey, and cream). The meal is served in an intimate dining room, made even more intimate by family antiques, paintings, and candela-bra. Lunch and dinner are available by request 24 hours in advance. ⊠ *8 km (5 mi) east of Belfast on A2, 60 Demesne Rd., Holywood, Co. Down BT18 9EX* ☎🖷*028/9042–5859* ⊕*www.rayannehouse.co.uk* ⤙*9 suites* ⟳*In-room: no a/c, Wi-Fi. In-hotel: restaurant, no elevator* ▤*MC, V* ⍾*BP, MAP.*

$ 🛈**Roseleigh House.** This charming Victorian guesthouse on a tree-filled avenue in residential south Belfast is a friendly option. Light-filled, spacious rooms decorated in calming blues with traditional floral bedspreads have modern comforts. Fresh flowers and daily newspa-pers adorn the coffee table in the residents' drawing room. Although Roseleigh is much renovated, stained-glass windows, elaborate fire-places, and period cornicing on the ceilings point to the late-Victorian date of the house. Evening meals can be requested with 24 hours' notice and breakfasts are healthy and robust. ⊠ *19 Rosetta Park, Belfast BT6 ODL* ☎*029/9064–4414* ⊕*www.roseleighhouse.co.uk* ⤙*9 rooms* ⟳*In-room: no a/c, Wi-Fi. In-hotel: restaurant, bar, no elevator* ▤*MC, V* ⍾*BP, MAP.*

UNIVERSITY AREA

$$ 🛈**Wellington Park Hotel.** Formerly a private residence and currently run by the Mooney family, this modern establishment is among the best in the University Area. The quiet, contemporary bedrooms are well designed, with built-in wood furniture; some have sleeping lofts. There's tradi-tional European food in both the bar and restaurant—though the menu in the restaurant is slightly more expansive and expensive than in the

bar. There's live music at the bar Friday and Saturday nights (soul, jazz, and Irish). ⊠ *21 Malone Rd., University Area, BT9 6RU* ☎ *028/9038–1111* 🖷 *028/9066–5410* ⊕ *www.mooneyhotelgroup.com* ⟿ *75 rooms* ⌂ *In-room: no a/c, Wi-Fi. In-hotel: restaurant, bar, laundry service* ⊟ *DC, MC, V* ⊚ *BP.*

$–$$ 🛏 **Ash-Rowan Guest House.** Thomas ★ Andrews, designer of the ill-fated *Titanic,* brought his bride to live in this spacious Victorian home after their wedding, then went off to work 14-hour days at the Harland and Wolff shipyard. Former restaurateurs Sam and Evelyn Hazlett now own, run, and cook for this outstanding B&B on a tranquil residential avenue. Every bedroom has its own style, all with Victorian overtones. Feel free to take advantage of the reading lounge, as well as the books around the house, and the conservatory. Breakfasts and dinners are first-rate. ⊠ *12 Windsor Ave., University Area, BT9 6EE* ☎ *028/9066–1758* 🖷 *028/9066–3227* ⟿ *5 rooms* ⌂ *In-room: no a/c, dial-up. In-hotel: restaurant, bar, no elevator, no-smoking rooms* ⊟ *MC, V* ⊙ *Closed Christmas wk* ⊚ *BP, MAP.*

$ 🛏 **Dukes Hotel.** Although this distinguished redbrick Victorian building has only 12 rooms, it has big-hotel amenities, including a spacious lobby, extensive exercise facilities, and two restaurants—one Chinese and one that serves healthy, local cuisine (traditionalists won't be disappointed, however, as fried food can be had). The hotel's color scheme is a distinguished, executive-style gray, enlivened with plenty of greenery, and a waterfall splashes down parallel to the stairway. Although not exceptional, the rooms are modern and comfortable, decorated in neutral shades. The lively bar is popular with staff and students from nearby Queen's University. ⊠ *65–67 University St., University Area, BT7 1HL* ☎ *028/9023–6666* 🖷 *028/9023–7177* ⊕ *www.welcome-group.co.uk* ⟿ *12 rooms* ⌂ *In-room: no a/c, Wi-Fi. In-hotel: 2 restaurants, bar, gym* ⊟ *AE, DC, MC, V* ⊚ *BP.*

$ 🛏 **Madison's.** A gracious hotel run by Botanic Inns, Madison's is in one of Belfast's liveliest spots—surrounded by the shops and cafés of lovely, tree-lined Botanic Avenue. The facade and public areas are decorated in a modish Barcelona-inspired take on Art Nouveau. Modern rooms—in primary yellows, reds, and rich blues—are stylish if sparsely furnished. The downstairs houses a restaurant that serves tasty contemporary cuisine at reasonable prices, and hip Club 33 fills the basement. Guests have discounted access to the extensive fitness facilities of Queen's University, including a pool. ⊠ *59 Botanic Ave., University Area, BT7 1JL* ☎ *028/9050–9800* 🖷 *028/9050–9808* ⊕ *www.madisonshotel.com* ⟿ *35 rooms* ⌂ *In-room: no a/c, Wi-Fi. In-hotel: restaurant, bar* ⊟ *AE, MC, V* ⊚ *BP.*

$ 🛏 **Old Rectory.** Mary and Jerry Callan's well-appointed house was built in 1896 as a rectory. Rooms are decorated in pastels and have good

> **HIDEOUT HISTORY**
>
> If you're lucky enough to stay in the oldest parts of The Old Inn, you still may be able to uncover a secret hiding place for contraband, as smugglers, like the famous highwayman Dick Turpin, made this one of their favored homes-away-from-home.

views of the mountains. Enjoy complimentary whiskey each evening in the parlor. Breakfast is hearty but healthy, a rarity in Ulster B&Bs: there's smoked salmon, scrambled eggs, fresh fruit salad, vegetarian sausages, homemade low-sugar jams, wheat bread, and freshly squeezed blended juices. ⊠*148 Malone Rd., University Area, BT9 5LH* ☎*028/9066–7882* 🖷*028/9068–3759* ➭*6 rooms* ♿*In-room: no a/c, dial-up. In-hotel: no elevator* ⊟*No credit cards* ❍|*BP, MAP.*

¢ 🖩**All Seasons.** Enjoying a superb location on the fashionable Lisburn Road in the south of the city, this spot has practically on its doorstep some of the city's most stylish boutiques and trendiest bars. Friendly owner Theodore McLaughlin has created a cozy home with a comfortable lounge, spacious dining room, and spotlessly clean rooms. Cranmore Park, a popular venue during the summer for sunbathers, is two minutes away on foot. ⊠*356 Lisburn Rd., University Area, BT9 6GJ* ☎*028/9068–2814* ⊕*www.allseasonsbelfast.com* ➭*5 rooms* ♿*In-room: no a/c, Wi-Fi. In-hotel: no elevator* ⊟*MC, V* ❍|*BP.*

NIGHTLIFE & THE ARTS

NIGHTLIFE
Belfast has dozens of pubs packed with relics of the Victorian and Edwardian periods. Although pubs typically close around 11:30 PM, many city-center–Golden Mile nightclubs stay open until 1 AM.

CENTRAL DISTRICT The **Apartment** (⊠*2 Donegall Sq. W, Central District* ☎*028/9050–9777*), beside City Hall, is the city center's trendiest bar, serving drinks and brasserie-style pub grub to Belfast's cool young things. Extensive but inexpensive wine and cocktail lists attract a good crowd. **Bittles Bar** (⊠*70 Upper Church La., Central District* ☎*028/9031–1088*), on Victoria Square, serves pub grub. Gilded shamrocks bedeck this interesting triangular-shape Victorian pub on the fringes of the Cathedral Quarter. Paintings of literary characters and local landmarks adorn the walls, while a high, wood-panel ceiling gives an illusion of spaciousness. **Kelly's Cellars** (⊠*30–32 Bank St., Central District* ☎*028/9024–6058*), open since 1720, has blues bands on Saturday night. The **Kremlin** (⊠*96 Donegall St., Central District* ⊕*www.kremlin-belfast. com* ☎*028/9031–9061*) nightclub is the city's oldest and most outrageous gay-oriented club. A massive statue of Lenin above the front door greets customers, and the over-the-top Soviet theme continues inside. Superstar DJs regularly fly in to perform.

Madden's Bar (⊠*Berry St., behind Castle Court, Central District* ☎*028/9024–4114*) is a popular pub with traditional tune fests on occasion. At **Magennis' Bar and Whiskey Café** (⊠*83 May St., Central District* ☎*028/9023–0295*) you get two pubs for the price of one: the quiet, 100-year-old bar frequented by older regulars, and the hip café, crowded with younger clientele. The free tapas on Friday evenings pull in the after-work crowd, who pop in for a quick pint and end up staying all night. Live folk music on Sunday afternoons is a great finish to the weekend. Regulars prop up the horseshoe-shape bar in the Victorian showpiece, the **Morning Star** (⊠*17–19 Pottinger's Entry, Central*

9

District ☎*028/9023–5968*), from noon until night. Strike up a conversation with some of the locals and you're guaranteed a bit of craic.

McHugh's (✉*29–30 Queen's Sq., Central District* ☎*028/9050–9990*), in Belfast's oldest building, dating from 1711, has three floors of bars and restaurants, and live music on weekends. **Pat's Bar** (✉*19–22 Prince's Dock St., Central District* ☎*028/9074–4524*) has first-rate sessions of traditional music on Saturday nights. The **Rotterdam** (✉*54 Pilot St., Central District* ☎*028/9074–6021*), which housed convicts bound for Australia until it became a pub in 1820, is filled with fascinating old junk. It hosts traditional Irish music on Monday and Thursday, jazz on Tuesday, and rock on Friday and Saturday. **Union Street** (✉*8–14 Union St., Central District* ☎*028/9031–6060*) is a gay-friendly bar near the Cathedral Quarter with charming staff and a wide selection of reasonably priced wines and imported beers. Housed in a converted 19th-century shoe factory, this three-story redbrick Victorian is one of the city's few "gastro-pubs," with a more formal upstairs restaurant that's popular with local foodies, and a simpler downstairs spot serving chili-fried whitebait-and-chips that you may wash down with a glass of chilled sauvignon blanc. **White's Tavern** (✉*2–12 Winecellar Entry, Central District* ☎*028/9024–3080*) claims to be the oldest public house in Belfast. In winter a roaring fire greets you as soon as you enter the bar. Friendly staff serve good pub grub, including the famous "champ," a creamy, buttery, cholesterol-laden concoction of mashed potatoes and spring onions. Downstairs, enjoy the traditional Irish sessions on Friday and Saturday nights.

GOLDEN MILE AREA   The glorious Crown Liquor Saloon is far from being the only old pub in the Golden Mile area—most of Belfast's evening life takes place in bars and restaurants here. There are a number of replicated Victorian bars where more locals and fewer visitors gather.

The **Beaten Docket** (✉*48 Great Victoria St., Golden Mile* ☎*028/9024–2986*), named after a losing betting slip, is a noisy, modern pub that attracts a young crowd. Here they play up-to-the-minute music, but it can get a bit boisterous, so some may prefer a quiet snug (booth) across the road in the famed Crown Liquor Saloon. **Benedict's** (✉*7–21 Bradbury Pl., Golden Mile* ☎*028/9059–1999*) is a bar, music venue, disco, 150-seat restaurant, and hotel. The faux-Gothic exterior of the hotel belies its modern origins. Straying from the model of the Victorian-style public house, the **Limelight** (✉*17 Ormeau Ave., Golden Mile* ☎*028/9032–5968*) is a disco-nightclub with cabaret on Tuesday, Friday, and Saturday, and recorded music on other nights. It's extremely popular with students, and books musicians as well as DJs.

Morrisons (✉*21 Bedford St., Golden Mile* ☎*028/9032–0030*) is a haunt of media types. It has a music lounge upstairs, and hosts discussions for film buffs arranged by local directors in conjunction with the Northern Ireland Film Council. **Robinson's** (✉*38–40 Great Victoria St., Golden Mile* ☎*028/9024–7447*), two doors from the Crown, is a popular pub that draws a young crowd with folk music in its Fibber

Magee's bar on Sunday and funk in the trendy BT1 wine and cocktail bar on weekends.

The stylish and modern **Bar Twelve** (✉ *Crescent Town House, 13 Lower Crescent, University Area* ☎028/9032–3349) is an excellent venue for some fashionable wine-sipping. On weekends, DJs spin 1960s and '70s soul and funk tunes. Settle into the comfortable leather armchairs for a long chat while you work your way through the impressive wine list. The **Botanic Inn** (✉*23–27 Malone Rd., University Area* ☎028/9050–9740), known as "the Bot" to its student clientele, is a big, popular disco-pub. The **Chelsea Wine Bar** (✉*346 Lisburn Rd., University Area* ☎028/9068–7177) is packed with affluent professionals determined to prove that life begins at 30. The contemporary cuisine is reasonably priced. **Cutter's Wharf** (✉*4 Lockview Rd., University Area* ☎028/9066–3388), down by the river south of the university, is at its best on summer evenings and during music performances on Sunday after 6. Spacious and light inside, it rarely gets too packed; if seating is limited, try the picnic tables and chairs on the wooden deck outside.

The **Eglantine Inn** (✉*32–40 Malone Rd., University Area* ☎028/9038–1994), known as "the Egg," faces the Bot across Malone Road. The **Empire Music Hall** (✉*42 Botanic Ave., University Area* ☎028/9032–8110), a deconsecrated church, is the city's leading music venue. Stand-up comedy nights are usually on Tuesday. The **Fly Bar** (✉*5–6 Lower Crescent, University Area* ☎028/9050–9750), with its over-the-top interior playing on the fly theme, is a lively spot for a cocktail in the evening.

Lavery's Gin Palace (✉*12 Bradbury Pl., University Area* ☎028/9087–1106) mixes old-fashioned beer-drinking downstairs with dancing upstairs. On the increasingly fashionable Lisburn Road, **TaTu** (✉*701 Lisburn Rd., University Area* ☎028/9038–0818) is a spacious homage to industrial chic filled with a cool, under-thirty crowd. It serves good casual food.

The **M-Club** (✉*23 Bradbury Pl., University Area* ☎028/9023–3131) is Belfast's hottest place for dedicated clubbers, with soap-opera celebrities flown in weekly to mix with the local nighthawks.

THE ARTS

The **Northern Ireland Arts Council** (☎028/9038–5200 ⊕*www.artscouncil-ni.org*) produces the bimonthly *Artslink* poster-brochure listing happenings throughout Belfast and the North. It's widely available throughout the city.

The **Belfast Festival at Queen's University** (*Festival office* ✉*25 College Gardens, University Area* ☎028/9097–2600 ⊕*www.belfastfestival.com*), which lasts for three weeks (usually late October into early November), is the city's major arts festival.

The **Promenade Concerts** (☎*028/9066–8798* ⊕*www.ulster-orchestra.org.uk*) are performed in June by the Ulster Orchestra in conjunction with the BBC.

ART GALLERIES **Bell Gallery.** This gallery in Nelson Bell's Victorian home shows many of Ireland's more traditional and representational painters from the 18th to the 21st century. ✉ *13 Adelaide Park, at Malone Rd., South University* ☎ *028/9066–2998* ⊕ *www.bellgallery.com* ☉ *Mon.–Thurs. 9–5, Fri. 9–3.*

Fenderesky Gallery. Under the same roof as the Crescent Arts Centre, Iranian philosopher Jamshid Mirfenderesky's gallery is one of the few in Ireland exhibiting the work of a stable of modern Irish artists known throughout Europe. ✉ *Crescent Arts Centre, 2 University Rd., University Area* ☎ *028/9023–5245* ☉ *Tues.–Sat. 11:30–5.*

FILM **Queen's Film Theatre** (✉ *20 University Sq., University Area* ☎ *028/9097–1097*), Belfast's main art cinema, shows domestic and foreign movies on its two screens. **Movie House Cinema** (✉ *14 Dublin Rd., Golden Mile* ☎ *028/9024–5700*) has 10 screens of major British and American box-office favorites.

MAJOR VENUES **Crescent Arts Centre.** Watch experimental dance and theater, witness provocative art in the Fenderesky Gallery, and listen to lively jazz concerts: it's all part of the Crescent. You can also take classes in this huge, rambling stone building, a former girls' high school off the campus end of Bradbury Place. ✉ *2–4 University Rd., University Area* ☎ *028/9024–2338* ⊕ *www.crescentarts.org.*

Grand Opera House. Shows from all over the British Isles—and sometimes farther afield—play at this beautifully restored Victorian theater. Though it has no company of its own, there's a constant stream of West End musicals and plays of widely differing kinds, plus occasional operas and ballets. It's worth going to a show if only to enjoy the opera house itself. ✉ *2 Great Victoria St., Golden Mile* ☎ *028/9024–1919* ⊕ *www.goh.co.uk.*

King's Hall. Pop and rock concerts take center stage at this venue that also serves as a conference center. ✉ *484 Lisburn Rd., South University* ☎ *028/9066–5225* ⊕ *www.kingshall.co.uk.*

Lyric Theatre. Set in south Belfast at King's Bridge, on the banks of the Lagan, this is the theater where Hollywood fave Liam Neeson made his stage debut. Traditional and contemporary Irish culture inspires the thoughtful dramas staged here and usually each new production is accompanied by a show, in the upper foyer lobby, of contemporary art by local artists. ✉ *55 Ridgeway St., South University* ☎ *028/9038–1081* ⊕ *www.lyrictheatre.co.uk.*

Odyssey Arena. Built to mark the Millennium and now home to the Belfast Giants—the city's first ice-hockey team (most of whom hail from North America)—the Odyssey complex also features the interactive science and technology center known as W5, a Sheridan IMAX theater, an indoor bowling alley, and the Odyssey Pavilion complex, replete with bars, restaurants, shops, nightclubs, and the Warner Village Cinemas multiplex. The latter kicks into high gear at night, while more family-oriented activities can be had by day. The center ring is the 10,000-seat Arena, Ireland's biggest indoor venue, which often hosts rock, pop, and classical troupes. Situated on Queen's Island, the Odyssey is close to the old Harland and Wolff shipyard and set along the banks of the River Lagan. ⊠*Queen's Quay, Central District* ☎*028/9045–1055* ⊕*www. theodyssey.co.uk.*

Old Museum Arts Centre *(OMAC).* A powerhouse of challenging, avant-garde theater and modern dance, OMAC also has a risk-taking art gallery. ⊠*7 College Sq. N, Central District* ☎*028/9023–3332* ⊕*www. oldmuseumartscentre.org.*

Ulster Hall. This, the main home to the Ulster Orchestra, has excellent acoustics and a splendid Victorian organ; however as of this writing, the orchestra will be playing at other venues indefinitely because Ulster Hall is undergoing a massive renovation (begun spring 2007)—check the orchestra's Web site for the latest performance locations. The classical music season runs from September through March; most concerts are on Friday. ⊠*Bedford St., Golden Mile* ☎*028/9032–3900* ⊕*www. ulster-orchestra.org.uk.*

Waterfront Hall. Everyone in Belfast sings the praises of this striking civic structure. From the looks of it, the hall is an odd marriage of *Close Encounters* modern and Castel Sant'Angelo antique. It houses a major 2,235-seat concert hall (for ballet and classical, rock, and Irish music) and a 500-seat studio space (for modern dance, jazz, and experimental theater). The Terrace Café restaurant and two bars make the hall a convenient place to eat, have a pint, and enjoy the river views before or after your culture fix. ⊠*Lanyon Pl., Central District* ☎*028/9033–4455* ⊕*www.waterfront.co.uk.*

SHOPPING

Belfast's main shopping streets include High Street, Royal Avenue, and several of the smaller streets connecting them. The area is mostly traffic-free (except for buses and delivery vehicles). The long thoroughfare of Donegall Pass, running from Shaftesbury Square at the point of the Golden Mile east to Ormeau Road, is a unique mix of biker shops and antiques arcades. All Belfast is abuzz watching the construction of the £300 million flagship Victoria Square complex, under construction at press time and due to be inaugurated in March 2008: a host of world-class designers are tipped to set up shop here, along with such popular stores as H&M, House of Fraser, Virgin Megastores, and RiverIsland.

MARKETS & MALLS

Castle Court (⊠*10 Royal Ave., Central District* ☎*028/9023–4591*) is the city's largest and most varied upscale shopping mall. Debenhams department store can fill many of your shopping needs, from cosmetics to kitchenware. Trendy stores like Gap can be found under Castle Court's glass roof, alongside British clothing chains like Miss Selfridge and Warehouse. Boys who like their toys will be in their element in the Gadget Shop. Plenty of parking makes shopping easy in the mall.

If you've an interest in bric-a-brac, visit the enormous, renovated **St. George's Market** (✉ *May St., Central District* ☎ *028/9043–5704*), an indoor market that takes place Friday and Saturday morning. Get there early on Saturday for an award-winning farmers' market, featuring organically grown fruit and vegetables, as well as treats such as homemade cakes and bread.

Occupying an eight-block site in central Belfast, **Victoria Square** (✉ *Chichester, Montgomery, and Ann streets, and Victoria Square, Central District* ⊕ *www.victoriasquare.com*) is changing the Belfast skyline with a Disneylandlike complex of shopping malls and residences, set to open in March 2008. One of the largest construction projects in Ireland, presided over by a vast geodesic glass dome eight stories high (replete with viewing platforms over the city), the complex will be a glossy steel-and-glass edifice of hypermodern design. Offering a delightful contrast, however, the complex also incorporates noted Victorian landmarks like the McErvel's Seed Warehouse and the Royal Belfast Ginger Ale Manufactury. Two department stores will be the main shopping anchors: H&M and the House of Fraser. In addition, a slew of other stores, including Virgin Megastore and Lunn's Jewelers will attract shoppers who previously just headed to Castle Court. Restaurants, cafés, and cinemas will round out this "day-out experience."

SPECIALTY SHOPS

Clark and Dawe (✉ *485 Lisburn Rd., University Area* ☎ *028/9066–8228*) makes and sells men's and women's suits and shirts.

Craftworks (✉ *Bedford House, 16–22 Bedford St., Golden Mile* ☎ *028/9024–4465*) stocks crafts by local designers. **Natural Interior** (✉ *51 Dublin Rd., Golden Mile* ☎ *028/9024–2656*) has Irish-linen throws, trimmed in velvet, by the designer Larissa Watson-Regan. It also stocks her vividly colored wall panels and cushions. **The Church of Ireland Bookshop** (✉ *61/67 Donegall St.* ☎ *028/9066–7754*) stocks rare books and manuscripts.

Smyth and Gibson (✉ *Bedford House, Bedford St., Golden Mile* ☎ *028/9023–0388*) makes and sells beautiful, luxurious linen and cotton shirts and accessories.

Looking for linen souvenirs? **Smyth's Irish Linens** (✉ *65 Royal Ave., Central District* ☎ *028/9024–2232*) carries a large selection of handkerchiefs, tablecloths, napkins, and other traditional goods. It's opposite Castle Court Mall.

The Steensons (✉ *Bedford House, Bedford St., Golden Mile* ☎ *028/9024–8269*) sells superb, locally designed jewelry. **Utopia** (✉ *Fountain Centre, College St., Central District* ☎ *028/9024–1342*) stocks intricate silver pendants and earrings made by up-and-coming local jewelry designer Abbie Dixon. Also worth a look are the hand-carved wooden and marble chess sets.

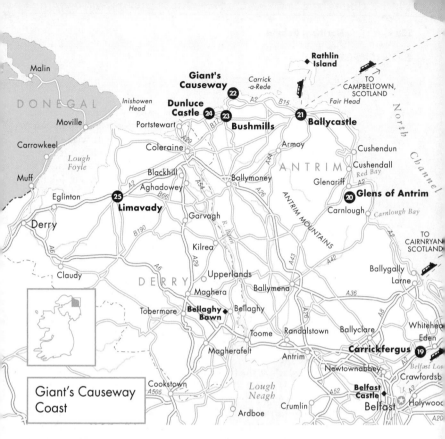

THE GIANT'S CAUSEWAY COAST

Starting in Belfast, stretching for 80 km (50 mi) along Northern Ireland's Atlantic shore, the Causeway Coast holds many of the province's "don't miss" attractions. The man-made brilliance of the castle at Dunluce, the endless string of whitewashed fishing villages along the sea, and the world-famous natural wonder that is the Giant's Causeway are just some of the delights to be discovered here. Once your car or mountain bike (ideal for the Causeway's flat terrain) makes its way past some fair-size towns, you'll enter the splendid Glens area—one of the more "gentle" (an Irish turn-of-phrase for supernatural) places in all Ireland. Here, ageless villages—still inhabited by descendants of the ancient Irish and the Hebridean Scots who hailed from across the narrow Sea of Moyle—are set in peaceful, old-growth forests that have become synonymous with Irishness. But once past the Giant's Causeway you'll find more cosmopolitan pleasures, including Bushmills—the oldest licensed distillery in the world—and the old walled city of Derry.

CARRICKFERGUS

 16 km (10 mi) northeast of Belfast on A2.

Carrickfergus, on the shore of Belfast Lough, grew up around its ancient castle. When the town was enclosed by ramparts at the start of the 17th century, it was the only English-speaking town in Northern Ireland. Not surprisingly, this was the loyal port where William of Orange chose to land on his way to fight the Catholic forces at the Battle of the Boyne in 1690. However, the English did have one or two small setbacks, including the improbable victory in 1778 of John Paul Jones, the American naval hero, over the British warship *HMS Drake.* Although a long way from home, this stands as the first naval victory of America's fledgling navy fleet. After this battle, which was waged in Belfast Lough, the inhabitants of Carrickfergus stood on the waterfront and cheered Jones when his ship passed the town castle, demonstrating their support for the American Revolution.

Carrickfergus Castle, one of the first and one of the largest of Irish castles, is still in good shape. It was built atop a rock ledge in 1180 by John de Courcy, provincial Ulster's first Anglo-Norman invader. Apart from being captured briefly by the French in 1760, the castle stood as a bastion of British rule right up until 1928, at which time it still functioned as an English garrison. Walk through the castle's 13th-century gatehouse into the Outer Ward. Continue into the Inner Ward, the heart of the fortress, where the five-story keep stands, a massive, sturdy building with walls almost 8 feet thick. Inside the keep is the Cavalry Regimental Museum, with historic weapons, and the vaulted Great Hall. These days Carrickfergus Castle hosts entertaining medieval banquets (inquire at Carrickfergus tourist information office or the Northern Ireland Tourist Board Information Centre). If you're here at the beginning of August, you can enjoy the annual Lughnasa festival, a lively medieval-costume entertainment. ⊠*Off A2* ☎*028/9335–1273* ⊕*www. ehsni.gov.uk/places/monuments/carrick.shtml* ⌨*£3* ⊘*Apr., May, and Sept., Mon.–Sat. 10–6, Sun. 2–6; June–Aug., Mon.–Sat. 10–6, Sun. noon–6; Oct.–Mar., Mon.–Sat. 10–4, Sun. 2–4.*

Old buildings that remain from Carrickfergus's past include St. Nicholas's Church, built by John de Courcy in 1205 (remodeled in 1614) and the handsomely restored North Gate in the town's medieval walls. Dobbins Inn on High Street, which has been a hotel for more than three centuries, is a watering hole that's popular with locals.

The **Andrew Jackson Centre** tells the tale of the U.S. president whose parents emigrated from here in 1765. This thatched cottage just outside of town is a reconstruction of an 18th-century structure thought to resemble their home. ⊠*2 km (1 mi) northeast of Carrickfergus, Larne Rd., Boneybefore* ☎*028/9335–8049* ⌨*£1* ⊘*Apr., May, and Oct., weekdays 10–1 and 2–4, weekends 2–4; June–Sept., weekdays 10–1 and 2–6, weekends 2–6.*

GLENS OF ANTRIM

 Beginning 24 km (15 mi) north of Carrickfergus at Larne.

★ Soon after Larne, the coast of County Antrim becomes spectacular—wave upon wave of high green hills that curve down to the hazy sea are dotted with lush glens, or valleys, first carved out by glaciers at the end of the last ice age. Nine wooded river valleys occupy the 86 km (54 mi) between Larne and Ballycastle. A narrow, winding, two-lane road (A2, which splits from the coastal at Cushendall) hugs the slim strip of land between the hills and the sea, bringing you to the magnificent Glens of Antrim run-

> **WATCH YOUR BACK**
>
> In the beautiful Glens of Antrim, locals often talk of "the wee folk," said to reside in and around the "gentle" (i.e., supernatural) places of Lurigethan Mountain and Tiveragh Hill. The fairies inhabiting these places are mischievous creatures who mostly mind their own business, but woe betide anyone rash enough to cut off a fairy thorn (a type of bush).

ning down from the escarpment of the Antrim Plateau to the eastern shore. Until the building of this road in 1834, the Glens were home to isolated farming communities—people who adhered to the romantic, mystical Celtic legends and the everyday use of the Irish language. Steeped in Irish mythology, the Glens were first inhabited by small bands of Irish monks as early as AD 700. Some residents proudly note that Ossian, the greatest of the Celtic poets, is supposedly buried near Glenaan. Given the original remoteness of the area, a great tradition of storytelling still exists.

The Glens are worth several days of serious exploration. Even narrower B-roads curl west off A2, up each of the beautiful glens, where trails await hikers. You'll need a full week and a rainproof tent to complete the nine-glen circuit (working from south to north, Glenarm, Glencloy, Glenariff, Glenballyeamon, Glenaan, Glencorp, Glendun, Glenshesk, and Glentasie); or you could just head for Glenariff Park, the most accessible of Antrim's glens. Tourist offices in the area, such as the one in Cushendall, sell a *Guide to the Glens*.

A little resort made of white limestone, **Carnlough** overlooks a charming harbor that's surrounded by stone walls. The harbor can be reached by crossing over the limestone bridge from Main Street, built especially for the Marquis of Londonderry. The small harbor, once a port of call for fishermen, now shelters pleasure yachts. Carnlough is surrounded on three sides by hills that rise 1,000 feet from the sea. There's a small tourist office inside the post office, which is useful if you need information on exploring the scenic Glens of Antrim and the coast road. ⊠*24 km (15 mi) north of Larne on A2.*

★ In **Glenariff Forest Park** you can explore the most beautiful and unsettled of Antrim's glens. Glenariff was christened "Little Switzerland" by Thackeray for its rugged combination of rugged hills and lush vales. The main valley opens onto Red Bay at the village of Glenariff (also known as Waterfoot). Inside the park are picnic facilities and

9

dozens of good hikes. The 5½-km (3½-mi) Waterfall Trail, marked with blue arrows, passes outstanding views of Glenariff River, its waterfalls, and small but swimmable loughs. Escape from the summer crowds by taking one of the longest trails, such as the Scenic Hike. Pick up a detailed trail map at the park visitor center, which also has a small cafeteria. ⊠ *7 km (5 mi) north of Carnlough off A2, 98 Glenariff Rd., Glenariff* ☎ *028/2175–8232* 🚘 *Vehicles £4, pedestrians £2* ⊗ *Apr.–Sept., daily 8–8; Oct.–Mar., daily 10–dusk.*

> ### ELIXIR OF YOUTH?
>
> The coastal caves of Cushendall have been used for various purposes, including housing. One of the more colorful residents was a lady called Nun Marry who lived in one cave for 50 years, supplementing her income as one of the region's better potion brewers. The damp and windy conditions obviously agreed with her—as did perhaps a taste of her own brew?—for she lived to the ripe old age of 100.

Turnley's Tower—a curious, fortified square tower of red stone, built in 1820 as a curfew tower and jail for "idlers and rioters"—stands in **Cushendall**, at a crossroads in the middle of the village. Another village of the picture-postcard variety, Cushendall is called the capital of the Glens due to having a few more streets than the other villages hereabouts. The road from Waterfoot to Cushendall is barely a mile long and worth the walk or cycle out to see the coastal caves (one of which had a resident called Nun Marry) that line the route. ⊠ *3 km (2 mi) north of Glenariff on A2.*

★ Off the main A2 route, the road between Cushendall and Cushendun turns into one of a Tour-de-France hilliness, so cyclists beware. Your reward, however, will be the tiny jewel of a village, **Cushendun,** which was designed by Clough Williams-Ellis, who also designed the famous Italianate village of Portmeirion in Wales. From this part of the coast you can see the Mull of Kintyre on the Scottish mainland. ⊠ *2 km (1½ mi) north of Cushendall on Coast Rd..*

EN ROUTE The narrow and precipitous Antrim Coast Road cuts off from A2 and heads north from Cushendun past dramatically beautiful Murlough Bay to Fair Head and on to Ballycastle. In this area is Drumnakill, a renowned pagan site; Torr Head, a jutting peninsula; and three state parks that allow for some fabulous hikes, fine hill-walking, and great views of Scotland from Fair Head. Or you can rejoin A2 at Cushendun via B92 (a left turn). After a few miles the road descends—passing ruins of the Franciscans' 16th-century Bonamargy Friary—into Ballycastle.

WHERE TO STAY & EAT

$$$ ✕🏨 **Galgorm Manor.** The manor house itself is photogenic, and the estate grounds—where you may go riding, practice archery, and shoot clay pigeons—cinematic. Full privileges at an 18-hole golf course, a mere five minutes from the hotel, is an added treat. The River Maine (good for brown trout) flows within view of many of the large rooms, which have wood beams on the ceilings above substantial dark-wood

beds. Gillies bar is decidedly Irish; the restaurant serves hearty portions of traditional Irish food ($–$$). Galgorm is off A42, 3 km (2 mi) west of Ballymena, 32 km (20 mi) inland of Larne, 40 km (25 mi) north of Belfast. ⊠ *40 km (25 mi) east of Larne on A36, 136 Fenaghy Rd., Ballymena, Co. Antrim BT42 1EA* ☏ *028/2588–1001* 🖷 *028/2588–0080* ⊕ *www.galgorm.com* ⌑ *24 rooms* ⌂ *In-room: no a/c, Wi-Fi. In-hotel: restaurant, bar* ⊟ *AE, MC, V* ⦿ *BP, MAP.*

$$ ✕🖼 **Londonderry Arms Hotel.** What awaits at Londonderry Arms are ★ lovely seaside gardens, ivy-clad walls, gorgeous antiques, regional paintings and maps, and lots of fresh flowers. This ivy-covered traditional inn on Carnlough Harbor was built as a coach stop in 1848. In 1921 Sir Winston Churchill inherited it; since 1947 it has been owned and run by the hospitable O'Neill family. Both the original and the newer rooms have Georgian furnishings and luxurious fabrics, and are immaculately kept. The restaurant serves substantial, traditional Irish meals that emphasize fresh, local seafood, simply prepared ($–$$). The hotel has an elevator and is wheelchair accessible. ⊠ *20 Harbour Rd., Carnlough, Co. Antrim BT44 0EU* ☏ *028/2888–5255* 🖷 *028/2888–5263* ⊕ *www.glensofantrim.com* ⌑ *35 rooms* ⌂ *In-room: no a/c, Wi-Fi. In-hotel: restaurant, bar* ⊟ *AE, DC, MC, V* ⦿ *BP, MAP.*

$$$ 🖼 **Ballygally Castle.** A baronial castle, built by a Scottish lord in 1625, rises dramatically beside Ballygally Bay. Attached to it is a modern extension that provides room for facilities but clashes a bit with the original. Bedrooms in the castle have retained beamed ceilings but have bland-if-comfortable furnishings throughout. Ask for a room in a turret—one comes complete with milady's ghost. On Saturday in the dining room, a decent set-menu dinner is served to musical accompaniment; a Sunday bistro meal is also available. ⊠ *274 Coast Rd., Ballygally, Co. Antrim BT40 2QZ* ☏ *028/2858–1066* 🖷 *028/2858–3681* ⊕ *www.hastingshotels.com* ⌑ *44 rooms* ⌂ *In-room: no a/c, Wi-Fi. In-hotel: restaurant, bar* ⊟ *AE, DC, MC, V* ⦿ *BP.*

9

BALLYCASTLE

㉑ *86 km (54 mi) northeast of Larne, 37½ km (23 mi) north of Carnlough.*

Ballycastle is the main resort at the northern end of the Glens of Antrim. People from the province flock here in summer. The town is shaped like an hourglass—with its strand and dock on one end, its pubs and chippers on the other, and the 1-km (½-mi) Quay Road in between. Beautifully aged shops and pubs line its Castle, Diamond, and Main streets.

Every year since 1606, on the last Monday and Tuesday in August, Ballycastle has hosted the **Oul' Lammas Fair,** a modern version of the ancient Celtic harvest festival of Lughnasa (Irish for "August"). Ireland's oldest fair, this is a very popular two-day event at which sheep and wool are still sold alongside the wares of more modern shopping stalls. Treat yourself to the fair's traditional snacks, "dulse" (sun-dried seaweed), and "yellow man" (rock-hard yellow toffee).

From Ballycastle town you have a view of L-shape **Rathlin Island,** where in 1306 the Scottish king Robert the Bruce took shelter in a cave (under the east lighthouse) and, according to the popular legend, was inspired to continue his armed struggle against the English by watching a spider patiently spinning its web. It was on Rathlin in 1898 that Guglielmo Marconi set

<table>
<tr><td>SHOOT THE CHUTE</td></tr>
<tr><td>If you summon up the nerve to cross the famous 60-foot-long Carrick-a-Rede rope bridge, which sways over a rocky outcrop and the turbulent sea, be mindful that you have to do it again to get back to the mainland.</td></tr>
</table>

up the world's first cross-water radio link, from the island's lighthouse to Ballycastle. Bird-watching and hiking are the island's main activities. Unless the sea is extremely rough, a ferryboat makes twice-daily journeys for £9. The trip can take up to 45 minutes; be mindful of the weather to ensure that you can return the same day. ⊠ *9½ km (6 mi) from Ballycastle.*

★ Off the Ballycastle coast in Larrybane you can see the **Carrick-a-Rede** rope bridge, which spans a 60-foot gap between the mainland and Carrick-a-Rede Island. The island's name means "rock in the road" and refers to how it stands in the path of the salmon that follow the coast as they migrate to their home rivers to spawn. For the past 150 years salmon fishermen have set up the rope bridge in spring, taking it down again after the salmon season ends. The bridge is open to the public and has some heart-stopping views of the crashing waves below. ⊠ *8 km (5 mi) west of Ballycastle on B15* ⊠ *Free (parking fee of £4)* ⊙ *Mid-Mar.–June and Sept., daily 10–6; July and Aug., daily 9:30–7:30.*

WHERE TO EAT

¢–$$ ✕**Wysner's.** Head chef Jackie Wysner has won several awards for both
★ this small family restaurant and the eponymous butcher shop next door. Menus vary daily, though the cooking emphasizes fresh local ingredients—from the hills and the sea. Specialties of the upstairs restaurant include North Atlantic salmon (caught nearby at Carrick-a-Rede), fillet of halibut with langoustine, and fillet of beef with mustard-seed cream sauce. A daytime menu is served downstairs in the informal café. ⊠ *16–18 Ann St.* ☎ *028/2076–2372* ⊟*MC, V* ⊙ *Closed Sun.*

GIANT'S CAUSEWAY

❷   *19 km (12 mi) west of Ballycastle.*

Fodor'sChoice
★   "When the world was moulded and fashioned out of formless chaos, this must have been a bit over—a remnant of chaos," said the great Thackeray about Northern Ireland's premier tourist draw, the Giant's Causeway. Imagine a mass of 37,000 mostly hexagonal pillars of volcanic basalt, clustered like a giant honeycomb and extending hundreds of yards into the sea. Legend has it this "causeway" was created 60 million years ago, when boiling lava, erupting from an underground fissure that stretched from Northern Ireland to the Scottish coast, crystallized as it burst into the sea, and formed according to the same natural prin-

ciple that structures a honeycomb. As all Ulster folk know, though, the truth is that the columns were created as stepping-stones by the giant Finn McCool in a bid to reach a giantess he'd fallen in love with on the Scottish island of Staffa (where the causeway resurfaces). Unfortunately, the giantess's boyfriend found out, and in the ensuing battle, Finn pulled out a huge chunk of earth and flung it toward Scotland. The resulting hole became Lough Neagh, and the sod landed to create the Isle of Man.

> **KEEP YOUR EYE ON THE ROAD**
>
> For excellent—and generally deserted—hiking, check with the staff at the Causeway Centre for tips on a dozen easy hikes in the area, including one that follows the pristine coastline toward the ruined tower of Dunseverick Castle, 5 km (3 mi) away—the impressive landscape along the way is the main reward.

To reach the causeway, you can either walk 1½ km (1 mi) down a long, scenic hill or take a minibus from the visitor center. West of the causeway, Port-na-Spania is the spot where the 16th-century Spanish Armada galleon *Girona* went down on the rocks. The ship was carrying an astonishing cargo of gold and jewelry, some of which was recovered in 1967 and is now on display in the Ulster Museum in Belfast. Beyond this, Chimney Point is the name given to one of the causeway structures on which the Spanish fired, thinking that it was Dunluce Castle, which is 8 km (5 mi) west.

Arriving by car at the Giant's Causeway, you first reach a cliff-top parking lot beside the modern **Causeway Centre,** a visitor center that has displays about the area and a superb audiovisual exhibition explaining the formation of the causeway coast, as well as a crafts shop. The nearby Causeway Hotel is a good place to stop off for lunch after any hunger-inducing walk. Word of warning: dress appropriately by taking a warm jacket and wear sensible walking shoes, as the causeway can be slippery on wet days. Small children will need to be properly supervised. ⊠ *44 Causeway Rd., Bushmills* ☎*028/2073-1855* ⊕*www.nationaltrust.org.uk* ✉*Visitor center movie £1, guided tours £2, parking £5* ⊙ *Visitor center Mar.–June, Sept., and Oct., daily 10–5; July and Aug., daily 10–6; Nov.–Feb., daily 10–4:30.*

BUSHMILLS

㉓ *3 km (2 mi) west of Giant's Causeway.*

Reputedly the oldest licensed distillery in the world, Bushmills was first granted a charter by King James I in 1608, though historical records refer to a distillery here as early as 1276. Bushmills produces the most famous of Irish whiskeys—its namesake—and what is widely regarded as the best, the rarer black-label version known to aficionados as Black Bush. During the guided tour you will discover the secrets of the special water from St. Columb's Mill, the story behind malted Irish barley, and learn about triple distillation in copper stills and aging (which happens for long years in oak casks).

You begin in the mashing and fermentation room, proceed to the maturing and bottling warehouse, and conclude, yes, with the much anticipated, complimentary shot of *uise beatha,* the "water of life." You can also have a light lunch in the Distillery Kitchen or pick up souvenirs in the distillery gift shop. If you're very lucky you could pick up a bottle of Bushmills Malt 21 Year Old, an extremely rare single-malt Irish whiskey, of which only a very limited number of bottles are available each year. Or if you really have a chubby wallet you could ask about the Bushmill's Malt Artist's Reserve—a mere £300 a bottle. One drop of this elixir and you'll realize that this small distillery is still top of its game four centuries after its founding. Children under 7 are not permitted on the tour. ⊠ *Off A2* ☎ *028/2073–3218* ⊕ *www.bushmills.com* ⊠ *£4* ⊙ *Tours Apr.–Oct., Mon.–Sat. 9:30–5:30, Sun. noon–5:30; Nov.–Mar., weekdays 10:30–3:30, weekends 1:30–3:30.*

WHERE TO STAY

$$–$$$$ 🏨 **Bushmills Inn.** Owner Roy Bolton oversees this cozy old coach inn. Stripped pine, peat fires, and gaslights warm the public rooms. Some of the bedrooms are quite small, so look before you decide. The livery stables now house the informal restaurant, which serves fresh and hearty food, and the bar. The staff can provide a baby-listening service—you leave the tot in the room with a baby monitor, and they alert you to cries. The distillery is a stroll away from the main square and the inn, as is the salmon-filled River Bush. Rooms in the less-expensive Coaching House section are smaller and overlook the road, perfect if you're on a budget. ⊠ *9 Dunluce Rd., Bushmills, Co. Antrim BT57 8QG* ☎ *028/2073–3000 or 028/2073–2339* 🖷 *028/2073–2048* ⊕ *www. bushmills-inn.com* ⇄ *32 rooms* ⚹ *In-room: no a/c, Wi-Fi. In-hotel: restaurant, bar* ⊟ *AE, MC, V* ⫷○⫸*BP.*

¢   🏨 **Causeway Hotel.** Owned by England's National Trust and flaunting a stunning location overlooking the Atlantic Ocean, this hotel is only a half mile from the celebrated Giant's Causeway. The hotel was founded in the 1840s then expanded in 1863 by one Mr. Trail (who masterminded the Giant's Causeway Tramway that ran along the coast), and in 1890 it became the first Irish hotel to be completely lighted by electricity. Alas and alack, they should bring back some of the candles. Nearly all the historic patina has long disappeared—both the exterior and the interior are largely comprised of white-on-white walls. Granted, the bar is welcoming, the dining room capacious, and the "high tea" a winner, but this spot will always be prized more for its setting than its mise-en-scene. One thing that hasn't changed much is the grub—nouvelle cuisine thankfully never caught on in this part of the world, so prepare yourself for what the locals call "a good feed" (featured throughout the day in myriad bed-and-board packages). Other hotels may offer posh facilities, but this one gives you the tranquillity and beauty of the glorious Antrim coastline right at your doorstep. ⊠40 Causeway Rd., Bushmills, Co. Antrim BT57 8SU ☎028/2073–1210 or 028/2073–1226 ☎028/2073–2552 ⊕www.giants-causeway-hotel.com ⌨28 rooms ☐In-room: no a/c, Wi-Fi. In-hotel: restaurant, bar. ⊟AE, MC, V ⑩MAP.

DUNLUCE CASTLE

㉔ 3 km (2 mi) west of Bushmills.

★ Halfway between Portrush and the Giant's Causeway, dramatically perched on a cliff at land's end, Dunluce Castle is one of the North's most evocative ruins. Even roofless, this shattered bulk conjures up a strength and aura that is quintessentially Antrim. Its long-storied history is filled with marvels, beginning with the fact that it stands on a 100-foot-high basalt rock, which contains the "Mermaid's Cave" (accessible by both land and sea). Originally a 13th-century Norman fortress, it was captured in the 16th century by the local MacDonnell clan chiefs—the so-called "Lords of the Isles." They enlarged the castle, paying for some of the work with their profits from salvaging the Spanish galleon *Girona*—note the two openings in the old gatehouse wall made for cannon that Sorely Boy MacDonnell rescued from the wreck—and made it an important base for ruling northeastern Ulster. Perhaps they expanded the castle a little too much, for in 1639 faulty construction caused the kitchens (with all the cooks) to plummet into the sea during a storm. Elsewhere on the grounds are the 1630 Manor House and the terraced Earl's Garden. From here, castle dwellers looked on in horror as the *Exmouth*—bound for Quebec—went down after fighting rough seas for three days in 1857. Exhibits at the castle detail this shipwreck, which caused the demise of 240 passengers. ⊠Coastal Rd., Portrush ☎028/2073–1938 ⊕www.northantrim. com/dunlucecastle.htm ☎£1.50 ⊙Apr., May, and Sept., Mon.–Sat. 10–5:30, Sun. 2–6; June–Aug., Mon.–Sat. 10–6, Sun. noon–6; Oct.–Mar., Mon.–Sat. 10–4, Sun. 2–4.

Dunluce Center is an entertainment complex with three floors of interactive play zones, shops, and a café near Dunluce Castle. ⊠10 Sandhill Dr., Portrush ☎028/7082–4444 ⊕www.dunlucecentre.co.uk ☎£8:50 ⊙Easter week, July, and Aug., daily 10:30–6:30; Apr. and May, weekends noon–6:30; June, weekdays noon–5, weekends noon–6:30; Sept.–Mar., weekends noon–5.

WHERE TO EAT

¢–$ ✕**Ramore Wine Bar.** On Portrush's picturesque harbor, this spot has
★ panoramic views, with daily offerings posted on a blackboard. ⊠The Harbor, Portrush ☎028/7082–4313 ⊟MC, V.

SPORTS & THE OUTDOORS

In a poll of legendary Irish courses, the **Royal Portrush Golf Club** (⊠ *Dunluce Rd., Portrush* ☎ *028/7082–2311* ⊕ *www.royalportrushgolfclub. com*) came out tops. The championship Dunluce is a sea of sand hills and curving fairways (£110 on weekdays, £125 on weekends). The valley course is a less-exposed, tamer track (£35 on weekdays, £40 on weekends). Both are typically open to visitors on weekdays, but it's best to call ahead. For more details, *see* the chapter *on Irish Greens.*

Portstewart Strand (⊠ *Coastal Rd., Portrush*) has some of Ireland's best surfing. It's signposted as "The Strand" on all major junctions in town.

LIMAVADY

㉕ *27 km (17 mi) east of Derry.*

In 1851, at No. 51 on Limavady's Georgian main street, Jane Ross wrote down the tune played by a traveling fiddler and called it "Londonderry Air," better known now as "Danny Boy." While staying at an inn on Ballyclose Street, William Thackeray (1811–63) wrote his rather lustful poem "Peg of Limavaddy" about a barmaid. Among the many Americans descended from Ulster emigrants was President James Monroe, whose relatives came from the Limavady area.

WHERE TO STAY & EAT

$$$ ✕🏨 **Radisson Roe Park Hotel & Golf Resort.** A country estate serves as the model for the deluxe modern resort amid 155 acres on the banks of the River Roe. The place is relatively large and impersonal, although the lobby is a feast of welcoming ruby-hued carpets and gilt lanterns. Regular guest rooms have simple, clean-line beds in woods and rich earth tones. Suite furnishings move a bit up the ornate scale with canopy beds and velvet armchairs. Green's restaurant is formal and international ($–$$$); the Coach House brasserie is a relaxed place where golfers congregate; and O'Cahan's bar takes its name from a local chieftain besieged on a riverside promontory, whose Irish wolfhound leaped an impossible chasm to bring relief—doubtless an inspiration to golfers flagging at the ninth. ⊠ *Roe Park, Co. Derry BT49 9LB* ☎ *028/7772–2222* ☐ *028/7772–2313* ⊕ *www.radissonroepark.com* ⇆ *118 rooms, 6 suites* ⏷ *In-room: no a/c, Ethernet. In-hotel: 2 restaurants, bars, golf course, pool, gym, public Wi-Fi* ⊟ *AE, DC, MC, V* ⏷⏷ *BP, MAP.*

DERRY

If Belfast were the Beethoven of Northern Ireland, Derry would be the Mozart—fey, witty, and a touch surreal. Every Halloween, for example, the entire populace of Derry—the second biggest city in Northern Ireland—turns out in wild homemade costumes, and pubs have been known to refuse a drink to anyone who hasn't made the effort to dress up. Despite the derelict factories along the banks of the River Foyle and a reputation marred by Troubles-related violence, the city has worked hard to move forward. Such efforts show in the quaint, bustling town center, encircled by 20-foot-tall 17th-century walls. The city's winding streets slope down to the Foyle, radiating from the Diamond—Derry's historic center—where St. Columba founded his first monastery in 546. Fine Georgian and Victorian buildings sit side by side with gaily painted Victorian-front shops, cafés, and pubs.

EXPLORING DERRY

Derry's name is a shadow of its history. Those in favor of British rule call the city Londonderry, its old Plantation-period name: The "London" part was tacked on in 1613 after the Flight of the Earls, and the city and county were handed over to the Corporation of London, which represented London's merchants. The corporation brought in a large population of English and Scottish Protestant settlers, built towns for them, and reconstructed Derry within the city walls, which survive almost unchanged to this day. Both before then and after, Derry's sturdy ramparts withstood many fierce attacks—they have never been breached, which explains the city's coy sobriquet, "The Maiden City." The most famous attack was the siege of 1688–89, begun after 13 apprentice boys slammed the city gates in the face of the Catholic king, James II. Inhabitants, who held out for 105 days and were reduced to eating dogs, cats, and laundry starch, nevertheless helped to secure the British throne for the Protestant king, William III. Whatever you choose to call it, Derry is one of Northern Ireland's most underrated towns. Derry, incidentally, has links to Boston that date as far back as the 17th and 18th centuries, when many Derry residents escaped their hardships at home by emigrating to that U.S. city and beyond.

26 To really experience Derry's history, stroll along the parapet walkway atop the ramparts of the **city walls,** built between 1614 and 1618 and one of the few intact sets of city walls in Europe. Pierced by eight gates (originally four) and as much as 30 feet thick, the gray-stone ramparts are only 1½ km (1 mi) all around. Today most of the life of the town takes place outside of them. You can join one of the guided tours given by the information center, or follow the sights below in a counterclockwise direction.

Walking tours of the city walls leave from the **Tourist Information Centre** and last just under two hours. They depart at 2:30 on weekdays year-round, as well as at 11:15 and 3:15 in July and August. ⊠44 *Foyle St., West Bank* ☎028/7126–7284 or 028/7137–7577 ⊕*www. derryvisitor.com* ✉*Centre free, tour £5* ⊗*Mid-Mar.–June and Oct., weekdays 9–5, Sat. 10–5; July–Sept., weekdays 9–7, Sat. 10–6, Sun. 10–5; Nov.–mid-Mar., weekdays 9–5.*

Thanks to **Open Top Tours,** you can tour Derry onboard a double-decker bus. Departing from the Tourist Information Centre and Guildhall Monday through Saturday, on the hour from 10 to 5, the bus ride lasts an hour, hits all the sightseeing spots, and has a guide with onboard commentary. ⊠*6 Pinetrees* ☎077/4024–9998 ✉*£9.*

9

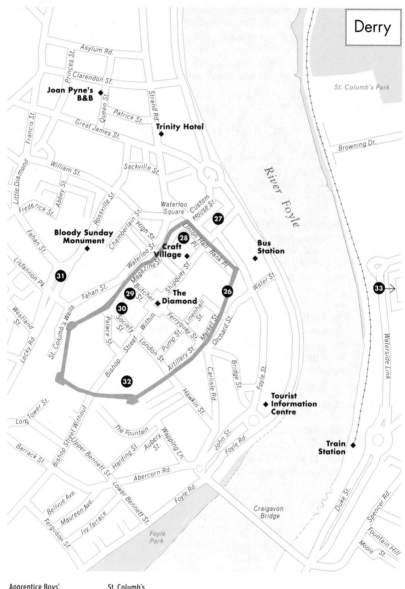

Derry

St. Columb's Park

Asylum Rd.

Princes St.

Clarendon St.

Joan Pyne's B&B

Queen St.

Strand Rd.

Patrick St.

Browning Dr.

Great James St.

Trinity Hotel

Francis St.

William St.

Sackville St.

Abbey St.

Little Diamond

Frederick St.

Rossville St.

Chamberlain St.

Waterloo Square

Custom House St.

Bloody Sunday Monument

Fahan St.

Lisnannon St.

High St.

Waterloo St.

Magazine St.

Union Hall Pl.

Bank Pl.

27

28

Craft Village

Shipquay St.

Bus Station

Water St.

River Foyle

31

Fahan St.

Butcher St.

29

The Diamond

Ferryquay St.

Linenhall St.

26

Orchard St.

Market St.

30

Society St.

Palace St.

Within

Pump St.

Artillery St.

33

St. Columb's Wells

Westland St.

Lecky Rd.

Bishop Street

London St.

Carlisle Rd.

Bridge St.

Foyle St.

Waterside Link

32

Hawkin St.

Tourist Information Centre

Lone Tower St.

Lower Tower St.

The Fountain

Wapping Ln.

John St.

Foyle Rd.

Barrack St.

Bishop Street Without

Upper Bennett St.

Harding St.

Aubery St.

Train Station

Bellvue Ave.

Maureen Ave.

Lower Bennett St.

Abercorn Rd.

Foyle Rd.

Craigavon Bridge

Duke St.

Spencer Rd.

Ferguson St.

Ivy Terrace

Foyle Park

Fountain Hill

Moore St.

Derry Taxis offers an alternative tour of Derry taking in local murals, monuments, and historic buildings. Find their taxi stands on Foyle and William streets. ☎028/7126–0247 ⊕www.derrytaxitours.com.

㉗ Derry city council meets monthly at **Guildhall,** an ornate Victorian stone and sandstone building dating from 1890. Some of the most beautiful glass creations in Ireland, the hall's stained-glass windows were shattered by two IRA bombs in June 1977 and rebuilt by the Campbell's firm in Belfast, which had installed the original windows in 1890 and still had the plans (now *that's* a filing system). Elsewhere, the eye is delighted by neo-Gothic strutwork, ornate ceilings, baronial wood paneling, a magnificent organ, and the fourth largest clock (modeled on Big Ben) in Ireland. The Guildhall also hosts occasional musical recitals. ⊠*Guildhall Sq., West Bank* ☎028/7137–7335 ☜*Free* ⊙ *Weekdays 8:30–5.*

㉘ Tall, brooding, medieval, and magical, a reconstructed granite-stone
★ O'Dohertys Tower contains the **Tower Museum,** which chronicles the history of Derry. The building was constructed in 1615 by the O'Dohertys for their overlords, the O'Donnells, in lieu of tax payments. Highlights of the museum include a small section on the eccentric Bishop Frederick Augustus Hervey (1763–1803), who conducted a lifelong affair with the mistress of Frederick William II of Prussia; built the now derelict Downhill Castle above the cliffs outside the city; and allegedly had his curates stage naked sprints along the beach while he horsewhipped them. The winners were awarded the most lucrative parishes in the district. There's excellent information celebrating the life and legacy of St. Columba. The vivid "Story of Derry" exhibition covers the city's history, from its origins as a monastic settlement in an oak grove up to the Troubles, beginning in 1969 after years of institutionalized discrimination in jobs and public housing. (A well-known Derry joke is that the skeleton in the city's coat of arms was actually a Catholic waiting for a house.) There's also an exhibition on the Spanish Armada. ⊠*Union Hall Pl., West Bank* ☎028/7137–2411 ☜£4 ⊙*Sept.–June, Tues.–Sat. 10–5; July and Aug., Mon.–Sat. 10–5, Sun. 2–5.*

㉙ The "Fifth Province" exhibition at the **Calgach Centre** provides a high-tech tour of the city's history, including its importance in creating the Irish diaspora of 17 million people. Sit in a comfortable armchair for virtual-reality time travel through the coming of the Vikings and the Normans, the flight of the Irish nobility from English persecution in 1601, and the famine of 1845–49, when 1½ million emigrated to the United States and a million died of starvation. ⊠*4–22 Butcher St., West Bank* ☎028/7137–3177 ☜£3 ⊙ *Weekdays 9:30–4.*

㉚ Imposing in its Scottish Baronial fortified grandeur, **Apprentice Boys' Memorial Hall** is a meeting place for the exclusively Protestant organization set up in 1715 to honor 13 apprentice boys who slammed the city gate in the face of the Catholic King James in 1688 and sparked the Siege of Derry, which has been a symbol of Protestant stubbornness ever since. Inside there's an initiation room in which 20,000 have pledged to uphold Protestant values, and a magnificently chaotic museum filled to

9

the brim with furniture, firearms, books, bombs, swords, and sculpture. It's a fascinating glimpse into a mostly closed world. An upstairs bar and dance hall—now used for meetings, initiations, and social events organized by the Apprentice Boys—has walls lined with 12 banners representing the lost tribes of Israel. (Some Protestants believe the lost tribes of Israel ended up in Northern Ireland and are their forebears.) ⊠*Society St., West Bank* ☎*028/7134–6677* ✉*Donations accepted* ☾*Tours by appointment; open to public 2nd wk of Aug.*

Walker Memorial, a statue of the governor of Derry during the siege, is a symbol of Derry's divided nature. It was blown up by the IRA in 1973, and the story goes that the statue's head rolled down the hill into the Catholic Bogside, where it was captured by a local youth. He ransomed it back to the Protestants for a small fortune, and today it sits on the shoulders of a replica of the original statue beside the Apprentice Boys' Memorial Hall. ⊠*Apprentice Boys' Memorial Hall, Society St., West Bank.*

㉛ At **Free Derry Corner** is the white gable wall where Catholics defiantly painted the slogan "You are now entering Free Derry" as a declaration of a zone from which police and the British Army were banned until 1972, when the army broke down the barricades. That year, 13 civil rights marchers were shot and killed by British soldiers in an event that rankles Catholics to this day. "Bloody Sunday," as it became known, is commemorated by a mural of the civil rights march. ⊠*Fahan and Rossville Sts., West Bank.*

㉜ **St. Columb's Cathedral** was the first Protestant cathedral built in the United Kingdom after the Reformation, and contains the oldest and largest bells in Ireland (dating from the 1620s). It's a treasure house of Derry Protestant emblems, memorials, and relics from the siege of 1688–89. The church was built in 1633 in simple Planter's Gothic style, with an intricate corbeled roof and austere spire. In the vestibule is the 270-pound mortar ball that during the Siege of Derry was fired over the wall with an invitation to surrender sent by King James. Legend has it that when it was read, every man, woman, and child in the city rushed to the walls and shouted, "No surrender!"—a Protestant battle cry to this day. The attached Chapter House Museum has the oldest surviving map of Derry (from 1600) and the Bible owned by Governor George Walker during the siege. Knowledgeable tour guides are on hand. ⊠*London St. off Bishop St., West Bank* ☎*028/7126–7313* ⊕*www.stcolumbscathedral.org* ✉*£1* ☾*Apr.–Oct., daily 9–5; Nov.–Mar., daily 9–4.*

NEED A BREAK? Derry is packed with agreeable pubs, but Badgers (⊠ **16 Orchard St., West Bank** ☎ **028/7136–0763**) has the best choice of wholesome food. It's also the watering hole for local media types, artists, writers, and musicians.

㉝ Across the River Foyle from the city walls, the **Workhouse Museum** was built in 1832 as an institution to alleviate poverty but became the end of the road for people who had tried in vain to make their lives better. During the famine years (1845–49), the city was the main emigration port for Northern Ireland, and many families came to Derry hoping to get on a boat. Instead, unable to afford the trip, they ended up applying for aid at the Workhouse, where hard labor earned a bed and food. Many families were separated once inside, and this was often the last time children saw their parents alive. From the beginning to the end of the famine, 1½ million people left Ireland and 1 million died. The museum details life in the Workhouse and has some thoughtful exhibits about famine in general.

> ### THE HIGH AND THE FLIGHTY
>
> Aviation fans, take note: Derry was where Amelia Earhart touched down on May 21, 1932, after her historic solo flight across the Atlantic. Local lore has it that the first man to reach her airplane greeted her in typically unfazed Derry fashion: "Aye, and what do you want, then?"

Many of the descendants of those who left came back during World War II: thousands of U.S. servicemen arrived in the city in 1942 to turn it into a base for the Battle of the Atlantic. Exhibits on the top two floors of the Workhouse chronicle the story of that battle, from the Yanks' arrival in the January rain (which prompted one of them to ask if the city's barrage balloons were actually there to stop the place from sinking) through the end of the war, when 64 U-boats lined up in the harbor to surrender. By 1946 the city's biggest export was G.I. brides. There's a space for traveling exhibitions that change regularly; call for details. ⊠ *23 Glendermott Rd., East Bank* ☎ *028/7131–8328* 🖃 *Free* ⊙ *July and Aug., Mon.–Thurs. and Sat. 10:30–4:30; Sept.–June, Mon.– Thurs. and Sat. 10–4:30.*

EN ROUTE For a delightfully rustic alternative to driving back to Belfast on A6, drive along the minor road B48, which skirts the foot of the Sperrin Mountains and reaches all the way to Omagh. Or, you may want to head north from Derry to explore the Inishowen Peninsula, the northernmost point of Ireland.

WHERE TO STAY & EAT

$–$$$ ✕ **Thompsons on the River.** This spot takes its name from the old Thompsons Mill that once occupied this historic building on the banks of the Foyle. Decor is airy and cool while the cuisine is stylish and hot: best bets include caraway-scented roast stuffed loin of pork or the fillets of red mullet in tomato-and-cumin sauce. Thanks to its popularity, reservations are recommended (and practically essential on weekends). Add in an impressive but not expensive wine list and this adds up to a fine place to chill with great views of the river. ⊠ *City Hotel on Queen's Quay, Central District* ☎ *028/7136–5800* 🖃 *AE, MC, V.*

$–$$ ✕ **The Exchange.** Overdressed twentysomethings lounge by the circular and ultramodern bar in this chic restaurant-cum-wine bar. It's become *the* place to be seen in Derry, so weekend evenings can be extremely busy. Unfortunately, reservations are not taken, so be prepared to wait at the bar—with a chilled glass of sauvignon blanc from the excellent wine list, it's no hardship. Locally caught seafood is delicious, and standouts include the halibut in shrimp sauce and the Hua Hin crab cakes flecked with coconut. Service is super-efficient but can be a touch brisk. ✉*Exchange House, Queen's Quay, Central District* ☎*028/7127–3990* ▤*AE, MC, V.*

$–$$ ✕**Spice.** It's worth the walk up the hill from town to this cozy restaurant with food that draws heavily on Pan-Asian influences. Main course highlights include crab claws and red Thai curry, served with plain or fried rice or noodles. ✉*162–164 Spencer Rd., East Bank* ☎*028/7134–4875* ▤*MC, V.*

¢–$ ✕**Fitzroy's.** This popular city center brasserie gives "quare packin" (Derry-speak for good value for money), with belt-busting portions of old favorites like burgers, steaks, and Caesar salads in the evening. Lunchtimes are busy, with weary shoppers and office staff stopping by for a turkey stuffing–and–cranberry panini sandwich or a big bowl of homemade leek-and-potato soup. The fully licensed bar stocks a good range of bottled beers and wines. ✉*2–4 Bridge St., Central District* ☎*028/7126–6211* ⊕*www.fitzroysrestaurant.com* ▤*MC, V.*

$$$ ▦**Beech Hill.** Journey past a fairy-tale gatehouse amid clumps of beech trees, and past streams and a duck pond to reach this grand 1729 country home. Beech Hill is very much attuned to the present with a number of conveniences to satisfy the demanding traveler (a trouser press, and tea and coffeemakers in-room). The vast honeymoon suite, with a four-poster bed, overlooks the gardens. Rooms in the old building are decorated in Georgian style; 10 rooms in a modern extension are larger and contemporary. A small museum celebrates the fact that Beech Hill housed a contingent of U.S. Marines during World War II. ✉*3 km (2 mi) southeast of town off A6, 32 Ardmore Rd., Beech Hill, BT47 3QP* ☎*028/7134–9279* 📠*028/7134–5366* ⊕*www.beech-hill.com* ⇆*28 rooms, 5 suites* △*In-room: no a/c, Wi-Fi. In-hotel: restaurant, bar, tennis court, gym, no elevator* ▤*AE, MC, V* ⫿⊙⫿*BP, MAP.*

$$ ▦**Tower Hotel.** The only hotel within Derry city's historic walls, this modern and comfortable hotel has more to offer than its unequaled location. Rooms are decorated in vibrant shades of red and blue, with pine furnishings and well-stocked bathrooms. The sleek oak-wood bar, with its low-hanging lights, is a favorite watering hole with locals as well as visiting guests. The bistro-style restaurant has won plenty of kudos, and the location is primo—just check out the view of the Bogside and the "Free Derry" corner from the upper bedrooms and the fourth-floor gym. ✉*Butcher St., Central District, BT48 6HL* ☎*028/7137–1000* 📠*028/7137–1234* ⊕*www.towerhotelgroup.com* ⇆*90 rooms, 3 suites* △*In-room: no a/c. In-hotel: restaurant, bar, gym, public Wi-Fi. In-hotel: no elevator* ▤*AE, DC, MC, V* ⫿⊙⫿*BP, MAP.*

¢ ▦**The Merchant's House.** No. 16 Queen Street was originally a Victorian ★ merchant's family town home built to Georgian proportions, then a rectory and bank, before Joan Pyne turned it into the city's grandest B&B. Garnet-color walls, elaborate plasterwork, and a fireplace make the parlor warm and welcoming. Little wonder the guestbook features some prominent names, including the late Hurd Hatfield, star of the movie *The Picture of Dorian Gray.* Joan also owns a similar but smaller building three minutes' walk away called the Saddler's House.

Charming and cozy, this Victorian jewel of a home (who can resist its faintingly pink living room parlor?) has been lovingly restored and is packed with interesting antiques and family portraits. It's also an excellent value for the money. Incidentally, many architecturally interesting homes occupy the neighborhood. ⊠*16 Queen St., West Bank, BT48 7EQ* ☎*028/7126–4223* 🖷*028/7126–6913* ⊕*www.thesaddlershouse. com* ⤳*6 rooms in Merchant's House; 7 rooms with shared bath in Saddler's House* ⊟*MC, V* ⦁⦁*BP.*

NIGHTLIFE & THE ARTS

ART GALLERIES The **Context Gallery** (⊠*5–7 Artillery St., West Bank* ☎*028/7137–3538*) shows works by up-and-coming Irish and international artists. The **McGilloway Gallery** (⊠*6 Shipquay St., West Bank* ☎*028/7136–6011*) stocks a broad selection of representational modern Irish art. Owner Ken McGilloway serves wine on Friday evenings until 9 PM during selected exhibitions. The **Orchard Gallery** (⊠*Orchard St., West Bank* ☎*028/7126–9675*) is known across Europe for its political and conceptual art.

PUBS & CLUBS The **Gweedore Bar** (⊠*59–63 Waterloo St., West Bank* ☎*028/7126–3513*) is a favorite for hip-hop and house music. Listen to traditional Irish music at **Peadar O'Donnell's** (⊠*63 Waterloo St., West Bank* ☎*028/7137–2318*). **Sugar Nightclub** (⊠*33 Shipquay St., West Bank* ☎*028/7126–6017*) is the place for dance music.

THEATER & OPERA The **Playhouse** (⊠*5–7 Artillery St., West Bank* ☎*028/7126–8027*) stages traditional and contemporary plays and also holds contemporary music concerts. The catch-all **Millennium Forum Theatre and Conference Centre** (⊠*Newmarket St., West Bank* ☎*028/7126–4455* ⊕*www. millenniumforum.co.uk*) presents everything and anything—from comedians to musicians to plays—on stage. The **Verbal Arts Centre** (⊠*Bishop St., Stable La. and Mall Wall, West Bank* ☎*028/7126–6946* ⊕*www.verbalartscentre.co.uk*) celebrates literature through performances and classes. It re-creates the great old Irish tradition of fireside tales at regular storytelling events.

SHOPPING

Shopping in town is generally low-key and unpretentious, but there are some upscale gems of Irish craftsmanship. Stroll up Shipquay Street to find small arts-and-crafts stores and an indoor shopping center.

Bookworm (⊠*18–20 Bishop St., West Bank* ☎*028/7128–2727*) is the best bookshop in Ireland, according to writer Nuala O'Faoláin.

Occasions (⊠*48 Spencer Rd., East Bank* ☎*028/7132–9595*) sells Irish crafts and gifts.

Stop at the gift shop **Pauline's Patch** (⊠*32 Shipquay St., West Bank* ☎*028/7127–9794*) for knickknacks.

Thomas the Goldsmith (⊠*7 Pump St., West Bank* ☎*028/7137–4549*) stocks exquisite work by international jewelry designers.

Off Shipquay Street, the **Trip** (⊠ *29 Ferryquay St., West Bank* ☎ *028/7137–2382*) is a teenage-clothing shop that specializes in knitwear.

THE WESTERN BORDER COUNTIES

While blissfully off the beaten track, this region contains some dazzling sights: the Ulster-American Folk Park; the great stately houses of Castle Coole and Florence Court; and the pottery town of Belleek. During the worst of the Troubles, the counties of Tyrone, Fermanagh, Armagh, and Down, which border the republic, were known as "bandit country," but now you can enjoy a worry-free trip through the calm countryside and stop in at some very "Ulster" towns, delightfully distinct from the rest of Ireland.

OMAGH

55 km (34 mi) south of Derry on A5.

Omagh, the county town of Tyrone, lies close to the Sperrin Mountains, with the River Strule to the north. Playwright Brian Friel was born here. Sadly, it's better known as the scene of the worst atrocity of the Troubles, when an IRA bomb killed 29 people in 1998. The town has two places of worship—a Church of Ireland church and a Catholic double-spire church. North of Omagh the country is pretty and rustic, with small farm villages.

34
★ Several miles north of Omagh is the big attraction of the region: the excellent **Ulster-American Folk Park** re-creates a Tyrone village of two centuries ago, a log-built American settlement of the same period, and the docks and ships that the emigrants to America would have used. The centerpiece of the park is an old whitewashed cottage, now a museum, which is the ancestral home of Thomas Mellon (1855–1937), the U.S. banker and philanthropist. Another thatched cottage is a reconstruction of the boyhood home of Archbishop John Hughes, founder of New York's St. Patrick's Cathedral. There are also full-scale replicas of Irish peasant cottages, Pennsylvania farmhouses, a New York tenement room, immigrant transport ship holders, plus a 19th-century Ulster village, complete with staff dressed in 19th-century costumes. Other exhibitions trace the contribution of the Northern Irish people to American history. The park also has a crafts shop and café. Last admission is 1½ hours before closing. ⊠ *Mellon Rd., 10 km (6 mi) north of town on A5, Castletown, Omagh* ☎ *028/8224–3292* ⊕ *www.folkpark.com* ☎ *£4.50* ☉ *Apr.–Sept., Mon.–Sat. 10:30–6, Sun. 11–6:30; Oct.–Mar., weekdays 10:30–5.*

BELLEEK

35 *42 km (25 mi) southwest of Omagh off A46.*

World-famous Belleek Pottery is made in the old town of Belleek on the northwestern edge of Lower Lough Erne, at the border with northwest Ireland. Other porcelainware makers are a few kilometers across the border.

On the riverbank stands the visitor center of **Belleek Pottery Ltd.**, producers of Parian china, a fine, eggshell-thin, ivory porcelain shaped into dishes, figurines, vases, and baskets. There's a factory, showroom, exhibition, museum, and café. On tours of the factory you can get up close and talk to craftspeople—there's hardly any noise coming from machinery in the workshops. Everything here is made by hand in the same method used in 1857. The showroom is filled with beautiful but pricey gifts: a cup-and-saucer set costs about £16, and a bowl in a basket-weave style (typical of Belleek) runs £69 and up. ☎028/6865–8501 ⊕www.belleek.ie ☑£4 ☉Apr.–June, Sept., and Oct., weekdays 9–6, Sat. 10–6, Sun. 2–6; July and Aug., weekdays 9–8, Sat. 10–6, Sun. 11–6; Nov.–Mar., weekdays 9–5:30.

WHERE TO EAT

$ ✕**The Thatch.** Housed in a lovely building dating back to 18th century, this simple café is well worth a visit—not just for the excellent soups, sandwiches, baked potatoes, and similarly light fare—but also because it's the only thatched-roof establishment in the entire county. Full of locals and rife with the sounds of easy banter, it's the perfect place to glean "local knowledge" and gossip about the surrounding area. ✉Main St., Belleek ☎028/6865–8181 ▤MC, V ☉Closed Sun.

ENNISKILLEN

③⑥ 5 km (3 mi) south of Devenish Island, Lower Lough Erne, on A32.

Enniskillen is the pleasant, smart-looking capital of County Fermanagh and the only place of any size in the county. The town center is, strikingly, on an island in the River Erne between Lower and Upper Lough Erne. The principal thoroughfares, Townhall and High streets, are crowded with old-style pubs and rows of redbrick Georgian flats. The tall, dark spires of the 19th-century St. Michael's and St. MacArtin's cathedrals, both on Church Street, tower over the leafy town center.

Among the several relaxed and welcoming old pubs in Enniskillen's town center, the one with the most appeal is **Blake's of the Hollow** on the main street, a place hardly altered since it opened in 1887. Its name derives from the fact that the heart of the town lies in a slight hollow and the pub's landlord is named William Blake. (Don't ask: he's not related to the English poet, painter, and engraver.) ✉6 Church St. ☎028/6632–2143.

Enniskillen's main sight is the waterfront **Enniskillen Castle,** one of the best-preserved monuments in the North. Built by the Maguire clan in 1670, this stronghold houses the local history collection of the Fermanagh County Museum and the polished paraphernalia of the Royal Inniskilling Fusiliers Regimental Museum. A Heritage Centre also stands within the curtilage of the castle. ✉Castlebarracks ☎028/6632–5000 ⊕www.enniskillencastle.co.uk ☑£2.50 ☉May, June, and Sept., Mon.

9

Beautiful Belleek

The origins of Belleek china are every bit as romantic as the Belleek blessing plates traditionally given to brides and grooms on their wedding day—that is, if you believe the legends. The story goes that in the mid 1800s, John Caldwell Bloomfield, the man behind the world-famous porcelain, accidentally discovered the raw ingredients necessary to produce china. After inheriting his father's estate in the Fermanagh Lakelands on the shore of the Erne River, he whitewashed his cottage using a flaky white powder dug up in his backyard. A passerby, struck by the luminescent sheen of the freshly painted cottage, commented on the unusual brightness of the walls to the lord of the manor. Bloomfield promptly ordered a survey of the land, which duly uncovered all the minerals needed to make porcelain. The venture was complete when Bloomfield met his business partners—London architect

Robert Armstrong and the wealthy Dublin merchant David McBirney. They decided to first produce earthenware, and then porcelain. And the rest, as they say, is history. The delicate, flawless porcelain (Bloomfield declared that any piece with even the slightest blemish should be destroyed) soon attracted the attention of Queen Victoria and many other aristos. Other companies tried to mimic the china's delicate beauty, but genuine Belleek porcelain is recognizable by its seashell designs, basket weaves, and marine themes. The company is now owned by an Irish-born American businessman, Dr. George Moore, and continues to flourish. It has become a favored tradition in Ireland to give a piece of Belleek china at weddings, giving rise to a saying: "If a newly married couple receives a piece of Belleek, their marriage will be blessed with lasting happiness."

and Sat. 2–5, Tues.–Fri. 10–5; July and Aug., Mon. and weekends 2–5, Tues.–Fri. 10–5; Oct.–Apr., Mon. 2–5, Tues.–Fri. 10–5.

At the Erne riverside, the 16th-century **Water Gate,** between two handsome turrets, protected the town from invading armies.

Beyond the West Bridge is **Portora Royal School,** established in 1608 by King James I. On the grounds are some ruins of Portora Castle. Among writers educated here are Samuel Beckett and Oscar Wilde, the pride of the school (until his trial for homosexuality).

WHERE TO STAY

$$ ⬛**The Manor House Hotel.** On the shores of Lower Lough Erne, this stately 19th-century manor harks back to a more tranquil age. Romantic canopied four-poster beds and traditional floral patterns await guests in the hotel's bedrooms, but be sure to ask for a room at the back so you can savor stunning views of the lakelands. Heavy linen napkins and silver cutlery add the finishing touches to the very good, if slightly formal, manor restaurant, presided over by the ambitious chef Jean-Michel Maquet. Why not take advantage of the excellent golf and fishing facilities and ask the friendly staff to book you a seat on the hotel's boat, the grandly named *Lady of the Lake,* for a cruise of Lough Erne? The idyllic location contributes to the hotel's

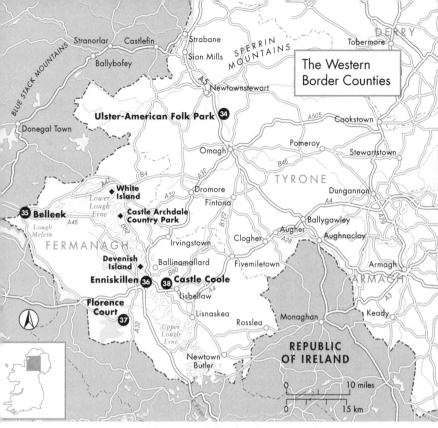

The Western Border Counties

laid-back relaxing air: sip a cocktail (or two) in the Belleek bar before dinner and you won't fail to unwind. ⊠*7 mi northwest of Enniskillen, Killadeas, Co. Fermanagh* ☎*028/6862–2200* 📠*028/6862–1545* ⊕*www.manor-house-hotel.com* 🛏*81 rooms* �*In-room: no a/c. In-hotel: restaurant, bars, golf course, tennis court, pool, gym, public Wi-Fi* ▤*AE, MC, V* 🍴�‌*BP, MAP.*

FLORENCE COURT

37 *11 km (7 mi) south of Enniskillen on A4 and A32.*

★

When it comes to Early Irish Georgian houses, there are few as magical as Florence Court. Less known than some showier estates, this three-story Anglo-Irish mansion was built around 1730 for John Cole, father of the first earl of Enniskillen. Topped off about 1760 with its distinctive two flanking colonnaded wings, the central house is adorably adorned with a positive surfeit of Palladian windows, keystones, and balustrades thanks to, as one architectural historian put it, "the vain-gloriousness of a provincial hand." Even more impressive is its bucolically baroque setting, as the Cuilcagh Mountains form a wonderful contrast to the shimmering white stone facade. Up until five years ago, the house—victim of a disastrous fire in the 1950s—was barely furnished, but a magnificent National Trust restoration, as well as a 1988 legacy left by the last countess of Enniskillen, have returned many family heirlooms to these interiors. Showstoppers in terms of decor are the Rococo plasterwork ceilings in the dining room; the Venetian Room; and the famous staircase, all ascribed to Robert West, one of Dublin's most famous stuccadores (plaster workers). For a peek at the "downstairs" world, check out the restored kitchen and other

> **LISTEN CLOSELY AND YOU SHALL HEAR...**
>
> Florence Court's ancestral park is one of Northern Ireland's glories—dotted with noted heirloom trees (including the Florence Court weeping beech), it also has nooks and dells where, legend has it, you can hear the "song of the little people."

service quarters. ⊠ *11 km (7 mi) south of Enniskillen on A4 and A32* ☎ *028/6634–8249* ⊕ *www.nationaltrust.org.uk* 💷 *£5* ⊙ *Grounds Oct.–Apr., daily 10–4; May–Sept., daily 10–8; mansion Mar.–May and Sept., weekends noon–6; June, weekdays 1–6, weekends noon–6; July and Aug., daily noon–6.*

CASTLE COOLE

🕘 *3 km (2 mi) east of Enniskillen on A4.*

★ In the 18th century and through most of the 19th, the Loughs of Erne and their environs were remote places far from Ireland's bustling cities. But it was just this isolated green and watery countryside that attracted the Anglo-Irish gentry, who built grand houses. This "uncommonly perfect" mansion (to quote the eminent architectural historian Desmond Guinness) is on its own landscaped oak woods and gardens at the end of a long tree-lined driveway. Although the Irish architect Richard Johnston made the original drawings in the 1790s, and was responsible for the foundation, the castle was, for all intents and purposes, the work of James Wyatt, commissioned by the first Earl of Belmore (whose family was related to the Counts of Enniskillen, who built Florence Court). One of the best-known architects of his time, Wyatt was based in London but only visited Ireland once, so Alexander Stewart was drafted as the resident builder-architect who oversaw much of the construction. The designer wasn't the only imported element; in fact, much of Castle Coole came from England, including the main facade, which is clad in Portland stone shipped from Dorset to Ballyshannon and then hauled here by horse and cart. And what a facade it is—in perfect symmetry, white colonnaded wings extend from either side of the mansion's three-story, nine-bay center block, with a Palladian central portico and pediment. It is perhaps the apotheosis of the 18th century's reverence for the Greeks.

Inside, the house is remarkably preserved; most of the lavish plasterwork and original furnishings are in place. On its completion in September 1798, the construction had cost £70,000 and the furnishings another £22,000, compared to the £6 million cost of a restoration in

1995–96, during which anything not in keeping with the original design was removed. The saloon is one of the finest rooms in the house, with a vast expanse of oak flooring, gilded Regency furniture, and gray scagliola pilasters with Corinthian capitals. The present earl of Belmore still lives on the estate and uses one wing of the house. He often attends the public concerts that are held here during the summer months. ⊠ *Dublin Rd., A4* ☎ *028/6632–2690* ⊕ *www.nationaltrust.org.uk* ⊠ *Grounds free, mansion £5* ⊙ *Grounds Oct.–Apr., daily 10–4; May–Sept. daily 10–8; mansion Mar.–May and Sept., weekends noon–6; June, Wed.–Mon. noon–6; July and Aug., daily noon–6.*

THE EASTERN BORDER COUNTIES

Home to St. Patrick's shrines of Armagh and Downpatrick and one of Ireland's best-known ranges—the Mountains of Mourne—Counties Armagh and Down make a fittingly moving finale to any tour of Northern Ireland.

ARMAGH

㊴ *74 km (42 mi) east of Castle Coole.*

The spiritual capital of Ireland for 5,000 years, and the seat of both Protestant and Catholic archbishops, Armagh is the most venerated of Irish cities. St. Patrick called it "my sweet hill" and built his stone church on the hill where the Anglican cathedral now stands. On the opposite hill, the twin-spired Catholic cathedral is flanked by two large marble statues of archbishops who look across the land. Despite the pleasing Georgian terraces around the elegant Mall east of the town center, Armagh can seem drab. Having suffered as a trouble spot in the sectarian conflict, though, it's now the scene of some spirited and sympathetic renovation.

The **Astronomy Centre and Planetarium** contains models of spacecraft, video shows of the sky, and hands-on computer displays. The Eartho-rium explores the world from three levels—its interior, surface, and atmosphere. The outdoor 30-acre AstroPark has a model solar system. You can also view the 16-inch telescope as well as the Robinson Dome, also known as "the 10-inch dome" for the 1875 Grub telescope it houses. ⊠ *College Hill* ☎ *028/3752–3689* ⊕ *www.armaghplanet.com* ⊠ *AstroPark and Robinson Dome free; Earthorium £1; special shows and other exhibitions £3* ⊙ *Weekdays 2–4:45.*

The pale limestone, Gothic **St. Patrick's Roman Catholic Cathedral,** the seat of a Roman Catholic archdiocese, rises above a hill to dominate the north end of Armagh. Inside, the rather gloomy interior is enlivened by a magnificent organ, the potential of which is fully realized at services. Construction of the twin-spire cathedral started in 1840 in the neo-Gothic style, but the Great Famine brought work to a halt until 1854. It was finally completed in 1873. An arcade of statues over the main doorway on the exterior is one of the cathedral's most interesting features. The altar is solid Irish granite and the woodwork is Austrian oak. ⊠*Hilltop* ☎*028/3752–2638* ⊕*www.armagharchdiocese.org.*

Near the town center, a squat, battlement tower identifies **St. Patrick's Anglican Cathedral,** in simple, early-19th-century, low-Gothic style. It stands on the site of much older churches and contains several relics of Armagh's long history, including sculpted, pre-Christian idols. Brian Boru (king of all Ireland) who visited Armagh in 1004—and was received with great ceremony—is buried here. In 1014, at the Battle of Clontarf, he drove the Vikings out of Ireland—but was killed after the battle was won. Inside are memorials and tombs by important 18th-century sculptors such as Roubilliac and Rysbrack. ⊠*Abbey St.* ⊕*www.stpatricks-cathedral.org* ☞*Free* ⊙*Tours June–Aug., Mon.–Sat. 11:30 and 2:30.*

Reopened in 2007 following a major renovation, **Palace Stables Heritage Centre** presents a diorama of everyday life—upstairs and downstairs—in the 18th-century days of the extremely wealthy Richard Robinson. Baron Rokeby was this man's ancestral title but he was best known as the region's archbishop of the Church of Ireland. He commissioned local architect Francis Johnston, who had designed much of Georgian Dublin, to create a new Armagh out of the slums into which it had degenerated. The archbishop gave the city a clean water supply and a sewer system then turned the city's racecourse into an elegant mall. He paved and lighted the streets; financed improvements to the Bishop's Palace and the Protestant cathedral; and endowed the public library, the observatory, the Royal School, and the county infirmary. The museum is located past the 13th-century Franciscan friary ruins, in the stables of the former archbishop's demesne. ⊠*Palace Demesne, Friary Rd.* ☎*028/3752–9629* ☞*£4.50* ⊙*June–Sept., Mon.–Sat. 10–5, Sun. 1–5.*

Just outside Armagh, **Navan Fort** is Ulster's Camelot—the region's ancient capital. Excavations date evidence of activity going back to 700 BC. The fort has strong associations with figures of Irish history. Legend has it that thousands of years ago this was the site of the palace of Queen Macha; subsequent tales call it the barracks of the legendary Ulster warrior Cuchulainn and his Red Branch Knights. Remains dating from 94 BC are particularly intriguing: a great conical structure, 120 feet in diameter, was formed from five concentric circles made of 275 wooden posts, with a 276th, about 12 yards high, situated in the center. In a ritual whose meaning is not known, it was filled with brushwood and set on fire. ⊠*3 km (2 mi) west of Armagh on A28* ☞*Free.*

OFF THE BEATEN PATH

Linen Green. Looking for a bargain? Venture north to Linen Green, an outlet mall where you can purchase clothing, lingerie, shoes, gifts, and furniture. You can buy woven items from well-known producers—such as Paul Costelloe, Ulster Weavers, Foxford, and Anne Storey—at a discount. ⊠*20 km (12 mi) north of Armagh off A29, Moygashel* ☎*028/8775–3761* ⊙*Mon.–Sat. 10–5.*

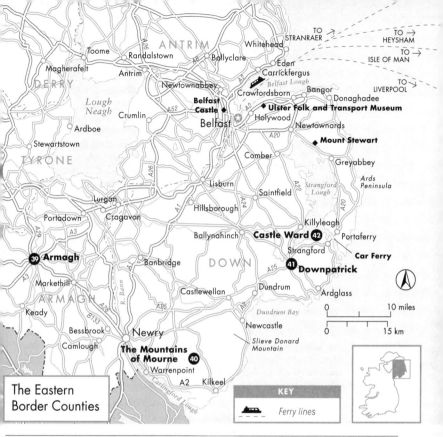

THE MOUNTAINS OF MOURNE

40 *52½ km (32½ mi) southeast of Armagh on A28, 51 km (32 mi) south of Belfast.*

Subjects of a song that is sung on every Irish occasion from baptism to funerals, the Mountains of Mourne must surely qualify as one of Ireland's best-known ranges. According to those lyrics by Percy French, the Mountains of Mourne "sweep down to the sea," from 2,000-foot summits. East of the unprepossessing border town of Newry, this area was long considered ungovernable, its hardy inhabitants living from smuggling contraband into the numerous rocky coves on the seashore. Much of the Mourne range is still inaccessible except on foot. The countryside is gorgeous: high, windswept pasture and moorland threaded with bright streams, bound by a tracery of drystone walls, and dotted with sheep and whitewashed farmhouses snuggled in stands of sycamore. It's the perfect landscape for away-from-it-all walkers, cyclists, and serious climbers. Climbers should inform their hotel when and where they're going before setting off.

The road to the **Silent Valley** reservoir park leads to mountain views and excellent photo-ops. ✉ *6 km (4 mi) north of Kilkeel off B27, right turn*

☎028/9074–6581 🖾Vehicles £3, pedestrians £2 ⏱June–Aug., daily 10–6:30; Sept.–May, daily 10–4.

Newcastle, a bracing Victorian cold-water bathing station, is the main center for visitors to the hills.

Looming above Newcastle is **Slieve Donard,** its panoramic, 2,805-foot-high summit grandly claiming views into England, Wales, and Scotland "when it's clear enough"—in other words, "rarely," say the pessimists. It's not possible to drive up the mountain, so leave your car in Donard car park. It should take roughly three hours to climb to the summit and no longer than two hours to descend. Experienced hikers should not find it difficult, but if you prefer an easier trek, follow the trails signposted in Tollymore Forest Park. Hiking boots are essential and, as the weather can be unpredictable, it's advisable to take an extra layer of clothing, even in summer.

> **WORD OF MOUTH**
>
> "If you like hiking, consider the Mountains of Mourne—wonderful scenery and very few other people other than walkers and locals know about their beauty. It is also the area where the Brontë family originated. The Silent Valley drive is wonderful."
>
> —Cambe

Covering 1,200 acres and entered through picturesque Gothic gateways, **Tollymore Forest Park** extends up the valley of the River Shimna. Many pretty stone bridges cross over the sparkling waters here. ⊠Tullybrannigan Rd., Newcastle ☎028/4372–2428 ⊕www.forestserviceni.gov.uk 🖾Vehicles £4, pedestrians £2 ⏱Daily 10–dusk.

A huge maze, grown to symbolize the convoluted path to peace, is the latest addition to **Castlewellan Forest Park,** which comprises 1,150 acres of forested hills running between the Mourne Mountains and Slieve Croob. With the maze, lake, secluded arbors, and arboretum, the park makes an excellent introduction to the area. ⊠Castlewellan ☎028/4377–8664 ⊕www.forestserviceni.gov.uk 🖾Vehicles £4, pedestrians free ⏱Daily 10–dusk.

WHERE TO STAY

$$$$ 🏨 **Slieve Donard Hotel.** A lavish redbrick monument to Victoriana, this turreted hotel stands like a palace on green lawns at one end of Newcastle's 6½-km (4-mi) sandy beach. The traditional furnishings may make you feel as if you're stepping back in time to the town's turn-of-the-20th-century heyday as an elegant seaside resort (though the rooms have modern comforts). Ask for a room overlooking the water. At the entrance to the grounds, the Percy French gatehouse restaurant serves adequate seafood dishes; there's music Friday and Saturday night. The Royal County Down Golf Club is next door, and the hotel has two exercise rooms. ⊠Downs Rd., Newcastle, Co. Down BT33 0AH ☎028/4372–1066 🖨028/4372–1166 ⊕www.hastingshotels.com ➬124 rooms ⚑In-room: no a/c, Wi-Fi. In-hotel: 2 restaurants, bar, pool, gym, spa ⊟AE, DC, MC, V ⏐◎⏐BP, MAP.

$$–$$$ 🏨 **Glassdrumman Lodge.** For those who wish to be pampered as well as immersed in the ancient Kingdom of Mourne, Graeme and Joan Hall's

eclectically simple and stylish lodge is the place. The outside of the house is less than spectacular, but the busy estate has more than enough drama to compensate, for the family grows their own crops, raises their own farm animals, churns their own butter, and bakes their own bread. Rooms are decorated in bright colors and have large windows with glorious views. ⊠*Mill Rd., Annalong, Co. Down BT34 4RH* ☎*028/4376–8451* 🖷*028/4376–7041* ⊕*www.glassdrummanlodge. com* ↦*10 rooms, 2 suites* ⑇*In-room: no a/c, Wi-Fi. In-hotel: restaurant, laundry service* ☰*AE, DC, MC, V* ⊙|*BP.*

SPORTS & THE OUTDOORS

Tollymore Mountain Centre (⊠*Bryansford, Newcastle* ☎*028/4372–2158*) provides advice on mountain climbing and trails. The **Royal County Down** (⊠*Off A2, Newcastle* ☎*028/4372–3314* ⊕*www.royalcountydown. org*) is considered by many golfers to be one of the finest courses in the world. Between April and October, a game on the Championship Links can run up to £115; the Annesley Links top at £35.

DOWNPATRICK

❹ *21 km (18 mi) east of Newcastle on A2 and A25.*

Downpatrick once was called "Plain and Simple Down" but had its name changed by John de Courcy, a Norman knight who moved to the town in 1176. De Courcy set about promoting St. Patrick, the 5th-century Briton who was captured by the Irish and served as a slave in the Down area before he escaped to France, where he learned about Christianity and bravely returned to try to convert the local chiefs. Although it's not true that Patrick brought a new faith to Ireland—there was already a bishop of Ireland before Patrick got here—he must have been a better missionary than most because he did indeed win influential converts. The clan chief of the Down area gave him land at the village of Saul, near Downpatrick, to build a monastery.

9

Down Cathedral is one of the disputed burial places of St. Patrick. In the churchyard, a somber slab inscribed "Patric" is supposedly the saint's tomb, but no one knows where he's actually buried. It might be here, at Saul, or, some scholars argue, more likely at Armagh. The church, which lay ruined from 1538 to 1790 (it reopened in 1818), preserves parts of some of the earlier churches and monasteries that have stood on this site, the oldest of which dates back to the 6th century. Even by then, the cathedral site had long been an important fortified settlement: Down takes its name from the Celtic word "dun," or fort. ⊠*Hilltop* ⊕*www.downcathedral.org* ⊠*Free.*

ⓒ For some hard facts concerning the patron saint of Ireland, visit the interactive exhibits of **St. Patrick Centre** next to the cathedral; It's housed, together with the Down Museum, inside a former 18th-century jail. The ancient myths and stories of early Christian Ireland are brought to life in this information center; you can explore how St. Patrick's legacy developed in early Christian times and examine the art and metalwork that was produced during this "Golden Age." Younger children will love the puppet shows detailing the life of the saint and can even paint their own *Book of Kells* with quills. The Grove art gallery exhibits jewelry, textiles, and paintings by local artists and craftsmen. If the weather is fine, have lunch on the terrace of the Cathedral Garden restaurant, with its dramatic views of Down Cathedral and the Mountains of Mourne. ⊠ *The Mall* ☎ *028/4461–9000* ⊕ *www.saint patrickcentre.com* 🖭 *£6* ⊗ *Oct.– Mar., Mon.–Sat. 10–5; Apr., May, and Sept., Mon.–Sat. 9:30–5:30, Sun. 1–5:30; June–Aug., Mon.–Sat. 9:30–6, Sun. 10–6.*

> ### A DAY LIKE ANY OTHER
>
> St Patrick's Day—March 17th—is a great time to visit Downpatrick, as the whole town turns out in carnival dress for the holiday parade. But why is St. Paddy fêted on March 17th? Legend has it he died on that date, perhaps in 461 AD. Others point to the fact that this date marked one of the great pagan festivals celebrating the onset of spring and the sowing of crops.

WHERE TO STAY & EAT

$ ✕ **Denvir's.** In this wonderfully atmospheric pub dating back to 1642, oak beams, stone floors, meat hooks hanging from the ceiling, and a large open fireplace testify to the antiquity. The bar top was crafted from the timbers of ships wrecked in Lough Foyle. Back in the mists of time, it was a member of the same Denvir family who gave the family name to a small settlement in Colorado, its name later modified to Denver. Solid traditional dishes dominate the menu—steak, roast chicken, spring lamb—complemented by a local delicacy called sloke, a species of seaweed. ⊠ *14 English St.* ☎ *028/4461–2012* ▤ *AE, MC, V.*

$ ✕🖭 **Dufferin Arms Coaching Inn.** Stewart and Morris Crawford preside
★ over this 1803 inn next to picture-perfect, grandly gracious Killyleagh Castle (reputedly the longest inhabited castle in Ireland and most probably the country's prettiest). Rooms in the low-slung, bright-red building are quaint, lush, and cozy, with four-poster beds. Downstairs, the original stables have been converted into the Kitchen Restaurant ($–$$), which sometimes hosts medieval feasts. It specializes in Irish cooking— the poached salmon and the roast duck in cherry sauce are two best bets. One of the bars has snugs, another an open fire. Diversions such as pub quizzes and Cajun and jazz music keep things lively. ⊠ *10 km (6 mi) north of Downpatrick, 31–33 High St., Killyleagh, Co. Down BT30 9QF* ☎ *028/4482–1134* 🖷 *028/4482–8755* ⊕ *www.dufferincoaching inn.com* ➪ *6 rooms* ⚷ *In-room: no a/c, dial-up. In-hotel: restaurant, bars, public Internet, no elevator* ▤ *AE, MC, V* ⦿ *BP.*

CASTLE WARD

❹❷ *11 km (7 mi) northeast of Downpatrick, 3 km (2 mi) west of Strang-*
★ *ford village on A25, on southern shore of Strangford Lough, entrance by Ballyculter Lodge.*

With a 500-acre park, an artificial lake, a neoclassical tempietto, and a vast house in Bath stone magically set on the slopes running down to the "Narrows" of the southern shore of Strangford Lough, Castle Ward must have been some place to call home. About 3 km (2 mi) from the village of Strangford, off the road to Downpatrick, this regal stately home was designed around 1760 in, rather famously, two differing styles. Bernard Ward, 1st Viscount Bangor, could rarely see eye to eye (gossip had it) with his wife, Lady Anne, and the result was that he decided to make the entrance front and salons elegant exercises in Palladian Neoclassicism, while milady transformed the garden facade and her own rooms using the most fashionable style of the day, Strawberry Hill Gothick. His white-and-beige Music Room is picked out in exquisite plasterwork (note how craftsmen decided to save a little money by taking objects, such as a tricorn hat and basket, and simply covering them in plaster), while

> ## AN EVENING OF THRILLS
>
> After Castle Ward fell into ruin (one Ward descendant had to resort to selling bread at the gate), the Victorian era ushered in new wealth, restoring the house to a sparkling state, never more so than during summer evenings when it becomes Ireland's Glyndebourne and hosts opera performances in its small private theater.

her Boudoir has an undulating fan-vaulted ceiling that conjures up the "gothick" medievalisms of King Henry VII's chapel at Westminster. In fact, the couple's contretemps were dinner-table hearsay and they actually got along famously and the Gothic style was used to beef up the ancestral image of a "Castle" Ward. Be sure to walk through the park (which has its own Wildlife Center) to enjoy the wonderful vistas overlooking the waters to the town of Portaferry and the Ards Peninsula. ⊠*1 mi west of Strangford on Downpatrick Rd., A25* ☎*028/4488–1204* ⊕*www.nationaltrust.org.uk* ⊠*£5.50* ⊘*July and Aug., daily 1–6; Sept.–June, weekends 1–6; grounds open May, Wed.–Mon., daily 10–8; June–Sept., daily 10–8, Oct.–Apr., daily 10–4.*

9

NORTHERN IRELAND ESSENTIALS

TRANSPORTATION

If traveling extensively by public transportation, be sure to load up on information (the best taxi-for-call companies, rail and bus schedules, etc.) upon arriving at the ticket counter or help desk of the bigger train and bus stations in the area, such as Belfast, Derry, and Armagh.

BY AIR

Scheduled services from the United States and Canada are mostly routed through Dublin, Glasgow, London, or Manchester. Several new routes have been introduced to Belfast International to great fanfare in recent years. Zoom offers low-cost direct flights from Toronto and Vancouver, and Continental offers direct service from the United States out of Newark.

Frequent services to Belfast's two airports are scheduled throughout the day from London Heathrow, London Gatwick, and Luton (all of which have fast coordinated subway or rail connections to central London) and from 17 other U.K. airports. Flights from London take about one hour. Aer Arann flies twice daily from Cork to Belfast on weekdays. British Airways flies to Belfast City Airport and Derry from Manchester and London's Heathrow and Gatwick. British Midlands, through its low-cost carrier BMI Baby, flies from Birmingham, Cardiff, Durham, Manchester and Nottingham to Belfast International. Jet2 flies from Belfast International to Barcelona, Leeds, and Prague. EasyJet flies from Belfast International to several European airports, including Alicante, Amsterdam, Bristol, Edinburgh, Glasgow, Liverpool, Luton, Paris, Rome, and Stansted. Eastern Airways flies from Belfast to Aberdeen. Flybe, also known as British European Airways, flies from Belfast City to Birmingham, Bristol, Edinburgh, Glasgow, Leeds, London Gatwick, Norwich, and Southampton, among others.

Carriers **Aer Arann** (☎ *081/821–0210 or 0800/587–2324* ⊕ *www.aerarann. ie*). **Aer Lingus** (☎ *0845/084–4444* ⊕ *www.aerlingus.com*). **British Airways** (☎ *0845/773–3377* ⊕ *www.britishairways.com*). **British Midland Airways** (☎ *0870/607–0555* ⊕ *www.bmibaby.com*). **Continental** (☎ *0845/607–6760* ⊕ *www.continental.com/uk*). **EasyJet** (☎ *0871/244–2366* ⊕ *www.easyjet.com*). **Flybe** (☎ *0871/700–0123* ⊕ *www.flybe.com*). **Jet2** (☎ *0871/226–1737* ⊕ *www. jet2.com*). **Zoom** (☎ *0870/240–0055* ⊕ *www.zoomairlines.com*).

AIRPORTS Belfast International Airport at Aldergove is the north's principal air arrival point, 30½ km (19 mi) north of town. Belfast City Airport is the secondary airport, 6½ km (4 mi) east of the city. It receives flights from U.K. provincial airports, from London's Gatwick and Heathrow, and from Stansted and Luton (both near London). City of Derry Airport is 8 km (5 mi) from Derry and receives flights from Dublin, Glasgow, and Manchester.

Airport Information **Belfast City Airport** (☎ *028/9093–9093* ⊕ *www.belfast cityairport.com*). **Belfast International Airport at Aldergove** (☎ *028/9448– 4848* ⊕ *www.bial.co.uk*). **City of Derry Airport** (☎ *028/7181–0784* ⊕ *www.cityof derryairport.com*).

TRANSFERS Ulsterbus operates a bus every half hour (one way £6, round-trip £9) between Belfast International Airport and Belfast city center, as well as between Belfast City Airport and the city center (one way £2). Contact Translink for information on all buses. From Belfast City Airport, you can also travel into Belfast by train from Sydenham Halt to Central Station or catch a taxi from the airport to your hotel. If you arrive at the City of Derry Airport, you may need to call a taxi to get to your destination.

Contacts **Delta Cabs** (☎ *028/7127–9999*). **Eglinton Taxis** (☎ *028/7181–1231*). **Foyle Taxis** (☎ *028/7126–3905*). **Translink** (☎ *028/9066–6630* ⊕ *www.trans link.co.uk*).

BY BOAT & FERRY

Norse Merchant Ferries has 11-hour daytime or overnight car ferries that connect Belfast with the English west-coast port of Liverpool every day. P&O European Ferries has a one-hour sailing to Larne from Cairnryan, Scotland; infrequent trains take passengers on to Belfast. The *SeaCat* high-speed catamaran sails between Belfast and Troon in Scotland, between Belfast and Glasgow, and between the Isle of Man and Belfast. The *StenaLine HSS* fast catamaran sails between Belfast and Stranraer, Scotland in 1½ hours.

Boat & Ferry Information Norse Merchant Ferries (⊠ *Victoria Terminal 2, W. Bank Rd., Belfast* ☎ *028/9077–9090* ⊕ *www.norsemerchant.com*). **P&O European Ferries** (☎ *0870/242–4777* ⊕ *www.poirishsea.com*). **SeaCat and Steam Packet Company Services** (☎ *0870/552–3523* ⊕ *www.seacat.co.uk*). *StenaLine HSS* (☎ *028/9074–7747* ⊕ *www.stenaline.com*).

BY BUS

Northern Ireland's main bus company, Ulsterbus, runs direct service between Dublin and Belfast. Queries about Ulsterbus service, or any other bus and rail transportation in Northern Ireland, can be answered by the national central reservation center, Translink. The republic's Bus Éireann runs direct services to Belfast from Dublin. Buses arrive at and depart from Belfast's Europa Buscentre; the ride takes three hours. Buses to Belfast also run from London and from Birmingham, making the Stranraer ferry crossing.

You can take advantage of frequent and inexpensive Ulsterbus links between all Northern Ireland towns. In Belfast, the Europa Buscentre is just behind the Europa Hotel. The Laganside Buscentre is around the corner from Belfast's Albert Clock Tower and about 1 km (½ mi) from Central Station. Within Belfast the city bus service is comprehensive. All routes start from Donegall Square, where there's a kiosk with timetables.

Bus Depot Europa Central Buscentre (⊠ *Great Victoria St., Golden Mile, Belfast* ☎ *028/9066–6630*). **Laganside Buscentre** (⊠ *Oxford St., Central District, Belfast* ☎ *028/9066–6630*).

Bus Lines Bus Éireann (☎ *01/836–6111 in Dublin* ⊕ *www.buseireann.ie*). **Translink** (☎ *028/9066–6630* ⊕ *www.translink.co.uk*).

FARES If you want to tour the north by bus, contact Translink: a Freedom of Northern Ireland Ticket allows unlimited travel on bus or train (£14 per day, £34 for 3 days, and £50 per week). An Irish Rover bus ticket from Ulsterbus covers Ireland, north and south, and costs £48 for 3 days, £109 for 8, and £156 for 15. An Emerald Card (bus and rail) costs £157 for 8 days and £271 for 15 days.

BY CAR

Many roads from the Irish Republic into Northern Ireland were once closed for security reasons, but all are now reinstated, leaving you with a choice of legitimate crossing points. Army checkpoints at approved frontier posts are rare, and few customs formalities are observed. The fast N1/A1 road connects Belfast to Dublin in 160 km

(100 mi) with an average driving time of just over two hours. In general, roads here are in much better shape and signposted more clearly than in the Irish Republic.

CAR RENTAL   You can choose among several rental companies, but renting a car won't be cheap. A compact car costs £150–£250 per week (including taxes, insurance, and unlimited mileage). If you're planning to take a rental car across the border into the republic, inform the company and check its insurance procedures. Main rental offices include Avis, Dan Dooley, Europcar, Ford, and Hertz. A £300 security deposit is required at the Ford agency in Derry, and a £500 to £750 security deposit is required by Hertz.

Agencies **Avis** (⊠ *Belfast International Airport, Belfast* ☎ *028/9442–2333 or 0870/606–0100* ⊠ *Belfast City Airport, Belfast* ☎ *0870/606–0100* ⊠ *Great Victoria St., Belfast* ☎ *028/9024–0404*). **Budget** (⊠ *Belfast International Airport, Belfast* ☎ *028/9442–3332* ⊠ *Belfast City Airport, Belfast* ☎ *028/9045–1111* ⊠ *96–102 Great Victoria St., Belfast* ☎ *028/9023–0700* ⊕ *www.budget.ie*). **Dan Dooley** (⊠ *Belfast International Airport, Belfast* ☎ *028/9445–2522* ⊕ *www.dooleycar rentals.com*). **Europcar** (⊠ *Belfast International Airport, Belfast* ☎ *028/9442– 3444 or 0800/068–0303* ⊠ *Belfast City Airport, Belfast* ☎ *028/9045–0904 or 0800/068–0303* ⊕ *www.europcar.ie*). **Ford** (⊠ *Desmond Motors, City of Derry Airport, Derry* ☎ *028/7181–2222*). **Hertz** (⊠ *Belfast International Airport, Belfast* ☎ *028/9442–2533* ⊠ *Belfast City Airport, Belfast* ☎ *028/9073–2451*).

PARKING   Belfast has many parking garages, as well as street meter-ticket parking. Before parking on the street, check the posted regulations: during rush hours many spots become no-parking.

TRAFFIC   Bad rush-hour delays can occur on the West Link in Belfast joining M1 (heading south or west) and M2 (heading east or north). Major roadworks will be underway in Belfast during 2008 and detours may be in place. On the whole, driving is quicker and easier in the north than in areas south of the border.

BY TAXI

Most taxis operate on the meter; ask for a price for longer journeys. You can order in advance. Most cabs will hold four people but you can pre-book a larger taxi that will hold six. Typical fares: Belfast International Airport to Belfast city center is around £25; Belfast City Airport to the city center is around £6; Derry City Airport to Derry city center is around £12. The minimum fare is usually £2.50 and £1.05 per mile thereafter although the larger multi-seater cabs are more expensive.

Taxi Companies **Value Cabs** (⊠ *27 Grosvenor Rd, Belfast* ☎ *028/9080–9080* ⊕ *www. valuecabs.co.uk*). **FonACAB** (⊠ *23a Botanic Ave., Belfast* ☎ *028/9033–3333* ⊕ *www. fonacab.com*). **Foyle Taxis** (⊠ *10a Newmarket St., Derry* ☎ *028/7126–3905*).

BY TRAIN

The Dublin–Belfast Express train, run jointly by Northern Ireland Railways and Iarnród Éireann, travels between the two cities in about two hours. Eight trains (check timetables, as some trains are much slower) run daily in each direction (five on Sunday) between Dublin and Belfast's misnamed Central Station—it's not, in fact, that central. A free shuttle bus service from Belfast Central Station will drop you off at City Hall or Ulsterbus's city-center Europa Buscentre. You can change trains at Central Station for the city-center Great Victoria Street Station, which is adjacent to the Europa Buscentre and the Europa Hotel.

Northern Ireland Railways runs only four rail routes from Belfast's Central Station: northwest to Derry via Coleraine and the Causeway Coast; east to Bangor along the shore of Belfast Lough; northeast to Larne (for the P&O European ferry to Scotland) and south to Dublin. There are frequent connections to Central Station from the city-center Great Victoria Street Station and from Botanic Station in the university area. A Freedom of Northern Ireland Ticket allows unlimited travel on trains (£14 per day, £34 for three days, and £50 per week). An Irish Rover train ticket provides five days of rail travel for £109.

Train Lines **Iarnród Éireann** (☎1850/366222 timetables ⊕ www.irishrial.ie/home). **Northern Ireland Railways** (✉28 Wellington Pl., Central District, Belfast ☎02/9066–6630 Translink ⊕www.translink.co.uk).

Train Stations **Botanic Station** (✉Botanic Ave., University Area, Belfast ☎028/9089–9411). **Central Station** (✉E. Bridge St., Golden Mile, Belfast ☎028/9089–9411).

CONTACTS & RESOURCES

EMERGENCIES

The general emergency number is 999. Belfast City Hospital and the Royal Victoria Hospital are the two Belfast hospitals with emergency rooms. Altnagelvin Hospital in Derry has an emergency room.

Contacts **Altnagelvin Hospital** (✉Glenshana Rd., on outskirts of East Derry ☎028/7134–5171). **Ambulance, coast guard, fire, police** (☎999). **Belfast City Hospital** (✉Lisburn Rd., University Area, Belfast ☎028/9032–9241). **Belfast's main police station** (✉6–10 N. Queen St., Central District, Belfast ☎028/9065–0222). **Royal Victoria Hospital** (✉Grosvenor Rd., West Belfast, Belfast ☎028/9024–0503).

MAIL, SHIPPING & INTERNET

In smaller towns, ask your hotel concierge if there are any Internet cafés nearby. It will typically cost about £1 for 15 minutes. Post office hours are generally weekdays 9–5:30 and Saturday 9–12:30. Smaller post offices still close at 12:30 PM on Wednesday; in larger city center areas post offices also are open 1–6 Sunday.

Internet Cafés **Revelations** (✉27 Shaftsbury Sq., Belfast ☎028/9032–0337 ⊕www.revelations.co.uk). **Bean-there.com** (✉20 The Diamond, Derry ☎028/7128–1303 ⊕www.bean-there.com).

Post Offices **Belfast GPO** (✉Victoria Sq., Belfast ☎028/2459–8466). **Derry GPO** (✉2 Boxland St., Derry ☎028/7609–3555).

MEDIA

The Irish News is a mainly Nationalist daily that covers Northern Ireland plus an all-Ireland section with some world news. Despite its name, *Belfast Telegraph* does not cover just Belfast but all of Northern Ireland. With both a morning and afternoon edition, this paper tends to have a slightly more Unionist editorial stance.

MONEY MATTERS

Main banks are open weekdays 9:30–4:30, smaller branches weekdays 10:30–3:30. Changing money outside banking hours is possible at Thomas Cook branches. The branch at Belfast Airport is open daily 6:45 AM–8 PM; the branch at Donegall Place is open from Monday through Wednesday, Friday, and Saturday 9–5:30, Thursday 10–5:30. You can also change bills at Travelex Worldwide Money.

Currency Exchange **Thomas Cook** (⊠ *11 Donegall Pl., Central District, Belfast* ☎ *028/9088–3900* ⊕ *www.thomascook.com*). **Travelex Worldwide Money** (⊠ *Belfast International Airport, Belfast* ☎ *028/9444–7500* ⊕ *www.travelex.co.uk*).

TOUR OPTIONS

BIKE TOURS Irish Cycle Tours organizes four- and eight-day tours of the Mournes, Glens of Antrim, and Causeway Coast, and the Sperrin Mountains and Donegal. The company closed its Belfast office in 2004 and is now based in County Kerry in the republic, hence the southern Irish phone number. Mourne Cycle Tours runs bike tours complete with hotel accommodations (bikes are delivered to the hotel), with rates for a two-night booking costing between £90 and £110.

Bike Touring **Irish Cycle Tours** (☎ *066/712–8733 in republic* ⊕ *www.irishcycletours.com*). **Mourne Self-Guided Cycling Breaks** (☎ *028/4372–4348* ⊕ *www.mournecycletours.com*).

BOAT TOURS On the Lower Lough Erne, Erne Tours operates an approximately 90-minute trip (£7) aboard the *Kestrel,* a 63-seat water bus, which leaves Round O Pier at Enniskillen Sunday May and June at 2:30, and daily July and August at 10:30, 2:15, and 4:15. Weekdays the boat stops for a half hour at Devenish Island. In September, tours leave Tuesday, Saturday, and Sunday at 2:30. Mid-May to end of August the company also has a Saturday evening dinner cruise departing at 6:30.

Contacts **Erne Tours** (⊠ *Round O Pier, Enniskillen* ☎ *028/6632–2882, 028/6632–4822 dinner cruise*).

BUS TOURS Belfast City Sightseeing runs an open-top bus tour (with shelter in case it rains) through Belfast. The Belfast City Tour (£8) covers the City Hall, Albert Clock, Shipyard, Titanic Quarter, Shankill Road, the peace line, the Falls Road, and past the Grand Opera House on Great Victoria Street. Tours leave Castle Place (opposite McDonald's) daily on the half hour from 9:30 to 4:30, and tickets are valid all day on a hop-on, hop-off basis. The entire route, without stops, takes about 70 minutes.

Ulsterbus operates half-day or full-day trips June through September from Belfast to the Glens of Antrim, the Giant's Causeway, the Fermanagh lakes, Lough Neagh, the Mountains of Mourne, and the Ards Peninsula. Ulsterbus has also teamed up with the Old Bushmills Distillery to run the Bushmills Bus: an open-top tour bus running from Coleraine (via Bushmills to observe whiskey making) to the Giant's Causeway and the coastal resorts. Contact Ulsterbus through Translink.

MiniCoach operates day tours of Belfast (£8–£16), and to the Giant's Causeway, Bushmills Distillery, and Carrickfergus.

Contacts Belfast City Sightseeing (☎ *028/9062-6888* ⊕ *www.belfast citysightseeing.com*). **MiniCoach** (✉ *22 Donegall Rd., Central District, Belfast* ☎ *028/9032-4733* ⊕ *www.minicoachni.co.uk*). **Translink** (☎ *028/9066-6630* ⊕ *www.translink.co.uk*).

TAXI TOURS Belfast City Black Taxi Tours do 75-minute tours in a London-style black taxi of either Loyalist or Nationalist sights. The cost is £25 for up to two people, £30 for three people, and £33 for four people. Black Taxi Tours provide a similar itinerary at £25 per taxi for one or two people and £8 per person after that. The Loyalist tours leave from North Street or Bridge Street and prices can vary depending on pick-up point; the Nationalist Tours, through West Belfast Taxis, pick you up at your hotel.

Contacts Belfast City Black Taxi Tours (☎ *028/9030-1832* ⊕ *www.all irelandtours.com*). **Black Taxi Tours** (☎ *028/9064-2264* ⊕ *www.belfasttours.com*). **Nationalist Tours** (☎ *028/9031-5777*).

WALKING TOURS Belfast Safaris offers tailor-made walking tours of Belfast city with a twist. All of the guides are local and passionate about their neighborhoods. Tours are organized according to each group's specific interests, and can include politics, art, or even soccer. Want to learn Irish or play the tin whistle? It can all be arranged. The Antrim Road trail starts at Duncairn Gardens, the birthplace of the artist John Luke, and finishes at Belfast Castle for a panoramic view of the city. The cost is £8 per person for a standard tour, more for longer, custom routes.

Historical Pub Tours of Belfast walking tours of the city's pubs leave on Tuesday at 7 PM and Saturday at 4 PM. The cost is £5. In Derry, walking tours (£4) are organized through the city's Tourist Information Centre.

Contacts Belfast Safaris (☎ *028/9022-2925* ⊕ *www.belfastsafaris.com*). **Derry Tourist Information Centre** (✉ *44 Foyle St., West Bank, Derry* ☎ *028/7126-7284 or 028/7137-7577* ⊕ *www.derryvisitor.com*). **Historical Pub Tours of Belfast** (✉ *Depart from Crown Liquor Saloon, 46 Great Victoria St., Golden Mile, Belfast* ☎ *028/9268-3665*).

VISITOR INFORMATION

The Northern Ireland Tourist Board (NTIB) Information Centre in Belfast is the main tourist information center for the whole of the north. The office incorporates the plush, comprehensive Belfast Welcome Centre—the main tourist office for Belfast city, run by the Belfast Visitor and Convention Bureau. It's open October to May, Monday 9:30–5:30, Tuesday to Saturday 9–5:30; and June to September, Monday

9:30–5:30, Tuesday to Saturday 9–5:30, Sunday noon–5. Year-round Tourist Information Offices (TIOs) are listed below by town. June to August many more towns and villages open TIOs.

NTIB Northern Ireland Tourist Board Information Centre (✉ *47 Donegall Pl., Central District, Belfast BT1 5AU* ☎ *028/9024–6609* ⊕ *www.discovernorthern ireland.com*).

Regional Tourist Information **Armagh** (✉ *40 English St., Co. Armagh BT6 17BA* ☎ *028/3752–1800* ⊕ *www.visitarmagh.com*). **Ballycastle** (✉ *7 Mary St., Co. Antrim BT54 6QH* ☎ *028/2076–2024* ⊕ *www.countyantrim.com/antrim_ballycastle. htm*). **Bangor** (✉ *Quay St., Co. Down BT20 5ED* ☎ *028/9127–0069* ⊕ *www. northdowntourism.com*). **Carrickfergus** (✉ *Heritage Plaza, Co. Antrim BT38 7DG* ☎ *028/9335–8049* ⊕ *www.carrickfergus.org*). **Derry** (✉ *Foyle St., Co. Derry BT48 6AT* ☎ *028/7126–7284 or 028/7137–7577* ⊕ *www.derryvisitor.com*). **Downpatrick** (✉ *53A Market St., Co. Down BT30 6L2* ☎ *028/4461–2233* ⊕ *www.downdc. gov.uk*). **Enniskillen** (✉ *Lakeland Visitor Centre, Shore Rd., Co. Fermanagh BT74 7EF* ☎ *028/6632–3110* ⊕ *www.fermanaghlakelands.com*). **Giant's Causeway** (✉ *Visitor Centre, Co. Antrim BT57 8SU* ☎ *028/2073–1855* ⊕ *www.moyle-council. org*). **Larne** (✉ *Narrow Gauge Rd., Co. Antrim BT40 1XB* ☎ *028/2826–0088* ⊕ *www.larne.gov.uk*). **Limavady** (✉ *Connell St., Co. Derry BT49 OHA* ☎ *028/7776– 0307* ⊕ *www.limavady.gov.uk*). **Lisburn** (✉ *53 Lisburn Sq., Co. Antrim BT28 IAG* ☎ *028/9266–0038* ⊕ *www.visitlisburn.com*). **Newcastle** (✉ *Central Promenade, Co. Down BT33 OAA* ☎ *028/4372–2222* ⊕ *www.downdc.gov.uk*).

Irish Greens

Portstewart, Londonberry, Northern Ireland

WORD OF MOUTH

"For great Irish golf, Ballybunion, Lahinch, Tralee, and Dingle all await, and they are easily reachable from Shannon airport. This is a pilgrimage that no golfer should miss. If I had only two days for golf I would choose Ballybunion and Lahinch. The natural dunes along the sea is links golf at its finest. Not only is the golf great, the west coast of Ireland is the best scenery that the Emerald Isle has to offer. Bring your raingear and a thirst for Guinness."

—39Steps

Updated by
Anto Howard

ASK MOST GOLFERS WHERE TO find the golf vacation of a lifetime—breathtaking and diverse courses, lovely settings, history seeping into every shot—and they'll probably say Scotland. Unless, of course, they've been to Ireland. The nation's oldest course dates from 1881, and the Golfing Union of Ireland is the oldest such establishment in the world. It started in 1891: all nine original clubs were in Ulster. Now the number of affiliated golf clubs is 4,002, with more than 200,000 members, and there are still more clubs that haven't joined.

Ireland is one of those remarkable places where mountains and sea often meet. Scraggly coastline and rolling hills of heather dominate the courses here, not the other way around. Real golfers are challenged, rather than deterred, by the vagaries of the elements—the wind, rain, and mist—and the lack of golf carts on courses in rougher terrain. Ireland's ever-beguiling (and often frustrating) courses attract players from around the globe. Tom Watson, winner of five British Opens, lists Ballybunion as his favorite course; so does the legendary writer Herbert Warren Wind—who, from an American viewpoint, put Irish golf on the map when he wrote, "To put it simply, Ballybunion revealed itself to be nothing less than the finest seaside course I have ever seen." And although Ballybunion is generally considered the Emerald Isle's prize jewel, many courses now rival it—from such classics as Portmarnock and Waterville to newer courses such as Mount Juliet, the K Club, and the Old Head of Kinsale.

There's more to Irish golf than its great links courses, though. Druids Glen features prominently alongside the likes of the K Club, Mount Juliet, Carton House, and Fota Island in every debate on the great inland golf courses. And although it's purely a matter of opinion—and, perhaps, your last scorecard—as to which is best, Druids Glen was voted European Golf Course of the Year at the prestigious Hertz International Travel Awards for 2000, and is considered one of the top 20 courses in Ireland by *Golf Digest*. The magazine has also moved up Ireland's Royal County Down to the number one spot on its list of top 100 courses outside the United States (replacing the Old Course at St. Andrews!). Carton House and K Club were home to several recent Irish Opens, where the giants of the U.S. and European tours go head-to-head for the old trophy during golf's greatest match-play competition.

The wonderfully alive, challenging natural terrain is one of the things that makes Irish golf so remarkable. Of the estimated 150 top-quality links courses in the world, 39 of them are in Ireland. Most of these leading courses were designed by celebrated golf architects, such as Tom Morris, James Braid, Harry Colt, and Alister MacKenzie, who capitalized on spectacular landscapes. Others—such as Severiano Ballesteros, with his new course at Killenard in County Laois—will continue in their steps.

The Weather Factor. You see all kinds of weather in Ireland—driving winds, rain, sleet, and sunshine—and you may see it all in one round. There are no rain-checks here. You play unless there's lightning, so pack your sweaters and rain gear, especially if you're planning your trip between fall and spring.

The Sunday Bag Factor. If you don't have a golf bag that's light enough for you to carry for 18 holes, invest in one before your trip. Electric carts are generally available only at the leading venues, so you usually have the option of using a caddy or caddy car (pull cart)—or of carrying your own bag. Many courses have caddies but don't guarantee their availability because they're not employed by the course, so you may have to tote your bag yourself. Be prepared with a carryall or a Sunday bag.

The Northern Ireland Factor. Some of the best and most beautiful courses are in Northern Ireland, where the leading venues—like Royal County Down and Royal Portrush—are less remote than in the republic. Remember that this part of the island is under British rule, so all currency is in U.K. pounds, although many clubs and businesses will accept the euro. There are no restrictions when traveling from one part of the country to the other.

The Private Club Factor. Unlike those in America, most private golf clubs in Ireland are happy to let visitors play their courses and use their facilities. It's important to remember, however, that such clubs place members first; guests come second. In some, you'll need a letter of introduction from your club in America to secure your playing privilege. There are often preferred days for visitors; call in advance to be sure that a club can make time for you.

NORTH OF DUBLIN

Carton House Golf Club. This just-outside-of-Dublin estate has quickly become one of the brightest stars in the Irish golfing universe. It's in a majestic 1,100 acre park that was the ancestral home of the earls of Kildare, presided over by an enormous and very grand 18th-century stately house. Two of the biggest names in golf designed the championship courses here. The parkland Mark O'Meara course makes use of the estate's rolling hills, specimen trees, and the River Rye. The highlight comprises the 14th, 15th, and 16th stretch: a pair of classy par-3s wrapped around a heroic par-5. The second 18 holes, created by Colin Montgomerie, make up an inland links-style course, which is flatter and virtually treeless. There's a good mix of long par-4s backed up with tricky short ones. Recessed pot bunkers lie in wait to pick up offline shots. ✉ *Maynooth, Co. Kildare* ☎ *01/628–6271* ⊕ *www.carton. ie* ⛳ *36 holes. Yardage: 7,006 (O'Meara), 7,301 (Montgomerie). Both courses: Par 72. Practice area, caddies, caddy carts, buggies, catering* 🏷 *Fees: Sun.–Wed. €115; Thurs.–Sat. €135* ⊗ *Visitors: daily.*

County Louth Golf Club. This course is better known by the name of its hometown, Baltray, and covers 190 acres by the Irish Sea at the mouth of the river Boyne. It's rated as "a hidden gem" among *Golf Digest*'s 100 best courses in the world, and, as such, this wonderful links course surprisingly even manages to keep a relatively low profile at home. Long hitters will love the atypical layout, a par-72 that features five par-5s, but beware the well-protected, undulating greens. ⊠*Baltray, Drogheda, Co. Louth* ☎*041/988–1530* ⊕*www.countylouthgolfclub. com* ⚑ *18 holes. Yardage: 6,936. Par 72. Practice area, caddies (reserve in advance), caddy carts, club rental, catering* ⊠*Fees: weekdays except Tues. €115; weekends €135* ⊙ *Visitors: Mon. and Wed.–Sun.*

Island Golf Club. Talk about exclusive—until 1960, the only way to reach this club was by boat. It was about as remote as you could get and still be only 24 km (15 mi) from Dublin. But things have changed. The Island has opened its doors to reveal a fine links course with holes that force you to navigate between spectacular sand dunes toward small, challenging greens. ⊠*Corballis, Donabate, Co. Dublin* ☎*01/843–6205* ⊕*www.theislandgolfclub.com* ⚑ *18 holes. Yardage: 6,236. Par 71. Practice area, caddies, caddy carts, catering* ⊠*Fees: €125* ⊙ *Visitors: daily.*

Fodor'sChoice   **Portmarnock Golf Club.** The hoo-ha and court battles over Portmarnock's
★   refusal to admit women members often overshadows the club's posi-
tion as the most famous of Ireland's "Big Four" (Ballybunion, Royal County Down, and Royal Portrush are the others). This links course, on a sandy peninsula north of Dublin, has hosted numerous major championships and Tom Watson often used it as a preparation for the Open. Known for its flat fairways and greens, it provides a fair test for any golfer who can keep it out of the heavy rough. ⊠*Portmarnock, Co. Dublin* ☎*01/846–2968* ⊕*www.portmarnockgolfclub.ie* ⚑ *27 holes. Yardage: 7,150, 3,449. Par 72, 37. Practice area, driving range, caddies (reserve in advance), caddy carts, catering* ⊠*Fees: weekdays €180; weekends €215* ⊙ *Visitors: Thurs.–Tues.*

Royal Dublin Golf Club. Links courses are usually in remote, even deso-late areas, but this captivating one is only 6 km (4 mi) from the center of Dublin—on Bull Island, a bird sanctuary. Royal Dublin is Ireland's third-oldest club. This links course has always been challenging but Martin Hawtree's ongoing redesign is making things even trickier. Watch out for the 5th, the 13th, and the infamous 18th—a par-4 dogleg with plenty of opportunities to shoot out-of-bounds. ⊠*Dollymount, County Dublin* ☎*01/833–6346* ⊕*www.theroyaldublingolfclub.com* ⚑ *18 holes. Yardage: 6,963. Par 72. Practice area, caddies, caddy carts, club rental, catering* ⊠*Fees: weekdays €150; weekends €170* ⊙ *Visitors: Thurs.–Tues.*

St. Margaret's Golf and Country Club. For those tired of getting blown off-course on Dublin's breezy links, this is 18 holes of pure bliss. The broad fairways on this parklands course are a little more forgiving than the likes of Portmarnock, but don't be lulled into a false sense of security—there are some real roller coasters along the way (like the awesome 12th). Two lakes and a babbling brook could bring your efforts on this hole to a watery end. ⊠*St. Margaret's, Co. Dublin* ☎*01/864–0400* ⊕*www.stmargaretsgolf.com* ⚑ *18 holes. Yardage: 6, 917. Par 73. Practice area, driving range, caddy carts, club rental, shoe rental, catering* ⊠*Fees: Mon. €50; Tues.–Thurs. €60; Fri.–Sun. €70* ⊙ *Visitors: daily.*

SOUTH OF DUBLIN

Fodor'sChoice   **Druids Glen Golf Club.** The beautiful Druids Glen course, 40 km (25 mi)
★   south of Dublin in County Wicklow, has hosted the Irish Open on four
occasions since it opened in 1995 and is known in golfing circles as
the "Augusta of Europe." The wonderful landscaping and the extensive
use of water in the layout explain the comparisons to the home of *The
Masters.* It's essentially an American-style target course incorporating
some delightful changes in elevation, and its forbidding, par-3 17th has
an island green, like the corresponding hole at TPC Sawgrass. A second
course, Druids Heath is a marvelous attempt to combine the best of links,
heathland, and parkland golf. ⊠*Newtownmountkennedy, Co. Wicklow* ☎*01/287–3600* ⊕*www.druidsglen.ie* ⚑*36 holes. Yardage: 6,560
(Glen), 6,833 (Heath). Both courses: Par 71. Practice area, caddies,
caddy carts, buggies, catering* ⊟*Fees: €80–€180* ⊘*Visitors: daily.*

The European Club. Tiger Woods used this elegant, Pat Ruddy–owned
and–designed links to prepare for the British Open at Muirfield, and
it does share some attributes with that great old course. The European
features 20 true links holes (two extra holes are in play most days) of
tumbling dunes with shockingly dramatic views of the Irish Sea from
16 of them. The small membership of 125 people makes it easier for
day visitors to get a tee time. The tournament-quality greens are tough
but fair. Like Turnberry and the Old Course at St. Andrews, there are
only two par-5s, one of which is almost 600 yards long. ⊠*Brittas
Bay, Co. Wicklow* ☎*0404/47415* ⊕*www.theeuropeanclub.com* ⚑*20
holes (2 extra holes). Yardage: 7,149. Par 71. Practice area, caddies,
caddy carts, catering* ⊟*Fees: €150* ⊘*Visitors: daily.*

★   **Heritage Golf and Country Club.** Millions of dollars have been spent on
developing this recent arrival to the Irish golf scene—and it shows. This
18-hole championship course is a challenge for the pros but somehow
manages to be forgiving to the amateur at the same time. Heritage has
second-to-none facilities including a 38,000-square-foot clubhouse.
A life-size bronze of Seve Ballesteros (by the renowned sports sculptor Paul Ferriter) greets you at the entrance to the course he designed
here, which is noted for its mix of challenging doglegs and water traps
(including five on-course lakes). Add four demanding par-5s to the mix
and the result is a truly world-class parkland course. The development
of luxury on-site accommodation has also increased the club's attrac-
tiveness to the visiting golfer. ⊠*Killenard, Co. Lais* ☎*0502/45040*
⊕*www.theheritage.com* ⚑*18 holes. Yardage: 7,319. Par 72. Caddy
carts, driving range, practice area, catering* ⊟*Fees: weekdays, €115;
weekends, €130* ⊘*Visitors: daily.*

The K Club. "Home to the 2006 Ryder Cup" says all a golfer needs to
know about the pedigree of the K Club. It remains Ireland's premier
luxury golf resort, with two full championship parkland courses. The
Palmer course is named after its designer, the legendary Arnold Palmer,
and offers a round of golf in lush, wooded surroundings bordered by the
River Liffey. The generous fairways and immaculate greens are offset by
formidable length, which makes it one of the most demanding courses

10

in the Dublin vicinity. Additional stress is presented by negotiating the numerous doglegs, water obstacles, and sand bunkers. The Smurfitt course is essentially an "inland links" course. The signature 7th hole wows visitors with its water cascades and man-made rock-quarry feature. The on-site facilities are terrific and include a 95-room resort with three restaurants, a health club, tennis and squash courts, a pool, and massage and other spa treatments. ⊠*Kildare Country Club, Straffan, Co. Kildare* ☎*01/627–3333* ⊕*www.kclub.com* ⌖*36 holes. Yardage: 7,337 (Palmer), 7,277 (Smurfitt). Both courses: Par 72. Practice area, driving range, caddies, caddy carts, club rental, shoe rental, catering* ⊠*Fees: €225–€370* ⊙ *Visitors: Sun.–Tues. (Palmer), daily (Smurfitt).*

Fodor'sChoice
★

Mount Juliet Golf Course. Attached to a magisterial country-house hotel, this Jack Nicklaus–designed championship parkland course, 19 km (11 mi) from Kilkenny Town, includes practice greens, a driving range, and, for those who feel a little rusty, a David Leadbetter golf academy. The heavily forested course has eight holes that play over water, including the wonderful 3rd hole—a par-3 over a stream from an elevated tee. The back 9 presents a series of difficult bunker shots. A sporting day out comes to a welcome end in the Hunter's Yard or Rose Garden lodge, which cater to both the thirsty and the hungry. Greens fees are above average, and although visitors are always welcome, a weekday round is best, since it's often crowded with members on weekends. ⊠*Mount Juliet Estate, Thomastown, Co. Kilkenny* ☎*056/73000* ⊕*www.mountjuliet.com* ⌖*18 holes. Yardage: 7,300. Par 72. Practice area, driving range, caddies, caddy carts, club rental, lessons, catering* ⊠*Fees: €94–€185* ⊙ *Visitors: daily.*

Powerscourt Golf Club. Set on the most spectacular estate in Ireland (once presided over by the Slazenger family), these two recently built courses are nestled in the foothills of the Wicklow Mountains on the ancient Powerscourt lands, home to a legendary 18th-century stately home and garden. Panoramic views to the sea and Sugarloaf Mountain—and all those 200-year-old trees—give the impression that the course has been here for years. The older East course is a largely parkland course, but some holes have certain links characteristics. The course's tiered greens will test even the best golfers. The more recently built West course is even more challenging and is designed with top-class tournament golf in mind. ⊠*Enniskerry, Co. Wicklow* ☎*01/204–6033* ⊕*www. powerscourt.ie* ⌖*36 holes. Yardage: 7,022 (East Course), 6,938 (West Course). Both courses: Par 72. Practice area, driving range, caddies, caddy carts, catering* ⊠*Fees: €130* ⊙ *Visitors: daily.*

SOUTHWEST

Adare Manor Golf Course. This parkland stretch is on the ancestral estate of the Earl of Dunraven. Its immediate success was virtually guaranteed by the international profile of its designer, Robert Trent Jones Sr. The grand old man of golf-course architects seemed far more comfortable with the wooded terrain than he was when designing the second links at Ballybunion. As a result, he delivered a course with the potential to host events of the highest caliber. The front 9 is dominated by an artificial 14-acre lake with a $500,000 polyethylene base. It's in play at the 3rd, 5th, 6th, and 7th holes. The dominant hazards on the homeward journey are the River Mague and the majestic trees, which combine to make the par-5 18th one of the most challenging finishing holes imaginable. ⊠ *Adare, Co. Limerick* ☎ *061/395–044* ⊕ *www.adaremanor. com* ⚑ *18 holes. Yardage: 7,125. Par 72. Practice area, caddies, caddy carts, catering* 🍽 *Fees: €145* ☺ *Visitors: daily.*

Fodor's Choice
★ **Ballybunion Golf Club.** President Bill Clinton will be eternally associated in Irish golfers' minds with this revered course. In fact there's even a brass statue of him teeing in the nearby village, to commemorate his visit there in 1999. On the shore of the Atlantic next to the southern entrance of the Shannon, Ballybunion has the huge dunes of Lahinch without the blind shots. It's no pushover, but every hole is pleasurable. Watch out for "Mrs. Simpson," a double fairway bunker on the 1st hole, named after the wife of Tom Simpson, the architect who remodeled the course in 1937. (Tom Watson did the same in 1995.) The Cashen Course, which opened in 1985, was designed by Robert Trent Jones Sr. ⊠ *Sandhill Rd., Ballybunion, Co. Kerry* ☎ *068/27611* ⊕ *www.ballybuniongolfclub.ie* ⚑ *36 holes. Yardage: 6,542 (Old), 6,477 (Cashen). Par 72, 70. Practice area, driving range, caddies, catering* 🍽 *Fees: €165 (Old); €110 (Cashen); €240 (both on same day)* ☺ *Visitors: weekdays.*

Cork Golf Club. If you know golf-course architecture, you're familiar with the name Alister MacKenzie, who designed Cypress Point in California and Augusta National in Georgia. One of his few designs in Ireland is Cork, better known as Little Island. There's water on this parkland course, but it's not the temperamental ocean; instead, Little Island is in Cork Harbor, a gentle bay of the Irish Sea. The highlight for most is the par-4 6th where a broad fairway narrows toward the green, nestled in former quarry. The course is little known, but it's one of the Emerald Isle's best. ⊠ *Little Island, Co. Cork* ☎ *021/435–3451* ⊕ *www.corkgolfclub.ie* ⚑ *18 holes. Yardage: 6,731. Par 72. Practice area, caddies, caddy carts, club rental, catering* 🍽 *Fees: Mon.–Thurs. €85; Fri.–Sun. €95* ☺ *Visitors: daily.*

10

Dooks Golf Club. On the second tier of courses in Ireland's southwest, Dooks doesn't quite measure up to the world-class clubs. It is, nonetheless, a completely worthwhile day of golf if you're touring the area, and it boasts stunning scenery, including views of the majestic Magillacuddy's Reeks. Built in the old tradition of seaside links, it's shorter and a bit gentler, although the greens are small and tricky. ⊠ *Dooks, Glenbeigh, Co. Kerry* ☎ *066/976–8205* ⊕ *www.dooks.com* ⚑ *18 holes. Yardage: 6,401. Par 71. Caddy carts, club rental, catering* 🍽 *Fees: €70* ☺ *Visitors: weekdays.*

Fodor's Choice
★ **Killarney Golf and Fishing Club.** Freshwater fishing is the sport here, for this club is among a stunning mixture of mountains, lakes, and forests. There are three courses: Mahony's Point, along the shores of Lough Leane; the Lackabane, on the far side of the road from the main

entrance; and the jewel in the crown, water-feature-packed Killeen. Despite the abundance of seaside links, many well-traveled golfers name Killarney their favorite place to play in Ireland. ✉ *Mahony's Point, Killarney, Co. Kerry* ☎ *064/31034* ⊕ *www.killarney-golf.com* ⚑ *54 holes. Yardage: 6,780 (Mahony's), 7,050 (Lackabane), 7,178 (Killeen). All courses: Par 72. Practice area, caddies, caddy carts, catering* ⊡ *Fees: €100 (Mahony's Point); €80 (Lackabane); €120 (Killeen)* ⊙ *Visitors: Mon.–Sat.*

Old Head Golf Links. Golf doesn't get much more spectacular than this. On a celebrated 215-acre County Cork peninsula, which juts out into the wild Atlantic nearly 300 feet below, you can find an awe-inspiring spectacle that defies comparison. The only golfing stretches that could be likened to it are the 16th and 17th holes at Cypress Point and small, Pacific sections of Pebble Beach, from the 7th to the 10th, and the long 18th. Even if your golf is moderate, expect your pulse to race at the stunning views and wildlife. ✉ *Kinsale, Co. Cork* ☎ *021/477–8444* ⊕ *www. oldheadgolflinks.com* ⚑ *18 holes. Yardage: 7,215. Par 72. Practice area, caddies (reserve in advance), caddy carts, catering* ⊡ *Fees: €295* ⊙ *Visitors: daily.*

Tralee Golf Club. Tralee is what all modern-golf-course architects *wish* they could do in the States: find unspoiled, seaside links and route a course on it that's designed for the modern game. This is an Arnold Palmer–Ed Seay design that opened in 1984, and the location is fantastic—cliffs, craters, dunes, and the gale-blowing ocean. Don't let the flat front 9 lull you to sleep—the back 9 can be a ferocious wake-up call. ✉ *West Barrow, Ardfert, Co. Kerry* ☎ *066/713–6379* ⊕ *www.traleegolfclub.com* ⚑ *18 holes. Yardage: 6,975. Par 74. Practice area, putting green, caddies, caddy carts, club rental, catering* ⊡ *Fees: €170* ⊙ *Visitors: Mon., Tues., and Thurs.–Sat.*

Waterville Golf Links. Here's what you should know about Waterville before you play: the 1st hole of this course is aptly named "Last Easy." At 7,184 yards from the tips, Waterville is the longest course in Ireland or Britain, and it's generally regarded as their toughest test. Now the good news: the scenery is so majestic you may not care that your score is approaching the yardage. Six holes run along the cliffs by the sea, surrounding the other 12, which have a tranquil, if not soft, feel to them. ✉ *Waterville, Co. Kerry* ☎ *066/947–4545* ⊕ *www.watervillegolflinks.ie* ⚑ *18 holes. Yardage: 7,225. Par 74. Practice area, caddies, caddy carts, buggies, catering* ⊡ *Fees: €165* ⊙ *Visitors: daily.*

WEST

Carne Golf Links. Clinging to the very northwest tip of County Mayo, this is literally the last golf course before you hit Boston. This Eddie Hackett–designed links ducks and dives among towering sand dunes next to what locals call "the wild Atlantic." From the elevated tees and greens you can see a string of Atlantic islands: Inishkea, Inishglora, and Achill. But don't be distracted by the amazing views—you'll need all your wits about you to beat the constant challenge of the high winds. ✉*Belmullet, Co. Mayo* ☎*097/82292* ⊕*www.carnegolflinks. com* ⛳*18 holes. Yardage: 6,119. Par 72. Practice area, caddies, caddy carts, buggies, club rental, catering* 💳*Fees: €60* ☉*Visitors: daily.*

Doonbeg Golf Club. Despite being held up for a time (due to government legislation to protect a rare local snail), Greg Norman–designed Doonbeg has arrived with a major splash on the Irish links scene. Physically stunning, this tough, unforgiving course stretches along nearly 2 mi of pristine Atlantic beach and dunes. The magnificent par-4 15th—with funnel-shape green surrounded by huge dunes—is at the center of the whole course. Gamblers beware: anything long could easily run off the green and never be seen again. If you make it to the tricky 18th, you'll be rewarded with breathtaking views of the ocean. ✉*Doonbeg, Co. Clare* ☎*065/905–5602* ⊕*www.doonbeggolfclub.com* ⛳*18 holes. Yardage: 6,885. Par 72. Practice area, caddies, caddy carts, catering* 💳*Fees: Mon.–Thurs. €190; Fri.–Sun. €200* ☉*Visitors: daily.*

Lahinch Golf Club. There's a real Scottish flavor to this venerable links course. The club was founded by members of Scotland's Black Watch regiment based in Limerick and the first course was designed by Old Tom Morris from St. Andrews in 1892. Then, in the 1920s, design maestro Alister MacKenzie created a wonderfully challenging 18 holes—full of undulating greens, huge bunkers, and maddening blind shots. Poorly thought-out alterations in the 1930s obliterated many of his innovations and it wasn't until 1999 that a four-year project to re-create the MacKenzie magic began. The Castle Course is less of a challenge to the experienced player but it has its moments: awkwardly placed bunkers and water hazards lie in wait. ✉*Lahinch, Co. Clare* ☎*065/708–1003* ⊕*www.lahinchgolf.com* ⛳*36 holes. Yardage: 6,882 (Old Course), 5,594 (Castle Course). Par 72, 70. Practice area, caddies, caddy carts, catering* 💳*Fees: €155 (Old Course); €50 (Castle)* ☉*Visitors: daily.*

Westport Golf Club. Twice this inland course hosted the Irish Amateur Championship. It lies in the shadows of religious history: rising 2,500 feet above Clew Bay, with its hundreds of islands, is Croagh Patrick, a mountain that legend connects with St. Patrick. The mountain is considered sacred, and it attracts multitudes of worshippers to its summit every year. All the prayers might pay off at the 15th, where your drive has to carry the ball over 200 yards of ocean. ✉*Westport, Co. Mayo* ☎*098/28262* ⊕*www.golfwestport.com* ⛳*18 holes. Yardage: 6,724. Par 73. Practice area, driving range, caddies, caddy carts, buggies, catering* 💳*Fees: Mon.–Thurs. €42; Fri.–Sun. €55* ☉*Visitors: daily.*

10

NORTHWEST

County Sligo Golf Club. Founded in 1894 on land leased from an uncle of W. B. Yeats, County Sligo is situated in the heart of Yeats Country at Rosses Point, a delightful seaside village 8 km (5 mi) north of Sligo Town. Ominous Ben Bulben mountain (best viewed from the par-5 3rd hole) dominates the northern views on this infamously windy course, which will test any player's ability to keep the ball low off the tee. The 17th is the signature hole—a long par-4 with a steeply uphill green. ⊠*Enniscrone, Co. Sligo* ☏*096/36297* ⊕*www.enniscronegolf. com* ⚑*18 holes. Yardage: 6,136. Par 71. Practice area, putting green, caddy carts, club rental, catering* ⊑*Fees: weekdays €70; weekends €85* ⊙*Visitors: weekdays; weekends by appointment.*

Donegal Golf Club. Recently named by *Golf World* as one of Ireland's top ten clubs, this is a course that has always rated high in the estimations of local golfers. On the shores of Donegal Bay and approached through a forest, the windswept links are shadowed by the Blue Stack Mountains, with the Atlantic as a backdrop. The greens are large, but the rough is deep and penal, and there's a constant battle against erosion by the sea. The par-3 5th, fittingly called "The Valley of Tears," begins a run of four of the course's biggest challenges, which could have you discreetly hiding your score card by the time you reach the 18th. ⊠*Murvagh, Laghey, Co. Donegal* ☏*074/973-4054* ⊕*www. donegalgolfclub.ie* ⚑*18 holes. Yardage: 6,753. Par 73. Practice area, caddy carts, buggies, club rental, catering* ⊑*Fees: Mon.–Thurs. €55; Fri.–Sun. €70* ⊙*Visitors: daily.*

Rosapenna Golf Links. The ghost of Old Tom Morris is alive and kicking on the first of the two courses at this recently revamped, old-school links. In 1891 the legendary Morris spotted the potential of this secluded stretch of Donegal coastline and staked out the original course himself. Long-dead greats such as Harry Vardon and James Braid played here, where the first 10 holes are classic links and the last eight actually play inland and uphill into high meadow. The priceless Atlantic views haven't changed since Morris's day, but the recent addition of the testing and tantalizing Sandy Hills links course has made this place a must-stop for the serious golfer. ⊠*Downings, Co. Donegal* ☏*074/915-53016* ⊕*www.rosapennagolflinks.ie* ⚑*36 holes. Yardage: 6,476 (Morris), 7,155 (Sandy Hills). Par 70, 71. Practice area, caddies (summer only), caddy carts, club rental, catering* ⊑*Fees: Morris €50; Sandy Hills €75* ⊙*Visitors: daily.*

NORTHERN IRELAND

Ballycastle Golf Club. Pleasure comes first here, with challenge as an afterthought. It's beautiful (five holes wind around the remains of a 13th-century friary), short (less than 6,000 yards), and has an unusual mix of both links and parkland holes. It's also right next to Bushmills, the world's oldest distillery. ⊠*2 Cushendall Rd., Ballycastle, Co. Antrim* ☏*048/2076-2536* ⊕*www.ballycastlegolfclub.com* ⚑*18 holes. Yardage: 5,927. Par 71. Practice area, caddy carts, club rental, catering* ⊑*Fees: weekdays £25; weekends £35* ⊙*Visitors: daily.*

Castlerock Golf Club. Where else in the world can you play a hole called "Leg o' Mutton"? It's a 200-yard par-3 with railway tracks to the right and a burn to the left—just one of several unusual holes at this course, which claims to have the best greens in Ireland. The finish is spectacular: from the elevated 17th tee, where you can see the shores of Scotland, to the majestic 18th, which plays uphill to a plateau green. The club also boasts the equally scenic 9-hole Bann course. ⊠*65 Circular Rd., Castlerock, Co. Derry* ☎*048/7084–8314* ⊕*www.castlerockgc. co.uk* ⚲*27 holes. Yardage: 6,747; 4,892 (Bann). Par 73, 67. Practice area, caddies (reserve in advance), caddy carts, catering* ▥*Fees: weekdays £50* ☺*Visitors: Mon.–Thurs.*

Malone Golf Club. Fisherfolk may find the 22-acre lake at the center of this parkland layout distracting because it's filled with trout. The golf, however, is just as well-stocked—with large trees and well-manicured, undulating greens, this is one of the most challenging inland tests in Ireland. Bring your power game—there are only three par-5s, but they're all more than 520 yards. However, for many, the feature hole is the par-3 15th. Water lies to the front and back of the small green and there are bunkers to the right; pinpoint accuracy is a must. ⊠*240 Upper Malone Rd., Dunmurry, Belfast* ☎*048/9061–2695* ⊕*www.malone golfclub.co.uk* ⚲*27 holes. Yardage: 6,706, 3,160. Par 72, 36. Practice area, caddies (summer only), caddy carts, buggies, club rental, catering* ▥*Fees: weekdays £55; weekends £60* ☺*Visitors: daily.*

Portstewart Golf Club. More than a century old, Portstewart may scare you with its opening hole, generally regarded as the toughest starter in Ireland. Picture a 425-yard par-4 that descends from an elevated tee to a small green tucked between the dunes. The greens are known for uniformity and speed, and seven of the holes have been redesigned to toughen the course. If you want a break from the grand scale of The Strand championship links, there's the Old Course and the Riverside, 36 holes of downsize, executive-style golf. ⊠*117 Strand Rd., Portstewart, Co. Derry* ☎*048/7083–2015* ⊕*www.portstewartgc.co.uk* ⚲*54 holes. Yardage: 6,895 (The Strand), 4,730 (Old Course), 5,725 (Riverside). Par 72, 64, 68. Practice area, caddies, caddy carts, buggies, catering* ▥*Fees: weekdays £70 (The Strand), £10 (Old Course), £20 (Riverside); weekends, £90 (The Strand), £15 (Old Course), £25 (Riverside)* ☺*Visitors: daily.*

Fodor'sChoice ★ **Royal County Down.** Recently ousting the Old Course at St. Andrews as the best course outside the United States in *Golf Digest*'s annual survey, Royal County Down is a links course with a sea of craterlike bunkers and small dunes; catch it on the right day at the right time and you may think you're on the moon. And for better players, every day is the right one. Harry Vardon labeled it the toughest course on the Emerald Isle, and if you can't hit your drive long and straight, you might find it the toughest course in the world. ⊠*Golf Links Rd., Newcastle, Co. Down* ☎*048/4372–2419* ⊕*www.royalcountydown.org* ⚲*36 holes. Yardage: 7,065 (Championship), 4,681 (Annesley). Par 71, 63. Practice area, caddies, caddy carts, catering* ▥*Fees: weekdays £120–135 (Championship), £30 (Annesley); weekends £150 (Championship), £35 (Annesley)* ☺*Visitors: Sun.–Tues., Thurs.–Fri. (Championship); daily (Annesley).*

Fodor'sChoice ★ **Royal Portrush.** In addition to Royal County Down, Portrush also makes *Golf Digest*'s top ten non-U.S. courses. A legend in Irish golfing circles, Portrush is the only Irish club to have hosted a British Open. The championship Dunluce course is named for the ruins of a nearby castle and is a sea of sand hills and curving fairways. Despite its understated appearance it poses many and varied challenges. "White Rocks," the par-5 5th hole, is quite literally a cliff hanger. It's a wicked dogleg with the green perched on the edge of a cliff. The Valley course is a less-exposed, tamer track. Both are conspicuous for their lack of bunkers. In a poll of Irish golf legends, Dunluce was voted the best in Ireland. ⊠*Dunluce Rd., Portrush, Co. Antrim* ☎*048/7082–2311* ⊕*www. royalportrushgolfclub.com* ⅃*36 holes. Yardage: 6,818 (Dunluce), 6,273 (Valley). Par 72, 71. Practice area, caddies, caddy carts, buggies, catering* ⊠*Dunluce: weekdays £110; weekends £125; Valley: weekdays £35; weekends £40* ⊙ *Visitors: Tues.–Sun.*

Ireland Essentials

PLANNING TOOLS, EXPERT INSIGHT, GREAT CONTACTS

There are planners and there are those who, excuse the pun, fly by the seat of their pants. We happily place ourselves among the planners. Our writers and editors try to anticipate all the issues you may face before and during any journey, and then they do their research. This section is the product of their efforts. Use it to get excited about your trip to Ireland, to inform your travel planning, or to guide you on the road should the seat of your pants start to feel threadbare.

GETTING STARTED

We're really proud of our Web site: Fodors.com is a great place to begin any journey. Scan Travel Wire for suggested itineraries, travel deals, restaurant and hotel openings, and other up-to-the-minute info. Check out Booking to research prices and book plane tickets, hotel rooms, rental cars, and vacation packages. Head to Talk for on-the-ground pointers from travelers who frequent our message boards. You can also link to loads of other travel-related resources.

■ RESOURCES

ONLINE TRAVEL TOOLS

The main web site for the Irish tourist board, Ireland Tourism, is ⊕*www.shamrock.org*; Fáilte Ireland (the National Tourism Development Authority) sponsors ⊕*www.ireland.ie* and ⊕*www.discoverireland.ie*. For lots of entertaining bits—Irish and otherwise—visit ⊕*www.irishabroad.com*. Some of the most popular sites are ⊕*www.browseireland.com* and ⊕*www.heritageireland.ie*. The Web site ⊕*www.ireland-information.com* is dedicated to providing as many free resources and as much free information about Ireland as possible on an array of topics from genealogy to shopping. For a central directory of links to all things Irish, log on to ⊕*www.finditireland.com*. Comhaltas Ceoltóirí Eireann is an association that promotes the music, culture, and art of Ireland and its Web site ⊕*www.comhaltas.com* has helpful news about the Irish traditional music scene. For listings of all music, film, and theater events, see ⊕*www.entertainment.ie*. Keep in mind that many of the leading newspapers of Ireland have Web sites, which can be gold mines of timely information. See, for example, the Irish Times' Web site, ⊕*www.Ireland.com*. For a weekly newsletter to keep Irish people abroad up-to-date on events at home, log on to ⊕*www.emigrant.ie*.

Officially designated Heritage Towns are featured on ⊕*www.heritagetowns.com*. A range of heritage attractions are flagged on ⊕*www.heritageisland.com*.For information on arts events of all kinds, try ⊕*www.art.ie*, which is affiliated with the arts councils of both the Irish Republic and Northern Ireland. For more information on counties in the west of Ireland, try ⊕*www.trueireland.com* or ⊕*www.irelandwest.ie*. A handy regional site is ⊕*www.southeastireland.com*. Portions of the Tourism Ireland's eloquent magazine, *Ireland of the Welcomes*, are available online at ⊕*www.irelandofthewelcomes.com*. For an eloquent site devoted to some of Ireland's most historic buildings, see ⊕*www.irish-architecture.com*, while ⊕*www.castlesireland.com* and ⊕*www.celticcastles.com* will please the castle lover. Green-thumbers will enjoy ⊕*www.gardensireland.com*, while food lovers should check out ⊕*www.bordbia.ie*.

ALL ABOUT IRELAND

Currency Conversion Google (⊕www.google.com) does currency conversion. Just type in the amount you want to convert and an explanation of how you want it converted (e.g., "14 Swiss francs in dollars"), and then voilà. **Oanda.com** (⊕www.oanda.com) also allows you to print out a handy table with the current day's conversion rates. **XE.com** (⊕www.xe.com) is a good currency conversion Web site.

Safety Transportation Security Administration (*TSA;* ⊕www.tsa.gov).

Time Zones Timeanddate.com (⊕ *www. timeanddate.com/worldclock*) can help you figure out the correct time anywhere.

Weather Accuweather.com (⊕ *www. accuweather.com*) is an independent weather-forecasting service with good coverage of hurricanes. **Weather.com** (⊕ *www.weather.com*) is the Web site for the Weather Channel.

Other Resources CIA World Factbook (⊕ *www.odci.gov/cia/publications/factbook/ index.html*) has profiles of every country in the world. It's a good source if you need some quick facts and figures.

VISITOR INFORMATION

For information on travel in the Irish Republic, contact **Tourism Ireland** (⊕ *www. discoverireland.com*), the international marketing authority for **Fáilte Ireland** (pronounced *fal*-cha), as the tourist information network in called within the Republic of Ireland. Information on travel in the North is available from the **Northern Ireland Tourist Board** (*NITB* ⊕ *www.discover northernireland.com*).

Information Fáilte Ireland (✉ *Baggot St. Bridge, Dublin 2* ☎ *01/602–4000, 1890/525– 525 toll-free within Ireland* ✉ *1 Amiens St., Dublin 1* ⊕ *www.ireland.ie*). **U.K.- Tourism Ireland** (✉ *Nation House, 103 Wigmore St., London W1U IQS* ☎ *020/7518–0800* ⊕ *www. discoverireland.com*). **U.S.- Tourism Ireland** (✉ *345 Park Ave., 17th fl., New York, NY 10154* ☎ *212/418–0800* ⊕ *www.discoverireland.com*).

NITB Northern Ireland (✉ *59 North St., Belfast BT1 1NB* ☎ *028/9023–1221*). **Canada** (✉ *2 Bloor St. W, Suite 1501, Toronto, Ontario M4W 3E2* ☎ *416/925–6368*). **U.K.** (✉ *24 Haymarket, London SW1 4DG* ☎ *020/7766–9920, 08701/555–250 info line*). **U.S.** (✉ *551 5th Ave., Suite 701, New York, NY 10176* ☎ *212/922–0101 or 800/326–0036*).

▌ THINGS TO CONSIDER

GOVERNMENT ADVISORIES

As different countries have different world views, look at travel advisories from a range of governments to get more

of a sense of what's going on out there. And be sure to parse the language carefully. For example, a warning to "avoid all travel" carries more weight than one urging you to "avoid nonessential travel," and both are much stronger than a plea to "exercise caution."

■**TIP**➔ **Consider registering online with the State Department (https://travel registration.state.gov/ibrs/), so the government will know to look for you should a crisis occur in the country you're visiting.**

The U.S. Department of State's Web site has more than just travel warnings and advisories. The consular information sheets issued for every country have general safety tips, entry requirements (though be sure to verify these with the country's embassy), and other useful details.

General Information & Warnings Australian Department of Foreign Affairs & Trade (⊕ *www.smartraveller.gov.au*). **Consular Affairs Bureau of Canada** (⊕ *www.voyage. gc.ca*). **U.K. Foreign & Commonwealth Office** (⊕ *www.fco.gov.uk/travel*). **U.S. Department of State** (⊕ *www.travel.state.gov*).

GEAR

In Ireland you can experience all four seasons in a day. There can be damp chilly stretches even in July and August, the warmest months of the year. Layers are the best way to go. Pack several long- and short-sleeve T-shirts (in winter, some should be thermal or silk), a sweatshirt, a lightweight sweater, a heavyweight sweater, and a hooded, waterproof windbreaker that's large enough to go over several layers if necessary. A portable umbrella is absolutely essential, and the smaller and lighter it is, the better, as you'll want it with you every second. You should bring at least two pairs of walking shoes; footwear can get soaked in minutes and then take hours to dry.

The Irish are generally informal about clothes. In the more expensive hotels and restaurants people dress formally for dinner, and a jacket and tie may be required in bars after 7 PM, but very few places operate a strict dress policy. Old or tattered blue jeans and running shoes are forbidden in certain bars and dance clubs.

If you're used to packing things or stowing dirty clothes in plastic shopping or drawstring bags, bring your own. About the only place you can find them here is in the closets of better hotel rooms (for on-site dry cleaning and laundry). Plastic bags carry a 15-cent government levy and can be sold by supermarkets, but it's illegal to give them away. So most stores use paper bags, or recycle boxes. Also, although salesclerks are good about wrapping crystal and pottery for travel, you can never be too careful with such items; bring along some bubble wrap.

PASSPORTS

All U.S. citizens, even infants, need a valid passport to enter Ireland for stays of up to 90 days. Citizens of the United Kingdom, when traveling on flights departing from Great Britain, do not need a passport to enter Ireland but it's advisable to carry some form of photo ID. Passport requirements for Northern Ireland are the same as for the republic.

We're always surprised at how few Americans have passports—only 25% at this writing. This number is expected to grow in coming years, when it becomes impossible to re-enter the United States from trips to neighboring Canada or Mexico without one.

U.S. passports are valid for 10 years. You must apply in person if you're getting a passport for the first time; if your previous passport was lost, stolen, or damaged; or if your previous passport has expired and was issued more than 15 years ago or when you were under 16. All children under 18 must appear in person to apply for or renew a passport. Both parents must accompany any child under 14 (or send a notarized statement with their per-

mission) and provide proof of their relationship to the child.

■TIP➔ **Before your trip, make two copies of your passport's data page (one for someone at home and another for you to carry separately). Or scan the page and e-mail it to someone at home and/or yourself.**

There are 13 regional passport offices, as well as 7,000 passport acceptance facilities in post offices, public libraries, and other governmental offices. If you're renewing a passport, you can do so by mail. Forms are available at passport acceptance facilities and online.

The cost to apply for a new passport is $97 for adults, $82 for children under 16; renewals are $67. Allow six weeks for processing, both for first-time passports and renewals. For an expediting fee of $60 you can reduce this time to about two weeks. If your trip is less than two weeks away, you can get a passport even more rapidly by going to a passport office with the necessary documentation. Private expediters can get things done in as little as 48 hours, but charge hefty fees for their services.

U.S. Passport Information U.S. Department of State (☏ 877/487–2778 ⊕ http://travel. state.gov/passport).

U.S. Passport & Visa Expediters A. **Briggs Passport & Visa Expeditors** (☏ 800/806–0581 or 202/464–3000 ⊕ www. abriggs.com). **American Passport Express** (☏ 800/455–5166 or 603/559–9888 ⊕ www. americanpassport.com). **Passport Express** (☏ 800/362–8196 or 401/272–4612 ⊕ www. passportexpress.com). **Travel Document Systems** (☏ 800/874–5100 or 202/638–3800 ⊕ www.traveldocs.com). **Travel the World Visas** (☏ 866/886–8472 or 301/495–7700 ⊕ www.world-visa.com).

BOOKING YOUR TRIP

Unless your cousin is a travel agent, you're probably among the millions of people who make most of their travel arrangements online.

But have you ever wondered just what the differences are between an online travel agent (a Web site through which you make reservations instead of going directly to the airline, hotel, or car-rental company), a discounter (a firm that does a high volume of business with a hotel chain or airline and accordingly gets good prices), a wholesaler (one that makes cheap reservations in bulk and then re-sells them to people like you), and an aggregator (one that compares all the offerings so you don't have to)?

Is it truly better to book directly on an airline or hotel Web site? And when does a real live travel agent come in handy?

▮ ONLINE

You really have to shop around. A travel wholesaler such as Hotels.com or Hotel-Club.net can be a source of good rates, as can discounters such as Hotwire or Priceline, particularly if you can bid for your hotel room or airfare. Indeed, such sites sometimes have deals that are unavailable elsewhere. They do, however, tend to work only with hotel chains (which makes them just plain useless for getting hotel reservations outside of major cities) or big airlines (so that often leaves out upstarts like jetBlue and some foreign carriers like Air India).

Also, with discounters and wholesalers you must generally prepay, and everything is nonrefundable. And before you fork over the dough, be sure to check the terms and conditions, so you know what a given company will do for you if there's a problem and what you'll have to deal with on your own.

▮ TIP → To be absolutely sure everything was processed correctly, confirm reservations made through online travel agents, discounters, and wholesalers directly with your hotel before leaving home.

Booking engines like Expedia, Travelocity, and Orbitz are actually travel agents, albeit high-volume, online ones. And airline travel packagers like American Airlines Vacations and Virgin Vacations—well, they're travel agents, too. But they may still not work with all the world's hotels.

An aggregator site will search many sites and pull the best prices for airfares, hotels, and rental cars from them. Most aggregators compare the major travel-booking sites such as Expedia, Travelocity, and Orbitz; some also look at airline Web sites, though rarely the sites of smaller budget airlines. Some aggregators also compare other travel products, including complex packages—a good thing, as you can sometimes get the best overall deal by booking an air-and-hotel package.

▮ WITH A TRAVEL AGENT

If you use an agent—brick-and-mortar or virtual—you'll pay a fee for the service. And know that the service you get from some online agents isn't comprehensive. For example Expedia and Travelocity don't search for prices on budget airlines like jetBlue, Southwest, or small foreign carriers. That said, some agents (online or not) *do* have access to fares that are difficult to find otherwise, and the savings can more than make up for any surcharge.

A knowledgeable brick-and-mortar travel agent can be a godsend if you're booking a cruise, a package trip that's not available to you directly, an air pass, or a complicated itinerary including several overseas flights. What's more, travel agents that specialize in a destination may have exclusive access to certain deals and insider information on things such as charter flights. Agents who specialize in types of travelers (senior citizens, gays and lesbians, naturists) or types of trips (cruises, luxury travel, safaris) can also be invaluable.

■ TIP→ **Remember that Expedia, Travelocity, and Orbitz are travel agents, not just booking engines. To resolve any problems with a reservation made through these companies, contact them first.**

A top-notch agent planning your trip to Russia will make sure you get the correct visa application and complete it on time; the one booking your cruise may get you a cabin upgrade or arrange to have bottle of champagne chilling in your cabin when you embark. And complain about the surcharges all you like, but when things don't work out the way you'd hoped, it's nice to have an agent to put things right.

Agent Resources American Society of Travel Agents (☎ *703/739–2782* ⊕ *www.travelsense.org*).

■ ACCOMMODATIONS

You should try to sample from Ireland's vast range of accommodations. In Dublin and other cities, boutique hotels combine luxury with contemporary (and often truly Irish) design. Manors and castles offer a unique combination of luxury and history. Less impressive, but equally charming, are the provincial inns and country hotels with simple but adequate facilities. You can meet a wide cross section of Irish people by hopping from one B&B to the next, or you can keep to yourself for a week or two in a thatched cottage. ITB-approved guesthouses and B&Bs display a green shamrock outside and are usually considered more reputable than those without. Hotels and other accommodations in Northern Ireland are similar to those in the Republic of Ireland.

Faílte Ireland has a grading system and publishes a list of "approved" hotels,

guesthouses, B&Bs, farmhouses, hostels, and campgrounds. For each accommodation, the list gives a maximum charge that can't be exceeded without special authorization. Prices must be displayed in every room; if the hotel oversteps its limit, don't hesitate to complain to the hotel manager and/or Faílte Ireland.

The lodgings we list are the cream of the crop in each price category. We always list the facilities that are available, but we don't specify whether they cost extra; when pricing accommodations, always ask what's included and what costs extra. Lodgings are assigned price categories based on the range from their least-expensive standard double room at high season (excluding holidays) to the most expensive. Lodgings marked ✕🖬 are lodgings whose restaurants warrant a special trip.

CATEGORY	COST
$$$$	€230
$$$	€180–€230
$$	€130–€180
$	€80–€130
¢	under €80

Republic of Ireland: All prices are in euros and are for two people in a standard double room in high season, including V.A.T. and a service charge (often applied in larger hotels).

CATEGORY	COST
$$$$	over £160
$$$	£115–£160
$$	£80–£115
$	£50–£80
¢	under £50

Northern Ireland: All prices are in pounds sterling and are for two people in a standard double room in high season, including V.A.T. and a service charge (often applied in larger hotels).

Most hotels and other lodgings require you to give your credit-card details before they will confirm your reservation. If you

Online Booking Resources

AGGREGATORS		
Kayak	www.kayak.com;	also looks at cruises and vacation packages.
Mobissimo	www.mobissimo.com	
Qixo	www.qixo.com	also compares cruises, vacation packages, and even travel insurance.
Sidestep	www.sidestep.com	also compares vacation packages and lists travel deals.
Travelgrove	www.travelgrove.com	also compares cruises and packages.
BOOKING ENGINES		
Cheap Tickets	www.cheaptickets.com	a discounter.
Expedia	www.expedia.com	a large online agency that charges a booking fee for airline tickets.
Hotwire	www.hotwire.com	a discounter.
lastminute.com	www.lastminute.com	specializes in last-minute travel the main site is for the U.K., but it has a link to a U.S. site.
Luxury Link	www.luxurylink.com	has auctions (surprisingly good deals) as well as offers on the high-end side of travel.
Onetravel.com	www.onetravel.com	a discounter for hotels, car rentals, airfares, and packages.
Orbitz	www.orbitz.com	charges a booking fee for airline tickets, but gives a clear breakdown of fees and taxes before you book.
Priceline.com	www.priceline.com	a discounter that also allows bidding.
Travel.com	www.travel.com	allows you to compare its rates with those of other booking engines.
Travelocity	www.travelocity.com	charges a booking fee for airline tickets, but promises good problem resolution.
ONLINE ACCOMMODATIONS		
Hotelbook.com	www.hotelbook.com	focuses on independent hotels worldwide.
Hotel Club	www.hotelclub.net	good for major cities worldwide.
Hotels.com	www.hotels.com	a big Expedia-owned wholesaler that offers rooms in hotels all over the world.
Quikbook	www.quikbook.com	offers "pay when you stay" reservations that let you settle your bill at checkout, not when you book.
OTHER RESOURCES		
Bidding For Travel	www.biddingfortravel.com	a good place to figure out what you can get and for how much before you start bidding on, say, Priceline.

don't feel comfortable e-mailing this information, ask if you can fax it (some places even prefer faxes). However you book, get confirmation in writing and have a copy of it handy when you check in.

Be sure you understand the hotel's cancellation policy. Some places allow you to cancel without any kind of penalty—even if you prepaid to secure a discounted rate—if you cancel at least 24 hours in advance. Others require you to cancel a week in advance or penalize you the cost of one night. Small inns and B&Bs are most likely to require you to cancel far in advance. Most hotels allow children under a certain age to stay in their parents' room at no extra charge, but others charge for them as extra adults; find out the cutoff age for discounts.

■TIP➜ Assume that hotels operate on the European Plan (EP, no meals) unless we specify that they use the Breakfast Plan (BP, with full breakfast), Continental Plan (CP, Continental breakfast), Full American Plan (FAP, all meals), Modified American Plan (MAP, breakfast and dinner) or are all-inclusive (AI, all meals and most activities).

APARTMENT & HOUSE RENTALS

Local Agents **Days Serviced Apartments** (☎01/639–1100 ⊕www.apartments-dublin.com). **Board Fáilte** (☎01/602–4000 ⊕www.discoverireland.ie).

ONLINE BOOKING RESOURCES

Contacts **At Home Abroad** (☎212/421–9165 ⊕www.athomeabroadinc.com). **Barclay International Group** (☎516/364–0064 or 800/845–6636 ⊕www.barclayweb.com). **Drawbridge to Europe** (☎541/482–7778 or 888/268–1148 ⊕www.drawbridgetoeurope.com). **Homes Away** (☎416/920–1873 or 800/374–6637 ⊕www.homesaway.com). **Hometours International** (☎865/690–8484 ⊕thor.he.net/~hometour). **Interhome** (☎954/791–8282 or 800/882–6864 ⊕www.interhome.us). **Suzanne B. Cohen & Associates** (☎207/622–0743 ⊕www.villaeurope.com). **Vacation Home Rentals Worldwide** (☎201/767–9393 or 800/633–3284 ⊕www.

vhrww.com). **Villanet** (☎206/417–3444 or 800/964–1891 ⊕www.rentavilla.com). **Villas & Apartments Abroad** (☎212/213–6435 or 800/433–3020 ⊕www.vaanyc.com). **Villas International** (☎415/499–9490 or 800/221–2260 ⊕www.villasintl.com). **Villas of Distinction** (☎707/778–1800 or 800/289–0900 ⊕www.villasofdistinction.com). **Wimco** (☎800/449–1553 ⊕www.wimco.com).

BED & BREAKFASTS

B&Bs are classified by Faílte Ireland as either town homes, country homes, or farmhouses. Many town-and-country B&Bs now have at least one bedroom with a bathroom, but don't expect this as a matter of course. The Irish farms that offer rooms by the week with partial or full board are more likely to be modern bungalows or undistinguished two-story houses than creeper-clad Georgian mansions. Room and part board—breakfast and an evening meal—starts at €260 per week. Many travelers don't bother booking a B&B in advance. They are so plentiful in rural areas that it's often more fun to leave the decision open, allowing yourself a choice of final destinations for the night. However, if you have discerning taste and enjoy meeting a variety of pleasant characters, check out the places listed by Friendly Homes of Ireland. Long weekends are the exception to this rule where B&Bs tend to be booked up far in advance, so keep an eye to the calendar for local holidays.

To qualify as a guesthouse, establishments must have at least five bedrooms. Some guesthouses are above a bar or restaurant; others are part of a home. As a rule, they're cheaper (some include an optional evening meal) and offer fewer amenities than hotels. But often that's where the differences end. Most have high standards of cleanliness and hospitality, and most have a bathroom, a TV, and a direct-dial phone in each room. Premier Guesthouses are generally small inns, run by the owner, and hard to distinguish from hotels.

Local Services **Bed & Breakfast Association of Northern Ireland** (☎28/4461–5542). **Irish Farm Holidays** (☎061/400–700 ⊕www. irishfarmholidays.com). **Town & Country Homes Association** (☎071/982-2222 ⊕www.townandcountry.ie). **Premier Guesthouses** (☎01/205-2826 ⊕www.premier guesthouses.com). **Friendly Homes of Ireland** (☎01/660–7975 ⊕www.tourismresources.ie).

Reservation Services **Bed & Breakfast.com** (☎512/322-2710 or 800/462-2632 ⊕www. bedandbreakfast.com) also sends out an online newsletter. **Bed & Breakfast Inns Online** (☎615/868–1946 or 800/215-7365 ⊕www. bbonline.com). **BnB Finder.com** (☎212/432-7693 or 888/547-8226 ⊕www.bnbfinder.com).

CASTLES & MANORS

Some of the most magical experiences on an Irish vacation are stays at some of the country's spectacular castle-hotels, such as Dromoland (Newmarket-on-Fergus), Ashford (Cong), and Castle Leslie (Glaslough). For directories to help you get to know the wide array of manor house and castle accommodations, including a goodly number of private country estates and castles, contact Ireland's Blue Book of Country Houses & Restaurants or Elegant Ireland.

Reservations Services **Elegant Ireland** (⊠15 Harcourt St., Dublin 2, Ireland ☎01/475-1632 🖷01/475-1012 ⊕www. elegant.ie). **Ireland's Blue Book** (⊠8 Mount St. Crescent, Dublin, South City Centre 2 ☎01/676-9914 ⊕www.irelands bluebook.com).

COTTAGES

Vacation cottages, which are usually in clusters, are rented by the week. Although often built in the traditional style, most have central heating and all the other modern conveniences. It's essential to reserve in advance.

Reservations Services **Irish Cottage Holiday Homes Association** (⊠Bracken Court, Bracken Rd., Sandyford, Dublin 8 ☎01/205-2777 ⊕www.irishcottageholidays. com). **Northern Ireland Self-Catering Holi-**

days Association (⊠63 Somerton Rd., North Belfast, Belfast BT15 4DD ☎28/9077–6174 ⊕www.nischa.com).

HOME EXCHANGES

With a direct home exchange you stay in someone else's home while they stay in yours. Some outfits also deal with vacation homes, so you're not actually staying in someone's full-time residence, just their vacant weekend place.

Exchange Clubs

Home Exchange.com (☎*800/877-8723* ⊕*www.homeexchange.com*); $59.95 for a 1-year online listing. **HomeLink International** (☎*800/638-3841* ⊕*www.homelink.org*); $80 yearly for Web-only membership; $125 includes Web access and two catalogs. **Intervac U.S.** (☎*800/756-4663* ⊕*www.intervacus. com*); $78.88 for Web-only membership; $126 includes Web access and a catalog.

HOSTELS

Hostels offer bare-bones lodging at low, low prices—often in shared dorm rooms with shared baths—to people of all ages, though the primary market is young travelers, especially students. Most hostels serve breakfast; dinner and/or shared cooking facilities may also be available. In some hostels you aren't allowed to be in your room during the day, and there may be a curfew at night. Nevertheless, hostels provide a sense of community, with public rooms where travelers often gather to share stories. Many hostels are affiliated with Hostelling International

(HI), an umbrella group of hostel associations with some 4,500 member properties in more than 70 countries. Other hostels are completely independent and may be nothing more than a really cheap hotel.

Membership in any HI association, open to travelers of all ages, allows you to stay in HI-affiliated hostels at member rates. One-year membership is about $28 for adults; hostels charge about $10–$30 per night. Members have priority if the hostel is full; they're also eligible for discounts around the world, even on rail and bus travel in some countries.

Information **Hostelling International—USA** (☎301/495–1240 ⊕www.hiusa.org). **Independent Holiday Hostels** (☎01/836–4700 ⊕www.hostels-ireland.com). **Irish Youth Hostel Association** (An Óige ✉67 Mountjoy St., North City Centre, Dublin 7 ☎01/830–4555 ⊕www.irelandyha.org). **Northern Ireland Hostelling International** (✉22–32 Donegal Rd., University Area, Belfast BT12 5JN ☎28/9032–4733 ⊕www.hini.org.uk).

HOTELS

Standard features in most hotels include private bath, two twin beds (you can usually ask for a king-size instead), TV (often with VCR), free parking, and no-smoking rooms. There's usually no extra charge for these services. All hotels listed have private bath unless otherwise noted.

Information **Ireland Hotels Federation** (☎01/497–6459 ⊕www.irelandhotels.com). **ITB** (⊕www.tourismireland.com). **Northern Ireland Hotels Federation** (☎28/9035–1110 ⊕www.nihf.co.uk).

■ AIRLINE TICKETS

Most domestic airline tickets are electronic; international tickets may be either electronic or paper. With an e-ticket the only thing you receive is an e-mailed receipt citing your itinerary and reservation and ticket numbers.

The greatest advantage of an e-ticket is that if you lose your receipt, you can

simply print out another copy or ask the airline to do it for you at check-in. You usually pay a surcharge (up to $50) to get a paper ticket, if you can get one at all.

The sole advantage of a paper ticket is that it may be easier to endorse over to another airline if your flight is canceled and the airline with which you booked can't accommodate you on another flight.

■TIP→ Discount air passes that let you travel economically in a country or region must often be purchased before you leave home. In some cases you can only get them through a travel agent.

Increasingly, airlines are quoting prices for one-way fares. Be sure to read the fine print to see if taxes are included or if there's a booking charge. The least expensive tickets must usually be purchased in advance. Airlines generally allow you to change your return date for a fee; most low-fare tickets, however, are nonrefundable.

CHARTER FLIGHTS

Charter carriers, such as Sceptre Charters, offer flights to Dublin and Shannon from various U.S. cities. Air Transat flies from Canada. Note that in certain seasons, usually fall and winter, their charter deals include mandatory hotel and car-rental packages.

Charter companies rent aircraft and offer regularly scheduled flights (usually nonstops). Charter flights are generally cheaper than flights on regular airlines, and they often leave from and travel to a wider variety of airports. For example, you could have a nonstop flight from Columbus, Ohio, to Punta Cana, Dominican Republic, or from Chicago to Dubrovnik, Croatia.

You don't, however, have the same protections as with regular airlines. If a charter can't take off for mechanical or other reasons, there usually isn't another plane to take its place. If not enough seats are sold, the flight may be canceled. And if a company goes out of business, you're out of luck (unless, of course, you have insurance with financial default coverage).

Charter Companies Air Transat
(☎877/872-6728 ⊕www.airtransat.com).
Sceptre Charters (☎800/221-0924 ⊕www.
sceptreireland.com).

▌ RENTAL CARS

When you reserve a car, ask about cancellation penalties, taxes, drop-off charges (if you're planning to pick up the car in one city and leave it in another), and surcharges (for being under or over a certain age, for additional drivers, or for driving across state or country borders or beyond a specific distance from your point of rental). All these things can add substantially to your costs. Request car seats and extras such as GPS when you book.

Rates are sometimes—but not always—better if you book in advance or reserve through a rental agency's Web site. There are other reasons to book ahead, though: for popular destinations, during busy times of the year, or to ensure that you get certain types of cars (vans, SUVs, exotic sports cars).

▌TIP➔ Make sure that a confirmed reservation guarantees you a car. Agencies sometimes overbook, particularly for busy weekends and holiday periods.

If you're renting a car in the Irish Republic and intend to visit Northern Ireland (or vice versa), make this clear when you get your car, and check that the rental insurance applies when you cross the border.

Renting a car in Ireland is far more expensive than organizing a rental before you leave home. Rates in Dublin for an economy car with a manual transmission and unlimited mileage are from €35 a day and €160 a week to €50 a day and €190 a week, depending on the season. This includes the republic's 12.5% tax on car rentals. Rates in Belfast begin at £25 a day and £130 a week including the 17.5% tax on car rentals in the North.

Both manual and automatic transmissions are readily available, though automatics cost extra. Typical economy car models include Volkswagen Lupo, Ford Focus, Fiat Panda, and Nissan Micra. Minivans, luxury cars (Mercedes or Alfa Romeos), and four-wheel-drive vehicles (say, a Jeep Cherokee) are also options, but the daily rates are high. Argus Rent A Car and Dan Dooley have convenient locations at Dublin, Shannon, Belfast, and Belfast City airports as well as at ferry ports.

Most rental companies require you to be over 24 to rent a car in Ireland (a few will rent to those over 21) and to have had a license for more than a year. Some companies refuse to rent to visitors over 74. Children under 12 years of age aren't allowed to ride in the front seat unless they're in a properly fitted child seat.

Drivers between the ages of 21 and 26, and 70 and 74 will probably be subject to an insurance surcharge—if they're allowed to drive a rental car at all. An additional driver will add about €5 a day to your car rental, and a child seat costs about €20 for the rental and will require 24-hour advance notice.

Your driver's license may not be recognized outside your home country. You may not be able to rent a car without an International Driving Permit (IDP), which can be used only in conjunction with a valid driver's license and which translates your license into 10 languages. Check the AAA Web site for more info as well as for IDPs ($10) themselves.

CAR RENTAL RESOURCES
Automobile Associations U.S.: American Automobile Association (AAA ☎315/797–5000 ⊕www.aaa.com); most contact with the organization is through state and regional members. **National Automobile Club** (☎650/294–7000 ⊕www.thenac.com); membership is open to California residents only.

Local Agencies Argus (☎499–9600 in Dublin, 048/9442–3444 in Belfast ⊕www. argus-rentacar.com). **Dooley Car Rentals** (☎800/331–9301 in U.S., 0800/282189 in U.K., 062/53103 in Ireland ⊕www.dan-dooley.ie).

Major Agencies Alamo (☎800/522–9696 1800/301401 in Ireland, 01/260–3771 in Dublin ⊕www.alamo.com). **Avis** (☎800/331–1084, 1890/405060 in Ireland, 01/605–7500 in Dublin ⊕www.avis.com). **Budget** (☎800/472–3325, 1850/575767 in Ireland ⊕www.budget.com). **Dollar** (☎800/800–6000 in U.S., 01/670–7890 in Dublin ⊕www.dollar.com). **Hertz** (☎800/654–3001, 01/676–7476 in Ireland ⊕www.hertz.com). **National Car Rental** (☎800/227–7368, 01/844–4162 in Dublin, 1800/301401 in Ireland ⊕www.nationalcar.com).

Wholesalers Auto Europe (☎888/223–5555 ⊕www.autoeurope.com). **Europe by Car** (☎212/581–3040 in New York or 800/223–1516 ⊕www.europebycar.com). **Eurovacations** (☎877/471–3876 ⊕www.eurovacations.com). **Kemwel** (☎877/820–0668 ⊕www.kemwel.com).

CAR-RENTAL INSURANCE

Everyone who rents a car wonders whether the insurance that the rental companies offer is worth the expense. No one—including us—has a simple answer. It all depends on how much regular insurance you have, how comfortable you are with risk, and whether or not money is an issue.

If you own a car, your personal auto insurance may cover a rental to some degree, though not all policies protect you abroad; always read your policy's fine print. If you don't have auto insurance, then seriously consider buying the collision- or loss-damage waiver (CDW or LDW) from the car-rental company, which eliminates your liability for damage to the car. Some credit cards offer CDW coverage, but it's usually supplemental to your own insurance and rarely covers SUVs, minivans, luxury models, and the like. If your coverage is second-

ary, you may still be liable for loss-of-use costs from the car-rental company. But no credit-card insurance is valid unless you use that card for *all* transactions, from reserving to paying the final bill. All companies exclude car rental in some countries, so be sure to find out about the destination to which you are traveling.

■TIP➔ Diners Club offers primary CDW coverage on all rentals reserved and paid for with the card. This means that Diners Club's company—not your own car insurance—pays in case of an accident. It *doesn't* mean your car-insurance company won't raise your rates once it discovers you had an accident.

Some countries require you to purchase CDW coverage or require car-rental companies to include it in quoted rates. Ask your rental company about issues like these in your destination. In most cases it's cheaper to add a supplemental CDW plan to your comprehensive travel-insurance policy than to purchase it from a rental company. That said, you don't want to pay for a supplement if you're required to buy insurance from the rental company.

■TIP➔ You can decline the insurance from the rental company and purchase it through a third-party provider such as Travel Guard (www.travelguard.com)—$9 per day for $35,000 of coverage. That's sometimes just under half the price of the CDW offered by some car-rental companies.

■ VACATION PACKAGES

Packages *are not* guided excursions. Packages combine airfare, accommodations, and perhaps a rental car or other extras (theater tickets, guided excursions, boat trips, reserved entry to popular museums, transit passes), but they let you do your own thing. During busy periods packages may be your only option, as flights and rooms may be sold out otherwise.

Packages will definitely save you time. They can also save you money, particularly in peak seasons, but—and this is a really big "but"—you should price each part of the package separately to be sure. And be aware that prices advertised on Web sites and in newspapers rarely include service charges or taxes, which can up your costs by hundreds of dollars.

■TIP➜ Some packages and cruises are sold only through travel agents. Don't always assume that you can get the best deal by booking everything yourself.

Each year consumers are stranded or lose their money when packagers—even large ones with excellent reputations—go out of business. How can you protect yourself?

First, always pay with a credit card; if you have a problem, your credit-card company may help you resolve it. Second, buy trip insurance that covers default. Third, choose a company that belongs to the United States Tour Operators Association, whose members must set aside funds to cover defaults. Finally, choose a company that also participates in the Tour Operator Program of the American Society of Travel Agents (ASTA), which will act as mediator in any disputes.

You can also check on the tour operator's reputation among travelers by posting an inquiry on one of the Fodors.com forums.

Organizations **American Society of Travel Agents** (*ASTA* ☎ *703/739–2782 or 800/965–2782* ⊕ *www.astanet.com*). **United States Tour Operators Association** (*USTOA* ☎ *212/599–6599* ⊕ *www.ustoa.com*).

■TIP➜ Local tourism boards can provide information about lesser-known and small-niche operators that sell packages to only a few destinations.

∎ GUIDED TOURS

Guided tours are a good option when you don't want to do it all yourself. You travel along with a group (sometimes large, sometimes small), stay in pre-booked hotels, eat with your fellow travelers (sometimes included in the price of your tour, sometimes not), and follow a schedule. But not all guided tours are a "If This is Tuesday, It Must Be Belgium" kind of experience. A knowledgeable guide can take you places that you might never discover on your own, and you may be pushed to see more than you would have otherwise. Whenever you book a guided tour, find out what's included and what isn't. The companies below all offer tours to Ireland on a "land-only" basis. A "land-only" tour includes all your travel (by bus, in most cases) once you arrive in the destination country, but not necessarily your flights to your destination. And remember that you'll be expected to tip your guide (in cash) at the end of the tour. Some of these companies also offer self-drive tours, which include car rental, pre-booked overnight accommodation, and customized touring advice. There are some good deals to be found in the self-drive sector, and the touring expertise included in the price can prove useful to first-time visitors when planning an itinerary.

GENERAL

CIE Tours International are one of the biggest and longest-established (75 years) tour operators in the Irish market. They offer a selection of fully inclusive, escorted bus tours, or independent fly-drive vacations. An eight-day itinerary with car rental and confirmed hotel bookings starts at $598 per person, with two people traveling. The Irish Odyssey is a 12-day bus tour, starting with two nights in Dublin, and taking in Bunratty Castle and Folk Park, Connemara, the Giant's Causeway, and the Ulster American Folk Park, among other attractions, with accommodation in top hotels.

12 Travel is a young company, set up by three friends on their return to Ireland from living and working in Philadelphia. They aim to create the best holiday experience by using enthusiastic local guides. A customized seven-day self-drive tour across Ireland starts from $407 per person, with two people traveling. The price includes six nights B&B, car rental, and toll-free calls to your vacation specialist. Escorted bus tours include the Irish Fling which could be combined with an independent stay in Dublin, as it includes the Ring of Kerry, Killarney, Waterford Crystal, and Kilkenny, and offers seven days, five nights, ten meals and accommodation in superior hotels and costs from $912 per person.

Contacts CIE Tours International (☎1800/243–8687 ⊕www.cietours.com). **12Travel** (☎1800/255–9302 ⊕www.12travel.com).

SPECIAL-INTEREST TOURS

BIKING

Irish Cycling Safaris pioneered cycling holidays in Ireland, and offer easy-going to moderate cycling trips along rural back roads with luggage transfer and accommodation in small family-run hotels and guesthouses. A weeklong tour of the Beara Peninsula in County Cork costs €630 per person sharing. Tour groups are accompanied by a local guide who drives the support van. Alternately, you can opt for a self-led tour which includes bike hire, itinerary, and pre-booked accommodation, also €630 per person sharing.

Walking Cycling Ireland is an association of Irish Tourist Board–approved specialty tour operators, offering guided and self-guided holidays in Ireland to hiking and biking enthusiasts. These do not just involve activity, but hotels, meals, and experiences.

■**TIP➔** Most airlines accommodate bikes as luggage, provided they're dismantled and boxed.

Contacts Irish Cycling Safaris (☎01/260–0749 ⊕www.cyclingsafaris.com). **Ireland Walking Cycling** (⊕www.irelandwalkingcycling.com).

CULINARY

Wonderfulireland.com offers the 7-day Waterford Gourmet Cycle with six nights' accommodation, and six nights' gourmet meals in addition to bike hire and itinerary for €995.

Contacts Wonderful Ireland (☎353/87761–3344 ⊕www.wonderfulireland.com).

CULTURE

Adams & Butler is Ireland's leading purveyor of customized vacations, with an unbeatable range of contacts in the upper end of the market. Most of their tours are customized for small groups in chauffeur-driven cars or on small, luxury buses. Their eight-day garden tour, for example, includes tours from owners of heritage gardens, and talks by horticultural experts, with accommodation in country-house hotels and castles, and starts at $5,250, including all admissions, all meals, and all guided tours and talks. There are similar packages available in interior design and antiques, literary Ireland, VIP horse racing, and even a ghost tour. Whatever your whim, Adams & Butler will be able to indulge it—or so they say.

Contacts Adams & Butler (☎1800/894–5712 or 353/86232–9932 ⊕www.privateluxurytravel.com).

GOLF

Executive Golf and Leisure, Scotland-based golf specialists, offer customized golf breaks, or packages such as a six-day golf tour of Ireland for $6,404 with luxury accommodation, transfers, and rounds on some of the finest courses: the K Club, Old Portmarnock, Royal Dublin, Waterville, Tralee, and the Old Head of Kinsale.

Golfbreaks.com will customize a golf tour for you, and also have tours of different regions of Ireland. Their Northern Ireland and the Northwest package includes rounds at the legendary Royal County Down and Royal Portrush courses.

Contacts **Executive Golf and Leisure** (☎1877/295–2247 or 044/1786–832244 ⊕www.execgolf-leisure.com). **Golfbreaks.com** (☎0800/279–7988 ⊕www.golfbreaks.com).

HIKING

Isle Inn offers self-drive holidays and escorted tours, and has an interesting range of activity holidays which include a Yoga Trek–gentle walking combined with day and evening yoga classes, and escorted hiking holidays averaging 10 to 12 miles a day, and staying in family-run guesthouses and characterful small hotels. The Yoga Trek starts at $1,405, escorted hiking holidays from $1,320, or cycling from $855.

Contacts **Isle Inn** (☎1800/237–9376 ⊕www.isleinntours.com).

RAIL TOURS

Railtours Ireland uses the Irish railway network for major transfers, and coaches for sightseeing at the destination, avoiding long, leg-numbing stretches of coach travel. The five-day tour starts with a train ride from Dublin to Cork (2 hrs, 45 mins) including breakfast, and continues with a bus tour to Blarney, train to Killarney, bus tour of the Ring of Kerry, and also visits Galway, the Cliffs of Moher, and Connemara, starting at $569 per person sharing with accommodation in B&Bs and modest hotels.

Contacts **Railtours Ireland** (☎3531/856–0045 ⊕www.railtoursireland.com).

▌CRUISES

Cruise Lines **Celebrity Cruises** (☎305/539–6000 or 800/437–3111 ⊕www.celebrity.com). **Costa Cruises** (☎954/266–5600 or 800/462–6782 ⊕www.costacruise.com). **Crystal Cruises** (☎310/785–9300 or 800/446–6620 ⊕www.crystalcruises.com). **Cunard Line** (☎661/753–1000 or 800/728–6273 ⊕www.cunard.com). **Holland America Line** (☎206/281–3535 or 877/932–4259 ⊕www.hollandamerica.com). **Mediterranean Shipping Cruises** (☎212/764–4800 or 800/666–9333 ⊕www.msccruises.com). **Norwegian Cruise Line** (☎305/436–4000 or 800/327–7030 ⊕www.ncl.com). **Oceania Cruises** (☎305/514–2300 or 800/531–5658 ⊕www.oceaniacruises.com). **Princess Cruises** (☎661/753–0000 or 800/774–6237 ⊕www.princess.com). **Regent Seven Seas Cruises** (☎954/776–6123 or 800/477–7500 ⊕www.rssc.com). **Seabourn Cruise Line** (☎305/463–3000 or 800/929–9391 ⊕www.seabourn.com). **SeaDream Yacht Club** (☎305/631–6110 or 800/707–4911 ⊕www.seadreamyachtclub.com). **Silversea Cruises** (☎954/522–4477 or 800/722–9955 ⊕www.silversea.com). **Star Clippers** (☎305/442–0550 or 800/442–0551 ⊕www.starclippers.com). **Windstar Cruises** (☎206/281–3535 or 800/258–7245 ⊕www.windstarcruises.com).

TRANSPORTATION

We've provided the fullest addresses possible for hotels, restaurants, and sights. Many of Ireland's villages and towns are so tiny they barely have street names, much less house numbers. If you're having trouble finding your destination, ask for directions—you're bound to get a hospitable response.

■ TIP→ Ask the local tourist board about hotel and local transportation packages that include tickets to major museum exhibits or other special events.

▌ BY AIR

Flying time to Ireland is 6½ hours from New York, 7½ hours from Chicago, 10 hours from Los Angeles, and 1 hour from London.

Flying into Ireland involves few hassles, although an increase in traffic in the last decade has caused a slight increase in flight delays and time spent waiting for baggage to clear customs. Flights within Ireland tend to be filled with business travelers. Increased competition on internal routes has led internal flights to be competitive with rail travel if you can travel outside peak business hours. However, given problems with passenger numbers and long lines for security clearance at Dublin Airport, rail is often preferable.

Checking in and boarding an outbound plane tends to be civilized. Security is professional but not overbearing, and airport staffers are usually helpful and patient. In the busy summer season lines can get long, and you should play it safe and arrive a couple of hours before your flight.

Airlines & Airports **Airline and Airport Links.com** (⊕www.airlineandairportlinks.com) has links to many of the world's airlines and airports.

Airline Security Issues **Transportation Security Administration** (⊕www.tsa.gov) has answers for almost every question that might come up.

AIRPORTS

The major gateways to Ireland are Dublin Airport (DUB) on the east coast, 10 km (6 mi) north of the city center, and Shannon Airport (SNN) on the west coast, 25 km (16 mi) west of Limerick. Two airports serve Belfast: Belfast International Airport (BFS) at Aldergrove, 24 km (15 mi) from the city, handles local and U.K. flights, as well as all other international traffic; Belfast City Airport (BHD), 6½ km (4 mi) from the city, handles local and U.K. flights only. In addition, the City of Derry Airport (LDY) receives flights from Dublin and Manchester, Liverpool, East Midlands, and Glasgow in the United Kingdom.

Airport Information **George Best Belfast City Airport** (☎028/9093–9093 ⊕www. belfastcityairport.com). **Belfast International Airport at Aldergrove** (☎028/9448–4848 ⊕www.belfastairport.com). **City of Derry Airport** (☎028/7181–0784 ⊕www. cityofderryairport.com). **Dublin Airport** (☎01/814–1111 ⊕www.dublinairport.ie). **Shannon Airport** (☎061/712–000 ⊕www.shannonairport.com).

GROUND TRANSPORTATION

TRANSFERS BETWEEN AIRPORTS

Contacts

FLIGHTS

From North America and the United Kingdom, Aer Lingus, the national flag carrier, has the most direct flights to Ireland.

Aer Lingus operates regularly scheduled flights to Shannon and Dublin from New York's JFK (John F. Kennedy Airport), Boston's Logan, Chicago's O'Hare, and LAX (Los Angeles International Airport). Delta has a daily departure from New York's JFK that flies first to Shannon and then to Dublin. Continental flies daily direct to Dublin and Shannon, departing from Newark Liberty International Airport in New Jersey. With the exception of special offers, the prices of the three airlines tend to be similar.

London to Dublin is one of the world's busiest international air routes. Aer Lingus, British Airways, British Midlands, and CityJet all have several daily flights. Ryanair—famous for its cheap, no-frills service—offers several daily flights from London Gatwick, Luton, and Stansted airports, while its low-cost rival, EasyJet, flies to many of these same destinations. With such healthy competition, bargains abound. British Airways, British Midlands, and low-cost airline EasyJet offer regularly scheduled flights to Belfast from London Gatwick, Luton, and Stansted airports. Aer Lingus provides service within Ireland to Dublin, Cork, Galway, Kerry, and Shannon. Aer Arann Express flies from Dublin to Cork, Derry, Donegal, Galway, Knock, and Sligo. British Airways has daily service between Dublin and Derry.

Airline Contacts Aer Arann Express (☎353/1844–7700 in Republic of Ireland, 0800/587–2324 ⊕www.aerarannexpress. com). **Aer Lingus** (☎800/474–7424 ⊕www.aerlingus.com). **American Airlines** (☎800/433–7300 ⊕www.aa.com). **British Airways** (☎800/147–9297 ⊕www. britishairways.com). **British Midlands** (⊕www.flybmi.com). **CityJet** (⊕www.cityjet. com). **Continental Airlines** (☎800/523–3273 for U.S. and Mexico reservations, 800/231–0856 for international reservations ⊕www.continental.com). **Delta Airlines** (☎800/221–1212 for U.S. reservations, 800/241–4141 for international reservations ⊕www.delta.com). **EasyJet** (⊕www.easyjet. com). **Northwest Airlines** (☎800/225–2525 ⊕www.nwa.com). **Ryanair** (⊕www.ryanair. com). **United Airlines** (☎800/864–8331 for U.S. reservations, 800/538–2929 for international reservations ⊕www.united.com). **USAirways** (☎800/428–4322 for U.S. and Canada reservations, 800/622–1015 for international reservations ⊕www.usairways.com).

▌BY BOAT

TO & FROM IRELAND

The ferry is a convenient way to travel between Ireland and elsewhere in Europe, particularly the United Kingdom. There are six main ferry ports to Ireland; four in the republic at Dublin Port, Dun Laoghaire, Rosslare, and Cork, and two in Northern Ireland at Belfast and Larne. The cost of your trip can vary substantially, so spend time with a travel agent and compare prices carefully. Bear in mind, too, that flying can be cheaper, so look into all types of transportation before booking.

Irish Ferries operates the *Ulysses,* the world's largest car ferry, on its Dublin to Holyhead, Wales, route (3 hrs, 15 min); there's also a swift service (1 hr, 50 min) between these two ports. There are several trips daily. The company also runs between Rosslare and Pembroke, Wales (3 hrs, 45 min), and has service to France. Stena Line sails several times a day between Dublin and Holyhead (3 hrs, 15 min) and has swift service to Dun Laoghaire (1 hr, 40 min). The company also runs a fast craft (1 hr, 45 min) and a superferry (3 hrs, 15 min) between Belfast and Stranraer, Scotland, as well as a fast craft (1 hr, 40 min) and a superferry (3 hrs, 30 min) between Rosslare and Fishguard, Wales. There are several trips daily on both routes.

Norfolk Line offers a Dublin and Belfast to Liverpool service (8 hrs). P&O Irish Sea vessels run between Larne and Troon, Scotland (4 hrs), a couple of times a day. The company also sails from Dublin to Liverpool twice daily (7 hrs) with a choice of daytime or overnight sailings. After a hiatus in 2007 service, Swansea Cork Ferries promise to once again travel between Swansea and Cork from mid-March to early November. The crossing takes 10 hours, but easy access by road to both ports makes this longer sea route a good choice for motorists.

WITHIN IRELAND

A 10-minute car ferry crosses the River Suir between Ballyhack in County Wexford and Passage East (near Arthurstown) in County Waterford, introducing you to two pretty fishing villages. The ferry operates continuously during daylight hours and costs €5.70 per car, (€8.25 round-trip) €1.20 for foot passengers. A boat from Tarbert in County Kerry leaves every hour on the half hour for Killimer in County Clare; return ferries leave Killimer every hour on the hour. The 30-minute journey across the Shannon Estuary costs €15 per car, (€25 round-trip), €4 for foot passengers. The scenic Cork Harbor crossing allows those traveling from West Cork or Kinsale to Cobh and the east coast to bypass the city center. The five-minute car ferry runs from Glenbrook (near Ringaskiddy) in the west to Carrigaloe (near Cobh) in the east and operates continuously from 7:15 AM to 12:45 AM daily. It costs €5.50 per car, €1 for foot passengers.

There are regular services to the Aran Islands from Rossaveal in County Galway, and Doolin in County Clare. Ferries also sail to Inishbofin off the Galway coast and Arranmore off the Donegal coast, and to Bere, Whiddy, Sherkin, and Cape Clear Islands off the coast of County Cork. Bere and Whiddy have a car ferry, but the other islands are all small enough to explore on foot, so the ferries are for foot passengers and bicycles only. Other islands—the Blaskets and the Skelligs in Kerry, Rathlin in Antrim, and Tory, off the Donegal coast—have seasonal ferry services running daily between May and September, less frequently outside these months. Fáilte Ireland publishes a free guide and map with ferry details, *Ireland's Islands*, or see ⊕*www.irelands islands.com*. Alternately, check with the nearest Tourist Information Office near the time of your visit, or see www.ireland. ie. In Northern Ireland in County Down a 10-minute ferry will take pedestrians and cars from Strangford to Portaferry on the Ards Peninsula. This ferry runs every half hour. It costs £1.80 for passengers and £8.50 per car.

Boating the Shannon River system is an appealing alternative to traveling overland. In some places bicycles can be rented so you can drop anchor and explore.

FARES & SCHEDULES

You can get schedules and purchase tickets, with a credit card if you like, directly from the ferry lines. You can also pick up tickets at Dublin tourism offices and at any major travel agent in Ireland or the United Kingdom. Payment must be made in the currency of the country of the port of departure. Bad weather can delay or cancel ferry sailings so it's always a good idea to call before departing for the port.

Information **Irish Ferries** (☎1890/313131 in Ireland, 08705/171717 in U.K., 0143/944694 in France ⊕www.irishferries.com). **Norfolk Line** (☎01/819–2999 in Ireland, 0870/600–4321 in U.K. ⊕www.norfolkline-ferries.co.uk/en/ is-passenger). **P&O Irish Sea** (☎1800/409049 in Ireland, 0870/2424777 in U.K. ⊕www. poirishsea.com). **Stena Line** (☎01/204–7777 in Ireland, 028/9074–7747 in Northern Ireland, 08705/707070 in U.K. ⊕www.stenaline.co.uk). **Swansea Cork Ferries** (☎021/483–6000 in Ireland, 01792/456116 in U.K. ⊕www. swanseacorkferries.com).

Boat Travel on the Shannon **Carrickcraft** (✉Banagher ☎0509/51187 ⊕www. cruise-ireland.com). **Emerald Star** (✉Connaught Harbor, Portumna ☎071/962–7661 ⊕www.emeraldsstar.ie). **Ireland Line Cruisers** (✉Killaloe ☎061/375–011). **Riversdale Barge Holidays** (✉Ballinamore ☎071/965–8964 ⊕www.riversdalebargeholidays.com). **Shannon Castle Line** (✉Williamstown Harbor, Whitegate ☎061/927–042). **Silver Line Cruisers** (✉The Marina, Banagher ☎0509/51112 ⊕www.silverlinecruisers.com). **Waveline Cruisers** (✉Quigley's Marina, Killinure Point, Glasson ☎0902/85711 ⊕www.waveline.ie).

▌BY BUS

In the Republic of Ireland, long-distance bus services are operated by Bus Éireann, which also provides local service in Cork, Galway, Limerick, and Waterford. There's only one class, and prices are similar for all seats. Note, though, that outside of the peak season, services are limited; some routes (e.g., Killarney–Dingle) disappear altogether. There's often only one trip a day on express routes, and one a week to some remote villages. Rural bus services shut down at around 7 or 8 PM. To ensure that a bus journey is feasible, buy a copy of Bus Éireann's timetable—€6 from any bus terminal—or check online. Many of the destination indicators are in Irish (Gaelic), so make sure you get on the right bus.

Numerous bus companies run between Britain and the Irish Republic, but be ready for long hours on the road and possible delays. All use either the Holyhead–Dublin or Fishguard/Pembroke–Rosslare ferry routes. National Express, a consortium of companies, has services from all major British cities to more than 90 Irish destinations. Buses are cheap but slow: the journey from London to Galway takes around 17 hours.

In Northern Ireland, all buses are operated by the state-owned Ulsterbus. Service is generally good, with particularly useful links to those towns not served by train. Ulsterbus also offers tours. Buses to Belfast run from London and from Birmingham, making the Stranraer–Port of Belfast crossing. Contact National Express.

Check with the bus office to see if reservations are accepted for your route; if not, show up early to get a seat. Note: prepaid tickets don't apply to a particular bus time, just a route, so if one vehicle is full you can try another. You can buy tickets online, or at the main tourist offices, at the bus station, or on the bus (though it's cash only for the latter option). A round-trip from Dublin to Cork costs €28 and Dublin to Galway return is €19.

You can save money by buying a multi-day pass, some of which can be combined with rail service. There are also cost-cutting passes that will give access to travel in both Northern Ireland and the Republic of Ireland. A Freedom of Northern Ireland ticket costs £47 for seven days' unlimited bus and rail travel—a really good deal when you consider that a one-day ticket costs £13. In the Republic, passes include the Irish Explorer Rail and Bus Pass, which gives you eight days' bus travel out of 15 consecutive days for €194. The bus-only Irish Rover Card costs €158 for eight days' travel out of 15 consecutive days across both Northern Ireland and the Republic. The Emerald Card is valid for both bus and rail in Northern Ireland and the Republic, and costs €228 for eight days' travel out of 15 consecutive days. Contact Bus Éireann or Ulsterbus for details.

Bus Information **Bus Éireann** (☎ 01/836–6111 in Republic of Ireland ⊕ www.buseireann.ie). **National Express** (☎ 08705/808–080 in U.K. ⊕ www.nationalexpress.co.uk). **Ulsterbus** (☎ 028/9033–3000 in Northern Ireland ⊕ www.ulsterbus.co.uk).

▌BY CAR

U.S. driver's licenses are recognized in Ireland.

Roads in the Irish Republic are generally good, though four-lane highways, or motorways, are the exception rather than the rule. In addition, many roads twist and wind their way up and down hills and through towns, which can slow you down. On small, rural roads, watch out for cattle and sheep; they may be just around the next bend. Reckless drivers are also a problem in the countryside, so remain cautious and alert. Ireland ranks third worst among the original 15 EU countries on road accident frequency and has the highest auto accident fatality rate in Europe.

Road signs in the republic are generally in both Irish (Gaelic) and English; in Dingle, the Northwest and Connemara, most are in Irish only, so get a good road map. On the new green signposts distances are in kilometers; on the old white signposts they're in miles, but recent legislation means the green signposts are here to stay. Knowing the name of the next town on your itinerary is more important than knowing the route number: neither the small local signposts nor the local people refer to roads by official numbers. Traffic signs are the same as in the rest of Europe, and roadway markings are standard.

There are no border checkpoints between the republic and Northern Ireland, where the road network is excellent and, outside Belfast, uncrowded. Road signs and traffic regulations conform to the British system.

All ferries on both principal routes to the Irish Republic take cars. Fishguard and Pembroke are relatively easy to reach by road. The car trip to Holyhead, on the other hand, is sometimes difficult: delays on the A55 North Wales coastal road aren't unusual. Car ferries to Belfast leave from the Scottish port of Stranraer and the English city of Liverpool; those to Larne leave from Stranraer and Cairnryan. Speed limits are generally 95 to 100 kph (roughly 60 to 70 mph) on the motorways, 80 kph (50 mph) on other roads, and 50 kph (30 mph) in towns.

GASOLINE

You can find gas stations along most roads. Self-service is the norm. Major credit cards and traveler's checks are usually accepted. Prices are near the lower end for Europe, with unleaded gas priced around €1.04 in Ireland and €0.87 a liter in Northern Ireland—more than three times what gasoline costs in the United States. Prices vary significantly from station to station, so it's worth driving around the block.

ROAD CONDITIONS

Most roads are paved and make for easy travel. Roads are classified as *M*, *N*, or *R*: those designated with an *M* for "motorway" are double-lane divided highways with paved shoulders; *N*, or national, routes are generally undivided highways with shoulders; and *R*, or regional, roads tend to be narrow and twisty.

Rush hour traffic in Dublin, Cork, Limerick, Belfast, and Galway can be intense. Rush hours in Dublin run 7 AM to 9:30 AM and 5 PM to 7 PM; special events such as football (soccer) games will also tie up traffic in and around the city as will heavy rain.

ROADSIDE EMERGENCIES

Membership in an emergency car service is a good idea if you're using your own vehicle in Ireland. The Automobile Association of Ireland is a sister organization of its English counterpart and is highly recommended. Note that the AA can only help you or your vehicle if you are a member of the association. If not, contact your car-rental company for assistance. If involved in an accident you should note the details of the vehicle and the driver and witnesses and report the incident to a member of the Garda Síochána (the Irish Police) or the Police Service of Northern Ireland (PSNI) as soon as possible. Since traffic congestion is chronic in Dublin, emergency services are more likely to be dispatched quickly to help you and to clear the road. If your car does break down, if at all possible try to stop it in a well-lighted area near a public phone. If you're on a secondary or minor road, remain in your car with the doors locked after you call for assistance. If you break down on the motorway, you should pull onto the hard shoulder and stay out of your car with the passenger side door open and the other doors locked. This will allow you to jump into the car quickly if you sense any trouble. Make sure you check credentials of anyone who offers assistance—note the license-plate number and color of the assisting vehicle before you step out of the car.

Emergency Services **Automobile Association of Ireland** (☎01/617–9999 in Ireland, 0800/887766 in Northern Ireland, 08457/887766 from cell phone in Northern Ireland ⊕www.aaireland.ie; www.theaa.com for Northern Ireland). **Police** (☎999).

RULES OF THE ROAD

The Irish, like the British, drive on the left-hand side of the road. Safety belts must be worn by the driver and all passengers, and children under 12 must travel in the back unless riding in a car seat. It's compulsory for motorcyclists and their passengers to wear helmets. Speed limits in Ireland are posted in kilometers per hour and in Northern Ireland in miles per hour, so if crossing the border be sure to make the adjustment. In towns and cities the speed limit is 50 kph (31 mph). On Regional (R) and Local (L) roads, the speed limit is 80 kph (50 mph), indicated by white signs. On National roads, the speed limit is 100 kph (62 mph), indicated by green signs. On Motorways, the speed limit is 120 kph (74 mph), indicated by blue signs.

Drunk-driving laws are strict. The legal limit is 80 mg of alcohol per 100 ml of blood. Ireland has a Breathalyzer test, which the police can administer anytime. If you refuse to take it, the odds are you'll be prosecuted anyway. As always, the best advice is don't drink if you plan to drive.

Speed cameras and radar are used throughout Ireland. Speeding carries an on-the-spot fine of €80 and if the Gardaí (police) charges you with excessive speeding you could be summoned to court. This carries a much higher fine and you will be summoned within six months (meaning you could be required to return to Ireland).

Note that a continuous white line down the center of the road prohibits passing. Barred markings on the road and flashing yellow beacons indicate a crossing, where pedestrians have right of way. At a junction of two roads of equal importance, the driver to the right has right of way. On a roundabout, vehicles approaching from the right have right of way. Also, remember there are no right turns permitted on a red light. If another motorist flashes their headlights at you they are not warning of a speed trap ahead, they are giving you right of way.

Despite the relatively light traffic, parking in towns can be a problem. Signs with the letter *P* indicate that parking is permitted; a stroke through the *P* warns you to stay away or you'll be liable for a fine of €20–€65; however, if your car gets towed away or clamped, the fine is around €180. In Dublin and Cork, parking lots are your best bet, but check the rate first in Dublin; they vary wildly.

In Northern Ireland there are plenty of parking lots in the towns (usually free except in Belfast), and you should use them. In Belfast, you can't park your car in some parts of the city center, more because of congestion than security problems.

▌ BY TRAIN

The republic's Irish Rail trains are generally reliable, reasonably priced, and comfortable. You can easily reach all the principal towns from Dublin, though services between provincial cities are roundabout. To get to Cork City from Wexford, for example, you have to go via Limerick Junction. It's often quicker, though perhaps less comfortable, to take a bus. Most mainline trains have one standard class. Round-trip tickets are usually cheapest.

Northern Ireland Railways has three main rail routes, all operating out of Belfast's Central Station. These are north to Derry, via Ballymena and Coleraine; east to Bangor along the shores of Belfast

Lough; and south to Dublin and the Irish Republic. Note that Eurailpasses aren't valid in Northern Ireland.

You should plan to be at the train station at least 30 minutes before your train departs to ensure you'll get a seat. It's not uncommon on busier routes to find that you have to stand since all seats have been sold and taken.

Ireland (excluding Northern Ireland) is one of 17 countries in which you can use **Eurailpasses,** which provide unlimited first-class rail travel, in all of the participating countries, for the duration of the pass. If you plan to rack up the miles, get a standard pass. These are available for 15 days ($588), 21 days ($762), one month ($946), two months ($1,338), and three months ($1,654). In addition to standard Eurailpasses, ask about special rail-pass plans. Among these are the **Eurail Youthpass** (for those under age 26), the **Eurail Saverpass** (which gives a discount for two or more people traveling together), a **Eurail Flexipass** (which allows a certain number of travel days within a set period), the **Euraildrive Pass** and the **Europass Drive** (which combines travel by train and rental car). Whichever pass you choose, you must purchase your pass before you leave for Europe.

The **Irish Explorer Rail & Bus Pass** covers all the state-run and national railways and bus lines throughout the republic. It does not apply to the North or to transportation within cities. An eight-day ticket for use on buses and trains during a 15-day period is €228. The **Emerald Isle Card** offers unlimited bus and train travel anywhere in Ireland and Northern Ireland, valid within cities as well. An 8-day pass gives you eight days of travel over a 15-day period; it costs roughly €158. A pass for 15 days of travel over a 30-day period costs about €235. Irish Rail International provides details on both passes.

In Northern Ireland, the **Freedom of Northern Ireland Pass** entitling you to seven days' unlimited travel on scheduled bus and rail services, April–October, is available from main Northern Ireland Railway stations. It costs £50 for adults (half price for children under 12 and senior citizens). Interrail tickets are also valid in Northern Ireland.

Train schedules are easy to obtain and available in a variety of formats. Irish Rail and Northern Ireland Rail have Web sites that produce a schedule in response to your input of an itinerary. Alternatively you can visit any train station to obtain a printed schedule or call either company's customer service line. Take special note of schedules when traveling on holiday weekends as schedules are usually changed. Both rail services print amended schedules well in advance.

Sample fares? A return ticket from Dublin to Cork will cost around €55; Dublin to Belfast is approximately €50.

Tickets can be purchased online or at the train station. Cash, traveler's checks, and credit-card payments are accepted. You must pay in the local currency. In Dublin, Connolly and Heuston stations have automated ticket machines that take either cash or credit-card payments, offering a convenient way to avoid long lines at ticket windows.

Many travelers assume that rail passes guarantee them seats on the trains they wish to ride. Not so. You need to book seats ahead even if you're using a rail pass. Seat reservations are required on some European trains, particularly high-speed trains, and are a good idea on trains that may be crowded—particularly in summer on popular routes. You'll also need a reservation if you purchase sleeping accommodations.

There's only one class of train travel in Ireland (with the exception of the Enterprise, the express train that travels from Dublin to Belfast, for which you can purchase a First Class or Standard Class ticket, and the Dublin to Cork train). All tickets bought online on the Cork-Dublin train include a seat reservation. Otherwise, specific seat reservations can only be made for trains deemed to be busy (ask when buying your ticket if they're taking reservations for your route). For example, the train traveling from Dublin to Cork on a Friday evening is considered a peak time, thanks to all the students and business travelers heading home for the weekend, and it would be advisable to have a seat reservation, and to board the train early. At peak hours and for popular routes, it's advisable to arrive early at the station to purchase your ticket (or buy it online) or you may find yourself standing for a significant portion of your journey.

Information & Passes CIE Tours International (☎800/243-8687 ⊕www.cietours. com). **DER Travel Services** (☎888/337-7350 ⊕www.dertravel.com). **Rail Europe** (☎800/438-7245 ⊕www.raileurope.com).

Train Information **Irish Rail** (Iarnrod Éireann ☎01/836-6222 ⊕www.irishrail.ie) is the rail division of CIE. **Northern Ireland Railways** (☎028/9089-9411 ⊕www.translink.co.uk).

Belfast Central Station (✉East Bridge St., Belfast BT1 3PB ☎028/9089-9400 ⊕www.translink.co.uk). **Connolly Station** (✉Amiens St., Dublin 1 ☎01/703-2358 ⊕www.irishrail. ie). **Galway Station** (✉Station Rd., Galway ☎091/564222 ⊕www.irishrail.ie). **Heuston Station** (✉Dublin 8 ☎01/703-3299 ⊕www.irishrail.ie). **Kent Station** (✉Lower Glanmire Rd., Cork ☎021/450-6766 ⊕www.irishrail.ie).

ON THE GROUND

■ COMMUNICATIONS

INTERNET

If you're traveling with a laptop, carry a spare battery and adapter. Most laptops will work at both 120V and 220V, but you will need an adapter so the plug will fit in the socket. In the countryside, a surge protector is a good idea.

Going online is becoming routine in Dublin, thanks, in part, to the Wi-Fi hot spots—which allow you to make a wireless connection from your laptop onto a network—popping up across the city. Nethouse has the most Internet cafés in the country, with nine locations in Dublin and one in Cork. There are also many independent Internet cafés across the country. Prices vary from the low end in Dublin of €2.60 per hour to €5 per hour in smaller cities. There are also new Wi-Fi hot spots in other major cities throughout the country, such as the Insomnia Coffee and Sandwich Bar chain in Galway. Dublin Airport and Dun Laoghaire Harbor have facilities to access wireless connection to the Internet. Hotels in Dublin that offer Wi-Fi access include the Conrad and the Four Seasons. A Wi-Fi connection will cost about €9 for an hour or €22 for unlimited access within a 24-hour period. In many cases, however, Wi-Fi access is usually free if you are using the facilities of the hotel or café.

Contacts Cybercafes (⊕www.cybercafes. com) lists over 4,000 Internet cafés worldwide.

PHONES

The good news is that you can now make a direct-dial telephone call from virtually any point on earth. The bad news? You can't always do so cheaply. Calling from a hotel is almost always the most expensive option; hotels usually add huge surcharges to all calls, particularly international ones. In some countries you can phone from call centers or even the post office. Calling cards usually keep costs to a minimum, but only if you purchase them locally. And then there are mobile phones *(⇨below)*, which are sometimes more prevalent—particularly in the developing world—than land lines; as expensive as mobile phone calls can be, they are still usually a much cheaper option than calling from your hotel.

Ireland's telephone system is up to the standards of the United Kingdom and the United States. Direct-dialing is common; local phone numbers have five to eight digits. You can make international calls from most phones, and some cell phones also work here, depending on the carrier.

Do not make calls from your hotel room unless it's absolutely necessary. Practically all hotels add 200% to 300% to the cost.

The country code for Ireland is 353; for Northern Ireland, which is part of the United Kingdom telephone system, it's 44. The local area code for Northern Ireland is 028. However, when dialing Northern Ireland from the republic you can simply dial 048 without using the U.K. country code. When dialing an Irish number from abroad, drop the initial 0 from the local area code. The country code is 1 for the United States and Canada, 61 for Australia, 64 for New Zealand, and 44 for the United Kingdom.

Public pay phones can be found in street booths and in restaurants, hotels, bars, and shops, some of which display a sign saying YOU CAN PHONE FROM HERE. There are at least three models of pay phones; read the instructions or ask for assistance.

CALLING WITHIN IRELAND

If the operator has to connect your call, it will cost at least one-third more than direct dial.

Directory Information Republic of Ireland (☎11811 for directory inquiries in the republic

LANGUAGE DO'S & TABOOS

In the old days, Ireland's native language was called Gaelic and some people chuckled that it was the world's most perfect medium for prayers, curses, and lovemaking.

These days, Gaelic is called Irish and no one is joking any longer.

In March 2005, legislation was passed to restore the sovereignty of Irish, originally a Celtic language related to Scots Gaelic, Breton, and Welsh, as Ireland's official national language.

English is technically the second language of the country but it is, in fact, the everyday tongue of 95% of the population.

However, the western coastlands of Ireland are still home to the Gaeltacht (pronounced *gale*-taukt). These Irish-speaking communities are found mainly in sparsely populated rural areas along the western seaboard, on some islands, and in pockets in West Cork and County Waterford.

Travelers to these western seaboard regions in Counties Donegal and Galway should note that new laws have mandated Irish as the sole language for signage.

In these Gaeltacht areas, English is now outlawed in road signs and official maps.

As the Associated Press reported, "Locals concede the switch will confuse foreigners in an area that depends heavily on tourism, but they say it's the price of patriotism."

The Gaeltacht includes some big tourist destinations. For instance, if travelers are in Killarney and now wish to go to Dingle, they will have to follow signposts that say "An Daingean," because that is Dingle in Irish.

Other instances include: Oileáin Árainn (Aran Islands); Corca Dhuibne (Dingle Peninsula); and Árainn Mhor (Aranmore Island).

As this changeover affects more than 2,000 other place-names, have an updated or Irish-friendly map if touring these Gaeltacht regions.

Don't rely on official Ordnance Survey maps, which can now only print Irish place-names in these areas.

This is even in cases where the English versions remain popular in local parlance (many hotels will retain their English names, such as the Dingle Bay Hotel).

Main place-names are given in both Irish and English in this guidebook for the affected regions.

Outside these Gaeltacht areas, Ireland remains officially bilingual in its road signs. "This will allow you to get lost in both Irish and English," as Mr. O'Reilly pointed out on Fodor's Web site.

With just 55,000 native Irish speakers in a population of 4 million, a major national debate has sprung up.

You can follow it if you Google Irish Place-names Act 2004, and local councils and tourist authorities have begun to protest the new laws.

For now, a good touring map will give both Irish and English names to places within the Gaeltacht.

And some basic Irish vocabulary certainly wouldn't hurt: *fir* (men) and *mná* (women) should prove useful when inquiring about public restrooms.

and Northern Ireland, 11818 for U.K. and international numbers, 114 for operator assistance with international calls, 10 for operator assistance for calls in Ireland, Northern Ireland, and U.K.). **Northern Ireland and the U.K.** (☎192 for directory inquiries in Northern Ireland and U.K., 153 for international directory inquiries, which includes the republic, 155 for the international operator, 100 for operator assistance for calls in U.K. and Northern Ireland).

To make a local call just dial the number direct. Public phones take either coins (€0.25 for a call) or cards, but not both. At coin phones just pick up the receiver and deposit the money before you dial the number. At card phones pick up the receiver, wait until the display tells you to insert the card, then dial. In the republic, €0.25 will buy you a three-minute local call; around €1 is needed for a three-minute long-distance call within the republic. In Northern Ireland, a local call costs 10p.

To make a long-distance call, dial the area code, then the number. The local code for Northern Ireland is 028, unless you're dialing from the republic, in which case you dial 048 or 004428, followed by the eight-digit number.

CALLING OUTSIDE IRELAND

The country code for the United States is 1.

The international prefix from Ireland is 00. For calls to Great Britain (except Northern Ireland), dial 0044 before the exchange code, and drop the initial zero of the local code. For the United States and Canada dial 001, for Australia 0061, and for New Zealand 0064.

Access Codes **AT&T Direct** (☎1800/550-000 from Republic of Ireland, 0500/890-011 from Northern Ireland). **MCI WorldPhone** (☎1800/551-001 from Republic of Ireland, 0800/890-222 from Northern Ireland using British Telecom, BT, 0500/890-222 using Cable & Wireless, C&W). **Sprint International Access** (☎1800/552-001 from Republic of Ireland, 0800/890-877 from Northern Ireland using BT, 0500/890-877 using C&W).

CALLING CARDS

"Callcards" are sold in post offices and newsagents. These come in denominations of 10, 20, and 50 units and range in price from €10 to €30.

MOBILE PHONES

If you have a multiband phone (some countries use different frequencies than what's used in the United States) and your service provider uses the world-standard GSM network (as do T-Mobile, Cingular, and Verizon), you can probably use your phone abroad. Roaming fees can be steep, however: 99¢ a minute is considered reasonable. And overseas you normally pay the toll charges for incoming calls. It's almost always cheaper to send a text message than to make a call, since text messages have a very low set fee (often less than 5¢).

If you just want to make local calls, consider buying a new SIM card (note that your provider may have to unlock your phone for you to use a different SIM card) and a prepaid service plan in the destination. You'll then have a local number and can make local calls at local rates. If your trip is extensive, you could also simply buy a new cell phone in your destination, as the initial cost will be offset over time.

■TIP→ **If you travel internationally frequently, save one of your old mobile phones or buy a cheap one on the Internet; ask your cell phone company to unlock it for you, and take it with you as a travel phone, buying a new SIM card with pay-as-you-go service in each destination.**

Contacts **Cellular Abroad** (☎800/287-5072 ⊕www.cellularabroad.com) rents and sells GMS phones and sells SIM cards that work in many countries. **Mobal** (☎888/888-9162 ⊕www.mobalrental.com) rents mobiles and sells GSM phones (starting at $49) that will operate in 140 countries. Per-call rates vary throughout the world. **Planet Fone** (☎888/988-4777 ⊕www.planetfone.com)

rents cell phones, but the per-minute rates are expensive.

■ CUSTOMS & DUTIES

You're always allowed to bring goods of a certain value back home without having to pay any duty or import tax. But there's a limit on the amount of tobacco and liquor you can bring back duty-free, and some countries have separate limits for perfumes; for exact figures, check with your customs department. The values of so-called "duty-free" goods are included in these amounts. When you shop abroad, save all your receipts, as customs inspectors may ask to see them as well as the items you purchased. If the total value of your goods is more than the duty-free limit, you'll have to pay a tax (most often a flat percentage) on the value of everything beyond that limit.

Duty-free allowances have been abolished for those traveling between countries in the EU. For goods purchased outside the EU, you may import duty-free: (1) 200 cigarettes or 100 cigarillos or 50 cigars or 250 grams of smoking tobacco; (2) 2 liters of wine, and either 1 liter of alcoholic drink over 22% volume or 2 liters of alcoholic drink under 22% volume (sparkling or fortified wine included); (3) 50 grams (60 ml) of perfume and ¼ liter of eau de toilette and (4) other goods (including beer) to a value of €175 per person (€90 per person for travelers under 15 years of age).

Goods that cannot be freely imported to the Irish Republic include firearms, ammunition, explosives, indecent or obscene books and pictures, oral smokeless tobacco products, meat and meat products, poultry and poultry products. Plants and plant products (including shrubs, vegetables, fruit, bulbs, and seeds) can be imported from other countries within the EU only, provided they are eligible under the EU's plant passport scheme. Domestic cats and dogs from outside the United Kingdom and live animals from outside

Northern Ireland must be quarantined for six months, unless they are traveling under the EU's Pet Travel Scheme.

Information in Ireland **Customs and Excise** (⌂ Irish Life Building, 2nd fl., Middle Abbey St., Dublin 1 ☎ 01/878–8811 ⊕ www.revenue. ie). **HM Customs and Excise** (⌂ Portcullis House, 21 Cowbridge Rd. E, Cardiff CF11 9SS ☎ 0845/010–9000, 0208/929–0152, 0208/929–6731, 0208/910–3602 complaints ⊕ www.hmce.gov.uk).

For details of the **Pet Travel Scheme** see (⊕ www.agriculture.gov.ie).

U.S. Information **U.S. Customs and Border Protection** (⊕ www.cbp.gov).

■ EATING OUT

It wasn't so long ago that people shared jokes about Ireland's stodgy, overcooked, slightly gray food. But in the last decade there have been changes in all aspects of Irish life, including food and drink. The country is going through a culinary renaissance, and Dublin chefs are leading the charge. They're putting nouvelle spins on Irish favorites. And, spurred by a wave of new immigration, ethnic eateries of all types have sprung up in most major towns and cities.

But change as the Irish menu may, many dishes remain the same. A typical Irish breakfast includes fried eggs, rashers (bacon), black and white puddings (black pudding is made with pork, pork blood, cereals, and seasoning; white pudding is similar, but without the blood), sausage, tomatoes, beans, soda bread, and a pot of tea.

Lunch might feature a hearty sandwich; dinners usually include meat, potatoes, and two vegetables. Some of the best food is found at family-run bed-and-breakfasts and in inexpensive cafés. Irish smoked salmon—usually served on brown soda bread with plenty of butter—is among the finest in the world, and many a wondrous dish has been created around the humble cockle and mussel, abundant in the clear Atlantic waters. Galway and the west are rapidly becoming famous for their oyster beds.

Of course there's the omnipresent potato, too. The Irish have many words for the humble spud, and they've invented plenty of ways to serve it. The best of these is "boxty," a traditional pancake of once- and twice-cooked potatoes: it makes the perfect bed for a beef-and-Guinness stew, or the equally hearty lamb casserole. *For more on the delights of the new (and old) Irish cuisine, see the introduction to the Where to Eat section in the Dublin chapter and "A Taste of Ireland" in Chapter 6.*

For information on food-related health issues, see Health below.

MEALS & MEALTIMES
Unless otherwise noted, the restaurants listed in this guide are open daily for lunch and dinner.

No longer will you "enjoy" your favorite tipple in the blue haze of a smoke-filled pub. The Republic of Ireland became the first European country to ban smoking in all pubs and restaurants in March, 2004. A smoking ban is to be introduced in Northern Ireland in 2007, but it is not expected to be as stringent.

The restaurants we list are the cream of the crop in each price category. Properties indicated by an ✕▣ are lodging establishments whose restaurant warrants a special trip.

Breakfast is served from 7 to 10, lunch runs from 12:30 to 2:30, and dinners are usually mid-evening occasions.

Pubs are generally open Monday and Tuesday 10:30 AM–11:30 PM and Thursday–Saturday 10:30 AM–12:30 AM. On Sunday, pubs are open 12:30 PM–11 PM or later on certain Sundays. All pubs close on Christmas Day and Good Friday, but hotel bars are open for guests.

Pubs in Northern Ireland are open 11:30 AM–11 PM Monday–Saturday and 12:30 PM–2:30 PM and 7 PM–10 PM on Sunday (note that Sunday openings are at the owner's or manager's discretion).

PAYING
Traveler's checks and credit cards are widely accepted, although it's cash-only at smaller pubs and takeout restaurants. Note that in Dublin and Southeast chapters prices are a few euros higher.

For guidelines on tipping see Tipping below.

CATEGORY	COST
$$$$	over £29
$$$	£22–£29
$$	£15–£22
$	£8–£15
¢	under £8

All prices are per person for a main course at dinner.

CATEGORY	COST
$$$$	over £22
$$$	£18–£22
$$	£13–£18
$	£7–£13
¢	under £7

In Northern Ireland: all prices are per person for a main course at dinner and are given in pounds sterling.

RESERVATIONS & DRESS
Regardless of where you are, it's a good idea to make a reservation if you can. In some places (Hong Kong, for example), it's expected. We only mention them specifically when reservations are essential (there's no other way you'll ever get a table) or when they are not accepted. For popular restaurants, book as far ahead as you can (often 30 days), and reconfirm as soon as you arrive. (Large parties should always call ahead to check the res-

ervations policy.) We mention dress only when men are required to wear a jacket or a jacket and tie.

Online reservation services make it easy to book a table before you even leave home. OpenTable covers most states, including 20 major cities, and has limited listings in Canada, Mexico, the United Kingdom, and elsewhere. DinnerBroker has restaurants throughout the United States as well as a few in Canada.

Contacts **OpenTable** (⊕ www.opentable.com). **DinnerBroker** (⊕ www.dinnerbroker.com).

WINES, BEER & SPIRITS

All types of alcoholic beverages are available in Ireland. Beer and wine are sold in shops and supermarkets, and you can get drinks "to go" at some bars, although at inflated prices. Stout (Guinness, Murphy's, Beamish) is the Irish beer; whiskey comes in many brands, the most notable being Bushmills and Jameson, and is smoother and more blended than Scotch.

▌ ELECTRICITY

The current in Ireland is 220 volts, 50 cycles alternating current (AC); wall outlets take plugs with three prongs.

Consider making a small investment in a universal adapter, which has several types of plugs in one lightweight, compact unit. Most laptops and mobile phone chargers are dual voltage (i.e., they operate equally well on 110 and 220 volts), so require only an adapter. These days the same is true of small appliances such as hair dryers. Always check labels and manufacturer instructions to be sure. Don't use 110-volt outlets marked FOR SHAVERS ONLY for high-wattage appliances such as hair-dryers.

Contacts **Steve Kropla's Help for World Traveler's** (⊕ www.kropla.com) has information on electrical and telephone plugs around the world. **Walkabout Travel Gear** (⊕ www. walkabouttravelgear.com) has a good coverage of electricity under "adapters."

▌ EMERGENCIES

The police force in the Republic of Ireland is called the Garda Síochána ("Guardians of the Peace," in English), usually referred to as the Gardaí (pronounced gar-dee). The force is unarmed and is headed by a government-appointed commissioner, who is answerable to the Minister for Justice, who in turn is accountable to the Dáil (the Irish legislature). Easily identified by their fluorescent yellow blazers in winter, or, if weather permits in summer, by a dark blue shirt and peaked cap, the Gardaí are generally very helpful. They, and all other emergency forces, can be contacted by dialing 999 (in the Republic of Ireland, 112, the European standard, is also in use). These numbers will connect you with local police, ambulance, and fire services. You can expect a prompt response to your call. The Garda Síochána Web site provides contact information for local stations. In Northern Ireland the police force is called the PSNI. They are distinguished by their dark blue coats and white shirts. They can be contacted by dialing 999 in Northern Ireland.

United States Embassies (⊠ 42 Elgin Rd., Ballsbridge, Dublin 4 ☎ 01/668–8777 ⊠ Queen's House, 14 Queen St., Golden Mile, Belfast BT1 6EQ ☎ 028/9032–8239).

General Emergency Contacts **Ambulance, fire, police** (☎ 999). **An Garda Síochána** (⊕ www.garda.ie). **Police Service of Northern Ireland** (⊕ www.psni.police.uk).

▌ HOURS OF OPERATION

Business hours are 9–5, sometimes later in the larger towns. In smaller towns, stores often close from 1 to 2 for lunch. If a holiday falls on a weekend, most businesses are closed on Monday.

Banks are open 10–4 weekdays. In small towns banks may close from 12:30 to 1:30. They remain open until 5 one afternoon per week; the day varies, although it's usually Thursday. Post offices are open weekdays 9–5 and Saturday 9–1; some of the smaller branches close for lunch.

In Northern Ireland bank hours are weekdays 9:30–4:30. Post offices are open weekdays 9–5:30, Saturday 9–1. Some close for an hour at lunch 1–2.

There are some 24-hour gas stations along the highways; otherwise, hours vary from morning rush hour to late evenings.

Museums and sights are generally open Tuesday–Saturday 10–5 and Sunday 2–5.

Most pharmacies are open Monday–Saturday 9–5:30 or 6. Larger towns and cities often have 24-hour establishments.

Most shops are open Monday–Saturday 9–5:30 or 6. Once a week—normally Wednesday, Thursday, or Saturday—shops close at 1 PM. These times do *not* apply to Dublin, where stores generally stay open later, and they can vary from region to region, so it's best to check locally. Larger malls usually stay open late once a week—generally until 9 on Thursday or Friday. Convenience stores and gas stations in both Dublin and rural Ireland are generally open until 8 or 9 PM.

Shops in Belfast are open weekdays 9–5:30, with a late closing on Thursday, usually at 9. Elsewhere in Northern Ireland, shops close for the afternoon once a week, usually Wednesday or Thursday. In addition, most smaller shops close for an hour or so at lunch.

HOLIDAYS

Irish national holidays in 2008 are as follows: January 1 (New Year's Day); March 17 (St. Patrick's Day); March 21 (Good Friday); March 24 (Easter Monday); May 5 (May Day); June 2 and August 4 (summer bank holidays); October 27 (autumn bank holiday); and December 25–26 (Christmas and St. Stephen's Day). If you plan to visit at Easter, remember that theaters and cinemas are closed for the last three days of the preceding week.

In Northern Ireland the following are holidays: January 1 (New Year's Day); March 17 (St. Patrick's Day); March 21 (Good Friday); March 24 (Easter Monday); May 5 (May Day); May 5 (early May bank holiday); May 26(spring bank holiday); July 12 (Battle of the Boyne); August 25 (summer bank holiday); and December 25–26 (Christmas and Boxing Day).

▌ MAIL

Outside of Dublin and Northern Ireland, postal codes aren't used; what's more important here is the county, so be sure to include it when addressing an envelope.

Letters by standard post take a week to 10 days to reach the United States and Canada, 3 to 5 days to reach the United Kingdom.

Airmail rates to the United States and Canada from the Irish Republic are €0.78 for letters and postcards. Rates are also €0.78 for letters and postcards to Europe. Mail to overseas can be sent economy or airmail. Letters and postcards within the Irish Republic cost €0.55.

Rates from Northern Ireland are 48p for letters and 54p for postcards (not over 10 grams) to continental Europe, and 54p to the United States and Canada, Australia, and New Zealand. To the rest of the United Kingdom and the Irish Republic, rates are 34p for first-class letters and 24p for second-class.

Mail can be held for collection at any post office for free for up to three months. It should be addressed to the recipient "c/o Poste Restante." In Dublin, use the General Post Office. The Irish postal service, known as An Post, has a Web site with a branch locator and loads of other postal information.

Contact **An Post** (⊕ www.anpost.ie). **General Post Office** (✉ O'Connell St., Dublin 1 ☎ 01/705–8833).

SHIPPING PACKAGES

If your package or letter absolutely has to get there the next day there are several overnight services available in Ireland. The most extensive and inexpensive service is the Express service offered by the national postal carrier, An Post. Letters and packages can be sent from main post offices to any destination in Ireland. International deliveries can be made to more than 200 destinations. The Courier service offers next-day prenoon delivery and it comes with a money-back guarantee for deliveries to Ireland and the United Kingdom. Sending documents to North America will take two working days, parcels three. This service is available from Dublin, Cork, Galway, Waterford, Limerick, and Shannon. Sending documents by Courier to U.K. cities and New York costs from €17 to €74. A 4.5-kg (2-pound) parcel will cost about €33 to send within Ireland, €70 to the United Kingdom, and €113 to New York. Familiar global carriers such as DHL, Federal Express, and UPS also operate services in Ireland.

Express Services **DHL** (☎ 800/725–725 ⊕ www.dhl.ie). **FedEx** (☎ 800/535–800 ⊕ www.fedex.com/ie). **SDS Courier** (☎ 1890/367–737 ⊕ www.sds.ie). **UPS** (☎ 800/575–757 ⊕ www.ups.com).

▌ MONEY

A modest hotel in Dublin costs about €130 a night for two; this figure can be reduced to under €90 by staying in a registered guesthouse or inn, and reduced

to about €45 by staying in a suburban B&B. Lunch, consisting of a good one-dish plate of bar food at a pub, costs around €8–€12; a sandwich at the same pub costs about €4. In Dublin's better restaurants, dinner will run €25–€40 per person, excluding drinks and tip.

Theater and entertainment in most places are inexpensive—about €18 for a good seat, and double that for a big-name, pop-music concert. For the price of a few drinks and (in Dublin and Killarney) a small entrance fee of about €2, you can spend a memorable evening at a *seisun* (pronounced say-*shoon*) in a music pub. Entrance to most public galleries is free, but stately homes and similar attractions charge anywhere from €4 to a whopping €8 per person.

Just about everything is more expensive in Dublin, so add at least 10% to these sample prices: cup of coffee, €1.80; pint of beer, €4.50; soda, €1.60; and 2-km (1-mi) taxi ride, €6. Travelers from the United Kingdom will find value when visiting Ireland. Due to the exchange rate, Canadians, Australians, New Zealanders, and—to a lesser extent, Americans—will find Ireland a little pricey when they convert costs to their home currency.

Hotels and meals in Northern Ireland are less expensive than in the United Kingdom and the Republic of Ireland. Also, the lower level of taxation makes taxable goods such as gasoline, alcoholic drinks, and tobacco cheaper.

Prices throughout this guide are given for adults. Substantially reduced fees are almost always available for children, students, and senior citizens.

▌TIP➔ Banks never have every foreign currency on hand, and it may take as long as a week to order. If you're planning to exchange funds before leaving home, don't wait till the last minute.

ATMS & BANKS

Your own bank will probably charge a fee for using ATMs abroad; the foreign bank you use may also charge a fee. Nevertheless, you'll usually get a better rate of exchange at an ATM than you will at a currency-exchange office or even when changing money in a bank. And extracting funds as you need them is a safer option than carrying around a large amount of cash.

■ TIP → **PIN numbers with more than four digits are not recognized at ATMs in many countries. If yours has five or more, remember to change it before you leave.**

ATMs are found in all major towns and are, by far, the easiest way to keep yourself stocked with euros and pounds. Most major banks are connected to Cirrus or PLUS systems; there's a four-digit maximum for your PIN.

CREDIT CARDS

Throughout this guide, the following abbreviations are used: **AE**, American Express; **D**, Discover; **DC**, Diners Club; **MC**, MasterCard; and **V**, Visa.

It's a good idea to inform your credit-card company before you travel, especially if you're going abroad and don't travel internationally very often. Otherwise, the credit-card company might put a hold on your card owing to unusual activity—not a good thing halfway through your trip. Record all your credit-card numbers—as well as the phone numbers to call if your cards are lost or stolen—in a safe place, so you're prepared should something go wrong. Both MasterCard and Visa have general numbers you can call (collect if you're abroad) if your card is lost, but you're better off calling the number of your issuing bank, since MasterCard and Visa usually just transfer you to your bank; your bank's number is usually printed on your card.

If you plan to use your credit card for cash advances, you'll need to apply for a PIN at least two weeks before your trip.

Although it's usually cheaper (and safer) to use a credit card abroad for large purchases (so you can cancel payments or be reimbursed if there's a problem), note that some credit-card companies *and* the banks that issue them add substantial percentages to all foreign transactions, whether they're in a foreign currency or not. Check on these fees before leaving home, so there won't be any surprises when you get the bill.

■ TIP → **Before you charge something, ask the merchant whether or not he or she plans to do a dynamic currency conversion (DCC). In such a transaction the credit-card** *processor* **(shop, restaurant, or hotel, not Visa or MasterCard) converts the currency and charges you in dollars. In most cases you'll pay the merchant a 3% fee for this service in addition to any credit-card company and issuing-bank foreign-transaction surcharges.**

Note that when using your credit card, check that the merchant is putting the transaction through in euros or pounds sterling. If he or she puts it through in the currency of your home country—a transaction called a dynamic currency conversion—the exchange rate might be less favorable and the service charges higher than if you allow the credit-card company to do the conversion for you. Be sure to ask at the time, and insist on being billed in euros to get the most advantageous rate and avoid the service charge.

Reporting Lost Cards American Express (☎800/992–3404 in the U.S. or 336/393–1111 collect from abroad ⊕www.american express.com). **Diners Club** (☎800/234–6377 in the U.S. or 303/799–1504 collect from abroad ⊕www.dinersclub.com). **Discover** (☎800/347–2683 in the U.S. or 801/902–3100 collect from abroad ⊕www.discovercard.com). **MasterCard** (☎800/622–7747 in the U.S. or 636/722–7111 collect from abroad ⊕www.mastercard.com). **Visa** (☎800/847–2911 in the U.S. or 410/581–9994 collect from abroad ⊕www.visa.com).

CURRENCY & EXCHANGE

The Irish Republic is a member of the European Monetary Union (EMU). Euro notes come in denominations of €500, €200, €100, €50, €20, €10, and €5. The euro is divided into 100 cents, and coins are available as €2 and €1 and 50, 20, 10, 5, 2, and 1 cent.

The unit of currency in Northern Ireland is the pound sterling (£), divided into 100 pence (p). The bills (called notes) are 50, 20, 10, and 5 pounds. Coins are £2, £1, 50p, 20p, 10p, 5p, 2p, and 1p. The bank of Northern Ireland prints its own notes, which look different from the English or Scottish Sterling.

Check out today's rates at ⊕*www.oanda. com*.

At this writing, one euro is equal to U.S. $0.73. One pound sterling is equal to U.S. $1.99. Rates fluctuate regularly, though, particularly for the euro, so monitor them closely.

■ TIP→ Even if a currency-exchange booth has a sign promising no commission, rest assured that there's some kind of huge, hidden fee. (Oh…that's right. The sign didn't say no *fee*.). And as for rates, you're almost always better off getting foreign currency at an ATM or exchanging money at a bank.

TRAVELER'S CHECKS & CARDS

Some consider this the currency of the cave man, and it's true that fewer establishments accept traveler's checks these days. Nevertheless, they're a cheap and secure way to carry extra money, particularly on trips to urban areas. Both Citibank (under the Visa brand) and American Express issue traveler's checks in the United States, but Amex is better known and more widely accepted; you can also avoid hefty surcharges by cashing Amex checks at Amex offices. Whatever you do, keep track of all the serial numbers in case the checks are lost or stolen.

American Express now offers a stored-value card called a Travelers Cheque Card, which you can use wherever American Express credit cards are accepted, including ATMs. The card can carry a minimum of $300 and a maximum of $2,700, and it's a very safe way to carry your funds. Although you can get replacement funds in 24 hours if your card is lost or stolen, it doesn't really strike us as a very good deal. In addition to a high initial cost ($14.95 to set up the card, plus $5 each time you "reload"), you still have to pay a 2% fee for each purchase in a foreign currency (similar to that of any credit card). Further, each time you use the card in an ATM you pay a transaction fee of $2.50 on top of the 2% transaction fee for the conversion—add it all up and it can be considerably more than you would pay when simply using your own ATM card. Regular traveler's checks are just as secure and cost less.

Contacts **American Express** (☎888/412–6945 in the U.S., 801/945–9450 collect outside of the U.S. to add value or speak to customer service ⊕www.americanexpress.com).

■ RESTROOMS

Public restrooms are in short supply in Ireland. They'll be easy enough to find in public places such as airports, train stations, and shopping malls, but if you don't find yourself in one of these locations your best bet is to look for the nearest pub (never more than a few minutes away in Ireland!). Restrooms are often labeled in Irish—Fir (men) and Mná. Pubs are increasingly putting up signs that restrooms are for customers only—but this is difficult to enforce. If it's outside of shopping or pub hours your last option may be the nearest hotel. Most gas stations will have toilets available. Only toilets in hotels or shopping centers will be up to a polished North American standard. Although many toilets look well-worn they are generally clean. Unfortunately, few toilets are heated and an open window is typically used for ventilation, making for uncomfortably cold restrooms in the colder months.

Find a Loo **The Bathroom Diaries** (⊕ *www. thebathroomdiaries.com*) is flush with unsanitized info on restrooms the world over—each one located, reviewed, and rated.

▌ SAFETY

The theft of car radios, mobile phones, cameras, video recorders, and other items of value from cars is common in Dublin and other major cities and towns. Never leave any valuable items on car seats or in the foot space between the back and front seats or in glove compartments. In fact, never leave anything whatsoever in sight in your car—even if you're leaving it for only a short time. You should also think twice about leaving valuables in your car while visiting tourist attractions anywhere in the country.

▌TIP➔ Distribute your cash, credit cards, I.D.s, and other valuables between a deep front pocket, an inside jacket or vest pocket, and a hidden money pouch. Don't reach for the money pouch once you're in public.

▌ TAXES

When leaving the Irish Republic, U.S. and Canadian visitors get a refund of the value-added tax (V.A.T.), which currently accounts for a hefty 21% of the purchase price of many goods and 13.5% of those that fall outside the luxury category. Apart from clothing, most items of interest to visitors, right down to ordinary toilet soap, are rated at 21%. V.A.T. is not refundable on accommodation, car rental, meals, or any other form of personal services received on vacation.

Many crafts outlets and department stores operate a system which enables U.S. and Canadian visitors to collect V.A.T. rebates in the currency of their choice at Dublin or Shannon Airport on departure. Some stores give you the rebate at the register; with others you claim your refund after you've returned home. Refund forms, known as a "Tax-Free Shopping Cheque," must be picked up at the time of purchase, and they must be stamped by customs, and mailed back to the store before you leave for home. It may take months for your refund to be processed. Many merchants work with a service such as Global Refund, which has offices at major ports and airports, and will refund your money immediately in return for a 4% fee. If a store gives you a refund at the register, you'll also be given papers to have stamped by customs; you'll then put the papers in an envelope (also provided by the store) and mail it before you leave. Most major stores deduct V.A.T. at the time of sale if goods are to be shipped overseas; however, there's a shipping charge.

When leaving Northern Ireland, U.S. and Canadian visitors can also get a refund of the 17.5% V.A.T. by the over-the-counter and the direct-export methods. Most larger stores provide these services on request and will handle the paperwork. For the over-the-counter method, you must spend more than £75 in one store. Ask the store for Form V.A.T. 407 (you must have identification—passports are best), to be given to customs when you leave the country. The refund will be forwarded to you in about eight weeks (minus a small service charge) either in the form of a sterling check or as a credit to your charge card. The direct-export method, where the goods are shipped directly to your home, is more cumbersome. V.A.T. Form 407/1/93 must be certified by customs, police, or a notary public when you get home and then sent back to the store, which will refund your money.

When making a purchase, ask for a V.A.T. refund form and find out whether the merchant gives refunds—not all stores do, nor are they required to. Have the form stamped like any customs form by customs officials when you leave the country or, if you're visiting several European Union countries, when you leave the EU. After you're through passport control, take the form to a refund-service counter for an on-the-spot refund (which is usually the quickest and easiest option), or mail it to the address on the form (or the envelope with it) after you arrive home. You receive the total refund stated on the form, but the processing time can be long, especially if you request a credit-card adjustment.

Global Refund is a Europe-wide service with 225,000 affiliated stores and more than 700 refund counters at major airports and border crossings. Its refund form, called a Tax Free Check, is the most common across the European continent. The service issues refunds in the form of cash, check, or credit-card adjustment.

V.A.T. Refunds Global Refund (☎800/566–9828 ⊕www.globalrefund.com).

▮ TIME

Dublin is five hours ahead of New York and eight hours ahead of Los Angeles.

▮ TIPPING

In some hotels and restaurants a service charge of around 10%—rising to 15% in plush spots—is added to the bill. If in doubt, ask whether service is included. In places where it's included, tipping isn't necessary unless you have received particularly good service. If there's no service charge, add a minimum of 10% to the total. Taxi drivers or Hackney cabs, who make the trip for a prearranged sum, don't expect tips. There are few porters and plenty of baggage trolleys at airports, so tipping is usually not an issue; if you use a porter, €1 is the minimum. Tip hotel porters at least €1 per suitcase. Hairdressers normally expect about 10% of the total spent. You don't tip in pubs, but for waiter service in a bar, a hotel lounge, or a Dublin lounge bar, leave about €1. It's not customary to tip for concierge service.

TIPPING GUIDELINES FOR IRELAND	
Bellhop	€1 to €2, depending on the level of the hotel
Hotel Concierge	€5 or more, if he or she performs a service for you
Hotel Doorman	€1–€2 if he helps you get a cab
Hotel Maid	€1–€3 a day (either daily or at the end of your stay, in cash)
Hotel Room-Service Waiter	€1 to €2 per delivery, even if a service charge has been added
Taxi Driver	10%, or just round up the fare to the next euro amount
Tour Guide	10% of the cost of the tour
Valet Parking Attendant	€1–€2, but only when you get your car
Waiter	Just small change (up to a euro or two) to round out your bill if service is included
Restroom Attendand	Restroom attendants in more expensive restaurants expect some small change or €1.

INDEX

PHOTO CREDITS

age fotostock. 20, *Joe Viesti/viestiphoto.com*. 21 (left), *Joe Malone/age fotostock*. 21 (right), *Joe Viesti/ viestiphoto.com*. 22 (top left), *Jane McIlroy/Shutterstock*. 22 (bottom left), *Marc C. Johnson/Shutterstock*. 22 (top right), *Ken Welsh/age fotostock*. 22 (bottom right), *Joe Gough/Shutterstock*. 23 (top left), *Matej Krajcovic/Shutterstock*. 23 (bottom left), *Vaide Seskauskiene/Shutterstock*. 24 (top left), *Thomas Barrat/ Shutterstock*. 24 (bottom left), *Wojtek Buss/age fotostock*. 24 (right), *Jean-Marc Charles/age fotostock*. 27 (left), *Kevin Galvin/age fotostock*. 27 (right), *Corbis*. 28, *Corbis*. 29, *J.D. Heaton/Picture Finders/age fotostock*. 31 (left), *Peter Adams/age fotostock*. 31 (right), *Richard Cummins/viestiphoto.com*. 33 (left), *Richard Cummins/viestiphoto.com*. 33 (right), *Kevin Galvin/age fotostock*. 40, *Danilo Donadoni/Marka/ age fotostock*. **Chapter 2: Dublin** 41, Liam White/Alamy. 42, Kevin O'Hara/age fotostock. 43, Richard Cummins/viestiphoto.com. 44, Jaap van der Beukel/Tourism Ireland. 45 (top), Danita Delimont/Alamy. 45 (bottom), Kevin Schafer/Alamy. 74, Kevin O'Hara/age fotostock. 75 (top left), Random House, Inc. 75 (top right), Roger Bamber/Alamy. 75 (bottom left), Mary Evans Picture Library. 75 (bottom left center), Beinecke Rare Book and Manuscript Library, Yale University. 75 (bottom right center), Arrow Books. 75 (bottom right), Macmillan. 76, Robert Harding Picture Library Ltd./Alamy. 77 (top), Joe Viesti/viestiphoto. com. 77 (bottom), Dublin Tourism. 78 (top and center), Mary Evans Picture Library/Alamy. 78 (bottom), Classic Image/Alamy. 79 (top), Popperfoto/Alamy. 79 (center), Lebrecht Music and Arts Photo Library/Alamy. 79 (bottom), Ida Kar Collection/Mary Evans Picture Library. 80 (top left), Richard Cummins/ viestiphoto.com. 80 (top right), Homer Sykes/Alamy. 80 (bottom), Pictorial Press/Alamy. 81, Peter Jordan/Alamy. 141 (top), Richard Cummins/viestiphoto.com. 141 (bottom left), Alvaro Leiva/age fotostock. 141 (bottom right), Richard Cummins/viestiphoto.com. 142, Joe Viesti/viestiphoto.com. 143, Joe Viesti/ viestiphoto.com. 144 (top left), Chloe Johnson/Alamy. 144 (top right), ImageState/Alamy. 144 (bottom left), Beamish & Crawford. 144 (bottom right), Murphy Brewery. 145 (top and bottom), David Sanger Photography/Alamy. **Chapter 3: Dublin: Environs:** 171, S. Howard/Alamy. 172 (top), Richard Cummins/ viestiphoto.com. 172 (center), Peter Titmuss/Alamy. 172 (bottom), Richard Cummins/viestiphoto.com. 173, Joe Viesti/viestiphoto.com. 174, Wojtek Buss/age fotostock. 175, Martin Norris/Alamy. 205 and 206 (top left), Department of the Environment , Heritage and Local Government, Ireland. 206 (top right), Richard Cummins/viestiphoto.com. 206 (bottom) and 207 (all), Joe Cornish/Dorling Kindersley. 208 (all) and 209 (top), Russborough. 209 (bottom), Web Gallery of Art. **Chapter 4: The Midlands:** 215–217, Richard Cummins/viestiphoto.com. 218, Nutan/Tourism Ireland. **Chapter 5: The Southeast:** 249, Steppenwolf/Alamy. 250, Peter Barritt/Alamy. 251 (left), Gavin Gough/Alamy. 251 (right), Richard Cummins/ viestiphoto.com. 253 (top), Richard Cummins/viestiphoto.com. 296 (top), Richard Cummins/viestiphoto. com. 296 (bottom), Wikipedia Commons. 297 , Richard Cummins/viestiphoto.com. 298 (top and bottom right), Wikipedia Commons. 298 (bottom left), Print Collection, Miriam and Ira D. Wallach Division of Art, Prints and Photographs, The New York Public Library, Astor, Lenox, and Tilden Foundations. 299 (top), Gavin Gough/Alamy. 299 (bottom), Wikipedia Commons. 300 (top), Mary Evans Picture Library/Alamy. 301, Mary Evans Picture Library/Alamy. **Chapter 6: The Southwest:** 307, Brent Bergherm/ age fotostock. 308 (left), Cork Kerry Tourism. 308 (right), Richard Cummins/viestiphoto.com. 309, Kevin Galvin/Alamy. 310 (top), Joe Viesti/viestiphoto.com. 310 (bottom), Jason Friend/Alamy. 333 (top), Marco Cristofori/age fotostock. 333 (bottom), Gubbeen Farmhouse Products. 334 (top left), Food Features/Alamy. 334 (top right and bottom), Ballymaloe Cooking School. 335 (top and bottom), Ballymaloe Cooking School. 336 (left), Belvelly Smoke House. 336 (right), Gubbeen Farmhouse Products. 337 (top left), John Minehan. 337 (top right), Urru Culinary Store. 337 (bottom), Gubbeen Farmhouse Products. 338 (left), Robert Harding Library Ltd/Alamy. 338 (top right), Richard Cummins/viestiphoto.com. 338 (bottom right), John Angerson/Alamy. 339, Richard Cummins/viestiphoto.com. 359 (top), David Lyons/ Alamy. 359 (bottom left), FAN travelstock/Alamy. 359 (bottom right), Jonathan Hession/Tourism Ireland. 360, Joe Viesti/viestiphoto.com. 362 (top left), Jiri Rezac/Alamy. 362 (bottom left), Philipp Mohr/ Alamy. 362 (right), Andrew Holt/Alamy. 363 (top), David Lyons/Alamy. 363 (bottom left), Michael Diggin/Alamy. 363 (bottom right), Peter Barritt/Alamy. 364 (top), Jonathan Hession/Tourism Ireland. 364(center left), Peter Horree/Alamy. 364 (center right), Cork Kerry Tourism. 364 (bottom), David Sanger Photography/Alamy. 365 (top), Adrian Muttitt/Alamy. 365 (bottom), nagelestock/Alamy. **Chapter 7: The West:** 407, Joe Viesti/viestiphoto.com. 408, Richard Cummins/viestiphoto.com. 409 (top and bottom left), Richard Cummins/viestiphoto.com. 409 (bottom right), Joe Englander/viestiphoto.com. 410, Matt Lombardi. 444, Joan Marcus. 445, Photodisc/Punchstock. 446, Jack Hartin. 447 (top), M.T.M. Images/Alamy. 447 (bottom), scenicireland.com/Christopher Hill Photographic/Alamy. 448, Jon Arnold/Agency Jon Arnold Images/age fotostock. 449, Jules Annan. 450 (top left and top right), Photodisc/Punchstock. 450 (center), Joe Viesti/viestiphoto.com. 450 (bottom left), Brand X Pictures/ Punchstock. 450 (bottom right), Photodisc/Punchstock. 451 (top), David Lyons/Alamy. 451 (bottom), Paul McCarthy. **Chapter 8: The Northwest:** 481, Gareth McCormack/Alamy. 482 (top and center left), Richard Cummins/viestiphoto.com. 482 (center right), PCL/Alamy. 482 (bottom), David Nixon/Alamy.

NOTES

NOTES

ABOUT OUR WRITERS

For our coverage of Dublin, Anto Howard has checked every fact, burnished every metaphor to the fine gleam of ancient brogues, and has so lovingly described the towns and villages found in the Dublin Environs chapter that even their natives will leave for the pleasure of coming back. Six post-graduate years of living in New York City recently convinced Anto of the charms of his native Ireland and he duly returned to take up residence in Dublin. He has written and edited books and articles about such far-flung places as Costa Rica, Las Vegas, and Russia, and has contributed to such publications as *National Geographic Traveler* and *Esat Online*. Anto (christened Anthony—Dubliners have a habit of abbreviating perfectly good names) is also a playwright, and his shows have been produced in Dublin and in New York.

Alannah Hopkin grew up in London but spent most of her childhood summers on her uncle's farm near Kinsale, where she learned two of the most important things in life: how to ride a horse and how to sail a boat. After graduate studies in Irish literature, she worked as a writer in London—but ancestral voices were calling her home, and she spent more and more time in County Cork, where horses and boats were easier to find. After publishing her first novel, *A Joke Goes A Long Way in the Country,* she made the big leap, and moved to Kinsale for a trial six months—and is still there 20 years later. Another novel was followed by a book on the cult of St. Patrick and an acclaimed guide to the pleasures of County Cork. She has written on travel and the arts for the London *Sunday Times,* contributes regularly to the *Irish Examiner* and the *Irish Times,* and is writing a book on West Cork. She has worked on *Fodor's Ireland* since 1985, and this year she updated the Southwest, West, and Smart Travel Tips chapters.

Born in "the kingdom" of Kerry, the urge to roam infected John Daly from an early age. Taking a two-week vacation in New York after university finals that morphed into a decade spent roaming the hinterland of America from Alaska to Texas, the lure of home eventually drew him back across the Atlantic. After stints as owner of a pub in Dublin and a restaurant in Cork, a midlife career U-turn into writing saw him settle in Kinsale. With a large extended family that's never seen him stuck for a bed anywhere from Cashel to Wexford, the task of updating the Midland, Southeast, Northwest, and Northern Ireland chapters provided an added bonus of visiting cousins and relations normally encountered only at weddings and christenings. A regular contributor to the *Irish Independent,* the *Irish Examiner,* and *Hibernia* magazine, he recently worked on a television project—a documentary on Calcutta's street children that premiered at last year's Galway Film Festival. Drawn inexorably homeward to his native Kerry, he's currently working on the next television production, a behind-the-scenes look at Puck Fair, Ireland's oldest festival.